Bonaparte

Bonaparte
1769–1802

Patrice Gueniffey

Translated by Steven Rendall

The Belknap Press of Harvard University Press
Cambridge, Massachusetts
London, England
2015

Copyright © 2015 by the President and Fellows of Harvard College
Printed in the United States of America

Second printing

First published in French as *Bonaparte: 1769–1802*, copyright © 2013 Éditions Gallimard, Paris, 2013

Library of Congress Cataloging-in-Publication Data

Gueniffey, Patrice.
  [Bonaparte. English]
  Bonaparte : 1769–1802 / Patrice Gueniffey ; translated by Steven Rendall.
     pages cm
  Includes bibliographical references and index.
  ISBN 978-0-674-36835-4 (alk. paper)
  1. Napoleon I, Emperor of the French, 1769–1821.   2. Emperors—France—Biography.
3. Heads of state—France—Biography.   4. France—History—Consulate and First Empire,
1799–1815.   I. Rendall, Steven, translator.   II. Title.
  DC205.G8413 2015
  944.05092—dc23
  [B]
                                                              2014034162

For Antoine, Arnaud, Caroline, Philippe, and Virginie

Contents

Color illustrations follow page 436.

MAPS

Bonaparte

One day in 1816, Napoleon was talking to the Count de Las Cases, his fellow exile on Saint Helena, about Britain's policies and his marriage with Marie-Louise. Suddenly, without seeming to remember that Las Cases was still there, he fell silent, "resting his head on one of his hands." After a moment he rose and said, "What a novel my life has been!"[1] These words are famous, often cited, and true. But Napoleon's life, no matter how novelistic it may seem, lends itself better to music than to literature. When Anthony Burgess decided to devote one of his novels to Napoleon, he called it *Napoleon Symphony: A Novel in Four Movements* (1974), making the different parts of the book correspond to the movements of the symphony that Beethoven had entitled *Buonaparte* before later renaming it, not without hesitations, *Sinfonia eroica per festeggiare il sovvenire di un gran Uomo*, the *Eroica*.[2] The direction placed at the beginning of the first movement indicates the tempo of the extraordinary destiny that Beethoven set to music: *Allegro con brio*.

People are sometimes astonished by the large—even enormous—number of studies that have been devoted to Napoleon: several tens of thousands, and the list grows longer every day. Instead we should be astonished by this astonishment. At what other time has such a profusion of unprecedented events, sweeping changes, and monumental collapses been packed into such a short time? Only a quarter of a century separates the beginning of the French Revolution—which made Napoleon possible, if not necessary, according to Nietzsche—from the end of the Empire.[3] From the meeting of the Estates General to the emperor's abdication, history did not simply move but raced forward. Napoleon traversed it like a meteor: from his entrance on stage in 1793 to the coup d'état of 18 Brumaire, six years elapsed; then three between the conquest of power and the proclamation of the Consulate for Life, and only two between the latter and the advent of the Empire in 1804. As Jacques Bainville points out, "Ten years later, less than ten years later, Louis XVIII will be there. . . . Ten years, when hardly ten years before [Bonaparte] had just begun to emerge from obscurity, only ten years, and then it would already be over. . . . A minor officer at twenty-five, here he is, miraculously, emperor at thirty-five. Time took him by the shoulder and pushed him forward. His days are numbered. They will fly by with the rapidity of a dream so prodigiously full, interrupted by so few pauses and respites, in a sort of impatience to arrive as quickly as possible at the catastrophe; loaded, finally, with so many grandiose events that this reign, in truth so short, seems to have lasted a century."[4]

During this very brief time, Napoleon played all these roles: Corsican patriot, Jacobin (but not too Jacobin) revolutionary, *Feuillant* (briefly), Thermidorian (but a defender of Robespierre's memory), conqueror, diplomat, legislator, "hero, imperator, patron of the arts," republican dictator, hereditary sovereign, maker and breaker of kings, and even a constitutional monarch in 1815 (if we take seriously the institutions created during the Hundred Days).[5] There was something of the magician about him. He changed not only roles and costumes, depending on the circumstances, but also his name and even his appearance. He began with a strange first name whose spelling and pronunciation were unclear, to say the least: Nabulion, Napolione, Napoléon, Napulion? No matter; he soon chose to use his patronymic alone, Gallicized from Buonaparte to Bonaparte. In Italy some people claimed that this name was no more authentic than his strange first name. He could invent cousins near San Gimignano, his courtiers could fabricate fantastical genealogies for him, but the skeptics said it had been demonstrated that far from being called Buonaparte, his ancestors had borne the name Malaparte. They saw the proof of this in his history, in their view more bad than good, often Mala-parte, rarely Buona-parte. These are fables, of course, but they had at least the merit of inspiring long afterward—perhaps on the advice of Pirandello, who could not fail to be attracted to such a story of onomastic and biographical doubling—the young Curzio Suckert's choice of Malaparte as his pen name.[6] In 1804 Bonaparte was crowned emperor and became Napoleon once again. Because this first name henceforth designated the founder of a dynasty—people assigned the name "Napoleonids" to the kings and princes he created—it had to be relieved of some of its strangeness. In Rome, where the pope did not want to quarrel with the man who had moderated the Revolution's hostility to the Church, lists of martyrs were searched, and because a

Saint Napoleon could not be found, they dug up a Saint Neopolis or Neapolis, whose existence was hardly less doubtful but who would serve the purpose. "Neapolis" was close enough to "Napoleo," and "Napoleo" to Napoleon. The Church chose as the feast day of this newly designated "Saint Napoleon" August 15, the day of the feast of the Assumption—and the emperor's own birthday.[7] Did Joséphine, who had always called him Bonaparte, change her habits? From then on he always signed his letters "Np," "Nap," "Napo," "Napole" . . .

As for Bonaparte's physical metamorphoses, Michel Covin has written an absorbing account of them.[8] He recalls something Bourrienne, Napoleon's secretary, said about him: "There is not a single portrait of the great man that looks absolutely like him." No doubt that is the case for most portraits: some certainly resemble their subjects more than others; they grasp better what the painter Gros called "the character of [the] physiognomy."[9] No portrait is true in the sense that it restitutes the *exact* face of Napoleon. A historian of representations of the emperor made that observation long ago: "Most of the portraits that would be made of Bonaparte [later, of Napoleon] are images very different from this figure that wears a mask full of mystery."[10] The abundance of effigies plays a certain role here: the French National Library alone holds more than 5,000 of them.[11] The emperor's features thus become a little blurred, even if one always immediately recognizes him. The conventional nature of many of these portraits doesn't help. Early on, art—especially painting and statuary— conformed to "a governmental style" that sought to display the office more than the man who held it.[12] Must we then prefer later representations to contemporary works, as Michel Covin suggests? We can agree that the great paintings by Gérard, Isabey, David, or Ingres representing Bonaparte as first consul, or Napoleon as emperor, hardly allow us to understand the enthusiasm that gripped Hegel when, in the midst of a crowd in Iena, he saw the *Weltseele* pass in front of him, or Goethe, who had the privilege of a conversation with Napoleon. So, Delaroche rather than David, Philippoteaux rather than Ingres? Must we even conclude that works of pure imagination contain more truth? Michel Covin attaches great importance to the somber *Saint Helena, The Last Phase* painted by James Sant at the beginning of the twentieth century. What do we know about Napoleon's physical appearance in his last exile? He had greatly changed and grown fatter, he no longer shaved, and Montholon's wife even referred to the "long beard" that made him unrecognizable. Far from the pious images showing the prisoner of Saint Helena wearing a hat and meditating on the sad fate of the slave Toby, Sant represented Bonaparte as he imagined him on the basis of accounts of the emperor's captivity: somber, sad, depressed, physically and psychologically used up. Although it is not based on any positive or verifiable evidence, the portrait is plausible, ever verisimilar. Would a photograph have been still more evocative? Not necessarily. There are several. In them one sees a man who is not, of course, Napoleon. They show his brother Jérome, photographed shortly before his death, during the Second Empire.[13] These daguerreotypes fascinated Roland Barthes: "I am seeing eyes that saw the emperor," he thought as he looked at them.[14] He could almost have seen the emperor himself in them, so much did Jérome resemble in these pictures what Napoleon might have become had he grown as old as his youngest brother did. It's he, no doubt about it. Fascinating photos. At the same time, we see only an old man who looks like Napoleon.

So let us give up the attempt to *see* him as he really was. His countless portraits compose—at least the best of them do, whether contemporary or later—a *psychological portrait* whose variety testifies to "the mysterious uncertainty that hangs over the character of the man."[15] The profiles dashed off by Gros and David, those on the medals by Gayrard and Vassalo, Ceracchi's bust, David's pencil sketches and especially his unfinished portrait of Napoleon, all depict the psychological rather than the physical Bonaparte. Just as Gros's *Bonaparte au pont d'Arcole* exalts the "symbol of individual energy" that Romanticism was soon to celebrate, Pierre-Narcisse Guérin's *Bonaparte* shows, better than any other portrait, the implacable element in him.[16] The emperor's admirers will choose Gros, his detractors Guérin.

Let us listen to Taine:

> Now, contemplate in Guérin the spare body, those narrow shoulders under the uniform wrinkled by sudden movements, that neck swathed in its high twisted cravat, those temples covered by long, smooth, straight hair, exposing only the mask, the hard features intensified through strong contrasts of light and shade, the cheeks hollow up to the inner angle of the eye, the projecting cheek-bones, the massive, protuberant

jaw, the sinuous, mobile lips, pressed together as if attentive, the large clear eyes, deeply sunk under the broad, arched eyebrows, the fixed, oblique look, as penetrating as a rapier, and the two creases which extend from the base of the nose to the brow, as if in a frown of suppressed anger and determined will. Add to this the accounts of his contemporaries who saw or heard the curt accent or the sharp, abrupt gesture, the interrogating, imperious, absolute tone of voice, and we comprehend how, the moment they accosted him, they felt the dominating hand which seizes them, presses them down, holds them firmly and never relaxes its grasp.[17]

So was Napoleon a name rather than a man? Was he like the hero of Simon Leys's *The Death of Napoleon*, whose name and history escape him? In Leys's novel the emperor has escaped from Saint Helena, where a double takes his place. If he had imagined he would be received as triumphally as when he returned from the island of Elba, he was mistaken. A few people look curiously at him, but who could believe he was in the presence of the true Napoleon? Isn't he a prisoner of the English? And hasn't his death suddenly been announced? The double, by dying too soon, not only compromises Napoleon's plans, but also deprives him of his destiny: "*His destiny was posthumous*. . . . An obscure noncommissioned officer, simply by dying like a fool on a deserted rock at the other end of the world, had managed to confront him with the most formidable and unexpected rival imaginable: himself! Worse still, from now on Napoleon would have to make his way not only against Napoleon, but against a Napoleon who was larger than life—the memory of Napoleon!"[18] It is impossible, and Napoleon has to face the facts when one evening a man who has recognized him—the only one—leads him to a house with locked doors where he finds himself in the presence of all kinds of Napoleons who look more or less like him and are making strange remarks and behaving in bizarre ways. He is no longer Napoleon; now he exists outside himself.

Napoleon is a myth, a legend; or rather: an epoch. He has so completely filled this epoch with his name that he and his time can hardly exist separately.[19] Historians have concluded from this that in his case the boundary between history and legend is so permeable that it would be impossible to write a biography of Napoleon. The emperor? A receptacle, an empty form, a metaphor valuable chiefly for the questions or representations it has successively shaped.[20] The idea that Napoleon does not exist is not a new one.[21] During the Restoration, Jean-Baptiste Pérès, a librarian in Agen, a small town in the south of France, claimed that this Napoleon people were talking about so much was a fiction: "He is only an allegorical image; he is the sun personified."[22] He found the proof of this in the name Napoleon, in the emperor's mother's first name, in the number of his brothers and sisters, and in that of the marshals, in all the phases of his history. For him, these were just so many signs that connected Napoleon with solar myths. But Pérès was not in earnest; he simply wanted to make fun of royal pretensions. Hadn't Louis XVIII dated his first orders in 1814 as issued in "the nineteenth year" of his reign, as if nothing had happened in France since the execution of Louis XVI? It wasn't Napoleon who didn't exist, of course, but rather the alleged first nineteen years of Louis XVIII's reign.

The hypothesis of Napoleon's nonexistence is a paradox; nonetheless, he does not easily lend himself to biography. Not to mention that there are many conflicting testimonies to almost every episode in this extraordinary life. As one writer put it, "If we are disposed to credit all that is told us, we must believe in the existence not only of one, but of two or three Buonapartes; if we admit nothing but what is well authenticated, we shall be compelled to doubt of the existence of any."[23] It is clear that every biography of Napoleon is more or less a history of his reign and vice versa. This is true of the monumental *History of the Consulate and the Empire* by Thiers, of Louis Madelin's sixteen volumes, and even of Georges Lefebvre's *Napoléon*, though Lefebvre denied that he was writing a biography of the emperor.[24] And in many cases the biographical approach is distinguished solely by the presence of chapters devoted to the hero's formative years. The relatively small number of biographies testifies to difficulties that are not, let us remember, peculiar to Napoleon: the biography of a king is necessarily a history of his kingdom, at least during his reign.[25] To be sure, no figure in history has had more biographers than Napoleon; but their number is not very high compared to that of studies of the period, as if many historians had shrunk from the difficulties of the enterprise or, in the end, were reluctant to choose between Napoleon and his time.[26] Today biographies of Napoleon have become still rarer, especially in French.[27] It is not that earlier studies have exhausted the subject; because any biography is simultaneously a reconstitution and a reinterpretation, the genre is not susceptible of a cumulative conception of knowledge. No biography can be "definitive" or instantly make all past work obsolescent or all future work superfluous; there is never a last word concerning the truth about a man. If biographies of Napoleon have become rare in recent decades, that is because both the genre and, in this case, the subject, have long suffered from a rather bad reputation.

Biography has been accused of being too close to literature, of granting too large a role to imagination, of being based on an "illusion"—life as destiny, one, continuous, coherent, and transparent—and of relying on an outmoded conception of history that exaggerates the efficacy of human will and the sovereignty of individuals. So much has been written about this "impure genre" that there is hardly any point in saying more, especially because the events of the tragic twentieth century ultimately destroyed illusions regarding the subordination of history to the action of imperious laws or of social forces alone.[28] A strange epoch, François Furet observed, in which "historical materialism reached its widest influence" at the precise moment when "it had the least explanatory power."[29] For in the end, Furet added, "there is nothing more incompatible with an analysis of the Marxist type . . . than the unprecedented dictatorships of the twentieth century. The mystery of these regimes cannot be explained by their dependence on social interests [the proletariat in the case of communism, big capital in the case of Nazism], because it has to do with precisely the reverse characteristic: their dreadful independence with regard to interests, whether they are bourgeois or proletarian."[30] In this context, in which the influence of interests on the behavior of individuals is overestimated and the efficacy of the individual will is underestimated, social history was obviously invested with a larger explanatory capacity than biography, which was considered entertainment or a more or less literary exercise in which a now obsolescent way of writing history survived in vestigial form. Beyond the influence of Marxism, liberal doctrines, or the predilection for collective processes and slow and silent transformations, the loss of the biographical genre's dignity, which has been so evident for a few decades, also testifies to a tendency which is that of democracy. Tocqueville pointed out long ago that since democracy succeeded aristocracy, the way of writing history had changed. The relationship between the particular causes and the general causes of events had been inverted: whereas aristocracy was inclined to give priority to the former and to explain history by "the will and humor of certain individuals," democracy had an inverse tendency to discover "great general causes" even for "the most insignificant particular facts." The former believed in individuals, the latter in collective forces, the former in the powers of the will, the latter in historical fatalities.[31] Because biography cannot by definition be a "doctrine of fatality," it had to give way so that history could transform itself from the psychological study of its actors' intentions into a science of the results of their actions, sometimes to the point of becoming "a narrative without a subject."[32]

If biography has since recovered its standing, Napoleon has little benefited from this rehabilitation. One does not need to be a great scholar to see why. If, as Michelet averred, the writing of history attains its most fully achieved form in "the annihilation of the great historical individualities," Napoleon was obviously the primary target.[33] He is the very incarnation of the history peculiar to aristocratic ages, in which the principal actors remain in the foreground and seem to dictate events, even if they do not always control their consequences. Whether victors or vanquished, all-powerful heroes or victims of "Fortune," they always testify to the power of the individual. The hagiographic nature of many books devoted to Napoleon is only a pretext used by the opponents to biography. After all, Napoleon has nothing to complain about; his historiographic pedigree is more than equal to that of many other historical figures. Stendhal, Chateaubriand, Taine, and even Nietzsche lean over his cradle, so to speak.[34] No, the real reason is precisely that he incarnates a kind of history that has become suspect. It is not that no attempt has been made to remove Napoleon from the picture, or in any case to make him less present, less visible. Thus historians have gradually passed from studying the emperor to studying the Empire. We should keep in mind, of course, that the movement inaugurated in 1977 by Jean Tulard's *Napoléon*, and even earlier if we recall the research of Louis Bergeron and Guy Chaussinand-Nogaret on the "blocks of granite" in the imperial period, has produced many valuable results.[35] People have started to take an interest in Napoleon's collaborators, his ministers, his officers, his allies and his enemies, to reevaluate the importance of what had been neglected in his history, to no longer consider solely what contributed to his glory but also what might tarnish its radiance.[36] Political, administrative, military, diplomatic, intellectual, legal, cultural history—it would be impossible to draw up even a brief list of the works that have recently enriched our knowledge of Napoleonic times. Napoleon's entourage, his collaborators, and his officers have emerged from the shadows; institutions and their functioning are better known to us; French society in particular has been, as it were, brought back into the spotlight, and for the past thirty years historians have in fact explored numerous "new paths."[37] The mistake, if it is one, was perhaps to have tried too hard to react against a tradition—notably a biographical tradition—that faced "bad press" and suffered from a pronounced hagiographic tendency. These efforts at renewal relied on studies of how the figure of the emperor was overshadowed: doing away with "the history of Napoleon" in order to write, finally, "the history of all the people of his time."[38] A difficult, perhaps impossible gambit. As in Noël-Noël's charming *La Sentinelle endormie*, which I read when I was a child, the emperor is present everywhere, even when you don't see him. As Aurélien Lignereux put it: "Writing a history of the Napoleonic period while absolutely refusing to focus on Napoleon would be like repeating Georges Pérec's literary experiment—writing a whole novel without using the letter 'e.' This disappearance might have the merit of depersonalizing historical narrative and even putting an end to it, but this authentically new history, having broken with the conventions of the classical theory of action, would doubtless have no posterity other than a conceptual one."[39]

Ralph Waldo Emerson was probably the first to have tried to imagine a history of the Napoleonic epoch without Napoleon. The emperor, he tells us, was great only with respect to qualities, and especially defects, that were those of his time. He was the democratic man personified, the true representative of the nineteenth century. Like the middle class of his time, he wanted to get rich, by any means, he had an extremely acute sense of reality, he was materialistic, positive in every way, concrete, a hard worker, unscrupulous, an enemy of lofty ideas and sentiments, a base soul, with vulgar tastes and coarse manners. What was Napoleon? He was "the agent or attorney of the Middle Class," a witness to a mediocre age, the contrary of a hero, the representative of the common man and thus the latter's idol.[40]

And Emerson himself? He was the anti-Stendhal, the anti-Nietzsche. For Nietzsche, Napoleon was, on the contrary, "like a last signpost to the *other* path"—the path opposed to the progress of democracy, "the most isolated and late-born man there has ever been, and in him the problem of the *noble ideal as such* [was] *made flesh*."[41] A late-born hero, according to Nietzsche, the first man of the modern era according to Emerson. Does he testify to a dying world? To a world about to be born? Both, no doubt; Emerson himself has great difficulty in coping with Napoleon's personal qualities, because he is forced to admit that if they were qualities common to the middle class, Napoleon possessed them to an *extraordinary* degree. It is not so easy to make Napoleon out to be inferior or to make him merge with his epoch by ignoring what is unprecedented in his story, to the point that one would seek in vain a parallel. Alexander? Perhaps, but Alexander was the son of a king. Caesar? The scion of a patrician family. From the outset, both of them were situated at the center of the world they were about to conquer. Napoleon's case is entirely different: he was of modest origin, he came from the periphery of the kingdom, and yet he was called not only to rise to the summit but to represent a universal figure that goes far beyond the sum of his achievements. What relation is there, in fact, between Napoleon's politics, which consisted in putting an end to the Revolution and enshrining its principles in institutions, and this exceptional figure who was basically so little in accord with his period? "Where is the peculiarity of the occasion? What sufficient reason is there for a series of events occurring in the eighteenth and nineteenth centuries, which never took place before? Was Europe at that period peculiarly weak, and in a state of barbarism, that one man could achieve such conquests, and acquire such a vast empire? On the contrary, she was flourishing in the height of strength and civilization. . . . Wherever we turn to seek for circumstances that may help to account for the events of this incredible story, we only meet with such as aggravate its improbability."[42]

Napoleon's work is part of the history of France, even if it had repercussions throughout Europe, whereas its author is in some sense universal. That is, moreover, one of the reasons Napoleon cannot be summed up by any of his portraits. There resides the limit of any biographical essay. "Countless psychological, intellectual, moral, portraits of Napoleon have been made, and as many judgments formed of him," Bainville said. "He always escapes by a few lines the pages in which authors attempt to confine him."[43] That is also the secret of the fascination that he continues to exercise, even as the world he helped to produce is rapidly slipping away from us and the change in mentalities has even tarnished its glory. The myth has shrunk: Napoleon's great military victories no longer have the same fascination for us that they had for Tolstoy's contemporaries. The myth is exhausted to the degree to which the passions that have maintained it have been extinguished: *glory, heroism*, and *war*, the latter having long been perceived as an education in virtue. The magic of war died with the atrocious slaughters of the twentieth century. However, something still speaks to modern imaginations: the belief—which was also that of the young Bonaparte, and is our own, or at least we would like it to be—*that our fate will not resist our will*. Bonaparte is, in a way, everyone's dream. That is probably why asylums used to be full of madmen who thought they were Napoleon: the man who, without famous ancestors or a famous name, created himself by force of will, work, and talent. He is the man who made his life a destiny, to the point of choosing the way it would end by returning from the island of Elba in 1815, this time without anything that justified his behavior, to give his story a fitting conclusion. He is the man who rose to unprecedented heights and who, through his genius, pushed back all known boundaries. Not a model, but a dream. In that respect—and here resides the secret of the fascination he still has for us—Napoleon is a figure of the modern individual. That is the subject of this book.

Regarding Napoleon, the biographical field is clearly marked out. Napoleonic historiography is a battlefield that has been worked over and traversed by so many armies that every historian is in some way a descendant of some other. That being the case, writing a new biography involves adopting a specific mixture of great systems of interpretation that arose in the nineteenth century, which I shall present briefly here.

Hippolyte Taine was the most profound representative of the interpretation of Napoleon's story as an *adventure*.[44] Taine's version of the story is organized around the figure of the Hero whose will dominates any form of necessity to the point of being conflated with the general history of the period: the latter is the history of an individual, almost the external manifestation of his character. History is absorbed into psychology. Taine saw the Napoleonic period as an interlude in the course of history, an anachronism without significance: without origins, without posterity. To him, Napoleon appeared to be a kind of reincarnation of the *condottieri*, a predator who had fallen upon a France exhausted by ten years of revolution and who made use of his prey to satisfy his ambition: "universal monarchy." The history of the Napoleonic period is nothing more than the history of the overweening Napoleonic *ego* and its external unfolding. This interpretation contains a kernel of truth: it is an attempt to conceive the obvious extravagance and strangeness of the figure of Napoleon in relation to postrevolutionary French society. Moreover, Taine does not deny the existence of a heritage: Napoleon gave France an administration, a currency, and institutions that were to shape it for more than a century. But according to Taine, this useful, positive, *necessary* part of Napoleon's legacy is precisely what bears least his personal stamp. What he did that was useful would have been done by others, not as fast, not as well, and perhaps in a more liberal spirit, but ultimately they would have done it. The role of necessity in the Napoleonic story lies in the deep movement of French history that has been represented, at least since the reign of Louis XIV, by centralization and the reduction, to the advantage of the state, of local liberties and the role of intermediate bodies. What makes Napoleon special and constitutes his grandeur (which Taine considered disastrous) is not that he takes up where the absolute monarchy and the Jacobins left off; instead, it is his pursuit, by means of war and conquest, of a dream of universal domination that is not in accord with either French history or the spirit of modern society, and that belongs to him alone.

In the opposite historiographic camp, everything from 1799 to 1814 was the outcome of necessity. Napoleon's story is a drama of fate, a tragedy, that of the will at grips with fatality. Whereas Taine dramatizes a Napoleon whose will triumphs over things, Jacques Bainville describes a Napoleon who is the victim of an implacable logic, simultaneously the heir and the prisoner of the Revolution, doomed to go round and round in a circle from which he cannot escape: continually seeking to force Europe to recognize French annexations and to sign, as people said, a "glorious peace," but without having the material means to achieve this goal. Without a navy, how could he force England to sign a peace treaty in conformity with France's interests? Napoleon exhausted himself trying to solve this conundrum, even imagining that the conquest of an *empire on land*—by means of a continental blockade—could make up for the impossibility of conquering an *empire on the seas*, over which Britain reigned alone. In this story there is, amid exploits that are beyond imagining, much monotony: no victory, no matter how brilliant, was of any avail in solving the problem. Finally, everything is attributed to the least free of the period's actors. "This absolute master was himself mastered by the circumstances," Mathieu Dumas wrote in his memoirs. "Therefore it is neither correct nor fair to attribute to a blind and mad ambition alone the gigantic expeditions that Napoleon boldly undertook and that have perhaps been too severely judged. This genius so vast, so profound, so meditative, this legislator so positive, this administrator with so much foresight, could not have allowed himself to be carried away by a frenzied imagination."[45]

The liberal interpretation is a composite of these two extreme theses: it associates adventure and necessity, and is actually closer to Taine than to Bainville, because it puts the stamp of necessity on the political and internal achievements, whereas it explains wars by the spirit of adventure. No figure has served more than George Washington to illustrate for liberals the merits and the faults of Napoleon. Chateaubriand, who inaugurated, along with Mme de Staël, this type of interpretation, wrote two very different parallels between Bonaparte and Washington, the first in 1822, just after the emperor's death, and the second in his *Mémoires d'outre-tombe* (published 1848–1850).[46] The first denounces the unscrupulous adventurer who sacrificed France to his ambitions, while the second develops an interpretation already defended by Benjamin Constant in *De l'esprit de conquête et de l'usurpation*: if Napoleon ended up as an adventurer, he had earlier been a man who emerged to meet an urgent need, in short, a French Washington, with genius to boot. At that time, between 1800 and 1804, he had wanted, like Washington, what he had to want, in accord with the interests and needs of his time. The French people had given him a mandate and even "elected" him, through their consent to 18 Brumaire, and he had "established a regular, powerful government, a legal code that was adopted in various countries, and a strong, active, intelligent administration"; he had also "restored order amid chaos and compelled furious demagogues to serve under him."[47] Chateaubriand recognized that Bonaparte was great because of his work, a work that was to survive him, and still more because of the personal qualities that allowed him to succeed where no one had been able to succeed before him, finding in his genius the support that he did not find in either laws or traditions. But if Bonaparte's genius permitted him to be for a time the representative of the French people's needs, it also enabled him to rapidly free himself from any kind of dependence with regard to the interests of his time, putting his period in the service of his desires after having put himself in the service of his period's interests. To do so, he did not have to resort to violence. Bonaparte had as his auxiliary the half-voluntary, half-forced consent of the French to their servitude. To put an end to the Revolution, or at least to suspend its course, a single man had to take the place of all, to make, as Mme de Staël put it, "the human race anonymous."[48] To that extent, neither Chateaubriand nor Mme de Staël fell into the trap that has caught so many liberals, beginning with Benjamin Constant, who, while approving the results, wish they had been obtained by means to which they themselves could subscribe. No, Chateaubriand replies, the Consulate was not solely a period of consolidation and construction—of the modern state—but a period in which society was "molded for passive obedience" and for "bastardized characters," and that thus paved the way for the adventurer.[49] From that time on, Napoleon is already visible behind Bonaparte. But for all that, the Napoleonic epic is not, as Taine believed, a pure manifestation of Napoleon's ego. The part played by adventure in Napoleon's career is not an effect without a cause. Napoleon, even as he escaped any dependency on the interests of French society, was still a representative of the latter, but this time he was the representative of French passions, and of the collective passion in which nineteenth-century liberals saw a national curse: the indifference to liberty, the consent to despotism provided that equality was flattered and the sacrifice of liberty compensated by grandeur.

The choice to publish this work in two volumes does not mean, any more than the decision to locate the dividing point in 1802, that I adhere to the liberal interpretation.

Contrary to an idea often expressed on the basis of the example of Stendhal's *Vie de Napoléon*, the biographer cannot advance at the same pace as the emperor, that is, as rapidly. In this respect, biography is a very different and more laborious exercise, because any life—even that of Napoleon, for whom to live was to act—has its dull and monotonous tracts. "In any strategic critique," Clausewitz said, "what matters most is to adopt exactly the actors' point of view."[50] How can we "know the circumstances in which [they] found themselves" without exploring some details or taking a few detours? If Napoleon can in many respects be considered the incarnation of the figure of the "great man" that is so central in Western political history, then we have to understand what it was in his personality that predisposed him to play this role; we have to describe the exceptional circumstances that allowed him to do so; we have to gauge the consent of public opinion without which he could not have done it; we have to identify the qualities—the understanding of the situation, the lucidity and audacity—that permitted him to take advantage of circumstances that in no way guaranteed his success; and finally, we have to determine the decisive moment, the one that can, as Borges said, sum up "every destiny, no matter how long and complicated it might be": "The [moment] in which the man knows once and for all who he is."[51]

I began work on this biography in 2004. François Furet had already urged me to write on Napoleon, suggesting that I devote a study to the episode of the Hundred Days, in which so many questions left unanswered at the end of the Revolution returned to the foreground. I therefore began my research on Napoleon from the end, though I did not complete this project. Perhaps I would not have persisted had not Georges Liébert asked me, shortly afterward, to write a biography of Napoleon. Without him, this *Bonaparte* would never have appeared. It is his name and that of François Furet that I take pleasure in putting at the threshold of this work that owes so much to them.

PART ONE
Napoleon and Corsica
1769–1793

ONE

An Italian Family in Corsica

*N*apoleon's family origins have long been a subject of debate. We now know that his ancestors came from Sarzana.[1] Since the thirteenth century the Buonapartes had been one of the leading families of this city between Tuscany and Liguria; they had produced administrators, governors, and ambassadors. In the fifteenth century, Sarzana was annexed by the Republic of Genoa. It was at that point—perhaps because life had become more difficult under the Genoese—that a Buonaparte decided to settle in Corsica. The Most Serene Republic had no plans to colonize the island, but it needed resident officials and magistrates, so it granted privileges to those of its citizens who agreed to move there. In 1483 a certain Giovanni Buonaparte went to Corsica, and his son Francesco, nicknamed "the moor of Sarzana," settled there permanently in 1529.

From Sarzana to Ajaccio

The date of the Buonapartes' arrival in Corsica has aroused no less debate than their origins. The nineteenth-century historian Hippolyte Taine suggested 1529, a date that we now know to be correct. Connecting this date with that of 1530, when on losing their independence to Charles V the republics of medieval Italy witnessed the end of "the great exploits of political adventures and successful usurpations," Taine saw Corsica as the key to the part of Napoleon that was foreign to his time: "Just at the time when the energy and ambition, the vigorous and free sap of the Middle Ages begins to run down and then dry up in the shriveled trunk, a small detached branch takes root in an island, not less Italian but almost barbarous, amidst institutions, customs, and passions belonging to the primitive medieval epoch, and in a social atmosphere sufficiently rude for the maintenance of all its vigor and harshness."[2]

Corsica. © 2015 The President and Fellows of Harvard College

For Taine, Napoleon was "a great survivor of the fifteenth century," the Buonapartes having emigrated to the rustic, untamed Italy that was Corsica, just when the mainland was entering a long slumber. Thus, through the generations of Buonapartes and of ancestors on his mother's side, the Ramolinos,[3] the spirit of the Middle Ages was supposed to have survived down to the century of the Enlightenment, finally to be reincarnated in Napoleon. In reality, the Buonapartes did not leave Sarzana for a wild country that had escaped the civilization of the mainland. The Corsica where they settled was not at all that of mountains and hereditary vendettas, but rather that of cities founded by the successive occupiers of the island, first Pisan and then Genoese. These presidios, as they were called, were small Italian enclaves established at intervals along the coast of the island. They were still Italy, a colonial Italy where the descendants of the first immigrants remained proud of their origins and did not want to be confused with the natives. But does that mean that we must conclude that in Corsica two distinct groups, one Italian, the other Corsican, lived alongside one another, very unequally divided between the cities on the coasts and the villages in the mountains? This distinction is not a myth, but it has to be qualified, because in Corsica things were in reality diverse. It probably holds true for Bonifacio, a city that long remained off-limits to native Corsicans, but it applies less well to the population of a Genoese colony like Ajaccio, whose people were entirely of Ligurian origin and soon mixed with Corsicans from the interior.

The Corsica of the presidios, at least in Ajaccio, was not an anti-Corsica but a different Corsica: different, to be sure, from that of the communities of the interior, but in no case a purely Ligurian bastion. If there was a sharp distinction, it was between those who lived in the city and those who lived in the country rather than between Italians and natives. It is true that the descendants of the Italian colonists were considered "foreigners" by indigenous Corsicans and were proud and even jealous of their continental origins. But nothing in fact connected them with the villages they considered the "homeland"—the land they had left to take up residence in Corsican cities. They may have presented themselves as continental out of a desire for honor and distinction, but this does not prove that they really were as foreign as Corsicans said, or as they themselves often imagined. In eighteenth-century Corsica, the descendants of the Genoese colonists were not the equivalents of twentieth-century French colonists in the

Maghreb. We might even say that they grew all the more attached to their Italian origins as they moved further and further away from them, becoming ever more deeply integrated into Corsican society through marriages. This was as true of the Buonapartes as of anyone else: related to the Genoese and Tuscan nobilities by virtue of titles that were, to tell the truth, suspect.[4] They were also relatives, by marriage and by birth, of the Pietrasantas, Costas, Paraviccinis, and Bonellis, all Corsican families from the interior. "I am more of an Italian, or a Tuscan, than a Corsican,"[5] Napoleon was to say; in fact, he could have said, as Paul Valéry did concerning his own origins, that he was the product of a "Corsican-Italian mixture."[6]

A Family of Notables

Travelers agreed unanimously that of all the colonies founded by the Genoese, Ajaccio was the most beautiful: "Three streets fanning out and intersected by a fourth, with houses of varying heights lined up one after another that one sees from afar jutting up among the bell towers, a tranquil harbor where a few sailboats lie quietly at anchor. Along the shore, beyond the ramparts, there is the suburb, . . . and all around, the countryside crowned with olive trees, with its vineyards and geometrical gardens."[7] Within Ajaccio's walls lived a whole group of common people consisting of craftsmen and fishermen, not to mention a swarm of ecclesiastics; higher up, there was a small group of bourgeois who eked out a living from the exercise of military or administrative offices on behalf of the Most Serene Republic. In the little society of Ajaccio—which counted hardly more than 4,000 inhabitants at the end of the eighteenth century—the Buonapartes occupied an honorable and occasionally underestimated position. The life they led is in fact too often judged by reference to the precarious economic situation in which they found themselves after the death of Charles Buonaparte in 1785. Even if they were hard up at that time, they had seen better days. We know next to nothing about how well off they were, but when Charles and Letizia married in 1764, their combined dowries amounted to almost 14,000 livres, and in 1775 the couple owned three town houses, lands, a mill, and a large herd of livestock.[8] These provided them with an average annual revenue of more than

7,000 livres, though Napoleon said that it amounted to 12,000 rather than 7,000.[9] It matters little whether their annual revenue was 7,000 or 12,000 livres if we consider that at that time a worker's salary hardly exceeded 1,000 livres per annum. In a society that was characterized by inequalities of wealth but in which the poor may have been a little less poor than on the continent, and the rich much less rich, the Buonapartes could at least maintain a respectable way of life, even if they were not part of the very closed world of the great landowners. In a country where the income of the most opulent rarely exceeded 20,000 livres, someone who had 7,000 was rich. It is true that this represented "wealth" only in comparison with the generally low standard of life prevailing on the island, and that the way of life enjoyed even by the most well-off remained modest and without luxury or ostentation. The fact that trade took place largely by barter attenuated the disparities in wealth. Napoleon was to recall, "In my family the main thing was to avoid spending money. Money was spent only on absolutely necessary objects such as clothes, furniture, etc., and not on food, except for coffee, sugar, rice, and other items that did not come from Corsica. Otherwise, everything was provided by the land. . . . What mattered was not spending money. Money was extremely rare. Paying for something in cash was a major event."[10]

Napoleon connected this past affluence with his ancestors' thriftiness and with a system of inheritance that favored keeping estates intact.[11] In addition, there was the Buonapartes' concern to make advantageous marriages. Their claim to belong to the class of notables was based not only on their possessions but also on their connections through marriage in a country where power was measured less by the bride's dowry than by the number of relatives who could be called upon in the event of difficulty. Their cousins in Bocognano, a mountain village on the road to Corte whose inhabitants were said to be particularly rough and larcenous, and those on Letizia's side, who lived in Bastelica, were as important as flocks and lands. "They were terrible people, these relatives, a great power on the island."[12] It was not nothing to be able, like the Buonapartes, to flaunt a cortege of some thirty cousins. Wealth was shown above all by the political influence and power that enabled a family to reach the top. Competition was ferocious; it required major investments, even if, when one succeeded, new opportunities to feather one's nest presented themselves. Land and relatives conferred power, and power in turn increased wealth. Whoever was master of the community's Council of Elders was master of the public wealth, and used it to benefit his own people, his relatives, friends, in-laws, and clients.

From Geronimo at the end of the sixteenth century to Giuseppe Maria, Napoleon's grandfather who died in 1763, each generation of Buonapartes had had a representative among the "Noble Elders" who administered the city. Until Napoleon's father reduced the family's wealth almost to nothing, the Buonapartes had been one of the first families in Ajaccio by their possessions, prestige, and influence. Their prestige probably did not extend far beyond the area around Ajaccio, which helps us understand why Napoleon and his brothers played only a secondary role during the first years of the Revolution. The family revenue having collapsed in the course of a few years, they no longer had the means indispensable for political action—the means that had allowed their ancestors to occupy an enviable position in local society.[13]

Corsica, a Simple "Geographical Term"

Until the period of Corsica's independence (1755–1769), the Buonapartes, like other notables in Ajaccio, had remained loyal to the Republic of Genoa, and then to the king of France after he landed his troops on the island to support his Genoese ally. Some historians see this as opportunism, or even "collaboration," accusing the notables of the presidios of having used the authority conferred on them by their fellow citizens to serve their own interests and those of the occupying power. However, it is far from clear that elected officials sought only to promote the interests of their respective clans. In any case, to accuse the members of this ruling elite of opportunism is to forget that legally they were citizens not of *Corsica* but rather of *Genoa*; in serving the doge they were serving their country, and they similarly remained loyal when they pledged allegiance to the king of France when the latter intervened at the request of the Genoese government. It is also to exaggerate the independence of Corsica's municipal institutions from the Genoese government: they were just one of the instruments through which the Republic exercised an—entirely relative—control over the island. Moreover, the local authorities showed their loyalty to Genoa as much through their status as through their self-interest: they owed their privileges and their influence to the government in Genoa, so their offices obliged them to represent that government more than the people of the island. Above all the accusation of collaboration presupposes the existence of a Corsican identity that was, in fact, foreign to the inhabitants of the presidios: even if they exaggerated their continental connections, they felt themselves to be less close to Corsica, whose sons they had become, than to Italy, where they sent their children to be educated.

The accusation of "betrayal" is ultimately based on a view of Corsican history that was shaped later on, after the French conquest of the island in 1769, and that is very different from the Corsica for which the young Napoleon made himself the spokesman in his *Letters on Corsica*: "The history of Corsica," he wrote, "is merely a perpetual struggle between a small people that wants to be free and its neighbors that want to oppress it."[14] In this unfinished work, Napoleon traced the heroic history of the Corsican people unified behind its "national" heroes in order to show how it had forged its collective identity in the constantly renewed struggle between the "earthenware pot and the iron pot."[15] Reacting against this orthodox version of Corsican history created by Enlightenment writers and subsequently cultivated by others, Franco Venturi once wrote that Corsica was distinguished, on the contrary, by the absence of a history of its own to which it could refer to find the elements of a common identity.[16] Let us be clear: nothing is more erroneous than the image of a Corsica untouched by the tumults of history, whose vicissitudes it certainly suffered. From the Romans to the Vandals, from the Saracens to the Holy See, from the Pisans to the Aragonese, from the Genoese to the French, all Europe marched through the island. How could it have been otherwise? As Seneca noted, the proximity of Italy made Corsica a tempting prey, while its poverty made it an easy one. Corsica could not belong to itself; it was a strategic stake in the struggle among European powers. To those who frowned and said that the conquest of that "useless pile of rocks" would be onerous for France, the partisans of conquest in 1768 replied that the possession of Corsica would enable France to become the dominant power in the Mediterranean region.[17] But it would be a mistake to suppose that Corsica had always been the victim of the "great game" played by European states. Its history is no doubt unfortunate; yet it is not a history of subjection in which Corsicans, attacked by superior forces, were utterly deprived of control over their own destiny. They helped shape that destiny, and even the legend created by the Enlightenment could not conceal this aspect of the matter. Was not even Voltaire, after recalling how the Corsicans had been invaded, sold, and ceded by the dominant powers, obliged to conclude that the Corsicans had always been to blame for their own subjugation?[18] Didn't Sinucello fight the Genoese on behalf of the Pisans, to whom he was indebted? Wasn't Vincentello d'Istria the liegeman of the king of Aragon? And two centuries after Genoa took legal possession of Corsica (in 1358), wasn't it Sampiero Corso who brought in the French to help liberate the island? Should this constant in the island's history be attributed to the Corsicans' desire to involve powerful and prestigious partners in their destiny, because they were aware that they could not exist independently?[19] This hypothesis might make us smile if we think about what kind of partnership such a poor island could have had with the Republic of Genoa at the height of its splendor, or with the kingdom of France: When in 1768 Matteo Buttafoco, who was negotiating with the French government on Paoli's behalf, asked Choiseul to sign a treaty of alliance and trade with Corsica, the French minister bluntly replied that "the Corsicans were not yet ready to deal with France on such a footing."[20] However, what the great powers' ministers considered a manifestation of inappropriate presumption had always underlain the Corsicans' behavior toward the outside world. But from the conqueror's point of view, it was simply a matter of obtaining the island's subjection in exchange for the formal recognition of a few rights and privileges. The agreement they signed with the Corsicans was at best an agreement between a suzerain and a vassal. The islanders' disappointment was necessarily proportional to their illusions. Because they did not have the power to set conditions, all they could do—and they did not fail to do it—was to throw off the present yoke and exchange it for another; they could change their master, but they could not live without one. The period of "revolutions" in Corsica—which began with the peasant uprising of 1729, ran through Pasquale Paoli's leadership, and ended with the French conquest that ousted him in 1769—is no exception. Like his predecessors, Paoli did not believe that Corsica would someday be independent, and although he proclaimed its sovereignty, he long remained uncertain whether to accept the "protection" of France or that of England.

Moreover, it was never "Corsica" or "the Corsicans" that called on this or that power for help; that would have supposed the existence of a people that was conscious of having common interests. The island had for ages been divided between parties devoted to the interests of various foreign powers, and that is the main reason Corsica had no history of its own, as Venturi suggested. The history of Corsica was the history of the competition between local factions acting as proxies for European states. There was no "Corsican" party, no "national" party, even in Paoli's time, but only a Genoese party, a French party, a Roman party, a Spanish party, a Venetian party, an English party, and even a party committed to the Order of the Knights of Malta. Corsican history was Italian, French, Spanish, and English; it was not Corsican. When the Corsicans looked back on their past, they could find no unity in the succession of invasions and revolts, conspiracies and betrayals, nor could they form a coherent idea of it. We might be surprised by the permanence and persistence of these divisions over centuries, and perhaps even more by the fact that the Corsicans never became aware of themselves as a nation. After all, the burden of foreign occupation—particularly by Genoa—had always been rather easy to bear. If Corsica had no history of its own, even though its Genoese master left it largely free to act, that is because it did not exist. It might have been said, as Metternich said of an eighteenth-century Italy, doomed to impotence by its political fragmentation, that it was only a "geographical term."[21] Nothing more.

The Law of Blood

To explain this situation, most historians of Corsica emphasize its internal divisions and its "tumultuous anarchy."[22] But a little more wisdom or a sense of the common interest would not have sufficed to put an end to these divisions. They were inherent in the island's geography, which has been described as an "aggregation of mountains crisscrossed by valleys of varying depths" in which communities lived in near-isolation and autarky, all the more alien to one another because routes of communication were few or nonexistent.[23] Here foreign domination was distant, its laws unknown or in any case ignored. Corsica had its masters, but it lived separately, under an imperious, immemorial, permanent law: that of blood, which dictates duties and obligations not only to those who dwell under the same roof but to all those—the "kin"—who see themselves as descendants of the same ancestor. Here there is no notion of the individual. Thus, in Paoli's view Napoleon, Joseph, and Lucien formed the un-differentiated set of the "sons of Charles," situated in a lineage whose merits and faults they accepted as their own. In this society in which nothing was ever forgotten, where an individual's offense contaminated his relatives, his allies, his clients, and his descendants, there was no place for any kind of autonomy. It was impossible to be oneself in a world that was closed and without exit, where endogamy exaggerated connections by blood, and where even generations did not pass away. Solidarity exists not only among the living but extends even to the dead.[24]

Along with geographical isolation, poverty, ignorance, and the absence of cultivated elites, family structures were among the most prominent obstacles preventing the formation of a national, or even simply a collective, identity. How could the idea of a community of interests and destiny be formed in a society in which "the idea of family is superior to any other social or governmental conception," in which the head of the family was seen as an absolute sovereign, in which solidarity with relatives and allies is complete and has priority over any kind of moral considerations, in which inexpiable hatreds doom whole clans to live in a combat-ready state "where the houses were crenellated like fortresses" and to emerge from their houses only in armed groups?[25] More than a few historians of Corsica refuse to mention realities—the law of silence or vendettas—that they consider to be part of the folklore popularized by Romanticism. While it is true that the gradual integration of Corsica into France that began in 1769 slowly reduced the intensity of the violence, though in a proportion that remained entirely relative, the "folklore" found in Prosper Mérimée's *Colomba* or *Mateo Falcone*, the folklore of the nineteenth century, was the hard reality of earlier centuries. Vendettas were responsible for the deaths of almost 29,000 people between 1683 and 1715, or more than 900 per year in a total population of a little over 100,000 inhabitants. It is true that the way in which Genoa dispensed justice on the island hardly helped pacify social conflicts, but the arbitrariness of the judgments handed down was the price to be paid for the impossibility of gathering testimony for the prosecution in a country where no one, not even the victims, would testify against the perpetrator. In the Corsica of old, people preferred misfortune to the dishonor implied by obedience to the laws that demanded that the guilty be handed over to the authorities. Napoleon himself was proud of this law of silence that forbade a Corsican to give up a cousin, no matter what his crime. "A Corsican cannot imagine abandoning his cousin," he said. "He thinks it sufficient to say: 'But he's my cousin. How can you expect me to abandon him?'"[26] Thus the Buonapartes, having chosen France, nonetheless helped their cousin Zampaglino, who had gone underground after the French conquest and attacked any Frenchman unfortunate enough to cross his path. As proud as Napoleon was of this "honorable outlaw," he nonetheless conceded that protecting the guilty in the name of ties of blood was incompatible with "a well-organized country" or with any notion of a fatherland, a state, or the impartiality of law.[27]

In its social structures, mentalities, or manners, Corsica in the old days was in no way unusual. We find much the same on other Mediterranean islands, such as Sardinia or Sicily, and even on the continent, in regions like Basilicate, which were still isolated and deprived at the beginning of the twentieth century and where Carlo Levi was relegated by Mussolini's regime, or on the Albanian plateaus where Ismail Kadare situates the vendetta he recounts in *Broken April*. These lines by Carlo Levi could have been written about the Corsica of yesteryear:

> Christ never came this far, nor did time, nor the individual soul, nor hope, nor the relation of cause to effect, nor reason nor history. Christ never came, just as the Romans never came, content to garrison the highways without penetrating the mountains and forests, nor the Greeks, who flourished beside the Gulf of Taranto. None of the pioneers of Western civilization brought here his sense of the passage of time, his deification of the State or that ceaseless activity which feeds upon itself. No one has come to this land except as an enemy, a conqueror, or a visitor devoid of understanding. The seasons pass today over the toil of the peasants, just as they did three thousand years before Christ; no message, human or divine, has reached this stubborn poverty. . . . But to this shadowy land, that knows neither sin nor redemption from

sin, where evil is not moral but is only the pain residing forever in earthly things, Christ did not come.[28]

The Paradoxes of the Age of Enlightenment

However, it seems to have been this people, whose culture and values prevented it from having any collective historical existence, that had the privilege of announcing the "age of revolutions" in the eighteenth century. Thus Corsica, fulfilling Rousseau's prophecy, "astonished the world." The idea grew that Corsica, rising up against domination by Genoa in 1729, had declared before all the world the sovereignty of the people, recognized the equality of all before the law, consecrated individual rights, and even instituted the separation of powers. Paoli achieved such fame that contemporary Pennsylvanians named a town in his honor, and when the father of the *patria* returned to his island in 1790 after twenty-two years in exile in London, the revolutionaries celebrated him as a precursor of their own revolution.

Myths die hard. An example of this is the myth according to which the successive revolutions on the island, from the peasant uprising of 1729 to Paoli's government (1755–1769), profoundly transformed Corsicans, to the point of replacing in their hearts the old feeling for the *patria* with that for the *nation*, "in the modern, democratic sense of the term."[29] To be sure, this interpretation of Corsican history in the eighteenth century arouses, even among those most inclined to support it, if not doubts, then at least questions: "What strikes the modern reader is the paradox," one of them writes, "between, on the one hand, Corsica's landscape and people, physical vitality and raw primitivity, and, on the other, her apparent promise as an advanced social experiment."[30] If we assume that the struggles of the eighteenth century had inculcated the principles of modern politics into Corsicans, then the history of the island would have repeated itself in a curious way at the time of the French Revolution, which other historians, basing themselves on evidence just as tenuous, present as the origin of precisely the same feelings.[31] In fact, the situation in revolutionary Corsica in no way differed from that of earlier times, and was just as incompatible with the ideas of law, citizenship, public interest, and a fortiori the nation.[32] In Corsica there was no more a national feeling in the French sense after 1789 than there had been before 1789, including during the time of Paoli's "generalship."

Nonetheless, one cannot say that nothing happened in Corsica in the eighteenth century. The turmoil it underwent starting in 1729 took on a particular character that turned a peasant uprising into a revolution. Genoa's inability to restore order played a role in this, as did the great powers' subsequent nonintervention, which rendered inoperative Corsica's old way of exchanging one master for another. In the course of the 1730s, appeals were made to the usual actors in Corsican history, all of whom failed to respond. However, the German emperor (1731–1733) and then France (1738–1741 and 1748–1753) intervened militarily to support the rights of the faltering Republic of Genoa. The conjunction of Genoa's impotence with international abstention had an unexpected consequence: around 1735 Corsica became de facto independent, because its Genoese masters now controlled only their maritime strongholds. The interior of the island was no longer governed by any external authority.

It is clear that between 1731 and 1735 unrest escalated. The peasant uprising of 1729 became an insurrection whose goal was to drive out the Genoese. The grievances presented in 1731, which demanded the restoration of the "traditional constitution of Corsica" (supposedly established by mutual consent in the fourteenth century), were replaced by a discourse advocating a definitive break with Genoa. The myth of Corsica's "ancient constitution" evaporated, with the result that the revolution could no longer take the form of a restoration of the old order, but could only take that of a new foundation with no real roots in the past. Thus eighteenth-century Corsica was forced to enter history and the contemporary world by the impossibility of finding the slightest vestige of a "natural" political order—in other words, by discovering its own lack of a history. An assembly that gathered at Corte in January 1735 took the plunge by giving Corsica its first "constitution," even if its promoters simultaneously tried to convince Spain to take over from Genoa. It matters little that this "constitution" never went into force. As a result of the disappearance of any external domination, an idea had been born: the idea that even if they had to find new protectors, the people of Corsica needed to provide themselves with institutions and leaders of their own in order to become, no longer a subject people, but a *peuple conventionné*, one that put itself contractually under the supervision of a state on the condition that it be accorded broad autonomy.

However, there is no reason to think that this project was endorsed by Corsicans in general. If there is one term that can describe the quarter of a century separating the revolt of 1729–1730 from Paoli's accession to power in 1755, it is surely "anarchy." Against the background of the foreign interventions and European wars whose repercussions battered Corsica, violence, private wars, and factional struggles rose to unprecedented levels. The Corsican "governments" of this period were no more than a juxtaposition of factions and clans whose murderous animosity toward one another was as intense as their common hatred of the Genoese occupier.

Legend claims that the Corsicans, weary of so much violence, then put power in the hands of Pasquale Paoli, thereby following the example of the communes of medieval Italy that named a *podestà* when their dissensions threatened them with total ruin. That is the meaning of the resolution adopted by the *consulte* in Casabianca on July 15, 1755, raising Paoli to the rank of "capo generale."[33] Seeking to consolidate "a common union," it declared that "the most proper and effectual means" of doing so was "the electing of one oeconomical, political, and general chief, of enlightened faculties, to command over this kingdom with full power."[34] The reality was somewhat different. In 1751, Corsica in rebellion had succeeded in appointing, in the person of Gaffori, a single leader whose nomination put an end to the system of collegial command. The Genoese, fearing Gaffori, had him assassinated in 1753. Corsica returned to anarchy and once again fell under the authority of a divided triumvirate. Paoli's return in April 1755, far from responding to general desire for peace, took place in the context of struggles between clans fighting for supremacy. Clemente Paoli arranged his brother's return to prevent Mario-Emmanuele Matra, the brother-in-law of Gaffori, from taking up Gaffori's legacy. Pasquale Paoli was so little expected to be the right man for the times that the *consulte* that had been immediately assembled to install him in office refused to grant him the title "general," so that he was forced to wait three months until another *consulte*, which met at Casabianca, conferred the desired title on him. But this *consulte's* legitimacy was doubtful, because only sixteen of the island's sixty-six *pieves* (cantons) had sent delegates to it. Paoli had hardly taken power before Matra called together another *con-*

sulte and obtained for himself the same title. Although Matra was killed in March 1757, the civil war lasted almost ten years, opposing Paoli to the clans that were jealous of his influence, to the feudal vassals who remained loyal to Genoa, and to the representatives of the pro-French party. Not until 1764 did Paoli become truly master of the island.

We could say about Paoli's "generalship" what Bonaparte was later to say about his proconsulate in Italy in 1796–1797: that the real sources of his power— "great activity and promptness in . . . punishing those who declared themselves our enemies"—were very different from what was to be found in the "romances" (newspapers and proclamations) that celebrated the people's love and the gentleness of their governors.[35] Similarly, the constitution that Paoli had promulgated in November 1755, which is often praised as having established "the first democracy of the modern era,"[36] was the "romance" that allowed him gradually to impose his authority by other means whose effectiveness redeemed their deviation from the principles of democracy and justice. Paoli's "dictatorship" was based primarily on an undeniable charisma that allowed him to overcome many obstacles, and on the exceptional means he employed. His rule depended on both respect and fear; as Boswell put it, he exercised a "despotism founded, contrary to the principles of Montesquieu, on the affection of love."[37] The reality of Paoli's regime has to be assessed less in the light of the constitutional principles that were supposed to have governed the island since 1755 than in that of Corsica's poverty and rural nature. The scarcity of resources explains many of the not strictly "democratic" aspects of his government, such as the widespread use of pardons and capital punishment, both of which spared the cost of maintaining prisoners. It also gave rise to the itinerant nature of the new state whose capital, Corte, was not able to support even a small bureaucracy, the "virtue" Paoli had made his supreme ideal because it was a cheap way of transforming a dreary reality into a positive value, and the social egalitarianism that was one of the axes of his politics because equality, even though it was relative, was already one of the characteristics of the island's society.[38] In the same way, the persistence of Paoli's dictatorship beyond the circumstances that had justified it was implicit in the nature of a power that was based more on the bonds of personal loyalty between the leader and the island's communities than on a legally defined and institutionalized superiority.

There was, of course, a constitution, whose democratic character cannot be denied, even if it has often been exaggerated. Drawn up in 1755, this constitution's goal was to confine force within the limits of the law by basing authority on common consent. In short, all authority came from the assembly representing the sovereign people, but Paoli was given full power on the condition that he justify his actions to the assembly every year and obtain its approval. It will be noted that the consolidation of Paoli's political power on the island around 1764 also was the signal for a series of constitutional reforms that sought to further strengthen his legal authority. The constitution had, so to speak, caught up with reality: it resided in the person and the will of Paoli. Despite the infringements on the institutions set up in 1755, the latter cannot be seen as merely a screen to conceal that the regime, far from being the product of the sovereign people, was no more than "the confederation of its numerous tyrants," as Buonarotti was to say after breaking with Paoli.[39] After all, Paoli himself was, like Napoleon, of mixed Corsican and Italian descent, not by blood but by upbringing. He was fourteen years old when he followed his father into exile in Naples in 1739, and there he had encountered the Italy of the Enlightenment. And he certainly became a man of the Enlightenment, though only in part. More in love with glory than with liberty, he was in certain respects a man less of the eighteenth century and the Enlightenment than of the seventeenth century and civic humanism, closer to Cromwell than to George Washington. It has been said that he was not very religious, but even though he fought the Church of Corsica because he suspected it of colluding with the Genoese enemy, even in his old age he spent much of his time in devotions. These contradictions make Paoli a character more fascinating than the pious legend created by the Enlightenment, according to which he was a philosopher struggling to regenerate a backward country. It is certainly true that he sought to make Corsica a modern nation. From this point of view the praise showered on him by the French revolutionaries of 1790 was legitimate. Like them, in fact, he had undertaken to bring the people together under a single law. He wanted to free Corsica from its immemorial divisions, to wrench it out of its violence and poverty, to develop it through participation, economic progress, and education to give it the political existence that would permit it to impose the indispensable guarantees of a free and worthy life on the partner, the great power, that its situation would not allow it to do without.

From Genoa to France

By prolonging his dictatorship, Paoli was betraying neither his ideals nor the goals he had set for himself, because the relative cessation of internal conflicts left unresolved the most important issue: that of relations between Corsica and foreign powers. Paoli had kept it in sight all along. Although he could not imagine signing an agreement with Genoa, which had been the "enemy" throughout his life, he had begun negotiations with London as soon as he took power.[40] But England had not responded to his overtures with the eagerness he had hoped for. Having emerged from the Seven Years' War (1756–1763) weakened, though victorious, it neither wanted nor could afford the risk of a confrontation with France. While the British remained quiescent, the French were active. Naturally, when the French-Genoese treaty of August 6, 1764, authorized French troops to land on the island to occupy the maritime strongholds for another four years, it was officially said to be so that France could enforce respect for Genoese sovereignty. But on reestablishing itself in the presidios, France was in a sense returning home. Its troops had already occupied the presidios from 1738 to 1741, from 1748 to 1753, and from 1756 to 1760. In Genoese Corsica, on which Paoli had never succeeded in imposing his authority, a powerful group supporting the king of France had arisen. Even if French policy with regard to Corsica was evolving in relation to the international situation, there had long been a plan for the conquest of the island. This plan involved the creation of a pro-French party that was supposed to get Genoa to cede sovereignty over the island to France, voluntarily and freely.[41] This policy had reached its apex in the early 1750s, when the Marquis of Cursay, who had been assigned to administer the cities occupied by the king's soldiers, used his talents to "make the name of France likable."[42] France's success among the inhabitants of the presidios, and particularly their elites, was all the greater because France had much more to offer than Genoa did—titles, pensions, jobs, investments—and because this Corsica that had never felt Corsican had refused to support Paoli and was moving away from Genoa as Paoli's star paled. It was as if Genoese Corsica were up for grabs. It is true that not everyone supported the king of France's party. Many people, such as the Buonapartes and the Ramolinos, had remained loyal to Genoa, and a few of them had even declared their support for Paoli. But in addition to the political choices made, the recurrent presence of the French in the port cities had accustomed their populations to French ideas, fashions, and customs. Boswell suggested this when he wrote that the residents of Ajaccio were "the genteelest people in the island, having had a good deal of intercourse with the French."[43] Paoli himself was aware of this; he did not care for the young people from Ajaccio or Bastia who came to see him, saying about them, "They have curled hair and smell of perfumes from the continent."[44] These little Genoese colonies had gradually become French colonies.

The British defection helped make France the necessary interlocutor, and in 1764 Paoli entered into negotiations with Choiseul. It was just at that point that the notables in the presidios began to rally to his side in large numbers. There were several reasons for this late-coming support. On the one hand, Paoli had finally subdued his enemies in the interior of the island, imposed his rule on the *pieves* in the south, which had long remained restive, and signed an agreement with the Roman Curia. On the other hand, the Genoese presence in Corsica seemed doomed, whereas the opening of negotiations between the general and the French, and the good relations he maintained with the Count of Marbeuf, the commander of the French occupying troops, suggested that an agreement would be signed that would put under French guardianship the Corsica Paoli governed. Paoli seemed to be firmly established in power, perhaps for a long time, and anyone who sought to play a role in the Corsica to come had to win his favor. Paoli and France were the future, Genoa the past.

Giuseppe Buonaparte died on December 13, 1763, having remained loyal to Genoa, and his son Carlo—Napoleon's father—set out for Corte in late 1765. One might suppose that Carlo had become a supporter of Paoli, like "everyone in his time who was not serving in the Royal-Corse regiment and had not had a taste of France."[45] But he was one of those who had "had a taste of France," and that was what he had in mind when he left for Corte. When he arrived in Paoli's capital, he was not able to see the general, but he sent to the Count of Marbeuf—his first contact with the man who was to make his fortune—a kind of report on the political situation on the island. The French commander politely declined his offers of service; to keep informed about what was happening in Corte, he had no need of Carlo. But in December 1765 Carlo was finally able to meet with Paoli and made himself part of the general's entourage. Did he perform some function for Paoli? Was he the "counselor" or "secretary" legend tells us he was? It seems that he was not, given that his name does not appear on any document from the period, except for a report filed by Marbeuf's police accusing him of spying for Paoli during his sojourns in Ajaccio.[46] The French governor did not want to employ him as an informer, so Carlo had entered Paoli's service.

In that same year, 1767, the negotiations between Paoli and Choiseul were nearing their end. In fact there had been no real negotiations, because neither side really heard what the other was saying. The general went so far as to demand that Corsica be an "entirely separate and independent state," whereas the minister asked him to recognize the purely nominal sovereignty of Genoa and to accept a French guarantee in exchange for a command or a title. On May 2, 1768, Choiseul broke off the talks. Two weeks later he signed in Versailles, with representatives of the Republic of Genoa, a treaty ceding Corsica to France. Both sides prepared for war. An impossible war, an absurd war, so immense was the disproportion between the forces involved. Buttafoco urged Paoli to accept the treaty of Versailles. In vain. Pommereul assures us that Paoli remained obstinate out of pride and vanity, preferring annihilation to any diminishment of his power, and that he was moreover convinced, wrongly, that the British would come to his aid or that the European powers, which opposed any increase in French power in the Mediterranean, would force Louis XV to withdraw his troops. Right to the end, Paoli probably pinned false hopes on international solidarity, but above all, as Voltaire said, "he was entrusted with the freedom of his country."[47] He preferred defeat to surrender, thinking perhaps that the court of public opinion that celebrated him as a hero would one day make it possible to take an entirely political revenge for the military defeat. Finally, if he made up his mind to go to war, whatever the cost, it was because he was convinced that France would sooner or later grow tired of its conquest and cede Corsica back to Genoa.[48]

On May 22, 1768, Paoli ordered mass conscription and issued a vibrant appeal to the youth of Corsica, promising that the young men would not sacrifice themselves in vain. Was Carlo the author of this proclamation? That is possible, but not certain. On the other hand, we know that he enlisted as a volunteer.

This was no doubt the period when he was closest to Paoli, following him everywhere and witnessing, like the general, battles in which neither of them participated directly. The war lasted almost a year. As long as French operations were directed rather halfheartedly by Marbeuf and Chauvelin, the Corsicans had a few successes, but after the Count of Vaux took command in April 1769, a few weeks sufficed to put down all resistance. On May 8, 1769, the Corsicans were defeated at Ponte Novo; on June 13, Paoli went into exile. The battle of Ponte Novo shows how little the efforts to make Corsica a nation had taken root on the island. According to legend, the Corsicans mounted a heroic resistance to the French on the bridge spanning the Golo, the attackers ceasing their fire only when all that was left of their opponents was a pile of bodies. The reality was worse: it is said that the mercenaries Paoli had brought in—Swiss, German, and Dalmatian—opened fire on the Corsican soldiers to force them to fight; that the latter lay down on the bridge to make the French think they were out of action; that several of Paoli's lieutenants ran off in a cowardly way; that Paoli himself proved inadequate to his task, prudently keeping his distance from the fighting and making no attempt to rally his routed troops.[49] The general's authority crumbled everywhere. What he thought he had united fell apart. The presidios, of course, hastened to pledge their loyalty to the king of France—Ajaccio did so on April 18, 1769, and the interior of the island soon followed suit: Rostino, Paoli's native village, submitted on May 9, and Corte, his capital, on May 21. Before, during, and after the lightning campaign of May 1769, a veritable decomposition of the Corsican "nation" took place. To this we must add the ferocious reprisals carried out by the French against rebellious villages, the declarations the French made assuring the Corsicans that they had not come to make them submit once again to the yoke of Genoa, and the "skepticism of many [of the Corsican leaders] with regard to a national independence that seemed to be purely utopian."[50]

The blood of the victims at Ponte Novo—500 or 20?—had hardly dried before a deputation of Paoli's officers went to declare their submission to the Count of Vaux. Carlo Buonaparte had the decency to wait until Paoli, abandoned by almost everyone, had boarded the ship that was to take him to Italy. Carlo accompanied the general to Porto-Vecchio and then, followed by his son Joseph and by his wife, who was pregnant with Napoleon, he returned to Ajaccio, where the Buonapartes and the Ramolinos had already pledged loyalty to the French. "I was at heart a good patriot and a Paolist as long as the national government lasted," Carlo said, "but that government no longer exists, we have become French, *evviva il re e suo governo!*"[51] Things had changed, and Paoli was far away. On July 37, 1769, two months after Ponte Novo, Carlo was invited to dine with the French intendant, Narbonne-Fitzlar. The "Corsican nation" was over.

TWO

A French Upbringing

*W*hen they returned to Ajaccio after Paoli's fall, Letizia and Carlo Buonaparte—who had changed his name to Charles when the French arrived—had been married for five years. Letizia had been fourteen or fifteen when her family forced upon her an eighteen-year-old husband whom she did not know and who, for his part, wanted nothing to do with her.[1] He had to be dragged, not to the church, because there was no religious ceremony, but to the notary, before whom the two families sealed their alliance. Almost immediately afterward, Charles abandoned his pregnant wife and went off to Italy, on the pretext of studying law, to have some fun before settling down. When he came back, his son was dead. Charles took off again. This time he went only as far as Corte. It was probably in late 1766, when Letizia was about to give birth to another child, that he asked her to join him in Corte and regularized their union by having a fraudulent marriage certificate included in the parish's marriage register.

What did the mercurial Charles and his shy wife share, apart from the pregnancies that produced twelve children in the course of twenty years of marriage? They began to be a real couple only in Corte. Joseph's birth on January 7, 1768, probably helped bring them together; he was a healthy child, and his parents showered affection on him. For Charles, the time for youthful indiscretions was over; he was now the head of a household, and its prosperity became his sole concern. Because in 1768 Paoli was still trying to maintain a kind of court life in Corte, Letizia acquired a certain ease, even if her shyness still prevented her from seeming graceful, despite her great beauty. She displayed the frivolity of a young woman of eighteen, being more preoccupied with her "court dress" than with the future of Corsica. After Charles and Letizia returned to Ajaccio and their second son—Napoleon—was born on August 15, 1769, ambition took the place of love, and the family divided its labors accordingly: Letizia ran the household while her husband focused on political intrigues and getting rich.

The Physiocrats in Corsica

Charles swore loyalty to the king of France and hurried off to Pisa to obtain a doctor's degree in law before returning to Corsica and joining the bar in Ajaccio. He had difficulties at first, but he was convinced that Corsica would derive many advantages from its union with France, and that France would not prove ungrateful to its most zealous servants. He was right. French domination was in fact to be very different from Genoese domination. And there was a reason for that: although Genoa was a considerable mercantile power, as a political power it was fragile and had neither the means nor the desire to make Corsica a part of Genoa; it had little interest in encouraging the formation on the island of an elite with which it would have to share honors and profits.[2] In contrast, France, as soon as it had eradicated in 1774 the last areas of resistance, started trying to make Corsica French. It is true that officially the king of France administered the island in the name of the Republic of Genoa, but in this respect the treaty signed on May 15, 1768, sought only to avoid wounding Genoese pride. No one was taken in by this arrangement; while maintaining the fiction of Genoese sovereignty over Corsica, the treaty of 1768 had ceded the island in perpetuity to France. Moreover, the French government immediately issued a series of regulations aiming at the complete and definitive integration of Corsica into the French kingdom. Thus the *Lettres patentes du roi concernant la soumission de la Corse* published on August 5, 1768, informed the Corsicans, in a language less ambiguous than that of the treaty of May 15, that having become "subjects" of the king of France they would henceforth have the same rights and duties as all his other subjects.[3]

This policy of integration was as much a threat as a promise, even if its goal was to free Corsica from a situation that was itself certainly not enviable. The French government wasted little time. It began by abrogating the laws and dissolving the institutions of the Paolist government, retaining only the traditional organization of the village communities along with their elected officials, and that of the *pieves* (cantons) along with their *podestàs*. Authority was concentrated in the hands of two royal commissioners, one of whom was the governor, in charge of military affairs, and the other the intendant, in charge of civil affairs. Corsica having obtained, like other provinces with marked particularities, such as Brittany or Languedoc, the status of *pays d'états*, an assembly with sixty-nine representatives of the three orders was created. A royal commissioner presided over this assembly, but it was limited to purely consultative functions. The judicial system was also reorganized into eleven royal jurisdictions—one of which was Ajaccio—and a Superior Council, an appellate court that was, not long afterward, to serve as a model for the "superior courts" that Chancellor Maupeou imposed on the kingdom as a whole in order to put an end to the parlements' privileges and opposition.

Once the government of the island had been set up, the French set about reforming Corsican society. The island became a laboratory in which the physiocratic ministers surrounding Louis XV and later his successor Louis XVI labored to advance the reforms they had found so difficult to apply on the continent. The royal officials imposed the Gallican doctrine of the king's independence from the pope on a Church of Corsica that was suspected of ultramontanism, and then they started in on community social structures. In 1770 they began a broad inquiry—the *"plan terrier"*—whose objective was not only "to establish order in property holdings and draw up a detailed description of the country" but also to define the main goals of a policy that would promote development.[4] The French authorities soon became convinced that the relative egalitarianism of Corsican society that had so much appealed to Enlightenment writers was preventing it from modernizing itself: "The most insurmountable obstacle that [Corsica] presents to civilization is perhaps the lack of a class of inhabitants who are not property owners," the Chevalier de Pommereul was to write.[5] Thus, it was thought, inequality had to be manufactured in this country where everyone or almost everyone was a property owner, and no one felt the need to work.[6] The community system became the chief target. The French administrators regulated the practices of transhumance, enclosure, hunting, and fishing, and reduced common lands to a minimum. Having demanded the presentation of written property titles—which did not exist—they confiscated numerous lands that were then added to the royal domain, from which vast "marquisates" were carved out for the benefit of about thirty beneficiaries.[7] The system was completed by the creation of a nobility—which did not, however, enjoy the fiscal privileges of its counterpart on the continent. "The French monarchy had understood that in order to balance the third estate and the clergy, they had to create and protect a class of men who would be attached to the government out of self-interest. Wouldn't inhabitants who had been given a few considerable advantages oppose any revolution that would strip them of their privileges?"[8] These measures—which were accompanied by others intended to conciliate the Corsicans, such as the establishment of a fiscal system more moderate than that on the continent, and that put heavy burdens on the royal treasury—were expected to transform Corsican society in depth. It would create not only an elite selected on the basis of merit and services rendered, but also "a class of men who were alien to landed property and would quickly devote themselves to manufacturing, commerce, and the arts, inaugurating the positive cycle of the modern way of producing wealth through enterprise."[9] No one in Corsica had ever seen a government impose the authority of law, try to transform mentalities and social structures, develop the country by building roads, and encourage the cultivation of fallow land and new crops. It was thus no surprise that in the end the king of France was no more successful in his enterprise than Paoli had been in his. Not only did many of these projects never get beyond the first stages or produce only minimal results, but Corsica remained, no matter what France did, "an ill-intentioned country."[10] It is true that the French and their friends on the island were far from being irreproachable. Nepotism, misappropriation of funds, and corruption were common, particularly because of the arrival in Corsica of dishonest officials whose ministers had found this an easy way of getting rid of them. As Albert Chuquet put it, they were the "dregs of the French nation," who landed in Corsica to pursue, first of all, their own interests.[11] But even making allowances for corruption, it was no easy task to transform what the Duke of Aiguillon called a "kingdom of poverty that is not cultivated and almost impossible to cultivate" into a showcase for enlightened policies.[12] Inertia overcame will. A handful of Corsicans seized the advantages offered by the monarchy, and when the monarchy collapsed, Corsica had hardly changed at all.

France's Liegeman

Charles Buonaparte could only be happy about the French conquest. The needy lawyer's career soon took off: in May 1771, he obtained a position as an associate judge in the royal jurisdiction of Ajaccio, and in September the Superior Council of Bastia declared the Buonapartes to have been noble for more than two centuries.[13] Charles soon took advantage of his elevation: elected the following year as representative of the nobility of Ajaccio in the Corsican assembly, he was immediately made a member of the council of the "Twelve Nobles" that performed the assembly's functions between sessions. On June 2, 1777, the assembly chose him as its representative in Versailles—a supreme but very expensive honor. In a few years he became one of the island's leading figures. A tireless petitioner who made his demands with an indomitable self-assurance and obstinacy, he furthered his own interests thanks to the reputation his official functions lent him, obtaining subsidies for the draining of *les salines,* the salt marshes near Ajaccio, the establishment and concession of a mulberry tree nursery, scholarships for his children, and the acquisition of an inheritance for which his family had been engaged in an interminable lawsuit.

Charles owed all this to the protection of the governor of the island, the Count of Marbeuf. Opinions have been divided about the count. In 1770 Marbeuf was fifty-eight years old; some writers assure us that he was witty, generous, and seductive, while others swear he was vain, hypocritical, and crude. He had a wife on the continent whom he concealed, and a mistress on Corsica—Mme de Varèse—whom he flaunted. He was hardworking, active, and authoritarian, showing consideration for neither the Corsicans nor his collaborators. Because he was constantly the target of cabals, he had to have his own party of supporters. Charles was one of this party's chief ornaments. The ties between the governor and the lawyer from Ajaccio had been formed in 1770 or 1771. From that time on, Charles became Marbeuf's liegeman. The count did everything he could to keep the flame of Charles's fidelity burning—he appointed him to offices, gave him bonuses, sponsored his children, and did not hesitate, any time there was an election, to ensure that he was the representative of the Ajaccio nobility. Marbeuf's protection was not undeserved: Charles was "witty, educated, eloquent"; a good-looking man, he impressed people. He was said to be "weak, frivolous, and luxurious," but he had no lack of flexibility, perseverance, or cleverness. Being aware of his own interests and knowing how to advance them, he was a valuable ally.

Did the favor the governor showered on the family have other motives? "Through his kindness, he had won the esteem and friendship of the patriots," Napoleon was to say, "and my father had positioned himself in the first rank of his partisans. It was to this that we owed his protection, and not, as some have falsely said, to his alleged love for my mother."[14] Although on this point most historians have agreed with Napoleon (who was in his heart of hearts convinced of the contrary), the objections made to the hypothesis of a love affair between Letizia and the governor are not very convincing: adultery, it is said, was impossible in a country where honor, and that of women in particular, was the supreme value, and affronts led to bloodshed. And it was no less impossible, they add, in a country where people lived, so to speak, on their doorsteps, with the result that it was difficult to hide anything. Thus the Buonaparte home is represented as open on all sides, with its gaggle of kids and swarms of aunts, servants, and gossiping women sitting on the sidewalk to enjoy the cool of the evening, watching and commenting on everyone's acts while they waited for the men to finish talking politics in the café, all the rest of their time being taken up by household tasks and childcare: the very image of Mediterranean life in an illustrated magazine. Where would Letizia have found the time to have a lover? How could she have had an affair without bringing ruin on the whole family? To make this image more plausible, Letizia has been presented as "Corsica personified."[15] The evidence? Several of her ancestors on her mother's side were from Sartène, the most Corsican part of Corsica. Letizia was a wife, it is said, not a mistress. She is depicted as austere, having experienced nothing but the yoke, having neither dreams nor feelings, intransigent regarding morals, superstitious and ignorant, obedient to her husband no matter what he said or did, seeking to make up for the latter's prodigality by an excessive sense of thrift. A Corsican Letizia, but also a Roman Letizia, simultaneously a matron and the "mother of the Gracchi," refusing to abandon Paoli after he had been betrayed by everyone, and replying to those who begged her not to persist in pursuing a hopeless path: "I won't go to a country that is the enemy of the fatherland; our general is still alive and all hope is not dead."[16]

All this is part of the legend. It was in 1770 that Letizia made the acquaintance of the Count of Marbeuf. No historian has denied the governor's assiduous attentions, the long periods he spent with her, the trips from Bastia to Ajaccio and back that he made more often than necessary for the sole purpose of seeing her. As early as the summer of 1771, they walked the *passegiata* before the eyes of all Ajaccio. Friendship, one-sided love, or a shared passion? Even the most determined defenders of Letizia's virtue have been forced to admit that it was neither her wit nor her conversation that attracted the governor and kept him at her side for so many years. Of wit she had none, and still less a gift for conversation. She spoke, Napoleon said, only her "Corsican gibberish." Marbeuf, for his part, was used to the manners and customs of the court, and anyone who knows the role played in that world by the art of conversation will understand that he could not have been dazzled by anything but the beauty of this woman who was forty years younger than he.

Although the supervision exercised by the rather difficult Mme de Varèse forced him to be relatively discreet, the affair became publicly known around 1775, when Marbeuf broke with his inconvenient mistress. Letizia resided at the governor's home and rode in his carriage, Charles following with the children in another carriage. Thus toward the end of 1778 a whole cortege, with Marbeuf and Letizia in the lead, accompanied Charles to Bastia, where he was to leave for the continent with Joseph and Napoleon. The latter, despite being only nine, was "extremely struck" by this scene.[17] When the ship had disappeared over the horizon, Letizia did not go back to Ajaccio; she went to Marbeuf's home in Bastia, and remained there for five months. The Buonapartes spent the end of each year and every summer in Cargèse, where Marbeuf owned a property. Everyone in Ajaccio was aware of this, and the memory of it did not fade away: a reference to the love affair between Letizia and the governor appeared in the indictment drawn up by the Paolists on May 29, 1793, in which the Buonapartes were accused of having been "born in the mire of despotism" and of having been "nourished and brought up under the supervision and at the expense of the luxury-loving pasha who was in command on the island."[18] Was Charles the only one who didn't know about the affair? That would be surprising. Cuckolds are often the last to discover that they have been deceived, but Charles might have seen some advantage in turning a blind eye to what was going on. Wasn't Letizia contributing in this way to the family's advancement? Hadn't she begun to respond to the governor's attentions at a time—August 1771—when Charles needed his support to have his nobility recognized? Besides, what would have been scandalous or extraordinary about such an affair, in the eighteenth century and in a city that was Corsican only by its geographical location, and that had passed from a not very prudish Italy to an even less prudish France? The French, while deploring the island's backwardness, were delighted by the ease with which the women of its cities, and those of Ajaccio in particular, adjusted to the continent's manners; it was almost enough to make them think that Corsica might not be hopeless. The Buonapartes were people of their time, and the public affair between Letizia and Marbeuf proves only that their assimilation into the society of the end of the Old Regime was rather successful. Finally, we may note that Letizia, who was prompt to reproach her daughters for their prodigality, never reproached them for taking lovers. She cared little for conventions regarding love affairs. Charles seems to have been no less indifferent to these conventions.

Letizia and Marbeuf's love affair came to an end in the early 1780s. After his wife finally died in 1783, Marbeuf remarried. He was seventy-one years old and his new wife was eighteen; Letizia was twenty-nine and had seven children. The young woman of 1770 had changed, and acquired the severe features we see in depictions of her. The governor founded a family—he had had no children, unless he was, as we have suggested, the father of Louis Buonaparte—and he distanced himself from Letizia. He died in 1786. In the Buonaparte home in Malerba Street, the Count of Marbeuf's portrait long hung in a place of honor, alongside that of Letizia.

The Obscure Years

It would have been surprising had this very French family spent its evenings talking about the battles of 1769 and independent Corsica. However, the claim has been made that it did, citing the "contrary loyalties" of the Buonaparte family, which had sided with France but was supposed to be nostalgic about the heroic years. Thus, Napoleon would have been telling the truth when he wrote to Paoli in June 1789 that his cradle had been surrounded by "the cries of the dying, the moans of the oppressed, and the tears of despair."[19] In reality Charles had put this part of his life behind him: not only was he bubbling with countless plans and projects focused on the future, not the past, but he had been no more sincerely a Paolist than he had sincerely become a subject of the king of France. In the end he was concerned only with the prosperity of his own family. But we cannot be sure of this, because we know so little about what was going on inside the Buonaparte family during the years between Napoleon's birth and his departure for school in Autun.

Here everything is subject to controversies and fictions: the obscurity enveloping Napoleon's birth led some people, and first of all Chateaubriand, to claim that he was born in 1768 and not in 1769, and others to assert that his biological father was none other than the Count of Marbeuf.[20] All the evidence regarding these obscure years is similar in kind. We follow the little Napoleon through a series of piously collected anecdotes that the emperor's biographers have more or less successfully arranged into a bouquet: the childhood surrounded by women in the big house on Malerba Street; the mother attentive to her brood's upbringing, not letting them get away with anything but, always pregnant or recovering from giving birth, leaving the task of playing games and taking the children for walks to the nursemaids, servants, grandmothers, and a multitude of aunts; the distant presence of the father, who was always busy and often not available; the close relationship with Joseph, the brother of whom he was most fond, and at first the only one (his second brother, Lucien, was born when Napoleon was almost six); the childish love affairs, the laughter and the tears, the secrets he told Joseph and the thrashings he gave him, the races through the streets of Ajaccio and the rambles in the nearby countryside, the tricks he employed to escape having to go to mass and his mother's slaps, the fights from which he returned bruised and with his clothes in tatters, his first studies with the Beguines in Ajaccio and then on the benches of the little school run by Abbé Recco, his precocious liking for calculation and mathematics: all this seems, if not authentic, at least plausible, even if on Saint Helena Napoleon said that the anecdotes told about his youth were completely false. We can also grant that he was authoritarian, brusque, difficult, and quarrelsome, to the point that Letizia thought him the most rebellious of her children. From the battles between Romans and Carthaginians in which Napoleon refused to be cast in the camp of the defeated party to his indigestion caused by eating figs and cherries, everything is plausible, or almost, because no one is going to believe that at his baptism—at the age of two—he cried out at the moment when the priest was about to baptize him: "Don't get me wet!"[21]

What lessons can we draw from these early years? Can we infer from such minuscule tales certain traits of the child's character, see in his agitation the desire to assert himself and attract the attention of a mother who was too occupied with her pregnancies, her love for Joseph, and her affair with Marbeuf? Maybe. Do we find here a few portents of a prodigious destiny? Not at all, even if there are many historians who, following their "program of being an apologist or a detractor," have claimed to discover in these little scenes harbingers announcing sometimes a "universal genius," sometimes a "ferocious despot."[22] The portrait of the child is too often a miniature version of that of the first consul or the emperor.

The Mystery of Irruption

Victor Hugo once said, speaking of Rubens: "A great man is born twice: the first time as a man, the second as a genius."[23] Anyone who has read the biography of one of the great actors in history—those figures who, for better or for worse, have changed its course by the sheer force of their will—should be struck by the truth of this observation. In such figures, the "great man," whether a monster or a hero, does not emerge from the individual as a butterfly emerges from its chrysalis, but is revealed all at once. The apparition of the great man is a kind of *springing up* or *irruption*. It is both a death and a birth, the death of the person he had been, and the birth of the person he will henceforth be. The break is so sudden and so complete that it becomes a delicate enterprise, to say the least, to understand retrospectively the man that the great man used to be. Conversely, it is difficult to grasp what there was in the man that may have foretold the great man. The passage from one to the other is always enigmatic: there is no continuity, not even an apparent one; it is as if we were dealing with two different beings, two distinct lives. The great man, once revealed, does not shed light on the personality of that other person he used to be, and the one he used to be does not allow us to divine the other person he is going to become. How can we stitch these two lives together? How can we find a common measure between the man who has now disappeared, even if he clearly had eminent qualities, and this figure who exists, as it were, beyond himself? Discussion of the early years usually serves as an ordinary introduction to a life destined to be extraordinary. Chateaubriand said that this discussion is most often composed of "puerile nonsense," and in any case of petty facts like those just mentioned, which are in themselves insignificant, but are presented as signs of future marvels.[24]

If we follow Chateaubriand's lead, the history of Napoleon as a child and a young man is not a preface to a legendary life. It is almost the history of another life, and in any case of an ordinary one. The past of great men speaks to us not only of men who have prematurely died; it underlines, *ex negativo*, how much what they have become depends on a greatness that resides chiefly in exceptional circumstances. Thus Chateaubriand tells us that "there is prelude to the emperor's life. An unknown Bonaparte precedes the immense Napoleon, [but] the idea of Bonaparte was in the world before he was there in person: it secretly shook the earth. In 1789, when Bonaparte appeared, people felt something tremendous, an anxiety they could not account for."[25]

The irruption of the great man into history does not depend on the birth of an individual endowed with uncommon abilities and on the efforts he later makes to dominate his period. The role played by Napoleon depends primarily, not on his existence, but rather on the crisis provoked by the French Revolution. Great men arise from times of crisis, from periods that allow talented individuals to make use of their capacities and especially their will, to an extent and with an intensity unknown in ordinary times when customs, laws, and institutions circumscribe the will's action within narrow limits. Peaceful times have no need for great men.

Nevertheless, it would be an exaggeration to present the appearance of great men as the outcome of a purely objective process, as Max Weber did in describing charismatic authority. According to Weber, charismatic authority is not based on a personal quality; it is a social relationship in which the personality of the leader is less important than the expectations of his adepts: the leader being a creation of the latter, it is of no great moment whether or not he actually possesses the qualities attributed to him. If we adopt this point of view, it is pointless to examine the youth of great historical actors: it tells us nothing. But common sense will object that not everyone can become a charismatic leader. All the great historical actors, whether heroes or adventurers, saviors or criminals, put a mark on history in which the age and the expectations of their contemporaries certainly played a role, but that ultimately belongs to them. Without them, without the accident that caused them to be present at this precise moment, history would have taken another direction. We have to acknowledge the role played by the coincidence of a situation and a man possessing qualities—or defects—that the age could both develop and endow with an unexpected influence. Had Napoleon been born not in 1769 but in 1789, he would surely have arrived too late. Would someone else have assumed the role of "savior" created by the revolutionary crisis and by the dead end to which it had led? Nothing is less certain. In any case, history would have been different: the person selected would have undertaken this task in his own way, depending on his abilities and in relation to his own objectives. The history of great men does not merge with the history of their time. That is, in a way, the paradox of the great man: he is caught up in history to the point of coalescing with it, in some cases completely, but we have to acknowledge that at the same time he gives it a character that is all his own and whose secret resides in him and in him alone.

That is why the search for signs prefiguring an exceptional destiny is not pointless: it is a way of coming to terms with the enigma always harbored by the lives of great men. Like everyone, great men are subject to the common rule: because nothing comes of nothing, the elements of this future greatness must have existed in these men very early on, perhaps from birth, even if they had to lie dormant until the moment when circumstances favored their development. Hence, there is a thread that leads from the man to the great man. Chateaubriand suggests this when, having said that there is "prelude to the emperor's life" and that "an unknown Bonaparte precedes the immense Napoleon," he adds: "Napoleon—who so rightly exclaimed: *Oh, if only I were my grandson!*—did not find power in his family, he created it: how many diverse abilities this creation supposes! Is it said that Napoleon was merely the person who implemented the social understanding surrounding him, an understanding that unprecedented events and extraordinary perils had developed? If we granted this supposition, he would be no less astonishing: in fact, what kind of man would be capable of directing and appropriating so many foreign superiorities?"[26]

Where did he get this astonishing ability? If he acquired it, how did he do so? And above all, how was he able to acquire it all by himself, given that he impressed everyone as the sole person capable of closing the book on the Revolution, of disentangling so many contradictory interests and opposing passions—Buonaparte, the little Corsican general, a priori the most improbable of the heirs to the French Revolution, the least predestined to achieve this implementation of "the social understanding surrounding him"? No one will ever discover completely the secrets of his various aptitudes. It is certain that these secrets lay within him, but it is difficult to find conclusive evidence or external signs of them before they became fully and brilliantly manifest. Here, much remains in the realm of the invisible; "youth, with its secret transformations and psychological mysteries, is a difficult study, and one on which very few certain ideas can be formed even by the most attentive observer."[27] Was he himself aware of this, did he even sense it? We won't ever know that, either: "The lips of the very great man," Nietzsche wrote, "are sealed regarding his inner life."[28] Just as Napoleon was to say that he had locked the door on his poverty at the time when, as a young lieutenant, he sometimes had to scrimp, it could be said that he kept the door to his inner life locked his whole life long. So we have to abandon at the outset the goal of drawing up a complete and exact genealogy of his faculties. On the other hand, it is not impossible to seek out, in his history as well as in his character and personality, some of the conditions that later allowed him to use so deftly the faculty Chateaubriand spoke of, when "Fortune" brushed him with its wing.

The Discovery of the Continent

In noble families, it was usual to expect the eldest son to pursue a military career and the youngest an ecclesiastical career. But all indications were that Joseph was too gentle, too quiet, to make a good officer, so his parents resigned themselves to going against tradition: the eldest would enter the Church and the youngest the army. The Count of Marbeuf took care of everything. He got the minister of war to reserve a place in a military school for little Napoleon, while Charles, so that his son would be given a scholarship, put together a voluminous dossier that included a certificate of indigence that had been granted without anyone's looking too closely into his resources: in that year he had actually received a comfortable income. Marbeuf also wrote to his nephew, the bishop of Autun, asking him to admit the two Buonaparte boys to the school in that city, where they would learn French before Napoleon went on to military school and Joseph to seminary.

They left the island on December 15, 1778. Napoleon never mentioned his feelings on separating from his mother, or the journey that took him through Marseille, Aix, Lyon, and Villefranche-sur-Saône on the way to Autun. He must have been struck by the change in scale in Marseille and Lyon, which were enormous cities compared to Ajaccio, by the change in the landscape as the carriage moved north, and by the change in the climate, as winter descended upon them. We know nothing about his stay at the school in Autun, except that four months sufficed for Napoleon to learn to speak and write passable French. Was he homesick for his family, disoriented, avoiding his classmates and "pouting"? He was not yet entirely alone. Joseph, his old companion, was there. It was no longer the world of his childhood, but it was not yet the unknown. However, he soon had to leave Joseph behind. Napoleon was entrusted to one of Bishop Marbeuf's friends, and on May 15, 1779, he was admitted to the Brienne military school. No longer seeing Joseph was surely painful for him. For the first time he found himself alone, and was moreover thrown into a world he knew nothing about. He had to don the blue uniform with red cuffs and white buttons, conform to the routine of strict schedules with fixed periods devoted to religious exercises, classes, and recesses, get used to the refectory and individual cells that were locked up every night by a monitor and not reopened until the morning, accustom himself to the discipline—in fact rather loose—imposed by the Minim Fathers. He was probably teased by his classmates because of his odd first name, his accent, and his ignorance—as he was one winter morning when, finding the water in his glass frozen, he asked who had dared put glass in it.[29] He had to endure the annoyances of every kind that await newcomers, and as such he suffered at first from the rigors of boarding school. Was life so hard for the disoriented little Corsican that he became "taciturn and unsociable"?[30] It has been suggested that this sad time, experienced as a kind of "deportation," made the distance separating him from his island even more painful—that it was his cultivation of the memory of his early years that caused him to form such a powerful attachment to Corsica and its heroes. Jacques Bainville assures us that this sudden passion expressed what he found hardest about his transplantation.[31] This picture is too dark. The young Napoleon was not easy to approach, that is true; he admitted as much later on, writing that "Bonaparte the schoolboy was out of touch with his comrades, and he was not popular."[32] Not because he was a Corsican, but because, being "good and very well-behaved,"[33] he preferred the library to his classmates' games. He had a tendency to want to be alone that in childhood constitutes a *casus belli*. It was this trait that caused his schoolmates to give him a hard time about his first name and his origins. They called him a Corsican, and he called them French, as he did when he told Bourrienne, after another quarrel: "I will do these French all the mischief I can!"[34] A mere jibe, which proves nothing. Should we take Bourrienne at his word when he assures us that Napoleon suffered from the situation of Corsica? Probably not. Nothing suggests that Napoleon was a "Corsican patriot" when he entered Brienne, or that he became one as a result of the ragging he endured there. The only thing we know for sure is that in the autumn of 1784 he left Brienne filled with these feelings, which he was to cultivate for almost a decade. The portrait sketched by Bourrienne is not implausible; it errs only in failing to pay enough attention to the length of time involved. At that age, the five years spent at Brienne were not trivial. Napoleon was almost ten when he was admitted to the school, and he had just celebrated his fifteenth birthday when he left it. The rather chubby boy who had left Ajaccio at the end of 1778 had turned into a sickly adolescent. It was at Brienne that he left his childhood. Napoleon recalled that a great change in his personality took place, and that having initially been "mild, quiet, and susceptible," he changed "on attaining the age of puberty" and became "morose."[35] Thus, it is around 1782 or 1783, three or four years after he entered Brienne, that we must situate a transformation due less to being uprooted than to the metamorphoses of adolescence. It was also at this time, in 1783 or 1784, that he turned in imagination toward his native island and conceived the plan of becoming the historian of its lost glory.[36] So it is to the same phenomenon that we must attribute the birth of a passion that is too often presented as the result solely of a difficult transplantation.

Besides, if the time he spent at Brienne had been marked by suffering and nothing else, would Napoleon have remembered it with the nostalgia he always showed when he referred to this period? Would he have so freely distributed gratuities and promotions to anyone who had been his professor or classmate there?[37] He said that it was in his "real homeland" in Champagne that he had "experienced the first feelings of a [grown] man."[38] In April 1805, on his way to Milan to be crowned king of Italy, he stopped in Brienne; he asked about the parish priest, received former school employees, and visited the ruins of the school. "Brienne is very important to me," he confided. He said no more, but mounted his horse and galloped off into the countryside and the woods, leaving his escort behind. Where was he going? What was he thinking about? The years that were gone forever? The road he had traveled since? Or about nothing at all, fully absorbed in the pleasure of revisiting the site of his youth? We don't know. When his aides-de-camp finally caught up with him three hours later, he laughed as he came up to them, saying only that he was proud of his "descampativos."[39] If he had known difficult times at Brienne, and he certainly did, he recalled only the moments of happiness, and these also certainly occurred. Brienne, with its joys and little miseries, was his lost childhood. And just as men used to recall fondly a military service they had often endured without pleasure, Napoleon remembered his school years as the happy twilight of his childhood.

The Champ-de-Mars École Militaire

It is said that Napoleon had initially chosen the navy. His father is supposed to have willingly accepted this choice; he was eager to see Napoleon leave Brienne so that little Lucien—who was then seven years old—could take over his elder brother's scholarship. But their mother is supposed to have been against this plan, and Napoleon exchanged the sailor's uniform for that of an artilleryman. Artillery was in fashion. It had undergone a general reevaluation in treatises on strategy, not only because of its tactical importance but also because it was, along with engineering, the only branch of the military in which merit counted more than birth, thus offering the children of the minor nobility or of impoverished families an opportunity for slow but real advancement that they would not find in either the infantry or the cavalry. Napoleon was preparing himself for the competitive examination for admission to a specialized school when he was chosen, along with three other students, to study at the prestigious École militaire in Paris.

The successful candidates arrived in the capital on October 19, 1784. Here again we do not know Napoleon's impressions. Travelers were generally dazzled by the city, and this fifteen-year-old youngster was scarcely prepared for what he saw. Having lived for five years within the walls of Brienne, he knew almost nothing about the outside world. What did he feel on seeing this city, which was immense for its time, populous, dark, dirty, full of sounds and odors, with its narrow streets, its crumbling buildings and, suddenly, enormous vistas opening out onto gardens, passersby leaping nimbly aside to avoid carriages, and the human swarm, the mixed population he could never have imagined? The only extant testimony is that of the future Duchess of Abrantès, whose family originally came from Cargèse and was well acquainted with the Buonapartes. One day her uncle Démétrius encountered the young Napoleon in the Palais-Royal gardens: "In truth," her uncle said, "he really did look like a newcomer. He stood there gaping, looking all around, blissfully unaware, just the kind of fellow that crooks would rob after taking one look at him, if he had anything to steal!"[40]

At the École militaire everything was different. From one day to the next he ceased to be a student and became an officer. Supervision was no longer provided by priests in cassocks but by noncommissioned officers who "gave brisk commands in a military tone."[41] The very splendor of the buildings designed by the famous architect Ange-Jacques Gabriel crushed him, and he once again had to get used to a completely new world. There were no more students than there had been at Brienne—fewer than 150 cadets—but they were different. The École militaire was in theory for the most deserving scholarship students from provincial military schools, but it also accepted paying boarders who came from wealthy and sometimes famous families. These students included scions of the Rohan-Guéménee, Montmorency, Juigné, and Polignac families who came straight out of the Old Regime's social register. This was reflected in the pomp and luxury displayed everywhere, in the very number of staff members assigned to see to it that the students lived relatively comfortably: "We were fed, served magnificently," Napoleon was to say later, "treated in every respect as officers who enjoyed great wealth, certainly greater than that of most of our families, and far beyond the wealth that most of us were one day to enjoy."[42] Some historians assure us that this exorbitant luxury pained him, especially when he compared it with his own poverty. It is true that young Buonaparte was not rich; he was no richer in Paris than he had been at Brienne: "At Brienne," he confided to Caulaincourt, "I was the poorest of all my schoolfellows. They always had money in their pockets; I never."[43] He is even supposed to have sent his father a veritable ultimatum, demanding that he be given what he needed to uphold his rank, or if that were impossible, that he be brought back to Ajaccio. In Paris, surrounded by wealthy young people, he is supposed to have had an increased sense of his poverty. But these are no more than hypotheses founded on bases that are fragile, to say the least. The letter sent to his father is apocryphal, and the regulations of the military schools strictly forbade students to receive money, clothing, or books from outside sources. No matter. All these testimonies seek to show that the discovery of late eighteenth-century French society was as painful to him as his discovery of France had been. Just as he had been mocked at Brienne because of his accent and his origins, he is supposed to have been snubbed in Paris for his poverty, thus experiencing the pangs of difference twice over: first cultural difference, then social difference. If we accept this view, then it is easy to conclude that he became resentful of monarchical France and its inequalities. This resentment would have further accentuated his Corsican patriotism, at the same time giving it a republican twist borrowed from the ideas that were arising everywhere. It would be to misunderstand the world of the schools, even the military schools, to imagine that the encounter with students from privileged backgrounds made Napoleon into a kind of Jacobin *avant la lettre,* or that it in any case disposed him to welcome the Revolution. Then as now, wrote Norvins, who studied at the prestigious Plessis-Sorbonne school,

all the inequalities of birth and wealth that were then so great disappeared as if by enchantment. The monosyllable *vous* was replaced on first acquaintance by the *tu* of comradeship. . . . Thus boys from the houses of Montmorency, Rohan, Tavannes, La Trémoille, Richelieu, Fitz-James, d'Harcourt, Duras, Séguier, d'Aligre, etc. attended the Du Plessis and d'Harcourt Schools where I received my classical education, sitting on the same benches in the church, in the refectory, and in the classroom as the sons of the craftsmen who worked for their families. . . . In the schoolyard, comradeship covered everything; in the classroom, it was work, and then the privileged boys were happy when their inferiors considered them their equals in their studies. . . . The noble boy was admired for working hard, since he didn't have to do so to ensure his future.[44]

If the students were conscious of inequalities, the ones that mattered to them had less to do with social status than with the forms of superiority that in these little republics guaranteed the boy who possessed them respect, admiration, or fear. In all schools and in all periods, these various kinds of superiority—which stood atop a hierarchy that was unofficial but known and accepted by good students, rebels, and bruisers alike—could also be combined in a single individual.

In Paris, Napoleon was no longer the loner he had been at Brienne. He was more convivial, though discussions with friends sometimes took a lively turn as soon as the subject of Corsica came up. At the same time, having been admitted to the class specially reserved for students who were planning to go into the artillery, he proved studious and diligent, driven by the sincere desire to pass the examination and to don the uniform of an officer of the king, dreaming of liberating Corsica as much as of serving the king who "oppressed" it. He spent less than a year at the École militaire. On September 28, 1785, he passed the final examination and was promoted to second lieutenant. A priori, his score was mediocre: he was forty-second out of fifty-eight graduates. But this is deceptive. Every year the minister of war drew up the list of the students in military schools who were authorized to take the artillery examination. Those who passed were in theory admitted to a specialized school where, after a further year of study, they took another examination to obtain their officer's commission. Nonetheless, some candidates for entry into the artillery schools were considered fit to enter active service immediately after passing the first examination; thus, they did not have to do an additional year of study. In 1785, 136 students from all over France took the competitive examination; 107 passed. Forty-nine of the latter went to artillery schools, while the fifty-eight others—including Napoleon—received the much-desired commission. Because most of those receiving the highest scores had gone to the prestigious school in Metz and only sixteen students from the Paris École militaire had taken the examination, Napoleon's rank appears to have been, contrary to what one might suppose, very honorable. It is true that on the national level he was only forty-second out of fifty-eight who passed, but he was third among the thirteen Paris cadets who passed, of whom only four obtained direct commissions as second lieutenants.[45] It was, in fact, a real success, and he was never to forget this day, recalling, with a precision that shows how dear the memory was to him, that he became an officer "at the age of sixteen years and fifteen days."[46] On October 30, 1785, Napoleon and his friend Des Mazis, who had been assigned to the La Fère-Artillerie regiment, set out for Valence.

A Child of the Enlightenment

In his memoirs, Bourrienne says that Napoleon's education had been greatly neglected. If we take this to refer to the military education of the future officer, we can go further and say that it was not so much neglected as deliberately nonexistent. Neither at Brienne nor in Paris had he acquired the slightest notion of tactics or strategy, and after reading Jomini he cried: "In our military schools, we were not taught anything like this!"[47] He was correct. When newly fledged officers left military school to go on active duty, they still had almost everything to learn. These schools were military only in name. As in other educational institutions, Latin and ancient history were the main subjects. "From all the windows and all the doors there seemed to escape a kind of jingle of Latin declinations and conjugations, of dactyls and spondees, of Ciceronian periods."[48] The teaching of grammar, literature, and French history came afterward. As it was taught, history was hardly more than a chronology mixed with genealogical tables that found its counterpart in the tedious lists of names in the geography class. French literature was reduced almost entirely to the seventeenth century,

Corneille and Racine, Bossuet and Fénelon, and especially Boileau. It was probably because of the weaknesses in the teaching of French that Napoleon was always a mediocre speller—to say the least. This is easy to understand if we add that French was not his mother tongue and that he learned it, probably too quickly, during his four-month stay at the school in Autun. But his brother Lucien insists that from this point of view Napoleon was in no way unique, and that he had had several schoolmates who were no better than his elder brother in this respect, even though they were French. We know that the eighteenth century was very critical of secondary education, and especially of its emphasis on Latin and the inadequate attention it accorded modern languages and modern history. The instruction given secondary school students was accused of teaching them a dead language "before they knew their own tongue" and of cluttering their minds with useless knowledge for which they would have no use later on. It was also accused of training citizens for a world that had ceased to exist a millennium and a half earlier and of inculcating in them principles and values that were in every respect contrary to those of the world in which they lived. Projects of educational reform multiplied around the middle of the century. The role granted French, history, and geography increased somewhat, but without challenging the preponderance of Latin and ancient history. The special schools served as laboratories. In them the role of Latin was reduced and teachers were allowed to use translations of classical authors rather than the original texts.

The teaching of modern languages underwent a more enviable change in the military schools than in other schools. At Brienne, Napoleon had suffered through German grammar because a minister who was a great admirer of Frederick the Great thought there was no army worthy of the name outside Prussia, and that no one ignorant of German could be a good officer. Napoleon forgot his German as soon as he left school, just as he did the English he studied in Paris. As for the sciences, although mathematics was competently taught— Napoleon had the good luck to have two excellent teachers in Father Patrault at Brienne and Louis Monge, the brother of the future member of the Convention, in Paris—the same was not true for physics, chemistry, or natural history, to which students were introduced when an itinerant technician came to present a few experiments.

Ultimately there weren't many subjects in which Napoleon was a brilliant student. Without aptitude for Latin, he was mediocre in French, "a dolt" in German, and the *arts d'agrément*—drawing, dance, fencing, riding, and music—offered him no more scope for distinguishing himself. Only in mathematics did he win a reputation as a good student. It is said that he was weak in literature, but the reference is only to his work in classes. When he wasn't working on mathematics, he would rush off to the École militaire's well-stocked library. It was there that reading became a passion. Although he constantly returned to Plutarch, he was probably reading everything he came across, without order but not without method. He read as others did in his time, with pen in hand, copying out extracts, drawing up summaries, and writing résumés.

Napoleon received an education typical of his period, even closer to the spirit of the time than the education offered in the schools, because it combined the two pillars of the scientific and the classical spirits, whose mixture, according to Taine, was to form the "poison" that swept away the world of the Old Regime in 1789. It is true that mathematics benefited from favored treatment in the military schools, first of all for its obvious utility in branches such as artillery and engineering, but also "because it was seen as a way of exercising the mind."[49] Although the directors of the military schools were wary of philosophy—it was taught little or not at all—they shared the philosophers' conception of the importance of mathematics: they saw it as the loftiest expression of the powers of reason. In the end, the education that Bonaparte got from his teachers and that he acquired on his own was not so inadequate. To be sure, he knew nothing about his future profession, but he had received from his education the best it could give him: not so much knowledge as the desire to learn. Utilitarian criticism of secondary education in the period fails to take into account the fact that education deliberately did not seek to be utilitarian. The real goal of the military schools was not to train officers but to cultivate gentlemen and loyal servants of the king. This was as much a matter of shaping the student's behavior as of instructing him. The schools sought less to provide a solid, comprehensive grounding in knowledge or immediately usable practical know-how than to form the student's judgment. According to Abbé Rollin, the purpose of good teaching was to "cultivate young people's minds" the better to turn them away "from idleness, games, and debauchery," to give them "gentler inclinations and manners," and to allow each of them, later on, to "be able to play their part, as in a great musical orchestra, in making perfect harmony."[50] That is why no plan for educational reform could deprive the classical humanities of their supreme place. The objective was not to train specialists in language and ancient history; it was to make students familiar with the models of greatness and virtue that abounded in the ancient world. That is why instruction really began only after the student left school: "Your classes are over, now your studies begin,"[51] Chancellor d'Aguesseau told his son. The education of that time has found few defenders. Refusing to believe that there was nothing good in this system, the philosopher Joubert was to regret the disappearance of the old schools:

> They were in fact small, elementary universities. In them, students received a very complete primary education. . . . There were chairs of philosophy and mathematics, subjects by which so much store is set; history, geography, and other branches of knowledge about which people talk played a role, not prominently and with fanfare, as they do today, but secretly and surreptitiously, so to speak. They were fused, insinuated, and conveyed with other subjects. . . . A little of everything was taught and . . . the chords of every disposition were sounded. Every mind was urged to know itself, and all talents to be developed. Taught rather slowly, with little ceremony and almost imperceptibly, students thought they knew little, and remained modest. . . . They left the old schools knowing they were ignorant and ignorant of what they knew. They departed eager to learn more, and full of love and respect for men they thought were learned.[52]

It is clear that this "secret and surreptitious" education did not always achieve its goal. The proof is that it created revolutionaries instead of loyal subjects and a crowd of deists instead of devout Christians. But that was less the fault of the teaching than of the spirit of the times, against which even the reclusion of the students was powerless. Rousseau was not on the reading list, but it was his books that the students secretly read. And like many young people of his generation, Napoleon lost his faith among clerics. His first communion took place at Brienne, his confirmation in Paris. But when he left school, he was no longer the pious boy he had once been. It is true that the Minim Fathers at Brienne were not very zealous in performing their religious duties. Father Château was proud that he could celebrate the mass in less than five minutes, and even the principal, Father Berton, performed it in no more than ten. But the teachers' lack of fervor would have had no effect had the spirit of the time not infused Brienne and the École militaire. Napoleon continued to submit to religious discipline, but as soon as he left the École militaire he stopped seeking the sacraments. He had formed his conviction. It was that of the century: religion was a support for morality, a factor in social stability, good for women and poor people, and had to be respected even when one had lost faith in its dogma, as he had. In this too, the young Corsican had received a French education. At the end of his years of study, he in no way differed from the generation that was, four years later, to plunge headlong into the Revolution.

THREE

The French Officer and the Corsican Patriot

*I*t was a newly fledged officer of sixteen whom the riverboat set down in Valence in late 1785. Napoleon was returning to the barracks of the La Fère-Artillerie regiment, where he had to receive basic training, stand guard, and do fatigue duty before he could don the uniform of a second lieutenant, of which he was to say on the day when, as first consul, he was to don that of a colonel in the grenadiers: "I know no dress more beautiful than my La Fère artilleryman's uniform."[1]

To judge by the way he always spoke of this period in his life, it seems that he had found a world that suited his temperament, almost a family, under the command of "paternal" leaders, "the bravest and worthiest people in the world."[2] And yet he had hardly put on his uniform before he began to long for his first "semester leave."[3] Finally, in August 1786, after less than a year of service, he returned to Corsica. Between the reunion with his mother and Joseph, making the acquaintance of brothers and sisters born since his departure, reading, and sorting out family matters, time passed quickly. Too quickly. His leave ended in March 1787. The following month, he requested and received a deferment. "What a happy time that was, when a young officer who had served only ten months could take a year's leave without losing a penny of his monthly pay!"[4] Napoleon used and abused ministerial generosity—it was only in May 1788, after spending twenty-one months in Corsica, that he went back to the barracks. In the meantime, the La Fère-Artillerie regiment had moved from Valence to Auxonne. Napoleon stayed there a little less than a year and a half; in September 1789 he was back in Ajaccio. A comparison between the time spent with his regiment and that spent in Corsica between 1786 and 1793 speaks volumes. Ten months in Valence in 1785–1786, twenty-three months in Auxonne between 1788 and 1791: a total of two years and nine months in the army—and five years and nine months on his native island.[5] He was a less than half-time officer.

Learning about Polite Society

In Valence, Napoleon lodged and took his meals in the home of a former button-maker, M. Bou, whose daughter, an old maid of fifty, obligingly engaged him in conversation and mended his shirts. He frequented M. Aurel's lending library and, sometimes, the theater. It was provincial life with its simple occupations, its regular hours, and its limited circle of acquaintances. It was, in short, a little boring, but Napoleon also felt for the first time that he was his own master, after six years of being confined within school walls.[6] His studies were not yet over, however: three days a week he worked on mathematics and learned to draw maps. His studies remained technical, though, and hardly touched on the principles of the science of artillery, which was at that time being completely revamped. When he left Valence a year later, Napoleon was still far from having a firm grip on the branch of the military in which he served.

His military service occupied relatively little of his time. His life was, as he later put it, very gay.[7] This boy of seventeen wore his uniform solemnly, but also enjoyed the typical amusements of the time. He has been described as "racked by poverty,"[8] eating only one meal a day and snacking on two little *pâtés* bought from a bakery in the morning. However, it was a very relative poverty. His annual salary amounted to a little more than a thousand livres, and he received a windfall of 1,200 livres when his family came into the possession of an inheritance it had had its eye on for a long time. "I ate very well and the food was good," he admitted on Saint Helena.[9] His situation changed in 1788, when he went back to Auxonne. He was no longer so well off; the legacy of 1786 had been spent, his salary had not been increased, and he was now helping to support his family. He had to count his pennies, to be sure, but he did not slip into poverty.

In a garrison city like Valence, officers, even at seventeen, were among the ornaments of local society. Napoleon appeared at the homes of Mme du Colombier and the Abbé Saint-Ruf, at balls, on excursions into the countryside, and so on. He discovered the France of the day, the France of a nobility and a bourgeoisie that were "not learned," Joubert tells us, "but [were] friends of knowledge, . . . in whom there was nothing exceptional, but everything was exquisite in its obscurity."[10] Immersed in a society where women had such an advantageous place, Napoleon himself grew more polished: he acquired manners and, to learn those he still lacked, he took lessons in dancing and deportment. He completed his education in the salons of Valence. Later on he recognized the importance of this period in his life, always recalling it with emotion, perhaps because it was at that time that he had his first love affairs. He had discovered a new world. Proud of his noble origins, he acquired a taste for the nobility. This confirms that his acquaintance with children from high society at the École militaire had not embittered him, even if he probably felt himself on a more equal footing with the minor provincial nobility in Valence than with the scions of the Polignac and Montmorency families.

If we limit ourselves to his stay in Valence, the story of Napoleon's youth seems to be that of a successful assimilation. It even constitutes a good illustration of the capacities of Old Regime France in this respect. Opening the doors of its schools to the little Corsican, it had made him a Frenchman. "Indelible impressions must have persisted in him and above all made him capable of understanding France and knowing how to talk to it."[11] Reacting against all those who, as heirs of the dark legend of 1814–1815, saw Napoleon as the very archetype of the *foreigner* who had never been assimilated, Jacques Bainville claimed that on the contrary, no one was more French than this young man of seventeen. Moreover, when Napoleon went back to Corsica in September 1786, he made a strange discovery: he no longer spoke his mother tongue. He even found it hard to relearn it. It was only during his second stay there in 1788 that he was able to use the language again, having worked at it. As Bainville also points out, "seven years in France had put their mark on him. He was already a little less a Corsican than he thought, even though he passionately labored to be one."[12]

A Singular Passion

He had already been working on this for some time: "Please have someone send me Boswell (*An Account of Corsica*), along with other histories or memoirs relating to that kingdom," he wrote to his father in September 1784.[13] These lines are the oldest extant trace of Napoleon's passion for his native island. He was then fourteen years old. The young man's "Corsicanism," which arose at Brienne, was manifested just as passionately the following year in Paris as it was later on in Valence and in Auxonne. Corsica was on his mind everywhere, and his imagination was full of it long after his adolescence. Neither military exercises nor regimental friendships nor evenings spent in the city caused him to forget it. Once he was back in his room and had closed the shutters, "in order to be more contemplative," he traveled in his imagination to his native island.[14]

Of course, he did not solely read works on Corsica. His taste for reading opened up vaster horizons to him. When he returned to Ajaccio in 1786, he got off the ship with a heavy trunk full of books that included not only Rousseau and Voltaire, Corneille and Racine, Plutarch and Plato, Cicero and Cornelius Nepos, but also Montaigne and Montesquieu, Raynal and the poems of Ossian. Some of these authors were old acquaintances he had made in the last years at Brienne, and a few of them—Plutarch, Corneille—accompanied him throughout his life. Others—the Abbé Vertot and the Abbé Rollin—soon came to seem to him "without talent or color."[15] There were also a few novels, particularly *Paul et Virginie*, which he never grew tired of reading. In addition, there were authors who were not on the school reading lists, especially Jean-Jacques Rousseau, in whose company, according to Joseph, Napoleon departed to live in "the ideal world."[16] He had read Rousseau's *Social Contract*, and *The New Heloise* made him weep. When he happened upon a book by Antoine-Jacques Roustan that attacked Rousseau's theories regarding civic religion, he took up his pen to write a *Refutation of Roustan* in which he adopted his hero's ideas and violently attacked the unfortunate pastor, denouncing his "ineptitudes" and accusing him of undertaking to criticize Rousseau without having read him.[17] Books were expensive, but nothing gave him more pleasure: "When by scrimping I had saved two six-livre écus, I made my way, with a child's pleasure, to the shop of a bookseller who lived near the bishop's palace. I often went to look over his shelves with the sin of envy; I coveted certain items for a long time before my purse allowed me to buy them. Such were the joys and the indulgences of my youth."[18] Thus he left Rollin's *Ancient History* and *Philosophical History of the Two Indias* for John Barrow's *History of England*, covering page after page with notes in his illegible handwriting, and then moving on to studies on the reign of Frederick the Great and the ministry of the Abbé Terray, closing

Mirabeau's *Lettres de cachet* to take up Buffon's *Natural History*, the Abbé Marigny's *History of the Arabs*, or Amelot de la Houssaye's book on the government of Venice, not to mention Lacroix's *Geography*, in which he underlined these words: "Saint Helena, a little island."[19] Was this, as Chateaubriand said, a sign of the "chaos" that reigned in his head?[20] Inspired by a few of these books he worked up his own stories, such as *The Count of Essex*, a ridiculous ghost story adapted from a page by John Barrow, or *The Prophetic Mask*, a little tale inspired by an episode in Marigny's *History of the Arabs*.[21] With the exception of the latter opuscule, which is better written than the others, these stories were no more than mediocre sketches. Napoleon's future style, laconic and dense, is little evident in these bombastic pages. Like the young Chateaubriand, Napoleon left a "hodge-podge" of juvenilia.[22] We will spare him the supposition often made that he aspired to become "the Rousseau of his generation."[23] The truth is more banal: he was a "scribbler," like most of the educated young people of his time.[24] Even if they didn't dream of winning glory with their pens, they couldn't help composing dissertations that smacked of both the schoolboy and the pathos of a philanthropic, vague, and sentimental age.

Although Corsica did not completely direct the young officer's choice of readings, he certainly considered himself Corsican from head to foot. "I drew my life from Corsica," he might have said, like one of the characters in his *Corsican Tale*, which he began writing in 1789, "and with it a violent love for my unfortunate country."[25] We are told that if he read with fervor the works of Rousseau and those of the Abbé Raynal, that is because they had supported Paoli. But this is to make the young man's thought too coherent. He was enthusiastic about Rousseau and the Abbé Raynal in the same way others were at that time. What matters is not that Napoleon was seized by a passion for Rousseau after reading a few lines devoted to Corsica in the *Social Contract*, but that he saw his island with Rousseau's eyes, as revealed by this fragment he wrote in April 1786, in which he wonders whether Corsicans have the right to throw off the foreign yoke:

> Either it is the people which has established [the] laws by submitting to the prince, or it is the prince who established them. In the first case, the prince is inviolably obliged to execute the conventions by the very

nature of his principality. In the second case, these laws must be aimed at the goal of government, which is the tranquility and happiness of peoples. If they do not do so, it is clear that the people returns to its primitive nature and that the government, not providing for the goal of the social pact, dissolves by itself; but we can say more: the pact by which a people establishes the sovereign authority in the hands of a body of any kind is not a contract, that is, the people can take back at will the sovereignty it had delegated. . . . Does not this reason come to the aid of the Corsicans in particular, since the sovereignty or rather the principality of the Genoese was merely conventional? Thus, the Corsicans were able, following all the laws of justice, to shake off the Genoese yoke and they can do the same with the French yoke.[26]

It is with the words and the abstract logic of Rousseau's *Social Contract* that the young Bonaparte pleads the cause of his homeland. Here there is no warmth, no feeling, no memory. He considers his island with a stranger's eyes. Should that surprise us? He was born in Corsica, but was very young when he left it, and did not really know it. If he loved it, it was with an *amour de tête* he had caught from books;[27] he talked about it like a Frenchman. This exacerbated patriotism was further evidence of the success of the education he had received on the continent. It was by becoming French that he had discovered Corsica; he considered himself all the more Corsican to the extent to which his education had erased in him everything that had originally been Corsican, even the language. Was it a pose struck by an adolescent delighted to be able to shock people by taking the side of the defeated while wearing the uniform of the victors, or was it the expression of deeper feelings? One thing the young officer wrote is well known: on May 3, 1786, a few days after having discoursed on the illegitimacy of the French conquest, he announced his intention of committing suicide. "Many young fools are obsessed with the idea of suicide, which they think proves their superiority," Chateaubriand coolly remarked.[28] The idea that it was a sort of pose seems all the more true because Napoleon had just read *The Sorrows of Young Werther*. Besides, at that moment he was joyfully looking forward to his return to Corsica, having received the "semester leave" he had requested. For the first time since 1778 he was going to rejoin his family and the country of his childhood. However, he could not help also dreading this reunion with a country he had experienced in his imagination with such intensity; the reality was in danger of disappointing him. If he feared discovering a Corsica different from that of his dreams, he feared no less having to depart when his leave was over. Even before he left, he was dreaming of coming back. Then, he wrote, he would have to resume a life that was not exactly exhilarating: "Life is a burden to me," he added, ". . . because the men with whom I live and will probably always live have manners as distant from my own as the light of the moon differs from that of the sun."[29] He was exaggerating the chasm that separated him from the French, but we can see that although his education had made him a Frenchman in his language, ideas, and manners, this in no way implied that his heart was deeply attached to France or that he could not conceive his future elsewhere. Incontestably French, he did not necessarily feel that he had duties to France. Until a very late point, in fact until fortune had singled him out, he did not exclude the idea of leaving France to pursue a career in a foreign country, wherever his talents might find full employment. Just as some children of exiled families reject their adopted country in favor of origins of which they retain no memory, Napoleon did not like the Frenchman he had become and tried to become the Corsican he no longer was.

The Love of Glory, a Passion of the Time

If Napoleon lived in Corsica in his imagination, that was also because the history of his island was, in his view, synonymous with heroism and glory. Its annals, full of figures of another time, seemed to him the modern equivalent of Plutarch's *Parallel Lives*. Finally abandoning the arguments borrowed from the *Social Contract*, in the *Letters on Corsica* he wrote in 1789 and 1790 he sought to reproduce the events of Corsica's history in the form of a gallery of portraits organized chronologically—portraits of the great men who had won fame in the history of the island. We cannot emphasize too strongly the attraction that the idea of glory then had for a young man of twenty. It was a passion of the time. If we underestimate it, we will understand neither the bitterness of the conflicts during the Revolution nor the Empire's military epic. Many people sought in literature what they later sought in politics, and finally in war.

It is no doubt an intoxicating pleasure to fill the universe with your name, to exist so much beyond yourself that it is possible to have illusions about both the space and the time of life, and to think you have a few of the metaphysical attributes of the infinite. The soul is filled with a proud delight by the usual feeling that all the thoughts of a great number of men are directed toward you; . . . that every meditation of your mind can influence so many destinies; that great events are developing inside you. . . . The acclamations of the crowd stir the soul, both by the reflections to which they give rise, and by the commotions they excite: all these animated forms, finally, in which glory presents itself must transport youth with hope and inflame its desire to excel.[30]

Like his reading of Plutarch, Corsica was a refuge in a world without glory. Military life was congenial, but it was not heroic. In 1789, working on an *Essay on Happiness* for a competition sponsored by the Academy of Lyon, he wrote these lines that might be taken as a summary of his own life:

When, on getting out of bed, a man does not know what to do and drags his boring existence from one place to the next; when, in contemplating the future, he always sees a dreadful monotony, every day resembling the other; when he asks himself: *why was I created?*, that man, in my opinion, is the most miserable of all. His body breaks down, his heart loses the energy so natural in man. How does it manage to exist, this empty heart? It is to lead the life of brutes with the moral faculties that are peculiar to our nature. How happy he would be did he not possess these faculties! Hence this man is discouraged by a trifle. The slightest setback seems to him an unbearable calamity. . . . [In] the void of solitude, an inner agitation will say to him: *No! I am not happy.*[31]

These lines would have been easy to understand in 1786 or 1788, when Napoleon was leading "the insipid life of a military officer in peacetime."[32] But they would have been much less so in 1791, when emigration was leaving gaps in the officers' corps that an ambitious young man might fill, when persistent rumors of a coming war were circulating, when France was throwing itself into political struggles, and when, turning its back on the values of modern society, it was espousing those of the ancient world in which Napoleon lived in his imagination. The "liberty of the ancients" reigned all around him in France, with its ideas of ferocious virtue, sacrifice, and heroism, but he did not see it, looking toward Corsica and admiring its patriots of another age. The reason for this singular blindness is perhaps simple: he was bound to Corsica by his family. How could he have conceived, even in 1791, an independent future in another place, while his family was counting on him?

A Burdensome Family

Charles Buonaparte died in Montpellier on February 24, 1785. Joseph, giving up his studies, returned home to his mother. She and his great-uncle Luciano soon understood that they could not rely on the eldest son. On the other hand, they could see in Napoleon's letters everything that set him far above his brother. There was much to be done. The family's position had reached its zenith in the late 1770s. But things changed after the Count of Marbeuf's remarriage and the departure of Intendant Boucheporn, with whom the Buonapartes maintained excellent relations. The facts had to be faced: they were short of money. Charles had spent lavishly and invested rashly. His travels on the continent and his stays at the court in Versailles, where, as we have said, he represented the nobility of the Estates of Corsica, had cost him dearly. He had obtained a concession for a mulberry tree nursery and another for the draining of the salt marshes near Ajaccio. The government had promised subsidies, but the latter were disbursed very irregularly, so Charles had accumulated costs: 30,000 livres for the draining of the marshes, according to his son.[33] He had died penniless and in debt. An inheritance made it possible to pay off a few debts and improve their everyday life, but this provided only a temporary reprieve. In May 1786 the government, noting that the mulberry tree nursery was not producing the anticipated results, decided to cut its losses and canceled the contract signed with the Buonapartes in 1782. Thus the family saw the hope of someday receiving the unpaid subsidies disappear, and worse yet, it had to pay back large sums to the government.

Napoleon returned to Ajaccio at just the right time. He set about writing up petitions and claims, and after a year of fruitless efforts, went to Paris, hoping to obtain from the clerks in the ministries what local officials refused to give him. He failed. Three years later, when Parisians were storming the Bastille, Napoleon's family affairs were still at the same point.

Even though he was only the second son, Napoleon had to watch over his family's welfare, compensating for his elder brother's indolence and relieving him of tasks that bored him, prevented him from sleeping in, and gave him headaches. Napoleon didn't demur. It was his duty as a son and a brother; he did it without complaint. If he hastened, as soon as he arrived in Valence, to take steps to obtain a leave, it was for the same reason. His family needed him, his diligence and his energy, and he soon donned the petitioner's garb that Charles had worn. Like his father before him, Napoleon besieged government offices and did not allow refusals to discourage him. "My family problems spoiled my youth," he was to say later.[34] There is some truth in that, and it was only the beginning. Right up to the end he was burdened by his family, whose demands increased with his notoriety and success. In 1795, even though his participation in putting down the insurrection of 13 Vendémiaire had raised him to the first rank, he still had to struggle to get Lucien out of the difficulties arising from his acquaintance with former terrorists, find a position for Louis, marry off his sisters, satisfy Fesch's dreams of grandeur, take care of the Ramolino clan, his relatives and the relatives of his relatives, not to mention the greediest of them all, Joseph, who could never make up his mind whether he wanted to settle near Paris and invest part of his wife's dowry in one of the church properties nationalized by the Revolution, serve as a diplomat somewhere in Italy, or seek his fortune in Constantinople. "I will fulfill all your desires," Napoleon wrote to him, asking only for "patience and time."[35] As in 1786 or 1787, he wrote letters of recommendation, did his best to ensure the success of a speculative investment in coffee, entered into communication with a merchant in Leipzig who was doing business with Joseph, went to visit properties he thought might interest Joseph but never pleased him, and sent money to his mother so that the family would be, as he put it, "provided with everything." He let nothing discourage him. "You know, my friend," he wrote to Joseph, "I live only for the pleasure I give my family, happy in their contentment."[36] And when Joseph told him for the thousandth time that he could not accept what Napoleon was offering him, Napoleon replied: "If you don't want to be consul, come here; you can choose whatever position suits you."[37] But there did come a day when he could no longer restrain himself and wrote at the bottom of a letter, after having reported on the countless matters with which he had to cope: "I cannot do more than I am doing for everyone."[38]

What did he think? He later acknowledged that he had been a "coward" in dealing with his own family.[39] Did his acts of duty also arise from love? It has been said that Joseph had always been his favorite brother because he remembered their early closeness. In any case, Napoleon was always indulgent with Joseph, pardoning him everything he didn't like, such as his indecisive and sensual nature, his irresolution, his laziness. He also saw good qualities in him, first of all Joseph's sincere friendship for him, his goodwill, his social talents. He certainly felt a genuine affection for him. Furthermore, he respected Joseph as his elder brother, always taking care to recognize the preeminence he had so little right to claim. But he didn't think highly of him, and admired him still less. His affection was mixed with a certain contempt when he said that Joseph would have been the best of men if he, Napoleon, hadn't tried to make him play a role that exceeded his abilities and "cast him outside his sphere."[40] These late comments, made at a time of disillusion and bitterness, probably do not faithfully reflect the young Napoleon's feelings with regard to his brother, but even then he already judged him severely.

As for the rest of the family, there is a coolness in his letters, almost an indifference toward the brothers and sisters who were like strangers to him, whom he had known little or not at all, and with whom he became acquainted only when he returned to Corsica in 1786. Lucien? Their first meeting, at Brienne in 1784, lacked cordiality; there was no complicity between them, and there was never to be any. Later on he became fond of Louis and took him with him to Auxonne in 1791. He hardly knew Élisa, who had left for Saint-Cyr in 1779; Pauline and Caroline had been born after his departure for the continent, as had Jérôme, the youngest child. Complete strangers.[41] He became acquainted with them in 1786–1788, and may have formed a kind of attachment to them. Back on the continent, he asked about them, advised Lucien to read ancient historians, and Jérôme to be good. He was, Masson tells us, "nostalgic about his childhood."[42] Long afterward, on Saint Helena, he was often to recall how badly his family had treated him, and sometimes mistreated him, how much they had harmed and poisoned his life, but he couldn't resist adding: "We sincerely loved each other. For my part, I never ceased to cherish fraternal affection for them all; and I am convinced that in their hearts they felt the same sentiments toward me."[43] Here too he was telling the truth, and perhaps he was still torn between the affection he felt for them because they were of his blood and the feeling that they were a very heavy burden to carry.

The Romance of Origins

We could go on forever quoting eloquent comments on the relations between Napoleon and his mother, about their love for each other, and about the debt he owed to her, which he willingly acknowledged: "It is to the way she brought me up as a child that I owe most of my rise. . . . I owe her a great deal. She had a wise influence on my character. . . . It is to her good principles that I owe my success and everything good that I have achieved." He added, pensively: "I owe everything to my mother."[44] There is no doubt that he respected her, but that he loved her or was close to her remains a hypothesis. It was only on the Isle of Elba in 1814 that there was genuine affection between mother and son. After all, as a child he had spent less time in her arms than in those of his nursemaid, whom he still called "Mama" in 1799, when he stopped in Ajaccio on his way back from Egypt. In the letters he wrote his mother, we find hardly any trace of genuine, strong feeling. "Take care of yourself. Love me always," he wrote to her in 1789.[45] In the course of seven years of study on the continent he saw her only once, in 1782, when she and her husband stopped at Brienne on their way to take the waters at Bourbonne-les-Bains.

That was also the first time he had seen his father since he left the island. He saw him once more, for the last time, in 1783, when Charles was taking Lucien to Brienne. In March 1785, Napoleon learned of his father's death. Did the news upset him? The letters he wrote to his mother and his great-uncle Luciano are hardly conclusive. To the archdeacon he wrote: "It would be pointless to tell you how strongly I felt the misfortune that has just befallen us. In him we have lost a father, and God knows what a father he was, his tenderness, his affection. Alas! We all see in him the support of our youth; in him, you have lost an obedient, grateful nephew . . . Ah! You know better than I how much he loved you. I dare even say that through his death the fatherland has lost a zealous, enlightened, and disinterested citizen."[46]

He was even more laconic with his mother, begging her only to "moderate her sorrow."[47] These letters came from a young man of sixteen who had just learned news that, without deeply affecting him, made it his duty to express the feelings of pain he thought appropriate.

He might have lost a protector, but surely not a model. By making Paoli his idol and vilifying the French oppressor, he made a choice opposite to the one made by his father, who had abandoned Paoli in order to enjoy the advantages offered by the new masters of the island. He is reported to have told the principal of Brienne: "Paoli was a great man, he loved his country; and I will never forgive my father, who was his adjutant, for having concurred in the union of Corsica with France."[48] It is hard to imagine that he was not thinking of his father when, in a letter to Paoli written on June 12, 1789, he denounced "the traitors to the fatherland, the vile elders corrupted by love for sordid gain."[49] A year later, in a memorandum written for the city of Ajaccio, he similarly stigmatized "those base souls who were the first to throw themselves into the arms of the French."[50]

For a long time he was obsessed by his father's "betrayal." Time did not attenuate these feelings, even if the word "betrayal" ceased to appear in the indictment he drew up against his father. The more he conformed, by becoming an officer of the king, to what Charles had wanted for him, the more he resembled his father, even becoming, like him, an indefatigable petitioner. And the more he sacrificed himself, like his father, to the happiness of his family, the more he believed and asserted that he was different from him. Conceding that his father was "a very fine man," charming, friendly, and intelligent, he reproached him at the same time for his lack of authority, his fanciful ideas, his womanizing, his sudden religiousness as death approached, and especially his prodigality. For a masculine model, he turned to his great-uncle Luciano, who, by economizing, "reestablished the affairs of the family, which had been much deranged by the extravagance of Charles."[51] Napoleon's great-uncle Luciano—"the father of us all"—had every virtue, his father every fault.[52] Napoleon once even admitted that he had always thought that had his father lived he would have barred his way.[53] When his father died, Napoleon could not have foreseen his own phenomenal destiny, but he experienced the death as a deliverance, and we can see that he did not want to associate the memory of his father with his own fortunes. In 1802, when the city council in Montpellier—where Charles had been buried—proposed to build a monument to the memory of the first consul's father, Napoleon had the council informed of his view: "Let us not disturb the repose of the dead, let their ashes remain in peace. I have also lost my grandfather and great-grandfather; why not erect monuments to them? This might lead too far. Had my father died yesterday, it would be proper and natural that my grief should be accompanied by some signal mark of respect. But his death took place twenty years ago: it is an event of no public interest, and it is useless to revive the recollection of it."[54]

This was, of course, a political refusal: it was advisable to spare republican sensitivities that remained alive. But there were also other reasons for this reluctance. He did not think he was an heir in any sense of the term; on the contrary, he was convinced that he owed his rise to himself alone, that he was the first of his name, and that in this respect he was free from the tyranny of the past. Perhaps, moreover, the father had died in his son's heart long before he was carried off by stomach cancer. It seems, in fact, that for years Napoleon had had doubts about who his biological father really was. We do not know at what point he conceived suspicions regarding the nature of the relationship between his mother and the Count of Marbeuf. Was it on the day in December 1778 already mentioned? Earlier, when Letizia, in Ajaccio, commanded her son to dress a little more quickly because he was going to dine at the governor's home? Later, at Brienne, when he was taken (according to a local legend) two years in a row to Callac, in Brittany not far from Guingamp, where he spent the summer vacation at the Marbeufs' château? Or still later, in Ajaccio, when he saw the two portraits of his mother and the governor hanging side by side on a wall in the living room?[55] In any case, there was a time when he imagined that he was an illegitimate child, a bastard, a time—which we are tempted to situate at Brienne or earlier—when the perfect, ordered world of his childhood exploded, when his parents ceased to be tutelary, quasi-divine powers that provided him with love and protection. We cannot say that he became convinced that he was Marbeuf's son. But he did ask the question, and continued to ask it for a long time. If his father was not his father, whose son was he? He went so far as to compare the date of his conception with those of Marbeuf's visits to Corsica and finally convinced himself he could not be the governor's son.[56] But then who was his father? In 1799, on the ship bringing him back from Egypt, he still confided his doubts to Gaspard Monge:[57] "He took up the unsavory question of his birth. Alluding to his mother's known liaison with M. de Marbeuf, and to the protection the latter gave her children, he explained how much he would have liked to be sure who his true father was. The reason he gave was that he was curious to know who had bequeathed him his military aptitude. . . . Treating the problem as a scientific question, he compared the times of the governor's departure and of his birth, and came to the conclusion that he was in fact Charles's son, . . . but then he no longer understood where he got his talent for leading an army."[58]

He had just celebrated his thirtieth birthday, and still didn't know for sure who his father was. Regarding his "legal" father, we can say that he was always "erased, dispossessed, castrated, denied, as it were, in every way conceivable" by Napoleon.[59] Ultimately he was replaced not by the most likely candidate for this position—Marbeuf—but by a sublime, purely ideal father adorned with the qualities Napoleon found lacking in Charles: Paoli. Did Napoleon know the *Life of Castruccio Castracani*? In that work Machiavelli makes an observation that seems to have been drawn from his own story: "It is astonishing to note . . . that all or most of those who have accomplished great things in this world and who have excelled among men of their time, have been of low birth or had humble and obscure beginnings, or have at least been greatly hindered by fortune; or they have been exposed to wild animals, *or had such a base father that out of shame they have declared themselves sons of Jupiter or some other god.*"[60] But this fabulous father whom he had adopted—but by whom he was never adopted in return; despite his efforts, Paoli always rebuffed him—was a hidden father, a father who did not really replace his true father. He was a model, but one to whose authority Napoleon was not subject and whom he could dream of not only imitating but even surpassing. Becoming the historian of the Corsican epic was a way of doing homage to its heroes and to the first among them, but it was also a way of authorizing himself to judge their errors and their weaknesses. Marthe Robert has shown that this "fable" of the bastard, though it does not exclude suffering, can become a source of creative freedom, the imagined father, who is always a king, a noble, or at least a powerful man, never really substituting for the fallen father and never actually occupying a place that is henceforth left vacant: The bastard, or at least the man who thinks he is or wants to be a bastard, "relegates his father to a realm of imagination, to a realm beyond the family that is a form of homage and still more of exile, because for the role that he then plays in everyday life this royal, unknown father, this eternally absent figure could also just as well not exist, he is a phantom, a dead man who can certainly be worshiped, but he is also someone whose place is empty and whom it is tempting to replace."[61]

Machiavelli said essentially the same: giving oneself a divine father to replace one's base father is a way of acquiring a freedom unknown to most people, of taking after no one, of being unrestricted, and of acquiring the power "to eliminate from one's biography every humiliating or undesirable element"; in short, of reigning "as absolute master over one's own destiny."[62] To be sure, because everything has its flip side, the "bastard" has to kill the unworthy father over and over and surpass the ideal father. Mastery over one's own fate comes at this price. The story of Napoleon confirms this: he wore himself out all through the first years of the Revolution trying to imitate, equal, or outdo Paoli and to obtain his recognition, until finally Paoli, having rejected him, was transformed into a base father in his turn, and finally, through his fall, gave Napoleon the freedom to which he aspired and that was finally to allow him to achieve things denied ordinary mortals.

Of all the factors at work in Napoleon's destiny, his father's early death, and still more the doubts Napoleon had about his descent, are not the least important. Of course, none of all this explains his extraordinary history. He did not become emperor of the French because he thought he wasn't his father's son. These factors provide only a possible psychological base for a disposition noted by everyone, from Chateaubriand to Taine, who autopsied the figure of Napoleon in the greatest depth. For Chateaubriand, he was "unparalleled," "unclassifiable," a figure who "came from on high [and] could belong to any time or any country";[63] for Taine, he was "cast in a special mould."[64] It is true that few people were as rooted in traditions, a history, a culture, a family past, as Napoleon was. This uncertainty as to his identity was no doubt very important, not so much for the freedom he actually had, but for his feeling of being free—if not of being his own son, then at least of having no ancestors, of being the inventor of his own history, the architect of his own destiny. He tolerated no subjection except to this "fortune" that he so often mentioned: not the blind goddess Fortuna who raises people up and strikes them down with indifference, not the endlessly turning wheel that rewards and punishes at random, but "fortune" in Machiavelli's sense, another name for the circumstances that a person who is far-sighted, prudent, and advisedly audacious, attentive to the slightest changes in the situation, can tame and use for his own ends. At a much later date Bourrienne saw in a book the words that were later so often attributed to Bonaparte when, arriving in Egypt, he feared that the British fleet pursuing him would not allow him time to disembark his troops: "Fortune, have you abandoned me? I ask only five days!" According to Bourrienne, Bonaparte could not have uttered these words: he did not believe in the "Fortune" of superstitious people; he very often spoke of "*his* fortune," but he never prayed to "Fortune."[65] In short, he yielded to a power that confirmed him in the certitude of his own sovereignty. Because this conviction was formed early on, Bonaparte's youth sheds light on the man he had not yet become: it allows us to glimpse a few of the threads that lead from the man to the great man. But we must not imagine that the future can be deduced from this disposition. The future was shaped by an unforeseeable series of circumstances and chances, by will, tenacity, ability, and, as Napoleon was to put it, a great deal of work and sleepless nights.

FOUR

The Revolutionary of Ajaccio

*I*t has been said that if Napoleon was not inattentive to the events that preceded the meeting of the Estates General, he observed them at most distractedly, being too full of Corsica to pay sustained attention to what was happening on the continent. His correspondence suggests the precise opposite: from late 1788 onward, the situation in France occupies an increasingly important place in his letters. He was already on the side of the "patriots." He had chosen this position not on the basis of his circumstances or ideals, but on that of a calculation. He embraced the cause of the Revolution out of love for Corsica. At the very moment that he was expressing enthusiasm for a "renascent" France, he was also putting to paper sentences that radiate a hatred of France and the French—for example, in his youthful work "A Corsican Tale," where one of his characters exclaims: "I have sworn on my altar never again to pardon any Frenchman. A few years ago I saw two ships of that nation sink. A few good swimmers managed to reach the island, but we killed them. After having helped them as men, we killed them as French."[1] Napoleon expected the France of 1789 to atone for the wrongs done by the France of Choiseul. It was in order to denounce these wrongs that he had undertaken to write a history of Corsica. The project was an old one; he had conceived it in 1786. The work was well advanced when Louis XVI announced, on August 8, 1788, that the Estates General would be convoked. Immediately understanding that this event could change the relationship between France and Corsica, Napoleon decided not to publish the manuscript. Only the first three chapters of it are extant. Retracing the history of the island up to the anti-Genoa rebellion of 1729, they probably formed the introduction to a book otherwise devoted to Corsica since the French conquest in 1769.[2] "I dealt with revolutions only in order . . . to give a clear idea of the current situation,"[3] he wrote to Joseph. A letter to his godfather, Laurent Giubega, written before the election of the island's delegates to the Estates General in June 1789 may be the only remaining trace of the original manuscript. It shows how recent events on the continent changed the way the young man perceived relations between Corsica and France, and how a question that had up to that point been purely historical, suitable for daydreams, was transformed into a political problem that opened up new horizons to him:

> While France is being reborn, what will become of us unfortunate Corsicans? As base as ever, shall we continue to kiss the insolent hand that oppresses us? Shall we continue to see all the employments for which natural law intended us occupied by foreigners as contemptible by their manners and conduct as their birth is abject? Shall we continue to see the military, giving free reign to its despotic humor, find no restraining dike and inundate us with its excesses right up to the highest summits of our mountains? Shall we continue to have as the arbiter of our properties and our lives a superior court without power, without energy, and badly constituted lower courts where a single man makes the decisions . . .? Shall we continue, monsieur, to see the head of the tax collectors usurp the rights of our Estates [of Corsica] and of our intermediate commission, issue decrees without right of appeal regarding challenges to their tax levies, govern at will the Estates' treasury, and oppress us all under the weight of his authority? I blush at this incredible degree of ignominy. . . . Shall we continue to submit to the triple yoke of the military, the magistrates, and the financiers, who, though so different in character, unite again and again to scorn us? Being scorned by those who hold the power of government in their hands—is that not the most horrible of the tortures our feelings can suffer? Is it not the most dreadful tyranny?[4]

Napoleon's Corsican patriotism had acquired a new face: it fed no longer solely on heroic tales of olden days, but also on personal experience and interests. He was now responsible for his family's affairs, and it was his inability to solve its problems that pushed him to side with the Revolution. This change should be located during the winter of 1787–1788, when, after the French administration in Corsica had dismissed his plea, he went to Paris to try to sort out the matter. There too he met with closed doors and refusals that were barely polite. We cannot say that at that point he realized the monarchy's advanced state of decay, but in any case he felt—as he says in his letters—that the lawsuits on which his family's welfare depended would have no favorable outcome so long as the financial crisis that was eroding the state was not resolved. He also became convinced, for the same reasons, that Corsica's freedom depended no longer on an uprising that would repeat the exploits of Paoli's day, but instead on the struggle that had begun on the continent between the defenders of the status quo and the partisans of reforms, which had not yet taken on the name "revolution." Finally, he acquired the conviction that the cause of Corsica's "misfortune" resided chiefly in the complete control exercised by the French over the island's political and administrative machinery. In a letter to his godfather he wrote that Corsica would recover its dignity on the day the French had been expelled from the island and their positions given to Corsicans. In the great upheavals to come he sensed the possibility, not of a break between Corsica and France, but of a redefinition of their relations in which Corsica would be offered a broad autonomy, beginning with what we would now call the "Corsicanization" of offices and employments. In his view, one figure—the intendant—symbolized the order to be overthrown, and if Napoleon espoused the cause of the Third Estate with such ardor, it was because the suppression of the intendants had a prominent place in the list of its grievances. The time seemed to him propitious, and in this same letter, written in the spring of 1789, he exhorted his godfather to join the movement that was under way, to endorse its principles, so that Corsica might gain not only the benefits promised all subjects of the kingdom, but also others peculiar to its situation. But Giubega was not cut out for that sort of thing, and any hope of seeing him play a role on the island soon dissipated.

Napoleon returned to his book. If he delayed its publication, it was not merely because he feared that events might force him to make certain revisions, but also because he wanted his book to appear under Paoli's auspices. On June 12, 1789, he had sent Paoli a letter that became famous, but to which the general did not deign to reply.[5] Napoleon then turned to another mentor, Abbé Raynal, who, having been so good as to receive him, advised him to make some improvements. "The novice historian," as he called himself, went back to work, even as he followed current events with passion. One day he feared that the "spark of patriotism" would go out too quickly, the next he regained hope. But let us not see the Napoleon of 1789 as a "hothead." The delegates' constitutional babble left him cold. He would have gladly accepted the limited reforms Louis XVI announced at the royal session of June 23, 1789. Hadn't the king promised to create provincial assemblies endowed with real powers? Didn't that imply the disappearance of the intendants and the transfer of their functions to the governed? Thus, he was at first frightened by the news of the Parisian insurrection on July 14: "I have at the moment received information from Paris. Two of my comrades have just left my room after having read me the news they received. This news is astonishing and singularly alarming. . . . The fermentation has reached a peak. It is impossible to say where all this will end."[6] Later he seemed to support the insurrection, and went so far as to borrow Barnave's quip: "Was the blood just shed really so pure?"[7] In fact, his reactions to popular violence varied depending on whether or not he had witnessed it. He had not witnessed the massacres of July 14; on the other hand, he was present, along with his regiment, when riots broke out on July 19 and 20 at Auxonne, where boatmen, porters, and peasants attacked the tax offices and the homes of the wealthy. This time Napoleon did not see these disorders as necessary for the birth of freedom; he reacted like an officer, deploring the weakness of General Du Teil: "They didn't want to fire or do too much harm. That's what's embarrassing," he wrote to his brother, and regarding the thirty-three rioters who had been locked up, he confined himself to remarking laconically: "The provost is going to hang two or three of them, I think."[8] Here we catch a glimpse of General Bonaparte behind the revolutionary.

The Choice of France?

Napoleon landed in Ajaccio in the last days of October 1789. Some historians say that the arrival of the young officer, who had already been won over to the Revolution, had a decisive influence on the course of events on an island that was still somnolent. Others object that we find no trace of such an influence, except perhaps his signature on a petition presented to the Constituent Assembly on behalf of the city of Ajaccio on October 31, 1789. Events support this objection, as Corsica had in fact joined the Revolution long before Napoleon returned from the continent.

The convocation of the Estates General had provoked a feverishness that the island had not experienced in many years. In the context of persistent rumors announcing the imminent retrocession of Corsica to the Republic of Genoa, the electoral competition had provided new reasons for rioting. The elections being held tardily—in early June—Corsica took no part in the great events that shook the kingdom between May and July, but it nonetheless reacted passionately to the news that the Bastille had been taken. As on the continent, people wanted to get rid of the current town councils and arm the citizens. The movement began in Bastia on August 14 and rapidly expanded, reaching Ajaccio on August 17, where a thirty-six-member committee—which included Joseph Buonaparte—was assigned to supervise the town council. The rioting spread to the countryside. Everywhere, the peasants were challenging the established authorities, questioning the confiscation of common lands that had occurred since the conquest, and even driving out parish priests they didn't like. Corsica was anything but peaceful when Napoleon returned.

The importance of Napoleon's contribution to the Revolution in Corsica has been exaggerated, and the truly revolutionary character of the riots that broke out almost everywhere may also have been exaggerated. There was certainly no general explosion. In Ajaccio, the pretext for the demonstrations was not the fall of the Bastille, but of all things the poor condition of the local cathedral. These diverse movements had little in common except the fear that Corsica would once again fall under the domination of Genoa. Although there was strong resentment against France, and more precisely against its representatives on the island, the hatred of Genoa was still more powerful. Twenty years of French rule had not extinguished this hatred. Were there in fact unacknowledged plans for retrocession? In the corridors of power, both around the king and in the National Assembly, some people were indeed thinking about ceding Corsica back to Genoa, and continued to do so after the vote on the decree of November 30, 1789, that declared the island to be fully French.[9] On October 11 a deputation from the nobility asked the minister of war to "beg" the king to publish "a declaration that would categorically disapprove the alleged project of ceding

Corsica to the Genoese."[10] It was because the danger seemed very real that Christophe Saliceti, one of the delegates for the Corsican Third Estate, sent his representative Barthélemy Aréna to London to invite General Paoli to reconsider his refusal to negotiate with the French government. Paoli yielded and sent two emissaries to Versailles. At the end of August, Saliceti succeeded in convincing the French intendant that the only way to restore calm to the island was to associate Corsicans more closely with its government. Saliceti advised him to form an assembly that would supervise the application of the National Assembly's decrees and could raise a militia.[11] This amounted to abolishing the system established in 1769 and granting the island significant autonomy, but it was also, in Saliceti's view, a way of binding Corsica to France by explicitly recognizing that it was, like all other French provinces, under the jurisdiction of the laws passed by the National Assembly. If we have to name the father of the formal incorporation of Corsica into France, he would be not Napoleon but Saliceti.

In the short run, however, Saliceti's efforts failed. He was opposed by the delegates of the Corsican nobility and clergy, who obtained the support of the council of the "Twelve Nobles"—the intermediate commission of the Estates of Corsica—which rejected the "Saliceti plan." The plan found no more favor with the government, which announced that the institutions established in 1769 would not be changed in any way, and decided to send to the island François Gaffori, the son of a hero of the war against Genoa, thinking that this would help to restore calm. Gaffori landed in September 1789. His mission turned into a disaster and threw Corsica, which the convocation of the Estates General had only stirred up, into the Revolution. He crossed the island escorted by troops and pronounced the dissolution of the town councils and militias that had been set up during the summer. One after another, the provinces of Corsica dissented, and Gaffori ended up taking refuge in the citadel of Corte.

Napoleon leaped into this fray and played a role that was far from negligible. On October 17, after the "Twelve Nobles" had rejected the "Saliceti plan," the revolutionaries in Ajaccio mobilized and asked Napoleon to compose an address to the National Assembly. It was clear that the Buonapartes, no matter how short of money, still had resources. They had supporters in Ajaccio: Joseph sat on the town council; a cousin, Jean-Jérôme Levie, would be elected mayor in March 1790; and on several occasions they made use of their family ties to have the city invaded by bands of peasants from Bastelica and Bocognano. Even so, lack of money remained their most severe handicap. More than the Buonapartes' notoriety, more than Charles's dishonorable behavior, lack of funds prevented them from rising to the level of the Salicetis and Peraldis. But turbulence offered hope. After all, aren't revolutions also an opportunity to reestablish damaged fortunes? On October 31, before about forty "patriots," including his brother Joseph and Charles-André Pozzo di Borgo,[12] Napoleon read the speech he had prepared:

> Deign, my lords [of the National Assembly], to consider our position. Torn away from freedom just when we were beginning to taste its sweetness [in 1769], for the past twenty years we have been incorporated into the monarchy. For twenty years, we had been living without hope, suffering under the yoke of an arbitrary administration when the happy revolution that restored their rights to men and their homeland to the French revived our spirits and caused hope to be reborn in our despondent hearts. . . . You, the protectors of liberty, deign to sometimes cast an eye on us who used to be its most zealous defenders; in losing it, we have lost everything, and we have found nothing but debasement and tyranny; an immense people [the French people] expects its happiness from you; we are part of it, we are more vexed than it is; cast an eye on us, or we shall perish.

The Ajaccio speech of October 31 foreshadowed the decree of November 30, in which the Constituent Assembly declared Corsica to be French. So should we attribute the paternity of this decree to Napoleon, even if indirectly? Certainly not. The delegates of the nobility and clergy of Corsica had already asked the king for a similar declaration, and at Versailles, Saliceti had long been laboring to achieve the same goal. If we except the party attached to the established order, Corsica was unanimous on this question: it wanted to obtain an explicit recognition that it was part of France in order to put an end to any plan of ceding the island to its former masters and to oblige the local authorities to bring Corsica the benefits of all the reforms initiated or announced by the Constituent

Assembly. Once again it was Saliceti who provided the decisive impulse. Noting that the Assembly's decrees were going unheeded, he wrote a letter exhorting the residents of Bastia to organize their national guard immediately. On November 5, blood was shed.

Was Napoleon in Bastia during this insurrection? An artillery officer, Félix de Romain, states in his memoirs that Napoleon hurried to Bastia after having had the Ajaccio address adopted on October 31. The skirmish being over, he is supposed to have inspired the letter from the residents of Bastia that asked the Constituent Assembly to formally confirm the integration of Corsica into the kingdom. It is true that this letter repeated the substance of the address, but perhaps the substance was already known in Bastia. Moreover, nothing attests to Napoleon's presence in Bastia on November 5, except perhaps an order he is supposed to have received from the governor (still according to Félix de Romain) asking him to come back to Ajaccio as soon as possible. It is likely that he played an indirect role in the November 5 riot, not by pulling strings behind the scenes, but by composing the October 31 address from which the people of Bastia took their inspiration when they requested incorporation, thus adding the wish of the main city of the southern part of the island to that of the capital of the northern part.

When the Constituent Assembly learned of the riots, it declared on November 30 "that Corsica is part of the French empire [and] that its inhabitants must be governed by the same constitution as other French people." All the ambiguities of the 1768 treaty were henceforth dissipated. Mirabeau had an amendment adopted that authorized the return to Corsica of Paoli and all those whom the conquest of 1769 had forced to go into exile. The island, as people said at the time, "illuminated" [*illumina*] when the decree was published a month later. In Ajaccio, Napoleon hung on the façade of his family's home a banner that read: "Evviva la Nazione! Evviva Paoli! Evviva Mirabeau!"

Did Napoleon make his definitive choice for France that day? Or did he long remain determined that Corsica would not become French? Opinions differ. Does the banner hung in Malerba Street lend support to the first view? "Evviva la nazione," "Long live the nation," it read. Yes, but which nation, Corsica or France? And if Mirabeau's name appeared on this banner, that of Volney, who had proposed the decree of incorporation, did not. If there are such differences in interpretation, that may be because the problem has been wrongly formulated. The choice confronting Napoleon after November 30 is too often presented as one between Corsica and France. In reality, the question was not framed in those terms, and the opposed interpretations may not be as incompatible as they seem. The meaning of the choice to side with France or remain faithful to Corsica was not the same in 1789 as it was in 1786. In 1786, choosing France, as his father had, meant embracing the cause of the conqueror; choosing France in 1789 meant declaring support for the Revolution. It was the latter that Napoleon celebrated; the November 30 decree had freed Corsica, not from France, but from Old Regime France. A few weeks later Joseph gave a speech in which he expressed feelings that were certainly shared by his brother:

> After having been the refuge of freedom under Paoli's generalship, the island was subjected by a minister's snares, at the mercy of the aristocratic administration of a few foreigners, governed by a mob of adventurers; [Corsican] nationals were scorned, demeaned by subaltern tyrants; but the Revolution . . . has destroyed despotism; patriotism and the fatherland are no longer empty words; our liberty is not uncertain and precarious; it no longer depends on the caprice of a favorite or the intrigues of a court; it is united by indissoluble bonds with the liberty of a great empire that is regenerating itself; a generous nation whose administrators were unjust has just undone all their wrongs by taking us in its arms as its children![13]

We can safely say that when Napoleon became "Corsican-French,"[14] ceasing to be "Corsican and nothing but Corsican," he did so willingly because France, by incorporating Corsica into the kingdom, was actually returning the island to itself. In fact, the November 30 decree meant that Corsica, freed from the authority of the governor and that of the intendant, would also soon obtain the right to administer itself. Not enough attention is given to the fact that this decree was published in Corsica at the moment when the island became aware of the laws of December 14 and 22 regarding the new administrative organization. These laws put an end to the monarchy's centralizing policy in favor of a decentralized system with its hierarchy of communal administrations, districts, and departments, all of which were elected and enjoyed de facto autonomy within the framework of the uniform laws passed by the National Assembly. With this law, all French provinces obtained what the Corsicans were demanding: the benefit of autonomy, on the condition that the common law was respected.

If Napoleon decided not to publish the *Letters on Corsica*, which had so greatly occupied him, it was because a logic of emancipation by breaking with France had been replaced by a logic of emancipation by integration into France. For a time he continued to work on his book, but the chapters he sent to Abbé Raynal in June 1790 were accompanied by a preface in which he declared that he was giving up his project:

> Convinced of the utility that it could have, . . . you sensed that the history of Corsica was lacking in our literature. Your friendship wanted to believe me capable of writing it; I eagerly accepted a task that appealed to my love for my unfortunate country, which was then debased, unhappy, in chains. I looked forward to denouncing to the opinion that was beginning to take shape the subaltern tyrants who were devastating it [Corsica], I listened solely to the cry of my powerlessness. . . . Here it is less a question of great talent than of great courage, I told myself. . . . Full of the flattering idea that I could be useful to my people, I began to collect the materials I would need; my work was quite advanced when the Revolution came to restore its liberty to Corsica. I stopped; I understood that my talents were no longer sufficient, and that to dare to take up the historian's pen, one had to have other capacities. When there was danger, courage was all that was required; when my work could be of immediate use, I believed my powers were sufficient; but now I leave the task of writing our history to someone who might not have my devotion but who will certainly have more talent.[15]

What should we make, then, of Lieutenant Buonaparte's "anti-French conduct" over the six or seven months that followed the publication of the November 30 decree? We must not forget that autonomy meant dismissing all the officials who had come to Corsica from the continent. They had been the target of numerous attacks in the island's lists of grievances; they had been accused of resisting the advancement of talented people in Corsica, their questionable morality had been condemned, their alleged incompetence and their ignorance of local customs criticized, and they had even been reproached for having brought to Corsica a hitherto unknown taste for luxury. These grievances revealed the resentment felt by young, ambitious people and no less a real aversion for "foreigners." It was no coincidence that the little colony of Greek migrants in Cargèse was one of the first victims of the rioting in the summer of 1789. Here, political cleansing often merged with ethnic cleansing. Bastia's walls were covered with posters threatening the French.[16] The time for the French to depart had come.

As we have seen, Napoleon was waiting impatiently for this moment. To be sure, one might argue that in demanding the departure of the officials from the continent who had been administering Corsica for years he was also serving the Revolution. But he clearly shared his compatriots' desire to live among their own. The ferociously Corsican Napoleon of Valence and Auxonne was not entirely dead. It was at Orezza, where he had gone with Joseph to attend a meeting, that he issued in the middle of April 1790 a manifesto calling for the expulsion of the French from Ajaccio. This document has disappeared, so we should remain prudent about what it actually said. The Ajaccio town council declared afterward that it contained nothing reprehensible. But the council was chaired by Napoleon's cousin Levie, and Joseph was a member of it. Better evidence is provided by the attack made on the two brothers shortly after their return from Orezza at the end of April 1790. They were taking a walk in the company of Pozzo di Borgo and Philippe Masseria, one of Paoli's lieutenants, when they were attacked by a group that accused Napoleon of having called for the massacre of the French. Things might have gone badly had Costa, a burly cousin from Bastelica, not happened to be there; he chased off the assailants. This incident, which occurred in early May and not in late July, as is claimed by those who want to relieve Napoleon of any responsibility for the events that took place in June 1790, proves that he was an active participant in the conspiracy that led to the expulsion of the French from Ajaccio on June 25.[17]

A few days after this attack, the town council led by Levie went on the offensive. A ceremony had been planned for May 10 to celebrate the newly signed pact of federation between Ajaccio and Bastelica (where the Buonapartes had numerous relatives). The residents of Ajaccio double-locked their doors and abandoned the streets to the people from the mountains. Backed by this mass assembly, the mayor demanded that the commander of the citadel, La Férandière, dismantle the cannons aimed at the city. Had the commander acceded to this demand, the citadel would have been taken by storm and either destroyed, as was advised by Masseria, or occupied by the national guard, as Napoleon wished. But because La Férandière refused to yield, the city council attacked again a few days later, publishing a violent diatribe against the French officials. The crisis came to a head on June 16, when the Ajaccio town council had a French engineer named Cadenol arrested. On June 23 the court ordered his immediate release, and Cadenol hastened to take refuge in the fortress. But on June 25 Commander La Férandière decided to hand over the unfortunate man to the municipal officials. He had hardly left the citadel before he was attacked, and got away with his life only by gaining asylum in a convent, where he was surprised to find the other French officials in Ajaccio, who had just been arrested. They were all soon expelled from Corsica.

Historians used to attribute the riot in Bastia to Napoleon, but tried to absolve him of responsibility for the violence in Ajaccio. They therefore told us that these spontaneous protests took the young man by surprise while he was working peacefully at home. He is supposed to have rushed out of the house, and because in such circumstances one must be able to overcome one's scruples, he assumed "the leadership of the people, which he was no longer able to refuse."[18] It is true that he kept in the background, but when the time came to explain what happened, he composed the town council's defense, blaming the violence on its victims and praising the calm shown by the residents of the city: "Once the people was satisfied [that is, once all the French officials were locked up and ready to leave forever], everyone went home, and order was rapidly restored."[19] The main objective had been achieved: Ajaccio had been "cleansed," just as Bastia had been at the same time. Paoli could return to Corsica.

Paoli's Return

One man then played a leading role in Ajaccio: Philippe Masseria. The son of one of Paoli's companions in arms who had been executed in 1763, he had joined Paoli in London, where he became one of the general's close associates and at the same time an agent of the British government. After his return to Corsica in late 1789, he had established a close relationship with the Buonaparte brothers.

Because they were always seen together, the people of Ajaccio considered the Buonapartes to be convinced Paolists, and it is probable that most of the two brothers' initiatives, starting with the call to drive out the French, were suggested to them by their good friend Masseria, that "bravissimo uomo," as Napoleon called him, who in 1793 was to push Paoli into the arms of the English.[20] The Buonapartes belonged to the "party of Paoli," as did anyone at that time who did not belong to the "party of Buttafoco," the delegate of the Corsican nobility at the Estates General. They all claimed Paoli's support, and they all adhered to the November 30 decree with the same sincerity and the same ulterior motives as the old leader.

"The pain of exile," Tocqueville observes, "is cruel because it causes great suffering and teaches nothing. It *immobilizes*, as it were, the minds of those who endure it. . . . It is like a clock that continues to show the time at which it was stopped, no matter what time it is now."[21] Paoli was a case in point. In July 1789 he was still saying that he would not consent to negotiate with the king unless Corsica's right to have its own government was recognized. Enormous pressure had to be put on Paoli to get him to agree to make contact with the new French authorities and even to give the November 30 decree his blessing. "Union with the free French nation is not servitude but participation by right,"[22] he wrote on December 23, 1789. Of course, this man of sixty-four would never be able to resign himself to seeing Corsica become a simple French department; for him it remained the "nation," distinct from France. He spoke of the Corsicans as his compatriots, and called the French his "fellows" (*confrères*). For him the incorporation decreed on November 30 was an unprecedented form of the contractual union between Corsica and a tutelary power that he had tried to establish in the 1760s. Many misunderstandings were to result from his inability to grasp the difference between incorporation and the establishment of a federal bond. But it remains that he sincerely accepted the November 30 decree and was not at that time thinking about England, even if, of course, he would have preferred Corsica to owe its liberty to England than to France. It cost him something to do homage to the enemy he had been fighting for two decades.

Nonetheless, he did not intend to leave his exile in London. He said he was sick; above all, he did not know these young people who were claiming to be his followers, and he certainly feared that he would no longer enjoy the undivided sway over his country that he had formerly exercised. Any idea of democracy was completely foreign to him, and he could imagine power only in an absolute form: because he was Paoli, he would be master or nothing. Moreover, the Revolution only half pleased him: "An attachment to the principle of authority, a hierarchical conception of human and social relationships, an insular traditionalism, an anti-French commitment to independence: these were the elements strongly rooted in Paoli's soul that prevented him from fully accepting everything that had happened since July 1789."[23] When in early 1790 he finally decided to leave his refuge in London, it was because there was once again talk of a retrocession of Corsica to Genoa. On March 6 he bid the king of England farewell.

Henceforth everything in Corsica was hanging on his return. Everyone tried to make himself indispensable. The competition promised to be stiff. It explains in part the escalating expressions of adulation of which Paoli was the object and the violence to which the partisans of the old order fell victim. People vied to be the most Paolist and the most intransigent toward those Corsicans and French who had incarnated the Old Regime. The Buonaparte brothers could not show the slightest moderation in this competition, as they had reason to fear that their father's behavior would prejudice the general against them. It was to demonstrate the sincerity of his "Paolism" that Napoleon fomented the plot that led to the expulsion of the French from Ajaccio. The diatribes against Gaffori and against Buttafoco with which he filled his writings had no other motive. But to attract Paoli's attention, one had to exist, take control of local strongholds, prove one's influence and legitimacy. The election of new town councils in the spring of 1790 provided an opportunity. Joseph Buonaparte, who had been a member of the municipal committee formed in August 1789, was a candidate, even though at the age of twenty-two he was ineligible.[24] Showing foresight, Napoleon had had false baptismal certificates made so that he could produce them if necessary, one attesting that Joseph had been born in 1765 and not in 1768, the other making Napoleon himself two years older. "Joseph has a good chance," he wrote to his uncle Fesch on February 10, 1790. "However, nothing is certain. People keep saying he should show his baptismal certificate. Thus it is indispensable that you do what I asked you to. . . . In that way, when we show Joseph-Nabulion's baptismal certificate, I can show mine from 1767, which will argue in his favor."[25] On March 7, election day, everything went off without a hitch: cousin Levie was elected mayor, Joseph a city official.

While the Buonapartes were accumulating reasons for Paoli to be grateful to them, the general was making haste slowly, being determined not to set foot on Corsica until a clean sweep had been made. He arrived in Paris on April 3 and stayed until June 22, celebrated, shown off like an icon, honored by Louis XVI and by the Constituent Assembly. Everywhere he went—to Lyon, Marseille, Toulon—there was the same enthusiasm for the hero who had, in Robespierre's words, "defended freedom at a time when we did not yet dare hope to achieve it."[26] But that was nothing compared to the delirious reception awaiting him in Corsica. Joseph was part of the deputation that welcomed him in Marseille on July 10. Napoleon himself did not meet Paoli until the beginning of August, in Bastia. If he had feared that he would be received coolly by Paoli, who had a long memory and held stubborn grudges, he must have been fully reassured, for although we know little about this encounter, there is every indication that Paoli gave him a warm reception, to the point that Napoleon remained in Bastia for more than a month, as part of the large entourage surrounding the *Babbo*,[27] and followed him when he went to Orezza to preside over the organization of the departmental administration: "He recollected with pride that when only twenty years of age, he had accompanied Paoli on a grand excursion to Porte di Nuovo. Paoli's retinue was numerous: he was escorted by upward of 500 of his followers on horseback. Napoleon rode by his side, and as they went along, Paoli pointed out to him the different positions and the places that had been the scenes of resistance or triumph during the war for Corsican liberty. He related to him all the particulars of that glorious conflict; and on hearing the remarks and opinions which fell from his young companion, he said, 'Oh Napoleon! There is nothing modern in your character! You are formed entirely on Plutarch's model.'"[28]

Despite the goodwill Paoli showed toward the Buonapartes, Joseph did not obtain the position as administrator of the department in Orezza that he wanted. This failure is often attributed to a hostility that Paoli concealed; as absolute master of these elections, he personally drew up the list of those elected.[29] In reality the Buonapartes were not "punished." The departmental administrations were the principal mechanisms of the new state, and to appoint to them a candidate whose eligibility was as suspect as Joseph's was to risk seeing the elections canceled. But when the time came to name the administrators of the districts, which were inferior jurisdictions and thus less prominent, with Paoli's benediction Joseph became the president of the directory of the Ajaccio district. It is often said that in Corsica Napoleon experienced nothing but failure and rejection. If we acknowledge the fact that Joseph's successes were also Napoleon's, we are forced to conclude that on the contrary, the overall outcome of this first year of political activity was more than positive; the future looked bright. It was with peace of mind and a satisfied heart that Napoleon returned in February 1791 to the continent and his regiment.

The Jacobin of Valence

In Auxonne, and then in Valence, where he was transferred on June 1, 1791, with the rank of lieutenant, Napoleon did not find the pleasant society he had frequented before the Revolution. Where he had not long before tried to learn the manners of the Old Regime's social world, he now more than once met with bitter comments from former friends, all hostile to the Revolution. A full-fledged "patriot," he bravely stood up to them, returning blow for blow, raising his voice, and was often saved by the mistress of the household's intervention, as the old ways had not entirely disappeared in the general crisis. "The same diversity of opinions, said the Emperor, was then to be met with in every part of France. In the saloons, in the streets, on the highways, in the taverns, everyone was ready to take part in the contest, and nothing was easier than for a person to form an erroneous estimate of the influence of parties and opinions, according to the local situation in which he was placed. Thus, a patriot might easily be deceived, when in the saloons, or among an assembly of officers, where the majority was decidedly against him; but the instant he was in the street, or among the soldiers, he found himself in the midst of the entire nation."[30]

Napoleon learned a great deal during this short stay—less than ten months. Just as in Corsica he had come to know "aiding and abetting, plotting, and contempt for legality,"[31] in Auxonne and Valence he saw what a society ripped apart by abstract political passions was like. Corsica could not have taught him this.

There, everything was tangible, composed of personal quarrels and specific interests; wealth and power were the only motives, and people didn't bother with abstract ideas. On the continent he discovered the fanaticism of opinions and how it can very quickly destroy customs and undermine relationships one had thought solidly established. In these same salons where before the Revolution he had been received gracefully, he was now treated with suspicion, just as he himself regarded as enemies these people whom he had shortly before seen as models. He witnessed at first hand the disaggregation of society, its shattering into irreducibly hostile parties under the impact of political passions and principles that were all the less open to negotiation or concession the more absolute and universal they were. He saw the effects, and even if the lesson bore fruit only later, he did not forget it. It was perhaps the sight of this society that had fallen into ruins that caused him to conceive his first doubts about the accuracy of Rousseau's theses. Up to then he had sworn by Jean-Jacques. Although he still wrote "O, Rousseau, why did you have to live only sixty years! In the interest of virtue, you should have been immortal!,"[32] he wondered whether he should really believe in the existence of "man according to nature." His youthful faith in man was shaken. By entering politics in Corsica, and then witnessing the disputes on the continent, he saw what a society that was going back to the state of nature was like: it was less a return to the golden age than an entrance into barbarism. Naturally, it was to take the experience of war, and that of the East as well, to make him declare that he was completely disillusioned with Rousseau, but he was already distancing himself from the "citizen of Geneva."

His revolutionary opinions were reaching their zenith. He had hardly arrived in Valence before he hurried off to join the local Jacobin club.[33] When Louis XVI and his queen were arrested in Varennes, Napoleon had, as he was to say, a "crisis of republicanism."[34] Although a few months earlier he had still associated, in an ecumenical homage, all the glories of 1789, lumping together moderate and advanced patriots—Bailly and Robespierre, Mirabeau and Pétion— henceforth he was to favor the republicans, and Brissot first of all. He was in their camp, along with the insurgents of the Champ-de-Mars who had shouted their demand that the treacherous king be overthrown, and when a new loyalty oath that no longer mentioned the king was required, he swore it, unlike many of his comrades who preferred to leave the army rather than betray the monarch. He became radical along with the Revolution. It is true that in doing so he was following a path taken by many of his contemporaries who had been royalists but became republicans after Varennes. But the transition was all the easier for him to make because he was, by his origins, "totally alien to the dynastic fidelity . . . that had shaped most of his comrades of the same age."[35] His loyalty was to his regiment rather than to the king, or indeed to the nation. However, this republican fever soon cooled: it was very strong toward the end of the Constituent Assembly, but was extinguished under the Legislative Assembly. Moreover, he retained a certain detachment; if he readily became heated, he was not so passionate that he forgot his duties. As republican as he had become, he nonetheless celebrated *la fête du roi* with his fellow officers on August 25, and even saved from lynching one of them who had gone to the window to sing "O Richard, O my king!"[36]

His republicanism was, however, sincere. The reason was still the same: the more France plunged into revolution, the better were Corsica's chances of freeing itself from any supervision. Even if Napoleon claimed to admire France more every day, it is not true that he cared less about Corsica. In Auxonne and Valence, he had reconnected with his old habits and passions. The only difference was the presence of his young brother Louis, who was thirteen years old and of whom he had become so fond that he undertook to educate him. He taught him French, had him study mathematics and geography, and took a paternal pleasure in the young man's progress and in the ease he showed in society. Louis, he said, was not only an excellent fellow, but the best and the most capable of his siblings.[37]

Between his exercises, political discussions, and supervising Louis's homework, he still found time to work. His workdays ran to fifteen or sixteen hours. He devoted his leisure time chiefly to writing an essay for a competition organized by the Academy of Lyon: "What truths and what feelings is it most important to inculcate in men for their happiness?" We are sometimes astonished that Napoleon, his head full of the tumults of the Revolution, would launch into an undertaking that seemed, in 1791, to belong to another age. It is true that it was no longer a time for academic jousts; but independent of the 1,200 livres promised the winner, it was also an opportunity for him to court Paoli. He dedicated the spring and part of the summer of 1791 to writing his essay.

His disappointment must have been great when he learned in November that the "Raynal prize" would not be given. Only one of the fifteen essays presented to the jury was awarded an honorable mention, and Napoleon's was ripped to shreds by the judges. One of them called it a "very pronounced dream," while another said it was "too poorly organized, too disparate, too disjointed and too badly written to capture attention."[38] It is true that it is not easy to read all the way to the end of this *Discourse on Happiness*, which is bombastic, sometimes ludicrous, often absurd, and always sentimental, full of flocks returning to the stable in the twilight, loving couples in their cottages, and sons prostrating themselves before their fathers—in short, it is full of "feelings that had never been in his heart."[39] If there are any things to remember in this "schoolboy amplification"—Napoleon was one day to throw into the fire a copy that Talleyrand had purchased somewhere—they are its republican profession of faith and its long panegyric to Paoli. The respective space devoted to the French Revolution and to Corsica clearly shows the hierarchy that existed between them in Napoleon's mind. Although the Revolution was mentioned before Paoli, Napoleon accorded only a few lines to the former, whereas he devoted several pages to the latter.[40]

It was to rescue the benefit of this eulogy of the "Father of the Country" that Napoleon, despite his painful failure, considered publishing his essay at his own cost. He finally abandoned the idea the following year, confiding to Joseph that this time he no longer had "the slightest ambition to be an author."[41] Did he still seek to be recognized by Paoli as one of his lieutenants? The general had on several occasions wounded Napoleon's self-esteem. First of all, the old leader, who said he loved Saliceti "like a son," had found a new favorite in the person of Pozzo di Borgo, whom the Buonapartes were offended to see receiving the favors that were refused them. Did Napoleon express his resentment with the frankness that Pozzo attributes to him?[42] Nothing is less certain, but this was the first crack in their friendship, the first sign of a rivalry in ambition that was soon to be transformed into hatred. Then, having learned that Pozzo di Borgo had publicly denounced Matteo Buttafoco, the former delegate of the Corsican nobility, Napoleon decided not to be outdone and to denounce him in turn. This *Letter from M. Buonaparte to M. Matteo Buttafoco, delegate for Corsica in the National Assembly*, which he had printed in Dôle in March 1791, probably satisfied his vanity as an author: for the first time, one of his works had been published. If we compare this letter with the disastrous *Discourse on Happiness,* it can only be to the advantage of the former. Although Buttafoco did not deserve all the insults Napoleon heaped upon him, the pamphlet was in no way inferior to those that appeared day after day in booksellers' display windows. It retraced, not without talent, the main stages in Buttafoco's "criminal life." This pamphlet sought not so much to detach Paoli from Buttafoco as to convince Paoli that he had no more devoted servant than Napoleon. His failure was complete. The general, to whom he had sent the printed version, was not happy with it. While he pardoned Masseria and Pozzo the violence of their denunciations of Buttafoco, he did not do the same for Napoleon. He wrote him a cold, curt letter: "Do not trouble yourself to contradict Buttafoco's impostures. That man cannot have any credit with a people that has always esteemed honor and has now reconquered its liberty. To name him is to please him. . . . He writes and speaks to make people believe that he is of some consequence. Even his relatives are ashamed of him. Leave him to the scorn and indifference of the public."[43]

Napoleon was put out. The rest of his correspondence with Paoli was not to calm him. Having once again begged the general to send him documents for the *Letters on Corsica* that he had told Raynal he was abandoning, Paoli replied with a flat refusal: "At present I cannot open my crates and search my writings. Moreover, history is not written when one is young." And when Joseph asked again, the reply was no more friendly: "I have other things to think about just now than looking through my writings and having them copied for him."[44]

At the end of the summer of 1791, there was no political disagreement between Napoleon and Paoli: the former was still an ardent Paolist and the latter was still faithful, at least on the surface, to the oath he had sworn before the Constituent Assembly in 1790. The Revolution had no more devoted auxiliary in Corsica. This became clear when the application of the Civil Constitution of the Clergy put an abrupt end to the apparent unanimity that had reigned at the time of his return. Personally, Paoli was favorable to this reorganization of the Church, but he was concerned when he saw the administration of the department, whose members he had chosen and over which he presided, advocating strict measures against priests who were hostile to the law. He would have preferred more moderation in order not to lose the support of the clergy and risk compromising his image in public opinion. But Aréna in Bastia and Saliceti in Paris urged him to be intransigent, and he ended up acting as they wished. Bastia rose up to defend its former bishop. Paoli's hand did not tremble. Troops patrolled the streets, the town council was suspended, and a few ecclesiastics were imprisoned. Prudently, the general transferred the seat of the departmental administration from Bastia to his fief of Corte. The rioters' defeat, easily accomplished, had shown that the general's authority remained complete. No one yet dared resist him. But by so openly taking the side of the enemies of religion, he had aroused mute resentments; above all, he had broken with the line of conduct he had adopted since his return: seize all powers but don't exercise any of them, stay above the melee as a recourse and an arbiter. Was this skill, or was it distrust of the young people surrounding him? It was more for the latter reason than out of aversion to revolutionary ideas that he rejected Napoleon's marks of respect and requests. It was not that in his view Napoleon was too revolutionary or too profane, but that he was one of those young people, so different from their fathers, who were too fond of lofty principles and who all sought the shelter of his name in order to climb more quickly the rungs of power. Wasn't this true of Barthélemy Aréna and the clique to which he had entrusted the departmental administration? As for these little Buonapartes who fixed elections and insulted Buttafoco—a defeated enemy who had been a friend of Paoli's before their break in 1768, as he could not help recalling—weren't they proving to be just as spineless and fawning toward him as their father had been toward the French? Decidedly, he didn't like "Charles's sons." Wasn't the eldest son, Joseph, now planning to be a candidate in the upcoming elections for the Legislative Assembly?

As he had in 1790, Paoli presided over the electoral assembly of September 1791. Once again, he had drawn up the list of future elected representatives. The main officials of the department, led by Aréna, imagined that they had a right to the *babbo*'s gratitude for the various services they had rendered. They were stupefied when Paoli imposed on the electors, first one of his nephews, Leonetti, and then two of his close associates, François-Marie Pietri and Pozzo di Borgo. Paoli was angry with Aréna for having compromised him in the religious matter. Pozzo had to intervene and Paoli finally consented to Aréna's election, but Aréna never pardoned him the affront. As for Joseph, his failure to become a delegate was compensated by his election to the directory of the department, in which half the seats were to be filled. We cannot suppose that Paoli felt a sudden surge of affection for the Buonapartes' eldest, so only one explanation seems plausible: because Ajaccio was losing the two men in whom Paoli had the most confidence—Pozzo di Borgo and Marius Peraldi were leaving to sit in the Legislative Assembly—he did not want to hand the city over to the Buonapartes. Napoleon could be on the island only intermittently, and Paoli was not averse to seeing Joseph forced by his new responsibilities to reside in Corte, where he could keep an eye on him. Ajaccio was finally going to be freed from the Buonapartes. It was at that point that Napoleon again returned from the continent. But this time it was not for a simple "semester leave"; he thought he had finally found a way to remain in Corsica for good.

A Failed "Coup d'État"

If, as is said, Napoleon had chosen France and the Revolution, why did he return to Ajaccio in October 1791 rather than take part in the war that was then considered so close? The proof that he had kept a cool head is that he didn't believe war was imminent: "Will there be a war? I've always thought there would not. . . . Europe is divided between sovereigns who command troops and sovereigns who command cattle or horses. The former understand the Revolution perfectly. They are frightened by it and would gladly make pecuniary sacrifices to destroy it, but they will never say so, for fear that their own countries might flare up in turn. . . . As for the sovereigns who command horses, they cannot grasp the whole of the Constitution, they despise it. They believe that this chaos of incoherent ideas will lead to the ruin of the French empire. . . . They will therefore do nothing. They are waiting for the moment when civil war breaks out, which according to them and their dull ministers is inevitable."[45]

Napoleon was right about this: one party was urging war, but the enemy was evading it. Even if we suppose that Napoleon saw the possibilities for promotion offered by the emigration of military officers, he would have continued to think that peace doomed the soldier to a monotonous existence. Under these conditions, Corsica was still the place where he had the best chance of making his mark. Furthermore, he had just become aware of a law passed on August 4 that authorized raising 97,000 volunteers for the army. These volunteers were to be organized into departmental battalions commanded by two lieutenant-colonels elected by their men (at least one of them had to have the rank of captain in the active army) and by an adjutant major chosen among the officers "currently on active duty" and named by "the general officer under whose orders the battalion would be."[46] Napoleon immediately saw in this an opportunity to serve in Corsica without losing either his rank or his pay. Because the general officer assigned to designate the chief warrant officer of each battalion was a family friend, Napoleon would return to Ajaccio with the hope, this time, that he would never have to leave again.

He arrived just in time to bury his great-uncle Luciano, who had died on the night of October 15. The family had been with the patriarch in his last hours, awaiting the moment to find out finally whether the old scoundrel had really hidden a nest egg in his mattress. Once Luciano was dead, the Buonapartes turned his bedroom upside down, but found nothing. The treasure on which they had so long counted did not exist. The uncle had used his patrimony to pay off, penny by penny, the debts Charles had left. It was a great disappointment. Were they going to miss the opportunity to buy the national properties that were about to be put up for sale? Joseph took matters in hand. He got an expert named to evaluate generously the amount of the improvements made to the properties for which the Buonapartes had received concessions. What Napoleon had been unable to obtain from the royal administration, Joseph obtained from his departmental colleagues: the costs that Charles swore he had incurred were reimbursed. Now that he had resources, "Napoleon brought Uncle Fesch before the authorities of the district to buy, along with him, the first set of national properties sold on the city's territory."[47] The envious spoke of misappropriations of funds, while the Buonapartes fought off suspicions by talking about the large inheritance the great-uncle had left them. When the time for the formation of the battalions approached, the Buonapartes were finally in a position to influence the electors' vote: that was what mattered. But an unexpected change in the law of August 4, 1791, forced Napoleon to give up the plan of having himself named adjutant major: on February 3, 1792, the Legislative Assembly prohibited officers on active duty from serving in these battalions. This time, war being imminent, the army needed all its officers. However, an exception was made for the lieutenant-colonels elected by their men. Napoleon no longer had any choice: if he wanted to stay in Corsica, he had to get himself elected.

The election had been set for April 1, 1792, in the presence of three departmental representatives. Two of the six candidates were serious competitors: Jean-Baptiste Quenza, a member of the departmental administration who was close to Paoli, and Mathieu Pozzo di Borgo, the brother of the delegate to the Legislative Assembly. To make things easier, Paoli had Quenza named one of the representatives (along with Murati and Grimaldi) responsible for seeing to it that the voting was conducted in accord with the rules. Napoleon immediately understood that he could never beat Quenza, and accepted the position of second lieutenant-colonel that Quenza offered him. On March 31 the volunteers arrived in the city, followed by the departmental representatives. The latter were not simple observers, but rather full-fledged actors in the voting. It was important for each candidate to show that he had their support. Napoleon could count on Quenza and Grimaldi. There remained Murati, who did not conceal his preference for Pozzo. He was staying with friends of the Pozzos, the Peraldis. He did not remain there long: he was dining when the Buonapartes' supporters broke in, seized him, and took him off *manu militari* to Malerba Street, where Napoleon greeted him with these words: "Here, you are at home" ("Ici, vous êtes chez vous"). Murati was so frightened that on the day of the election he voted with Quenza and Grimaldi. Pozzo and his supporters having been excluded from the assembly, Quenza and Napoleon were easily elected. The goal had been achieved, but at a high cost: this episode poisoned Napoleon's relationship with Pozzo di Borgo, and he had aroused the hostility of the powerful Peraldi clan.

As we have seen,[48] there was a strong animosity in Corsica between the residents of the former presidios and people living in the countryside: the presence in town of the volunteers, most of whom were from rural areas, had created a very tense climate. The soldiers of the Forty-Second Regiment, commanded by Colonel Maillard, maintained a prudent neutrality. Paoli, for his part, saw in the formation of battalions of volunteers an opportunity to put Corsican troops back in the citadels occupied by the "French" and thus to tighten his grip on the coastal cities. The departmental administration, henceforth directed by Saliceti, shared this point of view. So Napoleon was not the only one to conceive the idea of moving into the Ajaccio citadel; on this occasion he acted in concert with Saliceti, whose acquaintance he had just made. The same operation was attempted in Bastia, Calvi, and Bonifacio. Napoleon's initiative was part of an overall plan whose goal was to ensure, once the civil administration had been entrusted exclusively to Corsican elected officials, that security was put in the hands of soldiers who were natives of the island.

Quenza and Napoleon would probably have sent a warning to the commandant of the citadel, as had been done in Calvi and Bastia, demanding that he open the gates, had not serious incidents occurred on Sunday, April 8. On that day, a dispute between sailors and volunteer soldiers degenerated into a brawl in which an officer of the volunteers was killed. Napoleon and Quenza authorized their men to fight back, and they told Colonel Maillard that he had to hand over the citadel. The situation grew worse the following day. When Maillard ordered the volunteers to leave the city, the prosecuting magistrate of the district, an old friend of the Buonapartes, gave them a contrary order that Quenza and Napoleon used to strengthen their positions. "They fortified the houses they were occupying. . . . Napoleon rode on horseback through the advanced positions, haranguing his men, and told the 300 men confined in the Capucin convent that in their persons the whole nation had been outraged, but that it would know how to take its revenge and to make it proportional to the offense, that justice would be done, that the guilty parties would be punished. . . . Terrified, the residents of Ajaccio boarded up their homes to protect themselves against pillaging."[49]

Not having been able to make the commander open the gates of the citadel to him, Napoleon tried to incite a revolt among the men of the Forty-Second, but in vain. For a moment Maillard, recovering a bit of courage, decided to act aggressively and told Quenza and Napoleon that he would bombard their positions if they persisted in remaining in town. The two officers replied that they were prepared to fight.[50] The bombardment took place, but it amounted only to a warning, followed by further negotiation. The two officers had all the more reasons not to yield, because the department, having been alerted, was sending monitors and troops to Ajaccio. Napoleon and Quenza thought they had already won, but when the representatives arrived on April 16, they learned that Saliceti and Paoli were "abandoning" them. Moreover, Napoleon received an order to lead his troops to Corte. He refused, threatened, but finally gave in.

This not very glorious episode ended in a bitter defeat: the volunteers had not taken possession of the citadel and Napoleon had lost all his credibility. He could no longer dream of making a career in Ajaccio. What was even more serious was that he had displeased Paoli. The general, forgetting that he had encouraged the volunteers to seize the citadels, blamed the fiasco on those who had so badly executed his intentions: What do you expect, he wrote to one of his friends, "when the government is run by inexperienced youngsters [Saliceti], it is not surprising that little, inexperienced boys [Napoleon] are assigned to command the national guards."[51]

Complaints were accumulating, and Napoleon decided to plead his cause in Paris. This journey was all the more necessary because, his career as a lieutenant-colonel having been compromised, he had to be sure that he could resume, if necessary, a position on the continent. In fact, having the preceding year obtained a three-month leave that expired on December 31, 1791, he had been reported as absent, and on February 6, 1792, struck from the army's lists. Arriving in Paris on May 28, he did not make the rounds of the governmental offices in vain; he soon felt reassured. Paoli did not wish to publicize the events in Ajaccio, so Pozzo di Borgo, who was then in Paris, stifled his anger when Napoleon came to see him: "We seemed tense, but friendly," the latter wrote to Joseph.[52] Because Maillard, for his part, had proven no more courageous in his report than he had been during the crisis, the matter was settled.[53] Neither Quenza nor Napoleon was prosecuted. The minister of war, Lajard, referred the matter to his colleague in the Ministry of Justice: a few weeks later the monarchy was overthrown. Napoleon could now crow.[54] Not only was nothing done to him, but the anarchy was such that he obtained not only his re-entry into the artillery but also a promotion to the rank of captain, retroactive to February 6. The army, whose initial campaign had not been successful, needed all its officers, even those least worthy of confidence.

Napoleon in Paris

Napoleon's revolutionary career is awkward for his biographers. It offers no clear answer to the question that torments them: At what point did he choose France? Only the emperor's enemies have freed themselves from the obligation to make a decision on this point. For them, Napoleon never chose France; at most he was forced to become French when any possibility of remaining in Corsica disappeared, and at worst he never chose anything but himself. But most historians show more goodwill. The most indulgent of them opt, as we have said, for November 1789; others opt for his stay in Valence in 1791. But Napoleon's behavior afterward was so little in accord with this supposed choice that other historians resign themselves to situating Napoleon's voluntary naturalization later on, at the time of his stay in Paris in 1792. It is pointless to dwell on these differences: it is clear that on returning to Corsica in October 1792 Napoleon was the same man he had been when he left it the preceding May. Although the time he spent in the capital at the height of the crisis that led to the fall of the monarchy had an incontestable impact on his state of mind, it was by contributing to a perceptible cooling of his revolutionary enthusiasm. Frequenting the upper spheres of Parisian politics and, still more, witnessing the events of the *journées* of June 20 and August 10 created an aversion to the Revolution that the meetings of the Ajaccio club and the violence of April 1792 had not inspired in him.[55] If he lost his illusions, these concerned neither Paoli nor Corsica, but France and the Revolution. The delegates in the Legislative Assembly? They were "poor wretches."[56] The Jacobins? They were "madmen who lack common sense."[57] If anyone escaped the wreck of his illusions, it was La Fayette, who had protested against the *journée* of June 20, when a few thousand demonstrators had invaded the Tuileries palace and forced Louis XVI to don the red bonnet of the revolutionaries. After reading La Fayette's manifesto, Napoleon called it "very strong."[58] The Jacobin of Valence no longer belonged to the republican party, and if he was farther than ever from the counterrevolutionaries, he was certainly now among those who wanted to maintain "law, tranquility, and all the established authorities,"[59] including the king. Because he was in Paris and was seeing things close up, Napoleon henceforth tended to move in a direction opposite to that of the Revolution: the more radical it became, the more he moderated his stance. He had been a supporter of Brissot in Valence; in Paris he became a supporter of La Fayette.

We know his reaction to the *journée* of June 20, which he witnessed in the company of Bourrienne, an old classmate with whom he had recently reconnected. The sight of the riot offended the soldier in him, and when he saw the king appear at a window wearing the revolutionary bonnet, he could not restrain himself: "What a dolt! How could they have let that mob get in there?" This observation, as irreverent as it was toward the person whom the emperor was one day to call "my uncle," was good sense itself. But that was nothing. On August 10 he witnessed, from the vantage point of the furniture store run by Bourrienne's brother at the Carrousel, the taking of the Tuileries and the massacre of the Swiss guards:

> Never since has any of my battlefields given me such an image of dead bodies as the masses of Swiss guards presented to me, whether because the smallness of the space emphasized their number, or because it was the result of the first impression of this kind I felt. I saw well-dressed women behave with the greatest indecency on the bodies of the Swiss guards. I made the rounds of all the cafés in the neighborhood of the Assembly: everywhere the anger was extreme; rage was in every heart, it was seen on every face, even though these were not at all people of the common kind. . . . Although there was nothing peculiar about my appearance, or perhaps it was again because my face was calmer, it was easy for me to see that I was the object of many hostile and defiant looks, as if I were someone unknown and suspect.[60]

Napoleon had witnessed the most hideous aspect of revolutions. These *journées* inspired in him a permanent aversion to popular tumults. Did he lose his faith in the people at the same time? Had he once believed in it? That is doubtful.

"I am more undecided than ever," he had written Joseph on June 22, not sure whether he should remain in France or return to Corsica.[61] After he had rejoined the army, he thought for a time of staying on the continent, but in doing so he was merely yielding to his family's pressure. He said so as clearly as possible in a letter written on August 7: "Had I considered only . . . my own inclination, I would have come to Corsica, but you all agree that I have to join my regiment."[62] The Ajaccio affair having compromised his family, it was in his interest to keep discreetly out of sight for a while.

Let us therefore not imagine a Napoleon who chose France out of enthusiasm at the moment when "the great revolutionary ocean was about to overflow its shores."[63] If he had seen certain episodes of the Revolution, he had not experienced them personally. While everything around him was in tumult, he wrote to his brother some lines that testify to the pleasure he took in his studies: "I have devoted much of my time to astronomy while I've been here. It is a fine pastime and a splendid science."[64] The events themselves confirmed him in his conviction that his future lay in Corsica: "Everything here will end up leading to our independence," he wrote.[65] While pretending to yield to his family's dictate, he had made up his mind to take, at the first opportunity, his revenge for the defeat of April 1792. This opportunity soon came. The decree of August 11 convoking a National Convention changed everything. Now there was no question of rejoining his regiment, no question of remaining in France. He was heading back to Corsica: if the hour of independence had rung, then all hope of playing an important role was not lost.

FIVE

Lost Illusions

*W*hen Napoleon arrived in Ajaccio on October 15, he heard "bad" news: Joseph had not been elected to the Convention. Knowing that it would be a hard fight, Napoleon had continually urged his younger brother to cultivate Paoli's "friendship." But Joseph had lost. Paoli had nothing to do with his failure, because the general himself had suffered a defeat far more serious than Joseph's. Confined to his bed by illness, he had named his candidates, feeling sure that the electors would meekly follow his dictates. Everyone was expecting him to reward the directory of the department by making its principal members marshals. There was general astonishment when he let it be known that only one of its members deserved election: Saliceti. Had Paoli been present, the assembly might have yielded to his will. But he was absent, and Saliceti took control. He had himself elected, then his friends, and he awarded only two seats to the general's candidates. His triumph was complete, but he had inflicted on Paoli an affront for which he had to make amends.

The Birth of a Vendetta

When Napoleon returned to Corsica, the general was preparing to take his revenge. Distrusting the young man, he made him come to Corte, where he could monitor him more closely, on the pretext of entrusting him with the command of a few companies of volunteers. Because Paoli had recently been made head of the military forces on the island, Napoleon could not decline, and he spent a long, boring month in Corte, dreaming of seeking his fortune elsewhere, perhaps in Bengal, where the people, it was said, were fighting the British. He would continue to have these dreams of distant adventures for a long time; they came as quickly as they went when circumstances offered him opportunities that were, if less grandiose, at least more tangible. "I measure my reveries with the compass of my reason," he later said.[1] Like a dreamer awakened, he forgot Bengal, its elephants and its maharajahs, when he learned that Corsica was going to be called upon to supply troops for the more extensive military operations ordered by the Convention after the victory won at Valmy.

The war, which had begun on France's eastern flank, had spread to the south and the Mediterranean. The county of Nice had just been occupied, Savoy was about to be invaded, and the Convention wanted to pursue as far as Sardinia its actions against the Piedmontese monarchy. Paoli was supposed to provide a contingent to support the volunteers from southern France who had been assigned to carry out the attack, backed up by Rear Admiral Truguet's squadron. Toward the end of November, an exhilarated Napoleon was leading his volunteers to Ajaccio. He found the "casa Buonaparte" in a festive mood. Truguet had become a frequent visitor, as had Huguet de Sémonville, a former magistrate at the Parlement de Paris who was leaving for Constantinople, where he had been promised an ambassadorship. Truguet was courting Élisa, and Sémonville had promised Lucien to take him along to Turkey. On the other hand, there were brawls between the sailors in the port and the men the admiral had brought from Marseille. Several weeks went by, 1792 came to an end, 1793 began, and preparations for the expedition to Sardinia were not moving forward.

Napoleon was still in Ajaccio when he learned of the defeat—a real one, this time—suffered by Joseph in the new electoral assembly that had just reappointed the local administrations. Paoli had taken a devastating revenge. None of the members of the former administration—including Joseph—had been reelected, and the seats had gone to Pozzo di Borgo and his friends. For Pozzo, whose status as Paoli's favorite was thus made official, the time had come to settle accounts. He announced, loudly and clearly, that he was going to reveal the misuse of funds and misappropriations committed by the two previous administrations of Aréna (1790–1791) and Saliceti (1791–1792). There was talk of multiple salaries, favoritism, embezzlements, and fraud in the auctioning off of national properties. Pozzo was no less guilty than his predecessors, but he had the advantage of his position, and considering, as they had, that power is to be used to oppress one's enemies, he had presented himself as the "knight on a white horse" of the new administration. Paoli applauded him, and the former administrators trembled with fear. Not without reason: they had carved up Corsica. The prize was, to be sure, tempting: the national properties put on sale comprised almost 12 percent of the total area of the island. Some 500 Corsicans, out of a total population of about 150,000, had taken part in the looting. Compared to the Arénas and Salicetis, who had appropriated the lion's share, the Buonapartes were small potatoes. They nonetheless belonged to the clique that Pozzo had sworn to destroy and that was to be banished in May 1793.[2] This was the principal stake in the struggle triggered by the reappointment of the departmental administration in December 1792: it was a war between predators for control over power and local resources.

Saliceti, feeling threatened, counterattacked. Having been accused, he became an accuser. He nourished against the general "the icy hatred of a vendetta."[3] He had understood that the "old man's" affection was henceforth going to be given to Pozzo. Not being able to strike Pozzo without hitting Paoli, he launched, with the cold determination that always characterized him, a smear campaign. "You don't know how helpful that man could be in a difficult time," Napoleon later said. "He was one of those who always succeed."[4] Saliceti's allegations were all the more effective because the dispute had grown more serious, not between the Revolution and Paoli, but between France and Corsica. The Legislative Assembly, and then the Convention, had ordered investigations and commissioned reports; they all condemned the way the island was administered. Volney, who had gone to Corsica in 1792, said that there power had fallen "into the hands of the heads of families who, being poor, greedy, and inexperienced, [had] committed many errors and crimes, and [had] kept them secret out of fear and vanity."[5] The Revolution began to doubt whether the emancipation of Corsica was useful, just as in 1768 some people doubted the advantages of its annexation. Saliceti's accusations, which were conveyed to southern France by Aréna and Buonarotti, soon bore fruit. At the end of January 1793, General Biron mentioned the possibility of deposing Paoli. The members of the Convention on assignment in the south of France agreed. The Convention did not want things to come to this, but at Saliceti's request it decided first to put Corsica under the authority of General Biron, the commander of the army in the department of Var, and then to send three representatives to Corsica: Saliceti, Joseph-Antoine Delcher, and Jean-Pierre Lacombe-Saint-Michel. The Convention erred in entrusting the mission to Saliceti, but it did have more serious matters to deal with (on the same day it declared war on Britain). When second thoughts came, it was too late.

At first the aim was simply to take precautions. After all, nothing suggested that Paoli had the slightest desire to commit treason. He did have grievances against the Revolution and a certain bitterness with regard to the younger generation; Saliceti's "treachery" had wounded him and the way the Revolution was developing made him worry about the future of the union between Corsica and France. But he does not seem to have considered breaking his commitments. In April 1793 he still assured one of his supporters that he desired "the welfare of the Corsican homeland combined with that of the French republic."[6] Pozzo followed the same line: he was a royalist and as such hostile to the government established since the overthrow of the king, but he was in no way favorable to breaking with France or signing a treaty of "alliance" with Britain. Nevertheless, Paoli resumed contact with the British, probably in early 1793. Nothing emerged from these vague negotiations, but France's declaration of war on Britain, which was approved by the Convention on February 1, changed everything and lent credit to the accusations made by Saliceti and Aréna. The pair reminded people that Paoli had lived in London for more than twenty years; they disseminated letters in which Paoli, while assuring revolutionary France of his gratitude, swore more than ever that he would not participate in any action against Britain. The Convention came to agree with Saliceti; Cambon expressed the common opinion when he said that "Pitt has made [Paoli's] heart English."[7]

The Sardinia Expedition

What were the Buonapartes doing in Ajaccio? Did they participate, in the Ajaccio club, in the campaign organized against Paoli on the continent? They had to remain prudent. Saliceti and Aréna could talk all they wanted; they were far away, the one in Paris, the other in Toulon. The Buonaparte brothers were in Ajaccio, under the surveillance of Pozzo, who was looking for an opportunity to "reduce them to nothing."[8] If we must decide when Napoleon chose between France and Corsica, then it would have to be at this time, in early 1793, not because he was convinced that Paoli had committed treason, but because Joseph had been removed from the government and, like all former administrators, along with their relatives and allies, he was in danger of falling victim to Pozzo's revenge. Furthermore, it seems that by siding with Saliceti, Napoleon, who was in this case less lucid than Joseph, still believed, if not in the possibility of a reconciliation with Paoli, at least in that of imposing himself on him. The occasion? The planned campaign in Sardinia. If he performed brilliantly in this military campaign, Paoli would have to reckon with him.

We do not really know what made Napoleon put such stock in this project: the hope, despite everything, of still being able to play a role in Corsica, or the opportunity to prove himself under fire. For three months no progress was made, and then suddenly, in February 1793, the campaign got under way. Paoli had appointed its commanders: General Casabianca would lead the troops from Marseille in an assault on Cagliari, while Colonel Colonna-Cesari would carry out, with the Corsican volunteers, a diversionary maneuver on the little island of La Maddalena, off the northern tip of Sardinia. "The La Maddalena expedition was more than disastrous, it was shameful," Bainville was to write.[9] Nothing went as planned, neither the attack on Cagliari nor that on La Maddalena. A volley of bullets fired by the Sardinians sufficed to disperse the Marseille volunteers before Cagliari; the sailors on the ships carrying Napoleon and the Corsican volunteers doomed the effort to take La Maddalena, which the defeat at Cagliari had in any case made pointless. Colonel Colonna-Cesari's battalions had landed, and Napoleon had set up an artillery battery to bombard the village where a small Sardinian garrison was resisting, when the crew of the corvette *La Fauvette* refused to go under fire and mutinied, forcing the colonel to sound the retreat. On February 28 Napoleon was back in Bonifacio. Thus ended his first real experience of war. He bore no responsibility for the defeat; his own conduct in this affair had been exemplary.

Lucien and the Decree of April 2, 1793

Historians agree that Paoli was not to blame for this fiasco either; he had done everything he could to ensure that the expedition succeeded, even if he doubted that it would. But not believing in its success was already a crime, and the doubts

Paoli had expressed were added to the already long list of "proofs" that his republican feelings were only lukewarm. Aréna blamed the debacle on the general and repeated remarks he was supposed to have made to Colonna-Cesari: "Remember that Sardinia is our island's natural ally [and] that its king has always been a friend to the Corsicans; so try to see to it that this enterprise comes to nothing."[10] The Corsican volunteers themselves had indeed cried that they had been betrayed, and first accused Colonna-Cesari. But after they returned to Bonifacio on February 28, they signed—and Napoleon was one of the signers—an attestation of Colonna-Cesari's civic spirit, accusing only the crew of *La Fauvette*. On March 2, however, Napoleon did an about-face and sent the minister of war a report denouncing everyone—he mentioned no names—who had failed to take the necessary steps to equip and supply the expeditionary force: "The Republic's interest as well as its glory," he wrote, "require that the cowards or traitors who have caused us to fail be found and punished."[11] Who was he talking about, if not Paoli, who had been responsible for preparing the expedition and choosing its officers? The four days separating the return to Bonifacio and the report filed on March 2 are decisive: his break with Paoli coincides with these dates.[12]

Perhaps not enough attention has been paid to the dates: Napoleon's veiled denunciation of Paoli occurred on March 2; on March 14, in Toulon, his brother Lucien delivered a violent diatribe against Paoli that was immediately converted into an address at the Convention.

In late 1792, as we have seen, the Buonapartes had received Truguet at their home along with Sémonville, who was about to leave for Constantinople. Sémonville spent his leisure time at the Ajaccio political club, and Lucien offered to translate his speeches into Italian. In early February 1793 Sémonville received bad news: his mission to Constantinople had been postponed. No longer having any reason to remain in Corsica, he set sail for Toulon, and Lucien followed him. At that time Toulon was the headquarters of Paoli's adversaries. There Barthélemy Aréna and Buonarotti were conducting a smear campaign against the *babbo*. Saliceti soon arrived with his two colleagues. The group of former administrators was now complete. The campaign against Paoli grew more violent. On March 14 Lucien spoke at the Toulon club to denounce the general's "treachery" and to demand vengeance.[13] Did he provoke, that day, the fall of the whole family? We can set aside the quibbles made by François Pietri, who, in order to clear Lucien, states that he was not in Toulon, a claim the sources contradict.[14] But we cannot for all that take Napoleon at his word when he insists that Lucien alone was responsible for the break with Paoli. We can agree that given the difficulty of communicating between Corsica and the continent, neither he nor Joseph was behind their younger brother's speech. Lucien was urged to speak by Aréna and Saliceti. But at the same time Lucien thought he was acting in accord with the views of his elder brothers, and that is clearly the sense of the letter he wrote them a few weeks later when he learned that his speech had led to a vote to order Paoli's arrest: "Following an address given in Toulon, proposed and written by me in a small meeting at the club, the Convention ordered the arrest of Paoli and Pozzo di Borgo. Thus I struck a decisive blow against my enemies. You will have already learned of this from the newspapers. Weren't you waiting for that? Paoli and Pozzo are to be arrested and our fortune is made. Marseille has joined Toulon in sending addresses of the same kind to the Convention. But the effect has already been produced. I'm impatient to know what will become of Paoli and Pozzo di Borgo."[15]

For his part, Paoli was convinced that this was a concerted effort made by those "good-for-nothing" Buonapartes: "[Their] behavior would seem mysterious," he wrote the mayor of Ajaccio, "if we didn't know that they are completely dependent on Saliceti's will."[16] What Lucien, Saliceti, and Aréna could not foresee was the decision made by the Convention when it received the petition from the Toulon Jacobins. To be sure, it demanded Paoli's dismissal and indictment, but the Convention probably would not have acted on the petition had it not been, on that April 2, right in the middle of a debate about the treachery of General Dumouriez, who had threatened to march on Paris. Robespierre at the Jacobins and Chaumette at the Commune both demanded the elimination of the nation's enemies. Lucien's petition lent credit to the rumors of a conspiracy, and an order to arrest Paoli and Pozzo was issued. It stirred up a hornet's nest, taking by surprise even those responsible for it.

Napoleon Backs Down

The Convention's emissaries—Saliceti, Delcher, and Lacombe-Saint-Michel—had arrived in Bastia on April 6 completely ignorant of the arrest order that had been adopted four days earlier. In the political clubs Saliceti demanded Paoli's arrest while at the same time urging the Convention to be prudent. In fact he was hoping it would not be necessary to go so far, being well aware of the difficulty, and perhaps the impossibility, of arresting the general on his island. For most Corsicans, Paoli remained "the father of the country." Saliceti knew that; he wanted, not to overthrow Paoli, just to force him to separate himself from Pozzo, abandon the ongoing investigations of the administration he had directed, and agree to allow him to become once again, under the symbolic patronage of the old leader, the true "boss" of the island. Not despairing of success, he had a long conversation with the general on April 13, urging him not to separate himself from the Convention and inviting him to join the three emissaries in Bastia "to work together on the defense of Corsica and the pacification of the country."[17] Paoli neither refused nor accepted. It was far from a reconciliation, but it wasn't a flat refusal, either. The day after this conversation, the three emissaries received a notification of the April 2 decree ordering Paoli's arrest. They were thunderstruck. They immediately took up their pens to denounce this "precipitous" measure, but they could not refuse to publish the decree. On April 18 they finally resigned themselves and ordered Paoli's arrest. That done, they holed up in Bastia. Corsica was on fire. Hundreds of the general's supporters marched on Corte to protect him, bands of peasants attacked L'Île-rousse, the Aréna clan's fief, and although the members of the Convention were sure of Bastia and Saint-Florent, Bonifacio and Ajaccio were slipping out of their control.

Napoleon was getting ready to go see Joseph and Saliceti in Bastia when he learned of the April 2 decree. Although he was concerned about events, he was worried above all about a decree replacing the battalions of Corsican volunteers with regiments of chasseurs whose officers would be appointed by the executive power. Saliceti had forgotten to put Napoleon's name on the list of future officers. An awkward oversight: once again he was going to have to rejoin his regiment in Valence. He decided to go to Bastia to plead his case. He was about to leave when Joseph informed him of the decree. His reaction—a mixture of stupor and apprehension—was in no way unusual. Joseph and Saliceti had reacted the same way. They all understood that the decree was going to consolidate the alliance between Paoli and Pozzo, and that Paoli, backed by the support of the vast majority of Corsicans, would spare none of those he suspected of being his enemies. Napoleon hastened to draft the outline of a speech asking for the revocation of the decree. In it he protested against the offense done "a seventy-year-old man overwhelmed by infirmities" and rejected the accusations of conspiracy and ambition made against him.[18]

At the same time he wrote, in the name of the Ajaccio club, an address to the town council. But his initiatives did not have the effect he had counted on. The new mayor, Vincent Guitera, wanted nothing to do with the Buonapartes. As for the club where the Buonapartes still ruled the roost, it had lost much of its influence. The Paolists had founded another one called "The Society of Incorruptible Friends of the People, the Law, Liberty, and Equality"; it had its first session on April 1 and immediately denounced the Buonapartes as "seditious and incendiary men."[19] Napoleon tried to get the two clubs to merge, but the Society of Friends turned a deaf ear. Then he wrote to Paoli to assure him of his fidelity, but when the general had Napoleon informed that he "cared little for his friendship," he understood that the moment had come to burn his bridges. He may have attempted, on April 25, to get the citadel to open its gates to him, thus repeating the attempt made in April 1792. The episode is obscure and not entirely certain, but if it is authentic, the failure of this effort must have convinced him that there was no longer anything he could do in Ajaccio. He decided to join Joseph and Saliceti in Bastia.

Banishment

Napoleon called upon one of his cousins from Bocognano, Toussaint Bonelli, and on May 3 the two of them left Ajaccio at dawn. In the evening, when they had just passed Vivario, they met a relative who told them that Paoli's men were looking for them, and that people were talking above all about a letter that Lucien boasted had led to the April 2 decree. Napoleon and Bonelli decided to turn around. They found asylum in the home of the parish priest in Vivario. The next day they were back in Bocognano. Napoleon, who spent the night of May 4 with his relatives, planned to meet Bonelli in the hamlet of Corsacci, near Bocognano, from which he hoped to reach Ajaccio by evening. But when Napoleon arrived at the rendezvous point in the morning, Paolists took him by surprise and captured him. Bonelli called for help and after a few hours in detention, Napoleon managed to give his jailers the slip.[20] The next day, May 6, he quietly returned to Ajaccio and hid out at the home of Jean-Jérôme Levie, the former mayor. The gendarmes who showed up there on the evening of May 8 did not dare to search Levie's house, or to ask what the armed men he had brought in to guard its entrances were doing there. During the night Napoleon boarded a boat belonging to a fisherman friend. On May 10 he landed near Bastia.

So here was Napoleon, this time resolutely siding with Saliceti, a man who, even though he addressed them as "Dear friends," had recently written of the Buonapartes: "None of these petty intriguers will ever be my friends."[21] But Saliceti was in too delicate a position to be picky; he lacked the material means to put down the revolt that had taken over the whole interior of the island, and although he was now sure of Bastia, Saint-Florent, and Calvi, Ajaccio still eluded him. However, he had to be its master in order to control the island's lines of communication with the continent. Thus, he welcomed Napoleon with open arms when the latter coolly assured him that all the Convention had to do to make Ajaccio hang out the tricolor was to make a show of force. The decision to sail for Ajaccio was immediately taken. On May 24 four ships carrying 400 men left the port of Saint-Florent.

While Napoleon was sailing toward his native town, Paoli's partisans were not idle. More than a thousand of them gathered in Corte on May 27. They swore loyalty to the general, quashed the April 2 decree, revoked the mandate of Saliceti's delegate, and ordered the arrest of the "faction's cooperators." One speaker after another took the floor, some recalling the Buonapartes' connections with Marbeuf, others Lucien's actions. Finally, the *consulte* adopted the following resolution: "Considering that the Bonaparte brothers have aided all Aréna's efforts and abetted his impostures while at the same time joining forces with the Convention's representatives who are despairing of subjecting us to their tyrannical faction and threatening to sell us to the Genoese; considering on the other hand that the Corsican people's dignity does not obligate it to concern itself with the Aréna and Bonaparte families, we leave them to their private remorse and to public opinion, which has already condemned them to perpetual execration and infamy."[22]

While the Paolists were roaming the island, sacking and pillaging the properties of the "traitors," the Convention's naval squadron came within sight of Ajaccio. This, Napoleon's second military experience, was no more successful than the first. Fewer than fifty residents of Ajaccio, most of them civilians, joined the "patriots." The operation had failed. The squadron sailed away. The Buonapartes were sentenced to exile. Had Napoleon seriously thought it possible to take Ajaccio by force? Before boarding the ship at Saint-Florent on May 23, he had sent his mother a letter: "Preparatevi, questo paese non è per noi" (Prepare yourself, this country is not for us).[23] There are so many versions of the Buonapartes' last hours in Ajaccio, and they are based on testimony that is so unreliable, that it is impossible to give any of them precedence. Some writers tell us that Letizia remained in Ajaccio until the town council authorized her to rejoin the Convention's squadron; others that she took the initiative and withdrew to the Millelis family estate, under the protection of armed guards; still others insist that, learning of the approach of a Paolist group, she hurried off with her children to take refuge on the other side of the gulf, near the Capitello tower. In any case, Napoleon, who had landed, was able to find her: on June 4 the whole family was reunited at the home of their cousin Giubega; on June 9 they sailed for France.

The End of a Dream

In Toulon, where the Buonapartes landed on June 13, 1793, Napoleon composed a long indictment of Paoli. A few weeks earlier he had said that it was absurd to suspect the general of ambition; now he wrote: "What fatal ambition can lead astray an old man of sixty-eight? Paoli has kindness and sweetness in his face, and hatred and vengeance in his heart; he has unctuous feeling in his eyes and gall in his soul."[24]

Napoleon's farewell to Paoli, the hero of his youth, was also a farewell to the dream that had kept him chained to his native island for so many years. Must we conclude, with Jacques Bainville, that at the same time he turned his back on everything he had once believed in, "Jean-Jacques, Raynal, the Ideologues, and the *romance of the Revolution*"? Nothing proves that all this had been deeply rooted in him, or that the farewell was so absolute and sudden. Indeed, he continued to write sentimental anecdotes in the manner of Rousseau, such as *Clisson et Eugénie* (1795). But it is true that once he had been driven out of Corsica, he started down a new road. By rejecting Paoli after being rejected by him, he broke the final tie that attached him to the universe that he had imagined as the theater of his future glory. He had not yet "arrived at the age of feeling" but he had begun to "slough off his youth."[25] He had finished with the ideal fatherland of his adolescence.

Bainville also suggests that the lesson to be drawn from these Corsican years is only that they led the young Bonaparte to engage in illegal acts, and in so doing destroyed in him any scruples he might have had. If that were true, it would not be of negligible importance. In fact he arrived on the continent less destitute than he had been in 1789, when he had thrown himself into the fray in the Lilliputian theater of Ajaccio. Through his failures he had learned about "politics and men, trickery and action,"[26] and he had been well taught: his mentors were Paoli, Saliceti, and Pozzo di Borgo, all men of character and ability. With them he had made "a great study of the human heart," and Marmont is right, in his memoirs, to connect this study with the half-savage state of the society in which Napoleon lived, "where families are in a constant state of war with each other." The need for self-preservation, he explained, which is felt from infancy on, "develops in many people a particular genius: given equal faculties, a Frenchman, a German, or an Englishman will always be very inferior in this respect to a Corsican, an Albanian, or a Greek."[27] (Marmont had been governor in Dalmatia.)

But learning about politics, and about its means rather than its ends, is one thing, and showing a disposition for politics is another. From this point of view, Napoleon had not proven himself. If he had learned that dissimulation and prudence are virtues, he did not remember this when he tried to seize power in Ajaccio in 1792, making his attempt openly, at the risk of making powerful enemies who, he must have known, would never forget or pardon his offense.

The other part of his apprenticeship had taken place on the continent. There he had witnessed the Revolution and the passions and principles it put in motion. Because in Corsica political life was not driven by principles, he had arrived on the continent protected against the seductiveness of general ideas; he was not incapable of understanding them, or of gauging their power, but he was in no danger of becoming their victim. In witnessing passions he did not feel, he conceived an indifference or even a contempt for abstractions. His initial experience showed him that abstractions served as a pretext for powerful emotions, hatreds, and specific, personal interests, and it seemed obvious to him that politics is the art of manipulating people as they are and basing one's calculations more on their interests than on their convictions. This attitude guaranteed not only a realistic approach to human affairs, but also a wisdom and a moderation that were denied "people with principles." When Mme de Staël, meeting him for the first time in 1797, praised the "wisdom" he had shown in assessing the circumstances, noting that he had acted with tact and temperance in a situation where the Directory, claiming to act on its principles, was precipitous and violent, she revealed a certain blindness by accusing him at the same time of being lukewarm in his republicanism.[28] It was because he had learned early on not to believe in the sincerity of political professions of faith, to see words as snares, and revolutionary principles in general as barely good enough to put in "romances," and moreover because in his view people are neither good nor capable of improvement, that he was later able to govern them as they wanted to be governed and not as they should have been governed according to the *philosophes'* prescriptions. A profound skepticism learned in Corsica had taught him to be not only moderate but also indulgent with regard to some people's follies and other people's crimes.

> "I am well aware . . . of the influence which chance usurps over our political determinations; and it is the knowledge of that circumstance which has always rendered me very indulgent with regard to the party adopted by individuals in our political convulsions. To be a good Frenchman, or to wish to become one, was all that I looked for in any one." The emperor then went on to compare the confusion of our troubles to battles in the night-time, where each man attacks his neighbour, and friends are often confounded with foes; but when daylight returns, and order is restored, every one forgives the injury which he has sustained through mistake. "Even for myself . . . how could I undertake to say that there might not have existed circumstances sufficiently

powerful, notwithstanding my natural sentiments, to induce me to emigrate? The vicinity of the frontier, for instance, a friendly attachment,
or the influence of a chief. . . . Nothing more clearly proved the sort of
chance, the uncertainty, and the fatality which usually, in the laby-
rinth of revolutions, direct upright and honest hearts."[29]

For Napoleon, having started out in a peripheral theater like Corsica, far from
the great bursts of revolutionary fervor, was in the end a stroke of luck.

Stopover in Ajaccio

Napoleon was not yet done with Corsica, because one is never done with one's
childhood. In any case, how could he have stopped thinking about his native
island? On the one hand, the reconquest of Corsica, which Paoli had finally
handed over to the British, was one of the missions given the Army of Italy to
which he was assigned in 1794; on the other hand, he had not abandoned the
hope of someday recovering the family properties that had been confiscated,
whose value, according to a statement signed by his mother, amounted to 120,000
francs,[30] which was at that time a very considerable sum. He was concerned
about his family's interests, but he was also proud enough to want to triumph
over those who had banished him. Thus, he remained attentive to developments
on the island, watching for an opportunity to bring it back under the French
flag. In 1795 his superiors finally entrusted him with the preparation of a maritime expedition. A fleet was gathered in Toulon. It went to sea on March 11,
1795, encountered a British squadron on March 13, and, having lost two ships,
returned to its home base. It was not until the following year that Napoleon
added Corsica to the long list of victories won in Italy. To be sure, this victory
was the easiest of all: the fruit was ripe, and all he had to do was pluck it. The
alliance signed between France and Spain and the difficulties that assailed the
government of the "Anglo-Corsican Kingdom" on an island that had become
more ungovernable than ever after the forced departure of Paoli, who in October 1795 had gone into exile in England for the second time and was never to
return, led the British to leave Corsica. The rest was done by Bonaparte's lightning

victories in Italy, and especially by Murat's occupation, on June 27, 1796, of the port of Livorno, through which Corsica communicated with Italy. A handful of partisans recruited in Livorno and sent to Corsica sufficed. On October 19 the last British troops left Bastia. France had taken possession of the island again without meeting any serious resistance. The Bonaparte family recovered part of its property, but Napoleon did not make the trip.

He returned to his native island only once, on his way back from Egypt. The flotilla carrying him was sailing along the western coast of Corsica when a violent wind forced it to take refuge in the bay at Ajaccio. Learning that Bonaparte was aboard, the city authorities found themselves in an awkward situation. The rules required travelers who had come from the East to undergo a quarantine. But could they refuse to allow the national hero to disembark? The debate was lively: some speakers drew attention to the rules regarding plague, others to the residents gathering at the port and the boats going to sea to reach the ships lying at anchor. The latter finally won. "Nothing was so touching as the welcome given him," wrote Vivant Denon, who was accompanying Bonaparte, "cannons were being fired everywhere; the whole population was in boats and surrounded our ships."[31] Bonaparte and his officers climbed into rowboats. The Ajaccio authorities were waiting for them on the pier. It had been agreed that as a substitute for quarantine the travelers would wash their faces and hands with vinegar. The garrison formed an honor guard, and the town's bells rang as Bonaparte headed for his family home.

Six years had elapsed since his hasty departure in 1793. A strong wind out of the north kept Bonaparte in Ajaccio for a whole week. This involuntary stopover brought him back to his past, to his first years, to a time when he was still a nobody. He must have been moved on seeing once again the places and landscapes of his childhood. His walks took him through streets, where he shook people's hands and called them by name, asked about their wishes and listened to their complaints. He talked about harvests with the peasants, went to embrace his old nursemaid, and greeted shepherds who had helped him in 1793. But he saw the country of his youth almost with a foreigner's eyes. He was no longer the person who had walked these paths, passed through these streets, contemplated the sea. Bourrienne tells us that despite being sincerely touched, Napoleon was above all annoyed at seeing his arrival in France delayed, and also at these relatives of his who were continually popping up everywhere. "His great reputation had certainly prodigiously augmented his family . . . from the prodigious number of his pretended god-sons and god-daughters, it might have been supposed that he had held one-fourth of the children of Ajaccio at the baptismal font."[32] "I'm being deluged by family members," he grumbled.[33]

It was the resurrection of a past that, a fortiori, could turn out to be a handicap when he was getting ready to seize power. Corsica weighed on him. Already in 1796, when he had learned of the departure of the British, he had written to Joséphine: "Corsica is ours, good, good news for France, for the army, and for us."[34] It was good news for his mother, who was going to be able to return to the family home; it was good news for Joseph who, after having placed "in the new administration all his family members, his friends, his entire clan,"[35] got himself elected the island's delegate to the Council of Five Hundred (April 11, 1797); and it was good news as well for Lucien, who had proven so negligent in the various functions with which his brother had entrusted him that Napoleon ended up having him named war representative in Ajaccio: "He would be useful to the Republic in that country," Napoleon had written to Carnot, as if he were exiling his brother to prevent him from doing more damage to the Republic and his own reputation.[36] This kind of thing was worthy of his family; it was no longer worthy of him. He had accomplished so much in so little time that Corsica had become too small for him. On October 6, 1799, the wind finally calmed. That evening Bonaparte quietly slipped out of the family home. Passing through back streets, he reached the shore. At eleven a rowboat took him back to his squadron, which immediately set out to sea. He was never to see his native island again.

The Emperor and Corsica

Once he was in power, he cared very little about Corsica. "I have been ungrateful to the Corsicans," he once admitted, "I feel badly about that."[37] He was exaggerating: Corsica was not abandoned. It was administered by high-quality prefects, all of whom came from the country, and care was taken to apply the law there in a way adapted to local particularities. But it is also true that as early as the end of the year 1800, when uprisings broke out on the island, Corsica was declared to be "outside the constitution," and it remained so, on various pretexts, until the end of the Empire. The Corsicans repaid Napoleon his "ingratitude" with a mixture of indifference and hostility that was not always unjustified. They were never to forget, in fact, the iron hand of General Morand, the general administrator who "ruled" over the island from 1802 to 1811. During that time Corsica lived under a system of roundups and summary executions. As Miot de Melito, who was there as a representative, stated publicly, in Ajaccio the proclamation of Napoleon as First Consul for Life aroused more surprise than enthusiasm. The residents of Ajaccio, who had known the Buonapartes when their status was less flattering, could hardly believe it, and the two Corsican departments distinguished themselves by producing a particularly large number of negative votes. But there were other motives for this hostility. Corsicans remembered the events of 1793, and their resentment had not been extinguished; it had even increased in proportion to the unprecedented successes of the second of "Charles's sons." He had conquered Italy, taken back Corsica, and carried out a fabulous expedition to the East from which he had returned only to seize power and take up residence in the Tuileries, the former home of the ancient kings! This unimaginable ascension put an incommensurable distance between him and the Corsicans, as it had between him and other people. That was precisely what many Corsicans could not pardon; they weren't hostile toward him because he had succeeded beyond all expectations, but because he was one of them. Had Hoche been in his place, they might have applauded him; but that one of their compatriots should be there when they themselves were not—that was what they could not forgive. His successes were an insult, as if he had succeeded for the sole purpose of showing them how much he thought them inept. "Envy," La Rochefoucauld wrote, "is a fury that cannot endure other people's good fortune."

But if Napoleon proved "ungrateful" toward Corsica, it was not only in the way in which the island was governed under his reign, but also in the entirely political discretion he observed with regard to his origins. Naturally he had to be wary of petitioners who, claiming family or friendship ties with him that were sometimes very dubious, assailed him with requests for offices and favors. The burden of the cortege of relatives and friends that his family, beginning with his mother, brought along with it had already been quite heavy enough. It was completely understandable that he had taken care to give no ground, or the smallest possible ground, for the accusation that he was motivated by the clan spirit, especially because he was not above suspicion in this. More Corsican than he wanted to admit or even believed, he trusted only his compatriots. Most of his servants were natives of his island, and when he needed someone to carry out a delicate mission, he usually entrusted it to a Corsican. Nonetheless, the preference he showed Corsicans did not prevent him from confiding to Bertrand that "his foreign origin was a disadvantage that had to be concealed as if one were a bastard." And he added, not without cruelty: "One has to gloss over the weak parts." "You know the French mind and you have acted accordingly," Bertrand replied. "It was a disadvantage to be Corsican, it had to be hidden. The French have always gloried in being governed solely by Frenchmen, in having princes chosen among their own people."[38]

For a long time "pamphleteers had been saying [that he was] not French."[39] The image of the "fatal foreigner" had been born, first of all in England, as early as the campaign in Egypt. From caricatures to pamphlets, he had become, for the British public, "the Corsican ape, the Corsican worm, the Corsican tiger, the Corsican locust, the Corsican toad, the Corsican fox,"[40] even before this bestiary crossed the English Channel and spread all over Europe. The "dark legend" that swept through France in 1814 was already there, with all its ingredients, to denounce the foreigner who, taking advantage of the anarchy that reigned in France, had leaped upon his prey like a predator indifferent to its interests or to its children's blood, concerned solely with satisfying his dreams of domination. The legitimacy of his power was affected by his family origins. The problem became even more important as his power began to take monarchical forms. Every step toward supreme power required a further concealment of his ancestry. Just as he was to believe that by marrying an Austrian archduchess in 1810 he was facilitating his adoption by the European royal family, he had believed that by marrying Joséphine de Beauharnais in 1796 he was entering the French family; he had imagined that in this way he could acquire the nationality that even the education he had received in the royal colleges had apparently failed to confer on him. Although he had married Joséphine for love, he had not been impervious to the other good reasons that Barras had given him for marrying General

Beauharnais's widow: "He advised me to marry her, assuring me that she belonged both to the Old Regime and to the New, so that the marriage would give me good standing in society. Her house was known to be the best in Paris, and I should cease to be called a Corsican. In short, by this step I should become thoroughly Frenchified."[41] Thus, we can understand what he felt when his origins were mentioned in his presence: "Once in Lyon a mayor, believing he was complimenting me, said: *It's astonishing Sire, that not being French you love France so much and do so much for it!* It was as if he had hit me with a stick!"[42] Of all the insults showered on him by his enemies, "that of hearing [himself] called a Corsican" was the one that pained him most.[43]

A Wart on France's Nose

It would be pointless to inquire further into whether Napoleon sought to erase all suspicion regarding his origins after he took power or, a fortiori, when he was trying get the dynasty he had founded recognized in France and in Europe. But it was not in 1804 or in 1802, or even at the time of 18 Brumaire, that this question obsessed him; it preoccupied him as soon as he had taken his first steps on the public stage. The ink had hardly dried on the registry office document certifying his marriage to Mme de Beauharnais before he did away with the *u* in his name: they had married on March 9, 1796; on March 14, on his way to headquarters in Nice, where he was to take command of the Army of Italy, he wrote to her, signing his name, for the first time, *Bonaparte* and no longer *Buonaparte*.[44] Why did he fear tarnishing his glory by the foreign sound of his family name? It is all the odder because he himself liked to recall his Italian origins: "I had one foot in Italy, the other in France," he often said.[45] To be sure, he accepted with a smile the imaginary genealogies that were invented to flatter him. To those who claimed to have proof that he was descended from the Byzantine emperors of the Comnenus family or from the Roman *gentes* of Ulpia or Julia, he replied that "my titles are in my sword and in the Republic's confidence," and that the origins of his nobility were in the victories he had won at Montenotte and Lodi.[46] But he did not deny the possibility that his ancestors might have reigned over Treviso, and even took a certain pride in it. Similarly he considered it likely that he was related to the Medicis and the Orsinis. His ancestors, he said, had played an important role in Rome, and he owed his first name to the relations his Italian ancestors had maintained with "a Napoleon des Ursini who was famous in the chronicles of Italy."[47] He had an interest, of course, in making use of these aristocratic ancestors in the Italy he had conquered and of which he would later be president and then king: they were useful to him and contributed a great deal to the welcome the Italians gave him. Would he have made such a triumphal entrance into Milan and Bologna had their residents not seen in him a son of Italy and felt proud that their country had produced a figure "worthy of its lost grandeur"?[48] Bonaparte's Italian origins put the defeated in the camp of the victors, so to speak. In the "hero with Italian features who led the French phalanxes"[49] they could see, if not their own reflection, at least an image of their glorious past.

The "weak parts" that had to be covered up were not Italian, but Corsican. His Italian origins were illustrious and connected him with civilization and with Europe, whereas his Corsican origins set him apart from all this. It is true that his Corsican background had Italian associations, but the Italy they brought to mind was barbarous, poor, and obscurantist. For those who almost from the outset saw Napoleon as a *condottiere* or adventurer, a man *foreign* not only to France, to its history, and to its civilization, but also to European history and customs, his Corsican ancestry was a kind of admission that they were right.

The sympathy for Corsica's revolt against its Genoese masters that developed around the middle of the eighteenth century must not be underestimated. As Voltaire put it, at that time all of enlightened Europe was Corsican. Italian Enlightenment writers—from Joseph Gorani to Vittorio Alfieri—had been the first to celebrate the institutions founded by Paoli and the victories won by the Corsicans. And of course, the general's supporters had not been the last to show their enthusiasm. In 1758 the Neapolitan abbé Gregorio Salvini, Paoli's old friend, published a *Giustificazione della rivoluzione di Corsica* that was read throughout Europe. In it Paoli was presented "as an antique hero comparable to Thrasybulus, Epaminondas, and Timoleon, or to the great men of republican Rome."[50] The "Corsophilia" of the 1750s and 1760s spread from Italy to France. For a time Corsicans were honored guests in Parisian salons, at least metaphorically, since high society enjoyed their charms from afar. Madame du Deffand saw Paoli as the equal of Horace Walpole, who was in her opinion the greatest man in history, while Grimm put his pen in the service of these proud republicans, and Rousseau announced that because Corsica was the most backward of all the countries in Europe, and the only one still "capable of legislation," "someday this little island will astonish Europe."[51] From France the movement reached Britain, where it was to attain its greatest influence.[52] Catherine Macaulay praised the Corsican experiment in her *Short Sketch of a democratical form of government* (1767).[53] The young James Boswell—then twenty-five—became a passionate supporter of Corsica after reading Rousseau's *Social Contract*: having had the privilege of conversing with Rousseau, he went to Corsica in 1765. At first he nearly fainted, so impressed was he, and then, in the grip of "a sort of luxury of noble sentiment,"[54] he spent a few days in Pasquale Paoli's company, stunned by the nobility of the hero's features, his firmness of character, the virtue of his soul, his disinterestedness, his wisdom, his prudence, and also by the elegance of his manners and the love the Corsicans had for him, even though he was forced to observe that the great man lived surrounded by fierce-looking guards. Boswell left fully satisfied: "The contemplation of such a character really existing, was of more service to me than all I had been able to draw from books, from conversation, or from the exertions of my own mind. I had often formed the idea of a man continually such, as I could conceive in my best moments. But this idea appeared like the ideas we are taught in the schools to form of things which may exist, but do not; of seas of milk, and ships of amber. But I saw my highest idea realised in Paoli. It was impossible for me, speculate as I pleased, to have a little opinion of human nature in him."[55]

In Paoli, Boswell saw the reincarnation of the great legislators of antiquity, a new Solon, a new Lycurgus, and in the humble town Corte he saw the resurrection of the Athens of the century of Pericles. The success of his *Account of Corsica* (1768), which was soon translated into the main European languages, encouraged others to emulate him. John Symonds and a future bishop, Frederik August Hervey, Reverend Andrew Barnaby and Lord Pembroke, all discovering the Corsica they had imagined, were so enthusiastic about it that experience itself could not open their eyes. People flocked there just as, in another century, so many celebrities were to flock to Moscow.

No one, not even the most skeptical, quibbled about Paoli's right to admiration. Rightly, moreover, we can agree with Voltaire that "whatever one might say about him, it is not possible that this leader did not have great qualities."[56] The defense of Corsica was a cause that was all the more popular because in it the people were always associated with their leader and depicted in his image. The eighteenth-century *philosophes* believed that in Corsica they had finally rediscovered "Antiquity in the state of nature, an exemplary model of the persistence in modern times of the anthropological and moral characteristics of the classical age."[57] For a few years Corsica was the *tabula rasa* the Age of Enlightenment dreamed about, the new Promised Land where the ideal city previously confined to books would be realized. As Pierre Lanfrey was still to put it a century later, "Paoli was able seriously to dream of playing in his country the part of Solon and Lycurgus. . . . What in France was matter for speculation became in Corsica the programme of the statesman, and could be realised on the spot. . . . Corsica was in a situation only to be conceived as possible in any other country, on condition that everything existing should be swept utterly away."[58] For these writers it was because Corsica had remained outside European civilization that, thanks to Paoli's virtue and the help of his auxiliaries, the *philosophes,* it was very likely soon to arrive at the pinnacle of felicity.

But the enthusiasm that had spread as far as the European courts at Saint Petersburg and Potsdam—where Frederick the Great in person sent Paoli a sword of honor on whose blade were engraved the words *Patrias* and *Libertas*[59]—did not last. Enlightened opinion grew tired of it and soon found in the American insurgents other classical heroes to celebrate. It did so with all the more fervor because the Americans' rusticity, which was orderly and friendly, was free from the ferocity, primitive customs, and superstitious ignorance that stained the reputation of the inhabitants of Corsica and cast a shadow on admiration for them. An anecdote will clearly show this: When Boswell undertook to write an account of his pilgrimage to see Paoli, one of his friends advised him to talk less about Corsica, or the Corsicans, than about Paoli—at least if he wanted his book to be widely read. "Skim quickly over all the old-fashioned things," he told him, "the reader will get bored; it is the merits and exploits of their current leader that make the Corsicans an object of public curiosity."[60] The enthusiasm had never extended beyond the narrow circle of the salons and literary groups, and had it been possible to carry out an opinion survey, there is no doubt what the result would have been: despite Paoli and the sympathy and respect for the resistance mounted by a small, poor people, first to the soldiers of the Republic of Genoa and then to those of the king of France, the majority of the French still saw Corsica as Strabo or Livy had seen it: "Corsica is a harsh and mountainous land, and almost impracticable everywhere; it nourishes a people that resembles it. The Corsicans, who lack any civilization, are nearly as untamed as wild animals. Brought into captivity, they are hardly more domesticated when they are in chains. On the contrary, whether because they loathe work or slavery, they do themselves in; whether out of stubbornness or stupidity, they are unbearable to their masters!"[61]

Moreover, when the focus shifted from Paoli to the Corsicans in general, even the most favorably disposed expressed certain doubts. We may cite as examples Abbé Galiani, who saw the Corsicans as "poor, savage people who think liberty means impunity and who consider themselves fortunate not to be governed,"[62] and even Rousseau himself, whom Matteo Buttafoco had invited in 1764 to draft a proposed constitution for Corsica, or, more simply, a history of the island. Rousseau set to work, but the further he went, the more he felt the "necessity of studying on the spot the people to be legislated for, the soil they inhabited, and all the circumstances governing the application of new laws to the Corsicans." He wrote to Buttafoco, informing him of his intention to go to Corsica in the near future, and his preparations for this journey were well advanced when he met M. d'Astier, who had served in Corsica under Marshal de Maillebois (1738–1741). This meeting was critical: "He did all he could to dissuade me from the idea; and I admit that the frightful picture of the Corsicans and their country that he drew for me greatly tempered my desire to go and live among them."[63] Rousseau gave up his planned journey, worked a while longer on his plan for a constitution, and then lost interest in it. The future General Dumouriez, who had taken part in the military operations connected with the conquest of Corsica in 1768 and 1769, reports that everywhere people blamed Choiseul's initiative, and that one of his friends, who was nonetheless favorable to General Paoli, had told him that the Corsicans were so ungovernable "that we would be only too happy to find a large hole in the center of the island into which they could all be thrown."[64] Even the Abbé Raynal, another eloquent defender of the Corsicans, had mixed feelings about them, and when in 1787 he decided to dedicate to them the second volume of one of his novels, *La Négresse couronnée*, he did so in these pungent terms: "Dear citizens, I dedicate this book to you, because no one has ever dedicated anything to you, and I am eager to offer public homage to all those who have been consigned to oblivion; it seems to me that this is a way of avenging humanity's right. You will not be offended if it is only the second part; when it is a question of a Negro majesty, the swarthy have to yield precedence to the black."[65]

Paoli looked like a survivor from classical times who had at the same time cultivated the politeness and refined manners of the eighteenth century; the customs of the Corsican people appeared instead as "a remnant of barbarity that had survived within civilized Europe."[66] After conquering the island in 1769, the French very soon became convinced that Corsica was, as Napoleon put it, "a wart on France's nose."[67] The ephemeral renewal of fervor surrounding Paoli's return in 1790 did not change this image in any way, especially because the realities of the Revolution in Corsica were soon made known by reports that were, though not always free from polemical and partisan aims, uncontested in their factual observations if not in their conclusions. No one contradicted Volney when he asserted that "Corsica, by its physical constitution and its inhabitants' customs and character, differs completely from the rest of France," and that its population participated simultaneously, through its customs, in "the savage state and that of an incipient civilization."[68] Even the British were disillusioned when they took control of the island in 1794. They had once been among the most fervent admirers of Paoli and independent Corsica, but the experiences of the union of the British Crown and the island soon prompted them to make less favorable comments. It will be objected that these were prejudices. Nonetheless, Dupont de Nemours, learning that Bonaparte had been named to lead the Army of Italy in 1796, protested to his friend the Director Reubell: "My dear old colleague, it is said that you are entrusting the Army of Italy, our last hope if the war continues, to two Corsicans, Buonaparte and Saliceti. . . . Don't you know what Corsicans are like? For two thousand years, no one has ever been able to count on them. They are inconstant by nature; they are all out to make their own fortunes, and Pitt can give them more guineas than you can mint money. . . . The best thing to do would be to make peace. . . . If you are going to make war, then at least don't leave its outcome to Corsicans, and in Italy. Aren't there any Frenchmen any more? I greet you, embrace you, and pity you."[69]

In 1796 Corsica had been French for seventeen years. Napoleon had to free himself from this burden, and in the last days of his life he told Bertrand that had he been born in Berry rather than in Corsica, he would have had a palace built there.[70]

PART TWO

Entry on Stage

1793–1796

SIX

Toulon

$\mathcal{T}$he Buonapartes disembarked at Toulon on June 13, 1793, in a state of near deprivation; their possessions had been stolen, their goods pillaged. They found refuge in the nearby village of La Valette, but they soon had to flee; they had landed in the middle of the civil war that had been kindled by the proscription of the Girondins on June 2, 1793. All of southern France was ablaze. For two months Letizia drifted with the youngest of her children from Toulon to Beausset and from Brignoles to Marseille, where they finally found a safer retreat after the Convention's troops reconquered the city.[1] She had endured these trials without the help of her sons. Lucien had left to take up a modest job as the guardian of a supply depot in Saint-Maximin, while Joseph was in Paris asking the Convention to provide aid,[2] and Napoleon had rejoined his artillery regiment in Nice.

General Du Teil, who commanded the regiment, was glad to see him; the emigration of royalist officers had left such gaps that any reinforcement was welcome, even an officer known chiefly for his absenteeism.[3] Nevertheless, Napoleon did not get the active command he desired. Du Teil assigned him to organize convoys of gunpowder and materiel. He soon grew tired of this monotonous work and requested a transfer;[4] anything seemed to him preferable to the supervisory tasks to which he had been doomed. His assignment having taken him to Avignon, he witnessed the taking of the city by the army sent to fight the federalists in the south. We do not know what he did afterward, but at the end of August he entered Marseille on the heels of General Carteaux's victorious army.[5] On September 15 or 16, Saliceti and Gasparin, who were members of the Convention, came to his aid by naming him head of the artillery in Carteaux's army, which was now assigned to reconquer Toulon. Contrary to what Napoleon claimed later, a chance encounter with his brother Joseph and Saliceti played no role in his promotion. He had gone to meet them, and because he was complaining about the thankless assignments he had been given, Saliceti suggested that he attract the representatives' attention by writing something patriotic, since at that time anything coming from Corsica was a little suspect. Napoleon composed a republican profession of faith—*Le Souper de Beaucaire*— and arranged to have it printed. Saliceti took it upon himself to have a second edition printed at the army's expense, and next arranged for Joseph a lucrative position as "war commissioner first class."[6] Then it was Napoleon's turn. On September 7 Captain Dommartin, the commander of Carteaux's artillery, was wounded during the attack on the Ollioules defile, on the road to Toulon, and Saliceti and his colleague Gasparin gave the post to Napoleon.[7] "At least he's one of ours," Saliceti said.[8] He may never have liked the young Corsican—but he had not forgotten him.

Under Carteaux's Orders

The artillery entrusted to Captain Buonaparte was not impressive: about thirty small-caliber pieces and a few munitions. The rest of General Carteaux's army was no more prepossessing. It consisted of some 10,000 soldiers who were often disinclined to fight, and who had been taken from the Army of the Alps or even from the ranks of the federalist legion that had just been defeated at Marseille.[9] It lacked weapons, its salaries had not been paid, general indiscipline, waste, and lying were common, training was mediocre, and supervision incompetent.[10] Learning of the revolt in Lyon and in the south, the Committee of Public Safety had ordered the commanders of the Armies of the Alps and Italy, Kellermann and Brunet, to suspend their operations on the borders of Piedmont and to advance on the federalist bands. The two generals, reluctant to engage in civil war, took the importance of the first assignment with which they had been entrusted as a pretext for refusing to obey without an express order from the Convention. The Convention's representatives assigned to these armies insisted: Kellermann was forced to march on Lyon while part of his army, entrusted to General Carteaux, was to attack the rebels in the south. Kellermann willingly "lent" Carteaux, but refusing to direct the siege of Lyon himself, he assigned this task to General Doppet.

Carteaux had served in the army before beginning a career as an artist: he had produced, it is said, "acceptable paintings."[11] In 1789 he had enlisted in the

Parisian National Guard. Initially a supporter of La Fayette, he had later become a Jacobin. At heart he was a moderate, and although he tried to look like a Jacobin, with, as Jaurès said of the Hébertists, "a drooping mustache and a dragging saber," in private he was quite different: "He didn't want people to be too familiar with him," Napoleon recalled. "At table, only those in the middle, where he sat with the representative of the people, were well served; the guests at the end of the table got nothing."[12] Carteaux had risen to the summits of the military hierarchy thanks to his reputation as a *sans-culotte*, and knew nothing about war. The Revolution, which created so many talented officers out of thin air, also created some mediocre ones, and Carteaux was certainly one of the latter. However, he was completely ignorant only of real war, for concerning civil war he was very superior to Kellermann, as he demonstrated in the south—at least until the arrival of the British in Toulon put him in a theater where everyone could see his incompetence.

While Doppet was besieging Lyon, Carteaux marched on the federalists, and having defeated them in six weeks, he entered Marseille on August 24. Two days later the people of Toulon handed the port over to the Anglo-Spanish fleet. On September 29 Carteaux advanced on Toulon with a force of about 4,000 men. On September 7 he broke through the defile at Ollioules, while 4,000 soldiers from the Army of Italy under the command of General Poype approached from the east.[13]

Captain Buonaparte's Plan

The city of Toulon is nestled at the end of a double harbor. Access to the larger harbor is bordered on the east by Cape Brun and on the west by the Saint-Mandrier peninsula, while access to the smaller inner harbor is bordered on the east by the Great Tower and Fort Lamalgue, and on the west by the Le Caire promontory and its two forts, L'Éguillette and Balaguier. Impregnable by sea, Toulon is hardly less impregnable by land: backed up against Mount Faron, the city was defended by a dozen forts and redoubts constructed on both sides of the mountain, whose steep slopes separated General Carteaux's troops from those of La Poype. The allies—the British, Spaniards, Piedmontese, and Neapolitans—had 20,000 men, twice the number of the forces

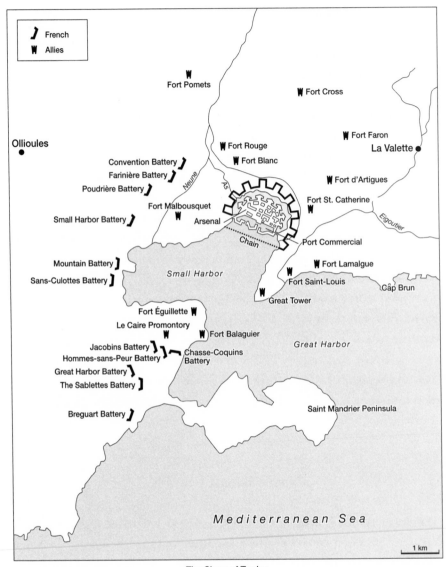

The Siege of Toulon

assembled by the Convention. They had occupied the heights and undertaken works of fortification.

Given the imbalance of the forces and the strength of the enemy entrenchments, how was Toulon to be taken? Napoleon studied the topography and drew this conclusion: The insurgents in Toulon could not resist for long without the support of the Allied fleet, so it was useless to try to take the city by making an assault whose success was doubtful; it sufficed to force the enemy fleet to leave by taking possession of the only point from which the passage between the small and the large harbor could be bombarded, thus breaking the British troops' connection with the high seas. This point was the Le Caire promontory. Napoleon repeated it indefatigably: "To control the harbor, we have to control L'Éguillette."[14] If enough firepower was assembled on this point, the allies would sail away rather than expose their ships to destruction. The artillery would play the main role in the operation, and the infantry could subsequently march into the city. The plan was realistic: it sought to compensate for the republicans' numerical and material inferiority by concentrating their means on a crucial point. The line of march to be followed was obvious: move on La Seyne and the Le Caire promontory after the penetration made at Ollioules on September 7 and install on its extremity powerful batteries that would, by threatening the two harbors, force the enemy fleet to run up its sails.

Many historians have refused to attribute this plan to Napoleon. They point out, for example, that it was so obvious, given the topography, that Napoleon "would have had little merit in discovering what everyone already knew."[15] The idea was in fact in the air. But it is a long way from an idea *in the air* to a precise plan. No one made the slightest mention of the Le Caire promontory or the preponderant role of the artillery.[16] Moreover, at this juncture the generals and representatives were in agreement in preferring an assault.[17] On September 10 the representatives were still talking in a confused way about attacking the forts held by the enemy or bombarding the city and the harbor in order "to burn the English fleet or force it to retreat."[18] The more precise plans were hardly more convincing; one of them, Albitte's, proposed "striking the port of Toulon and the fleet moored there" from "the little fort of La Seyne."[19] It has to be said, to Albitte's credit, that Carteaux had placed his artillery even farther from the shore, so far that the demonstration he had made, after a dinner where a great deal of wine had been drunk, to impress Napoleon on his arrival, did not at all convince him: none of the shots reached the harbor.[20] A naval engineer, Doumet-Revest, also envisaged the bombardment of the fleet, but as a secondary maneuver intended to support the movement of six infantry columns that would fall upon the city simultaneously.[21] A true specialist, Michaud d'Arçon, who was working with Carnot, proposed a plan in which we find Napoleon's very idea. But instead of designating the Le Caire promontory as the strategic position that had to be taken at any cost, he proposed to occupy the capes surrounding the two harbors, a gigantic task for which he estimated the number of men necessary at 150,000, whereas they had not even 15,000.[22]

I do not mean to suggest that Napoleon was the only person with eyes to see. That would be to insult the excellent officers who fought at his side in Toulon. Many of them probably shared his point of view but did not dare to say so. We cannot ignore the particularities of the time. In late 1793 it was risky, to say the least, to support a plan that gave the artillery the leading role. The mystique of the general conscription was then at its zenith; the revolutionaries favored bayonet charges. Enthusiasm was believed to be more important than military science, and the melee was considered preferable to clever maneuvering. Moreover, artillery was a suspect weapon because it was operated by technicians who had graduated from the Old Regime's best schools, and who were, it was said, motivated by an esprit de corps dangerous in a republic. The infantrymen from the volunteer battalions raised since 1791 were thought far better. Another factor was important: officers were in constant danger of being dismissed. No less than 1,300 of them were stripped of their functions in 1793; generals were imprisoned, and several were decapitated. The Revolution consumed a great many officers, punishing them when they were defeated, fearing them when they were victorious. The Convention's representatives were in no less danger: fifteen of them in the south denounced each other. Living themselves under the threat of a recall to Paris that augured ill, they had all the more tendency to sacrifice the demands of war to political imperatives and reality to rhetoric. How could they do otherwise when they were, day after day, assailed by governmental warnings requiring them to take "prompt and effective measures" to "exterminate all traitors"?[23] Forgetting that war obeys its own rules, they often saw in these reports in which the generals expressed their doubts and complained about the insufficiency of the means put at their disposition the expression of a culpable "modérantisme." Why didn't Napoleon do as others did, flattering General Carteaux or those emissaries who clung to the idea of an assault and, like Barras or Fréron, referred, perhaps without believing a word of it, to the tens of thousands of men they were going to send, bayonets fixed, to assault the rebel city? Because he put war above politics, considered for its own sake, without ever making any connection between his mission and the political dimension of the conflict. In his view Toulon was simply an objective, and he cared little whether the city had gone over to federalism or to counterrevolution. He happened to be in the camp of the Convention, but he would have studied with the same seriousness the possibilities of repulsing an attack by the Convention's forces had he been in the opposing camp. The political stakes in the conflict were not his concern.

The Siege of Toulon

On September 13—thus *before* Napoleon's arrival at Toulon on September 16 or 17—Saliceti and Gasparin adopted a new plan: "Far from us *to lay a regular siege* to the town of Toulon, *when we possess a surer means of reducing it, and this means consists in either destroying the hostile squadron by fire, or in compelling it to retreat in fear thereof. . . .* We are merely waiting for our heavy artillery to occupy a position whence we can reach the ships with red-hot ball, and *we shall then see whether we do not become masters of Toulon.*"[24]

Up to that point no one had considered control of the harbor as the key to the reconquest of Toulon, or, still less, mentioned the existence of a single position whose control would make it possible to take the city. Hence, it is likely—at least it is the most plausible hypothesis—that the two representatives had a conversation with Napoleon between September 11, the date of the previously adopted plan, and September 13, and that this conversation convinced them that it was impossible to conduct a classical siege. When Napoleon got there, he showed them precisely where to place the batteries. He knew Toulon well; he used to wait there for the ship taking him back to Corsica. The vessel's time of departure was at that time highly uncertain—a lack of wind, or too much wind, could delay it for hours or even days. The young officer had taken advantage of the wait to observe the surroundings. The topography was also familiar, because Toulon and Ajaccio, which is also located at the end of double harbor, greatly resemble each other. At Ajaccio, the first harbor is bound by the citadel and Point Aspretto, the second by that point and Point Porticcio. In the spring of 1793, shortly before he left Corsica, he had drawn up a *Plan for the defense of the Gulf of Ajaccio* in which he wrote that to prevent an enemy landing it would suffice to fortify the Aspretto promontory, which was situated at the junction of the two harbors, in exactly the same way that at Toulon he designated the corresponding promontory of L'Éguillette: "A battery placed on the Aspretto promontory would cross its fire with that of the fortress. . . . It would have absolute control over the entrance and the interior of the harbor, where the enemy could anchor only after having put a stop to the said battery's fire."[25] There is no doubt that it was Napoleon who inspired the plan the representatives sent to the Committee of Public Safety on September 26: "You know from our preceding communiqués the plan we had adopted: to burn or drive the enemy fleet out of the harbor and to limit ourselves, so far as Toulon is concerned, to cutting all lines of communication from the inside to the outside and from the outside to the inside. It was the only practicable one with the small number of men we have, because the situation of Toulon, whose only outlets lead through the two gorges, that of Ollioules and that of La Valette, does not require many troops to cut its lines of communication, and because the fleet would be taken care of by the artillery alone."[26]

However, winning the support of Saliceti and Gasparin was not nearly enough. It is true that without them, nothing would have been possible, and Napoleon never forgot what he owed them; they had, he said, "opened his career."[27] They protected him and backed his efforts to get his plan approved, but they could not invent what did not exist. The problem was that the means to realize his plan were completely lacking. With such a small number of artillery pieces it was impossible to set up the approximately ten batteries required.[28] Napoleon began by moving the existing batteries closer to the bay of Brégaillon, bombarding the ships anchored along the left flank of the Le Caire promontory to force them to move away. To be sure, "this was not enough to make the fleet think it was in danger."[29] But it did allow Napoleon to show that the only way to cause the allied fleet serious concern was to strike it from point-blank range. However, he needed more cannons, more shells, more powder; it was also necessary to give the artillery the "respect and independence in its operations without which it cannot serve usefully"; and finally the devotees of bayonet charges had to be convinced that "it is artillery that takes [fortified] places" whereas "the infantry is merely auxiliary."[30] Napoleon conducted a veritable war of harassment against his superiors. Every time he was asked, even by Carteaux in person, to lend horses or vehicles to transport the army's equipment, he abruptly refused, noting that the horses and vehicles assigned to the artillery could not be used elsewhere. That he had to fight so hard was partly because he was only a battalion leader.[31] The *sans-culotte* army of Year II was no less sensitive to hierarchy than any other. Thus Napoleon and his protectors asked that he be put under the direction of an artillery general who was "by his rank capable of contributing to respect and of impressing a bunch of ignorant members of the staff, with which it is always necessary to yield and dogmatize to destroy their prejudices."[32] General Du Teil did not arrive until November, and Napoleon fought alone to create an artillery on the basis of nonexistent resources, scolding his subordinates and harassing the military and civilian authorities until he had at his disposal the sixty artillery pieces he needed.

However, this relentless effort changed nothing essential. Carteaux refused to yield: Toulon would be taken by land. When Napoleon said, "That's where Toulon is," pointing to the promontory of L'Éguillette, the general-in-chief replied, "Am I dreaming? Aren't the steeples of Toulon there? And he tells me that Toulon is over there!"[33] As for Barras and Fréron, who did not believe in Bonaparte's plan and who, having hardly more confidence in Carteaux's military talents, despaired of seeing the siege end quickly, they thought up an alternative plan that consisted in raising the siege, no less, and then retiring behind the Durance River, carrying out a scorched-earth policy in order to starve the residents of Toulon and the British, who would give up after a few months. Then, "like a torrent, the republicans would push back the slavish horde and drive them out to sea."[34] The time of chimerical schemes was not yet over. Nonetheless, Carteaux could not flatly refuse Saliceti and Gasparin. Thus, Napoleon having moved up his batteries on La Seyne, Carteaux finally took the initiative of attacking the Le Caire promontory. Had he sought to prove that his plan was impracticable, he could have done no better. He "attacked halfheartedly and was thrown back."[35] This failed assault was not without consequences: the British landed reinforcements, occupied the promontory of L'Éguillette, and built a powerful redoubt there that bristled with cannons and was given the name of its builder, Lord Mulgrave. Saliceti exploded: "If our general has not grasped the only practicable plan for taking Toulon, the English have grasped the danger to them, and on Saturday evening (September 21) they landed troops, seized the heights, and placed forces around the large harbor. There was still time to drive them out . . . all that was required was to rush the position and take it by force at any cost. . . . That was not understood by either the general or the colonel commanding the attack. . . . We therefore consider that our common plan has failed, and that the Toulon expedition . . . is becoming a long-term affair that will succeed only with time and numbers."[36]

Carteaux and La Poype returned to their own concerns. La Poype, who was jealous of Carteaux, attacked Mount Faron: he hoped to take it, effect his junction with Carteaux's army, and then involve the latter, under his command, in an attack on Toulon. His failure was disastrous, as was another attack made on Cape Brun. This time it was too much. Saliceti and Gasparin decided to get rid of Carteaux and those around him, who were "even more ignorant and stubborn" than he was.[37] On October 12 they persuaded Barras and Fréron to sign a letter asking the Committee of Public Safety to replace the general-in-chief. Paris immediately responded to Saliceti's demand by replacing Carteaux by Dugommier, Doppet being assigned as interim commander pending the general's arrival. Napoleon, fearing that Carteaux's successors would be no more competent, had sent the minister of war a long report in which he once again set forth his plan.[38] But Dugommier's arrival on November 16 marked a turning point. A decorated officer—he was fifty-five years old and had taken part in the Seven Years' War and the American War of Independence—he was neither an egotist nor a charlatan, even though he owed to Marat his promotion to general. He restored order to the army, bringing it back from the brink of anarchy, and on November 25 he had the plan Napoleon had been advocating for months adopted.[39] The Council of War decided to focus the main effort on L'Éguillette and Mount Faron, the first objective being intended to force the enemy fleet's departure, the second to cut Toulon's lines of communication with the interior.[40] The offensive was set for December 8.

But the British, noting the preparations being made by the republican army, counterattacked from Fort Malbousquet on November 30. The 6,000 soldiers defending the republican lines scattered at the first charge. "The morning was too beautiful for me to forego telling you what happened," Napoleon wrote to his friend Dupin, one of the minister of war's assistants.[41] Although it turned out to be "beautiful"—Dugommier had finally turned a bad situation around and the British general O'Hara had been taken prisoner—it had above all revealed a lack of fighting spirit among some of the troops. The general attack was postponed for a few days. Finally, on December 11, everything was ready and the signal was given. The action began with a five-day bombardment of the enemy positions, and then, during the night of December 17, the republicans attacked, as planned, Mount Faron and the Le Caire promontory. Napoleon took part. The British were defeated. Driven out of Fort Mulgrave and the Le Caire promontory, they evacuated Toulon the next day.

Second Birth

"There will history take him up, never more to leave him; there commences his immortality."[42] That is a great exaggeration: Bonaparte was hardly mentioned after the fall of the city, and he himself later said that if the siege of Toulon had convinced him of his own talents, "all that did not go very far," not far enough for him to henceforth consider himself "a superior man."[43] He was known to a small group who were lavish in their praise of him, but beyond that circle he was still nothing, and Junot's father, tired of reading letters in which his son sang his superior's praises instead of relating news about himself, finally replied: "Who is this General Bonaparte? Where has he served? Nobody knows."[44] Even his promotion to the rank of *général de brigade* on December 22, 1793, did not mean that he had emerged from obscurity.[45] There was nothing exceptional about attaining such a rank at his age; like him, Marceau had been twenty-four when he had received his general's stripes, and Davout had been twenty-five.

The Revolution mass-produced generals: 962 of them from 1791 to 1793.[46] It could not do otherwise; 6,000 officers had emigrated or resigned by the end of 1791, and 10,000 by the summer of 1794. Promotions were numerous, advancement rapid, disgraces frequent. The Revolution, as has been said, did not always treat well those whom it raised to prominence. Napoleon had occasion to learn this only a few days after the victory at Toulon. The representative of the people, Maignet, asked him to inspect Fort Saint Nicolas in Marseille, the outer walls of which had been torn down by the revolutionaries. Napoleon advised raising them again in order to safeguard the gunpowder depot, and, if necessary, to "take control" of the city. This report caused a sensation in Paris. How dare he suspect the people? Maignet got scared. He denounced Napoleon, and the Convention summoned the "artillery commander." Such a summons was not to be taken lightly. Fortunately it was delivered to the wrong address, and it was Sugny, the artillery commander in Marseille, who set out for Paris. He had no trouble justifying himself. The affair might have stopped there had Maignet, who was clearly very frightened, not repeated his accusations. A new message was sent, this time to the right address. But the matter had dragged on too long. Napoleon had assumed new functions at the headquarters of the Army of Italy, where the representatives, Augustin Robespierre and Ricord, forbade him to leave his post. Thanks to the two representatives, the case was closed, but Napoleon had come close to finding himself, like so many others, thrown into prison.[47]

However, there is a kernel of truth in what Las Cases says. Even if Napoleon still did not know himself, in Toulon he appeared as the man he would continue to be. It is at that point that we must date the second birth we have mentioned. Everything is there, beginning with the imperious tone that does not brook disagreement, even when he is addressing someone more important than he is. Furious about the requisitions sent him by military agents and civil authorities, he wrote to the representatives to put them in their place: "One is just as guilty when one allows errors to be made as when one makes them. I beg you, representatives, to see to it that no weapon is taken away from its functions. One cannot know how to do what one has not learned and what one has never done."[48] With those of his subordinates whom he considered insufficiently zealous or incompetent, the tone, as one might imagine, is no gentler. In the

Army of Italy, where he took command of the artillery on March 1, 1794, there was an officer named Berlier. A veteran of the Old Regime's armies, he commanded the artillery at Antibes. Napoleon had hardly assumed his position before he noted grave errors of negligence in Berlier's service and fell upon him:

> That is not how the Republic is to be served; you have obviously compromised the service. . . . I am astonished that you take so long to carry out orders, it is always necessary to order you three times to do the same thing. . . . The notion has been spread around Antibes that the powder has been taken out of it; I hope it has not been spread by you or your guard, because things will go badly for those who sow alarm among the people. . . . I urge you, out of the interest I have in you, to never alarm anyone whomever. . . . I have been told that in an assembly of military men there was talk about the existing powder and the powder that was lacking for the supply of Antibes, that it was you who provided the information for these calculations; I hope that is false. . . . It is an imposture to say that you have only 28,000 pounds of powder in Antibes when you have 45,000, whether in barrels, in cannon charges, or in cartridges. The difference you mention can have no effect other than to alarm people. I therefore beg you to calculate better.[49]

He was hard on his subordinates, but protected them from others and defended their interests. When the representatives decided, applying the law to the maximum, to levy a tax of ten sous on the soldiers' salaries for every half-pound of meat provided to them, he opposed their decision: "Please issue an order that the war commissioner is authorized to levy the tax . . . only at the rate of five sous."[50] When Gassendi, whom he had known since Auxonne and to whom he had entrusted the direction of the arsenal of Marseille, was dismissed for having refused to take delivery of rifles manufactured, badly, by "revolutionary workshops," he hurried to Marseille and, not having been able to obtain Gassendi's reinstatement, took him under his protection and made him part of his own staff. Those who served under his command composed *his* army. During his period in Toulon he had already begun to establish relationships with his men that were based both on the protection he afforded them and on their allegiance to him personally. At that time an initial group of loyal followers formed, in which we find Gassendi and Victor, two old comrades from Auxonne, the ordnance officer Chauvet, Duroc, and especially Junot, Muiron, and Marmont. "I admired him profoundly," Marmont admitted; "I found him so superior to everyone I had already met in my life, his private conversations were so profound and had so much charm, there was so much future in his mind."[51] Like so many others later on, he would have followed him into Hell. Bonaparte was not, however, prepossessing; he was of medium stature,[52] frightfully thin, with a pale complexion—"yellow," witnesses say; he looked worn-out, his hair fell on his shoulders, he was unkempt, poorly dressed, his clothes were threadbare, he was awkward with his saber, seemed ill at ease on horseback, expressed himself with a strong accent that sometimes made him incomprehensible, and was moreover afflicted with scabies contracted during the siege. He looked ill, and in truth a little pathetic. And yet he impressed people. Napoleon was born in war. In it, he revealed qualities, a temperament, a charisma, even a style of which no trace is to be found earlier. Logically: it was at Toulon that he began his experience of war. "War is a singular art," he was to say, "I have fought sixty battles. Well then! I have learned nothing that I didn't know after the first one."[53] He was telling the truth. If one wanted to define what separated the battalion leader at the siege of Toulon from the general-in-chief of the Army of Italy, one might say that in Italy Bonaparte was precisely the same as he was in Toulon, only on a larger scale.

A Spring in Nice

"Extremely tired," as he acknowledged the day after Toulon was taken,[54] Napoleon did not have time to rest, no matter how much he deserved it. Assigned to inspect the coastal defenses, for two months he hurried back and forth from Toulon to Nice and from Marseille to Antibes. He was in Marseille when he finally obtained, on February 7, 1794, the command he had dreamed of, that of the Army of Italy's artillery. As soon as he had assumed his functions, at the beginning of March, he settled his mother in a little rural retreat near Menton and added Louis to his staff. The following months were certainly among the happiest of his life.

His superior, General Dumerbion, was no longer young. Courageous and learned, he suffered from a bad case of gout that often forced him to stay in bed; he could command the army so long as it did not move, but he would not have been able to follow it if it had gone on the offensive. He necessarily relied on his subordinates, and they thereby acquired an autonomy that would have turned into complete independence had they not been obliged to report to the Convention's representatives. There Napoleon was on familiar ground, because he found in Nice Augustin Robespierre and Jean-François Ricord, who had been at the siege of Toulon. Among these three young men—Napoleon was twenty-four, Augustin thirty-one, and Ricord thirty-five—there was esteem, trust, and perhaps friendship. People said Augustin was stupid and feared Napoleon. People were wrong. Gossips claimed that his head was a bell that rang when his brother Maximilien struck it. It is true that Augustin did nothing that would not have won his brother's assent. They had the same thoughts, and if one day, at the Jacobins, Maximilien brusquely interrupted his younger brother who had just criticized Dechristianization, it was simply because he had said out loud what Maximilien thought but considered still impolitic to declare. Augustin did not have Maximilien's aptitude for politics. He was indissolubly attached to his brother. He had been orphaned while still a child, and Maximilien had served as a father to him. On 9 Thermidor, he preferred to die with him rather than survive him. They were, however, as different as possible. Maximilien was cold and secretive, and led an austere, apparently chaste life, whereas Augustin was sociable and not well suited for the reign of virtue as his brother understood it; his entourage included men of doubtful character and pretty women.

After a year of near inactivity on the Alpine front, the time had come for the resumption of operations against the king of Sardinia, whose kingdom of Piedmont covered the Austrians, who had established themselves in Lombardy. Each of the two armies, of the Alps and of Italy, supported by the members of the Convention sent to them on assignment (Saliceti and Laporte for the Army of the Alps, Augustin and Ricord for the Army of Italy), demanded the leading role in the future offensive. The Army of the Alps wanted to attack in the direction of Turin, starting from Mont Cenis and supported on the right by the Army of Italy; the latter objected that entering Italy by the corniche offered "an easy passage to overthrow the Sardinian tyrant."[55] In Paris, approval of this plan was far from unanimous. Its advantages were recognized, the narrow plain bordering the sea was more practicable than the Alpine passes, but it was clear that it would involve a violation of Genoese neutrality. In order to overcome the government's hesitations, Augustin and Ricord needed a precise plan of operations. They entrusted its preparation to Napoleon. This kind of work did not, a priori, fall within the artillery commander's remit, but Augustin swore by this young general who had, he said, "transcendent merit."[56] Napoleon set to work. The campaign's objective was the fortified town of Coni, located at the beginning of the Piedmontese plain that extends as far as Turin. An initial phase was supposed to make it possible to drive the Piedmontese from all the positions they were occupying south of the Tanaro River. Whereas part of the Army of Italy would hasten along the coast, by way of the corniche, as far as Oneglia (Imperia), on Genoese territory, and would keep an eye on the Lombard plain where the Austrians were, the other part, which was also to enter by way of the corniche, would ascend the Roya, Nervia, and Taggia valleys and deploy on the right bank of the Tanaro along a line running from the heights of Limone in the west to Garessio in the east. Then the Piedmontese, established on the heights along the border, from Saorge to the Tende pass, seeing themselves attacked from behind and outflanked on their right, would abandon their positions and retreat to the north, toward Coni, in order to avoid the risk of seeing their line of communication with Cherasco and Turin broken.

This initial plan for a campaign written up by Napoleon has—in a larger theater—clear analogies with the maneuver he had directed in Toulon: in the latter case, to obtain the surrender of the rebellious city, he ignores it, moves around the harbor, and situates his cannons at the precise place from which, by threatening the fleet, he can force it to retreat. In Italy, to get the Piedmontese to abandon their mountain positions, he goes around the Alps and marches on their lines of communication. In both cases there is the same maneuver: a march on the flank and an attack from behind, the only difference being that in Italy, infantry divisions replace the cannons of Toulon. The offensive programmed by Napoleon was launched on April 6, 1794. Everything went as planned: Oneglia fell on April 9, Saorge on April 28, the Tende pass on May 7. Napoleon went back to his maps, considering the possibility of extending this initial success by launching a general offensive in which the left wing of the Army of Italy would give a hand to the right wing of the Army of the Alps. Whereas the former would move from the Tende pass toward Borgo San Dalmazzo, less than ten kilometers from Coni, the Army of the Alps, entering Italy via the Larche and Fenestre passes, would reach the valley of the Stura and march on Demonte, thus maneuvering behind the rear of the Army of Italy and playing a secondary role. Ricord was enthusiastic: the Italian campaign, he said, was going to be "a pleasure."[57]

Napoleon and Robespierre

This new plan was adopted on May 21, 1794.[58] At that point the Committee of Public Safety called a halt to the operations. Carnot was frightened by the "sudden extension of France," and "he perceived the difficulties we were going to encounter in assimilating so many territories all at once, the concerns that we were going to arouse in Europe that would prolong the war indefinitely, and finally the deflection of the revolutionary movement and the transformation of the national spirit into a spirit of conquest. Therefore he wanted to stop, at least for the moment, the extension of France."[59] He wanted this all the more because Robespierre had become a fervent partisan of offensive war. Carnot ordered the Army of Italy to suspend its operations.[60] To obtain, through Maximilien's influence, a counter-order, Augustin returned to Paris at the end of June, bringing with him the reworked plan of June 20 and, perhaps, a note from Napoleon, *Sur la position politique et militaire de nos armées de Piémont et d'Espagne* (On the Political and Military Position of Our Armies of Piedmont and Spain).[61] Napoleon had no doubt that Augustin would succeed: on July 11, without suspecting the imminence of catastrophe, he went to Genoa to reconnoiter the terrain and to inquire about the arrangements made by the Republic. He had hardly returned to Nice before he learned, on August 5, that Robespierre was dead. Two days later he wrote to Tilly, the French chargé d'affaires in Genoa:

> You will have learned of the conspiracy and the death of Robespierre, Couthon, Saint-Just, etc. [Robespierre] had on his side the Jacobins, the Paris city council, and the National Guard's staff, but after a

moment of vacillation the people rallied to the Convention. Barère, Carnot, Prieur, Billaud-Varenne, etc. are still on the Committee of Public Safety; that changes nothing. Ricord, after having been assigned by the Committee of Public Safety to notify the conspiracy, was called back to the Convention;[62] Saliceti is currently the representative to the Army of Italy. Our naval operations will be somewhat impeded, I think, and perhaps even completely changed. The artillery had been moved forward, and the Sardinian tyrant was about to receive a heavy blow, but I hope that it will only be delayed.... I have been somewhat moved by the catastrophic fate of Robespierre, whom I liked and thought pure, but had he been my father, I would have stabbed him myself if he aspired to tyranny.[63]

"Somewhat moved" (*un peu affecté*) is a euphemism. Was he moved because he found himself on the side of the defeated? Because he saw the collapse of the hopes he had founded on Robespierre's protection? Or because he was sincerely attached to Augustin?

Some people see in his conduct nothing but opportunism, saying that in 1793 he rallied to the Montagnards only after he had lost everything, counting on Saliceti to give him a boost. Napoleon's *Le Souper de Beaucaire*,[64] they continue, was "a self-interested and calculated act": "In short, the argument [of the *Souper*], is reduced to this, that it was an act of good citizenship to join the party of the Mountain, because the Mountain had proved itself to be the strongest."[65] An attentive reading of this little pamphlet hardly confirms this view. Napoleon did not claim that right and justice were to be found on the side of the Mountain; he even suggested the contrary. Far from showering the obligatory insults on the Girondins, he referred to their past "purity." His argument was different: the Girondins, he said, were guilty not because they were traitors but despite being victims—although they had been unjustly proscribed, they could expect to find their salvation only in civil war: "I do not ask whether these men who had served the people well on so many occasions have conspired against it; it is enough for me to know that since the Mountain, out of public spirit and out of party spirit, has been led to the furthest extremities against them, has decreed [against them], imprisoned them, and, I will grant, even slandered them, the

Brissotins [i.e., the Girondins] were lost without a civil war that put them in a position to impose their rule on their enemies."

Thus, Napoleon goes on, they have made themselves guilty of the "greatest of crimes" and are thus forced to seek aid from abroad and to join, even against their will, the counterrevolutionary camp. This condemnation of the Brissotins not for the imaginary crimes of which they were accused, but for the consequences of their calls for resistance, was not in any way singular at that time. It was the view of all those who, while disliking the Jacobins, feared civil war and counterrevolution more. Except in the south, the revolt was running out of steam. The movement had spread "more on the surface than in depth."[66] It was a revolt by bourgeois and elected officials who had soon grown frightened by its consequences. In the middle of the revolutionary conflict, in the middle of the foreign war, there was no possibility of a third way. The choice was between submission and treason. The leader of the "federalists" in Normandy, Puisaye, left for the Vendée; in Lyon the insurgents called upon the king of Sardinia for help, and in Toulon, the British. Those who had at first supported the Girondins soon abandoned them to their fate, thus sacrificing, with heavy hearts, the cause of justice to that of the homeland. They submitted to the Jacobins, who had sacrificed justice to the interests of their party.

Napoleon, for his part, espoused, not the cause of the Mountain, but rather that of the army, and he sided with the Mountain only insofar as the army remained loyal to it. He made a rational choice, not a choice dictated by passions he did not feel. He did not feel himself to be the compatriot either of those against whom he fought in Toulon or of those with whom he fought. Between him and them, there were none of the ties through which, in a civil war, the enemies involved remain, despite all their differences, fellow citizens sharing language, values, and history. The savagery of civil war has less to do with the absence of rules and customs that limit the violence of wars between states than with this proximity that has to be abolished, by any means, so that opponents are able to kill foes who are ultimately so close. Napoleon was involved in a quarrel that was not his own. "Amongst them [officers and soldiers]," Madelin writes, "the Corsican Bonaparte felt more than ever that he was French and took pride it."[67] That is incorrect. He did not feel at all "more French than ever"; he admired the *soldiers* whom he commanded, which is quite a different matter. It was in fact because he was fighting as an officer rather than as a revolutionary or a convinced Jacobin that he refused to take part in the terrible repression that followed the fall of Toulon. He preferred to leave the city, but it is said that before leaving he "successfully used his influence, several times, to save a few victims."[68] That is what makes him comparable to Augustin Robespierre. Maximilien's brother had signed the letter in which Barras and Fréron expressed their satisfaction with the massacres perpetrated after the reconquest of the city.[69] But like Napoleon, Augustin saved prisoners. He did so not out of compassion but as a matter of politics. Passing through Vesoul and Besançon a few weeks later, Augustin freed suspects arrested on vague pretexts and peasants accused of having gone to mass. Later still, in Nice, he and Ricord promised amnesty to the Barbets who laid down their arms.[70] Attacked as a "counterrevolutionary" by the Jacobins in Besançon who reproached him for his clemency, Augustin wrote to his brother, "There is nothing easier than to retain a revolutionary reputation at the expense of innocence. Mediocre men find in this means the veil that covers all kinds of turpitudes; but an upright man saves innocence at the expense of his reputation. I have amassed a reputation only in order to do good, and I want to spend it in defending innocence."[71]

In Napoleon's eyes, Augustin embodied a moderate, responsible Jacobinism that was opposed to the violent, anarchical Jacobinism of men like Fréron or Barras.[72] It is true that on the scale of his preferences, the Jacobins won out over the Girondins. He felt hardly any sympathy for the revolutionaries, whatever side they were on, but he could never speak too harshly about the irresponsible, cowardly conduct of the Girondins: "They did not want the death of the king," he said indignantly, "but they didn't dare say so. They voted for death, and then for the appeal to the people, in order to elude it. I prefer the conduct of the others."[73] In his view, the others—the Jacobins—at least had the merit of not being responsible for the situation that they had to cope with. But if he ranked the Jacobins above the Girondins, among the former it was Robespierre that he was thinking of in particular. Like Jean Jaurès, but for very different reasons, he would have sat alongside "the Incorruptible" had he had a seat in the Convention. He felt no admiration for the Robespierre of the early stages of the Revolution, the defender of great principles, the "political Tartuffe," as Michelet called him, with "his banal moral lessons, his appeals to virtue, his calculated

emotions, [his] frequent weepy soul-searching."[74] It was alongside the Robespierre of the end of 1793 and 1794 that he would have taken his seat, alongside the
proscriber of the Hébertists, the enemy of the Dechristianizers and the "rotten"
members of the Mountain, men like Fouché, Tallien, Barras, and Fréron who,
with an olive branch in one hand (the decree on the Supreme Being) and a sword
in the other (the "Great Terror"), were marching inexorably toward dictatorship.
Two men, and two only, would always escape the harsh judgments Napoleon
made regarding his contemporaries: Mirabeau and Robespierre. Napoleon never
ceased to say that Robespierre did not lack talent, even if he thought him inad-
equately endowed with the qualities necessary to do what Napoleon himself
had finally been able to do: put an end to the Revolution. But Napoleon was
convinced that this idea of ending the Revolution, which he held when he seized
power on 18 Brumaire, had already been Robespierre's before him. He saw himself as Robespierre's successor. He condemned the Terror but understood it:
Robespierre could not rely on the army, and political passions were still very
intense. Even if the Terror was an evil, the responsibility for it should be attributed not to "the Incorruptible" but to those who had begun the Revolution:

> Robespierre died because he tried to stop the effects of the Revolution,
> and not as a tyrant. Those who wanted to bring him down were cru-
> eler than he was: Billaud-Varenne, Collot d'Herbois, etc. He had against
> him Danton's party, which was powerful and immense. Probably he
> could not have acted otherwise. I believe that Robespierre was without
> ambition. . . . Everything I read in the *Moniteur* teaches me nothing,
> but it confirms me in the opinion that I had, and settles me in it even
> more. To be sure, Robespierre was not an ordinary man. He was very
> superior to everything around him. His discourse on the Supreme Being
> proves it. Disgusted by what he was hearing, he felt the necessity of a
> religious system among people who did not want anything, either reli-
> gion or morals. Morality had to be raised up again. He had the courage
> to do it and he did it. . . . That was great politics. No doubt he shed
> blood; that is the other side of the coin, but he is certainly less guilty
> than Tallien, who slaughtered Bordeaux, or Fréron whom I saw in
> Marseille taking poor unfortunates by the collar to have them shot.

Those men were real killers. Had he [Robespierre] not succumbed, he would have been the most extraordinary man who appeared. The moral of all this is no doubt that one must not begin a revolution. That is the truth, but when one does begin a revolution, can one expect that there will be no bloodshed? . . . It is the Constituent Assembly that must be accused of the Revolution's crimes, an assembly of long-winded authors of a ridiculous constitution.[75]

If he held the Girondins in contempt, Napoleon detested the members of the Constituent Assembly. Right up to the end, when he became indifferent to the antecedents of the former Jacobins that he took into his service, he refused to employ men whom he considered responsible for the Revolution. In 1809, when a British landing in Zeeland forced the government to recall retired generals to service, he still snapped at his minister of war, General Clarke, for having entrusted a command to Charles and Théodore de Lameth. "It's not that he lacks goodwill," he said about the former, "but he doesn't know how to move a battalion";[76] and about the latter: "General Théodore Lameth is a schemer with whom I want nothing to do."[77] He could not pardon them the thoughtlessness with which they had attacked the throne in 1789. In fact, his animosity was directed less at the members of the Constituent Assembly in general than at those in the nobility who had supported the new ideas, and whose motivations he suspected of being not exactly high-minded, but replete with sordid self-interest, vulgar ambitions, and pitiful resentments. He saw 1789 above all as a revolt by humiliated aristocrats. It was for that that he never forgave the Lameths, La Fayette, or Mme de Staël, who was the spokesperson for this faction. That was perhaps the reason for the admiration he professed a little later for the *Considerations on France*, whose author, Joseph de Maistre, excoriated the Revolution and revolutionaries of all allegiances, but reserved a special fate for the liberal nobility of 1789. De Maistre felt a genuine aversion to the liberal nobles who sat in the Constituent Assembly. According to him, these "rotten elements among the patricians" had played a role that was "more *terrible* (I do not say more horrible) than anything else we have seen in the Revolution."[78] The Revolution, a "mistake" in the people, was a "crime" in the liberal nobles.[79] Napoleon saw things the same way. He was not taken in by principles and ideals to which he did not subscribe. He had sided with the Revolution on the expectation that it, at least at that time, would lead to the emancipation of Corsica. He had rejoiced in it as people had in London and Vienna: by weakening the monarchy, the Revolution was bad for France, but it was good for his homeland. As for the rest, he soon became disgusted with it. Ultimately he became a supporter of Robespierre because he liked neither the Revolution nor the revolutionaries. He moved instinctively toward Robespierre because Robespierre was authority, dictatorship, power.

He never ceased to esteem that "honnête homme."[80] In 1797, when it was not very politic to praise him, Napoleon is supposed to have delivered at Ancona a veritable panegyric of "the Incorruptible," justifying Robespierre's conduct and his "alleged crimes," and asserting that on 9 Thermidor he was preparing to put an end to the Revolution by creating a "clemency committee" made possible by the elimination of the most deeply compromised terrorists.[81] But his esteem for Robespierre did not go so far as to compromise himself with a party that he could not hope to dominate at a time when factions were following one another to the scaffold. When in May 1794 Augustin proposed that he go to Paris to replace Hanriot, the commander of the armed forces, Napoleon refused. "The younger Robespierre wanted to take me with him—me, in whom he had great confidence: he never did anything in the army without having consulted me. I thought about it that evening. I didn't care to get mixed up in revolutionary plots that I had up to that point stayed out of. I went to see Ricord, spoke to him about the proposal that had been made to me, said that I could not go to Paris, that I was in the army. . . . Ricord agreed to dissuade the younger Robespierre, who, seeing that I was not eager to follow him, did not insist. Had I followed him, who knows what might have happened? I would probably have been drawn into their party and I would have commanded the Paris Commune in Hanriot's place, probably with a different result!"[82]

This is not certain. On 9 Thermidor Robespierre succumbed less because of Hanriot's drunkenness than because of his own indecision. If Napoleon hesitated a moment before declining the offer, he did the right thing.

SEVEN

In Search of a Future

*L*ess than two weeks after Robespierre's fall, Napoleon was relieved of his command and arrested. The order had been signed on August 6, 1794, by the representatives to the Army of the Alps, Albitte, Laporte, and Saliceti.[1] The latter's motives have been questioned: had a "pretty girl from Nice" come between him and Napoleon?[2] Had Saliceti been wounded by the unacceptable lack of respect shown him by Napoleon, who now trusted only Augustin Robespierre?[3] Or, on the contrary, did he have Napoleon arrested the better to protect him, telling the Committee of Public Safety that he would soon be transferred to Paris, but seeing to it that a preceding inquiry would clear him of all suspicions?[4] Had Saliceti really been in cahoots with his former protégé, however, Napoleon would not have held a grudge against him for what he did. A few months later, when Saliceti himself was in trouble, Napoleon, having learned where he was hiding, sent him a message in which, while assuring him of his discretion, he did not fail to remind Saliceti of his unjust conduct with respect to him.[5] In reality, Saliceti had Bonaparte arrested not in order to protect him but to save himself. The representatives to the Army of the Alps were not immune to criticism. Despite a few differences of opinion with their colleagues accompanying the Army of Italy, they had approved the offensive plan worked out by Napoleon, to which Carnot was, as we have said, hostile. They were thus no less suspect than Ricord, and in a threatening letter Carnot expressed his astonishment upon "seeing that Robespierre's system had found a certain favor among [them]."[6] Saliceti and his colleagues knew what the consequences of such an insinuation might be. A sacrifice had to be made, and even before he arrived in Nice, Saliceti informed one of his friends of his intention to have Napoleon arrested. He added, "It would be impossible for me to save Napoleon without betraying the Republic and without ruining myself."[7] He could hardly have been clearer. Was Napoleon incarcerated in Fort Carré in Antibes or simply put under house arrest at the home of M. Laurenti, his landlord?[8] The latter hypothesis seems more plausible. Having refused to escape, as Junot suggested,[9] Napoleon spent his spare time reading the history of Marshal Maillebois's campaigns in Italy[10] and writing a long, self-justifying memorandum addressed to the representatives in which, without saying anything against Robespierre, he reminded them of his past services and protested against a step taken on the basis of inchoate suspicions.[11] The ordeal did not last long; arrested on August 9, he was set free on August 20. Albitte and Saliceti wrote to the Committee of Public Safety: "Having examined his documents and all the information we have gathered, we have found no positive evidence that could justify detaining him any longer, . . . and we are convinced of the possible utility to us of this soldier's talents, which, we cannot deny it, are becoming very necessary in an army that he knows better than anyone, and in which men of this kind are extremely difficult to find."[12]

They needed him. After having been forced to evacuate the Tende pass in May 1794, the Piedmontese were expecting an attack on Coni, but when the French army failed to move, they grew bolder and tried to reconquer the ground they had lost. Above all, the Austrians began to move in their turn. The representatives had refused to reinstate Napoleon as commander of the artillery, so he rejoined the staff, where General Dumerbion gave him a hearty welcome: "'Young man,' he said, 'draw up a campaign plan for me, the kind you know how to make.'"[13] Napoleon wasted no time in preparing the plan; on August 26 he presented it to Dumerbion. The army, which was occupying positions on the banks of the Tanaro between Ormea and Garessio, was to descend onto the plain and occupy a line running from Bardineto to Loano. There, separating into two columns, one advancing through Carcare, the other through Montezemolo and Millesimo, it would march on Cairo-Montenotte in order to attack the rear of the Austrian forces.[14] Without waiting to receive Paris's agreement, the Army of Italy started to move on September 18. The enemy retreated toward Dego, where, on September 22, the French vanguard struck the Austrian rearguard, forcing the rest of the army to return to Acqui, its point of departure. The French could have exploited their advantage by turning left against the Piedmontese fortress of Ceva while the Army of the Alps attacked simultaneously in the direction of the Stura River, but Dumerbion and the representatives feared they would be disowned by the Committee; they were also worried about an Austrian counterattack, which was still possible, and ultimately they thought this plan perhaps too audacious. However, the main obstacle did not reside in Dumerbion's or the representatives' timidity. Ritter and Turreau, members of the Convention who reached the Army of Italy at the end of September 1794, supported Napoleon's proposals, but in vain. Carnot's response was final: the Army of Italy was to withdraw and limit itself to defensive operations.[15]

To keep the army busy, the Committee of Public Safety assigned it to reconquer Corsica. On March 11, 1795, a fleet of about thirty ships sailed from Toulon, encountered an Anglo-Neapolitan fleet on the thirteenth, lost two vessels, and returned to port. Napoleon took part in this expedition, whose failure must have reminded him of the unsuccessful landing on Sardinia two years earlier. Henceforth certain that there was no longer any glory to be garnered in the Mediterranean area, he requested a transfer to the Rhineland.

A General without an Army

He got what he wanted, but not in the way he expected: a decree of March 29, 1795, gave him the command of the artillery in the Army of the West. In the Vendée, the "dirty war" was not yet over, even though there was for the moment a provisional ceasefire. Napoleon was probably not enthusiastic about the prospect of going there, but he did not attempt to evade the assignment.[16] Far from resigning, as he later claimed, rather than "entering a service where he conceived he should only be concurring in mischief, without the probability of obtaining any personal benefit,"[17] he packed his bags as ordered and set off for the capital. It would be easy to see this assignment as a punishment. The fall of Robespierre had led to a purge of military men who had been involved in the "horrors committed under the tyranny."[18] Moreover, the government had decided to eliminate from the Army of Italy the numerous Corsicans it sheltered; they were accused of failing to do all they could to return the island to the Republic.[19] Joseph was struck from the list of war commissioners on the same day that Napoleon was transferred to the Vendée.[20] Most important, a policy of reducing and reorganizing the troops had been implemented. The state of public finances—

which was calamitous—no longer allowed the maintenance of an army whose numbers had swelled excessively since the beginning of the war in 1792. The remedy was harsh: the number of infantry battalions was cut from 952 to 420, and that of the cavalry squadrons from 323 to 178. The officers could not be spared: the majority (17,000 out of 32,000) were put on half pay.[21] In this context we can see that Napoleon was actually one of the privileged—at least for the moment.

His brother Louis, Marmont, and Junot went with him. Having left Marseille on May 8, they stopped for a few days in Châtillon-sur-Seine, at the home of Marmont's parents. Their son had spoken of the general with so much enthusiasm that they were astonished to see this taciturn young man who scarcely replied to questions and allowed painful silences to emerge. Mme de Marmont, in despair and reluctant to address this "Blue" who served a revolution she detested, called upon her neighbors for help. The neighbor's daughter Victorine—the future Mme de Chastenay—was assigned to make the young man more sociable. At first she didn't know what to say to this general, whom her neighbors considered to be almost an "imbecile." Thinking it would please him, she sang an Italian song, but when she had finished he told her only that her pronunciation was defective. Later on he warmed up and became more animated, speaking of war and politics, and literature as well, singing the praises of Ossian, criticizing *Paul et Virginie*, and reciting maxims by Condillac of which he claimed to be the author. The young lady was dazzled. She returned the next day. He made cornflower bouquets for her, murmured to her that a fan reflects "the emotions that move women," and with Marmont and Junot he sang, danced, and played "little games." And then, without saying good-bye, he left.[22]

On May 28 he arrived in Paris, where bad news awaited him. The artillery had also been hit by the reduction in officers. The number of its generals had been limited to twenty. Being one of the youngest and the most recently promoted, Napoleon was not on the list. He hurried off to see Aubry, who was in charge of this matter on the Committee of Public Safety. Historians have not been kind to this member of the Convention for having failed to understand what a man of the future he had in front of him. Because Aubry had served in the artillery without ever advancing beyond the rank of captain, historians have assumed that he was jealous. He had been imprisoned during the Terror for having protested against the expulsion of the Girondins, and many have consequently seen in his behavior an expression of the hatred inspired in him by this officer who was a "friend of Robespierre." It is true that Aubry liked neither the Republic nor the Jacobins, but he was simply doing his job, and to compensate Napoleon he offered to let him keep his rank if he moved from the artillery to the infantry. Napoleon protested, raged, objected that neither his age nor his length of service could count against him—there were generals-in-chief younger than he, and he had been an officer since he left the École militaire in 1785.[23] But it was all in vain: Aubry refused to yield. Napoleon approached, with no more success, Barras and Fréron, whom he had met in Toulon. On June 13 he received the order to proceed to his new assignment. Claiming that he was ill, he obtained a leave until the end of August. Perhaps he was hoping that the monthly reelection of the Committee would soon offer him an interlocutor more accommodating than Aubry. If so, he was mistaken: on August 16 he received a veritable summons ordering him to return to his position or, if his health did not allow him to do so, to inform the Committee so that his replacement could be appointed.[24] He had reasons to be unhappy about this—he was being forced to give up an independent position for the command of a brigade in which he would necessarily occupy a subordinate position. He had not protested his assignment to the Vendée, but the idea of serving in the infantry repelled him. A curious reaction, one might say, given that the infantry offered no fewer occasions to win glory than the artillery did. But to say that is to ignore the prejudices with which artillery officers were imbued:

> Those who have not served in the artillery cannot imagine the disdain artillery officers used to have for service in other branches: it seemed to them that to accept a command in the infantry or the cavalry was to lower oneself. . . . For a time I was, like others, under the sway of this prejudice; but I still cannot understand how Bonaparte, with his superior mind, such vast ambition, and such a remarkable way of foreseeing the future, could have been subject to it for even a moment. A career in the artillery is necessarily limited: this branch, which is always secondary, has great prestige in the lower ranks, but the individual's relative importance diminishes as he rises. The most illustrious

rank in the artillery is that of captain: there is no comparison between an artillery captain and a captain in any other branch. But an artillery colonel does not amount to much in the army, compared to a colonel commanding a fine infantry or cavalry regiment, and an artillery general in the army is only the very humble servant of a general commanding a simple division.[25]

It was then that Boissy d'Anglas, seeing this young man roaming through the corridors of the Committee of Public Safety and telling anyone who would listen to him about the "injustice" of which he was the victim, recommended him to Pontécoulant, his colleague responsible for military affairs.[26] Pontécoulant had joined the Committee in May, and the war in Piedmont had been one of the first questions he had had to deal with. At that time Kellermann was in command of the Army of Italy as well as the Army of the Alps. He had gone back on the offensive at the end of June 1795, but a few days later he had retreated, abandoning the positions taken in 1794 and falling back on Loano and the coast. He even threatened to evacuate Nice if he did not receive reinforcements. The news of Kellermann's retreat arrived in Paris on July 15. On hearing it, the Committee wrote to "all the deputies who had been with the Army of Italy to get information" and the deputies drew its attention to this general who was going from office to office trying to obtain his reassignment to the artillery.[27]

It is therefore probable that it was toward the end of July, and not, as is often said, on August 20, that Napoleon began to work with the Committee, and that he wrote for it a series of documents in which he elaborated on the conclusions he had drawn from the expedition against Dego the year before. Two letters, one dated July 30 and the other August 1, prove that at that time the Committee was already aware of his plans: "The peace treaty with Spain" (signed on July 22), he wrote in the first letter, "makes offensive war in Piedmont infallible. The plan I proposed is being discussed, and will infallibly be adopted."[28] Two days later he wrote: "The peace treaty with Spain, Naples, and Parma has been signed. . . . My plans for offensives have been adopted. We will soon have serious scenes in Lombardy."[29] I insist on this chronological point because Napoleon has often been depicted as living at that time in poverty and as depressed to the point of considering suicide, on the basis of an ill-interpreted letter of August 10. In this letter, in which he contrasted himself with his uncle Fesch—for whom, he said, the future was everything and the present nothing—he assured his brother Joseph that he was "constantly in the state of mind in which one finds oneself the day before a battle, convinced by feeling that when death is all around to put an end to everything, it is madness to worry." And he added: "Everything makes me defy fate and destiny."[30] He criticized Fesch's prudence, which he found so despicable, in order to oppose to it his own philosophy of life—live every moment as if it were to be the last—and not at all to open his heart and confide to Joseph his despair and his desire to put an end to it all. Besides, the preceding day he had told Joseph how "satisfied" he was with the Committee's reaction to his plans, or at least how satisfied he would have been had this business of the assignment to the infantry not poisoned his life.[31] He had in fact been briefly discouraged, but that was in June, when he had been informed of his transfer to the infantry; by August, those dark hours belonged to the past. Far from being at loose ends and making the rounds of the cafés and theaters with Junot and Bourrienne, his old classmate from Brienne whom he had recently run into again, he was working hard. His position in the Committee of Public Safety's war office was entirely unofficial, and though he was officially appointed to it around August 20, that was because of the summons he had received on the sixteenth: it was a way of preventing him from being struck from the army's lists for refusing to obey an order.

The creation of this "historical and topographical office" went back to 1793. It employed about twenty officers—including Lacuée, Dupont, and Clarke—most of them appointed by Carnot. They formed an expanded staff that prepared operations, followed the correspondence with army leaders, and gathered the necessary cartographic and topographic information. "It was not a mere sinecure that he had accepted," Pontécoulant was to say; "he sometimes worked fifteen hours a day, . . . and the considerable number of memoranda, reports, letters, and documents of all kinds that he wrote . . . would fill several volumes."[32] Napoleon wrote to Joseph: "I am swamped with work at the Committee from one in the afternoon until five, and from eleven in the evening until three in the morning."[33] It was then, in the middle of this period of feverish activity, that he wrote down his plan for the offensive campaign in Italy he had been thinking about for more than a year, since he had outlined it in his note *Sur la position politique et militaire de nos armées de Piémont et d'Espagne* (On the political and military position of our armies of Piedmont and Spain) submitted to Augustin Robespierre in June 1794.

Turin, Milan, Vienna: The Genesis of a Campaign Plan

Guglielmo Ferrero, whose study *Bonaparte en Italie* is often so valuable, detested Napoleon so much that he claimed that his contribution was nil. He asserted that the young general was not the author, or at least not the sole author, of the plan. It was in reality, he said, the collective work of "young officers"—including Bonaparte—"who were helping the government in military affairs."[34] It is true that the preparatory plans for the Italian campaign published by the editors of the emperor's correspondence, based on Coston or on documents from the war ministry's archives, were neither written nor signed by Napoleon—only one of these four documents has marginal annotations in his hand, according to the editors of the correspondence. But there is too much continuity between these plans written up in 1795 and the note from June 1794 addressed to Robespierre for there to be any doubt regarding Bonaparte's role in the conception of the 1796 campaign.

I have already delineated the movements Napoleon prescribed in April 1794 for the march on Oneglia and Coni and in September for the attack on Dego.[35] This attack—which was broken off on the orders of the Committee of Public Safety—played a decisive role in Napoleon's thinking. He had in fact accompanied the army, which from the heights of Loano and Finale had moved toward Carcare, Montenotte, and Cairo, where the Austrians had established their positions. After having driven them back toward Dego and beyond, the Army of Italy had taken up a position on the Cadibone pass, also called the Altare or Carcare pass. Napoleon had then seen two gaps opening up, one on his right, toward Acqui and Austrian Lombardy, the other on his left, in the direction of Ceva and the Piedmont plain. Was it then, and not in April 1794 as he was to say later,[36] that he conceived the plan for the campaign of 1796? J. Colin says it was: "In reality, the whole offensive plan for 1796 was already implicit in this situation, so clear, so striking, on September 23, 1794, and it is very natural that it was on that day, in Cairo, that Bonaparte conceived or completed the conception of [the] Montenotte maneuver." Occupying the "crossroads of Carcare and Cairo, between the two enemy rearguards"[37] and thus preventing their junction, would enable him to throw all his forces against the Piedmontese and threaten Turin.

When he left the Army of Italy at the end of 1794, it was in control of the coast as far as Savona, and from the Tende pass it held a line from the Tanaro River to Garessio. The following year was less successful, and it was then that Napoleon proposed to the Committee of Public Safety the plan for a counteroffensive to which he alludes on July 30, 1795, in the letter to Joseph already quoted. It was both a resumption and a development of the operations begun at Dego the preceding year. Napoleon spent the whole summer writing and rewriting his plan. "When I draw up a campaign plan," he was to say later, "I have no rest until I have finished, until my ideas are settled. I am like a woman in labor."[38] He prescribed a very different operation: First of all, the terrain lost along the coast as far as Vado had to be taken back. Only after that had been achieved would the army move in the direction of Carcare and Montenotte, driving a wedge between the Austrian and Piedmontese armies. Then, when the Austrians had been thrown back toward Acqui, as they had been in 1794, and the Piedmontese toward Mondovi, the army would march via Montezemolo on the fortress of Ceva that dominates the Piedmont plain, its movement being supported on the west by a division of the Army of the Alps, which, advancing through the valley of the Stura, would besiege Demonte. Napoleon assigned great importance to the conquest of the fortress of Ceva. Because this whole first phase of the operations had to take place before winter came, it was necessary to occupy a strong position—Ceva—that would make it possible to threaten Turin and prevent the Austrians from mounting any counteroffensive return during the winter truce.[39]

The second part of the plan could be implemented as soon as the king of Piedmont, fearing an attack on his capital, had asked for an armistice. The Army of Italy, then deploying as far as Alessandria, would go "into Lombardy to win the indemnities we would give the king of Sardinia for Nice and Savoy."[40] From Milan, whose conquest Napoleon scheduled for February 1796, the Army of Italy would then march on Mantua, where it should be "by the first days of spring": then it would be prepared, he wrote, "to seize the Trentino gorges and take the war, along with the army that would have crossed the Rhine, to Brisgau, right into the heart of the House of Austria's hereditary lands."[41] This plan was not Italian but Italian-German, and its ultimate goal was not Turin but Vienna. Italy, from Turin to Milan, was nothing more than a route toward the Tyrol and Austria. If the Montenotte maneuver was deduced from the observations made in Dego in 1794, the idea of a long march on Vienna through Italy was also born that year. Napoleon had developed it in his previously mentioned *Note sur la position politique et militaire de nos armées de Piémont et d'Espagne.*

In this note, Napoleon made the case for a great offensive executed by the Army of Italy, augmented by troops from the Army of the Alps and others brought back from the Pyrenean front. The war on the Spanish border and the one on the border of Piedmont, he argued, involved a dispersion of efforts that delayed that much more the end of the conflict with the main enemy, Austria. As the latter was the target, it had to be attacked on its home ground, and not in peripheral theaters of operations where the blows struck did not affect it directly. He then formulated this principle: "It is for systems of war as it is for sieges of fortified places: fire must be concentrated on a single point; once the breach is opened, the balance is broken; all the rest becomes pointless and the place is taken."[42] He had applied this principle to Toulon, and he was now applying it to Austria by proposing to "concentrate the attacks" through a combined march on Vienna by the Army of the Rhine, which would follow the Danube, and the Army of Italy, which would follow the Po after putting Piedmont out of action, and then cross "Ticino and the county of Tyrol."[43]

The originality of this plan has not been contested by Guglielmo Ferrero alone. Many others have pointed out that the invasion of Lombardy to "tie down" the Austrian troops in Italy, and even the conquest of the routes through Ticino and Trentino, had been advocated as early as 1793 by representatives of the people to the armies and by diplomats.[44] The idea even preexisted the Revolution, and more than a century ago a specialist objected to those who imagined that the plan for the Italian campaign had been engendered by Bonaparte's "genius" alone, maintaining that Napoleon had found its main lines in the memoirs that the Marshal de Maillebois wrote of another campaign in Italy, that of

1745.[45] The objective was then, as it would be in 1796, to break the Austrian-Piedmontese front and to force the king of Sardinia to make a separate peace. Maillebois had an ally, the Count of Gages, who commanded a Hispano-Neapolitan army. While Gages moved in from the east—he had left from Modena—the marshal had come into Italy by the Riviera route and, having occupied Finale, had marched on Acqui. The maneuver was in fact identical with the one outlined by Napoleon in 1795, except that in 1745 the Austrian and Piedmontese armies, separated at the point when the offensive was launched, had succeeded in regrouping on the left bank of the Tanaro; Bonaparte in 1796, by contrast, divided the two armies that had been united at the beginning of the operations. Another difference: whereas Bonaparte was moving on hostile territory, Maillebois could count on the support of Genoa and of the surrounding part of Italy. The difference in the context, like that of the result of the military operations in the region of Carcare and Montenotte, did not, however, prevent Napoleon from taking his inspiration from the plan implemented in 1745. As we have seen, after his arrest as a Robespierrist, he had read in Antibes the history of the Marshal de Maillebois's Italian campaign, and before returning to the headquarters of the Army of Italy in 1796 he asked the director of the topographic bureau to send him a copy.[46] So far as Maillebois's influence is concerned, the same conclusion can be drawn about the second phase of the 1796 campaign, namely the Lodi maneuver. In order to definitively divide the two enemy armies whose junction he had been unable to prevent at the end of the first phase, Maillebois had planned to send part of his troops along the Po to threaten Lombardy, draw the Austrians in that direction, and take advantage of their movement to throw the rest of his forces against the Piedmontese and drive them back toward Ceva, whose fortress he would then besiege. This time the operation had succeeded and the marshal achieved his objectives. The similarity with the operations carried out in May 1796 is striking, even if here, too, there are two important differences: as Maillebois saw it, the march along the Po was merely a diversionary maneuver, leading solely to a capitulation by the Piedmontese and not, as in 1796, to the conquest of Lombardy.[47]

Maillebois's influence is clear, but Napoleon had other models, too. It is said that he found useful material in the history of Prince Eugene of Savoy's Italian campaign of 1706.[48] Similarly, Bourcet's *Principes de la guerre de montagnes—*

Bourcet had served under Maillebois—played a crucial role in the young officer's thought: in this work he found the idea of invading Austria via Lombardy and the Alps. Bourcet, studying the Marshal de Villars's maneuvers in Italy in 1733, had stressed the advantage that could be drawn from an offensive that Villars, who had conceived it, had given up only in order to continue to keep the Austrian forces tied down in the peninsula.[49] Why should we be surprised by these various influences? Ever since he began his military studies, Napoleon had never ceased to read, reread, study, and meditate on "the history of the wars and the battles of great captains."[50]

Let us now return to an earlier period. It was in Auxonne, in 1788 and 1789, that Napoleon had received his real military education. In this respect the city in Burgundy played a privileged role: several of the officers in the garrison there were passionately interested in questions of strategy, and through them Napoleon discovered the most innovative theorists of the century. What did he read? *Éléments de la guerre*, by Le Roy de Bosroger (1773); *La Guerre de campagne à l'usage d'un officier général*, by Lloyd (1786), which had just been translated into French; *L'Usage de l'artillerie nouvelle*, by Jean Du Teil (the brother of the General Du Teil who directed the artillery school); *Essai de tactique générale*, by Guibert (1772); and Bourcet's *Principes*, which we have just mentioned. In these works he had discovered "war on a grand scale," the war of movement, vigorous and fast-developing, in which maneuvering prepared the battle, and in which the battle sought to drive the enemy to capitulation or total destruction. This renewal of the art of war had itself been possible only because of the technological revolution that had simultaneously increased the precision of firearms and the power of the artillery. Speed and surprise, lateral and turning movements, diversionary maneuvers and vast roundups could henceforth be given priority. This was especially true since the French army's adoption—in 1759—of the principle of organizing the army as complete divisions, which made it possible to form mobile army corps that were self-sufficient and could maneuver independently but could also be conjoined to attack the enemy, with the advantage of numerical superiority, at the weakest point in its deployment. In these works, especially *L'Usage de l'artillerie nouvelle*, the young officer had found most of the principles that later inspired his campaign plans: the concentration of effort, attacks on the flank and on the rearguard, the importance of surprise, speed of execution, and the principle to which he was one day to reduce the art of war: "Always have, [even] with an inferior army, more forces focused on the point that you are attacking or the one that is being attacked than one's enemy does."[51]

For all that, let us not suppose that Napoleon had, on the basis of his readings, deliberately broken with an "old," defensive way of waging war in favor of a new, offensive way, outlined in the treatises of the preceding century but not yet put into practice. It is true that the French Revolution gave the art of war a new face. Revolutionary armies, for example, tended not to follow the common practice of the Old Regime by seeking to "seize a province" at the end of elaborate maneuvers designed to dislodge the enemy. Rather, they took the enemy armies as their target and tried to destroy them or at least put them out of action.[52] But that does not mean that before 1789 strategists who were reluctant to go on the offensive did not dream of lightning attacks and decisive battles. Historians have put this idea of a theoretical rupture into perspective.[53] Political motives, first of all, and then technologies, often forced the generals of the Old Regime to prefer maneuvering to fighting battles and defense to offense. The transformation of political motives at the time of the Revolution imposed other choices on the revolutionary generals. In particular they had to cope with soldiers of a new kind, volunteers and requisitioned or conscripted men who were unlikely to be so passive and resigned that they would stand immobile in lines to receive an enemy's point-blank barrage, as had the poor devils who were enlisted by force in the old infantry regiments. Skirmishing as infantrymen, with all the freedom and initiative that presupposes, was certainly better suited to the temperament of these citizen-soldiers. Moreover, because everything depends on circumstance, Napoleon was not bound to a doctrine any more than Frederick systematically advocated offense or the Marshal de Saxe defense. He knew military history too well to imagine that from events so diverse in their causes, their development, and their outcome, general rules could be derived that would be applicable in all times and all places. The time when Roman armies always deployed in the same way was long past: "Among the moderns," Napoleon later said, "the art of occupying a position to hold it or to fight there is subject to so many considerations that it requires experience, an ability to assess the situation, and genius.... One cannot and should not prescribe anything absolute. There is no natural order of battle."[54] And also: "Everything depends on the character nature has given the general, on his good qualities, his defects, the nature of the troops, the range of the weapons, the season, and countless other circumstances that ensure that things never resemble one another."[55] This reminds us of *Le Fil de l'épee*, in which General De Gaulle stigmatizes the makers of military doctrines who claimed, in his period as well, to have found the absolute secret of the art of war that had previously been hidden, ignoring the fact that "the action of war takes on essentially the character of contingency."[56] Napoleon was well aware of that fact, and was scornful of all the "so-called systems of the art of war."[57] Though his judgment was shaped by his study of his predecessors, he adapted what he had learned from them to the new circumstances—"the enemy, the terrain, the distances, the personalities of his lieutenants, the value and condition of his troops"[58]—that on each occasion confronted him. He always tried, by subordinating his principles to what his "assessment of the situation" suggested to him, and not the reverse, to invent the maneuver best suited to achieve his objectives.

His reading of Maillebois and a few others, corrected by this "assessment"—in other words, tactical intelligence—concerning which Bourcet said that it had to be the primary quality of a military leader,[59] had thus allowed him to find the position that could decide the outcome of the campaign, as he had in Toulon two years earlier. He never ceased to repeat, in memorandum after memorandum: just as the point of L'Éguillette was to deliver Toulon, Lombardy would deliver Vienna. The first *Mémoire sur l'armée d'Italie* and the *Note sur la position politique et militaire de nos armées* echo the *Mémoire militaire* that completes them: "Once master of Lombardy, seize the Trentino gorges, penetrate into the interior of the Tyrol, join up with the Army of the Rhine and force the emperor, attacked within his hereditary lands, to make a peace that corresponds to Europe's expectations and to the sacrifices of all kinds that we have made."[60]

No matter how busy Napoleon was with preparations for a future offensive war in Italy or how flattered he was by the attention the government accorded him, he never ceased to consider his work for the Committee of Public Safety as temporary. He did not see himself closed up for long in an office and, having little hope that he would soon be given another active command—in the artillery, of course—he was on the lookout for any option that offered him some kind of future. That was when he learned about a request made to the Committee by the Ottoman government. Sending French military advisors to Constantinople was a tradition that began under the monarchy, but the requests made by Sultan Selim III had been rendered more pressing by the threats of war in Eastern Europe and the looming second partition of Poland.

For the moment France had nothing better to offer Bonaparte, so nothing kept him there, especially because his offensive plan, which had been approved by the Committee, had been rejected by Kellermann. Napoleon could therefore conclude that unless the general-in-chief was dismissed, which was unlikely, the great offensive in northern Italy would not take place. Furthermore, the moment had passed: "The true time to go to war [in Italy] and to strike powerful blows," Napoleon himself had opined, ". . . was between February and July," so as to avoid the oppressive heat of the summer and the snow of the winter.[61] Even if he were given another active command in the artillery, nothing would happen before the beginning of 1796. On the other hand, Pontécoulant's term on the Committee of Public Safety was to expire on September 1. Napoleon, who was still determined not to serve in the infantry but did not know whether Pontécoulant's successor would keep him at the topographic bureau, had a definite interest in "taking his precautions."[62] This was all the more vital because recent political events—the proscription of the Jacobins after the insurrection of 1 Prairial and that of the royalists after the failed invasion of Brittany, the adoption of a new constitution on August 22, and the peace treaties or alliances signed over the past few months—had persuaded him that France was taking a path that combined normalization within the country and pacification abroad. Since his arrival in Paris he had been observing events serenely, reassuring his correspondents by continually telling them that everything was "perfectly peaceful." The landing of the *émigrés* on the Quiberon peninsula in Brittany? "That causes no great concern here."[63] The food shortage? A temporary problem. The bloody settling of accounts between "reactors" and Jacobins in the south? "Unfortunate" events that would stop once there was "strong and better-organized government."[64] He saw the seeds of such a government in the constitution that was being written. It has been said that "rarely has a constitution [that of Year III] gone into effect amid such skepticism."[65] Napoleon himself appeared confident.

Was he, in that respect, at one with a public opinion that was weary of disorder and wanted to believe that the difficulties assailing the country were going to find a miraculous solution in the establishment of institutions in which informed people had no confidence? Perhaps. In any case, he repeated it: "People are generally very happy with the new constitution, which provides happiness, tranquility, security, and a long future for France. The peace treaty with Spain has caused the value of our currency to rise considerably. There is no doubt that everything will soon be back in order. It takes this country very few years to recover."[66]

The tone changes toward the end of the month, after the adoption of the "two-thirds" decrees (August 22, 1795). The Convention, which had reason to fear that the elections might bring to power men hostile to the Revolution and that the new institutions would be overthrown before they had even been tried out, had decided that the electors would choose as new representatives at least two-thirds of those who had served in the former assembly. The right-wing opposition, which was royalist or moderate, fulminated against this disguised perpetuation of the Convention. Napoleon notes a certain agitation, and predicts "storms," but soon returns to a serene tone. On September 3 he writes: "Everything is calming down. There will be no movement and the Constitution will make the people happy";[67] on the twelfth: "A peaceful day is dawning on the destinies of France";[68] and again on the twenty-third: "Everything seems to be going well. Within a month, the constitution will be established."[69] The political situation was propitious for traveling.

Still another reason encouraged him to leave. The Buonapartes all had a certain fascination with the Orient.[70] His brothers shared his passion. In 1793 Lucien had left with Huguet de Sémonville, who had promised to take him to Constantinople, where he believed he was about to be appointed as the French ambassador. Joseph had similarly been thinking for months about leaving the country to "exploit the vast domains of the Ottoman Empire."[71] He had married Julie Clary, the daughter of a wealthy Marseille businessman involved in trade with the Levant. After François Clary's death, Joseph had taken the family's affairs in hand.[72] In the course of the following weeks, his allusions to the possibility of taking up residence in Turkey had grown more precise. Napoleon had at first tried to discourage the plan, telling him that "making the rounds of the trading posts in the Levant would make you look a little like an adventurer or a fortune-seeker."[73] But on August 20, at the very time when he was assigned to the topographical bureau, Napoleon did an about-face: "I am requesting and will obtain an assignment to Turkey as an artillery general sent by the government to organize the Sultan's fleet, with a good salary and the very flattering title of envoy. . . . If the conditions, which I will deal with tomorrow, are as favorable as I want them to be and as I am led to hope they will be, I will not hesitate and will go to Turkey to see someplace new; escaping the failings of revolutions, being useful to the fatherland, earning money and acquiring a reputation is too fine a proposition to let it get away from me."[74]

Nonetheless he remained circumspect, fearing that the Committee might refuse and dispense with his services. On September 1 he submitted an official request, offering to go to Constantinople with six or seven officers "to make Turkey's military forces more redoubtable."[75] The Committee's consideration of his request at first confirmed his fears: Pontécoulant and Jean Debry refused to let such "a distinguished officer" go and proposed to compensate him by immediately reassigning him to the artillery.[76] What happened next is a little unclear. Merlin de Douai, who had joined the Committee after Pontécoulant's departure, refused to restore Napoleon to his rank in the artillery and asked the War Commission to prepare an order striking him from the list of the army's officers. The Commission on Foreign Relations was meanwhile considering the proposed mission to Turkey, on which no definitive decision had yet been made. On September 15 the Committee ruled on the first subject, dismissing the general on the grounds of "his refusal to go to the post to which he has been assigned."[77] Napoleon was probably completely unaware of this decision, of which no trace is found in his correspondence. On the other hand, he awaited impatiently the Committee's verdict on his proposal for a military mission. On September 27 he wrote to Joseph: "Now, more than ever, my journey to the Orient is under discussion. It has even been decided upon."[78] But nothing in fact had yet been decided: the Committee wanted to know more about the officers Napoleon wished to take with him. Napoleon was champing at the bit. "I don't know what I will do," he wrote on September 23. "It is, however, time to make up my mind. There are three options: Turkey, Holland, and going to the Army of Italy. I want to travel. I would therefore prefer the first option to the second, and the second to the third. Within ten days, it is likely that this will be entirely decided."[79]

He couldn't have said it better. Events put an end to his hesitations and dissipated, for the moment, his dreams about the Orient.

13 Vendémiaire

The rebellion provoked by the adoption of the two-thirds decree had spread to the majority of the Parisian sections. It would perhaps have abated, as Napoleon predicted,[80] had the Convention not stirred up a hornet's nest by creating, on October 3, an extraordinary commission headed by Barras and by ordering General Menou, the military commander of Paris, to dissolve by force the meeting of the Le Peletier section, which was organizing the rebellion. Menou, who was all the more reluctant to use force because some of his best friends were holed up in the Filles-Saint-Thomas convent, the headquarters of the rebellious section, refused after having obtained from the latter a vague promise to disarm and disperse. He was dismissed and replaced by Barras, who called upon volunteers from the *faubourgs* for help. But the revolt spread. On October 5 (13 Vendémiaire) 20,000 insurgents converged on the Tuileries via the quays and, coming from the boulevards, via Rue de la Loi (present Rue de Richelieu). On the left bank, they were unable to cross the Pont-Royal and the Pont-Neuf, while on the right bank they were driven back toward Rue Saint-Honoré, where, in the evening, the last groups were dispersed after violent combats around the church of Saint-Roch.

Napoleon's behavior on 13 Vendémiaire has been the subject of so many fantastic tales that it would be tedious to mention them all here. This is all the more astonishing because he himself provided an account of the events, even if it was laconic, in a letter written to his brother only a few hours after the insurgents' defeat: "Finally, it's all over: my first impulse is to send you my news. The royalists, organized into sections, are constantly becoming more audacious. The Convention has ordered that the Le Peletier section be disarmed, it has repulsed our troops. It is said that Menou, who was in command, betrayed us; he was dismissed on the spot. The Convention appointed Barras as commander of the armed forces; the committees appointed me as his second-in-command. We have deployed our troops; the enemies have attacked us in the Tuileries; we have killed many of them; they have killed 30 of our men and wounded 60. We have disarmed the sections and everything is calm."[81]

As is often the case, he is exaggerating. The Committee had not named him second-in-command of the Convention's forces. Not being able to rely on Menou's staff, Barras had appointed a new one composed of available Jacobin officers. Carteaux and Brune were thus back in office. Napoleon was one of the generals put back on active duty: "The Committees of Public Safety and General Security decreed that General Buonaparte would be employed in the army of the interior, under the command of the representative of the people Barras, the general-in-chief of this army," the decree explained.[82] But Napoleon was already considered Barras's protégé, and he willingly admitted this, saying that *he knew no one but Barras*. The latter had had an opportunity to see him at work in Toulon, and even if he later denied having entrusted the slightest responsibility to the young Corsican, he definitely took him on as his main lieutenant. How could it have been otherwise? Barras did not lack courage—as he had shown on 9 Thermidor—and it was for that reason that the Convention had placed him at the head of its troops. But he was too aware of how slender his military talents were not to employ a specialist, especially because this time he was not facing a mediocrity like Hanriot but instead General Danican, who, though he was not another Turenne, at least had some experience. Napoleon's first initiative, which proved to be decisive, was to immediately send a squadron leader, Murat (he became acquainted with him on this occasion), to seize the forty-odd cannons in the Sablons camp before the insurgents could get their hands on them. Thus he gave the troops loyal to the Convention a significant advantage, whereas the balance of power had initially been favorable to the sections. It is incontestable that he later contributed to the preparations for the defense of the Tuileries and the placement of the artillery and troops to counter the insurgents' attack, and even participated in the operations in the field as Barras's aide-de-camp. On the other hand, we know that the famous scene in which Napoleon had cannon fire directed at the insurgents gathered on the steps of the church of Saint-Roch is merely part of the legend.[83]

If Napoleon played an important role, it was not by being physically present, but by getting Barras to instruct the troops to fire real bullets and not just blanks, as the Committees had ordered. Napoleon said that he had great difficulty persuading Barras to disobey the Committee's order.[84] That is not impossible, because on the evening of 13 Vendémiaire, Barras felt he had to justify at length before the Convention the decision to "repel force by force."[85] Napoleon explained later on that he had tried in this way to spare the insurgents' blood:

> The reason there were so few killed,[86] was, that after the first two discharges, I made the troops load with powder only, which had the effect of frightening the Parisians, and answered as well as killing them would have done. I made the troops, at first, fire ball, because to a rabble, who are ignorant of the effect of fire-arms, it is the worst possible policy to fire powder only in the beginning. For the populace after the first discharge, hearing a great noise, are a little frightened, but looking around them, and seeing nobody killed or wounded, pluck up their spirits, begin immediately to despise you, become doubly outrageous, and rush on without fear, and it is necessary to kill ten times the number that would have been done, had ball been used at first. . . . It is a mistaken piece of humanity, to use powder only at that moment, and instead of saving the lives of men, ultimately causes an unnecessary waste of human blood.[87]

Although Napoleon's actions on 13 Vendémiaire remain controversial, one thing is certain: he did not offer his services to the insurgents before accepting the position proposed by Barras. On Saint Helena he himself lent credit to this accusation, which was later repeated by Barras.[88] Perhaps the emperor of the French, who claimed to have risen to the summits of power "without having committed a single crime,"[89] was loath to admit that he had had a hand in an episode of civil war, and especially one that worked to the advantage of the Thermidorians whom he overthrew four years later. But at the time, if he considered the possibility, as he says, it was only while he was on the way back from the theater where Barras's emissary had gone to get him.[90] Did he have to accept what he had refused in 1794 when Augustin Robespierre suggested that he go to Paris to help out Maximilien? At that time, he had thought it contrary to his personal interest to side with Robespierre against those—the future Thermidorians—who were planning to overthrow him; now he thought it was in his interest to defend the same Thermidorians against the "revolution" being prepared against them by the moderates. His personal situation had changed: in 1794 he was afraid of compromising himself, whereas in 1795 he no longer had much to lose. In 1794 he had a command, he was the inspiration for the representatives' strategy, and he could imagine a brilliant future for himself in the Army of Italy; one year later it was different: he was being offered an infantry command that he loathed and he was still waiting for a decision on his project of a mission. He reasoned like a gambler. Events were dealing him a new hand. Did he have better cards than he had had two or three days earlier? There was no guarantee of that. Throwing himself into the fray meant not only getting involved in a civil war, but also fighting on a side that he hated—that of the members of the Convention—and whose forces were notoriously inferior to those of its enemies. Thiers said that on 13 Vendémiaire Napoleon *seized the opportunity (saisit l'occasion aux cheveux)*. That expression is misleading, because it presupposes that he immediately gauged the advantage he could draw from it. But he didn't know whether he was going to win or lose. He gambled, and he won. It would be a mistake, however, to see nothing but opportunism in his conduct. His reasons for now siding with those who overthrew Robespierre were the same as those that had earlier led him to embrace "the Incorruptible's" cause. In both cases he was for the established authority, independently of any judgment regarding its conduct and principles, and against the supporters of another "revolution," no matter what its objectives might be. He had acquired the conviction that no new "revolution" could provide a solution to the problem raised by the Revolution. The only possible way to "terminate" it was through government, and not by upheavals that would inevitably prolong it. He is supposed to have said to Marmont, after having learned of Robespierre's fall: "If Robespierre had remained in power, he would have changed his ways: he would have reestablished order and the rule of law; we would have arrived at this result without upsets, because we would have arrived at it through government; people claim to be moving toward it by means of a revolution, and this revolution will lead to many others."[91] He had not changed his mind in 1795. His "doctrine" remained the same: "It established that changes had to come from above and not from below; that government had to be changed without leaving any gap in its exercise: and the present circumstance was much worse because at the time of the revolution of 9 Thermidor, the Convention, in which the principle of government then resided, had been preserved, whereas if today the sections were triumphant, there would be no recognized government anywhere."[92]

In this he shared the opinion that Benjamin Constant would develop a few months later. Constant argued that if the Republic that had emerged from the institutions founded in 1795 had to be considered legitimate, it was because, independently of justified reservations regarding some of its provisions, it had the merit of existing, and more precisely "of being what there is that is most established."[93] It represented a promise of order that had to be supported by all those who had so long awaited the ebbing of the revolutionary tide and the consolidation of its first principles and the interests to which it had given birth. The choice was between the established government and revolution, whether the latter took the form of another Jacobin swerve to the left or a royalist counterrevolution. "Counterrevolution," Constant stated, "would itself be only another revolution."[94] It was because he did not belong to the revolutionary camp that Napoleon supported Robespierre in 1794 and the Thermidorians in 1795, as paradoxical as that may seem. Moreover, as in Toulon, after Vendémiaire he refused to espouse the passions of the party to which he had rallied. He opposed it—insofar as he could—as soon as the victors let themselves be carried away by a spirit of vengeance that helped perpetuate the very divisions and hatreds it was their duty to end. He did not participate in the operations of cleansing and repression that took place on October 6 and 7, and regretting that he had not been able to save Lafond, the only Vendémiaire insurgent to be executed, he intervened on behalf of the unfortunate Menou, whom Barras wanted to put in front of a firing squad.[95]

When he got home in the early hours of 14 Vendémiaire, he found himself in the situation of a lucky gambler: "As usual," he wrote to his brother, "I am not wounded at all." And in a postscript, he added these gamblers' words: "I have luck on my side."[96]

Under Way

The dice had rolled on the green baize of the Revolution and he had won the jackpot. There were to be no more nights spent with Junot at the *Cadran bleu* on Rue de la Huchette or long strolls with Bourrienne; no more tattered clothes and muddy boots. This time he was really on his way. He owed it to Barras. He denied it, but he was lying.[97] It is true that Barras did not mention him when on October 10 he presented to the Convention the "volunteers of '89" who had cooperated in the victory. But Barras was in league with Fréron, who followed him at the rostrum. Courting Marie-Paulette (Napoleon's sister Pauline, then sixteen years old) and taking care to please the man who might soon become his brother-in-law, Fréron gladly participated in this little drama. He drew his colleagues' attention to Napoleon: "Don't forget," he said, "that the artillery general Bonaparte, who was named on the 12th to replace Menou, and who had only the morning of the 13th to make the clever arrangements whose happy effects you have seen, had been removed from his branch and put in the infantry."[98] Barras then took the floor again: "I shall call the National Convention's attention to General Buonaparte: it is to him, it is to his clever and prompt arrangements, that we owe the defense of these walls, around which he posted our forces with a great deal of ability. I ask the Convention to confirm Buonaparte's nomination as general second-in-command in the Army of the Interior."[99] The assembly applauded this general it knew nothing about and confirmed a nomination that had never been made. Barras resigned his post a few days later in order to have a free hand in the impending creation of the Executive Directory, and Napoleon succeeded him.

Though it cannot be compared with armies in combat, the "Army of the Interior" was not without importance. Created on July 12, 1795, and 40,000 men strong, its jurisdiction extended from the capital to about ten departments where it was supposed in particular "to protect the delivery of food supplies for Paris [and] maintain public tranquility."[100] Being primarily intended to perform policing tasks disdained by military men, its command offered few opportunities to cover oneself with glory, but the office carried certain advantages. Its head was provided with a personal vehicle and a town house, a loge at the Opera was reserved for him, and he received a salary of 48,000 livres paid for the most part in cash.[101] Napoleon performed these functions for a little less than five months, being "excessively busy"[102] with the consequences of the insurrection of 13 Vendémiaire and with the formation of the Directory: the National Guard having been compromised by its complicity with the insurgents, he dismantled it and transferred its powers to the army and to a police Legion in which so many former "terrorists" from Year II enlisted that it had to be disbanded a few months later. Confronted by a disarmed Paris, he armed the government by creating a Guard for the five directors and another for the deputies; both Guards were to provide him with valuable support on 18 Brumaire. The government having forbidden the singing of *Le Réveil du peuple*,[103] he made the rounds of theaters every evening to keep an eye on things and force the spectators to sing only *La Marseillaise*. He was seen as a terrorist, a Jacobin, but it was whispered that his staff included *muscadins*, men who had fought the Convention on 13 Vendémiaire, and without emotion on February 27, 1796, he went, at the Directory's order, to close the doors of the Panthéon club where the left was trying to recreate the Society of Jacobins. He was zealous about all this. Perhaps too zealous: Barras says that he often had to "moderate" his protégé by reminding him that a constitutional regime was hardly compatible with the arbitrary acts of which he was accused. Napoleon shrugged: "Pooh-pooh, could anything ever be done if one contented one's self with sticking to the law?" And he added: "I am not so particular as all that, and when I have committed some arbitrary act, I call on Minister [of Justice] Merlin [de Doubai] in the morning, so as to straighten out matters; he never fails to find for me in the laws some happy means of proving that we have not gone outside of them."[104] His correspondence from this period provides a different image of his administration. Although in fact he advocated the greatest firmness in dealing with the "Chouans" [royalist rebels] who were causing serious difficulties for the armed forces in Normandy, he advised the greatest moderation in dealing with the disturbances provoked almost everywhere by supply problems and steep increases in prices. That winter there had been suicides, mobs, riots. There are stories of Napoleon going to the markets in person to prevent the crowds from stealing the small amount of merchandise for sale, but the reported scenes are probably legends. On the other hand, on December 21 he gave the minister of war, Aubert-Dubayet, a regular lecture on politics regarding the grain riots:

> This temporary fever has to be monitored with the greatest attention, no doubt, but I do not think it should be met with force and thus give these movements a rebellious character that might have the most unfortunate consequences. Administrators who see armed force as the only

remedy for all these movements do not know how to govern. It was a failure to distinguish between sedition and rebellion that led to civil war. I therefore believe I should take no hostile measures against the suddenly arising and partial reactions in the communes of the department of Seine-Inférieure. I am writing to tell the department's administration to distinguish the instigators, troublemakers, and counterrevolutionaries who always try to take control of these initial popular movements, from the majority of the citizens, who are moved by need or by a moment of giddiness.[105]

These four months were far from being a waste of time: Napoleon learned to command and to administer, he discovered power and its hidden background, "he saw the little springs, the inchoate devices, the other side of the official decor, . . . what Mirabeau called the political pharmacy."[106] Many people say that the reason the Directory finally gave Bonaparte the command of the Army of Italy was that it was aware that over a few short months this little general had become a dangerous man. There is another hypothesis that is just as plausible, if not more so: this command was given him because he had previously served in the Army of Italy, because he was well acquainted with the theater of operations, and especially because he was the author of the plan that the Directory, having decided to resume operations in Germany and in Italy, had just adopted.

War and Peace in 1795

The time for war had in fact come, after several months during which the Thermidorian Committee of Public Safety had seemed to hesitate about what to do. Although the party in favor of "natural limits," which wanted to push the French border all the way to the Rhine and was dissatisfied with the border along the Meuse advocated by Carnot, remained powerful, the government then showed itself inclined to work toward a negotiated solution to the conflict. It did so prudently, and not without hesitations, because the Committee of Public Safety, even as it refused to annex the territories on the right bank of the Rhine in order to avoid compromising future negotiations with the German Empire,

Europe in 1789

simultaneously organized the pillaging of the occupied territories by creating, in May 1794, four "evacuation agencies" assigned to remove everything from them that could be removed. The war was financing the Revolution. At the same time the war itself was very costly, if only for the necessity of supporting 800,000 men in uniform. The government thus needed both war and peace. For a time it leaned toward peace because its efforts to reestablish a minimum of order within the country obliged it to seek at least a truce on the external front: "Every thing disposed people's minds to peace, and, in the same manner as they had gone over from the ideas of revolutionary terror to those of clemency, they now passed from ideas of war to those of a general reconciliation with Europe."[107] France, exhausted by the Terror, longed for rest. The situation was favorable; the coalition had been undermined by the dissensions provoked by the third partition of Poland (January 3, 1795). Negotiations were begun that led to the signature of treaties with Tuscany (February 9, 1795), Prussia (April 5), Holland (May 16), and Spain (July 12). Russia remained at war with France (though Catherine II, while speaking in violent terms, took care to avoid sending any troops to the front), as did Austria, Britain, and the Kingdom of Sardinia.

It did not seem impossible to arrive at an agreement with Sardinia, which was financially exhausted and unhappy with the negligible support it got from its Austrian ally. The failure of Kellermann, who was forced in July 1795 to surrender Vado and the crests of the Alps east of the Tanaro, had somewhat calmed the Piedmontese, but the offensive mounted by Schérer, who had reconquered in November the positions lost in July, seriously frightened them. The pessimists were not alone in advising the reopening of negotiations. In Turin there was a powerful anti-Austrian party, which was not unresponsive to the French government's informal propositions: Austrian Lombardy in exchange for Victor-Amadeus III's recognition of the French annexation of Savoy and Nice. The government in Turin might have consented—in early January 1796 it said it was prepared to sign a three-month armistice and then remain neutral—if Schérer had not, after the victory won on November 23 at Loano, suspended military operations on the pretext that he didn't have enough soldiers, and if the Directory had succeeded in getting the Republic of Genoa to agree to the alliance it sought to impose on it. At the beginning of February 1796, Victor-Amadeus had closed his door to the French negotiators and declared that he "would rather be buried under the ruins of his kingdom than listen to proposals contrary to his honor and his religion."[108]

French diplomacy had had no more success in Vienna. Here too people were weary of war, especially because Austria was paying for it by itself, or almost by itself. Emperor Francis II's German vassals were similarly tired and obviously turning toward Prussia. The latter had proclaimed its neutrality after concluding with France the Treaty of Basel authorizing the French occupation of the left bank of the Rhine until the meeting of a congress between France and the German Empire. In July 1795 it signed with the Committee of Public Safety a second accord establishing a line of demarcation between northern and southern Germany, the former adhering to Prussian neutrality. The states of southern Germany were not included in the agreement, but several of them did not conceal their desire to be federated with their neighbors to the north. France, seeing an opportunity to isolate Austria a little further, encouraged them, while at the same time trying to transform Prussian neutrality into a positive alliance. This would have posed a danger to Vienna, had Prussia not clung to neutrality for the sake of its commerce, and had it not seen the Treaty of Basel as fundamentally "an unfortunate concession imposed by necessity."[109] For its part, Austria could not so easily leave the coalition: that September it had signed a new tripartite pact with Russia and Britain. Moreover, the Convention had put an obstacle in the way of possible negotiations by decreeing, on October 1, 1795, the incorporation of Belgium into France, even taking the precaution of conferring a constitutional value on this decree. Austria would have willingly been consoled for the loss of Belgium by being given certain compensations she had long coveted: Bavaria, whose Tyrolean provinces would have facilitated its communications with Italy, and, on the peninsula, Venice or the pontifical legations of Bologna, Ravenna, and Ferrara, which would have given it access to the Adriatic and the eastern Mediterranean. The Directory was well aware of this, and in December 1795 it sent to Vienna an emissary named Poterat. It may be that France offered Piedmont to the Austrians at the same time that it offered Austrian Lombardy to the Piedmontese. In any event, Poterat met with a flat refusal. The reversals suffered at the same time in Germany by Pichegru and Jourdan, who were forced to retreat across the Rhine in September and even to abandon a pocket of territory around Mainz, did not encourage the Austrians to be conciliatory, and they made it clear to Poterat that France had nothing to offer that Austria could not obtain by itself or with the help of the Russians.[110] Poterat reported to the Directory: "There remains nothing for you to do but to pursue the war all-out and with the most extreme vigor."[111]

In the short run the Directory had planned to make its main efforts in Italy and in Germany, marching on Vienna along the Danube. The offensive of the Army of Sambre-et-Meuse and the Army of Rhine-et-Moselle would be supported by a combined attack of the Army of Italy against Piedmont and Austrian Lombardy as was proposed in the first part of the plan Napoleon had submitted to the Committee. Once it had adopted the plan, at least in part, the Committee asked Napoleon to write up a proposed set of instructions to be communicated to Kellermann. This text set forth in detail the plan for an invasion of Austria through Italy that Napoleon had already submitted to the Committee. After having gone into great detail regarding the arrangements to be made for the attack on Piedmont, he wrote: "Once Ceva has been taken, the fortifications will be repaired; the whole army will be assembled there as snow begins to obstruct the Alpine passes. Contributions will be levied on the whole

Piedmont plain; all the preparations will be made for beginning the campaign immediately after the rainy season. All peace overtures from the king of Sardinia will be entertained. In February [1796], if a peace treaty with the king of Sardinia has been signed, we will see to it that Alessandria is not occupied by the Austrians, and we will enter Lombardy, which we will seize. As soon as good weather begins in the coming campaign, we will cross the Trentino gorges and the mountains of the Tyrol."[112]

In less than a year the Army of Italy, which had up to that time hardly moved from the Riviera, was supposed to be massed before the walls of the Austrian capital. When he received these instructions dated August 30, 1795, Kellermann could hardly believe his eyes, and called their author a madman who ought to be locked up.[113] Schérer, who was arriving in Nice with reinforcements from the Army of the Pyrenees, replaced Kellermann, and on November 22 the Army of Italy attacked the Austrians. It threw them back to Acqui and the following day drove the Piedmontese toward Ceva. The objectives of the first phase of Napoleon's plan had been achieved: the French army was in Vado, Cairo, and Garessio, and the two allied armies had been separated. Schérer was supposed to plunge into the gap between the two armies and march on Ceva. In Turin, the Court thought it was doomed, but Schérer, considering his army too small, too poorly equipped, and too undisciplined, was afraid to venture too far from his bases and decided to go no farther. "We made a basic error by not forcing our way into Ceva while the defeated Austrians had been driven back beyond Acqui," Napoleon wrote. "The whole French army was available to defeat the Piedmontese, who, having not even twenty thousand troops, did not have forces comparable to ours, since we had thirty thousand. . . . General Sérurier's division, at Garessio and San Giovanni, was within range of Ceva; that of General Masséna, at Cairo, was only four leagues away." Napoleon, who at that point still commanded the Army of the Interior, was clearly keeping his eye on Italy, as this furious note proves. He even wrote up a new campaign plan, in which he carefully omitted making the slightest allusion to the final march on Vienna. In fact, although Carnot had finally adopted Napoleon's views, he certainly had no intention of giving so much importance to the operations in Italy. The main action was to take place on the Danube, with the Army of Italy assigned to *support* Moreau's and Jourdan's operations by forcing the king of Sardinia to lay down his arms and by driving the Austrians out of Lombardy. If the Austrians, who had massed their forces around Acqui, tried to reestablish their lines of communication with the Piedmontese, who had regrouped around Montezemolo and Ceva, then the Army of Italy was to march on Acqui via Cairo in order to force the Austrians to fall back to protect the road to Alessandria. If they did not move, then the Army of Italy was to proceed from Garessio to Montezemolo, defeat the Piedmontese, and move on Ceva, while the French division guarding the Tende pass would advance toward Mondovi and Coni. One part of the army would besiege Ceva, and the rest would then head "straight for Turin." Victor-Amadeus, Napoleon assured his superiors, would sue for peace. However, if he made any attempt to resist, "we will burn Turin without worrying about the citadel." Invading Lombardy would then be child's play: "We shall enter the Milan area as if we were in Champagne, without obstacles."[114]

When the Directory adopted Napoleon's new plan on January 19, 1796, on Carnot's proposal, General Clarke, who was responsible for military operations, had just written to Schérer deploring his inertia. Clarke's letter was not sent, and he was ordered to write another to Schérer to command him to attack (February 3).[115] But Schérer had no intention of obeying orders given by men who in his opinion were completely ignorant of the real situation of his army, and he told Masséna, one of his divisional generals, that he was "going to shut the mouths of [these] scribblers (and he mentioned Buonaparte by name) who, from Paris, claim that we could do much better than we have done."[116] In the end Schérer did not shut anyone up: he resigned. As Ritter, the Directory's representative to him and a former member of the Convention, put it, he refused to risk the destruction of the Army of Italy "because it has pleased a few maniacs to demonstrate on the map of a country of which there is no proper map that we could do the impossible."[117] Carnot took note and dictated this message to his secretary: "Buonaparte, general-in-chief of the Army of Italy. Accept Schérer's resignation; write him a kind letter." On March 2 the matter was settled: the Directory endorsed Carnot's proposal. Napoleon immediately procured maps of Italy and books about the country, and for a week he remained holed up in his office on Rue Neuve-des-Capucines, poring over his books or lying down to study maps that had been laid out on the floor. When he emerged on March 9, it was to go to marry Joséphine at the town hall on Rue d'Antin.

EIGHT

Happiness

From Eugénie to Joséphine

*L*egend or reality? A few days after Napoleon assumed command of the Army of the Interior (October 11, 1795), a very young man came into his office on the Place Vendôme. The fourteen-year-old Eugène de Beauharnais had been sent by his mother to request permission to keep her executed husband's sword, which she was supposed to hand over to the authorities in accord with a decree issued by the Convention disarming the residents of Paris.[1] Napoleon willingly gave his consent, and the next day Eugène's mother, Marie Josèphe Rose de Beauharnais, came to thank him. Napoleon went to visit her in return, but being "excessively occupied" by his new functions,[2] he did not repeat his visit often enough to satisfy Rose, as she was then known. On October 28 she reproached him for neglecting her.[3] He replied with a cordial note, and went to see her the next day—and remained there. When did he move from Rose's salon to her bed? Two weeks after their first meeting, as gossips claim? Or only in early December? It matters little. The affair advanced rapidly. Three months later they were married.

Prudish admirers of the emperor used to claim that he had lived chastely until he met Rose. Chastely, or almost, because they had to explain the prostitute he met at the Palais-Royal one evening in 1787 and who inspired him to write a short narrative.[4] There had been others: it was perhaps one of her counterparts in Toulon who in 1793 gave the general the "very nasty itch" from which Corvisart freed him only after 1800.

"He is the inverse of other men," he was soon to write about himself: "He began where ordinary men finish, and finished where others begin." Did he think he had lived backward, thrown into war before he had loved, more preoccupied with the joys of glory than with those of the heart?[5] In a short story sketched out around the same time—during the summer of 1795—he wrote about his hero, his literary double: "Clisson was born with a decided penchant for war. He read the lives of great men at an age when others read fables. He meditated on the principles of the military art at a time when other boys of his age were in school and chased girls."[6] That is not false of Napoleon himself. He had spent more time with Plutarch and Guibert than with girls, even if we know that he had had a few love affairs while he was living in garrisons. He picked cherries with Caroline du Colombier, became infatuated with a certain Emma whom he begged, in vain, to allow him "to know her heart"—at least if these letters, a few fragments of which have been preserved, are authentic.[7] None of this went very far. As young men often do at that age, he showed a scorn for matters of love that was proportional to his ignorance. "Harmful to society [and] to men's individual happiness," he had decreed in a *Dialogue sur l'amour* written around 1788.[8] In this little work he attacks his friend Des Mazis for being so infatuated with a girl named Adélaïde that he could not sleep, had lost his appetite and sense of friendship and duty, and was indifferent to everything that did not concern his heartthrob. Napoleon spoke of "disease," "madness," "depraved sentiment," and exhorted his friend to take as his models the Spartans, whose hearts were not, he said, occupied by "a single person" but "inflamed by the most sublime patriotism." All the same, he wept while reading Rousseau's novel, *La Nouvelle Héloïse*, and in 1791, after an excursion to the Alps from which he had returned in a dreamy state, he wrote that nothing could compare with the "sweet emotions of love."[9]

His youthful love affairs were not all as platonic as the old devotees of the Napoleonic cult liked to believe. However, we find hardly more credible his detractors who, animated by an equally narrow morality, described him as a kind of Casanova with an arriviste habit of sleeping with the wives of his superiors in order to climb the social ladder more quickly.[10] That would have been pointless: war and the shortage of officers at the time offered ample opportunities for promotion to anyone who had a little courage and talent. Napoleon certainly did not creep into the bed of General Carteaux's wife, but he might have passed through Ricord's. Charlotte Robespierre hints at this in her *Memoirs*. According to Charlotte, Marguerite Ricord, whose "coquetry at least equaled her beauty,"[11] was not stingy with her favors, distributing them equitably among her husband, Augustin Robespierre, and the young general commanding the artillery. Should

Charlotte be believed? It is possible that Napoleon had been Marguerite's devoted companion; whether he was more than that, we simply do not know. Moreover, it is as impossible to compare these little love affairs with the genuine passion that suddenly overwhelmed him after 13 Vendémiaire as it is to compare them with the bland feelings that Désirée Clary inspired in him during the months before he met Rose.

He was commanding the artillery of the Army of Italy and was returning from Genoa when, on August 1, 1794, Joseph married Julie Clary. Napoleon could not go to Marseille to attend the wedding, and it was only toward the end of the month, after he had been cleared of all suspicion of "Robespierrism" and released, that he met the Clary sisters. Bernardine-Eugénie-Désirée was sixteen years old. Unlike Julie, who was frankly ugly, Désirée was, if not pretty, at least charming, sentimental, and a little melancholy. Napoleon, who had spent his enforced leisure under house arrest in Nice at the home of a former Count Laurenti, flirting with his hosts' daughter, Émilie, also continued his flirtation with Désirée. The young woman, who was very romantic, fell in love with the general, and when they had to separate—she was returning to Marseille, he to army headquarters—she asked permission to write to him. He accepted. She wrote him tender letters to which he replied by praising her "inalterable sweetness" and her "charms," assuring her of his "friendship" and even of his "love."[12] All this was friendly banter with no real consequences, and did not prevent him from treating her basically as a little girl. The tone of his letters was that of a tutor to his pupil. Having noticed her fondness for singing, he advised her to buy a pianoforte, sent her sheet music, subscribed her to a "harpsichord journal," and considering her singing teacher not very competent, explained to her how she should perform her vocal exercises. He also drew up lists of books she should read, asking her to describe the effect they had on her soul: "Your reason will be further developed by reading, your memory will be furnished," he told her.[13] It wasn't very kind, it was even cold, at least enough that she felt it. She rebelled. "The most sensitive of women loves the coldest of men," she wrote to him. "If I sent you a daily record of my thoughts," he replied, "you would be still more persuaded that this time, good Eugénie [Désirée] is quite wrong."[14]

But he could not, in fact, send her "a daily record of his thoughts." It was not Désirée he was thinking about. For a few months he had been the lover of Louise

Turreau, the wife of the member of the Convention who had succeeded Saliceti with the Army of Italy. Younger than Marguerite Ricord—she was twenty-four, Marguerite thirty-one—she was as pretty and even more promiscuous. Napoleon was quite proud of this conquest, which had nonetheless cost him less effort than the conquest of Toulon. The lieutenant who had been bored by garrison life had stated that one had to choose between love and glory, but the happy general—he had just led the Dego expedition—was discovering that love and war go well together. "I was very young then," he confided to Las Cases, "I was happy and proud of my little success"[15]—so proud that, to be admired by Louise and to show her what a great captain he was, he organized for her benefit a combat that was simulated but nonetheless led to a few casualties. Was he in love, or was it merely a short-lived affair ("affaire de canapé"[16]) that did not involve feeling? All good things come to an end, and the two lovers soon had to separate. In March 1795, Turreau and his faithless wife returned to Paris. It may have been then, in order not to suffer from a "horrible solitude of the heart"[17] after Louise left, that he remembered the young woman to whom he was giving music lessons by correspondence. Désirée, whom Napoleon had not seen since their first meeting, was happy to find him so loving, and when they separated again, he sent her letters that were no longer teacher's letters: "You have been constantly in my memory. Your portrait is graven on my heart. . . . Forever yours."[18] There was a reason for this, the emperor was to say on Saint Helena: he had taken her "virginity."[19] It was hardly elegant on his part to say so, and it is false. If it had been otherwise, would he have later reminded Désirée "of those walks we took when love united us without satisfying us"?[20] He had perhaps tried; after all, he had scarcely left Louise, who had given him everything, but Désirée had not yielded. By telling Bertrand that he had deflowered her, he might have been affording himself the easy satisfaction of a final revenge on Bernadotte, Désirée's future husband, whom he had made a "marshal, prince, and king," he said, only to repair the wrongs he had done the young woman. Those who believe this fable see the proof of it in the "engagement" that is supposed to have been hurriedly celebrated just before Napoleon's departure for Paris. They even point to the date: April 21, 1795. Désirée certainly considered Napoleon her fiancé; her letters prove it. They had exchanged vows, he to love her forever, she to wait for him in Marseille for as long as necessary. Her mother knew about this, and so did Joseph. Had they talked about marriage? The idea was certainly in the air, but neither Mme Clary—whose husband had died in January 1794—nor Désirée's brothers, nor even Joseph, favored a possible marriage between the Buonapartes' youngest son and the Clarys' youngest daughter.

Was Napoleon really thinking about becoming his brother's brother-in-law? We have seen how mixed his feelings about Joseph were, combining a deep and sincere affection with a scarcely concealed contempt, but the relations between the two brothers never seemed better or closer than in 1795. A letter from Napoleon written on June 24 testifies to this. He had just learned that Joseph was going to Genoa: "You could have no better friend who is more dear to you and who desires your happiness more sincerely. Life is a frail dream that dissipates. If you leave and you think that it might be for some time!!! Send me your portrait. We have lived together for so many years, so intimately united that our hearts have fused. You know better than anyone how much what is mine is entirely yours. In writing these lines I feel an emotion I have seldom experienced in my life. I sense that we will soon see each other and I can no longer continue my letter. Farewell, my friend."[21]

Did he want to marry Désirée to be closer to his beloved brother and strengthen the intimate ties that would then have united them through the two sisters? Or, on the contrary, in planning this marriage and doing everything he could to impose it on Joseph, was he governed by the profound "hostility" that is supposed to have animated him, according to Freud, with regard to his elder brother?[22] For years he had been the de facto eldest son, providing for the family's needs by sending money taken out of his pay and taking care of administrative tasks that Joseph had neglected. Ever since his father's death, everyone had seen him as the head of the family. To be sure, Joseph had never ceased to enjoy the respect due the firstborn; he remained "the first of the brothers, the father's successor, the head of the family."[23] No one, and least of all Napoleon, contested the titles he held by right of birth. But in fact if not by right, Napoleon held the first rank. He had, as he was later to say, "disinherited" Joseph, and if, whenever he was asked his age, he always made himself older by two or three years, that was also because he wanted to make right and fact coincide, at least in the eyes of strangers. This situation had changed since the Buonapartes had arrived on the continent, and still more since Joseph's wedding. Joseph's marriage to Julie Clary was advantageous. The Clarys had made a fortune in trade with the Levant, and Julie brought with her a considerable dowry: 150,000 francs, perhaps. Joseph's marriage had nothing in common with the one the rascally Lucien had made three months earlier: he had married the daughter of an inn keeper in Saint-Maximin. No one mentioned that union, which was celebrated, moreover, against the wishes of the Buonapartes. The eldest son's marriage was quite a different matter. By marrying, Joseph had repaired, more than could reasonably have been hoped, the clan's financial situation. He had at his disposal an attractive amount of capital, and because his father-in-law was dead, he was even considered the head of the family. As a result, he had recovered the prerogatives of the elder son. At a time when Napoleon's career seemed compromised, Joseph once again became the support and the hope of his family. That being the case, it may be that Napoleon sought, by marrying Désirée, to challenge Joseph's hold on the advantageous position he had acquired, and to regain the de facto preeminence he had long enjoyed, even though he would never possess it de jure.

Love counted for little in these more or less unconscious calculations. The proof? Hardly had Napoleon set out for Paris on May 8, 1795, than his letters to his "fiancée" became cooler. She became once again a "good and tender friend" who inspired "affectionate sentiments" in him.[24] Désirée, who thought only of him and filled the pages of her music notebook with his initials, wrote him passionate letters: "You know how much I love you, but I shall never be able to express my feelings properly in words. . . . All my thoughts, my ideas, in a word, my existence, are yours. . . . Yes, my friend, you are never out of my thoughts, and my feelings for you will end only with my life."[25] Because he did not write to her often, she mixed with her passionate declarations of love an admission of "dark forebodings" and doubts regarding his sincerity and the depth of his love for her.[26] She suspected him of preferring to her the pleasures of the capital, and perhaps even of the "very amiable pretty women" he somewhat boorishly told her about.[27] She was jealous. Were his "walks in the Bois de Boulogne with Mme T***" going to make him forget the walk he had taken "along the bank of the river with good little Eugénie"? Her letters were waiting for Napoleon at the post office. He went by to pick them up only a week after his arrival in Paris. Their correspondence resumed, she accusing him of loving her with insufficient passion, he justifying himself halfheartedly. And then in June they suddenly exchanged roles: Désirée no longer wrote, and Napoleon was assailed by "dark forebodings" of his own.

What had happened? Désirée had followed Joseph and Julie to Genoa and dared not confess to her "fiancé" that she had broken her oath to await his return in Marseille. She finally summoned the courage to tell him everything. Her letter arrived on June 13, the very day on which Napoleon learned of his transfer to the infantry. With his career in ruins and Désirée escaping him, he had a moment of discouragement. He had his bad moments, too. To the young woman who had once again become for a few days his "fiancée," he wrote a letter in which he accused her in turn of no longer thinking about him since she had left Marseille. Their love was dead, he felt it, and he went so far as to wish her happiness with another man, since she no longer wanted to be happy with him.[28] From this letter of June 14 he drew a few weeks later the final scene of *Clisson et Eugénie*, giving the heroine the new lover he predicted for Désirée and dooming the hero to the death in battle that he had told Joseph he would seek for himself "if the Désirée affair did not work out."[29] But Désirée no more had a lover than he had any intention of getting himself killed. This moment of despair, though it was genuine, soon passed. Désirée no longer wrote, but Napoleon, who had begun to work with the topographic office, was no longer thinking about that. From time to time, he asked Joseph for news of "Eugénie." When in August he finally received a letter dated July 6, in which she swore that she still loved him and had left Marseille against her will,[30] he replied, addressing her as "Mademoiselle." It was no longer the letter of a lover, only that of a suitor.[31] The planned marriage with Désirée had become "the Eugénie matter," as he wrote to Joseph.[32] Still an option, to be sure, but only an option.

The Thermidorian Fete

When he arrived in Paris on May 28, 1795, Napoleon discovered a society of which his earlier sojourns in the capital in 1791 and 1792 could have given him no idea: "This great people is addicted to pleasure," he wrote to his brother on July 30. "Dancing, going to the theater, excursions to the countryside, and courting women, who are here the most beautiful in the world, is the great occupation and the great affair. Luxury, ease, theater: everything has resumed. People remember the Terror like a dream."[33] And a few days later he made this very acute observation: "One would think that they all have to make up for the time they suffered, and that the uncertainty of the future leads them to indulge unsparingly in the pleasures of the present."[34] The terrible hardships of the following winter, with which he was to be abruptly confronted when he commanded the Army of the Interior, did not darken this atmosphere of rebirth, at least for those who were not hungry. Napoleon, thanks to Barras, who had taken him under his wing, had a box seat for witnessing the "Thermidorian fete." Barras, on the strength of the role he had played in leading the operations against Robespierre, at that time stood at the top of the ladder. His terrorist past had been forgotten, and he had established himself, thanks to his presence and his total lack of scruples, as the rather villainous king of the period, at ease in this society where parvenus, more or less repentant revolutionaries, debris of the Old Regime, corrupt financiers, ambitious generals, and men of letters mixed. If Thermidorian society had a "king" and even a few princes—from Tallien to Fréron—it also had its "queens." Teresa Cabarrus was the most famous of these. Teresa was the daughter of a Spanish banker and had been sentenced to the scaffold; it was said that Tallien had headed the conspiracy against Robespierre in order to save her. Her admirers called her "Our Lady of Thermidor" (Notre-Dame de Thermidor), and her detractors the "new Marie-Antoinette." She was twenty-two years old. "When she entered a salon," the composer Auber recalled, "she made day and night: day for her, night for the others."[35] A swarm of pretty women buzzed around her: the scandalous Fortunée Hamelin, Juliette Récamier, Aimée de Coigny, Julie Talma—and General Beauharnais's widow. Teresa had married Tallien at the end of 1794 and chosen to live on Allée des Veuves (present-day Avenue Montaigne), where her "cottage" had become the most frequented rendezvous of Parisian high society. Here reputations were born and collapsed, fortunes were made, love affairs begun and others ended, but no one ever talked politics. Politics, for so many years the most common topic of conversation, was henceforth banished from this world devoted to elegance, money, and pleasure. The reign of the Incroyables and the Merveilleuses had replaced that of the Jacobins and the sans-culottes.[36]

Napoleon was more than impressed when he discovered the Talliens' "cottage" and its habitués: he was dazzled, intoxicated. To the point of losing all sense of propriety and foolishly making advances to the mistress of the house herself? Barras says that he did, and adds that Teresa put him firmly in his place.[37] Perhaps it was this rebuff that he alluded to when he wrote to Désirée: "Mme T[allien] is still just as amiable, but in my view by some fatality [her] charms have faded, she has aged a little."[38] Didn't he realize that he was a little too threadbare to be fully admitted to this society? He was like a poor relation, received only as a favor to Barras. His shapeless clothes, his long hair, his half-starved look, his foreign accent—none of that helped. He was more or less ignored. He took his revenge as he could; in a letter addressed to Désirée he mocked "the ugliest, oldest women" who surrounded Teresa.[39] In any case, he had understood that a marriage with Désirée would not give him the "social existence" he had to have to "assert his position."[40] Compared to the "old women" in the Allée des Veuves, Désirée was only a witless little provincial. Did he then set out to find a more "Parisian" wife, proposing marriage to two or three widows[41] and even to Mme Permon—the mother of the future Duchess d'Abrantès—an old family friend? Laure Junot claims that he did. If Napoleon really considered marrying her, it was probably at the beginning of October 1795, when Mme Permon lost her husband. But if he did, Mme Permon put an end to the matter with a burst of laughter, telling Napoleon that she would not make a fool of him by letting him marry a woman old enough to be his mother.[42] Was he so desperate that he ended up lending himself to a bad joke of Barras's, who wanted him to marry the sixty-five-year-old Mlle Montansier?[43] It is more likely that Napoleon, whose matrimonial campaigns were faltering but who was still in the grip of the "mad desire to get married," reactivated the "Désirée affair."[44] After all, at this time he was envisaging the possibility of going off to make his fortune in the Orient, for which purpose the daughter of the head of the Clary business firm regained a certain value. On September 5, 1795, he wrote to Joseph, who was still in Genoa, asking him to consent to his marriage with "Eugénie" and to obtain the Clarys' agreement.[45] He emphasized that "the Eugénie affair has to be completed or broken off,"[46] even though he knew all about his brother's reluctance and the Clary clan's opposition.[47] And then, suddenly, the "Désirée" affair vanished from his preoccupations.

Madly in Love

The marriage of Napoleon and Joséphine, François Furet wrote, "can be described like a vaudeville act," but it can also be described "in more touching ways that are just as true."[48] Regarding Napoleon, that is certainly so; regarding Joséphine, somewhat less. For him, it was love at first sight. Every evening he hurried off to Rue Chantereine, where she had just moved into a "folly" rented to Julie Talma. He was under her spell, so proud of his conquest that he took his friends to the restaurant where she was a regular to show her to them and to tell them that he was going to marry her; he was so taken with her that he agreed to share her bed with her pug, Fortuné, who was less accommodating than he was and bit his leg. He was so intoxicated with love that he had no sooner left her than he wrote her letters burning with passion that she read with amusement and laughed about with her girlfriends:

> Seven A.M. I wake up full of you. Your image and the memory of the intoxicating evening yesterday have left my senses no repose. Sweet and incomparable Joséphine, what a strange effect you have on my heart! Are you angry? Do I see that you are sad? Are you worried? My soul is racked with pain, and there is no rest for your friend . . . But is there any more for me when, yielding to the deep feeling that holds sway over me, I draw from your lips, from your heart, a flame that burns me? Ah! It was last night that I clearly saw that your image is not you! You leave at noon, and I shall see you in three hours. In the meantime, mio dolce amore, receive a thousand kisses; but don't give me any, for they burn my blood.[49]

For the first and the last time in his life, he was, at the age of twenty-six, madly in love, "in every sense of the word," as Marmont put it.[50] His personal successes further embellished his passion. After a year of uncertainty, he was getting everything all at once: an important position that opened the doors to the corridors of power and to the Thermidorian society that, not two months before, was still snubbing him—"a little kiss to Mmes Tallien and Chateaurenaud," he soon wrote, "to the first on the mouth, to the second on the cheek"[51]—the prospect of an imminent return to his cherished Army of Italy, and, last but not least, love. Not long before, a marriage of convenience had seemed to him the only way to escape from the dead end in which he found himself; now he was getting ready to marry for love.

He loved her so much, Françoise Wagener wrote, "that he renamed her, that he wanted to recreate her, as if she had been born from their meeting."[52] He had also renamed Désirée.[53] But Désirée, "his first inclination," was still a child; Rose was a woman, and moreover she was a "woman in the full sense of the term."[54] Everything about her was "incomparable": her clothes and her walk, her bearing and her voice—which was so much like a caress that later on, in the Tuileries, the servants stopped in the halls to listen to her—her smile and her look, "the equanimity of her temper and the easiness of her character, . . . the sweet expression of her face," and finally that "indolence natural to creoles, which made itself felt in her attitudes and in her movements."[55] On Saint Helena, Napoleon still spoke with emotion of her irresistible elegance: "Josephine was grace personified. Everything she did was with a peculiar grace and delicacy. I never saw her act inelegantly during the whole time we lived together. She had grace even *en se couchant*."[56] Grace overcame everything, her "sagging, flat" breasts, her bad teeth, and the skin of her face, which was already a little frayed; a grace that was so great that despite the twelve years that separated her from Teresa Tallien she could rival her, afford the luxury of appearing in her company at a party wearing the same "peach-blossom petticoat" and on her head the same "red kerchief knotted in the creole fashion, with three curls at the temples,"[57] without being in the least ridiculous. It wasn't that time had spared her more than others but, as Barras put it, that she knew how, "by consummate cunning and artifice," to make up for and even surpass what time had stolen from her.[58] She was fighting a war that had already been lost, but she was resolved to keep going as long as she could.

The very fact that she was six years older added to the *je ne sais quoi* that made her seem to Napoleon a "real" woman, *woman* incarnate. Although his imagination transfigured her, idealized her, he did not go so far as to see in her only an apparition: "She had the nicest little cunt imaginable," he confided. "The three isles of Martinique were there."[59] She liked sex and knew how to please. She revealed pleasure to him while making him think she was learning its secrets from him. He was delirious with happiness. There was pride in his passion, the pride of being loved by one of the most prominent women of his time, and also the pride of being loved by a great, a very great, lady. "My son-in-law is an enormous snob," the emperor of Austria said after having given his daughter to the emperor of the French. Just as in 1810 Napoleon thought he was entering the family of the *legitimate sovereigns* by marrying a Habsburg, a descendant of a line of Germanic emperors that went back to the Caesars, in 1796 he thought he was making a huge leap up the social ladder by marrying an adventuress whom he believed to be highborn. His own nobility, which was insignificant and doubtful, received from the marriage a brilliant confirmation. Even during the Revolution he had remained "susceptible and submissive to aristocratic prejudices."[60] But it was not merely a matter of a somewhat naive vanity: in his eyes Joséphine evoked the grandeur of a world that had disappeared and about which he was nostalgic, even though he had not known it. He loved not only the woman but the viscountess, and he was particularly fond of the intimate moments after most of the evening's guests had left and he and Joséphine remained with a few close friends, almost all of them vestiges of the Old Regime: "When the majority of the party retired, there usually remained M. de Montesquiou . . . the Duke de Nivernais, so celebrated for the graces of his wit; and a few others. They used to look round to see that the doors were all shut, and they would then say, 'Let us sit down and chat about the old court; let us make a tour to Versailles.'"[61] With Joséphine life became larger, and with his commission as general-in-chief of the Army of Italy in his pocket, he already saw himself winning victories to offer her.

Just as she made him think that she had been presented at the court, she pretended to be rich, displaying before his dazzled eyes the millions amassed by her family in Martinique and in Saint-Domingue. Did he have suspicions? Did he guess that she was struggling to meet her expenses? As a true son of an excessively economical mother, did he mentally calculate the cost of all the new dresses, baubles, and jewels she was constantly wearing? Had he heard about the discontent of her creditors, whom she could not pay? Did she inadvertently let him glimpse financial problems that she probably easily ignored but that must have darkened her mood when the bills came in? Doubt crept into his mind; she was lying to him. He decided to get to the bottom of the matter. He confided in Father Patrault, the former professor at Brienne whom he had met again in Paris. The priest sent him to see one of his businessman friends who had interests in the islands. This M. Emmery only partly reassured him: although Joséphine did in fact receive part of the family plantation's revenues, the amount was no more than 25,000 francs per annum. That was far less than the 500,000 francs she had talked about. However, Napoleon had to admit that in marrying her he was getting a better deal than she was. The marriage contract signed on March 8, 1786, testifies to this: while Joséphine brought to the marriage her annual income of 25,000 francs, Napoleon could offer his wife only a meager pension of 1,500 francs in the event that she became a widow, and even declared that he possessed nothing of his own, neither real property nor furnishings, with the exception of "his wardrobe and his military equipment," an admission he ultimately judged pointless and scratched out on the original.[62]

Still, he quarreled with her, not because she was not as rich as she had claimed—she was even less wealthy than these figures indicated, her accumulated debts having devoured her revenues for several years in advance—but because she had lied with an aplomb that made him suspect many other lies. She denied it, wept, accused him of not loving her for herself. He probably shouted at her as well, but the time had not yet come when, as he was later to aver, "he sometimes punished her in bed, when she went too far."[63] However, he was so much under her spell that after a night of recriminations he left Rue Chantereine in the grip of despair and immediately wrote to her to beg her to pardon him for having forced her to tell him the truth.[64]

Did he hesitate when the time came to commit himself? He confided in Barras, who thought his protégé certainly very foolish in everything unrelated to the military, but immediately calculated the benefits he could derive from a union that would make Napoleon obliged to him. He encouraged him, as we have seen,[65] and didn't have to try very hard to convince his protégé, who was only looking for a few additional reasons to do what he had, in his heart of hearts, already decided to do.

From Rose to Joséphine

Joséphine, for her part, was less resolved than her future husband. She had, to be sure, a few good reasons to hesitate. Her experience of marriage had left her with bitter memories. She had had a happy childhood in the soft cocoon of an almost exclusively feminine society—her grandmother, her mother, her two younger sisters, her nursemaid, and a few black servants—in which her father appeared only rarely. Indolent, carefree years spent in the shade of the frangipani and soursop trees of Martinique. The young girl knew nothing about her parents' financial difficulties. Unlike most of the colonists, who returned to the continent after having made a fortune in the sugar islands, Rose Tascher seemed doomed to remain there for a long time, leading a mediocre, almost impoverished existence. But life was sweet, and Rose grew up ignorant of the world's tumult. She was torn away from this little paradise in 1779, when she was sixteen years old. She landed in Brest one day in October, in the company of her father. There she discovered another world, gray and dreary, where everything was foreign to her, starting with the fiancé, Alexandre de Beauharnais, who was waiting for her on the dock. Alexandre was accompanied by his aunt Désirée Renaudin, who had been the best friend of the young man's mother and after the latter's death had taken over her role for her husband and her son. Because she could not marry the elder M. de Beauharnais, Mme Renaudin wanted at all costs to consolidate her position by marrying the son to one of her nieces. She had set her sights on the second of Joseph Tascher's daughters, but tuberculosis had carried the girl off prematurely. Of the two remaining daughters, Rose, sixteen, and Marie-Françoise, thirteen, the Marquis de Beauharnais preferred the younger to the elder, who was already too much a mature woman. But Marie-Françoise had wept so hard that in the end her mother refused to let her go. Mme Renaudin and de Beauharnais had to settle for Rose.

Once the wedding had taken place, on December 13, 1779, Alexandre rejoined his regiment in Brest and Rose moved into her father-in-law's town house in Paris, on Rue Thévenot. She found herself alone, bored in a city where she knew no one and where, moreover, she was hardly allowed to go out. Alexandre had made her promise to write to him every day, but she was lazy. The pen fell from her hand, as did the books he had recommended that she read in order to complete an almost entirely neglected education. To Rose, marriage seemed very dull; Alexandre, whom Rivarol summed up succinctly by saying he was "one of the most illustrious dancers of the old monarchy,"[66] found his wife very silly; he was even a little ashamed of this wife, who was, to be sure, pretty, but was ignorant and had nothing to say. Tired of spending such dismal evenings in her company, he resumed his bachelor's life. Quarrels grew frequent. Rose accused him of deceiving her, Alexandre reproached her for not loving him and suspected her of seeking happiness elsewhere. Nevertheless, two children were born of this shaky marriage, a boy, Eugène, on September 3, 1781, and a daughter, Hortense, on April 10, 1783. At that time Alexandre was far away, in Martinique, with a distant cousin of the Taschers, Laure de Longpré, who was consoling him for his conjugal problems and stoking his resentment toward his wife by insinuating that she was no longer a virgin when he married her and that he was not Hortense's father. Alexandre, who was suspicious by nature, believed her. Was he wrong to do so?[67] He almost went mad, and his rage, far from diminishing, was gradually transformed into an icy anger and hatred. When it was time for him to return to Europe, he notified his wife that the marriage was over, ordered her to retire to a convent, and told her he never wanted to set eyes on her again. Refusing to have any contact whatever with her, he moved in with his mistress, while Rose, entrenched in the family home, refused to leave it or to obey her husband's orders. She resisted for almost a year before giving up. She finally retired to the abbey of Panthémont, where the repudiated wives of high society found an asylum that, though not as licentious as the one Sade depicted in his *Histoire de Juliette,* was certainly not austere. In late 1785, after many crises—Rose had filed suit against Alexandre, and Alexandre had kidnapped Eugène—the couple formalized their separation before a notary. Alexandre agreed to pay Rose an annual pension of 6,000 livres and received custody of Eugène, while Rose received custody of Hortense.

The divorce—de facto if not de jure—was advantageous for Rose. She learned about high society, collected lovers, and spent a great deal of money. The Revolution took place while she was in Martinique, where she had hurriedly gone in late 1788 for reasons that remain mysterious: Did she want to see her mother again, as Hortense was to maintain? Was she escaping from an importunate lover? Did she want to conceal a pregnancy, and should her sterility be dated from that time? Fleeing the first disturbances that struck the island, she returned to France in the late summer of 1790. Her husband had become a powerful man, a deputy in the Constituent Assembly and a member of the Society of Jacobins. She ran into him, and though they did not resume their life together, they maintained a more peaceful relationship that was almost affectionate; they spoke about their children's education. Alexandre's celebrity opened the doors to fashionable salons for Rose. She was seen at Mme de Staël's salon and at the home of the Prince de Salm, as well as in Robespierre's entourage. She belonged to no party; politics left her cold. Moreover, she had no understanding of politics. But she was shrewd and was well aware that the friendship of powerful people, no matter what side they were on, was indispensable for her in the struggle with her creditors. Life was pleasant, punctuated by parties and balls. Because she was liberal with her favors, she always found someone to meet her needs. Living the high life thanks to her husband's notoriety, she was dragged down with him when he fell. The catastrophe occurred on July 23, 1793, the day Mainz was surrendered. The leaders of the Army of the Rhine were accused of treason. Custine and Dillon paid with their heads; Alexandre, who was more fortunate, was simply dismissed as the chief of staff for the Army of the Rhine. But that was only a temporary reprieve. Rose was frightened; she left Paris, finding in Croissy-sur-Seine a refuge where many revolutionaries came to take a break from political battles. There she became acquainted with Barère, Réal, and Tallien. If she thought she could escape danger by leading a discreet life, she was mistaken; Alexandre was soon arrested. She hastened to see Vadier, one of the members of the Committee of General Security she knew well. He promised her his protection and warded off the blows that were threatening her, at least until an anonymous denunciation drew attention to this aristocrat who was defying the law of suspects. On April 19, 1794, Rose was arrested in turn and locked up in the Carmes prison. Seven hundred prisoners were packed into the convent on Rue de Vaugirard, where her husband and many of her acquaintances had preceded her. Although in Carmes she was not on unknown territory, a feeling of terror gripped her soul when the gates closed on her. She wept a great deal. Too much, some of her fellow prisoners said, judging her behavior as lacking in dignity; they considered it their duty to resist misfortune by affecting a certain carelessness and lightheartedness. Beugnot recalled: "The proximity of the women provided us with pleasant distractions. We talked agreeably about everything without going into anything deeply. There, misfortune was treated like a naughty child, one to be only laughed at, and in fact we laughed wholeheartedly at Marat's divinity, Robespierre's priesthood, and Fouquier's magistracy. We seemed to say to these sanguinary knaves: 'You will kill us whenever you please, but you shall not prevent us from being pleasant!' "[68]

Rose was viscerally, terribly afraid of dying. Day after day she heard summoned to be sentenced people who would never be seen again. She witnessed devastating farewell scenes. Miserable, she fell into the arms of General Lazare Hoche, who had also been arrested. His transfer to the Conciergerie on May 17 increased her despair. Less than two months later her husband also left Carmes; he embraced Delphine de Custine, who had been his last mistress, and his wife, whom he had pardoned. Alexandre was not as fortunate as Hoche, who was saved by Robespierre's fall; he mounted the scaffold five days earlier. "I was attached to my husband," Rose admitted between two fits of weeping.[69] And then 9 Thermidor came. The relief. No doubt thanks to Tallien, she was one of the first to be set free. On August 6, 1794, she emerged to applause, crying.

Life, finally. She returned to her apartment on Rue de l'Université, to 50,000 francs of debt, and to the frightful dresses she had worn in 1793, cut from rough fabrics and decorated with tricolor ribbons, bonnets "à la Constitution," and iron jewelry. She got rid of all these horrors, dressed herself in silk, gauze, and lace, and hurried off to find Hoche, who had also been released from prison. She was in love, madly in love, and jealous of Hoche's wife, a silly little goose of sixteen whom the general, despite Rose's supplications, refused to leave. He also loved Rose, but the way a man loves a mistress, and he had no intention of getting a divorce in order to link his fate to that of this woman who gave him her peerless body, but a body that many others had also held in their arms. When he left to fight in the Vendée, she drowned her sorrows in the intoxicating Thermidorian fete and somehow ended up—in May or June 1795—in Barras's bed. The director was not a jealous lover; he reproached Rose neither for her affair with Hoche nor for the favors she granted the Marquis de Caulaincourt, the father of the future Grand Squire of the Empire. He consoled her when she wept and confided to him her problems with Hoche, who had betrayed her by getting his wife pregnant. Barras paid her debts and in August he gave her the funds she needed to sign a lease on the house on Rue Chantereine. But he was already tired of this affair, especially because he had just taken into his bed Teresa Tallien, whose marriage was on the rocks. Wanting to enjoy his new favorite in peace, he was also trying to get rid of Rose when Napoleon, telling him about his plans to get married, removed a thorn from his side.

Bad memories of her marriage to Alexandre were not the only reason for Joséphine's hesitations. The little general was "amusing," no doubt, and she was certainly flattered by his eagerness, which proved that she was still desirable and somewhat alleviated the fears that the flight of time inspired in her. But it had to be admitted that he didn't make her laugh much, and above all he didn't give her much pleasure, which she explained to her friends by saying that his semen had the consistency of water. Moreover, Napoleon wasn't even her type. She liked tall, well-built men like Barras and Hoche; Napoleon was of average height and puny. And then he was also very young. The years that separated them were not a problem, but might someday become one: "Being past my earliest youth," she is supposed to have written to a woman friend, "can I hope to maintain for a long time this violent tenderness that in the general resembles a fit of madness?"[70] She foresaw scenes, troubles of all kinds. All this was charming in a lover; it would be ridiculous in a husband. The greatest miscalculation in their relationship probably lay there. For her, marriage was a matter of convenience and proprieties, and all the more because the ideas inculcated by her upbringing and by her milieu were added to the memories of her failed union with Alexandre.[71] Love in marriage seemed to her unsuitable; she could not imagine that pleasure might bloom in the straitjacket of conjugal bonds. Her ideas about love remained those of the eighteenth century, whereas his were already those of the nineteenth. They belonged neither to the same century nor to the same world. Between them there was the difference that separated the aristocratic world he had not known from the bourgeois world whose manners she adopted without understanding or liking them. They were separated by a revolution, the one that had, since Rousseau, overturned the former order of the feelings. Joséphine was heir to the old world, where there was a more or less airtight barrier between pleasure and conjugality; Napoleon was a harbinger of a new world founded on the abolition of that barrier. One might see Joséphine as coming straight out of the pages of *Les Liaisons dangereuses*, and Napoleon out of those of a bourgeois novel. He could not conceive that one might get married without loving; he saw in marriage the natural outcome of passion, and imagined it as the ultimate degree of happiness. No doubt he had considered a marriage of convenience with Désirée, just as Joséphine had considered a marriage of love with Hoche. But once he was bound to Joséphine, Napoleon considered it no longer. The way in which he was always to speak about his marriage to her testifies to the misunderstanding between them: he saw his wife as a bourgeoise who had basically always been a "good woman," even if she loved diamonds a little too much and was not very faithful. For many years, he said, they had been "a completely bourgeois household, that is, one that was very tender and united, long sharing the same bedroom and the same bed."[72] And when he assessed those years, he said that his wife had "constantly provided conjugal happiness."[73] He dreamed about it even before he met her, and in *Clisson et Eugénie* he had given a description of conjugal happiness that anticipates a famous page in Tolstoy.[74] Let us recall the circumstances. Clisson, having known glory when he was still very young and having attracted the resentment it arouses, had one day felt "the need to meditate on his situation." He had been submerged by the desire for a simple happiness. Once Eugénie had entered his life, he had abandoned the joyless quest for glory:

> The months and years fled past as rapidly as the hours. They had children and were still lovers. Eugénie loved as constantly as she was loved. They had no sorrow, no pleasure, no care they did not share, it seemed that nature had given them the same heart, the same soul, the same feeling. At night Eugénie always slept with her head resting on her lover's shoulder, or in his arms, and during the day they were always at each other's side, raising their children, cultivating their garden, managing their household. Eugénie had well avenged the injustice men had done

Clisson, which now seemed to him only a dream. The world, people, the neighbors had forgotten, completely forgotten, what Clisson had been. Living in seclusion, enjoying love, nature, and rustic simplicity, . . . only the unfortunate appreciated and blessed them.[75]

This period piece evokes Rousseau and Chardin, of course, but it is true to Napoleon's character too in certain respects, for all through his life he was to feel, from time to time, the desire for married life, the ambition to "rest after completing a task—and to live simply,"[76] the nostalgia for a bourgeois happiness that he had never experienced and that he knew was not in his nature. After a few years, war tears Clisson away from this obscure and happy life in his cottage and in Eugénie's arms. That happiness was not for him. It was not for Joséphine, either.

If her proposed marriage with Napoleon was *also* a matter of convenience, for her there were additional reasons to hesitate. Barras might tell her that this apparently insignificant young man was an exceptional person from whom she could expect great things, but was that so sure? After all, the command of the Army of the Interior was no great position. Italy, Barras promised. But up to that point hadn't second-rate generals been sent to Italy? Even supposing that Napoleon was a hope, she could not live on hopes, she needed protection, and money. Besides, she had forgotten the very meaning of the word "future": "Because she had had so many troubles, because she had seen her world swallowed up, Joséphine had left forever *time that endures*, immemorial time, the immobile time in which she had been brought up, intangible, highly reassuring stability, in order to enter into immediate time, time without perspective, induced by the upheavals and threats that continue to weigh on people."[77]

She knew, however, that she had hardly any choice. She was thirty-three years old, with two grown-up children, debts, a body that would end up failing her, and a deplorable reputation. The time had come to stop. But she didn't like it. She feared reliving, fifteen years later, the years she had spent with Alexandre. Up to the last moment she hoped that Lazare Hoche would yield to her arguments. He had returned to Paris at the very time that she was becoming Napoleon's mistress. Hoche was told about this, and though he agreed to see her again, he did not pardon her this new relationship. However, he had known from the outset that she was not exactly a paragon of virtue. And although his own marriage had not prevented him from sleeping with her, his very recent fatherhood imposed duties on him: the birth of his daughter sounded the death knell for his love affair with Rose. On leaving Paris in January 1796 he said: "A man might for the time being indulge in having a trull as his mistress, but not for that take her unto himself as his lawful wife."[78] This time it was all over. Rose resigned herself to becoming Joséphine Buonaparte. On the evening of March 9, it was with a heavy heart that she went to the town hall on Rue d'Antin where the wedding was to take place.

Already an hour late, Napoleon had been tied up in his office, where he was preparing his departure for the headquarters of the Army of Italy in Nice. Joséphine and the witnesses—Barras, Tallien, and Calmelet, the notary—were waiting for him at the second arrondissement's town hall. Because the groom had not arrived, the registry official who was supposed to perform the marriage, a certain Leclercq, finally left. It was past ten when Napoleon, preceded by the sound of his saber striking the steps of the stairway, burst into the room, followed by one of his aides-de-camp, Captain Le Marois: "Marry us, quick!" To replace Leclercq, Barras called upon a commissioner from the Directory who was accompanying him. Less than ten minutes later they left the town hall, having signed a document in which everything was so mendacious and illegal that today such a union would be considered null and void. Collin-Lacombe, the Directory commissioner, could not substitute for the registry official, Le Marois was a minor, and both Napoleon and Joséphine had lied about their ages, he making himself eighteen months older, she making herself four years younger. The bride wore on her finger a gold ring decorated with a little sapphire. On the inside these words were engraved: *To destiny.* They said farewell to the witnesses and returned on foot to Rue Chantereine.[79] Their civil marriage was not in accord with the rules—so did the newly married couple have their union blessed by a non-juring priest?[80] Las Cases says they did, claiming to have learned this detail not from the emperor, but from Charles de Dalberg, the prince-primate of the Confederation of the Rhine, who might have heard it from Napoleon himself: "Madame de Beauharnais was married to General Bonaparte, by a non-juring priest; who by pure accident had neglected to procure the requisite authority from the curate of the parish."[81] Although most historians refuse to believe in the authenticity of this secret ceremony, it is far from implausible. Joséphine, like all great sinners, regularly said her prayers, whereas Napoleon, though he was hardly a believer, had no lack of reasons for putting religion on his side. In 1794 his brother Joseph had had his marriage to Julie Clary blessed by a non-juring priest, and it would not be surprising if Napoleon submitted to this formality too. Joséphine might have requested it, and her husband, in order to give such a ceremony a little value, might have granted her request all the more willingly because, though he had said nothing to his mother and to Joseph, whose reaction he could guess, he knew that he would soon have to tell them that he had married a widow who was older than he and encumbered with two grown-up children and a reputation as a promiscuous woman. God might be of some help. Perhaps Napoleon and Joséphine were married religiously in Croissy-sur-Seine the following day, March 10, on the way to or back from Saint-Germain, where Joséphine had insisted on introducing Napoleon to her daughter, Hortense, who was a boarder in the home of Mme Campan. In Croissy she had made friends with the former parish priest of Saint-Sulpice, Antoine-Xavier de Pancemont, who was hiding out in the house next to hers. Since then, Pancemont, without having sworn the oath, had gotten back into the government's good graces by signing a simple declaration of loyalty, and he had in exchange obtained permission to perform religious services.[82] It was because Pancemont had failed to obtain the previous authorization of the parish priest in Croissy that on the day before Napoleon's coronation in 1804, Fesch, by then Cardinal Fesch, is supposed to have been forced to perform a second religious marriage between his nephew and the empress. Perhaps his compliance should be seen as the origin of the favor Pancemont enjoyed after 18 Brumaire.

Baron de Frénilly maliciously said that this marriage was one "of hunger and thirst."[83] That is not entirely false, but on that day this apparently ill-matched couple was entering "into our mythology and our history, as one of the most complete and most indefectible couples there ever was."[84] Moreover, Joséphine was not the only one to receive a new name for a new love. Napoleon also celebrated the event by deleting the "u" from his name—the better to "Frenchify" it—and even by abandoning the use of the first name that puzzled people when it did not make them smile. Although on March 8 he had signed the marriage contract "Napolione Buonaparte," six days later, at the bottom of a letter addressed to his wife, he signed for the first time "Bonaparte."[85] Nothing else changed. Besides, there had not been time. As soon as he had returned to Rue Chantereine, he plunged back into his maps, his plans, his memoranda on Italy, but still found time to spend brief moments in Joséphine's bed. The honeymoon was short. It lasted two days. On the evening of March 11, Junot came by to pick him up: "Be patient, my dear, we shall have time to make love after the victory," he told Joséphine as he embraced her. He made her promise that she would soon join him on the peninsula. She promised and waved as the carriage drove away. She remained outside for a moment and then went into the house, relieved and thinking that she was finally going to be able to resume the usual course of her life.

PART THREE

The Italian Campaign

1796–1797

NINE

That Beautiful Italy

Montenotte

*L*ess than a year of fighting in Italy sufficed to carry Napoleon to the pinnacle of fame. He went to Italy an obscure general, unknown despite the siege of Toulon, 13 Vendémiaire, and even his command of the Army of the Interior. It all changed with a military campaign to which none of the Revolution's other campaigns can bear comparison.

Let us sum up. The Army of Italy's 30,000 men (8,000 others were guarding the Alpine borders) were distributed as follows:[1] Sérurier's division was in Garessio, while the others were strung out along the coast, Augereau at Loano, Masséna and Laharpe between Finale and Savona. They had few cavalrymen—but these were of little use on the mountainous roads in Piedmont—and no more than thirty light artillery pieces.[2] With more than 50,000 immediately operational men and almost 200 artillery pieces, the enemy was much better off. Twenty thousand Piedmontese were occupying a line from Coni to Millesimo, where they were supporting General Provera's liaison corps. Most of the Austrian forces—30,000 men—were grouped around Novi, Argenteau's division occupying an advanced position in the direction of Acqui. A priori, the allies had the numerical advantage, but what handicaps they had! Their line of operation, from Coni to Novi, was intersected by steep slopes that hindered communications; their leaders were old—the Austrian Beaulieu and the Piedmontese Colli were both over seventy—their armies were encumbered by baggage, the relations between the allies were terrible, and the staffs were in disagreement regarding the French general's intentions: Colli thought that Bonaparte would attack Turin, Beaulieu that he would march on Genoa to outflank the allied forces and invade Lombardy. Colli was right. The instructions given Bonaparte on March 6—he had had the initial text, dictated by Carnot, modified[3]—told him to put the Piedmontese out of action before driving the Austrians out of Lombardy. In order to do so, he was first to seize the fortress of Ceva. He scheduled the offensive to begin on April 15: while Sérurier marched from Garessio toward Ceva, the bulk of the army would leave Savona and break through the hinge of the Austro-Piedmontese position in Millesimo before turning back toward Ceva.

On April 9 Bonaparte was getting ready to go see Sérurier in Garessio when the Austrians suddenly launched an attack. They had been deceived by a French brigade's long-planned movement toward Voltri.[4] Thinking that the French army was about to fall on Genoa, they decided to cut it off by moving toward the coast. On April 10, while Beaulieu was marching toward the Riviera, Argenteau was descending through Dego and Montenotte toward Savona, planning to go around the French positions. Did this attack take Bonaparte by surprise?[5] In any case, he was strangely absent on the tenth and eleventh, when the French column, having evacuated Voltri, the small garrison occupying the heights of Monte Legino between Montenotte and Savona, saved the Army of Italy from disaster by stopping Argenteau. It was only then that Bonaparte went into action. While the Austrians were spending the night on the slopes of Monte Legino—despite having made three fruitless assaults, Argenteau had not given up hope of taking the position—Bonaparte was giving his orders. During the evening and the rainy night of April 11, his troops crossed the Apennines. The next day, at sunrise, the French counterattacked in the direction of Montenotte and threw Argenteau back toward the north. "The Battle of Montenotte was Bonaparte's first victory, and it already contained in germ the principles of the Napoleonic battle: pinning down the enemy by means of a frontal attack and an enveloping movement that threatens his natural line of retreat. Montenotte also testifies to Bonaparte's ability to obtain numerical superiority by the combined movements of different divisions. In this case, Laharpe's and Masséna's 18,000 men logically triumphed over Argenteau's 6,000 men."[6]

The Austrian defeat might have been even more severe—they lost about 2,000 men—had Augereau, who had been assigned to go around the enemy on the west to cut off its retreat, not been delayed. When he reached Carcare that evening, the Austrians had already fallen back toward Dego. The separation of the allies was not yet achieved, but a breach had been opened. Now "it was requisite, therefore, that, at one and the same time his left should force the gorges of

Millesimo, to make itself master of the Piedmont road, and that in front, he should take Dego, to open for himself the road to Acqui and Lombardy."[7] On April 13 the two vanguards set out, the first (Masséna) toward Dego, where Argenteau had taken up strong positions to cover Beaulieu's retreat from Voltri via Acqui, the second (Augereau) toward Millesimo. On the fifteenth, after hard fighting to dislodge Provera from the castle of Cossaria, Augereau took control of Millesimo and Montezemolo, where he joined up with Sérurier, who had left Garessio on the twelfth. Masséna, for his part, seized Dego, but not being able to prevent his army from breaking up to indulge in "all sorts of excesses,"[8] he was surprised by the Austrians' return offensive, which Laharpe was finally able to stop on the evening of the fifteenth. This time the separation of the two armies had been achieved: Beaulieu fell back on Acqui, Colli on Ceva. A gap of some forty kilometers separated the allied armies, and in order to reestablish their line of communication, they would have to follow the road seventy kilometers to the north that led from Acqui to Cherasco via Alba. Leaving Laharpe and Masséna in Dego to keep an eye on the Lombard plain, Bonaparte sent Augereau to assault the entrenched camp at Ceva.

The attack on the fortress ended up a fiasco, some say, because Bonaparte gave Augereau the absurd order to take by assault, with bayonets and without artillery, a fortified camp that could be conquered only after a regular siege.[9] In the first campaign plans he had drawn up in 1795, Bonaparte had called for a siege of Ceva, and even made the fortress's surrender the final objective of the first phase of the campaign: he believed that this would suffice to convince the Piedmontese to lay down their arms. The instructions of March 2, 1796, testify to a change in strategy—it was a question no longer of staking everything on the capitulation of the camp of Ceva but of pursuing the Piedmontese army, if need be by going around the fortress and continuing as far as Turin to force a surrender.[10] That is precisely what Bonaparte did next: on April 16 he attacked Colli, who had taken refuge in Ceva, and having dislodged him, went around the fortress and on the seventeenth resumed his pursuit of the Piedmontese army. Bonaparte was on the lookout for opportunities to fight a pitched battle. None of the actions that had taken place up to that point could be described as a battle. Even the combats on the twelfth, from Montenotte to Carcare, had been mere skirmishes.[11] Although these commonplace actions had proven to be strategically decisive, they had not sufficed to demoralize an enemy that, not having suffered any irreparable reverse, still thought it could redress the situation: "A great victory is always more significant than a series of small battles," Clausewitz observes, "even if the latter cause the enemy the same losses."[12] Moreover, these limited successes provided little material for triumphal victory bulletins, at least for the kind that might attract public attention to the Army of Italy and its leader. Seen from Paris, the maneuver at Montenotte was still only a small success won in a peripheral theater of action. There was nothing in it that might make Bonaparte the man of the day, or even to lend him importance in the eyes of the government. To exist, he needed the support of public opinion, and to put it on his side he had to distinguish himself in brilliant battles of precisely the kind that the circumstances did not allow him to fight or to win. That is why, on the eve of his movement on Ceva, he ordered Augereau to attack the castle of Cossaria, no matter what the cost;[13] and that is also why, on April 21, at Mondovi, he was perhaps to command—it has not been proven—the useless charge in which the leader of the cavalry, General Stengel, was killed.

At Mondovi the French won a true victory: the Sardinian army fell back toward Cherasco and Turin. In front of Bonaparte the plain stretched out as far as the eye could see, as far as Victor-Amadeus's capital. The general wrote to Barras: "One more battle and that will be the end of the king of Sardinia."[14] But the Piedmontese had not yet lost the war; their troops had not scattered and their artillery was intact. Besides, Bonaparte had no illusions about Colli's reasons for not making any attempt to prevent him from striking into the heart of Piedmont: "He knows that I lack everything and he is counting on time [to save him]," he said.[15] Time, and perhaps the Austrians. The latter could still turn the situation around by moving from Acqui toward Alba. The government in Turin had sent them an emissary to beg them to take action, but when on April 24 Beaulieu finally decided to aid his ally, it was to learn that the latter, who had already been thrown back beyond Cherasco, had asked for an armistice. Bonaparte was mistaken in thinking that the Sardinian leaders would mount a firm resistance. From the outset they had hesitated. Victor Amadeus III, who called himself Italy's "gatekeeper," did refuse to let the French enter, but his resentment of his Austrian ally was so bitter that he was reluctant to make the sacrifices necessary to drive out the small French army. Bonaparte's first successes, added to the blameworthy inaction of the Austrians, did the rest. In Turin the defeat at Mondovi seemed to foreshadow an imminent collapse, and the government authorized Colli to ask for an armistice.

It was almost midnight on April 27, 1796, when the king of Sardinia's emissaries appeared at the entrance to the castle of Cherasco.[16] "There were no guards defending the approaches to the building, which was almost unlighted," one of them was to say later. "We saw only a few soldiers sleeping on the threshold and on the stairway. No horses, no wagon or mules, no servants. Silence and calm seemed to reign in the rest of the city."[17] They walked through the empty rooms, looking for someone to talk to. They eventually found an officer who took them to Berthier; the latter went to tell Bonaparte, who made them wait for a long time:

> Bonaparte finally appeared. He was wearing the uniform and boots of the general in command, but he had no saber, hat, or sash; his bearing was solemn and cold. He listened in silence to the Piedmontese general's preamble, and in response he asked him only whether he didn't have a copy of the conditions he had proposed, whether these conditions had not been accepted by the king. And when a few complaints regarding the harshness of these conditions were made, he added: "Since I offered [those conditions], I have taken Cherasco, I have taken Alba. I am not increasing my initial demands: you should find me moderate." To the efforts made to show him how little he would gain from certain of the concessions he demanded, and particularly the passage over the Po at Valenza, he replied somewhat sharply: "The Republic, in conferring on me the command of an army, thought me sufficiently discerning to judge what suits its interests, without having to resort to seeking advice from my enemy." Apart from this slight sarcasm, in which he raised his voice and seemed bitter and hard, Bonaparte was constantly cool, polite, and laconic. . . . At one o'clock in the morning, he pulled out his watch, and seeing that the discussions were dragging on without producing anything decisive, he said to the emissaries: "Gentlemen, I warn you that the general attack is scheduled for two A.M., and if I am not sure that Coni will be handed over to me before the end of the day,

this attack will not be delayed by a minute. It may happen that I lose battles, but I shall never be seen losing minutes out of confidence or laziness."[18]

The Piedmontese plenipotentiaries, whom Bonaparte's feigned anger had frightened, granted him everything he asked for: the fortresses, free passage over the Po at Valenza, the demobilization of the Sardinians serving in the ranks of the Austrian army, and so forth.[19] Costa de Beauregard, one of the Piedmontese whom the general honored with a long conversation after a Spartan supper, was one of the first to see him up close: "The impression one gained of this young man," he was to recall, "was one of painful admiration; one's mind was dazzled by the superiority of his talents, but one's heart was oppressed. One sought in vain in him traces of that generous magnanimity that precedes trust and is the finest trait of the hero's character."[20] As they left, in the early hours of the morning, the Piedmontese emissaries felt they had been duped. "The sun was shining on the bivouacked troops of the French vanguard. Everything seemed to be in a state of extreme disarray; we saw no cannons and the horses were few, thin, and exhausted."[21] Seeing the pitiable condition of this army, the Piedmontese were ashamed to have yielded to such harsh conditions: "I have just spent a dreadful night," Costa confided to his wife. "I signed, on behalf of the king, a ceasefire with General Bonaparte on the most humiliating and dangerous conditions. . . . It's enough to make me die of resentment and shame. I would rather have done anything else; but we were so frightened that we thought we'd done the best thing in the world."[22] Bonaparte himself was surprised by a capitulation so easily obtained.[23] Politics, more than arms, had allowed him to win the first round.

Lodi

Although the Piedmont campaign had not given Bonaparte the great victory he dreamed of—the "battle" of Mondovi was in reality no more than a simple "retreat combat"[24]—he was soon to win one. After the armistice of Cherasco, the Austrians had pulled back to the left bank of the Po in order to establish

Battlefields of Italy (1796–1797)

three lines of defense before Milan, each supported by one of the river's tribu-taries.[25] Because Bonaparte had made Piedmontese give him the means of crossing the Po at Valenza, Beaulieu was preparing for a battle west of Milan. But the concentration of French forces around Valenza was a trick: although Sérurier was evidently undertaking preparations in that zone, the bulk of the French troops had already set out for Tortona. Bonaparte had two objectives: first, to spare the French army, which had no bridge-building equipment, the necessity of crossing three rivers to reach the Lombard capital;[26] and second, to overtake Beaulieu's army and cut off its retreat into the Tyrol. In order to do so, he had decided to move down the right bank of the Po as far as Piacenza, where he would cross the river and follow the Adda before falling back on Milan. In this way he would encounter no natural obstacle, and the Austrians' line of retreat would be cut off. Success depended entirely on the rapidity of the French march.

Once the army had caught its breath and incorporated 9,000 new men brought in from the Army of the Alps,[27] the vanguard set out on May 5. It reached

Piacenza on the morning of the seventh, having covered sixty kilometers in thirty-six hours. "We aren't marching, we're flying," Berthier wrote to a friend.[28] After seizing all the boats they could find, the first French troops landed on the left bank of the Po in the afternoon. Laharpe's and Augereau's division began to cross the river in turn, but Masséna's division was still far away, near Voghera, while Sérurier's rearguard was still farther away. Lannes was already moving rapidly toward the Adda. In Fombio, on May 8, he attacked the Austrian rearguard, which, being separated from the rest of Beaulieu's army, fell back on Pizzighettone. This time the Austrian general saw the full extent of the danger, and after evacuating on the eighth all his positions west of Milan, he returned to the combat zone the following night, trying to drive Laharpe back to the Po.[29] In vain. The only thing left for Beaulieu to do was to retreat beyond the Adda, leaving in Lodi a detachment assigned to cover his retreat. Bonaparte had hoped to cut off his route before he reached Lodi, but his troops were slow to get over the Po, Masséna crossing on the night of the ninth, Sérurier on the morning of the tenth. It was too late. When the French arrived in Lodi on May 10, the whole Austrian army had taken shelter beyond the Adda.

It may be that Bonaparte, seeing the bridge defended by an enemy detachment,[30] thought that Beaulieu's army was within musket range on the other side of the river.[31] In any case, a frontal attack on a bridge that was almost 200 meters long, under artillery fire, was "a bold operation."[32] Legends sprang up immediately after the attack, making it difficult to know exactly what happened.[33] Bonaparte had sent cavalry and light artillery upstream to look for a ford; they were then supposed to attack the Austrian right wing, whereupon the French infantry would rush the bridge. The infantrymen were waiting for the signal while taking shelter "behind the rampart of the city, which borders on the Adda."[34] The French artillery had been moved up to the entrance to the bridge, from which point it was firing on the opposite bank, and the enemy infantry had abandoned the other end of the bridge "in order to take advantage of a ridge that offered partial shelter."[35] According to the most plausible scenario, Bonaparte, who by 5 P.M. had received no news about the cavalry but had just learned of the arrival of Masséna's division, decided to go all out and make an assault.[36] The grenadiers attacked under volleys of grapeshot so intense that they stopped halfway across and began to retreat. Bonaparte did not then seize a flag and put himself at their head. That scene was invented post facto, but Bonaparte—let us do him this justice—never did claim that he had participated personally in the attack on the bridge. In the report he sent to the Directory the next day, and later on Saint Helena, he singled out those of his officers who, seeing the soldiers falter, put themselves at their head and led them to the other side of the river.[37] No doubt this "charge by the leaders"[38] would not have succeeded had some infantrymen not swum across the Adda and distracted the Austrians' attention. After a confused skirmish on the left bank, the arrival of reinforcements and then, belatedly, the cavalry, decided the outcome of the fighting.

"Even though since the beginning of the campaign we have had some very intense fighting," Bonaparte wrote the next day, "nothing approaches the terrible passage of the bridge at Lodi."[39] It was true: Bonaparte had finally waged the battle he had been waiting for ever since the beginning of the campaign. Nevertheless, it was only a half success: though Napoleon had thrown the Austrians back to the east of the Adda, Beaulieu had not been put out of action. The enemy had slipped away. These new successes in Lombardy were smaller than those Bonaparte had achieved in Piedmont. However, the Piacenza maneuver took on more importance than that of Carcare. In Piedmont Bonaparte had directed his efforts against the center of the enemy's lines in order to separate its two wings; the rest consisted of a march on the Piedmontese rear. In Lombardy he had just executed the enveloping maneuver against the enemy's flank that was to disconcert his adversaries for years: the Austrians having established their front west of Milan, he had, through a rapid movement, moved around their left wing, the one closest to their line of retreat toward Mantua, thus compelling them to fall back in disorder when they discovered, to their stupefaction, that they were about to be surrounded and, above all, forced to fight the enemy both in front of them and behind them. Everything is there: the flanking maneuver that creates the material and psychological conditions for a decisive attack, the rapidity of execution indispensable for the surprise effect, the latter leading in turn to "the preliminary demoralization of the adversary through the sudden appearance of armed masses blocking his line of retreat," and the quest for numerical superiority at the point when enemy is attacked.[40] The flanking attack launched at Lodi on May 5 nearly failed to achieve its goal: to form across the enemy's line of retreat "an unshakable barrier against which all the fleeing soldiers would crash pell-mell."[41] Had Bonaparte found better means of getting his army across the Po, Beaulieu would have been caught in the trap, and with his line of retreat cut off, he would have been forced to fight under disastrous conditions; had Beaulieu begun to retreat on May 9 instead of on May 8, the result would have been the same: Beaulieu would not have recrossed the Adda.

On May 13 Bonaparte gave up his pursuit of the Austrians: he could venture no further east, leaving Lombardy behind him without a government, especially because he knew nothing about the state of the negotiations with Piedmont (a peace treaty was to be signed on May 15). It was evident that if the negotiations failed, he would have to go back to try to find peace—this time in Turin itself. Augereau was thus ordered to occupy Pavia, and Masséna was ordered to occupy Milan.

Milan

All his life Napoleon was to remember the day of May 13, 1796, when he received out of the blue from the Directory an order to share with Kellermann the command of the Army of Italy. Since the beginning of the campaign he had taken care to give the government no reason to be dissatisfied with him, taking particular care not to exceed the limits of his powers, which forbade him, for example, to grant the enemy any "ceasefire" without having first obtained the Directory's consent.[42] Admittedly, by signing the armistice with Piedmont he had infringed upon these absurd instructions, but he was so afraid of the consequences that he had sent to Paris several letters justifying his actions at length, swearing that "in the military operations [he had] taken only [his own] counsel and in the diplomatic operations, [he had consulted] everyone."[43] He admitted to Barras alone how stupid he thought it had been to limit him to purely military functions: "If someone doesn't explain to me what is wanted, [if] I [am] constantly stopped for fear of not fulfilling your intentions and of being accused of trying to meddle in diplomacy, it will be impossible for me to achieve great things. At this point the war in Italy is half military and half diplomatic."[44] Because Bonaparte did not himself seek to set the conditions for peace with Piedmont, the Directory wiped his slate clean. But on May 13 his new instructions led to an initial conflict.

Seeing the general on the point of driving the Austrians out of Lombardy—these instructions were dated May 7—the government decided that the objective of the campaign had been achieved. It had never intended to authorize the Army of Italy to march on Vienna, so operations were henceforth to be confined to maintaining an observation corps around Milan to prevent any Austrian counterattack, while the rest of the army would head for central Italy. To that end the Directory decided to confer on Kellermann the command of the part of the army that would occupy Lombardy, while Bonaparte was to lead the other part toward the south. There was no mention of an expedition of this kind in the March 2 instructions. They did include a clause relative to the rest of the peninsula—"We are intimidating all of Italy and we are dissolving the coalition of the small powers that is in the service of the Austrian cause"[45]—but that referred only to a collateral benefit of the conquest of Lombardy. Since then, the Directors had been so surprised by the lightning defeat of Piedmont that they had begun to ask questions about this little general they had plucked out of the gutter. The young man had talent—perhaps too much of it. Who could swear that having defeated the Piedmontese in two weeks and preparing to do the same to the Austrians, he was not capable, as he had claimed, of leading his barefoot army right up to the walls of Vienna? The Directory was so afraid of seeing Bonaparte propose his Tyrolean plans again that it decided it had to express its opposition publicly: "The Directory must limit itself to a circle less extensive than the one you propose, and to which the imperious necessity of ending the war during this campaign returns it; it must fear everything in the way of disasters that a failure can entail. It counts on the Army of Italy's victories, but what might not be the consequences of an entry into Bavaria through the mountains of the Tyrol, and what hope of an honorable retreat in the event of defeat could be conceived? Moreover, with the forces you command and a few thousand men whom the Directory might add to them, how could so many countries subjected to our arms be contained?"[46]

But this general who did things so fast and so well had to be given something to do. There could be no question of leaving him in Milan: the Tyrol was too close. It was to get him farther away that the Directory replaced Bonaparte's "Italo-German plan" with an "Italian plan," or rather an "Italo-Corsican plan," of its own devising.[47] Kellermann being assigned to guard Milan, Bonaparte would set out for Livorno, where he would seize British merchandise and then prepare for a landing on Corsica. The Directory recommended that he not annoy the grand duke of Tuscany, or, for that matter, the magistrates of the Lilliputian Republic of Lucca. On the other hand, it authorized him to hold to ransom the Duke of Parma and the pope, demanding from the latter "his statues, his paintings, his medals, his libraries, his bronzes, his silver madonnas and even his bells":[48] "The Executive Directory is persuaded, Citizen General, that you regard the glory of the fine arts as attached to that of the army you command. Italy owes to them in large part its riches and its fame; but the time has come when their reign must pass to France to consolidate and embellish that of liberty.... The Executive Directory thus asks you ... to choose one or several artists who will seek out, collect, and have transported to Paris the most precious objects of this kind."[49]

The Directory did not lack reasons to justify this looting. According to the official interpretation of events, enemies of France were indirectly responsible for the Terror because of their plotting with the counterrevolution. According to this reasoning they were also responsible for the depredations that monuments had suffered in 1793; therefore it was up to them to "repair the ravages of the vandalism."[50] The assignment was clear: "Leave nothing in Italy that our political situation allows us to carry off and that might be useful to us."[51] The idea was in the air, and there had been precedents in Belgium, Holland, and the Rhineland; there, too, it had been claimed that the arts could not blossom without liberty, and France, the land of liberty, must therefore take in the whole world's art.[52] The anti-Austrian war in Italy was thus being transformed into an "expedition of freebooters."[53]

These instructions of May 7 went far beyond those given Bonaparte on March 2 before his departure. The earlier instructions ordered him to "subsist in and by means of the enemy countries."[54] This meant making the usual requisitions of food, forage for the horses, shoes for the army, and fabric to clothe it, and of imposing on the occupied countries heavy war levies in order to be able to buy what could not be taken by force. But from the first days of the campaign, Bonaparte took it upon himself to go beyond these instructions. The day after the Cherasco armistice he asked the French minister in Genoa for "a list of the pictures, statues, collections and curiosities in Milan, Parma, Piacenza, Modena, and Bologna" and assigned a young "artist attached to the legation of Tuscany," Jean-Pierre Tinet, to supervise the confiscations.[55] Then he immediately sent emissaries to the Duke of Parma to offer him the choice between war and a peace whose price was set at "two million [livres] and twenty paintings."[56] Among the latter were the "most beautiful paintings of Corregio," which left for Paris as soon as the armistice was signed.[57] At the same time, the Directory also named representatives to "transport to France all the transportable monuments of the sciences and the arts that they find worthy of entering into its museums and its libraries."[58] The pillaging thus arose from a convergence between the Directory's cupidity and Bonaparte's calculations. Bonaparte took the initiative for reasons from which politics was not absent. Even though the Directory, as we have seen, had finally given its blessing to the armistice signed with Piedmont,[59] Bonaparte sensed that he would soon have to resume playing a very subtle game with the government, since war and diplomacy could not be separated as rigorously as the Directory had ordered. How, without convincing them, could the directors be led to give him free rein? For an impecunious government, works of art and pieces of gold were more persuasive arguments than oaths of fidelity would ever be. Bonaparte gave the signal to pillage Italy because, thinking it likely to calm the government's suspicions, he hoped it would give him complete freedom in the conduct of operations. He believed he had found a way to become his own master. But when the May 7 instructions were added to Bonaparte's initiatives, the pillaging took on a dimension that was in fact "unparalleled in the history of modern nations."[60]

Bonaparte was so convinced that he had figured out how to free himself from the Directory's authority that he was astounded to receive the instructions that asked him to share his command with Kellermann. He recounted the scene so often that we can take it as authentic. He was in the village of Melegnano near Milan, waiting for Count Melzi, who had come with a deputation to hand over to him the keys to the capital of Lombardy:

> I was thinking about this letter [from the Directory], seeing the Army of Italy doomed by this crazy step. . . . I was in a room, near the hearth, close to a fireplace that was in the corner of the room, even though it

was already the warm season, there was a fire; apparently it had rained. I was absorbed in my thoughts when Melzi was announced. This moment has to be understood in relation to the opinion I had regarding my superiority. I felt that I was far more valuable, that I was stronger than the government that gave such an order; more capable of governing than it was; that there was an incapacity and a defect of judgment in this government concerning such important matters that it would doom France; that I was destined to save it. From that moment on, I could see the goal, and proceeded toward it.[61]

Lodi had left indelible impressions on him. Not without reason: it was there, on the bridge he did not cross, that his legend was born. For the past three days he had begun to see himself "in history . . . , no longer as a simple general, but as a man called upon to influence the fate of peoples."[62] And on another occasion he said: "I already saw the world passing beneath me as if I had been lifted into the air."[63] That was one of those formulas he knew how to coin to express feelings it was difficult to express in words. Naturally the Directory's dispatch brought him crashing down from the heights where his imagination had carried him. In it he saw the proof of the mediocrity, jealousy, and fear that characterized the "lawyers" in power. There was no question of handing command of Lombardy over to Kellermann: he refused, and threatened in no uncertain terms to resign, knowing perfectly well that his victory had already made him virtually untouchable:

> In the current position of the Republic's affairs in Italy, it is indispensable that the general commanding there have your confidence. If I were not that general, I would not complain. . . . Everyone has his own way of waging war. General Kellermann has more experience and will do it better than I; but both of us together would do it very badly. I can render essential services to the country only alone.[64]

Did the Directory really think it could impose Kellermann? Although it reconfirmed his nomination on May 18, it was already making concessions by not excluding the possibility of a future march on Vienna through the Tyrol.[65] On

May 21 it capitulated as soon as it received Napoleon's stinging reply of May 14. "You seem desirous," it wrote to the general, "of immediately continuing to conduct all the military operations of the current campaign in Italy; the Directory has given this proposition careful consideration and its confidence in your talents and your republican zeal have decided this question in favor of the affirmative."[66] Thiers is certainly right to say that had the Directory possessed the gift of prophecy, it would have accepted Bonaparte's proposed resignation.[67] That day, without knowing it, the directors suffered a first defeat that was heavy with consequences. It was only natural that the more victories Bonaparte won, and the more he sent gold and works of art home to France, the less control the Directory had over what was happening in Italy. The conduct of the war was in any case no longer within its competence, and it would not be long before Bonaparte would be disputing the Directory's last shreds of authority in the peninsula.

The time had come for him to enter Milan. Masséna had preceded him in taking possession of the Lombard capital, which had been abandoned by Archduke Ferdinand on the evening after the battle of Lodi.[68] Having arrived in a carriage, Bonaparte mounted a horse before entering the city through the Porta Romana. The city council was waiting for him and a crowd had gathered all along the route. Bonaparte finished the Lombardy campaign the way he had begun it: at a gallop, moving so rapidly that he passed by without seeing the authorities who had come to greet him. Realizing his mistake, he pulled his horse up short and turned around, while the magistrates, with Archbishop Filippo Visconti at their head, ran after him. Stendhal magnified the scene: "On May 15, 1796, General Bonaparte made his entrance into Milan at the head of this young army that had just crossed the bridge at Lodi and taught the world that after so many centuries Caesar and Alexander had a successor."[69] In the evening Bonaparte presided over a banquet at the Palazzo Reale, and having returned to the nearby Archbishop's palace, where a room had been prepared for him, he said to his aide-de-camp: "Well, Marmont, what do you think they're saying about us in Paris; are they happy? They haven't seen anything yet, and the future holds for us successes far greater than those we have already achieved. Fortune has not smiled on me today so that I might scorn her favors; she is a woman, and the more she does for me, the more I shall demand of her. In a few days we shall be on the Adige, and all Italy will be under our control. Perhaps then, if I am given means proportional to the scope of my plans, perhaps we shall soon leave it to go farther. In our time, no one has conceived anything great. It is for me to provide an example of greatness."[70]

The most astonishing thing is not that it was at Milan that he reached the "turning point of his life," but that he knew it.

TEN

An Italian Policy?

A few days after he entered Milan, Bonaparte set out in pursuit of Beaulieu. Once again the Austrian was almost caught in the trap. By a miracle he escaped and took refuge in the mountains of the Tyrol. Bonaparte was exultant: "The Austrians have been entirely driven out of Italy!"[1] That wasn't entirely true: the Mantua garrison was still holding out, and he knew he would have to force it to surrender before he could proclaim himself master of Italy. Nonetheless, temporarily freed from the Austrian menace,[2] he could focus on the expedition to the south prescribed by the government's instructions of May 7. The situation had deteriorated so much in the region that he himself now considered the expedition inevitable. The more the French army increased the number of territories it had conquered, occupied, or simply subjected, the more one question became urgent, that of their destiny: what was going to be done with Italy?

Italy in 1796

Without going so far as to endorse Leopardi's extreme opinion that Italy simply did not exist, we have to admit that at the time there was a multitude of little Italys, each of which had its own history, traditions, and interests.[3] For the majority of Italians, their country was the city or region where they lived. Few would ever think to speak of an "Italian nation." Patriotism was all the more inclined to be municipal because many states on the peninsula were either not very old or had shifting borders, or else had sovereigns (often of foreign origin) who had only recently taken power.[4]

The result of this mosaic of political entities of varying solidity was a juxtaposition of diverse peoples. This diversity was manifested in the differences between one region and another and, within a single region, state, or city, between

Italy in 1796

one class and another. Then as now, Umbria was the dividing line. North of it the countryside was relatively prosperous and there were industrious cities in which an enlightened elite, whether aristocratic or bourgeois, aspired to reforms. South of it was the poverty of the backward rural areas of Mezzogiorno and the deceptive splendor of the "parasitic cities" Rome and Naples, where a handful of powerful individuals, both clerical and lay, reigned over a mass of poor people and vagabonds. Vincenzo Cuoco, a contemporary, said that the gap between the highest and the lowest classes of Neapolitan society was like that between two species: incommensurable. "Two different nations" lived side by side in Naples, he wrote, "separated by two centuries of time and two degrees of latitude"—on the one hand, the thin stratum of the aristocracy and learned elites, on the other, the mass of the people. These two nations "had different ideas, different manners, and even two different languages."[5]

The contrast was less marked in the north than in the south, but it existed in Milan as well as in Palermo. On coming to know their dioceses, many Church dignitaries felt they were among savage peoples who had to be converted to Christianity, and called the country where their duty took them "our Indies."[6] The Italians had nothing in common but grandiose memories and an awareness of their present weakness (even if some of them saw this as an advantage, because it drew the great powers' attention away from the peninsula's affairs[7]). Mme de Staël said that in Rome she experienced "a deep melancholy" on contemplating the stark contrast between the "so admirable" monuments of the past and the pettiness of the "current state of affairs": "Here one is constantly aware," she wrote, "of the height from which man has fallen; what he is, and what he was."[8] For foreigners, Italy was a "metaphor of decadence," a "land of the dead" that had been slumbering for several centuries in a torpor that Stendhal called a "voluptuous tranquility."[9]

Happiness was perceived, along with political fragmentation and "foreign control over the territory," as another symptom of Italy's decline.[10] In unforgettable pages Guglielmo Ferrero described how Italians of this period dozed amid a "profusion of beauty."[11] This depiction is certainly overdone; it applies better to Baroque Italy, the Italy of Rome or Palermo, than to the Italy of Turin or Milan. Moreover, Italy, including its southern regions, was not so drowsy that it remained alien to its age. Its population had increased in a proportion comparable to France's, reaching eighteen million around 1800; thanks to its busy ports, it remained a maritime power; it had undertaken to modernize its agriculture, especially in the north, and it had also had its Enlightenment. In the 1760s, thanks to the alliance between the little groups of enlightened people and the leaders of the Habsburg and Bourbon possessions in Italy, a wave of reform had begun to swell in Milan, Florence, Naples, and, to a lesser degree, Turin. To be sure, the results were limited, because no decisive progress was made in removing the main obstacles to development pointed out by the reformers: the Church's moral and social influence and the corporate structure of society.

Ultimately—though any generalization regarding such a diverse country has to be treated with caution—Italy entered into a phase of decline marked by flagging growth, a decrease in industrial production, the ruralization of society, the accentuation of regional differences, and an increase of the already enormous proportion of property held by aristocrats and the Church. Not only had the reforms remained superficial, but after having allowed Italian sovereigns to augment their power on the pretext of modernizing the state, the changes had ended up destabilizing the very same rulers' authority by causing discontent among groups hostile to change.[12] Another reason there was so little resistance to the invasion was that Italian society had been weakened by this reformist medicine, which was sometimes administered abruptly. To borrow one of Ferrero's metaphors, it was because Italy's foundations were already shaky that it took only a single artillery shell to make it collapse: three months after the arrival of the French, nothing, or almost nothing, remained of the Baroque Italy of the eighteenth century.[13]

The Italians' sympathy for the Revolution of 1789 has been exaggerated. The Revolution certainly had its partisans on the peninsula, but its violence put off many Italians. The majority of those with "advanced" opinions, many of whom came from the patriciate, found repugnant the upheavals that accompanied a revolution: "Although most people wanted reform," Carlo Botta wrote, "the idea of a revolution had occurred to no one."[14] Moreover, Italians found it hard to comprehend the radicalism of a political movement that, though it claimed to be based on Enlightenment, clearly did not refer to the movement that had inspired the experiment with enlightened despotism in Italy. The Italian representatives of the Enlightenment did not understand why French reform of the state and society had involved such extreme measures as the abolition of the monarchy and the persecution of priests, or why to ensure the future it was necessary to abolish the past. The Italians had imposed reforms from the top down, whereas the French claimed to be rebuilding everything from the bottom up. This was an unbridgeable gap. The events of 1789, though they gave new impetus to the urban elites' aspirations to reform, were far from giving rise to a genuine revolutionary movement. The Revolution led to a break between the elites and the governments that halted reforms out of fear that the French disorders might be contagious. Paris soon acquired a small colony of Italian refugees. Misleadingly called "Giaccobini" (Jacobins), they were among the principal advocates of a French invasion of the peninsula. Some of them saw in such an invasion an opportunity to reconnect with the reformist politics that the autochthonous authorities had renounced; others who were more radical hoped that the invasion would give the signal for a general revolution in which Italians would find an opportunity to achieve both political unity and moral regeneration. In this they were inspired by the French Revolution: Hadn't it also transformed into a nation "one and indivisible" the aggregate of provinces and disparate customs called the kingdom of France? But unlike France, where the people had taken the initiative in national "regeneration," in Italy foreign intervention seemed indispensable if Italians were to be wrenched out of their torpor and thrown, despite themselves, into the maelstrom of history.[15]

The time for Italian revolutionaries came in early 1796, when the Directory decided to resume operations in Italy. Two of them, Buonarotti—a friend of Robespierre and Saliceti—and Cerise, submitted to the government a plan to incite a revolution in Piedmont before the arrival of the first French soldiers. At first the Directory seemed to encourage them, but the Italian revolutionaries soon had to face the fact that the French leaders wanted them merely to play the role of a "fifth column" in the shadow of the invading army, and had no intention of making the army the auxiliary of a Piedmontese revolution, or, a fortiori, of an Italian revolution.[16]

Subsequently the Directory seems to have momentarily supported the plan submitted by Buonarotti, who was authorized to go back to the border to prepare the insurrection.[17] Bonaparte had immediately sized up the Italian "patriots":

"Those people—not more than a 150 of them—will be of no use to us," he wrote in a report on April 9. "The notes on Italy signed by Buonarotti and Cerise are pitiful. . . . The Directory has been given false hopes. . . . It must count solely on our military forces and on the enemy's discouragement."[18] Two weeks later, when his soldiers were approaching Cherasco, he did allow Bonafous and Ranza to "revolutionize" Alba and Coni, but that was solely in order to increase the panic reigning in Turin: he had no intention of letting the partisans of a revolution take advantage of the circumstances. In any case, their isolation doomed them. Bonaparte had perceived that the mass of the population, which considered its nobles and priests "very good people," aspired so little to change that one must not, he said, "count on a revolution."[19] The Directory—after many hesitations, and because it had begun to react against the protosocialist followers of Babeuf, with whom the Italian refugees had maintained close relations in Paris—finally adopted the general's opinion. When the king of Piedmont signed the armistice, the Piedmontese revolutionaries suddenly lost all value, and Bonaparte abandoned them without remorse, even proposing to hand them over to the police in Turin—though he reserved the option of putting them back in the saddle if the circumstances required or permitted it.

In reality he had "abandoned" them not because he was hostile to their projects, but because his priorities had to be military. He later said he had reflected for a long time on whether a revolution in Piedmont—and Genoa—would be opportune, but finally concluded that it would not: given the weakness of the revolutionary party, it would have been risky to ignite behind his lines a civil war that could endanger the further pursuit of his operations against the Austrians.[20] Thus, it was for strategic reasons that Bonaparte put an end to the hopes of the "patriots," though he thought that once the Austrians had been expelled from the peninsula, politics would reclaim its rights.[21] One can see more clearly, then, why less than three weeks after having sacrificed the Piedmontese revolution on the altar of war, he changed his tune after the battle of Lodi, which sounded the death knell of the Austrian presence in Lombardy. Receiving Melzi in Melegnano on May 13, he declared that France desired the emancipation of Milan: "We will let you . . . determine your own destiny. Be what you want to be: provided that you no longer belong to Austria, that will be enough for France. A democratic republic, even if aristocratic, is what suits you best [and] if you show yourself worthy of liberty and you decide you want it, France will support you."[22]

Was he duped by the movement that his own agents, led by Saliceti, had incited in Milan with the help of the journalist Carlo Salvador? A popular group had been formed whose members wore a green, white, and red cockade, planted "liberty trees," and talked about storming the Sforzas' castle, where 2,000 Austrian soldiers had taken refuge. Not all the members of this political club were "hirelings," as Melzi later suggested.[23] And the crowds spontaneously acclaimed Bonaparte when he appeared on the balcony of the Palazzo Reale on May 15. It is difficult to disentangle the reasons for this warm reception: Were the crowds applauding the conqueror of the hated Austrian "occupier" or the general "of Italian origin [and] with an Italian face" who "led the French phalanxes"?[24] But if there was a real surge of popular support, it was neither universal nor enduring. The French were welcomed with acclaim solely in Milan and, later on, in Modena and Bologna, and even then only by some of the inhabitants. The common folk in the outlying areas and in the surrounding countryside uprooted by night the "liberty trees" that had been planted by day. When Stendhal says that the "thunderbolt of May 14 [1796]" had roused Italians from their torpor and soon made a new people rise up, he was espousing illusions that were, at the time, certainly those of the revolutionaries. In reality the three years of the initial French occupation left few marks on the area; instead, it was the subsequent fifteen years of French administration that revived aspirations to union and a national state in Italy.[25] Stendhal agreed: although the creation of a Lombard Legion testified to the reality of the Milan area's mobilization in 1796, it was only in 1809 that the viceroy Eugène mobilized 60,000 *Italians* against the Austrians.[26] All the same, the welcome received in Milan may have been sufficiently intoxicating to make Bonaparte dream of great upheavals on the peninsula. When Melzi begged him not to confuse the opinion of the people with that of a handful of Jacobins, he smiled "as if he felt sorry that [Melzi] was not aware of what was going on"[27] and immediately wrote to the Directory to ask this question: "If this [Lombard] people requests permission to organize itself as a republic, should the request be granted?"[28] Nevertheless, although he gave pledges to the people of Milan by distributing cockades of green, white, and red to the urban militia and by sending to the Directory a deputation "of good patriots who would like to establish liberty," he took care not to promise them independence.[29] So it is false that on the evening of his arrival he told them that they would soon form an independent state. He made that statement a year later, when the Cisalpine Republic was proclaimed.[30] At the time he limited himself to reassuring the people by saying that France would take away neither their property nor their beliefs, and in his proclamation to the Lombards on May 19, he abstained from making the slightest allusion to "liberty."[31] Not only did the Directory refuse to make a clear statement regarding Italy's future, but after four days of joy and illusions the time had come to return to reality.[32]

While swearing "fraternity with the peoples," Bonaparte estimated the price of that fraternity at twenty million livres. The Milanese authorities were placed under the supervision of a military agency, and the raiding began: levies in cash and in kind, the churches' gold and silver, pawned items, merchandise and credits belonging to Austria or England, paintings and manuscripts. If to this we add the untimely zeal of the Milanese Jacobins who, through their speeches, added fear to the irritation caused by the demands of the "liberators," we will hardly be surprised by the disturbances that soon broke out in Milan, and then in Pavia, as early as May 23. Two executions and the arrest of 200 hostages sufficed to restore calm in the Lombard capital, but unrest continued in Pavia, where insurgents had seized the castle. On the twenty-fifth, Bonaparte sent in his troops: they killed about a hundred peasants in Binasco and burned the village. Pavia was taken by assault, and there too, hostages were arrested, rebels were shot, and the city was pillaged for three hours.[33] But the fire had not been put out; it was already spreading to the "imperial fiefs" of Francis II scattered all across Liguria.[34] From Genoa to Tortona, a peasant uprising was threatening the rear of the French army. Bonaparte later said that he had realized these were uprisings of the common people, provoked by the requisitions made by the French and by their duplicitous language, which on the one hand "called [the Italian] nation to liberty" and on the other "took away its main resources."[35] But at the time he could not believe that they were spontaneous. He saw them as the result of a plan carefully orchestrated by Rome, London, and Vienna. Hadn't he learned that the pope was raising troops? Though not very dangerous in themselves, they might be reinforced by the 5,000 English troops currently occupying Corsica in order to open, with the help of the insurgents Genoa was surreptitiously encouraging, a second front, just when the Austrians returned from the mountains of the Tyrol to attempt the reconquest of Lombardy. Thus, the Directory's planned expedition in central Italy took on a new significance: it was now a matter not merely of looting the peninsula's riches, but also of pacifying the right bank of the Po in order to confront, in a month, or two at the latest, a new Austrian offensive. Bonaparte could not remain master of a part of northern Italy without becoming, directly or indirectly, by conquest or by armed negotiation, master of the whole peninsula.

The Directory exhorted its general to head south without delay. Bonaparte was furious: Didn't the government know that the warmest months of the year were approaching? Did it want to sacrifice an army in order to give itself the empty satisfaction of humiliating the pope? Finally, did it want the Austrians to return to Milan? If a defeat in the autumn was to be avoided, he wrote to General Clarke, it was absolutely necessary that the army "not be obliged to advance toward the south of Italy," and he even announced that he would not go beyond Livorno.[36] He left Tortona (where he had gone to supervise the repression of disturbances in the imperial fiefs) on June 17. A leisurely ten-day march allowed him to reach Livorno. The army passed by Modena on the nineteenth, entered Bologna on the twentieth, stopped off at Pistoia on the twenty-fifth, and occupied Livorno on the twenty-seventh. Nowhere, at least for the moment, did it encounter hostile reactions. On the contrary, inhabitants who hoped the French would improve their situation or bring them liberty came to applaud them. But the Lombardy scenario was invariably repeated, with curiosity and sympathy being soon replaced by hostility when comforting speeches were replaced by taxation and requisitions. The French had hardly left Bologna before revolts broke out, in Cesena on June 22, in Faenza on June 27, and in Imola on July 4. In Lugo the people, exasperated by the requisitions but also by a decree subjecting the commune to that of Ferrara, its hated neighbor, rose up and massacred the garrison. Had it not been for the resentment against papal domination felt by part of the population of the Legations, Romagna might have experienced disturbances as serious as those in Pavia.

Although this incursion toward the center of Italy sufficed to pacify the right bank of the Po, the governments of Rome and Naples still had to be disarmed—by taking advantage of the fear caused by the French army's lightning victories, because Bonaparte refused to move farther south. Even before he left Tortona, he had signed an armistice with an emissary of the king of Naples; as for Pius VI, Bonaparte had even less intention of going to threaten him in Rome, because the Spanish ambassador to the Holy See, Azara, had given him to understand that an accord was possible. Another detour via Lucca, where the gonfalonier, trembling with fear, agreed to provide 6,000 muskets and all the food the French army might need, an excursion to San Miniato to visit a canon named Buonaparte who claimed to be one of his cousins, a dinner in Florence on July 1 at the table of the grand duke of Tuscany, Ferdinand III—a dinner at which the grand duchess refused to appear in order to avoid meeting this revolutionary general—another stop at Bologna, and finally, on the thirteenth, Bonaparte was back at his headquarters in Roverbella.

Austrian Counterattacks

It was high time. Fifty thousand Austrians were descending the gorges of the Trentino to rescue the Mantua garrison, which was still under siege. Part of the Austrian army was following the left shore of Lake Garda under Quasdanovich's command, the other part the right shore under Wurmser's command. The Austrian assault, launched in the last days of July 1796, was so impetuous that the French defenses crumbled everywhere. Brescia, Salo, Rivoli, and Verona fell into the enemy's hands. The French generals, thinking the situation irreparable, advised retreat toward Milan, and to rally them to his offensive plan Bonaparte had to use all his influence at an extraordinary war council he had called for the evening of July 30. He willingly acknowledged the critical nature of the situation: the enemy was superior in numbers, the front had been broken at several points, their communications with Milan had been cut. So his lieutenants were stupefied to hear him declare that the Austrians were doomed. The Austrians had in fact committed an error that was going to prove fatal to them: "It was a mistake to put separately into action [two] corps without any communication between them [they were separated by the lake], confronted by a centralized army with easy communications."[37] It was a mistake, of course, if the two wings of the Austrian army were unable to effect a junction before

Mantua, and in order to prevent them from doing so, the French absolutely had to throw the totality of their forces against one of these wings before turning toward the other. That made abandoning the siege of Mantua, which immobilized several thousand French troops, inevitable. It was a hard pill to swallow for those who had been trying for two months to force the Austrian garrison to surrender, but Bonaparte was inflexible on this point. With heavy hearts the assailants dismantled their cannons, buried their stocks, threw into the Mincio the bullets they could not take with them, and abandoned the fortress, into which Wurmser entered in triumph on August 1. During this time the Army of Italy was marching on Quasdanovich and took Brescia back from him; it was a position they had to control to reestablish their communications with Milan. Just as in April Beaulieu had perceived too late the consequences of Argenteau's defeat at Montenotte, Wurmser did not immediately grasp those of the defeat suffered by Quasdanovich. On August 2, understanding that the junction of the Austrian army's two wings was in jeopardy, he flew to the aid of his colleague, but it was too late. The Army of Italy had taken up a position between Quasdanovich, who had been driven back toward Salo, and Wurmser, who was arriving from Mantua. August 3 was the decisive day: while Masséna was inflicting a new and bitter defeat on Quasdanovich at Lonato, Augereau was blocking Wursmer's route at Castiglione. The separation of the two Austrian armies had been achieved, and when Quasdanovich gave up and retreated north of Lake Garda, only Wurmser remained in action. Bonaparte attacked him on August 5 at Castiglione. For a moment it seemed that the Austrian was going to fall into Bonaparte's trap, but he finally succeeded in returning toward Trento, whence he had come. "The Austrian army," Bonaparte wrote as a kind of epitaph, "disappeared like a dream."[38]

In France, public opinion was so impressed by this new success that the Directory wondered for a moment whether it would not be judicious after all to send Bonaparte to attack Vienna, especially because in Germany French troops had finally crossed the Rhine, won several victories, and driven Archduke Charles beyond the Danube.[39] But the government soon lowered its sights: its luck was already turning. While Moreau was marching on Munich, Archduke Charles had counterattacked and defeated Bernadotte and Jourdan (August 23–24); the French generals, who did not get on well, had been forced to give up the terrain they had won and retreat toward the Rhine. Moreover, the fighting was not over in Italy, where Wurmser was getting ready to make a new attack. He had decided to draw Bonaparte in the direction of Trento and then, overtaking him, turn his flank on the east, free Mantua, and cut the route to Milan. The French, deceived by the false retreat undertaken by General Davidovich, one of Wurmser's lieutenants, headed north and were approaching Trento when, on September 5, Bonaparte understood that Wurmser was coming down the Brenta with the bulk of his forces. He turned around and set off in pursuit of the Austrians. On September 7 he fell upon the Austrian rearguard at Bassano. The Austrian line of retreat had been cut. Wurmser tried to take refuge in Verona, but having failed, he took the only road open to him, even farther from his bases: Mantua, where, having lost almost 30,000 men in three weeks, he holed up on September 15. Wurmser fell victim to the maneuver that he himself had devised to defeat Bonaparte: his army was caught in the trap, far from its bases, doomed to rely wholly on the hypothetical success of a third Austrian attempt. In this campaign, which was so short one hardly dares call it by that name, Bonaparte's military genius may have attained its zenith: Once he had understood the enemy's strategy, he never hesitated for a moment regarding the decisions to be made, and in perfect control of his means and his plan, he henceforth conducted the operations "with a dazzling vigor and rapidity that have never been equaled."[40]

Italy on the Edge of the Abyss

Wurmser's repeated failures had nonetheless revealed the fragility of the agreements Bonaparte had made with the Italian sovereigns. The ephemeral successes achieved by the Austrians on July 29 and 30 had been enough to revive rancor and discontent almost everywhere. The clergy had assumed the leadership of the resistance in Bologna and Ferrara, while in Rome "the streets were choked with long files of priests or monks, walking in procession"; followed by "enormous crowds," they implored divine protection against the barbarians.[41] From Rome to Florence, the people seemed ready to rise up, and even though some of the residents of Milan, fearing the return of the Austrians, asked to serve in the ranks of the French army, not far away a garrison was massacred, and Frenchmen were killed on Venetian territory, in Genoa, and in Piedmont. The sovereigns were not to be outdone. With the exception of those in Parma and in Tuscany, who observed a prudent neutrality, they all hoped, more or less openly, that an Austrian success would allow them to tear up the treaties they had signed with the invader. And all this agitation had been provoked by the simple news that the siege of Mantua had been abandoned! What would have happened had serious reverses taken place?

Bonaparte had feared the possible consequences of such reverses; on the other hand, he had not been sufficiently distrustful of victories that had been so brilliant and apparently so easy. Witnessing the spectacle of Italian sovereigns resigning and of Austrian impotence, Italy began to crack apart everywhere: "Was that what these governments that had been venerated for centuries amounted to? Governments incapable of defending against a handful of men honor, property, religion, and the laws? Public opinion and the government were suddenly being divorced; from one day to the next, Italy was detaching itself from the Old Regime, which was incapable of defending it, but in order to hate with redoubled fury the cause of all its misfortunes, the principles that the Revolution opposed to it: in the temporal order, it no longer believed in anything, not in the Old Regime and not in the Revolution, either; it was the void."[42]

The first symptom of the collapse of the "age-old edifice of legality" was the increased strength of the patriot party, which had been joined by "many wise and prudent men who were persuaded that . . . it was the duty of every friend of the fatherland to declare himself and to regularize as much as possible . . . the movements that were rocking hapless Italy."[43] The other symptom consisted in the symmetrical rise in power of the counterrevolutionary party, which "was exciting in the people a hatred of France and of the Revolution, helping the Austrian army [and] urging governments to go to war."[44] Was Italy on the brink of civil war? Bonaparte was worried about this. The double defeat inflicted on Wurmser did not blind him to the point of forgetting that Austria was powerful enough to send a new army against him in the near future. Neither had he given up the plan of marching on Vienna. But how could he enter Austrian territory if he left behind him an Italy that was plunging into anarchy and was guarded by forces insufficient in number? He had made his calculations: He had 32,000 men. That was few, too few, to resist Austrian assaults for long, and a fortiori for launching an attack on the Alps. Therefore he had to rely on the Italians themselves and "create in a crumbling Italy supports for the French army"[45] if he wanted to prevent Italy from flaring up behind him; and all the more because he feared the formation of a coalition among the states most hostile to the French presence—Rome, Venice, and Naples—which Piedmont and Genoa would certainly join. Even if he had not yet exhausted all the resources of diplomacy, he had to find sincere allies on whom the French could count. This role could not be assigned to either the grand duke of Tuscany or the Duke of Parma, both of whom were "absolutely useless in every respect."[46] So there remained only one solution: relying on the revolutionary party. Thus, it was neither out of love for the republican form of government nor out of sympathy for the Italians that after Bassano, Bonaparte decided to create republics in Italy. He considered republican government generally unsuited to modern nations; as for the Italians, he sometimes had little good to say about them. But he knew that the Austrians were not yet inclined to lay down their arms, and that was enough to impose on him a policy that was not guided by any long-term goal regarding the formation of a northern Italy that would be a satellite of France, or the creation of a unified, independent Italy. Instead, this policy, based on the probability of a third Austrian counterattack, responded solely to the imperatives of the military situation. When he returned to Milan on September 19, he had made up his mind to rely on pro-revolutionary Italy, and for that reason, to respond favorably to its demands.

The Policy of Sister Republics

Three days later, during a banquet in Milan, Bonaparte offered a toast "to the future liberty of Lombardy."[47] And the provisional administration followed suit by organizing an essay competition, the subject of which was the question: Which "free government would be most appropriate for Italy's happiness?" In this competition, the trend toward national unity was to manifest itself (timidly) for the first time.[48] But the French declarations and initiatives were deceptive; Bonaparte had no intention of setting Lombardy free so long as its geographical situation "on the French army's marching route" made necessary "the prolongation of the military regime" there.[49] One must have no illusions about this: the Austrians' departure had in no way increased the Lombards' autonomy, and when one day some of them criticized a proposal made by General Despinoy, the military commander of Lombardy, Bonaparte "got so angry that he struck the conference table with his sword and reminded the trembling municipal councilors that their function was only to register the victor's will."[50] He promised the Lombards that they would gain their liberty later on, after Austria had been defeated. He could not let them have it now—in November, the Milanese club would be closed once again for having demonstrated in favor of the constitution of a Lombard republic—but neither could he refuse it to them, because exciting patriotic feeling was also a way of multiplying the number of his Italian allies. On the other hand, he had chosen to create an initial republic in Modena and in Bologna, where he had been given a warm welcome in June. On that occasion he had protected the Duke of Modena, whom the "patriots" had wanted to depose; but in Bologna, which was a papal possession, he had gone farther by authorizing the senate of the city to cease obeying orders that came from Rome. In July Bologna had proclaimed the republic, and Reggio nell' Emilia had followed suit. On the basis of these precedents, Bonaparte declared on September 26: "The time has come for Italy to take its place of honor among the powerful nations. Lombardy, Bologna, Modena, Reggio, Ferrara, and perhaps Romagna, if it shows itself worthy of it, will one day astonish Europe and renew for us Italy's finest days."[51]

Abandoning his reserved attitude, he opposed the Directory's Italian policy. To the question he had asked in May—Would France support a revolution in Italy?—the government had finally replied in July that it would not.[52] The directors did not want to hear any more talk about an Italian revolution, and they wrote to Bonaparte to inform him that the Milan area would ultimately be either returned to Austria or ceded to the king of Sardinia in exchange for Savoy and Nice, or perhaps annexed to the duchy of Parma. In any case, they opposed the creation of republics, envisaging on the contrary territorial transfers that would have a better chance of obtaining Europe's consent.[53]

The Directory gave up any idea of exporting the Revolution for at least three reasons.

First, the policy of sister republics found ardent supporters among Italian refugees, many of whom were connected with Babeuf, whom the Directory had just had arrested, thus marking a turn to the right.[54]

Second, even in wartime the French and Austrian governments had been maintaining discrete contacts: though the Austrians continued to demand the restitution of Lombardy, they were showing increasing interest in Bavaria, and from this point of view it is obvious that the Directory's new instructions were connected with the prospect—which was at that point not chimerical—of a peace treaty with Austria: "Thus in Austria's plans as in those of the Directory, France would not establish itself in Italy, either by overt annexations or by creating a protégé state there. It would not cross its natural limits in the Alps, being satisfied to attain them on the Rhine. By allowing Bavaria to be reunited with Austria, it would create a large German state that would find its geographical unity in the Alps and its religious unity in Catholicism, and would be capable of preventing the absorption of southern Germany by Prussia."[55]

From that point on, and even if the negotiations with Austria bogged down in the summer of 1796, Bonaparte appeared as the successor to the former revolutionary messianism of the Girondins, at precisely the moment when the Directory, giving up any idea of exporting the Revolution, seemed inclined to return instead to the old politics of exchanges and compensations familiar to the European monarchies.

Finally—this was the directors' third motive—seeking a diplomatic solution to the crisis was also a way of regaining control of France's Italian policy by depriving Bonaparte of the total victory he hoped to win. It was not only because he feared the decomposition of Italy that Bonaparte turned a deaf ear to the warnings issued by the Directory, which kept telling him that "peace, our first wish, may depend on the fate of Milan, and it is [therefore] important to us to handle the object to be exchanged carefully."[56] It was also because he had decided to oppose by all possible means a policy of negotiation and compromise, which he had understood was also directed against him. The Directory, in fact, was trying for the last time to stand up to him. Knowing that Bonaparte was determined to put an end to the Republic of Genoa through a "revolution" or a coup d'état, it cut the ground out from under his feet by signing with the Genoese, on October 9, a treaty confirming their neutrality.[57] On the following day it made a further point by signing a peace treaty with Naples. Thus, the creation in October of an initial republic in Italy was not only a strategic measure dictated by the twists and turns of the conflict with Austria, but a kind of coup d'état through which Bonaparte claimed the power to define France's Italian policy as he pleased.

He crossed the Rubicon on October 2 by demanding that the Directory declare itself publicly in favor of the liberty of Italy and by announcing that the moment had come to "revolutionize" the duchy of Modena and the legations.[58] The government's response was, once again, negative: "The surrender of Lombardy or its cession may become the pledge of an enduring peace, and although we have made no decision in that regard, we think that it would be imprudent, in the current circumstances, to deny us the means of making [peace] at this price. . . . What we have said about the independence of Milan applies to Bologna, Ferrara, Reggio, and Modena, and to all the other little states of Italy, and we must redouble our circumspection and prudence in order to avoid compromising by too much facility the Republic's future interests."[59]

By the time the letter of October 11 had reached its destination, the Duke of Modena had already been overthrown and the republic proclaimed in Bologna. The very day on which the people of Modena carried out the "revolution" fomented by the French, Bonaparte ordered the meeting of a congress of about a hundred delegates from Modena, Reggio, Bologna, and Ferrara, who were assigned to set up "a kind of federation" for which Monge had invented a name, that of the "Cispadane Republic."[60]

There were new quarrels with the Directory: no peace with Austria without sacrifices in Italy, the government kept repeating, whereas Bonaparte struck back by threatening, as he had already done in May, to resign. "Every time your general in Italy is not the center of everything, you are running great risks," he warned. "This language must not be attributed to ambition; I have only too many honors, and my health is so ruined that I believe I shall be obliged to ask you for a successor."[61] The Directory broke out in a cold sweat: Was Bonaparte threatening to return to Paris and get involved in politics? This letter of October 8 was soon followed by another announcing the proclamation of the Cispadane Confederation.[62] What was to be done? And that is how the government, having already surrendered the direction of military operations, ended up letting the general determine France's Italian policy. Having lost all sense of shame, it approved the creation of the Cispadane Republic.

Bonaparte immediately took advantage of the Directory's capitulation to get rid of the representatives it had sent to him, whose supervision he sometimes found inconvenient. Appointed in late 1795, they were the heirs of the Old Regime's intendants to the armies and of the Convention's representatives. Initially invested with limited powers, they had seen these powers gradually increase, and they had been transformed from simple supervisors into important figures who had to be reckoned with. Bonaparte had had dealings with three of them: Saliceti, Pinsot, and Garrau. Although he had managed to get along with Saliceti, whom he had known for a long time, he was not pleased by the arrival of Pinsot. However, the latter did not remain long in Milan: because he had criticized the way in which the contributions were distributed and levied, the French military men and the Milanese revolutionaries joined forces to obtain his removal. Garrau succeeded him. From the outset Bonaparte took a dislike to this former member of the Convention, and the two men soon quarreled. "The Directory's representatives have nothing to do with my policies, I do as I wish," he told Miot."[63] He asked the Directory to rid him of Garrau:

> With a mediocre army [Bonaparte meant that he had an insufficient number of troops] I have to cope with everything: containing the German armies, besieging fortresses, guarding our rear, impressing people in Genoa, Venice, Tuscany, Rome, and Naples; we have to be everywhere in force. Thus, a unified military, diplomatic, and financial conception is necessary. In one place we have to burn, shoot, establish terror, and provide a striking example. In another there are things we have to pretend not to see and thus not say, because the time has not yet come. Diplomacy is therefore entirely military in Italy at this time. You can see that when each power, each municipality addresses itself indifferently to one of the three representatives and to me, and when each responds depending on his way of seeing things, it is no longer possible to have a single conception or to follow the same plan.[64]

The government had not responded, but as Bonaparte became more powerful it was forced to be more conciliatory, preaching moderation to its representatives and allowing the general to treat them more and more overtly as a negligible quantity. Bonaparte first got rid of Saliceti by assigning him to prepare the reconquest of Corsica. Garrau was next. As soon as the Directory had abdicated in favor of Napoleon, he transferred to the military authority the civilian responsibilities that had up to that point been reserved for the representatives. Garrau protested, but the Directory disowned him, and on December 6 the directors simply abolished the representatives to the armies. Bonaparte was now truly independent; he was "not only free, but controlled requisitions and contributions, as well as diplomatic relations."[65] He made all the decisions himself. In only six months he had gained full powers.

ELEVEN

On the Road to Vienna

*W*urmser's defeat—as we have seen, he had holed up in Mantua—had not deterred Austria from trying again. It assembled a fourth army and entrusted its command to General Josef Alvinczy, a veteran of the Seven Years' War. While his colleague Davidovich moved down the Adige to threaten Verona, Alvinczy would invade Italy through Friuli, and would then head, via Vicenza, toward Mantua, where Wurmser would try to fight his way out. The Austrians were all the more confident because Archduke Charles's offensive in Germany had been successful and the French army was known to be in poor condition: the soldiers were tired and morale was low; after seven months in the breach, they wanted to rest.

Bonaparte never ceased to repeat that he needed "troops, troops, if you want to keep Italy."[1] He had been reinforced by 19,000 men since the beginning of the campaign, and on paper his troops had increased from 40,000 to 60,000. But that did not take into account the losses—7,000 killed and wounded, and about 10,000 who were sick or had deserted.[2]

The reinforcements hardly compensated for the losses. As a result, many of the soldiers who were getting ready to face a new assault were the same men who had taken part in the first fighting in April. The same, less the dead and the wounded who were in no condition to return to the fray: almost 18 percent of the initial number of troops. This is an important figure, even if the Italian campaign cannot be compared to those under the Empire, which were to see immense armies collide with artillery shells raining down on them. Here artillery did not play a major role. It was an infantryman's war fought with the assistance of cavalry, a war of movement and rapid marches, skirmishes and ambushes, assaults and hand-to-hand fighting. In short, it was still an old-fashioned war in which death, far from being the result of chance that arbitrarily strikes one man and spares another, is often the price to be paid for courage and daring. The best men died first. In less than a year the Army of Italy had lost the cream of its officers and soldiers.[3] Bonaparte was well aware of that. Shortly before Alvinczy's offensive was launched, Bonaparte wrote to the Directory that given the weakness of his army, the loss of Italy could no longer be considered a simple hypothesis.[4]

Arcole

With his army so diminished in numbers and in fighting spirit, Bonaparte had to meet Alvinczy outnumbered two to one, and fight against a general whom he was later to consider the most talented of all those who had opposed him.[5] When the Austrian attacked, Bonaparte found himself in a situation even more delicate than he had faced in front of Castiglione. The Vaubois division that had been posted at Trento to stop Davidovich scattered, and would have left the road to Verona open had Augereau not come to the rescue. Masséna and Bonaparte, who had marched ahead of Alvinczy by heading for Bassano and Treviso, had to retreat in order to protect Verona (November 6). The Austrian's 30,000 men, driving 15,000 French troops before them, did not stop until they reached Caldiero, two days' march from Verona. The day of November 12 was terrible; the French exhausted themselves in attacks on the village of Caldiero, which was taken and retaken several times and at the end of the day remained in the hands of the Austrians. Considering the situation too favorable to the enemy for successful resistance in the event that Alvinczy connected up with Davidovich, Bonaparte decided to stake everything on forcing his adversary to fight where the latter's numerical superiority would give him no advantage. The Austrians' line of retreat was along the road between Verona and Vicenza, and Bonaparte chose to go around them on the south and cut it farther on, near Villanova, while Masséna attacked the enemy's left flank. If everything went as planned, Alvinczy, abandoning his attempt to seize Verona, would turn back toward Villanova, where he would be forced to fight in a marshy region intersected by a few narrow roads elevated like dikes. Here numerical superiority could even become a handicap.

Bonaparte left Verona as if he were retreating, and then, turning suddenly to the left, he hastened toward Ronco and crossed the Adige. The army then followed the path that runs along the right bank of the Alpone as far as Arcole, where a bridge twenty-five meters long and only four meters wide allowed it to rejoin the road leading to Villanova. Bonaparte reached the entrance to the bridge on the morning of November 15. A thousand Croats with two cannons were defending the bridge. As at Lodi, Bonaparte assigned one of his officers, General Guieu, to find a ford downstream and go around the Austrian defense; but then, again as at Lodi, not having received any news from Guieu, he ordered his troops to force their way across the river. What happened was the same as at Lodi, except that the bridge at Arcole was not crossed. Bombarded by the cannons and under heavy fire from the other bank, the attackers fell back, taking shelter however they could and refusing to renew the assault. Seeing this, the generals put themselves at the head of the troops, but with less success than at Lodi. Lannes, Verdier, Bon, and Verne were wounded. Augereau took over, rushing onto the bridge waving a flag. Did he call his men cowards?[6] "A few brave men followed him . . . but five or six having been unfortunately killed, they retreated and all took refuge again behind the dike."[7] Augereau was the last to leave the bridge. It was then that Bonaparte appeared on the dike. Followed by his staff, like Augereau he moved onto the bridge with a flag. "The soldiers saw him," Sulkowski reports, "[but] none of them imitated him."[8] All around Bonaparte, men were dying: his aide-de-camp Muiron, whom he had known since the siege of Toulon, General Vignolle, and two of Belliard's assistants collapsed, struck dead by enemy bullets. Miraculously, Bonaparte escaped, perhaps thanks to a ceasefire order issued by the Austrian commander who, seeing so many officers on the bridge, thought they were emissaries.[9] By the time he realized his mistake, Bonaparte had left the bridge. His retreat had triggered a general rout. Seeing their leader coming back toward them, the soldiers thought the order had been given to leave the position. They all started to run, scrambling so wildly that Bonaparte, knocked from the dike, landed "up to his neck" in the marshes, from which his brother Louis and Marmont had difficulty pulling him out.[10]

The army retreated toward Ronco.[11] The attack had failed. The panic that had gripped the army, though not the first, was certainly the most serious up to that point. It might even have had fatal consequences had the Austrians been able to exploit it, but they allowed the French officers to rally their exhausted soldiers, who said they no longer wanted to fight, and to use the night to re-form their ranks, reestablish a semblance of discipline, and prepare for a new attack. It still took two days to overcome the Austrians. After a day—November 16—when neither of the two armies succeeded in winning a decisive advantage, on the seventeenth Masséna and Augereau broke through the Austrian defenses and took possession of Arcole, reopening the road to Verona. Although Bonaparte had not been at his best, the third Austrian counterattack ended like the earlier ones—in a disaster.[12]

Bonaparte and His Army

The fact that Bonaparte obtained from his weary soldiers so many new sacri-fices would be astonishing if we did not recall that he had been able to estab-lish with them, in a few months, ties so close that they had no equivalent in any of the Republic's other armies.

We know what a deplorable material situation the 40,000 men entrusted to him had been in when he arrived in Nice. "The army is in a dreadful state of deprivation," he wrote after a first inspection.[13] The government did not have the means to feed, clothe, and pay its defenders suitably, so the Army of Italy lived by pillaging. Insubordination was chronic, and mutinies frequent. This sit-uation was, moreover, not in any way unique: it was the lot of all armies at a time when public finances were in a deplorable state, and Generals Hoche, Moreau, and Jourdan were in no better shape than Bonaparte.[14] The leaders knew that order could not be reestablished amid destitution. So they restrained the abuses more or less gently, trying less to forbid them than to limit their ex-tent. A few examples took the place of a policy. Bonaparte proceeded in the same way.

The image of particularly rapacious and plundering troops has nonetheless attached itself to the Army of Italy, which Melzi was later to compare to the lancers responsible for the sack of Rome in 1527.[15] It is true that since the be-ginning of the campaign, the exactions had become more numerous. Disgusted by this spectacle, General Laharpe is supposed to have considered resigning, whereas Bonaparte, while agreeing that it was enough to make one "blush to be a man," excused his troops' behavior by saying that they were thereby quenching their thirst.[16] All the same, on April 26, at the end of the first phase of the campaign, he decided he had to make a solemn appeal:

> Friends, I promise you this victory; but there is one condition that you must swear to fulfill, and that is to respect the people you are freeing, it is to stop the horrible pillaging in which scoundrels incited by our enemies indulge. If you do not, you will not be the liberators of peoples, you will be their scourges; you will not be the honor of the French people, they will disown you. Your victories, your courage, your successes, the blood of our brothers who have died in combat—all will be lost, even honor and glory. As for me and for the generals who have your confidence, we would blush to command an army without discipline, without restraint, which knew no law other than force. But invested with national authority, I shall know how to make this small number of men without courage and without hearts respect the laws of humanity and of honor that they are trampling. I will not allow brigands to tarnish your laurels; if necessary, I will have the rule that I have put in the order executed. Looters will be shot without pity.[17]

There were further executions and sentences to hard labor. "I shall reestablish order or I shall cease to command these brigands," Bonaparte said.[18] But he multiplied sanctions in vain; he was never able to put an end to pillaging and misappropriations. Three months later, he wrote: "It is often necessary to shoot [them], for there are intractable men who cannot be commanded."[19] The executions did not have the desired effect, so he increased their number, ordering investigations into the morality of the corps leaders and administrations, opening a register to receive complaints from residents of the Mantua region who had suffered particularly from the pillaging, and even considering the possibility of assuming some kind of dictatorial authority to have done with the thieves. He wrote to the Directory:

> Laws are insufficient; there is only one remedy . . . a magistracy that would consist of one or three people whose authority would last only

three or five days, and which during this short period would have the right to have an administrator of the army shot. This magistracy, sent to the armies every year, would result in everyone considering public opinion and maintaining a certain decency not only in morals and in expenditure, but also in everyday service. . . . However, do not conclude that I am soft and that I am betraying the fatherland in this essential part of my functions; I have employees arrested every day; I have their papers and their accounts examined; but in this I am aided by no one, and the laws do not accord enough authority to the general to allow him to impress a salutary fear on this swarm of scoundrels.[20]

However, we should not forget that at the beginning of the campaign he had encouraged pillaging in a way unlike that of any of his colleagues leading armies in Germany. He wrote to the Directory: "The poor fellows are excusable; after having sighed for three years at the summit of the Alps they arrive in the promised land and they want to enjoy it."[21] But he failed to mention that he himself had presented Italy as a "promised land" and aroused a rapine spirit by describing the "fertile plains" to which he was going to lead his men. "Rich provinces, great cities will be in your power," he had told them; "you will find there honor, glory, and wealth."[22] This proclamation became famous. In fact Bonaparte never wrote or uttered it, but it nevertheless faithfully sums up the spirit of the harangues he delivered in front of the troops before they took the offensive, and of which some trace has been preserved. Although he predictably made use of the usual rhetorical tropes about the fall of tyrants and the liberation of peoples, he galvanized his men by making them hope for booty that would compensate them for their sacrifices. "I know your sufferings," he declared to the men of the eighteenth demi-brigade. "I know that in order to obtain bread you have often had to sell valuable objects that you possessed. . . . On the other side of the Apennines, you will find a fertile country that will satisfy all your needs."[23] Such promises amounted to giving a destitute army a free rein. If he was subsequently never able to control pillaging, that is because the Army of Italy had so well acquired the habit and taste for it that it had become impossible to eradicate it totally, except at the cost of provoking seditions still graver than those that periodically broke out. At first Bonaparte preferred to permit what he could not prevent, for it would be quite wrong to imagine that it was easy for him, right from the outset, to impose his will on his subordinates. The army, one witness said, "could not trust the promises of a young man whose name it hardly knew."[24]

What is true of his relations with the troops was even more true of his relations with the leaders of the different divisions. How could Masséna, Sérurier, Laharpe, or Augereau not smile on seeing the "little runt" Paris had sent them? His service record could not impress men who had already fought so many battles. They were all older than their new leader. Masséna, the youngest, was eleven years Bonaparte's elder. Although Laharpe, who was from Switzerland, had joined the army only at the time of the Revolution—he had participated in the siege of Toulon—the others had extensive experience of war. Augereau had formerly served in the Neapolitan and Prussian armies, and Masséna, after an adventurous life, had distinguished himself in the Army of Italy. As for Sérurier, the eldest of them all (he was born in 1742), he was a career soldier. Later on Napoleon was to judge his old subordinates harshly, but at the time when he took his command they could only have impressed him. Augereau? "A great deal of character, courage, firmness, activity."[25] Masséna? "Active, indefatigable, bold, perceptive, and prompt to make up his mind." Sérurier? "Extremely hard on himself, . . . a steadfast friend of discipline, order, and the virtues most necessary for the maintenance of society."[26] This praise for Sérurier was a veiled criticism of the defects of his colleagues: Masséna's "sordid avarice," Augereau's insatiable appetite for "honors and riches."[27] Only one superior officer immediately put himself in Bonaparte's service: his head of staff. Alexandre Berthier was then forty-two years old. We do not know whether this veteran of the American War of Independence, who had commanded the National Guard at Versailles in 1789, felt from the outset the admiration for Bonaparte that was to make him his loyal follower for twenty years, but the general immediately took the measure of Berthier's strengths and weaknesses: a prodigious capacity for work and a peerless knowledge of "how to handle the details of the service," but associated with such a complete absence "of character and the qualities necessary for commanding"[28] that it would have been impossible to give him the command of even a simple battalion. Napoleon's judgment of a man who he said was doomed by nature to "subordinate positions"[29] was always harsh, but he nonetheless made him one of his closest collaborators. The relation between Berthier and Bonaparte was a curious one, consisting on the one hand of loyalty, even servility, and admiration, on the other of a disdain tempered by what has to be called friendship: "In truth," Napoleon was to tell Talleyrand, "I cannot understand how a relationship was established between Berthier and me that has to be seen as a kind of friendship. I care little for useless sentiments, and Berthier is so mediocre that I don't know why I would bother to be fond of him, and yet, down deep, when nothing turns me against him, I believe I am not entirely without a certain affection for him."[30] Berthier was not only Napoleon's man for files and forms, the person who knew better than anyone how to grasp and translate into precise directives his master's instructions, which were not always clear, but also the companion who lived, worked, traveled, and often even slept in the same carriage with him. He was even Napoleon's accomplice, because for a long time they were to be linked "by affairs with women, telling each other about their conquests, helping each other out, trading actresses and other theater women."[31] They were so close that Bonaparte made the faithful Berthier pay the price; the latter was often "overloaded during the day," Caulaincourt said, "and swamped with disagreeable tasks."[32]

Unlike Berthier, the generals patronized their new leader. But as Masséna told Chaptal later on, one staff meeting was enough for them to understand that appearances were deceptive:

When [Bonaparte] came to the Army of Italy, none of the generals knew him, and Masséna told me that the first time they visited him, they were initially unimpressed. His shortness and his puny body did not incline them in his favor. The portrait of his wife that he had in his hand and that he showed to everyone, and his extreme youth on top of it all, persuaded them that this appointment was another outcome of intrigues. "But a moment afterward he put on his general's hat and seemed to grow by two feet," Masséna added. "He questioned us about the position of our divisions, their materiel, their morale, and the number of troops in each corps, outlined the direction we were to follow, and announced that the next day he would inspect all the corps and the day after that they would march on the enemy to attack him." He spoke to them with so much dignity, so much precision, so much talent, that they withdrew convinced that they finally had a real captain.[33]

Aware of his disadvantage, Bonaparte adopted from the outset an air of command that he was never to abandon in any circumstance, and just as he did not allow any familiarity, he took care not to show any emotion. When the ordnance officer Chauvet, one of his oldest acquaintances, died suddenly a few days after his arrival in Nice, he confided his dismay to Joséphine.[34] But when the supplier Collot wept over the death of their common friend, he said severely: "This is not the time to grieve, we have to remain entirely devoted to the army."[35] Despite this self-discipline, Marmont recalls, confidence and obedience did not come right away. However, it took only a few weeks for Bonaparte to establish himself as a "leader surrounded by his subordinates,"[36] quite unlike his predecessors, Kellermann and Schérer, who had paid little attention to etiquette, content to be the "first among equals." When Miot de Melito saw him in Brescia two months after the campaign began, the roles were already clear: "He crossed the rooms adjoining that in which he had received me, and gave some orders to Murat, Lannes, and Junot, his aides-de-camp, and the other officers in attendance. Every one maintained toward him an attitude of respect, and I may even say of admiration. I saw none of those marks of familiarity between him and his companions that I had observed in other cases, and which was consonant with republican equality. He had already assumed his own place, and set others at a distance."[37]

He had been able to breathe a new pride into an army that was suffering less from its material situation than from having been forgotten by glory—up to that point it had been involved only in secondary combats. Bonaparte promised his men that they would soon be able to say with pride: "I was in the army that conquered Italy!"[38] He had kept his promise. These men who had not left the slopes of the Alps for three years were now, thanks to him, in Milan, Bologna, and Livorno. His eloquence elevated his victories and increased his prestige in the same measure. Rather than counting on blind obedience, he addressed himself to the soldiers' imagination, assigning to each combat, no matter how modest, a prominent place in the annals of history. Having witnessed the resentment elicited in the ranks by the attempts made in the last years of the Old

Regime to introduce Prussian discipline in France, he was well aware that his soldiers were in no way robots and that they would feel insulted to be treated as mercenaries. He knew how to talk to them. Sometimes he excited their cupidity, sometimes their sense of honor. Thus, he said to his *brothers in arms* on May 20, 1796: "You have accomplished much; but does there remain nothing for you to do? Shall it be said of us that we knew how to win, but did not know how to take advantage of our victory? Will posterity reproach us for having found Capua in Lombardy? But I already see you running to your arms: a cowardly repose wearies you; days that are lost for glory are lost for your happiness. Well then! Let us go! We still have forced marches to make, enemies to subjugate, laurels to garner, insults to avenge."[39]

To those who distinguished themselves he shouted: "Brave [soldiers of the] 18th, I know you; the enemy will not hold before you."[40] And if they proved unworthy, it was again to their sense of honor that he appealed to get them to rise up again. On the banners of two regiments in the Vaubois division, whose men had shown "neither discipline, nor constancy, nor bravery" in facing the Austrians, he had these words written: "They are no longer part of the Army of Italy."[41] That was the refined language of his orders of the day and of his proclamations, which was very different from the language he actually used to address his troops. The following episode took place during the Egyptian campaign, but there is no reason to think that Bonaparte expressed himself differently in Italy: "I said to the light infantrymen: You're assholes: one grenadier is worth sixty light infantrymen. To the grenadiers I said: You're nothing but big capons, good enough to eat, but as for fighting, long live the light infantrymen! With that, you can kill everyone. That's true military eloquence. In Acre, when the 69th returned to the attack—and if it had persisted, Acre would have been taken that day [I said]: I'll give you skirts. Take off their pants. You've got no cock between your legs, you've only got a hole. Take the pants off these women! I made them cross the desert holding their rifles upside down. Then they worked miracles at Abukir."[42]

Because he spoke to his soldiers using their own words, they thought him their equal, especially because he knew how to give of himself and provide an example; courageous under fire, he did not spare his efforts. He was "gaunt, thin, his skin stuck to his bones, his eyes shone with a constant fever."[43] But by strength of will he succeeded in making people think that he had "a body that can endure interminable riding without fatigue; the power to sleep at any moment, and to wake whenever he pleases; a stomach which can digest anything, and makes no complaint at being put on short commons."[44] Though he was capable of making the humblest of his soldiers believe that he was no different from them, he was also capable of putting himself beyond compare: he knew not only how to address troops, but also how to astonish them. He was not one of those war leaders who attract the respect of their men by proving that "they are just as demanding of themselves as they are of their subordinates, that their harshness is a rule of conduct that owes nothing to caprice, and that they can be trusted under fire," but one of those who "win the affection and the admiration of their troops through their unexpected reactions and their capacity for improvisation and initiative."[45] His men felt that for him, war was not only a vocation: he blossomed in it.[46]

He could be severe, even pitiless, the contrary of a leader "sparing" of his men's blood. He has been reproached, not without justification, for an insensitivity to which he once confessed by saying that the sight of a dog howling alongside its dead master on one of the battlefields of the Italian campaign had moved him more than the sight of the bodies he left behind![47]

At the same time he was attentive to his soldiers' needs. He forgot them neither in his proclamations nor in his reports, citing their courage, their devotion, their ardor in combat, saying, regarding a dangerous engagement on the eve of the Battle of Castiglione: "I was not worried, the brave 32nd demi-brigade was there," and congratulating the rifleman Pelard, who had driven through "three enemy squads and . . . personally killed thirteen men."[48] Neither did he forget the requests for promotion and compensations that he regularly sent on to Paris, having lists of those who had distinguished themselves drawn up in order to "make known to the nation the courageous acts that distinguish this memorable campaign."[49] Finally he took the initiative of reestablishing, in the form of *armes d'honneur*, the military distinctions that had been abolished in 1791.[50] Bonaparte, declaring that he wanted in this way "to testify to the country's recognition of the brave soldiers who have distinguished themselves by outstanding actions," had ordered "eighty grenadiers' sabers and six cavalry sabers with a Damas blade, gilt handle, and worked by the best Italian craftsmen." On one side of the blade was inscribed "Given by General Bonaparte on behalf of the Executive Directory of the French Republic," and on the other side a description of the "brilliant act for which this saber has been given."[51] In this way the general strengthened the ties he had made with the troops and at the same time stimulated esprit de corps and competition between the units. He recognized that victory relies less on the motives that led to war or that are supposed to animate the men in combat—love of country, of liberty, or of any other abstraction—than on the comradeship that makes it each soldier's duty not to abandon another member of his regiment or stain by his conduct the unit's honor.[52] Citations, inscriptions on flags, the homage done the dead, bonuses, and congratulatory letters for brilliant actions—all this helped strengthen the sense of belonging that was so powerful that the integration of reinforcements—when they arrived in early 1797—turned out to be delicate to say the least. There were "the men of the Army of Italy" and then there were the others.[53]

If victories rapidly accumulated under Bonaparte's authority, it was partly because the booty made it possible to improve the army's material situation, replace salt meat by fresh every other day, distribute brandy, make shoes and uniforms, monitor the hygiene of the hospitals, give the soldiers their back pay, and above all pay half of it in coin rather than in devalued bank notes. The Directory had promised to do this too but had not yet come through.[54] Bonaparte did it without worrying about the repercussions of a step that amounted to greatly increasing pay and thus aggravated the government's financial difficulties, aroused the jealousy of other armies, and ran counter to the policy of the government, which at the same time was trying to get rid of the bank notes by placing them abroad, precisely by using them to pay the troops. The measure did more for Bonaparte's popularity than his most flattering proclamations, and we should not be surprised that his men henceforth accorded him the fidelity and loyalty they refused to a government that was incapable of meeting their needs.

It was Bonaparte—and to some extent himself—that General de Gaulle was thinking about when he wrote about the "prestige" indispensable for those who claim to lead men in combat. He said that this "fluid of authority," also called "charisma," proceeds first of all from an "elementary gift" and is for that very reason impossible to explain, and the more it is shaped and perfected by attention and constant effort, the greater is its force and durability. Confronted by suffering, in defeats and even in success, there can be no giving in to emotion. There is no liberty for the leader of an army who, in the circumstances of war, which are by definition mobile, must retain his impassiveness, always observing the greatest reserve. He must dissimulate joys and disappointments, be sparing in words and acts, calculate his appearances and absences in order to maintain his men's confidence in their leader's "inner strength" and thus exercise over them the "magnetism" without which he cannot impose the hardest of trials. "Who then is as taciturn as Bonaparte?" de Gaulle asks. "When he had become emperor, he sometimes expressed his feelings more openly, but only regarding politics; in his functions as a general he remained, on the contrary, impassive."[55] And de Gaulle adds: "Ascendancy arises precisely from the contrast between inner power and self-mastery."[56] If reserve and character are necessary for the art of commanding, grandeur is no less so. It is even their indispensable complement:

> What the leader orders must take on . . . the character of elevation. He must aim high and judge broadly, thus contrasting with the common person who struggles within narrow limits. He has to personify scorn for contingencies, whereas the mass of people is devoted to concern about details. . . . It is not a matter of virtue, and evangelical perfection does not lead to empire. The man of action can hardly be conceived without a dose of egoism, pride, severity, and ruse. But he is forgiven all that and he stands out even more if he makes these the means of achieving great things. Thus by satisfying everyone's secret desires, and by thus compensating for the constraints imposed, he charms his subordinates and, even if he falls by the wayside, he retains for them the prestige of the summits to which he was trying to lead them.[57]

Was Bonaparte's prestige damaged by his fall into the marshes at Arcole? The bonds he had woven with the troops were all the stronger because he seemed to know each battalion and each regiment by its number, each officer and almost each soldier by his name. Was he already keeping his famous record books, regiment by regiment, which were to allow him to follow their movements almost from day to day and to tell their story better than they could have told it themselves?[58] Perhaps, as he already seemed to have "his whole army in his head."[59] The soldiers whom he called by name were probably aware that there was some artifice in this; there was even more than they could have imagined—in reality none of the military leaders of the time was as separated from his men as Bonaparte was: a personal guard already protected him from both the enemy and his own troops. No statute had provided for the creation of a corps of this kind, but on May 30, 1796, near Verona, Bonaparte had miraculously escaped from an Austrian squad, and after that Bessières and a company of "guides" specially assigned to protect the general accompanied him everywhere. This did not prevent the men in the ranks from being flattered by the attention and comradeship he showed them. Besides, he was less interested in flattering the troops than in taking advantage of this nearness to impress the generals, even as his victories were raising him a little higher above them. He applied a maxim he was never to abandon: show lower-ranking subordinates the rough familiarity he denied their leaders:

> [He] had divined, with the peculiar insight he had into passions that could be of service to him, that to humiliate the chiefs was an infallible means of pleasing those in inferior places; and he affected from that time as much familiarity with the common soldiers as reserve and coldness with the officers. If he had no difficulty in writing to Grenadier Léon Aune: "My brave comrade, I love you as my son" (January 15th, 1800), it was because that was an easy way of purchasing popularity at the price of a still easier formula; he knew very well that this language meant nothing, and that the grenadier would never take advantage of such familiarity. He took good care not to speak thus to those who just before had been his equals. On the contrary, he studied to keep them at a distance, and usually made a display before them of this preference for the common soldiers, which gave him popularity in the ranks, in order to make their officers feel that they were now nothing but what they were through him.[60]

It was for the same reasons that, paradoxically, he tolerated and even encouraged in the generals the pillage that he tried to stop in the troops. The more the leaders stole, the more they compromised themselves, and the greater his hold over them—on the condition, of course, that he appeared to be the sole honest man in his army. He worked at it. Thus, he is supposed to have refused several million offered him by the Duke of Modena in exchange for his protection,[61] other sums offered by the Republic of Lucca,[62] and even seven million collected for him by the Venetian senate.[63] But when Marmont admitted that he had refused bribes offered by the city councils of Pavia and Loretta, Bonaparte reproached him severely.[64] His integrity was proportional to the ascendancy that he sought to exercise over his subordinates. He had another reason to be scrupulous in this regard: the supervision the government's representatives exercised over him. That is why, in this domain as well, the autumn of 1796 marked a turning point.[65] As soon as he had gotten rid of the representatives, he launched a search for "scoundrels," which, though it did not prove useless, did not fulfill its promises either. Many escaped, and only a few important figures were caught, notably the administrators of the Flachat company, which was protected by the Director Reubell, a "bunch of scoundrels with no real credit, without money and without morality" who had obtained the contract for the army's supplies.[66] However, the purge had another objective: to replace one clan of wheeler-dealers by another that was no less greedy but more connected with the general-in-chief. In fact, men known to be close to him, such as the suppliers Collot and Caillard, the bankers Haller, Hamelin, and Vitta-Cohen, or again Regnaud de Saint-Jean d'Angély and several of his associates such as Périllier and André Briche, took over the positions formerly held by the "scoundrels."[67] Was it then that Bonaparte began to reward himself for his virtuous conduct up to that point? No historian has dared to claim that Bonaparte did not receive a share of the pickings. He himself admitted that he had returned to France with a nest egg of 300,000 francs, two-thirds of which went to buy and furnish a town house on Rue Chantereine (later renamed Rue de la Victoire).[68] Only 300,000 francs?, one is tempted to ask. It is plausible, because Joséphine, when her husband was off in Egypt later, could not rely on any war treasure: she was herself forced to engage in dubious speculations in order to pay her bills, and when she bought Malmaison, she had to borrow enough to make the first payment.[69] But Italy certainly brought Bonaparte much more than these 300,000 francs, which were soon spent. There were rumors, and accusations in a few newspapers—unverifiable, of course—relating to cases of misappropriated money and percentages levied on the take.[70] Romain Hamelin alone provides precise facts, regarding operations that concerned the mercury mines in Idrija, in Slovenia, in April 1797:

> The conquest of Trieste and the surrounding country drew attention to the value of the mercury mine in Idrija, in the Carniola region. Collot, a meat supplier who had at that time the general's full confidence in financial matters, was sent there. He found four to five million francs' worth of quicksilver ready to be marketed; it was sold to him by a fictive deal at the rate of eighty-four sous per franc, the going price being three francs. The result was that the army's coffers received 1,200,000 francs, and Collot 1,000,000 for handling the costs. The rest was for Bonaparte, but he handed out large bonuses to his officers. . . . I do not remember them all, but there was: 100,000 francs for Berthier, 50,000 francs for Bernadotte; as much for Murat; as much for Friant; 12,000 francs for each of the general-in-chief's aides-de-camp; 100,000 francs for the chief ordnance officer Villemanzy.[71]

This one operation may thus have brought in a million for Bonaparte. Should we believe then, with Bourrienne, that he left out a zero when he talked about 300,000 francs?[72] That is far from implausible. Starting in early 1797, once he had firm control over the Army of Italy, he is supposed to have systematized pillaging, taking his own share of the spoils. It is true that unlike Augereau or Masséna, who didn't quite know what to do with so much money, he invested in his future by purchasing the loyalty of his lieutenants, the goodwill of foreign diplomats, the passivity of the French government, and the brush or the pen of all the artists and journalists who were singing his praises, not to mention the princely way of life he adopted after the end of the military campaign in 1797. Most of the money was spent in Italy, and he probably returned to France with relatively little—henceforth all-powerful, or almost, but certainly less wealthy than his officers.

The Attack on the Alps

At the end of 1796, things had not yet progressed that far. The campaign was not over. In the report sent to the Directory after Arcole, Bonaparte stated that this battle "[had just] decided the fate of Italy."[73] In reality he needed another victory to make Mantua finally capitulate. He had only a short moment of respite, which he used to rest his exhausted army, and when he stopped Alvinczy's second attempt to relieve Mantua he was nearly as outnumbered as he had been at Arcole, with half as many troops as the enemy.[74] Alvinczy had stuck with the plan that had proven so unsuccessful in November: while he himself moved down the right bank of Lake Garda with 28,000 men, generals Bayalitch and Provera came up from the east and threatened Verona. Facing the attackers, General Rey watched over the left bank of Lake Garda while Joubert guarded, at Corona, the right bank, thus covering the bulk of the French troops, with Masséna at Verona, and Augereau between Arcole and Legnago. Joubert retreated before Alvinczy's drive on the thirteenth and fell back on the plateau of Rivoli, so Bonaparte thinned his center in order to reinforce him. He assigned Augereau to drive back Bayalitch, at the risk of letting Provera reach Mantua if the latter went around him on his right. Masséna, leaving Verona, made a forced march to Rivoli, where his arrival the next day changed the outcome of a battle that had not begun well for Joubert, who had been attacked by forces superior in number. The result of the Battle of Arcole had been indecisive, but the pitched battle at Rivoli ended with an Austrian defeat that was so definitive—a veritable "annihilation," according to Clausewitz—that it sealed the fate of Italy, this time for good.[75] Masséna immediately passed from the left wing to the right to support Augereau and repel Provera, who was approaching from Mantua. Wurmser, who was still holed up in the citadel, capitulated and surrendered the fortress on February 2. "Thus," Thiers wrote in summarizing the outcome of these ten months of campaigning, "fifty-five thousand French had beaten more than two hundred thousand Austrians, taken more than eighty thousand, killed and wounded more than twenty thousand. They had fought twelve pitched battles and more than sixty actions, and crossed several rivers, in defiance of the waves and the enemy's fire."[76]

Rivoli coming after Arcole, a triumph that repaired a near disaster, we can judge the power of Bonaparte's ascendancy and the confidence he inspired in his men by the fact that in this way he was able to send them once again, without respite or almost, to attack the enemy columns. "In Italy," he was to say, "it was always one against three, but the soldiers had confidence in me." And he added: "Moral force, rather than numbers, may decide a victory."[77] And this time the victory was final. When it was all over, the reinforcements finally arrived, almost 20,000 men coming from the armies of the Sambre-et-Meuse and the Rhine, under the command of Generals Bernadotte and Delmas. Thus the expeditionary corps of 1796 was transformed into a genuine army. At Rivoli Bonaparte had been able to oppose Alvinczy with only 25,000 troops; he was now going to be able to count on 80,000.[78] "From then on," he later said, "the Army of Italy was capable of undertaking anything,"[79] and in particular the march on Vienna he had been dreaming about from the outset. In Paris the wave of enthusiasm produced by the victory at Rivoli had done away with the last resistance, and the Directory itself was beginning to dream of a pincers movement directed against the Austrian capital. The commanders of the armies of Italy (Bonaparte), the Rhine (Moreau), and Sambre-et-Meuse (Hoche) would join hands under the walls of the city. As soon as it was informed of the capitulation of Mantua, the government sent Bonaparte instructions ordering him to invade Austria through the Tyrol and to coordinate his movements with those of the armies of the Rhine.[80] The time for the great expedition had finally come. The Army of Italy, called upon in the 1796 plan to support the operations of the armies of Sambre-et-Meuse and the Rhine, became co-responsible for the proper execution of the 1797 plan, and Bonaparte was put on an equal footing with Moreau and Hoche. The Army of Italy and its leader had imposed this change by stealing the limelight from the great armies that had obtained such mediocre results in Germany, and Bonaparte intended to take full advantage of it to confound these same armies. The poor tactical choices made by the Austrians contributed to his success. They had entrusted command to Archduke Charles, their best military leader, who had left the banks of the Rhine, where he had distinguished himself against Moreau and Jourdan, to head for Innsbruck with 40,000 men. Bonaparte feared that Charles would attack Italy via the Tyrol, because the proximity of the Rhine would then allow him to increase the size of his army with significant reinforcements that would inevitably submerge the Army of Italy. How could Bonaparte resist if 100,000 Austrians descended on Verona? So he was pleasantly surprised to find that the archduke, leaving a simple garrison of 6,000 men in the Tyrol, headed with the bulk of his forces toward Friuli, so far from his bases that reinforcements would have to march twenty days or more to reach him. Bonaparte decided to take advantage of the favorable situation by launching an assault on the Alps.

On March 10, 1797, after a detour via Tolentino, in the Marche, to put the pope in his place, and while Joubert guarded the Tyrol with 17,000 men, the Army of Italy set out to attack the Alpine passes, eleven months to the day after the campaign had begun. To understand this final phase, we have to recall that in Germany the French armies were still stalled at the Rhine. These reverses had not been without consequences for the operations in Italy, because they had allowed the enemy to send reinforcements to the Tyrol and to rebuild several times the armies Bonaparte had destroyed. But Bonaparte was perhaps not as unhappy about his colleagues' failure as he claimed. Jourdan's and Moreau's problems made his own successes seem more brilliant, and made him seem, more than ever, to be the Republic's main support, the man who provided its wealth and its glory—in short, the indispensable man. Not without malice, he constantly asked the government whether it knew when Moreau and Hoche (who had replaced Jourdan) were going to cross the Rhine and come to his aid by marching on Vienna. In fact he was in no hurry to see them arrive. On the contrary: he hoped to defeat Austria without their help. He feared that if the armies joined, he would have to submit to these generals, who had the advantage of seniority; and above all, he was determined to do everything he could to avoid having to share the glory of the victory with anyone. That was why he so boldly sent his troops to attack the Alps, even as behind him, Italy, and especially the territory around Venice, was catching fire. The operation was dangerous especially due to the Italian political situation, which he had to handle with only 20,000 men, because the rest were at that very moment either beginning to climb with Joubert the slopes of the Tyrol or, with Masséna and Sérurier, marching toward the Tagliamento River. So far as the material difficulty of the enterprise—reaching Vienna via the Alps—is concerned, it is an exaggeration to maintain, like Thiers, that this was "the boldest military march recorded in history."[81] Nonetheless, without being technically impossible, the undertaking was politically risky. Determined to reach Vienna before Hoche, Bonaparte staked everything on this venture, at the risk of losing everything—Italy, his reputation, his glory.

In Russia in 1812 he was to find himself in this situation again, but in 1797 success justified his imprudence. He attacked at the right time: Archduke Charles was still waiting for the reinforcements that were supposed to ensure that his army had a crushing numerical superiority, and the battle was fought with almost the same number of troops on each side, 30,000 on the French side, 35,000 on the Austrian side.[82] The confidence of the French, which had been very strong since Rivoli, and the doubt that had eroded the Austrians' morale after so many reverses, did the rest. Charles did not seem at any time capable of stopping Bonaparte, let alone defeating him. Forced to abandon the Piave line on March 12, and then that of the Tagliamento on the sixteenth, he had to surrender the Tarvis pass to Masséna on the twenty-third—"We were fighting above the clouds, in the middle of the cloud, and on sheets of ice"[83]—and then Villach and Klagenfurt, in Austrian territory, which the French entered on March 28. Bonaparte could breathe again: victory was at hand, and there was not the slightest risk that Hoche would show up to steal the limelight from him, because for lack of boats he had not yet crossed the Rhine! He began to move only on April 16, by which time hostilities between France and Austria had been suspended. Bonaparte was not unaware of the risks he had taken, and it was in order to cover himself, in the unlikely event that his troops were driven back to Italy, that he constantly warned the government regarding the consequences of Hoche's inaction: "All the emperor's forces are in movement," he wrote on March 22, at the moment when Masséna was attacking the Tarvis pass, "and all the House of Austria's estates are preparing to oppose us. If troops are late in crossing the Rhine, it will be impossible for us to hold out for long. I am waiting impatiently for the reply to my message to find out if the Rhine has been crossed. . . . If . . . the armies of the Rhine delay resuming the offensive, I shall see myself, left alone against all, forced to retreat into Italy."[84] On April 1: "The Rhine has no doubt been crossed by now. I am awaiting the news with the greatest impatience."[85] The day before, seeing how far he had ventured from his bases—he had covered almost 650 kilometers in three weeks—he had written to Archduke Charles to propose putting an end to the bloodshed: "This sixth campaign," he said, "is preceded by ominous omens: whatever its outcome, we shall kill a few thousand men on both sides, and we will end up having to come to an agreement, because everything comes to an end, even passionate hatreds."[86]

Napoleon was later to write, in his account of the Italian campaigns, that he had decided to propose peace to the Austrians after the Directory told him that he must not count on any help from the armies of the Rhine:

> The armies of the Rhine-et-Moselle and Sambre-et-Meuse were supposed to move out and cross the Rhine the same day that the Army of Italy passed the Piave; they were to advance at top speed into Italy; Napoleon, reporting on the Battle of the Tagliamento, announced that he would soon cross the Julian Alps and be in the heart of Germany; that from the first to the tenth of April he would be in Klagenfurt, the capital of Carinthia, that is, sixty leagues from Vienna, and before April 20 at Semmering pass, twenty-five leagues from Vienna; that it was therefore important that the armies of the Rhine move out and that he be informed that they had done so. On March 23 the government replied, complimented him on the victory at the Tagliamento, excused itself for the fact that the armies of the Rhine had still not taken the field, and assured him that they would move without delay. But three days later, on March 26, it wrote to tell him that Moreau's army could not take the field; that it lacked boats to cross the Rhine, and that the Army of Italy must not count on the cooperation of the armies of Germany, but must count solely on its own resources.[87]

Napoleon said he had received this dispatch from the Directory on March 31: "Not being able to count on the aid of these two armies, Napoleon could no longer hope to enter Vienna; he did not have enough cavalry to descend into the plain of the Danube. But he could easily get as far as the Semmering pass. He thought that the greatest advantage he could draw from his position was to sign a peace treaty."[88] He therefore wrote to Archduke Charles the letter of March 31 quoted above. In reality it seems that Bonaparte decided to negotiate, and thus took the risk of not obtaining the most advantageous peace treaty possible, even before he learned exactly what was happening on the Rhine. Six days after the Directory had allegedly informed him that Moreau and Hoche had not moved, he wrote to General Clarke, who was at that time (April 5) in Piedmont: "So here we are masters of three provinces of the House of Austria and thirty leagues from Vienna, but I have not heard that the Rhine has been crossed, and I confess that this worries me very much. . . . Every day I wait with impatience to learn whether the Rhine has been crossed, [because] no doubt I am not expected to guard Italy and overthrow the House of Austria with 50,000 men"[89]—which proves that his main objective was to finish the war against Austria by himself, whatever concessions his escapade might oblige him to make later on. He cared little about that: Hoche and Moreau, who had been guilty of inaction, would have to take the blame. His feigned concern about their movements, or rather their lack of movement, had no other source.

Archduke Charles did not dare take responsibility for responding to these overtures, so the war continued. Masséna resumed his march. Charles was defeated on April 2 at Neumarkt, and on the third at Unzmarkt. On the sixth, the French entered Judenburg, and on the seventh their vanguard reached the little town of Leoben, four days' march from Vienna. This time the alarm in the Austrian capital was so great that the archduke was ordered to respond favorably to the French general's offers and to ask for a ceasefire, which was immediately granted him. It was April 7, 1797. Bonaparte, who had come so close to catastrophe, had won a complete victory and the Italian campaign was over.

TWELVE

Mombello

$\mathcal{T}$he preliminary peace agreements with the Austrians were signed on April 18, 1797, and Bonaparte returned to Milan, where Joséphine had come to join him. They moved into a large villa situated north of the Lombard capital, at Mombello.[1] From the top of the hill on which it was perched, one could see the immense Lombard plain stretching away to the south, and to the north, the still-snow-covered crests of the Alps.[2] Bonaparte lived there for four months, until he left for Udine, where he was to resume peace negotiations with the Austrians. From Mombello he could easily reach Milan, where work awaited him, and several times, when the heat was too great, he took his wife, his officers, and his entourage on an excursion to the nearby lakes. On the shores of Lake Como and Lake Maggiore, the general rested from the ordeals of war. Miot de Melito accompanied them on the day they went to visit the Borromean Islands: "I was in Bonaparte's carriage, with his wife and Berthier. All the way he was gay, animated, told us several anecdotes about his youth, and told us that he had just turned twenty-eight. He was very attentive to his wife, and frequently took conjugal liberties with her that did not fail to embarrass Berthier and me; but these free manners were imbued with such a strong sentiment of affection and tenderness . . . that they could easily be excused."[3]

Joséphine's feelings for her husband were no stronger than they had been when they got married; their love had not entirely burned out (they never got to that point), but the passion that consumed Bonaparte had greatly cooled. They were moving, not without ups and downs, toward an equilibrium.

The Absent Wife

Bonaparte, we recall, had left his wife a few hours after marrying her. In the letters he wrote her almost every day he said he was racked by a fever that left him no peace, not even at night, especially not at night—"Adieu, adieu, I am going to bed without you, I shall sleep without you, I beg you, let me sleep."[4] And before he took the field he sent her one of the most beautiful letters ever written by a husband to his wife:

> I have not spent a single day without writing to you; I have not spent a night without holding you in my arms; I have not drunk a cup of tea without cursing the glory and ambition that keep me far away from the soul of my life. Amid my activities, at the head of the troops, in moving through the camps, my adorable Joséphine is the only woman in my heart, she occupies my mind, absorbs my thought. If I am moving away from you with the speed of the waters of the Rhône, it is the sooner to see you again. If in the middle of the night I arise to work again, that is because it might advance by a few days the arrival of my sweet friend. . . . Joséphine! Joséphine! Do you remember what I sometimes told you: nature made my soul strong and decisive; it has made you of lace and gauze.[5]

Joséphine's replies, which were infrequent and laconic, were so cold that on reading them he felt "the iciness of death." "Absence cures one of little passions and increases the great ones," he wrote to her, and though he said he loved her more every day, he reproached her for no longer thinking about him now that he was far away.[6] A month had not passed since their wedding before he accused her of being unfaithful to him. For her part, she was already weary. It wasn't that she regretted a marriage from which she was deriving such unexpected dividends; she owed to her husband's military successes the spectacular revival of her credit with bankers, and she even experienced a kind of apotheosis when on May 9, 1796, Murat and Junot delivered to the Directory the flags taken from the enemy in Italy. A large crowd attended the ceremony organized at the Luxembourg palace. Joséphine was radiant, Mmes Tallien and Récamier, with flowers in their hair, played the role of her ladies of honor. She was uneasy, however; Bonaparte never ceased to ask her to join him: "Hurry, come, come!"[7] It was annoying, she was so at ease; she was also reluctant to separate from Hortense; and above all, she was in love. The lucky man was a lieutenant in the hussars named Hippolyte Charles. He was twenty-eight years old, had an athlete's build, a magnificent mustache, a southern accent, and unfailing good humor, knew better than anyone how to tie a cravat, and had such a pretty face that "Mmes Récamier, Tallien, and Hamelin [lost] their heads."[8] In short, he was as pleasant to be around in bed as in a parlor. How could she, and especially why would she, resist him? Joséphine had fallen in love at first sight, and she was so mad about this "little figure for whores"—the expression is Napoleon's—that when she learned that her lover was going to leave for Italy she made every effort to see that he remained in Paris. As soon as she had achieved her goal, there was no longer any question of her going to Milan, and when Murat insisted, she ended up telling him it was impossible: she was pregnant. She had not thought about the consequences of this lie, but when she realized what she had done, she hastened to write her husband a letter that was "short, sad, and written in a trembling hand." Bonaparte believed her, gave up trying to persuade her to make such a tiring journey, and, worried by the tone of her letter, told her he was ready to do anything to make her happy: "Rather than know that you are melancholic, I would give you a lover myself."[9] He didn't realize how right he was.

Those were just words. Every day he hoped she would arrive in Milan. In vain. He felt he was foundering. He wrote her feverish letters to reproach her for her coolness and insensitivity; he assumed she had lovers and told her that because she no longer loved him, she could take back her freedom: "Adieu, my happiness, my life, everything that existed for me on Earth!!!"[10] Feeling that he was living "a nightmare,"[11] he set out for Tortona, where he had to put down the revolt of the imperial fiefs, and while the mobile columns were burning villages and shooting suspects, he awaited every evening the mail from Paris. But nothing came, nothing, despite his pleas: "My tears flow, no more peace nor hope."[12] A moment afterward, not being able to believe that "so much promised love" had already evaporated, he started hoping again. A letter from Murat saying that Joséphine was indisposed—her pregnancy, no doubt—sufficed to calm him. He felt himself come back to life, but ashamed to have been glad that she was ill, he was at the same time assailed by dark presentiments: What if she had died? He now begged her to take care of her health, to pardon him for having written such extravagant letters, and to further put off her departure.

But hardly had the letter been sent off than he was writing her another in which he implored her again to come without delay.

A surprise awaited him on June 13, 1796, on his return from the expedition to central Italy: Joséphine had arrived in Milan. Weary of resisting, she had finally resigned herself to going, and she had wept as she packed her trunks. "Poor woman," Arnault later said, "she broke down in tears, sobbing as if she were going to be tortured: she was going to reign!"[13] She had left Paris with a heavy heart, but followed by an imposing cortege of servants and friends, among whom Hippolyte Charles occupied a prominent place. She hoped that these familiar faces would make the exile to which she was doomed less trying. She had to submit to the attacks, reproaches, and oaths of her mad husband. He was so happy that he believed, or pretended to believe, the story she told him about a late menstruation that had led the doctors to think she was pregnant. Their reunion was fortunately as brief as the honeymoon in March: two days later he was on horseback, already far away, gone to fight the Austrians. But she had had to promise to follow him. He was once again very excited, and he sent her "a thousand loving kisses everywhere, everywhere."[14] He was mistrustful enough, though, to read her mail before having it delivered to her.[15] On July 25 she joined her husband in Brescia. These wanderings were not to her taste, and as if it weren't enough to be constantly on the road, she soon discovered that she had ended up in the middle of a war. Near Mantua, on the twenty-ninth, her carriage was fired upon. Terrified, but protected by a small escort, she fled as far as Florence. The only sunny moment of this dark summer occurred in Brescia on the night of August 17, when she managed to arrange a tête-à-tête with her lover Hippolyte.[16] This was not easy; she was never alone, and probably surrounded by spies who reported everything to the husband, whom she was, however, lucky enough to see only now and then. Bonaparte suffered from these separations, which he filled, as was his habit, with passionate, jealous, worried, and desperate letters in which by turns he expressed his love for his "sweet" and "adorable" Joséphine and called her "mean," "ugly," and "easy," sending her "a million kisses as ardent as the Equator," told her how much he was languishing in his "little dark forest," and threatened to return when she least expected him: "Who could this marvelous new lover be who absorbs all your moments, rules tyrannically over your days, and prevents you from thinking about your husband? Joséphine, beware, some fine night the doors will fly open and I'll be in your bed. You know! Othello's little dagger!"[17]

She did not receive this note sent from Verona on November 23: without saying anything she had left Milan for a journey toward Genoa, accompanied by Hippolyte, not knowing that at the same time her husband would come home sooner than anticipated in order to welcome General Clarke, who was arriving from Paris. It was as if Bonaparte had received a violent blow to the head. Finding the Serbelloni palace empty, he fainted, and for four endless days he felt, he said, "an incalculable unhappiness."[18] Perhaps it is from this episode that we must date the change that occurred in their relationship. Certainly it was following these events that Napoleon began the long series of his mistresses of a day or an hour. A former aide-de-camp recounts:

> The Marquise de Bianchi, who was eighteen or nineteen years old, appeared before the general-in-chief wearing a black silk dress, a garment allotted to Italian prostitutes, and demanded twenty-five horses belonging to her husband, which had been taken away from him in the Parma area; she obtained them by trading favor for favor. Then a virtuoso *di canto*, a woman named Ricardi, who had come specially from Venice to be the ornament of the Verona opera, was received at the Florentine academy. She pleased the general-in-chief, and the next day Duroc gave her a carriage and a team of six horses; but she refused a roll of a hundred louis that was also presented to her. . . . Mlle Campini, a seventeen-year-old dancer who passed for a virgin and was continually under her mother's guard, arrived in Milan from Genoa. She was supposed to dance in a ballet. . . . It was at one of these performances that Mlle Thérèse Campini's graces and large eyes conquered the conqueror of Italy. This intrigue, fed by a great deal of money and magnificent gifts, lasted more than a month. Mlle Campini was succeeded by a furrier's daughter from the south who had married a certain Caula, a Piedmontese patriot who had been hanged in effigy and who, having taken refuge in France, said rather gaily: *I was very cold on the day I was hanged.* . . . He went to Milan with his wife, who immediately

pleased the general. She was seen in Turin carrying the portrait of the hero on a gold chain around her neck.[19]

Napoleon later denied these fleeting affairs, telling Gourgaud: "What would have happened to a general of twenty-five if he had run after women?"[20] But he didn't have to "run." These moments stolen from work demanded little effort from him—for, as he also said, "all the ladies of Italy were at the disposal of the liberator of their country." He had only to choose among them.[21] The moments of despair he had experienced in Milan in November were also the last. The very tone of his letters changed, became less passionate and more affectionate. In only a few weeks he was to call Joséphine to his bedside: "I need you because I think I am going to be very sick."[22] These are the words of a husband rather than those of a lover. In short, it was the end of a passion that had lasted a year. Perhaps the scene in Milan was only the revelation of what the passion he had felt for Joséphine had fed on during her absence. It was a mental love in which imagination played a large role. He loved her all the more because she was far away, and to that rickety relationship he gave, through writing and imagination, proportions that it was far from possessing, so disappointing was it in reality. The love that united them existed in his head alone.[23] The end of the fighting also contributed to the calming of their relations. He loved her less, or differently, as soon as they began to be together for longer periods of time, and not just between two stays at the front. But at the same time, living alongside her he felt his esteem for his wife growing. That was when he understood everything that she could bring him: not the love she didn't feel, but friendship, tenderness, support he could count on, and the grace that won over everyone and enhanced his successes. With a wife like Joséphine, who was capable of conducting herself like a queen without anyone being tempted even for a moment to laugh at her, the general's glory seemed less recent. His wife's innate elegance gave her a kind of patina; with Joséphine on his arm, he looked less like a fortunate general who was also a parvenu. He was not to forget this. On the other hand, it is not clear that Joséphine understood that she had hit the jackpot. She was bored—"to death," she admitted shortly after her arrival in Milan[24]—and time did not change anything in that regard. The Italians bored her, Italy bored her; she had no taste for the contemplation of either landscapes or artistic masterpieces. She missed her children, her "friends from Chaillot," and especially Paris. She was inconsolable, especially because she no longer saw Hippolyte, who had left for Rome with Marmont. He alone could have comforted her. Her husband, although he spent "all day adoring [her] as if [she] were a divinity,"[25] could not play this role. So she longed for the end of this absurd war in this dreadful country, and it was without any joy that after the fighting ceased she moved into Mombello. Any small amount of pleasure she might have felt was immediately spoiled by the reunion of the Bonaparte family.

A Summer in Lombardy

Only Lucien was not present at the reunion. He had come to Italy to see his brother a few months earlier, but their meeting had been brief. Napoleon could not forgive the carelessness with which Lucien was meeting the obligations of his office as a war representative that he had obtained for him, while the younger brother reproached his elder for not having treated him as well as his other male siblings. Refusing to deal any longer with this "very bad person,"[26] Napoleon had taken advantage of the fact that Corsica had once again become a French possession to send the young man there. In Ajaccio, Lucien was impatiently fulfilling subaltern functions.

But Louis was with Napoleon—he was serving in the Army of Italy as an aide-de-camp, and so was Joseph. When the Italian campaign began, the eldest Bonaparte was in Genoa with Julie and their daughter Zénaïde, managing the affairs of the Clary family. He had gone to meet Napoleon, who had asked him to take to Paris the news of the Cherasco armistice. Joseph had taken advantage of this mission to introduce himself into the capital's political circles and to establish relationships that might someday prove useful to him: In October 1796 he got himself appointed resident minister of the French Republic in Parma, with a salary of 18,000 francs payable in cash. That wasn't bad, but it wasn't enough. Rather than going to take up his position, Joseph preferred to return to Corsica, following the republican troops. He recuperated what he could of the family's scattered property, had the house on Rue Malherba refurbished, and, on the strength of being in the camp of the victors, had himself elected delegate of the department of Liamone (Ajaccio) on the Council of Five Hundred. But just as he had not gone to Parma, he did not go to Paris for the opening of the legislative session; he returned to his brother in Italy. He didn't have to wait long to see himself rewarded as he thought he should be: on May 6, 1797, he was appointed "Minister Plenipotentiary of the Republic to the Court of Rome," a title that was replaced eight days later by that of ambassador, which sounded better and brought in more: 60,000 francs in cash. It was about Joseph that Frédéric Masson wrote these lines full of cleverness and truth regarding the emperor's brothers and sisters:

> They considered that what they received from him was their due: they had not the slightest taste for recognizing that they were obliged to him, not the slightest idea of attributing to him what they had become. They did not want to be pushed: they would say that they were self-made. . . . Besides, they were not at all surprised by what was happening to them, by the fairy tale in which they moved, by this marvelous adventure that, in only a few days, had freed them from all financial concern and opened all doors to them, carried them all the way along paths on which the day before they could hardly imagine ever setting foot; they were not worried about seeming out of place, they did not fear making mistakes or doing something silly; they had no concern for responsibilities; they had a self-confidence that was not even accompanied by a sense of the duties high position entailed. And this self-confidence sustained them despite everything, and so long as their luck held, it made easy for them things that to others seemed simply impossible. Their self-confidence lent them, in the elevated positions they occupied, a relaxed air that distinguished them from the common people, an ease of manners that prevented the two from being confused, an aplomb that one might think proceeded from an illustrious birth, a refined education, or a superior mind, a way of being generous and magnificent that cannot be learned, the ability not to be intimidated by anything or anybody, the audacity to attempt everything, the certainty of succeeding everywhere—in short, all the attributes of genius, except for genius.[27]

As for Pauline, she had also been in Italy for some time. She had come, chaperoned by Uncle Fesch, at Napoleon's request. Sixteen years old, she was a mixture of a spoiled child and a forward young girl who had grown up too fast. She was a birdbrain in a superb woman's body. She stuck out her tongue, made faces, kicked people under the table, and a moment later she would be found hidden in a corner giving herself to the first man who came along. Her brother wanted to get her out of the grip of Fréron, with whom—encouraged by Lucien—she had become infatuated to the point of talking about marriage. The former member of the Convention was nearly three times her age, his hands were dripping with blood, he had a dreadful reputation, and he wasn't worth a penny. Bonaparte vetoed the idea and asked Fesch to take Pauline to Italy, where, no doubt, she would forget her not very attractive suitor. When Joseph reached the Lombard capital after his interlude in Ajaccio, the family circle gradually reconstituted itself. Mme Bonaparte finally arrived on June 1, bringing with her Caroline, Jérôme, and Élisa, the latter accompanied by Félix Bacciochi, a distant cousin she had just married. She had come from Marseille and was in a hurry to get back to Ajaccio, where Joseph had made preparations for her return. Her reason for coming to Italy was not to make the acquaintance of her daughter-in-law. In March 1796 Napoleon had stopped off in Marseille, where he had told his mother about the marriage. One can imagine Letizia's reaction; it took her ten days to sign the—very dry—letter of congratulations to her new daughter-in-law that Joseph had written for her.[28] She hated her. In her view, Joséphine was the "Parisian woman, a woman of bad morals and expensive habits, untidy and wasteful, the great lady who would make people feel embarrassed and timid . . . a woman already matronly and who one [could] not believe would bear Napoleon children!"[29] Seeing her only encouraged Letizia in the silent war she henceforth waged against this "charmer" who had stolen her son from her.[30]

At present Letizia had another concern that justified her journey to Milan: Élisa—or rather her husband. For Letizia, Bacciochi had the immense advantage of being Corsican, and from Ajaccio to boot. But Napoleon had opposed the marriage on that ground as well. He was reluctant to see his sister marry a man who did not conceal his ties to the Pozzo di Borgo clan, which had been responsible for the family's proscription in 1793.[31] Madame Bonaparte did not allow herself to be intimidated, and having married her daughter in spite of Napoleon's opposition, she was now coming to "regularize" this union. Napoleon did not make a scene with either his sister or his mother; he consented, and even promised the young husband the command of the fortress of Ajaccio—a way of showing him that he considered him as a negligible quantity—but in exchange he demanded that Pauline give up Fréron and immediately marry General Leclerc. Had he surprised his sister and the officer in a compromising situation? Was Leclerc, who had long been in love with Pauline, waiting only until Fréron was out of the way to declare himself? In any case the matter was quickly settled, and on June 14 Pauline's wedding to Leclerc was blessed by the priest of a parish near Mombello. A month had not gone by before the family scattered again: Joseph went to Rome and his mother went to Ajaccio, taking with her Jérôme, Caroline, Fesch, Élisa, and Bacciochi.

The "King" of Mombello

There is no doubt that Mombello closely resembled a court, as is often said. Outside the private circle formed for a short period by Joséphine, Eugène, Louis, a few close friends, and the rest of the family, it was a hive of activity, an almost uninterrupted stream of "ministers of Austria, of the pope, of the kings of Naples and Sardinia, of the republics of Genoa and Venice, of the Duke of Parma, of the Swiss cantons, and of several German princes; of generals, the authorities of the Cisalpine Republic, and delegates of cities; couriers from Paris, Rome, Naples, Vienna, Florence, Venice, Turin, and Genoa who came and went at all hours."[32] The congestion was such that the villa's sitting rooms were not spacious enough, so that a vast tent had been erected in the garden, under which certain receptions took place. The guards commanded by Bessières had given way to a regiment of 300 Polish volunteers who protected the master from unwelcome visitors and escorted, every afternoon, the privileged persons authorized to watch him eat from an elevated gallery.[33] Bonaparte dined in public, an ostentatious practice even if his intention was to imitate, not Louis XIV, but rather the Italian princes who had established that custom in order to imitate the Sun King. Norvins is right: just as Bonaparte had acquired "the habit of absolute command" during the military operations of the campaign, "he contracted the manners of a monarch" at Mombello,[34] where the possibility of approaching him was not accorded equally to everyone, where his schedule was governed by strict rules, where a kind of etiquette was beginning to be established; where, in short, he was already living in the world of "omnipotence," separated from everyone and notably from "his most famous generals through their acknowledgment of his superiority."[35] The poet Arnault, who had come to Italy with General Leclerc (he was a witness at the latter's marriage to Pauline), is supposed to have told Regnaud de Saint-Jean d'Angély that Bonaparte seemed to him "a man apart."[36] Those who had known Bonaparte when he was less famous and less powerful reacted the same way. Unprecedented success had transfigured him. Thus, when Carrion de Nisias, a friend of Hippolyte Charles to whom Napoleon was later to entrust various diplomatic missions, saw him in Milan shortly after the Italian campaign began, he was greatly disappointed: "What!" he confided to his diary, "this is the Bonaparte whose name fills all Europe. . . . How different he is from the picture my imagination had painted of him! On these pale and withered cheeks, in this downcast face, under these staring and melancholic eyes, I seek in vain the physiognomy of the conquering hero I had imagined."[37] A year later, the magic had worked its effect, and it was no longer the same man that Nisias saw again: "I didn't have enough eyes, enough ears to grasp his features, his gestures, his looks, his least remarks," he wrote after a brief conversation with the great man on October 10, 1797. "There is Bonaparte in front of me! I touch him, I see him, I hear him! An inexpressible quiver, a religious shock causes my heart to beat faster, and I feel an unknown disorder throughout my being."[38] The diplomat Trouvé, who saw Bonaparte when he was returning to his post in Naples, said much the same in a letter sent to La Réveillière from Mombello:

> I write you from the residence of glory. . . . I am in the countryside with my little family, at the home of General Bonaparte, who made me an invitation too flattering and pleasant to be resisted, no matter how much I want to go quickly to my post. In embracing in him French and republican glory, I felt myself as penetrated by affection as I was by admiration. . . . The general-in-chief is outwardly very imposing. Although [he is] affable and gay, all his officers approach him only with

respect, because he is severe and allows no familiarity. He has around him his wife, his sister, a young brother, and seems to be a father to the family that everyone reveres. But he is not yet twenty-eight years old. . . . I had, based on your testimony, an elevated notion of his politics. I recognized, through his conversation, how much he is a true statesman. . . . General Clarke is also in this house; Berthier comes to dine there almost every day; all three of them are great workers; the most intimate union seems to reign among all these defenders of the Republic; but Bonaparte rises above them by his genius, by his great and powerful conceptions. The Marquis de Gallo [a Neapolitan diplomat] has just arrived here. . . . It is a treat for this young Fabricius to see this new Cineas coming to find him in the place where he is enjoying a little repose, and [to see] the pride of the courts bow down before the sublime simplicity of a republican hero. No day passes without a visit from the envoys of the powers, with whom, as one can easily see, he maintains perfectly the dignity of the nation that his exploits have so glorified. I seek in the annals of peoples ancient and modern models to compare with him for military, political, administrative talent, and I see no one who, even by uniting them all to the same degree as he does, has ever done so many great things in so little time.[39]

However, Marmont, who was then living in intimate contact with the general, has painted a different portrait, saying that once he had returned to his "interior," or to the company of the officers of his staff, Bonaparte was unaffected and always approachable as soon as he had finished with his work, liking to laugh and make "jokes that were gay and in good taste, never in any way bitter," and even taking part in the games of his entourage.[40] But if as soon as he arrived in Italy he had marked out his distance from other generals, what sort of familiarity should we now imagine with a man who had already been made so impressive in the eyes of his contemporaries by his natural disposition to command, the habit of exercising it that he had acquired, his constantly growing success, his influence and his power? In his presence, the generals were all a little awkward. We know how much he liked to get his familiars together for long conversations on a subject of his choosing, in which he not only "knew how to listen" but allowed his interlocutors the greatest liberty. Inevitably, most of them agreed with him. A kind of courtier-like behavior tinged these gatherings, and his favorite conversationalists, like Monge, were not the most insolent. But he could be contradicted. On the other hand, it was the sign of the dominance he already had over them that no one ever considered interrupting him. That was the misfortune of the army supplier Fortuné Hamelin:

> One evening when not many people were there, the general was sitting on the arm of a chair surrounded by a group that was listening to him respectfully. He was talking about astronomy with Monge and Abbé Oriani. In the course of the discussion, he happened to mention the parallax of the fixed stars. Everyone kept silent, but I, like a complete fool, interrupted him by saying that he was wrong, because of the length of the sides of the triangle, in proportion to which its base was negligible. Everyone lowered his eyes, and I had not finished my argument before I felt that I had done something stupid, and that I would have done much better to keep my mouth shut. Bonaparte looked at me with eyes that augured nothing good, but a moment later he came up to me and said to me: "So you've studied astronomy." "General, I have always tried to educate myself." "I wouldn't have thought so." From that day on, he treated me politely.[41]

If he did so, it may have been because, having learned his lesson, Hamelin didn't make the same mistake twice.

Clever Propaganda?

"The sublime simplicity of a republican hero": that was how Bonaparte appeared to Trouvé. The image was established after the battle of Arcole: "People everywhere admired that persevering genius, which, with fourteen or fifteen thousand men against forty thousand, had never thought of retreating; that inventive and profound genius, which had the sagacity to discover in the dikes of Ronco a new field of battle, that rendered numbers of no avail. . . . They extolled, in particular, the heroism displayed at the bridge of Arcole, and the young general was everywhere represented with the colours in his hand, amidst fire and smoke."[42] But Arcole did not create Bonaparte's glory: it had been growing apace since Lodi. From that point on, he was everywhere: in the newspapers, in the poems and songs dedicated to him, in the theater where the actors interrupted their performances to announce his victories, and everywhere his portrait was seen—painted, sculpted, engraved, reproduced even on dozens of medals struck in France, in Italy, and all over Europe.[43] "It was the first time since the Revolution," Mme de Staël observed, "that a proper name was in everyone's mouth . . . people talked about nothing but this man who was [soon] to put himself in the place of all and to make the human race anonymous by monopolizing fame for himself alone."[44] It has often been said that the unanimity of this concert of praise that rose, steadily more deafening, to honor Bonaparte—the conqueror of Italy, that new Hannibal, that new Alexander, or new Caesar—was a myth, its spontaneity a lie, the role played by fabrication and indoctrination being so manifest that nothing would be easier to explain than the formation of the Napoleonic legend. As Jean Tulard put it, "He forged his own legend. His genius was to have understood very early the importance of propaganda."[45]

Even if Bonaparte was the main author of his legend, the Directory would be his co-author, having done nothing to impede its rise. The Directory gave the Army of Italy's victories all the more prominence because the other armies had achieved few successes; and given that it could not itself announce to the French people good news about internal matters, which in all respects remained calamitous, it needed these successes abroad to add a few touches of light to a sky that was so dark. The directors themselves, as wary as they were of Bonaparte, succumbed to the enthusiasm that within a few hours consoled the country for the difficulties of all kinds that were assailing it. "Immortal glory to the victors of Lodi!" they had written to him. "Honor to the general-in-chief who was able to prepare the bold attack on the bridge!"[46] It was Carnot who told Bonaparte: "You are the hero of the whole of France."[47] The Directory called him the "great captain" and the "benefactor and legislator of a free people."[48] When the first ceremony was organized to pay homage to the "intrepid defenders of the fatherland" on May 29, 1796, Bonaparte's name was not mentioned.[49] But he was already the sole hero of a fete in honor of victories that everyone knew they owed to him, and to him alone: "Anyone else, in his place, would have been defeated," wrote Marmont to his father, "and he simply moved from triumph to triumph."[50]

All the same, let us agree that Bonaparte had a "genius for publicity."[51] Cynics will say that he had learned Machiavelli's lesson: the prince is judged on appearances rather than on his true nature, so he must cultivate the art of being a "great simulator and dissimulator" if he wants to be able to "manipulate people's brains by ruse."[52] Other people will point out—and this is not incompatible with the first explanation—that Bonaparte had grasped the power of public opinion in modern societies and understood that "the reign of opinion had [just] been substituted for that of birth."[53] For him it was not yet a matter of appropriating a political legitimacy that he could oppose to that of the government, but only of winning, along with popularity, the freedom of action and independence that, delivering him from the strict supervision of the Directory's agents, would allow him to carry out his military plan all the way to the end. He had to dazzle people in order to emancipate himself. He did not neglect any means of arriving at this goal. In order to be convinced of this, it suffices to read the proclamations and letters in which it was especially a question of himself, of *his* war, of *his* army, of *his* conquests. We just have to recall that on the day after Lodi, understanding that he now had the kind of exploit that pleases the crowds, he had asked a young artist to paint the scene;[54] to recall that he was soon to create in Italy newspapers that would play a significant role in the construction of his image as the "citizen general" and that, even if they were never very widely circulated in France, would find numerous echoes in the national press.[55] "Through Italy, Bonaparte imposed himself on France."[56] Must we then see in him above all the "fatal charlatan element" to which Thomas Carlyle referred?[57]

In the genesis of the myth, neither the role of fabrication nor that of propaganda should be exaggerated. Besides, the effectiveness of the latter generally depends on the consent of those to whom it is addressed; it does not have the power to govern minds, and even in the most authoritarian regimes it is to the police, rather than to propaganda, that the absence of any dissident voice must be attributed. Neither the Directory nor its police, and still less Bonaparte, had such a power in 1796. If there was propaganda, it responded to the public's expectations and desires. By overemphasizing the importance of artifice, one fails to see that the Army of Italy's victories seemed sufficiently extraordinary for contemporaries to admire them spontaneously, and after Lodi Bonaparte was not the only one who saw himself "in history": numerous artists, both Italian and French, also saw him that way and wanted to represent the hero.[58] We can hardly be surprised to see the passage over the Lodi bridge represented so often and in so many different ways: it was a brilliant action that no doubt violated "the geometrical laws of strategy," as Clausewitz put it, but touched on "the soul of war."[59] As for Bonaparte's entry into Milan as seen by Andrea Appiani, it summoned up Roman generals' triumphs, and it was not just once that such news arrived from Italy, but almost every day: "The rapidity of these successes, and the number of the prisoners, surpassed everything that had yet been seen."[60] All this counted in the shaping of public opinion, which was so powerful that even Bonaparte's detractors—and there were some—had to admit that what was happening on the other side of the Alps was not banal. These exploits were further magnified by the reverses suffered in Germany. From that moment on, the figures of Moreau and Bonaparte were contrasted with each other: Moreau the prudent, wise leader who spared his men's blood, and whose skillful retreat through Germany was admired; Bonaparte, the bold general who took immense risks but won astounding victories. Moreau made people feel safer, Bonaparte made them enthusiastic. If the vicissitudes of the war beyond the Rhine benefited Bonaparte, the epic tale of his battles was enhanced still further by the brilliant style of his reports, bulletins, and proclamations: "Bonaparte completed with his pen the conquests of his sword," Emil Ludwig justly observed.[61]

These reports were not as mendacious as one might imagine. In fact, there is nothing truer than the report addressed to the government after the Battle of Arcole. Bonaparte hides nothing, neither his troops' breach of duty nor the generals' bravery, nor Augereau's role. He does not present a travesty of reality, but he magnifies it; his style is that of a writer, not that of a military leader: "I am so exhausted with fatigue, Citizen Directors," he admits to them, "that it is impossible for me to tell you about all the military movements that preceded the Battle of Arcole."[62] The account that follows is lively, breathless, and uneven, like the fighting itself. It talks about fatigue, courage, cowardice, surprise, a surge of morale, sacrifice, suffering, and death in the midst of gloomy marshes. Under Bonaparte's pen, war, far from being "a mathematical operation," becomes a "passionate drama" in which horror mixes with grandeur, inhumanity with virtue.[63] The letters he wrote to Muiron's widow or to General Clarke, whose nephew had also lost his life at Arcole, are imbued with a grandeur—affected, no doubt—that touched the hearts of that era. This is true especially of the second of these letters: "He died with glory and facing the enemy. . . . What reasonable man would not envy him such a death? Who would not, in the vicissitudes of life, abandon himself to leave in that way a world so often contemptible? Who among us has not regretted a hundred times not having been thus spared the powerful effects of calumny, envy, and all the hateful passions that seem almost exclusively to direct human conduct?"[64]

Gros's *Bonaparte au pont d'Arcole* is a kind of pictorial transposition of these letters. The young painter, whom his teacher David had sent to Italy to perfect his art, was introduced to the general by Joséphine. Bonaparte received him kindly in Milan, flattered that a pupil of the great David would want to paint his portrait. Having told Gros that David wanted to paint the battle of Lodi himself, Bonaparte added that he had in mind "a few other good subjects,"[65] and Gros was soon assigned to represent the scene at the Arcole bridge. Bonaparte posed twice, if one can call posing the lightning visits he made to the painter, so agitated that Joséphine, it is said, took him on her knees so that he would hold still for a moment. Gros painted two copies of the picture and long before it was exhibited in the Salon of 1801 the work had traveled all around Europe. Let us grant this point to those who attribute the myth of Napoleon to clever propaganda: Gros, probably following his model's instructions, took a few liberties with truth: Bonaparte's appearance on the bridge, which had been a simple episode, became in the picture the *whole* battle.[66] In addition, Bonaparte's posture—his sword held in front of him, as if he were charging, his hair and the flag blown by the wind, his eyes looking backward—calls up another image: that of Bonaparte pulling the army behind him and victoriously crossing the bridge. But the important point lies elsewhere. Bonaparte fills the whole frame; we see neither the battlefield—except, perhaps, in the background, the sky being obscured by the smoke—nor the bridge, nor any soldier of either of the two armies. The picture does not represent another heroic scene like the many the Revolution had already inspired; it depicts the hero in person, and him alone.[67]

The French Revolution and Its Heroes

Gros's painting, which is so novel in its composition and its spirit, nonetheless participates in a heroic culture developed by the Revolution, a little in spite of itself. The Age of the Enlightenment had rebuilt the foundations of the cult of great men in order to make it really "the homage admiration renders to virtues."[68] Kings, saints, conquerors—too many false idols had been offered by the powerful to the adulation of the crowds. The enlightened century had therefore preferred men made famous by discoveries or actions useful for the happiness of humanity and for the progress of civilization. But in redefining the titles, the forms, and the objects of celebration, the Enlightenment did not challenge the principle of heroism. Moreover, it had not renounced—far from it—all the heroes of the past.[69] It saw in the cult of great men first of all the expression of a very human need to admire; secondly, a salutary support for the weakest citizens, who, modeling themselves on these sublime examples, would find in them the strength to behave virtuously; and finally, an institution that was becoming less dangerous in modern societies. In fact, because in these societies public opinion exercised a kind of sovereign magistracy, the praise addressed to great men, which formerly seemed to raise "a few men to the heights" only the better to lump all the rest together in an anonymous "herd," was now awarded by the free suffrage of citizens and thus no longer did anything but consecrate the omnipotence of opinion. Hadn't the public "crowned" Voltaire shortly before his death?[70] But as the century wore on, doubts arose: Could a society founded on the equality of rights celebrate alleged great men without creating fateful distinctions between citizens? Shouldn't it rather grant its homage to more authentic forms of grandeur? The acts of the virtuous citizen, of the good father—weren't they as good as the epic of Alexander? Wasn't the simple accomplishment of one's duty as worthy of respect as the most brilliant glory? Antoine Thomas, who did not share these doubts, nonetheless echoed them in his *Essai sur les éloges*: "Athens raised an altar to the unknown god; we might raise on Earth a statue with this inscription: to the virtuous men we do not know. Unknown during their lives, forgotten after their deaths, the less they sought acclaim, the greater they were."[71]

In 1784 Bernardin de Saint-Pierre made the "just citizen," a modest, anonymous, even obscure hero, the center of his "Elysium," a verdant, statue-studded pantheon in which this paterfamilias is accompanied by a wife and mother no less anonymous and, further, much further on, by the group of the illustrious defenders of the fatherland, men of letters and inventors.[72] Bernardin de Saint-Pierre challenged not only the traditional criteria of grandeur but also the inequality and separation that grandeur introduces among men. True grandeur, he said, does not separate men, it brings them together and makes them more equal, because it resides in each of them. So then, down with the great man of the classical age, who revealed exceptional gifts under extraordinary circumstances and who, though he did not become a great man or a hero solely by the freely expressed suffrage of public opinion, was nonetheless separated by an incommensurable distance from those who paid him their homage. To this grandeur that separates individuals, Bernardin de Saint-Pierre opposed another that brings them together, thus replacing the heroism of exceptional qualities with a heroism that is "without qualities, without attributes, perfectly ordinary."[73]

The French Revolution was at first on the side of Bernardin de Saint-Pierre.[74] It dreamed of establishing a society of equal citizens who, without being perfectly virtuous, would be virtuous enough at least to silence their particular self-interests. If a regenerated France had to pay homage to a great man, it would have to pay homage to the people itself.[75] Wasn't the Revolution the work of that collective being that was said to be endowed with sentiment, reason, and will? Michelet, whose history of the Revolution is, so to speak, written from the inside, so penetrated was he by its ideals and its representations, was the most profound of those who, from de Maistre to Marx, said of the French Revolution that it was "a great period without great men,"[76] in which the people led their leaders.[77]

The revolutionaries saw things the same way, and for a long time they tried to give material form to a collective and perfectly anonymous hero by resorting to bodily metaphors to represent the regenerated nation and demonstrate its power.[78] Their fete of the Supreme Being celebrated in Paris on June 8, 1794, even came very close to realizing Bernardin de Saint-Pierre's dream. The organizers had taken care to avoid any allusion to the upheavals of the Revolution, the better to offer the spectacle of a society reconciled with itself and freed from politics—where grandeur was everywhere because it was nowhere. And they had thrown away the busts of the *philosophes*, of the heroes of antiquity, and of the martyrs of the Revolution that had up to that point been exhibited in civic ceremonies, in order to draw out of anonymity Viala and Bara, two children killed in the revolutionary cause posthumously called upon to become the almost ordinary heroes of a Republic without heroes.[79] But to give regenerated France two heroes to admire and to imitate was to admit that Bernardin's dream would remain a utopia; it was to admit that virtue, far from being an innate quality, demanded efforts from every individual that not everyone is capable of making, at least without help. The Republic needed great men to offer as examples. In 1790 the idea had inspired the creation of the Pantheon; but knowing that it is only a step from admiration to idolatry, the revolutionaries reserved the nation's homage for the dead.

Nevertheless, nothing availed: the society dreamed of, so perfectly egalitarian that no one would be admired in it, remained in limbo. The Revolution—and this holds for any revolution—in fact entertained a relation to heroism that was no less close for being conflictual. If "the great man is one who breaches apparent fatalities,"[80] if heroism is in the end essentially transgressive, then what is more heroic than a revolution, than overthrowing the existing order to raise another one on its ruins? And regarding the Revolution of 1789, wasn't the cult of heroism a new kind of religion that, temporarily replacing the old one, tore the French away from "individual egoism, fostered heroism and self-sacrifice, and in many cases made them indifferent to all the petty goods that possess us" and ultimately allowed France to escape the tragedy of a complete and irreparable dissolution?[81] Still more, heroism is a constitutive trait of the character of the revolutionary, who is convinced that revolution is inherently necessary, but is incapable of imagining its achievement independently of his own intervention and his own sacrifice. Henceforth the revolutionary is less the purely passive agent of necessity than a hero who, because he sacrifices himself—even his life—to the cause, rises above other men, their desires, their sorrows, and the rules that govern their existence.[82] The French Revolution, from Marat to Robespierre, thus never stops giving birth to heroes: they are at once symbols of an anonymous collectivity exercising on itself a faceless power and the exemplars who have already run the whole course that their contemporaries have hardly begun to pursue. They receive, one after the other, the power to give material form to the sovereign people in its anonymity and to incarnate a people that does not yet exist. At the same time these great figures, by their very exceptional nature, recreate between themselves and the crowd of their admirers— even if, as in the case of Marat, in a monstrous, carnivalesque mode—the distanced, inegalitarian relationship peculiar to the heroes of the classical age that the Revolution had tried to abolish. Thus, at the same time the Revolution never ceased to honor its great men, though it later destroyed what it had adored, denouncing a popular penchant for "idolizing individuals."[83]

A New Hero for the New Century

Everything changed after 9 Thermidor. The denunciation of the crimes of the Terror immediately discredited the heroic conception of politics. "Drinkers of blood" who denied their crimes to save their heads, the ignorant and drunken despots represented in *L'Intérieur d'un comité révolutionnaire*, a famous play from the Thermidorian era: that is what these heroes were, once they were stripped of their costumes and their makeup, these heroes who were once celebrated with such fervor! It was then that the heroic values that had become useless in the political sphere recovered a new youth on a stage that had always been populated by heroes and heroic acts: war. In 1796 and 1797, in Italy, Bonaparte assumed a role that had fallen into escheat since the death of Robespierre, but he gave it a new form: the hero-figurehead of the Revolution's vanguard was succeeded by the "savior" to whom the country aspired.

Why a general? Not only was France bogged down in a crisis so complex and so deep that there seemed to be no way out, but people's minds remained so imbued with the monarchical idea that, given the difficulties and a Republic that seemed to many people an accident, many French people saw no remedy other than a return to a form of power that was absolute, if no longer by divine right, and that was naturally embodied by the generals. Why Bonaparte, rather than one of the other generals, of which France had no lack? Wasn't he a priori the least predestined to incarnate the collectivity? Wasn't there something foreign about him that should have set him aside when it came down to making a choice? Thiers replied subtly that the very traces of his foreign origin, which were still so visible, gave him an advantage: "Singularity always adds to the spell cast by genius, especially in France, where, with the greatest uniformity of manners, people are passionately fond of eccentricity."[84] The exploits of "the incredible Army of Italy," as Monge put it, were not irrelevant.[85] But Bonaparte could count not only on his astonishing victories, on the ascendancy he exercised over those who approached him, and on an incontestable talent for advertising himself, but also on his ability—and he alone possessed it to this degree—to reconcile in his person, or rather in the image of himself that he projected, the contradictory aspirations of Thermidorian public opinion. The French were tired of a Revolution that they wanted above all to have done with; but at the same time they refused to give up any of the material or symbolic goods that it had brought them. This was an equation that seemed insoluble, and that Bonaparte alone was capable of resolving, thanks to the fact that his character included both revolutionary and postrevolutionary elements.

He was a revolutionary figure first of all because of his youth, especially because the Revolution had grown old quickly, and badly. It had passionately loved youth. It had claimed to "mark a new departure for History, . . . to embody the youth of a world that would last forever."[86] Now that it was entering its winter, with its used-up actors and its faded ideals, the myth of its eternal youth was reincarnated in the army, and first of all in the Army of Italy. Its soldiers were so young, Stendhal was to say, that their leader, only twenty-seven years old, "was considered the oldest man in his army."[87] The campaign of 1796, even more than a masterpiece of strategy or politics, was a hymn to youth:

> We were all very young, . . . all radiant with strength and health, and devoured by the love of glory. Our ambition was noble and pure: we had no envy, no base passion found access to our hearts, a genuine friendship united us all, and there were examples of attachment that went as far as devotion: a complete security with regard to our future, a boundless confidence in our destinies gave us the philosophy that makes such a great contribution to happiness, and a constant harmony, never disturbed, brought warriors together in a genuine family; finally, the variety in our occupations and in our pleasures, the successive use

of our mental and physical faculties, gave life an extraordinary interest and rapidity.[88]

Bonaparte also incarnated the Revolution's belief in the power of the will—didn't he found states in Italy for which he wrote constitutions?—and the promise of equality. The spirit of the Revolution, the feeling of being able to accomplish the impossible, was all the more easily transferred to the military sphere because most of these twenty-five-year-old generals had, like Bonaparte himself, come up through the ranks. Their meteoric rise provided the Revolution with a confirmation that would be sought in vain in the civilian sphere, where notables of wealth had quickly replaced those of birth; it also explains why the army became "the revolutionaries' supreme refuge."[89] How could it have been otherwise in a group whose ambitions had so long been restrained by aristocratic rules of advancement? The army very logically feared a restoration that would have deprived it, to the advantage of the privileged, of the ranks won on the Revolution's battlefields. Nothing could make it accept demotion: this would be seen again in 1814 and 1815. The Revolution detested the émigrés, but the army hated them, because it was used to "seeing them in the ranks of the enemy."[90] The army was revolutionary not only out of self-interest but also, just as much, out of passion, and all the more wholeheartedly given that 1793 reminded them not of the Terror, as it did politicians mired in the past, but rather of a gigantic struggle against the invader that had been punctuated by battles and victories. Thus, the army could claim to adhere to the Revolution as a whole, including its darkest hours. In sum, and even if it had been involved in episodes of civil war—in the south, in the west—it incarnated the Revolution freed from the Terror. The defense of France's borders and the victories won over the armies of the "tyrants" blotted out everything else.

It is in this respect that Bonaparte, who was connected with the Revolution in so many ways, was at the same time postrevolutionary: he incarnated the Revolution, but not the civil war. The legitimacy that he claimed and was soon to oppose to that of the government was won on the fields of battle, outside the political arena. It is true that at Toulon, perhaps, and certainly on 13 Vendémiaire, he had a hand in episodes of civil war, but the epic campaign in Italy had erased all that. A son of the nation at war and not of politics, he received from it the power of embodying values that were stained neither by partisan interests nor by the memory of the recent schisms. Within two years he was able to draw from it the power, as Raymond Aron was to say of General de Gaulle in 1958, of "transcending French quarrels, of being simultaneously on the right and on the left, of uniting the former France with France after 1789."[91] Only a military man was capable of doing this. In fact, the armies that spread the Revolution's ideas outside French borders and threatened the old monarchies were reweaving, through their march across Europe, "the web of time": "In Italy and in the Rhineland, the republican armies were treading the same paths that had early been trod by the armies of Turenne and Condé. Across the centuries, brave men recognize each other and respond to each other. On his battlefield, the republican soldier discovered the values that constitute the value of the military occupation: courage, honor, devotion, loyalty."[92]

Reconnecting with values entrenched in the old aristocratic society, the Revolution followed in the footsteps of the Old Regime at the same time that it dispossessed it of the past and of the tradition that figured among its main titles to legitimacy. The war completed the expropriation of the old society by incorporating its values, particularly its military values, into the heritage of the Revolution. In a certain way it was up to the men of war to succeed where those of 1789 had failed: war allowed them to appropriate the values of the aristocracy that enabled them to achieve equality *from above*, whereas in the political order the attempt had been made to achieve it *from below*, at the price of destroying all the old values. Thus, the army realized the dream of a whole generation, which consisted, not at all in wiping out aristocratic culture altogether, but in providing a democratic version of it by replacing the criterion of birth by that of merit. The officers of the Army of Italy—their memoirs often dwell on this—tried to absorb the manners of the old societies they had vanquished by arms, relearning, with uneven success, how to be polite, to converse, and to dance. Without completely abandoning the inherent brutality of the Revolution, they succeeded in adapting fairly well—Bonaparte and Marmont managed this better than Masséna and Augereau—to the codes of the nobles who, in Milan, Bologna, or Florence, welcomed them in their salons. Their manners, the Marquis Costa later said, "occupied the middle ground between a republican lack of consideration and the old French courtesy."[93] The policy of "fusion" conducted by Bonaparte under the Consulate was ultimately only the political extension of what he had discovered when he was fighting in Italy: the marriage of democracy and aristocracy that was later, with the help of the imperial adventure, to remodel European society of the nineteenth century and, not without tensions and conflicts, set the figure of the military man alongside that of the bourgeois; the utilitarian morality of self-interest alongside honor, the brotherhood of combat, and sacrifice to the nation; the freedom of the Moderns alongside that of the Ancients. Rather than representing a strange, ultimate, and ephemeral resurrection of the ancient world, as Nietzsche thought,[94] Bonaparte embodied this association of contraries that characterizes the first century of the history of the democratic world. It is true that the nineteenth century was to see in Napoleon's fall the proof of the final defeat of the ancient hero at the hands of the modern bourgeois, but what was the later colonial adventure to be, if not the redeployment on a global scale of the passions, inextricably ancient and modern, aristocratic and bourgeois, that had been expressed in the revolutionary and imperial wars?

This association of the bourgeois and the hero fed the cult that took shape around Bonaparte, who was both an invincible conqueror and a modest reader of the poet Ossian. Even his marriage, which was simultaneously bohemian, aristocratic, and bourgeois, illustrates the telescoping or rather the interweaving of apparently antagonistic traditions that was to permeate the new century. Bonaparte is modern not only through his bourgeois side, because he loved his wife, shared her bed, and engaged in marital squabbles with her that would have been inconceivable in an aristocrat of the Old Regime, but also through his heroic side. What is apparently most ancient, almost antique, about him is perhaps at the same time what is most modern about him. Napoleon is a figure of the modern individual. Humboldt, who saw him in 1797 at a meeting of the Institute, remarked perceptively that Bonaparte "could contribute to the modern ideal."[95] Nothing is more accurate. What there is in him that speaks to the modern imagination is his conviction—and ours—that "his fate will never hold out against his will."[96] For his contemporaries, Bonaparte represented the man who, without famous ancestors or a famous name, created himself by force of will, by work and talent; the man who was, so to speak, born from himself, transformed his life into a destiny, and rose to unprecedented heights by transgressing all known limits. There is something existential in the life of this man who, seeing perfect happiness only in "the most complete development of [his] faculties," sought every day to realize it by not letting a single hour be lost, and who was, moreover, convinced that life has meaning only when it grows steadily larger and more grand. Like the amorous ideal described by Paul Valéry, who sought in love above all an "increase in general vitality" that would allow him to devote himself to something quite different,[97] Napoleon sought in glory, as in the love that Joséphine inspired in him, that very energy in which his life would find its meaning. That is the secret of the fascination exercised, even today, by the figure of Napoleon. He is the one who *does*, or, to adopt Carlyle's definition of the hero, the one who can do the most and the best,[98] an embodiment of the values—displayed in the celebration of energy and exceptional individuals—that were later to be those of Romanticism. In the course of his conversations with Eckermann, Goethe exclaimed: "Napoleon was the man! Always illuminated, always clear and decided, and endowed at every hour with energy enough to carry out whatever he considered necessary. His life was the stride of a demigod."[99] But that does not mean that his contemporaries dreamed of *doing* as Bonaparte did, because in that respect he was inimitable, incomparable, out of reach. "His destiny," Goethe added, "was more brilliant than any the world had seen before him, or perhaps will ever see after him. Yes, yes, my good friend: that was a fellow we cannot imitate!"[100] The hero offers himself for admiration, not imitation. On the other hand, that means that people dreamed of *being* like him, animated by the same vital energy that allowed him, from that time on, to transform the world surrounding him to make of it the subject and the setting of his destiny.[101] He was simultaneously exemplary and inimitable. But weren't the heroes of mythology themselves half human, half divine, both close to us and incommensurably distant from us?

THIRTEEN

Saving the Directory

A hero for revolutionary France—the Jacobins had not forgotten the "Vendémiaire general"—Bonaparte was no less a hero for "moderate" France. In the spring of 1797 the latter's representatives, whether conservative republicans or constitutional monarchists, had won a victory in the partial legislative elections (one-third of the Legislative Body was elected every year) so crushing that they began to think that they could take power. Even though they wanted to have done with the Revolution and reestablish the throne, they too had succumbed to the general enthusiasm provoked by Bonaparte's victories in Italy, to the point that the victor of Lodi and Rivoli erased in them the memory of the "Vendémiaire general." Lacretelle was to recall, "We *vendémiairists* could not at first see without pique so many exploits immortalizing the name of the man who had caused us to be fired upon in the streets of Paris, but this resentment could not hold out against the general admiration; it even seemed to us that our defeat was made glorious by the name of the victor."[1] The émigrés themselves applauded the exploits of the man whom Mallet du Pan still called, but now without finding much approval, "Mandrin's bastard."[2] Mallet was astonished by the admiration that the most rabid opponents of the Revolution professed for Bonaparte: Weren't they saying everywhere that "Caesar [was] a mere schoolboy compared to the modern conqueror of Italy"?[3] It was completely incomprehensible.

Neither Bonaparte's patriotism nor even his military talents suffice to explain by themselves an infatuation whose cause also resided in the moderation shown by the commander of the Army of Italy. Never before had a revolutionary general been seen to treat the established powers of the Old Regime with consideration. To be sure, he imposed harsh conditions on the Italian princes, and extorted millions from them, along with hundreds of paintings; but not once had he been heard questioning the privileges of the nobility or criticizing the misdeeds of "superstition." On the contrary: he did not hesitate to oppose those who, claiming to imitate France, spoke of overthrowing thrones and altars, and in his speeches, his proclamations, and his letters, he never forgot to defend religion. "Your properties, your religion, and your customs will be respected," he had promised the Piedmontese;[4] and a few days later he promised the people of Milan "respect for properties, for persons; respect for the peoples' religion."[5] Even if other military leaders, particularly Pichegru, had already made similar remarks,[6] people repeated these words, which were found strange coming from a general, and one reputed to be a Jacobin: "I seek far more to be known as the savior of the Holy See than as its destroyer," he declared to the French representative in Rome.[7] The contrast with the tone of the Directory could hardly be more striking. At the same time the Directory was telling him that "the Roman religion [would] always be the irreconcilable enemy of the Republic."[8] To please the government and the better to act as he wished, but also to avoid offending the very revolutionary Army of Italy—which would have preferred, like Monge, "to see the papal government, the center of lies and the damper of the human spirit," wiped from the face of the globe[9]—he liked to make fun of the "clerical crowd"[10] and said that a revolution would soon overthrow "the old machine."[11] But at the same time he wrote to Cardinal Mattei, the papal legate in Ferrara: "My particular concern will be not to allow any change to be made in the religion of our fathers."[12]

Bonaparte and the Pope

The Austrian counterattacks allowed Bonaparte to reveal his military genius, and the way in which he succeeded in imposing his own policy with regard to Rome revealed the extent of his political abilities, whose measure even he himself had not yet taken. As we have seen, in May 1796 the Directory had ordered him to threaten Rome and to demand that it hand over millions of francs as well as paintings and that the pope "immediately order public prayers for the prosperity and success of the French Republic."[13] Bonaparte had obeyed, and consequently adopted a bellicose tone toward the sovereign pontiff, swearing to his soldiers that he was going to "reestablish the Capitol" and "awaken the Roman people numbed by several centuries of slavery."[14] At the same time, but perhaps less for ideological or simply political reasons than for military ones, he refused to march on Rome, and, referring to the Austrian menace and the heat of the summer, he had not gone beyond Bologna.[15] Pope Pius VI had not waited for the Army of Italy to cross the borders of his estates before he contacted the unknown general who had, in a few weeks, defeated the Piedmontese and driven the Austrians out of Lombardy. He had asked the Spanish ambassador to Rome, Azara, to go to see Bonaparte. The latter received Azara on June 7, 1796. The Spanish mediator had first spoken with Saliceti, a not very accommodating interlocutor who couldn't find words harsh enough to criticize the "tyrant of consciences," but the reception Bonaparte gave him was no better. Like Saliceti, Bonaparte demanded fifty million francs, the expulsion of French priests who had taken refuge in Rome, and a papal bull exhorting French Catholics to accept the Republic. No agreement resulted from this first interview, but each of the interlocutors had already taken the measure of the other and understood that his adversary would be tough. One was as wily as the other, with the difference that Bonaparte was beginning his first real international negotiation, whereas Azara was an old hand at the secrets of diplomacy (he was sixty-six). Two weeks later Bonaparte was camping with his army on papal territory, in Bologna, and Azara was no longer in a position to make any demands. However, he stood fast against Bonaparte's fury and even won a kind of victory by getting out of Saliceti and Garrau the confirmation of what he already suspected—namely, that the French army was not capable of going as far as Rome. Although he was unable to set the tribute demanded of the pope at ten million francs, the sum to which he had initially been willing to agree, he succeeded in forcing Bonaparte to lower his conditions by reducing the indemnity from forty to twenty-one million francs.[16]

Financial bargaining was not the only motive for the quarrel: politics was also involved, and it seems that at this time—June 1796—Bonaparte had already determined the line that he was henceforth to follow in dealing with the Holy See. Historians have rightly drawn attention to François Cacault, the French chargé d'affaires in Florence, who turned out to be a valuable ally for Bonaparte. Cacault was very familiar with Italian affairs, concealed great moderation beneath the external appearance of an intransigent republican, and did not underestimate the spiritual and moral power of the papacy. He inspired at least part of the general's policy: "Be considerate of the clergy while at the same time treating it harshly, and impose the Catholic religion on the soldier while at the same time forcing the papacy to accept the agreement."[17]

In order to satisfy his government, Bonaparte demanded the release of about ten political prisoners held in Roman jails, and repeated that the Directory expected the sovereign pontiff to help calm religious quarrels in France by issuing a bull. This last step cost the pope and the Curia so little that a draft was soon ready that exhorted French Catholics to obey the laws of the Republic. But the bull, entitled *Pastoralis Sollicitudo*, was a mere draft that had received no official sanction and was communicated to the Roman diplomats who left to negotiate peace in Paris only to prove the pope's good intentions. Besides, had this draft been signed by the pope, it would still have been just one of those formal declarations that entail hardly any consequences, whereas Bonaparte had, for his part, given up another of the Directory's demands that was humiliating for Pius VI: the expulsion of the thousands of refractory priests—three thousand of them, it is said, perhaps even five thousand—whom the people and the authorities of Rome were not treating well, forcing them to live under very precarious conditions, but whom the pope, as Azara had told Bonaparte, could not expel from his estates without committing "a felony."[18] By giving up this part of his instructions, the revolutionary general spared the sovereign pontiff's pride, and from that moment on, despite French demands, the pope knew that he was confronting less an enemy than a partner, who was no doubt inconvenient but who resolved to stop at the gates of Rome. "Finally, we can breathe again," he is supposed to have said when he learned that the armistice had been signed in Bologna on June 23, 1796.[19] And certain perceptive members of Bonaparte's entourage understood that the destruction of the "throne of imposture" was not part of the general's plans.[20] Moreover, at this point the Directory had also given up the effort to put an end to the pope's temporal power.[21] But it is true that the government was not following a clearly defined line. Sometimes it dreamed of destroying the papacy, sometimes it resigned itself to negotiating, and when Pius VI's emissaries arrived in Paris to discuss the clauses of a peace treaty, they soon had to admit the obvious: the Thermidorian government of France was no less hostile to Roman power than its predecessors were, and because it now demanded that Pius VI recognize the 1790 Civil Constitution of the Clergy, the discussions that began on August 12 were broken off a few days later. They were resumed in Florence in September, in the presence of Saliceti, but were no more successful. The Directory then returned to its initial idea: the deposition of the pope. For his part, the pope had used the failure of the peace conferences as a pretext for breaking the Bologna armistice, making an appeal for general mobilization against the invader, and signing on September 25 a treaty of defensive alliance with the kingdom of Naples. In Rome, Austria's successive counterattacks had revived hope, despite their failure: people wanted to believe that the small French army could not resist these attacks indefinitely. Bonaparte had issued a warning by manhandling the pope's legate in Ferrara,[22] but for all that he did not wish to break with the Vatican, and when the negotiations in Florence failed, he was critical of the French negotiators' lack of flexibility. That was on October 8. As we have seen, a few days later the Directory, by approving the creation of the Cispadane Republic, put the conduct of French diplomacy in Italy in Bonaparte's hands. Bonaparte immediately wrote to François Cacault to ask him to reestablish the dialogue with Rome:

> Thus, you can tell the pope that Paris's reply has reached me; that through a series of feelings of moderation that the French government has adopted, it has assigned me to put an end to any kind of dispute with Rome, either by arms or by new negotiations. Wishing to give the pope a sign of my desire to see this long war end, and to see the misfortunes that are afflicting human nature come to an end, I offer him a honorable way to save his honor and the head of the religion. You can assure him overtly that I have always been against the treaty that was offered him, and especially the method of negotiation; that it is as a result of my particular and repeated requests that the Directory has assigned me to begin new negotiations. . . . You yourself know that regarding this subject we have always had similar principles, and, in view of the unlimited power of decision the Directory has given me, if Rome is willing to be moderate, we will take advantage of this power to bring peace to that beautiful part of the world, and to calm the timid consciences of many peoples.[23]

Despite his fervent desire to succeed, Cacault—even though supported by Cardinal Mattei[24]—also failed, but this time it was the fault of the Roman Curia: seeing Bonaparte battered at Arcole and refusing to believe that Naples had defected (it had secretly signed a peace treaty with France on October 10), the Curia had called on Austria for help. On January 10, 1797, a letter from Cardinal Busca to Monsignor Albani, the pope's ambassador in Vienna, fell into Bonaparte's hands, and thus he learned that Pius VI had actually entrusted himself "to the fortune of the House of Austria."[25] The latter had sent General Colli to Rome to organize the small Vatican army and to create a second front on the rear of the French army. The fighting on the battlefield of Rivoli was hardly over before Bonaparte announced his intention to march "straight to Rome,"[26] to sweep the pope's soldiers away, and to add the capital of the Church to the territories to be used to buy peace with Austria: Modena, Ferrara, and Romagna would form a republic allied with France—the Cispadane Republic—while Lombardy and Mantua would be restored to Austria, which would also receive Parma, for which Spain would be compensated by—Rome. It is true that in Paris the Directory, intoxicated by the victory at Rivoli, was starting to want everything, the left bank of the Rhine and part of northern Italy, Belgium, and the destruction of the pope's temporal power. On February 3, 1797, the French government asked Bonaparte to "destroy, if possible, the center of the Roman Church's unity . . . , either by putting Rome under another power, or, still better, by establishing there a form of internal government that would make the priests' government so wretched and odious that the pope and the College of Cardinals . . . would be forced to seek refuge in a place where at least they would no longer have any temporal power."[27] But in 1797 Bonaparte had no more intention of going as far as Rome than in 1796; and although he did not conceal from his interlocutors that he wanted to teach the pope a lesson for having broken the armistice and called on the Austrians to rescue him, he also let them know that he had no intention of overthrowing him: "Whatever happens," he wrote to Cardinal Mattei, "I beg you assure His Holiness that he can remain in Rome without worrying about anything. He is the Prime Minister of Religion, and as such he will find protection for himself and for the Church."[28] Bonaparte had not gone beyond Bologna in 1796; this time he proceeded as far as Urbino, Macerata, and Ancona. The occupation of the latter on February 9, 1797, led to the capitulation of the little pontifical army. In Paris people were already imagining the French in Rome, the Curia dispersed, and Pius VI forced to leave his capital, but in Rome, where Bonaparte's arrangements were known, the diplomats had already set out, with Cardinal Mattei at their head. They had been calmed by the French general's statements in Ancona, where he had once again promised that "no change in the Catholic, apostolic, and Roman religion"[29] would be made. He told the Directory that these were only words, and if the "clerical crowd" had "saved the Capitolinus," that was not the end of the matter: the financial drain he intended to inflict on the pope would soon provoke a revolution in Rome.[30]

The negotiation of the treaty signed on February 19 at Tolentino, near Macerata, was not the most difficult Bonaparte had had to conduct up to that point. He was eager to get back to Friuli in order to begin the march on Vienna, and the Holy See's envoys were in a hurry to reach an agreement that would constitute an official recognition of the pope's temporal power and force the French government to stop making threats. Bonaparte proceeded as he had many times before: he listened patiently to the very loquacious Cardinal Caleppi's "homilies," and then, when he decided his interlocutors had talked long enough, he brought his fist down on the table, threatened them with the worst reprisals, and imposed peace on them at the price of the definitive cession of Avignon and the legations, as well as that of Ancona "until there was peace on the continent," and an indemnity of fifteen million francs in addition to the sums required by the Bologna armistice. This peace treaty, Mattei declared, was "similar in every respect to the capitulation of a besieged fortress"; but, he added, in this way "Rome [had been] saved, along with religion."[31] Mattei owed this result less to his own skill than to the political choices Bonaparte made.

Waiting for Monk

The Directory was not deceived by the general's anticlerical diatribes, and was scandalized by the consideration with which Bonaparte treated "the colossus of fanaticism." La Révellière, the pontiff of the "theophilanthropists,"[32] was furious: "Fine things are happening in Italy," he grumbled. "A commander-in-chief of the republican armies calls the tyrant of Rome Holy Father, His Holiness!"[33] As usual the government let Bonaparte, whom it nonetheless considered a kind of "potentate" and usurper of its authority, do as he wished. Worse yet, the general, not content to treat Rome with kid gloves, seemed to be ignoring the laws against the émigrés. Having read an Italian translation of Joseph de Maistre's recently published *Considérations sur la France*, Bonaparte had the author informed that he could safely return to Savoy, where he could live under his personal protection. Having noted the wretched state of the French priests who had taken refuge on pontifical territory, he forced the Roman authorities to ensure that they had decent living conditions. And finally, when he referred to the pretender, the Count of Provence, who had been expelled from Verona at France's request, he called him "Monsieur, king of France."[34] He probably did so because everyone called Louis XVIII "king," out of habit and without malicious intentions, but such marks of respect seemed to confirm the point to which the little general was different from the men who were governing in Paris. As Mme de Staël was to put it, "Bonaparte's proclamations in Italy were intended to make people trust him. In them there prevailed a noble and moderate tone that contrasted with the revolutionary fierceness of the civilian leaders of France. The warrior spoke like a magistrate, while the magistrates expressed themselves with a military violence."[35]

The imaginations of the French, and not only of the counterrevolutionaries, were imbued by the English precedent of 1660. In his *Considérations sur la France*, de Maistre predicted that the Revolution would end in France as it had in England: with a restoration. When? How? It was impossible to say with certainty, but it was clear, he said, that the French would see a Monk appear.[36] The Revolution might even find its denouement at the point when all hope had disappeared, and perhaps the monarchy would not even be restored by a royalist, because "it is impossible to know when Monk began to serve the monarchy sincerely."[37] Many people, both moderates and émigrés, did not believe the royalists capable of reestablishing the throne; only a military man, they said, could overcome the obstacles and bring the nation safely home. A Monk was necessary to restore the monarchy, but a French Monk, a Monk from France. Many high-ranking military men had joined the counterrevolutionary camp: Dumouriez,

Pichegru, Willot, Rougé. Marceau was probably preparing to take the same step when he died. But their defection itself had made them émigrés, outlaws, and traitors. Bonaparte's name was being mentioned more and more frequently. "We were following him with deep attention and our predictions were not wrong," Lacretelle later said. "We were pleased to see in him a man who could put an end to a revolution of which we were mortally tired."[38] Emissaries of the princes approached Bonaparte. They proposed to make him constable of France if he agreed to play Monk's role. He did not turn them down, but smiled at their offers, like those of the Austrians, who dangled before his eyes a principality in Germany or Italy.[39] As Prosper de Barante wrote, "he could be offered nothing so great that it was not far surpassed by his imagination."[40]

Massacre in Verona, "Revolution" in Venice

I am not as sure as Thiers was that Bonaparte, having begun his career by fighting "the royalist faction" in Toulon, "was on bad terms with that group from the outset."[41] His constant conflicts with the Directory regarding Italy, the low opinion he had formed of the directors and also of the republican regime, everything, except perhaps the Jacobinism of his army, was pushing him toward the right. He had long since ceased to believe that the republican institutions founded in 1795 were capable of ending the Revolution, and when he spoke about them, it was with words that might have been used by a supporter of the royalist club on Rue de Clichy. Walking with Melzi and Miot de Melito in the gardens of Mombello one June day, he suddenly stopped and said to them: "Do you imagine that I triumph in Italy in order to aggrandise the pack of lawyers who form the Directory, and men like Carnot and Barras? What an idea! A Republic of thirty million men! And with our manners, our vices! How is it possible? That is a fancy of which the French are at present full, but it will pass away like all the others. What they want is Glory and gratified Vanity; but as for Liberty, they do not understand what it means."[42]

The temptation to establish connections with the right was all the greater because the Directory, after allowing him to march on Vienna, felt that it had been duped when it learned about the preliminary peace agreements signed on April 18, 1797, in Leoben, a few dozen kilometers from the Austrian capital. If we want to understand the sequence of events that led to the signing of these agreements, we have to turn to the Republic of Venice, which was directly concerned by the military operations, because the French army had not been able to drive into Austria without first crossing the Venetian "terra firma," which then extended from the city of the doges as far as Verona and Lake Garda.

Venetian neutrality had long been no more than a memory: since May 1796, the terra firma had become the scene of confrontations between France and Austria. Attacks and counterattacks had followed one another all during the summer, autumn, and winter, the French assuring the Venetians that they were only passing through and would respect the old Republic's neutrality, and the Venetians swearing in return that they deplored the anti-French protests that were becoming increasingly numerous. No one was deceived. The oldest republic in the world had no sympathy for its little French cousin. Its feelings were in fact so exclusively hostile that Bonaparte could write without exaggeration, "Of all the peoples of Italy, the Venetian is the one that hates us most."[43] Here, too, the French invasion had set in motion a revolutionary minority that counted on the support of the French to achieve its goals. This group was composed essentially of "provincial nobles" who were envious of the concentration of power in the hands of the aristocracy of the city of the doges. More than elsewhere, this revolutionary party was subservient to France, because with the exception of a handful of patrician families that were dissatisfied or ambitious, the bulk of the population, especially in the countryside, which was suffering from the soldiers' requisitions and exactions, was as hostile to these accomplices of the invaders as they were to the invaders themselves. As early as the end of 1796 the idea of "revolutionizing" Venice, as Modena and Bologna had been revolutionized, was in the air, in General Bonaparte's headquarters as well as in Paris.[44] However, it was only after signing the Treaty of Tolentino with the pope (February 19, 1797) and before beginning the march on Vienna (March 10) that Bonaparte decided to overthrow the Venetian government. It was a matter, on the one hand, of securing the rear of the French army when it was about to advance into Austrian territory, and, on the other hand, of taking an additional hostage with a view to future peace negotiations with Vienna.

On February 24, 1797, Bonaparte asked Clarke to enter into contact with the Austrians through their ambassador in Turin, Marquis Gherardini.[45] The two men met near the Piedmontese capital on the very day that Bonaparte began his final offensive against Prince Charles (March 10). Clarke declared that France was prepared to make peace if Austria ceded to it Belgium and the emperor's possessions on the left bank of the Rhine in exchange for Lombardy and Bavaria:

> "And what compensation for the Elector [of Bavaria] would you propose?" Gherardini asked. "None," Clarke replied, "I would say hello to him." . . . Gherardini declared that the Empire must not be touched, and that Italy alone would provide the indemnities. He scoffed at the republican farces of Milan and Bologna and brought up the subject of the legations. Then Clarke showed his hand: "Oh! As for the Cispadane [Republic], we shall not abandon it. . . . We shall fight for the Cispadane"; and in order to make that accepted, he added offer after offer: "We are prepared to accept your mediation in the peace treaty with Great Britain; you shall keep Mantua. . . . If you wish, you can seize Venetian Croatia, whose acquisition has always been desired by the House of Austria." Gherardini didn't frown, he simply said that [Venetian Croatia] was "a possession of a neutral power; it would be contrary to His Majesty's principles to take it away" and he returned to the legations. They separated without having concluded anything, but the crucial word had been uttered. Gherardini understood that they would have peace.[46]

Not only peace, but a peace in conformity with the secret desires of Austrian diplomacy. The latter ultimately cared little about Lombardy; nor did it regard Belgium or the Rhine as a matter of principle, provided that France compensated Austria suitably. Where? In Germany? France was offering Bavaria in exchange for Belgium, and a few ecclesiastical principalities in exchange for the left bank of the Rhine: the proposal did not appeal to the emperor, who feared the upheavals it would lead to in the Empire, and like his ministers he preferred to be compensated in Italy, where he coveted something far more precious than Lombardy, something that would give Austria access to the Mediterranean: Venice, and if not the city itself, then at least its territories touching on the Austrian border and its Balkan possessions. "It is to be desired that we establish ourselves in Venetia," the Austrian chancellor, Baron Thugut, had written a month before the discussions between Clarke and Gherardini.[47] However, an obstacle stood in the way of the realization of Austria's projects: the Republic of Venice was a sovereign state, independent, legitimate, enjoying an international recognition the Viennese government could not achieve except by right of conquest. The emperor had scruples. To avoid being accused of having destroyed the Venetian government, he preferred that these objectionable Frenchmen take the blame and then hand the remains of the doges' republic over to him.[48] Everything happened in accord with the scenario thought up by the Austrian chancellor and tacitly accepted by Bonaparte. Even before the outcome of the fighting had led them to begin negotiations, the parties already agreed on one thing, at least in principle: if peace had to be made, it would be made at the expense of the Venetians.

While Clarke was talking with Gherardini, Berthier is supposed to have gone to Milan to confer (on March 6) with the commander of the fortress, General Kilmaine, and one of his staff officers, Colonel Landrieux. He asked them to organize uprisings favorable to the French in several cities in the Venetian terra firma, on the model of the "revolution" that had made possible the overthrow of the Duke of Modena in October. Landrieux tells us this in his memoirs, even publishing the minutes of a second meeting held on March 9 in the presence of the principal Lombard officials to work out the final details of the operation.[49] It is abundantly clear that the uprisings that allowed the supporters of France to take control of Bergamo on March 12, Brescia on the fourteenth, Salo on the seventeenth, Crema on the twenty-eighth, and later Como and Verona, were aided by hired hands who had come from Milan and by the passivity of the French troops: the Venetian revolutionaries were too weak to succeed on their own, and nothing could be done in Italy without the consent of the French. Did Bonaparte himself give the necessary orders, or did the Milanese and Venetian revolutionaries, aided by certain parts of the army with which they maintained relations, take advantage of the circumstances—the concentration of the bulk of the French troops in Venetia—to launch a revolution in the terra firma? Learning of the events that occurred in Bergamo, Bonaparte condemned them as "very injurious" to French interests.[50] He was right: the pro-French agitators had hardly seized the cities before people in the rural areas rose up in turn, but they rose up against the French and their accomplices in an insurrection that soon began to look like "another Vendée."[51] In the same letter in which Bonaparte criticized the actions of the "patriots," he nonetheless said that he refused to intervene against these "Venetian citizens who liked the French army more than the imperial army." The next day he publicly defended the insurgents and threatened the Venetian government with reprisals if it associated itself in any way with the violence directed against the "Jacobins" and their French allies.[52] Supposing that the uprising of March 11 was premeditated and executed with the help and consent of the French, we will never know with certainty who gave the order for it, Bonaparte, Berthier, or Kilmaine.

Was the objective to provoke so much violence that the French would have grounds for intervening in the Republic of Venice's internal affairs? If so, it is likely that the French shared responsibility not only for the "revolution" of March 11, but also for the anti-French massacres in Verona. It was a poster that was dated March 20 and bore the signature of a Venetian magistrate that triggered these events. It called for a general uprising against the French and their supporters.[53] On April 17 and 18, conflicts broke out that were transformed, under circumstances that remain obscure, into a hunt for Frenchmen that resulted in three or four hundred victims. The poster responsible for all this is supposed to have been fabricated in Milan by the journalist Carlo Salvador,[54] and was moreover first published on April 5 in the newspaper published by the Milanese "Jacobins," *Termometro politico*. On the same day, and twelve days before the massacre, Bonaparte, who could not yet have seen a copy of the *Termometro*, alluded to this manifesto in a letter in which he denounced posters that were going to be put up in Verona only a several days later![55] Once we know that, how can we believe that he had nothing to do with this conspiracy, even if the instigators of these anti-French disturbances never imagined that they would lead to the death of more than 300 of their own men?[56]

The Preliminary Steps toward the Peace of Leoben

On April 17, while the disturbances in Verona were beginning, the preliminary steps toward a peace accord had only to be signed by the negotiators.

The emperor's representatives had arrived in Leoben on April 13. Agreement was rapidly reached regarding the fate of the left bank of the Rhine.[57] Bonaparte, who cared little about the future of the Rhineland territories, willingly granted that France would occupy them provisionally until, along with the representatives of the Holy Roman Empire, it ruled on their destiny (because the emperor refused to make a decision on this subject without the consent of the imperial Diet). On the other hand, the negotiations broke down regarding the annexation of Belgium. It was not that Vienna insisted on its restitution, but rather that Bonaparte offered nothing in exchange except compensations in Germany that Austria did not want. By arguing this point, it wanted only to force the French to raise the question of indemnities in Italy. It was finally the Austrians who, on April 15, laid down their cards and declared that they were authorized to sign the peace treaty immediately if France restored to them Lombardy and ceded to them either "all the countries of the Venetian territory between the Mincio, the Po, and the states of Austria," or the legations taken away from the pope.[58] Having the pertinent knowledge that Bonaparte would not give up either Milan or Bologna, the Austrians simply wanted to make him understand that they were ready to sign an agreement on the condition that France gave them Venetia, which belonged to neither of them.

Three days later the preliminary peace agreements, which were to serve as a basis for the discussion of the final treaty, were signed. Let us sum up: Austria ceded Belgium and Lombardy in exchange for the Republic of Venice's territory in the terra firma, Dalmatia, and Venetian Istria. Venice was to be compensated with the former pontifical legations of Bologna, Ferrara, and Ravenna. France would create an independent republic by combining Lombardy with the duchy of Modena (on the condition that the duke be compensated) and the part of Venetia "between the Adda, the Po, the Oglio, the Valteline, and the Tyrol," or, to the east of Milan, the provinces of Cremona, Crema, and Bergamo, as far as the Swiss border. Finally, the fate of the left bank of the Rhine, which was occupied militarily by the French, was referred to a congress at which representatives of France and the Holy Roman Empire would assemble to deliberate "on the basis of the integrity of the German Empire."[59] This initial accord between France and Austria was thus achieved at the expense of two states: the

Venetian republic, which was at first reduced to the city of Venice, and Cispadane Republic, which had just promulgated its constitution (March 27) and was already going to disappear, most of its territory (the former legations) being ceded to the Venetians, and the rest (Modena and Reggio) being destined to be part of the future Lombard or Cisalpine Republic.

The judgment issued against the Republic of Venice was immediately executed. On April 9, even before the beginning of the negotiations, Bonaparte had sent the Venetian authorities an initial ultimatum, demanding that they immediately stop the killing of French soldiers on their territory. The news of the death of the naval officer Laugier, whose ship had been bombarded in the waters off the Lido on April 23, made war ineluctable. It was when he learned of this that Bonaparte swore to be "an Attila for the state of Venice,"[60] to "destroy this atrocious and blood-thirsty government," and to "wipe the name of Venice from the surface of the globe," shouting that "the blood of all the Venetian nobles" had to flow "in order to appease the manes of the French they have had slaughtered."[61] In private he laughed with Junot, whom he had sent to take his ultimatum to the doge and who told him how he had been received by a "group of persons, most of them of a respectable age, wrapped in anachronistic garments and dying of heat."[62] On May 1 he declared war on the Republic of Venice, without for a moment thinking that as the simple head of an army, he did not have the power to do so. The next day the French army took up a position at Mestre; on the twelfth, the Great Council, manipulated by supporters of France and terrorized by a few rifle shots fired outside its compound, held its last meeting and abdicated; on the fifteenth, the French occupied the city, where on the sixteenth they installed a puppet government that immediately endorsed the trade of "terra firma for legations"[63] provided for in the preliminary agreements made in Leoben.

These preliminary agreements unleashed a storm in the Luxembourg Palace. The directors were divided. Carnot, who had long been hostile to any further territorial enlargement, would have willingly accepted this accord, even if Venice's fate bothered him somewhat. But Reubell wouldn't hear of it (though Barras and La Révellière initially approved it): he accused Bonaparte of having consented to an agreement that was entirely to Austria's advantage, whereas, not having the power to negotiate, he should have entrusted this task to the government's special emissary, General Clarke; and all that in order to sign a text that sacrificed the annexation of the left bank of the Rhine for the sole purpose of allowing Bonaparte to give himself the empty glory of having created "his" republic in Italy.[64] Reubell cried that this was treason, and even talked about a court martial. Bonaparte was aware that the preliminary agreements would trigger a chorus of protests, and just as he had done on the day after the Cherasco armistice,[65] he sent letter after letter to Paris to justify his actions, asserting that he had taken it upon himself to negotiate with the Austrians only because of the absence of Clarke, who was in Turin, and had not arrived in time (it has to be admitted that Bonaparte had deliberately notified him at the last minute). He recognized that this accord was no doubt imperfect but argued that it was certainly the best that could be obtained under the circumstances, in which, unlike himself, his colleagues on the Rhine had not fulfilled their part of the contract. And he concluded as was now his custom: by offering his resignation, which he knew would be refused.[66] Even if the directors had been able to agree to condemn the general's conduct, which was far from being the case, what could they have done against a man whom public opinion and the press were already lauding as the "peacemaker of Europe"? Nothing. The government ratified the preliminary agreements. Only Reubell, who was as ferociously hostile to Bonaparte's Italian policy as he was attached to the conquest of the left bank of the Rhine, was still bold enough to oppose them.

Many historians have agreed with Reubell that these preliminary agreements constituted a victory for Austria. Didn't one of the Austrian negotiators, the Marquis de Gallo, speak of a "miraculous peace"?[67] They point out that Bonaparte had ceded far more than he had gained, because he reinstalled Austria in Italy (and in a position more advantageous than its earlier one) without obtaining anything certain on the Rhine, and all that in exchange for the creation of a Cisalpine Republic, which, surrounded by hostile states (Austrian Venetia, Genoa, Piedmont, and so on), would have to be supported from a distance and at great cost. But to accuse Bonaparte of having substituted his own policy for that of the Directory is to assume that the latter had a policy, which remains to be proven. The French government's definition of its war goals had in fact constantly varied, depending on the circumstances, the development of the international and even the domestic situation, and the changing alliances among the five directors, who detested each other and each of whom tried to push French policy in the direction of his own convictions or interests.[68] How could their military or diplomatic agents have known what they were supposed to do? They were, in a way, obliged to interpret the government's intentions. In view of these incessant changes of course, it has to be admitted that Bonaparte navigated pretty well, except that instead of taking from Germany the compensation to be accorded the emperor, he took it from Italy. What about the left bank of the Rhine? Wasn't it being given up de facto by making its annexation depend on an arrangement with the Holy Roman Empire and, moreover, as an article of the treaty stipulated, "on the basis of the integrity of the Germanic empire"? Bonaparte proved to be very clever in deliberately ignoring all the Directory's instructions posterior to those of January 17, 1797, which were limited to two main points: obtaining the definitive cession of Belgium and the continuation of the occupation of the left bank of the Rhine until a final continental peace had been made. Thus, he declared himself obligated to carry out a program *a minima* whose main outlines Carnot had sketched in a letter sent to Clarke:

> The emperor cedes Belgium to France, along with all he possesses on the left bank of the Rhine. We evacuate Lombardy. We also give back the Palatinate and the electorates of Trier, Mainz, and Cologne, which we will, however, continue to occupy militarily on the current footing until there is a definitive continental peace. . . . These proposals are the Directory's ultimatum; you may perhaps find them too limited, but the need for peace is so great in all of France, this cry is so universal, [and] the penury of our means for continuing the war is so absolute, that we simply have to limit ourselves to them. The peace will still be glorious on these conditions and in my view it will be solid.[69]

The corollary was, of course, the abandonment of the Italian conquests, but Bonaparte was determined to forget about that, and all the more because one sentence in the Directory's instructions made the governmental choices subject to the approval of the leader of the Army of Italy; thus he acquired the means of concluding a peace more advantageous than the one expected of him.

18 Fructidor

It was at the moment when he was so close to breaking with the Directory that he himself was brutally rejected. Learning what had happened in Venice, right-wing opposition speakers and the newspapers that supported them railed against the so-called "revolution" in Venice. They denounced the violation of the treaties of neutrality and friendship that bound France to this ancient republic (and to that of Genoa, where the doge had also just been overthrown), the creation of "sister republics," and the ambition of France, which, by overflowing its "natural" borders, put Europe at risk of an endless war. Ardently desiring the peace without which the Revolution could not come to an end within the country, the right was hostile to the rhetoric of "natural borders," just as it was to any policy that sought to export the Revolution's ideas and institutions. "Have we forgotten," asked one of its orators, the representative Dumolard, "that this is no longer the time for Anacharsis Clootz's extravagances? That the French nation is not a sect of visionaries that seeks to expand, but a happy people that is proud of its constitutional liberty and wants to enjoy it while respecting the independence of other countries? . . . Is it a matter of our honor, of our self-interest, to revive [the coalition] from its ashes, by declaring perpetual war on established governments?"[70]

His adversaries accused the right of wanting France to return to its Old Regime borders. Even if France was no longer considering restoring Avignon to the pope or the county of Nice and Savoy to the king of Sardinia, it was in fact hostile to the annexation of Belgium or of the left bank of the Rhine, and that was one of the reasons Carnot, who would have willingly accepted the Meuse as France's northern border, had thought he could ally himself with the conservatives. As for Bonaparte's Italian conquests, the conservatives did not want to hear anything more about them. Their reaction to Bonaparte and his policy in Italy was all the more violent because, carried away by the size of their electoral victory a few weeks earlier, they believed that power was within their grasp, and consequently they were no longer as convinced that they needed a Monk, whoever he was, to put an end to the Revolution and restore the monarchy.[71] Furthermore, hadn't they found a Monk who openly supported their ideas in the person of General Pichegru, whom they had made president of the Council of Five Hundred? They gave free rein to the journalists, who depicted Bonaparte as a "visionary Jacobin," described him as an "avenging angel," said he was driven "by the madness of the greatest ambition," and accused him of being, like Janus, two-faced: "When his white demon prevails, he speaks the language of humanity, offers asylum to the victims of persecution, closes the lairs of anarchy, [but] when his black demon is triumphant, he violates the faith of treaties, allows the constitution to be trampled, and speaks the language of the factions."[72]

It would be a mistake to attribute Bonaparte's decision to side with the government to the bitterness he felt on reading newspapers that, he told his friends, "made him sick."[73] It is true that he found the slightest criticism intolerable: the preceding summer, perhaps as a result of the military defeats that, before Castiglione, had made people think that the Italian campaign was going to end in disaster, criticisms had been expressed in the press. Pierre-Louis Roederer, who was later to become one of Bonaparte's most fervent supporters, had distinguished himself in the *Journal de Paris* by warning the government against the growing autonomy of the generals.[74] Bonaparte had raged against the "wretches" who dared to reproach him for his way of conducting affairs in Italy, and faithful to his habit, he had threatened to resign if the press continued to "target" him.[75] For once the Directory had stepped up to defend its general, addressing to him a public letter of support and even getting one of his colleagues, and not the least of them—Hoche—to sing the praises of the Army of Italy's commander.[76] "Ah! You're a fine young man," Hoche wrote, "what republican soldier does not burn with the desire to imitate you? Courage, Bonaparte! Lead our victorious armies to Naples, to Vienna; reply to your personal enemies by humiliating kings, by giving our arms a new luster; and leave it to us to care for your glory!"[77] In 1797 Bonaparte reacted still more strongly against the attacks on him made by right-wing members of the legislature, demanding that the royalist club on Rue de Clichy be disbanded and that the newspapers that were "libeling" him be prohibited.[78] He was all the more furious because this time the Directory had avoided compromising itself as it had in 1796. On June 30 Bonaparte decided to respond publicly to Dumolard's accusations. He once again asked the government to find a replacement for him: "After having concluded five peace treaties and given the coalition the coup de grâce, I had the right, if not to civic triumphs, at least to live in peace, and to enjoy the protection of the Republic's first magistrates: today, I find myself denounced, persecuted, decried in every way, even though my reputation belongs to the fatherland."[79] As for the guilty parties, he threatened them directly in a note on the events in Venice that was enclosed with this letter, thus putting them on notice that in the test of strength about to take place between them and the government, he would be in the latter's camp:

> Ignorant and long-winded lawyers have asked, in the Clichy club, why we are occupying Venice's territory. . . . Ah! of course, we see what you have in mind! You are reproaching the Army of Italy for having sur-mounted all obstacles and traversed Italy, crossing the Alps twice, and for having attacked Vienna, being obliged to recognize this Republic that you, gentlemen of Clichy, want to destroy. It is clear that you are indicting Bonaparte for having caused peace to be made. But I warn you, and I speak in the name of 80,000 soldiers: the time when cow-ardly lawyers and miserable windbags had their soldiers guillotined is past; and if you force them to, the soldiers of Italy will come to the Clichy barrier with their general; but then you will be sorry![80]

The right-wing press campaign certainly helped bring Bonaparte closer to the Directory, but another event caused him to make up his mind: the arrest of Count d'Antraigues. This former delegate in the Constituent Assembly, who had emigrated, directed a network of spies. Having taken refuge in Venice and not having foreseen the French invasion—his information was not always very reliable—he had been arrested in Trieste on May 21, 1797. Bonaparte ordered that the count be brought to him in Milan, where the prisoner was secretly held in the Sforza castle. On June 1, Bonaparte interrogated him personally. One document had particularly caught his eye: the record of a conversation between d'Antraigues and another spy, Montgaillard, which revealed that the royalists had won General Pichegru over to their side. Bonaparte and his prisoner ar-rived at an agreement: d'Antraigues would copy this record, omitting certain passages in which, it is said, discreet contacts between Bonaparte and emissaries of the émigrés were mentioned; in exchange, he would be transferred from his dungeon to more comfortable quarters where his family could come to join him. The general did not need to be more precise. D'Antraigues had understood: he deleted the passages indicated, retaining in the end only the pages that accused Pichegru, who had in the interim become the very influential president of the Council of Five Hundred.[81] A few days later, d'Antraigues escaped with disturbing ease: no one, and Bonaparte least of all, had any interest in holding this inconvenient prisoner any longer.

From that point on the general was convinced that the right-wing legislators' opposition was the hostage rather than the accomplice of a royalist conspiracy seeking to overthrow the Republic with the help of part of the army: Pichegru's relations with the émigrés proved it, and Moreau's silence—Bonaparte had proof that he was aware of these relations—suggested the existence of numerous and influential complicities. He remained convinced of this: in their ineptness, frivolousness, and weakness, the supporters of the Rue de Clichy club, who were for the most part liberal royalists or conservative republicans, were unwittingly paving the way for counterrevolution.[82] It was not because he was still too much a "good-faith republican" that he decided to help the government defeat the party in favor of a return of the Bourbons: we know his opinion of the republican system in general and the Directory in particular. Moreover, he later said that he had coolly considered his options. Should he declare his opposition to both camps and present himself as the "regulator of the Republic"? "He did not think that the spirit of the times, and public opinion were such as to allow him to take so daring a step."[83] Should he back the royalist majority in the Councils? But the royalists, by attacking his policy, had themselves precluded that possibility, which was all the more improbable because he continued to think that the Revolution would be ended by governmental power and not by another revolution, no matter of what kind. And then it has to be said that the monarchy had much less to offer him than the Republic did: "What could a king do for his destiny? No matter how high he might be able to elevate him, that king would always be above him. Under the republic, on the contrary, no one would dominate him. Even if he did not yet dream of his unprecedented destiny, at least he foresaw in the republic an audacity and an immensity of enterprises that suited the audacity and immensity of his genius; whereas with a king France would be reduced to an obscure and limited existence. Thus, whatever he did with this republic, whether he served it or stifled it, Bonaparte could be great along with it, and through it, and he had to cherish it as his own future."[84]

Italy had revealed to him the extent of his own capacities. He had destroyed armies, negotiated with powers, governed, administrated, legislated, and, as "if he were already the dictator of that beautiful part of Europe," said a contemporary newspaper, he "held a sword in one hand and a pen in the other, occasionally laying down the latter to take up the baton that was the mark of supreme authority."[85] "High ambition" burned in him even more intensely since he had forced the Austrians to begin peace talks, but if he was already thinking of overthrowing the Directory, he refused to do it for the benefit of the royalists: "I am quite ready to weaken the Republican party," he said. "Some day I shall do it for my own advantage. In the meantime I must act with the Republican party."[86] Thus, he was resolved to defend a government that he scorned and institutions in which he did not believe, at least until he could overthrow them for his own benefit. He therefore donned once again the garb of the revolutionary and declared an "implacable war on the enemies of the republic and the Constitution of Year III,"[87] exhorting the government to use force against the royalist conspirators. On July 15 he wrote:

> The situation grows worse every day, and I believe, Citizen Directors, that it is high time you made a decision. . . . There is not a single man here who would not prefer to die in battle than to get himself killed in some alley in Paris. As for myself, I am accustomed to totally abdicating my own interests; however, I cannot be insensitive to the outrages, to the calumnies that eighty newspapers disseminate every day and on every occasion. . . . I see that the Clichy club wants to walk over my body to succeed in destroying the Republic. Are there no republicans left in France? And after having defeated Europe are we going to be reduced to seeking out some bit of earth where we can end our sad lives? With a single blow, you can save the Republic and perhaps two hundred people who are attached to its fate, and make peace in twenty-four hours: have the émigrés arrested; destroy foreigners' influence. If you need force, call upon the armies.[88]

At this time the Directory had already decided to overthrow the opposition by force. Not having had a parliamentary majority since the elections in April, Reubell, La Révellière, and Barras saw a dark future ahead. It didn't take a wizard to understand that all the quasi-majority on the right had to do was wait for the next partial election of the legislature, which was set for the spring of 1798, to gain a majority not only in the Councils but within the Executive Directory, to which Barthélemy had been elected after the elections of April 1797, replacing Letourneur. Another right-wing candidate—perhaps La Fayette, who, it was said, was about to be released by the Austrians—might come to further strengthen the duo already formed by Barthélemy and Carnot, and thus make the government lean in the direction of "reaction." The initiative for the coup d'état was left to Reubell, who feared seeing the majority challenge the policy of "natural borders," of which he was, within the government, the main defender. He had a hard time convincing the two colleagues he needed: the very anticlerical La Révellière-Lépeaux, who, exasperated by the right's proposals on behalf of the refractory priests, joined him in June, and Barras, who went over to his side after having hesitated between an alliance with him and an alliance with Carnot. However, the three directors were reluctant to lean on Bonaparte, whom they considered a potential agitator. Therefore, they chose to entrust the coup to Hoche, but a few untimely troop movements in the month of July sufficed to alert the parliamentary majority. The government had to send Hoche away. The conspirators were not happy about calling upon Bonaparte, but the republican petitions from the Army of Italy that he sent to Paris were at least a pledge that he would not hesitate to collaborate in the coup d'état.[89] For his part, Bonaparte had no intention of compromising his reputation by being involved in a risky operation to save a regime as discredited as the Directory. Remaining in Milan, he sent Augereau to Paris (July 27) and secretly also sent his aide-de-camp Lavalette. "See every one," he advised him, "keep clear of party spirit, give me the truth, and give it me free of all passion."[90] Lavalette conversed at length with Barras, who made a bad impression on him, and with Carnot, who convinced him of the necessity of adopting "a durable system of moderation" and of the impossibility of "pursuing any further the revolutionary route."[91] Whereas his army encouraged Bonaparte to side openly with the Directory, Lavalette constantly urged him to be prudent and to be wary of the risks he was running by associating himself with the "unjust violence" being exercised by the government.[92]

During the night of 17 Fructidor (September 3, 1797), soldiers under the command of Augereau—that "proud brigand," as Reubell called him—patrolled the streets of Paris.[93] General Pichegru and his friends in the legislature were arrested. Carnot hid out and then escaped abroad. On the morning of the eighteenth, the Directory issued a proclamation announcing to the country that a royalist conspiracy had been foiled and that any individual guilty of trying to reestablish the monarchy or the Constitution of 1793 would be summarily shot. The two Councils, or what remained of them, canceled the results of the elections in fifty departments out of ninety-eight (the election of 154 officials out of 262 was invalidated), deported to Guyana forty-two delegates of the Council of Five Hundred, eleven of the Council of the Ancients, two directors (Barthélemy and Carnot, on the run), several ministers, and a few dozen right-wing journalists. Barthélemy and Carnot were replaced in the Directory by Merlin de Douai and François de Neufchateau, the ministers of justice and the interior, respectively. An exceptional law ordered émigrés who had returned to France without authorization to leave within two weeks, on pain of death, reactivated the deportation measures voted in during the Terror against refractory priests, and muzzled the press by closing numerous opposition newspapers.

Bonaparte, affected by his aide-de-camp's warnings, henceforth refrained from publicly taking sides. From August onward he was as discreet as he had been vehement in July,[94] and when the coup d'état of 18 Fructidor had been carried out, he withdrew into a silence that the directors soon interpreted as a disavowal. "Your silence is very singular, my dear General,"[95] Barras wrote to him. Bonaparte put an end to his silence on September 22 by issuing a proclamation in which he halfheartedly expressed his pleasure in the defeat of the "enemies of the fatherland."[96] In private—and as always his remarks soon became public—he was not sparing with his criticisms. He praised Carnot's civic sense, deplored the deportation of the "Fructidorized" delegates, and condemned the reactivation of the decrees against the émigrés and the renascent religious intolerance. "It is currently to be hoped," he wrote to Augereau, "that the pendulum will not swing the other way and end up in the opposite party. It is only with wisdom and moderation of thought that the happiness of the country can be established in a stable manner."[97] The directors were so concerned that they sent Barras's secretary, Bottot, to see him; Bonaparte gave him an icy reception. Bottot left a report of these conversations: Bonaparte harshly criticized the Directory's Italian policy, the nomination as the successor of Hoche, who had suddenly disappeared, of his former lieutenant Augereau, whom the Directory was thus rewarding for his action on 18 Fructidor. Passing without transition to another subject, he accused the Directory of getting soft and, rather ironically, of allowing the generals to dictate to it, seemingly unaware that "military government [is] the worst of all." He went on to say that the government was attempting to conceal this weakness by means of unjust and arbitrary acts, and by the banishments that followed 18 Fructidor, which outraged public opinion, as was shown by the hundreds of letters received by his soldiers. In conclusion he even proposed to receive in Italy "all the men whom the Directory [considered] too dangerous to reside in Paris."[98] Finally, he admitted to Miot that he had sided with the Directory only in order to prevent a restoration that would have closed the gates of power to him. He had refused to play the role of Monk, but he also refused to allow anyone else, Pichegru or Moreau, to play it.[99] Between Monk and Caesar, he had made his choice. He was only waiting for his time to come.

FOURTEEN

Campoformio

Italy according to Bonaparte

*T*he negotiation of the final peace treaty with Austria began in Mombello a few weeks after the signature of the preliminary agreements made in Leoben (April 18, 1797). On the Austrian side, the minister of foreign affairs, Baron Thugut, had assumed the direction of operations, with the Marquis de Gallo representing him. On the French side, the situation was more complicated because Bonaparte did not hold a position comparable to Gallo's. Although Bonaparte did not always disagree with the Directory about the objectives to be attained, he often did. It added to the government's difficulty in making itself heard that General Clarke, its official representative in Italy, had become, through his own fault, less Bonaparte's supervisor than his auxiliary.[1] Furthermore, the Directory's Italian policy remained vague. On one subject, though, the government was consistent, that of the left bank of the Rhine. On this subject it had "absolute and obstinate views";[2] in particular, it was determined that in the final peace treaty priority would once again be given to French demands on the Rhine. In order to obtain Mainz and Cologne, it was prepared to make great concessions to Austria and to Prussia, trying to draw Prussia into its camp by suggesting that the time had come for it to acquire a preponderant influence in Germany, and even for the sovereign in Berlin to wear the crown of the German Empire. The Directory demanded the revision of several articles in the preliminary accords that it had reluctantly signed. First of all, it saw in the fifth article, which dealt with the meeting of a congress of all the German states, a major obstacle to French annexation of the left bank of the Rhine. The reference to "the integrity of the German Empire" as the basis for discussions seemed to rule out such an annexation.[3] Austria would no doubt agree to interpret this formula flexibly.[4] But it would do so in exchange for the Venetian terra firma, whose cession was awkward for the Directory, which would have far preferred to find in Germany rather than in Italy the indemnities promised Austria. It was offering the Austrians Salzburg, Passau, and Brixen, which were, of course, far less valuable than Verona or Vicenza. For his part, Bonaparte at first refused to go beyond the commitments made in Leoben, even though he had always thought that they were not definitive but simply a basis for discussion. The letter he sent to the Directory on April 22, four days after the signature of the preliminary accords, attests to this. As the outcome of "initial talks," the text signed at Leoben was open to "any kind of modification." Nonetheless, Bonaparte thought it capable of satisfying Austria's ambitions. In particular, the annexation of "the greater part of the states of Venice" would console Austria for the loss of Belgium and Milan.[5] I insist on this letter of April 22 because it does not yet mention ceding to the Austrians, in addition to the Venetian terra firma, the city of Venice itself.[6] Of course, we can sense that the general was annoyed by the later unification—foreseen by the preliminary accords—of Venice with the pontifical legations. He imagined another solution: attaching the city of Venice to the Cispadane Republic.[7] He clung to this idea for several weeks, as a plan sent to the Directory on May 19 shows. Instead of creating a single republic in Italy, as the (secret) article 8 of the preliminary accords foresaw, Bonaparte announced his intention to establish three republics: one (the Cisalpine) that would include Lombardy, Bergamo, Modena, Reggio, Massa, Carrara, and La Spezia; a second (the Cispadane) with Bologna, Ferrara, Venice, and Treviso; and a third with Genoa and the imperial fiefs.[8] But he doubted that this solution could be implemented, and he dreamed of another plan that would combine the legations with the Cisalpine Republic. The leaders of the henceforth tiny Republic of Venice would retain only "their island and the archipelago," without any further compensation."[9]

In the proposals communicated to the Austrian government somewhat later, on May 23, there was still no mention of ceding the city of Venice, because Baron Thugut, in his reply on June 16, protested "the establishment in Venice of a democratic government constantly occupied in disseminating and hatching antimonarchical feelings in provinces close to His Majesty's."[10] Thugut refused to see Venetia become an Austrian possession surrounded by republics that owed allegiance to France, one on the west (Milan), the other on the east (Venice). But in his heart of hearts, Bonaparte had understood that dismantling the Republic of Venice ultimately signed its death warrant. Whence his hesitations. It was in the last days of May 1797 that he began to think that sacrificing Venice was still the best way to lead Austria to agree both to the French annexation of the left bank of the Rhine and to the creation of a vast republic in Italy. No doubt this arrangement would give the emperor "an immense influence in Italy," but that was the price to be paid for reaching the Rhine without having to make any sacrifice in Italy.[11] There was one more thing. The sixth secret article of the preliminary accords stipulated that the fortress of Mantua, which Wurmser had surrendered in February, would be restored to the Austrians. But Bonaparte refused to give up Mantua. If he wanted to hang onto that fortress, he was going to have to offer the Austrians an additional compensation. That is why on May 27 he mentioned for the first time the possibility of the complete disappearance of the Venetian state:[12] "Venice, which has been in decay since the discovery of the Cape of Good Hope and the rise of Trieste and Ancona, can hardly survive the blows that we have just struck against it. Its people are inept, cowardly, and are not made for freedom; without lands, without waters, it seems natural that it should be left to those to whom we leave the continent."[13]

Bonaparte was now dreaming of a great republic. Sweeping across the northern part of the peninsula, it would extend from the Adriatic to the Gulf of Genoa, from Ancona to La Spezia, including Ferrara, Bologna, Modena, Milan, and Genoa.[14] It was because he wanted Ancona (a pontifical possession that France was provisionally occupying in accord with the Treaty of Tolentino) that he refused to let the legations go. The circumstances seemed propitious. It was said that Pius VI was ill, perhaps dying. If this news was confirmed, the moment was favorable, because the kingdom of Naples was planning to take advantage of the pope's death to make a few corrections in its boundaries. The king of Naples wanted Ancona, and he offered Napoleon Elba and Piombino in exchange. Napoleon turned him down—it was Ancona he wanted. However, he had understood that from then on, everything was negotiable. Although, contrary to what some historians have maintained,[15] he was not now envisaging putting an end to the pope's temporal power, any more than he had at the time of the treaties of Bologna and Tolentino. He had made up his mind that if Naples took advantage of the circumstances to seize part of the Roman state, he was also going to appropriate part of it. It was only when he received confirmation that the pope had recovered his health that he asked General Dallemagne, the governor of Ancona, to "promote as much as possible the establishment of a republican government in Ancona."[16]

Napoleon was no less preoccupied with the west side of the Italian peninsula than with the east. Although he was no longer thinking about overthrowing the House of Savoy—Piedmont was protected by the peace treaty signed with France on May 15, 1796—he had sought to draw it into an alliance that he said would inevitably lead to the fall of the monarchy. Regarding the equivocations of the Directory, which was refusing to transform the peace treaty into a genuine alliance, he wrote: "Is the problem that this would mean being allied with a king? . . . Is it the desire to revolutionize Piedmont and to incorporate it into the Cisalpine Republic? The way to do that smoothly, without violating the treaty, and without even impropriety, is to mix with our troops and associate with our successes a body of 10,000 Piedmontese, who would necessarily be the elite of the nation. Six months later, the king of Piedmont would be dethroned. It's like a giant who embraces a pygmy and holds him in his arms; he suffocates him, but cannot be accused of any crime."[17]

For a time he had considered adopting the same course with regard to the Republic of Genoa. Here he may have felt a resurgence of his Paolist youth: Bonaparte did not like Genoa, and felt as little sympathy for it as he did for Venice. At the beginning of the Italian campaign he had already envisaged the possibility of triggering a revolution in order to cleanse the Genoese senate of its members who were the most hostile to France. It was not only the Austrian counterattacks that had forced him to defer settling accounts with Genoa; he had also thought of transforming the peace treaty between France and Genoa signed on October 9, 1796, into an alliance that would make Genoa France's vassal. "Genoa's time has not yet come," he admitted with some regret.[18] Eight months after the signature of this treaty, when the war was over and the Venetian oligarchy had been deprived of its power, "the right moment" seemed to him to have come.[19] The Venetian senate abdicated on May 12, and an insurrection broke out in Genoa on the twenty-second. Was it spontaneous? Three days earlier Bonaparte was already using the past tense in referring to the Genoese government.[20] However, this uprising by supporters of France turned into a fiasco: its leaders were arrested and two Frenchmen killed. Bonaparte, furious about his supporters' "stupidities," sent the Genoese doge a warning, threatening to invade if he did not turn over the Frenchmen's killers and immediately disarm the port workers who had been roused against the revolutionary party.[21] Bonaparte was not considering wiping Genoa off the political map of Italy, as he was preparing to do with Venice, but he would have been pleased to see it dismembered, to leave intact its worm-eaten institutions but seize its eastern part and combine it, along with Massa and Carrara, into the Lombard Republic: the latter would then have access to the Gulf of Genoa via the port of La Spezia.[22] In all likelihood, at that point Bonaparte was preempted by Faypoult. The French ambassador, concerned to preserve the integrity and the independence of the Genoese state, persuaded its leaders that it would be more honorable for them to hand power over to the party favorable to France than to persist in a hopeless resistance, with the French army camped before the city gates. Bonaparte had to change his tactics. On May 30 he declared that he did not seek the disappearance of the Republic of Genoa, but only a change in its leadership and the reform of its institutions.[23] On June 6, at the end of discussions conducted with Faypoult and three Genoese representatives, a "Ligurian Republic" replaced that of Genoa, and Bonaparte gave it a provisional government that was assigned to write a new constitution. Having thus "rallied" the northwest of the peninsula to the French cause, Bonaparte, who had to be content with Massa-Carrara, giving up La Spezia, could now finish constituting the republic whose creation the Austrians had authorized at Leoben.

A new question now arose: Would this republic be a single political unit, or would it be a federation of formally independent states? The general had hesitated a great deal, and often changed his mind, fearing that "the childhood in which Italians still exist,"[24] and especially Italy's parochialism and ancestral rivalries, might make the creation of a large state impossible. He had no illusions about this. The following letter is late—he wrote it to Talleyrand on October 7, 1797—but it sums up well the remarks about Italians that Bonaparte often made to his interlocutors, remarks that are not very kind, even pessimistic, but mixed with a glimmer of hope:

> You know little about these peoples. They are not worth having 40,000 Frenchmen killed for them. I see from your letters that you are still operating on a false hypothesis: you imagine that liberty makes a soft,

superstitious, changeable, and cowardly people do great things. . . . Don't allow yourself to be fooled by a few Italian adventurers in Paris, or even by a few ministers . . . ; public opinion in France is strangely mistaken about the Italians. Only a little skill, a little dexterity, the ascendancy that I have acquired, and harsh examples can give these peoples great respect for the nation and an interest, though an extremely weak one, in the cause that we are fighting for. . . . I have the honor of telling you again: little by little, the people of the Cisalpine Republic will become enthusiastic about liberty; little by little, it will organize itself, and in four or five years it might have thirty thousand passable troops.[25]

The experience of the Cispadane Republic, far from dissipating his fears, had instead confirmed them. Since the meeting of the congress of Modena in October 1796, the Cispadans had been constantly tearing each other apart, to the point that Bonaparte finally had to appear in person to dissolve the assembly and call a new one. The recently created Cispadane Republic had no less than four provisional governments, the first in Bologna, the second in Ferrara, the third in Modena, and the last in Reggio; they bickered constantly and fundamentally did not want to coexist. On March 19, 1797, the congress finally adopted a constitution, modeled on that of France. On March 27 the Cispadane Republic was proclaimed, and was at the same time enlarged by the addition of the small principality of Massa and Carrara (on the other side of the peninsula, near Genoa). But the respite was brief. The elections organized a month later turned to the advantage of the supporters of the Old Regime, Bologna was already regretting its union with Modena, and Emilia was regretting having bound its fate to that of Romagna. In fact, the situation varied from one city to another. In Milan it was exactly the opposite: there, revolutionary tendencies had to be calmed, not "excited." The Milanese revolutionaries were demanding independence with increasing intensity, and some of them, having come together in a "Black League," even went so far as to demand that Italy be freed from the double yoke of the Austrians and the French. Bonaparte adapted his policy to the circumstances. He explained it this way:

The Cispadane republics are divided into three parties: first, the supporters of their former government; second, those of an independent, but rather aristocratic, constitution; third, those of the French constitution or pure democracy. I restrain the first, support the second, and moderate the third, because the second party is that of the wealthy property owners and priests, who in the final analysis would end up winning the support of the majority of the people, whom it is essential that we rally to the French party. The last party is composed of young people, writers and men who, as in France and in all other countries, do not change government and love liberty only in order to make a revolution. At this time, there are three parties in Lombardy: first, the one that allows itself to be led by the French; second, the one that would like liberty and even shows its desire with some impatience; third, the party favorable to the Austrians and hostile to the French. I support and encourage the first, I contain the second, and I repress the third.[26]

The mobilization in Milan was not entirely without advantages, because it had made it possible to set up a Lombard Legion whose 3,700 men wore on their hats the motto "Libertà italiana."[27] But it made it no longer possible to leave Lombardy under a provisional administration, and on March 24, the day after the adoption of the Cispadane constitution, Bonaparte wrote to the Directory: "The Lombards are very impatient; they want us to declare their liberty and also to allow them to write their own constitution."[28] This time the Directory approved the creation of a "Cisalpine Republic" and even suggested combining the Cispadane and the Cisalpine republics so as to constitute a more imposing state that would be better able to maintain and defend itself once a peace treaty with Austria was signed and the French left the peninsula. Thus it was the Directory that proposed a union that Bonaparte considered delicate to say the least, even though he thought it desirable. But these instructions of April 7, which were issued before the preliminary accords at Leoben (April 18), in no way meant that the Directory had adopted its general's Italian policy and was henceforth ahead of him. In fact, the French government still did not exclude the possibility of returning to the Austrians their Italian possessions. It simply wanted to believe, or pretended to believe, that proclaiming the independence of a large part of northern Italy, organizing it into a single state, and endowing it with institutions analogous to those of France, would lead to a "regeneration" of people's minds so complete that the Austrians, once their former possessions were restored to them, would have the greatest difficulty in making them obey again. In short, whatever conditions were set by the peace treaty, the seeds of a future emancipation would have been sown in Italy.[29]

Aware of the impossibility of further delaying the proclamation of an independent republic in Lombardy, Bonaparte authorized Milan to say that it was the seat of a "transpadane republic," and at the beginning of May he named several committees assigned to constitute the new state. He was not for the moment very favorable to the idea of attaching the Cispadane Republic to this new one, and afraid of displeasing both parties, he began by refusing.[30] But no sooner had he said that it was better not to rush things than he detached, on May 9, Reggio and Modena from the Cispadane Republic in order to add them to the Cisalpine.[31] Once the latter had been officially proclaimed, he annexed the Cispadane Republic to it.[32] The new republic thus extended from Rimini and Bologna to Modena and Mantua, from there to Milan, and from Milan to the borders of Tuscany and the Ligurian Republic, which had become a satellite state. A diplomat who talked with Bonaparte at Mombello later wrote: "He was already no longer the general of a triumphant republic; he was a conqueror in his own right."[33]

The Peace of Campoformio

In the meantime the peace negotiations with Austria, launched with great urgency, had hardly advanced. The preliminary accords had foreseen the signing of the final peace treaty in Bern, at a congress attended by the respective allies of the two powers; a different, Franco-German congress was to decide, as we have said, the question of the left bank of the Rhine. But Bonaparte and the Marquis de Gallo, Austria's representative, agreed to sign the peace treaty in Milan itself, without prior consultation with their two governments' allies, and also to arrive at an understanding regarding the Rhine so that the second congress, which was to meet in Rastatt on July 1, would only have to ratify formally the arrangements already made.[34] Would the peace be signed before summer arrived? Gallo hoped so, not as Austria's plenipotentiary, but as a Neapolitan diplomat. As strange as it may seem, it was in fact to the Neapolitan ambassador in Vienna that Austria had entrusted the defense of its interests. Bonaparte was well aware of that when, welcoming Gallo to Leoben, he bluntly asked him if he was going to be negotiating with Vienna or with Naples.[35] While acting as Francis II's loyal servant, Gallo could not forget that he was Italian, and the situation of Italy led him to seek a rapid solution that Austria's interests made it his duty to delay. Just as the French government was half obeyed by its general, the Austrians were only half seconded by their Neapolitan emissary: "The Marquis Gallo . . . , whose professional duty as a diplomat required him to remain cool, was so worried about the condition of Italy that he protested against the policy he was obliged to follow at Mombello and against the policy Vienna dictated to him. The Congress seemed to him an 'abstract fixation'; in his view, Vienna should hasten to make a separate peace and occupy Venetia. On June 24 he [wrote] to his minister in Naples: 'Italy is heading for ruin. Every day a government falls; every day democracy expands and establishes itself. If the pope dies, his state will be another prey for the French and a new cause of disorder, to the ruin of the Catholic religion and Italy's political system.'"[36]

Vienna saw things differently, and on June 19, as we have said, the reply to Bonaparte's offers arrived: a flat refusal. Thugut not only protested against the installation of a revolutionary government in Venice; he refused to sign a separate peace and demanded a meeting of the general congress provided for in article 4 of the preliminary accords. The Austrian foreign minister had another reason to delay the outcome of the discussions, which he achieved by making demands that were unacceptable in the French view: he knew how tense the political situation in France was, and because he could not predict whether the Legislative Body or the Directory would prevail, it was in his interest to wait. He even sent agents to Paris to inquire into the right wing's intentions. "If the party supporting *the old borders* triumphed in Paris," Albert Sorel commented, "it was immediate peace, and, after that peace, a government paralyzed by factions, without glory or prestige, a democratic Poland; Bonaparte would be disavowed, dismissed, or at least abandoned."[37] Thugut suspended the negotiations.

The Austrian was all the more eager to delay because the steps taken by the French led him to doubt the sincerity of their expressions of peaceful intentions.

It has to be said that Bonaparte had used the ceasefire following the signature of the preliminary accords to exploit his advantage, having the Ionian islands occupied, introducing revolutionary legislation in Venetia, which was supposed to become Austrian, and finally proclaiming the Cisalpine Republic without even waiting for the final peace treaty to be signed. Vienna had responded by occupying Istria and Dalmatia. Each side suspected the other of wanting war: the Austrians were making obvious military preparations, while Bonaparte was urging the Directory to get ahead of the enemy by attacking without further delay. It was not that Bonaparte wanted war at any price; on the contrary, it was in his interest to sign a peace treaty that France would owe to him. What glory would be attached to his name if, to the title of conqueror of Italy, he added that of Europe's peacemaker! That is why he had so imprudently rushed across the Alps, more intent on forcing Austria to negotiate than on entering Vienna itself. He was all the more eager to sign the peace treaty because, on the one hand, he still feared that if hostilities resumed he would have to share the glory with Hoche, and on the other hand, he knew that the political crisis raging in France would increase his room for maneuver. But he also belonged, perhaps by his profession, and surely by his situation, to the war party. Peace, he admitted to Miot de Melito, was far from being in his interest: "You see what I am, what I can now do in Italy. If the peace is made, I shall no longer be at the head of the army to which I have attached myself, I shall have to give up this power, this high position where I have placed myself, and go to court the favor of the lawyers at the Luxembourg Palace." What, in fact, would become of him once the fighting stopped? He would cease to be the "king of Italy" and become once again the general of a government he despised. That was impossible. But on the other hand, public opinion wanted peace so much that he could not refuse it without taking the risk of seeing the French turn their backs on him: "Peace," he went on, "may be necessary to satisfy the desires of our onlookers in Paris, and if it has to be made, it is up to me to make it. If I left that honor to someone else, this good deed would raise him higher in public opinion than all my victories."[38] This dilemma was to confront him with even greater force after his return to France, and as we know, he finally found a solution more in his predilections than in the long vacations he sometimes dreamed about: the expedition to Egypt.[39]

The Directory also hesitated to resume hostilities. The right, which was on a roll, had made peace one of its articles of faith. Public opinion, which supported it, would have reacted very badly to a breaking of the armistice. The government had to handle the opposition carefully, and it had even adopted a program more modest than the one announced at the beginning of the year: it still demanded "the limit of the Rhine, which nature seems to have indicated for the republic," but said it was nonetheless prepared to give up Mainz, Koblenz, and Cologne, if that made it easier to conclude the peace.[40] Moreover, Carnot never ceased to repeat that peace would not be made without important concessions to Austria.[41] On July 31, Austria finally used the pretext of Bonaparte's ultimatum threatening Francis II with the "ravaging of Germany" to request the resumption of talks.[42] Vienna gave up its demand for a meeting of the congress and declared that it was prepared to "provide its plenipotentiaries with all the powers necessary to negotiate, immediately and without further delay, in Udine, and to conclude and sign there, if the occasion presents itself, the definitive peace treaty between Austria and France."[43] The emperor had his reasons for going back to the negotiating table: he had just learned, on the one hand, that the English had restarted talks with the French and did not exclude the possibility of signing a separate peace;[44] and on the other hand, that in Russia Catherine the Great's successor, Czar Paul, was proposing to find a solution to the European conflict by offering his mediation—which Austria feared would be very favorable to Prussia.

On the French side, there was still the same uncertainty regarding the objectives to be attained. France was following, so to speak, three plans: Directors Reubell and La Révellière had one, their colleagues Carnot and Barthélemy had another, and, of course, Bonaparte had his own. The first one, dated August 19, enjoined Bonaparte and Clarke to take the preliminary accords as the basis for negotiation, but while seeking to "get the emperor out of Italy and to insist that he expand in Germany."[45] Two days before, Carnot had sent Bonaparte a letter telling him to do precisely the opposite: "What . . . seizes the attention of reasonable men who want to finally put an end to the ills of the country is the prospect of peace. They all have their eyes fixed on you, my dear general; you hold in your hands the fate of France as a whole: sign the peace and you will change its face, as if by enchantment. Even if you have to do it solely on the basis of the preliminary treaty of Leoben, sign it: it will still be superb; it will be superb for the emperor as well, it is true; but what do we care: could the peace be solid if he were too much injured?"[46]

As for the general, he set forth his plan in a letter sent to Talleyrand on September 12: "For us, the borders specified in our observations on article 4 of the preliminary accords, that is, Mainz, etc. For the emperor, Venice [including the city] and the Adige borders. Corfu and other islands are for us. The rest of Italy free, in the manner of the Cisalpine."[47] He was determined, this time, to hand over the city of Venice in exchange for the legations.

Bonaparte left for Udine, moving into a palace in Passariano that had belonged to Ludovico Manin, the last doge of Venice. The negotiations resumed, and were sometimes stormy, always tense. The Rhine, along with the legations, was the subject of disputes. Bonaparte claimed Mainz, Worms, and Speyer. The Austrians refused to cede lands belonging to the Empire without the consent of the imperial Diet, but they demanded Bologna and Ferrara, provoking Bonaparte's "feigned and artificial" rage.[48] He shouted: "How many leagues is your army from Paris?," assuring them that his army could be at Vienna in a week.[49] On September 13, after a week of fruitless discussions, the parties separated. Bonaparte was furious and blamed the failure on the Old Regime diplomats; he understood neither their starchy manners nor their fear of their superiors: "These people are so slow! They think a peace treaty of this kind has to be considered for three years. . . . They constantly refer to Thugut and their instructions. In private, they will tell you *sotto voce*, after looking all around to see if anyone can hear them, that Thugut is a scoundrel who ought to be hanged; but Thugut is the true sovereign of Vienna."[50] People began to talk again about war, and Bonaparte ordered his army to be ready to march on Vienna. It might have taken two or three more months to move beyond the deadlock, had the coup d'état on 18 Fructidor (September 4, 1797) not suddenly changed the situation.

Bonaparte heard the news on September 11. Henceforth he no longer considered breaking the armistice: the "peace party" having been overthrown, he could now incarnate all by himself the hope for peace by proposing, no longer the peace based on France's return to its former borders that was advocated by the royalists, but rather a "glorious" peace that would make permanent the annexation of Belgium and part of the left bank of the Rhine, and also see the foundation in Italy of a republic whose power would counterbalance the concessions made to Austria. He wanted, as he later said on Saint Helena, to add "to the glory of the conqueror and [the] peacemaker that of the founder of two great republics"[51]—the Cisalpine, of course, but also the French, whose new borders, which had been disputed for such a long time, would finally be recognized. He raised the flag of peace all the more willingly because the Directory, strengthened by the Fructidor crisis, now refused to make any concessions. The government already saw itself, Albert Sorel said, "the master of Europe, as it was the master of Paris,"[52] thinking itself so invincible that it ended the talks with England in Lille and rejected Russia's offer of mediation. Staking everything on a close alliance with Prussia, it wanted Austria to give up Italy altogether and accept as its only compensation Istria, Dalmatia, and the secularization, to its benefit, of the bishoprics of Salzburg and Passau. Knowing that Vienna would not agree to sign on such conditions, it planned to launch a winter offensive in Germany, under Hoche's command, that would drive to Vienna to steal the victory from Bonaparte. That was enough to make Bonaparte want to sign the peace treaty as soon as possible, especially because after Hoche died a few days later, on September 19, the best solution the Directory had been able to think of was to entrust his army to Augereau. The time when Bonaparte was inclined to sing the praises of his lieutenant was long past. Since Augereau had arrived in Paris to support the government against the attacks from the right, his vanity had swollen enormously; he seemed to have forgotten that he had served under Bonaparte, said to anyone who would listen that he would be able, if necessary, to oppose the ambitions of the commander of the Army of Italy, implied that his former boss had maintained suspicious relations with the people banished in Fructidor, and demanded that the Army of Italy reimburse him for his "extraordinary expenses" in the amount of 600,000 francs.[53] Bonaparte was revolted by the notion that he might have to share the laurels of victory and of the peace with his former subordinate. Thus he had to arrive at an agreement with the Austrians, and quickly. As soon as he had been informed of the results of 18 Fructidor, he submitted to the Directory the plan that he had already outlined in his letter of the twelfth to Talleyrand, which set conditions considerably less demanding than those now being made by the French government: "(1) The line of the Adige to the Emperor, including the city of Venice; (2) the line of the Adige to the French Republic, and thus Mantua; (3) the constitutional borders, as they were specified in the protocol of the 5th session, including Mainz; (4) that the Emperor would enter into possession of Italy only when we enter the ramparts of Mainz; (5) that Corfu and the other islands go to us; (6) that what we lack to reach the border of the Rhine could be arranged in the peace treaty with the Empire."[54]

If 18 Fructidor accelerated the conclusion of the negotiations, the arrival in Udine of a new Austrian negotiator, Count Ludwig of Cobenzl, also helped. He had his first discussion with Bonaparte on September 27. "The White Bear of the North," as Napoleon called him,[55] was forty-four years old. Marmont tells us that he was "very ugly and monstrously large,"[56] but also that he was an accomplished actor, almost without scruples, Voltairian with these Frenchmen whom he secretly feared, and obsequious with the princes. "Proud of his rank and his importance," Napoleon said, "he had no doubt that the dignity of his manners and his familiarity with courts would easily crush a general who had come out of the revolutionary camps; so he approached the French general with a certain insouciance."[57] The first collision was in fact a brutal one. In order to size up his adversary, Cobenzl brought up the question of the congress again; Bonaparte got angry, accusing the Austrian of bad faith and duplicity, swearing that he would no longer endure insults and threatening to march on Vienna; they argued about Venice, the Rhine, Germany—and parted very pleased with one another. They understood each other implicitly, and even as they continued to play cat and mouse, they soon became persuaded that they would be able to negotiate in a way satisfactory to both parties, if not to the French government. Bonaparte agreed to sacrifice the Venetians, as he had already implied at Leoben; the Austrians, for their part, were less afraid of the formation of a state that would be a French satellite than of Prussia's scheming in Germany. Bonaparte had sensed this, and what Cobenzl confided to him confirmed him in the notion that Austria wanted above all to avoid the threat that a Franco-Prussian alliance would represent for it.[58] Everything went very fast, even if not without difficulties. There were still, on both sides, shouts, threats, and even broken crockery: "It isn't easy to negotiate with Bonaparte," Cobenzl complained.[59] But although they quarreled, it was, as Sorel puts it, "on the same terrain, and through all these feints, they drew nearer to one another."[60]

The Directory continued to send Bonaparte menacing dispatches in which it demanded that he confront the Austrians with this choice: the cession of the left bank and the renunciation of Italy, or war. Bonaparte turned a deaf ear, claimed he was exhausted, and saying that he needed "two years of rest,"[61] asked to be replaced, knowing full well that the threat of his resignation, of which he had already made ample use, was a very effective way of getting the directors to back down. On October 8, after having received from Paris for the nth time, the order to reject Austria's annexation of Venetia, Bonaparte warned Cobenzl that if he wanted Venice, he had to sign without waiting for Vienna's permission.[62] The next day the agreement was ready.[63] On the eleventh there was a final incident that almost caused a complete failure. Bonaparte was aware that he was playing for high stakes, and because the destiny of the left bank of the Rhine remained officially dependent on the consent of the German Empire, at the last minute he tried to extract from his interlocutor guarantees regarding its cession to France. Cobenzl held firm, protesting against the modifications that had been surreptitiously introduced into the text that had already been approved by both parties:

> This project contained several new articles that were entirely inadmissible. . . . The first reading of this masterpiece written by Bonaparte had already given rise to a few rather sharp discussions in the course of which the French plenipotentiary, overheated by two nights without sleep, drank one glass of punch after another. We then proceeded to examine article by article the ones that could be adopted, and after having agreed on the first two or three, we came to the one that stipulated the limits of France in the Empire: I explained with moderation and the greatest calm its impossibility. . . . Bonaparte rose with the greatest fury, cursed like a rough soldier, scribbled his name in an illegible manner on a new copy of the declaration that had already been recorded once, and without observing that formality or waiting for our signatures, he put on his hat in the conference room itself and left, continuing into the street his shouting in a way that can only be attributed to drunkenness.[64]

Bonaparte broke a "porcelain tea service,"[65] shouting at an impassive Cobenzl, who kept repeating that the Empire's consent was necessary: "The Empire is an old servant used to being raped by everyone!"[66] His aides-de-camp and the Marquis de Gallo ran after him to try to calm him down. Was he play-acting? He later said he was: "M. de Cobenzl stood petrified; but M. de Gallo, who was of a more conciliatory temper, followed the French General to his carriage, endeavouring to detain him. 'He almost dragged me back by main force,' said the emperor, 'and with so pitiable an air, that, in spite of my apparent anger, I could not refrain from laughing in my sleeve.'"[67] Two days later the first snow appeared unexpectedly on the summits of the mountains. Bourrienne woke the general at 7 A.M., as he did every day, and told him that autumn, which had been very mild, had suddenly given way to winter. Bonaparte leaped out of bed and ran to the window: "Snow before the middle of October," he cried. "What a country! Well! we must have peace."[68]

The treaty was signed on the night of October 17 in Campoformio, halfway between Passariano and Udine, where Cobenzl was residing. "The general," one of his aides-de-camp later said, was in a "charmingly gay mood." The discussions were over. He no longer feared the arrival of a counter-order from the Directory. He signed with a light heart, so satisfied that he treated the Austrians to a few of the ghost stories he liked so much.[69]

Controversies regarding a Treaty

The Treaty of Campoformio was the object of vehement debate in the Directory on October 26, 1797. The directors refused to ratify the treaty, in which they saw not only "an impudent denial of the principles of the French Revolution" but also the threat of an endless war: this text was Bonaparte's, not theirs. Bonaparte, they said, had sacrificed the Rhine to Italy, and ultimately made a peace that was not only fragile but entirely to Austria's advantage.[70] Campoformio? Nothing less than a betrayal of France's vital interests.[71] Bonaparte anticipated their reaction so well that he had made the first move by justifying himself at length:

I have made use of the powers you gave me and the confidence you had in me to conclude the aforementioned peace. . . . If, in all these calculations, I have been mistaken, my heart is pure, my intentions are righteous: I paid no attention to the interests of my reputation, my vanity, my ambition; I have considered only the fatherland and the government; I have responded in a manner worthy of me to the unlimited confidence that the Directory has been willing to grant me for the past two years. I believe I have done what each member of the Directory would have done in my place. Through my services, I have deserved the government's and the nation's approval; I have received repeated tokens of its esteem. It remains for me only to return to the masses, to take up once again Cincinnatus's plow, and provide an example of the respect for magistrates and of aversion to a military regime, which has destroyed so many republics and caused the downfall of several governments.[72]

Naturally the government was not convinced by Bonaparte's protestations of loyalty, and still less reassured by his expressed desire to exchange Caesar's sword for Cincinnatus's plow. But what were they to do? In his memoirs La Révellière refers to this dilemma: to reject the Treaty of Campoformio was to lose the approval of public opinion, which wanted peace and had believed the royalists when they cried everywhere that the republican government wanted to "perpetuate the war" by any and all means. It was also to lose the services of the only general in sight, given that Hoche was dead and Moreau was in disgrace.[73] And finally, it was to risk Bonaparte's vengeance: they suspected he would leave the army and, out of spite, "prepare inevitable defeats for his successor . . . by sowing in the Cisalpine people and in the French army all the seeds of division, discontent, and sedition."[74] They were scared, and it was because they were scared, scared of Bonaparte and of the Legislative Body that they had, however, just cleansed, that they ratified, with heavy hearts, the Treaty of Campoformio, and pretended to be glad about it by having Talleyrand declare, during the ceremony of the official presentation of the treaty on October 31: "This is certainly not one of those servile peace treaties imposed by force. . . . No, it is victory that calls a halt; it is courage that restrains itself; it is a peace freely subscribed and

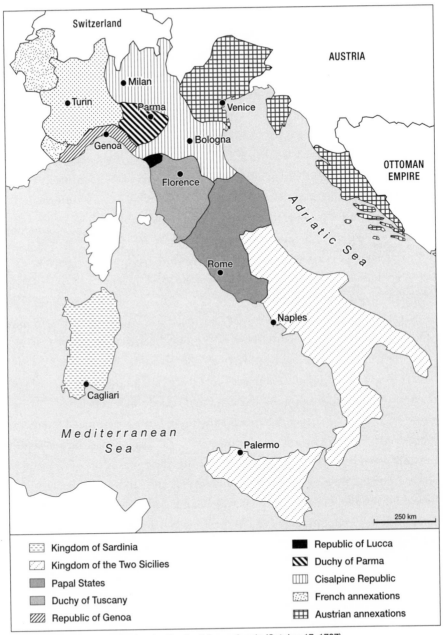

Switzerland

Milan

Turin

Parma

Genoa

Bologna

Venice

AUSTRIA

OTTOMAN EMPIRE

Florence

Adriatic Sea

Rome

Naples

Mediterranean Sea

Cagliari

Palermo

250 km

Kingdom of Sardinia

Kingdom of the Two Sicilies

Papal States

Duchy of Tuscany

Republic of Genoa

Republic of Lucca

Duchy of Parma

Cisalpine Republic

French annexations

Austrian annexations

Italy after the Treaty of Campoformio (October 17, 1797)

formally guaranteed which, by enlarging the domain of liberty, strengthens the Revolution, extinguishes the mad ambitions of external enemies, and . . . opens before us a future rich with all kinds of hope."[75]

Many historians have adopted the Directory's accusations in order to heap reproaches on Bonaparte. Is that justified? The Peace of Campoformio certainly had one victim: "the plans for a Prussian alliance that were so dear to all the men of the Revolution."[76] Austria had in fact obtained from Bonaparte that France would forego the annexation of Prussian territories on the left bank of the Rhine that it was occupying (the city of Cologne, in particular), and consequently that Prussia would not receive in Germany any of the indemnities promised to the princes of the left bank who were going to be dispossessed of their states. However, Prussia hoped that such territorial exchanges would allow it to round out its territory and at the same time increase its influence in northern Germany and in the imperial Diet. The peace treaty Bonaparte signed thus represented a defeat for Prussian diplomacy and a grave threat to the peace treaty signed with Berlin in 1795. In the end France was annexing all the territories located west of a line running from Basel to Mainz (the latter becoming French) along the river, and then from the mouth of the Nette to Julich and Venlo, in order to leave the (Prussian) region of Cologne outside the cessions decided upon in Campoformio.[77] This borderline was not, strictly speaking, set by the treaty, insofar as it was the subject of a secret article in which the emperor agreed to "use his good offices to see that the Empire consented" to cede the territories concerned to France. It was this restriction that angered the Directory. A priori, its anger was justified: if France went to war to conquer the left bank of the Rhine, then the war had not yet been won, because the consent of the Empire in "a congress composed solely of the plenipotentiaries of the Empire and those of France" still had to be obtained. This congress was to meet in Rastatt "to make peace between these two powers."[78] It is true that regarding the Rhine, Bonaparte, while insisting that Mainz become French, did not share the "absolute and obstinate views" of the Directory. Let us listen to Albert Sorel:

[Bonaparte] thought that whoever held Mainz would necessarily end up in Cologne. Time would do the job better than any treaty. Bonaparte shared neither the Paris politicians' infatuation with the greatness of

Prussia nor the deplorable mania that led Sieyès and his disciples to reform the German constitution. The treaties of Basel and Berlin stipulated in favor of the king of Prussia ample compensations intended to purchase his consent to the absorption of the left bank of the Rhine into France.[79] Compensations of the same kind would have to be given to the other lay princes holding possessions on the left bank. "To bring down the German Empire," he wrote on May 27, "is to lose the advantage of Belgium, and of the Rhine border; it is put ten to twelve million inhabitants in the hands of two powers of which we are equally wary. If the German entity did not exist, it would have to be created deliberately for our purposes."[80] France would not occupy the whole extent of Gaul, but Prussia would remain secondary and scattered, and France would be more secure in its supremacy than it would be all along the line of the Rhine in the presence of a Prussia that was concentrated and raised to the first rank. Prussia would thus return to its role, which was to be a counterweight to Austria. . . . France, by respecting the secondary states, would once again become the arbiter of Germany.[81]

Notwithstanding Bonaparte's ideas about Germany, we have to remind his detractors that he could not have obtained more at Campoformio, where he had made peace not with the head of the Holy Roman Empire, but with the king of Bohemia and Hungary, on whom war had been declared on April 20, 1792. We recall that Francis II von Habsburg was not only Archduke of Austria, and as such the head of the hereditary states of the House of Austria, king of Bohemia and Hungary, but also the elected German emperor (even if the office had in fact become hereditary in the House of Habsburg since the election of 1438). However, this latter title did not in any way give him the power to authorize alienations of territory, which could be decided upon only by the federated sovereigns within the empire as a whole. The emperor thus could not do more than he did: refer the final decision to a congress, while at the same time agreeing with France regarding the line of the new border, and committing himself to use his good offices with the congress, explaining that in the event of failure, that is, of the resumption of hostilities between France and the Empire, he would provide, qua Archduke of Austria, "only his contingent" of

7,000 men, and try not to do "any harm to the peace and friendship that [had just been] established between His Majesty and the French Republic."[82] This amounted to condemning in advance any possible German mobilization, and actually increased the chances of a negotiation in which the French would have the advantage of occupying de facto the territories they were claiming, and in which the Austrians would be all the more capable of pleading in favor of the necessary sacrifices because they would themselves have sacrificed their own possessions on the left bank, not to mention Belgium.[83] Thus, the Treaty of Campoformio not only marked the international recognition of the unification of Belgium with France, but created the conditions for an almost inevitable absorption of the left bank of the Rhine into the Republic. As Roger Dufraisse rightly observes,

> The Treaty of Campoformio was to find its fulfillment in the Peace of Lunéville (February 9, 1801), whose article 6 reads: "His Majesty the Emperor and King, in his own name and in that of the German empire, agrees that the French Republic henceforth possesses in all sovereignty and property the domains located on the left bank of the Rhine . . . in conformity with what had been expressly consented to by the Empire's deputation at the congress of Rastatt." Thus, the Rastatt congress [and consequently the Peace of Campoformio, from which it emanated] had not been merely a pointless meeting, because its results were to constitute the foundation for the Peace of Lunéville. The congress had been made possible only by the accords of Leoben and Campoformio, which in turn proceeded directly from Bonaparte's victories in Italy. It is thus unfair to accuse him of having sacrificed the Rhine to Italy.[84]

It is just as wrong to claim that the treaty was entirely to the advantage of Austria, even if the latter did not emerge from the conflict as a loser. In fact, if it had to recognize officially the Cisalpine Republic that had been established in its former possessions in Lombardy, as well as the attachment of the Cisalpine Republic to that of Mantua, it could be satisfied in other respects: in Germany, France agreed to "use its good offices to help His Majesty the Emperor acquire . . . the archbishopric of Salzburg and the part of the Bavarian circle situated between the archbishopric of Salzburg and the Tyrol";[85] in Italy it obtained the Republic of Venice, including the city, and its possessions of Istria and Dalmatia, which gave it the access to the Mediterranean it had long desired, even if France acquired for itself the Ionian islands and the Venetian trading posts in Albania.[86] Nevertheless, Bonaparte's detractors object that nothing was more fragile than this pax Italiana, and Guglielmo Ferrero, following Albert Sorel, even sees in it the germ of the wars that were to ravage Europe for almost twenty years.[87] The annihilation of the Republic of Venice and the creation of the Cisalpine Republic, he asserts, were "two enormous events that destroyed first of all the balance of the Italian system, and then, as a result, the balance of the whole European system," throwing "the Western world" into chaos. Regarding "the balance of the Italian system," Ferrero is exaggerating. It is true that the French intervention put a sudden and chaotic end to almost a century of peace in Italy, but the Italian states, their political systems, and their borders did not always have the antiquity that Ferrero lends them. Italy had been able to give the illusion that it was balanced and stable only because the great European powers had been indifferent to it since the Treaty of Aix-la-Chapelle (1748), in which its neutrality had been proclaimed. Moreover, can we really see in the destruction of the Republic of Venice the fatal blow that destroyed the European system of international relations established by the treaties of Westphalia (1648)?

Since the end of the Thirty Years' War (1618–1648) the international system had as its only legitimate actors a plurality of competing states that mutually recognized each other and thus existed in a relationship of equality that was independent of their real power. They were equal because they were sovereign, each holding the *summa potestas* over its territory, whether its lands were vast or minuscule, and over its resources, whether they were immense or limited. Legitimacy proceeded from sovereignty, not from real power. The treaties of Westphalia had thus established a kind of international law, though it did not go so far as to prohibit war. Military conflict remained the normal way of settling the differences that might arise between states whose sovereignty—each one considered itself as "emperor in its realm"—forbade them to recognize any supranational or supergovernmental system invested with the power to punish violations of rules that, though recognized by all the actors, were nowhere formally written down.[88] But this system had concrete effects: if it did not avoid war—from the War of the Spanish Succession to the French Revolution, warfare raged during almost the whole of the eighteenth century—it was accepted, notably, that it could not have as its objective the annihilation of the adversary. In general, war was waged for territorial gains, and the mechanism of indemnities and compensations generally made it possible to find a more or less satisfying solution for both parties; but the end of a conflict never resulted in the disappearance of one of the belligerents. The stronger party might deprive the weaker of a portion of its territory and its resources, but it did not put its very existence in question. The political structure of the international system remained unaltered, even when borderlines changed. Sometimes a sovereign was moved around, but his sovereignty was not destroyed.

Of course, the functioning of this system no doubt never attained perfection. It was always approximate, and to the extent that it worked, it relied on political and cultural developments that helped homogenize the European continent in the eighteenth century. The Westphalian system could not have lasted without the formation of a European civilization whose members—the cultivated elites—shared beliefs, values, customs, and tastes, and communicated, from Paris to Saint Petersburg, in the same language: French. This was so true that some people did not hesitate to say that the political divisions that fragmented European territory were like empty shells. Thus Rousseau wrote in 1770 or 1771: "Today there are no more Frenchmen, Germans, Spaniards, or even Englishmen, no matter what people say; there are only Europeans. They all have the same tastes, the same passions, the same customs."[89] Such optimism was only half justified, because the continent's growing cultural unity in no way determined in advance its political unity. At the same time that the *philosophes* were observing the formation of a European society unified by customs and interests, the continent's political fragmentation was more marked than ever, the birth of national identities even helping to damage another element that favored the sustainability of the Westphalian order: the "limited" violence of wars—limited insofar as wars were confrontations between governments and not peoples, though they certainly continued to lead to many deaths. "War," Rousseau could still write in *Le Contrat Social*, "is thus not a relation between man

and man, but a relation between state and state, in which individuals are enemies only accidentally, not as men or even as citizens, but as soldiers."[90] But in
1762, when Rousseau's work was published, this was already no longer entirely
true, and ten years later Guibert, deploring the situation described by Rousseau,[91] hoped for the appearance of a "people vigorous in its genius, means, and
government; a people that combines with austere virtues and with a national
militia a set plan of expansion," and that, "knowing how to make war inexpen-
sively and how to subsist through its victories," would not be reduced to laying
down its arms "out of financial calculations." This people, Guibert predicted,
"would subjugate its neighbors and overturn our weak constitutions."[92]

Was the disappearance of the very ancient Venetian republic, whose legitimacy had been recognized by all of Europe, the fulfillment of Guibert's prophecy,
as Ferrero thinks, triggering a war that could have no end because what was
only the effect of force could be undone and redone endlessly, by the same means,
not only in Italy, but everywhere? Must we then accuse revolutionary France,
the Directory, and Bonaparte of having overthrown the Westphalian system?
Or accuse them alone? After all, Bonaparte would not have sacrificed Venice if
Austria had not secretly encouraged him to do so; and Austria would probably
not have considered the destruction of a legitimate state if it had not earlier,
along with Prussia and England, thrice partitioned Poland (1772, 1792, 1795).
That was, moreover, Albert Sorel's thesis: the French Revolution merely followed
an impetus given much earlier, first during the terrible War of the Austrian Succession, and then on the occasion of the successive partitions of Poland, which,
taken together, led to the destruction of the system of the balance of powers
that had with great difficulty been set up after the end of the Thirty Years' War:

> Two episodes sum up Europe's custom on the eve of the French Revo-
> lution: the War of the Austrian Succession and the partition of Po-
> land. The first shows the importance attached to commitments made
> by the state; the second, the respect professed for established sovereign-
> ties. These iniquitous acts are the testament of old Europe; having signed
> it, all that remained was to die. . . . The Old Regime had arrived at those
> ambiguous limits where degenerate law becomes abuse. The example
> of past centuries, their own precedents, everything had inclined these

states to these acts and had imperceptibly led them toward these infringements of their principle. They did not understand that by infringing, they destroyed. Their law was only prescription, it was based on de facto possession. . . . They violently rent the veil that concealed the sanctuary of states and deprived the masses of the mystery of sovereignty. They showed nations that two things had priority over the law of sovereigns and the law of states: the force of states and the convenience of sovereigns. They opened the way to a revolution that to overthrow their thrones and to shatter their empires had only to turn their own conduct against them and follow their own examples.[93]

An accurate and profound text. To be sure, Ferrero's analysis is not very different, but Sorel understood, as Ferrero did not, that the annihilation of the Republic of Venice was not the cause but the effect of the collapse of the international order that had been painstakingly constructed almost two centuries earlier and whose death should be dated, not from 1792–1793, but from the years between 1740 and 1770. Even if we granted that the demise of the Republic of Venice was comparable to that of the Kingdom of Poland, it would be only a new episode in a history that was already several decades old. On the other hand, we can grant Ferrero that by giving republican France and monarchical Austria a common border in Italy, Bonaparte was creating the conditions for a confrontation so unlikely to be transformed into peaceful coexistence that war was, so to speak, written between the lines of the Treaty of Campoformio.[94] Besides, neither the Austrians nor Bonaparte had any illusions about how long the peace would last. This is shown by the ulterior motives that were troubling them as they were signing the parchment. The Austrian minister Thugut rubbed his hands with satisfaction while swearing to the English that he had yielded to force.[95] Not only had he obtained Venice and the promise of an expansion into Bavaria, but he had not given up hope that, with his armies reconstituted and with the help of the French government's deliquescence, he might be able to recover what he had had to cede in Italy as well as on the Rhine. Bonaparte had no more faith than Thugut in the sustainability of the partition of northern Italy. He was convinced that Venice would prove to be a poisoned gift that would soon escape Austria: "What opinion would the people of the world form of the morality of the cabinet in Vienna if they were to see it appropriate the lands of its ally, the oldest state in modern Europe, the one that nourished principles the most opposed to democracy and to French ideas, and do so without any pretext and merely because it is convenient! . . . That would present to Europe's eyes the satire of absolute governments and of the European oligarchy. What [could provide] more obvious proof of their senescence, their decadence, their illegitimacy[?]"[96] Thus, in his view the cession was temporary; inevitably Venice, and with it other parts of the peninsula, would amalgamate, sooner or later, with the Cisalpine Republic. The coexistence of French Italy and Austrian Italy threatened to be all the less durable because the conflict was not only territorial, but ideological; it was also, as Ferrero rightly says, a "conflict of political doctrines." Talleyrand saw its magnitude so clearly that only a few weeks after the signature of the treaty he declared that the war was far from over.

> In the situation in which a republic that has recently arisen in Europe, despite all the monarchies, and on the debris of several of them, and which is dominant there by fear of its principles and its arms, finds itself, can it not be said that the Treaty of Campoformio and all the other treaties we have signed are merely more or less splendid military capitulations? The conflict, momentarily dormant as a result of the defeated party's astonishment and consternation, is not of a kind that can be definitively terminated by armed force, the latter being temporary, whereas hatred persists. Because of the excessively great heterogeneity of the contracting parties, enemies regard the treaties they sign with us only as truces, not unlike those that Muslims limit themselves to making with the enemies of their faith, without ever daring to make commitments for a definitive peace.[97]

Peace? A truce, nothing but a truce.

FIFTEEN

Parisian Interlude

*O*n November 17, 1797, Bonaparte left Milan and, by traveling "at breakneck speed," reached the little town of Rastatt, where the German states' representatives to the congress called to rule on the fate of the left bank of the Rhine were beginning to arrive.[1] He had made a triumphal journey across Switzerland. People crowded around to see him, and his joy would have been unmixed had Augereau, whom he wanted to see in passing through Offenburg, where the Army of the Rhine had its headquarters, had not refused to receive him, on the pretext that he was bathing. In Rastatt, where he remained hardly a week, just long enough to extract from the emperor's plenipotentiaries the promise to evacuate the territories in the Rhineland by December 5 at the latest, he adapted testily to the diplomatic world's stiff rituals. Axel von Fersen, representing the king of Sweden at the conference, bore the brunt of his irritation. Bonaparte reproached him for his past and his intrigues on behalf of the French royal family, telling him that his person was "essentially disagreeable" to the French. When Fersen weathered the storm like a good courtier, Bonaparte cried: "No, Monsieur, the French Republic will not allow men well known to it through their ties to the old court of France . . . to come to taunt the ministers of the first people of the Earth!"[2] When the Directory's negotiators finally arrived, he very willingly left to them "all this diplomatic chit-chat" and headed for Paris.[3] Twenty-one months after his departure for Nice and Italy, he entered the city discreetly on the evening of December 5.

The Lessons of the Italian Campaign

However, he had not finished with Italy. What he had learned there was to remain with him for a long time. It was in Italy that he had done his apprenticeship in all domains—military, political, diplomatic, constitutional, legislative—and it was there that he had conceived some of the principles of the policy that he would apply to France once he had become first consul. The Italian campaign had, at least in the short term, more consequences for France than for the peninsula itself.

As we have seen, the events that marked the foundation of the Cispadane Republic had irritated and also disappointed him. On several occasions he had said that he was convinced that Italy could "achieve liberty without revolution and its crimes" as long as it did not imitate France.[4] Despite threats and warnings—he pointed out that to revolt is "to doom yourself to misfortune for twenty-five years" and announced that he would have all "anarchists" shot—he could not prevent civilian dissensions from arising in the new republics.[5] Left to itself, Italy did not seem able to escape a fate comparable to that of France. Only the presence of the French army protected it against a tragedy. But what would happen to Italy once the French had evacuated the peninsula? Thus, when he founded a Cisalpine Republic in Milan, Bonaparte was determined not to allow a repetition of the scandalous scenes that had stained the Cispadane congress's debates.[6] But despite the near absence of "elements of republicanism," as he put it, he maintained in Milan the same procedures that the constituent congress had already employed in Romagna.[7] He was reluctant to make changes, to the point that he did not dare return to the Lombard capital, where, as he knew, he could not long resist the electors' demands for a convocation. Similarly, the inevitable adoption of constitutions modeled on that of Year III, with its annual elections, made him fear the multiplied difficulties that the Cispadane electors had just exemplified in electing the candidates most hostile to the republican system and to France.

For once the Directory was in agreement with the general. It, too, feared that the defects of the French constitution from whose disadvantages it suffered every day might be transported to Italy. The annual election of one-third of the Legislative Body exposed the state to such frequent changes of majority that it was impossible to conduct a single policy for more than a few months. And the fact that the government had no way of legally opposing the delegates' resolutions—neither a legislative veto nor the right to dissolve the assembly—constantly confronted it with the choice between capitulating and using force. In France most observers doubted that the Thermidorian Republic could survive. Some thought that popular participation had gone too far when the right to vote was granted to more than five million citizens and annual elections established; others thought that the executive power was too weak, but all attempts to amend the constitution and to give the government a little more authority had failed. The idea of a constitutional revision surfaced from time to time, and at one point people had believed that the supporters of a revision, Barras and Reubell at their head, would seize the opportunity offered by the coup d'état on 18 Fructidor, which had momentarily freed them from the surveillance of the Legislative Body, to reform the institutions. They had launched a few trial balloons, but had soon given up, henceforth resigned only to seeking a better constitutional formula for the sister republics that were coming into being all around, in Amsterdam, Bologna, Milan, Genoa, and soon in Geneva and Rome as well. The Directory, alerted by him to events in Italy, advised Bonaparte to stop taking France as his model, because he was lucky enough to be in a country where it was possible to free oneself from the tyranny of principles without immediately arousing an outcry in public opinion. On April 7, 1797, it wrote to him an important letter that can be summed up as follows:[8] the Directory recommended that Bonaparte exercise, provisionally and exceptionally, a threefold power: constituent (he himself was to write the new republic's constitution), electoral (he was to make appointments to all the offices, whether or not they were elective in terms of the constitution), and legislative (he was to give the new state a complete set of laws). This anticipated precisely the procedure that was to be followed a little less than three years later when the consular system was set up—the final draft of the Constitution of Year VIII was to be jointly produced by Sieyès and Bonaparte, assisted by a committee of experts, and the delegates to the newly created assemblies were to be, on this occasion alone, appointed and not elected. The Directory invented for the use of Italy a political formula from which Sieyès and Bonaparte later drew their inspiration: the consular regime applied to France the system outlined in this letter of April 7, whose effectiveness could be measured by the creation of the Cisalpine Republic. Bonaparte agreed with the directors, and rather than convoke a congress full of agitations of every kind, he preferred to surround himself with a few experts to constitute a new republic, choose its leaders, and provide its first laws. Did that amount to betraying revolutionary ideals, in that "power, which must proceed from the people, fell upon him"? Guglielmo Ferrero thinks that it did.[9] "The formula of the sovereignty of the nation," Ferrero goes on, "was completely reversed, applied backward: instead of creating the government, the will of the nation was created by the government; government, which claimed to be legitimate through the will of the nation, in reality legitimized itself, because it fabricated, as it pleased, the will of the nation."[10] All this is incontestable, but Bonaparte, for once following the Directory's instructions, wanted to keep Italy from sinking into civil war, as France had. By becoming the only constituent, elector, and legislator, he thought he could neutralize the two parties that were everywhere ready to fight: the first represented by the "Jacobins" in Milan who considered Bonaparte too indulgent with regard to Rome and talked about burning the Vatican and throwing the Neapolitan Bourbons into Vesuvius;[11] the second represented by the "priests" who had dominated the recent elections in the Cispadane Republic. He saw in this the only way of restoring power to the partisans of an "aristo-democratic republic" that, though it had little support in public opinion, seemed to him the most suited to the realities of Italian society.[12] Besides, suspending the exercise of the "sovereignty of the people" was not as serious as Ferrero claims. After all, in France hadn't this "sovereignty" essentially amounted to coups d'état, violence, and illegality of all kinds, to the confiscation of the "general will" by more or less limited groups of activists? In Genoa, where the French were less present than in Milan or Bologna, the revolutionary party, which had emerged victorious from its battle against the senatorial oligarchy, had immediately attacked the bastion of religion, provoking disturbances and even an incipient uprising in the countryside during the month of September 1797. Bonaparte had then imposed on the Genoese a revised constitution in order to introduce into it a few additional guarantees in favor of religion. On this subject he remained loyal to the policy followed since the summer of 1796, and it is on the basis of documents whose authenticity is doubtful to say the least that intentions hostile to Rome have been attributed to Bonaparte.[13] It was only during the summer of 1798, almost a year after he had left Italy, that the authorities of the Cisalpine Republic launched into a vast enterprise of secularizing its society. After Tolentino, Bonaparte had deplored the impossibility of a concordat with Rome—"If I were master," he is supposed to have told Cardinal Mattei, "we would have a concordat tomorrow"[14]—not knowing, perhaps, that Pius VI had sought in vain to come to an understanding with revolutionary France. But on August 3, 1797, before he left Italy, he sent the Roman Curia and the French government a note seeking a compromise that neither the pope nor the Directory had the means, or the desire, to achieve and that finally materialized only in the Concordat of 1801:

> When the Treaty of Tolentino was signed, His Holiness's plenipoten-
> tiaries and their French counterparts glimpsed a moment when it might
> be possible to effect a rapprochement between the Holy See and
> France.... The current moment is propitious for beginning the exe-
> cution of this great work in which wisdom, politics, and true religion
> are to play such a great role. The French government has just permitted
> the reopening of the Roman Catholic churches, and granted this reli-
> gion tolerance and protection.[15] Either the clergy were to benefit from
> this first act of the French government in the true spirit of the Gos-
> pels, by contributing to public peace and by preaching the true prin-
> ciples of charity that are the foundation of the Christian religion, and
> then I no longer doubt that they will obtain a more special protection,
> and that this is a favorable start toward the so desired goal; or, if the
> clergy conducts itself in a completely opposite manner, it will be once
> again persecuted and expelled. The pope, as the leader of the faithful
> and the common center of the faith, can have a great influence on the
> conduct of the priests. He may think that it is worthy of his wisdom
> [and] of the most sacred of religions, to issue a bull or pastoral letter
> ordering priests to preach obedience to the government and to do ev-
> erything they can to strengthen its established constitution. If this bull
> is conceived in terms that are precise and suited to the great end it can
> produce, it will be a great step toward the good, and extremely advan-
> tageous for the prosperity of religion. After this first operation, it would
> be useful to know the measures that could be taken to reconcile the
> constitutional priests with the nonconstitutional priests, and finally the

measures that the Court of Rome might propose to remove all obstacles and that might return the majority of the French people to the principles of religion.[16]

Bonaparte's Italian experience had inspired in him a policy that the first consul was soon to apply in France, and that can be summed up as follows: authority and force in the service of moderation. It was opposed as day is opposed to night to that of the Directory, a weak government imagining that it could fool people with "angry measures." Before returning to France, Bonaparte sent the Genoese, on November 11, 1797, a long letter in which, on the pretext of offering the Ligurian Republic a little advice about government, he addressed a veritable manifesto to the French. In it he severely condemned the Directory's policy, at a time when the latter was falling back into the rut of cleansings and persecutions. "It is not enough to avoid doing anything against religion, we also have to give no cause for concern to the most timorous minds, or any weapon to malicious people," he wrote. And farther on: "Excluding all the nobles from public offices is a revolting injustice." It was no coincidence that a law of 9 Fructidor had banished émigrés' relatives and renewed the laws against the clergy. The rest could even be seen as a plea to turn away from "the revolutionary path" followed up to that point. Bonaparte, after aiding the Fructidor coup d'état, adopted the theses of the very people whom he had helped overthrow. How, then, can we not see in the following lines a condemnation of revolutionary politics as a whole, at least from 1790 on?

> The first impulses of fraternity and enthusiasm gave way to fear and terror. The priests were the first to rally around the tree of liberty; they were the first to tell you that the moral of the Gospels is entirely democratic. But men in the pay of your enemies . . . have taken advantage of the misdemeanors, and even of the crimes of a few priests in order to decry religion, and the priests went away. Part of the nobility was the first to arouse the people and to proclaim the rights of man. The misdemeanors, prejudices, or even the past tyranny of a few nobles has been taken advantage of; banishments have been made en masse, and the number of our enemies has increased. After suspicions had been aroused

in this way and people armed against one another, more was done: cities were opposed to other cities. . . . The alarming situation in which you find yourselves is the result of the hidden maneuvers of the enemies of liberty and of the people. Beware of any man who wants to concentrate love of country solely in members of his own coterie; if his language seems to defend the people, that is in order to exasperate it, to divide it. He accuses constantly, he alone is pure. These are men in the pay of tyrants, whose views they support so well. When in a state people get used to condemning without understanding, to applauding a speech in proportion to its fury; when virtues are called exaggeration and crime moderation, that state is close to its destruction. States are like a ship at sea and like an army: coolness, moderation, wisdom, and reason are necessary in the conception of orders, commands, or laws, and it takes energy and vigor to execute them. If moderation is a defect, and a very dangerous defect, in republics, it is when it is exercised in executing wise laws.[17]

No one was deceived, and the editor of the *Moniteur*—it may have been Maret—who had reproduced this long letter, declared in conclusion that these "wise counsels" were not addressed solely "to the people of the Cisalpine and Ligurian [Republics]."[18] Who would have believed that Italy would become a model for France?

The Ceremony at the Luxembourg Palace

Bonaparte had arrived in Paris alone on December 5. Joséphine, who had not accompanied her husband to Rastatt, was still in Italy. Overcome by a desire for excursions that was as sudden as it was unexpected, she had wandered about—ending her journey in the company of Hippolyte Charles, whom she had found in Nevers or in Moulins—and she reached the conjugal domicile in Paris only a month later. Did her husband know about her affair with Hippolyte? Junot is supposed to have heard him threaten to have that officer shot on the first pretext.[19] Some historians think that one of Joséphine's chambermaids had revealed the secret the preceding summer.[20] If Bonaparte knew or suspected something, he didn't let it show.

His first outings were reserved for official visits. The day after he got back, he went to pay his respects to the minister of foreign affairs, Talleyrand, who then accompanied him to the Luxembourg Palace where Barras and La Révellière gave him a warm welcome. On December 8, he went to the office of the Department of the Seine and to the offices of the ministers; on the ninth he received on Rue Chantereine the magistrates of the Supreme Court; and on the tenth he returned to the Luxembourg Palace, where a ceremony in his honor had been organized. This was one of those solemn occasions that "tortured" him.[21] The directors, ministers, and the diplomatic corps, all dressed up and plumed, were awaiting their guest in an amphitheater constructed in the court of honor and decorated with a forest of flags taken from the enemy. A crowd of spectators craned their necks to catch a glimpse of "the hero." An orchestra played patriotic airs. The last to arrive, Bonaparte advanced slowly amid applause as far as the foot of the amphitheater. Talleyrand was standing there, waiting for him. He had been assigned to greet the general. The two men, who had seen each other for the first time just four days earlier, had been corresponding since Talleyrand, who had formerly been the bishop of Autun, had succeeded Delacroix as the head of the Ministry of Foreign Affairs the previous July. They had exchanged flattering letters: "Rightly frightened by the office of whose perilous importance I am aware," the minister wrote to inform Bonaparte of his appointment, "I need to reassure myself by the sense of what your glory must provide in the way of means and facilities in negotiations."[22] The general replied: "I have studied the history of the Revolution too much to be ignorant of what it owes to you; the sacrifices you have made to it deserve a reward; you would not have to wait long for it were I in power. You ask me for my friendship; you already have it, along with my esteem; in return, I ask your advice, and I assure you that I will take it seriously."[23] Talleyrand added: "I shall see to it that you are sent all the views that the Directory may ask me to transmit to you, and fame, which is your usual organ, will often deprive me of the happiness of informing it of the way in which you will have fulfilled them."[24] Bonaparte praised the "great talents" and "civic spirit" of a minister "foreign to the aberrations that have dishonored the Revolution."[25] The tone had been set. If the courtier was already visible in the minister, as Sainte-Beuve put it, were Talleyrand and Bonaparte just trying to outdo each other in flattery?[26] The admiration professed by the former great lord for the general who had come up through the ranks was no less sincere than the secret fascination of the little provincial noble from Corsica for this authentic survivor of the grandeurs of the Old Regime. Talleyrand had immediately sensed that in this young man there were, as he was later to say, "great hopes."[27] Well before he became minister, he was enthusiastic about Bonaparte: this twenty-eight-year-old general, he wrote to a friend, "has every glory on his head—those of war and those of peace, those of moderation, those of generosity, he has them all."[28] For his part, Bonaparte had taken the measure of the talents of the new minister, who was so superior to his usual interlocutors. But each of them had pleased the other for further reasons: "With such a minister, Bonaparte understood that when he was in power, he could undertake everything and dare anything." And Talleyrand understood that Bonaparte represented an opportunity to make a very great fortune. They were made to get on with each other.[29]

Therefore without any need for long preliminary maneuvers, they agreed with each other and soon advanced beyond generalities to more personal subjects. Let us mention them before returning to the ceremony at the Luxembourg Palace.

A few days after 18 Fructidor, Talleyrand asked Bonaparte his opinion regarding institutions and how they might be improved. Bonaparte had given him his cue by writing in his first letter: "The fault of the Revolution is that it destroyed a great deal and constructed nothing, everything still remains to be done."[30] The general did not hide his opinion of the constitution: he often spoke about it with his confidants, with Miot de Melito, Melzi, Lavalette, and also the representative Pontécoulant, who, having been banished on 18 Fructidor, had taken refuge in Switzerland and was making an excursion to the Borromean Islands when Lavalette came to find him and take him to the general. Bonaparte told him: "France with a decent, strong government, that's what I want. An administration entrusted to [men with] clean hands, an executive power that has the authority necessary to make itself obeyed without exposing itself to the eternal chatter of journalists and lawyers, that's what our country needs; liberty will come later, if necessary. . . . France is strong enough to resist all of Europe risen up against it, but its government has to have all means of action at its free disposal. . . . In this respect the regime of the Convention was better than the Constitution of Year III; there was more unity in the government and therefore more strength."[31]

"In truth, the organization of the French people has still been only sketched out," he also wrote in his response to Talleyrand's question.[32] He attributed this lack of completion to the influence of *L'Esprit des lois*, a source of many "false definitions" for which Montesquieu was less to blame than his readers. In this book, in which Bonaparte saw only a "resume of notes taken during his travels or while reading," the literate audience of the eighteenth century thought they had found a constitutional doctrine, a political model valid in any time and any place, whereas in reality it was an analysis of the British constitution alone. The revolutionaries, falling victim to the same mistake, had concluded that a separation of powers was necessary that would ensure, as it had in England, the preponderance of parliament and the strict subordination of the executive. But if on the other side of the Channel the House of Commons was invested with such great prerogatives, particularly with regard to the system of taxes and war, that was because it was the sole elected representative organ in a system that associated three different social forces—the Crown, the aristocracy, and the people—the last of which was not the most powerful. "The English constitution," Bonaparte wrote, "is only a charter of privileges" in which the people must have the means to defend itself against the ambitions of the great: the people has to exercise control—Bonaparte grants this much—in the domains in which it is the main contributor: taxes and war. "Since the House of Commons is the only one that more or less represents the nation, it alone must have the right to tax; this is the sole limit they have been able to find to moderate the despotism and insolence of the courtiers." But in France, since the abolition of privileges in 1789, and especially since the abolition of the monarchy in 1792, nothing required the adoption of this model, which was adapted to an entirely different situation, and whose disadvantages—the parliament is not the best judge of the needs of administration or of foreign policy—found in England their sole justification in the specific characteristics of "mixed government": "In a government in which all authorities emanate from the nation, in which the sovereign is the people, why classify among the attributes of legislative power things that are foreign to it?" Why not see members of the executive as representatives of the nation? "The power of the government, in all the latitude I give to it," he wrote in this letter, "should be considered the true representative of the nation."

Consequently, Bonaparte went on to sketch out a new constitutional organization in which the executive took the lion's share. The legislative power would in effect be limited to making and reforming "the organic laws" necessary to implement the Constitution: "Impassive, blind and deaf to its surroundings, [it] would have no ambition and would no longer inundate us with countless laws of circumstance that cancel each other out by their very absurdity and constitute for us a lawless nation with three hundred *in folios* of laws." Ordinary legislative activity would be entrusted to the executive, the only organ capable of recognizing with precision the country's immediate needs. Because the delegation to the executive of the preparation and execution of the laws would require increased supervision of its actions, this supervision would not be exercised by the legislative power but by a "great council of the nation," a "very large" assembly composed of elected officials who had already held important public offices. This great council, "supervising and not acting," would form the second branch of the executive and would examine the constitutionality of the government's acts. Several of Bonaparte's proposals coincide with those of the proponents of a constitutional revision, from Sieyès to Mme de Staël, but in the importance he would give to the executive power, and in the more than subordinate role he assigned to the legislative authority, he was as far from them as he was from the revolutionaries. The misunderstanding of Brumaire, which was soon to lead some of his allies to regret their involvement, is, so to speak, already inscribed in this letter.

The first encounter between Bonaparte and Talleyrand, on December 6, only confirmed the feelings of respect and confidence that imbued the two men's correspondence. We do not know what they said to each other, but Talleyrand fell under Bonaparte's spell. "I had never seen him," he wrote in his memoirs. "When I first set eyes on him, he seemed to me to have a charming appearance; twenty battles won go so well with youth, a handsome face, a little pallor, and a kind of exhaustion."[33] All men, it will be said, have their weaknesses, even the coolest and wiliest; but it is true that Bonaparte, who was "naturally quick-tempered, decisive, impetuous, violent," had, said Count Melzi, "the astonishing power of making himself charming, and, by means of a measured deference and a flattering cheerfulness, to make the conquest of people he wanted to win over."[34] Talleyrand was not the only one to succumb to Bonaparte's charm.

So here we find the former bishop of Autun standing before the general and the crowd, celebrating the conqueror of Italy and Europe's peacemaker with a series of banalities, none of which would have been worthy of being passed on to posterity if, leaving the past, he had not projected himself into the future: "When I think of all that he has done to make us pardon him this glory, of the ancient taste for simplicity that distinguishes him, of his love for the abstract sciences, of his favorite readings, of the sublime Ossian who seems to detach him from the Earth; when no one is unaware of his profound scorn for brilliance, for luxury, for ceremony, those contemptible ambitions of common minds; ah! far from fearing what might be called his ambition, I sense that one day we shall perhaps have to appeal to him to tear himself away from the delights of his studious retreat. All of France will be free: perhaps he will never be, such is his destiny."[35]

It was Bonaparte's turn to speak. He was brief, "like a man who knows his elevation and wants to make his superiority felt."[36] He looked annoyed, almost irritated, as he always did when addressing any group other than the military audience he was used to. He was applauded even before he had finished, and perhaps his final words, which were the only remarkable ones, were not heard: "When the happiness of the French people is founded on better organic laws, Europe as a whole will become free."[37] A whole program was thus compressed into a sentence: the establishment of a stable political system, Bonaparte suggested, constituted the necessary condition for peace with Europe; and Talleyrand had provided the complement by insinuating that the future was in Bonaparte's hands. At the time, no one noticed the general's remarks, which in a normal situation and in the presence of a normal government would have seemed what they were, the words of a dissident general. This absence of reaction says a great deal about the state of decrepitude into which the regime had already fallen. The Directory limited itself to ordering the newspapers to delete the adjective "organic," which constituted a "patent reproach" directed at the institutions.[38] Next Barras spoke at length, not without singing the hero's praises in his turn: "Citizen general, nature, which is sparing with its miracles, gives great men to the Earth only from time to time; but it must have been eager to mark the dawn of liberty by one of these phenomena, and the sublime revolution of the French people, novel in the history of nations, must have presented a new genius in the history of famous men. The first of all of them, Citizen General, you have thrown off the yoke of parallels, and with the same arm with which you laid low the enemies of the Republic, you have set aside the rivals that Antiquity presented to you."[39]

Next a hymn written by Chénier and set to music by Méhul was intoned, in which a chorus of warriors, bards, girls, and old men sang: "You were long the dread, [now] be the love of the Earth, O Republic of the French!" Then there were more speeches, and in conclusion a banquet at which Bonaparte, fearing he would be poisoned, ate nothing.[40]

However, far from having been the signal for an effort to reform institutions, the ceremony of December 10, 1797, put an end to the hopes of the advocates of a revision. Besides, it is doubtful that Bonaparte and Talleyrand then thought reform possible, even if they did not conceal their poor opinion of the constitution of Year III. Judging that the political situation, a few months after 18 Fructidor, offered no opportunities for action—the Directory had come out of the crisis stronger than it had been before, at least temporarily, and attacking it would necessarily be tantamount to reviving the royalist party that had just been overthrown—they had instead taken advantage of the ceremony on December 10 to seal their alliance with a public event and set a date for the future. Was Sieyès already in cahoots with them? Michel Poniatowski says that he was, but if like them Sieyès was a partisan of a change in regime, he was also one of those who thought the repressive measures against priests and nobles adopted after 18 Fructidor were insufficient. He was then playing the Jacobin, and was foreign to the spirit of moderation that Bonaparte had just praised in his letter to the Genoese. However, Poniatowski is right concerning the general and Talleyrand:

> [They] also felt the same scorn for the Councils, for those little revolutionaries who had emerged from the swamps of the assemblies, for those long-winded and incompetent mediocrities. Bonaparte, like Talleyrand . . . , rejected a powerless and discredited regime whose ineptness contrasted with the glory of its army. Both were aware that republican and revolutionary France was a France surrounded and threatened. Its military power was a danger for Europe, and its

revolution increased the danger it represented. Attacked not only by a counterrevolutionary coalition but also by a [patriotic] reaction on the part of other countries, it had to be strong to resist. Its army was equal to its power, but its regime was not. The latter thus had to be changed; the civilian command had to be as strong as the military command. That was the price of an enduring peace. That was how Bonaparte's and Talleyrand's secret and shared thoughts proceeded. . . . They were going to take two years to realize them; that is the period of time separating, more or less, 18 Fructidor from 18 Brumaire.[41]

Some people suggest that Bonaparte, far from thinking about overthrowing the government, wanted on the contrary to join it by obtaining a dispensation regarding his age, because one had to be forty years old to become a director, and he was only twenty-eight. Steps are supposed to have been taken by people around him, his brothers, of course, and also Tallien, but the directors refused to make an exception. This is an improbable thesis, "a fable," according to Lavalette, who was very close to the general at the time.[42] It is all the less credible because Bonaparte, it is also said, is supposed to have considered the same idea after he returned from Egypt in 1799. Why would he have wanted to be in the Directory? Why would he have associated his name with a regime that he thought doomed and with men who feared and disliked him? "They're jealous of me," he said, "I know that, and despite all their flattery, I am not deceived by them: they fear me more than they like me."[43] The feeling was mutual: he had taken their measure in Italy and being often around them over these few months spent in Paris was not going to change his mind. But they courted him. La Révellière even invited him to dinner and introduced his wife and daughter to him; all three of them, the general said, "were masterpieces of ugliness." La Révellière, who set great store by the constitution—he had been one of its authors—tried to draw Bonaparte over to his side, and he thought the way to do it was to talk at length about the new religion of the "adorers of God and friends of man"[44] that he protected and encouraged, "theophilanthropy," even asking him to become one of its main dignitaries. Bonaparte, who was beginning to find the conversation "a little boring," replied that "on dark roads his principle was to follow those who had gone before him, and that he was therefore resolved to do in these matters as his father and mother had done," and he added coolly that if his interlocutor wanted something sublime, he had only to read the Paternoster. Things went no further, but from then on La Revellière, whom Bonaparte had rubbed the wrong way, no longer cajoled or fussed over the young man.[45]

The politicians were not the only ones who were seeking his favor; his family and friends were also dreaming of a great destiny for him, and were astonished to see him so prudent, even resigned, whereas it seemed that he had only to "reach out with [his] victorious hand to seize power."[46] He did not respond, or if he did, made only vague remarks. The generals present in Paris also wanted to know his intentions; he was approached by certain leaders of the Army of Germany, Kléber, Moreau, Desaix, Caffarelli—some of them on leave, others in disgrace, and all of them more or less badly treated by the government. "Kléber," he was to say, "proposed to make me the head of the government: 'You, Moreau and I—we'll get rid of these scoundrels, don't worry!'"[47] Bonaparte asked for time to think about it. He quickly understood that what they were unhappy about was less the sad situation of the country than the Directory's lack of consideration for them. "I wasn't sure where they wanted to go, perhaps they didn't know that themselves." He had meditated long enough on the failure of all the generals who, since La Fayette in 1792, had tried to overthrow the government, not to get carelessly involved with discontented officers. He was not like Hoche: the latter, he said, was the kind of man who would "come from Strasbourg with 25,000 men and seize the government by force, whereas I have never had anything but a patient policy, always guided by the spirit of the time and the circumstances of the moment."[48] He declined Kléber's offer and warned him against a reckless act: "Military government will never catch on in France."[49] The time of the Praetorians was past, and would not return. Kléber could act, of course, but he would do it without him, because Bonaparte would not at any price get involved in a conspiracy doomed to fail. He refused to be another Dumouriez.[50]

The Conquest of the Institute

Having decided that the moment was inopportune, he donned the garb of Cincinnatus, dressing in civilian clothes, with a bowler hat on his head, but was unable to prevent rumors from continuing to attribute to him the intention of overthrowing the government. He cultivated with care his image as "the most civilian of generals," and told anyone who would listen that he aspired to repose and obscurity. Joséphine found that amusing: "Don't believe a word of it," she said to a visitor to whom her husband had sworn that his ambition was now limited to becoming a justice of the peace somewhere in the countryside. "He has the most unquiet mind, the most active brain, the most fertile in projects, the most ardent imagination, and the most obstinate will in the world, and if he ceased to be occupied with great affairs, he would turn his home upside down everyday, it would be impossible to live with him!"[51] He went out little, leaving Rue Chantereine—it had just been renamed, in his honor, Rue de la Victoire—only to go to the theater, to attend, grumbling, a few evening parties, or to go see the elephants in the Jardin des Plantes. He avoided applause. He knew he was the current darling of the press and feared that his popularity—and even more, the genuine manifestations of idolatry of which he was the object[52]—would offend or frighten the directors. One evening when he was attending Mme Vestris's farewell to the stage, he insisted on sitting, in his loge, behind the old dramatist Jean-François Ducis.[53] The audience in the orchestra seats was greatly touched by this display of modesty, and gave the general an ovation: "We saw with delight this splendid homage that a man so young and so great paid to old age and genius."[54] On the other hand, he received many guests, "seeking in the crowd the useful and famous man to go and talk with him about the art or science in which he had distinguished himself."[55] In Italy he sought the company of scientists and artists, doing them small favors, attending to their welfare, and never failing to make them feel that he knew their works and was a modest admirer of them. The warrior who was supposed to eclipse even the greatest models, listened to them as if he were their pupil, and when they protested, reminding him of his incredible victories, he contrasted the useful works of artists and scientists with the trade—war—that circumstances, unfortunately, forced him to practice. When on December 25, 1797, the Institute made him a member of its mechanical arts section—appointing him to the chair left vacant by the banishment of Carnot—he sent his new colleagues a letter of thanks that provides a good illustration of the relationships he entertained with men of letters and scientists: "Before being your equal," he wrote, "I shall be your pupil for a long time." And he added, full of humility, that "true conquests, the only ones that cause no regret, are those that are made over ignorance."[56] This was not solely a pose: he really liked the company of artists, painters, musicians, as well as that of scientists. Even if his knowledge of the subjects the latter discussed with him was often superficial, he was in conversation as he was in war: "fertile, full of resources, quick to discern, prompt to attack his adversary's weak point," and above all endowed with an "astonishing ability to concentrate at will his attention on any given subject and to keep it fixed on it for several hours at a time."[57] His comments were sometimes banal, but his prestige elevated them and his interlocutors left these conversations with the feeling of having been distinguished by one of the greatest men in the universe, and they were ready to become the heralds of his glory. Thus in Italy he had enthusiastic supporters such as the astronomer Oriani, Canova, Gros, Berthollet, and especially Gaspard Monge.

Monge was a famous mathematician and geometer who was almost twice as old as the general when he was appointed, in May 1796, to the "Commission of the Sciences and the Arts" entrusted with supervising the seizure of works of art in the peninsula. In Milan the general gave him a welcome he had not expected, reminding him of the circumstances of their first meeting four years earlier, at a time when Monge was the First Republic's minister of the navy, and the young Bonaparte was making the rounds of the offices to obtain his reinstatement in the army. "Allow me to thank you for the kind reception that a young, unknown artillery officer who was somewhat in disfavor received from the minister of the navy in 1792; he has carefully preserved its memory. You see that officer in the present general of the Army of Italy. He is happy to offer you a grateful and friendly hand."[58] No doubt the young officer had remained in contact with the scientist after this meeting—Monge dedicated a copy of his *Description de l'art de fabriquer des canons* to Bonaparte in 1795—but the scientist, in addition to the surprise he must have felt on discovering what had become of the puny young man of 1792, was even more astonished and touched to see that despite his incredible ascension and his very recent exploits, the victor of Mondovì and Lodi had forgotten nothing of what he thought he owed him. Bonaparte, as we know, did not forget those who had in one way or another helped him in his ascent. Teachers at Brienne or the École militaire, officers in Valence or Ausonne, Corsican shepherds, representatives on assignment in 1793, all received the benefit of a gratitude that was manifested, sometimes to the advantage of their heirs, even in the emperor's last will and testament.[59] Monge, through the simple courtesy of his reception at a time when as a powerful man he could have ignored the young man and had not done so, now became forever a member of this group. But Bonaparte did not always esteem those to whom he paid homage. With Monge, it was different. His affection for him was sincere. He admired the scientist's work; he admired the authenticity of his republican convictions, which he honored by asking that the Marseillaise be played before every banquet at which Monge was present. However, he did not rank Monge very high as a politician. As Arnault was to say rather snidely, Monge was "simple like La Fontaine and hardly understood better what was going on in the world, although he was more involved in it."[60] But something in him touched Bonaparte, perhaps his contrast with the Army of Italy's perpetuation of the antireligious fanaticism of 1793. Monge himself was not very religious—though Bonaparte was hardly more—and was undoubtedly violently anticlerical, but he was nonetheless sensitive to the importance of religious sentiment and respected it. It was precisely because Berthollet, who was inseparable from Monge and Bonaparte at that time, proved inflexible on the subject of "superstition" that the general never showed him the affection he had for Monge. Finally, the latter was a delightful companion, enthusiastic, with encyclopedic knowledge, and never short of ideas, though he sometimes was of words to express them. As Arnault was to put it: "The sum of his knowledge was immense. He combined the faculty of learning with that of inventing, and with the faculty of understanding, that of making himself understood. He demonstrated things marvelously, yet I believe that in his whole life he never finished a sentence. He was eloquent, yet did not know how to talk; his eloquence, deprived of elocution, consisted in a mixture of gestures and words that drew strength from each other; a mixture from which there resulted a demonstration that, explained by the play of the physiognomy, arrived at comprehension through the eyes as much as through the ears. . . . It was a pleasure to see him talk. It is impossible to say how much wit there was in his fingers."[61]

Monge interested Bonaparte, and amused him. They played games of chess or snakes and ladders, and in the evening Bonaparte, presiding over an audience of officers, asked his dear Monge to explain to them the subtleties of his "poor descriptive geometry." Monge saw himself as the "spoiled child of the Republic."[62] He was happy. If we add to all that the disillusions resulting from the Directory's problems and the certainty that he was doing something useful by exercising the mission that Bonaparte had entrusted to him, we can understand why he soon formed for the general an "attachment that was total, definitive, absolute to the point of blindness," close to idolatry.[63] Supposing that he recognized this, he might have said, like the poet Arnault referring to his relations with the general-in-chief of the Army of Italy at the same period: "As jealous as I was of my independence, I did not seek, I admit, to escape a subjection of which I was proud."[64] The "terrible" Monge—of whom Napoleon was to say that he was in reality "one of the mildest and weakest men living"[65]—didn't know who scared him most, his wife or the general. When the latter was announced, Monge broke off a letter to his wife with an abrupt "The general is arriving, adieu!"[66]—and then immediately assured her that his "Italian indigestion" was such that he had "a great need to be in the Rue des Petits-Augustins for a little while to set his stomach straight," and for the hundredth time he swore to her that he was going to immediately ask the general for a leave.[67] If he dared to bring up the question with Bonaparte, the latter at once assigned him to a task so important that Monge gave in, terrified at the idea of having to explain to his wife this further delay, but secretly happy to be able to live a little longer close to the person he admired more than anyone in the world. Bonaparte needed Monge to provide entertainment in "his solitude."[68] But after the signature of the Treaty of Campoformio, it was to Monge, accompanied by Berthier, that he gave the signal honor of carrying the news to Paris, thus proving to him how much he esteemed him. This relationship of real affection, on the one side, and absolute subjection and devotion on the other, was to end only with Napoleon's exile and the death of the famous geometer in 1818.

Objectors were rare. There had been a few in Italy, such as Alfieri, who refused to have any relationship whatsoever with these French "anti-lyrical barbarians," and the castrato Luigi Marchesi, who refused to sing before Bonaparte in Milan. Even Ugo Foscolo, though shocked by the destruction of the Republic of Venice, could not help noting: "I admire him, perhaps more than he deserves."[69] In France itself there were even fewer who did not succumb. It was said that the general, having returned to Paris, talked about mathematics with Laplace and Lagrange, poetry with Chénier, metaphysics with Sieyès (even if it is doubtful that he had made Sieyès's acquaintance at that time), law with Daunou. Bernardin de Saint-Pierre, Arnault, Ducis, and Lemercier joined the group of panegyrists who added "the olive branch of civilization to the laurels of Mars" with which he was already crowned.[70] "That man is not like the others," Arnault said after making his acquaintance. "Everything bends under the superiority of his genius, under the ascendancy of his character; everything in him bears the imprint of authority. Just see how his [authority] is recognized by people who submit to it without realizing it, or perhaps in spite of themselves. What an expression of respect and admiration in everyone who meets him! He was born to dominate as others are born to serve."[71] We know David's exclamation when he met the general at this time: "Oh! My friends, what a physiognomy he has! It is pure, it is great, it is beautiful like the ancient! . . . In short, my friends, he is a man to whom altars would have been built in antiquity; yes, my friend, yes my dear friends! Bonaparte is my hero!"[72]

Bonaparte, who had come in contact with David in Milan through Gros, had asked the painter to join him in Italy. Did David refuse? Did the general forget his offer? They finally met again in the Louvre, in the studio where David had painted the *Oath of the Horatii*. David planned to represent the general presenting the Treaty of Campoformio to Emperor Francis II. The sitting lasted three hours—the painter had to be the great David, for Bonaparte to consent to pose for such a long time—giving the painter time to make a sketch of his head that is all the more expressive because the painting was later abandoned, Bonaparte not having returned to the Louvre, and David having resumed work on *The Intervention of the Sabine Women*. All the witnesses to the scene were struck by the youth of the model, his reserve, and his extreme impatience, "like that felt when one feels he is wasting his time."[73] Bonaparte did not see David again until after Brumaire: in any case, he had won him over, and the painter was as subjugated, perhaps even more than he had been by Robespierre a few years earlier.

In men of letters' eagerness to please Bonaparte, we find varying degrees of fascination with brute force and a taste for voluntary servitude. But they had other, more noble motives for gathering around the victorious general. After all, the "Ideologues" who sat in the Institute were Condorcet's heirs, and like him they did not, in their heart of hearts, really believe in democracy. In seeking to found a science of politics that would rationalize the government of modern societies, their preference, even if unavowed, was for the establishment of a strong government enlightened by philosophical reason that would make it possible to carry out, from above, what the Revolution had failed to achieve through the people. Bonaparte, who presented himself as a "civilian" general, never missed an opportunity to proclaim his attachment to the principles of representative government and his hostility to a military regime, thus seeming to them a possible instrument of the rational politics they dreamed about. A "warrior, legislator, philosopher, citizen," he might succeed where the people had failed. In any case, that is what the Ideologues wanted to believe, and Bonaparte had every interest in letting them believe that he was that man. Unless they found in this a convenient justification for abandoning their former ideals. How else can we interpret the sophisms that they would soon write, such as when Garat, one of the principal representatives of the Ideologues group, wrote in *La Décade philosophique*, "If the power of a great position and the power of military glory are combined to the highest degree in the same man, we must not fear [the power] of glory, but regard it as a guarantee and a barrier, for usurpers are never heroes and vice versa"?[74]

Mme de Staël, who considered the military mind incompatible with liberty and knew that even an army that is fighting for liberty "must have, to triumph, despotic customs and ideas,"[75] nonetheless courted the general. They met for the first time on December 6, 1797, at Talleyrand's home, she hoping to add him to her conquests, he already wary. It was a brief encounter that went nowhere, not because of their divergent political choices—Mme de Staël was among those who approved of 18 Brumaire—but because from the outset he was repelled by this woman so little in conformity with his idea of women. He was certainly not like the Schlegels, Constant, and other leading members of her "court" who jumped for joy "like schoolboys whose monitor is absent" when this woman who exercised over them "an inexplicable but very real domination" was away for a few days.[76] Her power never had any effect on Bonaparte, especially because in his view she had many other defects: At the beginning of the Revolution, she had frequented the liberal nobles he disdained, and on more than one occasion played a role that was ambiguous to say the least. She had been involved in the intrigues that preceded the insurrection of August 10, 1792, in the hope of raising to the first rank her favorite of the moment, the Count of Narbonne.

And recently she had been associated with the right before making an about-face and siding with the Directory at the time of 18 Fructidor. In his view she was the very image of the intriguer, the heir to the *Frondeuses* of the preceding century who had not hesitated to sacrifice the kingdom to their passions and to the ambitions of their lovers. Heinrich Heine summed up what happened next: "When the good lady saw that she would obtain nothing by all her persistence, she did what women do in such cases, she made great declarations of opposition to the emperor, fine arguments against his brutal and not very gallant tyranny, and went on reasoning like that until the police told her to get lost."[77]

In late 1797 it had not yet come to that. At that time Mme de Staël was liberal in her praise for the young hero. Lavalette recounts that having been sent to Paris before 18 Fructidor, he dined with her at Talleyrand's, where, carried away by her eloquence, she delivered a vibrant encomium of the general that had "all the intoxication, the disorder, and the exaggeration of inspiration." When Talleyrand showed his guests a portrait of Bonaparte that he had just received, Lavalette, as a gallant man, stepped back to allow her to go through the door before him. She refused, asking him, in a very excited tone: "How would I dare pass before one of Bonaparte's aides-de-camp?"[78] She is supposed to have written several letters to the general in Italy that were "full of wit, imagination, and metaphysical erudition" and in which she expressed to him "sentiments of enthusiasm worthy of her own *Corinne*."[79] Did she go so far, as Napoleon was to claim, as to reproach him for his marriage to "an insignificant little Creole"?[80] She might have had it in mind, as Heine maliciously suggests, "that the greatest man of the century had to be coupled, even if only ideally, with the greatest contemporary woman."[81] But she would not have made the faux pas of criticizing the woman to whom she knew he was so attached. Moreover, it is possible that Napoleon invented these expressions of enthusiasm and that Mme de Staël's letters had another purpose, such as obtaining his intercession on behalf of La Fayette—he was still being detained in Austria—whose return to France she desired. In any case, he didn't need her to write him to be prejudiced against her. His feelings about her father, Necker, were close to hatred. He considered him one of those responsible for the French Revolution, and when Bonaparte came back from Italy, he refused to stop and greet the former minister, who had left his château in Coppet to wait for Bonaparte along the road. Bonaparte's animosity against Necker extended to the whole of that "singular" family, the father, mother, and daughter "all three on their knees, regaling each other with reciprocal incense, for the better edification and mystification of the public."[82] When he met Mme de Staël in Talleyrand's antechamber, he hardly greeted her, telling her only that he was sorry not to have been able to speak with her father. Did he think he could get rid of her so easily? If so, he did not know her well. Mme de Staël was not one of those women who can be put off by coolness alone. She tried again. She was still there when Talleyrand gave, on January 3, 1798, a reception in honor of Joséphine Bonaparte. As the general was greeting the guests, she came up to him and spoke loudly enough to make herself heard by everyone present:

> Mme de Staël began by showering rather emphatic sentiments on Bonaparte, who replied with rather cold but polite remarks: another person would have backed off. Without paying attention to the annoyance that showed in his face and in his tone, Mme de Staël, determined to begin a real discussion, pursued him with questions and while at the same time assuring him that he was for her the first of men [she said]: "General, who is the woman you love most?" "My wife." "That's simple, but who is the one you esteem the most?" "The one who knows best how to run her household." "I can understand that, too. But for you, who is the first of women?" "The one who has the most children."[83]

And with those words he left her standing there. Had he answered her provocative question with a smile? "Thus placed and said *with a smile*," Sainte-Beuve remarks, "a riposte that might have seemed grossly impolite is nothing more than mischievous."[84] She remained dumbstruck for a moment, but being "capable of resisting discouragement," she soon recovered her spirits. She came to call on him, did not miss a dinner where he was invited, and ran into him at the theater, so that, Napoleon said, laughing, she ended up succeeding "in forming some degree of acquaintance, so far even as to be allowed to visit."[85] However, she said she had felt, though only later on, ill at ease in his presence:

> When I had somewhat recovered from the turmoil of admiration, a very pronounced feeling of fear succeeded it. . . . I had seen men very worthy of respect; I had also seen ferocious men; in the impression that

Bonaparte made on me there was nothing that might remind me of either the former or the latter. I perceived rather quickly, on the various occasions on which I met him during his stay in Paris, that his character could not be defined with the words we customarily use; he was neither kind, nor violent, nor sweet, nor cruel, in the way of individuals we know. Such a person had no peer, could neither feel, nor cause anyone else to feel, any sympathy: he was more or less than a man. . . .
I felt in his soul a cold and sharp sword that froze as it wounded.[86]

She had discerned in Napoleon, as Nietzsche wrote, the "synthesis of the *inhuman* and the *superhuman*" that made such a strong impression on everyone who met him.[87] However, Mme de Staël had concerns that justified her making a few efforts to overcome her fears. One of these concerns, in addition to the government's chronic ill humor with regard to her and the two million livres owed to her dear father, was the fate of Switzerland.[88] She feared that the French army would invade the little confederation and prompt the abolition of feudal rights of which her father was one of the main beneficiaries. It was to defend her father's interests that she finally obtained an audience with Bonaparte. Their private meeting lasted an hour. He listened to her, and then, when he had had enough, cut her off, saying curtly: "Yes, no doubt, but men have to have political rights, yes, political rights," and then, setting politics aside, he talked to her about the pleasure he took in retirement and in the countryside.[89]

Although he rebuffed Mme de Staël's advances, he began "to conquer, one by one, the most distinguished men in France."[90] He had understood the role played by public opinion in modern societies. That is why he was careful to appear to be the least military of the generals. If in his heart of hearts he ranked Turenne and Condé as the greatest military leaders of the past, in public he liked to mention Marshal Catinat (1637–1712). In fact, he considered Catinat "very inferior to the reputation he enjoyed."[91] But the marshal was said to have shown "the character of a sage at the head of armies," and to have brought to "the military profession the reason of a true philosopher and the feelings of a true citizen"; legend said that he saw in war "only a public crime [and] a calamity for peoples."[92] Bonaparte, as we have seen, had emulated Catinat when he wrote to Archduke Charles to ask him to put an end to a cruel war.[93] He knew his century. He knew how much, at a time when Voltaire and Rousseau were still alive in the memory of his contemporaries, the power of the mind won out over that of the saber. A citizen general and a philosopher, he combined "Caesar's fortune" with "Socrates' thought." He had made connections and arranged a rendezvous with the future. Because it was impossible to overthrow the regime and the generals were growing restless without knowing what they wanted, he began to think of ways of escaping.

PART FOUR

The Egyptian Expedition

1798–1799

SIXTEEN

The Road to the Indies

$\mathcal{B}$onaparte had sound reasons for wanting to leave Paris. Down deep he did not believe that the peace would last, either.[1] He feared that if hostilities resumed, he would have to accept the consequences. War was already looming on the horizon. When the Directory had learned of the death of General Duphot, who had been assassinated in Rome on December 28, 1797, it reacted by ordering Berthier to march on the Eternal City, drive out the pope, and proclaim a republic there—in other words, to carry out the orders Bonaparte had been eluding for the past two years.[2] Bonaparte wrote to his former head of staff to urge him to be prudent.[3] But the affair still risked provoking the Neapolitans to intervene, and perhaps also the Austrians. What would people say about the Treaty of Campoformio and his signing of it, if Italy burst into flames anew? Would they still celebrate him as the "Hero dear to Peace, to the Arts, to Victory," who had conquered "in two years a thousand centuries of glory"?[4] Or, on the contrary, would public opinion, which was firmly attached to peace, turn away from him? But he feared peace no less than war. Without war, was he in danger of being forgotten? Anyone who is not going up is going down: "The people of Paris do not remember any thing," he said. "Were I to remain here long, doing nothing, I should be lost."[5] Another peril: he was running the risk, by staying in Paris, of being compromised by his proximity to a discredited government. He had cause to fear just this when the Directory asked him to attend the ceremony on January 21, 1798, that commemorated the execution of Louis XVI. He refused to participate in this "dreadful mummery," but the directors and Talleyrand insisted, so he had to go, even if he was only in civilian clothes and lost among other members of the Institute. Should we conclude that for Bonaparte Egypt was only a "spectacular way of managing expectations," or, as Goethe said, that he left to conquer the Orient only "to fill up an epoch when he could do nothing in France to make himself ruler"?[6]

Destroying England

The Directory anticipated Bonaparte's desires by assigning him to invade England.[7] The war against the Austrians was over, but it continued against the British, and the government had declared its intention to attack them on their home grounds: "Europe's misfortunes are fabricated in London," he wrote in a "Proclamation to the French," "it is there that they must be ended."[8] To be sure, but how? Since the beginning of the conflict in 1793, the question had been how to strike this enemy so difficult to outclass at sea, where its superiority was not in doubt. The time was long past when, under Louis XVI, the French navy could still compete with its British counterpart. As a result of a lack of resources, the emigration of its officers, and a lack of discipline, the navy was in sad shape: its vessels were at best poorly maintained, and at worst ready for the junkyard, with improvised officers commanding sailors who had forgotten how to obey. Remedying this situation would have taken time, lots of time, and money, lots of money, and the government had neither. After five years of war, France had lost more than 200 ships, while England had lost less than half as many.[9] The reinforcement of the Spanish and Dutch fleets did not make up for the losses—far from it. The government considered resigning itself to negotiations. There had been negotiations in 1796 and again very shortly thereafter in Lille, during the summer of 1797, but nothing came of them. Some people said the British did not sincerely desire peace; others believed, on the contrary, in the sincerity of the British government. They pointed out that the conflict was expensive, and that if up to that point the British had been so little inclined to enter into talks, it was because French political instability deprived them of credible interlocutors. Was an agreement possible? Perhaps, had the bargaining concerned only colonies; but London also demanded the restoration of Belgium to the Austrians. For the British that was the essential point: to get France out of Antwerp, through which Britain communicated with Europe. What was not negotiable for them was no more negotiable for the French, and the Directory "declared clearly that article 332 of the Constitution prevented them from agreeing to any alienation of the territory set by the laws."[10] The war went on.

The French could not defeat the English at sea, so they considered ways of pursuing the struggle on land. Some people drew up plans for a tunnel under the English Channel or for an immense balloon capable of transporting by air an army of 12,000 men.[11] Others imagined striking a blow against England's commercial interests by denying it access to the European market: this was already tantamount to proposing a continental blockade.[12]

However, another project was then widely favored: that of a landing on the shores of England. But history lent it no support, because despite many attempts, no one had repeated the exploits of Julius Caesar and William the Conqueror.[13] The counsel of experience is seldom taken, and hardly had the war between France and Britain resumed in 1793 than plans drawn up more than twenty years earlier were exhumed, and in 1796 Hoche got the project of a twofold landing on the English and Irish coasts approved. "Only boldness and love of liberty are required to overthrow Pitt," he insisted. "Six months' thought has confirmed me in the conviction that a landing in England cannot be considered a mad fancy."[14] He had no doubt of success; even the Directory's decision to reduce the funds put at his disposal did not diminish his enthusiasm. There was, of course, no longer any question of landing two armies simultaneously. Hoche made no change in the plan concerning Ireland, but replaced the army intended to invade England with an expeditionary corps consisting of a few hundred men, most of them former *chouans* (counterrevolutionary rebels), who were supposed to land on the English coast and wage a guerilla war after having recruited supporters on site, among workers, poor people, and even "hooligans" (*mauvais sujets*).[15] The acts of violence committed by these men, who were to make surprise attacks and operate clandestinely, were intended to force the English to mobilize against them large forces that they would therefore not be able to send to Ireland, where the bulk of the French troops would land and join up with the thousands of rebel patriots whose leaders had promised their support. Nothing could make a dent in Hoche's determination. He was so sure of Irish collaboration that he finally decided to land in Ireland only half of the 22,000 troops called for by the original plan. By late 1796 everything was ready. Hoche was waiting for the signal. "Once the wind rises," he wrote, "everything, on land and at sea, is perfectly arranged; gaiety and tranquility are on every face; patriotism and confidence in every heart!"[16] The squadron sailed on December 15, 1796, but it had hardly gone to sea off Ouessant when a violent storm scattered it over the ocean. On January 1, 1797, what remained of the fleet was back in Brest. The humiliation was complete. The navy and the weather were chiefly responsible for the failure, but Hoche had been so sure of success that the venture's unhappy outcome showed him in an extremely poor light. The episode shows how little, in the end, he could have become a dangerous rival for Bonaparte. As Albert Sorel put it, his untimely death in 1797 conferred on him a greatness that had less to do with what he had been than with what he could have become: "Hoche benefited from the immense disappointment with the Empire. People preferred to recognize only his virtues and the promise of his genius. France adorned him with all its retrospective illusions; it imagined that had he lived, it could have broken with its bitter destiny. He offered the prospect of a different future for the Revolution."[17] Ireland was not his only lapse. Hoche had made his mark as a skillful general, and in the Vendée he had shown an incontestable political aptitude, but he had imprudently put himself at risk on 18 Fructidor. He was impressionable, irritable, suspicious, easily overwhelmed, subject to disappointment, to bitterness, and also—as in the case of the Irish affair—to irrepressible bursts of enthusiasm. He was not as profound a dissimulator as Bonaparte, who unlike Hoche had mastered the art of playing the lion or the fox, depending on the circumstances.

Mission Impossible?

The Directory seems not to have learned from Hoche's failure; moreover, it had serious reasons for making another attempt. The breaking off of the recent talks between France and Britain had convinced the Directory that there was no way out other than a total victory, and to those who dared to speak of a negotiated peace Reubell responded angrily: "What are you talking about, making peace with England? I know only one way to make peace with it, and that is to humiliate and subjugate it!"[18] In the end the Directory still wanted to believe that the enterprise would be successful, especially because it was going to be led by Bonaparte. Weren't his victories in Italy a pledge of his success?

For Bonaparte, the planned landing in England had certain advantages. For one thing, it would allow him to stay outside the current political turmoil. On the other hand, this command was no great prize. Having long since exchanged the role of a simple general for those of diplomat, legislator, and even sovereign, he could not once again become the executor of the government's will without demeaning himself. "I would leave Italy only to play a role in France more or less similar to the one that I play here," he had told Miot.[19] This projected landing clearly did not offer him that role. England was too close, and the operation was risky. However, Bonaparte did not consider it definitely impossible. Had that been the case, he would not have returned to the idea in 1803–1805. However, he certainly thought that it would be difficult to operate without a powerful fleet, and that it might not be the right time: Was it prudent to send an entire army to England when war was brewing on the continent? He did not conceal his doubts.[20] To the Directory's British project he opposed an Egyptian plan. In order "really to destroy England," he said, it would be necessary "to seize Egypt."[21] That did not mean that France had to give up the idea of striking England on its home ground; he simply wanted to convince the Directory that a landing was a very complex matter that could be executed only after months of preparation. When he wrote to Talleyrand, "Let us concentrate our activity on the navy and destroy England," it was to remind him that only the creation of a powerful navy would make it possible really to have done with England.[22] To the frontal attack favored by the government, he opposed an indirect strategy that might ultimately take the French as far as London. In fact, if he doubted the success of a landing, he thought it possible to proceed by stages, beginning by threatening the enemy on several fronts in order to force it to disperse its fleet. Egypt would be one of these fronts, Ireland another. Then, when England's naval superiority had been destroyed by the scattering of its ships, the landing would become possible. He already had in mind the plan he would adopt after the Peace of Amiens was broken in 1803. Bourrienne, who was then his closest aide, tells us, "His object was, having once secured the possession of Egypt, to return to Toulon . . . and next to combine with the fleet all the forces that could be supplied, not only by France, but by her allies, for the purpose of attacking England. . . . He always regarded a descent upon England as possible, though in its result fatal as long as we should be inferior in naval strength; but he hoped by various manoeuvres to secure a superiority on one point." And Bourrienne added: "He would have thought it sublime to date an order of the day from the ruins of Memphis, and three months later one from London."[23]

The Eastern Question

He had set his course, then, on Egypt. The idea was no more original than that of a landing in England.[24] Europe had been dreaming about the Orient for centuries. At first it had nourished the hope of reconquering the Holy Land. When the spirit of the Crusades flickered out, politics took over. The Turks had constantly expanded the borders of their empire—they had seized Constantinople, crossed the Bosporus, colonized the Balkans and later Hungary, and besieged Vienna (1529 and 1683); Europeans all the while thought of nothing but dismantling this colossus that, from the beginning of its history, had been considered an anomaly in the political order. Even if it was only in the nineteenth century that the Ottoman Empire earned the label "the sick man of Europe," for three centuries it had been common to predict its "ruin and overthrow."[25] However, European sovereigns avoided basing their policies on such predictions. The plans for conquest, even those written by men as famous as Sully (1607) or Leibniz (1672), were merely part of a stylistic exercise that contributed, with its obligatory figures and conventional formulas, to "the composition of the royal panegyric."[26] In particular, they invested the "very Christian" French monarchy with an oriental destiny, though neither Henri IV nor his successors had any serious intention of taking advantage of it. Nevertheless, this "prophetic repetition" had its uses. On the one hand, it allowed the king of France "not to abandon the field to other princes and to compete with them for the symbolic leadership of Christianity"; on the other, it served to support the claim to "French preeminence in the Levant."[27] In fact, verbal confrontation with the Infidels was not incompatible with maintaining good commercial relations and close political relations. Although the Turk remained the incarnation of the barbarian, he was also a commercial partner and an actor in his own right on the stage of European politics. It was unavoidable; he occupied, after all, a third of Europe's territory. Geography trumped ideology, and it was a pope—Alexander VI—who first took the initiative by establishing a rapprochement with the sultan.[28] Whereas Louis XI had refused to receive an emissary from the sultan for fear of compromising the salvation of his soul, Francis I did not hesitate to negotiate with Suleiman the Magnificent; he obtained advantageous conditions for French traders, and the system of "capitulations" was soon transformed into a genuine alliance. France's enemies never failed to denounce the pact that the king had signed with the enemies of Christianity, but the advantages of the alliance amply counterbalanced the doubt it cast on the French monarchy's religious orthodoxy. In the Levant, France benefited from its most-favored-nation status; its merchants controlled the outlet of the two trade routes of the Red Sea and the Euphrates, through which, until the sixteenth century, "everything that grows in Asia, Africa, and even the East Indies" came into Europe.[29] The sultan's friendship also allowed the French constantly to threaten the powers of continental Europe with an attack on their rear. All this was well worth accommodating Ottoman moods. Although Louis XIV did withdraw from Austrian Luxembourg when he learned that the Turks were once again besieging Vienna (1683), as Christian solidarity obliged him to do, the Turks had hardly been repulsed before he resumed the struggle. By falling on Spanish Flanders, he intended as much to relieve the Turks, who were then in complete disarray, by attacking the Imperial troops from the rear, as to take advantage of the fact that the empire was busy fighting the Ottomans in Hungary. France had no interest in weakening Turkey. But for the Ottomans the conflict with the emperor, which came to an end in 1697 with the signature of the Peace of Ryswick, merely delayed a military rout that had been foreshadowed by their failure before the walls of Vienna. The peace treaty they signed in Karlowitz on January 26, 1699, marked the beginning of a long century of decline and the ebbing of a power whose decrepitude was exaggerated no less in Constantinople than in the European capitals. After all, the Ottoman Empire survived for two centuries after the disaster at Vienna, and if there was a real decline, its causes were not exclusively military. Nonetheless, in Europe it was seen more than ever as being on the verge of collapse, whereas in Constantinople the time had come for harrowing changes.[30]

It was in fact becoming clear that Islam was farther than ever from the "Golden apple," the mythical city that was supposed to mark the end of the jihad. The defeats suffered by the Turks, the threats that now weighed on their Balkan and Caucasian possessions, Russia's expansionist intentions—all this showed them the weakness of their political structures and the obsolescence of their military instrument. Accustomed for centuries to seeing themselves as the bearers of a truth that it was their duty to make known to the rest of the world, they suffered a rude awakening. Superiority had clearly passed to the other side. It was not without repugnance that they said to themselves that they might have to learn from the "House of War."[31] Constantinople's first printing shop was established in 1729, a school of military engineering opened its doors in 1734, and toward the end of the century the Ottoman government tried to set up a genuine bureaucracy. These innovations did not meet with unanimous approval. The disdain for novelties and the faith in the superiority of Islamic civilization were so strong that resistance to change was widespread: the print shop was closed in 1742, the engineering school was dissolved, and it was only during the reign of Selim III that the Ottoman government opened—in London, in 1793— its first permanent embassy. The Ottomans finally resigned themselves to entering the concert of Europe, and at the same time to recognizing the legitimacy of infidel nations. This was the result of the decline of their power and a belated admission of their weakness. The Ottomans had long represented "a danger"; now they became "a problem."[32]

It was in this context that plans for military intervention in the east underwent a revival. For the French and the English, it was now a matter of keeping the Ottoman Empire alive in order to contain Russian expansion, which was heavy with portents of future conflicts. That is why they did not have to be asked twice to send engineers and military advisors to Constantinople, as well as to Persia, especially because they were able to charge a price: an increase in the privileges granted by the sixteenth-century capitulations. Louis XIV did not take the trouble to read the plan for the conquest of Egypt written for him by Leibniz.[33] But he did not exclude the possibility of going to Constantinople, if necessary, and in 1685 he sent one of his agents there, assigning him to study the city's defenses.[34] The Russians' later successes in the wars of 1768–1774 and 1789–1792 increased the general concern and propelled the "Eastern Question" to the first rank of chancelleries' preoccupations.[35] In France, diplomats wondered whether the occupation of Egypt did not, paradoxically, represent the best way of saving the Ottoman Empire.

Of the three main arguments given in favor of this conquest, the first had to do with the state of quasi-independence in which Egypt had existed for the past several decades. Although in 1517 the Turks had seized this ancient Mamluk sultanate, they had never been able to subdue the ruling caste of warriors; they had had to get along with them. Thus, alongside the pasha representing the sultan in Cairo there continued to be an "equestrian feudalism" consisting of emancipated slaves who had originally come from the Caucasus or the Balkans and converted to Islam.[36] It was among these Mamluks that the Ottoman authorities chose their governors, counting on the hatred among the different "houses" to which they belonged to keep control of these distant provinces. When the Ottoman Empire began to decline, the Mamluks tried to throw off the Turkish yoke. In 1768 one of the Mamluk leaders, Alî Bey, drove the pasha out of Cairo, minted coins bearing his own effigy, expanded his dominion to both shores of the Red Sea, and in 1771 launched an offensive against Syria. He made himself master of Damascus, but was forced to return to Cairo to defend his rule, which was being threatened by a revolt. Alî Bey's assassination in 1773 did not benefit the Ottomans, because his nephew, Abû al-Dhahab, pursued his policies, and Abû's successors (he died in 1775), Ibrâhîm and Murad Bey, allowed a representative of the sultan to return to Cairo only on the condition that he let them rule as governors of an Egypt that, though not independent de jure, was independent de facto.

A second reason for preferring Egypt was its strategic situation at the junction of Africa and Asia. On the one hand, it was close enough to Turkey that by occupying it, France could threaten Russian expansionist ambitions. On the other hand, through the Isthmus of Suez, Egypt would offer the French access to the Red Sea, and thus a maritime route to India, which would allow them to divert part of its lucrative trade.

That was the third argument. At that time the riches of the subcontinent traveled by the long route around the Cape of Good Hope. Reopening the old commercial route to the Mediterranean and Europe via the Red Sea and the Suez isthmus (where since the reign of Louis XIV the French had been thinking of digging a canal) would considerably reduce the time required for transport, and therefore the cost. Merchants, it was said, would not be able to resist such advantages and would soon abandon the route around the Cape for that through Suez, and Alexandria would once again become "the warehouse of a universal commerce."[37] These plans for gaining a stranglehold on world trade were backed by a conviction that Choiseul had expressed earlier in the century, namely that the Seven Years' War had sounded the eventual death knell of the European presence in the New World. However, Europe could not easily turn its back on the New World, because the sugar-producing islands in the West Indies were necessary to its prosperity. Choiseul and those who followed him believed they had found the solution: If America was Europe's past, the Orient would be its future. Travelers, merchants, and diplomats all swore that sugar cane and cotton could easily be grown in the fertile valley of the Nile. Moreover, the existence of a population reputed to be industrious and docile would make it possible to avoid resorting to slavery, which was denounced by the *philosophes* as immoral and by economists as being low in productivity. Then all the old commercial routes through the Red Sea, the Persian Gulf, and the Euphrates, which had been abandoned, would undergo a revival of activity.[38]

Choiseul's colonial policy was abandoned after he was disgraced in 1770. It still had supporters—including the minister of the navy, Sartine, whose predictions were soon confirmed when the United States achieved independence—but it met with the ferocious opposition of Charles Gravier de Vergennes, the secretary of foreign affairs from 1774 to 1787, who was well acquainted with Turkey because he had been ambassador there for fourteen years (1754–1768). In the mid-1770s the struggle between the "interventionists" and the "anti-interventionists" was bitter, if muffled. The former redoubled their efforts; Sartine dispatched to the Near East agents whose reports all concluded, of course, that immediate intervention was necessary.[39] But Vergennes refused to bend; he believed the maintenance of the Turkish empire was indispensable for the balance of Europe, and in order to tear it away from the Russians, he counted less on a permanent French presence in Cairo than on sending military advisors to Constantinople. He preferred cooperation to colonization.[40] After the end of the American War of Independence, which had diverted attention toward the west, the "Eastern Question" once again became a focus of interest: Baron de Tott advocated intervention.[41] Volney opposed it.[42] The debate would have gone on for a long time had the French Revolution not for a time put Ottoman affairs on the back burner.

The Revolution's successive governments remained faithful to the commitments France had made earlier; they provided help for "the fortifications of the Bosporus, naval construction, and the training of the officials and engineers necessary for the reforms that Selim was trying to make."[43] At the same time, the

Revolution had complicated relations with Constantinople, but in 1795 the two capitals had reestablished contact. The sultan officially recognized the French Republic, the two countries exchanged ambassadors, and the French government adopted the policy of cooperation that Vergennes had formerly advocated. "The Turks," the Directory was soon to write in its instructions to its ambassador, "are our most natural, oldest, most loyal, and most necessary allies."[44] However, in 1792 Turkey had suffered a reverse at the hands of the Russians that aggravated the effects of their defeat in 1774, and it seemed in worse shape than ever. Paris did not exclude the possibility of coming to the sultan's aid. How? Maybe, Delacroix, the minister of foreign affairs, suggested in early 1796, by occupying Rhodes, Crete, or better yet, Egypt. The latter, Delacroix said, "was of no use to the Turks"; and adopting the ideas of Choiseul, who was, however, accused of having tried to weaken Turkey the better to serve Austria's ambitions, he said Egypt was "in the hands of 6,000 brigands relentlessly devastating it." He insisted that "10,000 republicans would suffice to free it, restore peace and abundance, and make it an inexhaustible granary for the southern departments, a much shorter route to the East Indies, and consequently an advantageous commercial center." As for the sultan, "promising him an annual payment in the form of wheat to feed Constantinople could lead [him] to cede this country."[45] Revolutionary diplomacy was returning to the objectives and the means used by royal diplomacy.

Bonaparte and the Orient

Thus, the Directory was envisaging an Egyptian expedition long before Bonaparte proposed one in 1797. Delacroix's report proves it, and Napoleon himself was to confirm it by saying that "several campaign plans had been discussed for the year 1798."[46] The discord between the government and the general concerned the order of priorities: Egypt first, Bonaparte said; England first, the Directory replied, immediately adding that Egypt could be dealt with afterward.[47]

If Bonaparte insisted so fervently on the eastern option, it was not only because he had doubts about the success of a landing on the shores of England; the Orient was one of his old acquaintances. In his youth, as his notebooks show, he had studied ancient Egypt, its pyramids and pharaohs, Carthage, Assyria, and Persia. He had also read, pen in hand, Abbé Marigny's *Histoire des Arabes sous le gouvernement des califes*—a tedious catalogue of reigns grouped into dynasties[48]—and Baron de Tott's *Mémoires sur les Turcs et les Tartares.*[49] Later on, Junot confided, "When we were in Paris [in 1795], unhappy and unemployed, he spoke to me about the Orient, about Egypt, Mount Lebanon, the Druze."[50] Bonaparte's meeting with Volney in 1792 had played a crucial role. After the Constituent Assembly, of which he was a member, broke up, Volney had gone to Corsica. He said he wanted to retire there to devote himself to agriculture on a well-sited estate that he would make into his little personal Arcadia. Napoleon had been introduced to him in Corte in February 1792. The young officer of twenty-three was proud of the attention paid to him by such a famous man who was twelve years older than he, and perhaps even prouder of the fact that he wanted "to settle here and live peacefully among simple people."[51] The two men traveled together from Corte to Ajaccio "by the picturesque mountain road that climbs the dorsal spine of the island," and when they arrived at their destination, Bonaparte introduced Volney to his mother.[52] Did they talk only about the beauty of the landscape, figs, and honey from "Caccia"? Or also about the Orient, about Volney's *Voyage en Égypte et en Syrie* (which Bonaparte had not yet read, though he was soon to annotate a copy) and his latest work, *Les Ruines?*[53]

Seeing in Bonaparte's oriental ambitions "the connecting thread" that explains his policies as a whole, including even the policies he pursued as emperor, some people have taken him to be, in this respect, entirely extraordinary.[54] But the Orient was a passion of the age. The American War of Independence had made America fashionable, but the vogue of the Orient, which was older, was still going strong; in literature, in the theater, in the opera, in dress, and in interior decoration, "turqueries" were still all the rage. If the Orient inspired so much friendly curiosity, that was also because it was no longer a threat. The Oriental, who had formerly been the incarnation of the barbarous, cruel infidel, had been transformed, sometimes into a sort of noble savage who had remained close to the natural man, and sometimes into a kind of representative of a third estate of the antipodes oppressed simultaneously by a despotic political system and by backward religious ideas. Scholarly orientalism—the word, which had re-

cently appeared in English, was soon to enter the French language as well—
thus sought to tear down the wall that had separated Islam and Christianity
since the Middle Ages. The strongly contrasting descriptions of oriental customs given by Volney and by Claude-Étienne Savary (who had gone to Egypt
in the early 1780s and whose *Lettres sur l'Égypte* had enjoyed no less success with
readers than Volney's *Voyage*) are often cited. The two men had gone to the same
places, had witnessed the same scenes. Whereas Savary had contemplated "very
pretty girls" playing in the Nile "amid the waves," with "their braided hair floating
on their shoulders," Volney had seen wading in the muddy waters of the river
women whose bodies could not remind one of "naiads emerging from their bath,
unless one's desire has been inflamed by privation."[55] Savary's "cold, calm, [and]
taciturn Arab" who is "content with what he has" and enjoys "peacefully the
goods that nature offers him" contrasts with Volney's entirely different picture
of veiled women "like phantoms" and beggars dozing in dirty, abandoned
gardens.[56]

Savary saw everything through rose-colored spectacles; Volney saw everything through dark ones; one was enthusiastic, optimistic, and full of goodwill;
the other was cynical, pessimistic, and disenchanted. They differed not only in
temperament: Volney was a classicist who, not seeing Egypt as it was in the age
of the Pharaohs, found nothing to like in it, whereas Savary was a pre-Romantic
imbued with Rousseau and quick to confuse poverty with simplicity. But both
of them were pursuing the same goal: to wrench the Orient out of the irreduc-
ible particularism in which Montesquieu had imprisoned it by contrasting Europe, the "land of moderation and freedom," with Asia, the land of despotism.
Europe was said, however, to be indebted to Asia.[57] The Arabs were supposed
to be an important link in the "uninterrupted sequence" of the peoples who since
the origins of humanity had relayed with each other in carrying the torch of
civilization to ever greater heights; it was even claimed that they had revived "a
few sparks of the Greeks' genius," and that they might have added to this heritage had they not been subjected to "a despotism sanctioned by religion."[58] From
that point on, the Occident and the Orient had followed different paths, but it
was thought that they might converge again if the ills from which the oriental
world suffered could be identified with precision. From Savary to Volney, from
Turgot to Condorcet, the guilty party had a face: the Turk, who had emerged

from the outer reaches of the world to subject the land of the Byzantine emperors and the first caliphs to his cruel ideas, his brutal customs, his cupidity, his ignorance, and his thirst for domination. By spreading fear everywhere, the better to make himself obeyed, the Turk had snuffed out intelligence, creativity, and the spirit of initiative, turning the Orient away from the paths to progress and prosperity. The lexicon is that of the Enlightenment: the Ottoman world, poor, ignorant, and backward, illustrated the combined misdeeds of political despotism and religious oppression.[59]

This Orient, redescribed in ways familiar to the Enlightenment, ultimately appears as a failed Europe whose misfortune was largely due to its not having had a century of enlightenment to draw attention to the duties of princes and the rights of peoples. The Orient was Europe without Voltaire. The *philosophes* carried the comparison still further; following Boulainvilliers's version of the history of France, according to which the French nobility descended from the Frankish conquerors and the third estate from the conquered Gallo-Romans, they proposed a history of the Ottoman Empire based on the same model: "Thus, if modern Europe is the product of the Germanic invasions with aristocracies of barbarian origin and absolutist monarchies supported by religious institutions, the same holds for the great Oriental states, which have, more than Europe, undergone repeated major invasions (by Arabs, Turks, Mongols) and the manifestation of religious fanaticism. The constitution of the Ottoman Empire . . . is thus close to that of Europe. The Turks constitute a military aristocracy that exploits and oppresses a multiplicity of peoples."[60]

"The mechanisms of history being the same everywhere,"[61] this meant that oriental peoples could enjoy as much freedom as their European brothers. But they would need external intervention to achieve it, because they had to overthrow a political and religious regime that had remained intact, whereas Europe's monarchical-Catholic counterpart had been weakened by the attacks of the Enlightenment. Moreover, in Muslim society there was no intermediate class between the oppressed Arabs and the Turkish oppressors that was capable of leading the struggle for emancipation.[62] Volney, who ended up supporting this point of view, had at first doubted that such an intervention could succeed; but as Sainte-Beuve wrote, the French Revolution had put "that sober spirit in a state that was, so to speak, Pindaric".[63] The Revolution not only proved that nothing was impossible, but also attested to the illegitimacy of the Ottoman government: Was it not a living denial of the rights of man? In *Les Ruines*, Volney addressed to his oriental brothers a prophecy in which Bonaparte was to find a role that suited him:

> This nation and its leaders have ignored these sacred truths . . . Well, then! They will suffer the consequences of their blindness . . . the judgment has been made; the day is approaching when this colossus of power, broken, will collapse under its own weight; yes, I swear it by the ruins of so many defunct empires! The empire of the Crescent will suffer the fate of the states whose regime it has imitated. A foreign people will drive the sultans out of their capital. . . . In this dissolution, the peoples of the empire, freed from the yoke that held them together, will resume their former distinctions, and a general anarchy will follow . . . until among the Arabs, the Armenians, or the Greeks legislators arise who will reconstitute new states. . . . Oh! if only there were profound and bold men on Earth. What elements of grandeur and glory! . . . But the hour of destiny is already being rung. The war cry strikes my ear, and the catastrophe is about to begin. The sultan calls upon his armies in vain; his ignorant warriors are defeated, scattered; in vain he calls upon his subjects; their hearts are cold as ice. . . . In vain the true believers invoke Heaven and the Prophet: the Prophet is dead. . . . Let a virtuous leader emerge! Let a powerful and just people appear! And let the Earth raise it to supreme power: it awaits a law-giving people; it desires and calls for [such a people], and my heart awaits it. . . . Yes, a muffled sound already reaches my ears: a cry of freedom, uttered on distant shores, has resounded on the ancient continent. At this cry, a secret murmur against oppression arises in a great nation; a salutary concern warns it of its situation; it asks itself what it is, what it should be; and surprised by its weakness, it seeks to discover its rights, its means, how its leaders have behaved . . . Another day, another reflection . . . and [then] an immense movement will be born; a new

age will open up, an age of astonishment for the common folk, of surprise and terror for the tyrants, of liberation for a great people, and of hope for the Earth as a whole.[64]

Emancipated Europe had to come to the aid of the enslaved Orient. But Volney did not imagine this regeneration in the revolutionary mode of a popular uprising, even incited by French "missionaries" of the kind the Jacobins dreamed of sending more or less everywhere in the world, but rather in a mode directly inspired by the history of the Orient: that of the sudden appearance of a superman who would overthrow empires, unleash the apocalypse, and give birth to a new world. Volney dreamed of another Alexander, another Muhammad. Clearly, orientalism could not Westernize the Orient; when it dreamed of doing so, it returned the Orient to its foreignness. East of the Mediterranean began the land of unprecedented adventures, extraordinary conquerors, founders of empires, and great scoundrels. The history of the Orient had been full of them since time immemorial, but in the eighteenth century one man summed up all of them: Muhammad, the symbol of fanaticism, immoderation, cleverness, ruse, cynicism, cruelty, and ambition, but also of freedom. Voltaire, while at the same time condemning the charlatan who had not hesitated to spread "carnage and terror" in order to "change the face of the Earth," could not help admiring the child of the desert who had become "everything by himself and nothing by his ancestors."[65] Muhammad? An incarnation of the will to power.

That was, without any doubt, what appealed to the young Napoleon and never ceased to fascinate him. He cared little about the oriental "third estate"; what attracted him in oriental history and mythology was precisely the profusion with which they offered, in every age, people and episodes that might have been taken directly out of Plutarch. For him the Orient was both the homeland of great adventurers and a space that was, so to speak, virgin and full of infinite possibilities. The confidences he shared with Bourrienne when he was moping in Paris in 1797 are famous: "We have to go to the Orient," he told him, "all the great glories come from there."[66] The greatest of these glories was Muhammad's. Christ had been "a preacher," Napoleon said, whereas Muhammad was "a conqueror, a sovereign."[67] With a handful of Bedouins and the support of a religious credo that favored battle and sacrifice, he had conquered "half the world." More than the Rousseauist legislator and clever founder, he admired the qualities that had allowed Muhammad to obtain such great results with such small means.[68] Much later on he was to criticize Voltaire harshly for having presented Muhammad as a "scoundrel, worthy of the gallows," saying that if Muhammad had limited himself to intrigue and trickery, he would have achieved only "secondary results," whereas by "exciting the multitude" by his preaching, he had changed "the face of the universe."[69] However, in his youth Napoleon was not unresponsive to the figure of the charlatan Voltaire described, as is shown by a little tale he wrote called *Le masque du prophète* (1789), which he based on Marigny.[70] This work tells the story of an impostor named Hakem. Claiming to be invested with a divine mission, he raises an army of supporters made fanatical by his eloquence. He wins success after success until the day he is struck by a terrible illness. Disfigured, blind, and fearing that his misfortune will be seen as a divine punishment, he puts on a silver mask, saying that he wears it "to prevent men from being dazzled by the light that emerges from his face." Shortly afterward his army is defeated. Hakem has a broad ditch dug around his camp and filled with quicklime, into which the enemy is supposed to rush when it attacks. When night comes, he has his soldiers drink poisoned wine, throws their bodies into the quicklime, and finally leaps into it himself, so that neither he nor his soldiers could ever be identified. His imposture was thus forever concealed and his glory assured, because the belief soon spread that he and his men had been taken up into heaven. The tale's last sentence—"How far can the furious desire for fame lead?"—is often cited and opposed to the emperor's future conduct. But the story testifies to other things as well: first, his admiration for the wily skill of the false prophet; second, the conviction that trickery can become, if it succeeds, a source of legitimacy; and third, the fascination with the end of a figure who chooses, by means of a final deception, to live in men's memories rather than to continue an earthly existence without glory.

Such were the dreams of the young Napoleon. The Orient was his blank page at a time when the attention of most of his contemporaries was directed toward America. At that time the experiment most full of future promise seemed to be taking place in the West. The American War of Independence had made the New World fashionable. For a whole generation, Washington, Franklin, and Jefferson seemed to be revivals of the Plutarchan hero. As seen by Europeans, independent America presented the astonishing spectacle of a new nation established on virgin territory, freed of the weight of history, and knowing no inequalities. There, on the blank page of this empty land, new men were giving concrete form to the theories about the rational foundation of societies. America had, as it were, taken philosophy out of the books and embodied its ideas in a people of virtuous farmers and philosophers. Above all, America pleased philosophical minds, for which happiness consisted in escaping from society and history. The young Bonaparte's imagination—and this is one of his deepest personality traits—was not philosophical but historical. What led his contemporaries to admire the United States inspired in Bonaparte only indifference. His New World was not America but the Old World, not Europe, but the Orient, which was Europe's past, the origin of civilization, the area from which so many conquerors, from Tamerlane to Nadir Shah, had emerged and whose history offered an inexhaustible repertory of heroic actions, immense enterprises, and gigantic collapses. Before it became "the ideal time" of his life, the Orient was the imaginary country of his youth.[71]

The Sketch of a Mediterranean Policy

It was when Bonaparte arrived in Ancona on Italy's Adriatic coast on February 9, 1797, that he came into contact with the Orient for the first time. Beyond the horizon, there was Ottoman Albania; to the south, Corfu and the other Ionian islands; still farther on lay the coasts of the Peloponnesus and, through Albania and Greece, the land route to Constantinople and the maritime route to Egypt.[72] Ancona was a door opening on the Orient. From that moment on, he knew no rest. The general did not yet know the scenario for the next chapter of his life, but he was already preparing the ground and drawing up plans without worrying too much about how plausible or practical they were. He urged the Directory not to restore Ancona to the pope.[73] Having Ancona, he had to have Corfu; he sent a squadron to take possession.[74] Once the island was under French power, he decided to strengthen his control over the whole of the shores of the Adriatic. He sent messengers to the Ottoman pashas in Albania to assure them of his "genuine" friendship and to promise them that he would treat Muslims "with special partiality"; he paid homage to the "Maniots," a small Christian community at the southern tip of the Peloponnesus that the Turks had not been able to subdue and that was said to be descended from the Spartans.[75] Having made himself master of the Adriatic, he turned his eyes toward the Levant. His mind was already no longer entirely in Italy, while discussions with Austria were being pursued. However, it was not because conquered Italy was now incapable of satisfying his need for action that he looked toward the Mediterranean, but because the conquest of Italy, which was the consequence of the defeat of Austria, left France and England confronting each other alone. He was convinced that their quarrel would not be settled in the English Channel but on the Mediterranean. Just as the military operations against Vienna had suggested to him an Italian policy that he had not premeditated, the war with England suggested a Mediterranean policy to which everything contributed: the reconquest of Corsica, the Spanish alliance, the direct or indirect control over half of Italy, the domination of the Adriatic—it all led him to see the Mediterranean as a "French sea."[76] An absurd idea? It represented one of the main orientations of French foreign policy. For the Directory's diplomacy, which was focused on Belgium and the Rhine, Bonaparte proposed to substitute a policy—sketched out earlier by Choiseul, whose successor the emperor was to be in this respect[77]—that would make French influence in the Mediterranean its priority.

A hundred years ago historians were so obsessed by the German peril that they gave the location of national borders an excessive importance. In accusing Bonaparte of having given Italy priority over the Rhine at Campoformio, they forgot that conquering the left bank of the Rhine meant strengthening Prussia by reducing Germany's political fragmentation. And how can we believe in the viability of this borderline, which was supposed to extend the Republic to include Mainz, Koblenz, and Venlo in Holland? France could not indefinitely retain these territories, whose populations had no liking for the French or their Revolution any more than the Belgians did. Moreover, this accusation forgets that France already had borders that could protect it from invasions—knowing that no border offers absolute protection—a fact that in 1748 had led Louis XV to return to Austria the Belgium his armies had just seized, saying that the security of the kingdom in no way required that its limits be expanded. Finally, this accusation rests on associating power with size and assumes that strength increases with the acquisition of a few acres of land, forgetting that the bases of wealth had begun to change; Britain, more than any other nation, was providing an example of an essentially industrial, commercial, and colonial power. In six years of war France had lost, to the benefit of the British, most of its colonies, and its commerce had been ruined. The activity and prosperity of the great port cities were no more than memories. The Directory's policy, which was turned toward the interior of the continent and not toward the seas, had left these cities in economic stagnation. The policy advocated by Bonaparte sought to revive them by opening up new commercial routes: in this case, toward the Orient, given that the French colonies in the Caribbean had been lost and were unlikely to be reconquered directly. Obtaining the restoration of the colonies was the ultimate goal of the war, and there was only one way to achieve it: threatening the very sources of England's wealth. Whereas the Directory continued the "borders policy" of Louis XIV and Vauban, Bonaparte sought to reestablish France's status as a commercial power.[78]

Monge, Talleyrand, and the Others

Bonaparte was not alone in dreaming about setting foot on Egyptian soil. His entourage echoed his dream. Between games of chess and conferences with the Austrians, the general talked to Monge about his projects, and took up the subject again during his "long evening walks" through the "magnificent grounds" of the Villa Manin in Passariano.[79] It was there that he made a remark that became famous: "Europe is a molehill," he exclaimed. "There have never been any great empires and great revolutions except in the Orient, where six hundred million people live!"[80] Monge was the more enthusiastic; he already saw himself walking in the footsteps of Herodotus in Bonaparte's company. In addition to Bonaparte's usual companions, there were also visitors, such as Raymond Verninac, a former ambassador who was returning from Constantinople, where he had asked one of his aides for (still another) plan for the conquest of Egypt. The Italians themselves dreamed of recovering, thanks to Bonaparte, their former influence in the Mediterranean region.[81]

Monge had had books, reports, and maps sent from Paris, and Bonaparte devoted a great deal of time to poring over the details of an expedition that he still considered not "decided upon" but only "possible."[82] In any case, the project was taking on clearer outlines. When Desaix came to see him in Passariano, Bonaparte made him stay and explained the operation at length and in all its details: "Ideas about Egypt, its resources," Desaix wrote in his notebook after the conversation. "Sail from Venice with 10,000 men, 8,000 Poles for Egypt. Take it. Advantages. Details. With 5 divisions, 2,000 horses."[83] If Bonaparte left the decision to be determined by events, he did not finally exclude any hypothesis, and in his heart of hearts Egypt was already no longer merely an option.

It has to be said that he now had a powerful ally in Paris: Talleyrand, who had recently been made minister of foreign affairs. Without having consulted one another at all, they were toying with the same projects. Whereas Bonaparte and Monge were talking about going to raise the French tricolor over the pyramids, at the Institute Talleyrand was proclaiming himself the heir to the oriental policy of Choiseul, whose protégé he had been. Like Choiseul, he considered the American colonies lost to Europeans and called for the establishment in the Orient of colonies "whose ties to us [would be] more natural, more useful, and more enduring."[84] Praising Egypt's fertility, the "means of wealth and prosperity" to be found there and its geographical situation, which made it the "natural center of the trade of three of the four parts of the world," he added, referring to the opening of a new trade route through Suez and the Red Sea: "Trade with India would infallibly leave the long and expensive route around the Cape of Good Hope and follow that of Suez. . . . This event would bring about a revolution in Europe's trade that would affect mainly England. It would destroy its power in India, the sole foundation of its greatness in Europe. The resumption of the Suez route would have an influence on it as fatal as the discovery of the Cape of Good Hope had on the Genoese and the Venetians in the sixteenth century. . . . Neither should we lose sight of the fact that sooner or later, the peoples of Europe will lose their Western colonies. The possession of Egypt will suffice to amply compensate the Republic for this loss."[85]

He had, it is said, other reasons for being interested in Egypt and India, notably the project of an "Indian bank in Paris" from which he hoped to realize considerable profits.[86] We cannot say with certainty whether Bonaparte or Talleyrand was the first to propose the Egyptian expedition. The colonial policy advocated by the new minister of foreign relations was already well known when Bonaparte first came out publicly in favor of an oriental expedition:[87]

> The islands of Corfu, Zante [Zakynthos], and Cephalonia are more interesting for us than all of Italy taken together. I believe that if we were forced to choose, it would be better to return Italy to the emperor and keep the four islands which are a source of wealth and prosperity for our commerce. The Turkish empire is collapsing daily; the possession of these islands would put us in a position to support it as much as possible, or to take our share of it. The time is not far off when we will feel that in order truly to destroy England, we have to seize control of Egypt. The vast Ottoman Empire, which is steadily wasting away, obliges us to begin thinking about measures to preserve our trade with the Levant.[88]

Was this a belated commitment? It was the end result of several months of reflection and many conversations. Talleyrand, glad to meet someone who shared his views, expressed his approval by writing to the general to say that Egypt would in fact be "of great utility someday."[89] They had understood each other. Like Monge, Talleyrand showered Bonaparte with reports and memos that confirmed him in the conviction that, Egypt being more or less independent, the Porte would not object to a French intervention that would be all the easier because it would be supported by the majority of the population and would encounter opposition only from the Mamluks—who constituted a very small minority.[90] In turn, Bonaparte never ceased to remind Talleyrand that the route to Alexandria passed by way of Malta.[91] In the fief of the Knights Hospitaller he saw a stage on the way to the Orient, a lock to which it was all the more important to hold the key because the Treaty of Campoformio had introduced a new actor in the Mediterranean region, Austria. Indeed, Austria had just won an initial success by getting its candidate elected to the position of grand commander of Malta left vacant by the death of its former incumbent—a Frenchman.[92] At the end of September, the Directory, which was being "worked upon" by both Bonaparte and Talleyrand, yielded and approved the organization of an expedition against Malta. Poussielgue, whose talents the general had already had an opportunity to assess, was ordered to go to the island to reconnoiter its fortifications, make connections, and prepare for the arrival of the French. But Poussielgue had hardly set out before the Directory reoriented its foreign policy toward England alone. Bonaparte gave in; he recalled Poussielgue and devoted himself to preparations for crossing the Channel, lying on maps spread out on the floor, "a compass and pencil in his hand."[93]

He had not yet left Italy when he gave the first orders for organizing the return to France of the thousands of soldiers who were to be assembled on the shores of the Channel; he speeded up the manufacture of muskets and cannons, and oversaw the organization of the fleet and the restoration of the ports that were to receive the warships and transports.[94] We know almost nothing about the work done under his direction, but every indication is that it was considerable, because by the middle of January 1798 almost 50,000 men were already waiting to embark. The secrecy surrounding these preparations was so tight that Grouchy's request to take part in it because he had served under Hoche was unceremoniously refused: "The expedition to England," the minister of the interior, Letourneur, wrote to him, "is being secretly prepared by the Directory and the *immortal* general; it is impossible for me . . . to propose you [for a position] in a work in which no one is allowed to participate."[95] As a result, we do not know exactly when Bonaparte definitively rejected the idea of a landing.

The month of January was certainly decisive. Bonaparte had continued to work on this project with Caffarelli, Andréossy, the engineer Forfait, and the minister of war, Schérer, and on the twelfth he submitted to the Directory his plan for the invasion and the list of officers he wanted to take along. But events in Switzerland and Italy led him to be circumspect. Although he continued to transfer troops from the Mediterranean to the Channel, he did not exclude the possibility of sending them to the Rhine, if necessary. The Directory was still confident and was busy gathering the funds necessary for the expedition by asking for a loan of eighty million francs. Did Bonaparte hear that there were few subscribers (less than one-fourth of the capital was covered)? Or that the fleet's deplorable condition was poorly disguised by the minister of the navy's reassuring reports? He had not forgotten Egypt, of course, and even if he had,

Talleyrand would have reminded him of it, because it was more than ever on his mind. In his ministerial correspondence Talleyrand even went so far as to speak as if it were an expedition that had been officially authorized. In the first days of January Talleyrand arranged for Bonaparte to meet with the Ottoman ambassador in Paris, Ali Effendi, and then he sent to him multiple reports in favor of an immediate intervention.[96] Dubois-Thainville, who had worked under Verninac, Charles Magallon, the former consul in Cairo, and Joseph Félix Lazowski, who had returned from Constantinople a few days earlier, all assured Bonaparte that Egypt, weary of the Mamluk tyranny, was waiting for its liberators. Nothing seemed easier than taking control of Egypt; and nothing, moreover, would be more profitable, because the valley of the Nile would soon be transformed into a garden. There was no need to take a great army there, or to foresee a long campaign: Bonaparte would be back before winter to undertake, if it was still on the agenda, the assault on England—unless he decided to go to India via the Red Sea to help out the sultan of Mysore, Tipû Sâhib, who was putting up a ferocious resistance to the English in the southern part of the subcontinent. The expedition was without risks. Besides, the pretext had already been found: Egypt was "in the grip of anarchy" and the sultan's *firmans* were so little respected that foreigners were exposed to violence even though they were supposed to be protected by the capitulations. Thus, France could claim to be intervening in Egypt to reestablish the sultan's authority, which had been defied by the Mamluks. As for Turkey itself, the partisans of intervention insisted that the Porte was prepared to cede Egypt to a friendly nation provided that the latter helped it oppose the Russians' expansionist aims, and now those of the Austrians as well. This absurd idea was supported in particular by Talleyrand, both with Bonaparte and with the Directory; he did not hesitate to claim that the establishment of French colonies in the Orient would strengthen the Franco-Turkish alliance and would be so profitable that there must be no hesitation to risk war with the Russians.[97] "The conquest of Egypt," Magallon wrote in the conclusion of one of his reports, "is easy and even infallible."[98] Talleyrand went even further: "I can guarantee, based on the assertions of the men who know Egypt best, that its conquest will cost almost no French blood."[99]

Much later Bonaparte was indignant about this, saying that he would never have gone to Egypt if he had not been taken in by these stories about the wealth of the country and the friendliness of its inhabitants.[100] Everything in these reports was false, and after he returned from Egypt he angrily annotated one of Talleyrand's reports, punctuating whole passages with: "That is false!" "A plan good for a trading caravan!" "To the madhouse!" "What folly!"[101] In fact, if he had been deceived, it was by himself: he was no less persuaded than Magallon of the certain success of the enterprise, whereas from the outset he had doubted the possibility of landing an army in England. Talleyrand didn't have to make a great effort to convince him to set out for Egypt when they met, discreetly, on January 26, 1798. They separated satisfied with each other. Talleyrand, wanting to prove how dedicated he was to this project, had even promised to go to Constantinople in person to obtain the Turks' consent to the French occupation of Egypt. Bourrienne is clear on this point. In the last days of January the general told him: "Bourrienne, I don't want to stay here, there is nothing to do. They [the directors] don't want to hear anything about it. I see that if I remain I will soon be sunk. Everything is worn away here, I no longer have any glory; this little Europe doesn't offer enough of it."[102]

It remained, of course, to convince the Directory. While Talleyrand was besieging the government—to which he submitted an initial report on the Egyptian expedition on January 27, and a second on February 14—Bonaparte undertook to provide proof that the landing in England could not succeed, at least as things currently stood. From February 8 to February 19 he traveled along the coasts of the North Sea, from Boulogne to Antwerp. He observed ships at anchor, asked about supplies, forage, and weapons, visited ports, and drew up a list of repairs and arrangements that had to be made before the crossing; everywhere he went he excited the ardor of some people and threatened others. This gave a new impetus to the preparations. However, there could no longer be any illusion: the landing was impossible; the ports were in too bad shape; and the ships were too few, poorly maintained, poorly armed, poorly manned. As he wrote to Caffarelli, who had been assigned to inspect another part of the coast, nothing was irremediable, everything, both ports and ships, could be put back in satisfactory condition, but there wouldn't be enough time.[103] A crossing of the Channel could be attempted only during a favorable period, when the nights are long. In two months that time would be over, and the preparations could not be completed by then. Bonaparte no longer believed in the landing, at least in 1798. That was, in substance, what he explained to the Directory in the long report he submitted when he got back:

> No matter what efforts we make, it will be several years before we can acquire superiority at sea. Carrying out a landing in England without having control of the seas is the boldest and most difficult operation that has been made. If it is possible, it would be by making the passage by surprise, either eluding the squadron that would block Brest or Texel, or using small boats to cross in six to eight hours during the night, and landing at one of the points of the province of Kent or Sussex. For that operation, long nights would be required, thus winter. After the month of April, it is no longer possible to do anything. . . . Our navy is currently as little advanced as it was at the time when the Army of England was created, that is, four months ago. . . . The English expedition thus does not seem possible before next year; and then it is likely that hindrances arising on the continent will prevent it. The right time to prepare ourselves for this expedition has been lost, perhaps forever.[104]

Bonaparte proposed three solutions: invading Hanover (which was still under the control of Britain's Hanoverian dynasty); resuming talks with the British government; "or undertaking an expedition in the Levant that would threaten trade with the Indies." The first two proposals were obviously there only for form's sake. However, the Directory was not impressed, and instead of giving Bonaparte the blank check he was asking for, it granted him—on paper—the exceptional funds he had said might still allow him to successfully invade England. The Directory thus put all powers—military, administrative, financial, and political—in Bonaparte's hands, and allotted him a considerable budget. If he pretended to return to the preparations for the landing, it was not for long, because as early as March 3 the government asked the minister of the navy to suspend the execution of the orders issued a few days earlier.[105] In the meantime, Bonaparte had met with Desaix, who had just returned from a tour of Brittany and who painted such a deplorable picture of the situation that there could no longer be any doubt: whatever was done, nothing would be ready in time.[106] Of the thirty-four ships of the line present in the harbor at Brest, ten were not in condition to go to sea, only ten were armed, and none had a complete crew.[107] The operation was all the more compromised because at the same time it was learned in Paris that the ships commanded by Brueys in Corfu were in too poor condition to sail back to Brest, and the number of ships available for crossing the Channel was much smaller than had been predicted.[108] The only good news had come from Poussielgue. Not having received Bonaparte's counter-order, he had gone to Malta, and when he returned to France he sent a report favorable to the conquest of this "other Gibraltar" that was so essential for the domination of the Mediterranean.[109] This report arrived at the right time, just as Bonaparte was getting ready to make a new attempt to persuade the directors not to invade England. By then the directors themselves no longer believed in the landing. Was Reubell once again the only one who opposed Bonaparte, as he had been after Campoformio? In any case, the others consented with varying degrees of enthusiasm. Their motives have been much discussed. Did they resign themselves all the more willingly because by sending Bonaparte to Egypt they would rid themselves of his inconvenient presence, at least for a time? That would suppose that they were in principle hostile to this expedition, or at least that they thought it useless. But as we have said, since 1795 they had repeatedly mentioned it, and the difficulties it posed were not the kind that would impress them: "They were in the spirit of the Revolution," Bainville was to say, "those shining illusions for which neither difficulties nor distance counted."[110] Because the British could certainly not be attacked on their home ground, they would be attacked in India. What finally convinced the directors was not the pressing desire to keep all these more or less openly dissident military men busy, nor the desire to get this troublesome general out of their way, but rather the promise Bonaparte made to return to France as soon as he had Egypt well in hand, by the end of 1798 at the latest, to take command of an expedition to England that they would in the interim have had time to properly prepare. The government had in fact not given up on the landing; they had postponed it. And so it was that Bonaparte, who arrived at the Luxembourg Palace on March 5, 1798, emerged from it as the general-in-chief of an entirely new Army of the Orient.

SEVENTEEN

The Conquest of the Nile

*I*t took only two months to assemble, arm, and supply the formidable armada that set out from Toulon and Marseille, and from Corsica, Genoa, and Civitavecchia, on May 19, 1798. From the top deck of *L'Orient*, a gigantic three-decker vessel, one of only three in the French navy, Bonaparte watched the ships in the Toulon convoy leave the harbor to the sound of cannon fire and fanfares.[1] "It is seven o'clock in the morning," he wrote in a note addressed to the Directory. "The light squadron has set out . . . , and we are hoisting anchor under very fine weather."[2] More than 330 ships of war and transports sailed with almost 38,000 troops aboard—infantrymen, artillerymen, and cavalry (most of them without mounts)—plus a large group of workers representing all the arts and crafts, 3,000 sailors, and 167 scientists that Bonaparte had insisted on including in the venture.[3] In sum, 54,000 men, whereas the expeditionary corps sent to America at the time of the War of Independence consisted of less than 10,000.[4] When all the convoys had rejoined the flagship, the fleet looked to the passengers like "an immense floating city."[5]

The Toulon Rendezvous

If the preparations for the Egyptian expedition required so little time, it was first of all because Bonaparte had set to work on them even before the Directory had given its approval.[6] When the Directory finally adopted his proposals, he was thus able to submit a plan that gave a list of the regiments to be mobilized (along with their numbers), the officers to be assigned, the details of the artillery pieces to be taken along, and an estimate of the necessary budget—eight to nine million francs.[7] Nor was it irrelevant that the general staff had worked on the English expedition.

The circumstances also proved to be favorable. Money had been lacking for the English project, but it flowed freely for the Egyptian project, whose launch coincided with the proclamation of the Roman Republic and the fall of the Helvetic Confederation. To Berthier, who had been assigned to attack Rome in reprisal for the death of General Duphot, Bonaparte gave this advice: "Make money on everything, in order to provide for your army."[8] His former chief of staff replied: "I'll try to fill the money box."[9] As for Switzerland, its days had been numbered since the signature of the Treaty of Campoformio. Having created a satellite republic in northern Italy, France naturally coveted the roads that led there, and they all passed through Switzerland. Bonaparte had already taken advantage of disturbances troubling the canton of Graubünden to deprive it of the Valtellina region, attach it to the Cisalpine Republic, and in that way open up for France the Simplon route to Italy. The Directory had pursued this policy by having part of the bishopric of Basel occupied, annexing Mulhouse, and finally, massing on the borders troops that the Swiss "Jacobins" in Basel and Bern were calling on to help their own "revolution." Bonaparte, whose support for the revolutionary cause changed with the circumstances, was entirely on its side in this case. His respect for the head of the Church had been eclipsed by a pressing need for cash, and for monetary reasons he was similarly glad that "Vaud and the other Swiss cantons" wanted to adopt "the principles of liberty, equality, and indivisibility."[10] The conquest of Switzerland did not require of the French any more effort than the conquest of Rome. The government in Bern tried to resist, but on March 5, 1798—the same day the Directory adopted Bonaparte's Egyptian plan—the city was occupied. Its treasury was seized to fill the expedition's coffers, which were empty again, and its bears, the symbol of the city, went to the zoo at Paris's Jardin des Plantes.[11] Many other obstacles, insurmountable when the invasion of England was planned, disappeared as if by enchantment. Not only money but also ships were found, and the transport fleet that could not be assembled to cross the Channel soon sailed to take control of the Mediterranean, escorted by about fifty warships.[12]

Nonetheless, it seems surprising that a government as disorganized as the Directory was efficient enough to carry out in only two months a project of such scope,[13] but we have to remember that the coup d'état of 18 Fructidor, by temporarily freeing the government from any kind of opposition from either the left or the right, allowed it to succeed in many domains where it had up to that point obtained only mediocre results. Just as it gave Bonaparte the means to complete the preparations for the Egyptian expedition in record time, it stabilized the financial system by means of a two-thirds devaluation of the currency, a veritable coup d'état against rentiers that would have been impossible to perpetrate as long as the government had to reckon with a public that was hostile or distrustful.

Another sign testifies to the—momentary—surge that followed the Fructidor crisis: the secrecy surrounding the preparations. It had been decided, in fact, that the decrees creating the Army of the Orient and defining its objectives—the conquest of Malta, the occupation of Egypt, and the expulsion of the British from the Red Sea—would not be made public, and that the government would act as if nothing had changed in the plan for invading England. Bonaparte recommended that his subordinates observe "the deepest silence,"[14] and the government repeated, with a great deal of publicity, its orders regarding the assembly in Brest of the fleet for the invasion of England. The result was that many members of the expedition did not learn its objective until after the fleet's stop in Malta.[15] "We don't know what our destination will be," the captain of a ship wrote; "it's the mystery of the Incarnation."[16] Even Monge's wife didn't know.[17] And although her husband had been fully informed from the outset, many of his colleagues at the Institute wondered where this "simultaneously scientific and military expedition" they had been invited to join was going.[18] Dolomieu recalled that Berthollet "couldn't tell us to which country we would go because it was a great secret. I asked him if in this country there were mountains and rocks. 'Lots,' he replied. 'In that case, I'll go with you,' I told him, laughing." Like Dolomieu, most of those invited were satisfied with the assurance that Bonaparte would take care of them, and, as Arago was to write, "the mathematician Fourier, left his much sought-after post at the École polytechnique to go . . . he knew not where; to do . . . he knew not what."[19] Of course, the troop movements toward southern France and the renewed activity in the Mediterranean ports did not go unnoticed. In addition, there were the inevitable indiscretions, and the most perspicacious observers soon guessed the goal of these armaments.[20] The press repeated their conjectures, the *Moniteur* going so far as to report that the expedition had been prepared "with the consent of the sultan himself."[21] But the government's denials maintained confusion, and still more importantly, the leaders of the army and the navy kept silent—so silent that the rumors never entirely became certainties, and the British, whose agent in Livorno had informed them in April of the expedition's objective, long refused to believe that the French had really decided to land in Egypt.

The idea of combining a scientific expedition with the military expedition was Monge's. When he was in Rome in 1797, he had been struck by the "singular contrast between the monuments of the Romans and the Greeks and those of the Egyptians. . . . If the latter did not have the former's elegance, grace, and variety, they had simplicity, regularity, grandeur, and especially durability. The geometer wondered about the audacity, strength, and knowledge of the people who had so perfectly shaped imposing masses of stone; he would have liked to rediscover their astronomical and mathematical knowledge, the procedures of their art, the customs of their public life, and the meaning of their political and religious ceremonies."[22] Thus, he proposed to associate "with the army a body of educated men whose sole mission would be to visit and make known to European scholars and scientists a country that has always been seen as the cradle of human knowledge."[23] Besides, the idea was in the air.[24] Hadn't the *Encyclopédie* declared that Egypt was "a country to be studied"?[25] Hadn't the Institute taken as its mission to combine all the branches of knowledge into a single system, and wasn't Egypt, presented as the original homeland of the sciences and the arts, the ideal place to pursue that quest? For his part, Bonaparte did not need to be pushed much to adopt this project as his own. As the preamble to *La Décade égyptienne* (written by Tallien but inspired by Bonaparte) put it, he knew that "we no longer live in the age when conquerors knew only how to destroy the places where they bore their arms."[26] Bonaparte's election to the Institute only confirmed him in this conviction. It pleased him to return to Egypt the civilization that was born there, and while doing so open the door to a new empire for France. The Directory had given its consent—La Révellière was enthusiastic—and it ordered the minister of the interior to "put at General Bonaparte's disposition the engineers, artists, and other subordinates of his ministry as well as the various objects [that he] might request to aid in carrying out the expedition with which he was entrusted."[27] Monge (who was soon ordered to go to Rome), Berthollet, Caffarelli du Falga and the mathematician Fourier went hunting for participants. "You will probably be surprised," Vivant Denon wrote to a woman friend, "to learn that I am leaving and don't know where I'm going. My relations with General Bonaparte have caused me to join the expedition he is going to make."[28] The notoriety of these recruiters and Bonaparte's prestige led more than one person to sign on. Geoffroy Saint-Hilaire, Malus, Conté, and Dolomieu responded to the general's call. But there were also refusals. That was predictable: Were the fortunate elect being asked to give up everything for an adventure about which they were told nothing? Many of the leading figures in the world of science and the arts proved to be the least enthusiastic. Laplace, Cuvier, Lacépède, and David turned down the invitation, as did the poet Legouvé, the botanist Thouin, and the engineers Isnard and Prony; Ducis gave his age as the reason for refusing, Méhul his duties, and the singer Lays his fragile throat. Lays's refusal annoyed Bonaparte: "I'm angry that he doesn't want to go with us," he is supposed to have said, "he would have been our Ossian. We need one, we need a bard who sings at the head of our columns when we need him to, his voice would have had such a good effect on the soldiers!"[29] Villoteau, who was Lays's understudy at the Opéra, refused to leave him, and the composer Rigel refrained from accepting an offer that the great Méhul had not found it necessary to accept.[30] Some of those who declined the invitation later prided themselves on having opposed the new Caesar,[31] but it is more likely that they feared what they might lose in this mysterious enterprise. They probably no longer had the insouciance of youth, and one can hardly be surprised if in the end most of the recruits were young, novices in their careers; most of them were graduates of the newly established École polytechnique. It has been said that Bonaparte took with him a "living encyclopedia."[32] That is true, but it was less prestigious than he had hoped when he said he would leave with "a third of the Institute."[33] In the shadow of a few men who were famous and coddled by the Republic, it was an intellectual corps drawn from the second and third ranks that went off into the unknown "as if on a picnic,"[34] their heads full of dreams of glory and fortune.

In Toulon, in Civitavecchia, where the troops assembled, the effervescence was extreme. "The goal of our expedition is still covered with a veil of mystery," one of the participants wrote to his parents, "but the love of change and extraordinary enterprises inspires a noisy gaiety in everyone. The idea that we are going to fight England, or any country whatever, suffices to excite enthusiasm."[35] For Bonaparte as well, these were weeks of intense activity. "The earth seemed to be burning his feet," La Révellière said.[36] He kept an eye on everything: troop movements, supplies, naval armaments, the recruitment of scientists, the collection of a specialized library like the one he had established in Passariano, not to mention the eclectic "portable library" whose catalog he had drawn up himself, and that Horace de Say, an officer on General Caffarelli's staff, was putting together for him.[37] "Orders and instructions succeeded each other, with extraordinary rapidity," and if an order was lacking, Bonaparte rushed over to the Luxembourg to get it out of the directors.[38] He did not forget that the scientists would need a great many instruments for their work, and because the army's destination had to remain secret, he wrote personally to Monge, in Rome, to ask him to seize "the Arab print shop" of the Vatican's propaganda office.[39]

Obstacles and Hesitations

In the "whirlwind of decisions to be made and orders to be implemented,"[40] Bonaparte still had to set aside a few moments for his household. The weather was stormy on Rue de la Victoire. Joséphine, who had been so miserable in Italy, had not rediscovered happiness in Paris. "My life is a continual torment!" she wrote to *her* Hippolyte. She was tired of playacting. Through Hippolyte's mediation, and especially that of Barras, she had gone into business with the Bodin brothers, suppliers who, though less well known than those of the Flachât company, were no less dishonest. This whole little world was speculating on supplies for the armies, and it had just learned a bit of news that gave it great joy: with Barras's help, the Bodin company's bid for supplying the Army of Italy had been accepted.[41] It was the prospect of juicy profits that were to allow her to pay off some of the debts that she had such trouble concealing from her husband. She made use of countless tricks to escape to the Faubourg Saint-Honoré, where her lover and his associates were living in the same private home. It was then that the storm broke out. Napoleon was too busy to keep a close eye on her, but his clan did it for him. She was surrounded by spies, and through one of them Joseph learned that his sister-in-law was involved in Barras's schemes. He hurried over to Rue de la Victoire where, glad to be for once able to play the elder brother's role, he revealed everything, appealing to the family honor and his younger brother's self-interest. Napoleon called Joséphine in and made a scene. Was it true that she spent a great deal of time in the Faubourg Saint-Honoré? Was she involved in the affairs of those Bodin scoundrels? Was she taking advantage of her relations to see Captain Charles? She denied everything, claimed that she was "the most unfortunate and the unhappiest of women," and because there is no better defense than attack, pretended to be outraged and screamed louder than he did. Did he want a divorce? Fine, good riddance! Back in her room she wrote a long letter to Hippolyte in which she vilified the whole tribe—her husband, her mother-in-law, her brothers-in-law, all of them:

> Yes, my Hippolyte, I hate all of them; you alone have my affection, my love. The dreadful state I've been in for the past several days must show how much I abhor them. They see the regrets, the despair that I feel from being deprived of seeing you as often as I want. Hippolyte, I shall kill myself. Yes, I want to end [a life] that will henceforth be a burden to me if it cannot be devoted to you. Alas, what have I done to these monsters? But no matter what they do, I shall never be the victim of their atrocities. Tell Bodin, I beg you, that he must say he doesn't know me, that it is not through me that he got the contract for the Army of Italy.... Ah! They will torment me in vain, they will never separate me from my Hippolyte: my last sigh will be for him.... Adieu, my Hippolyte, I send you a thousand kisses ardent as my heart, and as loving.[42]

She was worried. What if Joseph succeeded in convincing her husband to divorce her? Did she have reason to be afraid? A few days after this scene took place, Napoleon bought, for 180,000 francs to be paid on credit, the private town house on Rue de la Victoire that she had been renting from Julie Talma since 1795. Some people saw this as a threat: whereas he used to live in her house, now she would live in his. Was he preparing separation this way? But if he had not forgotten what had just happened, he had at least pardoned it, and it was, on the contrary, in order to protect his wife against the schemes of Joseph and the rest of the clan that he bought the house on Rue de la Victoire. Whatever happened while he was away (he thought his departure imminent), she would at least have a roof over her head. He got Joseph to agree—he could hardly refuse—to see that the payments were made. Besides, the conjugal sky had cleared. They talked about buying a residence outside Paris and visited an estate, Malmaison, but postponed the purchase; they were also seen at Mme Campan's pension in Saint-Germain-en-Laye, where Joséphine's daughter, Hortense, and Napoleon's sister Caroline were studying. Once again, they were completely in love, though they were both wary. Joséphine finally tried to pull off a coup. She begged her husband not to leave her alone in Paris. Why couldn't he take her with him? He talked about the harshness of the climate, the dangers of the expedition, the difference in customs. She cried out, secretly horrified by what he told her about these dreadful countries, and in any case fully resolved not to leave either France or her handsome Hippolyte. As always, he yielded; he was glad she would accompany him as far as Toulon and even wanted to believe that she really would join him later in Egypt. He was resolved not to listen to anything further his brothers might say to him. He was not finished dealing with domestic problems. This time, though, the problem was Monge's wife. Like the general, the scientist was incapable of saying no to his spouse. When Monge began organizing the scientific expedition, it was understood that he would be part of it; he had no greater desire, and as we have seen, it was in order to supervise the preparations for the expedition that he was sent to Rome. But as soon as he was far away from Bonaparte, Monge's determination wavered; he was afraid of telling his wife that he was leaving. On March 15, trembling, he wrote to Bonaparte to beg him not to force him, "at his age," to "go on adventures."[43] The letter did not amuse the general, who replied brusquely: "I'm counting on you, even if I have to come up the Tiber with a squadron to get you."[44] Monge was simultaneously delighted by this response, because it proved that he was still "the Republic's spoiled child," and very worried about Mme Monge's possible reprisals. To reassure him, Bonaparte did what he would have done for scarcely anyone else: he made several visits to Monge's wife to extort her consent. She finally resigned herself to her husband's departure, in exchange for a promise that Gaspard would be back within four months.[45] The scientist was ecstatic, and as he was about to embark at Civitavecchia, he wrote this enthusiastic letter to Bonaparte: "So here I am, transformed into an Argonaut! This is one of the miracles performed by our new Jason, who is not going to cross the seas to conquer a golden fleece whose material could not much increase its value, but who is going to carry the torch of reason to a country that light has not reached for a long time. . . . I am very eager to join you, my dear general, and the winds, which at this point oppose us, will probably cause me great impatience."[46]

He had to wait three long weeks, because it was only on Malta, on June 9, that he finally rejoined "his" general.

The time for departure had come, and Bonaparte was getting ready to set out for Toulon when an unexpected incident almost compromised everything.

On several occasions there had already been talk of his abandoning the preparations for a landing in England or those for the Egyptian expedition in order to go to Rastatt, where negotiations regarding the cession of the left bank of the Rhine were making no progress. But at the end of March, the Germanic Empire's plenipotentiaries having finally agreed to this cession, the trip became pointless. The agreement, which recognized France's unqualified victory, aroused a strong feeling of humiliation in Austria, and on April 13, while the diplomats in Rastatt were congratulating one another, the Viennese attacked the residence of the new French ambassador, Bernadotte, and burned the French tricolor. There was outrage in Paris. People talked of mobilization, of taking revenge for the affront. Bonaparte, who had just sent to Toulon the order to embark, countermanded it. At an initial meeting with the directors on April 23 he denounced Bernadotte's provocations and praised, on the contrary, the Austrian government's moderation with such fervor that Barras and Reubell wondered whether Bonaparte had not become, without their noticing it, the Austrian ambassador in Paris.[47] Barras, who tells us of this scene, says that Bonaparte later changed his mind and, not being happy about the prospect of another war, even considered canceling the Egyptian expedition. Miot de Melito, who unlike Barras cannot be suspected of wanting to sully Bonaparte's reputation in his memoirs, ventures that Bonaparte, who always had several cards in his hand, believed for a moment that the incident in Vienna might open for him a shorter path to power than the long detour through Egypt: "For, by entrusting him with the negotiations occasioned by the Vienna affair, the Directory replaced him in the position he coveted; once more the fate of France and her Government was in his hands. He was the arbiter of peace and war, he commanded the one or made the other, according as his interest rendered peace or war necessary. Lastly, either as the conqueror of Austria for the second time, or as a worshipped peacemaker, he would return to Paris with his power increased by all the moral influence either title would have given him over the nation, and he would then carry out what, in fact, he did afterwards put in execution on the 18th Brumaire."[48]

It is not impossible that he hesitated, fearing he would miss an opportunity to do what he had been unable to do on his return from Italy. Because he was waiting to see what would happen before making up his mind, he limited himself to writing to Count von Cobenzl, the Austrian negotiator at Campoformio, a letter very peaceful in tone,[49] and prepared to leave for Rastatt. But in Vienna there was no desire for war, and after a few days of tension the affair turned out to be less serious than it had seemed. False alarm. It was time to get back to the Egyptian expedition. Although Bonaparte was still talking about going to confer with Cobenzl in Rastatt, he was already asking Admiral Brueys to sail for Genoa and wait for him there.[50] On May 2 everything finally fell into place and Bonaparte, accompanied by Joséphine, left Paris on the night of the third. Passing through Chalon and Mâcon, his carriage reached Lyon, where it was loaded onto a boat and descended the Rhône as far as Avignon. On May 9 Bonaparte arrived in Toulon—where, less than five years earlier, everything had begun.

To the Orient

"The French are delighted with the Egyptian expedition," Chateaubriand noted indignantly, "and they don't see that it injured probity as much as political rights: in complete peace with France's oldest ally, we attack it, we seize its fertile province of the Nile, without a declaration of war; [it is] as if the Algerians, in one of their disputes, had seized Marseille and Provence."[51] The idea that the conquest of Egypt was contrary to all principles had occurred to neither the Directory nor Bonaparte, except perhaps in Talleyrand's promise to secure the sultan's agreement as a fallacious pretext for the invasion and to present the appearance of respect for Ottoman sovereignty. It is here that we see how much Bonaparte, despite his meager support for the Revolution, wholly belonged to it. He was its son. Like the revolutionaries who had overthrown the secular order of the monarchy and its privileges in the name of liberty and justice, he also subordinated established law to will enlightened by reason. Like them, he was convinced that tradition had no particular authority when it violated principles or simple appropriateness; and, like them, he was reluctant to sacrifice the interests of the Great Nation in the name of commitments, treaties, and diplomatic customs that belonged to the history of the Old Regime. Why should revolutionary France have to measure its ambitions by the yardstick of a tradition it disdained? Why did it have to spare the Turks because it had pleased Francis I to sign a treaty of alliance with Suleiman the Magnificent in 1536? Was it responsible for commitments made before 1789? A profound question, with vast consequences, which has to be answered by all regimes emerging from revolution, and which must have had a considerable influence on French diplomacy down to the fall of the Empire. It is one of the legacies of the Revolution. The glamor of the Egyptian expedition spoke more to contemporary imaginations than did scruples about morals or the good faith of treaties. The aggression perpetrated against France's oldest ally shocked public opinion no more than the sacrifice of the Venetian oligarchy.

The Egyptian expedition was not merely a crime, but a folly. It led to an inconceivable alliance between sworn enemies, the Turks and the Russians. It deprived France of 40,000 seasoned soldiers at a time when war was looming on the continent. No one could be unaware that this army, even if it was victorious, would not be seen again any time soon. An aggravating circumstance was that this force was sent to the other end of the Mediterranean with just enough ships to carry it there. As for bringing it back, that depended on the fleet escaping British squadrons. The secrecy of the preparations has no other explanation: the ships could not defeat the Royal Navy, so they had to escape its surveillance. A risky gamble. The new minister of the navy, Admiral Bruix, did not conceal his fears; he even tried to get the government to postpone its projects long enough to provide France with a navy worthy of the name.[52] But his voice did not carry, especially because events seemed to be confirming the views of the bold, and the British government seemed to be lost in conjectures regarding the renewed activity in Toulon and in Rome.

However, Henry Dundas, the British Secretary of War, suspected the truth early on. Studying with care the reports from Europe and India, he soon solved the puzzle.[53] The French were heading, not for the coasts of England, but for those of Egypt, with the intention of moving next on the Red Sea in order to hook up with the squadron in the Indian Ocean and with Tipû Sâhib.[54] Dundas besieged Pitt and his colleagues, but in vain; they did not take this information seriously. They did not believe the minister when he told them that the French occupation of Egypt could pose a grave threat to India and its trade: not so much because it would allow the French to attack India, as because they would then be in a position to reopen the old trade route via the Red Sea and divert part of the Indian trade toward Suez. Pitt refused to believe it, and it took many more events for the British to finally understand that they could not remain the masters of India and its trade without taking control of Egypt.[55] Their government even asked Nelson, who was in Gibraltar, to reconnoiter the situation. When the admiral entered the Mediterranean on May 9, Bonaparte was arriving in Toulon. The Englishman managed to approach the harbor without being seen and observed the fleet's final preparations before its departure; but on May 20 a violent storm dispersed his squadron. When he returned to Toulon after repairing his damaged ships in Sardinia, Admiral Brueys's fleet had disappeared. Nelson searched the Tyrrhenian Sea for it in vain. By the time he headed south, the French were already within sight of Malta.

Aboard the French fleet, the enemy was expected to appear at any moment. Were those sails on the horizon friendly or hostile? Was it true or false that ships that had lagged behind had been boarded and searched by the British? And if nothing was seen ahead, wasn't that simply because Nelson had hidden his ships farther on, near Cap Bon, where he was patiently waiting for Bonaparte? Every time a suspicious sail was sighted, one or two frigates left the convoy to hunt them down, and more than once ships that the French feared might alert the British were forced to join the convoy. Such worries helped break the monotony of the voyage. Headwinds, storms, and holds that were too heavily loaded slowed down the convoy's progress. People passed the time as best they could. During the day there were conversations from one ship to another when they were close enough, military exercises, navigational incidents, broken masts, or sailors who fell overboard, whom launches tried to save accompanied by shouts of encouragement from the passengers. In the evening there were improvised shows, card games, and the contemplation of the sun sinking into the sea; and, always, reading. There were also "many arguments and shouting matches," often led by members of the scientific expedition. They were unhappy: first with the general-in-chief, who had thought he could divide them, for comfort, food, and pay, into several classes, members of the Institute being treated like superior officers, the others like subaltern officers; and then with the military men, who never missed an opportunity to make them feel unwelcome. Bonaparte had thought he had found in each of them another Monge; he was disappointed by so much pettiness. Some of them, judging the food inedible, talked about leaving the expedition at the first opportunity. There was no need to tell them where they were going: they already detested it! Bonaparte, who had at first been familiar and accessible, ended up closing his door to all those whose functions or rank did not give them the right to approach him. Only Admiral Brueys and Berthier dined with him. He spent his days in bed, battling seasickness with the help of Bourrienne, who read to him; like many Corsicans whose villages turned their backs on the sea, he did not have sea legs. When he emerged from his cabin, it was to scold the ship's officers and thump those he found reading "chambermaids' novels" like *Werther* or *Paul et Virginie*.[56] He himself plunged into Homer with Arnault, the Bible and the Quran with Bourrienne: he was slipping into the skin of the new character he was going to play. After having eaten supper and taken a walk on the deck, he would assemble a few officers and scientists to discuss a subject he had chosen: "One day, he asked if the planets were inhabited; another, how old the world was; then he proposed as a subject for discussion the probability that our globe would be destroyed, either by fire or by water; and finally whether premonitions were true or false and the interpretation of dreams."[57] As he had done in Passariano, he listened, spoke little, and served as an umpire when the discussion got heated, as it did the night when Caffarelli put forth his criticisms of private property. When Junot, bored by all this talk, started to snore, Bonaparte called an end to the entertainment and sent everyone to bed.

The convoy that had left Civitavecchia had been cruising for three days off Malta when, on June 9, the bulk of the squadron hove into view. The Maltese had been worried about these ships that approached the shore during the night and moved off during the day, but they had neither the means nor even the intention of trying to repulse them. The order of the Knights of St. John had long been a mere shadow of its former self, and the island of Malta had become a prey fought over by France, Austria, and Russia. In an order of April 12 the Directory had commanded Bonaparte to seize it, even stating that "honor and the national interest" overrode the obligation to make a preceding declaration of war.[58] This shows the contempt in which Paris held these descendants of the Crusaders. Although the minister of the navy had mentioned the possibility of strong resistance if the French attacked, Bonaparte was persuaded that the conquest of Malta would cost France only a little money. The knights, he said, were only waiting for an opportunity to get a good price for the island.[59]

He was not mistaken. Naturally the knights couldn't disappear without putting up a show of resistance. When the French asked to be resupplied with fresh water, the knights began by refusing to allow more than four vessels to enter the port at a time. Bonaparte interpreted these restrictions as a hostile act and gave the order to land. The knights, faced with a choice between fighting and submitting, made a token resistance, already thinking of how to get the most out of a surrender that was all the more inevitable because Bonaparte's troops were already besieging Valetta. Opinion in the city was far from unanimous: some wanted to fight, while others, led by the bishop himself, emphasized the futility of making a gallant last stand. The Grand Master, Ferdinand von Hompesch, asked for a ceasefire and soon received a visit from the mineralogist Dolomieu, himself a former Hospitaller, to whom Bonaparte had given these instructions: "Tell the knights that I will offer them the most advantageous conditions; that I want to buy their island from them; that I will pay them whatever they want; either in cash or the treatment I accord them."[60] The surrender was signed on June 12: Hompesch got a pension and the promise of a principality in Germany, the knights got a more modest pension and, for those who were French nationals, the removal of their names from the list of émigrés. The raiding had, of course, already begun; Berthier took care of it, having the mint seized, along with all the objects of value in the churches, except those "necessary for religious services," because Bonaparte had guaranteed "the free exercise of the Catholic religion."[61]

He remained less than a week in Malta, but as the future general Belliard said, half with admiration and half with irritation: "When this little fellow comes, one cannot rest easy."[62] Reforms showered down on the somnolent island like a hailstorm. The Order of Malta's property was seized, knights and priests who were not French in origin were expelled, prisoners held "because of their opinions" released, the island's government and courts reorganized on the French model, titles of nobility and privileges abolished, the powers of the Church strictly limited, and priests deprived of their civil status; the Orthodox and Jewish religions were granted a status, several hundred Muslim slaves were emancipated, and an end was put to the old institution of the "buonavogli," which allowed freemen to enlist as galley slaves, as contrary to human dignity. To defend the island, a national guard was created, and the better to ingrain the spirit of the time, primary schools and a "central" (secondary) school were established, along with the stipulation that every year sixty young people from the wealthiest families would go to France to be educated there. Emissaries were already sent out to announce in Albania, Greece, and North Africa that France had returned in force to the Mediterranean. The last decree had hardly been signed before Bonaparte ordered the fleet's departure, and on June 19 it sailed away from Malta. It left General Vaubois behind, along with a garrison of 3,000 men and a few sick. About thirty knights had gotten on board, not to mention the Muslim slaves, who had hardly been freed before they were enlisted as sailors.

The Army's Rancor

It was time to leave. Nelson's squadron was approaching; on the day on which Admiral Brueys's fleet left Malta, Nelson was passing through the Strait of Messina. This time the British knew what was going on: the expedition was heading, not for Gibraltar or the Atlantic, but for the eastern Mediterranean. They set out in pursuit, so rapidly that during the night of June 22 the British fleet passed the French fleet without seeing it. On the twenty-fifth Nelson was sailing along the coasts of Cyrenaica, and on the twenty-eighth he caught sight of Alexandria. He was very surprised not to find the French there; he thought he had been following them. He could not have known that he was ahead of them. Fearing that he might be caught in his own trap if the imposing French fleet showed up unexpectedly, and even wondering if he hadn't been mistaken in designating Alexandria as its objective, he decided to leave the next day to look for the French farther to the north. "Fortune" was on his side that day. What would have happened had Bonaparte found him a few hours earlier with his rear to the coast, confronting an enemy superior in firepower?[63] The future British victory at Abukir would have been a French victory. Fate, or destiny, decided otherwise. By moving away from the shores of Egypt, Nelson allowed Bonaparte to make his landing unimpeded, but he saved his fleet, setting up the conditions for a future revenge. He went to Cyprus (July 3), sailed down the coasts of Anatolia and Crete, and finally returned to Sicily. When he dropped anchor in the port of Syracuse on July 20, the French were arriving at the gates of Cairo.

On leaving France, Bonaparte did not think he was going to land at Alexandria. He remembered having read in Volney that the city was perched on a coast so arid, backed up to a desert so inhospitable, and separated from the Nile by a distance so great that it was not very tempting as a prey, unlike Rosetta and Damietta, from which Cairo could easily be reached by following the banks of the Nile or by moving up the river itself—which was navigable on this side—after having loaded men and materiel onto boats. The important thing, as Bonaparte realized, was to reach Cairo as quickly as possible. He had meditated on the failure of St. Louis; although the latter had a considerable army, it had taken him eight months to cross the Nile delta. When he had finally seized Mansoura, the final obstacle on the way to Cairo, it was too late. The Saracens had had the time to bring up reinforcements and weapons, and to organize a counterattack, and that great king but "poor general" had experienced the supreme humiliation of being taken prisoner.[64] Bonaparte knew that to avoid such a misadventure he had to hasten to meet the Mamluks, disperse them, and take control of Cairo.[65] That is why he had planned to land at Alexandria only a small contingent assigned to secure the port, while the bulk of the troops would land at Rosetta and Damietta, whence, via the navigable branch of the Nile, he would

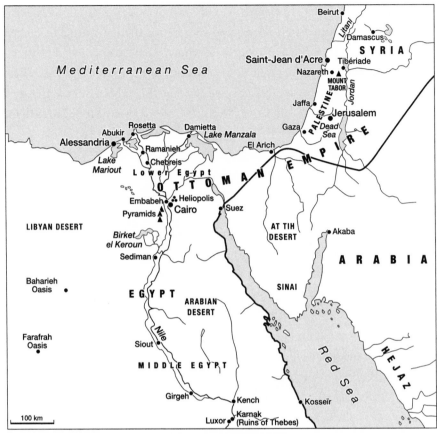

Egyptian Campaign (1798–1799)

then move up the river. But having learned, as he was approaching Alexandria, that Nelson had passed by the day before, and fearing that the British would return, he gave up his initial plan and decided to land without further ado.

There were high seas on the night of July 1. Launches, threading their way blindly between rocks and reefs, carried Menou's, Kléber's, and Bon's divisions to the beaches of the cove of Marabout. Bonaparte spent the night on the beach, in an area that looked, in the moonlight, as if it were "covered with snow."[66] In the early hours of the morning the troops set out in the direction of Alexandria, about ten kilometers to the east; facing into the sun, they followed the narrow strip of land that separates the sea from Lake Mariout. In this white landscape spotted with a few palm trees and dried-out bushes, the soldiers saw small groups of horsemen in the distance who fired a few shots at them. Because they had not yet landed the artillery—they were waiting until the ships had taken refuge in the port—and because Bonaparte considered it necessary to display his power, they attacked. The general-in-chief observed the scene from Pompey's column, south of the city.[67] The ramparts were guarded by a crowd of defenders whom the city's people were urging to fight. Under a hail of projectiles, the French scaled the walls, sabering and shooting at point-blank range those who refused to give up. "No one ran, they all had to be killed in full cry," Vivant Denon notes (though he was not there).[68] Berthier (who was there) wrote: "This people fought like desperate fanatics."[69] The Ottoman soldiers, driven off the ramparts, lay in ambush in the narrow streets and doorways, with the help of some of the residents. The soldier Laporte wrote: "There was firing in the streets, at the crossings, through doors and from terraces; we lost a great many men almost without being able to fight back; but fortunately the regiment's engineers managed to break down a few doors, we took over the houses, and from the terraces we leveled a deadly fire on the inhabitants and drove them back from house to house and from street to street. Everybody in the streets was killed."[70]

"The soldier's fury was extreme," the same witness adds, "and if Alexandria had not been such an important point for us and so necessary for the army, this city and its inhabitants would have experienced all the horrors of a fortress taken by assault." If the massacre that Vivant Denon and a few others mention did not take place, it almost did.[71] On the French side there were about 100, perhaps 200, casualties; many more on the Ottoman side, 700 to 1,000.[72] The attack on Alexandria involved a kind of violence to which the Italian campaign had not accustomed the victors, but it was going to become familiar to them. This "slaughter" was only the first of a long series.[73] It is true that the attackers, to combat thirst, had drunk large quantities of alcohol,[74] which may explain the brutality of the fighting and the number of French troops who lost their lives in an operation that was dangerous but certainly not extraordinary. After all, the Ottoman force was not a first-class opponent. There is another explanation, though, for the violence following the sudden scaling of the walls. These enemies may have been mediocre, but they were different from all those the expedition's soldiers had encountered up to that point. From the outset the foreignness of the place and their opponents aroused in the French a feeling of fear that was to continue to grip them and to aggravate the brutality inherent in war. For their part, the Ottoman soldiers guarding the ramparts of Alexandria were no less afraid than the French; they were afraid of the invaders, of course, but they were still more afraid of their own officers. To the officers, these peasants torn away from their wretched farms on the Anatolian plateau or from their villages in the Balkans or the Caucasus were cannon fodder of little value, because they could be easily replaced. They counted them for nothing, mistreated them in every possible way, and reduced them to the level of beasts of burden. The Ottoman soldiers were redoubtable without wanting to be or even being aware of it, especially because, in addition to fearing that they would be punished by their officers if they retreated, they were afraid of being run through with swords if the enemy won, "for among them that is the terrible law of war."[75]

Far from celebrating their victory, the victors showed the greatest consternation. To properly understand the expeditionary corps's stupor and dejection, from the humblest soldier to the highest-ranking generals, it has to be recognized that perhaps no army was ever less prepared for the kind of war it was going to have to wage. When the Army of Italy began its campaign, its leader had told the men that there would be hard fighting before they could enjoy the booty they had been promised. Here, secrecy having obliged him not to reveal the expedition's goal, Bonaparte had not been able to name the enemy and use the resources of his eloquence or of propaganda that could have prepared the men for combat. No doubt Bonaparte talked, as he had in Italy, about the battles and the fatigue to be endured and about the glory and the riches to be gained, emphasizing the latter more than the former, and referring less to the "new dangers" that awaited them than to the "six acres of land" they would all, without exception, have the means to buy when they got home.[76] But he hadn't told them where they were going to get that money, nor against whom or what they were going to fight. Things became no clearer once the fleet's destination was known, because the fiction of a friendly intervention implied that it was being made with the consent of the very people they were going to have to fight. The general referred vaguely to a few thousand Mamluks so hated by the Egyptians that the latter were impatiently awaiting their liberators, whoever they might be. Rather than dwell on a victory considered "infallible," he thought it more useful to exhort his men to be "tolerant" of beliefs and customs "different from those of Europe," or to whet their curiosity by reminding them that they were going to walk in the steps of Alexander the Great and, after him, move from astonishment to wonder.[77]

They had landed with images straight out of Savary dancing in their heads: "caravans to be looted . . . and seraglios to be conquered."[78] Many of them had imagined Egypt as another Italy, more exotic but no less rich and sensual. They were brought abruptly back to earth. Where were the splendors of the Orient, then? Was this "pile of ruins" and its dirty little streets really the Alexandria they had heard so much about?[79] Could this wretched, ignorant, wild, "hideous," "imbecile and barbarous," "dreadful and moronic," "villainous mob" be the Arab people whose refinement was so much praised?[80] They had been plunged into the unknown and the abject. They all used the same words to express what is not even disappointment but rather a genuine shock: "ruins, barbarity, abasement, and poverty everywhere."[81] And just as they had lauded Savary's *Lettres* before seeing Egypt, they now swore only by the somber descriptions in Volney's *Voyage.*[82]

They had just arrived, and they were already longing for home, and even more for that beautiful Italy whose splendors and pleasures had amply compensated them for the suffering they had endured there. They cursed the politicians of the Directory, and Bonaparte, who had taken them to Egypt, unless their general was also the victim of the perfidious intentions of a government that, in order to get rid of him, had not hesitated to "deport" its best army to this inhospitable and barbarous country.[83] They felt tricked. Basically, an uncomfortable situation that was in no way unusual for an army on campaign was made unbearable by the embellished memory of the Italian campaign, whereas the exotic image of the Orient made them find the "sad and sobering reality"[84] that confronted them seem horrible. The generals, who had taken even greater advantage of Italy's delights than their men had, felt the same way. They concealed their thoughts so little that more than once their leader had to threaten them with a firing squad, and when those he passed by on the route asked him if he was going to lead them as far as the Indies this way, he replied furiously: "I wouldn't make the journey with such soldiers."[85] However, they had to move out nonetheless and reach the Nile, marching straight across the desert. On the evening of July 3, Desaix's division left Alexandria and the coast, followed at one day's march by the troops of Generals Reynier, Vial, and Bon. A staff officer wrote: "On leaving Alexandria to reach the river, we assembled and passed across a desert as naked as one's hand, where we found, every four or five leagues, only a wretched well with muddy water. Imagine an army forced to cross these arid plains under the blazing sun, the soldiers marching on still hotter sand, all loaded with packs and dressed in wool, and each carrying enough food for five days. After an hour's march, overwhelmed by the heat and the weight of their belongings, they lightened their loads by throwing away their food, thinking only of the present and forgetting the morrow. Soon suffering from thirst and hunger, they found neither bread nor water."[86]

On this mineral, petrified "ocean of solid ground,"[87] on this dead land, the horizon was indeterminate, vague, floating, drowned in hot vapor or in clouds of dust raised by the wind. The men seemed to march without advancing an inch, as if space kept closing in around the long column. "The army's effort could have been compared," Sulkowski said, "to that of an irresistible mass that is making its way through an elastic body, with the latter immediately closing up again after it. Nothing was ours except what was within reach of our weapons."[88] To the troops, it felt as if they were "in the maw of a very hot oven."[89] When they arrived at one of the rare water sources, they rushed toward it, and there was a ruthless struggle, fights, even murders, sometimes all in vain: the regiments that had passed before them had left them nothing, or the well was dry, or it had been filled in, or the water was "brackish and dark like the water in a marsh."[90] Some soldiers committed suicide, and a few went mad.[91]

In the rear, things looked even worse. The lame, the laggards, those who were slowed by their burning eyes, drew on their last strength to keep from being left behind. They had been warned: isolated men ran the risk of being "cut to pieces by the Arabs"![92] The Bedouins suddenly appeared out of nowhere and rushed on their prey in a whirlwind of dust. It was soon learned that they treated "their prisoners as Socrates is said to have treated Alcibiades" before mutilating and killing them.[93] When they did not put them to death, they demanded a ransom. Bonaparte, who had himself taken the step, in Alexandria, of giving money to Bedouins who brought in a few prisoners, now forbade yielding to their threats. How many soldiers died of exhaustion, by the Bedouins' hands, or by their own? Did Desaix's division really lose 1,500 men during this crossing of the desert that lasted hardly a week?[94] The figure of 500 to 600 casualties given by Niello Sargy seems more plausible, but it remains frightening.[95] It was an exhausted army on the edge of revolt that finally reached the banks of the Nile at Ramanieh on July 10 and 11 and—after having entirely burned down the village, whose inhabitants had fled, taking everything with them—dove into the waters of the river.

A Western Way of War?

The disorientation from which the troops suffered, along with the depression that struck them—"disgust, discontent, melancholy, despair, and spleen," Napoleon was to say[96]—were certainly more dangerous enemies than the Ottoman janissaries or the Mamluks.

The alert among Egypt's defenders had first been sounded in Cairo after Nelson stopped at Alexandria. The news that he had gone back to sea restored calm, but on July 4 there was general astonishment when it was learned that a second fleet, a French one this time, and much larger, had dropped anchor at the same place, landed its troops, and attacked Alexandria. The Mamluk leaders hastened to come to an agreement with the religious authorities:

> They . . . assigned Murad Bey to organize an army and to go to meet the French.[97] . . . Five days later Murad Bey left the city after Friday prayers and went to Djesser el-Essoued. He camped there for two days. When his army was complete, he moved out. He had with him a large number of cannons and a great quantity of munitions. He divided his troops into two parts: The cavalry took the land route. The infantry, including the Turkish and Maghrebin foot soldiers, were transported on the river in little boats that the emir had had built. . . . Thanks to all these preparations, Murad Bey thought he could hold out a long time while waiting for reinforcements to come from Constantinople. But what happened was the contrary.[98]

While deliberations were taking place in Cairo, the French forces had carried out their rendezvous at Ramanieh: those who had come over the desert joined the Dugua division that was coming from Rosetta and the flotilla of about fifteen ships that the division head Perrée had formed with vessels borrowed from the fleet or found on site. On July 12 the army resumed its march to the south. The first encounter with the forces assembled by Murad took place the following day, near Shubra Khit. About 4,000 Mamluks, supported by a flotilla on the Nile, tried to stop the French, offering first the magnificent spectacle of horsemen "covered with gold and silver, armed with the best rifles and pistols from London, the best sabers in the Orient, and mounted on what might have been the best horses on the continent."[99] The fighting took place both on land and on the river, where the Turkish ships long threatened those of Captain Perrée. The French having finally gotten the upper hand in this artillery duel, the Mamluk cavalry went into action. Their way of fighting was well known. Because they were not a disciplined army under a single command, but rather a feudal equestrian order, they cared little about common tactics. The only tactic they agreed to observe was that of the "circle": "Surround the enemy on all sides by separate platoons, find his weak point, and then concentrate on it with all the rapidity of their horses"[100] in order to open a breach, pour into it and strike the adversary with their scimitars, so sharp that one soldier of the expedition said he saw "arms, wrists cut cleanly off, thighs also cut cleanly off and separated from the body."[101] Then each horseman, followed by one or two footmen and armed with a rifle, javelins, pistols, and a saber, fought on his own, and the battle was reduced to a series of individual duels in which each combatant tried to surpass his neighbor in valor, skill, and rapidity. Expert, fiery horsemen, they threw themselves headfirst into the fray, but broke off the combat just as suddenly if they thought it was going badly.

Such an enemy was redoubtable if allowed to get close, but not very dangerous if held at a distance. It has been wrongly maintained that the unsuccessful assaults the Ottoman forces launched against the French lines inspired in Bonaparte the formation in squares against which the Ottoman cavalry was to exhaust itself on the day of the Battle of the Pyramids. In fact it was the Russians who, confronted by the Ottoman cavalry in the campaigns they had conducted against the Porte in the Caucasus, had imagined the formation in squares with artillery at the angles, protecting the baggage placed in the middle and mutually supporting each other: on the plain, this arrangement made it possible, by firing straight on and from the flanks, to mount an effective defense of the sides and rear of the divisions against the attacks of a cloud of cavalrymen.[102] It was not without disadvantages: the squares—rectangles six ranks deep—maneuvered slowly, lost their cohesion whenever the slightest unevenness in the terrain was encountered. Within them "men bumped into each other, pressed together [and very quickly raised] a terrible cloud of dust, concentrated in a small space into which air could not penetrate to dissipate it," transforming the test into a torture.[103] But the result was there: these squares made it possible to oppose the cavalry with unapproachable, mobile citadels:[104] "A few brave men came to skirmish; they were received by the fire of the platoons," Bonaparte wrote after Shubra Khit, and after several hours of fruitless attacks, the cavalry turned around and disappeared. A simple skirmish, no doubt, but important for its psychological effects: the Mamluks, who at first had not believed in the reality of the danger and had been convinced that the infidels would be crushed beneath the hooves of their horses, began to have doubts. Hadn't the "Franks" seized Alexandria and the Delta without firing a shot, and hadn't they just victoriously resisted the cavalry's charges? Having gotten his fingers burned, Murad decided to await the French not far from Cairo, and there to throw the whole of his forces into a decisive battle. He placed his troops on the left bank of the Nile, near Embabeh, while Ibrahim Bey, on the right bank, was fortifying the area around Bulaq.[105]

On July 21, at dawn, and after a three-day march "in one of the hottest climates in the world,"[106] the French army came within sight of Cairo: "The sight that then met [Bonaparte's] eyes seemed to defy the imagination. To his right, in the distance and vibrating with the heat, the pyramids of Gizeh raised their triangles toward the sky. To his left, beyond the Nile, hundreds of dentate minarets rose from Cairo, along with the crenellated ramparts of Saladin's citadel. In front of it lay the village of Embabeh, with its shapeless retrenchments . . . and farther on, along the river bank . . . the whole Mamluk cavalry, dazzling under a sun that made the steel of their armor and the gold of their garments sparkle."[107]

The scene must have been impressive. The Mamluk cavalry, supported on the right by an infantry corps entrenched at Embabeh and 300 ships assembled on the Nile; on the left, a platoon of Bedouin cavalrymen posted toward Gizeh forming a line that was, people said, more than ten kilometers long.[108]

Nonetheless, this "Battle of the Pyramids" turned out to be nothing other than a repetition on a larger scale of the battle of Shubra Khit. Once again the Mamluks sent their horses at a gallop against the French army formed into squares, and with just as little success, each wave of cavalry screaming as it came up and then retreating, leaving behind it horses and riders cut down by lethal gunfire. On the right, Desaix and Reyner were repelling the cavalry, while on the left, half of the Bon and Vial divisions had been formed into an attack column that was marching under the command of General Rampon toward Embabeh, where most of the fighting took place, sabering the terrorized Mamluks, Ottoman infantrymen, and Arab militiamen and throwing them back on the Nile.[109] When the Mamluk chieftains had taken the measure of the disaster, they fled, Murad in the direction of Upper Egypt, along with 3,000 horsemen, Ibrahim toward Bilbeis, some fifty kilometers northeast of Cairo, on the road to the Sinai, with 200,000 other survivors. Had this scene not taken place in such a grandiose setting, had it not marked the return of a European army to the Orient for the first time since the Crusades, and had it, finally, not been magnified by painters— from Gros to Hennequin and Vincent—it would certainly not be remembered as a battle of Titans, because in truth one hesitates to call a "battle" what was ultimately only a skirmish. "We had only two battles and three or four skirmishes," Lacuée de Cessac wrote to his uncle, "or rather, we had only two slaughters. The Mamluks had only bravery on their side; we were trained and disciplined."[110] The epitaph is cruel but correct, so obvious was the superiority of the French army.[111] The two societies whose armies were confronting each other, the French and the Egyptian, were so distant from one another in organization, technology, and especially values that they could not even come to grips under conditions that might have given the Egyptians—if we can give that name to the mosaic of ethnic groups and "castes" that populated the banks of the Nile—some chance of winning. European technological superiority was not the only factor involved.[112] After all, artillery had played a fairly secondary role since the landing; as for the cavalry, it was almost absent: for lack of horses, 600 or 700 cavalrymen were playing the role of riflemen on board Perrée's flotilla! The crushing victory won by the French had more to do with the cohesion and discipline of their infantry during the fighting, as is clearly shown by the squares that were, a priori, so difficult to maneuver. Beyond that, the quality of management comes into play, and the quality of these soldiers who were, to be sure, inclined to complain and pillage, but who at bottom cultivated the feeling of being the depositories of a glorious military heritage—which embraced centuries of the monarchy—and the Revolution's civic values. Of all its battles, the Battle of the Pyramids is perhaps the one that illustrates best Victor Davis Hanson's theses regarding the existence, since the Greek hoplites, of a "Western way of war."[113] However, and to qualify what has just been said, we must not forget that at Shubra Khit, as at the Pyramids, there were, so to speak, two battles quite different in kind: not only a Mamluk cavalry charge in both cases, but at Shubra Khit a battle on the river, which the French had a difficult time winning, and at the Pyramids the frontal clash between the two infantries around Embabeh. It was there, on the Nile and at Embabeh, that the victory was won, and not during the cavalry charges, which were assuredly very colorful and for that reason have been given priority by history, but they were gratuitous and without any consequence other than to amplify the Ottoman defeat. The episode symbolized not only the collision of two civilizations (though the infantry combat that followed showed that the activity of the European military advisors who had for decades been sent to Constantinople had not been in vain) but also the fairly incongruous encounter between two epochs, two centuries. Whereas the Mamluks' flotilla on the Nile and the Ottoman infantry at Embabeh waged modern war with weapons brought from Europe, the cavalrymen were waging a war from another age, the one that, at the beginning of the sixteenth century, had already led to their defeat at the hands of the Turkish conquerors.[114] To the Turks' muskets and "bombards" they had opposed the virtuosity of their cavalry. They were mowed down by Turkish bullets but fell with contempt for these enemies so cowardly that they fought with weapons that would have allowed—and this was the height of scandal—even a woman to win![115] More than three centuries later, nothing had changed. At the Pyramids the Mamluks put up the same resistance to Bonaparte in a gallant last stand that was also their farewell.

From Rousseau to Voltaire

French troops crossed the Nile on the night of July 21, and the next day they moved into Cairo. The city was in chaos. Brigands were pillaging houses abandoned by the Mamluks and holding their occupants for ransom. Many of the Mamluks fled, taking with them as many of their possessions as they could, because they feared not only that the pillagers would rob them, but also that the "Franks" would kill them. As they left Cairo, the French troops passed close to the battlefield, where a quite different sight awaited them:

> The [French] divisions that had taken the Embabeh camp found themselves amid abundance; they had discovered a great many food supplies, canteens full of preserves and sweets; all the baggage of the beys and kashifs, their carpets, porcelains, and silverware; the hope of rich booty had revived the soldiers' strength, and most of them were fishing the corpses of their enemies out of the river, where they had drowned. The large sums of money the Mamluks customarily carried on their persons . . . their magnificent clothing, their precious weapons set with gold and silver and decorated with beautiful engravings all encouraged the troops to search their bodies. They were auctioning off the booty that had been taken in combat; the battlefield had become a market. Amid the corpses, horses, weapons, clothing, saddles, and barding were being sold.[116]

Did this pillaging compensate the French for the suffering they had endured since their arrival in Egypt? Whether or not the victories at Alexandria, Shubra Khit, and the Pyramids had been easy, no one really celebrated them. The troops' state of mind remained the same as it had been the day after the conquest of Alexandria. The crossing of the desert had not, as one can well imagine, made things better. Cairo itself inspired in none of them "the enormous astonishment" that still gripped Flaubert half a century later.[117] All of them would have subscribed to the few words uttered by Captain Perrée: "This country is not to my taste."[118]

It wasn't to their leader's taste, either. He couldn't find words harsh enough to describe his conquest and its inhabitants. In his account *Campagnes d'Égypte et de Syrie*, he spoke of a "barbarous people." He called the peasants that he'd seen on the banks of the Nile "as stupid as their buffalos." He described the Bedouins as "horrible men of the desert, so ugly, so ferocious, [with] their women, who were still dirtier."[119] As soon as he had arrived in Egypt, he too had begun dreaming of going home. He wrote his brother Joseph to this effect, asking him to find him an estate in the countryside: "I'm weary of human nature. I need solitude and isolation; grandeurs bore me; my feeling has dried up. Glory is dull at twenty-nine; I've exhausted everything."[120] This disgust probably had still another cause: Junot had just informed him of Joséphine's infidelities—"I have much, much domestic sorrow, for the veil has been entirely lifted."[121] But whatever he may have read in Volney's *Voyage* that warned him against the seductions of the Orient, he had not expected what he found after landing at Alexandria. Volney's *Voyage en Égypte et en Syrie* had communicated to him its faith, in spite of everything, in the goodness and purity of the human race, even when corrupted and degraded by despotism, superstition, ignorance, and poverty. Bonaparte was part of the immense cohort of Rousseau's disciples, even if, very early on, he had expressed a few doubts regarding the historical reality of the state of nature Rousseau described, without, however, challenging the postulate of a naturally good man corrupted by history, society, and inequalities. That is why the time spent in Egypt was crucial: Italy had not destroyed his faith in Rousseau's ideas; Egypt made them repellent to him. "Above all, I am disgusted with Rousseau since I have seen the Orient," he was to say later, "the natural man is a dog."[122] In the Arabs he did not see, as Volney had, victims of history and injustice, or, like Savary, noble savages miraculously protected from the misdeeds of civilization: "It is the spectacle of the most hideous natural man one can imagine."[123] This time Bonaparte had chosen Voltaire over Rousseau.[124] As for his army, it was never really reconciled to the Orient and constantly dreamed of going home, even after all hope of a rapid return had sunk in the waters off Abukir along with Admiral Brueys's squadron.

Abukir

On July 28, 1798, one month after passing by Alexandria, Nelson received, in Syracuse, the confirmation that the French had landed in Egypt. Without delay he sailed for Alexandria, intending to attack the French fleet. On August 1, as he was approaching his goal, the *Zealous*'s lookout signaled the presence of enemy ships in the bay of Abukir: "After being pursued for seventy days, over 4,611 nautical miles, his prey was at anchor."[125] He did not let the opportunity escape him. Of the thirteen French ships of the line boxed into the bay of Abukir, only two, the *Guillaume-Tell* and the *Généreux*, were able to get away, followed by the frigates *Diane* and *Justice*. The *Orient* exploded, four other ships of the line as well as a frigate sank, and six ships struck their colors. Admiral Brueys had been killed, along with many officers and 1,500 to 1,700 sailors and soldiers, for a total of perhaps a third of those who were on board. A disaster and a slaughter.

Bonaparte learned the news only on August 13. The information was not very precise, but one thing was certain: Admiral Brueys's squadron had been destroyed. It was a heavy blow.[126] Bonaparte could not gauge its consequences, but in public he appeared unmoved. Did he deliver in front of his officers the long speeches that were reported later?[127] Or did he limit himself to an about-face: "We shall have to die here, or come out of it as great as the Ancients"?[128] In any case, he forbade them to refer to an event that aggravated the army's "morale," threatening even to cut the tongues out of those who talked too much.[129] In private, things were different: he remained angry, and the more detailed the information he received, the more he condemned his "friend" Admiral Brueys. A month afterward he still wrote to Kléber: "We must recognize that in the battle [of Abukir] it was our generals who were defeated rather than the squadron, because though we have as many ships as the English, they had an advantage of three or four to one [Brueys' decisions had resulted in only one-fourth of the French forces being able to fight]."[130] In the reports he sent to the Directory—the first one is dated August 19—he denounced the incompetence of Brueys, who instead of mooring his fleet in the safe harbor of Alexandria's Old Port or retreating to Corfu, had preferred to expose his fleet in the bay of Abukir, deploying it in a manner contrary to all good sense and failing to cover it with coastal batteries of sufficient power.

Historians long shared Napoleon's judgment and condemned the unfortunate Brueys, but since the publication of studies by Clément de la Jonquière and Georges Douin[131] they have held Bonaparte mainly responsible for the disaster. Here the pendulum swings too far: if the general was in fact at least partly responsible for the loss of the fleet, no one can seriously deny that Brueys committed errors that are hard to understand, given that he was such an experienced sailor. He had referred to the bay of Abukir as an anchorage that made his position formidable, whereas the shelter was "illusory," given that the natural harbor was largely open to the sea and the waters along its shores too shallow for ships to be able to approach them. On July 13 he had repeated that he was "impregnable," whereas on the seventeenth he received a report from the brigade leader Poitevin that mentioned all the many disadvantages of this position. And although he took care to establish a battery on the point of Abukir and to fortify the little Dessouki Island that continues it, he anchored the head of his line too far from the coast for it to be covered by the cannons, and also too far from the four-fathom line to prevent enemy vessels from slipping between the coast and the French ships and taking the latter in a crossfire. Finally, despite his personal preference for fighting while under way, he yielded to his lieutenants who recommended fighting while at anchor, and connected the ships by cables that on the day of the attack exposed the French fleet to murderous enemy fire by not allowing it to maneuver.[132]

Above all, Brueys underestimated his adversary. Because he had miraculously escaped during the voyage from Toulon to Alexandria, and there had been no sign of Nelson's squadron, he had ended up concluding that the British had not been ordered to attack him. Once freed of this worry, he thought all he had to do was find an acceptable anchorage so that he could finally devote himself to the task of replenishing supplies, which he considered primary. He did not know—and Bonaparte was not unjustified in reproaching him for his "timidity"—that his English counterpart was driven by feelings different from his own. Little inclined to interminably weigh circumstances and risks, Nelson followed a simple strategy: "straight ahead." He threw himself on the head of the French line and passed it, determined to "anchor side by side with each of his adversaries in order to fight them to the death, in a methodical and systematic way, at point-blank range."[133]

Was the defeat the sailors' fault, and theirs alone? Certainly not. Although they made poor choices, they were also in an unenviable situation. It will be said that they had more guns than their adversaries—1,182 vs. 1,012.[134] But several of their ships were in bad condition; their crews were incomplete, discipline was deficient, the exercises were irregular, the esprit de corps of their officers, who had often come from commercial seafaring, was insufficient, and some of them were more attentive to logistical questions than to the necessities of war. Moreover, even if they had possessed in the highest degree the qualities required of combatants, they would still have had to adjust to Bonaparte's demands. The latter was by temperament wholly absorbed by what he was doing at the present moment, so that what was to become of the fleet ceased to be central to his preoccupations as soon as he had landed on Egyptian soil. The proof? He had drawn on his stores of weapons, munitions, and provisions to equip the Nile flotilla, and he had taken with him 600 of the ships' sailors—so that had he wanted to, Brueys could not have left Egypt.[135]

Where would he have gone? Corfu? Bonaparte constantly repeated that he had ordered Brueys, if he could not shelter his ships in Alexandria's Old Port, to send them without delay to Corfu:[136] "On 18 Messidor [July 6]," he says in the report for August 19, "I left Alexandria; I wrote to the admiral, telling him to enter the port of that city within twenty-four hours, and, if his squadron could not enter there, to promptly unload all the artillery and all the goods belonging to the land army, and to go to Corfu."[137] This order exists. It bears the date July 3, the day that Alexandria fell.[138] But its authenticity is contested, and many historians now agree that it was written after the fact in order to shield from responsibility a Bonaparte "tormented . . . by the impression that this naval defeat would make on the public," and much later, in 1807, he is supposed to have had destroyed a number of original documents relating to the Egyptian expedition.[139] In reality it is impossible to decide. Although those who claim there was falsification do not lack arguments, it is still hard to understand why Bonaparte would have waited until 1807, eight years after the events, to eliminate the compromising documents from the file; and it is difficult, to say the least, to explain how a forgery such as the order for July 3 could appear, in identical form, in Berthier's register.[140] Ultimately, it matters little whether or not Bonaparte mentioned on July 3 the possibility of leaving for Corfu. Even if we consider the order of July 3 authentic, we can see that Corfu was only a last-resort solution.[141]

Brueys was looking for an anchorage, and refusing to put the fleet in the shelter of the Old Port at Alexandria because the access to it seemed to him too narrow and too shallow, he thought he had found a much better position in the bay at

Abukir. When he understood that it was not without risks, Bonaparte was already far away, and he did not dare take it upon himself to change a plan of action that had obtained the general's approval before his departure for Cairo. In fact, Bonaparte, while preferring the anchorage at Alexandria, had not vetoed the departure of the vessels for Abukir.[142] He even considered, on leaving Alexandria, that they might stay there for some time.[143] He probably left it up to the result of the soundings ordered by Brueys, and when he set out for Damanhur and the Nile, it was with the conviction that Brueys was going to solidly fortify the position at Abukir, and later on, if possible, move to the port in Alexandria. But Captain Barré's report, which concluded that it was possible to protect the fleet in the Old Port, even if maneuvering was difficult, did not convince the admiral and he asked for an additional investigation.[144]

While awaiting the result, he preferred to stay in Abukir. After the tragedy, Vice-Admiral Blanquet du Chayla accused Bonaparte of having left Brueys without orders other than the inapplicable one of anchoring his fleet in Alexandria, while at the same time implying that the fleet should under no circumstances leave the Egyptian coast.[145] This is, in fact, where Bonaparte's responsibility lies.

But let us return to Cairo, where the general was unaware of everything that was going on in Alexandria. The first mail he received, on July 27, was precisely Barré's report; he concluded that Brueys had followed Barré's recommendations and taken his ships to Alexandria.[146] Thus, he was stupefied when, on July 30, he finally received several letters from Brueys and learned that the squadron was still anchored in the bay of Abukir. He called in one of his aides-de-camp, Captain Jullien, and asked him to go to the admiral as quickly as possible and urge him either to move the fleet to the port of Alexandria, as he had been asking him to do for the past month, or to load supplies of water and food and to leave for Corfu. This was no doubt the first time that he seriously considered the departure of the fleet, but still without really wanting it.[147] Jullien never made it; he was caught in an ambush. But if he had reached Abukir, it would have been too late, at best the day after the battle, and in any case Brueys could not have sailed for two weeks, long enough to receive the supplies Bonaparte had sent him from Cairo. Nothing could have saved Brueys, especially not the minor adjustments to his plan that, having recognized his vulnerability, he had made a few days before the catastrophe.[148] Still later, finally realizing the extent of the danger, Brueys is supposed to have returned to the Alexandria hypothesis, writing in great haste a letter to warn Bonaparte that they had finally found a more secure passage and that he was currently having it marked out: "Once the squadron is anchored in the Old Port," he added, "we can sleep in peace."[149] Nelson didn't give him time to do that.

Ultimately neither Bonaparte nor even Brueys bears the chief blame for the disaster. By inquiring into their respective responsibilities, we too often forget that what was truly responsible for the French defeat was first of all the French sailors' deep conviction that they were outclassed by the British, a feeling of inferiority that played an important role in the defeat, in spite of the courage of many of them; and second, Nelson. It is not certain that anyone other than the English admiral, finding himself in the same situation, would have made such a bold attack. But Nelson had a powerful motive for going all out: he wanted to do battle with this fleet that had so narrowly escaped him off Alexandria a month earlier. Above all, his success was the expression of a strategic revolution in naval combat comparable to the one that in 1796 had allowed Bonaparte to outclass his Piedmontese and Austrian adversaries: the British at sea, like the French on land, gave priority to surprise, offensive action, rapidity, the concentration of forces, and the desire to annihilate the enemy. Nelson fought like Bonaparte, and Brueys, unfortunately, fought like the Austrian Beaulieu. But Brueys's tactics were those endorsed by the French navy, of which the commander of *L'Orient*, Casabianca, who was killed in the battle, said had become, since the Revolution, "a disgusting cadaver."[150] The defeat at Abukir marks the beginning of a long and tragic history: it anticipates not only Trafalgar—the actors were to be the same—but also the escapades to which Napoleon was to be doomed in order to erase its long-term consequences and to conquer on land the English who were henceforth uncontested masters of the seas.

1. Henri-Félix-Emmanuel Philippoteaux, *Napoleon Bonaparte in Lieutenant-Colonel Uniform at the First Battalion of Corsica in 1792*, 1834. Châteaux de Versailles et de Trianon, Versailles.

2. Jacques-Louis David, *Sketch of Napoleon Bonaparte*, 1797. Musée d'Art et d'Histoire, villa Masséna, Nice.

3. Étienne-Barthélémy Garnier, *Napoleon Bonaparte, Commander in Chief of the Italian Army*. Châteaux de Malmaison et de Bois-Préau, Rueil-Malmaison.

17. Antoine-Jean Gros, *Louis Alexandre Berthier in the Uniform of a Maréchal de Camp*, 1834. Châteaux de Versailles et de Trianon, Versailles.

18. Anonymous, *Paul François, Vicomte of Barras*.

19. Jacques-Louis David, *Emmanuel-Joseph Sieyès*, 1817. Fogg Art Museum, Harvard University.

20. Marie-Éléonore Godefroid, *Germaine Necker, Baroness de Staël-Holstein Known as Mme de Staël*. Châteaux de Versailles et de Trianon, Versailles.

21. Pierre Paul Prud'hon, *Charles-Maurice de Talleyrand-Périgord, Prince of Bénévent*, 1817. The Metropolitan Museum of Art, New York.

22. Louis-François Lejeune, *The Battle of Aboukir, July 25, 1799*. Châteaux de Versailles et de Trianon, Versailles.

Credits
1. Chateau de Versailles, France/Bridgeman Images. 2. Musée d'Art et d'Histoire, Palais Massena, Nice, FranceGiraudon/Bridgeman Images. 3. © RMN-Grand Palais / Art Resource, NY. 4. Musée National de la Légion d'Honneur, Paris, FranceGiraudon / Bridgeman Images. 5. Musée de l'Armée, Paris, FranceGiraudon/Bridgeman Images. 6. Photo12 / Pierre-Jean Chalençon. 7. De Agostini Picture Library / G. Nimatallah / Bridgeman Images. 8. Château de Versailles, France / Bridgeman Images. 9. Château de Versailles, FranceGiraudon / Bridgeman Images. 10. © RMN-Grand Palais / Art Resource, NY. 11. Musée National du Château de Malmaison, Rueil-Malmaison, FranceGiraudon / Bridgeman Images. 12. © RMN-Grand Palais / Art Resource, NY. 13. Louvre, Paris, FranceGiraudon / Bridgeman Images. 14. © Musée de l'Armée/Dist. RMN-Grand Palais / Art Resource, NY. 15. © RMN-Grand Palais / Art Resource, NY. 16. Musée Marmottan Monet, Paris, France / Bridgeman Images. 17. © RMN-Grand Palais / Art Resource, NY. 18. Rue des Archives / The Granger Collection, New York. 19. Jacques-Louis David, Emmanuel-Joseph Sieyès (1748-1836), Harvard Art Museums / Fogg Museum, bequest of Grenville L. Winthrop, 1943.229. Imaging Department © President and Fellows of Harvard College. 20. Château de Versailles, FranceGiraudon / Bridgeman Images. 21. The Metropolitan Museum of Art. 22. Château de Versailles, France / Bridgeman Images.

EIGHTEEN

Governing Egypt

*I*n London, Nelson's victory seemed so complete that people thought the expedition's fate was settled.[1] It is easy for historians to object that the campaign was far from over. "No matter how profound, how important the consequences of the Battle of the Nile might be," one of them opines, ". . . they did not prevent Bonaparte from continuing, or even gaining strength in his conquest."[2] Bonaparte himself was determined to believe the same, repeating that "this setback, no matter how considerable it is, would be overcome."[3] He wasted no time: the sea was still washing debris and bodies onto the shores while he was giving orders and instructions to reestablish communications with France, and as early as August 18 he announced to the Directory that the French squadron in the Mediterranean would soon have as many vessels as it did before the catastrophe.[4] Did he really believe that, or was he only pretending to be so confident in order to keep up the army's morale, knowing that the disaster at Abukir would inevitably have consequences?[5]

The first of these consequences was the interruption of communications between Egypt and France. Nelson had left Commodore Hood behind; his two ships of the line and several frigates sufficed to prevent almost all contact with the rest of the world. Bonaparte's correspondence is full of complaints that he has received no news from Europe since his departure from Alexandria on July 6.[6] "No news from Europe," he wrote on October 4 to Desaix.[7] And on the eleventh to Barras: "We are eager to know what you are doing in your Europe."[8] To the Directory the following month: "We are thirsty for news from Europe."[9] And in December: "We are without news from France; no mail since Messidor [July]; that is unprecedented, even in the colonies!"[10] All he received were, in November, a few newspapers, the most recent of which was dated August 10 and gave him no information he did not already have.[11] He tried to establish a direct line of communication with Benghazi and Tripoli via the desert and Derna,[12] and asked the couriers he assigned to carry his messages to Malta or Corfu to bring back to him all the newspapers they could find. No blockade is ever hermetic. A few of these messengers slipped through the net and reached Italy or France.[13] In the opposite direction, from Paris to Cairo, communication was even more difficult. However, the Directory spared no effort to remain in contact with the Army of the Orient; it sent numerous agents, but few arrived.[14] Those who preferred to travel by sea rather than across the desert were probably no more successful.[15] The advice Bonaparte lavished on the Directory shows what precautions had to be taken if one wanted the slightest message to have a chance of reaching its addressee:

> Make six copies of each of your dispatches, all in code. . . . Send the first through Ancona, whence a small neutral ship will sail for Damietta; the second through Toulon and Genoa, which will come directly to Damietta; the third to Naples, overland: the minister will send a ship to Tripoli, whence a ship will be sent to Derna, where an Arab will be sent across the desert; the fourth for Constantinople, overland, whence it will be sent by a Tartar to Aleppo, and from there to Latakia, and from there by ship to Damietta; the fifth, by a corvette that is to enter Alexandria when there is a fresh breeze and with a pilot who knows the port; the sixth, a frigate sent to Damietta: if it learns that the enemies are there, it takes the precaution of having a large, decked dinghy with a sail, a howitzer, and four guns; it comes at nine in the evening to within four leagues from Damietta, lowers its dinghy to the sea, puts its dispatch in it, and goes back out to sea, disappears, comes back more than ten days later to Cap Bourlos, where, waiting for it, the answer will be delivered to it.[16]

The Army of Egypt, cut off from its bases and deprived of reinforcements, was the prisoner of its own conquest.

Egypt, Another Italy?

Some say that this was, in the end, a stroke of luck for Bonaparte: not being able to return to France within "two months," as he had intended,[17] he could devote himself entirely to organizing Egypt. Once again, as in Italy, he played simultaneously the roles of military leader, "enlightened despot, and reformer."[18] He was still learning his craft, but he led with more brilliance—the immense difference in the circumstances, customs, and beliefs required of him "more resources and creations."[19] Because it had become almost impossible to cross the Mediterranean, he had greater freedom of action: the British blockade absolved him of the obligation to report to the government. That is why he did more than govern in Cairo. There, in the isolated Egyptian arena, he played the role of sovereign: he "rehearsed the exercise of sovereignty and empire," as Sainte-Beuve put it.[20] Indeed, Sainte-Beuve went further, saying that Bonaparte's policy under the Consulate was not to be fundamentally different from the one he implemented in Egypt, where, more than in Italy, he had to reconstruct a society from its scattered debris, as he would have to do in France as well: "[In Egypt] one saw unveiled an old society being reconstructed by a powerful hand, an old civilization with its essential parts being put back together like a great ship. . . . By addressing himself to these Arab chieftains, to these ulemas and revered doctors, to these *honnêtes gens* of the country, trying out on them his policies of respect and reparation for those great interests of every society—religion, property, and justice—the young conqueror was practicing for the far more delicate tasks he was going to have to perform elsewhere. Soon he would return to us better prepared."[21]

In the age of triumphant colonialism, between 1880 and 1940, it was a commonplace to say that Bonaparte had laid the foundations for a policy that later inspired Gallieni in Madagascar and especially Lyautey in Morocco.[22] He had in fact reflected at length on ways to establish France in Egypt. To do so he had to carry out a project simultaneously military and civilian, a work of pacification and administration that could succeed only by showing the greatest respect for customs and religious beliefs, on the one hand, and by involving the people in the work of colonization, on the other. "There is no doubt," he later told Bertrand, "that the conquest was a combination of war and politics."[23] His very first proclamation in Egypt set the tone: "You will be told that I come to destroy your religion; don't believe it! Reply that I come to restore your rights, to punish the [Mamluk] usurpers, and that I respect, more than the Mamluks, God, his prophet, and the Quran."[24]

It has been written without exaggeration that "no European colonizer ever presented himself to Islam with more tolerance and even deference."[25] Did the religious authorities hesitate to celebrate the Prophet's birthday or, later, that of Hussein, the third Imam? Bonaparte urged them to make no changes in the calendar of religious festivals and paid a subsidy to "ornament the neighborhoods with torches, garlands, and lamps."[26] Prayers took place at the accustomed hours, and the French were ordered not to approach the mosques, to pay a fair price for the things they needed, to respect women, to take care of the pilgrims who stopped at Cairo on their way to Mecca, and to adapt themselves to Islamic customs. He constantly gave his generals the same instructions: "Protect the muftis, the imams, the religion."[27] He was hardly exaggerating when he wrote to the pasha of Acre: "I have reassured the people and protected the muftis, the imams, and the mosques. The pilgrims going to Mecca have never been welcomed with greater care or friendship than I have given them, and the feast of the Prophet has just been celebrated with more splendor than ever."[28] He himself referred to the consideration he showed for the sheikhs and religious dignitaries: "They were old men venerable for their morals, their knowledge, their wealth, and even their birth. Every day, at dawn, they and the ulemas of al-Azhar acquired the habit of going to the palace before prayer time. . . . The French guard presented arms and rendered them the greatest honors. When they had arrived in the rooms, the aides-de-camp and interpreters received them with respect, had sorbets and coffee served to them. Shortly afterward, the general entered, sat down among them, on the same divan, and tried to inspire confidence in them through discussions of the Quran, having them explain the main passages to him, and showing great admiration for the Prophet."[29]

Did he go too far? He did not hesitate to proclaim the superiority of Islam over Christianity, and listed his claims to Muslims' sympathies: "Qadis, sheikhs, imams, shorgagis [officials], tell the people that we are the friends of true Muslims. Is it not we who have destroyed the pope who said war must be waged against Muslims? Didn't we destroy the Knights of Malta, because those madmen believed that God wanted them to make war on Muslims?"[30] On September 12 he even wrote to the pasha of Saint-Jean d'Acre, Ahmed Jezzar: "We are no longer the barbarians of barbarian times who came to fight your faith; we recognize it to be sublime, we adhere to it, and the time has come when all Frenchmen, regenerated, will also become true believers."[31] Playacting, it has been said, "unscrupulous opportunism," shameless masquerades! The soldiers of the Army of Egypt were not the last to blame their general's initiatives or to laugh at his declarations. Those of them who were indifferent in religious matters did not understand why the leader of a republican army showed so much consideration for the representatives of a religion that was neither more nor less harmful than others; and those "who had retained the principles of the faith in which they had been brought up (there were very few of them, but there were some) judged still more severely this conduct on the part of a victorious general lowering himself to feign religious sentiments contrary to his conscience."[32] Bonaparte was playacting, but in a way entirely different from that of General Dupuy, the commander in Cairo, who made fun of himself welcoming the caravan of pilgrims on their way to Mecca,[33] or the "madman" Menou,[34] who converted to Islam, married a woman who claimed to be a descendant of the Prophet, and signed his orders "The victorious, judicious administrator General Abdallah Jacques Menou,"[35] but who laughed when his friends asked him whether he was going to take several wives, as the Quran allowed him to do. He replied that a second "Turkish female" would certainly endanger his health.[36] Bonaparte, in contrast, was playing a role in which he saw nothing funny. As in Italy, state interest guided his conduct. That was what led him to handle believers with care, to speak their language, and even to flatter them by begging them to instruct him in the religion of the Prophet. If he always had five coffeemakers on the fire,[37] it was not for the pleasure of conversing with the ulemas of the great mosque of al-Azhar, but for political advantage. Al-Azhar, the "Sorbonne of the Orient,"[38] where the Quran and Aristotle were studied, had a powerful clergy and 14,000 students, an immense power to form opinion and create a cadre of intermediaries with the population. There must be no mistake about the meaning of the consideration he showed for Islam: it is not the sign of any preference for or intellectual proximity to a religion that, some witnesses assure us, he secretly preferred to Christianity.[39] He had studied its history and its principles, he had reflected on its effects on social life, for that is what attracted his attention. He considered it without prejudices and with equity, but coolly, thus showing how foreign he was, in the end, to any passion of a religious nature.[40] In the library he took with him to Egypt, hadn't he classified the Quran, along with the Old and the New Testaments, under the rubric "Politics"?[41] Islam interested him only insofar as he had to govern a Muslim country. His personal convictions had no influence on his political behavior.

This politics seemed to impose itself on him with all the greater force because he had meditated on Volney's warning regarding the resistance, which might be "invincible," that the Muslims would put up to any attempt at colonization.[42] Bonaparte did not underestimate the specificity of Muslim societies, and that is why he considered it indispensable to do everything he could to escape "the anathemas of the Prophet [and] not allow [himself] to be ranked among the enemies"[43] of a religion that, far from preaching "submission and obedience," like Christianity, taught "intolerance and the destruction of infidels."[44] That is why his religious policy could never be in Egypt what it had been in Italy. There he had limited himself to reassuring and protecting the Catholics, and he had never claimed to be recognized as Pius VI's vicar; here he had to persuade the Muslims to support his policy. He had not only meditated on Volney; he had had long conversations with the former consul Magallon and with Venture de Paradis, who had served as his interpreters with the Egyptians. They had explained to him how the Mamluks had freed themselves from the Ottoman yoke after 1750, to the point of envisaging, in the 1770s, the possibility of creating an independent state, adding Palestine and Syria to their possessions, and how, after the death of the great Mamluk chieftains Ali Bey and Abu al-Dhahab, the Turks had landed in Egypt with the intention of reestablishing the sultan's authority there. That was in 1786. To succeed, they had thought to turn the population against the Mamluks by accusing them of being enemies of Islam. Once in Egypt, the Ottoman leaders had courted the Muslim clergy and invested it with political responsibilities that the Mamluks had refused it. When the Ottoman army was obliged to leave to fight the Russians, the imams had not given up hope of someday regaining what the Turks' premature departure had lost them.

Bonaparte understood: it was pointless to try to establish himself in Egypt without the support, or at least the neutrality, of the religious authorities. Besides, he had no choice. He had to maintain order in Cairo with less than 1,000 men. Not being able to impose anything without risking a religious war that his army might be incapable of winning, he had to seduce and convince, or failing that, use cunning and trickery. The possession of Egypt was worth a few sacrifices and a little "charlatanism." Hadn't Henry IV said, upon embracing the Catholic faith, that Paris was well worth a mass? In exchange for his friendship Bonaparte expected the authorities to exhort the people to swear obedience to the French. To obtain obedience, was he prepared to convert to Islam, and take his army along with him? He said he had considered it a possibility, should events keep him in the Orient.[45] Would he have converted? Convinced that nothing repels people more than religious conversion, he would probably not have taken that step. Because circumstances did not require him to choose between conversion and departure, he limited himself to promises. He began laborious negotiations with the ulemas to overcome various obstacles, the most important of which concerned circumcision and drinking wine. He finally got what he wanted—the French who converted to Islam would be spared circumcision and could drink wine in exchange for a few alms—but for all that he did not convert: he simply promised to do so after a year had passed, and the better to calm the imams' impatience, he also promised to have constructed an immense mosque large enough to contain the whole expeditionary force on the day of the ceremony.[46] He had gained time—in his view that was what mattered—and bought, or at least he thought he had, the right to be proclaimed God's emissary. The authorities in Cairo wrote him letters in which they called him "the pillar of the weak and the wretched, the protector of the sciences, and of those who cultivate them, the friend of the Muslim religion and of those who profess it, the support of orphans and the oppressed, the regulator of the affairs of empires and armies," "very great, very glorious, very valiant prince of the French army . . . endowed with boundless intelligence."[47] That was already pretty good, and on September 1 he obtained from the same authorities an official declaration that included these words: "[Bonaparte] assured us that he recognized the unity of God, that the French honored our prophet, as well as the Quran, and that they regarded the Muslim religion as the best religion. The French have proven their love for Islam by setting free the Muslim prisoners held in Malta, by destroying the churches and breaking the crosses in the city of Venice, and by driving out the pope, who commanded Christians to kill Muslims."[48]

Opportunistic Adhesions and Unconquerable Distrust

"A great lesson in politics," according to Sainte-Beuve, especially given that it concerns only one aspect of a complex game.[49] Bonaparte, like the Turks before him, was trying to establish his domination over Egypt by exploiting the rivalries, divergences of interest, and enmities among the different ethnic, religious, and social groups that constituted the Egyptian population. The natives were in fact divided against themselves. Well received by the Christians of Greek and Syrian origin who had suffered the consequences of the war waged by the Turks against Orthodox Russia, the occupiers had not been received with as much enthusiasm by the Jews, whose customs and religion the Muslims respected in exchange for the payment of a tithe, and still less by the Copts, who traditionally administered the country for the Mamluks and did not rally to the French cause until after their masters had fled.[50] If religion united the Muslims, their interests divided the sheikhs, the imams, the craftsmen of Cairo, of Rosetta or Alexandria, the "fellahs" of the banks of the Nile, the Turks, and the Bedouins. The fall of the Mamluks, who were rightly suspected of religious indifference, must have been welcomed by the religious leaders, who probably deplored the fact that these infidels had been driven out by other infidels, but saw in it an opportunity to increase their own influence. As for the notables in Cairo and elsewhere, they accepted French invitations to collaborate all the more willingly because they had witnessed the general dissolution that had followed the Mamluks' defeat at the pyramids, and feared the return of those "terrifying" hours.[51] Moreover, the peasants of the Nile valley, who were regularly attacked by Bedouins, might accept the army of occupation on the condition that the latter ensure their security and act equitably:

> The political situation resulting from the different interests and different races that inhabited Egypt did not escape Napoleon, as he was to say on Saint Helena, and it was on it that he built his system of government. Not very eager to administer justice in the country, the French couldn't have done it even if they had wanted to. Napoleon left that to the Arabs, that is, to the sheikhs, and gave them full predominance. From that point on, he spoke to the people through the channel of these

men, who were both nobles and legal scholars, and in this way he involved the Arab national spirit and the religion of the Quran in his government. He was waging war solely on the Mamluks. . . . He sought, by the same policy, to get a hold on the Copts. They had the additional link of religion with him, and they alone were experienced in the administration of the country. But even if they had not had that advantage, the French general's policy was to give it to them, in order not to depend exclusively on Arabs, and not to have to fight with 25,000 or 30,000 men against the power of the national and religious spirit. The Copts, who saw the Mamluks destroyed, had no choice but to attach themselves to the French; and in that way our army obtained, in all parts of Egypt, spies, observers, monitors, and financiers who were independent and opposed to the nationals. As for the janissaries and the Ottomans, the policy called for consideration to be shown them as representatives of the Great Lord; the sultan's flag was flown in Egypt.[52]

From the outset, the policy of pacification sought both to prevent any return of the Mamluks and to put an end to Bedouin tribes' raids by driving them back into the desert if it proved impossible to negotiate with them. This policy did not fail to produce results. Desaix, sent to Upper Egypt in pursuit of Murad Bey, did not succeed in killing the cavalrymen who had escaped with him from the battlefield at the pyramids, but for almost a year he prevented them from approaching Cairo. If some Bedouin tribes turned out to be inflexible, others gave in: Kléber won an initial success by concluding an accord with the main tribes of the Damanhur region. Later on, after the military adapted to the particular conditions of warfare against nomadic peoples, Bonaparte succeeded in rallying the powerful Aydy and Henadi tribes to his cause.

The religious neutrality that he observed seemed to him to increase the chances of success of his policy, which sought simultaneously to exploit divisions of interest, reduce the influence of minorities, and satisfy the demands of a majority that he thought was "neutral" by nature, ready to support anyone who would make its fate less harsh and give it a glimpse of a better future. For the first time in history, Europeans were coming to the Orient without any religious ulterior motive, animated on the contrary by purely secular values, and bearing ideas of progress in which the general hoped Muslims would see "the secret of Europe's success and [a way] to provide a remedy for the weakness, poverty, and decline of their country."[53] One of the most solid foundations he was counting on was the Porte's consent to the French intervention in Egypt. If he did not actually obtain it—he thought that Talleyrand was working on it in Constantinople—it was indispensable that the people believed he had. That is also why he was so eager to keep the squadron on the Egyptian coast: he wanted to prevent any contact with Turkey, at least until an accord was signed with the sultan, and he never missed an opportunity to remind people the goal was to obtain the consent of the Great Lord himself.

For all these reasons he had no difficulty finding collaborators to sit on the nine-member council—to which the Turkish name of "divan" was given—created in Cairo on July 25, to dispense justice, collect taxes, administer the country, and maintain order. All the same, the number of those who rallied to his side must not be exaggerated; there were at most a few hundred of them. Nor should we conclude that ultimately religion was not an insurmountable obstacle in Egypt. In fact, only a few of the people who collaborated with the French were Muslims: these included the notables called upon to sit in the divans, of course, and also a certain number of the agents and the religious leaders for whom the general showed such consideration. The former collaborated in order to prevent the country from falling into anarchy; the latter were thinking about the future, after the infidels had gone home. However, the majority of the collaborators came from the Christian minorities: the main Egyptian financial officer, Jârkis al-Jawharî, was a Copt, as was the famous Ya'qub (Jacob) who acted as an intendant for General Desaix, and the head of the police, Barthélemy Serra, came from the Greek island of Chios. We know which of them left Egypt with the French in 1801 and were later incorporated into the Mamluks of the Imperial Guard: they were Georgians (like the famous Rustam Raza, whom Bonaparte took into his service in 1799), Armenians, Greeks, Hungarians, and especially—this was the case for most of them—Syrians, to whom we must add a few Africans who had come from Sudan or Abyssinia with the caravans involved in the slave trade, such as Abdel-Talut, who had been kidnapped in Ethiopia, sold as a slave in Cairo, and died in 1812 during the retreat from Russia. These were the true supporters of an expedition that was far from popular with Muslims, even if a few Albanians donned the uniform of the "Oriental chasseurs." When we try to gauge the impact left by this brief encounter between East and West, the same names always come up: Sheikh al-Mahdî—a Copt who converted to Islam—and Sheikh Hasan al-Attâr (1766–1835).[54] These are exceptional cases, in the literal sense of the word, because for almost all the Muslims who cooperated, to differing degrees, with the French, political collaboration never signified adhesion or conversion.[55]

During the first weeks, however, Bonaparte and his generals thought the contrary, betting on the gradual adhesion of a people they could not believe would remain unmoved by the advantages of the French presence. Although in September the general-in-chief was still talking about the "barbarity" of the Egyptian people, he immediately added: "A change in customs is taking place, and in two or three years everything will look very different."[56] Had the French confused resignation with support? At first the defection of the governor of Alexandria, whom they had left in office, seemed to them an isolated event from which no hasty conclusions should be drawn, but they were soon disillusioned.[57] The French could show as much respect for Islam as they wanted, but from the first to the last day of the occupation they confronted the insurmountable distrust of the Muslim population. No matter what they did, in the eyes of Islamic natives they remained invaders and "Crusaders." For every Attâr, there were many more men like al-Sharqâwî, who, even though he had collaborated with the French at the highest level, described them as "a sect of philosophers who reject the Law . . . and put human reason above all else."[58] Confronted by this hostility that nothing could diminish, the French, after having congratulated themselves on the population's malleability, denounced its duplicity.[59]

Let us make no mistake. This mute hostility did not prevent life from resuming, more or less, its usual course. Businesses reopened their doors after the invasion, they welcomed French customers who readily paid inflated prices, and cordial relationships were even formed, individually, between the soldiers and those they dealt with every day. As one soldier was to say, many Egyptians were "good people" who saved more than one Frenchman during the revolt in Cairo.[60] Egyptians, all the same, were shocked by the French, by the bad manners of these foreigners who got drunk, fired shots in the streets, scaled the walls of harems, or strutted through the streets of Cairo arm-in-arm with the women who had followed the expedition—300 of them, it is said—or those whom the Mamluks had bequeathed to them. The immodesty of the French was not the only scandal. Although they respected the mosques and the exercise of religion, they blasphemed by pretending to believe in God or imitated, in an Arabic that was often incorrect, the speech of Muslims. The Islamic discourse of which Bonaparte was so proud? It was nothing but an "incomprehensible gibberish."[61] The discourse was less to blame than the author. The proclamations in which Bonaparte, claiming to be the Prophet's emissary, threatened the recalcitrant have often been mocked. For example, this famous address "fulminated" after the Cairo revolt:

> Sherifs, ulemas, orators of the mosques, tell your people that those who blithely declare themselves my enemies will find no refuge in this world or in the next. Is there anyone so blind that he does not see that destiny itself guides all my actions? . . . Tell the people that since the world has been the world, it was written that after having destroyed Islam's enemies and had the crosses pulled down, I should come from the depths of the West to fulfill the task that was imposed on me. Make the people see that in the holy book of the Quran, in more than twenty passages, what is happening was foreseen, and what will happen is also explained. So let those who are prevented from cursing us only by the fear of our arms change: for in calling upon the heavens to oppose us, they are calling for their own condemnation; let true believers pray for the success of our arms. I could ask each of you to account for the most secret feelings of your hearts, for I know everything, even what you have said to no one; but a day will come when everyone will see clearly that I am guided by superior orders, and that no human efforts can avail against me.[62]

This proclamation left a man like al-Jabartî cold: "It is long and full of pretension," he wrote, "inspired by a false idea, as can be seen on first glance."[63] The incomprehension was complete, especially because despite the assurances he gave Muslims, Bonaparte had in fact not forgotten the expedition's ultimate objectives, which were neither to punish the Mamluks nor to temporarily threaten British interests in Italy, but to lay the foundations on Egyptian soil for a new colonial empire. Egypt was supposed, not to be the object of later diplomatic bargaining, but to become permanently French. It was a question of bringing the West into the East, not the other way around. It was written black on white in the prospectus announcing the publication of the first issue of the journal *La Décade égyptienne:* The intellectual goal of the expedition was to enrich the history of humanity by rediscovering its pharaonic origins, but its political goal was to make the Egyptians benefit from Western civilization, though this might require the conquerors to promise to act with prudence and even to respect, for as long as necessary, the natives' "prejudices."[64] The oath that Bonaparte had his troops swear on the anniversary of 13 Vendemiaire (October 4, 1798) made this explicit: for the first time in history the conquerors refrained from adopting the ideas and customs of those whom they had conquered, but made it their duty to acculturate among them their own ideas and customs, whose alleged superiority was the basis for the enterprise's legitimacy. That marked all the difference from Alexander's Oriental expedition, of which Arago was to say that he had had the philosopher Callisthenes accompany him "solely for the purpose of collecting . . . scientific documents that would be violently taken from the vanquished nations." Bonaparte by contrast took with him Monge, Berthollet, Fourier, and other scientists so that they might help him "carry the fruits of European civilization into the heart of [these] barbarous populations bent under the yoke."[65] Even if we suppose that Bonaparte had waged in Egypt, as Edward Saïd wrote, a "uniquely benign and selective war" of a kind never before seen in this part of the world, it was nonetheless directed against Islam, because it sought to transport "the Orient into modernity."[66]

These ambitions were wrecked by the population's incomprehension and indifference. "The people has neither curiosity nor a desire to emulate," Dolomieu said. "Its absolute indifference to anything foreign to its condition, to its beliefs, or its customs is perhaps what seemed to me most extraordinary in its way of life. Nothing astonishes it because it pays no attention to what it does not know."[67] For example, the divan. It is true that Bonaparte had invested this assembly of Muslim dignitaries with restricted, essentially consultative powers.[68] But he also saw in it a means of introducing into the Orient Western principles of representative government, and an opportunity for the Egyptians to learn about them. This was a first step, and the assemblies created in Cairo and in the main cities during the summer were soon followed, in October, by a "general divan" in which about 200 representatives were called upon to participate. It was conceived as a sort of assembly of the states-general representing not only the provinces but also the different "estates" or social groups constituting the population of Egypt. Once assembled, they were asked to name, on the Western parliamentary model, a permanent committee assigned to make proposals regarding the political and administrative reorganization of Egypt—of its judicial and fiscal systems—and the reform of property law.[69] Thus Bonaparte laid the foundations for what he conceived as a project of regeneration. The experiment was a failure, not only because the Cairo insurrection led to the dissolution of the general divan, but also because the members of these assemblies did not see the utility, and still less the interest, of these assemblies. The local Cairo divan soon stopped meeting, and if the country's Grand Divan replied to the questions Bonaparte asked, it was not exactly in the way he would have hoped, as its members showed above all a desire not to change anything. The very idea that they might have the power to legislate, to conceive and impose new rules established to serve the general good, was foreign to them. Their faith denied any possibility of a human legislative power, and, forbidding them to create anything, it allowed them only to preserve the divine will and make it respected. It was solely because the meaning of the divine prescriptions was not always very clear that the leaders granted themselves a limited power, not to deviate from these prescriptions, but to interpret or complete them "by customary law or simply by the will of the ruler."[70]

The Institute of Egypt, which was created by Bonaparte after his entry into Cairo and which was to play a capital role in the exchange of knowledge and the diffusion of Western science among the local elites, did not spare its efforts, seeking to attract Cairo's educated elite by its library or the public experiments conducted by its chemists, its engineers, and its balloonists. The public came. Those who came to the library and were astonished by the friendly welcome given them were shown "all sorts of printed books," most of them illustrated, maps of the world, astronomical instruments, clocks, the chemistry and pharmaceutical laboratories, and so forth. "Astonished by the sight of all these fine things," they were not, however, disturbed, and still less convinced: these were simple magic tricks that "minds like ours," al-Jabartî noted, "could neither conceive nor explain."[71] The success of an experiment on electricity was no more consequential than the failure of several hot-air balloons that fell a few minutes after they were launched. Even music—Grétry, Haydn, Mozart—had no effect, to the point that Monge, beside himself, could not help crying: "These brutes are not worthy of the effort you are making!"[72] None of these "tricks," as al-Jabartî called them, fooled the citizens of Cairo,[73] who, instead of establishing a causal connection between European technology and the occupier's military power, concluded that these Frenchmen were decidedly very conceited. To the Enlightenment policy advocated by the French, religion posed an obstacle that was all the more powerful because the French occupation and the fall of the Mamluks benefited essentially the religious "party."

Must we conclude that Bonaparte's "high politics" was a complete failure? In the short term, no doubt; the expedition left few marks on Egypt in the first years of the nineteenth century. But all was not lost. After a long "latency period" the influence of the brief French occupation made itself felt when Mehemet Ali, who had seized power in 1805, undertook to modernize the country by taking his inspiration from some of the reforms imagined by Bonaparte.[74] More than fifty years after the departure of the French, Flaubert noted that they were still "respected" and that Bonaparte was regarded "almost as a demigod."[75] Moreover, the initial resistance of the native populations to the novelties that the French sought to impose on them cannot be assessed without recalling the simple fact of the occupation. The French were in the situation of all "armed missionaries."[76] Leaving aside the obstacle presented by differences in religion and customs, those the French wanted to make happy saw in them invaders rather than liberators, and by instinct refused what the French offered.

"In a Climate Not Our Own"

In the end the occupiers were never able to convince the Egyptians that France was going to stay in their country for a long time. The French themselves had a hard time believing it. When Kléber addressed the garrison at Alexandria after the destruction of the squadron at Abukir, he told them that for lack of a fleet to take them back to France, they would have to resign themselves to living for what might be an extended time "in a climate not our own."[77] Neither he nor his soldiers imagined that they would stay long, but in a matter of months they found themselves establishing winter quarters. One officer remembered: "We found the life we led very boring . . . it was so different from the one that we had led in Europe that we found it very hard to get used to it. The heat was considerable; we couldn't go outside; besides, where would we go to walk? Over the sands, amid the ruins, we would have needed an escort; at the gates of the city we were attacked by Arabs. We had few books. . . . Our outings sometimes consisted in riding donkeys; we went to race through the streets of the city, where the sun doesn't beat down. . . . We spent our evenings playing *bouillotte*."[78]

Card games and money! They come up on almost every page of the memoirs written by members of the expedition. The men played everywhere, and soon gravitated to the "Tivoli," a gathering place opened in November thanks to a subscription. The great thing was, of course, women. Many of those who could not take advantage of the company of the French women who had followed their husbands on the adventure, and who hoped for encounters with women other than the hundreds of prostitutes who plied their trade in the Bâb-al-Lûq quarter, founded temporary homes. Thus Geoffroy Saint-Hilaire wrote to his father: "I am living very peacefully here, occupying myself by turns with natural history, my horses, and my little black family, to which I have temporarily transferred my affection useless to my European family."[79] It was a flourishing trade. A black woman cost 500 francs, 800 if she was a virgin, the price to be negotiated when the caravans arrived from Abyssinia. The price of white women soared in proportion to their rarity; the engineer Le Père bought a Caucasian woman for 3,600 francs, but the sum demanded might exceed 8,000 francs. Opportunities spread by word of mouth: Father Félix, from the Capuchin convent, rented mothers and their daughters by the day.[80] Women were the cause of continual disputes. The soldiers accused the subaltern officers, and the latter accused the superior officers, of having seized the most appetizing women—"in the name of the nation," one of them adds[81]—all of them claiming, moreover, that Oriental women did not have such slender figures as those they were used to. And then they got tired of everything and, despite the festivities organized to celebrate the annual breaking of the dikes of the Nile or the anniversary of the victory at Rivoli, the excruciating desire to see Europe and France again came back. The witnesses are unanimous in this: the celebration of the Republic on September 21 took place in a glacial atmosphere, the soldiers keeping stubbornly quiet instead of shouting the required hurrahs when Bonaparte proposed a toast to "the year 500 of the French Republic!"[82] The certainty of a rapid return home helped the more optimistic adapt to a stay that several were to remember as "the saddest time of [their] life."[83] Even if most of those who made "gloomy conjectures" and dreamed of escaping their Egyptian prison did not go so far as to risk getting themselves "fucked by the Barbaresques," as Kléber elegantly put it in a letter to Dugua.[84] Nonetheless, it was necessary to take steps to prevent some men from taking advantage of the presence of commercial ships flying neutral flags to escape. Bonaparte did not absolutely forbid any departure; he discussed this with Berthier after he had learned that the doctors were distributing false certificates to those who wanted to leave Egypt: "It is not my intention . . . to keep in the army men who are not sensitive to the honor of being among our companions in arms; let them leave, I shall facilitate their departure: but I do not want them to mask, by feigned illnesses, the real motive for not sharing our travails and our perils."[85] The geologist Dolomieu left, and the ordnance officer Sucy, and the adjutant general Beauvais, and General Dumas, whose departure Bonaparte was never to forgive and which he interpreted as a betrayal, and others as well. For a time Kléber considered leaving.[86] Berthier himself, who missed his Italian mistress, la Visconti, so much that he had set up a little altar to her always adorned with flowers and lit by a candle, ended up begging his boss to let him go back to Europe. We do not know what Bonaparte felt on seeing himself abandoned by his most faithful lieutenant on the eve of the beginning of the Syrian campaign. Bitterness, no doubt, but, perhaps weary of the "idiotism" to which passion sometimes led his chief of staff, he signed the requested leave, even going so far, in recognition of services rendered, as to disguise this authorization as an order for a secret mission. But Berthier, who already could no longer imagine living far from his great man, finally gave up his plans to leave.

Bonaparte also wanted to go back to France. It was not that he was bored; he didn't know the meaning of the word, and had he known it, the work to be done would not have left him time to languish: "We have here an enormous task: it is an unparalleled chaos to be untangled and organized," he wrote.[87] Between staff meetings, conversations with the notables of Cairo, and work sessions with Bourrienne or Berthier, his days were very full. There was no question, of course, of leaving details to his aides, any more than there had been in Italy. Thus, on September 21, after ordering various troop movements, reading a large number of reports on the ongoing military operations, combing through the accounts drawn up by the financial officer Poussielgue, dictating the order of the day for the army, sending food supplies to Salheyeh, and reorganizing the command at Damietta by replacing General Vial, who was suspected of embezzlement, with Dugua, he still found time to write to Poussielgue: "I see, on the report for storehouse no. 2, that 251 livres of candles were put in and taken out; who took them?—There are seven coffee mills that have to be put at the disposal of the ordnance officer [Sucy]; four pairs of pistols that have to be given to the head of brigade Bessières; two saddles, as well as the tents, which have to be given to the director of clothing."[88] Having only three or four servants, he was surrounded by a small number of close collaborators.[89] Fewer than twenty. There was, of course, his secretary Bourrienne. For military affairs, his chief of staff General Berthier, the heads of the engineers (Caffarelli), the artillery (Dommartin), the cavalry (Dumas), and his aides-de-camp (Junot, Duroc, Lavalette, Sulkowski, Croizier, Guibert, his son-in-law Eugène, and the son of Director Merlin de Douai).[90] Caffarelli du Falga, whose acquaintance Bonaparte had made after his return from Italy, played a role that went well beyond employing his military skills. This former Hébertist, suspected of being a follower of Babeuf, had become one of the general-in-chief's confidants, and his death during the siege of Saint-Jean d'Acre was a loss that sincerely affected Bonaparte. Caffarelli, about whom he was later to write that he "understood perfectly the details of his weapon" and "[also] excelled in his moral qualities and by the extent of his knowledge," was probably the sole "ideologue" to whom Bonaparte ever paid homage.[91] Sucy (who succeeded Daure), Poussielgue, and Estève took care of administrative and financial affairs. General Dupuy, who was replaced by Dugua, was in command at Cairo. Bonaparte also worked with Girgès al-Gawhari, the intendant-general al-Shaqâwi, the president of the divan, the mathematician Fourier, who provided the liaison with the divan, Monge, who handled relations with the Institute, Tallien and Jean-Joseph Marcel, who were concerned with newspapers and the print shop, and the Orientalists Magallon and Venture de Paradis. The latter in particular, who had been an interpreter at the embassy in Constantinople and had since become a professor of Turkish at the École des langues orientales, played a major role in teaching Bonaparte about the Orient, serving as an interpreter during his conversations with Arab leaders, and, in a nutshell, exercising in Egypt the role of unofficial minister for everything that concerned Arab affairs.[92] His death, during the Syrian campaign, deprived Bonaparte of a first-rate collaborator whom Jaubert, who succeeded him, could not fully replace.[93] Bonaparte had a hand in everything. He liked to live in a whirlwind, and sometimes drove his collaborators to despair: overwhelmed by work "until dawn" and called upon to do everything "with order, precision, without delay," they nonetheless had to be ready to "ride horseback at any time [in order to] second the activity of a man who regarded as lost any time that was not used for his projects."[94] It was in this way that Egypt was to remain in his memory as the "finest time" of his life, "because . . . the most ideal." Not because he could dream at will about that "land of poetry" and imagine himself, as he told Mme de Rémusat, "on the way to Asia, riding an elephant, a turban on [his] head and a new Quran in [his] hand"; nor even because in the Orient he found himself "freed from the restraint of a hindering civilization," but because here, and more than in Italy, he found himself invested with a power as absolute for civilian affairs as he had for the conduct of the war.[95] Surprisingly, the fact that the government could exercise no control over him at such a distance played little or no role in this. His omnipotence had more natural causes: it was a consequence of the scarcity of water. It was not solely their religious blinders that made the local populations indifferent to the representative system whose praises the Westerners sang. It was also the fact that a country that was nine-tenths desert and depended for its subsistence on the annual flooding of the Nile required a very concentrated power capable of supervising the politics of water with the help of an administration that was decentralized and informed about local circumstances. Water was the one precious resource that everyone, for reasons that are easy to understand, was tempted to seize. Referring to the Nile canal at Alexandria, which had water in it only a few weeks per year, the engineer Le Père wrote: "During the time when Alexandria's needs require that the waters of the river reach it directly without being diverted, the *kashif* or lieutenant of the bey, who has the command [of the province], makes his rounds and sets up along the canal to prevent the anticipated breaks and diversions, and to see to the maintenance and repair of the dikes; his supervision was so strict in this regard that any infraction of the regulations was punished by death."[96] An iron hand was necessary to forestall an increase in conflicts and disorders, of which there were already many. In addition to the lack of water, which varied depending on the height of the Nile's annual rise, there was the permanent threat posed to the inhabited areas by nomadic warriors, which forced the authorities to be constantly ready to go to war.[97] Napoleon said it: nowhere else did the need for government make itself felt so strongly: "In no country does the administration have so much influence over public prosperity. If the administration is good, then the canals are well dredged and well maintained, the regulations for irrigating are enforced fairly, the flooding is most extensive [an allusion to the practice of breaking the dikes to irrigate lands at the time of the Nile's flooding]. If the administration is bad, vicious, or weak, the canals are obstructed with silt, the dikes poorly maintained, the irrigation regulations are disregarded, and the principles of the system of flooding are violated by sedition and the particular interests of individuals or localities."[98]

That says it all: under such conditions, how could the transfer to Egypt of institutions and guarantees invented for the use of the inhabitants of fertile, temperate Europe be considered? On the banks of the Nile one could not govern in the same way as on the Seine or the Po.

Repression: A "Regress of Civilization"?

That is why the question of repression has to be approached prudently. In his memoirs Barras reproduces, over several pages, a sinister anthology of extracts from Bonaparte's correspondence. They solely concern mobile units sent all over Egypt, villages seized, men shot, heads cut off and put on pikes, beatings with truncheons, roundups of hostages, camps razed to the ground, houses burned down, flocks confiscated, peoples deported.[99] All these documents are authentic, and nearly a whole volume could be filled with orders of this kind. Barras sees in them overwhelming evidence against Bonaparte and his reputation as a "civilizing genius"; it has also been called evidence of a "regress of civilization."[100] The repression was incontestably brutal and incommensurable with what it might have been in Italy. We recall the pillaging of Pavia, the destruction of Binasco, and a few other similar scenes in Italy, but these were the exception; in Egypt, such scenes occurred daily and probably resulted in hundreds of victims. The army was involved, and so were the companies of janissaries placed in Cairo under the twofold authority of the divan and the local commander, General Dupuy. Barthélemy Serra was in charge of them. With a "silken plume" on his hat, "a rich fur on his back," and a scimitar at his side, Serra imposed a reign of terror. Prancing at the head of his *Mustahfizân*, he arrested, tortured, and executed, and in the evening he was seen returning with the heads of his victims attached to his saddle. The French and their agents had no monopoly on violence or cruelty. The war waged against them by the Bedouins, Mamluks, and fellahs in revolt was atrocious; the wounded were killed and decapitated, prisoners were raped and mutilated, sometimes burned alive and even skinned. This began as early as the march to the Nile, on July 7, and from that time on never ceased. Isolated Frenchmen were murdered, patrols were assaulted, boats on the Nile attacked and pillaged. "On July 18," a supply officer reports, "a food-storehouse guard was sent into a village to buy wheat. The Arabs captured him along with his servant, tied them both to a tree, and burned them alive. We saw their still-smoking bodies. Confronted with this barbarity, Bonaparte's indignation was so great that he ordered the village burned and all its inhabitants shot or run through. This very severe example did not prevent us from finding along the road, at every step, unfortunate victims that these ferocious peoples had mutilated in various ways. I saw one with the head taken off, others with the skin of the face torn away and the soles of the feet burned."[101] The behavior of the French army in Egypt was in no way exceptional: it shows the excesses a regular army can commit when it is disoriented by the confrontation with irregular forces that are omnipresent but invisible, appearing out of nowhere, striking and disappearing without respecting any of the implicit codes common to military professionals. The sequence of actions and reactions was governed by the dynamics of the rise to extremes in which Clausewitz saw the profound reality of war.[102]

To many members of the expedition, it seemed that they were reliving the war in the Vendée, where they had fought alongside Kléber or Menou. A man named Rozis wrote to a friend: "The enemy is all around us, in front, behind, and on the sides; exactly as in the Vendée!"[103] As in western France in 1793, the soldiers of the Army of the Orient saw in the enemy, not Bedouins or rebellious peasants, belligerents, combatants protected by the laws of war and the *droit des gens*—the international law of the time—but instead vulgar "brigands" who had placed themselves outside the law by refusing to submit to French authority, which was legitimate by the law of conquest. Their enemies appeared to them at best as rebels, at worst as highwaymen who were to be attacked and summarily hanged. In fact, they were no longer considered delinquents subject to criminal law, a status that would have required an investigation, a trial, formalities, delays: "The *droit des gens* offered, for cases of this kind—and Egypt is one of them—a third method that combined the advantages of war and penal repression: the recognition of the state of war, but a state of war outside the *droit des gens*. Against pirates at sea, against brigands on land, against those who, living on the margins of society, attack the very foundations of civilization, the sovereign makes war without being subject to the ordinary laws of war, because it is only just to strike outside the law those who have voluntarily gone beyond it. All jurists made this distinction between *hostes* and *proedones*, enemies and brigands."[104]

The difference of language and religion, the difference in customs, and more generally the feeling of being far away from the civilized world, all helped increase fear as well as scorn, and ultimately increased the brutality of the repression by weakening the prohibitions and inhibitions connected with the use of violence. After all, wasn't the expeditionary corps in a country where "a man's blood is shed like that of an ox," where "the population of the interior is made up of different kinds, all accustomed to being beaten or beating, tyrants or tyrannized?"[105]

They all knew about the "exploits" of the current pasha of Acre, Jezzar, a Bosnian who had been bought in the slave market by the Mamluk chieftain Ali Bey and who had risen, in the Oriental manner, to the highest ranks. He was called "the butcher," because he had, as Lockroy puts it, "the dilettantism of murder": "He took pleasure in blood, which he knew how to shed artistically. . . .

He liked his power to be a hindrance and a threat to everyone. He made it felt at every moment, to foreigners and to his subjects, as if he himself needed to witness, through the horror he inspired, the magnitude of the power he had acquired."[106] His subjects respected him because they feared him, and this fear even took on the aspect of a quasi-religious terror when Jezzar, having foiled still another conspiracy—in 1790—had all the women in his harem drowned and eviscerated with his own hands his favorite Circassian wife. This massacre marked a turning point in his life. "Up to that point he had killed; now he began to systematically mutilate his subjects."[107] He cut off their noses, put out their eyes, cut off their ears or tongues; he bought women and walled them up alive. But he also had his good sides: he was compassionate, gave alms to the poor, saw to it that fair prices were asked in the bazaar—if a seller went too far, he nailed his tongue to the counter. He liked to sit at the harbor, his ax alongside him, contemplating the sea, in his garden he cultivated rare flowers, and he spent his spare time weaving tapestries, unless he was using it to mangle the hands of some wretch picked up on the street. "He's fair," the people said.

After that, we will not be surprised to read these words written by Bonaparte: "The Turks can be guided only with the greatest severity; every day I have five or six heads cut off in the streets of Cairo. We have had to treat them with consideration up to this point to destroy the reputation for terror that preceded us: now, on the contrary, we have to adopt the tone required to make these peoples obey; and for them, to obey is to fear."[108] Bonaparte was even convinced that the Orientals were so used to being afraid that they could not be made to obey without constantly giving them further reasons for fear. A feeling dulled by habit had to be revived in them so that "the right lessons . . . remain in their heads."[109] As for punishments, the French adapted to the local customs. Beatings were administered for simple infractions, because this penalty, which later inspired in Flaubert a few juicy remarks, was the most common one.[110] Heads were cut off for more serious crimes. As for women—this was the custom— they were thrown into the Nile, sewed up in a sack.[111] Had a village revolted? "Have the most rebellious people's heads cut off," Dugua recommended; "if they have escaped, burn down their houses."[112] Was one of his aides-de-camp killed near another village? Let it be burned: "[If the officer in charge of the operation] can manage to arrest the sheikhs, he shall take them to Cairo as hostages.

He shall let the village be pillaged, in such a way that no house remains untouched."[113] Do the Bedouins refuse to listen? Let "five or six hundred" of them be killed, as this is the only way to subject "those people."[114] Are the Aydy and Hautât tribes continuing their attacks and raids? Their camps have to be attacked, Bonaparte had Murat told; he must "seize their camels, women, children, old men, and take them to Cairo, and kill everything he can't take with him."[115]

Nevertheless, one cannot conclude from all this that the French had completely sold their souls. One element was missing that was so important in the story of someone like Jezzar: the imagination, the caprice, the art. Even in the orders quoted by Barras, Bonaparte took care to keep the repression from turning into outbursts of unmotivated violence. A crime had to have been committed for a mobile unit to be sent to punish the presumed guilty parties, to attack a Bedouin camp, or to burn a village. It was always a matter of making an example, no doubt terrible, but limited, so that on the one hand the accustomed penalties deterred the local populations from continuing their offenses, but on the other hand the victor's clemency astonished them enough to make them reflect that after all, obeying him might turn out to be the lesser of two evils. The heart of Bonaparte's policy in this domain was to get the heads of the tribes or of the villages to designate hostages they cared about and send these to the French to guarantee good relations with the occupying forces. The general saw in this the best way to diminish, little by little, the frequency of recourse to force: "The method of taking hostages is the best," he wrote to General Lanusse; and to Murat: "It is useless to make any arrangement with the Arabs if they do not give hostages; it would be a waste of time and leave us open to further events. . . . You shall have them told that if they want to live on good terms with us, they have to send me fifteen hostages, assuring them that no harm will come to them; without which these brigands will slaughter, at the first opportunity, the boats on the Nile."[116] And to Lannes: "Scatter the groups, arrest the sheikh *al balad*, take the leading personages hostage, and let the village know that the first time a boat is attacked we will burn down the village and cut the hostages' heads off."[117]

It was all a matter of intuition and circumstance. Kurayyim, the emir of Alexandria, was executed, but Hassan Tubar, the powerful sheikh of Menzaleh who had taken up arms, was finally spared.[118] And though revolts were still harshly repressed, Bonaparte nonetheless refused to strike back against the inhabitants of Tantah, "a place very revered by the Muslims" that had put up armed resistance to the tax collectors.[119] Bonaparte boasted of having three heads cut off per day.[120] But he was exaggerating and made this claim only in order to forestall any fit of weakness among his generals. When, on the contrary, the generals went beyond his orders or judged the situation with too little discernment, he did not hesitate to correct them. He did not have words harsh enough for those of his subordinates who forgot that "pacification" sought, not to make the silence of the tomb reign in Egypt, but rather to lead to the formation of a "party" favorable to the French presence at least out of self-interest, which would never be obtained by blind violence. He condemned the use of torture, as he reprimanded General Zayonchek for having had arrested without good reasons, and then freed with the same carelessness, the members of the divan of Menouf and the Copt intendant of the city:[121] "I did not enjoy seeing the way you behaved toward the Copt; my intention is that we show those people consideration and respect. . . . Neither do I approve of your arrest of the divan without having determined whether or not it was guilty, or of your release of it twelve hours later: that is not the way to conciliate a party. Study the people around you; distinguish those who are the best suited to be employed; sometimes make fair and severe examples, but never anything that approaches caprice and thoughtlessness."[122]

Kléber acted no differently from Bonaparte. They are, however, often contrasted. The former, it is said, was as merciful as the latter was implacable. When Bonaparte learned of the uprising that bloodied Alexandria on July 13, he asked Kléber to disarm the population, have the guilty decapitated, raze their homes, and take fifty hostages.[123] Kléber showed, in fact, great moderation. Judging that the blame lay in the poor behavior of his troops, he reprimanded them. He had the man who had seriously wounded a French soldier arrested and executed, but did not allow the destruction of his house: "May this example of French magnanimity convince Muslims that in coming to free them from the oppression of the Mamluks," he declared, "we desire nothing so much as to maintain with them the good terms and harmony that politics and reason require of both nations."[124] But he also knew how to be ruthless. When the inhabitants of Berket Ghitas diverted the waters of the Nile canal at Alexandria with the help of Bedouins from the tribe of Awlad 'Ali, the "gentle" Kléber sent a mobile unit there with these instructions (September 13): "You shall go to the village of Berket Ghitas. You shall seize everyone who resists you and you shall arrest and guard carefully the women, old men, and children. The Arabs of the village who perish in this affair shall be decapitated . . . and their heads put on a few pikes that shall be exposed to the view of passersby, after which you shall set fire to the village and destroy it completely. For you must know that these miserable inhabitants have no goal other than to divert the waters of the khalig [canal] and to prevent their arrival in Alexandria. This example will no doubt contain the other towns situated along the canal."[125]

If Kléber and Bonaparte did not like each other, their forms of repression had nothing to do with it.

The Cairo Revolt

For all the differences between Egypt and Italy, it was true in both places that the harsh necessities of occupation constantly impeded the achievement of French policy objectives. As in Italy, the shortage of money was extreme. Maintaining the army was very expensive—1,300,000 francs per month—and, as in Italy, Bonaparte said he was surrounded by thieves: "I am hard pressed here to find money," he confided to Kléber, "and in a wood full of thieves."[126] There soon remained nothing of the war treasury brought from Toulon and Rome, and by September 1798 the soldiers' pay was already two months in arrears, and constantly fell further behind, even though money was being coined hand over fist in order to cope with the most important payments due. The instructions were clear: it was up to everyone to find a way to ensure that the army would lack for nothing. They had to resort, and with fewer scruples and less consideration than in Italy, to requisitions, forced contributions, "loans" that would never be repaid, confiscations of goods, and even to holding to ransom prisoners suspected of hiding a treasure. When these extraordinary resources had been exhausted and everything that could be raided had been taken, there remained nothing but to hope that ordinary taxes—the *miri*—would produce revenues sufficient to pay the soldiers.[127] But the country was poor, war had paralyzed its commerce, and the peasants, like their peers throughout the world, hid their money and put up a fierce resistance to the tax collectors, so that it was necessary to go to great lengths to squeeze a few *talaris* out of them.[128] It is hard to assess the impact of these measures. All we can say is that the French were generally met with hostility, whether it was of religious origin or provoked by fiscal exactions. Nonetheless, it varied depending on the place and the social groups concerned. The discontent arising from the collection of taxes was directed not solely toward the French but also, as always, toward the Copt employees; and the terrible war that the French waged against the nomadic tribes to some extent served the interests of the sedentary population.[129] Tension was highest in the capital, Cairo, where the fiscal measures were aggravated by a deluge of decrees intended to improve hygiene or to better supervise urban space.

An initial incident went unnoticed by the French: on September 15 a hostile mob booed Bonaparte when he came to visit Sheikh al-Sâdât, not far from the great mosque: "At that moment, Bonaparte came out . . . when he passed through the crowd, there was a general outcry and loud quotations of verses from the Quran. Bonaparte asked what was going on, but the truth was hidden from him, and he was told that the crowd was applauding him and wishing him well. This was a critical moment that could have had very serious consequences."[130] The day after this warning shot, the French announced that from then on property owners would have to register their titles and pay a registration fee. This was not merely to provide a new source of revenue but also a better basis for the property system, given that "properties in Egypt [were] only temporary concessions by the government that could be renewed or withdrawn upon the holder's death, just as was formerly the case in Europe for fiefs in the early period of feudalism": "The divan had approved this measure, which it said was entirely in conformity with the letter and the spirit of the Quran, but in vain; it nonetheless aroused a general discontent. The concessionaires saw in it nothing other than a means of taking away their money through a tax, and in their view it was simply a disguised vexation."[131] The creation on the same day of a trading license for businessmen and craftsmen did nothing to calm the waters. Bonaparte did not understand that with his measures he was permanently alienating both property owners—fearing disorder, they had up to that point observed a prudent neutrality—and the poor hangers-on who lived on their alms. "Then the imams, seeing the hatred they had long kept alive among the lower classes of the people spreading to the upper classes, thought the moment had come to call true believers to a holy war."[132] The establishment on October 16 of a tax on buildings was the final straw.

On Sunday, October 21, Bonaparte left the city early in the morning to inspect the fortifications being built in Old Cairo and on the island of Rudah. He had no inkling of what was to happen, any more than did General Dupuy, the commander of the citadel, who was the first to be astonished when he was informed that demonstrators had emerged in large numbers from the mosques and were heading for the seat of the *qadi*, the highest Ottoman magistrate, shouting "Let God give victory to Islam!"[133] Dupuy got on his horse and went straight toward the crowd. The rioters, who were for the most part students at the al-Azhar mosque and inhabitants of the poor quarters of the city, and who were led by the sheikh of the al-Azhar brotherhood of the blind, threw themselves on Dupuy and killed him. The news spread like wildfire: the leader of the French—Bonaparte's name was given—was dead. The crowd then grew larger, receiving reinforcements from all over the city. The insurgents attacked the houses inhabited by the French or by Christians, and the scientists from the Institute who were besieged in their palaces escaped with their lives only because of their courage. Bonaparte, who had been informed, hurriedly returned to Cairo: "We were met with a hail of stones," one of those who accompanied him reported; "having finally managed to return through the Bulaq gate, we found the city in the most cruel situation: musket fire was heard from all sides, and we began to see dead bodies frequently."[134] Bonaparte named General Bon to succeed Dupuy and mobilized all the available forces, beginning with Barthélemy Serra, whose courage was admired that day by all the French. Then he started helping the Christians, without trying to move into the quarters strongly held by the insurgents. During the night he prepared a counterattack, and on the twenty-second, after the failure of a mediation attempt made by the sheikhs of the divan, the powerful batteries placed on the heights of the citadel began to pour heavy fire on the al-Azhar mosque and the surrounding neighborhoods, which the insurgents had turned into an armed camp: "This bombardment was so terrible that the inhabitants of the city, who had never seen anything like it, began to cry out, begging Heaven to save them from these misfortunes. The rioters stopped firing; but the French continued to fire."[135] It was only around

8 p.m., after eight hours of uninterrupted bombardment, that Bonaparte, yielding to the divan's requests, ordered a cease-fire. His troops regained possession of the rebellious quarters, destroyed the barricades, and moved into al-Azhar; the French, Jabartî reports, "broke the lamps and the student's desks; they stole everything they found in the cupboards; they threw books and the Quran on the floor and trampled on them with their boots. They urinated and spat in this mosque, they drank wine there, and broke bottles that they threw in all the corners."[136] We do not know exactly how many casualties resulted from these two days of rioting: between 200 and 300 Frenchmen are supposed to have perished, with ten times as many deaths on the Egyptian side. About 2,000 suspects are said to have been arrested and taken to the citadel. Among them were the hundred or so "imams, muezzins, and leaders of the Maghrebins, all people of the lower class" who had formed a "divan of defense" and put at their head the powerful sheikh al-Sâdât.[137] About ten leaders "of a violent and irreconcilable spirit" were executed along with insurgents captured with arms in their hands. None was executed in public. The executioner did his work within the walls of the citadel. That night the decapitated bodies were carried to the Nile, and those of the sheikhs who were condemned to death on November 3 were buried in a place kept secret.[138] "The wretched inhabitants of Cairo," Geoffroy Saint-Hilaire wrote with satisfaction, had just learned "at their expense" who the "world's tutors" were.[139] Many of the French thought, however, that 2,000 dead and 100 executions were far from enough. Hadn't Bonaparte scandalously spared al-Sâdât, whose responsibility was nonetheless well-known? Denon and most of his friends from the Institute could not get over their anger:

> Perhaps all those whose eyes had seen the retreat of companies of French should have been put to death without exception, Denon was to say, but clemency had preceded repentance: thus the spirit of vengeance had not been snuffed out by consternation; that was what I saw the next day in the attitude and the expression on the faces of the malcontents; I felt that if before [October 21] we were already surrounded by a circle of Arabs, a smaller circle had just closed around us, and henceforth we would move only through our enemies. A few traitors were arrested and punished, but the mosques that had been the asylum of the crime

were returned; and the pride of the guilty was nourished by that condescension: fanaticism was not destroyed by terror; and whatever danger Bonaparte could be made to envisage, nothing could alter the feeling of generosity that he showed in this circumstance: he tried to be as merciful as he could have been terrible; and the past was forgotten, whereas we were counting numerous and important losses.[140]

Bonaparte had in fact decided that the executions that had followed the reconquest of the city would not be continued, and when the repentant al-Sâdât came to kiss his hand, he received him in the usual way. Why transform into a martyr this old man, who was undoubtedly deceitful but respected? When Kléber expressed his astonishment that he had not been killed, Bonaparte said to him: "No, this people is too foreign to us, to our habits. It needs leaders. I prefer that it have leaders like this one, who can neither ride a horse nor wield a saber, than ones like Murad Bey. . . . The death of this powerless old man would produce no advantage."[141] Because the officers and scientists continued to look grim, he inserted a clarification in the *Courrier de l'Égypte*. The revolt, he said, had been fomented by "religious subordinates"; if they had seduced "the populace," "a large part of the population" had still remained loyal to the French or neutral:

> It would therefore have been sovereignly unjust and cruel to crack down en masse without taking the trouble to discern the guilty individually; such passions can carry away weak and cowardly governments that during the calm relax all the bonds of order and would like to sacrifice the human race to their fear as soon as the slightest danger threatens them; these [passions] cannot suit the French, who are naturally disposed to clemency and are full of courage. The French strike their enemies with vigor, but they are not governed by a blind anger. They act under the eyes of history, and know with what severity it has punished the cruelties committed in America and in India by the Spanish and the English.[142]

The authorities in Cairo had learned their lesson. The victims were buried, worship resumed, al-Azhar was returned to its imams and to the students. To the proclamations in which the ulemas called upon the population to submit, Bonaparte replied by establishing a new divan. Niqula al-Turk celebrated the end of these events with an "Ode to Bonaparte" in which we read: "The leader who marches at the head of the French is impetuous in war and magnanimous in peace. His name terrifies kings. The latter bend their haughty heads before the invincible Bonaparte, the lion of battles. His courage dominates irrevocable destinies and the heavens of glory bow down before him."[143]

Relaxations

Calm had finally come, and almost order. The defeat of the insurgents had not put an end to prejudices and hatreds, but it had been so shattering that the enemies of the French presence were not able to recover for several months. Bonaparte was going to have three months—November, December, and January 1799—during which he could devote himself to the tasks of government. He allowed himself a few recreations. They had been rare up to that point, even if he had been seen at the pyramids before the revolt in Cairo. He had amused himself by making Berthier, who was afraid of heights, climb to the top of Kheops by asking him to go see if his darling was not awaiting him there; when Bonaparte arrived at the summit in his turn, he remarked laconically to Monge that with all those stones one could build around France a wall one meter wide and three high.[144] Did he yield to the soldiers' infatuation with Free Masonry? We have no proof of that, but he may have been initiated into an improvised lodge of the Scottish rite.[145] Finally, on December 24, 1798, he left for Suez to locate the remains of the ancient canal. Monge had never ceased saying how much the general would add to his glory by reestablishing communication between the Mediterranean and the Red Sea:

> He crossed the isthmus and went to visit, Bible in hand, the Springs of Moses; going along the end of the gulf, he was almost carried away by the tide . . . ; that was, he said, the explanation for the Pharaoh's misadventure when he was pursuing the Hebrews, who had, no doubt, passed over at low tide. Assigning the engineer Arnollet and two engineering officers to explore the two shores of the gulf in a gunboat, he

went back north to explore the isthmus; having found vestiges of the pharaonic canal, he was excited: "Monge! Monge!" he cried, "We are right in the canal!" His companions shared his enthusiasm: "We have found the famous canal," Berthier wrote triumphantly; we have followed it for five leagues starting from the gulf of Suez, and we have also found it near Belbeis."[146]

Back in Cairo he was seen at the Institute, where he was a member of the mathematics section, over which he presided starting on December 16; in the evening he received visitors in the vast residence recently constructed on Ezbehkieh Square by a Mamluk chieftain. There, underneath the trees in the garden and to the sound of the fountains, he even hosted a few balls, and like the others, and with all the fewer scruples because he now considered his marriage over, he enjoyed the local beauties. It is said that he had several Circassian slave-girls presented to him. Later he was to mention, laughing with Rustam, the memory of these "beautiful sultanas" whom he in fact sent away, finding them too fat and especially leaving much to be desired in the matter of cleanliness, which he considered so important.[147] Did he console himself for his wife's infidelities with Sheikh al-Bakrî's daughter Zaynab? We cannot affirm it, but after the departure of the French the poor woman was almost certainly killed for having had criminal relations with the occupier. He ended up following Geoffroy Saint-Hilaire's example, inventing a substitute household, not by buying a black woman but by putting in his bed the wife of one of his officers, the lieutenant of the chasseurs Fourès. Her name was Pauline, she was twenty years old, and she had long blond hair and the accent of her native Languedoc. A milliner in Carcassonne, she had followed her husband, dressed as a man. Bonaparte met her at the end of November. Things moved fast, because on December 17 Lieutenant Fourès was given an important mission that was to take him to Paris, from which the two lovebirds hoped he would not soon return. Unfortunately the ship that was conveying him was captured by the British, who, whether because he seemed to them of negligible value or because they had gotten wind of the general-in-chief's love affair, authorized their prisoner to return to Egypt. Bonaparte had to go to greater lengths. A war representative, transformed for the occasion into a registry official, pronounced the divorce of the Fourès couple. We do not know what happened to the husband, who did not in any case seem much bothered by his misfortune.[148] As for Pauline, who became once again Pauline Bellisle—Bonaparte called her "Bellilotte"—she got used to her role as mistress of the general-in-chief's household and "sultana." She did the honors of the headquarters, got angry when the guards forgot to present arms to her, harassed the servants and aides-de-camp, and teased her great man of a "husband," who was amused by her jokes and liked her good humor. Was there something serious between them? Did he promise to divorce his wife and marry her if she gave him a child? Bourrienne says he did.[149] "Bellilotte" was his wife of the antipodes, his white negress, and the idea of returning to France with her probably never occurred to him. For he had not given up hope of soon returning to Toulon and France. He was convinced that Abukir had merely delayed his departure.[150] It was a matter of a few months, and if he was awaiting news from Europe with such impatience, it was because he feared he would return too late. He admits as much in a letter to the Directory written on December 17: "We are still without news from France . . . it is a strong need for our souls, for if the nation's glory needs us, we would be inconsolable not to be there."[151] But when he left Cairo on February 10, 1799, it was not to return to France, but to cross the Sinai and invade Syria.

NINETEEN

Jaffa

*T*he naval battle of Abukir had produced an international turnabout that was as complete as it was sudden. On the French side, it dissipated many an illusion. Three weeks earlier, Talleyrand had been saying that the French occupation of Egypt was going to strengthen the Franco-Ottoman alliance. He saw the French helping the Turks take Crimea back from the Russians and the Turks lending France a hand in the event of another war with Austria.[1] We would laugh at these fancies if they did not appear in a report that was supposed to define the main orientations of French diplomacy. A month later, not one line in this document was still valid. There remained nothing of Admiral Brueys's squadron, and the expeditionary corps sent to Ireland had surrendered. Disaster in Alexandria, failure in Ireland—and the collapse of the dream of a Mediterranean under French influence: the British were threatening Malta, the French were preparing to evacuate the Ionian islands, and the Neapolitans were taking up arms again and marching on Rome.[2] The Peace of Campoformio was doomed, and the way was open to the formation of a new coalition against France.

The Porte had known of France's designs on Egypt since the spring and had issued a warning: the occupation of one of its provinces would lead to a breakup of the alliance and a rapprochement with Britain. Some people said that the conflict could have been avoided if the Directory had had a representative in Constantinople who was "capable of negotiating in its name, informing the divan of the causes and objectives of the expedition to Egypt, soothing its irritation, and keeping it neutral."[3] Since the death of the ambassador, Aubert-Dubayet, in December 1797, France had been represented in Constantinople by a simple chargé d'affaires named Ruffin, who was "very well-informed about questions of the Orient."[4] It is not clear that someone else would have had more success. Nonetheless, fearing that Ruffin was not up to the task, the Directory had decided to send a special emissary to the sultan, and Talleyrand, as we have seen, had volunteered for the post.[5]

People have wondered about the behavior of the minister, who in the end never did leave his town house on Rue du Bac. Had Bonaparte been so insistent that Talleyrand ended up promising, but without any intention of keeping his promise? Or had he really considered, for a moment, leaving France? That is not impossible: as one of the five directors was replaced every year, it was usual that the departing director became a minister. Talleyrand, fearing that the departing director might have his heart set on Foreign Affairs, might then have asked to be named ambassador to Vienna or Constantinople; whence the commitment made to Bonaparte. But in the end the departing director, François de Neufchâteau, chose the Interior portfolio and Talleyrand kept his position. He no longer had any reason to leave France. Had he wanted to, the Directory would in any case have forbidden it. Relations with the United States had become so strained that a war was feared, and Talleyrand, who had lived in that country during the Terror, was considered to be *the* specialist on it; thus, his presence in Paris was judged indispensable. As for his successor as ambassador to Turkey, Descorches de Sainte-Croix, he did not leave either. The defeat at Abukir made the journey pointless. In Constantinople, where the news of Nelson's victory had arrived on August 12, French diplomats and residents had been interned. This time relations were broken off. On September 9 the Ottoman Empire officially declared war on France and opened talks with the British and the Russians.[6]

The Assault on Syria

As we have seen, in Cairo Bonaparte was unaware of what was going on in Paris or Constantinople; he had had no news since leaving Toulon. Had he believed in Talleyrand's promises? In any case, for several months he continued to ask about the progress of the minister's mission and, refusing to believe that Talleyrand had deceived him, wrote again on August 22 to "M. Talleyrand, Ambassador of the French Republic in Constantinople."[7] In October he finally had to face the facts: Talleyrand had not kept his promise.[8]

On the other hand, so far as Constantinople was concerned, Napoleon soon knew how matters stood. In his *Campagnes d'Égypte et de Syrie*, he implies that Talleyrand would have succeeded in his mission had he taken the trouble to go to Constantinople, because Selim III did not really want to break with France, for fear of becoming dependent on Russia. The sultan was prepared to lose Egypt, Napoleon says, as long as the French played by the rules. Selim even sent to Cairo "an official of the harem."[9] Held up in Alexandria, this "secretary of the vizier" finally left for Cairo only on September 3.[10] He is supposed to have made an agreement with the French, but according to Napoleon, when the Turk got back to Constantinople the Ottomans had decided to break with France and were getting ready to enter into an alliance with the British and the Russians.[11]

Bonaparte had understood that the defeat at Abukir, by striking a heavy blow to the prospects of the French enterprise, had greatly diminished the chances of an agreement with the Porte. As soon as he heard about the battle, he wrote to the Grand Vizier, the sherif of Mecca, and the pashas of Damas and Acre to assure them of his desire to be "on good terms."[12] Receiving no reply, he sent two emissaries to the governor of Acre: Jezzar refused to receive one of them, and later had the other killed. When the first of these messengers returned to Cairo on September 7, Bonaparte understood that it would be difficult, to say the least, to persuade the sultan to consent to the French occupation of Egypt. A few days later the previously mentioned Ottoman emissary came to see him, but he had left Constantinople with instructions that the battle of Abukir had made obsolete.

Several hostile Ottoman manifestos reached Bonaparte, and in October Turkish ships bombarded Alexandria. This time he knew where he stood. However, he made several further attempts to contact the Ottoman leaders. On November 9 he wrote to the Grand Vizier: "I repeat this third letter to let your Excellency know the French Republic's intention to be on good terms with the Sublime Porte."[13] But he was well aware that he would soon have to fight on three fronts: internally against the remains of the Mamluk armies, encouraged by Abukir to reject his peace offers; externally against the British, without having a squadron worthy of the name; and finally against the Turks, without any hope of receiving reinforcements. The Directory, confronted by the rapid deterioration of the situation in Europe, had decided to leave the expeditionary corps to its own resources: "You understand," it wrote to Bonaparte on November 4, 1798, "that so long as the Mediterranean is occupied by the English and the Russians, it will be impossible to establish regular communications with you and to send you reinforcements in men and munitions. . . . Hence you must, at least for the time being, make arrangements to be self-sufficient."[14] Bonaparte did not receive this letter until six months later, but he already knew that he was in a precarious situation. His journey to Suez, from which he returned on January 6, did not change his mind. On the contrary; there, on the shores of the Red Sea, he learned that the Ottomans were preparing a combined attack on Egypt, one army taking the land route—its vanguard had reached El-Arish, in the Sinai—and another coming by sea. He could not wait any longer. The situation was, moreover, favorable for launching an offensive: order reigned in Cairo, Desaix was completing the pacification of Upper Egypt—it was reported that Murad Bey was dead[15]—and an attack seemed all the less likely from that quarter because in India Tipû Sâhib and the Afghan leader Zahman Shah, who was marching on Delhi, were occupying the British forces. He decided to head for Syria. Bonaparte explained his decision in a letter sent to the Directory on the eve of his departure for the Sinai: "I have . . . three goals: (1) to ensure the conquest of Egypt by constructing a fortress on the other side of the desert [Bir Qatia], and then keeping armies of whatever nation so far from Egypt that they cannot join up with a European army that might land on the coasts; (2) to force the Porte to explain itself . . . ; (3) finally, to deprive the English fleet of the food supplies it gets from Syria (in Jaffa and Acre) by using the two months of winter that remain to me to make, by war and by negotiations, this whole coast favorable to us."[16]

Far more ambitious goals have been attributed to Bonaparte. He discusses them at length himself in his *Campagnes d'Égypte et de Syrie*, speaking of a march on the Indus starting from Damas, the plan for which is supposed to have been elaborated with such care that even the date of the operation's launch had been set, for "the autumn of 1799," so as to arrive "amid the Sikhs and Mahrattas," who were enemies of the British, by spring 1800. Napoleon states that he could easily have found the necessary 40,000 men in sub-Saharan Africa, Syria, and Lebanon. The Porte's hostile activities only delayed the execution of this vast project. The plan was to repel the Ottoman vanguard, take Acre, arm the Christians of Syria, and instigate an uprising of the Druze and Maronites so that he could still set out on the great adventure, make himself master of Damas in June 1799, and "arrive on the banks of the

Indus by March 1800."[17] Few historians have found credible these remarks made much later.[18] Were they vain dreams in which he indulged all the more willingly because the defeat at Abukir had narrowed the horizons around him? In Bourrienne's presence he had developed another plan: it was no longer a question of crossing Persia to reach India, but of marching on Constantinople and returning to France by way of Vienna: "I stir up and arm all of Syria. . . . I march on Damas and Aleppo. As I advance through the country, I enlarge my army with all the malcontents; I announce to the people the abolition of slavery and the tyrannical governments of the pashas. I arrive in Constantinople with armed masses. I overthrow the Turkish empire, I found in the Orient a new and great empire that will establish my place in posterity, and perhaps I shall return to Paris via Adrianople or Vienna, after having destroyed the House of Austria."[19]

Was he serious? Perhaps. After all, who could have imagined, three years earlier, that this young artillery general was soon going to reign over Egypt? No one could have sworn that circumstances would not one day lend themselves to his plans, however chimerical they might have looked in retrospect. Bonaparte himself didn't know where Fortune might lead him. He set out to learn the geography of Asia, just as he had studied with care maps of Egypt before leaving Paris. The British, who had long thought absurd the hypothesis of a French landing in Egypt, now believed Bonaparte capable of anything; forgetting Abukir, they feared that after Cairo he might set his heart on Calcutta.[20] For his part, Napoleon had certainly mentioned these distant expeditions to the directors before leaving Paris, and they allude to them in their instructions of November 4, 1798, where the government admits its inability to help the Army of the Orient, and offers its leader three options: "Remain in Egypt, creating there an establishment that is safe from attacks by the Turks . . . advance into India . . . finally, march toward Constantinople to meet the enemy that is threatening you."[21] There is perhaps another echo of these conversations: a curious article published in the *Moniteur* for November 19, in which Volney tried to imagine what Bonaparte was going to do. March on India? Volney did not believe that possible, or even useful: the fleet had been destroyed, India was far away, and its conquest would certainly not suffice to ruin England:

He will not budge from Egypt during the winter, and if he leaves in the spring, it will not be to go to India. He cannot do so by sea, he lacks ships, and the enemy, forewarned, is in a defensive posture. He can do so still less by land, because that route via the Euphrates, the deserts of Persia, and the Indus is a folly that not even a caravan of Arabs would undertake, and a French army demands more. Even if he could go by sea and by land, he would no longer want to, because events have changed his whole situation. The Abukir affair, the sultan's declaration of war, the entry of the Russians into the Mediterranean, their coalition with the English, which puts the Turkish fleet, and soon the city of Constantinople, in their hands, places Bonaparte in a new world of circumstances.[22]

On the other hand, he could very easily imagine Bonaparte returning to Europe via Turkey: "The theater of war must be brought back to Europe," Volney had Bonaparte say, "and since the Turk has imprudently raised his standard, it is in Constantinople that I want to tear it from his hands." He imagined Bonaparte entering the Turkish capital "in a whirlwind of cavalry" after having stirred up along the way the Arabs, Druze, Maronites, and even the Kurds, Armenians, and Persians. He saw him crossing the Bosporus, liberating Poland and wrenching Greece away from Muslim domination, threatening Russia on his right and Austria on his left, and finally forcing continental Europe to break with Britain.[23] This is a singular, even prophetic text, because the emperor's continental policy, around 1809 or 1810, would not be so different from the one Volney imagined in 1798. But with regard to the present situation, Volney neglected a factor that Bonaparte himself made central to his calculations: he was going to enter Palestine with only 13,000 men—even if they were elite troops.[24] The proof that he was not seriously considering an attack on the British in India, or seizing Constantinople, is that in his correspondence we find no allusion to plans of this kind: We have already quoted his letter to the Directory of February 10, 1799; a few days earlier he wrote to Desaix that his only goal was to "drive Ibrâhîm Bey out of the rest of Egypt, scatter the troops gathering in Gaza, and punish Jezzar for his bad behavior."[25] On April 8, when he was in front of Saint-Jean d'Acre, he again told Marmont that he expected, "in the next month, to be in Egypt and to have completely finished [the] operation in Syria."[26] That is the proof that Syria was his sole objective.[27] By this military demonstration, he sought only to impress the Ottomans and force them to enter negotiations. He may have had another motive: punishing Jezzar, the pasha of Acre. He later said that Jezzar had sent several men to Cairo to assassinate him, an attack that failed only because of the vigilance of the members of the divan.[28] That is why, while preparing for war, he sent to Constantinople an emissary, the astronomer Beauchamp, who was supposed to demand the liberation of French citizens and remind the sultan that the French had not come to Egypt with hostile intentions, but on the contrary in order "to punish the Mamluks and the English, and to prevent the partition of the Ottoman Empire that the two emperors (of Austria and Russia) had decided upon." The emissary was even authorized to mention the departure of the French as soon as the two sovereigns gave up the "project of dividing European Turkey."[29] Did Bonaparte still believe in the possibility of an arrangement? Beauchamp had left Alexandria when Bonaparte set out for Syria. Nothing was ever heard from his messenger; captured by the British and handed over to the Turks, he was interned.

The general had another reason for wanting to undertake only a limited campaign. He intended to be back in Cairo before summer, so that he could either repel a landing that seemed unlikely during the winter months or leave for France if war resumed in Europe. In October he had already informed the Directory that if he learned "that the continent [was] not yet pacified," he "would resolve to go."[30] He had in fact just received news from France, the first since his arrival in Cairo. He was getting ready to rejoin the army when the arrival of two French businessmen was announced; they were coming from Trieste after a long journey of three months. Bonaparte knew one of them well, Romain Hamelin, a former war representative in Italy who was a friend of Joséphine's. He received him on February 8. Since Hamelin had sailed in October, what he knew he had learned by chance in the ports of call: it was said that the Neapolitans were marching on Rome and that Corfu was under a Russo-Turkish blockade.[31] Was France at war with Naples, Russia, and Turkey? Hamelin's report was not very precise, and often false.[32] The day after this conversation Bonaparte confided to Marmont, "Citizen Hamelin arrived yesterday; I found a great deal of contradiction in everything he learned en route, and I find not very credible all the news he brought."[33] Nonetheless, he wrote to the Directory, in code: "If, in the course of March, Citizen Hamelin's report is confirmed and France is in arms against the kings, I shall come to France."[34] The next day, having entrusted the command of the army to General Dugua, he left to rejoin the troops that had set out for the Sinai on February 6.

The Crossing of the Sinai

They were moving fast: three days had sufficed to cross the Sinai from west to east and reach El-Arish, where the first Ottoman forces were barring the way to Palestine. The vanguard had even advanced so fast that its leader, General Reynier, did not see the following division, Kléber's, arrive until February 14. Thinking himself then strong enough not to wait for the bulk of the troops, he gave the order to attack the enemy fortifications constructed in front of the fort. The attackers routed the Ottomans. Thanks to Reynier's initiative, the French army was no longer in danger of being flanked and cut off from its bases; it now had only to attack the fort, which would capitulate sooner or later, and enter into Palestine without further delay. However, Bonaparte upbraided Reynier when he arrived on February 17, accusing him of having unnecessarily put his men in danger. He did not like Reynier, Moreau's former chief of staff, whom he had added to the expedition only on Desaix's recommendation. He liked still less Kléber, who had seconded Reynier during the February 14 assault. The tension reflected a continuing deterioration of his relations with his generals, which had been bad ever since the landing in Alexandria. The decision to invade Syria had further poisoned them; the majority of the superior officers did not understand why Bonaparte insisted on it rather than negotiating the expeditionary corps' return to France. Not without reason, Kléber was considered the leader of the malcontents. He had not pardoned Bonaparte for having assigned him in July to the command of Alexandria, which he considered an "exile" and a disgrace. Wasn't he first of all a fighter? He refused to be transformed into a bureaucrat! Moreover, Kléber had quickly seen how thankless the task was: Bonaparte left him without instructions, and even worse without funds. The letters in which he asked for money and orders remained unanswered, as did his requests for a transfer. Bonaparte eventually snapped, accusing Kléber of poor management and reminding him that he had to obey orders, like everyone else.[35] The Alsatian, who was not impressed by the Corsican, replied tartly: "You forgot, when you wrote that letter, that you held history's chisel in your hand, and that you were writing to Kléber"—and he slammed the door.[36] Bonaparte, while pretending to regret this "misunderstanding," did not forgive it.[37] Although he forgave everything to those who had done him the slightest favor, he was vindictive toward soldiers he thought had wronged him (he scorned civilians too much to hold a grudge against them for long). The revolt in Cairo led to a reconciliation, but only an apparent one. In private Bonaparte was already sketching the falsely flattering portrait of his subordinate that is found in the texts he wrote on Saint Helena, concealing beneath the praise awarded "the handsomest man in the army"[38] insinuations concerning his honesty and his talent.[39] Kléber for his part wrote to his friends and in the notebook that never left his pocket his poor opinion, all the more pronounced now that he saw him every day, of the "so-called" great man:

> At the age of eighteen, he thought himself a great man; when that happens, a person rarely becomes one. There are men who have to be judged only by their achievements; they would lose everything if the means by which they arrived at them were scrutinized, B*** is one of these. Turenne won his glory because he fought against Montecuculli, the greatest general of the century. B*** obtained his fame by fighting against the most imbecilic generals the House of Austria had. . . . Is he liked? How could he be? He doesn't like anyone; but he thinks he can make up for that by creating creatures by promotions and presents. . . . He knows neither how to organize nor how to administer, and yet, wanting to do everything, he organizes and administers. The result is disorder, waste of all kinds; and hence, absolute deprivation, this poverty even amid abundance.—Never a set plan, everything goes by fits and starts, the day settles the day's affairs. He claims to believe in fatality.

Farther on, however, we find this admission: "What is his greatest quality, then? Because, after all, he is an extraordinary man. [This quality] is to dare and dare again, and in this art he goes so far as temerity."[40] Did Bonaparte fear Kléber, his outspokenness, his anger, his ascendancy over the troops? The fact remains that at El-Arish, not daring to attack the Alsatian, he showered abuse on Reynier. But the latter, perhaps encouraged by Kléber, fought back; he even put his response in writing.[41] Bonaparte feared a scene and preferred not to reply, but he did sanction Reynier by moving him from the vanguard to the rearguard. These disputes did not bode well for future operations. Most of the generals involved in the venture doubted it would be successful, as did many soldiers, who had lost all hope of ever seeing their country again, to the point that they responded with almost complete indifference to the sacrifices demanded of them and the dangers that threatened them. When Kléber's division mutinied a few days later, it was because it lacked water, but Bonaparte, suspecting its leader of having stirred up his men, could not restrain himself. He blew up: "You won't remedy your ills by mutinying!" he shouted. "At worst, it would be better to stick your heads in the sand and die with honor than to yield to disorder!"[42]

The quarrels in El-Arish left their mark. Reynier was champing at the bit and joined the rearguard, but Bonaparte, now fearing that his generals might be hatching some plot behind his back, gave up the idea of taking the initiative without waiting for the fall of the fort at El-Arish; he decided that rather than begin a siege that could go on for a long time, he would offer the besieged forces generous conditions in exchange for their capitulation. He proposed that the Turkish commander lead his men to Egypt, whence they would be sent back to the Ottoman port of their choice, provided that it was not in Syria. He also promised to let the thirty principal officers of the garrison keep their weapons and even withdraw into Syria after they had promised to no longer fight against the French.[43] The Turkish commander still refused the French offers, and the artillery went into action, bombarding the fort while Bonaparte sent the Ottomans a final offer: in exchange for their capitulation and the surrender of their weapons—the thirty leaders still being authorized to keep theirs—the garrison could withdraw either to Egypt or to Baghdad if they promised to no longer take part in the current war.[44] The fort capitulated on the evening of February 20:

"We . . . agree to hand over to you the fort of El-Arish; we will travel over the desert to Baghdad. We are sending you the list of the Agas of the fort, who promise you under oath, for themselves and for their troops, to no longer serve in Jezzar's army, and not to go to Syria for one year counting from today. We will receive from you a safe-conduct and a flag. We will leave in the castle all the provisions that are there."[45]

Did the French fail to keep their promise? Henry Laurens says they did, mentioning the disarmament of the 1,100 men of the garrison.[46] But this was stipulated by the terms of the surrender. On the other hand, the forced enlistment in the French ranks of a few hundred Mahgrebins and the return to Egypt of soldiers who were natives of that country, which had not been previously mentioned, could indeed be interpreted by the Ottomans as a violation of the agreements.[47] The vanquished withdrew and had hardly arrived in Syria before they violated their own oaths and rejoined Jezzar's troops in Jaffa.[48] Had they really intended to stop fighting? And did they, anyway, have a choice? As for those who were enlisted, they soon deserted. Having taken control of the crucial fortress of El-Arish, Bonaparte moved on, and leaving Africa, entered Asia. The landscape changed: the stony desert of the Sinai had given way to more attractive horizons, and on approaching Gaza one would have thought, Bonaparte said, that one was near Béziers (where he had never set foot).[49] The weather had also changed: now there was heavy rain, day and night, without respite. The sky was dark, the wind whipped the sea into waves "as high as mountains."[50] It was cold, the men sank up to their hips in the mud, horses and camels died by the dozens. A brief skirmish on February 24 sufficed to take Gaza, where supplies of powder and food were found in large quantities. The rain still had not stopped when the army set out again on the twenty-eighth. By way of Ramla—where it found once again great stores of provisions left behind by the Turks—it headed for Jaffa. These were no longer landscapes like those of Languedoc but rather "an immense plain covered with hills of moving sand" (a "lake of mud," one soldier said) where moving forward was as difficult for the men as it was for the animals, permanently threatened by "parties of Arabs" who were harassing the army.[51] On March 3, Kléber's and Murat's men finally arrived within sight of the little fortified port of Jaffa, located at the seaside in a setting of "delicious and quite varied" greenery.[52]

The city, most of whose population was Christian, was an important stopover on the road to Acre: if the enemy seized it, he could land troops behind the French rearguard. The French had to take control of it if they wanted to maintain their line of communication with Egypt and receive reinforcements. Moreover, it was at Jaffa that Bonaparte was to rendezvous with Admiral Perrée who was conveying, with three frigates that had escaped at Abukir, the heavy equipment needed to besiege Saint-Jean d'Acre. Jaffa was built on a hill shaped like a sugar cube and crowned with a small citadel surrounded by a crenellated wall without a moat, only four meters high and not more than a meter thick—hardly more than a "garden wall," as Volney put it.[53] It was defended by several thousand well-armed janissaries, but despite several vigorous sorties, they were unable to prevent the French from occupying the fortress. On March 7, the defenders having refused to lay down their arms and a breach having been made, the French attacked.

The Massacre

It was in this countryside planted with wine grapes and shaded by fig, apricot, and almond trees but soaked by the storms, that one of the most tragic episodes of the Egyptian campaign occurred. After heavy fighting, "the Lannes division . . . entered the streets, massacring everyone who tried to stop it." At the same time the Bon division was arriving at the port: "The whole army rushed into the city with a fury that is difficult to describe."[54] The mathematician Malus was there: "The soldiers . . . were slaughtering men, women, old men, children, Christians, Turks; anything with a human face fell victim to their fury. The tumult of the carnage, the broken-in doors, the houses shaken by the sound of fire and weapons, the screams of the women, the husband and the child tumbled one on the other, the daughter raped on her mother's body, the smoke of the dead burned by their clothing, the smell of blood, the moans of the wounded, the cries of the victors fighting over the spoils of an expiring prey, the furious soldiers responding to the cries of despair with cries of rage and redoubled blows . . . that was the spectacle offered by this unfortunate city until night came."[55]

lives. There was formed, since it has to be said, a terrible pyramid of dead and dying men dripping blood, and the bodies of those who had already expired had to be moved aside in order to finish off the unfortunates who, being protected by this dreadful, frightful rampart, had not yet been struck. This description is exact and faithful, and memory makes tremble my hand that does not render all its horror.[66]

No one denies that this episode was one of the cruelest in Bonaparte's life.[67] It is less clear whether it should be described as a crime, according to Bonaparte's own definition—"in war as in politics, every evil, even if it abides by the rules, is excusable only insofar as it is absolutely necessary: everything else is a crime."[68]

The soldiers, most of whom were in favor of the execution, referred to the "laws of war," but the *droit des gens*, which tried to subject relations between states to common rules and customs, was not as clear as they claimed. Let us examine, for instance, Vattel's treatise, one of those most widely read in the eighteenth century.[69] The philosopher conceded that in war, necessity is law. A state that is waging a "just" war can use every means to disarm the enemy, if necessary by killing him. The principle, however, was quickly limited: killing the enemy, Vattel explained, is conceivable only in the heat of action, never when he has "laid down his arms." Bonaparte's defenders can object that at Jaffa this was not the case for the enemy, because it had refused to lay down its arms and had even killed the emissary who had come to propose an armistice. Perhaps the garrison thereby fell under the exception made by Vattel: "There is, however, one case in which one may refuse to spare an enemy who surrenders . . . that is when this enemy has been guilty of some enormous violation against the *droit des gens*, and in particular when he has violated the laws of war."[70] But the philosophy of the age of Enlightenment did not imagine that, to punish a crime ultimately imputable to the supreme leader of an army, ordinary soldiers would be condemned to death—soldiers whose only offense was to have obeyed their superiors' orders.[71] Was a mass execution consequently inexcusable?

Bonaparte had invoked this same law of war when, in order to force the commander of El-Arish to surrender, he wrote him that "among all peoples, the garrison of a conquered city must be killed."[72] Did the unwritten law of war authorize putting to death soldiers whose sole crime was, ultimately, that they had obeyed orders and done their duty? Vattel said it did not, but on this point he was far in advance of his time. He was aware of this, saying that the "so-called law of war" authorizing the mass execution of a whole garrison" had "not [yet] been entirely abandoned."[73] The proof of this is the letter we have just quoted, addressed to the commander of El-Arish. Is more proof desired? Consider the debate on the defense and surrender of fortresses conducted in the Legislative Assembly in July 1792, in which the representatives, not being able to imagine that the soldiers of a free country might capitulate before having been attacked by the enemy, wanted to prohibit, on pain of death, surrendering the fortress "before there has been an accessible and practicable breach [in the defenses]": several speakers pointed out that such a rule was to be imposed only in fortresses that had an interior retrenchment in which the defenders and inhabitants could take shelter, because "every time that a fortress is taken by assault the law of war calls for . . . not only the garrison, but even all the inhabitants be put to death."[74] And the speaker—it was Carnot's brother—even cited the sad examples of Bergen-op-Zoom in 1747 and Ochakov in 1789.[75]

Vattel, who was so concerned to protect the rights of the defeated, nonetheless allowed one major exception to the rules he was trying to promote, and it almost looks like it foresaw Jaffa: "When one has such a large number of prisoners that it is impossible to feed them, or to guard them securely, does one have the right to put them to death, or must one send them back to strengthen the enemy, at the risk of being overwhelmed by them on another occasion? Today, the matter is not difficult: these prisoners are released on parole, imposing on them the rule that they must not take up arms again until a certain time or until the end of the war."[76]

Bonaparte had chosen clemency after El-Arish was taken, releasing the prisoners on the condition that they promised to return to Damas without going through Jaffa or Acre. But the day after the conquest of Jaffa, it was perceived that several hundred of the captured fighters were men who had been paroled at El-Arish and had come to reinforce the Jaffa garrison. They could not be released a second time without danger: "These men will immediately go to Saint-Jean d'Acre to reinforce the pasha," Bonaparte is said to have told Bourrienne, "or else they will go into the mountains of Nablus, do a great deal of damage to our rearguard and our right flank, and kill us for the price of the life that we have left them." If freeing them would have been irresponsible, another solution was to deport them to Egypt. Bonaparte was not against this solution: he allowed 500 janissaries who had come from Egypt to benefit from it, assigning a battalion to escort them as far as Gaza, where forty camels took them the rest of the way. But from the repatriation of these Egyptians we cannot conclude that it would have been possible to deport 3,000 prisoners. Although the former were unlikely to resist—they were going home—could the same be said about the latter, most of whom were from Albania? And then, how many men would have to be assigned to this transport, which would necessarily be over land, because there were no available ships and because the sea, in any case, was no longer free. One witness insists that it was only when Bonaparte had realized that mass deportation was impossible, that he resigned himself to killing the prisoners.[77] But, it will be said, given that they could be neither released nor deported, couldn't they be incorporated into the French regiments? This could hardly be done; it is difficult to imagine the French putting any trust in "such comrades" who had already broken their promise—or, in any case, how they could be fed. Benoist-Méchin, who is very critical of Bonaparte's conduct, objects that large quantities of food had been found in Gaza, Ramla, and now Jaffa: no less that 400,000 rations and 2,000 quintals of rice.[78] Enough to feed the prisoners, he says. But if the French had found food supplies, that did not mean that they always would, and the problem was all the graver because Bonaparte had given insufficient attention to supplies. Finally, there was the matter of hygiene. On March 6, three deaths attributed to the plague were recorded; five more the following day, and six the day after that.[79] The appearance of plague was not a surprise: it had been raging since late autumn in the Nile Delta, where it had already killed more than 200 men.[80] Bodies encumbered the ramparts and the streets of Jaffa, causing concern, of course, about the rapid spread of the disease. The overpopulation occasioned by the surrender of these 3,000 men did nothing to improve the situation. If Bonaparte had read Vattel, he could have referred to another passage to justify the extermination of the prisoners: "When our security is incompatible with that of an enemy, even one who has surrendered, there is no choice."[81] Not enough food, too few soldiers, no ships, a perfidious enemy, the beginning of an epidemic—in his view, that was enough to silence the scruples that his promise to let the soldiers live might have inspired in him. The betrayal of the fighters of El-Arish was his soundest argument.[82] He thought he could infer from the conduct of the men paroled at Jaffa that these prisoners would behave similarly, and punish them, not as guilty, but as potentially guilty. His first duty as the leader of the army, Marmont insists in his memoirs, was to preserve it; as the general, the blood of even one of his men had to be more important to him than "that of a thousand enemies." Moral objections? "False philanthropy," Marmont replies.[83] Cheap sentimentality, Stendhal adds. The most convinced of the apologists for the massacre at Jaffa asserts that in this circumstance Bonaparte behaved as a "father" to his army, applying to its benefit the old Roman maxim *Salus populi suprema lex esto*: "To save his army, does a general have the right to put his prisoners to death, or to put them [his soldiers] in a situation that will necessarily lead to their deaths, or to hand them over to barbarians from whom they can expect no mercy? Among the Romans, there would have been no question about that. . . . What is most certain is that the necessity has to be clear and urgent, and it cannot be denied that there was necessity in the case of Jaffa. It would not have been wise to release the prisoners on parole."[84]

Most contemporaries agreed that Jaffa responded to a "horrible necessity."[85] But it will be said that the general did not execute his prisoners solely because he feared that releasing them would increase his enemies' power. He also did it because the Egyptian campaign, its violence, and the enemy's cruelty had accustomed him, and not him alone, to quick solutions. Even if Bonaparte tried to contain violence, it seems clear that in Egypt the French did not accord life, including that of their compatriots, the same value that it was accorded in Europe. Some people accuse Bonaparte, even before the Syrian campaign, of having soldiers who showed signs of the plague strangled.[86] Others say that the execution of the prisoners was not the only massacre perpetrated in Jaffa: Bonaparte is also supposed to have executed an unknown number of women the soldiers had seized by force, taken into the camp, and subjected to an odious trafficking. We do not know whether this claim is authentic, but some have said that Bonaparte, seeing only the disorders that these unfortunate women caused entirely in spite of themselves, decided that their elimination was once again the simplest way of putting an end to these disturbances.[87]

But let us come back to the prisoners in Jaffa. They were not put to death solely because "it was more convenient," but also "to produce an effect."[88] Bonaparte hoped to spread such terror that it would dissuade the enemy from continuing the fight. The massacre of the garrison at Jaffa was also a message addressed to the garrison at Acre: "Lay down your arms or you will all die." In all that, Bonaparte was convinced he was acting in conformity with local mores. There was no lack of precedents. Notably, just fifteen years earlier Abû al-Dâhâb, a Mamluk chieftain who had tried to conquer Syria after assassinating his protector Alî Bey, had ordered the massacre of the garrison and the inhabitants of Jaffa after more than forty days of siege.[89] The proclamation Bonaparte addressed to the inhabitants of Gaza, Ramla, and Jaffa on March 9, while blood was still being shed, testifies to the same intention: "You should know that all human efforts are useless against me, for everything I undertake must succeed. Those who declare themselves to be my friends prosper. Those who declare themselves my enemies perish. The example that has just occurred in Jaffa and in Gaza should make you understand that if I am terrible to my enemies, I am generous to my friends, and especially clement and merciful for the poor people."[90]

The strategy of terror is not an Oriental specialty, and Bonaparte could have taken his inspiration from many precedents drawn from European history, even if we have to go back to the wars of the reign of Louis XIV to find a case comparable to that of Jaffa. Like the massacres at Swammerdam and Bodegrave in Holland, which were wiped off the map by Marshal Luxembourg in 1672, the execution at Jaffa was an example made—in part—in cold blood.[91] Did it attain its objectives? It is not easy to say. In Saint-Jean d'Acre, the effect of the massacre in Jaffa was to galvanize the resistance of the men in the garrison, who preferred to fight on to the end, running the risk of a *possible* death, rather than surrender and thus see themselves doomed to a death they believed to be *certain*.[92] On the other hand, at Abukir a few months later, the same feeling of terror felt by the Ottoman soldiers led them to throw themselves into the sea in order to escape the French, thus giving Bonaparte the victory.[93]

In the end, the effects of the massacre in Jaffa were above all deferred. Whatever its necessity, this mass execution had shown what Bonaparte was capable of. His hand had not trembled as he ordered the prisoners put to death. He made it clear, should any have doubted, that he would not shrink from any shedding of blood he considered necessary. Perhaps we must see in this terrible episode what allowed him later on to govern France by means that were essentially moderate. He no longer needed to demonstrate that he could be brutal, so much did the memory of Jaffa suffice to disarm many of his rivals and opponents.

The Wonder-Working General

On March 11, the day after the execution of the prisoners, Bonaparte visited the soldiers who were ill with what the surgeon Larrey still called "the prevailing sickness."[94] Growing more numerous every day, they had been gathered together in a monastery transformed into a makeshift hospital.[95] Despite the denials of the superior officers—the doctors themselves did not agree as to the nature of the disease—concern was growing along with the number of the sick and dead. Bonaparte, wanting to reassure the troops and persuade them that they could avoid contagion by means of "moral courage" alone, decided to go to see the sick men.[96] In Gros's painting, which won "enormous success" at the Salon of 1804, Bonaparte, accompanied by Generals Berthier and Bessières (one of them pressing a handkerchief to his mouth), the chief ordnance officer Daure, and the physician Desgenettes, touches the buboes of a patient who is standing up, half naked.[97] Beside him, a moribund soldier is being bandaged by a kneeling Turkish doctor; in the foreground, another sick man is succumbing, lying on the knees of Masselet, a young French surgeon who was a friend of Gros's and was soon to be carried off himself by the disease. Desgenettes is holding Bonaparte's arm, trying to pull him away. On the left side of the picture, we see other sick men lying on the floor. The imploring eyes of the ill reply to the terror shown by the general-in-chief's entourage. We have three accounts of this visit: Bourrienne says that Bonaparte took care not to touch any of the sick men, and limited himself to passing through the halls, "lightly striking the yellow cuff of his boot with the riding crop he held in his hand."[98] Desgenettes describes a bolder Bonaparte:

> The general-in-chief, followed by his staff, came to visit the hospitals. . . . The general walked through the two hospitals, spoke to almost all the soldiers who could hear him, and spent more than an hour and a half examining all the details of a good and prompt administration; finding himself in a small and very crowded room, he helped lift up the hideous cadaver of a soldier whose ragged clothes were soiled by the opening up of an abscessed bubo. After having tried to gently urge the general-in-chief back toward the door, I explained to him that staying any longer was becoming more than useless. This did not prevent it from being

frequently grumbled in the army that I should have more forcefully opposed such a prolonged visit by the general-in-chief: anyone who believes that there are easy ways of changing his mind or intimidating him by a few dangers know little about him.[99]

As for the ordnance officer Daure, he wrote that "with the help of a Turkish nurse, General Bonaparte lifted up and carried away a plague victim who was lying across the door of one of the halls."[100] This news soon made its way around the camp and seemed to all to be of "a deep policy."[101] Above all, it was enriched with details that, though not necessarily false, are not attested by any direct witness: Bonaparte, it is repeatedly said, touched "the principal sick men," and went so far as to press a bubo to extract the pus from it: Detroye reports this as a certain fact, and Geoffroy Saint-Hilaire, who had not left Cairo, repeats it in a letter to his father dated June 23, 1799.[102] Through this act, from which Gros took his inspiration and which rapidly entered into the legend,[103] this visit acquired another meaning. In visiting the plague victims, Bonaparte was not just a general who was trying to keep his army from succumbing to panic, even if that was his initial intention, but a leader who was manifesting superior, even superhuman powers.[104]

One has to admit that it took a certain audacity simply to go to the sickbeds of these dying men. Goethe, discussing the scene with Eckermann, saw in it the very paradigm of everything the will is capable of. Bonaparte's will was so strong, and fear so alien to his soul, he explains, that he ran the risk of contagion with the imprudence of the unaware, but certain that the danger diminished "when one is capable of triumphing over fear": "It is incredible what power the moral will has in such cases. It penetrates the body, and puts it into a state of activity that repels hurtful influences. Fear, on the other hand, is a state of indolent weakness and susceptibility, which makes it easy for every foe to take possession. This Napoleon knew well, and he felt that he risked nothing in giving his army an imposing example."[105]

Inaccessible to evil, he "touched" the plague victims as kings used to touch the scrofulous.[106] He was walking in the steps of St. Louis, who on this same Oriental soil had buried with his own hands the victims of various epidemics.[107] The scene of Bonaparte's visit to the plague victims in Jaffa reproduces, more or less, the one Joinville describes: "King Louis helped bury the dead with his own hands. Hardly could anyone be found who wanted to touch them. The king came to the place every morning after his mass, for the five days it took to bury the dead, and he said to his people: 'Let us go bury the martyrs who have suffered for Our Lord, and do not be wearied of doing this, because they have suffered more than we have.' There were present, in ceremonial garments, the archbishop of Tyre and the bishop of Damietta and their clergy, who were saying the service for the dead. But they stopped up their noses because of the stench; but the good king Louis was never seen to stop his, so firmly and devoutly did he do it."[108]

In Jaffa, in the Holy Land, Bonaparte's act revived in his soldiers memories from a childhood in which religious matters had a place they had perhaps forgotten. Perhaps then they recalled the Scriptures and the leper imploring Jesus: "If you will, you can make me clean," and Christ replying: "I will; be thou made clean."[109] Each evening, in this city full of the putrefying bodies of the soldiers and the inhabitants killed during the assault, Monge pulled a Bible from his pocket and read from the Gospels, while the oldest of the soldiers, who had formerly been educated by priests, "sang Jeremiah's canticles and lamentations."[110] The two scenes of the massacre and the visit to the plague victims, which are symbolically strong, complement each other. One is inseparable from the other: Bonaparte inflicts death, and the next day he defies it and promises healing. Deliberate or not, it is a late and singular imitation of the ritual that attested to the sacred origin of the royalty and contributed to the assertion of the king's sovereign authority over the barons and other great lords who were sometimes more rich and powerful than he was.[111] The healing power attributed to the king was the complement of the power of judging and punishing: the two sides of sovereignty.

The emperor's entourage always refused to mention events such as the massacre that nonetheless played a major role in his ascension; they wanted the ascent of their idol not to be sullied by any crime or moral violation. Doctor O'Meara, having succeeded, after many efforts, in leading General Bertrand onto this slippery terrain, got this response: "Napoleon arrived at the summit of human greatness by upright means, and without having committed any private action that morals might disavow. In this respect, his elevation is unique in history; for in order to reign themselves, David destroyed the house of Saul, his benefactor; Caesar destroyed the government of his fatherland; Cromwell caused his master to die on the scaffold; Catherine II had her husband murdered."[112]

In his *Napoleon* (1921), Élie Faure points out that three "crimes against public morals" punctuated Bonaparte's march toward supreme power: first, Jaffa; then 18 Brumaire; and finally, the execution of the Duke of Enghien.[113] If the last two "crimes" raised Bonaparte above his contemporaries by giving him respectively the Consulate and the Empire, it was the first that made the others possible: the Bonaparte of Jaffa was not yet *above the others*, but he was already alone, *separated from the others* by the "crime" that he had just committed. It was because he was henceforth *apart* that he could, finally, dare to overthrow what was most sacred in the Revolution: the figure of the Law. This separation from others assuredly has its origin in his consciousness of his own genius, and in the recognition of it by those whom he commanded. But the "crime" of Jaffa also contributed to it. From that day onward, he became "a being more apart from men."[114] In this respect, Jaffa not only preceded 18 Brumaire but made it possible. In Jaffa, Bonaparte experienced *the other side of things*. Now he was ready.

TWENTY

The Return from the Orient

*B*onaparte arrived under the walls of Acre on March 19, 1799, and abandoned the siege sixty-two days later, on May 21, without entering the fortress. Kléber summed up the episode in a cruel but accurate remark: "We attacked in the Turkish manner a fortress defended in the European manner."[1] It is not one of the military splendors of Napoleonic history. For two months, Bonaparte persisted, despite repeated failures, in directing his attacks on one of the best-defended points of the ramparts that protected the city, which Caffarelli had indicated to him.[2] After a week devoted to laying the groundwork, he ordered the first assault on March 28:

> Twelve light field guns and four mortars set up as a battery began to bombard a tower that was located in the middle of the enemy's defensive line. At three in the afternoon, the breach appeared to be practicable, and the grenadiers demanded an assault with such insistence that we were obliged to yield to their wishes. They rushed forward; but to their great astonishment they found, ten feet from the breach, a moat fifteen feet wide, with a good counterscarp whose existence had not even been suspected. This unexpected obstacle only slowed the movement of the French troops without diminishing their ardor. Ladders were put in place, the grenadiers descended into the moat; a few of them reached the breach. On their approach, a movement of terror had gripped the besieged. They were already abandoning the tower to flee toward the port; but seeing that they were not being pursued, they returned, led by Jezzar. The grenadiers had not been able to take the advantage of this first movement that it was so important to seize. When they arrived at the breach, they had found it ten feet high, and the troops commanded to support them had stopped before the fatal moat, for lack of means to cross it. Struck down by fire from the fortress, crushed by

a rain of stones, grenades, and flaming materials that were thrown on them from the top of the tower, they retreated, trembling with disappointment, into the covered path.[3]

The tone was set. The Ottomans, who up to that point had thought the French invincible, were taking heart and trying to make vigorous sorties, but Bonaparte had learned nothing from this first failure. On April 1, Lannes resumed the assault, with no more success. The general-in-chief sent his troops against the walls of Acre seven more times. The duel turned into a slaughter. The French used the bodies strewn in the trenches as a rampart.[4] Each side shot, skewered, butchered the other. "It's death, always death," Miot was to say.[5] On May 7 the attackers finally thought success was within reach. On that day Lannes broke through the first line of fortifications. But the time when the Ottomans would have fled was past. Led by Jezzar, they threw the attackers back beyond the walls. Two days later Kléber made two more attempts; he was disgusted by so much blood shed for nothing and full of indignation against the man he called the "ten thousand men a day" general.[6] This time it was over; there was no longer any hope of taking Acre by force. That evening Bonaparte gave the order to retreat.

The Failure at Acre

It is hard to recognize at Acre the officer who, at Toulon, had immediately discerned the cracks in the enemy defenses. Here it was the contrary. Why so much blindness and obstinacy? Had his easy successes at El-Arish, Gaza, and even Jaffa blinded him? Was he mistaken about the consequences of the massacre at Jaffa, thinking that he had terrified the enemy to the point of making him incapable of fighting, whereas in reality fear had increased his combativeness? Did he believe that "the crenelated towers, the squat bastions and covered paths," Acre's fortifications, which were in fact poorly maintained, would be incapable of resisting him for a long time because Volney, in his account of his journey to the Orient, had declared them indefensible?[7] Was he seeking, at whatever price, an exploit suitable to ornament his legend—he who had just told a stunned

Kléber that he lived only to fill the pages of history with his name?[8] Had he underestimated Jezzar and the support the British were providing him?

He had certainly understood that the battle would be more complicated than foreseen. Acre was covered by the fire of two British ships that his own flotilla, formed of ships that had escaped at Abukir, was incapable of attacking, so it was impossible to land materiel and artillery near the French camp. The proof? The ships that were supposed to carry them as far as Haifa had not been able to turn around soon enough, and the British had stopped and boarded them, so that the French began the siege without heavy artillery.[9] They had to wait more than a month for a new convoy to deliver to Jaffa cannons that were then towed to Acre.[10] By then it was too late for this reinforcement to reverse the course of events. The siege began badly, then, without cannons or munitions in sufficient quantities; whereas, thanks to the protection provided by the British ships, the Ottomans were receiving reinforcements, food supplies, and munitions. But Bonaparte refused to give up. He was not unaware that Jezzar, having had Christian inhabitants of Acre suspected of colluding with the French strangled and thrown into the sea, had called for a holy war.[11] But he also knew that the Shi'ites of Lebanon had risen up against the "Butcher" of Acre, and in addition he believed he could rally to his cause the Druze in the Chouf mountains, Maronite Christians, and Shi'ites in the Bekaa valley. He cajoled their chieftains, hoping to convince them not to limit themselves to making money by supplying his army with food, but also to further commit themselves by putting their militias at his disposal. The failure of the first assaults toward the end of March thwarted his calculations. The Ottomans regained their courage; the Lebanese chieftains decided it might be wiser to wait and see how things developed before taking sides.[12] As for the British, who had at first been skeptical about their allies' combativeness, after Jezzar's resistance they decided to come to his aid.[13]

History has recorded the names of two of the advisors who were active around Jezzar: Phélippeaux, a former schoolmate of Bonaparte's at the École militaire, who, once he was on site, had the fortified wall doubled before falling ill and dying during the siege; and Sidney Smith, who was to play such an important though underestimated role in Bonaparte's ascension. After a nomadic and adventurous youth—he had joined the Royal Navy while still very young, and then served under the king of Sweden and the Turkish sultan—Smith had returned to his homeland to take part in the battle against revolutionary France. At Toulon his path crossed Bonaparte's for the first time. Deliberately ignoring his superiors' orders, he set fire to the French ships at anchor in the harbor. He fell into the hands of his enemies two years later, when his ship was sailing up the Seine under the fire of French batteries. Imprisoned in the Temple and despairing of being released or exchanged someday, at the end of 1797 he sought intercession from the hero of the moment. Bonaparte turned a deaf ear to him, not out of hostility but because it was said that the Englishman was a spy. On April 24, 1798, Smith himself put an end to this not very amusing chapter in his life by making a spectacular escape with the aid of several émigrés, including Phélippeaux. On May 10, while the Army of the Orient was preparing to sail from Toulon, Smith returned to London, where the people and the king himself gave him a triumphal welcome. In July he was given command of the *Tiger* and ordered to go to Constantinople to work on Anglo-Ottoman rapprochement, with a twofold military and diplomatic mandate that gave him full control over the organization of the struggle against the French. Nelson, who did not like this rather unruly officer, was furious, but he had to give in. It was fortunate that he did, because Smith, a specialist in bold and risky strikes, showed at Acre that he also had a leader's temperament and even a strategist's qualities.[14]

Once the British had entered the fray, a kind of routine was established. The British and the Ottomans constructed new defensive works, while the French dug trenches and subterranean passages; the two sides sent volleys of bullets at one another, and from time to time the besieged attempted a sortie that the attackers repelled after heavy hand-to-hand fighting. During the intervals there was a kind of truce: the men talked from one camp to the other, and Sidney Smith is even supposed to have received Junot and Kléber on board the *Tiger*.[15] It was a siege like so many others, with its deadly monotony and its phases of inaction. Bonaparte detested this kind of war, which left no room for improvisation and still less for imagination, where everything went according to rules as in the theater, where the besieged knew what was going to happen, even if they didn't know when the adversary would act or what the outcome of the conflict would be. The confrontation could last for weeks, even months.

The diversion came from Galilee, where soldiers, most of them from the Nablus region, and contingents raised in Damascus were gathering. Kléber, sent to see what was happening, tried to rout the enemy by cutting off its line of retreat toward Damascus. This imprudent act could have had serious consequences—by making this turning movement on the enemy's rear, Kléber might have been cut off from Acre himself if Bonaparte and General Bon's division, which had left Acre on April 15, had not come to his rescue and driven the Turks back toward the Jordan. The mood in the French camp was so morose that the victory won near Mount Tabor helped lift—temporarily—the troops' morale. This brief stay in the cradle of Christianity had at least the advantage of allowing Bonaparte to quit his "Islamic disguise"[16] and don for a few hours that of the Crusader. He attended a mass, kneeling in the convent of the Récollets, glared at those of his officers who sniggered when a priest took them to the grotto where the Virgin received the angel Gabriel's visit and showed them where Judith decapitated Holophernes.[17]

The victory at Mount Tabor was not advantageous in every respect: it also revealed to the French their irremediable weakness. When he went to Nazareth on April 17, Bonaparte had a meeting with representatives of the Druze and Maronites that proved to be decisive: without flatly refusing his offers, they were hesitant, saying they needed time, a great deal of time, to raise the militias he was asking for. Bonaparte understood that he wouldn't make it to Damascus and that he would have to return to Cairo even if he succeeded at Acre.[18]

Attacks and sorties resumed. Bonaparte could not ignore the sufferings of his men, though he pretended to be indifferent, showing compassion only to Caffarelli, who died as a result of his wounds on April 27, and to Monge, who was sick with dysentery, and whom he visited every day. Nor could he overlook the decreasing number of his men. Victims of the fighting or the plague, they were fewer every day. Many of the officers had died: Generals Rambaud and Bon, the aide-de-camp Horace Say. Morale had fallen to its lowest level yet. Several generals made themselves the spokesmen of their men: "You're killing your own soldiers!" Murat is even supposed to have shouted at him.[19] One battalion mutinied.[20] But Bonaparte refused to face the facts. Between him and Jezzar, it was "a duel to the death."[21] And it was completely pointless: as Sidney Smith wrote to Nelson, Bonaparte could not have held Saint-Jean d'Acre for long, because he could not prevent the British squadron from continuing to bombard the city.[22] It was not until May 10, after another failure and another quarrel with Kléber,[23] that he finally accepted that he would never take "that miserable dump" whose defense had just received the reinforcement of a rescuing army from Rhodes.[24] The time had come to go home.

Now Bonaparte wanted to return home: the news from Europe he had received from Hamelin in February had since been confirmed by various sources and was about to be confirmed again—on May 13—by Ottoman prisoners.[25] First there had been the visit in the last days of March of an emissary sent by Joseph. His name was Bokty. Having left Genoa in February, he landed in Egypt a month later, accompanied by a messenger from the Directory, Mourveau, whom he had met on the way. Upon their arrival in Cairo, the two men learned that Bonaparte was in Syria. They were given a camel, and that was how they reached Saint-Jean d'Acre on March 26. We do not know what message Bokty was carrying. He had left Europe in February, so what could he tell Bonaparte other than that the international situation was deteriorating? Mourveau brought still older dispatches dated November 4 and December 26, 1798. Nothing really new, therefore, in relation to what Hamelin had told him two months earlier. On April 5 Bonaparte wrote to General d'Alméras that he could still not say with certainty whether or not war was going to resume in Europe.[26] In the end it was the enemy who provided him with fresh news. In April, Phélippeaux informed the French, "in talks that often took place in the trenches," that France was facing a new coalition. Several days later, it was Vice-Admiral Perrée's turn to tell Bonaparte about the entry of the French into Naples.[27] The Ottomans arriving from Rhodes having confirmed this information, there could no longer be any doubt: war was beginning again in Europe.

It was then that Bonaparte confided for the first time his intention to return to France. Not only did he have to fall back to his Egyptian stronghold, but without hope of receiving reinforcements, he had to recognize that the Egyptian adventure no longer had any possible outcome other than capitulation. His army was drained of blood and his Oriental dreams were at half mast. However, it should not be thought that Egypt had been merely a diversion, that he had undertaken this campaign "merely to fill up an epoch when he could do nothing in France to make himself ruler."[28] In fact, and Bainville emphasizes this, "there as elsewhere, he was entirely engaged in what he was doing at the present moment."[29] But Egypt held his attention only so long as it lent itself to vast projects; as soon as that was no longer the case, he turned away from it. Egypt became a "molehill"—worse yet, a prison: and it was precisely that captivity from which he intended to escape. And soon. As Sainte-Beuve puts it, "he took his spirit to transport it elsewhere."[30] Acre seemed to him already far away, as did Egypt, where he nonetheless knew that he still had things to do. He was to recognize this: "The general-in-chief now thought only about how to get back to France. Syria, Galilee, Palestine were no longer of any importance; the army had to be brought back to Egypt, where it was invincible; then he could leave it and throw himself into that ocean of events that presented itself to his mind."[31]

The Retreat

Having sent the Directory a report in which he cut the number of casualties in half, stated that he had transformed Acre "into a pile of stones," and declared the occupation of its ruins to be useless, he made a triumphal proclamation to his troops—intended less for his soldiers than for their comrades who had remained in Egypt and for the local authorities—and gave the order for departure.[32]

The army followed in the opposite direction the route it had taken on the way to Acre. It was like "a foretaste of 1812," thirteen years before and on a smaller scale.[33] It was not the Cossacks who were harassing the routed army, but the inhabitants of Nablus; there was no snow, but sand; instead of cold, temperatures above 40 degrees Centigrade. In a different setting the scene was identical: the same procession of harassed and haggard soldiers, the same disarray—moving at a rate of forty kilometers a day—whose hallucinatory portrait Bourrienne painted, showing the wounded who were abandoned by the wayside in order to go faster and the lack of pity felt by those who, hearing the supplications of these wretches, passed on without even looking at them.[34] Kléber brought up the rear, burning crops, looting villages, and stealing the livestock.[35]

Before lifting the siege, Bonaparte had taken steps to evacuate the sick and wounded. He had asked Vice-Admiral Perrée to take back to Egypt "four to five hundred wounded."[36] But the commander of the flotilla not only refused to approach the coast but took advantage of the opportunity to sail away and take his ships to France, so that Bonaparte, no longer being able to consider an evacuation by sea, decided to requisition wagons and horses, not excepting those of the staff. They all went on foot, led by Bonaparte. He did not want to leave any of his men behind, but there were men who could not be moved and those suffering from plague.[37] "Out of 200 sick in the hospital, only 50 could be evacuated on mounts," according to the chief doctor Desgenettes: "The rest could not be [moved] except on vehicles and stretchers," and for a great number of these there was no hope of healing.[38] What to do? Did Bonaparte decide to finish them off?

The affair exploded after the return of the French army in 1801, when a British diplomat posted in Constantinople, James Morier, revealed that Bonaparte was suspected of having poisoned a certain number of the sick men. Morier did not indicate a number, and even recognized that the evidence did not allow him to draw any certain conclusions.[39] Robert Wilson, whose *History of the British Expedition to Egypt* was published the following year, gave a very precise figure: 580.[40] Napoleon denied it, without convincing. For those who had been in Egypt, it was not a revelation. The army had hardly left Jaffa before the rumor was making the rounds among the men: Bonaparte had had poisoned the soldiers who "could not have henceforth rendered any service to the general-in-chief, even if they had gotten well."[41] Sometimes he admitted having had opium given to a few incurable men—seven, he says, or maybe eleven—leaving them free to commit suicide in the unlikely case that they survived until the departure of the rearguard twenty-four hours later; sometimes he flew into a rage against what he called gossip fabricated by the English. Sometimes, without explicitly admitting that he gave the order, he justified it, saying that he himself, were he in the place of these poor fellows who could not survive and were in danger of falling into the Turks' hands, would have blessed the hand that offered him poison.[42] The testimonies are too numerous for there to be any doubt.[43] As at the time of the massacre at Jaffa, Bonaparte consulted his staff, and the physicians.[44] In his notebook, Kléber wrote in abbreviated fashion: "On propose aux o. d. s. d. d. l. aux f. et b.d." ("Health officers are being advised to give laudanum to the feverish and dangerously wounded men").[45] Desgenettes had mentioned the affair laconically in the first edition of his *Histoire médicale de l'armée d'Orient*, published in 1802.[46] He returned to it at greater length in a new edition published after the emperor's death and augmented with "a few notes that could not appear before 1821." One of these notes concerned the plague victims:

> Late in the morning of the same day, [May] 27, General Bonaparte had me summoned to his tent, where he was alone with his chief of staff. After a short preamble concerning our situation, he said to me: *"If I were you, I would put an end to both the sufferings of our plague victims and the dangers they pose to us by giving them opium."* I replied simply: *"My duty is to save them."* Then the general developed his view with the greatest calm, saying that he was advising for others what he would ask for himself in a similar case. He begged me to observe as well that he was, more than anyone, entrusted with saving the army, and consequently with preventing our abandoned sick from falling alive under the scimitar of the Turks. "I am not trying to overcome your reluctance," he said, "but I believe that I will find people who will better understand my intentions."[47]

Bonaparte is supposed to have finally turned to the head pharmacist, Jean-François Royer, who made the lethal poison.[48] Did he really administer it to the sick men? We don't know even approximately how many victims there were: Wilson proposes the figure of 580, Niello Sargy that of 400 to 500; others say it was less than a hundred: 60, Bourrienne tells us, 50, says Lacorre, not more than 30 according to Captain François; Desgenettes speaks of 150 untransportable sick men without saying, however, that they were poisoned.[49] The very day the decision was made, May 27, Bonaparte organized the evacuation of 191 wounded men remaining in Jaffa,[50] and in the end he was able to repatriate more than 1,000 wounded men across the desert and with the help of a few ships found in the port of Jaffa.[51]

None of this would have been necessary if Bonaparte had relied on the generosity of the enemy, or that of the British, in any case, for the care of the sick and the untransportable wounded. Sydney Smith would not have refused to do this. Indeed, following not far behind the French army in retreat, he picked up along the road a large number of injured men.[52] But Bonaparte had forbidden any relationship with that man, whom he had publicly called mad and accused of inoculating French prisoners with the plague.[53] Could he change his mind and begin with the victor talks that he considered humiliating? A prideful reaction for which his soldiers reproached him during the retreat, being well aware that many of them were paying for it with their lives.[54]

The debris of the army finally reached Egyptian soil. How many of them were present when roll was called on June 7? Out of the 13,000 men of the expeditionary corps, almost 1,500, or about 12 percent, were reported missing.[55] The number was 2,500 if we believe other calculations: to the 1,200 men killed in combat, we must add 1,000 victims of disease,[56] about 100 amputees, and 200 soldiers blinded, or about 20 percent of the total.[57] The men were allowed a few hours of rest, and then, on June 14, the defeated army, led by Bonaparte, returned as victors to Cairo:

> The inhabitants had gone out to meet [the army]. . . . The deputations of the craftsmen's and merchants' associations had prepared magnificent gifts, which they offered to the sultan El-Kebir [Bonaparte]: beautiful mares with superb harnesses, beautiful camels famed for their speed, finely worked weapons, lovely black slaves and beautiful negresses, handsome Georgian men or beautiful Georgian women, and also rich carpets of wool and silk, cashmere shawls, caftans, the most precious moka coffee, pipes from Persia, caskets full of incense and aromatic herbs. . . . The general-in-chief entered the city through the Gate of Victories, preceded by the heads of the militia, the corporations, the four muftis, and the ulemas of Gâma al-Azhar. . . . For their part, the French who were in Cairo had had prepared in the middle of a field a banquet to celebrate the arrival of their comrades; they embraced one another and spent several hours drinking.[58]

Bonaparte himself was thinking about leaving, and even if he still did not know *when* and *how* he would depart Egypt, he ordered the initial preparations to be made, asking Admiral Ganteaume to keep the frigates *La Muiron* and *La Carrère* ready to go to sea.[59] But he could not leave after such a bitter failure.

He needed a victory, not only to erase the bad memories of Acre, but also to reestablish his authority, which had been quite seriously damaged. The soldiers, "harassed and discontent," had not limited themselves to "murmuring" against the general who had led them so far for such a mediocre result. From "murmurs," some had moved on to "threats," and when he returned to the Sinai, Bonaparte preferred to leave his men behind.[60] But he was still grappling with resentment among the troops, who during a review in Cairo applauded the doctor Desgenettes, who had dared to stand up to Bonaparte at the Institute. When the general was trying to explain the failure of the siege of Acre by referring to the epidemic of plague, thus casting, at least indirectly, all the responsibility on the physicians, Desgenettes had rebelled. As Bonaparte was calling the doctors "charlatans and grave diggers," Desgenettes interrupted him and retorted that "charlatanism in politics and in the art of war were far more pernicious and fatal to humanity than charlatanism in the art of healing." Sensing the support of some of his colleagues, he grew bolder: "After adding that contempt for the principles of morals led to criminal actions, he let it be seen that he had nobly refused to make himself the murderer of those whom he was entrusted with saving, alluding to the poisoning of the sick in Jaffa and at the same time to the massacre of the Turkish prisoners. The general, livid with anger, wanted to shut up the energetic speaker; but in vain; Desgenettes continued in the same vein, despite the brotherly pleas of the presiding officer and the warnings of the general, who was imperiously enjoining him to shut up."[61]

The most astonishing thing is not that this scene took place but that it had no consequences. Desgenettes continued to benefit from the goodwill of the general, who, once things had calmed down, seemed not to remember anything about it.[62] Nonetheless, Bonaparte understood that he could not leave Egypt before having reestablished an authority and a prestige that the failure in Syria had damaged. He prepared to repel the Ottoman attack that the retreat from Syria made inevitable.

The Victory at Abukir

Bonaparte began by putting the army back on a war footing, finding the ranks so greatly thinned that he wrote to Desaix to ask him to buy "two or three thousand negroes who are over sixteen years old," and to the Directory to warn it that unless reinforcements were forthcoming it would have to resign itself "to making peace."[63] No doubt some convalescents would rejoin their units, but the hospitals were full of wounded and especially sick men, many of whom were suffering from venereal diseases. The latter were numerous enough to make Bonaparte take the matter seriously. During his absence the divan of Cairo, on the pretext of fighting the spread of plague, had expelled the prostitutes, but they continued to ply their trade at the gates of the city.[64] Bonaparte had hardly returned before Dugua submitted the file to him. Dugua would probably have preferred to "diminish the number" of prostitutes "without employing the Turkish expedient"—the traditional drowning of unmarried mothers—but after consultation with the local authorities, he came back to Bonaparte and proposed to "drown [prostitutes] caught in the barracks."[65] Bonaparte acquiesced, though he asked that the operation not be entrusted to French soldiers. How many women were rounded up, knocked out, sewn up in sacks, and thrown into the Nile? Four hundred, the future General Belliard says.[66] Several generals refused to execute this measure, considering it "contrary to French honor."[67] They might have added that it was ineffective, because they could not round up all the thousands of prostitutes active in Cairo and in its environs. But Bonaparte considered the measure so necessary that he did not think he had to waste his time on what he certainly deemed untimely scruples.[68] The situation, he said, demanded it.

Although Dugua had not done a bad job during his superior's absence, the country was far from calm. The Mamluks had reappeared in the Nile Delta, high officials who had rallied to the French, like the "emir of the pilgrimage," had gone over to the enemy, and more seriously, a man who had himself called "the Angel Mahdi" had stirred up the inhabitants of the Damanhur region. His supporters were so fanatical that it had been necessary to go to great lengths to convince them, as Bonaparte put it, "that God no longer performs miracles."[69] The fire was smoldering under the ashes. Murad Bey himself was attracting attention again. Leaving his refuge in the oasis of Kharguèh, west of Luxor, he was moving toward the delta with "two or three hundred ill-armed, lame men."[70] If Murad was no longer a real military danger, Bonaparte feared that because of his charisma he might succeed in federating revolts and resentments whose failure was due only to a lack of coordination. There was a danger that Murad might organize a second front on the French army's rear. Bonaparte also feared another revolt in Cairo. That is why, very shortly after he returned to his "capital," wanting to spread a climate of terror there, he had prisoners executed in such large numbers that Dugua finally asked him to authorize hiring a headsman.[71] Bonaparte hoped above all that the generals sent to search for Murad would bring back his dead body: "I strongly desire," he wrote to Friant, "that you add to the services that you have not ceased to render us the far more important one of killing Murad Bey or causing him to die of fatigue; let him die in one way or the other!"[72] But Murad was playing with his pursuers, and when his presence was reported near Giza, Bonaparte decided to hunt him down himself.

He was at the pyramids on July 15 when a message informed him that two days earlier an Anglo-Ottoman fleet had dropped anchor in the harbor at Abukir and begun to unload 10,000 to 15,000 soldiers.[73] Bonaparte prepared to confront the attack. He either had to surrender or throw the Ottomans back into the sea, and to do so, to strip Egypt of its riches. He had no choice. By combing through the whole of Egypt, he gathered together an army of some 10,000 men and returned to the Nile Delta on July 19. Two days later he had more or less managed to concentrate his troops: one week had passed since the Turkish landing. In fact, Bonaparte was three days behind developments.[74] That was the reason that he made the men march so fast and ordered the regiments to make special efforts to reach their positions as soon as possible: he had to make up for a delay that might at any moment be transformed into a catastrophe if the enemy moved before the French army arrived. He peppered Dugua, who was in Cairo, with urgent and worried questions: Had Lagrange's division moved out? What was Rampon doing? Why had he still not joined him? What about the laggards? And the subordinate officers who were unduly extending their leaves? And Reynier? And Dugua himself? Didn't he know that at least 2,000 pairs of boots and 300,000 rations were needed here?[75] July 18 to 20 was a dangerous time when everything could have gone the other way if the Ottoman staff and its British "advisors" had decided to march on Alexandria (defended by Marmont) or on Rosetta (where Kléber arrived only on the twenty-third, the day before the battle). It is unlikely that the advance of the Ottoman troops would have provoked an uprising among the people of the delta, but it might have hampered or even prevented the regrouping of the French troops and thus forced Bonaparte to fight under difficult conditions. Instead the Turks chose to dig in on the Abukir peninsula. The cavalry Murad Bey had promised had not shown up, and their own cavalry not having arrived, they did not dare to drive farther into the delta. On July 22 Bonaparte, noting that the enemy seemed reluctant to leave its positions, decided to attack. During the night of the twenty-fourth he left Alexandria and advanced as far as the Canopic branch of the Nile, a few kilometers from the Turkish positions.

The Ottomans had established two lines of defense to protect their main camp, which was backed up against the Abukir fort, at the extremity of the peninsula. The first line consisted of two forward positions protected by high dunes; the second—behind the village of Abukir—consisted of a redoubt that the Ottomans had extended on their right as far as the sea, but that they had not had time to fortify on their left. Several dozen small gunboats flanked the two shores of the narrow peninsula.

The French assault began at dawn. When the signal was given, Destaing's and Lannes's troops attacked the forward posts. Murat's cavalry waited, ready to charge. In all, counting the reserves, Bonaparte had scarcely 8,000 men. But with his 1,000 cavalrymen he had a major advantage. The soldiers raced across the kilometer of sand that separated them from the Turks and charged up the dunes. The Ottoman defense crumpled, then gave way. At that point Murat's cavalry roared in to cut off the enemy's line of retreat. Being unable either to advance or to withdraw, the Turks sought refuge in the water, trying to swim out to the boats anchored at sea or to the gunboats that were guarding the coast. Several hundred drowned before they could reach the open sea. In a few minutes, or in any case in less than an hour, 3,000 Turks were put out of action.

Without stopping to catch their breath, Destaing's and Lannes's divisions pounced on the village of Abukir, which was guarded by 2,000 Ottomans. Destaing launched a frontal attack, while Lannes and the cavalry flanked the Turkish positions to surround them. Now sheltered behind the village's houses, the whole French army could see the redoubt bristling with cannons and defenders. It could also see the fortifications built on the left as far as the shore.

Bonaparte saw the difficulty, but the absence of fortifications on the right opened up a space a few hundred meters long. He ordered the artillery brought up and placed along the seaside, in order to bombard the enemy's right flank. In this way he wanted to persuade the Turks that the French attack would be made on the redoubt and its fortifications.

The French batteries went into action. With the cannonballs passing over their heads, the men of Lanusse's division, who had taken over, rushed the redoubt, engaging the Turks in hand-to-hand fighting with bayonets. There were many casualties on both sides, and the French were even on the brink of defeat. The Ottoman soldiers took advantage of this moment to emerge from their fortifications to decapitate the dead and wounded, before the eyes of their adversaries. That was the Turks' first mistake: the sight galvanized the French troops, who renewed their attack. The second mistake: seeing the cannonballs landing on the redoubt and the grenadiers trying to take it by frontal assault, the Turks massed their forces on their right, thinning their defenses on the left. Murat seized the opportunity and sent in his cavalry, which rushed into the breach, going around the redoubt and sowing indescribable panic among the thousands of soldiers there. Lannes's division followed, firing on the fleeing Turks; it moved beyond the redoubt and marched toward the Ottoman camp, above which the vizier's flag was flying.

Napoleon was later to say that the fighting at Abukir had been "the most horrible" he had ever witnessed. Hundreds of Turks, probably thousands (since only 3,000 prisoners were taken) rushed into the sea. "In this part of the harbor," Marmont explained, "the water is not very deep, so the fleeing men had to wade far out into the sea before their bodies were in the water." As they were splashing through the shallows "we shot them at will, mowed them down." However, panic and the topography of the place—there was no possibility of a real retreat—do not suffice to explain by themselves the fact that half the Turkish army preferred the risk of drowning to falling into the hands of the French. The memory of what happened at Jaffa, where Bonaparte had had more than 2,000 captives shot, probably played a determining role: the Turks preferred a perilous attempt to escape over the certain death awaiting those taken prisoner by the French. Many of the fleeing men would probably have escaped death if the gunboats that were cruising a short distance away had helped them. But "instead of saving these unfortunate men," Marmont wrote, "[they] fired on them to force them to get out of the water and return to the fight."[76] The sultan's army sank into the sea. It is said that thousands of turbans gradually floated up to the surface.

The battle was over. Almost nothing remained of the Turkish army. The estimate of Ottoman casualties—10,000 to 12,000 dead—offered by Bonaparte the day after his victory does not seem exaggerated when one knows that the sea was to wash up 6,000 bodies, that more than 1,000 soldiers were killed in battle, that almost 2,000 bodies were found in the fort, and that 400 prisoners who surrendered on August 2 were to die in the following days "from having drunk too much and eaten too greedily."[77] The figure of 10,000 killed is a minimum. It corresponds to a loss of almost eight-tenths of the men involved, a rate that has no equivalent in the military history of the period. The disproportion between Ottoman and French casualties is spectacular: at most 250 French were killed.[78] But for all that, the loss of 250 French soldiers and officers—not to mention 1,000 wounded—was not negligible, because it came on top of all the losses the expeditionary force had suffered over the past year. Sydney Smith got it right when, on the day the last Turkish combatants surrendered, he wrote to Nelson that it would take only a few more French victories of the same kind to finish off Bonaparte's army.[79]

Bonaparte had said before the battle that a victory would ensure "France's possession of Egypt."[80] Instead it gave the French presence there only a short reprieve. On the other hand, it "saved" Bonaparte, even determined his destiny—by allowing him to return to France as a victorious general, it kept him from having to sign a surrender himself. That is why this battle was a "battle of extermination," a sort of Waterloo in reverse on which Bonaparte staked everything. If he lost, he could say farewell to his ambitions; he had to win, at any price. He was counting on this victory, which was going to "decide the fate of the world," as he told Murat.[81] Miot, who witnessed this conversation, saw in this the proof that the decision to go back to France had already been made: A victory obviously could not "decide the fate of the world," but it would acquire a quite different import by enabling Bonaparte to return to Paris.[82] July 25, 1799, a date of secondary importance for the history of France, is a capital date in the history of Napoleon.

The Call of Destiny?

Back in France, Bonaparte gave his version of the circumstances of his departure, saying that the idea imposed itself on him the day after the battle of Abukir.[83] Negotiations on an exchange of prisoners had begun after the British handed him a bundle of newspapers in which he learned, he assures us, of the reverses the French armies had recently suffered in Germany and in Italy.[84] He says that he immediately summoned his principal lieutenants, telling them: "I have made up my mind to leave and return to France. . . . The state of affairs in Europe forces me to make this important choice; our armies are being overwhelmed by reverses. . . . And then what can the incompetent people placed in charge of things do? Among them there is only ignorance, foolishness, or corruption. It is I, I alone, who have borne the burden, and, by means of continual successes, given substance to this government which without me would never have been able to be set up and maintained. If I were absent, everything was going to collapse. Let us not wait until the destruction is complete: the problem would be irremediable."[85]

Should we believe Bonaparte, a fortiori, when he claims not to have calculated "the dangers"? "I would have wrapped myself in my overcoat and left in a small boat had I not had frigates."[86] This sentence seeks to describe in the simplest terms the man of destiny responding to his country's call. It says nothing about the complex way in which the plan to return was really conceived and carried out. Looking into this question is all the more legitimate because the decision to leave Egypt, abandoning the army there, was heavy with consequences. It is difficult to imagine Bonaparte staking his future on the authority of a few old newspapers and exposing himself, without any kind of protection, to the perils of a voyage that, if it went badly, could have put an end to his extraordinary adventure.[87] Could he lightly run the risk of being captured by a British ship or arrested as a deserter on his arrival in France? Could he stake his glory on the flip of a coin? Could he rush, under the influence of a moment of indignation, into the abyss in which La Fayette and Dumouriez had earlier disappeared after they had lost popular favor by failing, for lack of preparation, in their moves against the government? He was aware of the danger, telling Monge on the ship that took them back to France that he would not let the

English capture him and make him a "vulgar deserter."[88] His supporters claim that he returned "without being summoned and without premeditation."[89] Many others doubted it. Some of the latter say that he came back only after he had received from one of his brothers a signal that the way was clear.[90] Others suspect not only the existence of internal accomplices but also foreign intervention.

His brothers? They were now living it up. Joseph, who owned a town house in Monceau, had just enriched his patrimony by buying the vast estate of Mortefontaine, near Ermenonville. Lucien was lodged no less grandly: he had just bought a town house on Rue de Miromesnil, then called Rue Verte. The two brothers had gone into politics. Lucien in particular was making a great fuss in the Council of Five Hundred, where he had been representing Corsica for the past year. He was frequenting Jacobin revenants of doubtful respectability whose convictions were still more doubtful, and not a day went by without him attacking the government—at least until July 14, when he changed sides. It has to be said that the government had also changed, with the entry into the Directory of Sieyès, who did not conceal his intention to revise the constitution at the first opportunity. By putting himself at the disposal of the new director, Lucien thought he had bet on a winning horse. No doubt he did not forget that Napoleon had given him a leg up, but his future no longer depended on that brother of whom he was in any case not very fond, and moreover, no one could say whether he would return anytime soon, or ever. Besides, Lucien did not consider himself in any way inferior to his elder brother: he wanted to believe, he did believe, that "equitable nature, imparting to his brother the genius of war, had suited him, as a compensation, for civil government."[91] Thus, he was far from working for Napoleon's return, and perhaps even from wishing for it.

As for Joseph, though he sent a messenger to his brother, as we have seen, nothing proves that he was entrusted with organizing his return to France. The elder Bonaparte devoted most of his time to improving his properties, to literature, and to social life. Educated, likable, speaking with ease, he had made his salon a fashionable meeting point for the Paris of politics, letters, and the arts. Joseph was at the center of a large circle of relations of which it would be hasty to say that it was intended to be used in the service of Napoleon. It was so used in the end, but that does not mean that was its purpose from the outset. The elder Bonaparte took pleasure in his new life as a lord. He had just published a little short story in the style of Ossian, *Moïna ou la villageoise du Mont-Cenis*. In truth, he hardly thought about his brother. Furthermore, he was cultivating a new friendship, that of Bernadotte, who had just married his sister-in-law Désirée. Did he support the ambitions of his brother-in-law, who had recently been named minister of war? Assuming that Joseph had indeed teamed up with Bernadotte, the help he gave was certainly disinterested, so much was his character passive and indecisive. Joseph encouraged Bernadotte in the same way that he dreamed of a brilliant future for Napoleon, with a certain indifference that was faithful, ultimately, to the maxim placed at the head of *Moïna*: "Independent of external events, happiness lies in domestic affections."

Foreign accomplices? Mario Proth, a virulent opponent of the Second Empire, expressed "strong and legitimate suspicions":[92] "Were the English inept as sailors or as politicians? Were they incapable of capturing Bonaparte, or did they fatuously think it preferable not to capture him? . . . The Mediterranean lake was being crisscrossed in every direction by British fleets, it was monopolized, occupied, monitored, surrounded by the English, who were the best sailors in the world, so armed, so farsighted, so invincible, and yet they allowed two little Venetian boats carrying Bonaparte and his companions to flee Egypt, a prison, and to hasten toward 18 Brumaire, an apotheosis."[93]

Here we rejoin Sidney Smith, who, after his success at Saint-Jean d'Acre, thought it was his task to defend Britain's superior interests in the region.[94] He did not forget the mission that had been entrusted to him: forcing the French to evacuate Egypt. Giving Bonaparte newspapers and distributing them to the French army were part of a strategy whose aim was to incite French soldiers to rebel and desert. By telling them that war had resumed in Europe and by assuring them that their government would not come to their aid, Smith hoped to persuade them to surrender to the British, who would send them home. Even before Bonaparte had lifted the siege of Acre, Smith had distributed a manifesto in which the Ottoman government offered guarantees to those who surrendered, and repeated the already widespread claim that the Directory had sent the elite of the French army to the Orient in order to get rid of it.[95] This disinformation campaign had little effect. The executions, mutilations, and atrocities perpetrated by the Ottomans were not likely to reassure the many French soldiers who wanted to go home. Smith had tried the same tactic on

General Dugua and the troops who had remained in Egypt.[96] But he was not discouraged; he thought it still possible to arrive at an arrangement with Bonaparte, in spite of the insults that they exchanged in public; he knew that Egypt would support the French only so long as they were victors, and that once they left it would capitulate. After Bonaparte had been defeated at Acre, it was just a matter of time. "One does not catch flies with vinegar," he wrote, "therefore I offer them honey; and it is not to Buonaparte alone that I offer this *pont d'or*, but by other channels indirectly to all individuals of his army."[97] To that extent, although the destruction of the Ottoman army at Abukir was a terrible blow for Smith, it was also a profound satisfaction, because it set the stage for what he had been seeking for such a long time: Bonaparte's departure.

It was not after reading the newspapers given him by the British that Bonaparte decided to leave, but after a secret meeting he had in Alexandria with John Keith, Sidney Smith's secretary, on August 5.[98] In a letter to Admiral Nelson dated September 7, Sidney Smith reports that the conversation dealt at length with the European situation.[99] Keith is said to have proposed that "the general evacuate his conquest and go to win Italy back from the Russians."[100] Niqula al-Turk, a direct witness to these events, which he experienced as part of Bonaparte's entourage—the Christians of Lebanon had sent him as their envoy—also states that the talks led to an agreement in due form.[101] Did Bonaparte ultimately seize power with at least the indirect help of the British? So long as the British squadron was cruising off Alexandria, any departure remained dangerous. The British had to "open the door"; without their complicity, there could be no departure. That is why, through a deliberate "indiscretion," Sidney Smith let Bonaparte know that the British squadron would soon be leaving Alexandria to replenish its supplies of fresh water in Cyprus.[102] In itself this agreement is hardly surprising: Bonaparte wanted to leave and Smith had long desired his departure. The failure of the Syrian campaign and the victory at Abukir favored the conjunction of these two interests. On August 9, four days before the conversation between Bonaparte and John Keith, Smith wrote to the British minister Lord Spencer: "Admiral Ganteaume . . . , I have reason to believe, will attempt to sail with two frigates, a corvette and a brigantine. Perhaps Bonaparte himself will slip his neck out of the collar, leaving Kléber in command. If he does, Kléber will yield to the army's clamor and negotiate with a view to returning to France, when a force sufficient to justify such a step is assembled against him. . . . I have acquired proofs of this in the course of the relations we have recently had with them, and it is unfortunate that we cannot exercise on them a pressure strong enough to persuade them to evacuate."[103]

What better way to say that, in Smith's view, to authorize Bonaparte's departure would be to hasten the end of the French occupation of Egypt? Moreover, it is certain that Smith's only goal was to defend his country's interests. Wasn't it also in France's interest that he consented to Bonaparte's departure? He not only allowed Bonaparte to leave Alexandria but did everything he could to get him to France safe and sound. On this point, he lied to his superiors when he told them, on August 9, that he had sent west two warships, the *Theseus* and the *Cameleon*, which had been assigned to intercept Bonaparte.[104] In reality these two ships were far away when the French sailed, and it was only on October 3 that they occupied the positions that had been assigned to them on August 9: at that time, Bonaparte was making a stop in Corsica.[105] He had a head start of more than a month, which was amply sufficient. Had Smith wanted to "cover himself" while at the same time not guarding Bonaparte's return route, he would not have acted otherwise.[106]

My goal here is not to construct a fiction involving the British government: this strategy was developed solely by Sidney Smith, whom Napoleon considered "capable of any folly."[107] It is true that in 1799 Britain had an interest in making peace; but believing it was impossible to negotiate with a government as unstable as the Directory's, it staked everything on the formation of a new coalition that this time, with the assistance of Austria and Russia, would be able to overcome revolutionary France. The second coalition was no more successful than the first, but so long as the operations begun in the spring of 1799 went well, the allies thought they could put an end to the war by war, and they were no longer focusing on Bonaparte. Thus, on July 23, 1799, the British secretary of war, Henry Dundas, wrote to a correspondent: "Our public situation is most brilliant in every respect and I don't conceive it possible that the French monster can live much longer. . . . We have now forgot Buonaparte."[108] That is the proof, certainly, not only that in London people had been concerned about Bonaparte, but also that they stopped thinking about him as soon as they imagined that France was close to capitulation.

The British would not have given Bonaparte an "exit permit" had Sidney Smith not been so fond of France—the France of the Old Regime—or shared the royalists' illusions. He was deeply francophile; he spoke French and had formerly lived in France, where he later chose to live out his old age and be buried—in the Père Lachaise Cemetery in Paris. He was very attached to the royalist cause and a friend of many émigrés; it is not inconceivable that he developed a policy of his own that corresponded to the interests of both Britain and France. Working out an agreement with the man who might someday play the role of Monk was not only a way of defending British interests in the Orient, but also, as he saw it, a way of helping to put an end to the Revolution and restoring the legitimate monarch. Thus, no extraordinary conspiracy presided over Bonaparte's return. There was no overall accord among certain French political leaders and the British cabinet, but rather an agreement negotiated directly between the French general-in-chief and his British counterpart.

The Departure

Having returned to Cairo on August 11 after talks with the British, Bonaparte made no changes in his schedule or his habits. Directives and reprimands began raining down on his subordinates again, as if the victory at Abukir had opened a new chapter in the history of the French presence in Egypt; as if, especially, Bonaparte were planning to preside over the destiny of the new colony for a long time to come. On August 13 he attended the ceremonies in honor of the Prophet. But he had already drawn up a list of those whom he was taking with him. None of the elect knew about this, save those who had been told at the time of the agreement. Nonetheless, how could leaks be avoided? On August 13 the engineer Jomard said that "a vague rumor, or rather a suspicion" had reached the Institute of Cairo: it was said that in Alexandria two ships were ready to sail for France.[109]

Bonaparte had begun to make arrangements for his departure by writing to General Lanausse that he would come to see him in Menouf "in two days' time," as the first stop on an "inspection tour" he said he planned to make in the region of the delta.[110] The same day, he told Admiral Ganteaume, who was in Alexandria, that he would leave Cairo on the fifteenth and be in Ramanieh on the nineteenth, where he would await the signal to embark. But on the day specified he had to delay his departure: Ganteaume informed him that the ships would not be ready to go to sea before the twentieth, which meant that the enemy fleets, Turkish or British, were still cruising the waters off Alexandria. Bonaparte replied that he would set out on the eighteenth, and rejoined the guests whom he had invited to celebrate his thirtieth birthday with him.

On the evening of August 17 he finally received from Admiral Ganteaume the message he was waiting for: the enemy ships had sailed away. This time the door was open. Bonaparte decided to leave Cairo that very night. Around 10 P.M. the general-in-chief's carriage went to the Institute of Cairo to pick up Monge and Berthollet, who were waiting with their bags backed, awkwardly trying to reassure their colleagues regarding the goal of this precipitous departure. Monge, who had never been able to hold his tongue, lived up to his reputation once again, because when Fourier renewed his questions, he sheepishly replied: "My friends, if we are leaving for France, we knew nothing about it before noon today."[111] When the two scientists arrived at Bonaparte's residence, the latter was nonchalantly talking with his guests, and when he spotted Monge, he launched a scientific discussion, going out from time to time to give an order. Finally, around midnight, after having said goodbye to Pauline Fourès, he left his headquarters.[112] When he started down the Nile at 3 A.M., General Lanusse and the aide-de-camp Merlin told him about the rumors that were circulating: "It is said, general," Merlin remarked, "that you are going to embark at Abukir and return to France. If that is true, I hope that once you are back in our country, you will think about your army in Egypt."[113] Even though Merlin was to sail along with him, which he did not yet know, Bonaparte flatly denied that he was departing. But the news had gotten out: Bertrand had given Lannes letters for France, and Lanusse had told Bourrienne that Bonaparte was leaving Egypt.

Bonaparte spent the day of August 19 in Menouf. He took advantage of this stop to ask Kléber, who was in Damietta, to meet him in Rosetta on the twenty-fourth: "I need to consult with you about some extremely important matters."[114] Ganteaume having informed him that he had to leave before noon on the twenty-fourth, he set out again on the same evening. The following evening he reached Ramanieh, where he wrote to Menou to ask that he and Kléber meet him "at the spring between Alexandria and Abukir."[115] On August 21 he left the river and headed for Alexandria on horseback. That evening, when he stopped at Berket-Gitas, he told his escort the true goal of this journey. "Joy was pictured in every countenance," Bourrienne wrote.[116]

The next day they were within a dozen kilometers of Alexandria when Bonaparte suddenly ordered a turn toward the right to reach the sea without passing through the city. It was there, on the beach, that he received Menou. "I am leaving this evening for France," he told him.[117] He entrusted to him instructions for Kléber, who had not arrived on time at the rendezvous and was supposed to replace him as the head of the expedition, a proclamation for the army, and several letters addressed to the officers he was leaving in Egypt. "When you receive this letter," he wrote to Junot, "I shall be far away. I have regretted not being able to take you with me: you were too distant from the place of embarkation."[118] He promised Dugua that he would bring the army home before the spring of 1800, and he promised the authorities in Cairo that he would come back within three months. The embarkation began after sunset. "When the launches arrived," Merlin wrote, "everyone, without distinction of social or military rank, hastened to get on the ships and to do so went into the water up to their knees, so impatient were they, and so much did they fear being left behind. Each sought to be the first on the *Muiron*, pushing and shoving with little care or attention for his fellows."[119]

At 8 A.M. on August 23, 1799, the flotilla sailed, and by noon it had lost sight of the Egyptian coast. But a few hours later the wind shifted and began to blow out of the northwest, slowing the advance of the four ships. For almost twenty days they slowly drifted along the African coast. Bonaparte, who doubted the sincerity of the British, had asked Ganteaume to do this as a matter of security: "This long route spared them the danger posed by the enemy fleets; always staying between 32 and 33 degrees latitude, and not far from the coasts of Africa, we were in an area that was, if not unknown, at least very little frequented by sailors, and very far away from the route that ships usually followed when going from Europe to Egypt."[120] No ship noticed the flotilla sailing along the Egyptian and Libyan coasts or was seen by it. And for good reason: there was none.

Finally, on September 11, the equinoctial wind rose. On the sixteenth the flotilla rounded Cap d'Ocre (Libya). During the night of the twenty-second, precisely one month after departure, and while the crew and passengers were celebrating the seventh anniversary of the proclamation of the Republic, it passed by Lampedusa. The following night it rounded Cap Bon, and on the twenty-fourth, around noon, it was off Bizerte. Once Cap Bon had been passed, the danger increased: Sidney Smith could not protect Bonaparte from the threat posed by the British ships cruising the western Mediterranean. A perilous encounter could not be ruled out. Bonaparte might fear it all the more because the newspapers Smith had given him had informed him that Nelson's fleet had entered the Mediterranean. On the other hand, what he did not know, and which was to ensure the success of his enterprise, was that the French, Spanish, and British fleets had left the Mediterranean: the Franco-Spanish fleet had returned to the Atlantic on July 8, and the British had followed on the thirtieth. There remained in the Mediterranean only a few British ships at Malta, two more at Civitavecchia, one at Livorno, and a few more at Gibraltar: Bonaparte's flotilla was crossing a sea that was virtually empty. Luck had not played such a great role in the success of his departure from Alexandria, but it favored him during the second part of his voyage. As Bonaparte was fond of saying, "In a great affair, some role always has to be granted to chance."[121] It is true that for a long time Fortune, that auxiliary indispensable for great enterprises, remained faithful to him.

PART FIVE

Crossing the Rubicon

1799

TWENTY-ONE

The Conspiracy

*W*as Bonaparte a deserter? If we stick to the facts, there is no doubt: he departed Egypt without permission and left his army behind.[1] However, as Thiers was to say, this "desertion" was "one of those rash acts by which the great ambitious tempt Heaven."[2] He staked his destiny on it. As General Thiébault put it, either a "throne" or a "scaffold" was awaiting him in France.[3] Historians sometimes pointlessly maintain suspense regarding Bonaparte's intentions: He is supposed to have returned in order to seize power, and for no other reason; he told General Menou so before he left: "I shall arrive in Paris, I shall drive out that pile of lawyers who care nothing for us and who are incapable of governing the Republic, and I shall put myself at the head of the government."[4] He sensed that this time the fruit was ripe, and that the time had come for him to undertake what he had not dared when he returned from Italy. It will be said that he knew almost nothing about the situation in France and in Europe. That is true: he knew only that war had resumed and had gone badly for the French armies; but that was already a great deal. Military victories—his in particular—had prolonged the existence of the regime by casting a little glory on it, so it didn't take a wizard to understand that defeats, far from being blamed on the generals, would be attributed to the government and its carelessness. Moreover, because victories provided the regime's only solid support, it was clear that defeats would lead to its downfall. But he still had to get to France, and in time, to take advantage of the situation. That is why the very slow crossing of the Mediterranean was a torture for him. He was obsessed by the idea that he might arrive too late. Finally, on October 9, 1799, after a voyage of more than forty days and a week's stopover in Ajaccio, the convoy dropped anchor in the bay of Saint-Raphaël.[5] There Bonaparte learned the latest political and military news; it was then that the project that had led him to leave Egypt ceased entirely to be one of those "pipe dreams" that his imagination generated in such profusion. The future and the circumstances he would confront were no longer a secret for him.

The Death Throes of the Directory

In the spring of 1799 war had resumed with Austria and its Russian ally. Jourdan had been defeated in Germany and Schérer in Italy, where Moreau, called upon to rescue him, had done no better. Only Masséna had distinguished himself, by stopping the Russians in front of Zurich. But Italy was lost and the Rhine frontier was threatened. The situation seemed so desperate that the directors had finally recalled Bonaparte, a step they had up to that point refused to consider. When Barras proposed it a few weeks earlier, they had replied by asking whether they did not already have enough generals who wanted to usurp authority without adding Bonaparte. We are not sure why Barras was so eager for the general to return: did he believe Bonaparte was the only one capable of turning the military situation around, or anticipating the fall of the regime, did he want to have his former protégé at his side? A few defeats later, Barras renewed his proposal, this time successfully. The order recalling Bonaparte—with "part of his army"—was signed on May 26, 1799, and immediately sent to Admiral Bruix so that he might head immediately for Alexandria.[6] But the mission fizzled out. Storms, damage to the ships, and the ill will of the Spanish, whose fleet was supposed to accompany Bruix's, thwarted the admiral's hopes: on July 10, instead of sailing toward the eastern Mediterranean, the ships put under his command headed for the straits of Gibraltar and the Atlantic![7]

The directors did not try again. They now had other worries. Once again the annual election of a third of the assemblies had not strengthened the government's position. The coup d'état of 18 Fructidor had not helped matters either. The opposition on the right had been muzzled, to be sure, but that on the left had taken over, to the point that in 1798 the operation carried out the preceding year against the right had to be repeated against the left. The assemblies lent themselves to the operation but did not forgive the government for having made them play such a humiliating role. As the elections of 1799 approached, the Directory sensed that it would be impossible for it to perpetrate its third coup d'état—in three years—in order to "correct" the outcome of the voting. Refusing to use force and no longer being able to count on the support of the members of the Legislative Body, it decided this time to let the voters decide. The failure of most of the candidates supported by the government surprised no one, but the Directory emerged from this new trial so weakened that the Legislative Body thought the time had come to take its revenge.

The Council of Five Hundred, headed by the "neo-Jacobin" representatives, led the rebellion. Who were these "neo-Jacobins" who were going to shake the foundations of the government and who were going to be, on 19 Brumaire, the last obstacle on Bonaparte's path to power? They formed, not a party, but rather an ill-defined coalition: they claimed to be picking up where their predecessors had left off in 1793, at a time when the country's borders were again being threatened, but it would take a clairvoyant to say what they really wanted. Among them there were a few revenants from the period of the Terror. There were some republicans—they were the most numerous—who sincerely believed that France had returned to the time of "the fatherland in danger" and also wanted to reestablish the rights of the national representative body against the "usurpations" of the executive branch. There were neo-Jacobin generals—Augereau, Jourdan, Brune, and a few others—who thought they had been poorly rewarded for their services to the government and disapproved of the latter's timid attempts to regain control over its armies.[8] And finally there was a handful of "politicians eager for fame and in a hurry to rise to power," of whom Lucien Bonaparte was assuredly the prototype.[9]

Every year, the Legislature replaced one of the five directors, and this time it was Reubell, one of the pillars of the government, who lost his seat. Barras may have been behind this "stroke of fate." It is said that he hoped to replace Reubell with one of his cronies, General Lefebvre; but the Councils stood up to him and elected Sieyès. The ex-abbé was in Berlin, where he was representing the Republic—and freezing to death—but in Paris a group of "Véritables" including neo-Jacobins and partisans of institutional reform paved the way for his return to politics. The neo-Jacobins remembered the role played in 1789 by the author of the resounding pamphlet *Qu'est-ce que le tiers-état?* (*What Is the Third Estate?*); and they had not forgotten that after 18 Fructidor he had deplored what he regarded as an excessively moderate repression of the royalists. The partisans of institutional reform thought the time had come to give a chance to a man who, well-informed people said, already had among his papers a new constitution that was so carefully considered and so well constructed that it would supply a definitive response to all the problems that had up to that point not been solved. Thanks to Sieyès it would be possible to do away with the institutions created in 1795 that inspired in him a contempt he made no attempt to hide: he had called them childish, a "*ba be bi bo bu* constitution" (referring to the classroom mnemonic for the five vowels). At a time when in perilous circumstances everyone was looking for the "savior" capable of preventing the Republic from going over the cliff, many people remembered Sieyès. "No one but [he]," they said, "can govern the Republic and make it prosper."[10] This phrase seemed to recur in every conversation, and Benjamin Constant was not the last to put his money on the ex-abbé. On the day after the election he wrote to Sieyès: "I regarded your nomination as the last hope of the Republic, of that poor Republic that for the past eighteen months has had to struggle so hard against immorality and foolishness . . . It is not surprising that the man who created public opinion in 1789 should be the same one who resuscitates it ten years later . . . You will be more powerful than any man has been since the Revolution, more supported by the general will, more invested with universal confidence, all France is weary of mediocrity and corruption, all France thirsts for virtues and enlightenment."[11]

Director La Révellière-Lépeaux had a different opinion. Attached to the constitution of Year III as if it were his child, he understood that when Sieyès replaced Reubell, the hour of the regime's liquidation had sounded.[12]

The crisis exploded the day after Sieyès's return to Paris. After several days of extreme tension, rumors, and agitation, on 30 Prairial (June 16–17, 1799), the Councils forced three of the five directors—Treilhard, Merlin de Douai, and La Révellière—to resign. The neo-Jacobins in the Council of Five Hundred, who had led the attack, intended to make the most of this first victory. The conquests of two seats on the Directory (for Generals Gohier and Moulin), of the position of the military commander of Paris (Marbot), and of the portfolios of the Police (Bourguignon), Finances (Lindet), and War (Bernadotte), were not negligible, but it was only a start. They began by imposing a radical change in policy: mass mobilization (June 27), the arrest of hostages in departments where disturbances occurred (July 12), the cancellation of the celebration of 9 Thermidor (July 26), and the imposition of a tax of 100 million francs on the rich (August 6). It almost seemed that the terrible days of 1793 had returned. Even the Jacobin club had been revived at the Manège, the former seat of the National Assembly, where the "friends of liberty and equality" demanded a proclamation that the country was in danger. But it was no longer 1792 or 1793. Aristocratic mobs fought in the streets with adherents of the Manège; the mass uprising increased the number of rebels fleeing the city and joining bands of brigands; borrowing the wealthy's money immediately made money disappear and paralyzed what remained of economic activity. Sieyès, turning his back on his neo-Jacobin allies, decided to reach out to Barras, whom they had been constantly attacking. The regime might not have surmounted this crisis if at that point the Directory had not received the support of two heavyweights: Lucien Bonaparte and Fouché. The youngest Bonaparte brother, who since his election to the Council of Five Hundred in 1798 had become one of the leaders of the neo-Jacobins, had until then not spared the government, but suddenly—it was July 14, 1799—he sought to defend those who were, he said only a day before, hardly fit to be hanged. Did he fear that the Republic would collapse before his brother returned? That is doubtful.[13] Had Barras threatened to reveal the real nature of a few shady affairs from which Lucien had escaped through his intervention?[14] It is not impossible. Had Sieyès made him see that he had more to gain by supporting him than by remaining in the camp of the loudmouths? That is probable. The fact remains that the Directory now had an influential ally in the more hostile of the two assemblies. This was a welcome reinforcement, but perhaps less important than that of Fouché, whom Barras had just made minister of police.

Fouché was a revenant from the "extreme Terror," the man who carried out the massacres in Lyon and the author of the famous formula inscribed on the pediment of the cemetery of Nevers: "Death is only an eternal sleep." But *that* Fouché now belonged to the past, which does not mean that the new Fouché, full of unction, moderation, and indulgence, was more authentic than the old one. It is true that he had never been violent out of fanaticism. He had been violent by chance, because of events, choosing to be violent so long as the violent were in charge. He had endured a long exile from power. Even though he had been largely responsible for Robespierre's fall, the memory of his crimes was too vivid for him to escape disgrace. Fouché was definitely too compromising as an ally. Although he was not harassed, he owed this to the protection provided by Barras, who made use of him in his secret police, though he avoided being seen in his company. Fouché lived wretchedly, half starving to death, until 1797, when Barras got him involved in trafficking in military supplies. Fouché did very well in these shady dealings, and laid the foundations of a great fortune. Having become rich, the former pupil of the Oratorian clergymen was somewhat more presentable. He emerged from his den after 18 Fructidor, and in late 1798 Barras decided to get him out of purgatory: the Directory entrusted him with secret missions in Italy and Holland, which he carried out well, and in July 1799 the need for a man with an iron hand got him appointed minister of police. Moderates regarded his return with horror, the Jacobins regarded it with joy. In a few days the former were reassured and the latter disenchanted. As Stefan Zweig put it, Saul had been transformed into St. Paul.[15] He received with an Old Regime politeness the ladies of the Faubourg Saint-Germain who had come to plead the cause of a relative who had emigrated—sometimes enlisting them in the intelligence service he had immediately begun creating, along with his criminals (Vidocq) and his elegant debtors (Joséphine)—reassuring, cajoling, preferring to warn rather than punish, but making people feel that he had an eye on everyone and everything, that the police would become the heart of a failing state and that he was going to be the strong man in a weak government.

When the worried directors asked Fouché what he planned to do regarding the Manège club, he replied laconically: "Close it." On August 14 it was done. The neo-Jacobins were staggered by the blow. They needed a few days to regroup, and on August 20 they launched the offensive that was to be their swan song. They demanded the heads of Sieyès and Barras and called for a government of public safety. Paris hummed with rumors, not entirely unfounded, of an imminent coup d'état. The fall of the regime seemed so certain and so near that many people contemplated precipitating the event, in the hope of better controlling its consequences. Sieyès seriously considered this possibility. He had worked out a plan with Lucien, made contacts, and even chosen a "sword": General Joubert, who had been in Italy with Bonaparte and attracted attention there. But Joubert had just been killed at Novi by an Austrian bullet, and Sieyès had to postpone the operation that was supposed to finally allow him to constitute the republic on solid bases. In the opposing camp, preparations were also being made. Jourdan and Augereau were on the lookout for an opportunity, and did all they could to bring along the minister of war. They were wasting their time. Bernadotte was indecision personified. The living image of the intrepid Gascon, inclined to be rebellious and insouciant, seductive, open, and cordial, loved by his soldiers and by women, he was in reality of a pusillanimous nature. "He seemed at first ready to try anything, to assail anything, and then his tempestuous energy dissolved into mere words."[16] Was he a Jacobin? Like so many other generals, beginning with Bonaparte, he was ambitious, and jealous to boot; not being the first, he could not bear anyone else being first in his place. It was Barras who best explained Bernadotte's Jacobinism, by saying that he "seemed to believe he had a special mission to combat the ambition of others."[17] Wanting to join the Directory, he listened carefully to the proposals made by his fellow generals, encouraged them, but postponed a response that he would never give. Although there was a Jacobin conspiracy in early September 1799, it failed for lack of Bernadotte's support. The directors nevertheless took the threat seriously enough to meet on the night of September 13. Sieyès persuaded them to dismiss Bernadotte, and sent him a letter that freed him from his ministerial functions "in response" to his frequently expressed desire to return to active command. Bernadotte replied, not without wit, "I have received, Citizen President, the order issued yesterday and the cordial letter that accompanied it. You are accepting the resignation I have not made."[18] Deprived of their most influential ally in the government, Jourdan and his Jacobin friends beat a retreat.

A Triumphal Return

The government was far from saved, but it had won a reprieve, especially because the successes on the internal front—the royalist uprisings in the Toulouse region and in the Vendée had ended in failure—were accompanied by victories won by Brune in Bergen, North Holland, on September 19, and, once again, by Masséna in Zurich on September 25–27. Sieyès and Barras could breathe more easily. The directors were even so cheered that, after having signed at the high point of the crisis in early September a new order recalling Bonaparte to France, they told themselves that after all, the general's return was not perhaps as necessary as they had thought.[19] The horizon had cleared without him. Why complicate the situation by reintroducing him into the political game? A third letter was therefore sent to him on October 10, to advise him not to rush his return.[20] Barras and Siboth were unaware that the general had not only left Egypt but had landed the preceding day at Fréjus.

If Bonaparte had feared that he would return to France too late, and if he also believed, for a moment, that the situation was no longer what he had expected and perhaps hoped it would be, the welcome he received from the authorities and residents of Fréjus must have reassured him. When the flotilla approached the port, the people gathered on the dock, a cannon was fired, and the sea was full of small boats going out to meet the ships. "Vive la République!" the commander of the port cried, "the savior of France has arrived in our harbor."[21] Bonaparte, Bourrienne assures us, was literally "picked up and carried to land."[22] Did he kneel down and kiss the soil of France? The newspapers claim he did. He refused to discuss politics and even seemed uncomfortable when someone said to him: "Go, General, go and defeat and drive away the enemy, and then we will make you king, if you want."[23] He left Fréjus that same evening, beginning a journey that was certainly one of the "finest periods" of his life.[24]

If there is one episode that is not controversial among historians, it is surely this one. Virtually no one has denied the enthusiasm that accompanied him as far as Lyon. At most we must add that he was preceded by couriers who announced his arrival and organized the festivities. But the fact remains that the people responded massively to the call, without its being necessary to force them. Church bells chimed; villagers came down from the mountains to line the road almost all the way, and the crowd was so dense "that the carriages had difficulty moving forward."[25] At night, fearing an attack by the robbers that infested the region—Bonaparte's baggage had already been pillaged in Aix—men carrying torches took turns running alongside the carriage; fires burned on the mountains, the cities were lighted and hung with the Republic's colors; the municipal authorities came to meet him and garrisons presented arms. After having crossed Aix-en-Provence, Bonaparte arrived in Avignon on the morning of October 11. The future general Boulart wrote that "on seeing the great man, the enthusiasm reached its apex, the air resounded with acclamations and the cry: *Vive Bonaparte!*" He adds: "It was the first time I saw that prodigious being. I contemplated him with a kind of avidity, I was in a state of ecstasy."[26] Then it was Montélimar, Valence on October 12, and on the thirteenth, Lyon, which gave him a triumphal reception. The future general Marbot and his father, who were on their way to Nice, were approaching the city when they learned of Bonaparte's return: "The houses were all illuminated and beflagged, fireworks were being let off; our carriage could hardly make its way through the crowd. People were dancing in the open spaces, and the air rang with cries of 'Hurrah for Bonaparte! He will save the country!' "[27] A play, *Le Héros de retour*, had been improvised in the general's honor. Despite his fatigue, he was taken from his lodging and led to the theater of the Célestins, where the actors, not having had enough time to learn their lines, mumbled their way through the play amid general indifference—those who had succeeded in following Bonaparte into the theater had eyes only for him. He was then accompanied back to his lodging, on the Place de la Comédie, where the crowd was chanting his name. He had to appear on his balcony two or three times to wave to the multitude. The following day, October 14, he set out for Chalon. The triumphal march continued.

Once again luck had been on his side. First of all, news of the victory at Abukir having reached France just before he did, the general was on the front page of the newspapers even before he landed. While he was making his way toward Paris, the French could read the very embellished account of his exploits in the Orient. What would have happened had he been preceded by the accusatory reports written by Kléber after Bonaparte left Egypt?[28] Second, he was returning with victories. Not his own victories, it might be objected, but those won by Masséna and Brune, which had put an end to the risk of immediate invasion and thus took on an importance quite different from that of the "little" victory at Abukir won over a notoriously inferior enemy in a peripheral theater of operations. However, Bonaparte's triumphal bulletins filled the newspapers so much that Brune's and Masséna's victories seemed to "ornament" those of the Army of Egypt, as if Bonaparte himself had repelled the enemy. He benefited from battles he had not fought. Finally, far from returning too late, he came back at the precise moment when the French were ready to welcome him.

It will be objected in vain that in 1799 the situation was not as serious as Bonaparte and his sycophants were later to claim, the better to justify the coup d'état. If the question were merely academic, we might in fact recall that the Republic of the Directory, which was said to be inefficient, powerless, and without imagination, was nonetheless strong enough to pave the way for the future stabilization of the financial system by liquidating the *assignats* (the banknotes used during the Revolution)—at the price, of course, of a disguised bankruptcy that ruined most savers[29]—and that in many domains, from administration to education, it laid the foundations for the reforms on which the Consulate was to pride itself after having carried them out.[30] But that is just the point: the men of the Directorate never had the political means, or even the will, to fully implement most of these reforms. Public opinion judged the Thermidorians not on their intentions but on their results. It did not hope for any benefit from this weak government that was violent by fits and starts, and it took badly everything that proceeded from it, even refusing, Thiers adds, to believe in the good that the government sometimes did.

Some people will also point out, on the basis of the study of the major trends in the economy, that the people were suffering from difficulties that were essentially transitory, and to which the impending return of the growth characteristic of the eighteenth century was to put an end. That is true: growth resumed in 1802. But the problem is that a macro-economic analysis or one bearing on long-term development does not allow us to understand the immediate implications of an economic situation, for a simple reason: contemporaries cannot perceive the major trends of an economy; they are living, concretely, in a short-term, not a long-term, framework. There is no point in telling them that everything is going fine on the scale of half a century or a century; they see only that everything is going badly: not enough money, few products to buy, the return of bartering, impassable roads, the plague of brigandage, rising taxes, unending war, a government that inspires no confidence, fortunes amassed by a handful of privileged people and profiteers of the Revolution.

Even the government's recent successes could provide no confidence in the future: "It is absurd to say that [Masséna's victory at Zurich] had saved France," Thiers observed. "Zurich was but an accident, a respite."[31] When the winter was over, war would resume under the direction of an unstable government whose lack of credibility and weakness constituted just so many obstacles to peace. As for the neo-Jacobins, they might rise up again: the right being proscribed, they had every chance of winning the elections of April 1800 and, thanks to the retirement of Barras, whose five-year term would then come to an end, of seizing the seat on the Directory that they needed to control the executive. It was the fear of a return of the Jacobins—in other words, of the Terror—that weighed most heavily on the Directory. The royalists wrongly imagined that the fear of the "blood-drinkers" of Year II served their cause, for even if the majority of the French were weary of the Revolution, of its disturbances, its violence, and its injustice, they remained attached to what it had brought them— equality, nationalized property, the victories of the republican armies—and were united in their rejection of the Old Regime, even if they had to admit that life was easier before 1789 than it had become since. The obsession with the past, a disgust with the present, the fear of the future, scorn for the government and for those who sought to replace it: The French not only lived "apart" from their leaders, the assemblies, and the constitution.[32] They no longer believed in politics. The latter had been one of the great passions of the Revolution, which had invested political action with an unlimited power to transform things, but the Terror, and then the disappointments of the Thermidorian period, had overcome this belief. Passion had changed to a disgust that spared nothing and was manifested in a massive disengagement, a turn toward the private sphere, an almost absolute indifference to everything that concerned the state, ideas, or party struggles, and an unqualified skepticism regarding the possibilities of transforming the present or taking control of the future. No longer believing in the Revolution, the French watched the Republic collapsing but did not believe that things would go better if it were replaced by a monarchy. If many of them gave Bonaparte a triumphal welcome, that was because he seemed to be a symbol, not of a freedom that the French no longer cared much about, but rather of victory, peace, and order. Victory? Wasn't he returning from the Orient, crowned with victories all the more fabulous because little or nothing was known about them? Bonaparte *was* victory: he was also peace. His name evoked not only Rivoli but also Campoformio, that ephemeral peace that the Directory's irresponsible behavior—everyone was convinced of this—had destroyed. At that time, who was lucid enough to state, loud and clear, that the Treaty of Campoformio, which was unacceptable even for its signatories, carried war within itself as a cloud carries a storm?[33] If Bonaparte's return seemed to be a promise of peace, it was also a promise of a peace that his unprecedented victories guaranteed to be "in conformity with honor"; in other words, France's enemies would lay down their arms without France being obliged to sacrifice any of the Revolution's conquests. Finally, Bonaparte was a symbol of order. It is true that he had participated in 18 Fructidor, but if he had remained faithful to the camp of the Revolution at that time, he had deplored the excesses the coup d'état perpetrated against the royalists. Neither another revolution nor a counterrevolution, neither left nor right: he seemed to carry the flag of a Republic that was the enemy of both the Old Regime and the Terror, which the directors, who had taken it as their watchword, had not been able to defend. Above all, he gave this politics of the golden mean the support of force, a force that was henceforth imposed on others as well as on himself. Miot de Melito, who visited him after his return, testifies to this: "I thought his tone in conversation firmer and fuller than before. His naturally strong mind had gained in vigour under the strain of the perilous expedition to Egypt, and he was full of courage."[34] Everyone sensed in him something implacable, in which the cruelest episodes of his Oriental escapade certainly played a role. He had proven that there was no limit to what he was capable of.[35] Later this would often allow him to avoid being violent. His Oriental adventure had made him grander. It had also added a touch of the marvelous to his character. He was no longer a mere general who was returning from the mists of the mysterious Orient, but already a legendary figure, a new Alexander, "a phenomenon" as Mme de Staël put it,[36] all the more imposing because all around him everything now lay in ruins. Whereas people and things seemed to have grown smaller during his absence, he returned new, washed clean even of what his past might contain that was murky or unavowable. The general collapse made him seem greater.

Another factor operated in his favor. The Revolution had run through the whole spectrum of known political forms. Constitutional monarchy had disappeared with Louis XVI, the democracy of 1793 had sunk into violence and terror, and the Directory's failures had confirmed the old axiom of eighteenth-century political philosophy: the impossibility of a republic in a large country. How could the French not have believed that, the wheel having made full circle, a restoration of the monarchy was inevitable? The cries of "Vive le roi!" that were heard with increasing frequency in 1799 meant that this time there was no longer any question of the revolutionary utopia of perfect democratic power, of the vain quest for a government whose "impersonality" would be diametrically opposite to the personalization characteristic of the monarchical system. The French were ready, or at least resigned, to see rise again "the only great role in the history of France": that of the king as a figure of power incarnate.[37] The Revolution had tried every way of substituting the people for the king. In vain. From one usurpation to another, the crown had fallen from the people's head into the hands of increasingly improbable beneficiaries, until the little Corsican general, basing himself on the glory won on the battlefield, finally came to raise it up by recovering for his own benefit the legitimacy that the feeble institutions of the Thermidorian Republic had lost. Mme de Staël, referring to Bonaparte's return to France, summed it all up in a few words: "It was the first time since the Revolution that the name of an individual was heard in every mouth. Till then it was said—the Constituent Assembly has done so and so, or the people, or the Convention; now there was no mention of any but this man, who was to be substituted for all and leave the human race without a name."[38]

Bonaparte, as a royalist agent put it no less profoundly, had returned "to give France a new face,"[39] and to give the Revolution, along with a king of a new kind, an end that fulfilled its promises, even if it was in a form that the revolutionaries could not have imagined. How else can we understand the kind of consent that surrounded him upon his return? He was to mention this later, in a passage worthy of Tacitus, in which he no doubt exaggerates, but which is basically true:

> When a deplorable weakness and an endless inconstancy are manifested in the halls of power; when, yielding by turns to the influence of contrary parties, and living from day to day without a set plan, without a firm step, it has given the measure of its inadequacy, and when the most moderate citizens are forced to agree that the state is no longer governed; when, finally, to its internal nullity the administration adds the gravest fault it can have in the eyes of a proud people, I refer to external debasement, then a vague uneasiness spreads through society, the need to preserve itself troubles it, and, casting its eyes on itself, it seems to be seeking a man who can save it. This guardian spirit is always contained within a numerous nation; but sometimes it is slow to appear. In fact, it does not suffice that it exist, it must be known; it has to know

itself. Until then all attempts are vain, all maneuvers powerless; the inertia of the masses protects the nominal government, and despite its incompetence and its weakness, its enemies' efforts do not prevail against it. But when this impatiently awaited savior suddenly makes a sign of his existence, the national instinct divines him and calls him, obstacles are smoothed out before him, and a whole great people, hurrying to see him pass, seems to say: Here he is![40]

Bonaparte was clearly not the "hero" of all French people: there is no unanimity in this world. But what matters lies elsewhere. If he was not acclaimed by all the French, he was acclaimed by the peasants of the Rhône valley and by the residents of Lyon and Paris, and the Jacobins proved to be as satisfied with his return as were the royalists, even though for different reasons. It is true that not *all* the Jacobins and *all* the royalists cried "Vive Bonaparte!" But it is because *some* Jacobins, *some* royalists, and some people of all social strata cried together "Vive Bonaparte!" that he was to claim that on his return to France he was received not as a citizen, nor as a general, but as a "sovereign returning to his estates."[41]

Conjugal Scenes

Bonaparte arrived in Paris early on October 16. In order to escape acclamations, he had taken a route through Nevers and Montargis rather than the more direct route from Lyon to Paris via Chalon. It was not that he feared the Directory's reaction, but he thought it pointless to provoke it by making too ostentatious a return to the capital. Everything went well: the directors had momentarily considered court-martialing him as a deserter;[42] instead they received him with solemn faces; they were resigned to eating humble pie, given that they could not, as Sieyès had wisely pointed out, show themselves to be "more severe than France."[43] The ice was hard to break and the accolade that ended the interview "was not given or received very fraternally."[44]

Bonaparte's mind was elsewhere: he had found his house empty when he arrived there. As he approached Paris, was he still thinking about separating from his wife, as he had written to Joseph the preceding year after Junot had spoken to him about Captain Charles? Time had gone by since then, and there had been "Bellilotte." Did he imagine Joséphine obediently waiting for him at the fireside, like the virtuous wife she was not? The fact remains that not finding her in the house on Rue de la Victoire reminded him of the painful hours he had endured in Milan, and revived the idea of divorce. The first visit he made, after meeting with the Directory, was to Barras. After all, he was the director who had advised him to marry Joséphine. Barras listened to the account of his conjugal misfortunes and then, like the true centrist he was, cried: Divorce? For such trifles? Isn't life made of transactions and concessions? What about the gossip? And the jokes? Had he thought about that? And finally, he added subtly, did Bonaparte really regret this marriage that had not disserved him, far from it: hadn't Joséphine helped make him what he was today? Couldn't she still be useful to him?[45] Bonaparte refused to listen to him, but the next day he told Collot about his problems, and the financier gave him the same advice as Barras, and received the same response: "No! I've made my decision; she will no longer set foot in my house."[46]

Joséphine arrived on the night of October 18, bringing Hortense along with her. For four days she had been roaming the roads of France looking for Napoleon. It had been eighteen months since she had heard from him. She had not longed too much for this husband whom she said she "liked well enough, despite his little defects."[47] After having accompanied him as far as Toulon, she had sojourned a long time at the Plombières spa before returning to Paris, where she had resumed the expensive habits and the life that she liked so much, attending balls, spending hours with her dressmakers, putting her relations in the service of anyone who asked it of her, without ever refusing, fleeing her creditors, borrowing in order to buy—on credit—the half-ruined house and the grounds of Malmaison, with which she had fallen in love.[48] Did she see Hippolyte again? Did she reconnect once or twice with Barras, who had remained faithful to her in his own way? Did she become infatuated with one of the director's aides-de-camp? The rumors regarding her husband's death that regularly agitated Paris troubled her hardly at all. After all, she was also waging war, and on an enemy still less convenient than the Turks: her mother-in-law, her brothers-in-law, and her sisters-in-law, who never missed an opportunity to denigrate her. She had found a new protector: Director Gohier, who courted her discreetly and came every day, at four o'clock sharp, to offer her his homage and spend a little time in the light that she shed all around her. This was a welcome reinforcement against Joseph's and Lucien's scheming. She was dining at Gohier's home on October 13 when her husband's landing at Fréjus was announced. "I am going to meet him," she said to Gohier's wife.[49] Rising from the dinner table, she hurried off to Saint-Germain to get Hortense. That same evening she left Paris. Joseph did the same, taking with him Lucien, Louis, and even his brother-in-law Leclerc, as if it were indispensable that the family overwhelm Napoleon by its numbers in order to have a small chance of competing with the unfaithful wife. Joséphine's carriage passed through Sens, Joigny, and Auxerre. At Chalon she learned devastating news: Bonaparte was returning via Nevers.[50] She was worried, she panicked. He must already be at Rue de la Victoire, perhaps surrounded by the whole group. She turned around. When she finally got back to Paris, she found herself alone. Bonaparte's brothers had also gone the wrong way.[51] They had come back before her and Lucien had been able to speak with his elder brother. Did they talk about Joséphine? It is not clear, but it seems probable that Napoleon would not have told this younger brother he didn't much like what he willingly confided to Barras.

Bonaparte had given orders not to allow Joséphine to come in. She pushed the doorman aside and entered . . . to find his trunk in the vestibule. Then she made a great scene, weeping and begging before the closed door to the bedroom, calling Hortense and even Eugène to come add their tears to her own, until Bonaparte, defeated or thinking he had done enough to make her understand what a catastrophe she was escaping, opened the door and let his wife throw her arms around his neck. The next morning it was a radiant Joséphine lying in bed alongside her husband who greeted Lucien, who had come to see if "the old woman," as he called her, had finally cleared out. A few hours later Bonaparte whispered to Collot, who had come to lunch: "What do you expect me to do? To be human is to be weak."[52]

If Joséphine boasted of having found Bonaparte "more loving than ever,"[53] things did not, despite everything, completely return to the way they were before. Joséphine never forgot how close she had come that night to being repudiated. She learned to be prudent, but she also lost, in part, the irresistible ascendancy she had exercised over her husband. Perhaps the danger paradoxically helped her have new feelings toward this "Bonaparte" whom she had up to that point loved in her own way, that is, distractedly. Above all, he had changed, and it was perhaps at this moment that she finally understood that she had, as François Furet says, "hit the jackpot" by marrying him.[54] As for Bonaparte, he had ended up yielding, perhaps secretly satisfied with the victory won by his wife, because it freed him of a worry at a time when politics required all his attention. But he was also, and from then on, marked by the memory of that empty house, which told him a great deal about the reality of their marriage. If Joséphine henceforth felt a new attachment to her husband, Napoleon did not rediscover for her a love that he had already ceased to feel long before. A "habitual tenderness" replaced it.[55]

The Reasons for a Coup d'État

With regard to the public, Bonaparte adopted the same rule of conduct he had followed when he returned from Italy: adhere to a very republican discretion that, without preventing him from being suspected, at least sheltered him from any formal accusation. So he went out infrequently; but though he did not seek out the crowd, the crowd came to him. His brothers, first of all, followed by the veterans of the Italian campaign and Talleyrand, whom he received without seeming to remember that the former minister—who had in the meantime resigned his post—had failed to fulfill his promise to go to Constantinople to negotiate the cession of Egypt. Then Joseph brought to Rue de la Victoire his friends who were representatives in the Legislature and writers: as Taine put it, "the intelligent Republic" passed through Bonaparte's house. The "booted Republic" was not to be outdone. There was an uninterrupted parade of uniforms. The dinner table was open to all. Lunches and dinners were eaten at a rapid pace, presided over by a smiling Joséphine and a Bonaparte who was sometimes reserved and sometimes hurled accusations at the Directory. He kept an eye on his guests' reactions and whispered to the military men who agreed with him, as if they were already on his side: "Go give your address to Berthier!" The government itself seemed to have transferred its offices to the general's house, and Roederer rightly observed that "without balking at the idea of handing over superior authority to him, everyone granted it to him; he had it really; he did not exercise it, but no one else exercised it without his consent."[56] The government no longer governed; the parties themselves held their breath and looked to this man whom everyone saw, according to Marmont, as "the rising sun." Everything depended on the initiatives he would take. It was tacitly admitted that he and he alone held the secret of the future.

However, it would be a mistake to imagine that 18 Brumaire was "easily achieved."[57] Power was not given to Bonaparte; he had to seize it. If a coup d'état was inevitable, this was first of all because legitimacy, no matter how strong it is, does not automatically confer authority. There was still a government, which, no matter how weak, was unlikely to spontaneously abdicate its powers; and there was a constitution, which, even if it was contested, even if it was weakened by repeated power plays, continued to draw a boundary between what was legal and what was not, between what was legitimate and what was not.

Furthermore, the constitution prohibited any institutional reform for another five years. The rigidity of the procedure for revision, it will be said, justified the coup d'état in advance, as soon as there was a near consensus in favor of a constitutional change. Under these conditions, can one really speak of a "coup d'état"? Instead, it was a matter of finding a way around the legal obstacle in order to make changes that everyone agreed could not wait another five years. This forced revision was illegal only from the point of view of a legality that was inapplicable and even harmful to the preservation of republican institutions. It was in this spirit that Sieyès had worked all summer on the preparation for a coup d'état that he saw as a simple revision intended to renovate the Republic and not overthrow it, undertaken at the initiative of the legal political authority and executed by the parliament, while the army—General Joubert filling the role of "sword"—would intervene to overcome, if necessary, any possible attempts at resistance.

Given Bonaparte's personality and reputation, the revision achieved by exceptional means became a veritable coup d'état. The rather easy success of 18 Brumaire has retrospectively attenuated the difficulty of the enterprise. But, it will be objected, the law had been violated so often during the Revolution that no one could take offense at an additional infraction. That is to forget that the people and its elected representatives had always scoffed at the law. Hence, violence could appear to be *legitimate* because it was a matter of the people (or the active minorities that took its place) exercising through exceptional means, and under circumstances that were usually extraordinary, its fundamental right to make and unmake the laws. Each revolutionary coup d'état had taken on the appearance of a return to the constituent power of the people. A strange spectacle: the attacks on the new principle of legitimacy—the Law—did not destroy the idea of law. The idea had survived all its violations, it remained the supreme value, the horizon toward which the Revolution tended and the anchoring point to which it sought to attach its acts. Even the Terror had not been able to erase the prestige of the law. After the crimes committed by the Committee of Public Safety and the countless illegalities during the period of the Directory, it remained the condition of any legitimacy, the principle in relation to which every decision had to be justified, no matter how contrary it might be to any kind of legality or morality. Thus the ovations did not protect Bonaparte against the accusation of having usurped power. The army could not take the place of the people as a few thousand militants from the Paris sections had been able to do in the past. Bonaparte could not base himself on the "will of the sovereign people" because he did not occupy any official position in the government, and neither could he count on the support of sections that had long since ceased to play the slightest political role. To seize power, he had to overthrow the Law with a capital letter, but without being able to base his actions on any of the justifications used by his predecessors. The most civilian of the generals nonetheless remained a general, who could not be unaware of how much the Revolution had lived in fear of the day constantly prophesied when Caesar, Cromwell, or Monk would overthrow liberty. Even surrounded by general recognition, if in his turn Bonaparte attacked institutions in a way that was too clearly military, he had to reckon with the risk of becoming, in the view of public opinion, a seditious general like La Fayette, Dumouriez, and Pichegru before him: not because he would be attacking the institutions, but because he would then seem to be attacking the principles—liberty and the sovereignty of the people—that at least in theory supported them. Thus, he was aware of the necessity of obtaining the support of at least some of the directors of the Republic. In order to give a civilian aspect to his coup d'état, he even had to show himself to be very punctilious with regard to the apparent respect for legal forms. For all these reasons, the preparation of the coup d'état cost Bonaparte many sleepless nights and travails, in any case more than he wanted to admit after he had won.

Maneuvers, Preparations, and Negotiations

All the parties sought him out on his return. Did that mean that he had his choice of allies? Barras? Too compromising. The Jacobins? Too unpopular: "After having won with them," he was to say later, "I would have immediately had to win against them."[58] Sieyès then? Sieyès did not come empty-handed, but with the plan he had worked out over the summer with Lucien when the two men were considering overthrowing the Directory with Joubert's help. With a proposed constitution and a large number of supporters who had a majority in the Council of Ancients and were powerful at the Institute, he could be seen as constituting the "national majority." From the outset, Bonaparte leaned toward Sieyès and Sieyès leaned toward Bonaparte. Upon learning of the general's return, the Old Regime abbé had told Lucien: "It is around your brother, now, that we all have to gather."[59] The two men needed one another, and knew it: the general to seize power, the director to establish his constitution. If Bonaparte put off making a decision, it was because he did not want to alarm those with whom he had already decided, in his heart of hearts, he would not ally himself. He wanted to let everyone entertain the hope that he might finally go over to their side. Another reason for this slow and gradual rapprochement: the two men did not know each other well and didn't much like each other. Between them, there was first of all the difference in age: Sieyès was over fifty years old, Bonaparte was thirty: the former represented the past, the latter the future. In addition, Sieyès had always been secretive, whereas Bonaparte could live only in the full light of day. No one symbolizes better than Sieyès the passion for abstraction and the spirit of system that characterized the Revolution; Bonaparte, skeptical and realistic, detested theories and theoreticians. "An old man with his head in the clouds," he was to say about Sieyès: "A young adventurer," retorted Sieyès, "who sleeps with the Republic when he needs to find her in his bed."[60] Between them there was enmity, and pride. As Jacques Bainville wrote, they were both "figures too great" to be able to meet in a simple way and seal their alliance with a handshake.[61] It was a question of vanity that at the same time involved something still more decisive: How can we imagine one of the two taking the first step that would make him dependent on the other? For Bonaparte there was no question of joining the conspiracy that Sieyès had been weaving since June: on the contrary, he had to make Sieyès understand that he, Bonaparte, was accepting the director's help. When Lucien came to advise his brother to meet Sieyès, Bonaparte replied that things were not yet ripe: "It does not suit me to take on the color of a party," he told him.[62]

Convinced that he would finally arrive at an agreement with Sieyès, Bonaparte sought chiefly to gain his competitors' trust. If General Moreau spontaneously promised him his help—not without a certain hypocrisy—none of the other heavyweights in the army showed the same eagerness. Neither Augereau, nor Jourdan, nor Bernadotte—especially not Bernadotte, Joseph's brother-in-law—made the pilgrimage to Rue de la Victoire. Bonaparte's and Bernadotte's respective entourages were working in the wings to facilitate a rapprochement, but the conversation finally arranged on Rue de la Victoire on October 27 went nowhere. An "accidental" meeting arranged the next evening on leaving the Théâtre français yielded no greater result, and the two men parted on cool terms after a long interview at Mortefontaine, Joseph's home. Bonaparte went back to Paris on October 30. Another meeting awaited him: with Barras.

It is not easy to disentangle the director's feelings during these crucial days that were to end with his fall. He seems to have been confident, certain that Bonaparte would not betray his former mentor, and he was all the more sure of himself because he held several key cards in his hand: Lefebvre, the commander of the capital's troops, and Fouché and Réal, the two chiefs of police.[63] He could afford to stay in the background to some extent, certain that he could put a quick end to any enterprise that did not have his approval, and perhaps he would have waited still longer to make up his mind had Réal not told him that the general was on the brink of making an agreement with Sieyès. Barras, worried, decided to have a frank discussion with Bonaparte as soon as possible. As for Bonaparte, he could not forget that Barras had always "shown friendship toward him." And Barras was a former solider: they belonged to the same world, they understood one another. On the other hand, Barras was the detested symbol of a discredited regime. Whereas the weight of habit acted in his favor, reason pleaded against him. Bonaparte knew that breaking with him would not be easy, but Barras himself facilitated things. He proved to be clumsy, thinking he could patronize his guest. When he declared himself in favor of creating a president of the Republic on the American model and proposed, half seriously, half jokingly, the obscure General Hédouville for this office, Bonaparte got up from the table, slammed the door, and went to see Sieyès: "I stayed there only five minutes, because I couldn't be seen, and I told him that I was coming to tell him that I would go with him.—Is it a deal, then? Sieyès said.—Yes. We shook hands.—Tomorrow, we'll agree on the means. And I left."[64] However, Bonaparte was not quite done with Barras, whom Réal succeeded in persuading to go to Rue de la Victoire the next day to try to glue things back together. Bonaparte recounts the meeting: "Barras was announced at my home; he came with his big hat on askew as usual, and his cane. I was in bed. He is announced, he comes in. . . . I thought last night, Barras says, about what you said to me yesterday [I listened]. I think what would be best is for you to take power.—I have not been well, I said, since I endured the heat of the tropics. For three months I have not been good for anything, and other remarks of the sort. My decision was made, and my commitments were elsewhere."[65]

As soon as Barras had left, he added: "The man is sunk!"[66] He was sunk, but had to be treated carefully. Bonaparte let the director believe that a last-minute agreement was still possible. He even returned to the Luxembourg Palace on November 4: "My interests are yours; our causes are so bound up," he is supposed to have told Barras.[67] What mattered was to prevent him from having any suspicions. Thus, on the sixth, an impressive delegation appeared at the Luxembourg, with Joseph and Talleyrand at its head, to assure Barras of Bonaparte's goodwill. Bonaparte himself came the following morning to see the director one last time. Their conversation was brief. Bonaparte promised to come back that evening. Barras waited for him in vain. Late that night Bourrienne appeared instead to inform him that the general had been held up. It was as if everything were suddenly collapsing around the director: "I see Bonaparte is deceiving me," he said. "He won't return. It's over. But I'm the one to whom he owes everything."[68] Bonaparte had definitively escaped him. This time the "old lion" was truly dead. A void opened around him. Réal abandoned him without hesitation and, power attracting power, on November 3 Fouché presented himself at Bonaparte's home on Rue de la Victoire to make his change in allegiance official.

The Plan for the Coup d'État

Bonaparte had made a brief stop at Sieyès's home on the evening of October 30. The decisive meeting took place on the night of November 1, at Lucien's home on Rue de Miromesnil. Even though marked effusiveness was hardly to be expected, Lucien was uncomfortably affected by his brother's coolness. At first Bonaparte made a few efforts, saying that he was confident that Sieyès's genius could give France the constitution it needed, but the conversation soon took a sudden turn that surprised the director. "The time to act has come," Bonaparte told him. "Have you decided on everything you're going to do?" Sieyès tried to lead the discussion onto constitutional terrain, the only one on which he could exercise a certain ascendancy over the general, but the latter was not to be deceived, and without letting his interlocutor finish his remarks, he interrupted him:

> I know all that through what my brother told me; but surely you are not intending to present France with a new, ready-made constitution without its being discussed calmly, article by article. That cannot be done quickly and we have no time to lose. Thus we have to have a provisional government that will take authority the very day of the transition, and a Legislative Commission to prepare a reasonable constitution and propose it to a vote of the people; for I will never accept anything that has not been freely discussed and approved by a universal, properly certified vote. . . . So concern yourself solely with the move to Saint-Cloud and the simultaneous establishment of a provisional government. I approve the limitation of this government to three persons; and because it is considered necessary, I consent to be one of the three provisional consuls along with you and your colleague Roger Ducos. As for the definitive government, that is another matter; we shall see what you shall decide with the Legislative Commission. I shall support your

decisions; but I reserve for myself the right to be part of the executive power or to command an army. That will depend on what arrangements you make.[69]

Sieyès was staggered. Bonaparte had referred to the formation of a constitutional commission: wasn't that intended to limit Sieyès's work and give Bonaparte himself the means for amending it? He had also demanded that the definitive text be presented to the people for its approval: that was not compatible with the principles of the former member of the Constituent Assembly. He was not pleased by all this. Seeing Sieyès looking sulky, Bonaparte lost his temper: "You wouldn't want to submit your plan to a commission? As for myself, without going any further, I tell you frankly that in that case, you must no longer count on me. Look here, give it some thought. We can see each other again when you want to." And he went away, letting the ex-abbé express his resentment in front of Lucien.

Once the agreement between the leaders was finally made the following day, it was time for the intermediaries to speak. Going back and forth between Rue de la Victoire and the Luxembourg, Talleyrand and Roederer made sure the necessary support had been gained and set about making the material preparations for the coup d'état. Jacques Bainville called this plan a "project full of holes."[70] That is certainly true so far as the imprecision of its objectives is concerned—Sieyès and Bonaparte, and especially the latter, had carefully avoided defining too clearly the outlines of the regime that would succeed the Directory. The same cannot be said of its means. It is true that the preparation for the coup d'état was rapid, but it was not as casual as is affirmed by those who have, since Tocqueville, ridiculed the "civilians" and "intellectuals" who took the initiative. A few days sufficed because the plan had been worked out at the time when Sieyès was preparing "the Joubert operation." It would be a mistake, moreover, to attribute the plan's imperfections to the short deadline: they resulted from the will to act as legally as possible and to use force only as a last resort. The respect for legality could be only apparent. Not only did the Constitution of Year III prohibit any constitutional modification before 1804, it also stipulated that the constituent power could not be exercised by the ordinary Legislature. To that extent, the revision could be carried out only by violating the Constitution, and all the more so because the power relationship in the two councils was not favorable to the conspirators. Although they were fairly sure of the Council of Ancients, that was far from being the case for the Five Hundred. Nonetheless, it was not in order to force the Five Hundred to carry out the revision that the army's assistance was indispensable, but rather in order to prevent them from finding aid outside the parliamentary compound. The memory of the great revolutionary *journées* was still present in people's minds, and the conspirators feared an uprising in the faubourgs, even though this was unlikely. They considered it necessary to isolate the Councils.

The Constitution of Year III itself offered the solution: to forestall any repetition of the events of May 31 and June 2, 1793, when the Convention had been besieged by the sections, it authorized the Council of Ancients to transfer the Legislature outside the capital. On the pretext of an imminent plot, they would resolve to transfer the Legislature to Saint-Cloud and would entrust its defense to the army. In terms of the Constitution, this decree, once adopted, was irrevocable, and could be abrogated neither by the Five Hundred nor by the Directory, and the session of the Legislature would be adjourned until it had gathered in the place designated by the Ancients.

This plan had the advantage of paralyzing the Five Hundred during the interval separating the adoption of the transfer decree and the extraordinary meeting of the assemblies in the château of Saint-Cloud, which had been chosen for its proximity to the capital and the ease of controlling access to it with a relatively small number of troops. But the plan did have one major downside: it spread the coup d'état over two days, the first for the transfer, the second for the regime change. It would probably have been better to rush things and take advantage of the representatives' astonishment to get them to do what was wanted. The intervening time was certainly a drawback, but it could have been avoided only by executing a purely military strike during the first hours of 18 Brumaire; a formal, purely parliamentary procedure, even if it was illegal, required this interval, no matter how dangerous it was. It was the price that had to be paid to save appearances.

A Final Summit Meeting

Three or four days had sufficed to refine the plan and assign roles. The conspirators' movements back and forth, even though precautions were taken, could not pass totally unnoticed. Rumors were beginning to spread.[71] In fact, the success of the coup d'état had less to do with unavoidable ignorance of what was brewing than with the government's desire not to know what every informed person knew. Bernadotte had told Barras, Dubois-Crancé knew, Moulin understood nothing, and Gohier did not want to know. Bonaparte was so little concerned about the possible reactions of the men in power that the date of the coup d'état having been initially set for November 7 (16 Brumaire), at the last moment he asked for a delay of two days. The reason? He had invited Jourdan to dine with him on the seventh. He wanted to have a last chance to convince his colleague, if not to join the operation, at least not to oppose it. This final attempt was well worth a small delay.

Jourdan was not an adversary to be scorned. The left recognized him as its leader, and despite his recent defeats in Germany, for many French people he remained the victor of Wattignies and Fleurus. Moreover, he was considered to be sincere in his political convictions, which gave him—paradoxically, perhaps—increased influence over a group in which convictions were generally uncertain. Jourdan was influential because he was respected. And he was respected, by all parties, because even though he was seen as the leader of the Jacobins, he lacked neither moderation nor good sense. From that point of view, he had nothing in common with Augereau or Bernadotte. Jourdan, who knew he was the leader of the opposition, accepted the associated responsibilities and duties. But of course he had his own interests to defend; since the time when he had fought as a simple soldier in America, he had risen so high that he feared choosing the wrong horse and taking a vertiginous fall. He was bound to his party, and honor forbade him to abandon it, but he would have liked his party to be conciliatory, and he wished an agreement could have been worked out with Bonaparte.

Most of the Jacobins were not hostile—on the contrary—but the conspirators had to reckon with Bernadotte and especially Augereau, who repeated to anyone who would listen that he would take the "escapee from Egypt" down a peg or two.[72] On October 30, the evening Bonaparte dined at Barras's home, Bernadotte, who had also returned from Mortefontaine, had called a meeting of the leading Jacobins. The session was stormy. Jourdan had to fight hard to get a strategy of conciliation adopted. Against Augereau's advice, he succeeded in persuading his interlocutors to approach Bonaparte and offer him the Jacobin party's support in order to raise him to power. Jourdan went to Rue de la Victoire, but Bonaparte had gone out. Told about Jourdan's visit, Bonaparte invited him for lunch on November 7.

On that day, after lunch, the two men went into the garden, and Jourdan told Bonaparte about his friends' proposals. Was he expecting his host's very sharp response? "I can do nothing with you and your friends, you don't have a majority. You have frightened the Council [of Five Hundred] by proposing to declare that the country is in danger, and you are voting with men who dishonor you. I am convinced of your good intentions and those of your friends, but on this occasion I cannot work with you. However, don't worry, everything will be done in the interest of the Republic."

Jourdan pursued the matter no further. As he was leaving, he mentioned to Bonaparte that he did not want civil war: that was a way of promising to remain neutral, in any case so long as fate did not turn against the conspirators. Now nothing was holding Bonaparte back.

The preceding evening he had gone to the Temple of Victory (the church of Saint-Sulpice), where the Councils had organized a gala dinner for him and for Moreau. Seven hundred guests were waiting for him when he arrived around six o'clock. Despite the forest of flags hung on the walls, music, hymns composed for the occasion, and toasts proposed by the two special guests—"To the union of all Frenchmen!" for Bonaparte, "To all the Republic's faithful allies!" for Moreau—the mood was solemn, icy, and dark. As the editor of the *Gazette de France* put it: "The dinner was short, silent, and not very gay. The musical instruments took the place of conversation. Moreover, most of the guests had already eaten, people said. They sat down to table out of politeness; and in general there was in this meal a diplomatic manner, an air of constraint that proves that one can voluntarily attend the same banquet, break the same bread and not have the same political opinion, be guests at the same table without being close friends."[73]

Neither Augereau nor Jourdan nor Bernadotte had accepted the invitation. But the directors were there, as were 500 representatives, those who were anxiously awaiting the time to go into action sitting alongside those who did not suspect that the regime was living its last moments. Lavalette, Bonaparte's aide-de-camp, wrote, "Those who were in on the secret of the plot preferred not to speak rather than to risk dangerous conversation with neighbors who might differ in opinion with them."[74] Bonaparte did not try to conceal his uneasiness among these legislators whom he knew so little and detested so much, or the annoyance he felt at playing a secondary role in a play that was approaching its last act. "Let's get it over with, and quickly," he seemed to be saying. After two hours, without having touched his food and having shaken a few hands, he slipped out. The Thermidorian Republic had just given its last performance: it had no more than two days to live.

TWENTY-TWO

Brumaire

Citizen Gohier, the sitting president of the Executive Directory, slept badly on the night before 18 Brumaire (November 9, 1799).[1] He was peacefully dozing in the apartment he occupied on the ground floor of the Petit-Luxembourg—the official residence of members of the government—when a servant awakened him: Citizen Beauharnais was asking to see him. Gohier got up. What could Eugène possibly want at one o'clock in the morning? The day before Gohier had visited, as he always did, Joséphine, Eugène's mother, who told him that she and Bonaparte would dine at his home the following day. Was the young man going to tell him they couldn't come? If that were the case, he had chosen an odd time to do it. Eugène handed him an envelope. It was a note from his mother: "My dear Gohier, come eat breakfast with me tomorrow at eight, and bring your wife. Don't fail to do so, I have to talk with you about some very interesting matters."[2] Once Eugène had left, Gohier returned to his bedroom, pensive. Why did Joséphine want to see him so early, when she and her husband had promised to come to the Luxembourg around 2 P.M.? What could she have to tell him that was so "interesting"? Had he been a more suspicious person, Gohier would have remembered the warnings given him by the minister of war, Dubois-Crancé, who had accused Bonaparte of fomenting a coup d'état. It was a matter of days, he said, maybe of hours. But Gohier refused to believe these rumors that were buzzing all through Paris. There was no ministry, no salon, no café where the same thing had not been said repeatedly ever since the general, back from Egypt, had returned to the capital on October 16. Gohier had heard many such rumors. Experience had made him skeptical. Assuming that Dubois-Crancé's report might have troubled him, the fact that the general was coming to dine with him on 18 Brumaire would have fully reassured him.[3] He was certain that nothing would happen the next day.

The Last Day of the Revolution

How long had he slept? The noise had awakened him. A great commotion, the clatter of weapons, footsteps, orders shouted to no one in particular, the sounds of boots and the whinnying of horses . . . He got up, opened the window, threw open the shutters and saw with astonishment the guard assigned to protect the Directory getting itself into marching order. Amid the foot soldiers and cavalrymen he saw General Jubé, the commander of the guard, and shouted: "Citizen-general, what are you doing there?"—"Citizen-president, you see well enough what I am doing; I am assembling the guard."—"No doubt I see that very well, Citizen-general; but what are you assembling them for?"—"Citizen-president, I am going to make an inspection of them, and to command a great manoeuvre."[4] It was incomprehensible. He hadn't been informed of anything. He let it go. He watched the troops leave the Luxembourg and remained a moment at the window, listening to the sound of the men's footsteps and the clatter of the horses' hooves. Then he went back to bed, wondering whether he was going to be allowed to finish his night.

While Gohier was trying to go back to sleep, candles were burning in the Tuileries, where, behind the drawn curtains of the offices of the Council of Ancients, the quaestors (*inspecteurs de salle*) were wide awake. They were important figures: the constitution gave them the power to convoke the assembly, and also the power to requisition the Legislature's guard. It was on their orders that the guards had been doubled; and it was on their orders that in the early morning, armed men surrounded the Tuileries. With the aid of a few clerks, they had drafted the convocations for a session set for an unusual hour: seven in the morning. The list of representatives to be informed had been drawn up with care.

At Bonaparte's home on Rue de la Victoire, candles were burning as well. Alexandre Berthier, his chief of staff, was putting the final touches on the letters addressed to the officers of the Paris garrison and the National Guard to ask them to present themselves at the general's residence at 6 A.M., in uniform. There again, as at the Tuileries, some were told what was going on, others were sent away. Bonaparte himself had written several of these letters—the one addressed to General Lefebvre, commander of the Paris military division, and those sent to Generals Moreau and Macdonald. The officers who had returned from Egypt with Bonaparte had been asked to help draw up the list of their colleagues who could be counted upon: Marmont for the artillerymen, Murat for the cavalry, Lannes for the infantry, Berthier for the general officers. While Jubé was leading his troops out of the Luxembourg, the officers of the Legislative Body's guard and Bonaparte's aides-de-camp were knocking on doors, awakening representatives and military men.

On Rue Taitbout, three men jumped into a carriage that set out for the Place Vendôme. They were Roederer, his son Antoine, and Talleyrand, whom they had come to pick up at his home to go to the seat of the administration of the Department of the Seine, whose head, Réal, was waiting for them.

Finally the troops began to move. Around 5 A.M., the soldiers of the Ninth Regiment of Dragoons, commanded by Colonel Sebastiani, left the Hôtel de Soubise, in the Marais quarter, defying the orders of the minister of war, who, suspecting that something was up, had confined them to their barracks. Most of the troops moved down the boulevards toward the Place de la Révolution, while the rest headed for Rue de la Victoire. The Eighth Dragoons moved out a little later, followed by the Twenty-First Chasseurs, led by Murat. The two regiments, one coming from the Champ-de-Mars, the other from the Quai d'Orsay, took up positions from the Chaussée d'Antin to the Tuileries. In all, almost 3,000 men, most of whom had served under Bonaparte in Italy, were involved. The coup d'état was beginning.

The previous night's rain had given way to icy weather. The members of the Council of Ancients were already hurrying to the Tuileries. They sat in the hall formerly occupied by the Convention, the "Salle des Machines" in the Tuileries. The galleries reserved for the public were empty. The president, Lemercier, immediately gave the floor to the head of the commission of the quaestors, Mathieu-Augustin Cornet. He referred in vague terms to the existence of a plot against the Republic.[5] A deathly silence prevailed in the assembly. The time had come to indicate the remedy: the transfer to Saint-Cloud of the two legislative councils and the Executive Directory. In parliamentary language, the motion elicited "diverse movements." Despite the care with which known opponents had been excluded, not all the representatives present were prepared to swallow this. Regnier, one of the conspirators, spoke up: "Representatives of the people, have no concern about the execution of your decree: first of all, it is drawn from the Constitution itself, to which everything must be subject; second, it will have the public's confidence as its guarantee. . . . If you need something more, I would say to you that Bonaparte is there, ready to execute your decree as soon as you have asked him to do so. This illustrious man, who has deserved so much from the country, is eager to crown his noble works with this act of devotion to the Republic and national representation."[6]

Some representatives demanded proof, while others invoked the Constitution, which gave the Executive Directory, and not the Council of Ancients, the power to name the commander of the troops assigned to defend the government. There was shouting, but the opponents were reduced to silence and the decree voted upon and adopted without discussion: the Legislature was adjourned and convoked for the following day at the château of Saint-Cloud, and all the troops in Paris and its environs would be placed under Bonaparte's command as soon as he had been sworn in before the Ancients. Two of the quaestors, Cornet and Barailon, were assigned to present the decree to the general. It was over. The session had lasted less than an hour.

Facing the People's Representatives

The quaestors arrived at Bonaparte's home around 8:30 A.M. The street was full of soldiers, the garden and the reception room full of officers in full dress. They had been there since six o'clock, some eighty men who did not know what was brewing. Some had been told that Bonaparte was organizing a review on the Champs-Élysées, others that he wanted to say goodbye to them before leaving Paris. They waited. The general was nowhere to be seen. He did not show himself until he had received the decree naming him to head the troops. Berthier undertook to greet the officers. Only a few high dignitaries in the army received particular favors. Lefebvre, one of the first to arrive, was immediately taken in to see Bonaparte. If the commander of the Paris military division still had a few scruples about abandoning his friend Barras, Bonaparte relieved him of them by informing him of the substance of the decree that would soon be delivered to him. Lefebvre, his conscience at ease, promised to help "throw the lawyers into the river."[7] Moreau and Macdonald also spoke with the general, as did Bernadotte. Joseph Bonaparte had gotten his brother-in-law out of bed. The latter had agreed to go to Rue de la Victoire but refused to put on his uniform. "What! You aren't in uniform?" Bonaparte asked as he greeted him.[8] Bernadotte replied that he was not on duty. Bonaparte retorted that he would be on duty in a moment, and then, calming down, took him aside and said: "The Directory is governing badly, it will destroy the Republic if we don't watch out. The Council of Ancients has named me commander of Paris, of the National Guard, and all the troops of the division: go put on your uniform, and join me at the Tuileries, where I am going right now." The conversation took a turn for the worse, it is said, when Bonaparte forbade Bernadotte, who persisted in his refusal to join him, to leave Rue de la Victoire before the official reception of the Ancients' decree. Did the Gascon put his hand on his sword-cane, as Barras says? That is doubtful. Did they insult each other? Possibly. There was a silence, and then Bonaparte said, adopting an amiable tone:

> —All I ask of you, General Bernadotte, is that you should pledge me your word of honor that you will not undertake anything against *me*.
> —Yes, as citizen, I give you my word of honor not to act.
> —What do you mean [by that]?
> —I mean that I shall not go into the barracks and public places to work on the minds of the soldiers and of the people; but should the Legislative Body or the Directorate give me the order to defend them, and entrust me with the command of their Guard . . .
> —Oh, I feel quite easy on that score . . . they will not employ you; they dread your ambition more than mine; as for myself, I feel sure of having no other than that of saving the Republic. I wish to go into retirement [afterward] at Malmaison with a few friends.[9]

Joseph was waiting in the antechamber. Bonaparte, wary, asked his brother to take Bernadotte to lunch at his house; that way, at least for several hours he would not have to worry about what Bernadotte was up to.

The quaestors of the Council of Ancients having finally arrived, Bonaparte was officially invested with the command of the troops and went out to speak to the officers. Lefebvre went with him. He read the text of the Ancients' resolution and then, mounting a horse lent him by Admiral Bruix, he set out for the Tuileries, followed by a brightly colored escort that was soon reinforced by 1,500 cavalrymen Murat had assembled on the boulevards.

Bonaparte did not go into the Council of Ancients alone; he was followed by his whole staff, an unusual and vaguely threatening cortege in a parliamentary space. He was appearing for the first time before the representatives. They were there, in front of him, these "lawyers" he detested, in their long blue robes, wearing broad scarlet sashes around their waists and velvet caps on their heads, several dozen unknown faces, their eyes fixed on him. He was brief:

> Citizen Representatives, the Republic is dying; you have recognized it, and your decree has just saved it. Woe to him who wants disturbance and disorder! I shall stop them, with the help of General Lefebvre, General Berthier, and all my companions in arms. Do not seek in the past examples that might slow your march! Nothing in history resembles the end of the eighteenth century; nothing in the end of the eighteenth century resembles the present moment. Your wisdom has rendered this decree; our arms will be able to execute it. We want a Republic based on true liberty, on civil liberty, on national representation. We shall have it, I swear it; I swear it in my name and in that of my companions in arms.[10]

He was assuredly exceeding his role by referring to measures belonging to the domain of the Councils alone. The Ancients kept silent, perhaps beginning to wonder about the consequences of this decree they had approved in haste, especially when they heard Bonaparte's escort shout even before he had finished speaking: "We swear it!"[11] Bonaparte explicitly recognized the preeminence of the civilian power by swearing to apply its decisions, but he refrained from swearing fidelity to the Constitution of Year III. Although he cited a few general principles, he did so to avoid explicitly committing himself to defend the established institutions; on the contrary, by speaking of "the republic as we want it," he did not conceal the fact that in his view the Directory was no longer useful. The Ancients understood him perfectly. Once again there was a moment of concern; Garat rose to ask Bonaparte to swear loyalty to the Constitution, but Lemercier refused to allow him to speak, as he did, it seems, in the case of other representatives, saying that the decree of transfer having been adopted, any further debate was adjourned until the meeting of the Councils at Saint-Cloud. The session was declared closed.

The End of the Directory

"Gohier didn't come, too bad for him,"[12] Bonaparte said as he left for the Tuileries. He believed he could persuade the director to follow him by suggesting that the coup d'état's goal was to "regenerate" the regime by excising from it Barras, its rotten part. In Bonaparte's view, Gohier's support was essential. First of all, he represented, along with General Moulin, the Jacobins within the Executive Directory. If he joined the conspiracy, a threat of resistance would disappear. And then Bonaparte feared depending too much on his allies, Sieyès, Ducos, and the moderate majority on the Council of Ancients. If he succeeded in drawing Gohier to his side, and at the same time at least part of Gohier's political friends, his dependence on Sieyès, who was at the origin of the coup d'état, would be diminished. The more his allies were of differing opinions, the more he would have a free hand. Finally, if Gohier rallied behind the coup d'état, the majority of the Directory would be on the side of the conspirators. If Sieyès, Ducos, and Gohier were with Bonaparte, it would be all the easier to get rid of the two other directors, Barras and Moulin, and move gradually, without an abeyance of the executive, toward regime change. But Gohier didn't see things that way, and although it is true that he let the opportunity of his life escape him on 18 Brumaire, his fall was not without grandeur. Refusing to violate the Constitution to which he had sworn loyalty, he "hitched his star to the constitution of Year III and like it went down rather gracefully."[13]

We do not know whether the furtive departure of the Directory's guard finally made him realize what was happening or if the new information he received in the early morning from the minister of war aroused his suspicions. In any event, as he was leaving for Rue de la Victoire, to which Joséphine had asked him to come in the early hours of the morning, he changed his mind and asked his wife to go on alone. She had just left the Luxembourg when Fouché turned up. Impassive, the minister of police told Gohier about the decree transferring the Legislature to Saint-Cloud and giving Bonaparte command. The director was flabbergasted and flew into a rage, accusing Fouché of incompetence, of not having foreseen, discovered, or said anything. Fouché did not reply. Fouché left the Luxembourg and never set foot in it again. Then Gohier summoned General Lefebvre and demanded an explanation. Lefebvre replied curtly that because he had been placed under Bonaparte's authority, he no longer took orders from the Directory.

Gohier called in his colleagues, but he was told that Sieyès had already left; and if Sieyès had disappeared, there was no point in seeking Ducos. Gohier then asked Moulin to meet him as soon as possible in the conference room and sent the same request to Barras. But that morning Barras had decided to take a very long bath. So he had Gohier told that he needed at least an hour to finish dressing. The two directors, instead of seeing their colleague arrive, received from him a laconic message: "I sense, as you do, everything that this crisis in which we find ourselves demands of us. I am going to send Bottot [his secretary] to find out. Let us meet in the conference room, and count on me."[14] In his memoirs Gohier candidly admits that he was "satisfied" with this response. While Barras was peacefully taking his bath, waiting for news, and perhaps still thinking that a revolution was impossible unless he had approved it, Gohier and Moulin were waiting for their colleague, and they would have waited still longer had they not received from the Council of Ancients' quaestors a letter asking them to go to the Tuileries to confer with Sieyès and Ducos, who needed the signature of a third director for the decree of transfer to be applied. In fact, no law could be promulgated without the signature of at least three of the five directors. Neither Gohier nor Moulin considered refusing their signature: they knew the Constitution and were aware that a refusal would have constituted an "attack on the safety of the Republic"; but at least they could delay it or sign the decree not with Sieyès and Ducos but with Barras. Didn't the three of them constitute the majority of the Directory—on the condition, of course, that Barras decided to get out of his bathtub? Still hoping to see Barras arrive, Gohier resolved not to leave the conference room, and above all not to respond to the summons from the Council of Ancients.

He was all the more determined because he had finally received news from his wife. She had arrived early at the rendezvous set by Joséphine. The house was full of officers. She was entering when she saw the general and Bernadotte. Bonaparte had greeted her and asked where her husband was: "He absolutely must come," he had told her. She had pretended to consent and had had this letter delivered to her husband: "You did well not to come; everything that is going on here tells me that the invitation was a trap."[15] The Director's bitterness was no doubt great when he understood, rather late, that Joséphine had tricked him.

During this time Barras's secretary, Bottot, hurried off to the Tuileries. He got there just as Bonaparte was reviewing the troops. The two men then had a private conversation. According to some reports, the secretary asked what his employer could expect from the general, and Bonaparte replied harshly: "Go tell Barras that the name of the Republic has been abused to put its finances in disorder and insult the people's rights long enough; he has only one choice, and that is to resign."[16] According to other reports, he took Bottot by the arm and whispered to him: "Tell Barras that I am inviolably attached to him and that, so long as I live, I shall oppose the attacks of all his enemies, and defend him against them."[17] Bottot returned to the Luxembourg.

The emissaries Bonaparte sent to Barras—Admiral Bruix and Talleyrand— were already on their way.[18] They arrived at the Luxembourg at the same time that Mme Gohier got back from Rue de la Victoire. Bonaparte having left for the Tuileries, Joséphine had detained the director's wife as long as she could. She had repeated to her that her husband was wrong not to join the general, that the latter respected him and wanted to make him "one of the members of the government that he proposed to establish," and so on. She even begged her to persuade her husband by telling him that because Barras's resignation had been obtained, he no longer had a majority within the Directory, and that he had to join Sieyès and Ducos at the Tuileries.[19] Mme Gohier thus informed her husband that Barras had resigned. Gohier rushed to his colleague's home and found the door closed: Barras was conferring with Bruix and Talleyrand.

Barras, to whom Bottot had reported the substance of his conversation with Bonaparte, was getting ready to sit quietly down to breakfast with the banker Ouvrard when the two emissaries sent by the general arrived. They informed him that Sieyès and Ducos had resigned (in fact, they were to do so a little later) and demanded that he do the same. Talleyrand laid before him a letter of resignation prepared in advance by Roederer. Barras didn't need to think about it long: the Directory's guard had left its post, the army was under Bonaparte's orders, Sieyès and Ducos had left the government. It was over. He had already known it for several days, since the moment when he had understood that Bonaparte no longer needed him. When Dubois-Crancé came to ask him to order Bonaparte's arrest, he had already replied: "I don't give a damn what happens, don't bother me again."[20] Stoically, he took a quill, dipped it in the ink, signed the letter, and then withdrew in order to prepare his departure for the château of Grosbois, where it was agreed that he would go "to rest."

It has rightly been said that Barras "escaped" from power without trying to keep it. However, he had just made an inestimable contribution to the success of the coup d'état: without his resignation, Gohier and Moulin would have had the third vote they were counting on to put Sieyès and Ducos in the minority. So it was actually Barras who gave the regime its coup de grâce: "The daring undertaking of Bonaparte," Gohier was to say, "hung by a thread—by a thread that the resigning director tied into a knot by his defection."[21] It is likely that Barras did not sacrifice himself out of goodwill. It is not clear whether he took the money offered as compensation by the conspirators or if Talleyrand succeeded in keeping it. It remains that Barras, whether compensated or not, did nothing to hinder Bonaparte's projects, even though he knew that he had no role to play in them. The attachment he felt for the general whose Pygmalion he had once been was perhaps still determinative.

After Barras resigned, further resistance became pointless. Gohier and Moulin reluctantly signed the Ancients' decree. At the Tuileries, where Bonaparte had set up his headquarters, they found Sieyès, Ducos, and all the ministers with one exception: Dubois-Crancé. The general greeted Gohier warmly; he congratulated him on joining him "to save the Republic." Once again Gohier did not understand that Bonaparte was throwing him a lifeline: he retorted that the Republic was not in danger. Boulay de la Meurthe, a member of the Council of Five Hundred and Sieyès's confidant, intervened to say that the danger was internal and not on the borders, and the discussion then degenerated. Too bad for Gohier! Bonaparte brusquely turned toward Moulin and, referring to the reports of suspicious movements in the Faubourg Saint-Antoine, threatened to have Santerre, the former commander of the Parisian National Guard who was said to be one of his relatives, shot. Moulin's reply—"Santerre is not my relative, but he is my friend, he's a good citizen incapable of causing any trouble"[22]—was lost, because after Gohier mentioned "the Directory's legitimate authority" that remained in his hands, Bonaparte barked at him: "There is no longer any Directory! Sieyès and Ducos are resigning; Barras has sent his resignation."[23] Adopting a peremptory tone, Bonaparte asked Gohier and Moulin to follow Barras's example. But they refused, even declaring that they would denounce in the Councils the unconstitutional nature of the command conferred on Bonaparte by the Ancients and ask them to provide for the filling of the three vacant positions in the Directory. With that, they set out for the Luxembourg to draft a formal protest that was to be their political testament.[24] But the Luxembourg was already surrounded. Bonaparte had dispatched 300 men under the command of Moreau—who henceforth played the not very rewarding role of jailer—on the pretext of guaranteeing the "protection" of the two directors. Gohier and Moulin were taken prisoner, Barras had resigned, and there was no longer any government.

On the Razor's Edge

If the first act had gone off as planned, "in the simplest way in the world,"[25] the same cannot be said of the second, which took place the next day, 19 Brumaire (November 10). Bonaparte was well aware that nothing was over yet. When he left for Saint-Cloud that morning, as the carriage was crossing the Place de la Révolution, he told those who accompanied him: "We shall sleep tonight in the Luxembourg or we shall end up here."[26] As the decisive moment approached, the conspirators, and still more the Ancients who had made their task easier the day before, were no longer so sure of themselves. Conversely, the long hours of the evening and the night had given their colleagues in the Five Hundred time to recover. The Jacobins had met and, after interminable debates, agreed on the necessity of trying in every way, the next day at Saint-Cloud, to bar Bonaparte's way to power.[27] The session in Saint-Cloud began so badly that at first they thought that victory was within their reach.

At that time, two roads led from Paris to Saint-Cloud, one going through Auteuil, the other through Passy. They both ended at the entrance to the bridge of Saint-Cloud. On the far bank of the Seine, the village was on the right; on the left, a long ramp that passed between the pavilion of the Guards and the pavilion of the Valois led to the main courtyard framed by the impressive château with its north and south wings in a horseshoe shape. Behind it was the Orangerie; because of the slope of the terrain, it was on the same level as the second floor of the building and the north wing that contained the Apollo gallery.

When Bonaparte arrived, nothing was ready. Only the Apollo gallery, where the Ancients were to hold their session, was finished. In fact, it had been decided that the Five Hundred would sit in the gallery in the south wing, so that the two Councils could not communicate too easily, but then it had been noticed that that the part of the gallery designated for the Five Hundred no longer existed; Marie-Antoinette had divided it up into apartments. Only one other space could hold the 500 representatives, along with the spectators whose exclusion no article of the constitution permitted: the Orangerie. But it was in a lamentable state and so long that most of the audience would be able to hear nothing that was said from the rostrum. So it had been decided to use only half of it by building a dividing wall across the middle of the room, but tiered seating and a platform for the president and the speakers still had to be constructed. It was noon and the carpenters were still at work. Representatives, curious onlookers, and soldiers were waiting in the courtyard. To reach the château's entrance, Bonaparte had to make his way through the crowd. He heard a few hostile cries. The Jacobins, who had turned out in force, were trying to win over those who had the day before voted for the transfer decree.

It was almost 2 P.M. when the representatives were finally able to enter their respective meeting halls. It had been agreed that the Ancients, noting the resignation of three of the five directors, would propose the nomination of three provisional consuls and the creation of a commission assigned to work on institutional reform. But as soon as the session was opened, everyone could see that things would not go as planned. While the Five Hundred were getting ready to resist by requiring that each representative be called to swear an oath of fidelity to the Constitution of Year III, the Ancients no longer seemed to know what to do or what side to choose, to the point that although the preceding day they had still been determined to change the Constitution, they were now going so far as to consider completing the Directory by giving Gohier and Moulin three new colleagues! "The zealots," Napoleon wrote later, "became neutral; the timid ones had already changed sides."[28] Should we be astonished by this? The paradox is that the established regime was necessarily to see the number of its supporters, which was almost zero so long as it continued to exist, increase as soon as it was really threatened. It was not that the flame of constitutional loyalty flared up at the last minute or that the charms of legality were abruptly discovered by those who had scoffed at it for such a long time; the reason for this sudden nostalgia for institutions almost universally held in contempt had to do with something more instinctive: each individual's concern for his own security. The fall of the Thermidorian Republic was necessarily going to lead to a plunge into the unknown, but an unknown whose forms could be logically predicted on the basis of what had happened under analogous circumstances in 1792, 1793, and 1797. Experience was hardly reassuring in that regard—each upheaval had been followed by acts of vengeance and proscription. No one could imagine that a coup d'état would not inevitably be followed by arrests, arbitrary trials, deportations, and even executions, simply because such an outcome had never happened. Because the current coup d'état would necessarily be carried out by one group of politicians against another—the former justifying themselves by reference to the threat posed by the latter—those fated to be its sacrificial victims necessarily saw their final protection in the institutions they had previously scorned. Thus, a constitution that no longer had any supporters was to find defenders when its death was imminent.

Bonaparte's decision to speak before the Councils in order to do away with them more quickly has often been described as inopportune. But it is not asked often enough what other choice he had. Should he have let things run their course? Lucien, who was presiding over the Five Hundred, was to reproach his brother for having compromised everything, but how long could he have held out in an assembly where his supporters had abandoned him by proclaiming their fidelity to the Constitution? It was not very probable that the power drifting toward opponents of the coup in the two assemblies would be reversed. The passivity of the coup's supporters left Bonaparte hardly any choice other than to rush things in order to reawaken Sieyès's friends from their strange torpor. But if, by deciding to appear before the Council of the Ancients, he did the only thing he could do, he was completely mistaken about the way in which to deal with the representatives.

He began by ordering silence and reminding his audience that he had taken command of the troops in response to their invitation. And "as a reward for the devotion we showed yesterday," he exclaimed, "today we are showered with calumnies! People talk about a new Caesar, a new Cromwell, it widely said that I want to establish a military government!"[29] He noted that his "comrades" in the army had made proposals of this kind when he had come back from Italy: Why suspect him of wanting to do now what he had refused to do in the past? He exhorted the Ancients to save "the two things for which we have made so many sacrifices, liberty and equality." But when a representative, Lenglet, shouted at him, "What about the Constitution?," he could no longer restrain himself: "The Constitution? Is it fitting that you should invoke it? And can it still be a guarantee for the French people? You violated it on 18 Fructidor, you violated it on 22 Floreal, you violated it on 30 Prairial. The Constitution? It is invoked by all the factions and it has been violated by all of them; it is scorned by all; it cannot be a means of salvation for us because it is no longer respected by anyone. The Constitution? Isn't it in its name that you have exercised all kinds of tyrannies?" Then, more calmly, and perhaps aware of the negative effect of his words:

Representatives of the people, do not see in me a wretched intriguer who wears a hypocritical mask! I have proven my devotion to the Republic, and any dissimulation is of no use to me. I am speaking to you in this way only because I don't want so many sacrifices to be wasted. The Constitution, the rights of the people, have been violated on several occasions; and because we are no longer allowed to render to that Constitution the respect it should have, let us save at least the foundations on which it rests, let us save equality, liberty! Let us find means to assure each man the liberty due him, which the Constitution has not been able to guarantee. I declare to you that as soon as the dangers that have caused extraordinary powers to be granted me have passed, I shall give up those powers. With regard to the magistracy that you have named, I wish to be only the arm that will support it and cause its orders to be executed.

Several representatives then asked Bonaparte to name the authors of the conspiracy the threat of which was being brandished. He threw them as a sop, at random, the names of Barras and Moulin, but seeing that that produced hardly any effect, he flew into another rage, pointing at those who now claimed to be defending the institutions: "The various factions came to knock on my door; I did not listen to them, because I belong to no coterie, because I belong only to the great party of the French people. And these men who insolently call themselves the sole patriots came to tell me that the Constitution had to be set aside and, to cleanse the councils, they proposed to exclude men who are sincere friends of the country. That is their attachment to the Constitution!"

Then he attacked the Five Hundred. There was a burst of protests when he swore to set things in order there, shouting: "And if some orator paid by foreigners spoke of putting me *outside the law,* may the thunderbolt of war crush him at that instant! If he spoke of putting me *outside the law,* I would appeal to you, my brave companions in arms! . . . Remember that I advance accompanied by the god of victory and the god of good fortune!"

Did he say that, or rather, as Frédéric Masson thinks, did he utter this variant with a still more deplorable effect: "Know that I am the god of war and the god of good fortune"?[30] Whatever the precise version, the words were inappropriate and ridiculous. He was to agree with this judgment, saying in his own defense: "The French have a sense of the fitting, and hardly had I uttered these words than a murmur of protest made me feel that. But what do you expect? They had spoiled me all along the way. They had so often repeated those words between Marseille and Paris that they remained with me."[31] In fact, these words remind us less of those he had heard after having landed at Fréjus than of those he used in his Egyptian proclamations. Though the "god of victory" and the "god of good fortune" left them cold, the Ancients felt very sure that as he addressed them the general was thinking: "You are all a pack of wretches, and I will have you shot if you do not obey me."[32]

He had no experience in dealing with assemblies. He did not like them. The audience he knew so well how to speak to, for whom it was easy to find formulations that hit the target, was quite different: when addressed by their leader, the soldiers always responded with cheers. He was familiar only with "passive silence in the ranks"; he knew how to command but did not know the art of carrying along a parliamentary assembly. He had mounted the Ancients' rostrum under circumstances very different from those of the preceding day. Then, he had been assured of the approval of these same representatives; now, he was trying to rouse them from their torpor and force them to do what he and Sieyès expected of them. Favorable the day before, they were now, if not hostile, at least hesitant. When he had to address these men whom he despised, he was seized by the stage fright felt by an inexperienced actor, and was incapable of controlling himself as soon as they failed to fulfill their commitments. In any case, the damage was done. He was booed as he went out.

People have wondered, a fortiori, about the motives that led Bonaparte, as he left the Council of Ancients, to take with him two grenadiers as he hurried off to the Council of Five Hundred, where he burst in without even having himself announced. Had he lost his head? Did he want to reveal the import of his last conversation with Jourdan to put the opposition in a difficult position and allow the Ancients time to recover? Did he want to help out his brother, who was being given a hard time by the Five Hundred? There again, to understand what he did it suffices to analyze the different choices he faced. He had not succeeded in winning over the Ancients. His supporters in that Council had remained silent, and the opposition, even though in the minority, had pursued its attacks with renewed vigor. How could he have believed that what had failed with the Ancients could succeed with the Five Hundred, where his adversaries were both more numerous and better organized? With the defection of the Ancients, the support on which he and Sieyès had counted to lend the coup d'état a parliamentary appearance had disappeared. From that point on, he could either let parliamentary procedure take its course, hoping that the presidents of the two assemblies, Lemercier and Lucien, would finally regain the upper hand, or he could precipitate the resolution. Lucien later maintained that the first option had to be chosen because it was the only one that made it possible to achieve the desired result without blackening the birth of the new regime with violence.[33]

But again, how could he have believed that this would lead to a legal and peaceful outcome? Nothing suggested that the representatives colluding with them, after flinching when they had to act, were now going to get a grip on themselves. On the contrary, each passing moment increased both their indecision and the determination of their adversaries, who despite their numerical inferiority no longer despaired of being able to elect new directors and have the session adjourned until the next day. It was especially the latter possibility that frightened the conspirators. The coup d'état absolutely had to be completed the same day; otherwise they would have to resign themselves to defeat. The solution was obvious: they had to call in the army that was surrounding the château of Saint-Cloud. They had to resort to force, even though they had resolved not to do so, having persuaded themselves that the discredited institutions would find no defenders. One sentence Bonaparte had used in speaking to the Ancients allows us to suppose that he had already decided to confront their colleagues in the Five Hundred: "I did not count on the Council of Five Hundred, which is divided; on the Council of Five Hundred, where there are men who would like to return us to the Convention, the revolutionary committees, and the scaffolds; . . . on the Council of Five Hundred, from which emissaries have just left to organize a movement in Paris."[34]

Bonaparte assured his audience that with the help of his "comrades in arms" he would be able to defend the Republic against agitators. Wasn't that to insinuate that the Council of Five Hundred was not free? To publicly acknowledge this he went immediately to the Orangerie and entered without having himself announced: he was seeking an incident that could justify recourse to the army. But just as he had been mistaken in addressing the Ancients with an inappropriate kind of eloquence, he was mistaken about the Five Hundred, not suspecting for a moment what was going to happen. He expected cries of derision, a storm of protest, but not the "vulgar fistfight" his irruption triggered.[35]

We have to imagine the Orangerie to understand this famous scene. It was entered through a revolving door at the château end of the hall. Because the building had been divided into two parts by a wall, it was indescribably crowded. Had one wanted to prevent the deliberations from being conducted calmly, one could not have done better. The representatives—few of them were absent—were packed into the tiered seats lined up all along the window side of the room, and they filled the narrow space between these tiers and the rostrum placed on the opposite wall. The Jacobin speakers had left their seats and were milling around the base of the presidential platform. There were also spectators in the few free places. The entrance of Bonaparte and the two grenadiers accompanying him was probably initially noticed only by those who were near the revolving door. The agitation it provoked led people to look in that direction as Bonaparte advanced toward the platform along the tiers of the representatives. Shouts were heard: "Death to the tyrant! Down with the dictator! Long live the Republic and the Constitution of Year III!" The representatives climbed onto the tiers to see better. The Jacobins and Lucien spotted Bonaparte only when he drew close. We can imagine the president's astonishment on seeing his brother about to mount the platform. The Jacobins were no less astonished. They rushed toward the general as the representatives began to chant: "Outlaw! Outlaw." There was a violent and brief scuffle. Bonaparte was grabbed, pummeled with blows, and, without having been able to say a word, had to retreat, the two grenadiers protecting him with their bodies and returning blow for blow.

The scene had lasted only a few seconds. It was without grandeur. To justify the intervention of the troops, Bonaparte later claimed that several of the representatives were armed with daggers. If that had been the case, this vulgar scuffle would have taken on an antique character, but it did not. No one had done what Tallien did when on 9 Thermidor he brandished a dagger—which he did not intend to use—at the Convention, swearing that he would kill himself rather than submit to Robespierre. The only "casualty" of 19 Brumaire was the grenadier Thomé, who in the fight lost a sleeve of his uniform.

On this occasion the Jacobins proved to be unequal both to the circumstances and to their own reputation: "Where then were Brutus, Cato, Scaevola, Sydney? Where were these great speakers for liberty, virtue, and public safety?"[36] Once Bonaparte had left, it was worse. Lucien refused to put to a vote the outlawing of his brother. Why didn't they knock him down? Why didn't they seize the chair and why did they limit themselves to shouting, thus losing precious time? By declaring Bonaparte outside the law, they might have been able to make the Ancients come over to their side and sow confusion among the soldiers, in particular among those of the Legislative Body's guard, in whom the conspirators had so little confidence that they had thought it necessary to add regular troops to their ranks the better to keep an eye on them. Mme de Staël says that even the most loyal of them would have been shaken by a decree outlawing Bonaparte: Hadn't they "constantly abandoned for the past ten years those of their generals whom the legislative power had proscribed"? It was true that the representatives of the nation had lost some of their luster, but, Mme de Stael adds, "the similarity of words often prevails over the diversity of things."[37]

Unfortunately for the Jacobins, their leaders were absent. Jourdan and Augereau had traveled to Saint-Cloud but did not participate in the session. They were walking in the courtyard, hiding their uniforms, it is said, under their overcoats, ready to act against Bonaparte in the event that he found himself in difficulty. If that is true, then they were far inferior to their pretensions, because neither of them took the smallest step to exploit the situation. They disappeared at the moment when their friends needed them the most. Jourdan in particular proved mediocre. His failure was complete. He had promised Bonaparte not to do anything that might lead to a civil war, but now that Bonaparte had gotten into difficulty, Jourdan was obligated to support those who had put their trust in him. He did not do so, and quickly left Saint-Cloud.

Through their ineffective agitation, Lucien was to say, the Jacobins "erased the error made by the general in violating our space."[38] In any event, they gave him time to recover. Witnesses say that Bonaparte left the Orangerie in a pitiful state. He is even supposed to have fainted, coming to only to speak incoherently and address Sieyès as "General." Clearly Bonaparte was badly affected by the scuffle in the Orangerie. Perhaps he even thought, as Sieyès did, that "the coup had failed." But he quickly got a grip on himself, telling Sieyès, who wanted to call in the troops immediately, that the attack absolutely had to be covered by "a scrap of legality."[39] No decision had yet been made when a messenger who had been sent, it seems, by Talleyrand arrived to tell Bonaparte that he had been proscribed by the Five Hundred. Was that the case? If we read attentively the reports of the session, we see that the Five Hundred made several decisions after Bonaparte left: the continuation of the Council; its immediate return to Paris; Bonaparte's dismissal and the transfer of his powers to Bernadotte. On the other hand, it does not seem that the proscription was adopted by a formal vote. It doesn't matter, in any case: the news, even if false, had as its only result to advance by a few minutes a military intervention that was now ineluctable: "Since they are putting you outside the law," Sieyès remarked, "put them outside it yourself."[40]

It was amid the greatest disorder that Bonaparte mounted a horse to address the troops. His speech, which we know only from reconstructions after the fact, was no less disjointed than the preceding ones. Bonaparte denounced the assassins who had tried to strike him, the "agitators who want to reestablish their bloody domination," the "muddleheads" who thought themselves better "friends of liberty" than the soldiers; he spoke of the humiliations inflicted on the army and the sacrifices he had constantly made in favor of the Republic. "Has my good fortune triumphed over the most redoubtable armies only to fail against a handful of agitators?" he cried.[41] Was he interrupted by shouts of "Vive Bonaparte!"? If the regular troops applauded the general, it seems that the Legislative Body's guard did not show the same enthusiasm. Its men were clearly reluctant to intervene against an assembly they had sworn to protect. It was at this point that the conspirators were in the greatest danger. What would have happened had the Councils' grenadiers sided with the Five Hundred?

Meanwhile, a few members of the Five Hundred, friends of Lucien, left the Orangerie to inform the general that his brother was a prisoner of the "agitators." The decision to "liberate" him was immediately made: the president of the Five Hundred, who was struggling, believing that he was about to be arrested by order of his colleagues, was briskly taken away *manu militari* despite the clamor of the representatives and delivered to his brother.[42] The "liberation" of the president of the Five Hundred, coming to seek the army's protection against the "agitators" who had seized control of the assembly, gave the troops' intervention the "scrap of legality" that Bonaparte had just been seeking. Lucien represented the Law personified coming to authorize the violation of the "sanctuary of the laws." Napoleon's brother addressed the troops in his turn: "Citizen soldiers, the president of the Council of Five Hundred declares to you that the immense majority of this Council is at this moment subject to the terror of a few representatives of people armed with daggers who are attacking the rostrum, threatening their colleagues, and making the most dreadful decisions, and . . . I tell you that this small number of madmen have put themselves beyond the law by their attacks on the liberty of this Council. In the name of the people who, for so many years, has been the plaything of these wretched children of the Terror, I entrust to the warriors the task of delivering the majority from these representatives so that, once freed from daggers by bayonets, it might deliberate on the fate of the Republic."[43]

It has to be admitted that on this occasion Lucien showed a firmness that his brother had lacked. On that day he did Napoleon the kind of favor that people who receive it rarely pardon. For these two brothers who didn't like each other very much, Brumaire didn't help matters. Napoleon was never to forget that he owed his elevation to Lucien, and Lucien paid a heavy price for this, even if the repeated falls from grace he had to endure had other motives as well.

It was 6 P.M. The drums were beating the charge, the first soldiers appeared at the door, and the Five Hundred understood that the end was imminent. "Long live the Constitution of Year III!" they shouted. Because they refused to give way, Murat moved forward and said laconically: "Citizens, you are dissolved." Legend tells us that, the representatives not having obeyed as quickly as he thought they should, he added "Get everybody out of here!"—and that then there was a real scramble: the frightened representatives rushed out the French windows and fled into the garden, leaving togas, caps, and the insignia of their office caught on the bushes. The reality was different: the representatives withdrew through the French windows, which were at the same level as the garden, because it was the only way to get out of the Orangerie. General Petiet, who was there, later told his son that when Murat declared the Council's dissolution, "everyone went out of the room without saying a word, and that it was false that anyone jumped out the windows to get away more quickly."[44]

The curtain had fallen, and the actors went home. The Republic did not go out in glory, that is certain, but neither did it end with a shameful scene—invented by the victors—of the flight of hundreds of representatives so scared that some of them didn't slow down until they were back in the capital.[45] It fell to Réal to utter the last line. Meeting a representative of the Five Hundred, he cried: "The farce is over!"[46]

Parliamentary Epilogue

It was not yet quite over. As Bourrienne says, "the day for destroying a government was over, the night had to be devoted to building a new one."[47] The coup could in fact not end with the army's intervention. It required an act that respected the forms and attenuated the violence. Were they going to return to Paris without having decided anything and thus accept the idea that the new regime would be based on the use of bayonets? That was unthinkable. Thus, the Five Hundred had to be reassembled and the deliberations had to be continued from the point where they had been broken off, especially because the declared opponents would undoubtedly not dare reappear. The session had not only to resume but to take place in the presence of a significant number of representatives: according to article 75 of the already defunct Constitution of Year III, to be valid the deliberations had to be based on a quorum of 200 members. But when the session was reopened, it was noticed that most of the representatives of the people had disappeared. In the Apollo gallery a few dozen members of the Council of Ancients were patiently awaiting the outcome of the action in which they had been involved, but the Orangerie was empty, with the exception of a few representatives who had taken part in the coup d'état and various soldiers who had taken shelter from the cold. Many of the Five Hundred had holed up in taverns, some of them shouting, others silent, some "mentally and physically harassed," others still displaying "a rather great insouciance regarding what had just happened."[48] But all of them were ruminating on the events and perhaps recovering, as they ate, a little of the courage they had so sorely lacked at the crucial moment.

"Bring them back in," Lucien ordered. Easier said than done. The grounds were searched, then the château; they made the rounds of the taverns and inns to roust out all the representatives they could find. How many were there who started back to the château after 8 P.M.? We do not know; no attendance records were kept. "A large number," "the majority of the council," said the *Moniteur* and, later on, Napoleon. But the name by which this nocturnal assembly came to be known is "the Council of Thirty": most of the witnesses and contemporaries say that there were no more than about thirty representatives present, fifty at most. Thibaudeau gives the highest number, 100, and some historians have estimated 200 by reference to the number of members of the Council of Five Hundred who, because they later had seats in the Consulate's assemblies, had probably not offended the victors by their behavior on 19 Brumaire.

The session resumed. Lucien, his spectacles on his nose, presided over "this senate of automatons, in the shadows of a hall that was three-quarters empty":[49]

Imagine a long, wide barn full of overturned benches; a podium set up in the middle against a bare wall; under the podium, and slightly far-ther forward, a table and two chairs; on this table two candles, and as many on the podium; no chandeliers, no lamps, no other light under the vaults of this long enclosure. See on the podium . . . Lucien reading the new constitution, and in front of the table, two representatives giving a report. Across from them, in a narrow, tight space, a group of repre-sentatives indifferent to everything they were being told; most of them were lying on the three benches: one served them as a seat, the second as a footrest, the third as a pillow. Among them, in the same posture and scattered about at random, were ordinary people interested in the day's success. Not far behind them one saw a few lackeys who, driven indoors by the cold, had come to seek shelter and were sleeping while waiting for their masters. Such was the strange areopagus that gave France a new government.[50]

In a silence disturbed only by the shuffling of feet, coughs, and the sputtering of the candles, Lucien solemnly called upon his colleagues to finally give the principles of the Revolution the stable "constitutional organization" that France had been seeking in vain since 1789. And in conclusion he exhorted them to prove themselves worthy of "the public jubilation" that was already being manifested upon the announcement of the failure of the agitators who had oppressed the national representation. No one applauded. A representative of the department of the Drôme, Bérenger, followed him to praise Bonaparte's devotion and the army's selfless restraint. Then, amid indifference, the "Council of Thirty" de-clared that General Bonaparte and the troops put under his command deserved the country's gratitude. A commission was then named to draft a proposed res-olution; this was taking a long time—an hour, then two, had passed—so Lucien returned to the rostrum, this time to deliver a long and violent diatribe against the "assassins," the "children of the Terror," the "bloodthirsty men," and even the "fury-like women" who had tried to stab his brother. The time had to be spent somehow until the commission had put the finishing touches on its pro-posal. Finally it appeared. It was 11 P.M. Procedure was followed to the letter: when one of the commissioners had presented the list of steps to be taken, a new commission, chaired by Boulay de la Meurthe, was assigned to examine them. There was a pretense of a debate in which only the supporters of the coup d'état spoke. Cabanis had written an interminable speech that he read before a drowsy audience. Finally the resolution was put to a vote. Need it be said that it was adopted unanimously? The Directory was dissolved, and in the same order Sieyès, Ducos, and Bonaparte were named provisional consuls, and the Legislative Body was adjourned on February 20, 1800.

A last formality remained to be completed: to have these decisions ratified by the Council of Ancients, about sixty of whose members were still in session when, late at night, they were brought the text adopted by the Five Hundred. "Three or four" of the Ancients—we do not know which ones—refused to engage in this farce. The provisional Constitution had been adopted in accord with the forms established by the overthrown constitution; that was the essential point. It took another two hours before Sieyès, Ducos, and Bonaparte, preceded by a drum roll, were able to appear before the Council of Five Hundred to swear an oath of "inviolable loyalty to the sovereignty of the people and to the French Republic, one and indivisible, to equality, to liberty, and to the representative system." Lucien Bonaparte, who gave the final speech, had the last word:

> Representatives of the people, French liberty was born in the Jeu de Paume at Versailles. Since then . . . it has labored along as far as you, prey by turns to thoughtlessness, weakness, and the convulsive disorders of infancy. Today it has donned virile dress. All the convulsions of liberty have come to an end today. . . . You have just founded it on the confidence and love of the French people and already the smile of peace and abundance shines on its lips. Representatives of the people, listen to the benedictions of this people and of these armies who have so long been the playthings of domestic factions, and let their cries reach deep into your souls. Listen, too, to posterity's cry: if liberty was born in a tennis court at Versailles, it was consolidated in the Orangerie at Saint-Cloud. The constituents of '89 were the fathers of the Revolution; but the legislators of Year VIII were the country's peacemakers.[51]

It was about 3 A.M.: Lucien Bonaparte arranged for the representatives to meet on February 20 to resume a parliamentary session that he knew would be the last. The candles were blown out.

Endgame

Sieyès and Ducos set out for Luxembourg Palace again. Bonaparte and his secretary got into another carriage. Through Boulogne, Passy, and Chaillot, it returned to Paris. At the Ursulines barrier, the soldiers on guard presented arms. The two men remained silent. "Bonaparte," Bourrienne tells us, "was extremely tired after so many trials and tribulations; a new future was opening before him, and he was completely absorbed in his thoughts and said not a single word as we rolled along."[52] He hardly noticed the soldiers who were also returning from Saint-Cloud to their barracks, singing *Ça ira!* Then, by way of the former Cours de la Reine, the carriage reached Rue de la Victoire and stopped in front of the passageway that led to the little private town house.

There was still light upstairs. Joséphine was waiting for her husband to return. Bonaparte, not being able to fall asleep after such a day, talked for a long time with his wife and his secretary.[53] Joséphine asked what would happen to Gohier. "What do you expect," Bonaparte replied, "it's not my fault. Why did he refuse [to follow me]? He's a good man, [but] he's a fool. He doesn't understand me! ... The poor man! ... And these people think they're statesmen! ... Out of the question!" From Gohier he moved on to his family, asking his wife if they had not been too worried. She told him how, during the evening, his mother-in-law and Pauline had burst into the house, frightened out of their wits: they were at the Feydeau theater when the play, *L'Auteur dans son ménage*, was suddenly interrupted by the author, Antonio Bartolomeo Bruni, who had come in person to announce, in a solemn voice, that the general had just escaped an assassination attempt. Pauline became hysterical, and her mother tried in vain to calm her and make her drink a glass of water brought by an usheress. When they arrived at Rue de la Victoire, Pauline constantly sobbed and finally left only after receiving reassuring news regarding Napoleon. But

Bonaparte was worried less about his own family than about Bernadotte. He said he had learned a thing or two about him. Not only had Bernadotte refused his offers, he had talked about "getting on a horse and coming with the troops he would be given to command," even saying that if it was necessary to proscribe Bonaparte, he would see to it if he received an order to do so. Joséphine said that Bernadotte and his wife had left Paris in great haste, and that no one knew where they had gone.[54] The discussion was casual. Bonaparte sat on the bed. He stuck to the subject of Bernadotte, saying at one point that he had to be distanced from the coteries that surrounded him, and at another exclaiming: "I can't take revenge on him, Joseph likes him, I would have everyone against me. Oh! What a stupid thing family considerations are!" Finally he sent his secretary to bed: "Good night, Bourrienne. . . . By the way, tomorrow we shall sleep in Luxembourg Palace."

PART SIX

A King for the Revolution

1799–1802

TWENTY-THREE

First Consul

*I*n one of Tocqueville's unpublished chapters on the end of the Revolution, he observes that nothing is more "curious" to follow than "the army's gradual march toward sovereign power." And he adds:

> At first, [the army] collapses when faced by unarmed groups or rather is dissolved in the rapid movement of public opinion. For a long time, it is foreign, as it were, to what is going on inside [the country]. . . . However, the Revolution follows its course. As the ardor it had elicited dies down . . . its government becomes softer. . . . During this time the army is organizing itself, becoming harder, winning fame; great generals are shaped by it. It retains a common goal, common passions, when the nation itself no longer has any. The citizens and the soldiers form, in a word, . . . two entirely different societies. The bond holding one together loosens as that holding the other together grows stronger. . . . Starting on 13 Vendémiaire, it is no longer possible to govern without [the army]. Soon afterward, it is possible to govern only through it. When it arrives at that point, it will want to govern itself.[1]

For the preceding ten years there had been no lack of Cassandras: the situation was so unstable, they said, and the impotence of the government so extreme, that the Revolution would end with a military coup d'état. Mirabeau and Robespierre had both warned of this, and so had others.[2] Foreign wars and internal disturbances, meanwhile, lent substance to a different prophecy inspired by English history: in 1660 General Monk had overthrown the republic that Cromwell founded and restored the monarchy. The question had to be asked after Brumaire: Had the French Revolution just seen an epilogue like that of its English predecessor? General Thiébault feared an outcome of this kind so convinced me more than ever that in everything he does he sees only his own elevation."[8]

As for the royalists, the more visionary began to see in Bonaparte a French Monk.[9] Others interpreted the "revolution" of Brumaire as another illustration of the weakness of republican institutions. The wheel continued to turn and would someday bring France back to monarchy: nothing in these events justified despairing of the royal cause. Hyde de Neuville, who was involved in all the conspiracies seeking to restore the throne, said so in his memoirs: "The accession of Bonaparte to the Consulate seemed [so much] a new phase in the life of the Republic rather than its end" that "the question of monarchy seemed not decided for all that."[10] Just as in the republican camp Constant was one of the rare people who realized the importance of the events, among the royalists Mallet du Pan was almost the only one who understood that they were compromising the chances of a restoration.

The former editor of the *Mercure de France* was then publishing a new periodical, the *Mercure britannique*, in London (where he was to die a few months later). In the issue for December 10, 1799, one month after 18 Brumaire, his readers could find one of the most astonishing texts ever written about Bonaparte.[11] Mallet had so well taken the latter's measure that he had no words harsh enough to qualify the thoughtlessness of his royalist friends, that "swarm of starlings" and "very fine imbeciles" who imagined that so "extraordinary" a man had used so much ruse, patience, and skill, and taken such great risks, just to restore the Bourbons.[12] "It is on his [own] head that he would place the crown," wrote Mallet, "if it were a matter of putting the crown back together."[13] Moreover, if the restoration of the monarchy was compromised, it was not Bonaparte's fault alone; the situation made its contribution as well. Bonaparte, Mallet said, was doomed to conduct a policy of reparation, reconciliation, and pardon if he didn't want to fall prey to the defeated Jacobins once again. France would gain a beneficial respite and Bonaparte would gain such strong support in public opinion that he could give his power a solid and durable foundation. Mallet was convinced that the new regime would not be liberal in any way; but wasn't the mass of the French people ready to trade a liberty it had never really enjoyed anyway since 1789 for the advantages of genuine security and a guarantee of equality? Mallet concluded that 18 Brumaire was soon going to appear to have been the signal for a "political metamorphosis" as complete of that at the beginning of the Revolution: it would see the destruction of "all the dogmas of 1789" and the ascension of a strong government, no doubt invested "with a greater power to do evil" but, by the same token, "with a greater independence for doing good." Pessimist by nature, Mallet du Pan did not see the future as bright. If the French could reasonably hope that the new government would depart from the route laid out by the preceding "revolutionary tyrannies," Mallet was lucid enough to understand that the problem now lay in the personality of the beneficiary of the coup d'état. In a well-organized republic, he said, "such a citizen is thrown off the Tarpean rock"; in any case, he is not allowed to seize the leading role: "In a republic such as France," he went on, "this citizen ascends to the Capitol with the power to set it afire if he is forced to descend again, or if the consular scepter does not suffice to [guarantee] either his security or his domination." The danger was all the greater because in Bonaparte's case, ambition was a matter not only of calculation and self-interest, but also of imagination: "Bonaparte's head is in the clouds; his career is a poem, his imagination a storehouse of heroic romances, his theater an arena open to all the frenzies of the understanding of ambition. Who could determine the point at which he will stop?"

Three Consuls and Four Ministers

The general himself didn't know the answer to Mallet's question when, at 6 A.M., his carriage left Rue de la Victoire to take him to the Luxembourg Palace, where Sieyès and Ducos were waiting for him. "In the beginning, under the Consulate, true friends sometimes asked me where I wanted to end up: I answered that I didn't know. They were struck by this, perhaps unhappy about it, and yet I was telling the truth. It was that I was not master of my acts, because I was not so mad as to want to twist events to my system: on the contrary, I bent my system to the events."[14]

The weather was mild and rainy. Through almost empty streets—it was *décadi*, a holiday—he went over to the Left Bank. "A new order of things is beginning," one read on a poster; on another poster Bonaparte said: "All the parties came to me, told me about their plans, unveiled their secrets, and asked for my support; I refused to be the man of a party. . . . Frenchmen, you will no doubt recognize in this conduct the zeal of a soldier for liberty, of a citizen devoted to the Republic."[15]

It was as a "citizen," wearing a "greenish" frock coat and a bowler hat, that he made his entrance into the Luxembourg. The Consulate was going to use the Directory's furniture; it had even retained its appearance: the five directors were replaced by three consuls and the Councils of the Ancients and the Five Hundred, and two legislative commissions of twenty-five members each that had emerged from them, an article of the law of 19 Brumaire specifying that "the commission of the Five Hundred [would exercise] the initiative, [that] of the Ancients the approval," just as they had before. In reality everything was different, and the "consular commission" that replaced the Directory for a transitional period of three months was "invested with full directorial power, specially entrusted with organizing order in all parts of the administration, restoring domestic tranquility, and obtaining an honorable and solid peace."[16] As for the two phantom assemblies that remained, while the law accorded them the power of ruling on "all the urgent matters of police, legislation, and finances," it was solely at the "necessary and formal proposition of the consular executive commission." A "pastime" was—temporarily—given the surviving representatives: preparing a civil law code. There were certainly more urgent matters to be dealt with.

The task awaiting the consuls was immense, and time was short. The situation of the public finances was catastrophic (on the morning of 20 Brumaire, the state had only 167,000 francs, the remains of an advance of 300,000 granted the preceding day by the banker Collot), the coalition's armies were camping on the borders, and those of the Republic were no longer being resupplied or paid. The rebels in the Vendée and the *chouans* had taken up arms again, and nothing guaranteed that the Jacobins thwarted the day before would not try something, or that the army would unreservedly and unanimously applaud the coup d'état.

However, the history of the Consulate began with a farcical scene. After having talked with Sieyès, Bonaparte entered the hall where the new government's sessions were to be held, and where Ducos, the third consul, and Lagarde, the former secretary of the Directory, were already present. Ducos suggested that Bonaparte preside over the meetings. Did he do so guilelessly, or in order to tell the general that he could count on him henceforth? Bonaparte, who was worried about offending Sieyès by accepting the offer, refused, and ultimately it was decided that the chairman would be changed every day in alphabetical order, which allowed Bonaparte to preside over the first meeting.[17] Was it because Sieyès was obviously unhappy that Bonaparte declined the offer to share with the two former directors—and perhaps Lagarde—the money used to compensate the member of the Directory who was designated by lot each year to resign his office before the end of his term? By refusing to accept his share of the money, was he affording himself the pleasure of humiliating Sieyès, who not only was incapable of resisting the temptation, but also bickered with Ducos in order to pocket the greatest part of the sum?[18]

Once these preliminaries were settled, they moved on to designate the ministers, and if Sieyès had thought Bonaparte would agree to share the tasks, reserving war for himself and leaving internal government to the former director, he was quickly disabused of this hope. It was as he was emerging from this first session that he is supposed to have said to Talleyrand and Roederer: "Messieurs, you have a master! That man knows everything, wants everything, and can do everything!"[19] Of the ministers who were retained in their positions or appointed that morning,[20] four were called upon to play a particularly important role: the ministers of war, foreign relations, police, and finances.

Had the Directory's last minister of war, Dubois-Crancé, been less closely connected with the Jacobins he would still have lost his portfolio: not because on 18 Brumaire he had been almost the only person who tried to oppose the coup d'état, but because Bonaparte did not intend to entrust to anyone but himself the direction of military affairs.[21] The latter task had to be assigned to a minister, so Bonaparte entrusted it to Berthier, who Bonaparte said was like "a ready quill that divines [his] thought."[22] Sieyès no longer tried to argue with Bonaparte about the choice of the minister of foreign affairs. Moreover, it had been agreed that Talleyrand, who had been forced to resign this office in July, would be reappointed to it as soon as possible.[23] Bonaparte knew how delicate negotiations would be with the enemy whose armies had been stopped at the gates of France by Masséna but had not been defeated. He was therefore eager to entrust these talks to an experienced diplomat with a famous name who would have a better chance of gaining the attention of European diplomats than the excellent Reinhard, who had learned his trade in the school of the Revolution: "It was a kind of delicate regard for European diplomacy to present to its members, to negotiate with them, a man of a rank at least equal to theirs."[24] Because Reinhard could not be replaced without giving him some sort of compensation, they had to be on the lookout for an opportunity: it presented itself in the form of an ambassadorship to Switzerland, and on November 22 Talleyrand moved back into the town house on Rue du Bac.

Although Sieyès approved of the choice of Talleyrand, he was not in favor of keeping Fouché as the head of the police. It was true that the former member of the Convention had rendered important services to the Directory during the summer, at the height of the battle with the Jacobins, but Sieyès could not help but see in Fouché the former terrorist and the friend of those Jacobins of whom he was himself so afraid. By keeping him as the head of the police, weren't they running the risk of leaving at the heart of the state a representative of the party that had just been rightly overthrown? Bonaparte insisted: "We [are beginning] a new epoch: of the past, we must remember only the good and forget the bad."[25] Was he trying in this way to prevent Sieyès from gaining control of the police and to entrust it to a minister "capable of keeping him on his guard" against this "cheat"?[26] Bonaparte had not been acquainted with Fouché long: they had never met before the preceding November 3, when the minister, sensing that his protector Barras was about to fall, had come to Rue de la Victoire to pledge his allegiance to the general. But though Bonaparte had not known the men of the Revolution well, he knew how to judge men in general and needed no more time to take the measure of the advantage he could derive from the former artilleryman from Lyon.

Stefan Zweig described this first interview in a misleading way by depicting two giants face to face and writing that "superior people who are on their way up always recognize each other."[27] It is certain that the two men carefully examined one another: Fouché understood that the future was there, along with power, influence, and money; Bonaparte recognized in his visitor, as Zweig says, "a useful man who could be employed to do anything." But that also means that the relation between the two men was not a relation between equals. Bonaparte had plumbed Fouché's soul, gauged his talents, and also perceived the limits of a figure who was basically subaltern and inspired neither esteem nor liking. In this respect Fouché cannot be compared with Talleyrand. Bonaparte liked the former bishop; he admired in him the old world of which he was, by birth and manners, a living memory; he enjoyed his intelligence, his vast knowledge, his conversation, to the point of being amused by his indelicacy and of forgiving him for not having kept his promise to go to Constantinople to obtain the Porte's consent to the conquest of Egypt.[28] An unusual infatuation: Talleyrand seemed to incarnate everything Bonaparte detested. He was "immorality personified," Bonaparte was to tell Gourgaud.[29] Lazy, nonchalant, careless, secretive and dissembling, greedy and venal. There was filth in him, "hidden ugliness" beneath "a gracious or imposing exterior," Sainte-Beuve says; but the old bishop, like a good courtier, did not spare his flattery. Who went into greater raptures over the "miracles" and other "marvels" for which France was, according to him, indebted to Bonaparte? The latter was not surprised that he was addressed the way Louis XIV had formerly been: "Now that every day restores me to greater health and strength, I feel ready to rejoin you if you think that suitable," his minister wrote to him a few months later; "and I daresay that if your absence were to be further prolonged, I should not only desire to be with you but feel the need of it."[30] Or this: "I am not complete when I am far away from you," which sounds, according to Sainte-Beuve, like Voltaire "during his honeymoon with Frederick the Great."[31] But flattery would not have succeeded so well had Talleyrand's name been less prestigious. In the eyes of the son of Charles Bonaparte, "that erased everything."[32] Did Talleyrand imagine that Bonaparte, knowing nothing about the art of governing, needed a principal minister, to use the Old Regime term, and did he think he was to play that role? That seems possible if one knows that he had hardly returned to Rue du Bac before he asked to work only with Bonaparte.[33] But Bonaparte did not yield to Talleyrand's charm to the point of succumbing to it and letting his minister do as he pleased.

After his return to France, Talleyrand was part of the inner circle, which also included Roederer, Réal, Regnaud, Monge, and a few others. Bonaparte often made him stay to have one of those long, rambling conversations that gave him an opportunity to talk about all kinds of things—but never about nothing—to refer to his past, which was still so short but had been so well used, and to reveal to his listeners what he called his "pipe dreams." Fouché was never allowed to join in such conversations: "I never spoke with Fouché about what I planned to do, about my projects. The same was not true of Talleyrand," he said.[34] Bonaparte considered his minister of police as "a man who engaged in base intrigues," useful and even necessary, but the kind of person one is a little reluctant to acknowledge.[35] That was unfair, to be sure—Fouché admired the general no less than Talleyrand did; moreover, his admiration was more sincere, because he saw in Bonaparte the best obstacle to the return of the Bourbons, whereas Talleyrand, who was convinced that a restoration was inevitable, thought Bonaparte useful only until the Bourbons had been converted to liberal and moderate ideas.[36]

The general disliked Fouché not only because he had blood on his hands, starting with Louis XVI's, but because he was a little too plebeian for his taste. Even though he was rich and powerful, he lived simply, surrounded by a few old friends he had known since they had been schoolmates, and when they left, he went to bed with his wife in a room they shared with three of their children.[37] Basically, he remained a man of Year II: a good husband, a good father, an implacable citizen. What he retained of the revolutionary distanced him from Bonaparte, but at the same time it gave him a value Talleyrand lacked: through his past, Fouché belonged entirely to the Revolution. He could not hope to be pardoned by the Bourbons, so something stronger than material interests attached him to the Revolution, and if he had fought the Jacobins the preceding summer, that was because he thought that by replaying 1793 they were making themselves the involuntary instruments of a counterrevolution. He had rallied to Bonaparte for the same reason, knowing that he was on the side of the Revolution, no matter how harshly he criticized it: it had made him a successful general and carried him to the top; the Bourbons' supporters had nothing comparable to offer him. Thus, politics drew Bonaparte toward Fouché, while his inclinations pushed him toward Talleyrand. Fouché embodied a period Bonaparte did not much like, but to which he owed everything, whereas in his view Talleyrand, a holdover from the older France, represented a world whose disappearance he regretted but that could not return without depriving him of his gains and, worse yet, of what he might still gain. He needed Talleyrand *and* Fouché, and if we must apply to someone the expression invented to designate the other two consuls—"the two arms of the chair"—we should apply it to these two men, representing the two Frances, the old and the new, which the Revolution had separated. Even if each of them symbolized what was least palatable, in different ways, in the old and the new regimes, Talleyrand was no more "the natural medium" with the Old Regime than Fouché incarnated the Revolution as a whole.[38] Just as Talleyrand would probably have played no major role without the Revolution, the Revolution triumphant, orderly, and thus stale would have discarded Fouché. Both of them were children of disordered times, and they embodied the transition from the old to the new more than one of them embodied the old and the other the new.

Sieyès had to be compensated, so Bonaparte made no objection when his colleague proposed to make Martin-Michel Gaudin finance minister. Gaudin had learned his trade in the administration of royal finances, where he had become, on the eve of the Revolution, one of the most important officials. "Endowed with an upright rather than a broad mind, precise, industrious, orderly in everything, in his business as in his grooming, assiduously going to the Opéra, scrupulous regarding social duties, unshakable in his habits, very reverential toward the government, a little reluctant to accept novelties, in the Old Regime he would have provided the perfect model of those senior civil servants who were neither born nor died, because from generation to generation they were found always to be the same."[39]

Attached to the Old Regime more by the spirit of order than by an implicit loyalty, he would probably have embraced the revolutionary side had it not, as he saw it, struck an irreparable blow to public finances by abandoning the distribution of tax revenues to the communes by abolishing sales taxes and by creating *assignats* (banknotes).[40] He had nonetheless agreed to serve as a commissioner of the National Treasury created in 1791, but in 1795 he declined the office of minister of finance offered him by the Directory, and declined it again in 1799 when Sieyès, his protector, was elected as a director.[41] The conditions for effective action, he said, did not prevail.[42]

Gaudin later wrote that Bonaparte's entry into the government seemed to him to inaugurate a period of stability favorable to reforms.[43] In fact, on the morning of 20 Brumaire no one could say whether the new government would hold up or not. What is most likely is that Sieyès, receiving Gaudin before Bonaparte arrived, gave him assurances regarding the two points he cared most about: the reorganization of the administration of the country's finances and the reestablishment of indirect taxation. Then Bonaparte received him. According to Gaudin, he limited himself to a few words of encouragement, giving him two hours to get settled and go to work.[44] Did he also give Gaudin assurances? It is possible but not certain, because a few months later the first consul firmly opposed the reestablishment of taxes on salt and beverages, and Gaudin threatened to resign.[45]

However, this first meeting marked the beginning of a relationship "of intimate confidence" that was to end only with the Empire.[46] Napoleon, who on Saint Helena denigrated most of the people who had served him, continued to praise Gaudin: "He is a man of integrity and a fortress impervious to corruption. I always approved of his assistance, and I have for him a friendship that I take pleasure in recalling."[47] As for the minister, he said in his memoirs that his only goal in writing them was "to make the memory of the Great Man loved as much as it is admired."[48] Between them, there was not only trust and, on Gaudin's part, admiration, but also a convergence of opinions. Gaudin was a man of the age before 1789 in matters not only of dress but also of finance; he was attached to the maxim that was also Bonaparte's, who was upset by the slightest allusion to credit: "The fortune of states is governed by the same principles as that of individuals."[49] With Gaudin, the Old Regime's ideas and techniques of financial management made at least a partial comeback.

Discreet Opponents, Skeptical Supporters

If we had to establish a hierarchy among the ministers, the first place would be Gaudin's, because the stabilization of the financial situation certainly required more effort and burning of the midnight oil than did the maintenance of order. The opponents of 18 Brumaire—and there were some, beginning with the sixty-one representatives who had lost their seats—remained largely silent.[50] All the resistance, if we can use that word, amounted to a few individual resignations and the refusal of about ten departmental administrations to register the law establishing the provisional Consulate.[51] The most serious warning came from Toulouse. When the fall of the Directory was announced, the Jacobin club there called for resistance. Everywhere in France clubs reacted, but most were promptly dissolved. In Toulouse the garrison had to be called out. For several days people were frightened by the rumor that those defeated on Brumaire were planning to converge on Toulouse and set up a rival government there.[52] The consuls took this threat seriously. They sent General Lannes to Toulouse, decided to dispatch to the provinces commissioners assigned "to instruct the people regarding the causes of the events of the eighteenth and nineteenth and the fortunate results they will bring about," and in conclusion resolved to make an example that would put officials tempted by this sort of adventure back on the right path.[53] The thunderbolt landed on the head of a certain Barnabé, the president of the criminal court of the Yonne, who had refused to record the law of 19 Brumaire on the court's registers. He was suspended, indicted for abuse of authority, and put under house arrest in Orléans, and all his property was sequestered.[54] This example produced the desired result. One week after 18 Brumaire, only thirteen of the eighty-three departments had approved the coup d'état. That was not many. Ten days later, only twenty had not yet adhered to the new government, and after a month, only three departments had still not done so: Haute-Garonne (which included Toulouse) and the two Corsican departments. All opposition, or at least overt opposition, had ceased without a single drop of blood having been shed. Purges were limited: although two-thirds of the municipal staff in Paris was replaced, in the provinces only a few dozen elected officials and government employees were dismissed or transferred. Military men were also involved. Bonaparte perhaps found the most detractors in the ranks of the army—among officers and soldiers who had remained loyal to the ideals of Jacobinism, generals who resented seeing one of their own rise to power and destroy at the same time the equality that was supposed to exist among them.[55] If only a few dozen superior officers were cashiered, how many were there who disapproved of 18 Brumaire but, being accustomed to obey or fearing a civil war, chose to remain silent? Perhaps they were more numerous than we think. Their acquiescence allowed Bonaparte to avoid confronting a military revolt; nonetheless, in some of the armies a mute distrust was to persist for a long time.

The importance of the events just mentioned must not be exaggerated. The most astonishing thing is not that the coup d'état met with some opposition, but that opposition was not stronger.[56]

Although it did not encounter any real resistance, the coup d'état did not elicit any extreme enthusiasm. To be sure, there was approbation, a few vengeful attacks on the defeated Jacobins, and even a tangible sign of unmixed satisfaction, that of investors: the stock exchange, where prices had been falling for months, made a spectacular recovery.[57] At the theater, royalists and moderates applauded the mention of Bonaparte's name and booed the Jacobins represented in topical plays entitled *The Sailors of Saint-Cloud*, *A Day at Saint-Cloud*, and *The Weathercock of Saint-Cloud*. A few newspapers echoed them, calling openly for a "reaction against the principles."[58] All over France the faithful were coming together to demand the reopening of churches that were still closed and the restoration of the Sunday mass.

More than civil war, the consuls feared seeing the "muscadins" (aristocratic mobs) appropriate 18 Brumaire and make it the pretext for a wave of reaction. They feared another "White Terror." They knew from experience that they would suffer the Directory's fate in their turn if they gave the rancors and hatreds accumulated over so many years the slightest opportunity to express themselves. Bonaparte repeated it on every occasion: 18 Brumaire was not another "revolution," but the "revolution" that would put an end to the deadly mechanism of "revolutions."[59] Because "reaction" was a more pressing danger than Jacobinism, it was that phenomenon the government prepared itself to confront; but before unleashing Fouché against it, the government published, a week after the coup d'état, a sort of manifesto in which Cabanis, its author, asserted that there would be no reaction.[60] The police set to work, a few books were prohibited, a few plays withdrawn; the theaters' repertories were made subject to prior authorization, and at almost the same time that the opponents of the coup d'état were abandoning their attempt to prevent the establishment of the new government, those who had hoped it would espouse their resentments calmed down.

The Outline of a Politics

As for the great majority of French people, assuming that it is possible to know what they thought, they were probably waiting to see what the consuls' first acts would be. Prudence was called for. This "revolution" could very well be followed in a week, or a month, by another one in the opposite direction. France had been unstable for a long time, and in early 1800 Talleyrand was still to say about Bonaparte: "If he goes beyond a year, he will go far!"[61] Neither was there any guarantee that this "revolution" that had so far proceeded without deaths or banishments would not end up resembling its predecessors. Experience had taught the French to stop thoughtlessly trusting people. Made blasé about "revolutions"—over the past ten years, they had been through four constitutions and at least fifteen more or less successful coups d'état—they were even more blasé about promises. People could say all they wanted about how Bonaparte's presence in the government would ensure that real change would take place; prudence was called for.

Nonetheless, the day after the coup d'état, a proclamation promised that there would be change: the new government was going to put an end to the injustices committed by the "hateful factions" that had led France.[62] This time, acts followed. Put end to end, they outlined a new politics of the return to order, of reparation and reconciliation. The obligatory loan inflicted on a quarter of those who paid the most taxes was canceled.[63] And so was the law of hostages; Bonaparte went in person to the Temple prison to free those detained there: "An unjust law has deprived you of freedom," he told them, "my first duty is to restore it to you."[64] The newspapers reported this statement and all others attributed to the general. He said he refused to take on "the color of a party."[65] "To govern by a party is sooner or later to become dependent on it. You won't catch me doing that; I am national. I make use of all those who have ability and the desire to go along with me. . . . I like good people of all colors."[66] He also declared, referring to the future government: "Positions will be open to all Frenchmen of all opinions, provided that they are enlightened and have ability and virtues." This declaration made a sensation. "If this new and bold statement is true, and if the one who uttered it keeps his promise," a newspaper commented, "we are in fact at the end of the Revolution."[67] Not content with formulating such little remarks, the victor of Brumaire asked the *Ami des lois* to publish his political breviary: "By liberal ideas, Bonaparte means everything that can embellish the republic and make it loved; everything that tends to moralize the revolution; to remedy its faults and errors; he means the victor's magnanimity toward the vanquished; he means the indulgence that cannot harm the strengthening of the Republic; he means the recall to the laws of men who have gone astray; he means beneficial institutions, political and religious tolerance, and trust in repentance; he means, finally, the forgetting of offenses."[68]

The *Moniteur universel* even published an astonishing and in any case unprecedented manifesto demonstrating that only a weak government could fear reversing itself to repair its errors, and that a strong government, which could make mistakes just as anyone can, has on the contrary a duty to "reverse itself" if it has taken the wrong road. "It is trust that makes the strength of governments," the author of this text wrote, "and it is justice that creates trust."[69] It was by virtue of this new maxim that from its first days in office the provisional Consulate multiplied measures of clemency: priests under oath who were still being held on the isles of Ré and Oleron were freed, negotiations with the rebels in the Vendée were begun, émigrés caught on French soil and threatened with execution were expelled from the territory. These gestures had a resounding effect, and it is not certain that the less liberal comments that sometimes escaped Bonaparte's mouth had less success, so weary of disorder was the public: "I have blazed a great path forward," he said one day; "anyone who marches straight down it will be protected; anyone who veers off to the right or left will be punished."[70]

The policy followed by the consuls would not have been disavowed by the "Feuillants" of 1797, but in playing this game they were in great danger of appearing as the heirs of those defeated in Fructidor and the instruments of their revenge. And so, because they refused to follow in the wake of any party, they had to provide assurances to those whose work they were dismantling. Successive measures favoring the victims of the Revolution were adopted, and official speeches were full of warnings intended to reassure their former persecutors: the government had no intention, the consuls said, of reestablishing the old system of weights and measures, or the Gregorian calendar, or Catholic holidays. For his part Fouché asserted that the Republic would never go back on the ban on Catholic worship or grant émigrés the rights of citizens; but Fouché also considered with goodwill requests presented by those who wanted to return.[71] As a result the government seemed to be tergiversating, taking back with one hand what it had given with the other. A necessary duplicity, but one that was certainly prejudicial to the establishment of trust, especially because a misstep was always possible.

On November 20, ten days after the coup d'état, there appeared in the *Moniteur* an order decreeing that thirty-seven opponents would be deported to Guyana and twenty-two more would be put under house arrest. The list of the outlaws included, along with the representatives who had opposed the coup d'état, "men covered with a righteous opprobrium."[72] This lumped Destrem, Delbrel, and even General Jourdan together with people involved in all the past riots and massacres, and with Gabriel Mamin, who in 1792 had disemboweled the Princess of Lamballe.[73] Who was the initiator of this measure? We do not know.[74] Sieyès was convinced that by taking such steps earlier they would have disarmed the adversaries of the coup d'état before the sessions at Saint-Cloud, and Bonaparte had still not forgotten the "brawl" in the Orangerie. Bourrienne says that at that point the general feared the royalists' actions more than the Jacobins' vengeance.[75] If this was so, he felt with respect to the "anarchists" a distrust mixed with fear that disappeared only after the assassination attempt on Rue Saint-Nicaise, when he finally rid himself of the principal leaders. Later, on Saint Helena, acknowledging that the decision had been made in common, he said that the consuls wanted only to disarm the "anarchists" in the capital by scaring them, without really intending to deport them.[76] But that is a post facto, mendacious version: preparations were even made for executing the order.[77] The minister of justice, Cambacérès, immediately hurried to Bonaparte's home to protest against a measure that betrayed the promises of pardon and reconciliation. As soon as it became known, the deportation order of November 12 had provoked a reprobation so general and complaints so numerous that the consuls hastened to strike several names off the list.[78] On November 25 Cambacérès got the deportation changed into simple house arrest. Bonaparte had not waited to shift the responsibility for the decree entirely onto Sieyès. "It was Abbé Sieyès who had this order issued," he told Fouché, who had come to request that Jourdan's name be taken off the list. "I do not approve of this measure. Had I agreed to believe these fearful people, there would have been bloodshed."[79] He even wrote to Jourdan to assure him of his friendship and to tell him how much he hoped to see "the victor of Fleurus" join him.[80] He made public another letter addressed to one of the representatives struck from the list on 21

Brumaire, in which he repeated that all his efforts sought to heal the Revolution's wounds and to mobilize all good citizens in the interest of France and it alone.[81] Comparing these letters and the decree of November 12 made the lesson clear: Bonaparte was the man of change and the future, and Sieyès the man of continuity and the past.[82] He had just scored a point in his struggle with Sieyès.

From Sieyès's Dictation to Bonaparte's Constitution

Sieyès probably knew from the beginning of his alliance with Bonaparte that he was performing the last act of his public life. The events of the coup d'état, and even more the first days of the Consulate, had certainly relieved him of any illusion in that regard, but he did not intend to fade away without having done everything he could to impose his conditions on Bonaparte, especially because on the constitutional terrain his knowledge and savoir-faire were very superior to the general's. Did he think his time had come? He was in the government, he was—finally—going to be able to give France the institutions he had been thinking about for such a long time. Everyone was expecting him to deliver the result of his meditations. When he seemed reluctant to do so, his friends at first thought he was being coy, but they had to face the facts: if the oracle had his constitution all ready, like the lazy person he was, he had it in his head and had written nothing down. Boulay de la Meurthe, one of his confidants, took up his pen.

Because Sieyès divided the organization of the state along two axes, one "ascending," the other "descending," let us do the same to present his proposal as succinctly as possible.[83]

The foundation is the system of "lists of confidence" (*listes de confiance*). For the preceding two years at least, annual elections and universal suffrage had been the target of all the attacks. They were blamed for the failure of the Directorial regime, the repeated coups d'état, instability, the factions' grip on the Republic. To remedy this situation, most of the revisionists proposed to lengthen the duration of terms of office, and especially to establish a system of suffrage based on the payment of a certain amount of taxes sufficiently selective to exclude those who were not property owners. Sieyès had a different idea: instead of limiting suffrage, he chose to empty it of its substance by substituting for the power to make decisions a simple right to make proposals: citizens would no longer invest their officials with a precise function; they would limit themselves to drawing up the list of those eligible for the various public offices. "The confidence comes from below, authority comes from above," he told Boulay de la Meurthe. Thus, he proposed to establish a pyramidal system: six million citizens would choose 600,000 candidates for communal "lists of confidence," and the latter would be reduced to 60,000 to form departmental lists that would finally be reduced to 6,000 names on the national list. These lists, which would serve as lists of candidates eligible for the offices at the corresponding level, would be updated every year and especially cleansed of those who had lost, for whatever reason, the citizens' confidence. As for the election proper, the system was complex: the authorities of the commune were to be chosen from the communal lists by the department's notables, and the authorities at the level of the department or the country as a whole were chosen by a "College of Conservators"—the Senate—which had, moreover, the power to exclude a tenth of the citizens on the national list.

The College of Conservators invested with the electoral power was France reduced to eighty electors. It was formed by cooptation; each member held his office for life and received a sumptuous income—Sieyès allotted them an annual revenue of 100,000 francs based on an allocation of national property. They named the departmental officials, the members of the two assemblies exercising legislative power—the 100 representatives composing the Tribunate and the 400 representatives composing the Legislative Body—and finally the head of state Sieyès called the "Grand Elector." In addition to these functions, the College of Conservators examined the constitutionality of laws, revised the constitution, and exercised a kind of right of ostracism in having the power to call to sit on it "any man who by his talents, services, popularity, and ambition would be likely to disturb the public peace and the maintenance of the established order," at the same time making him permanently ineligible for any other office.[84]

The Grand Elector, appointed for life by the College of Conservators, was to be still better rewarded than the members of the latter: lodged in "a national palace," he was to receive a revenue of five million francs. This was, in a way, a compensation for his political quasi-nullity: his functions were limited to representing France with dignity abroad and naming two government leaders—one "for the interior," the other "for the exterior"—who, in their turn, would name ministers to aid them, a Council of State, and a Chamber of Justice concerned with administrative disputes.

Ultimately this bizarre plan sought to conciliate the three classic political forms: democracy resided in the mechanism of "lists of confidence," aristocracy in the College of Conservators, and monarchy in the largely honorific office of the Grand Elector. But in reality the Conservators held most of the power, because in appointing individuals to almost all the offices, they still retained the authority to *co-opt* any official whom they no longer deemed suitable, including the Grand Elector.

What place could Bonaparte have in this strange edifice? In his memoirs Lucien says that Sieyès invented the Grand Elector when he was obliged to associate himself with Bonaparte for the coup d'état.[85] Sieyès took the constitutional question too seriously to see it from an exclusively political point of view. He was convinced he had constructed an edifice that would last for centuries, and as for the man most capable of holding the office of Grand Elector, he may have been thinking of himself. As Paul Bastid says, "old age now created in him aspirations to solemnity and splendor."[86]

When he first presented the result of his labor to the constitutional sections of the two legislative commissions created on 19 Brumaire, Sieyès was fully reassured: his listeners cried that he was a genius. But their opinion counted for little. Only Bonaparte's view mattered, and it was to win him over that Sieyès had Roederer offer him the position of Grand Elector: "Bonaparte took a very long time to understand this system; finally he grasped the important point: "Do I understand you correctly?" he asked me. "I am being offered a position in which I would name everyone who has something to do, and in which I myself could not be involved in anything! . . . I will not play such a ridiculous role. I want to be consul . . . or nothing. Rather nothing than ridiculous."[87]

The general and Sieyès met again on December 1. The meeting went badly: Sieyès, convinced that nothing could be changed in his beautiful mechanism without completely destroying it, refused any compromise, while Bonaparte refused as unworthy of him the sham power the ex-abbé offered him. Bonaparte rejected the right of co-option that Sieyès accorded the Senate, and considered the Grand Elector's office ludicrous: "Your Grand Elector would be merely an idle king. The time for idle kings is past. What man of spirit and heart would want to be subjected to such idleness? Six million and the Tuileries to strut like a king on a stage, put his signature on the work of others, and do nothing himself! All that is impossible and an illusion. You'd have for a Grand Elector nothing but fattened pig, or you'd have a master all the more absolute because he'd have no responsibility. You should know that if I became your Grand Elector, I'd pay no attention to you and do what I wanted."[88]

The two men parted angry with each other. The whole day of December 2 was spent in confabulations. Sieyès threatened to withdraw; Bonaparte replied "Let him leave!" and said that he would have Roederer draw up a constitution that suited him.[89] And then, being well aware that he could not act like a Praetorian, he proposed another meeting. It took place that same evening and went very well, because each man carefully avoided touching on practical questions and kept to "general outlines."[90]

It was then that Bonaparte beat Sieyès to the punch. On the evening of December 3 he invited the members of the two constitutional sections to his home. Sieyès could not escape. Once again he set forth his plan. Bonaparte listened to him in silence. And when there was a pause in the conversation, he played his ace. "That's all very fine and profound," he said, "but there are several points that are worth serious discussion." Then, pointing out that the discussion would be clearer if Sieyès's proposals were written out in the form of articles, he proposed that Daunou be assigned to carry out this task. Bonaparte was departing here from the procedure defined by the law of 19 Brumaire. The latter gave legislative commissions the power to modify, in response to a proposal made by their constitutional sections, the Constitution of Year III. Nowhere had it been foreseen that such changes would be made in the course of more or less informal evening meetings in Bonaparte's parlor. And in asking Daunou to put Sieyès's project in written form, Bonaparte was sure that Daunou, who thought himself no less expert than Sieyès in this domain, would propose a plan of his own, very different from that of "the oracle."

The following evening Daunou, his work completed, went to the Luxembourg. His plan restored elections, created two assemblies modeled on those of the Directory, a Council of Two Hundred and another of Five Hundred, proposed a "jury" entrusted with monitoring the constitutionality of laws, a Council of State and three consuls who were elected by the councils to a term of ten years and were eligible for reelection. On the one hand, he had not forgotten Bonaparte: the promulgation of the laws, the appointment of state councilors, ministers, military leaders, prefects, subprefects, mayors, and so on, were the exclusive domain of the first consul, who would not need to request the consent of his two colleagues. The government and the new Council of Five Hundred were given the right to initiate legislation. But on the other hand, the consuls' actions were narrowly restricted, notably with regard to the proclamation of a state of emergency; the prerogatives of the assemblies were protected, and one article, which obviously concerned Bonaparte, even provided for the replacement of a consul who took command of an army.[91]

Bonaparte now had two proposed constitutions. He had only to take from them what suited him best. Assuming direction of the proceedings, he said to Daunou: "Citizen, take your pen and sit there."[92] Daunou read an article, Bonaparte opened the debate, sometimes participating in it, sometimes putting an end to it when he thought they had talked enough, put proposals to a vote, and dictated the final text. The writing of the Constitution of Year VIII, begun on December 4, was completed on the twelfth.

The lists of notables were adopted without much debate. All the participants were tired of elections, and Bonaparte himself, even if he was later to say that he had never approved of this system, did not find it so bad. He knew it, moreover, because it was the one that had been employed in the army at the time when its officers were elected, the soldiers drawing up a list of candidates for each position, from which the superiors chose.

The creation of the assemblies—the Tribunate, the Legislative Body, the Council of State—proved no more difficult. The only amendments to Sieyès' plan consisted in reducing the number of the members of the Legislative Body from 400 to 300, and especially in depriving the Tribunate, to the exclusive benefit of the government, of the power to propose laws. The atmosphere was less serene when the time came to decide what to do with the College of Conservators, which was now called the "Conservator Senate." Once again Bonaparte opposed the principle of co-option, saying that the Senate, equipped with such a weapon, "could disorganize the government whenever it wanted by suddenly depriving it of the most essential men"; and, growing more vehement, he even ended up shouting: "That shall not be done! Instead, there will be blood up to the knees!"[93] No one dared reply. When Mme de Staël reproached one of the participants in this debate for his lack of courage, he responded: "Oh! Madam, we are come to such a point, that we must think of saving, not the principles of the Revolution, but the men who have been concerned with it."[94] There is another explanation: all these new positions went to their heads. Already thinking about the future, they didn't care whether they offended the general. Even Boulay de la Meurthe had ended up abandoning Sieyès, and no one spoke up to mention the Grand Elector. In Daunou's plan, the latter was replaced by three consuls elected for ten years and eligible for reelection. But the first of the three was no longer the preponderant figure Daunou imagined; he alone was in command, exercising all the—immense—powers attributed to the executive, his two colleagues playing only a decorative role. "What do you expect!" Bonaparte later said to La Fayette. "You know Sieyès had put nothing but shadows everywhere: a shadow of legislative power, a shadow of judicial power, a shadow of government; there had to be substance somewhere . . . Well! I put it there."[95]

To preserve the appearance of respecting the procedure foreseen by the law of 19 Brumaire, the proposed constitution was referred to the legislative commission of the Council of Five Hundred during its daily session on December 12. Boulay read the first part of a long report, postponing the rest until the following day.[96] At the appointed time he reappeared on the rostrum to say laconically that "changes" made since the day before obliged him to further postpone the reading of the rest of his report.[97] On the evening of the twelfth there had been a meeting at Bonaparte's home, as usual. Several questions remained to be examined, notably those concerning a possible declaration of rights and the organization of the administration and the judiciary. But Bonaparte, seeing that the discussion was becoming heated, and thinking, besides, that what mattered most had been done by organizing the principal powers of the state, rose, interrupted the discussion, and adjourned the meeting until the next day. His decision had been made: the Constitution would be adopted as it stood, unfinished, and what it lacked would be the object of organic laws adopted later. On the evening of the thirteenth, Sieyès, Ducos, and the members of the two intermediary commissions came to

Bonaparte's home for a last session. He informed them that the debate was over, had the text read, and asked each of them to sign it. The fifty representatives present did as he asked. One formality remained to be attended to: the election of the three consuls, concerning which it had been decided that, this time, they would be named by the Constitution. This was against all the principles, but because this Constitution did not say how the consuls were to be elected, that avoided many difficulties.

Ballots had been prepared and put on a table on which a large vase stood. Bonaparte seemed to take no interest in the voting. With his back to the fireplace, he was warming himself. The voting was over, and the counting was beginning when he suddenly rushed over to the table, swept the ballots off it and, turning toward "that imbecile Sieyès," as he called him,[98] said calmly: "Instead of counting votes, let us once again express our gratitude to Citizen Sieyès by giving him the right to designate the three first magistrates of the Republic, and let us agree that the men he designates will be considered to be those we have just proceeded to nominate."[99] In the course of the day, after many hesitations and consultations, Bonaparte had made his choice of those who were to exercise the offices of second and third consuls. All the participants having immediately approved the general's proposal, Sieyès uttered the three expected names: Bonaparte, Cambacérès, and Lebrun were, in that order, named consuls of the Republic. There was applause and the ballots were thrown into the fire.

TWENTY-FOUR

First Steps

"The Two Arms of the Chair"

*A*ccording to François Furet, Bonaparte could not have chosen his fellow consuls better: "Their names," he writes, "bridge the gap between the present and the two great national memories: Cambacérès, a man of the Revolution, and Lebrun, a servant of the Old Regime. The former had been a member of the Convention and a regicide (but he had voted for a deferment), the latter was a former secretary to Chancellor Maupeou, the last great defender of royal authority against the *parlements*. . . . Through them, the two Frances of yesteryear formed the young hero's cortege."[1] Was Cambacérès really a man of the Revolution, and Lebrun a man of the Old Regime? According to Napoleon, "Lebrun, who was a fervent defender of the Third Estate, could not stand the nobility." Regarding Cambacérès, "he would have also moved closer to the Bourbons if he hadn't voted [to execute the king]." He was the opposite of Lebrun in his views regarding the nobility and was the great defender of all [the] abuses of the Old Regime.[2]

Lebrun was less insignificant than people say. Long after his association with Maupeou, whose fall returned Lebrun to literature—he translated Homer and Tasso—he sat in the Constituent Assembly and played an important role in the obscurity of its committees in charge of finance and the liquidation of feudal rights. Imprisoned under the Terror, by some miracle he escaped the scaffold, and under the Directory he was twice elected representative, in 1795 and 1799. In his ideas Lebrun resembled his friend Malouet. An admirer of the English constitution, from which he would have liked to see the French take their inspiration in 1789, he was first of all an enemy of the *parlements* and intermediary bodies, dreaming of the advent of a monarchy that, freed from these obstacles, would have a free hand to carry out the indispensable reforms. He was a *ministeriel*, as they said, above all a supporter of a strong and effective government. Sixty years old, he was a man of earlier times, but in whom the Old Regime, and especially its institutions, inspired very little nostalgia. Bonaparte had chosen him for his authority in financial matters, for the contacts he had retained with the members of the Constituent Assembly of 1789, and also, perhaps, because he was said to be informed about what was being said and done in the court of the Pretender in exile.[3]

Cambacérès shared with Lebrun a talent vital in revolutionary times: the art of surviving in a hostile environment. A former member of the Convention, he had more ties with the world of the Revolution than his colleague did, but he cultivated more the men of the Revolution than its ideas. He had voted for the king's death, as we have seen; that was enough to make him feel remorse and, especially for the mere hypothesis of a restoration, to keep him awake nights. Bonaparte teased him: "My poor Cambacérès, I can't do anything about it, but your case is clear: if the Bourbons ever return, you'll be hanged!"[4] Cambacérès adhered to the Revolution solely because of this burden that he was doomed to bear forever. So far as the rest was concerned, he longed for the Old Regime. A former magistrate, he missed the days of the provincial estates and the rule of the magistrature that Lebrun had fought against. Just as Bonaparte was henceforth to have access, through Lebrun, to the men of the early days of the Revolution, he was to have access, through Cambacérès, to the men of the Mountain and the revenants from the Old Regime.

Cambacérès had other merits that made it well worthwhile to overlook aspects of his character that seemed to the general a little ridiculous. He was a "diner by nature," as Thibaudeau put it, spending hours at the table, dressing as people dressed around 1775, so covered with lace and baubles of all kinds that the children of the Palais-Royal quarter had a good laugh when they saw him taking his daily walk in the garden, followed by a cortege of "subaltern courtiers" led by his friend, the former Marquis d'Aigrefeuille.[5] He was, in addition, a very solemn man, and if his dinner table was the best in Paris, it was also the most boring. But Cambacérès was more than all that. He was, all by himself, Rambuteau later said, "a great school of government."[6] He was a "learned jurist," Molé adds—in 1793–1794, and then again in 1796, he had written the first versions of the *Code civil*—and a "consummate businessman."[7] In 1798 he had opened a law office whose main client was none other than Ouvrard.[8]

He admired Bonaparte and was sincerely devoted to him; perhaps he even felt a kind of attraction to him—he was in any case very fond of the general's hands, saying he had never seen such beautiful ones—and Bonaparte loved him in his own way. Having no prejudices in matters of morals, provided that no scandal erupted, Bonaparte joked with Cambacérès, asking him one day, after the latter had said he had employed a woman for a diplomatic mission: "My compliments, so you have come closer to women?"[9]

It is difficult to say what role Lebrun played in relation to Bonaparte. The latter esteemed him. He visited him, played hide-and-seek with the third consul's children.[10] Lebrun was probably consulted on financial questions, appointments—particularly when prefects were being designated[11]—but all that matters little compared to the role played by Cambacérès. The latter was not only one of Bonaparte's favorite partners in conversation, but also one of the few, perhaps the only one, he listened to and whose advice he followed. Cambacérès really played the role of a vice president: knowing that he would never be the first, he had chosen to be a little more than a second.[12]

Two Constitutions in One

The proclamation of the Constitution of Year VIII on December 15 was a non-event. It was the fourth constitution in less than ten years, and that was enough for it to be granted hardly any importance. It had been a long time since people thought that any constitution could solve all problems, and this one was unusually terse and riddled with gaps The text adopted on 22 Frimaire was an outline of a constitution, dominated by one office and one man. When they were asked what was in the Constitution, idle onlookers replied: "There's Bonaparte."[13] The regime of Year VIII juxtaposed, in fact, two different systems: a juridical order and a political reality enclosed only in the constitutional articles relating to the executive. In these articles there was an almost complete constitution. If we leave aside the lists of notables and the maintenance of assemblies with limited powers, an obvious return to monarchical forms was marked by the immense prerogatives accorded the executive, the first consul's absence of responsibility, and the creation of a Council of State.[14] Necker was not deceived:

"The first consul is thus everything, absolutely everything," he wrote. Freed from the people and the assemblies, protected against them—"the only armor is given to the government"—he had such power to do both good and evil that freedom would depend on "what the consul wishes."[15]

18 Brumaire marks, more than anything else, the fall of the parliamentary assemblies. "We have to consider the spirit of the times," Napoleon was to say later, "people were tired of assemblies."[16] The time had come for the executive's revenge. The idea that there would be an imminent reestablishment of representative government, a fond hope cherished by the *politiques* who had sided with Bonaparte on 18 Brumaire, was becoming all the more improbable. Deceptive constitutional forms, Bonaparte's popularity, the destruction of all the existing powers except for the army, public opinion's scorn for the old ideas and the old principles—everything conspired to give the new age a new face.

The coexistence of these two regimes, one de jure, the other de facto, was almost palpable. Sieyès and Ducos, members of the Senate's right wing, had named an initial contingent of twenty-nine senators, and all of them together were to choose the twenty-nine other senators.[17] Then together they would name the 300 members of the Legislative Body and the 100 representatives of the Tribunate. Napoleon said later that he left the formation of the assemblies to Sieyès. The ex-director took advantage of this to fill the Senate, the Legislative Body, and the Tribunate with survivors of the Revolution. Bonaparte named at most a few generals; he was primarily occupied with preventing his brother Lucien from entering the Tribunate. Napoleon preferred to keep an eye on him; Lucien had shown, when he was a member of the Five Hundred, how affected he was by speeches from the rostrum and how much he had the qualities of a leader of the opposition. The astronomer Laplace was appointed the day after the coup d'état as minister of the interior to please the Institute.[18] He had proven so mediocre—Napoleon said that he "brought the spirit of the infinitely small into the administration"—that Bonaparte seized the opportunity provided by the new constitution's going into effect to replace him with Lucien.[19]

There were several reasons for letting Sieyès do as he wished: First of all, Bonaparte didn't know the actors of the Revolution well enough to choose several hundred representatives by himself.[20] In addition, these assemblies were Sieyès's invention, and Bonaparte was all the more disposed to let him put his friends and relatives in them because they were going to play a rather limited role. Finally, he may not have been displeased by the unprecedented spectacle offered by these appointments: ever since 1789 political officials had owed their positions to the electors, even if the voters had not always made their choices with complete liberty. For the first time hundreds of positions were going to be filled by appointment. As a result, in a moment a whole world of courtiers emerged to besiege those who currently held power in order to obtain a precious legislative term in office. The case of Benjamin Constant is often cited; in order to win a seat in the Tribunate, he ran from Bonaparte to Sieyès, swearing to the former that he would retain the latter, and to the latter that he would be able to block the former's ambitions.[21] The *Moniteur* for December 24 devoted a half-amused, half-indignant article to this rush to get positions: "Since the Constitution has created a large quantity of richly rewarded positions, how many people are bustling about! . . . How many Brutuses making requests! How many small talents are being praised! How many minor favors are being exaggerated! How many bloody stains are being disguised!"[22] The publication of the list of the new assemblies' members aroused general indignation. It was a *tableau vivant* of the Revolution, a museum of its successive generations.[23] The "perpetuals" whose retirement had been desired for the past five years seemed this time to have attained immortality: "Redo the nominations, that is a general wish," the newspaper *Le Diplomate* wrote. Even before they had met, the new assemblies had been debased.

At the same time, the real legislative power passed from the assemblies, the Tribunate, and the Legislative Body to the Council of State, whose prompt startup presented a striking contrast with the painful birth of the other assemblies. The Constitution gave Bonaparte power to appoint the state councilors who were to work under his direction—he presided over the Council—and who would work with the ministers to draft laws or offer opinions on questions submitted to them by the government. In short, these councilors played a merely technical role in relation to the ministers, serving as a little parliament that would examine not only the legal conformity of the bills but also their appropriateness and content.[24] The constitutional effacement of the political assemblies threw the Council of State into still sharper relief. Whence the importance of the choice of its members. Bonaparte made use of his entourage, asking

Regnaud, Roederer, and Cambacérès for lists.[25] A few days sufficed to choose the first twenty-nine councilors. Most of them had also come from the revolutionary personnel—Fructidorians and Fructidorized mixed together, a few Jacobins, and a handful of overt royalists[26]—but unlike Sieyès, Bonaparte knew how to make them look like new men. Bonaparte had wanted more than anything, Molé was to say, men who were competent in their domains and who had "such varied knowledge that they could serve him as living dictionaries."[27] The Council of State illustrated the kind of principles that inspired his politics: fusion, beginning with that of men from the various periods of the Revolution, and the priority accorded to competence over opinions.

The Councilors had hardly been named when they met on December 25, and the work of forming the assemblies had not yet begun when the Council rendered, on the twenty-seventh, its first opinion. It abrogated the laws depriving former nobles and relatives of émigrés of their political rights, on the ground that such an exclusion was not provided for in the new Constitution. The government and the Council of State, by acting without waiting for the new powers to become active, acquired an image of efficiency that the assemblies certainly could not claim. It could already be sensed that the Council of State would very quickly become the place where "great affairs of state" were discussed and "the most favorable theater for ambition."[28]

The order of December 27 closely associated the Council with the measures of reparation and clemency that the newly installed government was multiplying, like so many "happy advent" gifts: amnesty in favor of former members of the Constituent Assembly, from La Fayette to La Rochefoucauld-Liancourt, from fructidorisés and "terrorists," Carnot, Boissy d'Anglas, and Portalis, on the one hand, to Barère, Vadier, and Billaud-Varenne, on the other; the suppression of all national holidays with the exception of July 14 and 1 Vendémiaire;[29] the reopening of churches and, even though it was not said explicitly, the reestablishment of the Sunday mass—except in cases when it coincided with the Sunday that was part of the *décadi* during which no work was done; the suppression of the oath required of priests, which was replaced by a simple promise to obey the Constitution; the decision to grant funereal honors to the remains of Pope Pius VI, who had died in captivity in Valence on the preceding August 29; amnesty for the insurgents of the West. All these steps were taken by the government, not by the parliament. The lesson was clear: the reign of the assemblies was over.

The Unhappy Brumairians

Could it be that with time, political life would resume a more "normal" course and constitutional practice would return to forms more in harmony with the principles proclaimed in 1789? All hope had not disappeared; it subsisted in particular among those who had come to politics via the assemblies, even if they were supporters of 18 Brumaire. They could not believe that they were really disappearing—especially now, more than a month after the fall of the Directory. They already missed the rostrum. They were afraid, and fear had thrown them "into the arms of the first consul to find shelter there against the storms."[30] The coup d'état had succeeded, the Jacobins no longer posed a threat, the rebels in the Vendée were on the point of laying down their arms, and all that people talked about was order and peace. In short, the maintenance of an exceptional regime was no longer justified, and the time was close when everyone could go back to their old cherished habits. The Revolution, which everyone was tired of, had become such a permanent state of affairs that it was difficult to imagine that things could be done otherwise. How could they give up speeches, action, the illusion of making History? For many people that was impossible, and if some of the supporters of 18 Brumaire—Cambacérès, Roederer, Réal, and a few others—had linked their destinies with Bonaparte's, the others hoped to be able to continue the game where they had broken it off long enough to repel the Jacobins. To be sure, the Constitution had established a new set of rules, but really, who could seriously imagine that it was the last one? As for Bonaparte, who could say what would happen? Countless circumstantial factors could ultimately change the situation, and perhaps even replace the de facto regime that had been imposed after 18 Brumaire with the regime that the Constitution of Year VIII had created de jure.

Thus it happened that as early as December, the "Brumarian party" split. On one side were Bonaparte's supporters, who, though they were not yet pushing him toward personal power, at least encouraged him in everything that went in the direction of an authoritarian interpretation of the Constitution. On the other side were their former liberal allies at the Institute and many representatives from the defunct Councils, who, though they no longer hoped to reform the regime, still thought they might be able to give it a more liberal twist. If they had overthrown the Directory, they had done so not only to reestablish order, "but to create at the same time a regime of liberty and guarantees." They regretted that they had allowed "a constitution that gave too much power to authority" to be extorted from them; they felt they had been swindled.[31]

The Senate having been confined to a function that was primarily electoral, the Legislative Body having been silenced and its session cut to four months, the Tribunate became their refuge. It is true that in the collapse of parliamentary forms, the Tribunate came out rather well: it was the only assembly in permanent session, and also the only remaining deliberative organ. It examined the proposed laws transmitted by the government after consultation with the Council of State, expressed a positive or negative wish, and designated "orators" who were to debate it, along with those of the Council, before the silent Legislative Body.

It is certain that Bonaparte's animosity toward the Tribunes greatly harmed their reputation. But in fact there probably had not been a meeting of so many talented persons since the Constituent Assembly, and anyone who takes the trouble to read the debates that took place in the Tribunate can only agree: in their seriousness and decorum, they compare well with the Council of State's discussions and even with some of the most remarkable debates in the revolutionary assemblies.

In the Tribunate's very first meetings a scandal occurred when Duveyrier attacked the assignment of the Palais-Royal to the Tribunate: Had the body been located there amid gambling dens and brothels in order to discredit it? His speech would not have attracted much attention if, after recalling that in 1789 it was at the Palais-Royal that Camille Desmoulins had called upon the residents of Paris to revolt, he had not then addressed himself to the government: "I thank [it] for having had us see this place where, if monarchical ambition were to make satellites armed against liberty reappear, we could remind people that liberty enrolled under its banners, which were then still new, the monarchy's veteran soldiers; where, if someone dared to speak of a fifteen-day-old idol, we could remind him that a fifteen-centuries-old idol was overthrown!"[32]

Scolded by the "fifteen-day-old idol," whom he had known in Italy, where he was dealing in supplies for the army, Duveyrier quickly retracted his statement, but the damage was done. From that day forward Bonaparte was convinced that the Institute, to which Duveyrier belonged and of which Bonaparte was still a member but for which he already no longer felt his former affection, was surreptitiously stirring up a nest of agitators. As Bourrienne says, the Institute was "a body" capable of debating, and thus criticizing. Moreover, the title "Member of the Institute," which Bonaparte affixed to his signature when he was in Egypt, gave him colleagues—too many colleagues, for now "he detested colleagues."[33] So he no longer courted the favor of the members of the Institute whom he had hastened to greet upon his return to France, nor did he continue to visit the widows of Helvétius and Condorcet in Auteuil.[34] Didn't all the learned people in Paris attached to the Revolution attend their salons? Garat, Destutt de Tracy, Cabanis, Volney, Chénier, Ginguené—all people Bonaparte was soon to describe as "nebulous metaphysicians"[35]—frequented Auteuil. It had been a power to which consideration had to be shown; now it was a coterie that had to be monitored.

Hardly had Duveyrier's sally been forgotten than another, more serious incident occurred regarding a proposed law establishing the modalities of the presentation and discussion of proposed laws. This proposal, which became law on 19 Nivôse (January 9), granted the government the power to set the date at which the speakers of the Council of State and of the Tribunate would present their conclusions before the Legislative Body. The latter could, of course, ask for additional time, but the Tribunes saw in this proposal a maneuver intended to deprive them of the time necessary to examine the texts. The goal, Benjamin Constant said on January 5, was "to elude our alleged resistance by beating us to the punch, by presenting us with proposed laws on the wing . . . and to make them pass through our examination like an enemy army, in order to transform them into laws without our having been able to catch them."[36]

When she returned to Paris on the very day of 18 Brumaire, Mme de Staël had immediately reopened her salon, applauding the coup d'état, which she hoped would lead to the adoption of the ideas she had expressed in 1798 in a work she had finally decided not to publish, or at least the ideas expressed by

government has to give it impetus, and this impetus must be everywhere the same."[51]

Just as the designation of the *Moniteur* as the official organ had prepared the way for bringing the press to heel—on January 17, sixty of the seventy-three newspapers published in Paris were suppressed, and censorship was reintroduced[52]—the market had to be put under government control and the "loudmouths" in the assemblies had to be, if not silenced, at least closely monitored.

Finally, Bonaparte did not know how fragile his power was because his legitimacy was so connected with the circumstances. In this domain he shared the view Necker expressed a little later: he was "the necessary man," the dictator France needed, but whom it would need only long enough to remedy the situation.[53] Bonaparte knew that the fear of Jacobinism—a terror inspired by a "phantom," Mme de Staël said[54]—had won him the support of the political establishment, but also that the establishment would return to its principles and habits when that fear disappeared. Were his opponents in the Tribunate the only ones who thought this? Did Bonaparte's supporters really believe in his power? He was doomed to subjugate people, again and again, if he wanted to endure: "A newborn government has to dazzle and astonish," he told Bourrienne. "As soon as it no longer awes, it falls."[55] This was all the more true because the new constitution hardly supported him. Not that Bonaparte cared much about the constitution; he did not conceal from his visitors the indifference and contempt it inspired in him.[56] At heart, he was convinced that he was the son of his exploits and that he would find the secret of his power in that fact. "My power depends on my glory, and my glory on the victories I have won," he said to Bourrienne. "My power would decline if I did not continue to found it on glory and on new victories. Conquest has made me what I am; conquest alone can maintain me."[57] He drew from this a power that was immense, but at the same time too "rigorously *magical*" not to be precarious.[58]

In the Palace of the Kings

That is why the plebiscite to endorse the Constitution took on a certain importance, even if the government did not wait to learn the result before promulgating the text.[59] The process continued until January 1800. The small number of negative votes—1,562 in all—is hardly surprising. In elections themselves unanimity was not rare at the time, and in earlier constitutional referenda held in 1793 and 1795, although the no votes were more numerous—12,766 and 49,979, respectively—they represented a negligible fraction of the votes cast (0.7 percent and 4.5 percent). On the other hand, the government was disappointed by the number of positive votes, which scarcely exceeded a million and a half. That was more than in 1795 (1,107,369), but less than in 1793 (1,854,912): between 26 and 28 percent of the voters, less than a third. Lucien Bonaparte, who had just assumed his office as minister of the interior, decided to improve the score by adding a bloc of 556,061 yes votes that were supposed to express the unanimous wish of the armies, which had not been consulted, and a second bloc of 900,000 votes at a ratio of 7 to 14,000 per department: in more than a third of the departments, the number of voters was at least doubled.[60] On February 7, 1800, the consular regime was able to announce that the Constitution had been approved by 3,011,007 votes, a record rate of approval amounting to more than half of the voters. The outcome was triumphal—the Constitution of 1793 had been approved by only 34 percent of the voters, and that of 1795 by 20 percent—but it was also false.

All the same, it was something to be able to claim the "massive" support of public opinion when it was becoming difficult to keep the support of a revolutionary oligarchy that was worried by the taming of the Tribunate and, since then, by the suppression of the majority of Paris's newspapers. *L'Ami des lois* was upset: Were the republicans soon going to have to "cross the seas, flee to American lands and ask for hospitality from a people whose magistrates [were] models offered to free peoples," or could they still hope "to find a young Washington in France and not be obliged to ask the old Washington and America for asylum"?[61]

People had just learned of George Washington's death, and the news came at the right time. Bonaparte seized the opportunity on the fly: he ordered the army to go into mourning and announced that a ceremony honoring the president would take place two days later in the church of the Invalides.

In the nineteenth century Washington was to be the hero of liberals, the antithesis of Napoleon. At the time of his death, his reputation was already well established: he illustrated the marriage, a priori improbable, of grandeur with the values of modern society. After forcing the British to grant his country independence, he had laid down his arms, abdicated his powers, and, like a modern Cincinnatus, gone home to Mount Vernon. Perhaps he would never have left his solitary retreat had the crisis of the Confederation not led him to participate, a few years later, in the Constitutional Convention held in Philadelphia, and then to become the first president of the Union. But after two terms he had addressed to his compatriots a farewell speech that had surprised and saddened those imagined him presiding over the destiny of the United States until his death. For the second time George Washington entered into the obscurity of private life. If he was a hero celebrated throughout the world, it was because his virtues were civic and his grandeur not excessive. He had been the servant of his time and his country, nothing more, expecting his reward from posterity and never seeking to take undue advantage of his glory: "A retired magistrate," Chateaubriand wrote, "he went peacefully to sleep under his own roof, amid the regrets of his compatriots and the veneration of all peoples."[62]

The sobered revolutionaries who had made 18 Brumaire dreamed of a French Washington who would put an end to the Revolution while respecting its principles, and would then be virtuous enough to withdraw from public life. Washington's modest glory did not impress Bonaparte very much. He considered the American president a good patriot, an honest general, and a scrupulous governor, but he thought his success was explained less by his personal qualities than by circumstances easy to control: a rustic society of peasants, a country cut off from the rest of the world, an enemy—Britain—that ultimately did not really wish to make the sacrifices necessary to keep its colony.[63]

It had been suggested to him that Chénier and Ginguené write the eulogy.[64] Not very enthusiastic about the idea of offering a rostrum to these opposition orators, Bonaparte was wondering who to turn to when Maret proposed Louis de Fontanes.[65] This "big man with the head of a wild boar,"[66] who had recently returned from emigration abroad, where he had traded the Voltairean lightness of his youth as a poet for a pompous style that he put in the service of his hatred of liberty, played on that day for the first time the role of official eulogist that he was never to abandon, at least so long as his master remained powerful. His master was in a hurry: he gave him two days to compose the eulogy.

Fontanes was well aware that he was being asked not only to praise Washington but also to slip in, beneath the roses, a few thorns; he knew his trade.

The victories Washington won? "More solidity than brilliance."[67] The hero? Very different from those "prodigious men who appear from time to time on the stage of the world with the character of grandeur and domination."[68] "His ideas were more wise than bold; he did not win admiration, but he always maintained esteem,"[69] he added. The time had come to bring the "French Washington" on stage: "The man who, while still young, surpassed you in battles, O Washington, will heal, as you did, with his triumphant hands, the country's wounds. Soon, we have his will as our pledge, and his military genius, if it were unfortunately necessary, soon the hymn of peace will resound in this temple of war; then the universal feeling of joy will efface the memory of all the injustices and all the oppressions: the oppressed are already forgetting their woes, entrusting themselves to the future; the acclamations of all the centuries will finally accompany the hero who will give this boon to France, and to the world that it has been troubling for too long."[70]

People's minds also had to be prepared for the consuls' moving into the Tuileries. Bonaparte had taken the initiative. "Solemn like grandeur," he is supposed to have murmured upon looking around the place. No doubt, but there was no question of remaining in the Luxembourg Palace, which in his view lacked the majesty indispensable in the residence of a head of state. It is no less certain that given "the disposition of many to find in him a Caesar, a Cromwell . . . this removal to the palace of kings was a bold and delicate step, not on account of any resistance that it could provoke, but of the moral effect which it might possibly produce."[71] It was to avoid providing any occasion for hostility that he had organized the homage to Washington.

The move into the Tuileries took place on February 19. The former royal palace had been allotted to the consuls by a law of December 24. Although Lebrun agreed to become Bonaparte's neighbor, Cambacérès refused, not because this prestigious residence shocked simple tastes he didn't have, but because he feared that he would no sooner move in than he would be turned out by the first consul.[72] He had obtained a house called the Hôtel d'Elbeuf, near the Place du Carrousel. Moreover, the Tuileries were in poor condition. In 1789 when the royal family, under pressure and forced, had chosen it as their domicile, the dauphin had said to his mother when he saw the palace: "Everything here is very ugly, Mama." Things had not gotten better in the interim, to say the least. The scene of most of the great revolutionary *journées,* the palace bore their scars. It had been sacked and pillaged on August 10, 1792. The spaces then occupied by the Convention and its committees, and later by the Council of Ancients, had been restored, but the rest had a sad air of neglect. The roof leaked, the floors were collapsing, the cracking walls threatened ruin, the plumbing no longer worked, and an army of rats had taken up residence. Bonaparte had inspected his new apartments. In the gallery of Diana, pointing to the graffiti, liberty trees, and Phrygian bonnets that stained the walls, he said to the architect Lecomte, who was accompanying him: "Get rid of all that, I don't want such abominations!"[73]

February 19 was a gray day. Women were not involved in the spectacle. Joséphine and Mme Lebrun, with their entourages, had gone to the palace at an early hour and had set themselves up at the windows of the Pavillon de Flore. On the Place du Carrousel, 3,000 infantrymen and cavalrymen were awaiting the arrival of the cortege. The latter left the Luxembourg at 1 P.M., the cavalry preceding a cortege whose appearance was less splendid: in place of carriages, the new regime's dignitaries had gotten into rented cabs "whose numbers had been hidden beneath a strip of paper," according to Albert Vandal.[74] There were still no servants, no liveries, no powder on people's hair, but rather an air of improvisation, "poorly concealed poverties," and, in short, a very republican simplicity. A monarchy cannot be restored in a few days. The sole luxury was a team of six white horses that drew the consuls' carriage. They had been given to Bonaparte by the emperor of Austria in 1797, after Campoformio. Lebrun was seated in front, Bonaparte in back, with Cambacérès at his side. When they arrived at the Tuileries, Bonaparte got out of the carriage without waiting and jumped on a horse to review the troops. Lebrun and Cambacérès had joined the women. They were not needed. In the evening there was a gala dinner.

That morning Bonaparte had said to his secretary: "Well, Bourrienne, so here we are in the Tuileries! . . . Now we have to stay here."[75] He was there now; he would have time, the next day, to worry about how to stay there. When the dinner was over and the guests had gone, he went to the bedroom that he was going to share with Joséphine, in the part of the building where the royal family had lived. They were alone. He showed her the bed and told her, perhaps with a laugh, and surely with pride: "So, little Creole, come get into your master's bed."[76]

TWENTY-FIVE

From the Tuileries to Marengo

*C*itizens, the revolution is attached to the principles that began it. It is finished."[1] With these words the consuls announced to the French the adoption of the new constitution. "Representative government, the sacred rights of property, equality, [and] liberty" forming its bases, the Revolution that had been carried out in the name of these principles was "finished," according to Bonaparte, in the twofold sense of "ended" and "accomplished."[2]

It was not the first time this had been said. These words had been heard in 1791 after the promulgation of the first revolutionary constitution, and again in 1795 after the adoption of a third constitution. The illusion lasted as long as dreams last. It was different this time, and though no one dared predict the future, it could at least be assumed that it would little resemble the past. The proclamation the first consul addressed to the French people on the evening of his "election" testifies better than any other document to the reality of the change:

> To make the Republic cherished by its citizens, respectable abroad, and formidable to its enemies, those are the obligations that we have contracted by accepting the first magistrature. It will be cherished by its citizens if the laws, the acts of authority, are always marked by the spirit of order, justice, moderation. Without order, administration is no more than chaos. . . . Without justice, there are only parties, oppressors and victims. Moderation gives governments and nations an august character. . . . On these principles depend the stability of the government, the success of trade and agriculture, the grandeur and prosperity of nations. By developing them, we have outlined the rule by which we must be judged. Frenchmen, we have told you what our duties are; it will be you who shall tell us whether we have fulfilled them.[3]

resumption of operations, he did not hide the fact that peace, which he admitted was the country's first need, would be imposed on the enemy by force of arms.[11] It was for military men to speak, rather than diplomats. As soon as Berthier had retaken possession of the Ministry of War, the order to attack was given. But in Germany Lecourbe had been forced to withdraw from the right bank of the Rhine, and in Italy Championnet had not been able to save Coni. The distress was such—"The army [of Italy] is absolutely naked and shoeless," Masséna was still to write in February 1800—that the troops were incapable of going into combat.[12] If we except a sum of around eight million francs collected to cover part of the soldiers' back pay and to cover various urgent expenses, recourse to expedients had to be made to maintain a semblance of order in the ranks. Seditions, desertions, and the insubordination of new conscripts had reduced the French forces to fewer than 400,000 men. Considerable sums would have been required to set things right. The state did not have them.

That is why the diplomatic path was clearly the only way to defer the resumption of operations after the winter truce. The situation was hardly encouraging. France had as allies the continent's two other great maritime powers, Spain and the United Provinces, but no one could say how far it could count on them. The Egyptian campaign had shown how reluctantly Spain fulfilled its obligations, and the Dutch were beginning to fear the consequences of their alliance with France: the British had tried to land on their shores and had seized the Cape of Good Hope.

Bonaparte reserved his main attention for the court of Berlin. Since 1795 Prussia had taken advantage of the peace treaty signed with France to advance its pawns in Germany, without, however, accepting the formal alliance proposed by the French government. Prussian goodwill varied in relation to French power. Luck having changed sides in 1799, Prussia now proved less inclined to guarantee the French occupation of the right bank of the Rhine. Therefore, what had been obtained in 1795 had to be confirmed, if not redone. Bonaparte sought to rebuild confidence with Berlin and to make clear to the European capitals that under his direction France was going to reestablish the customs of diplomacy and become once again an interlocutor with whom one could negotiate. The conduct of the authorities of the free city of Hamburg, who had handed over several Irish refugees to the English, provided him with an opportunity.

Two of these refugees having formerly served in the French army, Bonaparte denounced Hamburg's behavior as an unacceptable violation of international principles, to which the preceding French governments had paid little attention but which he said he now wanted to adopt as a rule of diplomatic conduct.[13]

A competent and respected ambassador, Otto, was representing France in Berlin, where he had been trying, not without a certain success, to make the Prussians forget the abrasive Sieyès. Bonaparte nonetheless decided to send there a personal emissary, his aide-de-camp Duroc, whose visit would demonstrate the importance he attached to Prussia's friendship. Duroc made a good impression in Berlin. He was a well-mannered soldier, elegant and energetic, but he obtained nothing but smiles and friendly words. The king said he was happy to meet "the aide-de-camp of the greatest man [he] knew,"[14] and asked him if he had seen crocodiles on the Nile, but took care not to make the slightest commitment. After having tried several months earlier to tear up the Treaty of Basel, Prussia was resuming the "wait-and-see policy" so irritating to the French.[15]

The mission entrusted to Duroc did not consist solely in obtaining the confirmation of the Franco-Prussian agreement; he was also to exploit, with the aid of Prussia, the dissensions among the coalition's partners. The Russians in particular had reason to complain about the Austrians. In order to have a free hand in northern Italy, the Austrians, who coveted Piedmont, which had just been "liberated" by Suvorov's army, had sent the Russians to Switzerland, where Masséna tore them to pieces. The defeats inflicted on the Russian forces at Zurich and Bergen led the czar to withdraw the troops that he had sent west. Meanwhile, the French, attacked on the continent by forces superior in number, evacuated Egypt, and the Austrians, busy in Italy and in Germany, left the czar free to act as he wished in the Balkans.[16] Some of Suvorov's regiments were already retreating toward Prague, and Suvorov himself probably was not sorry to put a great distance between himself and this Bonaparte, whom he considered a "sorcerer."[17] Duroc was therefore assigned to get in touch with the Russians through the Prussians, suggesting to the latter that they would reap major rewards if they contributed effectively to a successful rapprochement with the czar. Russia thus entered into French strategic calculations and would remain there until 1812. Bonaparte was not inventing anything new: he was adopting a plan found in the Directory's papers, according to which a France allied with the czar would dominate the European continent.[18] He knew little about Paul, an unstable Romanov who had no desire to move closer to his former enemies even if he was disgusted with his present allies. In any case, the first consul tried to cajole him in the hope of weaving a vast alliance that might someday reach from Madrid to Amsterdam, and from Milan to Berlin and Moscow. He showed himself obliging toward the Knights of Malta, and when Paul was declared their protector sent him the Grand Master's sword, which he had brought back from his brief stay on the island.

The steps taken to detach Russia from the coalition remained for the moment unfruitful—Paul I prudently waited to make his decision until the new French government had proven its stability. The proposal to open negotiations, which was simultaneously addressed on December 25 to the British and Austrian sovereigns, fared no better.[19] Did Bonaparte believe that it was possible that he might get a hearing, as some people suggest?[20] That is unlikely; he contented himself, Driault said, with "shaping his image [as the friend of peace] for his contemporaries and for posterity."[21] Wasn't the important thing to see his offers rejected as publicly as they had been made, and thus to force Vienna and London to assume the responsibility for the resumption of hostilities? As foreseen, his overtures met with a flat refusal. At the end of December William Pitt set forth the British government's position:

> It is, however, very material, in my opinion, to speculate on the probable terms, as I think we have nothing to do but to decline all negotiation at the present moment, on the ground that the actual situation in France does not as yet hold out any solid security to be derived from negotiation; taking care at the same time to express strongly the eagerness with which we should embrace any opening for general peace, whenever such solid security shall appear attainable. This may, I think, be so expressed, as to convey to the people of France that the shortest road to peace is by effecting the restoration of royalty, and thereby to increase the chance of that most desirable of all issues to the war.[22]

Pitt declared himself all the more in favor of a restoration because he knew that it was improbable; he was particularly pleased about the "revolution" of 18

Brumaire, which he thought would further weaken the French government and increase the coalition armies' chances of success when the moment came to resume operations. The Austrians, who controlled most of Italy and who had returned to the banks of the Rhine, saw things the same way. Nonetheless, Chancellor Thugut's reply was not quick in coming. Archduke Charles, whose defeat in 1797 had convinced him of Bonaparte's talents, expressed doubts so serious concerning the outcome of the next campaign that he had to be replaced as the head of the army before the French proposals could be rejected. The diplomatic chapter was closed. "The kings of Europe may well regret not having wanted peace," Bonaparte is supposed to have said.[23]

The Spirit of War

"These two attempts," Talleyrand wrote, "led to no reconciliation, and could not lead to any, but they had a happy effect upon the internal peace of the country, because they announced dispositions which ought to be agreeable to the people, in revealing as a skillful statesman the great general who had become the head of the government."[24] This period of the beginning of the Consulate is remembered as that of a dictatorship that was firm, judicious, and beneficial—to borrow Lacretelle's words[25]—and that did more in a few months than had been done in ten years, the government carrying out under the direction of the first consul reforms so well conceived and implemented that most of them were to pass the test of time successfully. Without going so far as to claim, following Las Cases, that the "nation in dissolution was magically reconstituted in a few instants" thanks to Bonaparte's genius, it cannot be denied that there are few moments in French history that can bear comparison with the beginnings of the Consulate.

After five years of Directorial paralysis, everything was moving very fast: four months sufficed to create the Amortization Fund and the Bank of France, to set up a new administration of direct tax payments and the prefectoral system, and to reorganize the judiciary.[26] Historians have long presented these reforms as if they had emerged directly from the head of an omniscient Bonaparte capable of conceiving and executing everything all by himself. Going to the other extreme, many now suggest that he had little or nothing to do with any of this, except as a kind of CEO or manager who knew how to choose his collaborators and get the most out of them.[27] But although he played a role that went far beyond mere encouragement, he also benefited from a favorable context: 18 Brumaire had left the various parties so disoriented that even if they had wanted to oppose the government's policy, they could not have done so effectively. Bringing the assemblies to heel—adding to their constitutional marginalization—had also removed one of the principal obstacles to the speed of reform. In his memoirs Gaudin pretends to be astonished by the ease with which such a fundamental and complex reform as that of the administration of tax collection could be carried out within only a few weeks:

> The operations . . . were made much easier by the existence of two legislative commissions that replaced temporarily, and until the promulgation of the new constitution, the two councils that the day of 18 Brumaire had destroyed. I devised, along with a section of each of these commissions, the arrangements requiring a legal authorization. The law was drafted immediately, and from one day to the next it was submitted. The instructions necessary for its execution were prepared in the meantime; so that they arrived in the departments at the same time as the law itself. This kind of dictatorship in finance forestalled great misfortunes. . . . Thus, on the one hand the extraordinary arrangements demanded by the perilous situation of the public treasury, and on the other the fundamental bases of the financial system, were decreed in twenty days.[28]

This was the result of the combination of the effacement of the assemblies following the coup d'état and the leveling produced by ten years of revolution. Nothing remained of the society bristling with privileges that in the eighteenth century had so often defeated the monarchy's reform-minded ministers. Village communities, corporations, *bonnes villes* (cities with privileges guaranteed by the king), provincial estates, *parlements*, exemptions, rights and liberties based on custom—all that had disappeared. In the reports that he had sent ten years earlier to the court, Mirabeau had seen a good reason for Louis XVI to support the Revolution. Hadn't the Revolution just rid him of his worst enemies by creating a situation that favored "liberty," to be sure, but favored "the exercise of power" even more? "Is it nothing to be without *parlements*, without *pays d'états*, without a body of clergy, privileges, or nobility? The idea of forming a single class of citizens would have pleased Richelieu. . . . Several reigns of an absolute government would not have done as much for royal authority as a single year of liberty."[29] In reality this first year of the Revolution, like those that followed, had done more for "liberty" than for authority.[30] Far from increasing the state's grip on society, it had largely shielded society from the state's authority. Decentralization, the limitation of the central government's powers and jurisdictions, the generalization of the elective principle to all offices with responsibility—the revolutionaries had tried to replace the Old Regime with a society of equal citizens governing itself by means of elected representatives; they saw in governors chosen by election a more effective protection for citizens than the privileges that had formerly shielded them, more or less, from royal or administrative arbitrariness. The sequel had shown that this was not true, and that an elected government could ultimately prove more dangerous to individual liberty than an old monarchy so sure of the future that it had become good-natured. Anarchy, Terror, the instability of the Directorial period: the democratic ideal of a society in which everyone would be simultaneously or by turns governors and governed had collapsed. The formation of the revolutionary government in 1794 had already established the bankruptcy of the idea of self-government, but in 1795 the Republic had tried, without success, to reconnect with the momentum of 1789. The death knell of this experiment was sounded by 18 Brumaire. With the exception of the little phalanx of the "Ideologues," almost no one still believed in the virtues of voting or the merits of deliberation.

The reforms implemented in 1800 testify to the distance that had been covered, in reverse, over a few weeks. Everything that in 1789 had escaped the king's hands to be entrusted to the citizens or to their elected representatives now fell once again within the orbit of the government.

This was true for taxes, whose roles the municipalities determined and whose collection had been entrusted since 1789 to "occasional" bidders;[31] for justice, which was rendered by elected magistrates; and for local administration, which was entrusted to elected executives flanked by deliberative assemblies that held the real power. Taxes were the concern of taxpayers, justice the concern of citizens, and government the concern of the governed. Taxes were poorly collected, the tribunals' actions left much to be desired, incompetence and corruption were found everywhere. No doubt these realities were the consequence less of the system than of the circumstances, but after a decade of experimentation it was clear that the innovations of 1789 had reached their limits. The new government thus decided to reexamine "certain ideas . . . that, though they may be very good in theory, are bad in practice."[32]

An agency handling direct tax payments and in charge of 1,000 inspectors and comptrollers was assigned to distribute tax income, tax collection being entrusted to collectors, who had to make a deposit guaranteeing the anticipated payments they would make to the Treasury out of the revenue from the taxes to be collected. This "fiscal army"[33] had its counterpart in the "judicial army"—the Revolution's elected judges were replaced with magistrates appointed for life by the government in order to guarantee an independence that promotion at the will of those in charge made rather theoretical[34]—and in the "battalion" of prefects and subprefects.

It was another revolution. It returned, in some respects, to monarchical absolutism. After all, the prefects and subprefects were the direct descendants of the intendants and subdelegates of the end of the Old Regime, with this—considerable—difference: although all-powerful so long as they were executing the will of the government that had appointed them and could dismiss them, they could no longer act like the earlier intendants who, with the help of a strong personality, sometimes behaved as if they were genuine viceroys. The prefects were in the government's hands, and the country was in the hands of the prefects. Despite these analogies between the new and the old regime, the consular institutions were in no way participating in a counterrevolution. The reign of the tax farmers was really over, as was that of the magistrature, whose independence in the eighteenth century had so often led to collisions with a monarchy whose ministers encouraged it to become absolute in fact as well as in theory.[35]

The Consulate adopted as its own, ultimately, the great project of rationalizing the state that had failed over the last two decades of the Old Regime. In

1800 it was promoted by men—Lebrun, Gaudin, Dufresne—who, as we have seen, had often supported it in the past. If it succeeded, ten years after the failure of the liberal and decentralizing experiment of 1789, it was because the French Revolution had realized the other side of the program of the Old Regime's reforming ministers: the modernization of society indispensable for the rationalization of the state. Through force and through violence, the Revolution had achieved this modernization; the Consulate could go to work.

But the way in which the obstacle of privileges had been removed changed the very nature of the project. The reforms of the consular period gave France a face that was neither that to which the reformers of the 1760s and 1770s aspired, nor what the members of the Constituent Assembly dreamed about in 1789. Whereas the former thought they had found the solution in the association of the elites with the exercise of royal power through representative assemblies, the latter imagined that they could come very close to the idea of the government of the people by itself. In both cases, society benefited rather than the state.

The spirit of the institutions established in 1800 is very different: they testify, Marx said, to the abdication of society confronted by the state. Marx even drew a comparison between the Terror and Bonaparte's advent, saying of Napoleon that he had revived and continued the revolutionary government of Year II after "modern bourgeois society" had, in 1799 as in 1793, admitted its inability to constitute a state that was the expression of the society of self-sufficient individuals created by the Revolution of 1789. Neither the Constituent Assembly nor the Directory, which were creations of "modern bourgeois society," had found the secret of institutions that were both effective and stable. The bourgeoisie, confessing its impotence as Louis XVI had earlier confessed his own by convoking the Estates General, had fallen back on dictators, Robespierre in 1793, Bonaparte in 1799, and was ready to pay the price: the emancipation of the state with regard to social interests: "Napoleon represented the last battle of revolutionary terror against the bourgeois society. . . . He still regarded the state as an end in itself and civil life only as a treasurer and his subordinate which must have no will of its own."[36]

Of course, these analogies have only a relative import. Marx himself acknowledges this when he explains that Bonaparte, unlike the Jacobins of 1793, "already discerned the essence of the modern state; he understood that it is based on the unhampered development of bourgeois society, on the free movement of private interest." The first consul even understood this so well that he resolved, Marx adds, "to recognize and protect this basis."[37] In this respect Bonaparte is in fact an anti-Robespierre. It is precisely the care with which he protected the interests of the property-owning, patriarchal France that had both won and suffered from the Revolution that made it so attached to him until the collapse of the regime. But—and this is the essential point—the state created by Bonaparte in 1800 was the servant of these interests, not because it was their expression—the bourgeois government of a bourgeois society—but because he needed an orderly, prosperous France from which to draw the money and men he needed for his foreign policy. The coincidence of the interests of society and those of the state was real, but when the former were finally revealed to be contrary to the latter, under the Empire, Napoleon never hesitated to sacrifice them.

As early as 1800 Bonaparte put in place what was to constitute the most durable part of his heritage: the modern administrative state. Would it have been born without him? Probably, insofar as absolute monarchy had laid the foundations for it and it was already present in germ in the revolutionary advent of a society of individuals with equal rights, abstracting from all actual social determination: "From a society in ruins centralization emerged," Royer-Collard was to say in 1822, even before Tocqueville became the historian of administrative centralization in France.[38] It is probable, however, not only that the process would have been slower, but also that the result might have taken on forms that were a little less liberal. Under Bonaparte's influence, centralization in fact took a military turn—Gabriel Ardant compared it to "setting up an army on campaign"[39]—that in the long run was not without consequences. Because obedience to orders was ranked above all else, the agents of the central power sometimes manifested a lack of initiative that sometimes proved damaging. In this connection, the example of General Malet's conspiracy in 1812 is often cited: Napoleon being absent, the government was taken aback by an event that had not been foreseen, and that he had left no instructions for dealing with.[40] From this it has been somewhat hastily deduced that an inability to improvise was one of the effects of an administrative centralization so exaggerated that it was becoming counterproductive.[41] But this episode occurred much later, like all those that can be cited in support of this thesis. It is taken from a period when the leader's growing authoritarianism was becoming increasingly burdensome, and aggravated to boot by an obvious decrease in the quality of the men employed by the emperor: the Montalivets and Pasquiers had succeeded men who had been shaped by the trials of the Revolution and who had made the Consulate's heyday. At that time, energy, talent, and ability were accompanied by an enthusiasm that recalled that of the beginning of the Revolution, and the feeling of being, once again, at the dawn of an epoch. There was so much to do under Bonaparte's leadership, and so much to gain.

The idea that the productivity of administrative centralization reached its limit very early on also ignores the future: what happened after Napoleon was gone showed how well the mechanism had been conceived. He had probably exercised on it a domination so powerful that its functioning was sometimes affected, but as Tocqueville says, "since 1789, the administrative constitution has always remained intact amid the ruins of one political constitution after another."[42] And in a note he adds:

> The perfection of the administrative machine built by Bonaparte is proven by the ease with which it functions almost without a motor, as has been demonstrated by the revolutions that have taken place since, or functions in the infirm hands of mediocre scoundrels . . . almost as well as it could under the impetus of the greatest minds; it produces its work, independently of the value of the workman.[43]

On the other hand, on one point there is widespread, if not unanimous, agreement, and it reconciles fervent defenders of the emperor's memory and his detractors: the centralization of Year VIII accentuated, or perhaps even inaugurated, the "illiberal trend "in French history. Albert Vandal, Alphonse Aulard, and Hippolyte Taine said it: the great reforms of 1800, which related everything to the state and required everything to be done by the state or its agents, led to the destruction of any trace of local autonomy and, later on, the atrophy of the aptitude for freedom among the French.[44] Post-Napoleonic French society? An "impoverished, inert, or languid" body, Taine says, "in brief, human dust or mud." The accusation is so common, proceeding from both the left and the right, that it is useless to insist upon it, except to object that such an assessment ignores the weight of history. Taine basically judges France in the early nineteenth century by comparing it, with regret, to the path followed by England, and much the same can be said of all those who deplore the despotic aspects of French history. According to this argument, the two nations were in the same situation around 1783. England had undergone, after the American War of Independence, a financial crisis that was even more serious than that of public finances in France; but unlike France, it had been able to resolve this crisis without a revolution and without sacrificing its liberal traditions. It is sometimes said that if Louis XVI had been capable, like George III, of supporting against public opinion a French William Pitt determined to impose the unpopular measures indispensable for financial recovery, France might have avoided the Revolution.[45] In reality, England was able to overcome the crisis because its government could count on the support of the people. It was not because the government was more capable or stronger, but because England's population was three times smaller than France's.[46] It was a more homogeneous society under the control of an elite that held in its hands a threefold social, economic, and political influence. This ruling class descended from "ancient castes," as Napoleon said, from a "gentry" France did not possess and never had. France had an upper class in which, at the end of the eighteenth century, wealth brought nobles and well-off bourgeois together, but this social and economic elite was never at any time a ruling class. Turgot, Necker, and Calonne had certainly tried to involve it in the exercise of power by setting up assemblies that would have been reserved for them, but their failure had been complete. The Revolution broke out in 1789 because society had always been too weak in France to impose on the Crown limits of the kind that the barons and the communes proclaimed in England as early as 1215, and because the Crown's legitimacy was too fragile for it even to think about relinquishing the smallest amount of its power, finding in its privileged connection with religion and in the support of a bureaucracy that long remained embryonic the authority and the strength that compensated for its uncertain legitimacy. The Revolution destroyed the French upper class, which had almost become a ruling class in 1789, but on the other hand it accelerated the development of an administrative class that was all the more competent because, having been born in the offices of Versailles, it had completed its education in the disorders of the Revolution. In 1799 and 1800 the rout of the deliberative assemblies handed power to the administrative class, which took possession of the Council of State, the *Cour de Cassation*, the prefectures, the administration of finances, the Ministry of the Interior, and so forth, prolonging and accentuating a development that was already notable under the monarchy. Hence, Taine's criticism must be understood as a manifestation of his regret on contemplating the spectacle of a history that could hardly have turned out differently. The "damage," if damage there was, had been done long before Bonaparte seized power, and even well before the French Revolution broke out.

Difficult Beginnings

The reforms carried out in 1800 could not produce their effects immediately. The nomination of judges and the organization of new tribunals, the designation of prefects and tax collectors-general took time, not to mention the fact that the new institutions, which collided with a good many habits and interests, were not always well received. Their effect was deferred especially in the financial domain. Not until 1804 did all the tax collectors become state employees. Many departments benefited from reprieves or rescheduling of payments on back taxes, and because doubts about the duration of the new regime persisted, the bonds given by tax collectors-general were long bought and sold at exorbitant prices.[47]

While asserting that reforms led to an improvement in the financial situation as early as June 1800, Gaudin admits that for some time it remained necessary to resort to the same expedients to which the Directory had owed its survival.[48] These took the form of extraordinary measures applied with a firmness that would have recalled the bad old days of 1793 had they not had such positive effects, because even before fiscal reform had borne fruit, a consular order was able to announce, on August 11, 1800, the resumption of the payment of annuities in cash. The government had also succeeded in finding the money it needed, notably to finance the resumption of the war, without raising taxes, which permitted it to retain the support of a large part of the population. Despite Bonaparte's popularity, the authority of the new regime was so fragile that there was no solution other than to intimidate all those who were capable of contributing, within in France or without: "The new government holds out its hand. . . . Collot throws 500,000 francs into it, according to Bourrienne, 800,000 according to Marmont; 2 million francs are squeezed out of Genoa, 4.5 million out of Hamburg. . . . Flessingue is sold to the Batavian Republic for a few million. In Nivôse Year VIII [January 1800], the situation is sufficiently precarious that officials begin to look toward Holland, which is so often the resource for governments that are short of funds: Marmont, a man who can be counted on, is assigned to go there to negotiate a loan of 10 to 12 million, and if necessary to give as a pledge to get it, the Regent's [diamond]: the attempt is not successful."[49]

"Gifts" were obtained from a few large provincial cities, such as Lyon, Marseille, and Nantes. Purchasers of national properties were required to pay sales costs immediately. The banker Portal lent a million francs at a rate of 1.5 percent. Money was drawn from the mass of national properties that had not yet been put on sale, and Bonaparte, who wanted to make the bankers and suppliers whom the Revolution had made wealthy pay, called them in to command them to get together a sum of twelve million, which they later reduced to three.[50] No doubt the rest was promised in the form of security for a loan that succeeded so well that it produced the desired sum, but Bonaparte, furious about the reduction, decided to make an example by putting Ouvrard, the former auctioneer of naval supplies and the most prominent of the bankers, under house arrest.[51] The "attack" worked, despite a protest by "the commerce of Paris," which merely earned the capital's bankers and financiers another summons to the Luxembourg Palace to face the ire of the first consul, who was scandalized that they had been offended by the arrest of a dishonest "state employee." On February 17 Ouvrard agreed to the revision of certain clauses in the contract between him and the Ministry of the Navy, and lost, in exchange for his freedom, about ten million francs that went to refill the Treasury's coffers.[52]

About the Consulate's great works, Jacques Bainville wrote that they reflected "the period" and the "chicken in every pot" side of Bonaparte,[53] as if the latter had relaxed after coping with thorny and crucial international questions by putting a little order in the country. This is not the most intelligent thing Bainville ever wrote. Not only was the restoration of order within the country indispensable for the pursuit of the war, but Bonaparte also agreed with Machiavelli that "of all men who have been eulogized, those who deserve it most"—after the founders of religions but before "those who have commanded armies, and have extended the possessions of their kingdom or country, their own territory or that of the country"—are "such as have established republics or kingdoms."[54] A reputation for conquest alone does not suffice to make a man renowned; he has to add to it the glory reserved for those who achieve something enduring. More than in the urban development or the construction of monuments that were going to occupy much of his time after his encounter with Percier and Fontaine in late 1800, it is perhaps in the institutional work of 1800 that we can best see how he valued his role as a civilian leader at least as much as his role as a military leader, and also how well he was able to combine the grandiose and the useful. There coexisted in him an uncommon sense of grandeur and what Bourrienne rightly calls "administrative wisdom."[55]

The End of the Wars in the Vendée

War had resumed in the departments of the west. It had never completely stopped, even after the terrible repression of 1794. The La Jaunaye accords, concluded in February 1795, and then the policy of military "pacification" skillfully conducted by Hoche in 1795 and 1796, had reestablished only a precarious calm. The people remained "ill-intentioned" toward the Republic, and the Republic was itself little inclined to respect its commitments. After Stofflet, the Vendéean leader, was shot in Angers in February 1796, and Charette in Nantes in March, new leaders had appeared. The situation grew more tense after 18 Fructidor. The fall of the moderate, royalist right, whose successes had given rise to the hope that a restoration might be brought about by peaceful means, was like an alarm. Vendéean rebels and *chouans* thought the time had come to take up arms again, especially because the Directory, having struck a shattering blow to the left, was no longer showing itself inclined to make concessions. The resumption of hostilities and the French defeats in the spring and summer of 1799 persuaded the royalists in the west, in consultation with émigrés in London, to begin the uprising without further delay.

It exploded in mid-October, at the moment when Bonaparte was returning to France. Not knowing that the republican armies had halted the Russian and Austrian offensive, the insurgents attacked the principal cities. The surprise effect alone allowed a few of them to be seized, Le Mans on October 15, Nantes on the twentieth, Saint-Brieuc on the twenty-seventh. It quickly became clear that this was not a repetition of the events of 1793, but only the "last rumbling of a storm that is moving away."[56] People mention about 40,000 men under arms, but distributed from the Vendéean Bocage to Normandy, and commanded by six or seven leaders who disagreed with each other and paralyzed the sometimes close connections that they maintained with the émigrés—who were themselves as indecisive—and with the princes, who remained little desirous of owing a restoration to these half-savage peasants. General Hédouville, sent to the area with reinforcements, quickly assessed the situation, whose most prominent characteristic was no doubt the weak mobilization of the old military Vendée: the rebellion involved the *chouans* more than the Vendéeans. Without neglecting military action, Hédouville sought above all to enter into contact with the royalist leaders. His efforts were greatly facilitated by the news of 18 Brumaire, which arrived in the west at this point and, when added to the victories won by Masséna and by Brune, seemed almost to annihilate the insurgents' determination.

Bonaparte's moderate statements, his declared wish for reconciliation and forgiveness, the conciliatory instructions he gave Hédouville—even if he forbade him to sign a "diplomatic treaty" with the rebels[57]—and also the feeling that things might be going to change all had an effect. They certainly played a part in the decision made on November 23 by Autichamp, Châtillon, and Bourmont, who were commanding, respectively, the insurgents on the left bank of the Loire, the right bank of the Loire, and in Maine, to sign a one-month ceasefire.

Had they, too, conceived a few illusions about Bonaparte's intentions? Did they take him for Monk, as Louis XVIII did when he wrote to him from his exile in Mitau [modern Jelgava] to demand from him his throne? But they knew nothing specific about the general's plans, and to get to the bottom of the matter they sent one of their men, d'Andigné, to Paris.

Through Hyde de Neuville, who knew the diplomat Bourgoing, who knew Talleyrand, d'Andigné was able to obtain an audience with the general. On December 27 he went to the Luxembourg in Hyde's company. The interview began rather well. Bonaparte had known d'Andigné's brother, first in Auxonne, then in Egypt. This tie provided a starting point. After having praised the brother, Bonaparte looked at the proposed treaty the royalist had brought and began to examine its terms. D'Andigné and Hyde were amazed: The exemption from conscription in the departments of the west? A discount on back taxes? The removal of the royalist leaders from the list of émigrés? Bonaparte accepted everything. As for the free exercise of religion, he said, smiling as people do who understand one another: "I will reestablish religion, not for you, but for myself. . . . It is not that as nobles, we are very religious; but it is necessary for the people, and I shall reestablish it." The two royalists were already rejoicing when Bonaparte declared out of the blue that he would not sign anything! They cried out, asking him what guarantee he was offering? His word, he replied drily, only his word, because so long as he lived, no treaty would be signed with rebels. The discussion went on a long time, mostly courteously, sometimes tensely.[58] "He told us several times," Hyde reported, "that if the royalists did not come over to him, they would be exterminated." His interlocutor having asked whether, in exchange for their submission, he would restore the Bourbons, he replied that they should not count on that: the Bourbons were finished.[59]

"We separated without having negotiated," wrote Hyde de Neuville, "but the main point [a possible restoration] was only too clear after that conversation."[60] The next day a proclamation appeared that was obviously Bonaparte's response to the proposals that had been made to him, a clever mixture of concessions and threats.[61] In any case, there was nothing left to negotiate: the public orders on the occasion of the Consulate's move into the Tuileries—the restoration of the Sunday mass and freedom of religion, the suppression of the oath of loyalty to the Civil Constitution of the Clergy, the decision to grant funereal honors to the remains of Pius VI, and the suppression of the January 21 holiday—satisfied the insurgents' demands concerning religion. Hence, at the same time that the Consulate sent to the west the proclamation of December 28 announcing the restoration of freedom of religion, an amnesty, and several other measures, orders went out to form an army of 60,000 men under Brune's command and assigned to liquidate the last centers of resistance. This was triple the number of soldiers in 1793, for an uprising one-third the size. Bonaparte explained that it was necessary "to make the rebels feel the whole weight and horror of war."[62] That was when Abbé Bernier entered the scene. In 1793 Bernier, a curate, had led his parishioners in an attack on republican soldiers in the Vendée; it was even said that he had killed several of them with his own hands. He was venerated or detested, and Charrette said that he was a scoundrel combined with a traitor. Few people could resist this priest, who had, however, the misfortune to look like a brigand, "short, stocky, squint-eyed, rough-skinned and frizzy-haired."[63] He "knew how to inspire fanaticism in his peasants, without sharing it."[64] Seductive, intelligent, and persuasive, he exercised a certain ascendancy over his interlocutors, and not only because of his past as a champion of the Catholic and royal cause. His heroism, though, was ultimately only a pose. Bernier was "a politician who had wandered into heroism" and who was looking for a way to get out of a role that only half pleased him. He was above all "a diplomat, go-between, and politician."[65] That is why Charrette despised him, but it is also why he was able to break down, not only the gates of power, but more modestly, those of the corridors of power. Having succeeded in making his way into Hédouville's entourage, he had made contact with Bonaparte and ended up establishing himself as the necessary intermediary between royalist and republicans. He traveled all over the region, running from one leader to another and from there to Hédouville's and Brune's headquarters, so effectively that these talks, along with the military operations vigorously carried out by Brune, led Autichamp to surrender on January 18. The war was over on the left bank of the Loire. On the right bank, Bourmont and Cadoudal were resisting the disarming of their troops, and Frotté refused to surrender. The first two, pursued by Brune, ended up capitulating. Frotté did not: captured in Alençon on February 17, he was executed at Verneuil the following day.

Frotté's execution has ever since raised questions. Hyde de Neuville and Barras started a rumor that Bonaparte had Frotté killed to prevent him from talking.[66] The first consul and the *chouan* leader are supposed to have known each other at the École militaire, and the general, on his way back from Egypt, is alleged to have contacted his former classmate to make the royalists believe that he was returning with the intention of playing the role of Monk, intending to soothe them at a time when the Jacobins still seemed a real threat. It is because he wanted to conceal these compromising relations with the royalists that he is supposed to have ordered Frotté's death. It is certainly possible that Bonaparte wanted to protect himself from royalist unrest by making a few vague promises. But why would he have chosen as an interlocutor a *chouan* whom he did not really know, who had gone underground, and who had no authority beyond the bands he commanded in the Norman bocage?[67] If Bonaparte had in fact decided that Frotté had to die, it was for very different reasons: at a time when his mind was turning toward the next campaign, he wanted the last rebels eliminated. He said so to Brune, a few days before Frotté was captured:

> We are already in February; time is extremely precious. My intention is that within ten days all the armed groups of the Morbihan be dissipated and their disarming carried out by agreement or by force. During that time I shall do the same thing in the fourteenth military division [Orne]. It is only by taking this step that it will be possible for us to have half of your troops available by the end of March. . . . Peace within the country and the success of the next campaign are both connected with how you perform in this circumstance. The government must not be the dupe of a few miserable émigrés or a few peasants.[68]

Frotté, who refused to lay down his arms, was shot in accord with the laws of war. There was no reason for the first consul to spare him. Indeed, he had just set a similarly severe example, in Paris itself, by ordering the execution of an eighteen-year-old émigré, the Chevalier de Toustain, whose only crime was to have come to the capital without authorization to see his brother, who was being held in the Temple. With Bourmont and Cadoudal having surrendered, and Frotté dead, the main objective had been achieved: the war in the Vendée was over. The lives of a handful of *chouans* did not weigh heavily in the scales. The Constitution, which had been suspended for a moment in the departments of the west, was put back into force, and on March 6 Bonaparte received in the Tuileries Abbé Bernier and the main leaders of the uprising. With the exception of Cadoudal they were all nobles, so he pretended that the peace was a gentlemen's agreement, though he could not resist telling Bourmont, who had been insolent, that he would "break his head."[69] He succeeded less well with Cadoudal. During the reception on March 6 he had paid hardly any attention to this "big

Breton" who had, however, been described to him as the most intelligent and most dangerous of his adversaries.[70] So he received him again a few days later:

> The interview was long. General Bonaparte made the words "country" and "glory" resound in Georges [Cadoudal]'s ears, and he even tried, also in vain, the allure of ambition on the heart of this ferocious soldier of the civil war; he did not succeed, and on seeing his interlocutor's face was himself convinced that he had not succeeded. Georges, leaving him, left for England with Hyde de Neuville. Several times, as he was recounting his interview to his traveling companion, he cried, showing him his vigorous arms: "What a blunder I committed in not strangling that fellow!"[71]

The Great St. Bernard Pass

Bonaparte did not wait until he had finished with the civil war to begin preparing for war abroad. The provisional Consulate had hardly been set up before he was issuing orders for the creation of a reserve corps and reorganizing the command of the armies. Command had been entrusted to Brune in Holland and Masséna in Switzerland, while Lecourbe and Championnet were temporarily in command in Germany and Italy. Augereau now replaced Brune, Masséna took command of the Army of Italy, his Army of Helvetia being combined with the Army of the Rhine entrusted to Moreau a few days before 18 Brumaire.

Was Moreau retained at the head of the imposing Army of the Rhine—150,000 men—because he had to be rewarded for his support on the day of the coup d'état? He had played such a subordinate, almost humiliating role—he had been assigned to guard the directors held prisoner in the Luxembourg—that Bonaparte may have thought he owed him compensation, especially because their relations had not always been serene. Moreau had not forgotten how Bonaparte, as head of the Army of Italy, had violated courtesy by arriving first at the gates of Vienna in 1797. The memory of his recent defeats in Italy, which had been compared with Bonaparte's "brilliant successes" in Egypt, didn't help matters. Victor or vanquished, Moreau remained popular in public opinion and

Campaign of 1800 in Italy

in the army; even the suspicions that he had colluded with the royalists had not damaged his reputation. Everything suggested that he should be treated with the greatest consideration. Moreover, with Jourdan sidelined because of his opposition to 18 Brumaire, Moreau was the only man, except for Bonaparte himself, who was capable of commanding an army as large as that of the Rhine.[72] Masséna was certainly a bolder and more talented military leader than Moreau: the latter was "not much in the first line of generals," Bonaparte was to say, whereas the former had the ability of the greatest captains, if only amid danger and under fire. In other words, in Bonaparte's view Masséna was very capable of leading into battle a division or a little army but was hardly up to commanding a behemoth of 150,000 men.[73]

Moreau on the Rhine and Masséna in Liguria led armies that were poorly supplied and decimated by desertion and insubordination. Confronting them were two Austrian forces: in Swabia, 120,000 men commanded by Archduke Charles (who was soon replaced by Field Marshal Kray); and in Lombardy, 130,000 men under the orders of the old Field Marshal Melas. The two French armies, Moreau's, which had fallen back on the left bank of the Rhine, and Masséna's, driven back toward Genoa and the Riviera, were separated by the Alps and by Switzerland, whose importance Thiers explained well, especially since revolutions and military interventions had made the young Helvetian Republic dependent on France:

> When Austrian armies advance towards France, they are obliged to ascend the valley of the Danube, on the one hand, and the valley of the Po, on the other, divided into two acting masses by the long chain of the Alps. While they are in Bavaria and in Lombardy, these two masses can communicate across the Alps by the Tyrol, which belongs to the emperor; but, when they arrive in Swabia, on the Upper Danube, in Piedmont, on the Upper Po, they find themselves separated from one another, without any possible communication across the Alps, because Switzerland, independent and neutral, is usually closed against them.[74]

The gates of Switzerland were the pivot of the French plan of action. There, on December 5, less than a month after 18 Brumaire, Bonaparte ordered the assembly of a reserve corps capable of coming to the aid of both the left wing in Germany and the right wing in Italy.[75] The final composition of this army of 40,000 men was decided only on March 8, when it was certain that the war in the west was over.[76] Battalions that had come from Brittany and the Vendée, soldiers drawn from the Army of the Orient's supply depots, men taken from the Army of Italy—to Masséna's great dismay—gradually arrived in Dijon, Saulieu, Beaune, and Bourg-en-Bresse. The cavalry assembled at Dôle, the artillery at Auxonne, where Bonaparte had gone to school. Only 4,500 men had come by the end of March; 32,000 had arrived by the end of April; and the force stood at 36,000 when Bonaparte arrived in Switzerland on May 8.[77] Berthier, who was to command them, arrived in Dijon at the beginning of April, having handed the War portfolio over to Carnot.

Allowing the return to France of the former director, who had been exiled along with royalists on 18 Fructidor, had been one of the new government's first initiatives. It cannot be said that Bonaparte was one of the admirers of the "Organizer of Victory"; he had not forgotten the part Carnot had played in the fall of Robespierre or the ambushes he had strewn along the route of the young general of the Army of Italy in 1794 and 1795. Moreover, he thought Carnot's talents as a strategist were overestimated. Carnot had been trained in fortification at the school for military engineers, and the kind of war that he preferred was that of the age of Vauban, which Bonaparte loathed. But Carnot was hardworking and honest. Bonaparte had established trusting, if not cordial, relations with him, though this hadn't prevented him from abandoning the director to his fate at the time of 18 Fructidor. It is true that he later disapproved of Carnot's proscription, even if, stopping in Geneva on November 21, 1797, he had ordered the arrest of one of Carnot's "accomplices" who had been denounced to him; he did not push his zeal so far as to order a search for the former director himself.[78] Carnot did not hold it against him. As soon as he had been granted amnesty, on November 26, 1799, he set out for Paris. Bonaparte welcomed him with many expressions of friendship: Carnot, a living symbol of the Revolution, incarnated the political realism that Bonaparte intended to make the basis of his own policies. Appointed minister of war on April 2, Carnot restored order to a military administration infected by corruption, and he contributed effectively to the preparation for the campaign of 1800. But the relations between the two men, though courteous, were inevitably to turn sour. Carnot was too great a figure, too conscious of what he represented, to let himself be scolded and rebuffed. "An honest man, and very industrious," Napoleon agreed; but impossibly "self-opinionated."[79] And Carnot did not see war the way Bonaparte did: he didn't like it, or if he liked something about it, it was only what lent itself to the illusions of science. Sixteen years older than Bonaparte, he was in matters of war more a man of the eighteenth century than the first consul, dreaming of freeing war from its element of chance and giving it a character of certitude peculiar to mathematical things. He was interested in war as a scientist, whereas Bonaparte loved it as an artist. From the very first weeks of their collaboration it was evident that this marriage would last only as long as the campaign. Carnot was an interim solution.

The final plan focused the main effort on Germany. The left wing of the Army of the Rhine would leave its positions between Strasbourg and Basel and fall back on the right wing, hiding its movement "behind the curtain of the Rhine." The army would then move en masse toward Schaffhausen, where, throwing "four bridges at once" across the river, it would cross in twenty-four hours and march immediately on the Danube, going around the Austrian left wing posted on the right bank. If Kray let himself be taken by surprise, he would be cut off from his bases and lost; if he turned around to try to stop the enemy from cutting his line of retreat, he would have to fight under unfavorable conditions. Once Kray was defeated or thrown back beyond Ulm, Moreau would move on Regensburg and Linz, following the Danube. In the meantime Masséna was to persevere in Italy in order to "immobilize" Melas and prevent him from marching on Bavaria over the Tyrol to threaten the right flank of the French army marching toward Vienna.[80]

All the glory of these operations was reserved for the Army of the Rhine; Bonaparte willingly agreed that it alone held the keys to the peace, which in 1800 as in 1797 could be decided only in Germany, not Italy.[81] However, it is not clear that in the first consul's mind Moreau was to draw the main benefit from the victory. He even considered taking command of the Army of the Rhine himself, or at least going to join it without any official title but supervising the operations from a little higher up and a little farther away than he later did with Berthier's reserve army, because he had to take care not to wound Moreau's pride.[82] Another reason encouraged him to stay in the background: "The consular magistrature being essentially civilian," he was later to say, "the principle of the separation of powers and the responsibility of the ministers does not allow the Republic's first magistrate to be in direct command of an army."[83] Was this a sincere scruple on his part? Or was it an awareness of the fragility of his power? The Constitution was in fact silent on this subject: its authors had even rejected an amendment proposed by Daunou that sought to prevent the first consul from taking command of the armies. Bonaparte probably did not want to arouse concern among the touchiest of republicans; but as he also said, "no arrangement, and no principle, was opposed to his being present (with the army),"[84] and he expected all the more to benefit from it because a large part of public opinion could not imagine him remaining in Paris while Frenchmen were fighting on the borders.[85]

In Bonaparte's view it was clear that the plan could not succeed without him. He demanded close coordination among the three armies, and thus a single command, and Bonaparte did not imagine that anyone other than himself could perform the functions of the "generalissimo."[86] Moreau? Bonaparte knew his prudence, the care he took with the army's supplies and baggage. He was admired as much for his skillful retreats as for his victories. But the plan demanded audacity and speed: audacity, because the Rhine had to be crossed at a single point and without being seen by the enemy; speed, because the final victory depended on the rapidity of the march on the Danube. Not only did Bonaparte refuse to leave Moreau the laurels of victory, but he was convinced that commanded by Moreau alone, the Army of the Rhine would never reach Vienna: wasn't that what had happened in 1797?

Unsurprisingly, Moreau refused to fight as second-in-command; he refused with no less vehemence to cross the Rhine at Schaffhausen when there were, in Strasbourg, Neuf-Brisach, and Basel, several points where his army could cross the river with complete safety. For him there was no question of "attempting the passage at one point only with the chance, it is true, of a much more brilliant advantage, but also with the possibility of incalculable disaster."[87] He was furious. He confided his grievances to his chief of staff, Dessolle, who went to Paris, and even threatened to resign.[88] The real negotiations took place over three days, among Bonaparte, Carnot, and Dessolle, in the middle of March, as if

Dessolle were the representative of an ally rather than a simple head of an army, and they tell us a great deal about the influence Bonaparte attributed to Moreau. A treaty in due form was even drafted, according to which Moreau was allowed to cross the Rhine at the points he chose, with only his right wing building bridges at Schaffhausen; in exchange he agreed to send part of that right wing to support the reserve army's operations in the Alps.[89] After making these concessions, Bonaparte decided to stake everything on the reserve army and Italy. The campaign plan, which had been German, now became Italian.[90] "You are right," he is supposed to have told Dessolle. "Moreau is not capable of appreciating and executing the plan which I have conceived. Let him do as he pleases. . . . What he dares not do on the Rhine, I will do on the Alps. He may, by and by, regret the glory which he relinquishes to me."[91] New orders were sent out.[92] Reconnaissance was carried out at the principal points of passage toward Italy. Of the earlier plan, nothing remained but the first phase: Moreau's assignment was to defeat the enemy or at least to "hold him down" in Swabia in order to prevent him from going to the aid of Melas in Lombardy. Then the reserve army, commanded by Bonaparte, would cross the Alpine passes and fall on Melas, who would be caught in a pincers movement between it and the Army of Italy concentrated around Genoa.[93]

Did Bonaparte at the same time surrender the hope of winning the war, given that it could not be won in Italy? Did he prefer to a decisive success a brilliant stroke that was inconsequential on the military level but would increase his glory and consolidate his power? In reality the new plan had little of the brilliance of the first: it replaced a lightning maneuver on the enemy's rear, which was intended to lead to a general peace, with a limited maneuver in Italy that was inspired by the same tactical schema, but from which Bonaparte could not expect a comparable military and political benefit. If he had been able to choose, he would certainly have preferred the Ulm maneuver to that of Marengo. Peace was postponed as soon as he gave priority to the Italian theater, but if someone was responsible for this situation, it was Moreau. He was the one who had refused to cross the Rhine at Schaffhausen, a refusal that by itself led to the abandonment of the initial plan. Thibaudeau is right when he says that in this matter, Bonaparte showed great indulgence: "Far from showing himself to be, as has been said, envious and jealous, [the first consul] was overflowing with consideration,"[94] going so far as to silence Berthier, who advised him to be firmer,[95] and never failing to close his letters to Moreau with warm expressions of friendship and confidence that must have cost him something: "with a fond farewell," he still wrote to him in May.[96]

On April 6, 1800, the Austrians took the initiative in Italy, and Masséna soon found himself in difficulties. Not only was he facing forces superior in number, but he had increased this disadvantage by retaining the division of his little army of less than 40,000 men into two parts. One of these, commanded by Suchet, was guarding the French frontier from Nice to the Tende Pass, and the other, placed under Soult's orders, occupied the area around Genoa. Masséna had been constantly asking for supplies, weapons, and reinforcements. In vain. A few days before hostilities began, he had even received a strong reprimand, Bonaparte telling him curtly that all that could be done for him had been done, that he must not count on any additional reinforcement, and that instead of recriminating he should think about how to get the most out of the positions he was occupying and prevent the Austrians from cutting his army "into two separate bodies."[97] The first consul was right. The Austrians easily separated the two poorly connected parts of the Army of Italy, throwing Suchet back to the Var and Soult to Savona.[98] Masséna was forced to fall back toward Genoa, and then to take refuge in the city: a failed attempt to break out on April 9 marked the beginning of the siege. Masséna now had only one task: to hold on, while making a sufficient number of sorties—his position was not bad, provided that he could bring in supplies[99]—to immobilize the Austrians long enough for the reserve army to pass over the Alps.

The beginning of the maneuver depended on the operations of Moreau, who had not yet made any movement at all. It took a veritable ultimatum from Bonaparte, on April 24, to get him to decide to cross the Rhine.[100] As he had wanted, he sent most of his troops across the river at Strasbourg, Brisach, and Basel, and then moved along the right bank as far as Schaffhausen, where the right wing (Lecourbe) crossed in its turn. On May 1 the whole Army of the Rhine was bivouacking on the right bank; Lecourbe took Stockach on May 3, Moreau took Messkirch on the fifth, but then he let Kray retreat to Ulm by the right bank of the Danube, without trying to throw him back on the left bank. Kray reformed his troops in Ulm (May 11–12), and Moreau decided not to give battle but moved farther east, toward Augsburg and Munich, where, Thiers tells us, he "confined himself to a calculated inaction."[101]

Napoleon was to judge Moreau's campaign very harshly.[102] However, Moreau had achieved the designated objectives, even if he had done so in a way that lacked brilliance and could not please Bonaparte. To be sure, he had not destroyed Kray's army or fought to take Ulm, but "he had fulfilled the essential condition of the plan of the campaign; he had passed the Rhine without accident, in the teeth of the Austrian army; he had fought two great battles with it . . . notwithstanding his *fumbling* before Ulm, he had shut up the Austrians around that place, and kept them blockaded there, cutting them off from the route to Bavaria and the Tyrol."[103] Moreau did not think he could or should do more. At the time he was beginning his movement toward Munich, Carnot had personally delivered to him the formal order to detach Lecourbe and 25,000 men to the St. Gotthard and Simplon passes, without even waiting, as had been agreed, until he had "obtained an advantage over Kray considerable enough to give him superiority."[104] Once again the discussion was intense. Moreau yielded, sick at heart. He wrote Bonaparte this simultaneously insolent and bitter note: "The detachment you ask of us upsets us, but we shall do our best. . . . I have hope in your successes, which I regard as certain. You shall be able to conduct this year a campaign as brilliant as the one you conducted in Italy. I wish you all possible success; your arrival at the reserve army has given the greatest pleasure to us all; it is the harbinger of victory."[105]

Moreau resisted a little more and finally sent fewer than 14,000 men, commanded by Moncey, to the St. Gotthard Pass. Bonaparte was satisfied. In any case the time had come for him to make his entrance on the stage.

While the battalions of the reserve army, which had officially headed for Dijon, had secretly gone to Geneva and Lausanne in order to avoid alerting the Austrians—this disinformation campaign was carried out masterfully by Berthier and Carnot—reports on the best way to enter Italy had come in one after another.[106]

Bonaparte had at first given priority to the route that leads from Zurich to Milan via the Splügen Pass and Lake Como.[107] He had also sent someone to reconnoiter the St. Gotthard Pass, which could take him to Milan via the valley of the Ticino.[108] Bonaparte needed the help of Moreau's right wing, because he gave priority to this maneuver in upper Italy.[109] It was only toward the end of March that he included the possibility of a passage farther to the west that would make it possible, in case of need, to come rapidly to Masséna's rescue. For all that, nothing had yet been decided; the Splügen Pass was soon excluded, and the St. Gotthard route, which was supposed to be the easiest, came to be preferred. But the bad news from Genoa and the Riviera—Melas, who had left Ott to besiege Genoa and had marched against Suchet, was going to occupy Nice on May 11—finally forced Bonaparte to move westward over the passes in the Valais.[110] Mont Cenis was certainly the most accessible route, but given the circumstances it had the disadvantage of preventing a priori any maneuver on the enemy's rear. The Simplon Pass and the Great St. Bernard Pass thus remained in contention. The former was without any doubt easier than the latter, but to reach it the troops would have to cover about forty kilometers of roads in poor condition. The Great St. Bernard Pass, which began at the easternmost extremity of Lake Geneva, was easier to reach; the access route as far as Bourg-Saint-Pierre was passable. That is what determined the decision. The most difficult part on either side of the summit, between Saint-Pierre and Saint-Rémy, was only about twenty kilometers long. The St. Bernard Pass also had the advantage of leading to the intersection of two roads, leading to Lombardy on the east and to Piedmont on the south. Thus, it would be possible to decide at the last minute which direction to take, depending on Masséna's situation.[111] Stretched out on the floor of his office to examine "Chauchard's big map of Italy," with Bourrienne at his side, Bonaparte stuck into it, with serious attention, pins whose heads were daubed with red or black wax. He called his secretary, who didn't understand what he was doing, an "imbecile" and then showed him, "with a triumphant air" as if he had defeated him, the point: "the plains of Scrivia"—where he hoped to fall upon the rear of a Melas as dumbfounded as his secretary.[112]

Having left Paris on May 6 on the pretext of going to inspect the army in Dijon, Bonaparte made a stop in that city the next day, just long enough to visit the garrison, whose small number of men were presented as the bulk of the reserve army, and then headed for Geneva, where he arrived on the eighth. Necker, whom he had not seen when he passed through the city in 1797, came to greet him: "The first consul," Bonaparte said laconically, "was not very satisfied with his conversation," finding in the former minister to the king more conceit than real knowledge, including in the financial domain.[113] Necker was followed by a delegation of notables:

> [Bonaparte] spoke of nothing but peace, humanity, the end of Europe's misfortunes, the century of happiness that was beginning for it. . . . [He] said that he would be happy to die, provided that he saw the world at peace. His pallor, dejection, thinness, and the state of exhaustion to which his earlier travails had reduced him were such that one would have said he ought to hasten to sign a peace treaty if he wanted to enjoy his work. Then he kindly asked about Saussure, Bonnet, and Sennebier (he said nothing about Rousseau), declaring that he wanted to restore respect for the sciences and letters. . . . The citizens of Geneva admired the warrior's pacific sentiments; but they did not see what was in his heart; they did not perceive that he was going along with the times only in order to make himself their master.[114]

Bonaparte was already entering Lausanne. He left it on the sixteenth, first for Villeneuve, then for Martigny, whence the vanguard under the command of Lannes had departed the day before to climb the slopes leading to the Great St. Bernard Pass. The ascent was steep—more than 2,000 meters in altitude— and the descent abrupt.[115] It took eight hours to reach the pass, and two hours to come down from it; the horses were slow, and the artillerymen were even slower. A whole day was necessary to lug the cannons up to the summit. They were disassembled, the smaller parts were numbered and then loaded, along with the munitions, onto the backs of mules. As for the barrels, they were at first placed on specially fabricated sledges fitted with wheels, but these proved unusable. The men ended up cutting down trees, hollowing out their trunks, and placing the two-ton cannon barrels in them; a hundred men then dragged the loads to the summit.[116] Peasants from the surrounding area had been re-cruited for the task, but the work was so hard that most of them fled after a few hours.[117] The divisions of the various corps—those of Lannes, Duhesne, Victor, Lecchi, and Murat's cavalry—were following each other at one day's dis-tance. The passage over the Alps lasted until May 20, with the consular guard bringing up the rear. Bonaparte crossed the pass on the twentieth, on mule-back, and then began the descent, "falling down in the snow," as far as Étroubles, and reached Aosta the next day.[118]

The greatness of this exploit by the reserve army has been contested. Stendhal was no doubt the first to do so. Having followed the army with the supply services, he wrote to his sister Pauline a few days later: "All I can tell you is that the difficulty has been extraordinarily exaggerated."[119] Legend, or propaganda, probably both, immediately seized upon the episode. Long before David painted his *Premier consul franchissant les Alpes au col du Grand-Saint-Bernard*, the scene had been reproduced in countless etchings, engravings, prints, and lithographs, sometimes showing the soldiers pulling the cannons, sometimes their leader in different situations, observing the progress of his men, dictating orders, or mounted on a horse that replaced to dramatic advantage the mule on which he really made the ascent. The crossing of the Great St. Bernard Pass recalled other exploits of the same kind, those of Frederick Barbarossa, Charlemagne before him, and long before Charlemagne—via the Montgenevre Pass—Hannibal and his elephants.

While refusing to believe that Hannibal had encountered as many difficulties as Livy claims he did, Napoleon willingly admitted that he had been in a less delicate situation than the Carthaginian leader.[120] A road led to the Great St. Bernard Pass, and once Saint-Rémy had been passed, another went down to Aosta. The efficient administration of the kingdom of Piedmont, he said, had made his task easier.[121] He was probably not insensitive to the impression that the passage of a whole army over a snowy mountain pass would make on the Austrians and on public opinion in France, but it was not for that reason alone that he chose this route. If we recall that at the same time other French columns were moving toward Italy—Thureau over the Mont Cenis Pass with 4,000 soldiers, Chabran over the Little St. Bernard Pass with 5,000 more, General Bethencourt's division over the Simplon Pass, Moncey and his 12,000 men from the Army of the Rhine over the St. Gotthard Pass—we can see that by coming out of the valley of Aosta Bonaparte was going to occupy a position "in the center of the semicircle," capable of turning toward Turin or toward Milan, and well placed, if he failed in his maneuver to cut the Austrians' line of retreat, to fall back in good order through one of the passes over which he had taken control.[122]

The important thing was to occupy Ivrea as soon as possible, especially because on the way Bonaparte had received bad news. The Austrians had entered Nice, and Masséna, in Genoa, found himself in increasing difficulties. Having left Martigny on the fifteenth, the vanguard of the reserve army had run into 1,000 Croatians in Étroubles, whom it had thrown back on Aosta and from there toward Châtillon, which it entered on May 18. Following the valley of the Doire, Lannes still had to overcome one obstacle before reaching Ivrea: the fortress of Bard, which blocked his way. The French knew it was occupied by an Austrian garrison, but not that it was well defended—by 400 men and twenty-six cannons—and they were especially mistaken about the possibility of taking it by occupying the surrounding heights. On May 19 Lannes attacked the obstacle. He quickly saw that men and horses could bypass it by taking a mountain path sheltered from enemy fire, but it was impossible to move the artillery, without which he could not even think about pursuing the campaign. Bonaparte grew impatient.[123] Berthier feared the worst; he already saw the campaign compromised, the war perhaps lost.[124] It was Marmont who found the solution after the reserve army had taken control on May 22 of the only road that crossed the hamlet located at the foot of the fortress and that lay under the fire of its cannons. He had the road covered with manure and wrapped the wheels of the gun carriages with straw in order to muffle sounds, and after two fruitless attempts, the artillery got through under cover of darkness.[125] On May 22 Lannes entered Ivrea, on the twenty-eighth he reached Chivasso and the banks of the Po. Bonaparte could write triumphantly to Joseph:

> The greatest obstacles have been overcome; we are masters of Ivrea and the citadel. . . . We have fallen on them like a lightning bolt: the enemy was not expecting it and can hardly believe it. Very great events are going to take place. They will have great results, I hope, for the happiness and glory of the Republic.[126]

The first phase of the campaign ended with a success that the Austrians could probably have prevented had they left a bigger garrison at Bard,[127] and had they not previously razed Ivrea's fortifications and neglected the Swiss frontier out of a belief that Bonaparte was going to come down the Rhône valley in order to defend Provence from attack and take back Nice.[128] They were waiting for him in the area of Suse, and he popped up behind them.

Victory or Defeat?

The Austrian leader, General Melas, had been informed of the movement over the Great St. Bernard Pass on May 21. Could he still throw the French back toward the Alps? Lannes was by then approaching Ivrea, but the artillery was still blocked in front of Bard. Perhaps Melas might have been able to stop the French if he had reacted immediately, but hoping that Genoa would soon fall and preparing himself to attack the Var, it was not until May 28, when the French were reaching the line of the Po, that he moved on Coni with about 10,000 men, still convinced that the passage over the Alps was a mere diversion.[129] Once the French had arrived in Chivasso, he had to face the facts: they were threatening his line of retreat via Mantua. He assembled 30,000 men to defend the right bank of the Po.

Bonaparte waited until the last minute to decide whether to head for Genoa to help Masséna, for Turin to threaten the Austrians who had crossed the French border, or for Milan. On May 19 he still didn't know what he would do after taking Ivrea.[130] Masséna's appeals for help grew more and more pressing, and they were, moreover, justified—the people were starving and on the brink of revolt, the exhausted army lacked munition—but Bonaparte accorded them little importance, being convinced that Genoa was a place so easy to defend that no Austrian assault could take it. Masséna therefore had to hold on at whatever price, so that the port did not fall into the hands of the Austrians, or those of the English who were cruising off the coast.[131] As for moving toward Turin, Bonaparte ruled it out: he could not yet count on all his divisions, and the delay occasioned by the transportation of the artillery exposed him to the danger of confronting the enemy army under unfavorable conditions. There remained Milan. He knew that he would be welcomed in the Lombard capital as he had been in 1796; he also hoped that the reestablishment of the Cisalpine Republic would sow terror in the Austrian camp to the point that Melas, in danger of being cut off from his bases, would order the immediate end of the siege of Genoa and try to make his way, with the whole of his forces, toward the Tyrol and Austria. But Bonaparte had not forgotten Genoa, and he has been wrongly accused of having sacrificed the Ligurian capital.[132] He was not going to Milan for the sole pleasure of being applauded, but instead to cut the Austrians' line of retreat. This accusation also forgets that Masséna, even if it would have been preferable for him to hold out, had achieved the objectives assigned to the Army of Italy: to "immobilize" the Austrians during the crossing of the Alps and to weaken them by fighting a war of skirmishes. Indeed, the combats against Masséna and Suchet cost them a third of their men.[133]

Melas, finally understanding the situation in which he found himself, in fact ordered the immediate return of the troops that had ventured into France, the lifting of the siege of Genoa, and the general regroupment of the Austrian forces around Alessandria. But Masséna was out of resources: on June 4 he capitulated with full military honors. No doubt the debris of his army, which were allowed to go back to France, could not be made available before a certain time. But they would come to reinforce Suchet who, seeing the Austrians evacuating Alpes-Maritimes, regained possession of the Riviera, from Nice to Savona, and thus helped confine the enemy in a Piedmontese refuge from which it could emerge only by trying to fight its way out against the reserve army, which was moving from Chivasso and Milan toward the river Po to control its crossings.[134] Duhesme had reached Lodi on June 3, and Murat had reached Piacenza on the fourth, while Lannes was moving from Pavia toward Belgiojoso. On the sixth the army crossed the river. Bonaparte had decided to concentrate his forces in Stradella, a choice that Thiers would call worthy of "being for ever admired."[135]

> As a result of the curve that [the Alps] form to include the Gulf of Genoa, they move north and throw out foothills that hug the Po very closely, from the position of Stradella to the area around Piacenza. In this whole part of Piedmont and the duchy of Parma, the foot of the mountains approaches the river, to the point of leaving only a very narrow place for the main road to Piacenza. An army placed before Stradella, at the entrance to a kind of defile several leagues long, with its left wing on the heights, its center on the road, and its right wing along the Po . . . is difficult to dislodge. . . . One sees immediately that

placed at Stradella, and controlling the bridges of Belgiojoso, Piaceza, and Cremona, General B was in position at the most crucial points, for he blocked the main road, that from Alessandria to Piacenza, and at the same time he could, by making a strong march, either hasten to the Ticino, or go back down the Po as far as Cremona, and fly toward the Adda.[136]

However, Bonaparte could not wait until Melas made an attempt to force his way through to reach Mantua and the escape routes of the Tyrol and Friuli. On June 8 he learned the "distressing news" of Masséna's capitulation[137]—not without anger but without regarding it as a defection or an unpardonable breach of duty.[138] He feared that Melas might take refuge in Genoa, from which it would then be difficult to dislodge him—Bonaparte had not forgotten Saint-Jean d'Acre—or that he might try to take a route farther north to reach the lake region. He was therefore less confident regarding the outcome of his operations than he let on to Carnot, to whom he said that Melas was doomed, whatever he did.[139] He ordered a move forward. Twenty-four thousand men advanced toward Voghera, halfway to Alessandria. Other detachments were guarding the line of the Ticino, that of the Oglio, and the Milanese capital, thus reducing the main army's number of troops.[140] On June 9, while Bonaparte was leaving Milan to rejoin his troops, Lannes, with only 8,000 men, was driving back to Montebello General Ott's 18,000 soldiers who had just arrived from Genoa. Ott retreated in disorder toward Alessandria.[141] Bonaparte, who had just received his artillery and welcomed General Desaix on his return from Egypt, advanced on the thirteenth. No trace of the Austrians, except for a few thousand men—the rearguard?—who were easily dispersed before Marengo. Had Melas left for the north? Some reports suggest that he had.[142] This was not false intelligence, just premature. Melas would indeed consider this option, though he eventually decided against it. Having regrouped his army in Alessandria, Melas had finally decided to fight. Despite the reverses that Ott had suffered, he had earlier considered several options: forcing his way out, retreating toward Genoa, or returning to Piedmont before marching on Milan. The latter option was favored by several of the Austrian general officers. With reference to these discussions, Neipperg wrote:

Losing a battle would jeopardize the security of Italy and the army.
Many of the general officers and the general staff thought that a battle
should be avoided, arguing that doing so could only result in an advantage for us and a disadvantage for the enemy. The dominant opinion
was that we should cross the Po at Casale, and then turn right toward
the Ticino, where the enemy was no longer present in force, and to put
it, by this new position, between us and our strongholds in Piedmont,
such as Tortona, Serravalle, Valenza, Alessandria, Turin, Coni, Ceva,
Arona, and Milan, all of which were well supplied with everything.[143]

Bonaparte had been only half deceived by these reports, which forced him
to divide his forces for fear that the enemy, which he felt was within his grasp,
might escape. Desaix left to look for the enemy around Novi, and La Poype
did the same around Valenza.

It has often been said that Bonaparte committed an obvious error by dividing
his forces at the moment when Melas was gathering his together in Alessandria. Not only were Desaix's and La Poype's divisions away, but others were far
from the theater of operations: Chabran was in Verceil, Bethencourt near the
Lago Maggiore, Longe was far from Piacenza. The result was an imbalance of
forces—31,000 Austrians backed up by about a hundred cannons, against scarcely
20,000 French troops and only twenty-five cannons. The imbalance was all the
more dangerous because Bonaparte was completely unaware of how the enemy
was deployed and what his intentions were. But how could he have acted differently? He would have had to know exactly what movements the Austrians
were going to make before he could concentrate his troops at one point in the
immense space between the Ligurian coast and the Alps that he had to monitor. Furthermore, it is doubtful, anyway, that all his forces were ready to be in
the Marengo plain on the morning of June 14, when a sustained barrage signaled the beginning of the battle.

The Austrians, with O'Reilly on the right, Melas in the center, and Ott on
the left, had come out of Alessandria and crossed the Bormida, heading toward
the Fontanone river, behind which, and before the farms of Marengo, the French
had taken up positions. Victor was on the left, Lannes in the center, and Mon-
nier farther back on the right. The battle long remained undecided. The French

had to abandon the Fontanone line and fall back toward Marengo, but the Austrians hardly advanced at all, as Lannes and Kellermann's cavalry drove the assailants back. In the early afternoon the situation changed abruptly when General Ott launched an enveloping maneuver from the north against the French right wing. Ott seized the village of Castelceriolo, which put the left and the center, under Victor and Lannes, in danger of being outflanked. They fell back, retreating stage by stage as far as the village of San Giuliano. Shortly before 5 p.m. the whole French army was regrouped in this area, far behind the lines it had occupied that morning. Had the Austrians launched a decisive attack at that point, there is no doubt that they would have thrown the French back on Stradella. But the Austrians were tired after a day of fighting and had been abandoned by Melas, who, certain of victory, had handed command over to his lieutenants and started back to Alessandria, where a repose that he believed he richly deserved was awaiting him. So they limited themselves to following the French retreat, as if the battle were over. The arrival of Desaix, whom Bonaparte had summoned in the late morning, changed the situation. We do not know what instructions were given after the brief council of war held by Bonaparte: to counterattack, or to conduct a rearguard action to give the bulk of the troops time to reach the shelter of Stradella.[144] The skirmishing continued. When he was leading the Ninth Light Demi-Brigade against the enemy, Desaix was killed by a bullet to the heart. It seems that his death led to a new panic in the ranks, and his return to the battlefield might have changed nothing if Kellermann—the son of the future marshal—had not then sent his dragoons to attack the Austrians. The sudden irruption of his brigade produced an indescribable panic in the ranks of the enemy, which lost in a few minutes all the gains of the day and fell back in the greatest disorder toward the Bormida.[145]

The victory left a bitter taste in Bonaparte's mouth. In private, Bourrienne tells us, he was far from showing the same satisfaction he showed in public.[146] He knew he had come very close to a serious defeat, and he was exaggerating when he later said that of the two battles of Marengo that took place on June 14, he had lost the first but won the second.[147] Moreover, he was lying when he claimed that he had never doubted that he would succeed and had always maintained control of the situation. The retreat during the afternoon? A simple "conversion movement," he said.[148] "Confidence in victory was always complete in the head of the leader who was guiding them," Berthier was to claim.[149] However, before Desaix's arrival he was described as "gloomy and silent," perhaps thinking about the consequences of the defeat.[150]

If Melas had been of little help to his men, we cannot say that Bonaparte did much better on that day. Still thinking that he was dealing with a delaying action intended to mask the movement of the bulk of the Austrian forces, he had remained until a late hour at a considerable distance from the battlefield, in Torre Garofoli, between San Giuliano and Tortona, too far away to have a clear view of what was happening or to react quickly. He owed the victory first of all to the panic that had seized the Austrian troops and to the mediocrity of the enemy command, and then to his lieutenants. It is true that he had taken the initiative in calling Desaix, but it was Kellermann's impromptu charge that decided the day's outcome. Contrary to what many historians say, Bonaparte did not seek to hide the role played by Kellermann. Besides, the whole army knew about it, and so did the Austrians. The *Bulletin de l'armée de réserve* does not conceal the extent to which the charge made by Kellermann's dragoons contributed to the victory, even if it claims that Kellermann launched it at Bonaparte's express order.[151] Was Bonaparte sulky when he received Kellermann after the battle? "Without asking him for any details concerning what he had just done, and putting on his dignified and imperious air, [Bonaparte] limited himself to telling him: *You made a rather good charge*. Indignant, Kellermann could not help replying: *I am happy that you appreciate it, since it puts the crown on your head*."[152]

Bonaparte may have received the great Kellermann's nephew coolly, but it is not true that he persecuted him and prevented him from gaining honors, as Bourrienne assures us. The following July 6, Kellermann was promoted to *général de brigade* and from that point on, as Thibaudeau says, "his fate was linked to that of the conqueror of Italy."[153]

Marengo was a battle without a victor. In the end the Austrians lost the ground they had gained, but the French did not recover the ground they had lost earlier. Melas still had sufficient means to continue the struggle. The victory was not military but political, insofar as the Austrian commander hastened to ask for an armistice that nothing really required him to seek. By virtue of the text signed the next day by Melas and Berthier, the Austrians promised to retreat to the line of the Mincio and to hand over the fortified positions they were occupying all over northern Italy.[154] The victory at Marengo was no doubt not as brilliant as the propaganda claimed it was, not by a long shot, but for the first time in two years the French were victors in Italy. That was enough to eclipse the names of Bonaparte's unfortunate predecessors, Scherer, Joubert, Championnet, Macdonald, and Moreau. The situation at the time of Campoformio had been restored. Once again Bonaparte was master of Italy: he had gained the success that would, he told those close to him before he left, "leave him free to do whatever he wanted."[155]

TWENTY-SIX

Works and Days

*B*onaparte did not want a triumphal return.[1] On the one hand, he wanted to avoid any ambiguity about his intention to devote himself henceforth to his civilian duties: he did not want to offend sensitivities that he knew were still acute. On the other hand, the reconquest of Italy did not mark the end of the war, even if the first consul, all the more content with his victory because he had come so close to defeat, began to dream about making peace with Austria without having to await the outcome of operations in Germany. He had written to the emperor a letter like those he wrote in 1797, in which he condemned the war and asked Francis II to sign a new treaty based on that of Campoformio.

It was all the more natural for Bonaparte to be thinking about peace because he had just relived the happy days of the first Italian campaign. Milan had again welcomed him as "the unique man, the peerless hero, the incomparable model."[2] He reconnected with the role of "liberator" of Italy, restoring the Cisalpine and Ligurian Republics, setting up a provisional administration in Turin, and even opening negotiations with Rome.

In the meantime, war continued in Germany. On July 15, following maneuvers that allowed Moreau to establish himself in the heart of Bavaria and drive the Austrians back behind the banks of the Inn, the general and his Austrian counterpart signed an armistice that in no way proved that Chancellor Thugut's government had peaceful intentions. At the very moment when Thugut agreed to send to Paris the emissary Count Saint-Julien—Bonaparte believed the latter could help him "explain [to the Austrians] the articles of the Treaty of Campoformio that experience had proven necessary,"[3] that is, that required clarification—he was signing with the British a new treaty providing for subsidies and secretly committing himself to sign no separate peace with France. Was Bonaparte deceived? In any case, for several days he hoped to be able to transform the half-victory of Marengo into a diplomatic triumph so complete that it would reduce to silence all those—who were numerous—who were waiting, hopefully or fearfully, for Bonaparte to make a mistake.

Tensions, Doubts, and Intrigues

On leaving for Switzerland and Italy, Bonaparte had advised his fellow consuls and the minister of police to remain vigilant. The "discontented Brumairians" were not the greatest of his worries: the parliamentary session had ended in calm. Even *La Décade philosophique*, their organ, had congratulated the government on its action. It is true that its editor, the dramatist Andrieux, had protested a few of the measures ordered by the consuls. The challenge to the principle of the equality of inheritances seemed to him an unacceptable attack on the Revolution's heritage,[4] and though he wanted to believe that Bonaparte would ultimately recognize the benefits of a constructive opposition, he was also concerned to see the growing influence in the first consul's entourage of flatterers who were pushing him steadily farther from the ideas and men of the Revolution. However, despite these reservations, Andrieux wrote, on the eve of the campaign: "the positive changes that have been made have to be seen within the country."[5]

The Jacobins were more to be feared, at least the hardcore hotheads who had not gotten over the "tumble" they had taken in Saint-Cloud, and on whom the police were keeping a close eye.

And then there were the royalists. The departments of the west had been subjugated; but had they really been pacified? Bands of *chouans* had been reported here and there, and it was said that Cadoudal was already back on the moors of Brittany. The return of the émigrés was a challenge of a quite different order. The list of proscribed émigrés, which still included more than 140,000 names, had been declared closed when the new Constitution went into force. The conditions set for obtaining removal from the list were so easy that émigrés everywhere were beginning to pack their bags.[6] In order to cope with this "invasion,"[7] a commission had been set up on the Place Vendôme under the authority of the minister of justice and assigned to deliver the precious certificate that would allow some émigrés to recover part of their property, and others to hold offices.[8] The Marquis de la Tour du Pin said how easy it was to come to terms with this tribunal "when one didn't come with empty hands."[9] Shady deals and bribes were legion, as were recommendations from the powerful—Joséphine willingly gave her signature, her husband more rarely, whereas Réal, who had moved from the leadership of the department of Seine to the Council of State, played the role of an unofficial "minister of pardons."[10] But wasn't the essential point that the émigrés were returning and that, owing their rehabilitation to the goodwill of the new government, they would have an interest in preserving it?[11] Bonaparte wished to close the wounds opened by the Revolution and to allow the return of all those who had left France since 1789, on the condition that they had not "divorced themselves from the country" by taking up arms against it.[12] But he also thought he could make all these grateful returnees a bulwark that would diminish his dependency on the men of the Revolution. This was above all a political choice, because he had no real affection for these revenants, "bad citizens" and "adversaries of their country."[13] He esteemed them hardly more than "Louis XVI's assassins."[14] But he was so aware of the need to avoid dependence on any one party that he overcame this very personal repugnance, one that many people in his entourage shared.[15] Talleyrand was perhaps most opposed to the return of those who had been defeated in 1789. He had his reasons; he knew that in their milieu he was detested more than any of the other actors of the Revolution, and paradoxically it was Fouché who, following Réal, supported Bonaparte's efforts most strongly. Reconciliation and "fusion" also produced, however, an element of illusion and numerous difficulties. The beneficiaries of the policy were not always grateful to the government. Some did not understand why, their civic existence having been restored, their possessions were not restored to them as well; they complained and threatened those who had purchased their former properties. Others—whom Bonaparte had allowed "to work without demeaning themselves," as Count Damas wryly put it[16]—brought to their new functions the solemnity of the "great figures" they had formerly been or the memory of the passions and resentments they had never shed.[17] For the moment, the amalgam Bonaparte sought was often reduced to a simple "forced marriage." Mme de Staël said that the probable advantage was "to force the parties to rub shoulders with one another," but that didn't make them like each other any more.[18] This was the case, of course, when revolutionaries had to rub shoulders with former émigrés, but also when the winners and the losers of Fructidor were in the same room. For example, Bonaparte named Siméon, who had been proscribed in 1797, to the Supreme Court, but he refused to remain there, deeming himself to be "in bad company" with the former director Merlin. Bonaparte indulgently gave him a seat in the Tribunate: "When Siméon made his first appearance in the Tribunate, Chénier looked daggers at him. Bailleul fidgeted on his bench, asking: 'Where is this going, then?' Daunou, who had helped make Siméon's exile easier to bear, avoided him, for fear of looking like a *chouan*. And Siméon was astonished by this reception—he who had rejected with such bitterness and scorn any contact with a man like Merlin!"[19]

Almost everything would have to be rebuilt.

Thus, Bonaparte had not been wrong to be uneasy on leaving Paris, especially because just a month before his departure a mysterious incident had suggested that a plot was afoot. There had been talk about an assassination attempt to be carried out on April 5 at the Théâtre-Italien. Bonaparte had intentionally gone there alone, without an escort. Nothing had happened, but Fouché received a stinging reprimand. Bonaparte—urged on by Lucien, who accused Fouché of negligence and even of being indulgent toward the most diehard Jacobins—had demanded the heads of men "accustomed to live on revolutionary movements." Fouché had assured him of his loyalty, and added, looking at Lucien with "his lifeless, terrifying eyes": "I would arrest the minister of the interior himself if I learned that he was involved in a plot."[20] We will never know if Lucien was conspiring against his brother or, what is more likely, had simply been listening to the recriminations of the other jealous member of the family, Bernadotte, who was at that time staying with his friend Sarrazin and constantly brooding over his resentment of Désirée's former fiancé.[21]

In the end, symbolic steps were taken: censorship of the theaters was restored and a few émigrés who had returned to Paris without official permission were expelled. Fouché had won, but he had been humiliated. A few days later he took revenge[22] by dismantling "the Paris agency," a small royalist office that had organized, in collusion with Hyde de Neuville and the émigrés in London, the demonstrations of January 21.[23] This allowed him to regain his master's confidence, and Bonaparte, once in Italy, relied on him to maintain order in the capital.[24] Calm was not really in danger, but those who had fomented trouble in March were just waiting for an opportunity to do it again.

On June 20 the rumor of a French defeat in Italy—it was even said that Bonaparte was dead—stirred up the little group that frequented the halls of power, not only the ambitious and jealous, malcontents of all kinds, but also some of Bonaparte's supporters. The latter had good reasons to be worried about the consequences of Bonaparte's death.[25] If everything rested on his shoulders, if the Constitution of Year VIII was no more than a legal fiction intended to cloak the power of a single man, what would happen if he was killed? Not all of these so-called conspirators aspired to succeed Bonaparte, and few were running around Paris looking for a new sort of government—no more than thirty or forty, according to Roederer, all of them habitués of Auteuil, where Helvétius's and Condorcet's widows lived.[26] Writing to his brother, Lucien is supposed to have accused Carnot, La Fayette, and Sieyès:[27] "The intrigues in Auteuil have continued. There has been much hesitation between C*** and La F***. . . . I do not yet know whether the high priest decided for one or the other; I think he was using both for d'Orléans, and your friend in Auteuil was behind the whole thing."[28] The names of Talleyrand, Fouché, Benjamin Constant, and Bernadotte have also been mentioned as candidates, along with those of the clan of "discontented Brumairians" and even Cambacérès.[29] But Lucien may never have written this letter that Bourrienne attributes to him.[30] Neither is it proven that La Fayette and Carnot encouraged those who were thinking of them as Bonaparte's successors, or that to recover the compromising evidence of this "Marengo plot," Fouché commanded the kidnapping of his friend Clément de Ris, to whom he is supposed to have entrusted it.[31] Ultimately the whole affair amounted to a few secret meetings that were ended by confirmation of the victory at Marengo. The time for speculations was over. As Fouché put it in his memoirs, "The battle of Marengo, like that of Actium, made our young Triumvir triumph, and raised him to the pinnacle of power, equally fortunate, but not so discreet as the Octavius of Rome. He had left us in the character of the first magistrate of a nation, still free, and he was about to reappear in the character of a conqueror. In fact, one might have said that, at Marengo, he had less conquered Italy than France."[32]

If Bonaparte was concerned about a disturbance regarding which he had certainly been informed—he had five different police organizations, not to mention the reports submitted by Cambacérès and Lebrun[33]—events had settled the unrest and left him time to finish what he had to do in Milan. He left the Lombard capital on June 24, returning to Paris via Turin and Lyon, where he stopped to lay the first stone for the restoration of the façades on the Place Bellecour that had been destroyed in 1793. He was acclaimed at every point along the way. He had to spend a night in Sens—the carriage had broken down and on the Montereau-Fault-Yonne bridge it tipped over—but during the night of July 2 the first consul returned to the Tuileries.[34]

When he asked Cambacérès, half in jest, half in earnest,[35] if he had made arrangements in case the Austrians killed him or took him prisoner, he was told that the second consul had in fact conceived a backup plan: replacing him with Joseph. Bonaparte understood the message: the plots were the logical consequence of a situation from which they would emerge only by clarifying the nature of the regime. Cambacérès did not conceal his thinking, telling Bonaparte that if Joseph had succeeded him and been invested by the Senate, "the public would have learned simultaneously that the first consul no longer existed and that he had a successor."[36] Bonaparte did not mention this allusion to the formula "The king is dead, long live the king"; he limited himself to replying, while tapping his interlocutor's forehead: "I am well aware that you are a resourceful man."[37] But wanting to know exactly what had happened during his absence, he pursued his investigation, questioning Roederer and even Sieyès.[38] Did he quarrel with Fouché, threatening to "crush all those ungrateful men and traitors into dust"?[39] Around him, everyone was trying to magnify the events of his absence. Fouché himself was proud of having halted a wave of panic;[40] Bonaparte heard confidences and accusations, some people exaggerating their loyalty, others the dishonesty of their friends. By listening to them the first consul understood that in imposing punishments for disloyalty he would end up, as Albert Vandal put it, having to rely on "others who were less intelligent and no more loyal."[41] He put it all behind him. However, Fouché said, and after him so did many historians, that Bonaparte remained wounded, suspicious, irritable. "Confidence disappeared," Sorel says.[42]

Was Carnot the sacrificial victim who paid for those whom the first consul had decided not to punish? This is often said, but another explanation is possible. The incompatibility of the two men's characters doomed their collaboration more than any alleged "conspiracy"—and if there was any such, it did not involve the minister of war. Bonaparte had put up with Carnot because he needed his name, and because he needed Berthier in nominal command of the reserve army; once the war was over, he no longer needed Carnot. The latter, for his part, refused to play the role of first lieutenant, especially in the service of a man whose republican convictions seemed to him suspect. Bonaparte was perhaps not entirely unhappy to get rid of the minister, the memory of whose exploits would always make him seem a possible alternative. Thus it was by tacit agreement that once Bonaparte returned, Carnot moved toward the exit. There was a certain pretense of reluctance: on September 1, Bonaparte refused to accept Carnot's resignation.[43] But a month later he accepted it, and on October 8 Berthier moved back into his office at the War Ministry.[44]

Although he had refused to allow the celebration of his return, Bonaparte nonetheless received applause at the balcony of the Tuileries and even a sort of triumph in the Roman style that was repeated each time one of the great state bodies came to assure him of the French people's gratitude.[45] "Disgusting and servile flattery"?[46] No doubt, but that does not prove they lacked sincerity. Even those who deplored the regime's growing authoritarianism fell under the spell of Marengo. We have already cited Andrieux; Mme de Staël was not to be outdone: far from wishing Bonaparte to be defeated in order "to halt the progress of his tyranny," as she was later to claim,[47] her correspondence in this period was full of praise for "the very great man" from whom she expected "something extraordinary" every day and about whom she said, on the eve of Marengo: "This man has a will that elevates the world and himself."[48] And it was with unfeigned enthusiasm that she wrote about the regime to Dupont de Nemours after the general's return to Paris: "It is a glorious dictatorship of arms, in comparison to which nothing exists and nothing appears. But how can one not be enthusiastic about so many memorable exploits!"[49]

The policy of reconciliation that had been pursued for the past six months was officially celebrated on July 14 by a *fête de la Concorde* over which Bonaparte presided in person, and the arrival in Paris a few days later of an emissary from the court of Vienna seemed to be the prelude to a peace treaty. Everything was going the first consul's way. That was well worth a few compliments.

Musical Intermezzo

Bonaparte had gone back to work. There was so much to do that he later said he had never worked so hard as at this time.[50] The administration of the armies represented, as it always did, the most burdensome task, even without the work of directing military operations. There was also diplomacy, the administration of domestic affairs and justice, the previously mentioned return of the émigrés, the financial situation, the problem of food supplies, which Lucien had neglected so much that at the doors of Parisian bakeries people were complaining about the high price of bread. "[The price of] bread has risen in Paris, dear minister," Napoleon wrote to his brother. "I beg you to focus your attention on this interesting subject and to write a report for the government."[51] To this must be added the sessions of the Council of State, of which he was the nominal president, setting up and getting under way the commission entrusted with drafting a civil law code, and several ceremonies that required his presence: the fete of Concord on July 14, the transfer of Turenne's ashes to the Invalides on September 22, and the homage to Kléber and Desaix the following day.

We can understand why Bonaparte hardly had time to leave Paris. He granted himself only two short stays of two days each at Mortefontaine, his brother Joseph's home near Senlis.[52] The first was toward the end of July, the second the following month.[53] Because Stanislas de Girardin had come to visit as a neighbor—his château was at Ermenonville, about twenty kilometers away—Bonaparte asked him to show him Rousseau's tomb. He saw the Île des Peupliers and the tomb, now empty, where René de Girardin, Stanislas's father, had had Jean-Jacques interred.[54] Was he thinking about his youthful passion for the author of the *Social Contract*? Probably. But that was far in the past. He turned away, saying: "It would have been better for the peace of France that that man had never existed." Girardin asked him why, and he replied that Rousseau had "paved the way for the French Revolution."[55] When his interlocutor asked whether he could sincerely complain about a revolution without which he could not have risen so high, he is supposed to have said, before walking off: "Well, the future will tell if it wouldn't have been better, for the peace of the Earth, that neither Rousseau nor I had ever existed!"[56] The retort was no doubt invented after the fact, but it is true that Bonaparte already saw himself as occupying a place in history. He was joking when he said he had done just enough to deserve a few lines in books.[57] Ever since Lodi, he had been living on heights where the air was too thin for any of his contemporaries.

He also made a few visits to Malmaison. They were rather rare.[58] The construction work going on there under the direction of Fontaine and Percier—the dining room had just been finished—does not suffice to explain this.[59] Bonaparte had his reasons for remaining in Paris. They were rather comical. Although it is true that the reconciliation between Bonaparte and Joséphine in October 1799 was not feigned, it had consisted chiefly in an alliance. At a time when Bonaparte was getting ready to overthrow the Republic, he needed Joséphine; for her part, she had understood, this time, everything she could gain from this marriage that she had so often regretted since 1796. She had ceased her misbehavior, ended her affair with Hippolyte Charles, and put all her grace in the service of her husband's ambitions.[60] Bonaparte probably no longer felt his old passion for her, but with him less in love, and she more attached to this husband with a future, they formed a more harmonious couple than they had at the beginning of their marriage. In the Tuileries they shared the same bedroom, the same bed, and this very bourgeois intimacy prevented them, Napoleon later said, from becoming complete strangers to one another.[61] There were also Joséphine's children, whom Bonaparte had come to love almost as if they were his own. That was not hard, since they formed such a pleasant contrast with his own family, where there was a mere appearance of manners, a lack of gentleness, a hardness of character, a boundless greed. Among the Beauharnais everything was softened by the delicacy of manners. No one could resist the charm of Hortense, who was now seventeen years old, or that of Eugène, who was approaching his twentieth birthday and looked dashing in his uniform as a captain of the chasseurs of the consular guard. He had followed his stepfather to Italy, to Egypt, to the Great St. Bernard Pass. He was brave and chivalrous, and his sister was "sweet, affable, and elegant."[62]

Although Joséphine had turned over a new leaf and broken off an affair that she had in reality long wanted to end, she still had a few secrets from her husband. Still fond of beautiful jewels, she bought them now, and consequently continued to go into debt; there were still, and were always to be, problems with creditors. There were even a few dalliances in which we no longer encounter the familiar figures from the time of the Directory, but new men like Rouget de Lisle, the author of the *Marseillaise*.[63] For his part, her husband did not deny himself a few pleasures with women whom Frédéric Masson calls "passersby."[64] The most recent was an Italian woman who had spent a night with him in Milan on June 3 or 4, shortly before Marengo. Giuseppina—Joséphine—Grassini had just sung before him at La Scala. He knew her because he had already met her, in the same venue, three years earlier. She had been seventeen years old and making her debut. Had she offered herself to the conqueror of Italy then and there? Even if she did so, she is not on the list of his conquests during his first Italian campaign.[65] Did he find her more to his taste three years later? Mme Vigée-Lebrun, who was to paint no less than six portraits of the young woman, praises, in addition to the timbre of her voice, which made her the most celebrated contralto of her time, her beauty, and her extreme "kindness."[66] This time Bonaparte was so sensitive to Giuseppina's talent that he immediately decided she would accompany him to Paris. But he feared Joséphine's reaction. He had begun writing to her, helped by the excitement of the war, a few passionate letters in the style of those he wrote in 1796, asking her to see to it that "the little cousin" (her vagina) behaved herself.[67] So he summoned Berthier to his bedroom, where he was eating breakfast with Giuseppina,[68] and dictated to him a bulletin to the Army of Italy that ended this way: "The people of Milan seem very inclined to resume the tone of gaiety that they had while the French were here. The general-in-chief [Berthier] and the first consul attended a concert that, though improvised, was very pleasant. Italian singing has a charm that never grows old. The famous [female singers] Billington, Grassini, and [the castrato] Marchesi are expected in Milan. It is said that they are going to leave for Paris to give concerts there."[69]

He saw Giuseppina again after Marengo. Just before leaving, he assigned Bourrienne to arrange for the young woman's journey to Paris.[70] So that she would not suffer financially from the change in residence, he ordered that she sing at the July 14 festivities. The faithful Berthier was supposed to choose the singer who would have the privilege of singing "an Italian piece on the liberation of the Cisalpine": "General Berthier informs me that he expects to send either Mme Billington or Mme Grassini," Bonaparte wrote, casually, to his brother Lucien.[71]

Giuseppina Grassini was his "passerby" of the summer. She herself, however, did not see things exactly that way. She imagined herself the favorite and did not much appreciate the furtive meetings or the indifference feigned in public by her lover the consul, and to avenge herself she took another lover, the first violin at the Paris Opéra.[72] This time it was over. But the affair, which had lasted a few months, left Napoleon more than bitter memories.[73] In 1806 he brought Giuseppina back to France with the title of His Majesty the Emperor's *première cantatrice*. It is true that by then she was acclaimed all over Europe. She had just had a brilliant success in London; that was reason enough to bring her again to Paris. It is also certain that the emperor did not hold the past against her; if he had, would he have allowed her, one evening when she was playing Cleopatra in Handel's *Caesar in Egypt*, to interrupt the performance to turn toward him and sing a fashionable air composed by Félix Blangini: *Adora i cenni tuoi questo mio cuor fedele; Sposa sarò se vuoi non dubitar di me. Ma un sguardo sereno, ti chiedo d'amor?*[74]

It is difficult to believe that Joséphine did not suspect this affair. "She followed, understood, guessed everything," her husband was to say.[75] But she knew how to distinguish between inconsequential flings with singers or actresses and affairs with women who, occupying a higher rank in society, could hope to draw a more substantial benefit from their intimacy with the first consul. She was, Bertrand said, "jealous by politics" more than by feeling.[76] She was not deceived by her husband's enthusiasm for contraltos, but she was not much concerned by it. No doubt it was different when Bonaparte had a brief affair with Mme Mollien, whose husband ran the Amortization Fund.[77] And she was certainly alarmed when a few months later he took to his bed Adèle Duchâtel, the wife of the head of the Registration Office.[78] Joséphine would patrol the corridors of the Tuileries, in person or through the intermediary of her servants, trying to catch her husband, who went to his mistress in the middle of the night and returned before dawn, barefoot, holding his slippers in his hands, in order not to make any noise. It was a time of guile, suspicion, sidelong glances, and tips generously distributed to valets to purchase their discretion.[79]

This bourgeois part of the hero's life would be "vaudevillesque" if Bonaparte's mind could avoid investing the smallest things with the greatest ideas. His interest in music was not unconnected with the decision to bring Mme Grassini to Paris. He intended not only to prolong in this way the pleasures of his Milanese court, but also to make French opera benefit from her talent. We know how sensitive he was to music, in particular vocal music—more than to painting, and much more than to poetry or literature.[80] In 1796 he had enriched French museums with works taken from Italian palaces and churches, and it was entirely natural that he should do the same for music.

On music, his ideas were those of his century; he was clearly sensitive to its political virtues: "Of all the fine arts," he wrote to the directors of the Paris Conservatory of Music in 1797, "music is the one that has the greatest influence on the passions, and the one that the legislator must encourage the most. A piece of music that is moral and composed by a master inevitably touches our feelings and has much more influence than a good [written] work on morals, which convinces the reason without having an influence on our habits."[81] The fact that he was aware that music could become the auxiliary of a politics and a system of government, does not mean that he did not love it for its own sake. Composers, authors of librettos, and journalists eagerly reciprocated, some to glorify him, others to track down the slightest allusions that could offer a parallel with the hero. Under the Consulate, music, and particularly lyrical music, resumed the functions it performed under the monarchy; but this was less the sign of a strategy or deliberate propaganda than one more testimony to the tendency that since Brumaire had gradually been leading France back to monarchical forms.[82]

In 1800 Mme Grassini's arrival inspired a whole group of Italian musicians, singers, and composers—the troupe of the "Théâtre-Italien," Spontini, Fioravanti, or the Neapolitan Paisiello, long Mme Grassini's favorite—to come to Paris, not only because the first consul was a lover of bel canto, but also because after the period of the Directory, Paris, where Cherubini had preceded them long before, had once again become a great capital of music and in particular of the art of the lyric.[83] Grétry, Méhul, Lesueur, and soon Boieldieu, whose names are not familiar today, were all the rage at that time. If Bonaparte exercised an influence, it was by reviving the role of the princely patrons of earlier times and by fostering, with considerable discernment, "the profound transformation of tastes and sensibilities that led, a generation later, to the advent of the great French Romantic opera in 1830."[84] All the same he mistrusted works that were too new in tone, and he was not always fair to the French school.[85] The Duchesse d'Abrantès exaggerates when she says that he did not like French music.[86] But imbued with the theories Rousseau set forth in his *Letter on French Music* regarding the superiority of melody over harmony—the former being the Italian specialty, the latter the French—he certainly considered it too intellectual, too cold, in a word, very inferior to the works of the transalpine school.[87]

Servants and Collaborators

The public side of this bourgeois life has been depicted so often that I hesitate to describe it again here.[88] We know all about how Bonaparte spent his days, the men he surrounded himself with, the setting in which he worked at the Tuileries: the antechamber separating the office from the second-floor bedroom where he did not sleep—it had been transformed into work space, because most of the time he slept with his wife on the ground floor.[89] In the office there were a few chairs, a fireplace, and in a corner two tall bookcases separated by a pendulum clock; farther on, a long, low armoire containing boxes; in the center, a rolltop desk that had belonged to Louis XVI but to which Bonaparte preferred the settee placed next to the pedestal table where the day's correspondence awaited him, and, in the embrasure of the window looking out on the garden, his secretary's table.[90] Adjacent were first the "outer office," a former boudoir furnished with only two tables, where Bonaparte worked with his collaborators, and then another antechamber, called the *guichet du portefeuille*, which was under the constant guard of an usher who saw to it that no one entered this veritable sanctuary.[91] The furnishing was Spartan. The only luxury was the decoration, which dated from the reign of Louis XIV: on the walls, landscapes in the style of Poussin; on the ceiling, Minerva crowned in glory.

Bonaparte's life was reclusive, "serious and full," "frugal and solitary."[92] Baron Fain, his last secretary, went so far as to say that there was something of the soldier-monk in Bonaparte.[93] Like all great workers, he was a man of habit, not to say routine, and just as nothing was ever to change in the arrangement of the places or the classification of his papers, he did not much like new faces. He still had relatively few servants. In 1800 we are still far from the 176 employees of the first consul's "household" on the eve of the proclamation of the Empire, and still farther from the 3,381 staff employed on January 1, 1812![94] At this time there was still just a handful, most of them old acquaintances:[95] his valets, Jean-Joseph Ambard and Jean-Baptiste Hébert, who had been in his service since 1796; the intendant Pfister, who had held his position since 1794; the maître d'hôtel Fischer, who had held his position since 1796; the cooks who had accompanied Bonaparte to Egypt; and, of course, the Mamluk Roustam, who followed him everywhere, carried his new boots, and slept across the threshold to his bedroom.[96] There were a few departures: Ambard, a somber, melancholic man, had developed a persecution complex that made him difficult to get along with, and his assistant, Hébert, was so timid and fearful that he dared not shave the first consul.[97] It was then that Constant Wairy made his appearance: He was initially in Joséphine's service, but Bonaparte took him along when he left for the Great St. Bernard Pass, and Wairy ended up occupying the position of first valet. This "funny rascal," as Bonaparte would call him while pummeling him, was close to his master in the way valets often are.[98] Though it may be true that no man is a hero to his valet, Wairy derived from his proximity to Bonaparte such a feeling of importance that he managed to impress people to the point that soon everyone called him only "Monsieur Constant." The future emperor had all the more need of the services of this young Belgian—he was only twenty-one—because he was born, his master said, "to be a valet."[99] Bonaparte had always been able to rely on servants for his daily needs, in any case since 1974 when he had assumed the command of the Army of Italy's artillery. He did not know how to shave himself—he learned after Ambard left—and in the evening, when he was going to bed, his clothes, which he had strewn all over the room, had to be picked up and put away.[100] When he awoke, around 7 a.m., he had the newspapers or a novel read to him, and threw them into the fire if they displeased him.[101] Once he had washed, shaved, and dressed, he went up to his office, crossing the little antechamber guarded by two ushers in turn.[102] They were not strangers, either, any more than were the men to whom the first consul entrusted, from the outset, his security: Duroc, his favorite aide-de-camp, who could almost be called a friend if Bonaparte had had any friends, and the latter's assistant, the future General Reynaud, whom he had known in Italy and who was to be joined successively by Clément—a former officer on Desaix's general staff—and Philippe de Ségur, not to mention Lannes, who commanded the consular guard. Bonaparte had known his cartographer, Bacler d'Albe, in Toulon, and his two librarians—Ripaul and Abbé Denina, a Piedmontese formerly employed by Frederick II—in Italy, as he had his doctors, the surgeon Yvan and Jean-Noël Hallé, with whom he quarreled because the scientist did not like to have his ears pinched in public.[103]

And then there was, of course, his secretary, Bourrienne. The two men had known each other at Brienne, and Bourrienne had rejoined Bonaparte in Italy in 1797.[104] When they met again face to face, there was certainly strong emotion on both sides, one admiring what the other had become, and the latter gauging how far he had traveled by looking at the former. But Bourrienne understood immediately that nothing between them would ever be the way it had formerly been: "Here ceased my relations with Bonaparte as an equal and a comrade. . . . I no longer approached him as I usually had before: I was too aware of his personal importance; his position had put too much social distance between him and me for me not to feel the need to adjust my approach to him. I did so with pleasure, and without regrets; the sacrifice was very easy, first of all the sacrifice of familiarity, of addressing him with the familiar *tu*, and of other little intimacies. When I entered the room where he was surrounded by the most brilliant general staff, he said to me in a loud voice: *There you are, finally!* But as soon as we were alone, he made it clear that he was pleased with my reserve, and was grateful for it."[105]

Hardworking, devoted, discreet: Bourrienne did not lack good qualities, and Bonaparte was unjust when, trying to sum up his secretary, he said he had "nice handwriting."[106] In ceasing to be a comrade, Bourrienne had not become a servant. Bonaparte always complained about not being able to find his collaborators when he needed them.[107] Exhausted, they sometimes hid to escape for a moment from his tyranny.[108] But when he wanted to have a bell installed on his desk, Bourrienne protested, and Bonaparte, aware that he had gone too far, backed off.[109] He had too much need of this secretary, who was far superior to his predecessors, Junot and Jacoutot. And they had known each for so long. Bourrienne was to some extent the civilian counterpart of Berthier. His assignments were considerable.[110] He sorted the mail, supervised the translation of foreign newspapers, kept in order the files and registers in which the papers of each ministry were stored, put together dossiers for appointments, and transmitted to the first consul everything that had been delivered to him by the state secretary, not to mention the portfolio bound in red Moroccan leather entitled "Foreign Periodicals," which actually contained reports from the minister of police and copies of letters opened by the postal administration's *Cabinet noir*.[111]

Bonaparte and Bourrienne worked in private, as if cut off from the world. But there were frequent interruptions: each morning, a work meeting with Cambacérès and Lebrun, the former repeatedly complaining that it was held so early;[112] the audiences with the ministers; a quick lunch, which Bonaparte ate at about 10 A.M., always alone; in the afternoon, sometimes a council, sometimes a session of the Council of State, and then another meeting with the consuls. But let us return to the morning. The first consul finished with the *répondu*—the letters and reports to which it was thought pointless to reply and that covered the floor.[113] Then he started in on the *courant*, that is, the dossiers that were to be dealt with the same day and that were piled up next to the matters—the *suspens*—that deserved reflection. Going from the desk to the settee where he liked to read, he studied the dossiers, asked for information, signed a paper that he threw to Bourrienne, telling him "Send," or else, rising and beginning to pace back and forth, he said "Write." Everyone who had to write down the master's words, under the Consulate and the Empire as on Saint Helena, said what a torture it was. And although Bonaparte willingly admitted that his thought moved so fast that it did not leave him time to write, he would not have understood, and still less allowed, being interrupted or asked to repeat something.[114] The scribe, who also had to replace the malapropisms that escaped the consul's mouth with the correct words, had to leave numerous blank spaces in his text so that he would have room to make corrections when he had time to recompose a dictation of which he had been able to seize only fragments.[115] Méneval, who succeeded Bourrienne in 1802, was never to forget his first dictation: "He finally arrived, holding a paper in his hand. Without seeming to pay attention to my presence in his office ... he dictated to me a note for the minister of finances, with such volubility that I could hardly understand him and write down half of what he was dictating to me. Without asking me if I had understood him and if I had finished writing, he took the paper out of my hands and did not allow me to try to reread it; when I pointed out to him that it was an illegible scribble, he went into his salon with my note, saying that the matter was familiar to the minister and he would be able to figure it out."[116]

The exercise, when prolonged, was exhausting. Sometimes the secretary had to read back what he had taken down, and if the first consul was not happy with the result, he began over again.[117] When Bourrienne was busy, Bonaparte called on one of his aides-de-camp, preferably Duroc or Lauriston, or General Clarke, whom he had set up in the bedroom transformed into an office in order to supervise from the Tuileries the War Office's work.[118]

Bourrienne was exhausted, but happy. Living in the shadow of the great man, he could believe that he was, even if all familiarity had ceased, his confidant, the depository of his plans and his secrets, perhaps even his indispensable auxiliary. Because he accompanied Bonaparte to Malmaison, took part in the household's games, acted out plays with Hortense,[119] and listened to Joséphine's confidences, he had ended up thinking he was important, that he was indispensable and untouchable, which he wasn't. His appointment to the Council of State in July 1801 could only confirm him in these views. He was not a member of the family, but almost; he derived a few benefits from this, some of them symbolic, others in hard cash. He liked money—in fact, he was mad about it, to the point, the emperor was to say, that his face changed when large sums were mentioned in his presence.[120] He was engaged in business with Joséphine, with Talleyrand, with suppliers to the armies.[121] Bonaparte was certainly not ignorant of this; besides, everyone else around him was getting rich. Bourrienne was no exception. Unfortunately for his career, he eventually got mixed up with the Coulon brothers, whose bankruptcy in 1802 had caused a stir: one of the brothers committed suicide, and Bourrienne, who had imprudently stood security for him, was involved to the point that it was not impossible that he might be picked up one morning and put before a law court.[122] He could not remain a second longer with the first consul, who fired him on the spot.[123]

Did he do so unwillingly? In reality he saw Bourrienne leave without much emotion. His relations with Bourrienne had been deteriorating for a long time, and the Coulon affair gave him the pretext he had been looking for to get rid of him. In early 1802 Bonaparte had fallen ill, seriously enough for his mood to be affected. A dispatch sent to Talleyrand had not arrived on time, and this so enraged him that he insulted Bourrienne and almost knocked him out by slamming the door in his face.[124] Bourrienne, furious, resigned. Bonaparte, far from excusing himself, told Duroc that he would henceforth replace Bourrienne; but Duroc, though he was able to take dictation, had none of the skills a secretary needed, and after a few days the facts had to be faced: Bonaparte had no one who could take Bourrienne's place. He did what he was so good at doing—Bonaparte had a certain talent for acting:[125] he took a hon-eyed tone, pinched Bourrienne's ear, asked him if he was still sulking, and, sensing that he was already yielding, told him that he expected him the next day at the usual time.

Bourrienne resumed his duties, but he soon realized that his days as the first consul's secretary were numbered. Bonaparte, who was so indulgent to those who had done things for him, did not pardon those who failed him. Bourri-enne, who belonged to him, could not leave him without paying a price.[126] A month had not gone by before Bonaparte told Bourrienne that he looked tired, and adding that he could not continue without his aid, he announced that a young man, Méneval, who had up to that point been in the service of his brother Joseph, would henceforth help him.[127]

Méneval, whom Bonaparte had received on April 2, 1802, began his new job the following day, not at Bourrienne's table but in an adjacent office, where the official secretary soon realized that Bonaparte was trying to teach him the trade.[128] When the Coulon bank went bankrupt in October 1802, Méneval was ready: Bourrienne had no choice but to leave.[129] His successor spent ten years in the service of Napoleon, who later said that in separating himself from Bour-rienne he had acted like Louis XIV when, after Mazarin's death, he decided to no longer have a prime minister: similarly, Bonaparte decided to have a "first secretary" no longer. No one could be more suitable in the diminished position than Méneval: "A gentle air, modest habits, great reserve, a timid exterior that the appearance of delicate health made seem even younger, seemed to be perfectly combined in the person of M. Méneval, to make of him the *little secretary* to which Napoleon wanted to reduce him."[130]

At 5 p.m. the usher announced Maret. The state secretary was no doubt the most important minister in the government.[131] "The minister of ministers," Napoleon called him, "the great notary of the Empire."[132] Everything passed through his hands, and it was his signature, and not that of the first consul, that informed ministers what had happened to the proposals they had transmitted to him.

Contemporaries were not fond of Maret, and historians have not been fond of him either. Talleyrand mocked his lack of wit.[133] Mme de Chastenay saw in him "something subaltern."[134] In many people's eyes this former journalist—he had founded the *Moniteur* in 1789—whom Bonaparte came to know through diplomacy,[135] was the prototype of the servile lackeys of whom Savary, who had also just joined the inner circle, was another example. However, Maret had numerous good qualities: "He was kindly, and could be counted on. Along with pedantic and starchy manners, and with a clumsy and pretentious imitation of the ways of the high aristocracy, he had a great deal of tact in his relations with others," Barante recalled.[136] Yet Barante does not conceal the fact that with Bonaparte Maret was "the most obsequious of servants."[137] Not out of ambition or fanaticism, but because his limited abilities, Pasquier snidely suggests, predisposed him to hold a position in which what was expected of him was "the literal execution of the orders given" and nothing else.[138] If he had no ideas other than those of the first consul, that was also because it never occurred to him that he should. Maret thus seems to have been a kind of civilian Savary, wholly devoted to his master, and a little narrow-minded. An underling.

Tocqueville saw two kinds of servants around Napoleon: The first, he said, had neither scruples nor morality. They were tired of being revolutionaries and were now in a hurry to enjoy themselves. They were the scum of the Revolution, hardly distinguishable from some former émigrés eager to make up for what the Revolution had cost them by acquiring new titles, new offices, and emoluments. But Napoleon, Tocqueville added, was also surrounded by a different class of "upright, punctilious, honest" servants for whom virtue was not just an empty word. The author of *The Old Regime and the French Revolution* did not spare his admiration for these men. But he did not like them, seeing in them the embodiment of a French tendency to idolatry and servitude that had formerly favored absolutism and whose objects the French Revolution had changed, but not their substance. Just as these "statesmen" had formerly bowed down before the absolute monarch, they had then revered the abstract idol of the sovereign people, and now that the government was coming to resemble the former monarchy, they submitted to Bonaparte, abdicating once again their consciences and free will, "without eyes, or ears, or guts," as soon as it was a matter of carrying out plans they had neither conceived nor discussed.[139]

Tocqueville developed this analysis in the speech he gave on the occasion of his entrance into the French Academy, where he succeeded one of the emperor's former ministers, Gérard Lacuée. Molé, who had also served as a minister under Napoleon, was assigned to give the response. Tocqueville's remarks had wounded him, and he rightly noted—a point that is too often forgotten—that Napoleon's regime had been based not solely on a handful of immoral men leading a mass of disenchanted men who were prepared to endure anything, but also on a generation that sincerely believed that by serving the first consul and then the emperor, they were "repairing so many ills, erasing the memory of so many crimes, rehabilitating so many eternal truths [and] embracing a sacred and noble crusade."[140] They felt that they were at the dawn of a new age that offered vast prospects, even if the revolutionary belief in the omnipotence of the will had collapsed. To these two categories of servants—former revolutionaries of all parties whose security Bonaparte guaranteed in exchange for obedience, and whom he often employed provided that they were competent,[141] and the smaller number of blindly loyal henchmen of whom Savary is certainly the model—we have to add this third category of servants described by Molé. It was the largest of the three, and in it Molé rubbed shoulders with Lacuée, Gaudin, Mollien, Cambacérès, Clarke, Bigot de Préameneu, and so many others.[142]

An Enlightened Despot?

Bonaparte liked having power less than wielding it. For this reason alone, those who worked for him lost, if not their importance, at least their luster. His ministers were in the same position with respect to him as the ministry's employees were with respect to them. Seeing them as simple servants, even though he did not allow others to treat them as negligible quantities, he received them only when necessary. Talleyrand was the only exception to this rule; he had the privilege of working tête-à-tête with the first consul almost every day.[143] As for the other ministers, Bonaparte simply wrote to them, and later on he admitted that he had abused this peremptory system.[144]

There was no cabinet, properly speaking—first of all because the ministers, in conformity with the principles in force since 1789, did not compose a council that had a collective existence and that could have had responsibility, and second because the Wednesday afternoon meetings, which became regular under the Empire, were not yet regular under the Consulate.[145] Bonaparte preferred to work one-on-one with his ministers or in the framework of the administrative councils that focused on a specific dossier or domain and included, along with the first consul, the relevant minister, his main collaborators, and in some cases technicians, civil engineers, or naval construction specialists.[146] Each minister came with his files, presented them, answered any possible questions, and then submitted his papers to the state secretary. He was never told the first consul's decision immediately: as Baron Fain says, Bonaparte "did not feel obliged to sign during the council."[147] He made his decision later, when the minister concerned was no longer present; the latter was informed of the decision by Maret.

This system was the diametrical opposite of the one set up at the beginning of the Revolution, in which each decision was, at every level, the product of a debate that was not only required by the principle of collective sovereignty but expected to lead to decisions that were more fair, more enlightened, and based on a broader consensus than if they had been dictated from on high. At every level, from the municipalities to the National Assembly, collective deliberation was the source of decisions whose application was then left to magistrates of the king or the mayor, who were closely supervised. With Bonaparte's accession to power, a completely new system emerged. Contrary to the revolutionary principle of separating deliberation from execution, it put both in the same hands. The government was now not only authorized to participate in the making of the laws, it could even propose them; and if it was entrusted with applying them, who knew better what the realities and needs of the country were than it did?

Revolutionary doctrine had separated deliberation and execution in order to prevent "ministerial despotism," as people said in 1789, by making the government a simple executive in the service of the country's will. The revolutionaries had given priority to collective debate among the representatives of the citizens, not only to remain faithful to the principle of popular sovereignty, but also because the royal state had suffered from the absence of representative assemblies; these would have kept the monarchy better informed about political realities and given it the support it needed to overcome the resistance to reform. All the ministers who had succeeded one another since the 1750s had proposed such bodies, and in the absence of truly representative assemblies that could stand up to the oligarchy of the corporative assemblies and *parlements*, the *philosophes* had argued that the free press was another means of informing the government and the public about the necessary reforms.

Bonaparte wanted neither assemblies nor a free press. Regarding the latter, he had made up his mind long ago. He had been able to see during the Revolution that one of the causes of increasing violence had been journalists' attempts to outdo each other in making radical recommendations. In 1797 he himself had been the victim of a negative press campaign because of his policy toward Venice. The suppression of sixty of the seventy-three newspapers published in Paris had been one of the first steps the consular government took—on January 17, 1800—and unanimously, because Cambacérès had also been convinced that the return to stability would involve the suspension of freedom of the press.[148] "If I give it free rein," Bonaparte said, referring to the press, "I shall not remain in power for three months."[149] The newspapers that had escaped the purge fell under the direct control of the government or its allies. Maret's *Moniteur* became the official organ.[150] Maret also bought shares in the *Journal de Paris* edited by Roederer, who was himself very close to the first consul.[151] Fiévée was given a position on the Bertin brothers' *Journal des débats*; Fouché bought the *Journal des hommes libres*.[152] Bonaparte even ended up founding his own periodical, the *Bulletin de Paris* (March 11, 1802), whose editorship he assigned to Regnaud, but it never succeeded in establishing itself.[153] Each evening Bonaparte and Maret wrote the program for the following day's newspapers. The first consul indicated the articles that were to be published, sometimes dictating outlines for them. He knew so well what was in the newspapers, and how true it was, that he told Bourrienne not to bother reading him the periodicals published in France.[154] This situation had disadvantages as well as advantages. Because Bonaparte could not derive any useful information from the newspapers, or from the assemblies created by the constitution of Year VIII, whose function was above all to provide pensions for retired revolutionaries, he was forced to rely on his ministers, state councilors, all those with whom he conversed, and even the "*friends* who were paid a few thousand francs a month to write frankly about everything that was going on, what was being said, and what they themselves thought about it."[155] Mme de Genlis, Montlosier, Barère, Desrenaudes, Fiévée, and a few others thus compensated, but very imperfectly, for the absence of genuine representative assemblies.

Work with the ministers, discussions with the Councils, and ministerial and administrative meetings had only one function: to inform the first consul so that he could make his decision without their contributing to it in any formal way. Whatever their titles were, his collaborators were all technicians assigned to constitute or to enrich by their knowledge dossiers complete enough to allow the first consul to make a final decision.[156]

This does not mean, of course, that Bonaparte was the source of all the bills that were passed at that time. Most of these reforms were "in the air, in the atmosphere of events and ideas."[157] Each of them might be given the name of the person or persons who conceived them and guided them into law: Gaudin for the finance bill, Roederer and Chaptal for the local administration bill, for which Sieyès had provided the first sketch,[158] Abrial, Boulay de la Meurthe, and probably also Cambacérès for the justice bill,[159] whereas the Bank of France took over from the Current Accounts Fund set up in 1796 by bankers, several of whom helped work out the plan for the new establishment.[160] Albert Vandal, who often allows himself to be carried away by his enthusiasm as soon as his hero is involved, says rightly concerning the first consul that if he was not the demiurge depicted by legend, he was "the person who extracted solutions, the great realizer," thanks to his ability to grasp "what was in the air," to understand the needs of the moment, and to give concrete form to what were often only confused or poorly formulated aspirations.[161] That is how we must interpret a comment Roederer made: "The first consul needed only ministers who understood him, never ministers who stood in for him."[162] This was true not only for ministers, but also for the Council of State, where Bonaparte long put up with a freedom of expression that he rarely tolerated elsewhere: "Under the Consulate, which was a period of organization in which all the great questions were discussed under the chairmanship of the first consul, he gave the debate free rein. When it seemed to bog down, he sometimes even revived it. . . . The Council was composed of men with very diverse opinions: each one freely defended his own. The majority was not oppressive. Far from giving his own opinion, the first consul encouraged the minority. He let go on for hours discussions that he could have ended after a quarter of an hour."[163]

But Bonaparte gave the councilors free rein precisely because the Council of State was a council *of the government*, its auxiliary, and not a *governing* council that had its own power of initiative and decision.[164] Even though he had enough confidence in this group of technicians to consult it almost systematically regarding proposed laws and numerous other questions, some of them very political, it made no decisions and did not examine any matter without having been asked to do so.

> [The Council of State] was advisory, only advisory . . . his secretary Locré was to say, a necessary instrument in the hands of the government for the writing or discussion of laws and regulations of public administration; for permitting or refusing authorization to indict an official of the administrative order or its own members: a voluntary instrument when it pleased the head of state to consult it on other subjects; but always just an instrument, a passive instrument, having no movement except at the head of state's impetus; deciding nothing, only expressing an opinion; giving only its view; informing the head of the government regarding the advantages and disadvantages of the proposals made by his ministers; indicating the amendments and improvements that might be made in them; writing and ordering nothing but simple plans; having, in a word, no power except the moral power that reason exercises when it is listened to and is on one's side.[165]

Thibaudeau, who was a member of the Council of State, says this in his own way when, having reminded his reader that the first consul allowed the councilors to contradict him, he observes that the situation was completely different when Bonaparte had announced his decision: "Once he had said in public, 'This is the way it is,' it was useless to contradict him; he yielded neither to figures nor to facts."[166] The order he issued he had considered without anyone's help, and if it happened to be in conformity with the majority opinion, it was certain that it was not a product of the latter. The discussions in the Council of State were a kind of background music that helped him think. Because he knew he was among supporters, he let himself go:

> Sunk in the armchair from which he presided over the Council of State, contemplative, absorbed in his meditation to the point of forgetting where he was, and even those who were listening to him, his mind far away and distracted, continually, mechanically opening the little golden snuffbox to take pinches of tobacco that he aspirated without sound, most of it falling on the white cuffs of his uniform and remaining scattered there, and finally the mechanical movement of his arm to hand the aforesaid snuffbox to the chamberlain on duty, who handed it back to him full, all that made him look so much the man meditating in solitude that all eyes were fixed on his face, observing him ... and everyone avoided making any noise for fear of disturbing the inner labor of which they were awaiting with curiosity the end and the product. Little by little, as his thought was being formed, he let it emerge from his mouth without being concerned about the form it took. The subject he was thinking about made little difference to him; disdaining all rules, placing himself above all proprieties, he considered it the privilege of his superiority over other men to be able to think out loud and let his brain freely produce and his mouth utter, counting on the attention and respect with which his slightest words would be received by his listeners, the most eminent of whom felt so inferior to him. He had no fear of contradicting himself; ingenious in finding subtle and plausible reasons to support any opinion, he set less store by choosing well among them than by proving that his mind had considered all sides of questions and that there was not a single idea that they could suggest that had not already occurred to him.[167]

State councilors, consuls, ministers, secretaries, or generals, all were like the "booklets" in which "each compartment in his memory had its supplement."[168] There were compartments for war, the navy, food supplies, finances, civil engineering projects—instruments necessary for the exercise of power and from which he tried to get the most. As for this latter talent, it is incontestable: Napoleon was always the ultimate master of the art of "getting the most out of the men [he had] chosen."[169] He was, for example, fond of referring to the immense task performed by Dufresne as the head of the Treasury, even though he was, Bonaparte said, "more or less stupid on any subject other than finances."[170]

The enormous amount of work Bonaparte did to remain informed at all times on all the subjects he had to deal with has not been sufficiently emphasized. His well-organized brain—in which "the diverse objects and diverse matters were filed away as they might have been in an armoire"[171]—probably helped him in this regard. Capable of concentrating for hours on end without a single moment of distraction, he was also capable of moving without transition from one question to another without the one he had just left having the slightest influence on the one to which he was currently devoting himself: "When I want to interrupt something," he said, "I close its drawer and I open another one. . . . If I want to sleep, I close all the drawers, and then I'm asleep."[172]

His sovereign exercise of power obliged him to know everything; but that was not the only reason for the prolonged work sessions that kept him glued to his desk for almost eighteen hours a day. The care with which he kept his notebooks up to date had to do with his desire not only to be always aware of the latest state of the situation in each domain, but also to know at least as much about it, and preferably more, than his collaborators did. His knowledge was not the least important part of the power he exercised:[173]

> One can understand . . . how the emperor, in the depths of his office, could occupy himself with so many diverse things, and at the same time prove so meticulous, so exact, and yet so rapid. With such an armory of positive information in his head and in his hands, he was never caught unprepared, and on the contrary acquired at will superiority over his entourage in all areas and at all times. If people were talking in the Council and in his presence regarding the necessity of moving troops

to a point within the country where disorders were to be feared, immediately after having glanced at his notebook he himself told his minister of war which troops were closest and to which generals orders should be sent. . . . If he was reviewing a body of troops, he knew where to find the personal things he wanted to say to the general or the colonel. When he paused in front of veterans, he knew which battles and which campaigns to talk to them about. . . . If a marshal wrongly complained about not having enough men, the emperor wrote to him, letter for letter, to point out resources he hadn't mentioned, this or that corps he had forgotten, this or that reinforcement whose arrival the minister was supposed to have announced to him. On entering a fortress, he knew better than the commandant how the place's armaments were arranged, how many 12-pounders there were on the ramparts, how many 24-pounders, how many eight-inch howitzers, etc., and in the magazines, how many quintals of powder, how many bullets of a certain caliber, how many artillery pieces without carriages, etc. If a prefect talked to him about conscription, he knew better than this prefect the number of deserters there had been in the last contingent; if he went to visit public works, he calculated for the engineer the funds already employed, and knew how to judge the work done in relation to the expenditure.[174]

It was at the cost of extraordinary work that he could do away with any kind of deliberation that would inevitably have reminded people of the Revolution and even the interminable discussions in the royal councils. Can this be called a system of government? It must first of all be related to the hatred of parliaments and of assemblies, with their displays of eloquence and their sluggishness, a hatred that explains in particular the invincible repugnance that the Tribunate inspired in Bonaparte. He could not imagine a great people that was not driven forward by a leader in a perpetual state of "illumination."[175] And he certainly could not look with favor on a parliamentary regime that gave priority to deliberation simply because it considered nothing more important than healthy slowness and wise moderation.

Bonaparte's military education contributed no less, and indeed in a decisive way, to forging his conception of the exercise of power. We must look here for the importance he accorded to collecting information that was as reliable and complete as possible before making a decision that, once made, was final and could no longer be questioned by anyone. That is why he gave as much attention to the most minute details as he did to great questions. This maniacal surveillance surely had something to do with a desire to control everything, just as his reluctance to rely on his subordinates was a way of refusing to grant them the slightest independence. This was the manifestation of a despotic temperament. But Bonaparte was also convinced that everything has its importance and that it is not demeaning—on the contrary—to accord equal attention to conception and to execution. He was, as Mollien says, "patient with details"[176]—because he knew that war is a serious matter in which the realization of strategic objectives depends on a judicious use of resources that have to be known with precision at every moment, in the interest of effectiveness, of course, but also because war does not allow one to make mistakes. Here the sanction is immediate and potentially lethal, and the responsibility falls on the man who, by virtue of the hierarchical principle itself, bears the burden of defeat just as he receives the benefit of victory. In short, it is the exact contrary of politics, where the consequences of an erroneous assessment of the circumstances are often deferred, rarely irreversible, and, because the decision is usually made by several people, the responsibility is proportionately diluted. When the sanction is immediate and potentially irreversible, everything becomes important: the tiniest factor affects the future.

Bonaparte governed as he made war. That is why he thought he had to get to the bottom of every subject before making a decision. He learned fast. No one has better or more completely described this aspect of the training peculiar to military men than Thiers did:

> The art of war may be the art that exercises the mind most. . . . It puts the whole person into action and on display. In this respect, the only art similar and equal to that of war is the art of governing . . . because one governs and one fights with one's whole soul. A man called upon to command others on the battlefield has first of all . . . to acquire scientific knowledge. . . . An engineer, an artilleryman, a good officer, he must also become . . . a profound geographer who is in full command

of the map, of its design, of its lines, of their relationships, of their value. Then he must have precise knowledge of the strength, the interests, and the character of peoples; he must know their political history, and particularly their military history; and he must especially know men, for men at war are not machines; on the contrary, [in war] they become more sensitive, more irritable than elsewhere; and the art of managing them, with a tactful but firm hand, was always an important part of the great captains' art. To all this superior knowledge, the man of war must also add the administrator's more commonplace knowledge, which is no less necessary. He has to have an employee's sense of order and detail; for it is not enough to make men fight, they also have to be fed, dressed, armed, and healed. All this vast knowledge has to be deployed at the same time, and amid the most extraordinary circumstances. At every moment one has to think about the day before, the day after, one's flanks, one's rear; take everything along: munitions, food supplies, hospitals; reckon at the same time with the atmosphere and the men's morale; and all these elements that are so diverse, so mobile, that change and constantly become more complicated, have to be combined amid cold, heat, hunger, and cannonballs. While you are thinking about so many things, the cannons are booming, your head is in danger; but what is worse, thousands of men are looking at you, seeking in your face the hope of their salvation; farther on, behind them, is your country and its laurels or cypresses; and all these images have to be driven away, you have to think, think quickly; because one minute more and the finest scheme has lost its relevance, and instead of glory, it is shame that awaits you. All that can certainly be done in a mediocre fashion, as all things can; it is possible to be a mediocre poet, scientist, or speaker as well; but to do it with genius is sublime. To think strongly and clearly in the depths of one's office, is undeniably very fine; but to think just as strongly and clearly amid cannonballs is the fullest exercise of human faculties.[177]

One expression inevitably comes to mind when Bonaparte's work methods are mentioned: *enlightened despotism.* Many historians have seen in the regime founded in 1800 the ultimate incarnation of the political system with which philosophers were infatuated in the eighteenth century. They had been enthusiastic about Frederick II, Catherine II, and even, like Roederer, the Chinese imperial system.[178] They saw in the alliance of political authority with philosophical reason the formula most favorable to progress and to the accomplishment of the reforms that did not necessarily win the assent of the majority, however good in themselves and even indispensable they might be.[179] More than Peter the Great, more than Frederick the Great, Bonaparte is the paradigm of the enlightened despot, the "sovereign who is instructed and informed about all the parts of his task, who employs and consults competent men, and finally who thinks before he decides."[180] In France in 1800, as in Prussia around 1740 or in the Austria of Joseph II, the goal was to liberate the political will in the service of reforms that, instead of being realized by the people, would be realized from above, with better chances of success and at a lower cost.

Did the Consulate mark the return to a formula that had had its hour of glory half a century earlier? Even if we leave aside the question of the nature of the—republican—consular regime, and despite the obviously monarchical form of Bonaparte's government, it was not the former monarchy that the Consulate revived. Now that the reign of revolutionary daydreams was over, Bonaparte was fond of suggesting the comparison by presenting himself as a sort of distant successor to Louis XIV, who had been called upon to reestablish certain eternal verities regarding politics. When Mollien praised economic freedom and suggested that political freedom is inseparable from it, Bonaparte replied: "The great order that rules the whole world has to govern each part of the world; the government is at the center of societies like the sun: the diverse institutions have to follow their orbit around it without ever deviating from it. Thus the government has to regulate the combinations of each of them in such a way that they all contribute to the general harmony."[181]

Mollien pushed the same comparison further when he wrote about the Council of Ministers that it "resembled that of a king," adding: "It was, in fact, entirely in a single man."[182] Nonetheless, this is where the difference lies: Bonaparte sought so jealously to ensure that he retained a monopoly on decision making not, or not only, because his temperament incited him to want to do everything and control everything; it was also because the monarchy had, if not perished, at least suffered terribly from the anarchy that reigned at its summit. Absolute monarchy, which in theory had only one head, had in reality several. Depending on the king's temperament, whether or not he was inclined to handle business by himself, the ministers had more or less power, and because they could not be everywhere at once, the reality of power gradually descended into the hands of their senior clerks, who in the eighteenth century were in many cases the true heads of state, while the King's Council retained some of the power in order to make use of it in a way that was not subject to any genuine supervision.

> Everyone conceived, executed, and supervised the others, Napoleon was to say. They could act contrary to one another, because the kings limited themselves to signing the projects or legalizing only their orders, the state secretaries [i.e., the ministers] could execute or fill them out as they wished, without being in danger of having material responsibility. Add to this that they had the power of signature, which they had tried to make me adopt, and that I had rejected as the weapon of do-nothing [Merovingian] kings. Among these ministers, some might have money that was not used, while others were unable to do anything because they hadn't a penny. [There was] no central power that could coordinate their movements, meet their needs, guide their execution.[183]

This was, moreover, the reason Bonaparte was careful to see to it that the ministers' action—and thus that of the bureaucracy—was backed up by that of the Council of State,[184] and the latter by his ministers and by the meetings of the various councils that he convoked.[185] Ultimately he was seeking a middle path between a monarchy that was de jure absolute but had ended up abandoning the reality of power to its servants, and the Revolution, which by giving priority to freedom over effectiveness, dreamed more about hobbling the government's exercise of power than about making its task easier.

The Consulate resumed the attempts at reform made at the end of the Old Regime, but with one difference: Turgot wanted to create representative assemblies so that the king would be better informed when it came time to decide, while not according these assemblies any real authority, so that they could not hinder the exercise of royal power. Tocqueville said rightly that it was an illusion characteristic of people who had had no experience of either politics or the human heart to believe that it was possible to create deliberative assemblies that would confine themselves voluntarily and permanently to a purely consultative role.[186] Bonaparte sought to return to the tradition of enlightened despotism, but in a form that took into account the lessons learned from the Revolution. Basically, if Turgot and the "economists," the last reformers of the Old Regime who tried to modernize the monarchy by making the minimum concessions to liberty, formed one of the main branches of the flourishing tree of the Enlightenment, then the Consulate can appear as the Enlightenment's revenge on the Revolution. The Revolution had failed to transform society from below, through the people. Bonaparte gave new life to the project that had been that of Turgot and of most of the *philosophes*: a reform of society carried out from above, by the prince.

An Evening at the Tuileries

Dinner, which was served around 6 P.M., lasted hardly longer than lunch. Hortense was a little apprehensive about it; although her stepfather could be kind and teasing, he could also be taciturn, sitting there without saying a word. After having dipped his bread in the gravy and eaten with his fingers, he might get up from the table even before dessert had been served.[187]

The evening, or what took its place, did not extend beyond 10 P.M. If no outing to the theater or the Opera was planned, and no council meeting was set for a late hour, Bonaparte spent a few moments in Joséphine's salon, where, not caring for gambling—he was a bad gambler, cheating and refusing to lose[188]—he looked instead for someone with whom he could have one of the long conversations he liked so much. They were often monologues. Then he would take Joséphine's arm for a walk in the Tuileries garden. "Not yet ready?" he asked her. Hortense says she heard this question as often as ten times a day.[189] Everything always went too slowly for his taste. When his wife could not accompany him, Duroc or Bessières replaced her.[190] At 10 P.M., after a last visit to his office, he retired to his bedroom, often getting up again at 2 A.M. In a dressing gown, and warming himself at the fireplace, even in the summer, he studied his files and checked the accounts, taking advantage of what he called "the presence of mind after midnight"; he called in a drowsy minister, drank a glass of chocolate, requested sherbets for his secretary. Around 5 A.M. he went back to bed, unless he asked his valet Constant to draw a bath for him, where he spent two hours, claiming that for him they were the equivalent of a whole night's sleep.[191]

Inevitably the question arises as to where Bonaparte had learned his trade, so naturally and spontaneously, without trial and error. How did things seem to come to him, as if he had always known them? He had, of course, undergone an initial apprenticeship in Italy, and then in Egypt. He had tried his hand at the art of governing even before he had seized the reins of government. War had made a great contribution to his education. He also had models, starting with Frederick II, whose workdays resembled his own.[192] He may have learned from him the discipline without which he would certainly not have been able to accomplish so much and over so long a time. But this does not completely answer the question. One is tempted to agree with Goethe that in the end it is impossible to explain how Napoleon, "while still so young, [knew how] to deal with the world's greatest problems with such skill and assurance that he seemed to have had numerous years of practice and experience."[193] Doesn't it suffice to say that "Napoleon handled the world as Hummel handled his piano," and that the former's talents are as little capable of being explained as the latter's?[194] It is the mystery of the Romantic hero, "always in his element, always equal to the circumstances," always doing things with a disconcerting facility.[195] At least, so long as his body allowed him to continue this incredible expense of energy, which was repeated day after day, month after month, almost without interruption, for more than twenty years. His mother worried about it: "You're working too much," she said to her son the first consul. He retorted: Did she think he was just "the lucky one," and that he could behave like that do-nothing Joseph, who spent his days "lazing around at Mortefontaine"?[196] That would have been impossible for him, and he would not have wanted that kind of life: What would he have done with his days, he who was so intensely aware of how fast time passed?

Constant, his valet, said that only one portrait really resembled him: the one painted by Horace Vernet in *Une revue du Premier consul sur la place du Car-*

rousel.[197] He is seen on a white horse, wearing a blue coat and white trousers tucked into his boots, in profile; he is still thin, with hollow cheeks, as in Italy in 1796, but he has cut his hair and given up the *oreilles de chien* (long locks) that did not become him. On contemplating this painting, one senses how much his fragile physique is supported by an iron will. Again, Goethe said it: he could not have inflicted such severe tests on his body, over so many years without giving it either respite or repose, if his "moral will" had not been so strong that it penetrated his whole body and put it "into a state of activity that repels hurtful influences."[198] The body itself was often on the verge of breakdown. There were few moments when Bonaparte was not suffering from some illness. He is supposed to have had bouts of malaria early in the Revolution.[199] In 1793 he got a case of scabies, which developed into an eczema that only hot baths relieved.[200] He caught colds easily, complicated by coughs and fever; he had come back from the East with a nasty "pulmonary inflammation" that Corvisart finally cured with the help of poultices.[201] In July 1801 he was so ill that he was thought to be dying.[202] In early 1802 he began to suffer from stomach trouble, with violent crises that took his breath away and provoked vomiting: "From the beginning of 1802, Napoleon felt sharper pains in his right side. I often saw him at Malmaison, during the evening work session and as midnight approached, lean on the right arm of his chair, unbutton his coat and shirt, and heave a sigh of pain. I spoke to him, and he replied: How I suffer! And a few moments later I accompanied him to his bedchamber. Several times I was obliged to support him on the little stairway that led from his inner office to the corridor where the apartments were."[203]

He attributed this problem to overeating and was on a permanent diet.[204] His valet offered a similar explanation.[205] Volney, who finally became concerned about Bonaparte's physical appearance, attributed it to poor hygiene, advising him to eat better and sleep more.[206] Bonaparte was probably already suffering from the ulcer that, cancerous or not, killed him in 1821.[207] But even when Napoleon was ill, Constant entered his bedroom every morning and opened the curtains. A new day was beginning.

TWENTY-SEVEN

The Turning Point of 1801

*T*he advent of the Consulate had opened the door to new diplomatic initiatives, to which the victory at Marengo gave fresh impetus. Talks with Austria had to be initiated,[1] contact with Prussia maintained, the tranquility of northern Italy assured, the alliance with Spain restored, and finally an end had to be put to a squabble between France and America. Provoked by the measures the Directory had taken against ships flying neutral flags, this squabble had degenerated into a "quasi-war." The Americans had taken the initiative toward reconciliation.[2] President Adams's envoys refused to deal any longer with Talleyrand, whose rapacity had left a bad impression on the other side of the Atlantic.[3] So the first consul assigned his brother Joseph to direct the French delegation; he knew Joseph had connections, polite manners, and moderation.[4] Bonaparte seemed sincerely to desire peace, and the signature of two treaties crowned this first diplomatic act, from which the regime emerged stronger: the Treaty of Mortefontaine (September 30), which restored the entente with the United States by reaffirming the principles of the "right of neutrals," and the Treaty of San Ildefonso, signed with Spain on October 1.[5]

France's Return to America

Since the signature of a treaty of alliance in 1796, relations between France and Spain had been marked by more downs than ups. France despised its neighbor and ally, considering it weak and decadent; for its part, Spain loathed an alliance that had been imposed on it by force of arms, faced strong opposition in public opinion, and only made more obvious and painful the country's decreased diplomatic status. The Spanish had some justification. Strictly speaking, the two countries were bound not by an alliance but by a treaty between a suzerain and a vassal, in which Spain was reduced to the role of an auxiliary of the French republican armies, an instrument of French foreign policy. It could not refuse what was imposed on it, but neither did it have much to gain; in fact, it had much to lose in this fool's bargain. If it made common cause with France, it would clearly pay a heavy price in America, where the English would take advantage of Spain's preoccupation elsewhere to strip it of its empire. Therefore, Spain, while abiding by the treaty of 1796, tried to be such a mediocre ally that the English enemy would be grateful. Never vetoing French demands, Spain nonetheless fulfilled its obligations poorly, half out of ill will and half out of an inability to do better. For its part, France had overestimated Spanish naval power and noted again and again the poor condition of its ships and the second-rate quality of their crews. In early 1798 the planned landing in England had to be abandoned, and in 1799 the French government found itself incapable of transporting reinforcements to Egypt. Clearly, the Spanish government was not able to act otherwise. Its alliance with France was unbalanced, and as the weaker party it hoped to escape this unwelcome bond someday; in the meantime it tried to do as little as possible.

However, the news of 18 Brumaire led to a change in Madrid. Charles IV and Queen Maria Luisa remembered Bonaparte's lightning conquest of Italy in 1796. Just as the Austrians coveted Venice, the king of Spain coveted for his daughter, who was married to the Duke of Parma's heir, not a simple duchy but a kingdom. If someone could help the Bourbons in Madrid satisfy their Italian ambitions, it was certainly Bonaparte.[6] The first consul felt only indifference toward Spain: it was not part of his imaginary geography. But his interest in the Mediterranean was enough to make him prize the alliance of 1796 and to do everything he could to maintain and strengthen it, particularly by making clear to the Spanish that his government was going to break with the past, even in formal terms. His first act was to send Alquier to Spain. Alquier was a revolutionary with a great deal of experience—he had sat in all the assemblies except the Legislative Assembly. He was said to be timid and not very industrious, but he at least had the merit of belonging "to the old French bourgeoisie that amid the brutalities of politics and despite the jargon of the time, had retained a taste for good manners and polite language." "Alquier was one of those who had easily adopted the title of Citizen and the familiarity of tone imposed by the Jacobins, but who understood that this was a language that could not be exported and who would have no difficulty returning to the habits of good society that formerly prevailed."[7] Bonaparte counted on him to erase the memory of his predecessor, Guillemardet, who had been crude and incompetent, and to establish contact with Manuel Godoy, Queen Maria Luisa's favorite, who was known as the Prince of the Peace. Having been driven out of power on the orders of the Directory in the spring of 1798, Godoy had not only kept the ear of the queen, who was as enthusiastic as ever about him, and that of her indulgent husband, but had also become the leader of a "Catholic" or "religious" party.[8] Because this party opposed the policy hostile to papal power pursued by the current prime minister, Urquijo, Godoy had become the ally of choice when Bonaparte began to negotiate with Rome. Nonetheless, in the first consul's view, the paramount reason for consolidating the alliance with Spain was Egypt.

Bonaparte foresaw what his soldiers would think when his departure was announced, which was why he preferred to leave on the quiet, without even meeting Kléber at the rendezvous he had set with him. Kléber, to whom he had entrusted the destiny of the Army of the Orient, had been furious on arriving at Rosetta too late and discovering that "the bird had flown the nest."[9] Before the troops he had officially justified his predecessor's departure, but at the same time he denounced his desertion to a government that he believed was still the Directory.[10] Bonaparte could not limit himself to imposing silence on events in Egypt. Before he left, he had sworn that he would not forget his old companions in arms. He even claimed to have returned to France to force the government to provide reinforcements and weapons; and in fact one of his first steps had been to get together the funds necessary to cover the soldiers' back pay, to order Berthier to establish regular communications with Egypt, and to write to Kléber and the Army of the Orient to tell them that help was on its way.

An expedition was being prepared. Breaking through the blockade of Brest, it would head for the Mediterranean, and after landing reinforcements in Egypt, turn around and unblock Malta. The preparations were moving forward slowly. At the end of February 1800, Bonaparte was still so confident that he increased the naval forces entrusted to admirals Bruix and Ganteaume, and even called upon the Spanish for help. As they had the preceding year, Admiral Gravina and his colleague, Mazaredo, the Spanish ambassador in Paris, were dragging their heels: "In military operations," Bonaparte finally told the latter, "hours decide the outcome of campaigns."[11] Time was passing, and on March 20 Bonaparte learned that the English had reinforced the blockade off Brest; forty ships were now preventing any breakout. The facts had to be faced: "If the equinox passes without the squadron dispersing, then no matter how much interest we have in unblocking Malta and getting reinforcements to Egypt, we shall have to give it up," he wrote to Bruix.[12]

Up to that point no one in Paris knew the situation in Egypt, where Kléber, having repelled another attempted landing by the Ottomans in November 1799, had been waiting in vain for a sign from Paris, and even more for the promised reinforcements. An Ottoman army was approaching through the Sinai. Judging his forces inadequate, noting the collapse of his troops' morale, and never having believed in the possibility of success himself, Kléber made contact with the enemy. On January 23, 1800, he signed a convention of evacuation with Sidney Smith.[13]

Bonaparte learned of this only when the rescue operation had failed. In a letter to Desaix he seems resigned and fatalistic, while at the same time wondering how "16,000 to 18,000 French troops" could possibly fear 30,000 Turks.[14] The information passed to him by Menou, who wanted to be Kléber's successor, revived his anger, to such a point that he asked Talleyrand to have published in the *Moniteur* documents proving that nothing justified a convention that he considered no less than a betrayal.[15] Was he thinking about prosecuting Kléber? Later he said he was,[16] but at the time, perhaps for fear of provoking revelations that he did not want, he remained quiet about the loss of a colony that destroyed his Mediterranean policy.[17]

Egypt was no longer on the first consul's mind. It has to be admitted that he now had other preoccupations: the preparation of the second Italian campaign monopolized so much of his time that he paid hardly any attention to the news that was filtering in toward the end of May (he was then in Italy). The British government had refused to back Sidney Smith and validate the Convention of El-Arish, so war had resumed in Egypt. Contradicting Kléber's pessimistic prognoses and confirming Bonaparte's optimism, it had turned to the advantage of the French expeditionary corps, which, after defeating the Turks at Heliopolis on March 20, was about to retake control of the country. As for sending reinforcements, that was impossible before "sometime in the winter,"[18] especially because the failure in March had shown that Spanish support had to be secured, and the chaos in the naval administration remedied, before anything could be done.

Marengo produced a sudden improvement in French-Spanish relations: because Bonaparte had once again become the master of northern Italy, Charles IV and his wife began to hope that he would help them accomplish their projects in Italy. Bonaparte sent Berthier to them, and the terms of an agreement were soon ready, even if it proved impossible to draw Spain into an intervention against Portugal.[19] In exchange for making the duchy of Parma a kingdom and expanding its territory, Spain would cede Louisiana back to France and put part of its war fleet at France's disposal.[20] The second treaty of San Ildefonso was signed on October 1. Charles IV thought he had driven a very good bargain by paying for the reinforcement of Bourbon influence in Italy—his brother Ferdinand IV ruled over Naples and his nephew over Parma—with a colony that France had ceded during the Seven Years' War, and over which Madrid had since exercised an authority that was intermittent at most. Bonaparte was convinced that he had paved the way for an American policy that he saw as the complement to, or if necessary the substitute for, his Mediterranean policy, in the event that Egypt escaped him. In any case, the retrocession of Louisiana marked the return of France to the American continent, from which it had in large measure been expelled, retaining a presence only in Guyana, Guadeloupe, and Saint-Domingue, part of the island of Hispaniola.[21] France's control over the latter was, however, entirely theoretical: metropolitan France had in fact already lost the "Pearl of the Antilles." After years of revolts, civil wars, anarchy, and atrocities of all kinds, Saint-Domingue was about to become orderly again under the control of the most gifted of the insurgent leaders.

The sad end of Toussaint Louverture at the Joux fortress in 1803 contributed as much to his transfiguration as did his fight against slavery. It is hard, perhaps impossible, to know what he really was.[22] Many biographers have made the attempt. But when one has said that he was born a slave sometime between 1739 and 1746 and was later set free, one has said almost everything we know. The rest is supposition. Was one of his ancestors an African prince? That is not impossible. Had he had a good education? Was he even the "profound thinker" described by his most fervent admirers?[23] We do not have a single line written by his hand, and he probably didn't know how to read or write, the Bible serving him as his intellectual viaticum.[24] But his abundant correspondence, dictated to secretaries, reveals an intelligent and capable man. He had judgment, a political instinct developed to the highest degree, and a mixture of ferocity and practical wisdom that allowed him to rise to the first rank and to overcome rivals and enemies who, though no less brutal, remained inferior. He had played his role well amid civil disturbances and foreign interventions, first by the Spaniards, then by the British, allying himself with each side before abandoning them and never losing sight of the goal: making the French part of the island, and if possible the whole island, a free state that would nonetheless retain privileged ties with France. That is why, although he had accepted from the Directory the rank of general in the French army, in 1797 he got rid of the government's representative and the following year forced General Hédouville's expeditionary corps to get back on its ships and leave. He had just crushed his last adversary—the half-blood General Rigaud—when Bonaparte took power.[25] Toussaint had tried to restore order in the former colony, and especially to restart the production of sugar and coffee, without which the treasuries remained hopelessly empty. He had signed trade agreements with representatives of Britain and the United States.[26] Not believing any more than the colonists did that there was a viable alternative to the plantation system, he had reduced the former slaves, who had just become free men, to forced labor.[27]

If this new system did not quite mark a complete return to the former state of affairs, it did revive a still older reality, that of the *encomienda*, by means of which the first Spanish colonists had enslaved the native populations.[28] Order returned little by little, under the iron rule of Toussaint, his lieutenants, and an army of 30,000 men. Toussaint was so proud of his work and the first results it produced that he sent out a call to white planters asking them to return and help him restore the former prosperity.

The Consulate, which had just been established, sent ships to cruise off the island to show the French flag, and then three commissioners were assigned to deliver the Constitution of Year VIII to the local authorities and to receive their oath of loyalty.[29] Four thousand men were supposed to follow them, but as we can easily imagine, their ships were never able to depart.[30]

However, something had changed. The colonists' "party" was regaining the upper hand in France.[31] The new constitution, breaking with the heritage of the Convention and the Directory, which had declared the complete integration of the colonies into the Republic, declared that the colonies were subject to a special system.[32] The experiment of transforming former colonies into departments subject to a common law was thus over. The minister of the navy, who had traditionally been in charge of this sector, became its administrator again and urged the first consul to restore the old system of "the Exclusive," which limited colonies to trading with France.[33] The navy men were not alone. Cambacérès and Lebrun, Talleyrand and Barbé-Marbois in the government, Regnaud de Saint-Jean d'Angély and Malouet, a former member of the Constituent Assembly, were among those trying to get Bonaparte to abandon the "false philanthropy" that had inspired the decree abolishing slavery issued on February 4, 1794.[34] The ranks of the opposing camp, that of the philanthropists, were getting thinner and thinner. Even Abbé Grégoire regretted the sudden abolition of slavery in 1794, believing that the abrupt passage from slavery to freedom had led to a catastrophe.[35] Admiral Truguet, Volney, and Fouché were the only ones around Bonaparte who defended the heritage of the Revolution. The first consul received visitors, informed himself, and listened.

The question of the blacks' condition did not torment him. He knew about slavery; he had seen the slave market in Cairo, approved the purchase of young Sudanese men to fill out his army's regiments, and accepted the slave, Roustam, given him by Sheikh el-Bekri; he was not scandalized. Slavery was a fact, an institution; therefore it had to be judged, like every institution, solely by the yardstick of utility. Was it advantageous for the nation, its prosperity, its power, or not? Ultimately he did not understand the compassion of the "Friends of the Blacks"; he saw it as an abstract passion that probably flattered their "amour-propre" because it allowed those who shared it to flaunt their "humanity," but was deeply imbued with hypocrisy and injustice. That explains his virulent reply to Admiral Truguet when the latter was making the case for the blacks: Wasn't the admiral, completely absorbed in his compassion for the victims of slavery, indifferent to the sufferings of the victims of the slave revolts? Didn't he consider the colonists, whose property had been stolen and who had been the victims of countless atrocities, unworthy of his pity? Bonaparte said the Friends of the Blacks were like a Frenchman who preferred Italians to his compatriots during the invasion of Italy, and added: "If it had been necessary to choose between destroying all Italy and sacrificing two of my soldiers, I would have destroyed all Italy; because, above all, I am part of my army and for my army!" He was in fact the leader of his army, the leader of his state, and responsible for the lives and the interests of his fellow citizens. That is what he meant when he said to Truguet: "I am for the whites, because I am white; I have no other reason, and that is the right one!" The conflation of morals and politics could prove immoral in its effects, he thought, as had been shown by the fate of the colonists in Saint-Domingue since 1794.[36] They had received neither compensation nor a restoration of their rights. But for a long time he hesitated between two policies: Hadn't the former slaves become citizens for whom he was now accountable, just as he was for the colonists, even if, in his heart of hearts, he did not believe that Africans "without civilization" could be so easily transformed into citizens?[37] He had two options, he said later, neither of which foresaw the reestablishment of slavery where it had been in fact abolished, and both of which sought to satisfy existing interests, even if the first was to the advantage of the former slaves and the second to that of the former colonists: "The first option consisted in giving the black Toussaint-Louverture civil and military authority, and the title of governor-general of the colony; in entrusting command to black generals; in consolidating and legalizing the order of work established by Toussaint . . . ; in obliging black farmers to pay a poll tax or license fee to the former French property owners; in retaining for the home country the exclusive trade of the whole colony. . . . The second option consisted in reconquering the colony by force of arms, bringing back to France all the blacks who had held ranks superior to that of a battalion leader, in disarming the blacks and ensuring their civil liberty, and in restoring their property to the colonists."[38]

Thus, different options were being examined, as is proven by a note addressed to Forfait, the minister of the navy, in the spring of 1800.[39] Bonaparte began by turning his back on the colonists and their advocates, and sticking to positions opposed to those who supported the reestablishment of the old colonial system.[40] Naturally he could not entertain the idea of cooperating with Toussaint without confirming the decree of 1794, and his first proclamation to the inhabitants of Saint-Domingue made them this promise: "The consuls of the Republic . . .

declare to you that the sacred principles of the liberty and equality of black people will never be violated or modified among you."[41] Nine months later he had not changed his mind, as is shown by the speech he delivered before the Council of State on August 16, 1800:

> The question is not whether it is good to abolish slavery. . . . I am convinced that this island would belong to the English if the Negroes were not attached to us by the interest of their liberty. They will make less sugar, perhaps; but they will make it for us, and they will serve us, if needed, as soldiers. If we have one less sugar refinery, we shall have one more citadel occupied by friendly soldiers. . . . Thus I shall speak of liberty in the free part of Saint-Domingue; I shall confirm slavery in Île de France [Mauritius] [and] even in the [Spanish] slave part of Saint-Domingue; reserving to myself the right to make slavery gentler and to limit it where I shall maintain it; to reestablish order and introduce discipline, where I shall maintain liberty.[42]

The confirmation of the abolition of slavery in Saint-Domingue, in Guadeloupe, and in Cayenne, the reestablishment of slavery in Martinique, where the decree of abolition had not been promulgated: the program was risky, but remained in place at the end of the year, when he decided to name Toussaint Louverture "captain-general of the colony."[43] And he did not deviate from it, at least not until Toussaint himself put an end to the negotiations by invading the Spanish part of Hispaniola (ceded to France in 1795), which Bonaparte had just given up as a gesture of friendship toward his ally. On the other hand, it is hard to disentangle the first consul's true intentions. In addition to the letter to Forfait already cited, we also find, very early on, references to Toussaint's army that present it as a "national guard."[44] Thus it was necessarily limited to secondary functions and subservient to regular troops from metropolitan France: perhaps the 4,000 men that Lacrosse had not been able to take to Saint-Domingue in the spring of 1800; perhaps 3,000 others whom an expedition being prepared was supposed to take to Port-au-Prince at the end of the same year.[45] If reducing Toussaint's army to the status of a national guard was the real objective concealed behind the—exaggerated—homage paid to him and his men, what would remain of the broader promises made once the objective had been attained? Wouldn't Bonaparte then move from his first plan to the second, from an autonomous protectorate associated with France to a pure and simple reestablishment of the colonial regime?

It is too often forgotten that in his calculations Bonaparte was still taking Britain into account. It was a question not only of re-creating, behind Britain's back, strong French positions in America, but also of preparing for the peace treaty that would inevitably be signed when the British could no longer rely on any ally in Europe. That is why the French presence in Egypt had to be consolidated as soon as possible and the home country's authority reestablished in the colonies before the beginning of the great bargaining. How could it be believed that the British would put up with the abolition of slavery in part of the French possessions, when they were well aware that this measure had been taken to stir up trouble in their own colonies? And how could one believe in the viability of a system that made slave and free zones coexist side by side, as was the case in Saint-Domingue, where slavery would be maintained in the old Spanish part of the island and abolished in the French part? Finally, and this argument was a weighty one, if Bonaparte and the whole government were so eager to retake control of Saint-Domingue, it was in order to draw from it the profits that the production of sugar and coffee had earlier provided for France: at that time they represented around 4 percent of the kingdom's revenues—a sum that was not unconnected with the plantation system based on slavery.[46] As we have seen, Toussaint had taken steps to reestablish production.[47] It was still too early to gauge the effects. It was not yet known that forced labor was not going to allow production to be returned to even a tenth of its level before the Revolution.[48] After ten years of disturbances, Saint-Domingue was divided between a population reduced to forced labor and an army of 30,000 men that monopolized almost all its resources. Not only could the French government not accept this, but it could not resign itself to depending on a military clique that constantly threatened massacres to impose its will. Henceforth, even supposing that Bonaparte had not yet made a final choice—especially given that at the end of 1800 the reconquest of Saint-Domingue remained a hypothesis— the range of possible choices was already not very broad, and tragedy was already nearing.[49]

The acquisition of Louisiana might prove valuable in this context. It would serve as an operational base for the reconquest of the French islands, while logs floated down the Mississippi would make it possible to undertake naval construction on site that would improve the defense of this distant empire. On a strategic level, it would make it possible to strengthen the ties that had just been reestablished with the United States thanks to the Treaty of Mortefontaine (President Jefferson's negative reaction to the recovery of Louisiana was not yet known in Paris), to threaten the British with an attack on their rear, and last but not least, to help Spain keep its American colonies.[50] The idea that France needed to assist Spain was widely shared. Spain's power had fallen so low that it hardly had the means to prevent the emancipation of its colonies in California, Central America, and South America, whether they proclaimed their independence, as the United States had done in escaping British domination, or whether the British or the Americans seized them. Bonaparte was worried in particular about American expansionism and also saw in Louisiana a barrier to the young republic's advance toward the west and the south.[51] The stakes were crucial: Bonaparte had acquired the conviction that the Spanish would remain France's allies so long as they retained their American empire. William Warden, who often spoke with the emperor on Saint Helena, reported:

> In one conversation I had . . . concerning the emancipation of the Spanish colonies, I understood that Napoleon believed that the emancipation of these colonies would be of the greatest advantage to Great Britain, for the following reasons: because, so long as Spain's principal policy aims to retain and administer its colonies in America, it will consider any power that has control of the seas as its natural enemy and will unite with France to counterbalance England's maritime dominance, but now that America has been emancipated, Spain's policy is becoming purely continental, and consequently it is becoming a rival for France, [the latter] being the only power in contact with or in opposition to it on the continent.[52]

This was one of the most important reasons for the efforts made to reconstitute a colonial empire at the pivot of the two Americas. In the interim, the treaties signed one after the other with the Spaniards and the Americans opened a new front against Britain, and provided the means of turning to America if the projects of colonization in Egypt finally failed. They also solidly connected— or at least so Bonaparte wanted to believe—Spain to France, giving grounds for hope that the offensive against Portugal that it had been impossible to carry out in 1798 would really be on the agenda this time. In Egypt, Bonaparte had announced Menou as the successor to Kléber, who had been assassinated in Cairo on June 14, and as he was writing to him to tell him that reinforcements would soon be sent,[53] French troops were occupying Austrian Tuscany,[54] which the first consul had decided to seize with a view to an arrangement very different from the one that he had just made with the Spaniards.[55]

Sovereign, Not Yet a Monarch

The eighth anniversary of the Republic had just been celebrated. On September 22 Bonaparte had presided over the inauguration of a monument erected on the Place des Victoires to the memory of Kléber and Desaix. The ceremony was both imposing, with flags flying and soldiers in their dress uniforms, and boring. The inexhaustible Garat, who had in the course of his long life composed eulogies and speeches for the most diverse masters, had not been able to restrain his pen, and inflicted on his audience a speech 107 pages long in praise of the deceased generals, and especially of the one who was very much alive but half asleep and looking daggers at him. "Can you imagine an oaf like Garat?" Bonaparte asked when he got back to the Tuileries. "What a blabbermouth! I had to listen to him for three hours!"[56] The next day there was a different speaker: Lucien in person had been entrusted with the task of celebrating Turenne, Louis XIV's great marshal, under the dome of the Invalides, as the predecessor and model of the other "greatest captain of his century" who was sitting in the front row before him. The cortege that transported the marshal's mortal remains— which the revolutionaries had expelled from Saint-Denis and relegated first to the Jardin des Plantes, and then to the Museum of French Monuments—the decoration of the former church, which had been renamed the Temple of Mars, the attendance of the soldiers, the large crowd of the people, and even Lucien's long speech did not lack a certain panache. Those who heard the minister of the interior proclaim the birth of a new *Grand Siècle* and celebrate France's reconnection with its past, with today's hero offering his hand to yesterday's hero, had the feeling that they were experiencing an important moment. This homage to the marshal seemed to illustrate Bonaparte's policy in favor of reconciliation and the restoration of values and authentic embodiments of greatness. "What was once great, and what is great today," Lucien cried, "the living heroes and the illustrious dead, are assembled in the same place to celebrate the day France changed its laws without interrupting the course of its great destinies."[57] The festivities at Mortefontaine, organized ten days later to celebrate the reestablishment of peace with the Americans, showed on the contrary, by their improvised and disordered nature, how much the two societies, military and civilian, had followed divergent paths.

Joseph had thought big at Mortefontaine: banquet, music, theater, fireworks. He had brought in a master of ceremonies, Despréaux. Married to a former star of the dance, Marie-Madeleine Guimard, and himself not only a dancer but also a singer, a silhouette artist, and a composer of comic operas—he was the author of *Syncope, reine de Micmac*—Despréaux had no peer, it was said, when it came to organizing a fete. But in this case, no matter what he did, everything went wrong. When the table settings were unpacked, it was discovered that the knives had been forgotten. There were no decorations for the table. The wine tasted of vinegar, and the workers assigned to set up the stage had drunk half of it anyway. It rained hard all day and the guests had to wade through mud while waiting for the guards to check the playing cards that had been handed out to serve as passes. People finally sat down at the table, pell-mell, actresses next to solemn Americans. The orchestra, which didn't know quite what to play, treated the guests to *Ça ira* and other revolutionary songs. When the meal was over, Despréaux was unable to get the actors to go on stage: they refused to be treated as servants. As for the pyrotechnists, they were dead drunk. The show finally began at midnight.[58] Almost a year after 18 Brumaire, the regime was far from having rid itself of its revolutionary origins.

However, Bonaparte's aim from the outset had been to put distance between himself and the Revolution. The establishment of the consuls in the Tuileries had no other purpose. The general was certain that the more the government returned to the splendor and spectacle found in most states, the more respect, and thus authority, it would have. In Italy he had noted the astonishment of diplomats and ministers when he received them without the slightest ceremony and without observing the usual formalities. These formalities, which in Paris were considered outmoded and peculiar to monarchical regimes, had their importance as they eased the search for a compromise between diplomats who, while defending contrary interests, spoke the same language and observed the same customs. The Directory had been less concerned to reestablish the old forms of diplomacy because its goal was not to make alliances with the powers of the old continent but to impose on them the will of the Great Nation. On coming to power, Bonaparte knew that he would have to play a strong diplomatic game, and he intended to behave as courteously as he had done, to everyone's great surprise, toward the pope during the Italian campaign. That is why one of his first acts was to restore a minimum of ceremony when he received ambassadors.

Something important was at stake: France's reintegration into the "concert of nations." The time had come to relearn the language of diplomacy. But how? No one knew how to speak that language anymore; the Revolution was only ten years old, but it seemed like a century. Did Talleyrand advise Bonaparte? Probably. The most difficult task was to find a "chamberlain" to introduce the ambassadors. The problem was that this was considered a servant's function. A volunteer was found, however: state councilor Benezech, a former minister of the Directory, a strange fellow who thought nothing better than the Versailles of the *ancien régime*. So to the amusement and scorn of his colleagues, he agreed to play the role of chamberlain, holding his usher's baton at ceremonies that owed their solemnity chiefly to the intimidating presence of Bonaparte himself. Once the diplomats had been introduced, everyone formed a circle; they talked standing or seated, depending on the mood of the moment; at table, where women were only rarely present, there was neither protocol nor etiquette, and an ambassador might well be seated next to a general, a member of the Institute, a state councilor, or even a subordinate officer or soldier who had been decorated at the morning inspection. The same was true for the dinners to which were invited, each "decade"—the revolutionary calendar remained in force— sometimes senators, sometimes members of the Legislative Body, sometimes

Napoleon had probably brought up the question and expressed a few doubts regarding Joseph's abilities, because the latter thought it necessary to remind his younger brother that his incontestable "moderation" was in no way the expression of a weakness of character: "You would misjudge me," he even explained, "if you thought I do not have a strong will in decisive matters."[71]

If Napoleon rejected one hypothesis, it was certainly that one. It is not that he refused to consider the future; he knew how much the question of his succession obsessed his supporters, and had he not known it, the "Marengo crisis" would have brought it to his attention. He confided to Cabanis that there was a gap in the current social contract that had to be filled.[72] If we believe Miot, his entourage had been thinking about this for several months.[73] Nevertheless, Bonaparte hesitated to raise the question, even if in his view the extension of his term as first consul was a foregone conclusion. La Fayette said later that he had understood this when he spoke to him about the proposal made by several members of the Philadelphia Convention to create a president for life in the United States.[74] Not only did the first consul fear that referring to the future would unleash ambitions, but he also did not see whom he could propose as his successor. Carnot? He told Roederer that the minister of war was probably the best candidate.[75] Of course, he didn't think that at all. Everything he said at that time was intended to make his interlocutors understand that he was the necessary man, the savior without whom France would plunge back into chaos.[76] It was in fact in danger of falling back into chaos if questions were brought up that he was convinced public opinion was not yet prepared to debate. He never ceased to repeat that there was no inherited power or monarchy without a nobility, but were the French ready, eleven years after 1789, to consent to the creation of a new nobility? When the Council of State considered the creation of the lists of nobility foreseen by the Constitution of Year VIII, Bonaparte seized the opportunity to clarify his thought on the subject. When Roederer proposed that a "notable" could be removed from the list only by an absolute majority of registered voters, Bonaparte opposed him: "We have to recognize that if we require half of the citizens with the right to vote, plus one, in order to remove a name from a list of notability, the notability will be a real nobility; this institution will offend the mass of the people. There are two things for which the French nation is not yet ripe: the heredity of offices and nobility."[77]

He had another reason for prohibiting any discussion of heredity: he did not want to wound Joséphine. It was out of tact that he replied to the insistent Roederer, who was speaking to him about the necessity of having a natural heir: "I don't have a child; I don't feel the need or the necessity of having one. I have no family spirit."[78] But whatever he did, he could not prevent commentaries from proliferating. His state of health was closely watched and—this was a sign that many people were already considering the idea of a return to monarchy— rumors were circulating: some said that he was going to proclaim himself king on the anniversary of the Republic,[79] others that he was going to get divorced and remarry, and still others that he was already king because he was a direct descendant of the Man in the Iron Mask, who was said to be Louis XIV's brother.[80]

Joséphine was obsessed with the possibility of a divorce. It was unlikely that she would give her husband a child, and she lived in fear that one of his mistresses would become pregnant.[81] She trembled when she was told that she would be the new queen of France. If her husband's power became hereditary, it would mean the end of her marriage. She also sensed that the clan was on the watch. At about this time Lucien, who hated her, made her a rather odious reproach: "You are going to take the waters," he said as she was leaving for Plombières, "you'll have to have a child by someone else, because he can't give you one." When she protested, he insinuated that perhaps it was she who couldn't give Napoleon one, and that in that case maybe he ought to find himself another woman, whose child she would adopt. "It's in your interest," he concluded, "and you must know why."[82] That is the reason she listened so attentively to the supporters of the Bourbons. When Bonaparte received, through the intermediary of Lebrun, two letters that Louis XVIII had written to him from Mitau in December 1799 and in February 1800 to ask for the return of his throne, she and Hortense besieged the general in an attempt to stop him from replying to the king with a curt refusal.[83] In vain. Bonaparte pinched their ears and told La Fayette, referring to the royalists: "They promise me a statue, in which I would be represented offering the crown to the king. I replied that I should be afraid of being shut up in the pedestal."[84] He sent Louis XVIII a friendly letter, but in which he begged him to abandon these fantastical ideas if he did not want to have on his conscience the death of 100,000 Frenchmen.[85]

Joséphine did not give up the fight. At the same time that she was receiving the princes' more or less secret emissaries, she was moving closer to republicans hostile to any idea of inherited power.[86] She had sensed that she had to be wary of Talleyrand, and that she had no more reliable ally in the government than Fouché.[87] She knew that Fouché was opposed to a restoration of the monarchy, whoever the beneficiary, and she expected him to support her against the very numerous neo-royalists in her husband's entourage, whether they believed, like Talleyrand, that from a King Bonaparte it would be easier to return to the Bourbons,[88] like Roederer that monarchy went hand in hand with strong, stable, and conservative government,[89] or like many others that the French people had to get used to monarchy again before putting the Duke of Orléans on the throne.

It was a quiet struggle, with everyone trying to draw the first consul into his camp. The republican "party" was organized around two bastions: the Institute and *La Décade philosophique*. At that time *Décade* exercised a genuine intellectual domination, at least over the part of public opinion that remained attached to the Revolution and to the philosophical rationalism of the eighteenth century. The friends d'Andrieux and Guingené, its editors, dominated the Institute and had many supporters, starting with Fouché, in the first consul's entourage. Like all the "parties" of the period, this one had many nuances. There was more criticism of religion at Sophie de Condorcet's salon in Auteuil than in Germaine de Staël's, and more criticism of the first consul among Benjamin Constant's friends than among people who frequented his muse's salon.[90] But everyone hoped to keep the new government in the Revolution's camp.

And first of all Mme de Staël, who counted Lucien and especially Joseph Bonaparte among her friends. As for the first consul, she had mixed feelings about him. Here one can fully agree with Fontanes, who said that in her there was a continual tension "between the movements of her soul and the opinions of her mind."[91] Bonaparte's rejection of her in 1797 was in the distant past, the incidents that had marked the beginning of the session of the Tribunate were forgotten, and Benjamin Constant would surely not have read without disappointment these words, which say a great deal about how little importance she accorded to an assembly that Constant considered the last rampart of liberty: "The true tribune, the true senator, the true legislator, is Bonaparte. The country is all the better for it," she wrote.[92] She could not help admiring Bonaparte, and even being subject to his ascendancy: "What can I say?" she asked Lucien one day. "I become stupid in front of your brother because I want so much to please him."[93] She hadn't succeeded in doing so up to that point, but she refused to give up. In *Dix années d'exil*, she describes herself as a longtime opponent, even stating that in 1800 she hoped the French armies would be defeated.[94] But in reality she still believed that Bonaparte might be converted to liberal ideas. "I am convinced that Bonaparte likes enlightened ideas," she wrote to Dupont de Nemours on August 6.[95] La Fayette, who was more farsighted than she in matters of politics, agreed with her on this point, and when Bonaparte asked him if he had found the French "cooler toward liberty" when he returned from captivity, he had replied: "The French are more than ever in a state to receive it; it is for you to give it to them, it is from you that they expect it."[96]

De la littérature, which Germaine published in May 1800, was in no sense an occasional work, and contrary to a common view, it was far from being an opposition manifesto. Instead it testifies to the illusions that its author still cherished. To be sure, she took a few shots at the regime and its leader, but the book's vigorous denunciation of military government merely takes up a theme that Bonaparte himself liked to expound upon.[97] And wasn't her eulogy of the poet Ossian a way of courting the first consul, since everyone knew how much he liked the songs of the false bard?[98] Defended by Fauriel in *La Décade*, lauded by Daunou in the *Clef du cabinet des souverains*, the book was torn to shreds by Fontanes in the *Mercure de France*.[99] Fontanes attacked Mme de Staël's style, anticipating Sainte-Beuve by accusing her of not writing as well as she spoke, or rather of not knowing the difference between spoken language and written language, and he denounced her advocacy of the doctrine of "perfectibility"—scientific, moral, and social progress advancing at the same rate—as a pernicious ideology inherited from the Enlightenment through the intermediary of Condorcet, and whose inanity had been proven by recent history.[100] Chateaubriand, who entered the ring after Mme de Staël, reaffirmed her belief in the doctrine of "perfectibility,"[101] but attacked her deism, which was a way of saying that she was opposed to the religious pacification sought by the government.[102] Fontanes, indicting the dead ends of modern philosophy and calling for a return to the wisdom of the ancients, presented her as an avowed enemy of the policy that attempted to reconnect with France's thousand-year-long history.

The polemic was philosophical, and more profound than is usually said, but it also had obvious political connotations.

This neo-Catholic, neo-monarchist, conservative "right wing" was born after 18 Fructidor and its persecutions. In its ranks were found former Voltairians like Fontanes and Mathieu de Montmorency, *philosophes* who had become reactionaries, like Michaud and Fiévée, and outright reactionaries like Louis de Bonald. Kept at a distance from the Institute, they had their bastions, including the *Mercure de France*; their muses, Juliette Récamier and the Countess of Clermont-Tonnerre playing here the same role that Sophie de Condorcet and Germaine de Staël played in the opposing camp;[103] and their powerful protectors—Fouché for one side, Élisa and Lucien Bonaparte for the other.

Historians have painted, and are still painting, Lucien Bonaparte in highly fanciful poses. He has been described as a man with convictions, as the family's revolutionary and republican, indeed as a perpetual rebel.[104] It is pointless to seek the slightest coherence in the youngest Bonaparte's political itinerary. His older brother knew this so well that, fearing to see him transformed into an opposition orator, he made him minister of the interior. That involved paying a high price for Lucien's neutrality, as he can hardly be said to have performed brilliantly in his new office.[105] A good speaker, he proved to be a poor administrator; paperwork bored him. Although he helped choose prefects—he knew many of the men who made the Revolution—he willingly left the everyday work to an entourage that was not above all reproach. He was preoccupied with Juliette Récamier, with whom he was less intimate than he desired, but who enabled him to establish ties with Fontanes, La Harpe, and the whole reactionary camarilla that surrounded her. Lucien liked to see himself as a protector of the arts and letters. That was opportune, because Fontanes dreamed of restoring "the ancient alliance between the republic of letters and public power."[106] Moreover, Fontanes was to some extent a member of the family. Lucien lost his wife, Catherine, on May 14, and his sister Élisa, who was dreadfully bored with Bacciochi, came to console her brother. She remained at his home to take care of the children, Charlotte and Christine, and soon fell into Fontanes's arms. Lucien financed the launch of the new *Mercure de France*, and when, as minister of the interior, he had to organize the July 14 festivities, it was very natural for him to turn to Fontanes. The latter must have had powerful protection to be able to speak about the Revolution the way he did in a song Méhul set to music:

Ô souvenirs d'horreur! Ô jours de l'espérance!
Déplorons le passé! Célébrons l'avenir!
La nuit de la douleur couvrit dix ans la France.
Dix ans d'adversités en ce jour vont finir.[107]

[O memories of horror! O days of hope!
Let us deplore the past! Let us celebrate the future!
For ten years painful darkness covered France.
Ten years of adversity shall end this day.]

The battle with the party of the Institute and Fouché was ferocious. Fouché and Lucien hated each other. The regime's future was only one of the questions on which they disagreed. Lucien did not like seeing the police escape the control of the Ministry of the Interior, and he tried to have the minister of police dismissed, in the hope of obtaining his portfolio for himself.[108] Fouché was on the lookout for the slightest opportunity to counterattack, and although he had been unable to defeat his rival, he had at least scored points by dismantling the Royalist Agency of Paris. Furthermore, Bonaparte refused to give reaction free rein: when Fontanes and his friends attacked the Institute and tried to reestablish the old French Academy, he thwarted them. It was not that the Institute remained as dear to his heart as it had been in the past, but even if the trend was carrying him toward monarchy, he wanted to move at his own rate, while reviving only the parts of the Old Regime that seemed to him useful. The French Academy was not one of them.[109]

On November 1, 1800, a pamphlet entitled *Parallèle entre César, Cromwell, Monck et Bonaparte* was published in which the question of the succession was raised publicly for the first time: "There are men who appear at certain times to found, destroy, or repair empires. Everything bends under their ascendancy.... Our revolution had up to this point given birth to events greater than the men.... It seemed to be impelled by some blind force that drove and overthrew everything in front of it. For ten years we have been seeking a firm and skillful hand

end, of course, and Saint-Julien was disavowed and arrested on his return to Vienna. The Austrians then proposed—perhaps in agreement with the British, who were trying to gain time and especially to bring the Russians back into the coalition—a general congress with which the British would be associated. Bonaparte, who did not want to take responsibility for a resumption of the war, pretended to accept and sent the diplomat Otto to London to inquire into British intentions. He had never believed that the mission could succeed. War was therefore once again on the agenda. Brune replaced Masséna in Italy.[121] In Germany, Moreau prepared to attack.

The fall of the Austrian chancellor, Thugut, who was succeeded by Ludwig von Cobenzl, the Austrian negotiator at Campoformio, deferred the resumption of hostilities. Less intransigent than his predecessor, he proposed a separate peace with the French on the condition that it remain secret until February 1, 1801, the date on which the agreement Vienna had signed with London expired. He went to Lunéville, where he met with Joseph Bonaparte, who then took him to Paris to speak with his brother. Nothing came of this conversation, however, except an ultimatum that the Austrian rejected.

Thiers's description of the second campaign of 1800 is so magisterial that it will suffice here to give a brief summary of it.[122] In particular, he gives an excellent explanation of why Bonaparte, who this time had no intention of going in person to the site of the fighting, divided his forces, not into two great masses—one in Germany, the other in Italy—as he was to do in 1805 and again in 1809, but instead into two main armies, Moreau's in Bavaria, and Brune's in Friuli, one of them supported by Augereau in Franconia and the other by Murat in central Italy, with Macdonald's corps occupying the Grisons and threatening both the Austrian and the Italian Tyrol. The double march on Vienna along the Danube and through Klagenfurt required an audacity he thought neither Moreau nor Brune possessed. Hence, it was better to adopt more traditional arrangements.

On November 28 Macdonald began the hostilities by invading the Italian Tyrol, while Moreau crossed the Isar and headed for the Inn. That is where the first skirmishes with Archduke John of Austria took place. The latter counterattacked with such spirit that Moreau, taken by surprise, preferred to have his troops take shelter in the dense forest of Hohenlinden. There he fought, on December 3, the greatest battle of his career and, Thiers adds, "surely one of the greatest of this century which has seen such extraordinary [battles]."[123] The Austrian defeat was disastrous: the archduke's army lost 20,000 men, its artillery, its baggage, "and, what was still more serious, all its morale."[124] Moreau crossed the Inn on December 9, and the Enns on the twenty-first, which put him within two days' march of Vienna. Refusing to humiliate the enemy by occupying his capital, he stopped. Archduke Charles, on whom the emperor had called for help, considered the war lost. On December 25 a new armistice was signed; it was complemented on January 15 by another signed with Brune in Italy. This time the war with Austria was over, and Bonaparte, it is said, jumped with joy on learning the news about the victory at Hohenlinden.[125]

This military triumph was enhanced by France's diplomatic successes: the discussions between Joseph and Cobenzl had resumed in Lunéville, and although no accord had yet been signed with the Russians, relations between the two countries were gradually improving. For Paul I, breaking with the coalition was easier than abandoning the Bourbons, of whom he had declared himself the protector; in the first case, it sufficed to invoke Russia's interest, whereas in the second he had to silence his own self-esteem. Thus, while receiving more than coolly General Dumouriez, Louis XVIII's envoy, he accepted the king's other ambassador, M. de Caraman. At the same time, he asked his ambassador in Berlin, Krüdener, to transmit his conditions to the French, and sent General Sprengporten to Paris to meet with the first consul and to take charge of eight thousand Russian prisoners of war whom the French government had decided to release.[126] The return of these prisoners, along with the proposal to cede to Russia the island of Malta—where General Vaubois was to capitulate on September 3—were a few of the "marks of respect" that Bonaparte wanted to give the czar to detach him completely from Britain.[127] With unalloyed satisfaction he received the news that Paul was going to embargo British vessels and merchandise.[128] Bonaparte received Sprengporten as soon as he arrived in Paris. The two men got along so well that the general had hardly left before Bonaparte wrote an enthusiastic letter to Paul proposing a formal alliance: "I desire to see the two most powerful nations in the world promptly and irrevocably united," he told him.[129] The czar was the first European sovereign to engage voluntarily in a rapprochement with a country that he detested as the creator of the Revolution, but Paul admired the leader that France had just given itself. Bonaparte was not completely deceived by these bursts of enthusiasm. To La Fayette, who was speaking to him about the czar's sudden passion, he replied: "That's true, and since we don't know how long it will last, we have to take advantage of it."[130] Yet his head was still somewhat turned, because it was in fact with Bonaparte, and not with France, that Paul, the son of Catherine the Great herself, was infatuated. After all, it was not the same as being admired by the French, that bunch of beggars Paul would not have considered fit to polish his shoes. There resides, perhaps, the enthusiasm with which Bonaparte was always to speak of the czar's "friendship" and the immense possibilities it contained.[131] Did Paul really intend to ally himself with revolutionary France, which in his heart of hearts he detested? In any case, he had approved a plan for partitioning the Ottoman Empire—another one—drawn up by his chancellor, Rostopchin, who planned to associate France, Prussia, and Austria in the operation.[132] In Paris, meanwhile, people were dreaming of a joint expedition of the Russian and French armies in the direction of British India.[133] Such plans were no more than talk at diplomatic negotiations that were to prove more difficult than suggested by the enthusiastic comments of Bonaparte, who had an interest in portraying rapid progress, or by the fits of enthusiasm manifested by the czar, whose unstable mind, Sorel tells us, moved without transition from "a pathological concern with minutiae" to "obscure abstractions."[134] In any event, Paul took an additional step by expelling the king's representative, Caraman. Louis XVIII understood immediately that his turn was next: on January 22, 1801, in fact, he received the order to leave his exile in the Latvian city of Mitau. He set out, along with his last loyal companions, for Warsaw, not knowing where he would find a new asylum, while an experienced Russian diplomat, Kolychev, headed for Paris.

Above all, the exactions made by the British navy on ships flying neutral flags had contributed to the rapprochement between Russia and France. Paul I had struck back by ordering the seizure of British cargos, and on December 16 he took the fatal step of forming with Sweden and Denmark the Second League of Armed Neutrality, which Prussia joined on the eighteenth. France did not belong but had just expressed support for the right of neutrality by signing the Treaty of Mortefontaine with the United States.[135] The birth of this representative coalition was obviously a first-rate asset in the conflict with Britain.

Brutus's Dagger

The consolidation of the consular regime led to a revival of the conspiracies that had succeeded one another ever since Bonaparte's accession to power. They were, in the end, the logical consequence of events: the more that authority was concentrated in the hands of a single person, the greater was the temptation for the regime's enemies to overthrow it by cutting off its head. During the Revolution, the idea of striking at the regime's heart by killing one of its main actors had indeed occurred to some people.[136] But it remained marginal: the Revolution had so many heads that it didn't have any at all. Cutting off one, a hundred, or a thousand would have no effect. Robespierre's execution marked a turning point and revived the old doctrine of tyrannicide. Bonaparte's conquest of power strengthened it further, both among the royalists, whose hopes he had not fulfilled, and among the most diehard Jacobins who saw in him nothing but a traitor, "a Caesar who ought to fall under the dagger of a Brutus."[137]

Hardly a month went by without some new conspiracy being talked about. One day it was men lying in wait on the road to Malmaison to kidnap him, the next there was a plan to make use of a tunnel to take control of the Tuileries palace, or to assassinate Bonaparte in the theater or during a public ceremony.[138] Jacobin or royalist plots fomented in Paris, or hatched by spies in England or Switzerland—it was bewildering. There were as many plots as there were historians, beginning with Ferrero, who doubted whether they were real and saw in them the result of police machinations intended to justify the restrictions that were slowly strangling most of the freedoms achieved by the Revolution.[139] One oft-cited case is the "daggers conspiracy." It is a rather banal story. A former soldier named Harel had become acquainted with a little group of bitter republicans, some of whom opposed the regime, and others Bonaparte; two of them, Giuseppe Ceracchi and Joseph Aréna, had known Bonaparte personally.[140] It all amounted to big talk in a cabaret, and nothing might have happened had Harel, who needed money, not informed on them to a war commissioner he knew, who passed the information on to Bourrienne.[141] When Bonaparte was told, he instructed Bourrienne to pay Harel and let things run their course. He wanted to put Fouché in a difficult position by using this conspiracy, which the minister knew nothing about—and for good reason—to prove that he had not been sufficiently vigilant. Encouraged by Harel, Ceracchi, Aréna, Demerville (Barère's former secretary),[142] Topino-Lebrun, and a few others gradually transformed themselves into conspirators and on October 10 they were caught as they were getting ready to assassinate Bonaparte, who knew exactly what was going to happen that night at the Opera.

However, the plots were not all fabricated or left to develop by the police. Less than a month after the "discovery" of the dagger conspiracy, Fouché's agents arrested another Jacobin, Chevalier, who was making a bomb in Meudon from which the royalists were later to take their inspiration in an attempt to kill Bonaparte on Rue Saint-Nicaise.[143]

Among the émigrés, Louis XVIII was almost the only person who still pretended to believe that Bonaparte might finally restore him to his throne. Hyde de Neuville and Cadoudal, who had met the first consul, did not think he was the kind of man who would so easily give up spoils won by hard fighting. The capitulation of the Vendée and the victory at Marengo had naturally led them, or at least Cadoudal, to consider a kidnapping or assassination. It is certain that these possibilities were discussed in high places, even in the entourage of the Count of Artois, toward whom all the hotheads turned after they had not received a warm welcome from Louis XVIII, who disdained vulgar plotting, as his royal blood required. Later on, in his conversations with James Fox, Bonaparte accused the British government of having fomented the attack on Rue Saint-Nicaise.[144] It is impossible to prove that the British were involved in this plot. But the idea was in the air. In 1798 British secret agents had planned to assassinate the members of the Directory; the attempt was not carried out because its instigator, James Talbot, who directed the "Swabian Agency," had been sharply reprimanded by Lord Grenville, who refused to allow the use of means contrary "to the sentiments of honor and humanity that befit a civilized nation."[145] For some émigrés, these scruples were irrelevant. Was Cadoudal, who had returned to Brittany, involved in the attack on December 24? He always denied it, explaining that he wanted to kidnap the first consul, not kill him or, a fortiori, innocent passersby.[146] However, one of Cadoudal's most fanatically devoted lieutenants, Saint-Réjeant, had no such hesitations. He traveled with his servant Carbon to Paris, where Fouché got wind of his arrival; but being familiar with going underground, Saint-Réjeant escaped the police and went to melt into the anonymity of the slums found in every large city. Was it there, thanks to contacts and meetings between people who shared the same resentments and the same hatreds, that he learned of the device being constructed by Chevalier and his accomplice Veycer? Saint-Réjeant seized the idea and on December 24 put it into action.[147]

That evening Bonaparte and Joséphine were going to the Opera, where Haydn's *Creation* was to be performed for the first time. On Rue Saint-Nicaise, Saint-Réjeant was waiting for Carbon to signal the arrival of the first consul's carriage before triggering the bomb. Suddenly, without having received the expected signal, he saw the carriage pass in front of him. He set off the explosion a few seconds too late, thanks to which Bonaparte, whose carriage was already turning the corner of Rue de Malte, was not killed.[148] Seven dead and about thirty wounded were reported.[149] Bonaparte refused to return to the Tuileries, and at the Opera he showed an impassive face, while the news of the assassination attempt was spreading all around him. But when he got back to the Tuileries, he exploded in anger. Fouché was there, of course, and Bonaparte's wrath fell on him. It was said that he was protecting the Jacobins, to whom Bonaparte had already attributed the responsibility for the explosion. Did Fouché retreat into a prudent silence, or did he allow himself to tell the first consul that he was mistaken, that the royalists had made the attack and that he would prove it?[150] Whatever his reaction was, Bonaparte had made up his mind: the remnants of Jacobinism were going to pay for this.[151] The Council of State immediately went to work. Because it was examining the proposal to create special tribunals to fight brigandage, it suggested adding two amendments to the text, one assigning these special courts to try those accused of crimes committed against members of the government, the other giving the consuls the power to banish from Paris individuals whose presence there was considered dangerous, or even to deport them if they tried to escape the order of banishment. Bonaparte opposed these changes on the ground that the punishments proposed were not severe enough:

> There are 400 to 500 men, either in Paris or scattered over France, steeped in crime, without home, without occupation, and without means. These men form an army in constant action against the

government. . . . They are the enemies of every form of order, no matter what its principles, of every liberal idea, of every kind of government. . . . This horde of hungry wolves scattered through the whole of society . . . keeps alive a constant state of terror. What must Europe think of a government under which such wolves live and flourish? What confidence can she have in a government that either does not know how or else is not able to protect its own capital?—a government under whose eyes an infernal plot that brings ruin and desolation on a portion of the inhabitants of that capital is carried out? It is impossible that these things can continue; it is time to rid society of this scourge; before five days have passed, 20 or 30 of these monsters must die, and 200 or 300 must be deported. As for me, I am ready to take upon myself all the weight and all the opprobrium in such a measure of public safety.[152]

When Truguet dared to say that there was no certainty regarding the identity of the guilty parties, Bonaparte outshouted him for more than half an hour, and then, furious, his voice hoarse, he declared the session closed and left, slamming the door behind him. The next day, December 27, it was Cambacérès who, with a very ecclesiastical unction, called together at his home the sections of the Council concerned with legislation and internal matters to ask them to revise their text and prepare one that authorized the government to expel from the territory, without trial, a certain number of brigands, and even to put to death those of them who were thought to be involved in the attack on Rue Saint-Nicaise. The Council was reluctant to be associated with this arbitrary act, and also to associate the assemblies with it: so it proposed to write an order that would be signed by the consuls alone. Bonaparte refused: the whole apparatus of the state, he said, had to be associated with this act of public safety. Was it Roederer who finally proposed resorting to the Senate, or was it Cambacérès, or Talleyrand?[153] It was decided that there would be no law, but only a simple order that the Senate would examine to decide that it was not contrary to the Constitution: "With the help of this expedient," Lanfrey comments, ". . . the Senate, the guardian of the Constitution, was going to be transformed into a veritable constituent power modifying at will the pact entrusted to its vigilance, and invested with the right to legalize all arbitrary acts."[154] The voting machine of the *sénatus-consultes* was now ready to go into action. Bonaparte himself wrote the order that was to be issued by the Council of State.[155] The Council made a last attempt to oppose the first consul's will. It had good reasons for hesitating: on December 30, Réal revealed that the police now had proof that the assassination attempt was the work of "*chouans* paid by England."[156] Roederer, though he was very close to Bonaparte, could not help but ask for explanations: What if, he asked, "the men affected by the proposed measure belonged to one party, and the guilty ones to the other party?"[157] Did that mean, Bonaparte retorted, that they would have to be spared on the pretext that they were innocent of this crime, whereas they had probably committed others or were preparing to do so?[158] Debate was closed, and Fouché was assigned to draw up the list of individuals to be deported.

The Senate, of course, did not put up the slightest resistance; on January 4, 1801, it pronounced the deportation of 130 suspects as a "measure to preserve the Constitution."[159] At the same time that these deportees were setting out for Nantes, whence they were to be transported to the Seychelles, heads fell: first, on January 11, those of Chevalier and Veycer, and then, on the sixteenth, that of a Jacobin named Metge, the author of a pamphlet entitled *Le Turc et le militaire français* calling for the assassination of the first consul, and finally, on the thirtieth, those of Joseph Aréna, Ceracchi, and their accomplices. The true perpetrators of the attack on Rue Saint-Nicaise had been arrested, Carbon first, Saint-Réjeant a little later.[160] The minister was triumphant: he went to Malmaison to show the records of the interrogations that proved that he had been right from the outset. But Bonaparte was no less satisfied: because there had been a royalist plot, he said, he had been able to take advantage of it to decapitate "the Jacobin general staff."[161] The benefit was twofold.

In the following weeks, however, the opposition to Bonaparte's crackdown appeared to be stronger than ever. The proposed law on special courts, which was finally adopted on February 7, 1801, met with a veritable outcry in the Tribunate.[162] Had these events not occurred, the creation of exceptional jurisdictions to cope with the scourge of brigandage might not have aroused so much opposition, but the consequences of the attempted assassination had reminded people of the dark days of the Terror. Ginguené denounced the return of the exceptional measures justified by the alleged circumstances. Constant, Daunou,

Chénier, and others echoed this denunciation, and after two weeks of debate the proposal was adopted by only 49 votes to 44. Even the Legislative Body, usually docile, resisted by approving the proposed law by *only* 192 votes to 88, an unprecedentedly small margin. Once again Bonaparte was furious. He threatened to govern without the assemblies, by decree, and to appeal to public opinion. After Ginguené's speech he cried: "These are twelve or fifteen metaphysicians fit to be drowned. They are vermin I have on my garments; but I will not allow myself to be attacked like Louis XVI; no, I will not put up with it!"[163]

He was, however, in no danger of being subjected to harassment by the assemblies as the monarchy had been at the beginning of the Revolution. The peace negotiations had been advancing rapidly, and the end of the war with Austria sheltered him, if not from assassination attempts, at least from any challenge or even any criticism. Joseph Bonaparte and Cobenzl had resumed their talks after Hohenlinden, and on December 31 the emperor authorized the Austrian minister to sign the peace treaty without further concern about the British. This was the end of the new coalition formed in 1799. If the break between Austria and Britain made peace virtually certain, the path leading there was still full of pitfalls. Bonaparte proved intransigent, forcing the Austrians to accept humiliating conditions.[164] A cool observer who had not been caught up in the momentum would probably have thought that the kind of peace Bonaparte wanted was unacceptable for the Austrians, and that the latter would sign it without having any more intention of respecting their commitments than they had at Campoformio. Joseph had tried to get his brother to accept a few amendments, particularly in favor of the grand duke of Tuscany, who was going to be deprived of his possessions without receiving any compensation. In vain. Cobenzl protested, but he was no longer as pugnacious as he had been in 1797. At that time he had not yet come to know Bonaparte; now he was negotiating with the feeling that there was nothing he could do. The treaty was signed on February 9. France expanded on the right bank of the Rhine, Austria officially recognized the French annexation of Belgium; in Italy, Tuscany became a possession of Parma, that is, of Spain; the Cisalpine Republic extended along the whole course of the Po, and Austria retreated behind the Adige and lost in addition the bishopric of Salzburg, which Bonaparte had marked out for the grand duke of Tuscany.[165] Finally, the princes who lost their possessions on the right bank of the Rhine had to be compensated in Germany, which clearly meant an enormous territorial upheaval in the German empire. Peace? It was a "peace on paper."[166] The conditions imposed on the vanquished amounted to canceling the benefit of the military victories won in 1800. Marengo and Hohenlinden had put an end to a nine-year-old conflict; consular diplomacy set the stage for another war, sooner or later.

Before Marengo, Bonaparte had declared that a victory would make him capable of doing whatever he wanted. The assassination attempt on December 24 was just as useful for him as the victory and the peace treaty. Whereas the latter confirmed his legitimacy, the former now allowed him a free hand: first because the twofold purge that followed it, aimed at the Jacobins and then royalists,[167] had eliminated any risk of conspiracy, and also because the creation of special tribunals and especially the revision of the Constitution to the benefit of the Senate gave him new ways of defeating opponents. The Consulate was being transformed into a "definitively provisional" dictatorship.[168] This "institutionalization" of the exception was, moreover, in the air at the time. From this point of view, the Consulate merely continued what had been begun by the Directory, which had not hesitated, starting in 1797, to generalize the use of exceptional means to put down its enemies and attack various scourges, of which brigandage was not the least serious.[169] But if the government gained control of the majority in the Senate, it would henceforth be able to escape all rules, to suspend them or change them by means of *sénatus-consultes* forced on a docile Senate, or even modify, by the same means, the form of the institutions themselves. The conspiracies of late 1800 paved the way for the Consulate for Life and the Empire:

> Recognizing that he had equally formidable enemies in the two extreme parties, the Royalists and the Terrorists, [Bonaparte] became persuaded that Supreme Power alone could save him from plots against his life, and the unexpected docility displayed by all the bodies of the State convinced him that thenceforth there was nothing he might not attempt with great probability of success. Not, however, that those bodies or the citizens were already prepared to confer on him the absolute Sovereignty which he acquired two years later; but the public imagination

was so deeply impressed with the idea that he was the necessary man, and so terrified at the abyss into which the nation must fall if he failed it, that no sacrifice was thought too costly to preserve a life on which the existence of France herself depended. Bonaparte was therefore greatly indebted to his enemies. By aiming at his life with the assassin's dagger they had revealed to him the secret of his strength, and enforced on him, so to speak, the necessity of exerting it.[170]

TWENTY-EIGHT

Peace with the Church

The day the peace treaty of Lunéville was signed, Bonaparte was in Picardy, where he had summoned the engineer Prony and five of his colleagues to examine on site the construction of the Saint-Quentin Canal.[1] The project was an old one: the decision to link navigation on the Seine and the Oise with that on the Somme and the Escaut went back to the reign of Louis XIV, but the financial and technical difficulties—two tunnels were necessary—had slowed the work. The Revolution had interrupted it. This abandoned project reflected the country's condition after a decade of turmoil. Chateaubriand left us a famous description of France as he found it on his return from exile in the spring of 1800. From Calais to Paris, he saw nothing but "dilapidated châteaus," "damaged perimeter walls," "abandoned churches," "bell towers without bells," "cemeteries without crosses." "One would have said that fire had passed through the villages, they were pitiful and half-demolished: everywhere there was mud and dirt, muck and ruins."[2] His forced exile in England had certainly made Chateaubriand more sensitive to the poverty that had already struck Arthur Young during his travels in France fifteen years earlier.[3] Chateaubriand was not much inclined to make an equitable assessment of revolutionary France, so his testimony would have little weight if it were not supported by the reports written in 1801 by the state councilors assigned by the new government to assess the state of the country.[4] What they saw was catastrophic. They wrote of anarchical, incompetent, corrupt administration; salaries, pensions, and wages paid irregularly or not at all; a disastrous judicial system; dilapidated schools; orphanages in which infant mortality approached 99 percent; roads full of potholes, canals silted in for lack of maintenance, ruined bridges, forests that had not been cared for, public buildings damaged and ransacked, and so on. Everywhere the marks left by the Revolution, civil war, and the invasion of 1793 were still visible; nothing had been repaired. A few additional details could be added to this picture: there was a shortage of money, a return to bartering, and, everywhere, the scourge of brigandage. No doubt the new regime inspired more confidence than its predecessor: it had not been inactive since it was established, but if it had not imposed peace on Austria, the benefits of the change in government would certainly have appeared doubtful. It was impossible to reduce poverty quickly, especially because the resumption of normal economic activity had not yet made itself felt.[5] Poverty did not decrease until 1802, when the return of growth made it possible to erase the last traces of the Revolution at the same time that it carried Bonaparte to the pinnacle of power.

The First Consul's Great Works

On the whole, the country looked as if it had been failed by the authorities, mismanaged, damaged, and generally impoverished.[6] The textile mills Bonaparte visited in Saint-Quentin could hardly have made any other impression on him. Did they really employ, before the Revolution, 70,000 workers who produced fifteen million francs' worth of fabric, most of which was intended for export? In one decade their activity had decreased by over 80 percent, a stagnation that Bonaparte attributed, not solely to a general decline in demand, but also to consumers' preference for English muslins.[7] In economics as in other domains, Bonaparte believed in the power of the will, especially because he may have divined behind the general poverty and dilapidation the existence of intact forces, the stimulation of which would suffice to change France quickly. Dean Paul, one of the Englishmen who hurried to France in 1802, put it this way: France was a century behind England in everything, but at the same time the people were of a gaiety unknown in his own country and displayed "an air of independence" that was found nowhere before 1789; the French were not a very attractive people, to be sure, but there was not one of them who did not consider himself "as a man of high importance."[8] The Revolution had passed through France, but had not left it entirely in ruins: Europe was soon to learn this at its own expense.

Bonaparte was not as ignorant in matters of finance and economics as has sometimes been said.[9] Although it is true that he was not very receptive to pleas like Mollien's in favor of the freedom of financial transactions, that was because he did not understand, and could not accept, that the stock exchange could serve interests other than those of the state.[10] He was nonetheless interested in economic questions and liked to talk about them with Mollien, Gaudin, or Chaptal. While feeling for businessmen a distrust bordering on aversion, he was aware how much foreign trade contributed to France's influence and power. In economics, as in everything else, he was primarily interested in political implications. Prosperity was the precondition for order and stability inside the country, and for power and domination abroad. He cared little about promoting the development of a society of citizens who were rich, hence egoistic, and hence soft—there was still a little Rousseau in his head—but he knew that to resume its rank in world affairs, France had to become rich again.

In most domains his ideas were those of the century in which he had been born. He did not like credit; he rejected—and on this point he never wavered— paper money, preferring a good, solid metallic money that inspired confidence.[11] As a good follower of the physiocrats, he ranked agriculture above industry, and industry above commerce. There was nothing original in all this. Like most French people, he had gotten his fingers burned by the Revolution's experiments and adventures; and again like them, he was a protectionist, fully convinced that there could be no power without industry, or industry without tariff protection.[12] By adhering to the enduring principles of protectionist politics that the Franco-British free-trade treaty of 1786 had put in question—leaving behind it very bad memories—Bonaparte was responding to the aspirations of many French people, but not all: the regime was never to be very popular in the port cities open to the world. On the other hand, he satisfied the demands of industrialists concerned above all about protection against English competition, which had the advantage of its technological head start, its sources of supply in raw materials, and its lower manufacturing costs.

Here we see the importance of Chaptal's appointment as minister of the interior, replacing the inept Lucien. Under the direction of the famous chemist, this ministry was about to gain a new weight. Chaptal had, unlike his predecessor, not only a taste for applying himself to complex problems and the competence necessary for dealing with them, but also ideas and a plan for a new industrial policy that immediately caught the first consul's attention. A physician and a chemist, Chaptal had made a name for himself before the Revolution, less by his own discoveries than by presenting to the public the recent discoveries that were then revolutionizing chemistry. He had conceived the policy that he was to implement later on. Distressed to note France's industrial backwardness and French industry's growing dependency on other countries for raw materials, and seeing how advances in chemistry could make it possible to find products to substitute for these materials that France did not have and to improve various manufacturing processes, he sought to "free [his] country from the onerous tribute it was paying to England and Holland."[13] In his view, science and politics were inseparable, or rather he saw in science a means of diminishing the French economy's dependence on its imports and of augmenting the competitiveness of its manufactured products on the international market.

By marrying a rich heiress from Montpellier, Chaptal had entered the powerful and closed circle of financiers and textile producers in Languedoc who, through men like Cambon, Cambacérès, and Ramel-Nogaret, played a crucial role during the Revolution.[14] In 1801 it fell to Chaptal to embody one of the great "parties" that since the early eighteenth century had been trying to impose their views on how to ensure French power. There were three such parties. The first relied on the alliance with "Spain, which provided money, America, whose tobacco and sugar were predominant in Europe [and] the Netherlands, which were better organized from the point of view of banking," a system of alliance that France had tried to set up at the beginning of the eighteenth century. The second, championed by Necker, wanted "above all peace with Britain [and] free trade on all the seas." The third essentially represented the interests of the textile industry, which was "threatened by the progress of the British industrial revolution": it agreed "to import, if necessary, raw materials (Indian white cotton goods, for example), but on condition of reserving dyeing and processing for itself: [it] preferred to manufacture locally and export finished products. . . . [It] was protectionist and even aspired to autarky."[15] Textiles from Montpellier occupied a key position for this third party. Two men represented successively the policy it advocated: Cambon under the Convention and Chaptal under the Consulate. Chaptal, whose ideas associated the conquest of independence with the conquest of power, could not fail to please Bonaparte, and though relations between the two men had their ups and downs, right to the end he remained the economic counselor to whom the emperor listened most.

The resumption of work on the Saint-Quentin canal was, along with the launching of other large construction projects, one of the first results of this collaboration.[16] Naturally these great public works were not by themselves sufficient to reactivate economic activity, but as Thiers rightly points out, "in public evils there are always a real evil and an imaginary evil, the one contributing to render the other insupportable." He adds: "It is a great point gained to do away with the imaginary evil; for you diminish the sense of the real evil and inspire him who has to endure it with the patience to await the cure."[17] Even if confidence was not as great as it is sometimes imagined to have been— the personalization of the regime increased questions about its future and duration—the efforts of the new government and its leader, the victories, the end of the civil war, and the first measures to restore order everywhere, presented such a striking contrast with the impotence of its predecessor that the majority surely did not wish to see the first consul retire. This was all the more true because France, which was slowly moving away from the revolutionary shore, was now approaching lands that were in many respects unknown.

A Society in Preparation

At this point everything was disconcerting: a new society was taking form that was neither what the eldest remembered nor what the revolutionaries had dreamed of, nor even the product of their juxtaposition that the increasingly massive return of the émigrés might have provoked.[18] It was something else, the result of an improbable hybridization that Chateaubriand described as a "bizarre hodgepodge":

> Disguising themselves by mutual agreement, a large number of people became persons they were not: each one wore his pseudonym or borrowed name hung about his neck. . . . One was supposed to be Italian or Spanish, another Prussian or Dutch: I was Swiss. The mother passed for her son's aunt, the father for his daughter's uncle; the owner of a

property was only its manager. This movement reminded me, in a contrary sense, of the movement of 1789, when monks and religious left their cloisters and the old society was invaded by the new: the latter, after it replaced the former, was replaced in its turn. Meanwhile the ordered world was beginning to be reborn. . . . The old republican generations that were retreating were distinguished from the imperial generations that were advancing. Generals who had been conscripted, poor, speaking roughly, with severe faces, and who, from all their campaigns had brought back nothing but wounds and tattered clothes, passed by officers wearing the brilliantly gilded uniforms of the consular army. The émigré who had returned chatted peacefully with the assassins of a few of his close relations. . . . Men who had participated in the September massacres, having changed their names and their neighborhoods, had become merchants hawking baked apples on street corners; but they were often forced to clear off because the people, who recognized them, overturned their stalls and tried to beat them up. Revolutionaries who had grown rich began to move into the great town houses they had bought in the Faubourg Saint-Germain. On their way to becoming barons and counts, the Jacobins spoke of nothing but the horrors of 1793, the necessity of chastising the proletarians and repressing the excesses of the populace. . . . Amid all this there emerged a vigorous generation sown in blood that would henceforth shed only the blood of foreigners: day by day, the metamorphosis of republicans into imperialists and from the tyranny of all to the despotism of a single man was being carried out.[19]

On reading this page we see why as soon as he returned from Italy Bonaparte launched other great projects—political and juridical this time—intended to shape this new world, define the relations among its members, impose rules on it, and subject it to laws that could transform this legacy of the Revolution into a viable and ordered community. The creation of the commission entrusted with drawing up a proposed civil law code was contemporary with the first work on the reform of the public education system inherited from the Directory, with discussions about the establishment of the "lists of notability" foreseen by the

Constitution of Year VIII, and the opening of negotiations with Rome. The first consul had firmly laid out the route to be followed in matters of reform by declaring before the Council of State that: "We have finished with the romance of the Revolution: now we have to begin its history, seeing only what is real and possible in the application of the principles, and not what is speculative and hypothetical. To follow a different path today would be to philosophize and not to govern."[20] What was true for civil law was also true for religious affairs, the thorniest of all problems.

The religious revival, in which Fontanes and his friends rejoiced and that Chateaubriand's *Atala* and then his *Génie du christianisme* were soon to consecrate in literary form, was manifest long before 18 Brumaire. It had begun as early as 1794, in the middle of the Terror, after Robespierre, having put an end to Christianity, established the cult of the Supreme Being. This civil religion, which was more or less inspired by Rousseau but smelled strongly of Catholicism, had appeared to many people to foreshadow an imminent religious restoration, God implying worship and worship that there would be priests. Repression let up after 9 Thermidor, and this was enough to elicit aspirations that were all the more fervent for having been so long and so harshly restrained. The clandestine life to which the Catholic Church had been condemned for three years—clandestine because it was not, of course, to the priests who had sworn loyalty to the Civil Constitution of the Clergy that the faithful turned—had not been without its effects. It had taken the community of the faithful back to the time of the catacombs. The persecutions revived a faith that had become, as is well known, no more than lukewarm by the eve of the Revolution: oppression had turned into fervent believers many who had been Catholics by tradition more than by conviction. Chateaubriand, Mathieu de Montmorency, Fontanes, and La Harpe illustrate these conversions to a Catholicism that was all the more eager to reclaim souls because it was new and, in truth, less orthodox. These revitalized Catholics, however, faced opponents who retained a certain fervor of their own; passion had not entirely deserted the revolutionary camp, where some proved all the more attached to the battle against obscurantism and superstition because it was about all that remained of the great hopes of 1789. The return of the émigrés and the priests also created multiple opportunities for conflict. One side wanted to bring God back to the nation that had long been "heaven's most favored," while the other sought to defend to the last breath achievements that they saw as the legacy of the Enlightenment or as the welcome outcome of a secular Gallican politics.

The Heritage

It would be an exaggeration to claim that with regard to religion the Constituent Assembly merely followed a furrow the monarchy had plowed long before. But it would be no less an exaggeration to see in the Civil Constitution of the Clergy of 1790 an effort to break with Catholicism. For the most part, the representatives in the Constituent Assembly were Christians in the way people tended to be Christians at the time. Their intention was not to weaken dogma: they believed in the social utility of religion and, confirming Catholicism's status as the state religion, they had even refused to include the principle of the freedom of religion in the 1789 declaration of rights. However, faithful to the Gallican tradition that insisted the nation play a role in religious affairs, they intended to place everything that had to do with the Church's "discipline" under the control of the state. They were inspired less by the policies of the French monarchy, which had been consecrated by the Concordat of 1516 and the Gallican Declaration of 1682, than by the policy pursued in Austria, Germany, and the Habsburgs' Italian possessions by the man who reigned in Vienna at the time, Emperor Joseph II. Like him, they wanted to nationalize the Church, not religion. They considered the Church as exercising, in its spiritual mission, social functions that had to do with what was called the "police of the kingdom." It seemed to them legitimate that the state, on which the Church depended for everything that did not concern the government of souls, assure itself of the Church's fidelity and prevent it from constituting itself as an independent power, as its association with Rome gave it a tendency to do. The expulsion of the Jesuits, the war declared on monastic orders, the oath of loyalty demanded of priests—Joseph II had already gone a long way down that road.[21] But even though Joseph had as his councilors philosophers who were little inclined to moderation toward Rome, he had always cooperated with the clergy, who, not being at all hostile to imperial policy, were in a good strategic position to moderate it.

In 1789 and 1790, circumstances were different in France: the episcopacy had put itself out of the game altogether by opposing the common meeting of the three estates in May and June 1789. Thus, religious reform was planned almost exclusively by Gallican jurists with almost no input or interference from the clergy.

This reform, which had moreover been made inevitable by the nationalization of the clergy's property and the prohibition on monastic vows, consisted in the almost complete integration of the Church into the system of public offices. Dioceses were redistributed to make them coincide with departments; the clergy were put on the national payroll and at the same time required to make an oath of loyalty and recruited under the same rules as other agents of the state: parish priests would be elected for five years, bishops for fifteen. But the members of the Constituent Assembly, carried away by the certainty that no principle could prevail over the sovereignty of which they were jealous guardians, had crossed a line that Joseph would never have crossed: priests and bishops would be elected by a body of voters that included Protestants and Jews by virtue of the laws of emancipation dating from December 1789 and January 1790. As for the pope, he was deprived of a power that no Catholic nation had ever denied him: the power to appoint bishops. Henceforth, parish priests would receive their investiture from their bishop and the latter from a metropolitan or, if necessary, from another bishop.

The stubbornness of the members of the Constituent Assembly and the intrigues of Cardinal Bernis, the French ambassador to the pope, and of prelates who had emigrated in 1789, no doubt contributed to the failure of the talks with the Roman Curia, as did the specifically theological implications of the law, which had the greatest influence on the pope's decision. Temporal questions played their part too—not least the fate of the papal possession of Avignon, though this was certainly secondary in the pope's decision on March 10, 1791, to condemn the Civil Constitution and in the refusal of at least half of French ecclesiastics to swear the oath demanded by the Constituent Assembly.[22]

The new church, called "constitutional," never really took root, especially because in 1793 it was itself persecuted, its ministers harassed, its places of worship closed, and its—rare—worshippers scattered. After the end of the Terror, the Thermidorian government, which knew that the Constituent Assembly's religious policy had led to numerous disorders and sufferings, decided to turn over a new leaf: the Civil Constitution was abrogated and replaced by a system of separation between church and state. However, there was no question of proclaiming the religious neutrality of the state. The regime was resigned to the resumption of worship only because of the failure of de-Christianization in 1793, but would insist that it be narrowly restricted and closely monitored. Separation meant above all that priests would be left to their own resources and would receive no further subsidy from the state. The Thermidorians hoped in this way to obtain by impoverishment what the de-Christianizers of 1793 had not been able to obtain by violence: the triumph of Reason, whose worship they entrusted at the same time to a new church, that of the "theophilanthropes," which failed to recruit any more believers than the mass celebrated by priests who had sworn the oath in 1791 or 1792, or the festivals dedicated to the goddess Reason in 1793.

Only through an abuse of language could the Directory's religious policy be seen as an initial attempt at separation, Albert Mathiez even going so far as to speak, apropos of the years 1795–1801, of "seven years of liberty and tolerance" in the domain of religion.[23] The regime's experiment with separation took place later on: it began with the first measures of pacification taken by the provisional Consulate in the last days of 1799, when several decrees restored to religion the churches that had not been sold, authorized a free choice between *décadi* and *dimanche* (Sunday), and above all replaced the oath still required of priests with a simple promise of "fidelity to the constitution."[24] From that moment on, Jules Lanfrey said, "the legal condition of France" was a system of "full and complete freedom of religion."[25] And he goes on to express surprise that Bonaparte did not stop there. Why did Bonaparte think he had to come to an understanding with Rome? The system of separation, accompanied by a complete freedom, kept the various religions from having any political influence and, in exchange, left them unlimited latitude to regain a moral influence whose impact must not be exaggerated, according to the same author. If there was a religious renaissance, it was more mundane than social and led by men, Fontanes and Chateaubriand at their head, whose faith was vacillating, to say the least.[26] Why, under these conditions, did Bonaparte take the risk of a new marriage with Rome, which awakened in the Church "dormant ambitions" and "desires he could not and would not satisfy"?[27]

nations and lead the pope to break with Louis XVIII and the royalists. "Is nothing, then, to oblige the pope and the clergy to declare themselves opposed to the Bourbons' legitimacy?"[48] he asked La Fayette, who also grimaced at the idea of an entente with Rome.

He had decided what he was going to do. "What will it take to pacify the Church of France?" he had asked. "One decisive step: the resignation of all the bishops. All the sees have to be declared vacant; instead of these émigré prelates who are constantly conspiring on behalf of the royalty in their dioceses, I name bishops who are devoted to the new order, and I have the pope give them bulls."[49] As for the rest, he had no intention of putting in question the principle of religious freedom, the closure of the convents, or, of course, the sales of ecclesiastical property.

Bonaparte knew that his task would not be easy. He would have to reckon not only with the remains of the constitutional clergy but also with his own supporters, the majority of whom were all the more attached to the Revolution's religious policy because they had repudiated, one after the other, almost all of its other ideals. In addition he would have to reckon with Rome, where the prelates who favored a restoration of the monarchy or who supported Austria were not inactive. It cannot be too strongly emphasized how much audacity the first consul showed by pursuing, almost alone, a path that he would certainly not have taken had he been thinking solely of his immediate interests. Both the political group that emerged from the Revolution and the one associated with the Institute—which was dominated, as Barante says, by "sensationalist philosophy"—opposed any accord with Rome, and tended to discourage Bonaparte from embarking upon a project in which he had little to gain and that might cost him many of his supporters.[50] Wouldn't it have been easier to let things run their course and rely on the police to deal with the disorders that the prevailing anarchy could not fail to provoke? Of all the achievements of the consular government, the concordat is undoubtedly the most notable. The Civil Code was in the air, but the concordat collided with many prejudices, especially among the establishment. It took great wisdom to recognize how essential religious peace was in order to emerge from perpetual revolution, and it took a still greater will to transform this idea into action.[51]

The First Milestones

Of the three obstacles we have mentioned, the last was the least difficult to surmount. The papacy's situation was not promising: Pius VI had lost his papal states, which had been transformed into an ephemeral Roman Republic, and then he had been exiled in France, where he had just died. Once the French were driven out of the Eternal City, the Neapolitans had established themselves there, and when the French subsequently had to evacuate the three papal legations of Bologna, Ferrara, and Ravenna, the Austrians had taken possession of them. That was not all. The Spaniards were now seeking to impose on the pope a concordat compared to which the one proposed by Bonaparte looked almost lenient.[52] Thus, the cardinals who gathered in Venice in March 1800 to choose a successor to Pius VI met in full disarray. After many hesitations, the conclave was unable to assemble a majority of votes in favor of any of the leading candidates. It finally chose unanimously the bishop of Imola, Barnaba Chiaramonti, whose fragile health made him a priori a transitional pope. Even if Chiaramonti, who remained loyal to Roman policy, hastened to announce his election—under the name of Pius VII—to Louis XVIII,[53] the French republicans and their supporters in Italy still had a few reasons to be happy about this choice. The new pope, after all, exhorted the peoples of the territories incorporated into the Cisalpine Republic to submit, explaining to them that the republic and democracy were not necessarily contrary to the teachings of the Gospels.[54] And as if he had wanted to show that he expected a great deal from the new French government and from the "very extraordinary young man" who presided over it, Pius VII announced his intention to return to Rome and his desire to see the Neapolitans evacuate his capital.[55] He had just left Venice when Bonaparte won the victory at Marengo.

The first consul hastened to pave the way for the future concordat by convoking an assembly of Milan's priests. He delivered a veritable Catholic confession of faith, asserting that the Roman Catholic religion was the "anchor" that held back from the edge of the abyss modern societies, which were always threatened by the clash of interests and passions, and that no other religion could compare with it from this point of view or lent itself more naturally to the establishment of a republican government. Dismissing out of hand the theories of "modern philosophers" and firmly condemning the Directory's anticlerical policy, he declared that he wanted to reestablish Catholicism on its old footing, said that he took pleasure in the religious revival in France, and ended by expressing his desire to soon "talk with the new pope."[56]

The bishop of Verceil, Monsignor Martiniana, who was a friend of Pius VIII, served as an intermediary; Bonaparte met with him before he left Italy. He is supposed to have more or less repeated what he told the Lombard priests. In any case, Martiniana thought that the first consul was disposed not only to reestablish the Catholic religion in France, but also to put the Church on its former footing. Was it going to recover, after a decade of persecutions, part of its property and its status as the state religion or, as it was phrased, the "dominant religion"?[57] On that day Bonaparte made use of all his talents as an actor, promising more than he could or would do. The important thing was to entice the pope. Martiniana was enthusiastic:

> His intentions seemed to me definitely sincere; I base this . . . on his promise, if he is successful, to use all his power to ensure that the Holy See recovers all its States. He would like to make a *tabula rasa* of the Gallican Church. According to him, the bishops who have emigrated are no longer suitable for France, because for the most part they are said to have left, not because of pure zeal for religion, but because of temporal views and interests. As for the interloping bishops, he does not want to hear anything about them. It seems to him that the new bishops must be chosen by the authority that will exercise sovereignty in the nation, and that they must be canonically instituted, receiving from the Holy See their mission and bulls. In addition, because for so many years of revolution there has been a total alienation of the property owned by the Gallican Church, and because getting it back would be absolutely impossible, these bishops [would] receive a small temporary share allocated from the national finances.[58]

If Pius VII responded favorably to the bishop of Verceil's report, he prudently abstained from committing himself too much.[59] Prepared to make great sacrifices, he was nonetheless reluctant to depose the old bishops who had preferred exile to a "schismatic" oath. Nor did he want to make a hasty decision at a time when Bonaparte's troops, having won at Marengo, were spreading through Italy, retaking possession of the legations and even threatening to march on Rome to drive out the Neapolitans. And if the French really wanted to sign a new concordat, wasn't there some way to make them pay for it by giving back the legations? The Curia, informed of the first consul's proposals, proved no less prudent than the pope. It even stipulated new conditions, rejecting any forced deposition of bishops, refusing to recognize the confiscation of ecclesiastical property, and asking the question, which had not been raised with Verceil, of the status of the Catholic religion in France and of the Catholicity of the French government. Moreover, it was on the basis of the reply given to this latter question that the pope's envoy in Paris, the archbishop of Corinth, Monsignor Spina, was to determine his own responses.[60] It was understood, moreover, that he would not sign anything without having previously referred it to Rome.[61]

Bonaparte had also chosen his own representative: the Abbé Bernier, whom we have already seen at work in the Vendée. Bonaparte had understood that as a defector from the rebellion and as a flexible, redoubtably intelligent man who had sincerely rallied to the regime, from which he expected honors that neither his parish nor services rendered to the Bourbons would have won him, this "scoundrel" was an ideal intermediary to rely on.[62] This was especially so because, though he did not want to keep Talleyrand out of the discussions, he could not rely exclusively on the former bishop of Autun, who in addition to having the disadvantage of having been excommunicated, was thought in Rome to be the person mainly responsible for the schism of 1791.

Delicate Negotiations

The talks advanced slowly.[63] The blame for this resided not solely in the instructions given Spina, who arrived in Paris on November 6, but also in real divergences that Bonaparte, in a hurry to conclude a concordat, had perhaps underestimated. The archbishop, who was prepared to accept a reduction in the number of dioceses, began by opposing the rigorous steps the pope was supposed to take against bishops who refused to resign. The sovereign pontiff, he emphasized, did not have the power to depose a bishop unless the latter had committed a very serious crime proven by a court judgment. Were the prelates who had remained faithful to their religion criminals? The new concordat's clauses thus could be applied only to sees that had been declared vacant, and although Spina agreed that the new bishops would be named by Bonaparte, he refused to allow him to choose the members of the constitutional Church. Furthermore, even this power of nomination was a problem: Spina was willing to believe that the first consul was a professed Catholic, but what about his successors? If Bonaparte wanted to exercise the rights conferred on Francis I in 1517, he had to proclaim Catholicism the "state religion." Bernier resisted, argued, disputed, notes being added to notes, proposals succeeding reservations; it was a discussion between priests accustomed to squabbling, and Bonaparte, though he was furious about the exasperating slowness of the negotiations, abstained from getting involved. But he was annoyed to see time passing without anything concrete being achieved. Austria had been put out of action at Hohenlinden, and a peace treaty was no longer a wild dream. Thus, he had to hurry and proclaim the reestablishment of peace on the continent at the same time as religious peace. Bernier had finally scored some points: Spina agreed to replace all the bishops, and as the Italian still rejected the demand that the pope depose the recalcitrant bishops, it had been decided that "the former bishops who had not been reelected by the government in agreement with the Holy See [would be] considered to have resigned." But something had to be given in exchange, and Bernier, while rejecting any demand aimed at restituting ecclesiastical property, promised the reestablishment of Catholicism as the state religion. The end of the year 1800 was approaching. Bernier said he was confident that the negotiations would be concluded.[64] But they were to continue for a long time yet. At the moment when Abbé Bernier thought the conclusion near, the situation grew more tense. Talleyrand had intervened to rewrite the text that had so laboriously been worked out, replacing in particular the expressions "dominant religion" and "national and dominant religion" by a formula he considered more compatible with the spirit of the Revolution: Catholicism would be declared "the religion of the majority of the citizens"; and it was in the same spirit that he extended to the constitutional bishops the papal exhortation to resign that was supposed to be addressed only to bishops who had remained loyal to Rome. After all, the

This is playacting, to be sure. Bonaparte wanted to conclude the negotiations at least as much as Pius VII did; but he wanted to conclude them rapidly. Not only did Roman dilatoriness exasperate him, but he now accorded increased importance to the treaty. He hoped it would not only put an end to religious disputes in France but also consolidate his position in Europe right at a time when it had been suddenly compromised.

Diplomatic and Military Reverses

Bonaparte's position had never been as favorable as it was at the moment he signed the Peace of Lunéville with Austria, on February 9, 1801. The time of coalitions that united almost all of Europe against revolutionary France seemed far away; now it was Britain's turn to be threatened by diplomatic isolation. It could now count on only three allies, the kingdom of Naples, Portugal, and the Ottoman Empire.

As for Naples, its fate was soon settled.[78] Portugal was next to find itself on the hot seat. In Madrid, Manuel Godoy's return to government had been followed by a change in policy. Whereas in 1798 the Prince of Peace had refused to support a second French intervention in Portugal, he now proved willing, but on the condition that Portugal would gain rewards proportionate to its sacrifice. The queen, who trusted him and no one else, besieged her virtuous husband, who felt a little reluctant to strike his cousins the Braganzas, especially if it was a matter not only of forcing them to break with the English but, as he had reason to fear, of permanently weakening the Portuguese kingdom.[79] Lucien Bonaparte, who had just succeeded Alquier as ambassador, had a proposal to make, secretly conveyed to him from Paris: instead of transforming the old duchy of Parma into a kingdom that at the duke's death would revert to Prince Louis of Parma and to Crown Princess Marie-Louise, France would cede them Tuscany, which the Habsburgs had just lost by the Treaty of Lunéville.[80] As the kingdom of Etruria, Lucien said, it would considerably enlarge the house of Bourbon's influence in Italy. The first consul was so concerned about Spanish "lethargy" that he was even prepared to go further by giving the Spanish Bourbons the kingdom of Naples, if Tuscany did not seem to them sufficient.[81] This bargaining went on for almost three months. Then, on January 24, 1801, the Convention of Madrid endorsed the plan for a joint offensive against Portugal, and on March 18 the Treaty of Aranjuez confirmed the agreement on Tuscany. Godoy, convinced that he had made a good deal, had in reality been duped. In fact, the territorial enlargement of the duchy of Parma and its erection into a kingdom would have constituted a genuine manifestation of friendship with Spain. Instead Bonaparte seemed to be giving alms to his allies by ceding to them a brand-new kingdom created with his own hands out of the remains of the Austrian possessions, and to be taking advantage of this exchange to seize Parma for France.[82] This humiliating gift says a great deal about the respect that Bonaparte professed for the Spanish monarchy. But Godoy was no less wily than his ally. Hoping to carve out a principality in Portugal for himself by aiding the French, he did not intend to help them to the point of breaking all contact with the English. He sought to get himself named generalissimo of the Spanish army, and without waiting for the French contingent commanded by General Gouvion-Saint-Cyr to arrive, he marched on the Tagus. When he arrived on the banks of the river on May 16, he attacked the Portuguese forces without encountering any serious resistance; the next day, May 18, he reached Elvas and that same evening received a request for an armistice: the war was over. Spanish and Portuguese sovereigns, the ministers of the two countries, and ambassadors—Lucien was one of them—met at Badajoz, where a treaty was signed on June 6 that infuriated Bonaparte. Portugal, instead of ceding a fourth of its population to serve as a guarantee of Britain's restitution of Malta, Minorca, and Trinidad, as had been agreed in Madrid in January, sacrificed only the province of Olivenza and promised to close its ports to British ships.[83] "Rosewater diplomacy!" Napoleon cried.[84] When he refused to sign the treaty, instead ordering his troops to occupy Porto and even threatening to dethrone the Spanish Bourbons if they dared to oppose his will, Lucien reacted angrily.[85] It has to be said that because Lucien had received twenty paintings and 100,000 écus for his role in the cession of Tuscany, Spain's interests had become very important to him. He resigned, then helped renegotiate the treaty, which in the end was only slightly amended.[86] Lucien's discovery, on his arrival in Madrid, of "the abjection of all these grand people" was long past: he now refused to lend his hand to his brother's aggressive diplomacy, which was so humiliating for "a court that is a sincere friend of France" and of which he had become the most ardent defender.[87] When he left the Spanish capital a few months later, he did not leave empty-handed: he carried off in his baggage, it was said, "a collection of little sacks of uncut diamonds from Brazil and a portrait of Charles IV whose frame was made of rolls of paper full of diamonds."[88]

Let us return to the spring of 1801: Europe was in the process of closing itself to the British. Perhaps Bonaparte would have gone still further had he not been obliged to be careful not to offend the emperor of Russia. That is why he had granted the king of Naples rather lenient peace terms and refused to decide the fate of Piedmont occupied by his troops. He must have been concerned that Paul would proclaim himself the protector of the two dynasties and the guarantor of the integrity of their states.

While all this was going on, talks with the Russians were being pursued in Paris. The first consul hoped they would lead to a formal alliance. The czar's new representative, Stepan Kolychev, was cooler toward the first consul than was his master during his moments of enthusiasm. He arrived in Paris with negative prejudices, and refusing to be taken in by appearances, never ceased pointing out that this regime was no more solid than those that had preceded. Moreover, he said, its leader was inclined, by self-interest and by passion, to wars and conquests that would never end: out of self-interest, because peace would bring back to France armies that were too accustomed to war to adjust to peace and were commanded by ambitious, jealous officers; out of passion, because far from asking Russia for its help in pacifying Europe, Bonaparte wanted its help to set the whole world afire. "There is no sincerity in the rapprochement between France and Russia," he concluded.[89]

The talks were not easy,[90] but they were moving forward, and this intense diplomatic activity was not good news for the British. Their increasing isolation was accompanied by internal difficulties that arose in part from the increasingly elevated cost of this endless war. William Pitt knew he could not long oppose the general wish for peace, and he wished to acquiesce to the demand all the more because he did not believe it possible to put together a new coalition, given the current state of Europe. Britain's allies were defecting one after another. Everywhere, people were tired of war. Fearing that he would end up with a minority in Parliament, Pitt decided to make the first move: he preferred to go down on a question of domestic policy—the bill in favor of religious emancipation intended to complete the Act of Union with Ireland.[91] That would be less likely to jeopardize his chances of an eventual return to government when the war with France, which he was sure was far from over, would return to the agenda. It was also a way for him to prepare his succession and keep control over the new cabinet. On February 8—the day before the signature of the Peace of Lunéville—he resigned, leaving his office to Addington and Hawkesbury, who, after watching developments for a month, informed the French minister, Otto, that they were prepared to begin talks. But Britain had not had its last word, and if there were to be negotiations, it intended to begin them from a position of strength. At the very time that Addington's ministry was advertising his desire to break with the diehard belligerency of his predecessor, he was attacking on two fronts: Egypt, where he hoped to finish driving the French out of the Mediterranean (they had lost Malta in September 1800), and the Second League of Armed Neutrality, where he sought to open a breach on the continent.

In the Mediterranean, a new French expedition intended to rescue Egypt— where Menou had recently succeeded Kléber—had just failed. Admiral Ganteaume was no more successful than his predecessor, Bruix, and the Spanish no more cooperative.[92] In the meantime the British had landed on the coasts of Egypt. On March 21, at Canopus, the battle had turned to the advantage of the invader, and Menou had found himself once again blockaded in Alexandria. Belliard succeeded in holding on for a few more weeks in Cairo before surrendering on June 27. In Alexandria, Menou had not yet capitulated, but it was only a question of weeks, or days. This time the adventure was truly over.[93] Menou has often been reproached for his incompetence, his lack of firmness, his conceit. Bonaparte protected him against everyone and everything because, it was said, Menou had never expressed the slightest criticism of any of his former boss's initiatives.[94] In private the first consul was less kind; he willingly admitted that Menou, though no doubt fit to administer a province or even a colony in peacetime, was not at all fit to cope with an invasion: "Our friend Menou," he said with fatalism, "has done many foolish things."[95] But for all that, he did not speak of having him shot, something he had expressed the desire to do to Kléber as a punishment for his "betrayal." Although Bonaparte was a good judge of character, he also had blind spots and a singular indulgence for the incompetent or treacherous. He said to Menou when the latter returned to France: "You've done all that could be expected of a man of courage and experience; your misfortunes were assuredly great; but they have not lowered my opinion of you."[96] There is nothing more stupefying than the casual way Bonaparte consoled himself for the loss of Egypt, even if he told Thibaudeau a few weeks later: "We will return there someday."[97] Egypt and the Mediterranean had been central to his preoccupations ever since the first campaign in Italy. He had reacted the same way in 1800 when he learned of the agreement Kléber had made with the British. Was it because he had long known that the enterprise was doomed, or because he guessed that the loss of Egypt, after that of Italy, was going to remove the last obstacles to the signature of a treaty with Britain?

The British government had been doing everything it could to amass the maximum number of pledges before the talks opened. As its soldiers were winning the Battle of Canopus, it was also delivering an ultimatum to the Danes insisting that they leave the Second League of Armed Neutrality. On March 28, when a British fleet bombarded Copenhagen, thereby causing the breakup of the League, the Russian emperor had been dead for four days.[98] Was his assassination inspired, if not backed, by London? Bonaparte was immediately convinced that it was, and remained so:[99] "The English missed me on 3 Nivôse," he said, "they didn't miss me in Petersburg!"[100] No one has ever been able to prove that Britain was directly implicated in the czar's assassination.[101] Was it just a fortunate coincidence? That is the most probable hypothesis: Paul fell victim to a banal conspiracy in a system in which, as Voltaire put it, despotism was tempered by assassination, in this case an assassination plotted by nobles with the help of Paul's own son and successor, Tsarevich Alexander. Bonaparte heard the news on April 12.[102] He was all the more appalled by the "attack of apoplexy" that Paul had suffered, as he said in his letters, underlining these words,[103] because the difficulty of the discussions with Kolychev did not in any way prevent him from already seeing "England blockaded, the continent formed into a coalition against it, Europe divided between himself and the czar, and the czar, mad and magnificent, led by him like an enfant terrible whom one entertains with shadow figures, amuses with phantasmagorias, busies with toys, and puts to sleep with fairy tales."[104] Virtually everything now had to be redone, especially because, just as Bonaparte learned of the czar's death, he received news of the defeat in

Canopus, which no longer left any doubt concerning the outcome of the Egyptian venture.

A few weeks later the future royal couple of Etruria visited France on their way to take possession of their kingdom, which made it possible to throw a veil over the sudden turnaround in the international situation. There were dinners, theatrical performances, and operas to which these two degenerates had to be taken, the heir to Parma who didn't know what to say in reply to the questions asked of him and his ugly wife, who was hunchbacked and lame—but a good mother and a nice woman, according to Bonaparte's valet Constant. It was a sad image of a Spanish monarchy that remained, in the end, France's most reliable ally.[105] However, Bonaparte was not unhappy to have to appear alongside this awkward couple, who hardly magnified the image of the Bourbons: "You see that these are princes who have issued from an old family," he told several of his ministers. "How can the government of peoples be entrusted to them? Moreover, it is not a bad thing to have been able to show the French this sample of the Bourbons. They can judge whether these old dynasties are up to coping with the difficulties of a century like ours."[106] The signature of the concordat with Pius VII became all the more urgent to improve the balance sheet of this not very encouraging diplomatic season, even if the disappointment of French ambitions in the Mediterranean was going to pave the way for a peace that was no less desired in Britain than in France.

Consalvi in Paris

Cacault had communicated Bonaparte's ultimatum on May 29. The pope and the cardinals, meeting together to examine the French proposals, were not impressed. The cardinals held firm, refusing to make any new concessions. "We are obliged to tell you," Pius VII wrote to Bonaparte, ". . . that we absolutely cannot make any further concession. . . . We have received the faith from hands of our predecessors, pure and intact, and we wish, following in their glorious footsteps, to transmit it just as intact and pure to our successors."[107] Cacault, who was fully familiar with Roman rhetoric and customs, understood that the negotiations were going to break down if they continued to rest entirely on

Spina's and Bernier's shoulders, and that it was necessary to find a way of putting the pope and the first consul in direct contact. It was he who had the idea of advising the pope to send to Paris an emissary invested with full powers to negotiate and sign a treaty. Instead of acknowledging the pope's refusal to make new concessions and leaving Rome, as Bonaparte's ultimatum instructed him to do, he went back to see Pius VII and persuaded him to send his state secretary to Paris.

Bonaparte was delighted: Cardinal Consalvi's arrival boded well for an early signature, especially because deep down—he had not hidden this from Bernier—the alternative draft of May 13 and the text of the pontifical brief proposed by Pius VII suited him reasonably well. The pope had compromised on two essential points, the complete replacement of the bishops and the recognition of the sales of ecclesiastical property.[108] If the text, along with a few minor additional notes written by Bernier, could have waited to be presented to Consalvi when he arrived on June 20, there was no doubt that the accord would have been signed at that point. But it was impossible to prevent Talleyrand from finding out about it, and when he did he was furious, telling Spina that he had to disavow the text revised in Rome and adhere immediately to the draft Bonaparte had written in January, in which he had had a hand.[109]

Of course, it was no longer in Spina's power to decide anything; he had been relegated to the background, and everything was now awaiting Monsignor Consalvi's arrival in Paris, which was almost a turning point. In any case it was an event, and there was a crowd at the Tuileries on June 21 when Bonaparte, in full ceremonial dress, received the cardinal, who had also put on his most formal garments. Such a spectacle had not been seen for so long a time that it felt unprecedented. The cardinal described it this way:

> The honor guard, lined up along the stairways and in the reception rooms, saluted me. In the rooms I was received by various gentlemen (I shall call them by that name); I know neither their offices nor who they were. In the last antechamber, I was received by the minister of foreign affairs, Talleyrand, who accompanied me into the great hall where the first consul was. He was in full dress, surrounded by his ministers and a very large number of persons occupying high offices, all in

gala dress. I was wearing a black habit, red stockings and skullcap with a biretta, as is the custom in Rome. The first consul came forward a few steps to meet me. At a short distance from his whole entourage he stopped, and standing with the minister of foreign affairs at his side, granted me an audience that lasted no less than three-quarters of an hour and perhaps more.[110]

Bonaparte courteously but firmly told Consalvi that he consented, as a sign of appeasement, to submit a new draft to him, but that this would have to be approved within five days; otherwise he would be forced to adopt "a national religion."[111] This opening gambit was mainly intended to impress the prelate, because the points of disagreement were no longer so numerous. Rome had resigned itself to the loss of the former bishops, almost forgotten its ties with Louis XVIII, and even accepted the prospect that Catholicism would no longer be the "state religion" of France. In return, the pope and his envoy demanded from the French leaders a profession of Catholic faith and also agreement that all the concessions made up to this point—and they were immense—would be compensated at least by the reestablishment of the public nature of Catholic worship. Once again Bonaparte might have yielded had Talleyrand not interceded, flatly refusing Consalvi's two demands.[112] Bernier had put on paper a new version, the seventh, and the cardinal, considering it unacceptable as it stood, had decided to write a new, eighth draft. Were they heading for a new impasse? Bonaparte's ultimatum expired on June 27. One day, two, then three went by without any advance being made, and on July 1, Consalvi's alternative draft was, as might have been expected, refused. This situation could have gone on forever had Talleyrand, who was not so tormented by the question of the concordat that he neglected his health, decided to go as planned to take the waters at Bourbon-l'Archambault. He left very precise instructions with d'Hauterive, but the latter was not Talleyrand, and above all he did not have the same influence with the first consul. Once Talleyrand had left, Bonaparte felt he had more elbow room. Nothing is more curious than the deference he had shown to his minister all through this long negotiation, believing he could not take any initiative without first submitting it to him. Did he feel so insecure that he needed Talleyrand's advice? Did he fear him? Above all, he needed him, counting on the former bishop of Autun to justify his religious policy for his revolutionary friends. Talleyrand did not grant his support free of charge, and he was fully resolved to hold up the negotiations until he obtained the absolution that would return him to lay status.

Talleyrand had hardly left Paris before Bonaparte received Consalvi at Malmaison. Here we see how well he had learned Talleyrand's lesson. Without concealing the fact that he had to reckon with a body of opinion—that of the former revolutionaries—that he knew was hostile to any agreement with Rome, he explained to Consalvi that he could not compromise on the guarantee of religious freedom, on the question of ecclesiastical property, or even on that of the Catholicism of the consuls: What would people say if he were to make amends by swearing to be Catholic? Consalvi would have to be content with a *presumed* confession of faith—none of the consuls having publicly repudiated the religion of their childhoods, they were all considered Catholics. Moreover, Bonaparte added, wasn't it absurd to suppose that a French leader could not be Catholic? Therefore he refused to commit himself to a humiliating declaration by the leaders of the Republic. In exchange he would withdraw his ultimatum, authorize Consalvi to take the necessary time to study the proposed agreement, and, finally, give his consent.[113]

Final Disputes

This time the end really was near.[114] About ten days sufficed for the cardinal to put the finishing touches on the text of the last alternative draft, and on July 12 Bonaparte received the dossier at Malmaison. The cardinal had misinterpreted the first consul's intentions; he had thought he could amend the text, while suspecting that these new changes would later be the object of intense negotiations. Bonaparte understood the situation differently. In his view it was up to him to make the final decision regarding the text revised by Consalvi. He had already explained that it was no longer a question of resuming the cycle of drafts and alternative drafts that had been going on now for more than eight months. The first consul did not want to draw up the final text of the concordat without involving Cambacérès and Lebrun in the process, and it was with them that he re-read and reworked Consalvi's text. The cardinal had definitely gone too far. Bonaparte struck out and modified several articles:

> His corrections all tended to support the state's rights. He did not ac-
> cept the government's profession of faith; he rejected any restriction on
> the external regulation of worship. The government's approval of the
> choice of parish priests [by the bishops] was reestablished. . . . A new
> aggravation was introduced into the two articles concerning ecclesias-
> tical property. Up to that point, in order to maintain the Church's right
> to own property, the authorities in Rome had counted on the restitu-
> tion of the properties, including religious buildings, that had been nei-
> ther sold to private parties nor assigned to public use. Today, in exchange
> for striking a few words in the article, Bonaparte reserved the right to
> arrange the sales or ulterior assignments, to give the latter in future
> the benefit of pontifical indulgence, though that was applicable only to
> the past. Finally, no brief for married priests, but a special article in
> their favor.[115]

Bonaparte set the signature for July 14 and assigned his brother Joseph, assisted by Bernier and state councilor Emmanuel Crétet, to organize with the
Italians the final meeting for the exchange of signatures. Consalvi was astonished to receive the final text on the afternoon of the thirteenth.[116] He had a
feeling that he had been tricked. He announced that he would not sign it. Joseph succeeded in getting him to come to his house, accompanied by Spina and
Father Caselli.[117] The meeting went on all night and continued until noon, July
14.[118] Through sheer stubbornness, Consalvi got satisfaction on several points,
in any case enough to decide that, having no hope of obtaining anything more,
he had to sign without further delay, before the confounded French changed
their minds. But Joseph, aware of having been more flexible than his brother
would have been in his place, feared putting his signature at the bottom of the
document, as the powers granted him prescribed, without having obtained Napoleon's assent. He hurried to the Tuileries, where the first consul had just returned after presiding over the July 14 ceremonies. Joseph had not been worried without reason. Bonaparte exploded in anger: "If you had signed that," he

shrieked, "I would have torn up your paper in your face! I want my text or it's over! Tell them that, if they don't want to sign it, they can leave right away. They'll have only themselves to blame for what will happen then."[119]

Joseph had hardly left before Napoleon had Consalvi notified that he did not want to break off the discussions, and that they were to be resumed at the home of his brother. The next day, another dozen hours were necessary to arrive at an agreement. This time it was over, and because the negotiators put the finishing touches on the document after midnight, the concordat was dated July 15, 1801. Bonaparte finally had the success he had wanted for so long, which he considered the most important of all he had achieved up to this point. Rome had yielded almost all the way down the line: Catholicism as the religion of "the great majority of French people," the deposition of the bishops, the new circumscription of the bishoprics, the recognition of the sales of ecclesiastical property, the principle of a clergy that would be paid by and promise loyalty to the state and even report to the government anything that might harm it, the principle of the state's religious neutrality, the ratification of the revolutionary legislation regarding the civil registration of births, marriages, and deaths, divorce, and the return of married priests to lay status. More than that: the concordat was a genuine humiliation inflicted on the European powers, who were from now on forced to admit into their company the revolutionary France whose legitimacy they had contested. They had been disavowed de facto by the pope, who had not only rehabilitated France but absolved its "sins," beginning with the regicide of 1793, and they were forced to abandon, again de facto, the cause of Louis XVIII.[120] This victory was greater than those of Marengo and Hohenlinden combined. What had the pope obtained in exchange? Permission for Catholics to create foundations—in the form of investment income—to help the Church, the reference to "the particular profession" of Catholicism that the consuls were to make, the presence of a papal legate in Paris, the reestablishment of the religion as a closely monitored public freedom rather than merely a private one, and finally—this was probably the most important for the sovereign pontiff—the suppression of the constitutional Church, the end of the schism, and the resumption of a regular pastoral life in France that laid the foundations for a future spiritual reconquest. That was also a major achievement, as Consalvi, ultimately satisfied with the accord, confided to a friend.[121] On the

French side, it was not a time for triumphalism. Bonaparte was unsure enough of his victory that he took precautions in presenting the text to the Council of State.[122] He was so worried about the reaction of this assembly, the most faithful to him of all, that he decided there would be neither debate nor vote. The reception was icy. As Thiers put it, the state councilors "remained gloomy and silent, as if they had seen perish along with the schism one of the works of the Revolution the most [to be mourned]."[123] The concordat, far from appearing to them as the accomplishment of its religious policy, seemed instead to be a "veritable abjuration."[124] As might have been expected, the exchange of signatures took longer than anticipated: only on August 15, after having hesitated for a long time—so little remained of his initial demands—did Pius VII finally sign the bull proclaiming the new concordat between Rome and the French Republic. Bonaparte signed in turn on September 8. The time had passed. There was no longer any hurry: Bonaparte decided that the formal proclamation of the text could wait for a better occasion. He could, in any case, be satisfied. He had succeeded, almost alone, in this enterprise that he considered the most important of all and that he never repented, contrary to what a legend claims, even at the height of his quarrels with the pope.[125] He realized the gravity of these quarrels, but he always considered them to be an accident that proved nothing against the wisdom of signing the concordat. He would certainly have been able to subscribe to Abbé Pradt's assessment:

> The concordat of 1801 was national, because France had been deprived of the freedom to exercise its religion. This violation of its rights was an infinitely great hardship on it. It maintained within it the greatest of evils, which is division. To put an end to it was therefore to do what was most in the interest of the state. . . . Peace was reestablished, discords ceased, people's ways of thinking grew closer. In all these respects, the 1801 concordat was an eminently national act. To convince oneself of this, one has only to refer to the time of this event. Let us remember the feelings that it unleashed not only in France but in all of Europe. This act was not only French but also European, because it was eminently social. The reconciliation of France with the religion of its fathers hastened the reconciliation of Europe with France; Europe no

longer feared reaching out to a nation whose members could unite their people with its people on the same altars. From that time on, some of the barriers separating Europe from France were lowered. With religion, it was seen to re-enter the social order.[126]

Perhaps down deep, Bonaparte had been proud not only to have put an end to religious discords but also to have brought Catholicism, "the religion of his fathers," as he put it, back home. However, he also had a vague feeling, and maybe a little more, that by reestablishing the Church he was paving the way for the reestablishment of the throne. He considered the "marvelous" aspect of religion indispensable for royal power.[127] But he also thought religion, and the Catholic religion in particular, had a close connection with monarchy, and certainly he was fully convinced that by becoming the pope's ally he had moved the Bourbons a little farther still from the throne.

TWENTY-NINE

The Top of the Ladder

*I*n 1801 foreign policy was an abiding concern. In Russia, Prussia, northern Italy, Spain, Rome, Naples, not to mention the colonial projects, the treaties signed with the governors of North Africa, the new constitution that was soon to be imposed on the Dutch,[1] and the plans for reorganizing the Helvetic Republic:[2] everywhere, the goal was to draw the consequences of the Austrian defeat and prepare as well as possible for the now-imminent negotiations with the British, even if Bonaparte remained convinced that London did not sincerely desire peace. He had said this to Roederer, not without exaggerating French influence: "[England] cannot desire it because we are the masters of the world. Spain is ours. We have a foot in Italy. In Egypt, we hold the area in their rear. Switzerland, Holland, Belgium.... There is one thing that has been irrevocably decided, and for which it has been declared to Prussia, Russia, and the Empire that we would, if necessary, wage war alone against all of them: that there will be no stadtholder in Holland, that we will keep Belgium and the right bank of the Rhine.[3] Having a stadtholder in Holland would be like having a Bourbon in the Faubourg Saint-Antoine."[4]

But did he believe more sincerely than the British did in the chances of an enduring peace? Did he even want it? Nothing is less certain; but he was convinced that a ceasefire, if not a peace treaty, was on the horizon, so he sought to enter discussions in a favorable position by repairing as much as possible the damage caused by the death of the Russian emperor and the dissolution of the Second League of Armed Neutrality. He was concerned that the Prussians, seeing the French more vulnerable than at the time of the Treaty of Lunéville, might distance themselves from France, following the example of Denmark and Sweden, which had signed treaties with England. The king of Prussia had to be kept in the neutral camp.[5] It was also urgent to resume the dialogue with Russia: Duroc had gone to Saint Petersburg to inquire into the intentions of Paul I's successor.

whom he esteemed—the esteem was mutual—the first consul entrusted him with a project that, under his guidance, advanced quickly, to the general's great satisfaction. The first draft of the code was ready in January 1801, less than six months after the creation of the commission, whose work was immediately communicated to the Supreme Court and the Court of Appeals. The magistrates' observations were then sent for review to the legislation section of the Council of State, over which Boulay de la Meurthe presided, before the whole dossier was submitted to the councilors assembled in plenary session.[13] No less than 109 sessions were then devoted to the Civil Code: Bonaparte presided over 57 of them.[14]

Bonaparte often participated in the debates; the record of the discussions published in the *Moniteur* testifies to this. It has been asked how many of the speeches attributed to him were in fact his own. Thiers had no doubts on this subject, depicting a Bonaparte who, having been rapidly initiated into the thorny questions of civil law by Cambacérès, had assimilated them so well that he quickly became "the master" for the "learned men around him," promptly drawing from their debates "the most natural and most reasonable conclusion," skillful at "summing up" and "settling with one word" the longest and most arduous discussions.[15] All this, of course, was seen quite differently by the emperor's detractors:

> Desirous of attributing the honor of the enterprise to himself, he had wanted people to see his hand in it. . . . Initiated into the knowledge of these subjects as he had been into canon law, by means of a few hasty readings and many conversations with Cambacérès and Portalis, addressing an audience composed of his supporters and associates, contradicted only insofar as it might bring out and excite his eloquence, sometimes he seemed to be directing the debates, sometimes he suddenly intervened in the discussion with a burst of peremptory and sententious phrases; his decision, like one of those halfhearted blows struck in tourneys in honor of sovereigns, usually tipped the scales . . . and he left his naïve listeners dazzled by his newfound erudition and convinced of his omniscience. The next day, Locré [the secretary of the Council of State] cleaned up these improvisations for the benefit of posterity.[16]

Thibaudeau reproduced several of Bonaparte's speeches with the published version on facing pages. A comparison of the two texts shows that Guillaume Locré was not "the first consul's cleanup man."[17] It is true that the secretary adjusted the form of speeches that Thibaudeau recognizes were "without artifice, without inhibitions, [and] without pretension," but he took care not to change the substance, even when Bonaparte had expressed ideas that were not very orthodox or made comments that proved that it would have been very difficult to take him for a jurist, even an inexperienced one.[18] In his secretary's version, the first consul's remarks lose more color than authenticity.[19] The discussion was free; Bonaparte did not always win out. For example, on the subject of adoption, he wanted to give it more solemnity, whereas the State Councilors were satisfied with a judgment confirming the act of adoption. Bonaparte spoke at length on this question, teasing Cambacérès, who had defended the right of bachelors to adopt children, and then opposing the majority of the councilors by demanding that each adoption file be submitted for approval to a "political body" rather than to a tribunal or even a simple notary. This speech is characteristic of the way in which he approached the questions raised in the Council:

> Adoption is neither a civil contract nor a judicial act. What is it then? An imitation through which society wants to ape nature. It is a kind of new sacrament: I cannot find in the language a word that can well define this act. The son of flesh and bone passes, by the will of society, into the flesh and bone of another person. That is the greatest act one can imagine. It gives filial sentiments to someone who did not have them, and those of the father reciprocally. Whence must this act proceed, then? From on high, like a thunderbolt. You are not the son of this man, the legislative body says; but you will have a son's feelings. . . . The legislator, like a pontiff, will provide the sacred character. Let us suppose that there are quarrels between the unadopted and adopted sons? The latter will reply: The same authority certified the marriage from which you were born; it is the law itself that made me your brother. It has been objected that adoption is revocable; but I would not want it to be revocable. Divorce is cited as an example. How can what dissolves be compared with what creates? Once a political body has pronounced an

adoption, certainly we cannot think of permitting it to be revoked. It would be different if it proceeded from a tribunal. It would no longer be anything but a sentence. . . . The imagination has to be strongly struck. If there are discussions between the natural father and the adoptive father; if, being in the same ship, they are in danger of dying, the son has to declare himself for the adoptive father. Only the will of the sovereign can impress this sentiment. . . . The vice of our modern legislation is not to have anything that speaks to the imagination. Man can be governed only through it; without imagination, he is a brute. If the priests established adoption, they would make it an august cere-mony. It is a mistake to govern men as if they were things. . . . We are not dealing with the question, we are doing geometry. We are envis-aging it as lawmakers and not as statesmen. The imagination has to consider adoption in the context of the misfortunes of life. . . . If the natural father of the adopted son becomes wealthy, the latter will abandon his adoptive father. He must be bound to him forever, other-wise he is nothing but an heir. Who takes the place of God on earth? The legislator. Who is the father's son? No one is sure. It is the legisla-tor's will. The adoptive son must be like the son of flesh and bone. If there is the slightest difference, you have missed the target, and I no longer understand anything.[20]

Was he so active in this debate, as in the discussion of divorce, because he did not exclude the possibility that he would some day have to get a divorce or adopt the son that Joséphine had not given him?[21] Maybe. It had been under-stood from the outset that the Civil Code would carry out a synthesis of the Old Regime's legal traditions and those of the Revolution, and Portalis had wished that the latter be retained as little as possible and the former as much as possible. And Portalis was not alone in this. Bonaparte did not get what he wanted on the question of adoption, because the procedure was entrusted to the courts.[22] On the other hand, divorce by mutual consent was adopted over the objections of numerous councilors. He was not in favor of this arrangement, and not even of divorce, but he saw it as a necessary counterpart of the early age of marriage, eighteen for boys and fifteen for girls, and also as a consequence of the secularization of marriage, as a way of adapting the law to the evolution of manners and, perhaps still more, as a way of resolving delicate situations without dishonor.[23] When Portalis said that a "new people" would have no need for divorce, he replied that even in that case it would remain indispensable so long as young people of fifteen or sixteen were authorized to get married. Although they were considered incapable of making most decisions or taking care of themselves, they were allowed to make the most difficult choice there was.

> An individual who gets married as a minor, at an age when he does not have much foresight, will later realize that he has made a mistake, that he has not found in the person he chose the qualities he hoped for, and he will not be able to dissolve his marriage without blackening that person and without dishonoring himself? . . . You say that divorce for incompatibility is disastrous for spouses, for children, and for families. For my part, I find nothing more disastrous than a bad marriage or a dishonoring divorce. . . . If the marriage is unhappy, mustn't a civil law foreign to sacramental notions provide for the happiness of individuals? . . . Most unions are marriages of convenience. Only time can sanctify them. Prohibit divorce after a certain time, when the couple has got to know one another, when there has been an exchange of love and of blood, for instance after ten years of marriage, fine. I see the reason for that. One mustn't abandon a woman from whom one has had children, unless she commits adultery. . . . But before ten years, incompatibility has to suffice, let the matter be dealt with before a family council presided over by a magistrate, and let no one be allowed to divorce twice, for that would be absurd and would debase marriage. Divorced individuals must be able to marry again only after a period of five years, so that it is not the prospect of another marriage that leads them to get divorced. Then you will have done all that morals requires. . . . The happiness of individuals has to be considered, too.[24]

For example, was it necessary to force the scorned spouse to reveal his or her misfortune before a court, when divorce by mutual consent would offer a way of settling the problem without dishonor? The law is made for manners, not maintained there.[40] When Bonaparte heard this news, he revoked Toussaint's appointment. A few weeks later, in October 1801, Vincent returned from Port-au-Prince to tell Bonaparte that a Constituent Assembly had given Saint-Domingue a constitution: although it did not contest Saint-Domingue's membership in "the French Empire," the reunified island now had a governor appointed for life who had given himself, in addition to full powers, also the right to name his successor. This was a challenge to the home country's authority; could Bonaparte accept a de facto autonomy that would sooner or later lead to the end of the monopoly on trade with the colony and perhaps ultimately to the governor's signing of treaties of alliance and trade with other powers?

Toussaint's fate was sealed. That of Saint-Domingue as well? Officially it was still only a question of retaking possession of the island, without reestablishing slavery there but putting an end, this time, to the power of the "black Jacobins," who had to be, by trickery or by force, disarmed, deprived of their command, arrested, and sent to France. Their troops, meanwhile, would be sent back to work on the plantations, which would be restored to their former owners.[41] Bonaparte could not ignore the colonists' demands, especially at a time when he was trying to reestablish legal rules in metropolitan France. Moreover, because the great majority of the colonists were descended from old noble families, he saw in the restoration of their property a kind of compensation for the property they had lost in France, for which there was no question of indemnifying them. Nonetheless, how could the return of the plantation system fail to entail that of slavery? How could abolitionist and slaveholding territories coexist on the same island? Was the promise that Bonaparte repeated to Toussaint's own sons, Isaac and Placide, who had come to study in France,[42] a ruse intended to conceal the expedition's real objective, when it was clear that it would encounter ferocious resistance? We will never know what Bonaparte and Leclerc said to each other before the latter left to take command of the troops in Brest, but the reestablishment of slavery was probably in the cards from that moment on. It is true that the law of May 20, 1802, concerning the "maintenance" of slavery in the "colonies returned to France by virtue of the peace treaty [with Britain]" was not to change anything in Saint-Domingue and Guadeloupe, where the law abolishing slavery was not to be called into question. But as Pierre Branda and Thierry Lentz have shown, the statement of the motives written up by the new minister of the navy, Admiral Decrès, announced in veiled terms the reestablishment of slavery "in all our colonies and within a short time," and on July 13, Richepanse, who had landed on Guadeloupe, received the order to suspend the application of the law of 1794.[43] It was probably because the reestablishment of the former colonial regime was the secret goal of the expedition that the British government, which was at first very concerned about the assembly in French ports of about fifty warships, more than 20,000 men, and 20,000 sailors, ended by consenting to an operation that violated the inaction that the signers of the preliminary peace agreements were generally observing until the final treaty was signed. Fearing that the abolition of slavery unilaterally decreed by the French would end up endangering slavery in its own colonies, Britain limited itself to sending a squadron to observe the movements of Admiral Villaret-Joyeuse's fleet which, having been kept on the coast by a violent windstorm, left France on December 14, 1801.[44]

Fouché later accused Bonaparte of never having believed in the success of an operation whose true instigators had been the representatives of the colonists, though he took advantage of it to get rid of generals and soldiers whom he distrusted, especially those who had come from Moreau's old army.[45] Had the first consul deliberately sacrificed an army whose opposition he feared, he would not have entrusted it to his brother-in-law, General Leclerc, even if it is true that he didn't much like him, and he certainly would not have insisted that Pauline, his wife, accompany him, along with their young brother Jérôme. The Saint-Domingue expedition aroused an enthusiasm comparable to that provoked in 1798 by the announcement of a great expedition whose destination—Egypt—was then unknown. This time the goal was known. The outcome of the intervention seemed beyond any doubt, to the point that adventure lovers, fortune seekers, and speculators of all kinds rushed to take part in it.[46]

The British were wary. They were right. If Bonaparte was pushing so hard the implementation of clauses in a peace treaty that had not yet been signed, it was because he also wanted to take advantage of this interval to fulfill the clauses of another treaty—a secret one—concluded with Spain regarding the retrocession of Louisiana. That is why he hoped for a rapid conclusion of the talks in Amiens, and was furious that the Spanish were slow to send a representative to the congress, and moreover threatened to exclude Holland from the negotiations if it persisted, as it had indicated it would, in refusing to cede Ceylon to the British: he hoped to sign the peace treaty before the British understood the scope of his American ambitions—and before he strengthened his grip on Italy.

He had been working on this for several months, both with officials of the Cisalpine Republic and with Talleyrand. Before assigning Melzi to write a new constitution, he had had to overcome the reluctance of his minister of foreign affairs, who was worried to see the first consul adopt the policy of sister republics whose failure had contributed to the fall of the Directory.[47] Talleyrand would have much preferred to replace this republic, whose allegiance to France upset any equilibrium in Europe, with a principality or a kingdom ceded to the grand duke of Tuscany, to a Habsburg in any case, from which the legations would be detached in order to return them to the Holy See. This was, as Thiers put it, "a state more or less under the direct domination of the French Republic," and thus offered another chance to make the peace more acceptable to Europe.[48] But could Austria be brought back into Italy so soon after it had been expelled, when Spain had just been established in Florence, and Piedmont attached, de facto if not yet de jure, to France? Talleyrand had argued against the policy of expansion that he saw getting a hold on Bonaparte's mind. In vain.

The Opposition's Last Stand

It was at this triumphant juncture that the opposition, which had been dormant since its first attacks at the beginning of the Consulate, though momentarily awakened during the voting on the law on special tribunals, redoubled its efforts. It was, Thiers said, a new episode—and the last—in the struggle between the heirs of Brumaire. Some of them had not given up on the project of founding, with or without Bonaparte, a "democratic, moderate republic like the one Washington had just established in America," while others wanted to establish "a monarchy . . . less the old prejudices, less the feudal system, and plus grandeur." These two parties "continued exaggerating each other by their very contradiction": "Some of them were becoming almost violent revolutionaries again, seeing what was happening, seeing the first consul's authority growing, monarchical ideas spreading, a court being formed at the Tuileries, the Catholic religion being restored or almost restored, the émigrés returning in large numbers. Others were becoming almost old-fashioned royalists, so eager were they to react and reconstruct a monarchy, and so inclined were they to accept even an enlightened despotism as the whole result of the Revolution."[49]

The former were all the more resolved to do battle because contentment was not universal or unmixed among the French. The return of the émigrés, the restoration of religion and other forms from the Old Regime, and even the restoration of order led to unrest. Interests were offended, habits were disturbed. People get used to everything, even disorder. In a little more than ten years, revolutionary agitation and war had become for many people an almost natural state, as obvious and necessary as the air they breathed.

The concordat signed with Rome crystallized certain resentments. Since its ratification in August and the publication of the bull requiring bishops to resign, matters had not advanced far enough for Bonaparte to be able to do as planned and make the official proclamation coincide with the ceremonies organized on November 9 to celebrate the second anniversary of 18 Brumaire and announce the imminent signature of the peace treaty with Britain. Rome had named a legate, Cardinal Caprara, who was not expected to arrive in Paris for several months, and Paris, as we have seen, had named as director-general of religion none other than Portalis. But not all the bishops had yet submitted their resignations, and Bonaparte preferred to wipe the episcopal slate clean before officially proclaiming the concordat. He did not want Rome to be able to renege on its commitments, while the proclamation of the accord made with the Church was supposed to accompany that of the Organic Articles reaffirming the principles of Gallicanism. Another motive led him to delay the proclamation once again: the imminence of the legislative session, which was set to open on November 22. It was expected to be turbulent, the opposition having decided to counter the government in every way it could to show its hostility to the reconciliation with Rome. Cabanis had already unleashed a tremendous storm at the Institute, where, Bernardin de Saint-Pierre having dared to mention God, he shouted: "I swear that there is no God and I ask that his name never be uttered on these premises."[50]

The quarrel was fierce. It began with the election of Dupuis, the author of the bitterly antireligious tract *L'Origine de tous les cultes*, as president of the

Legislative Body, and continued during the consideration of a peace treaty that had just sealed the reconciliation with Russia.[51] About twenty people in the Tribunate, and about thirty in the Legislative Body, refused to ratify the treaty because it stated that the signers were committing themselves "not to allow any of their *subjects* to maintain a correspondence of any kind . . . with the internal enemies of the current governments of the two states."[52] This article, by virtue of which Russia promised no longer to support the Bourbons and France promised no longer to support the Polish refugees in Paris, caused an uproar: it was thought that the citizens of the Republic were being called "subjects." The dispute was absurd but that only made it more violent. Although the treaty was finally ratified by a strong majority, Bonaparte remained angry at the "muddleheads," "defrocked priests," and "Jansenists" in the assemblies.[53] His opponents repeated their attacks with even more vigor, and this time they were successful when it came time to appoint someone to the first of the three vacant seats in the Senate. Bonaparte proposed a general—Jourdan, La Martillière, or Berruyet.[54] The Legislative Body proposed Grégoire, a living symbol of the Revolution and of opposition to the concordat.[55] The senate, where Sieyès, seized by a renewed revolutionary ardor, was surreptitiously inciting the malcontents, rejected the government's candidates and chose Grégoire. This was a serious slap in the face for the executive branch, but it was nothing compared to what was to follow. Although the maintenance of capital punishment, which the Convention had promised in 1795 to abolish, passed without too much difficulty, the government had to give up a proposed law that reestablished punishment by branding.[56] This was a bad omen, coming before the debate on the first chapters of the Code Civil.

The tribunes had decided to examine this text very carefully. They had no shortage of reasons for attacking it: it was a product of the Council of State, which was increasingly associated with the executive exercise of power and aroused many resentments and jealousies. Bonaparte was particularly attached to it; its promulgation was not so urgent that a short delay could compromise France's future. Thus, the members of the Council of State saw here an opportunity to exercise a final pressure to force the first consul to agree to share a little of his power with the assemblies, of which they were, in a way, the representatives, these assemblies that had run the government for a decade and which they considered the ultimate bastion of liberty. Despite all the reverses they had suffered since Brumaire, they did not believe they had definitively lost the battle. They even thought that the end of the war, added to the domestic recovery, would soon make the dictatorship of the first consul feel too burdensome, revive aspirations to liberty, and restore to the assemblies the popularity that, admittedly, they did not currently enjoy. They did not fear a coup d'état, knowing full well that Bonaparte was taking care not to appear to be the head of a military government; they did not believe that the assemblies would be dissolved, because the Constitution of Year VIII did not provide for that possibility. They were, if not confident regarding the outcome of the battle, at least convinced that in the event they failed, as they had in 1800 and 1801, they would have another chance.[57]

Bonaparte, who suspected what would happen, had asked that the Civil Code be presented as a whole to prevent the assemblies from examining its provisions in detail, but Tronchet, who very rightly did not believe that such an important text could be adopted in haste, succeeded in convincing him that they had to present it title by title.[58] In the Tribunate, Andrieux began by attacking the preliminary article of the Code relating to the way in which laws would be promulgated and their nonretroactivity. It was rejected by a very large majority of the Tribunate and a much smaller one of the Legislative Body,[59] making it clear that they intended similar treatment for the texts to come on "The enjoyment of civil rights" and "The form of civil status records." To make the rebellion a little more striking, the Tribunate first examined the second project, which was less controversial because, taking the certification of births, marriages, and deaths away from the clergy, it could be presented as another victory won over "superstition": it was therefore adopted.[60] The article on the exercise of civil rights was then rejected on January 1, 1802.[61] The slap in the face was all the more painful because the election for the second seat vacant in the Senate seemed to be going badly: the government was pushing the appointment of an obscure general, La Martillière, and the opposition, whose relations with Bonaparte had been deteriorating for the past two years, was supporting Daunou. The former Oratorian easily won a majority in the Tribunate; in the Legislative Body, La

Martillière had tied the rebels' candidate in the first round of voting, but in the second he had lost ground; everything suggested that the Senate, having given Grégoire a seat, would give another to Daunou.

Bonaparte was indignant, less because one of his adversaries was entering the Senate than because of the bias the opposition showed by rejecting two of the three first titles of the Civil Code.[62] He convoked the Council of State after the rejection of the first title and announced that the government would go into its "winter quarters" if another text was rejected: "What can you do with people who, before the discussion, said that the Councilors of State and the consuls were mere asses, and the work should be thrown at their heads? I've read Portalis's speech to the Legislative Body, in response to the orator of the Tribunate; he has left them with nothing to say. But however eloquent one is, and even if one spoke nonstop for twenty-four hours, one could make no headway against a prejudiced assembly resolved not to listen to anything."[63]

His anger was magnified because everywhere other than in the assemblies, he was being acclaimed. His supporters were weaving laurel crowns for him that were perhaps a little too loaded with rhetorical flourishes.[64] But the enthusiasm was not all false. In a little more than two years he had achieved everything he had promised: peace abroad, order at home. The record was impressive, and it is not without reason that historians are generally amazed by it. Contemporaries were no less amazed. No one had ever seen before, or ever would see again, so many ills remedied in so little time. People from all over Europe hastened to catch a glimpse of this extraordinary man to whom so many benefactions were attributed. A remark made by Thiers will suffice to sum up this record: "Security had been reestablished on the highways, and whereas in January and February 1801 one could hardly travel from Paris to Rouen, or from Paris to Orléans, without running the risk of being killed, at the end of this same year it was possible to cross all of France without being in any danger."[65]

The "dogs" of the assemblies, as Bonaparte called them, would have to wait if they wanted to attack the Code Civil further.[66] Cambacérès had pointed to the solution: put the assemblies on "a diet of laws" and withdraw all the proposals under discussion until a definitive decision was made.[67] On January 2, while a message from the consuls was informing the assemblies of the withdrawal of the proposals, Bonaparte was receiving at the Tuileries a deputation from the Senate.[68] Referring to the failure of General La Martillière, he asked: "You don't want to appoint any more generals? You owe them the peace, you know: this would be the time to show them your gratitude. . . . I warn you that I would regard the appointment of Daunon to the Senate as a personal insult. You know that I have [never] put up with one."[69] The threat was enough to make the senators cringe.[70] The tribunes and members of the Legislative Body backed down; canceling their votes in favor of Daunou, they all gave their votes to the government's candidate. But it was too late, the session had been suspended and a plan for doing away with the opposition once and for all was being studied. Cambacérès had found a suitable juridical artifice. He pointed out to Bonaparte, who was already imagining the troops dispersing the tribunes as they had the Five Hundred on 19 Brumaire, that articles 27 and 28 of the Constitution of Year VIII stipulated that the first reelection of one-fifth of the assemblies— that is, twenty tribunes and sixty representatives in the Legislative Body—would take place sometime "in the course of Year X [1801–1802]": Why not before spring? And since the Constitution was no more precise about the way in which those who would lose their seats would be designated, Cambacérès proposed that the Senate designate those who would keep their seats, instead of drawing lots to choose the names, as was the custom in such cases. Those who were not retained thus finding themselves excluded de facto, it would remain only to replace them by men considered favorable to the government, or who were simply more docile.[71]

That was one thing Bonaparte liked about lawyers, at least when they were on his side: they could find a good reason for anything. Cambacérès emphasized that by this subterfuge, they were reestablishing the right to dissolve assemblies that they had not dared to give the government in 1799. He failed to mention, of course, that the change in the Senate would result, not from a free, popular election, but from a designation made by the Senate itself. The first consul was satisfied; that would take care of the opposition for twenty years, he said.[72]

Basically, he hadn't changed his mind since 1797, when he told Talleyrand his views regarding institutions. An opposition was useful, he explained to the Councilors of State gathered on January 7 to discuss Cambacérès's plan, only to counterbalance the influence of an aristocracy and a monarchy that were still powerful, as in Britain. In France, where the government represented the sovereign people directly, it would be not just useless, but harmful, and all the more so because unlike England, postrevolutionary France was not an old society in which political struggles took place under the auspices of the constitution, but a new society in which, nothing yet being entirely legitimate, the adversaries of the new order still hoped to achieve their ends, whether they were royalists advocating a return to the past or Jacobins seeking another revolution. As for the government, he added, it would be a mistake to believe it was all-powerful: like the reputation of individuals or works in modern societies, its authority was at the mercy of public opinion. The government could act and maintain itself only with the support of public opinion, and in accord with it. Compared to that, how important were the restrictions and counterweights with which the revolutionary constitutions had been stuffed, and some of which—the Tribunate, of course—had subsisted in the Constitution of Year VIII? Were 100 tribunes and 300 representatives really capable of representing the nation and speaking in its name as if it had expressed itself directly? The supposition was absurd. Counterweights were useful in England, useless in France. What the country needed was a government invested with the people's confidence and aided in the exercise of its functions by assemblies and organs that, far from being restrictions and barriers to its action, would be associated with it as so many points of support.[73] In his view, it ultimately mattered little that, prior to this final show of resistance, the assemblies had been particularly moderate for the past two years. Out of ninety bills that had been submitted to them, they had rejected only four.[74] That was four too many.

A Republican Crown

The time had come for Bonaparte to go back to Lyon, where he had convoked the Italian representatives entrusted with drafting a new constitution for the Cisalpine Republic. Since its reconquest, Lombardy had been administered by a provisional government, while Bonaparte undertook the reform of its institutions, which worked hardly better than those of the defunct Directory on which they were based. Francesco Melzi and a few others had drawn up the outline for a new constitution, based this time on that of the Consulate, taking care not to give Italians the equivalent of the Tribunate and substituting for the three consuls of the Constitution of Year VIII a president of the Republic— with a vice president at his side—elected for ten years and eligible for reelection.[75]

Bonaparte claimed that at first he had not thought of being president himself; he had sought a potential candidate in Italy, but not having found any genuine "statesman"—except Melzi, who would make a very acceptable vice president—he turned to his brother Joseph. Joseph acknowledged later that he had been asked, but said he had refused an offer that was in fact unacceptable because his brother intended only to make him play the role of a "political mannequin." Then Napoleon made the decision that he had no doubt already taken: he would be the first president of the Italian Republic.[76] How could it be thought that he might have considered another solution? Italy was, after all, his second home, and it had been the scene of his ascension and his greatest victories. The meeting of the 450 representatives of the Consulte of Lyon was going to be the occasion for a veritable plebiscite whose object was less the constitution of the Italian Republic than Bonaparte himself. He was expecting a consecration, a kind of rehearsal for what he desired in France itself and wanted to "try out" first on these Italians, whom Carlo Botta said were likely to be more docile than the French, having been defeated by him on the battlefield. In France there were still a few vestiges of republicanism, but there was not the slightest trace of them in Italy. "Thus, after having conquered Italy by France's force of arms," Botta concluded, "he was going to conquer France by Italy's willing submission."[77]

Between two banquets and two balls that Joséphine honored with her graceful presence, and at which her husband made a brief appearance, the necessary cajoling took place. Talleyrand, to whom Bonaparte had entrusted the chairmanship of the Consulte,[78] knowing that his minister did not approve of his Italian policy, and Murat, who had come with the Italians, questioned the representatives about their intentions, examining the possible choices with them, pointing out various people's inadequacies, weaknesses, and defects, and, without suggesting any name, guiding them little by little toward Bonaparte's own choices: himself as president and Melzi as vice president. On January 25 Bonaparte was proclaimed president by the unanimous acclaim of the assembly. The next day he appeared before the representatives who had elected him, surrounded by his wife, ministers, generals, and officials, a royal ceremony for a republican investiture.[79]

Bonaparte returned to Paris at the end of the month to put the finishing touches on the peace treaty with Britain and to finish off the opposition.

The conclusion of the peace treaty with Britain was in theory a simple formality: the two countries had arrived at an accord in London the previous autumn. However, six months of discussions were still necessary. In Britain the atmosphere had changed. The fervor and joy of October had given way to disappointment. The French government was not showing any intention of resuming with its partner the trade relationships that had been very favorable to Britain before the Revolution. Except for the cessation of hostilities—but the British had never directly suffered from the fighting—the benefits of the peace treaty had still not made themselves felt. Commercial activity had not resumed, and the taxes levied to finance the war were a heavy burden. As for the British government, it had been displeased to learn of the impending return of the French to Louisiana, which made it regret having agreed to the departure of the expedition assigned to retake possession of Saint-Domingue. And there was more. Bonaparte, by having himself elected president of an Italian Republic, was not only proceeding effectively to annex northern Italy to France, which suggested that a similar fate awaited Piedmont, but also implying through the very name of this new state that it would expand. Were the French thinking of driving the Bourbons out of Naples and politically unifying the whole Italian peninsula? And wasn't that a clear sign that the first consul, even if he had been forced to evacuate Egypt, had not given up on his Mediterranean project? What worried the British most was that the French were offering the king of Etruria the principality of Piombino, which the Neapolitans had just ceded to France, in exchange for Elba.[80] From then on their suspicions grew: What if the French, having returned to the Mediterranean via Italy and the island of Elba, tried to retake Malta, which the British had just given back to the not very redoubtable Knights of St. John? A compromise had been found, but distrust remained.[81] In London there was concern that Bonaparte might, furthermore, take advantage of the truce to prepare for future battles. The violation of the Peace of Amiens was in a sense programmed even before it was signed.

"This coolheaded politician was driven by a prodigious imagination," Chateaubriand observed. "He would not have been what he was, had the muse not been there; reason realized the poet's ideas. All these men with great lives are always composed of two natures, because they have to be capable of inspiration and action: one gives rise to the project, the other accomplishes it."[82] In Bonaparte the relations between imagination and reason were not always so harmonious. Many examples of this could be found, among the clearest being these new Mediterranean projects, where imagination definitely triumphed over reason. Georges Lefebvre observed, with less style than Chateaubriand but perhaps more accuracy, that in Bonaparte's view a success amounted to nothing if it was not followed by another. Hardly was the goal achieved before he was already looking farther ahead, higher: "Bonaparte's ambition was not at all of the kind we can all feel: achieving a certain goal that satisfies us; his was an ambition that had no final goal."[83] Did he feel a kind of terror at the prospect of the life—leisurely, or at least more ceremonial than active—to which the reestablishment of peace abroad and at home condemned him? He had ended the Revolution, he had defeated the coalition: What more could he do? Being aware that the Revolution and war had brought him to power, did he fear that peace would soon make him less necessary in the eyes of his fellow citizens? He did not have to be a wizard to see the great benefits he would receive from the peace, but was he already thinking about the still greater benefits he would gain, when the time came, from war?

The Political Consequences of the Peace

The British had considered refusing their signature if, at the very least, the king of Sardinia was not compensated for the loss of Piedmont. But Bonaparte had refused to discuss this point, and the British did not want to bear the blame for a break. So Lord Cornwallis and Joseph Bonaparte signed the peace treaty on March 25.

Now everything was ready for doing away with the opposition without having to fear the slightest criticism. Kept in check so long as the war was not over, the opposition could not survive the peace. At the very time when Bonaparte was leaving Paris to go to Lyon, a message from the consuls had asked the Senate to reelect one-fifth of the seats in the Tribunate and the Legislative Body, as called for in the Constitution. A few days later the Senate, circumvented by Cambacérès, who had spared no efforts, decided not to designate those who would lose their seats or to choose them by lot, but instead to designate the four-fifths who would keep their seats.[84] About fifteen senators protested, including Garat, Lanjuinais, and Grégoire; Sieyès remained silent. As might be expected, the Senate's balloting eliminated the most virulent opponents: Benjamin Constant, Ginguené, Say, Daunou, Marie-Joseph Chénier, and Andrieux.[85] When the assemblies met on April 5, a few days after the signature of the Peace of Amiens, the change was obvious, even if subsequent discussions showed that the cleansing did not suffice to put an end to all debate. There were certainly no more obstructive maneuvers or attacks on the government by a minority that had not given up hope of transforming the regime of Year VIII into a representative, parliamentary system.

This was clear when the concordat was presented to the assemblies, after several delays, at the session of April 5. Bonaparte, still fearing the representatives' dissatisfaction—he remembered the icy reception in the Council of State the preceding August—had taken the precaution of reserving a not inconsiderable place for the constitutional priests in the new episcopacy.[86] Caprara protested in vain; the first consul did not yield: "I have not come to make one party win out over the other," he told him, "I have come to reconcile them by maintaining an equal balance between them. . . . I shall therefore mix a few constitutional bishops with the bishops you call faithful; I shall choose them well, I shall choose few; but there will be some."[87]

The same went for the addition to the concordat of seventy-seven "Organic Articles" written by the director-general of religions, Portalis, who reestablished the *Déclaration des Quatre Articles* of 1682, reaffirmed the principle of the concordat Church's obedience to the government in all matters concerning discipline, organized the liberty of religions and their coexistence, restricted public demonstrations of the Catholic faith, and confirmed the secularization of civil status and the abolition of monastic orders.[88] These two laws—regarding the concordat and the Organic Articles—plus a third on the Protestant religion, were adopted without enthusiasm but also without any marked opposition in the assemblies.[89]

Monsignor Caprara became the Holy See's official representative to the French Republic, and on Palm Sunday the first bishops under the concordat were consecrated in Notre Dame—among them were Cambacérès's brother and Abbé Bernier.[90] On Easter, April 18, a *Te Deum* celebrated both the return to peace and the reestablishment of religion. For the first time in years, Paris woke up to the sound of the bells of Notre Dame. A curious throng, which was not always disciplined or contemplative, had invaded this former Temple of Reason and crowded along the avenues where the cortege was to pass: Bonaparte, his fellow consuls, and the great state bodies went to the ceremony in carriages, preceded by troops and accompanied by their servants. The new archbishop of Paris, old Monsignor de Belloy, awaited the first consul under a canopy to present the holy water to him.[91]

This sight was absolutely new for the youngest spectators; for others, it was a resurrection of the past, but with entirely different actors who were a little ill at ease, and often skeptical. People were no longer used to this kind of ceremony, and though Bonaparte had required all generals who were in Paris to attend—he had rebuffed Augereau, who asked him in their name that they not be forced to participate in this "tedious moralizing" (*capuçinade*)—the organizers had forgotten to assign seats for them. Proving the power now possessed by the first consul, they were all there, with the exception of Moreau, who was ostentatiously strolling through the Tuileries gardens smoking a cigar. No fewer than sixty generals, gathered in the middle of the crowded nave, "didn't know where to go or what to do, and finding on their right more than sixty priests comfortably seated and looking at them and almost sniggering at these officers who were the honor, the glory, and the aegis of their country. One understands the grumbling that began and the oaths that were mixed with it."[92] An official came and presented his excuses, saying that he could do nothing: "'Go fuck yourself,' Masséna told him, and then, seizing and shaking the chair of the priest sitting in front of him, he made him clear off and took his place. This example, which was immediately followed, rather abruptly substituted officers who should not have had to seat themselves for the priests and neophytes."[93]

The sermon was given by Boisgelin, the archbishop of Tours, who had officiated at the coronation of Louis XVI. We do not know whether the audience paid him much attention. On the other hand, all eyes were fixed on Bonaparte kneeling on a prie-Dieu; behind, also on their knees, were Talleyrand and Fouché, who amid the vapors of the incense "were cleansing their old sins."[94] Méhul and Cherubini directed the instrumentalists and the choirs. Cardinal Caprara celebrated the mass. The generals sniggered, talked, and drew attention to themselves, but when Bonaparte raised his eyes to look daggers at them, they all shut up.[95] When he returned to the Tuileries after three hours of ceremony, he took to task General Delmas, who happened to be there, reproaching him for his attitude. Delmas retorted: "A fine *capuçinade!* All that was lacking was the 100,000 men who got themselves killed to do away with all that!"[96]

Although the assemblies had been tamed, the military had not. Moreau, whose wife never ceased to tell him that Bonaparte had taken the place that should have been his, had already been sulking for several months, and the first consul had resigned himself to dealing with him. After Moreau had not come to a dinner to which he had been invited, Bonaparte did not invite him again.[97] But Moreau was prudent, and moreover undecided; he let the malcontents talk about him as a recourse, but took care not to compromise himself. The first consul's relations with Bernadotte had not improved, either; the Gascon felt humiliated by the appointment of Leclerc to head the Army of Saint-Domingue, while he was dying of boredom with the Army of the West. But he had refused every other assignment—the French Indies, Guadeloupe, an ambassadorship in Constantinople, and even Louisiana. He was ruminating and listening more or less distractedly to the malcontents in the army, who were all the more numerous because the return of peace meant a reduction in the number of troops and, for many of them, half pay or a retirement pension. Moreau, Bernadotte, and Masséna were considered the leaders of the military opposition. They were aware that Bonaparte was having them watched, and they were not scatterbrained enough to get involved in a conspiracy like the one that had been formed, it was said, to assassinate Bonaparte at Notre Dame.[98] There were, however, private discussions; generals were regularly sent away from Paris—Bernadotte, Macdonald, Augereau, Gouvion-Saint-Cyr, Brune.

We do not know how far the discontent went, but it is certain that it increased after the April 18 ceremony at Notre Dame. General Delmas, who had been rebuffed by Bonaparte, was mixed up with Oudinot in a "conspiracy of Polangis" that may somehow have been connected with another conspiracy called "the conspiracy of Patience," which was more serious because its chief instigator, the squadron leader Donnadieu, intended to assassinate Bonaparte. Donnadieu was arrested, Delmas was sent away from Paris, and Oudinot was pardoned. Still in the month of May, the police foiled another plot, this time in Rennes, where General Simon, Bernadotte's chief of staff—we do not know how far Berna- dotte himself was involved[99]—had posters put up inciting the troops of the west to revolt. Simon was arrested, and a few battalions were sent to the colonies. Bernadotte did what he had done on 18 Brumaire: he hid, this time in Plom- bières, and eventually asked Rapp to intercede on his behalf. Bonaparte began by refusing, telling his aide-de-camp: "Don't mention that man, he should be shot!" However, Bernadotte was Joseph's brother-in-law, Désirée's husband, and once again he managed to escape without damage, even recovering his command at Rennes. Bonaparte was well aware that many generals would remain discon- tented, no matter what he did to satisfy them: "Just as there isn't one of them who doesn't think he is [Bonaparte's] equal and doesn't claim to have the same right to the highest rank," Royer-Collard wrote in one of his reports to Louis XVIII, "neither is there one who doesn't regard [Bonaparte's] elevation as a wrong done to him personally."[100]

This rebellious climate was all the more intense because the first consul's pop- ularity continued to grow in the country. The nation, which had already for- gotten the Revolution, was grateful to him for peace and for the order that had finally returned, and for church bells that rang once again every Sunday. Bonaparte thought there was no point in taking the slightest risk, and the am- nesty for the émigrés, the first of the important steps he had decided to take after the Peace of Amiens, was discussed between the Council of State and the Senate without being subjected, as the Constitution of Year VIII stipulated, to examination by the Tribunate and the Legislative Body.[101] However, it was not always possible to avoid the assemblies. The law on public education that created the lycées, which had been prepared by Roederer, passed without too much difficulty.[102] But the creation of the Legion of Honor was the pretext for a last stand made by those who, having remained faithful to the Revolution, had suffered so many reverses and saw with dismay courtly customs being revived at the Tuileries, the émigrés hastening to the borders, cassocks reappearing in the streets, and government speakers praising distinctions, decorations, and titles. Bonaparte sought in vain to explain that this new elite was entirely civic and not military, that it substituted the reign of merit for superiorities of birth or fortune.[103]

The project's adversaries saw only one thing: the Legion of Honor was not a purely military reward, it would be awarded to civilians, to *citizens* who would, ipso facto, form a new aristocracy no less incompatible with the equality proclaimed in 1789 than the old one.[104] Bonaparte was so attached to this institution that he had deferred its creation until there was no danger of its being rejected. It was, along with the Civil Code, the cornerstone of his politics: "Everything has been destroyed; now it is time to recreate," he had said. "There is a government, powers, but the rest of the nation, what is it? Grains of sand. We have among us the former privileged people, organized by principle and interests, and they know exactly what they want. I can count my enemies. But we, on the other hand, are scattered, without system, without connection, without contact. So long as I am here, I can answer for the Republic; but we have to think about the future. Do you believe the Republic is definitively established? You would be very mistaken to think so. We can make it, but we don't have it, and we won't have it if we don't lay a few blocks of granite on the soil of France."[105]

"Meritocracy" may well have been part of 1789's heritage, but it was one thing to decree free access to all positions and to all offices "without any distinction other than that of talents and virtues," to borrow the words of the Declaration of Rights of 1789, and another to consecrate this process by creating a permanent body with titles, decorations, and pensions. The reestablishment of distinctions, and moreover distinctions associated with an idea, honor, on which the old aristocracy liked to pride itself, could not be imposed without encountering resistance. If the adversaries of such a measure dared to oppose it, then it was to some extent Bonaparte's fault, because he had entrusted the defense of the text to Roederer, who had once boasted about wanting to "dishonor honor."[106] As close as he was to the first consul, Roederer did not like him very much. Bonaparte esteemed his conversation, his vast knowledge, and even his advice, but he pardoned him neither his close ties with the clique surrounding Joseph nor, especially, his reservations regarding the concordat. Making him defend a law that reminded him of a past that he would prefer to forget was a way of putting him in his place, but it was also taking a risk. The bill passed the Tribunate and the Legislative Body, but by weak majorities: 56 votes to 38 in the former, 166 to 110 in the latter, while in the Council of State ten of the twenty-four members dared to vote against it.

Consul for Life

The defenders of the Revolution and the parliamentary system had fired their last ammunition. Bonaparte was resolutely advancing toward absolute power. He had brought back many of the forms, if not the spirit, of the Old Regime The servants at the Tuileries now wore liveries; a large consular guard watched over the first consul; Benezech, the master of ceremonies who had introduced ambassadors since Brumaire, had been replaced by chamberlains; and palace ladies surrounded Joséphine. There were military reviews, audiences, dinners and soirées; silk stockings and powdered wigs were back in fashion. Only women, Thibaudeau says, resisted the return of the old fashions because they feared that "dresses that showed figures" in the Greek or Roman manner would be abandoned in favor of the hoop-skirts of Louis XV's reign.[107]

Mary Berry, who had come to France in the spring of 1802, saw the first consul at a review at the Tuileries on April 5, and again in Joséphine's salon three days later. On April 5 she saw "a small man, who rode his horse well," with a "yellowish complexion," a "long nose," "close-cropped hair," and a "serious face," who disappeared as soon as he had passed the troops in review, without seeming to notice the curious crowds outside the fences.[108] On April 8 she saw an entirely different man enter the salon where Joséphine received her guests—taller than he had seemed to her at the review, with broad shoulders, light gray eyes, a smile that, Fiévée was to say, "deserved to become historic,"[109] and an intelligent face that breathed "frankness" and "calm." "The man of the review" and "the man of the salon" seemed to be two different persons:

He made the rounds of the room, speaking to each of the ladies for two or three minutes. M. de Luçay [one of the chamberlains] held in his hand a sheet of paper on which were written the name and the nationality of each lady. . . .

We had time to observe his manners and his way of approaching people; he is very simple and without affectations. He spoke to the Italians in their own language, repeating *riens royaux* of the same kind. My turn came. . . . Bonaparte asked me if I had been in Paris a long time. I replied: "More than three weeks."

"How do you like the opera? Were you satisfied with it?"

"Oh! Very lovely! But we have seen so many operas!"

This response seemed to make him feel that he could have spoken to us about something else. . . . Then he moved on to our neighbor, who happened to be Russian, and asked the same kind of questions: *did she ride, etc.* . . . When he had spoken to all the women, he addressed a few words here and there to the men grouped in front of the window, and then slipped out the door through which he had entered.[110]

He was not really at ease with women, not knowing quite what to say to them, and Chaptal reported a few of his blunders. He was more comfortable dealing with men—Chateaubriand, for example, who was presented to him a few days after the vote on the concordat and the publication—on April 14, 1802—of the *Génie du christianisme*:

Bonaparte noticed me and recognized me, I don't know how. When he came toward me, no one knew whom he was looking for; the crowd parted as he advanced; everyone hoped that the consul would stop and talk to him: he looked as if he felt impatient with these misunderstandings. I hid behind my neighbors; Bonaparte suddenly raised his voice and said to me: "Monsieur de Chateaubriand!" Then I was standing all alone in front of him, for the crowd drew back and soon reformed in a circle around the interlocutors. At first, Bonaparte approached me in a simple way: without complimenting me, without idle questions, without preliminaries, he immediately spoke to me about Egypt and the Arabs, as if I had been one of his close friends and as if he were merely continuing a conversation we had already begun. "I was always struck," he told me, "when I saw the sheikhs fall on their knees in the middle of the desert, turn toward the east, and touch the sand with their foreheads. What was the unknown thing they worshipped toward the east?" Bonaparte interrupted himself, and moving without transition to another idea, he said: "Christianity! Haven't the ideologues tried to make it into a system of astronomy? If that were true, do they think they [can] persuade me that Christianity is small? If Christianity is the allegory of the movement of the spheres, the geometry of the stars, freethinkers can talk all they want, despite themselves they still left enough grandeur to *l'infâme*." Bonaparte immediately walked away. Like Job, in my darkness, *a spirit passed before me, and the hair of my flesh stood up. It paused, but its likeness I could not discern; a figure was before my eyes, and I heard a still voice* [Job, 4:15–16]. . . . I noticed that as he moved through the crowd, Bonaparte gave me looks deeper than those he had given me as he spoke to me. . . . Fontanes and Mme Bacciochi told me about the satisfaction the consul had had from *my conversation*: I hadn't opened my mouth; that meant that Bonaparte was content with himself.[111]

Bonaparte was learning how to be a king without sacrificing to these new obligations any more time than necessary. Around him discussions had resumed regarding the future of the regime and his own future. Joseph and Lucien—the latter had returned from Madrid at the end of 1801—Talleyrand and Roederer were exhorting him to reestablish the monarchy for his own benefit.[112] Bonaparte was hardly more talkative on this subject than he had been in 1800; he pretended to be modest, refused to allow a monument to be erected in his honor, said that his ten-year consulate was all he needed to make him happy. He restrained his supporters, but all the while Cambacérès worked to increase the number of those who wanted to strengthen his power, if they couldn't make him a king right away. The two men understood each other without there being any need to say more.

Cambacérès—the third consul, Lebrun, supported his colleague—had made sure of the complicity of the purified Tribunate, where Lucien now played a leading role in favor of his brother. It was a tribune, Siméon, who took the initiative by asking his colleagues to express the wish that a "splendid token of national gratitude" be given the first consul. Bonaparte, of course, proved equal to the circumstances, thanking the tribunes who had come to communicate their deliberations to him, but replying that "the affection of [his] fellow citizens" sufficed to make him happy.[113] There was heavy traffic at Cambacérès's home, where the members of the Senate came one after another to inquire about the kind of reward most likely to please Bonaparte. Cambacérès thought the first consul took the matter too lightly; he urged him, if not to explain himself, at least to tell the Senators a little more clearly what he wanted. Bonaparte made fun of these fears, saying that from now on the Senate was prepared to do everything he asked of it and more.[114] Roederer, who was less worried than Cambacérès, took the initiative, calling upon the Senators, in an open letter published on May 8, to give Bonaparte "time to make France happy": "Give him the century that begins with him," he concluded, a transparent allusion to the Consulate for Life.[115]

Not everyone was ready for this, and it is to Fouché's maneuvering in the wings that historians attribute the decision the Senate made the same day, to accord the first consul only an extension of his term for an additional ten years.[116] Perhaps the Senators were playing a subtle game. In taking a step that was clearly a violation of the Constitution, which did not give them the power to increase the duration of the first consul's term, they were letting Bonaparte know that they would support his ambitions, but by granting him only another ten years, they were trying to make him understand that he should show some consideration for them in return.[117] As one might imagine, this "token of national gratitude" far from satisfied Bonaparte, and if the Senators had wanted to make him understand that he had to reckon with them, subsequent events showed them that the first consul could get along without them.[118] It is not that he considered this extension of ten years—until 1819—as too short for him; he would then be fifty years old. But because the Constitution already declared the first consul eligible to be reelected for another term once the first expired, he was expecting to be offered much more than what merely amounted to an early confirmation. This so-called reward seemed to him almost an insult. He "concealed his strong annoyance," Bourrienne says, "with that profound skill that he possessed in the highest degree when he could not do otherwise."[119] Cambacérès was called in to help. Just as he had found the legal artifice that made it possible to cleanse the assemblies, he came up with a subterfuge that allowed Bonaparte, by presenting the Senators' proposal to the people itself, to obtain from the citizens, with impressive effect, what the Senators had refused him.

> "The Senate offers you an extension of power," Cambacérès told him, "reply that you are grateful for such a proposal, but that it is not from [the Senate] but from the suffrage of the nation that you hold your authority, and it is from the nation alone that you can receive the extension, and that you want to consult it by the same means that were adopted for the consular Constitution. . . . Then we will have the Council of State draw up the formula that will be submitted to the national sanction. By making in this way an act of deference to the sovereignty of the people, we will succeed in substituting one proposal for another. We will raise the question, not whether General Bonaparte should receive an extension to ten years in office as consul, but whether he should receive the consulate for life."[120]

Cambacérès took care of everything, and Bonaparte retired to Malmaison. He was therefore absent on May 10 when the Council of State met to draft the question that would be put to the French people. The opponents—and they were few—preferred remaining silent to making empty protests, so it was easy to come to agreement on this question: "Shall Napoleon Bonaparte be consul for life?"

The referendum organized in the last days of 1799, three years earlier, had not involved more than 1.5 million Frenchmen.[121] This time participation approached 60 percent, and the yes votes almost 100 percent—apparently without rigging, if not without pressure[122]—since there were only 8,374 no votes. If we recall that the Constitution of 1793 had been approved by 34 percent of the French, that of 1795 by less than 20 percent, and that of 1799 by about 25 percent, the progress was spectacular, even if the regime was caught in its own trap.[123] Having artificially raised the score achieved in 1799, it could boast of only a small advance of less than ten points, whereas in fact the numbers of voters was higher

longer have any illusions. France willingly accepted Bonaparte's yoke. It was subjugated by the beginnings—brilliant in many respects, it is true—of the new government, which, for the first time in ages, satisfied its instincts for order and preservation. . . . Abroad, the Treaty of Amiens ensured the general peace that was so earnestly desired; at home, the émigrés had returned in large numbers . . . and everywhere the pact between the country and its new leader seemed to have been signed."[135]

On August 15, 1802, Bonaparte's birthday—the thirty-third—was celebrated like that of a king: "Solemn expressions of gratitude were offered to God," said a bitter, soon to be dismissed Fouché, "for having given France a man who had graciously consented to exercise supreme power all his life."[136] An orchestra of 300 performed a great concert, the Tuileries and Notre Dame were illuminated, a statue dedicated to peace was erected at the Pont Neuf, and receptions and a formal dinner were organized at the Tuileries.[137] A week later the first consul was seen, accompanied by his wife, taking possession of the loge that had been prepared for him at the Théâtre-Français. Mlle Duchesnois and Talma were playing *Andromaque,* and when the curtain went down, Bonaparte, who was wearing "a very richly embroidered blue jacket," rose and saluted the applauding audience three times before leaving.[138] The next day, August 21, he went to the Senate to swear the oath of office. From the Tuileries to the Luxembourg Palace, troops lined both sides of the street. For the first time Bonaparte did not share his carriage with Cambacérès and Lebrun. Drawn by eight horses, like the carriage of the kings of France, it was escorted by a numerous staff on horseback, in full dress uniforms, and followed by the regiments of the consular guard and the cortege of the major state bodies. A deputation from the Senate awaited Bonaparte at the entrance to the Luxembourg and led him to the armchair, which rather resembled a throne, that had been prepared for him.[139]

Was this still the republic? The question of inherited power had been only halfway decided by the *sénatus-consulte* of August 4, which accorded the first consul the right to designate his successor. Bonaparte had begun by refusing to allow the question to be asked publicly, even if from time to time he made a few offhand remarks, saying, for example, to Roederer that kings had been very lucky, that they were respected because the crown was seen as a property transmitted from father to son.[140] Nonetheless, when the Council of State had taken the initiative of adding the question to the text that was to be submitted to the vote of the French people, Bonaparte had struck it out, reducing the plebiscite to the establishment of the Consulate for Life alone.[141]

He had no lack of reasons for not wanting any allusion to a future that he did not allow himself to think was imminent: only thirty-three years old and set to hold office until he was forty, he thought the time had not yet come to raise that question. It has been said that he feared the stability characteristic of the monarchical system, and feared still more that the latter might take a constitutional form that would inevitably involve the limitation of his powers.[142] Even supposing that he had sought a monarchy, was it possible to achieve one without observing any transition, without considering the sensitivities of those whom the very word threw into convulsions? Wasn't it wiser to leave things as they were, so as to allow the French to reacquire the habit of absolute power, even if it meant later taking advantage of the uncertainties weighing on the future of the regime to impose, finally, the reestablishment of hereditary monarchy?

Bonaparte's opposition to the question of hereditary power was not a matter of principle. But assuming that his authority was transmitted to his heir, who would be the lucky chosen one?

He no longer believed that Joséphine would bear him a child. She had also lost all hope, and for that reason showed herself, supported by Fouché, resolutely hostile to any reform of the institutions. She was satisfied with her role as the first consul's wife, and she feared that the role of queen, or empress— since Charlemagne's empire was being talked about—would signal the beginning of difficult times. For a while she had believed she could persuade her husband to make himself the instrument of a monarchical restoration on behalf of the Bourbons, but she had to face the facts: "Bonaparte" (as she continued to call him) would never agree to play the role of *connétable* (commander-in-chief) that had been proposed for him in London.[143] Thus, she had to persuade her husband—with the aid of Fouché, in whom she had found an ally—to cease thinking about taking up the succession of the Bourbons. If no child was born of their marriage, to whom could they turn? Bonaparte feared above all opening the Pandora's box of family ambitions. Joseph was already a candidate to succeed him. The idea was grotesque.[144] He sometimes mentioned Cambacérès, and Carnot as well, but immediately changed his mind. If he excluded one choice, it was certainly to name an heir in his will: the fate Louis XIV's last will and testament had met with in the Parlement de Paris was there to show him how much wills, and the dead, were worth: "One cannot fail to see that a dead man is no longer anything," and his last will not much more, he explained to the state councilors who had met to revise the Constitution of Year VIII.[145]

However, an idea was taking shape in his mind. Roederer says that it was as early as the end of 1800 that Joséphine, increasingly tired of pursuing treatments that made no change to her situation, conceived the project of marrying her daughter Hortense to her brother-in-law Louis, whom Napoleon had earlier cared for as if he had been his own son.[146] This marriage, reinforcing the bonds between the Bonapartes and the Beauharnais, would make her position stronger, and the birth of a child would allow Napoleon to adopt the heir that she now knew she could not give him. The question of the succession, if it ever came up, would be less difficult. But it was not so easy to obtain the consent of Hortense, who had become infatuated, to her mother's great dismay, with Duroc, the general's aide-de-camp. Joséphine dreamed of a marriage that was more politically useful, if not more brilliant. As for the sullen Louis, he was hardly more enthusiastic. He was in love with one of Hortense's cousins, Émilie de Beauharnais. The combined efforts of Joséphine and Napoleon, who had been won over to the project,[147] finally overcame the young people's reluctance: the wedding took place before the first consul left for Lyon.

Ultimately, it was the success of the plebiscite held in the summer of 1802—and the numerous appeals written on the voting registers favoring the first consul's right to designate his successor[148]—that caused him to change his mind and accept what he had refused in May.

And there was something else.

Louis and Hortense's marriage lasted hardly longer than the wedding ceremony. The couple were not going to grow old together. Louis, jealous, suspicious, taking out on his wife the hatred he felt for Joséphine, quarreled with her; she wept and two months had not gone by before he abandoned her. But when the young woman took refuge in the Tuileries, she was pregnant. The conception dated from the first days of the marriage. Despite the dates—Napoléon-Charles was born on October 18, 1802—a rumor soon spread, peddled by the

NOTES

Translator's Note

I would like to thank first of all my wife, Lisa Neal, who read the whole draft and made many crucial suggestions for improvement. I would also like to thank the author, Patrice Gueniffey, and my editors: Ian Malcolm, Joy Deng, and Kate Brick at Harvard University Press, and Kimberly Giambattisto at Westchester Publishing Services, for all their help. Any blunders or infelicities that may remain are, of course, entirely my own.

Every effort has been made to locate quotations from the original French text in English editions. Where this was not possible, I have cited the French work and translated the quotation.

Introduction

1 Las Cases, *Mémorial*, 2:893.

2 "Heroic Symphony, Composed to celebrate the memory of a great man." On the change in the title of Beethoven's third symphony, see the account by his friend Ferdinand Ries (Wegeler and Ries, *Notices biographiques sur Ludwig van Beethoven*, 104–105). On Beethoven's hesitations, see Solomon, *Beethoven*, 157–167; see also Lentz, *Cent questions sur Napoléon*, 53–54.

3 Nietzsche, *Oeuvres philosophiques complètes*, 13:123 (fragment from autumn 1887).

4 Bainville, *Napoléon*, 250.

5 The phrase is from the subtitle of Annie Jourdan's book *Napoléon: Héros, imperator, mécène*.

6 Serra, *Malaparte*, 132–135. The anonymous pamphlet mentioned above is quoted by Maurizio Serra. It was published in Turin in 1869 and was entitled *I Malaparte ed i Bonaparte nel le centenario di un Bonaparte-Malaparte*.

7 Hazareesingh, *La Saint-Napoléon*, 16.

8 Covin, *Les Mille visages de Napoléon*.

9 Letter of December 7, 1796, quoted in A. Dayot, *Napoléon: Raconté par l'image*, 39.

10 Ibid., 24.

11 In a valuable work, Armand Dayot has reproduced a large number of portraits, busts, and medals depicting Napoleon that allow us to follow his metamorphoses and to see the infinite diversity of the representations of him. This rare work can be consulted at the following Web address: http://gallica.bnf.fr/ark:/12148/bpt6k63053579.r=armand+dayot .langFR.

12 Foucart, "Les Salons sous le Consulat."

13 http://www.robswebstek.com/2010_11_01_archive.html.

14 Barthes, *La Chambre claire*, in *Oeuvres complètes*, 3:1111.

15 Whateley, *Historic Doubts Relative to Napoleon Buonaparte*, 1.

16 "symbol of individual energy": see Tulard, *Le Mythe de Napoléon*, 6, and Bloom, "Napoleon and Prometheus." The Guérin portrait, engraved by Jean-Gabriel Fiésinger, was deposited in the National Library on 29 Vendémiaire, Year VII (October 20, 1798).

17 Taine, *The Origins of Contemporary France*, 1:13–14.

18 Leys, *The Death of Napoleon*, 79–80.

19 Georges Lefebvre observes that Napoleon established himself so firmly "at the center of universal history" that "despite the profound unity that binds his reign to the revolutionary tragedy, the traditional division founded on his advent cannot be recommended" (*Napoléon*, 2).

20 Prendergast, *Napoleon and History Painting*, 20–32.

21 See also Bouthillon, "Comme quoi Napoléon n'a jamais existé" (1988).

22 Pérès, *Comme quoi Napoléon n'a jamais existé*, 5. Gérard de Nerval also makes use of this solar metaphor in his *Napoléon et la France guerrière* (1826); compare Tulard, *Le Mythe de Napoléon*, 8.

23 Whately, *Historic Doubts Relative to Napoleon Buonaparte*, 8; Peter Geyl, in his *Napoleon: For and Against*, rightly concluded from the multiplicity of judgments and portraits of Bonaparte that the historiographic debate about him could never come to an end (16).

24 Lefebvre, *Napoléon*, 2.

25 To mention only a few great successes, see J. Le Goff, *Saint Louis*, and J.-C. Petitfils, *Louis XIV* and *Louis XVI*.

26 A list can be found in the bibliographies by R. J. Caldwell, J. A. Meyer, R. Martin, and A. Pigeard cited in the bibliography, and a presentation of the most important, with the exception of the most recent, can be found in Geyl, *Napoleon: For and Against*, and Petiteau, *Napoléon, de la mythologie à l'histoire*.

27 See the bibliographies cited in the preceding note. In the twentieth century, most of the biographies have been written in English, including those of J. Holland Rose (1934), H. Butterfield (1939), J. M. Thompson (1951), F. Markham (1963), V. Cronin (1971), B. R. Jones (1977), P. Johnson (2002), S. Englund (2004), Ph. Dwyer (2007), and others. Even the "biographies" published on the occasion of the bicentenary of the proclamation of the Empire are not really biographies, with the notable exception of Luigi Mascilli Migliorini's *Napoléon*. Steven Englund claimed to have written "a *political* life, not a military or an intimate life" (*Napoléon: A Political Life*, 471), and Philip Dwyer focused on the figure of Napoleon especially from the point of view of a cultural history of the politician.

28 "impure genre": I refer the reader to Madelénat, *La Biographie*, Dosse, *Le Pari biographique*, and especially Loriga, *Le Petit X*.

29 Furet, *Le Passé d'une illusion*, 199–201.

30 Ibid.

31 Tocqueville, *Democracy in America*, 569.

32 See in particular Loriga, *Le Petit X*, 9–12.

33 Ibid., 39. On this turning point in methodology and its effects, see also Julliard, *Que sont les grands hommes devenus?*, 8–11.

34 See Regent, "Nietzsche's Napoleon: A Renaissance Man."

35 See in particular Bergeron, *L'Épisode napoléonien*, vol. 1, *Aspects intérieurs*; Bergeron, *Banquiers, négociants et manufacturiers parisiens* (1978); and Bergeron and Chaussinand-Nogaret, *Grands notables du Premier Empire* (30 vols., published 1978–2011).

36 The *Dictionnaire Napoléon* edited by Tulard (1999), Woloch's *Napoleon and His Collaborators*, and J.-O. Boudon's works on the episcopacy of the concordat represent a few of the results owed to this broadening of our perspective. We may add to them the works of Th. Lentz, from his *Le Grand Consulat* (1999) to his extensive *Nouvelle histoire du Premier Empire* (4 vols., 2002–2010).

37 Petiteau, *Voies nouvelles pour l'histoire du Premier Empire*; Petiteau, *Napoléon, de la mythologie à l'histoire*, 11–25. For a recent survey of this historiographic renewal, see Lignereux, *L'Empire des Français*, 7–14.

38 Lignereux, *L'Empire des Français*, 10.

39 Ibid., 17.

40 R. W. Emerson, "Napoleon: Man of the World," in *Representative Men*, 144–146.

41 F. Nietzsche, *Genealogy of Morals*, §16.

42 Whately, *Historic Doubts Relative to Napoleon Buonaparte*, 13–15.

43 Bainville, *Napoléon*, 607.

44 Taine, *The Origins of Contemporary France*, 1:110–150.

45 M. Dumas, *Souvenirs*, 2:226–237.

46 Chateaubriand, *Voyage en Amérique*, in *De l'Ancien Régime au Nouveau Monde*, 95–98 (this parallel, published in 1827, had been written in 1822); Chateaubriand, *Mémoires d'outre-tombe*, 1:414–418.

47 Chateaubriand, *Mémoires d'outre-tombe*, 1:1552–1553.

48 Staël, *Considérations sur la Révolution française*, 357.

49 Chateaubriand, *Voyage en Amérique*, 100.

50 Clausewitz, *La Campagne de 1815 en France*, 16.

51 Borges, "Biografía de Tadeo Isidoro Cruz, (1829–1874)."

1. An Italian Family in Corsica

1 Galantini, *Napoléon et Sarzane: Les origines italiennes de Bonaparte*.

2 Taine, *The Origins of Contemporary France*, 1:4.

3 The Ramolinos, who came from Lombardy or Tuscany—it is not clear which—had also settled in Corsica in the sixteenth century.

4 In 1661, more than a century after the family had settled in Corsica, one of the Buonapartes, Sebastiano, obtained from the Republic of Genoa official recognition of his noble and Genoese ancestry. His great-grandson Giuseppe succeeded in extorting from the grand duke of Tuscany letters that certified the noble and Tuscan origin of the Buonapartes, recognizing their right to claim the rank of patricians. (Chuquet, *La Jeunesse de Napoléon*, 1:42–44.)

5 Gourgaud, *Talks of Napoleon at St. Helena*, 38.

6 Valéry, *Cahiers*, 1:52.

7 Versini, *M. de Buonaparte ou le livre inachevé*, 33.

8 See Tomi, "Les biens de la famille Bonaparte."

9 Gourgaud, *Talks of Napoleon at St. Helena*, 36. It is impossible to say what the modern equivalent of these sums would be. Bernard Simiot (*De quoi vivait Bonaparte*, 12) speaks of an annual revenue of 1.5 million 1950 francs, and Frank McLynn (*Napoleon*, 4) of a revenue

equivalent to 90 pounds sterling, or about 135,000 euros. But these figures are mere approximations.

10 Bertrand, *Cahiers de Sainte-Hélène*, 3:64.

11 In Corsica, "property is divided from one generation to the next in such a way that each of the heirs receives as his lot a little of the property of all his ancestors, both paternal and maternal. Are there three children and three houses to be shared? A Corsican inheritance will never give one house to each of the children: tradition demands that each one inherit one-third of each of the three houses" (Vergé-Franceschi, *Histoire de Corse*, 1:26–27).

12 Ibid., 1:177, 2:316, 2:418.

13 From more than 7,000 livres, the family revenue fell to less than 1,500 livres at the end of the 1780s (McLynn, *Napoleon*, 32). These "fortunes" were fragile: the system of inheritance made it difficult to transfer capital, most of the revenue from landed property was received in kind, and liquid assets proceeded chiefly from emoluments connected with the exercise of administrative and judicial functions. Just like the Buonapartes were thrown into financial difficulties by the death of Charles, the Pozzo di Borgos experienced the same in 1781 after the death of the father of Charles-André (Napoleon's future rival). The latter had to take a position as a public prosecutor to support his family, which nevertheless owned twenty-two landed properties (Carrington, "Les Pozzo di Borgo et les Bonaparte," 107–109).

14 Napoléon Bonaparte, *Manuscrits inédits*, 395.

15 Montholon, *Récits de la captivité de l'Empereur Napoléon à Sainte-Hélène*, 2:16. The reference is to a fable of Aesop's (and La Fontaine's) whose moral is that the weaker party should beware of the stronger.

16 Venturi, *Rivoluzione di Corsica*, 7–8.

17 Chuquet, *Jeunesse de Napoléon*, 1:5.

18 Voltaire, *Oeuvres historiques*, 1544.

19 Hypothesis put forth by Michel Vergé-Franceschi, *Histoire de Corse*, 1:28–29.

20 Article "Buttafuoco" in *Dictionnaire Larousse du XIXe siècle*, 1446.

21 Quoted in Pillepich, *Napoléon et les Italiens*, 13.

22 Voltaire, *Oeuvres historiques*, 1546.

23 Vergé-Franceschi, *Paoli*, 12–13.

24 Ph. Meyer, *Dans mon pays lui-même . . .* , 101.

25 Taine, *The Origins of Contemporary France*, 1:4. Compare the delightful and so accurate chapter on Corsica in Edmond Demolins's book published at about the same time: *Les Français d'aujourd'hui*, 163–199.

26 Bertrand, *Cahiers*, 2:218, 315.

27 Ibid.

28 Carlo Levi, *Christ Stopped at Eboli*, 4.

29 Englund, *Napoleon*, 9.

30 Ibid., 6.

31 See, for example, Casanova and Rovère, *La Révolution française en Corse*, 146–161.

32 See Pomponi, "Sentiment révolutionnaire et esprit de parti en Corse au temps de la Révolution," 56–87.

33 *podestà*: similar to a chief magistrate. The *consulte* was an institution peculiar to Corsica, a large assembly convoked to resolve a general problem.

34 Quoted in Boswell, *An Account of Corsica*, 128.

35 *Correspondance générale*, no. 2149 (to Talleyrand, October 7, 1797), 1:1244–1246.

36 Defranceschi, "Corse," in J. Tulard, *Dictionnaire Napoléon*, 1:519.

37 Boswell, *An Account of Corsica*, 162.

38 This point is emphasized by Venturi, *Rivoluzione di Corsica*, 30–40.

39 Quoted in A. Rovère, "Paoli dans son temps: La naissance des mythes," in Cini, *Nascita di un mito*, 17.

40 Graziani, *Pascal Paoli*, 14.

41 See the instructions given by the secretary of state for foreign affairs, the Marquis de Chauvelin, to the French representative in Genoa, Campredon, on April 26, 1735, in Pomponi, *Mémorial des Corses*, 2:282.

42 Arrighi, *Histoire de la Corse*, 78–79.

43 Boswell, *An Account of Corsica*, 25.

44 Quoted in Charles Napoléon, *Bonaparte et Paoli*, 83.

45 Masson, *Napoléon et sa famille*, 1:10.

46 Report filed September 11, 1767: "In this city [Ajaccio] there are writers who favor General Paoli, and I strongly suspect Monsieur Buonaparte, the brother of the Consul's wife [Gertrude, Carlo's sister, had married the French consul, Nicola Paravaccini], who resides in Corte with his wife, and who remains here only as a spy" (Caratini, *Napoléon, une imposture*, 60).

47 Voltaire, *Oeuvres historiques*, 1552.

48 On September 11, 1767, he wrote that he would prefer "the choice of arms to losing freedom forever by yielding to the desires of the French, with a strong probability of eventually finding ourselves once again under Genoa's yoke" (A. M. Graziani, *Pascal Paoli*, 246–247. [The translation of the French quoted from Graziani is my own.—Trans.]

49 See Jollivet, *La Révolution française en Corse*, 15; Carrington, *Napoleon and His Parents*, 44–45; and Vergé-Franceschi, *Paoli*, 374–379. Some say that the mercenaries opened fire on the Corsicans at the order of an officer, Giocante Grimaldi, who is supposed to have been in the pay of the French (Antonetti, *Histoire de la Corse*, 372–373).

50 Antonetti, *Histoire de la Corse*, 374.

51 "Long live the king and his government!" Quoted in Chuquet, *Jeunesse de Napoléon*, 1:55.

2. A French Upbringing

1 Because the parish registers for the years 1745–1750 are not extant, there remains some doubt regarding the year of Letizia's birth.

2 Pomponi, *Histoire de la Corse*, 291–293.

3 *Code corse*, 1:128–130.

4 On this land plan or "plan terrier," which was completed only in 1795, see Willis, "Development Planning in Eighteenth-Century France: Corsica's Plan Terrier."

5 Pommereul, *Histoire de l'île de Corse*, 1:39–47.

6 "The right granted everyone to rely on hunting and gathering freely over the whole island, to fish in the sea, the rivers, and the lakes along the coast, to take from the common resources all the wood and materials necessary for lighting, the construction of his house, his plowing implements, etc., to graze his flock on all the open lands of the island, and finally to practice an itinerant agriculture on the common lands on the sole condition of restoring

the parcel to the community after cultivating it for three years, made each inhabitant of the island a small independent property owner, to the point that those who owned land . . . found no one to work it and had to either cultivate it themselves or bring workers in from the continent (generally from Lucca) to do the agricultural work" (J. Defranceschi, "Corse," in Tulard, *Dictionnaire Napoléon*, 1:557).

7 These "marquisates" received by people such as the Count of Marbeuf and Buttafoco comprised more than 10 percent of the island's surface (Casanova and Rovère, *La Révolution française en Corse*, 42–44).

8 Chuquet, *Jeunesse de Napoléon*, 1:19.

9 Mascilli Migliorini, *Napoléon*, 20–21.

10 Chuquet, *Jeunesse de Napoléon*, 1:39.

11 Ibid., 26–31.

12 Quotation from Antonetti, *Histoire de la Corse*, 376.

13 Seventy-six other families were declared to be noble. We do not know the exact number of Corsicans who benefited from the edict of 1770 creating a nobility on the island, but it must not have been negligible: the recognition accorded the Pozzo di Borgo family alone created thirteen nobles in Ajaccio; that accorded the Pietri de Sartène family, forty-three; and that accorded the Ortoli family, fifty-six—all the inhabitants of the village of Olmiccia (Carrington, "Les Pozzo di Borgo et les Bonaparte," 112–113). If we assume an average of fifty ennoblements per act of recognition, we obtain a figure amounting to about 4,000 nobles, or slightly less than 3 percent for a population of 150,000.

14 Montholon, *Récits*, 2:18.

15 Bartel, *Jeunesse inédite de Napoléon*, 25.

16 Quoted in Chuquet, *Jeunesse de Napoléon*, 1:45–51.

17 See Carrington, *Napoleon and His Parents*, 102–108.

18 Quoted by Defranceschi, *Jeunesse de Napoléon*, 209.

19 *Correspondance générale*, no. 29 (to Paoli, June 12, 1789), 1:76.

20 Chateaubriand, *Mémoires d'outre-tombe*, 1:1091–1093.

21 Chuquet, *Jeunesse de Napoléon*, 1:76.

22 Lévy, *Private Life of Napoleon*, 11.

23 Quoted in Leys, *Protée et autres essais*, 59.

24 Chateaubriand, *Mémoires d'outre-tombe*, 1:1097.

25 Ibid., 1101–1102.

26 Ibid., 1088.

27 Lanfrey, *The History of Napoleon the First*, 1:6.

28 Nietzsche, *Fragments posthumes (été 1882–printemps 1884)*, 80.

29 His first name was odd in Brienne and Paris, but relatively common around Genoa and in Tuscany. The first name of one of his paternal uncles was Napoleon; this uncle was buried in Cortre in 1767 under the name "Lapulion Bonaparte" (Vergé-Franceschi, *Napoléon, une enfance corse*, 31–33).

30 *Buonaparte et sa famille, ou confidences d'un de leurs anciens amis* (1816), quoted in Simiot, *De quoi vivait Bonaparte*, 18.

31 Bainville, *Napoléon*, 19–21.

32 Quoted by Lévy, *Private Life of Napoleon*, 12.

33 Bertrand, *Cahiers*, 2:67.

34 Bourrienne, *Private Memoirs*, 1:32.

35 Las Cases, *Journal*, 1:115–116.

36 As is proven by a letter written to his father on leaving Brienne: *Correspondance générale*, no. 2 (to Charles Bonaparte, September 12 or 13, 1784), 1:45.

37 See Chaptal, *Mes souvenirs sur Napoléon*, 64–66.

38 Montholon, *Récits*, 2:19.

39 Norvins, *Mémorial*, 3:117–128. He was referring to a risqué game of outdoor hide-and-seek played most famously by Marie Antoinette in the gardens of Versailles.

40 Abrantès, *Souvenirs sur Napoléon*, 25.

41 Bertrand, *Cahiers*, 3:70–71.

42 Las Cases, *Journal*, 2:114.

43 Quoted by Lévy, *Private Life of Napoleon*, 12.

44 Norvins, *Mémorial*, 1:10–12.

45 Picot de Peccaduc (ranked 39th, with the highest score in the group from the Paris École militaire), Phélippeaux (41st), Buonaparte (42nd), and his friend Des Mazis (56th) (Carrington, *Napoleon and His Parents*, 181–182).

46 Quoted by Bainville, *Napoléon*, 27.

47 Quoted by Chuquet, *Jeunesse de Napoléon*, 1:207.

48 Sicard, *Études classiques avant la Révolution*, 47.

49 Hahn, *Le Système du monde*, 23.

50 Rollin, *Traité des études*, 1:17–28.

51 Quoted by Delbeke, *Action politique et sociale des avocats au XVIIIe siècle*, 45.

52 Joubert, *Pensées, essais et maximes*, 2:384–390 (letter to Fontanes, June 8, 1809).

3. The French Officer and the Corsican Patriot

1 Quoted by Simiot, *De quoi vivait Bonaparte*, 29.

2 Las Cases, *Journal*, 2:286.

3 "I won't have my semester leave until next September," he moaned in a letter of November 25, 1785 (*Correspondance générale*, no. 7, 1:49).

4 Simiot, *De quoi vivait Bonaparte*, 37.

5 Including two long stays in Paris, the first in 1787, the second in 1792.

6 "At last, I'm free," he is supposed to have exclaimed upon leaving the École militaire (*Cahiers d'Alexandre Des Mazis*).

7 Las Cases, *Journal*, 1:127.

8 Madelin, *Histoire du Consulat et de l'Empire*, 1:61.

9 Bertrand, *Cahiers*, 3:71; Las Cases, *Mémorial*, 1:92–93.

10 Joubert, *Pensées*, 2:390.

11 Bainville, *Napoléon*, 16–19.

12 Ibid., 32.

13 *Correspondance générale*, no. 2 (to Charles Bonaparte, September 12 or 13, 1784), 1:45. James Boswell's book, published in 1768, had been translated into French the following year.

Some scholars say that Napoleon read it in Italian translation (Ettori, "Pascal Paoli, modèle du jeune Bonaparte," 94).

14 Las Cases, *Mémorial*, 2:338–339, 459.

15 Ibid.

16 Joseph Bonaparte, *Mémoires*, 1:32.

17 The Genevan pastor Antoine-Jacques Roustan's book is entitled *Défense du christianisme considéré du côté politique où l'on répond en particulier au chapitre VIII du quatrième livre du Contrat social.*

18 Quoted by Simiot, *De quoi vivait Bonaparte*, 40.

19 Napoléon Bonaparte, *Manuscrits inédits*, 367.

20 Chateaubriand, *Mémoires d'outre-tombe*, 1:1138.

21 I will return to this story later.

22 Ibid., 1101.

23 Martin, *Napoleon the Novelist*, 10.

24 Bainville, *Napoléon*, 28–29.

25 Napoléon Bonaparte, *Manuscrits inédits*, 384.

26 Ibid., 2–4.

27 Bainville, *Napoléon*, 32.

28 Chateaubriand, *Mémoires d'outre-tombe*, 1:1100.

29 Napoléon Bonaparte, *Manuscrits inédits*, 6.

30 Staël, *De l'influence des passions*, 56–57.

31 Napoléon Bonaparte, *Manuscrits inédits*, 536–537. This paragraph does not appear in the final version of the *Essay on Happiness*.

32 Tulard, *Napoléon: Ou le mythe du sauveur*, 42.

33 *Correspondance générale*, no. 14 (to Loménie de Brienne, November 24, 1787), 1:57–58.

34 Quoted by Madelin, *Histoire du Consulat et de l'Empire*, 1:53.

35 *Correspondance générale*, no. 317 (to Joseph, July 30, 1795), 1:242–243.

36 Ibid., no. 337 (to Joseph, September 6, 1795), 1:261–262.

37 Ibid., no. 389 (to Joseph, January 1, 1796), 1:287–288.

38 Ibid., no. 349 (to Joseph, October 11, 1795), 1:270.

39 Las Cases, *Mémorial*, 3:372.

40 Ibid., 2:662.

41 The Saint-Cyr-l'École boarding school for young noblewomen had been founded by Louis XIV in 1684, at the request of Mme de Maintenon.

42 Masson, *Napoléon et sa famille*, 1:35.

43 Las Cases, *Journal*, 4:78.

44 Larrey, *Madame Mère*, 1:73–74; Bertrand, *Cahiers*, 2:315; O'Meara, *Napoléon dans l'exil*, 2:67.

45 *Correspondance générale*, no. 25 (to Letizia, April 15, 1789), 1:72.

46 Ibid., no. 4 (to Archdeacon Lucien Bonaparte, March 28, 1785), 1:47.

47 Ibid., no. 5 (to Letizia, March 28, 1785), 1:48. In order to attenuate the impression of coldness and indifference, some historians claim that the letters written by students were corrected by their teachers. However, it seems that no one went over these letters. Would the

professors have let pass turns of phrase as incorrect as "j'ai été sensible au malheur *qu'il vient* de nous arriver" or, speaking of his deceased father, "tous nous désignons en lui," instead of "tous nous désignions en lui"? Probably not.

48 Quoted by Bourrienne, *Private Memoirs*, 1:32.

49 *Correspondance générale*, no. 29 (to Pascal Paoli, June 12, 1789), 1:76.

50 This memorandum of the municipality of Ajaccio written by Napoleon is reproduced in Nasica, *Mémoires sur l'enfance et la jeunesse de Napoléon Ier*, 98–99.

51 Las Cases, *Journal*, 1:107.

52 *Correspondance générale*, no. 23 (to Archdeacon Lucien Bonaparte, March 28, 1789), 1:70.

53 Bertrand, *Cahiers*, 1:178.

54 Las Cases, *Journal*, 1:106.

55 He had Marbeuf's portrait taken down when Paoli returned to Corsica in 1790 (see *Correspondance générale*, no. 35 [to Joseph, 1790], 1:83). Paul Bartel (*Jeunesse inédite de Napoléon*, 42) states that in this letter to Joseph, Napoleon added, after "Remove Marbeuf's portrait," the following: "Also remove Mama's portrait," a phrase that does not appear in the recent edition of the *Correspondance*. Is this connected with the "three or four illegible words" mentioned by Ernest d'Hauterive in the edition of these youthful letters, which he was the first to publish ("Lettres de jeunesse de Bonaparte [1789–1792]," 788) on the basis of a copy of the original preserved in the National Archives (400 AP 137), and which also includes this phrase? Was Bartel able to consult the original document, which seems now to have been lost?

56 He was still talking about it on Saint Helena (Las Cases, *Mémorial*, 1:80).

57 Monge (1745–1818) was a brilliant mathematician and longtime friend of Bonaparte.

58 Bartel, *Jeunesse de Napoléon*, 43.

59 Robert, *Roman des origines*, 59.

60 Machiavel, *Oeuvres complètes*, 913 (emphasis added).

61 Robert, *Roman des origines*, 51.

62 Ibid., 56–57.

63 Chateaubriand, *Mémoires d'outre-tombe*, 1:1093.

64 Taine, *The Origins of Contemporary France*, 1:2.

65 Bourrienne, *Private Memoirs of Napoleon Bonaparte*, 1:142.

4. The Revolutionary of Ajaccio

1 Napoléon Bonaparte, *Manuscrits inédits*, 387.

2 Natalie Tomiche (*Napoléon écrivain*, 113–119) is, to the best of my knowledge, the only historian who has been sufficiently attentive to see that the text published by Masson and Biagi (Napoléon Bonaparte, *Manuscrits inédits*, 383–445) was at best no more than a fragment of the one Napoleon wrote in 1787–1789.

3 *Correspondance générale*, no. 26 (May 1789), 1:73.

4 Ibid., no. 28 (April or May 1789), 1:74–76. This letter is generally dated to June 1789, which is too late, considering its content.

5 In the letter, Bonaparte pleaded with Paoli to support his book, writing: "If you deign, General, to approve a work in which you will often appear; if you deign to encourage the

efforts of a young man whom you saw born, and whose relatives were always attached to the good party, I shall dare to predict its success. . . . Whatever the fate of my work, I sense that it will arouse the hostility of the numerous cohort of French employees who govern our island, and whom I attack; but what does that matter, if the interest of the fatherland is at stake?" *Correspondance générale*, no. 29, 1:76.

6 Ibid., no. 30 (July 15, 1789), 1:77–78.

7 Ibid., no. 25 (April 15, 1789), 1:72; no. 31 (July 22, 1789), 1:78–79.

8 Ibid., no. 31 (July 22, 1789), 1:78–79.

9 A further decree, that of January 21, 1790, was necessary to put an end to the debate (Graziani, *Pascal Paoli*, 297–298).

10 Quoted by Vergé-Franceschi, *Paoli*, 424.

11 Defranceschi, *Corse française*, 38–39.

12 The Buonapartes and the Pozzo di Borgo family had long been close. Charles-André, Napoléon's future adversary, had been Joseph Fesch's schoolmate. A friend of Napoléon's brother Joseph, Charles-André had become Napoléon's friend as well during the latter's stay in Corsica in 1786–1788 (McErlean, *Napoleon and Pozzo di Borgo*, 13–22).

13 Quoted in Chuquet, *Jeunesse de Napoléon*, 2:109.

14 Ibid.

15 Napoléon Bonaparte, *Manuscrits inédits*, 396–397.

16 See Defranceschi, "Le rôle du lieutenant Bonaparte aux débuts de la Révolution française en Corse."

17 Albert Chuquet states, following Nasica, that this incident took place on the last Sunday of July 1790, and thus he presents it as the result of the events at the end of June 1790 (*Jeunesse de Napoléon*, 122–123). In reality, it occurred in early May after Napoleon and Joseph's return from Orezza, around April 23 or 24 (McErlean, *Napoleon and Pozzo di Borgo*, 46): The *Giornale Patriottico di Corsica*, recently founded by Buonarroti, reports these events in its May 22, 1790, issue (70–71).

18 Nasica, *Mémoires sur l'enfance et la jeunesse de Napoléon*, 85.

19 Ibid., 87–99.

20 On Masseria, see McErlean, "Between Paoli and Bonaparte: Philippe Masseria, an Anglomaniac in Corsica, 1789–1793." Nonetheless, in August 1790 Napoleon made remarks about Masseria to his brother Joseph that were not very obliging: "Masseria is writing a great deal here, but his letters, like his face, are not persuasive; they repel. The man has no tact" (*Correspondance générale*, no. 41 [August 22, 1790], 1:87). The expression "bravissimo uomo" is found in O'Meara, *Napoléon dans l'exil*, 1:232.

21 Tocqueville, *De la démocratie en Amérique: Souvenirs—L'Ancien Régime et la Révolution*, 1119.

22 In a letter to his friend Nobili Savelli, quoted by Defranceschi, *Jeunesse de Napoléon*, 134.

23 Mascilli Migliorini, *Napoléon*, 51.

24 The minimum age required was twenty-five.

25 *Correspondance générale*, no. 37 (February or March 10, 1790), 1:84.

26 Quoted by Defranceschi, *Jeunesse de Napoléon*, 136–137.

27 A nickname given Paoli that means "grandfather."

28 Las Cases, *Journal*, 2:343–344.

29 Saliceti was named the general prosecuting magistrate of the department, but because he had a seat in the Constituent Assembly, Aréna replaced him. The assembly in Orezza was in fact under Paoli's thumb. Not content to choose those whom he designated, it made him, completely illegally, commander in chief of the national guards of the island's nine districts. It even went beyond what he wanted by attributing to him, as to a monarch, and with a praiseworthy generosity, a civil list (funds and property granted by the state to the sovereign) amounting to 50,000 livres—in a department that produced only 180,000 livres in tax revenues (Graziani, *Pascal Paoli*, 308).

30 Las Cases, *Journal*, 3:141.

31 Bainville, *Napoléon*, 42.

32 In his *Discours sur le bonheur* (Napoléon Bonaparte, *Manuscrits inédits*, 560).

33 Alexandre Des Mazis, who was his comrade in Valence, implies the contrary. He is clear-sighted about Bonaparte's "republicanism," so his testimony should not be dismissed: "Republican ideas were beginning to sprout in people's minds, and they had sprung up spontaneously in Buonaparte's head when he was a child, but its theater did not extend beyond Corsica; thus, when after the Federation [of July 14, 1791] an attempt was made to force officers to attend popular assemblies, he refused. The political movements operating in France made him hope that one day Paoli, who was his hero, would return to his country and that he might join him to found in Corsica the Spartan republic of which he had always dreamed" (*Cahiers*).

34 Madelin, *Histoire du Consulat et de l'Empire*, 1:118–119.

35 Mascilli Migliorini, *Napoléon*, 52.

36 An air from *Richard Coeur de lion*, an opera by Grétry (1784), which had become the royalists' hymn.

37 See *Correspondance générale*, no. 49 (April 24, 1791), 1:100.

38 Quoted in Chuquet, *Jeunesse de Napoléon*, 2:217.

39 Lanfrey, *The History of Napoleon the First*, 1:15.

40 Napoléon Bonaparte, *Manuscrits inédits*, 545–546).

41 *Correspondance générale*, no. 68 (to Joseph, August 7, 1792), 1:116.

42 "Napoleon expressed some regret to see me always ahead of him in the competition for the distinctions that the circumstances of the time offered. He told me rather pointedly that our union would not last long if I intended to continue in the same way" (quoted in Carrington, "Les Pozzo di Borgo et les Bonaparte," 123).

43 Quoted in Chuquet, *Jeunesse de Napoléon*, 2:145.

44 Paoli's letters are quoted in Masson, *Napoléon dans sa jeunesse*, 258–260.

45 *Correspondance générale*, no. 67, 1:115. This letter to Jean-Marie Naudin is dated by the editors of this volume July 27, 1792. In view of its content and the place where it was composed (Valence), it can have been written only during the summer of 1791.

46 *Réimpression de l'ancien Moniteur*, 10:303–304.

47 Defranceschi, *Jeunesse de Napoléon*, 155–157.

48 See Chapter 1.

49 Chuquet, *Jeunesse de Napoléon*, 2:278.

50 "The firing of the cannon will be the signal for rioting and disunion. It will no longer be possible to restrain the paid national guards and those from the interior who have come to help. We are at the point of seeing the arrival of the departmental commission, which is said to have arranged everything. The prosecuting magistrate [Coti] has presented you with a requisition that you must not resist. If there are disorders when the cannon fires, we will hold you responsible" (ibid., 357).

51 Ibid., 292.

52 *Correspondance générale*, no. 60 (to Joseph, May 29, 1792), 1:108.

53 See the reports, reproduced by Albert Chuquet, of the department's directory, of June 13, 1792 (*Jeunesse de Napoléon*, 2:361); of the Ajaccio district, on April 17 (365); of the royal commissioner, Grandin, of April 18 (366–369); and of Colonel Maillard (369–374). See also the justifying memorandum of the volunteer battalion, of April 19, written by Napoleon, which rejects all these accusations (Napoléon Bonaparte, *Oeuvres littéraires et écrits militaires*, 2:237–257).

54 "The case of the Ajaccio battalion, with which I did not concern myself because it does not interest me much at a time of combustion like this one, was sent from the war office to the minister of justice because it did not involve any military offense. That was what I really cared about. So this matter is closed" (*Correspondance générale*, no. 68 [to Joseph, August 7, 1792], 1:116).

55 Masseria and the Buonaparte brothers had started a political club in Ajaccio, the Globo patriottico, in early 1791.

56 *Correspondance générale*, no. 66 (to Lucien, July 3, 1792), 1:114.

57 Ibid., no. 65 (to Joseph, June 22, 1792), 1:113.

58 Ibid., no. 66 (to Lucien, July 3, 1792), 1:114.

59 Ibid., no. 64 (to Joseph, June 18, 1792), 1:112.

60 Las Cases, *Mémorial*, 1:101.

61 *Correspondance générale*, no. 65 (to Joseph, June 22, 1792), 1:113.

62 Ibid.

63 Michelet, *Histoire de la Révolution française*, 1:762.

64 *Correspondance générale*, no. 68 (to Joseph, August 7, 1792), 1:116.

65 Ibid., no. 64 (to Joseph, June 18, 1792), 1:112.

5. Lost Illusions

1 Quoted by Regenbogen, *Napoléon a dit*, 45.

2 Out of the sixty-five families that were forced to leave Corsica, fifty-nine of them had bought almost half of all the national properties sold since 1791 (Defranceschi, *Corse française*, 90).

3 Marcaggi, *Genèse de Napoléon*, 386.

4 Cited in Chuquet, *Jeunesse de Napoléon*, 3:75–76.

5 See the delegate Louis Monestier's report to the Legislative Assembly (*Compte rendu des opérations des commissaires civils envoyés en Corse*, [1792]); Clavière's speech given on February 1, 1793 (Marcaggi, *Genèse de Napoléon*, 388); and the articles Volney published in the *Moniteur* on March 20 and 21, 1793 (*Réimpression de l'ancien Moniteur*, 15:738–739, 746–747).

6 Letter to Andrei quoted in Chuquet, *Jeunesse de Napoléon*, 68.

7 Quoted in Defranceschi, *Jeunesse de Napoléon*, 198.

8 Quoted in McErlean, *Napoleon and Pozzo di Borgo*, 103–104.

9 Bainville, *Napoléon*, 50.

10 Quoted in Chuquet, *Jeunesse de Napoléon*, 3:54–55.

11 *Correspondance générale*, no. 77 (to Paoli, March 2, 1793), 1:122–123.

12 It has also been said that Napoleon went to see Paoli, but nothing proves that this meeting actually took place: see Bertrand, *Cahiers*, 2:143–144, 3:73–74.

13 Lucien Bonaparte, *Mémoires*, 35–38.

14 Pietri, *Lucien Bonaparte*, 39–45. According to Pietri, Lucien did not leave Ajaccio until April 26, 1793; but a letter from the mayor of Ajaccio, Guitera, dated April 5 proves that Lucien had left with Sémonville in February and that he had not returned since (Marcaggi, *Genèse de Napoléon*, 405).

15 N. Bonaparte, *Napoléon inconnu*, 2:426.

16 Quoted in Chuquet, *Jeunesse de Napoléon*, 3:126–127.

17 Quoted in Marcaggi, *Genèse de Napoléon*, 396–397.

18 *Correspondance générale*, no. 79 (to the National Convention, a letter written after April 18, 1793), 1:124–125.

19 Quoted in Marcaggi, *Genèse de Napoléon*, 405.

20 Ibid., 413–416.

21 Quoted in Franceschini, "Saliceti et Napoléon," 140.

22 Quoted in Chuquet, *Jeunesse de Napoléon*, 3:140–143.

23 Ibid., 143–144.

24 "Position politique et militaire du département de la Corse au 1er juin 1793" (Napoléon Bonaparte, *Oeuvres littéraires et écrits militaires*, 2:286).

25 Bainville, *Napoléon*, 54.

26 Ibid., 42.

27 Marmont, *Mémoires*, 1:53.

28 Staël, *Considérations sur la Révolution française*, 336–341.

29 Las Cases, *Journal*, 1:219–220.

30 Barbaud, "La maison Bonaparte: L'immeuble et le mobilier."

31 Denon, *Voyage dans la Basse et la Haute Égypte*, 290–291.

32 Bourrienne, *Private Memoirs*, 1:216.

33 Proth, *Bonaparte comediante tragediante*, 300.

34 *Correspondance générale*, no. 1005 (to Joséphine, October 17, 1796), 1:638.

35 Masson, *Napoléon et sa famille*, 1:149.

36 *Correspondance générale*, no. 1012 (to Carnot, October 25, 1796), 1:642.

37 Bertrand, *Cahiers*, 1:42–43.

38 Ibid., 43–44.

39 Ibid.

40 Ibid.

41 Gourgaud, *Talks of Napoleon at St. Helena*, 56.

42 Ibid., 2:273.

43 Pillepich, *Napoléon et les Italiens*, 26.

44 *Correspondance générale*, no. 414 (to Joséphine, March 14, 1796), 1:298–299. He had already Gallicized his first name in 1794, abandoning the "Napoleone" or "Nabulion" of his youth in favor of "Napoléon" (Lentz, *Napoléon*, 5).

45 Gourgaud, *Talks of Napoleon at St. Helena*, 87.

46 Gourgaud, *Mémoires*, 2:196.

47 Bertrand, *Cahiers*, 2:419.

48 Mascilli Migliorini, *Napoléon*, 100.

49 Giuseppe Pecchio, *Vita di Ugo Foscolo* (1830), quoted in Mascilli Migliorini, *Napoléon*, 101.

50 Pomponi, *Histoire de la Corse*, 272.

51 Rousseau, *The Social Contract*, 77.

52 Venturi, *Rivoluzione di Corsica*, 168–208.

53 The full title of Macaulay's book is *Short Sketch of a democratical form of government: Loose remarks on certain positions to be found in Mr. Hobbes's Philosophical rudiments of government and society. With a short sketch of a democratical form of government, in a letter to Signior Paoli.* The 1767 London edition was titled "Loose remarks on certain positions to be found in Mr. Hobbes's Philosophical rudiments of government and society: with a short sketch of a democratical form of government, in a letter to Signior Paoli."

54 J. Boswell, *Account of Corsica*, 297.

55 Ibid., 330.

56 Voltaire, *Précis du siècle de Louis XV* (in *Oeuvres historiques*, 1550).

57 Mascilli Migliorini, *Napoléon*, 14.

58 Lanfrey, *The History of Napoleon the First*, 1:5.

59 Antonetti, *Histoire de la Corse*, 362.

60 Pomponi, *Mémorial des Corses*, 2:374.

61 Norvins, *Histoire de Napoléon*, 1:16.

62 Graziani, *Pascal Paoli*, 132.

63 Rousseau, *Confessions*, trans. Cohen, 599.

64 Dumouriez, *La Vie et les mémoires du général Dumouriez*, 1:138.

65 Raynal, *La Négresse couronnée*, vol. 2.

66 Cini, *La Nascita de un mito*, 144.

67 Bertrand, *Cahiers*, 3:79.

68 Volney, "Précis sur l'état de la Corse" (*Réimpression de l'ancien Moniteur*, 15:738–739, 746–747). Not long afterward Volney also wrote that the Corsicans were to Europe what the "savages" were to America (*Tableau du climat et du sol des États-Unis d'Amérique*, 2:483–488).

69 Quoted in Guyot, *Le Directoire et la paix de l'Europe*, 159n1. Saliceti had been appointed the Executive Directory's representative for the Army of Italy.

70 Bertrand, *Cahiers*, 3:144.

6. Toulon

1 Masson, *Napoléon et sa famille*, 1:85.

2 On July 11 the Convention allowed a deputation of Corsican refugees, including Joseph, to attend its session, and voted to provide initial support in the amount of 600,000 livres (*Réimpression de l'ancien Moniteur*, 17:95–96).

3 Jean Du Teil was the brother of the brigadier commanding the artillery school at Auxonne and the author of the treatise *Usage de l'artillerie nouvelle*, which will be discussed later on.

4 The minister of war, Bouchotte, did not reply, but on September 1 he asked the Convention's commissioners to see this young, "patriotic" officer and to "promote him" if they considered him capable (Madelin, *Histoire du Consulat et de l'Empire*, 1:223–224).

5 We have no letter written by him from July 30 to September 14, inclusive. Those of September 15 were written in Marseille.

6 Masson, *Napoléon et sa famille*, 1:76–78.

7 See Saliceti's letter to the Committee of Public Safety on September 26 (Aulard, *Recueil des actes du Comité de salut public*, 7:79).

8 Bertrand, *Cahiers*, 3:27.

9 Saliceti and Gasparin to the Committee of Public Safety, October 12 (Aulard, *Recueil des actes du Comité de salut public*, 7:392–393).

10 Saliceti to the Committee of Public Safety, September 26 (ibid., 7:80).

11 Monteagle, "Première rencontre de Barras et de Bonaparte," 142. In particular, he had painted a *Louis XVI équestre* in 1791.

12 Bertrand, *Cahiers*, 2:183.

13 Krebs and Moris, *Campagnes des Alpes*, 1:374.

14 *Correspondance générale*, no. 111, 1:142. The Le Caire promontory ends in two points known as the Point of L'Éguillette and the Point of Balaguier.

15 Krebs and Moris, *Campagnes des Alpes*, 1:373n3.

16 Let us nonetheless note that at least one man had grasped, before Napoleon, the importance of the Le Caire promontory: an administrator of the department of L'Hérault named Brunet, who was in Toulon at the time and spoke about it to Gasparin on September 4 (Havard, *Histoire de la Révolution dans les ports de guerre*, 1:220–221).

17 See Barras's letters to the Committee of Public Safety (September 6) and those of Gasparin, Saliceti, and Albitte (September 7) (Aulard, *Recueil des actes du Comité de salut public*, 6:320–321, 350).

18 Ibid., 6:413.

19 Ibid., 6:393.

20 Marmont, *Mémoires*, 1:38.

21 *Projet d'attaque de l'infâme ville de Toulon par tous les points dont elle peut être susceptible de défense, par le citoyen Doumet-Revest, ingénieur de la marine résidant à Grenoble* (in Colin, *Éducation militaire de Napoléon*, 195).

22 Ibid., 195–201. On October 15, d'Arçon added a postscript that came closer to Napoleon's point of view, not by changing the strategic plan of action, but by recognizing that blocking the harbor would make it possible to avoid an assault (ibid., 394).

23 Aulard, *Recueil des actes du Comité de salut public*, 6:319, 378.

24 Quoted by George Duruy in his introduction to Barras, *Memoirs*, 1:lxxxviii.

25 Napoléon Bonaparte, *Oeuvres littéraires et écrits militaires*, 2:269–270.

26 Aulard, *Recueil des actes du Comité de salut public*, 7:79. On September 20 Saliceti had already sent to the Committee of Public Safety an initial report written by Bonaparte, asking the government to "read [it] to the Convention" (Colin, *Éducation militaire de Napoléon*, 184).

27 Las Cases, *Journal*, 1:144; *Correspondance de Napoléon Ier*, 29:10.

28 *Correspondance générale*, no. 111, 1:143–144.

29 Madelin, *Histoire du Consulat et de l'Empire*, 1:232.

30 *Correspondance générale*, no. 111, 1:145; no. 105, 1:139.

31 Since September 29.

32 *Correspondance générale*, no. 105 (to the Committee of Public Safety, October 25, 1793), 1:139.

33 Bertrand, *Cahiers*, 2:428.

34 *Réimpression de l'ancien Moniteur*, 18:623–624. This letter was presented to the Convention on December 9 by Barère, a member of the Committee of Public Safety, who spoke of a letter "fabricated" by "plotters and slanderers." Barras and Fréron declared, after Toulon was taken, that this letter was a forgery (ibid., 19:63–64).

35 Madelin, *Histoire du Consulat et de l'Empire*, 1:232.

36 Aulard, *Recueil des actes du Comité de salut public*, 7:80.

37 Ibid., 79–80 (letter of September 26).

38 *Correspondance générale*, no. 111, 1:142–148.

39 There were two competing plans, one worked out by Carnot in the Committee of Public Safety, the other by Napoleon and signed by Dugommier. In the latter we read: "There is no one who, knowing Toulon and its defenses, does not see that its weak spot is the one from which the combined squadrons could be approached, and shells and red-hot cannon balls directed upon them. There is no one who, being familiar with the navy, does not know that ships never expect them. The position that most easily affords us this advantage is incontestably the promontory of L'Éguillette. . . . Once masters of L'Éguillette, we will imperatively order the enemies to leave the port and the harbor" (quoted in Colin, *Éducation militaire de Napoléon*, 203). Carnot, who had taken his inspiration in part from the notes sent by Saliceti and Napoleon over the past two months, also stressed the importance of the promontory of L'Éguillette's position. However, he advised an attack on all fronts: on the Le Caire promontory "to deny the enemy entrance into the small harbor," on the Sainte-Croix peninsula to strike the large harbor, at Fort Lamalgue to prevent an enemy landing on Cape Brun, and finally on Mount Faron (Aulard, *Recueil des actes du Comité de salut public*, 7:222–223).

40 "Procès-verbal de la séance du conseil de guerre tenu au quartier général d'Ollioules," written by Napoleon (*Correspondance de Napoléon Ier*, no. 8, 1:20–21).

41 *Correspondance générale*, no. 113, 1:148–149.

42 Las Cases, *Journal*, 1:138.

43 Bainville, *Napoléon*, 61.

44 Ibid., 60.

45 Captain Buonaparte had been promoted to the rank of *chef de bataillon* on September 29, and to that of *adjudant général chef de brigade* on October 7.

46 Blaufarb, *French Army*, 104–105.

47 *Correspondance générale*, no. 139, 1:159–160 (report of January 4, 1794). On Saint Helena, Napoleon referred to this affair, briefly with Las Cases (*Mémorial*, 1:110) and at length with Bertrand (*Cahiers*, 2:185–186). He also recounts the incident in his *Précis des opérations de*

l'armée d'Italie, but places it during the winter of 1794–1795 (*Correspondance de Napoléon Ier,* 29:36). Napoleon also talked about it with Chaptal (*Mes souvenirs,* 71–73). Coston provides an exact account (*Biographie des premières années de Napoléon,* 1:306–309). Maignet's accusations are in Aulard (*Recueil des actes du Comité de salut public,* 11:206–209, 545–548).

48 *Correspondance générale,* no. 96, 1:134.

49 Ibid., nos. 163, 172, 204, 205, pp. 1:171, 174, 186–187.

50 Ibid., no. 110, 1:141; Marmont, *Mémoires,* 1:60–61.

51 Marmont, *Mémoires,* 1:60–61.

52 In his *Campagnes d'Égypte et de Syrie,* Napoleon says that he was in French measurements five feet two inches tall (*Correspondance de Napoléon Ier,* 30:27). Very precisely, "five feet, two inches, and four lines," that is, 1.686 meters, or in Anglophone measurements slightly taller than five feet six inches, according to the measurements taken by Antonmarchi after his death (Marchand, *Mémoires,* 2:338).

53 Quoted in Mistler, *Grand livre de Napoléon,* 1:68.

54 *Correspondance générale,* no. 127 (to Dupin, December 24, 1793), 1:154.

55 Letter from Augustin Robespierre to the Committee of Public Safety, November 2, 1793 (Robespierre and Robespierre, *Correspondance,* 1:207).

56 Ibid., 274 (letter from Augustin to Maximilien Robespierre, April 5, 1794).

57 Quoted in Colin, *Éducation militaire de Napoléon,* 259–260.

58 A movement carried out by the Army of the Alps, which had reached the Barricades, on the road to Coni, required that a few adjustments be made, and a new version was presented to the Council of War on June 20, 1794 (*Correspondance de Napoléon Ier,* no. 30, 1:44–53; Colin, *Éducation militaire de Napoléon,* 273–285).

59 Colin, *Éducation militaire de Napoléon,* 286.

60 Reinhard, *Le Grand Carnot,* 1:132–133.

61 Either this note was submitted to Augustin Robespierre before he left for Paris, or Napoleon sent it to him, at his request, around July 6 or 7, to reply to objections raised by the Committee of Public Safety against the June 20 plan (Colin, *Éducation militaire de Napoléon,* 295).

62 By a decree issued by the Convention on August 2. Ricord was not to be bothered, at least not immediately.

63 *Correspondance générale,* no. 232, 1:196. Jean Tulard doubts the authenticity of this letter (*Napoléon,* 68), which the editors of the *Correspondance générale* accepted as authentic despite the absence of the original (it was published for the first time in Coston, *Biographie des premières années de Napoléon,* 2:286–287).

64 Napoléon Bonaparte, *Oeuvres littéraires et écrits militaires,* 30:291–308.

65 Lanfrey, *The History of Napoleon the First,* 1:23–24.

66 Furet and Richet, *La Révolution française,* 224.

67 Chuquet, *Jeunesse de Napoléon,* 3:252.

68 Marmont, *Mémoires,* 1:45.

69 "The nation's vengeance is unfolding: large numbers of people are being shot; all the naval officers have already been exterminated; the Republic will be avenged in a manner worthy of it; the *mânes* of the patriots will rest in peace" (*Réimpression de l'ancien Moniteur,* 19:64).

70 "Barbets" was the name given to the insurgents in the county of Nice who had remained loyal to their former sovereign, the king of Sardinia.

71 Robespierre and Robespierre, *Correspondance*, 1:253. A little later he also wrote: "I have not followed the system of those immoral and perverse men who affect philosophism in order not to let it be seen that they are without morals and without virtues, who pull down a cross to prevent people from paying attention to their misappropriations and their crimes" (ibid., 270).

72 Englund, *Napoleon*, 67–68.

73 Bertrand, *Cahiers*, 1:163.

74 Michelet, *Histoire de la Révolution française*, 2:1019.

75 Bertrand, *Cahiers*, 1:175–179.

76 *Correspondance de Napoléon Ier*, no. 15701 (to Clarke, August 23, 1809), 19:388.

77 Ibid., no. 15750 (to Clarke, September 5, 1809), 19:427.

78 "pourritures du patriciat": Maistre, *Discours à Madame la marquise de Costa*, 37; Maistre, *Considerations on France*, 101.

79 Maistre, *Considerations on France*, 203.

80 O'Meara, *Napoléon dans l'exil*, 2:111.

81 The authenticity of this speech is somewhat suspect, but we find in it ideas that Napoleon continued to repeat right up to the end of his life (Tulard, "Robespierre vu par Napoléon," 38).

82 Bertrand, *Cahiers*, 2:273. According to Lucien's memoirs (56–57), Augustin's proposal is even supposed to have been discussed in a kind of family council. There is a somewhat different version in Las Cases, where the role attributed here to Ricord is attributed instead to Dumerbion (*Mémorial*, 1:229).

7. In Search of a Future

1 Coston, *Biographie des premières années de Napoléon*, 2:285–286.

2 Madelin, *Histoire du Consulat et de l'Empire*, 1:248.

3 Mauguin, "Saliceti et l'arrestation de Bonaparte," 262.

4 That is Marmont's opinion (Colin, *Éducation militaire de Napoléon*, 305). The inquiry was entrusted to the ordnance officer Denniée, who proved, it is said, to be very accommodating (Coston, *Biographie des premières années de Napoléon*, 2:285n1).

5 *Correspondance générale*, no. 304 (June 18, 1795), 1:229–230.

6 Colin, *Éducation militaire de Napoléon*, 308.

7 Mauguin, "Saliceti et l'arrestation de Bonaparte," 262.

8 Garros and Tulard, *Napoléon au jour le jour*, 74.

9 *Correspondance générale*, no. 235, 1:197.

10 *Histoire des campagnes de M. le maréchal de Maillebois* had been published, with a valuable atlas, in 1775 by Masson de Pezay.

11 *Correspondance générale*, no. 236, 1:197–198.

12 Aulard, *Recueil des actes du Comité de salut public*, 16:328.

13 Coston, *Biographie des premières années de Napoléon*, 2:292–293.

14 *Correspondance*, 29:34–35; and "Dispositions de marche pour la division de droite de l'armée d'Italie, 17 septembre 1794" (Colin, *Éducation militaire de Napoléon*, 457–459).

15 Ibid., 323–328.

16 *Correspondance générale*, nos. 291 and 293, 1:222–223.

17 Las Cases, *Journal*, 4:114–115.

18 Law of April 10, 1795 (Blaufarb, *French Army*, 135).

19 Marmont, *Mémoires*, 1:59.

20 Girod de l'Ain, *Désirée Clary*, 53.

21 Blaufarb, *French Army*, 140–149.

22 Madelin, *Histoire du Consulat et de l'Empire*, 1:310–312.

23 *Correspondance générale*, no. 319, 1:244–245.

24 Iung, *Lucien Bonaparte*, 1:55.

25 Marmont, *Mémoires*, 1:63–64.

26 On this whole subject, see Le Doulcet de Pontécoulant, *Souvenirs*, 1:322–347.

27 *Correspondance de Napoléon Ier*, 29:43.

28 *Correspondance générale*, no. 317, 1:242.

29 Ibid., no. 318, 1:243.

30 Ibid., no. 322, 1:249.

31 Ibid., no. 320, 1:246.

32 Le Doulcet de Pontécoulant, *Souvenirs*, 1:338–339.

33 *Correspondance générale*, no. 329, 1:254.

34 Ferrero, *Bonaparte en Italie*, 15n.

35 See Chapter 6.

36 Camon, *Quand et comment Napoléon a conçu son système de manoeuvre*, 10–12.

37 Colin, *Éducation militaire de Napoléon*, 321–322. In early 1795, in Nice, he is supposed to have set forth his plan at length for Volney and Turreau (Chaptal, *Mes souvenirs*, 73–74).

38 Bertrand, *Cahiers*, 2:170.

39 *Correspondance de Napoléon Ier*, no. 49, 1:65.

40 Ibid., 67.

41 Ibid. This calendar is set in the "Mémoire militaire sur l'armée d'Italie" (ibid., no. 50, 1:68–70).

42 Napoléon Bonaparte, *Oeuvres littéraires et écrits militaires*, 2:311.

43 Ibid.

44 Reinhard, *Le Grand Carnot*, 2:112–116; Colin, *Éducation militaire de Napoléon*, 232–235.

45 Pierron, *Comment s'est formé le génie militaire de Napoléon Ier?*

46 These documents are quoted by Pierron, ibid., 8–9. The topographic bureau was unable to send Bonaparte the volume he requested; it did not have the *Histoire des campagnes de M. le maréchal de Maillebois*, and did not have enough money to buy a copy.

47 See Pierron, *Comment s'est formé le génie militaire de Napoléon Ier?*; the reply of an anonymous officer (*Comment s'est formé le génie militaire de Napoléon Ier? Réponse au général Pierron*); Sismondi's account of Maillebois's operations (*Histoire des Français*, 28:386–391); and, of course, Masson de Pezay, *Histoire des campagnes de M. le maréchal de Maillebois en Italie pendant les années 1745 et 1746*.

48 Having left from Trento and going along the left bank of the Adige River, he "crossed the lower Adige, the lower course of the Po, went back up the right bank of this river through Modena and Stradella, passed the Tanaro after having joined up with the Duke of Savoy,

and established himself between the Doria Riparia and Stura Rivers, on the French army's line of operations" (Anonymous, *Comment s'est formé le génie militaire de Napoléon Ier? Réponse au général Pierron*, 11).

49 See Colin, *Éducation militaire de Napoléon*, 14–15.

50 Napoléon Bonaparte, *Dix-huit notes sur l'ouvrage intitulé "Considérations sur l'art de la guerre"* (*Correspondance de Napoléon Ier*, 31:365). These notes were dictated by Napoleon on Saint Helena.

51 *Correspondance de Napoléon Ier*, no. 1976 (reply to Duverne de Presle, July 1797), 3:163.

52 See Anonymous, *Comment s'est formé le génie militaire de Napoléon Ier? Réponse au général Pierron*, 21.

53 See Heuser, *Evolution of Strategy*, 76–110.

54 Napoléon Bonaparte, *Dix-huit notes sur l'ouvrage intitulé "Considérations sur l'art de la guerre"* (*Correspondance de Napoléon Ier*, 31:330–331).

55 Ibid., 365.

56 De Gaulle, *Le Fil de l'épée*, 43.

57 *Dix-huit notes sur l'ouvrage intitulé "Considérations sur l'art de la guerre"* (*Correspondance de Napoléon Ier*, 31:364).

58 De Gaulle, *Le Fil de l'épée*, 124.

59 Bourcet, *Principes de la guerre de montagnes*, 37.

60 *Correspondance de Napoléon Ier*, no. 50, 1:69.

61 Ibid., no. 49, 1:66–67.

62 Le Doulcet de Pontécoulant, *Souvenirs*, 1:342.

63 *Correspondance générale*, no. 309, 1:233.

64 Ibid., no. 312, 1:238.

65 Gauchet, *Révolution des pouvoirs*, 189.

66 *Correspondance générale*, no. 318 (August 1, 1795), 1:244.

67 Ibid., no. 335, 1:259.

68 Ibid., no. 341, 1:265.

69 Ibid., no. 343, 1:266.

70 I will return to this question later. See Chapter 16.

71 Masson, *Napoléon et sa famille*, 1:81, 96–97, 120–124.

72 Girod de l'Ain, *Désirée Clary*, 15–37, 385–400.

73 Joseph Bonaparte, *Mémoires*, 1:129.

74 *Correspondance de Napoléon Ier*, 1:84n2; Le Doulcet de Pontécoulant, *Souvenirs*, 1:343–344.

75 *Correspondance de Napoléon Ier*, 1:84n2; Le Doulcet de Pontécoulant, *Souvenirs*, 1:343–344.

76 Ibid.

77 The order was signed by Cambacérès, Berlier, Merlin de Douai, and Boissy d'Anglas, but not by Letourneur, as Pontécoulant claims (Le Doulcet de Pontécoulant, *Souvenirs*, 1:345–346).

78 *Correspondance générale*, no. 344, 1:267.

79 Ibid., no. 343, 1:267.

80 Ibid., no. 344 (to Joseph, September 27), 1:267–268.

81 Ibid., no. 346 (14 Vendémiaire, October 6, 2 a.m.), 1:269.

82 Zivy, *Treize Vendémiaire*, 76.

83 See Zivy's analysis, ibid., 90–91.

84 Carrot, "Napoléon Bonaparte et le maintien de l'ordre," 18.

85 *Réimpression de l'ancien Moniteur*, 26:132–133.

86 The figures vary from 200 to 400 killed and wounded.

87 O'Meara, *Napoleon in Exile*, 1:270–271.

88 Barras, *Mémoires*, 1:250–251.

89 O'Meara, *Napoleon in Exile*, 1:154.

90 Las Cases, *Mémorial*, 2:356–357.

91 Marmont, *Mémoires*, 1:56.

92 Ibid., 83–84.

93 B. Constant, *De la force du gouvernement actuel*, 38.

94 Ibid.

95 "I've seen it all, they want to destroy you," Bonaparte wrote to him. "But I will do all I can to save you, despite certain representatives' raging desire to blame their foolishness on the generals" (*Correspondance générale*, no. 347, 1:269).

96 Ibid., no. 346, 1:269.

97 Bertrand, *Cahiers*, 2:276; 3:85–86.

98 *Réimpression de l'ancien Moniteur*, 26:175.

99 Ibid., 177.

100 Ibid., 25:222. Its jurisdiction covered the six departments of the military's Seventeenth Division (Seine, Seine-et-Oise, Seine-et-Marne, Oise, Loiret, Eure-et-Loir) as well as the Somme, the Seine-Inférieure, and the Eure.

101 Reinhard, "Le général Vendémiaire," in Mistler, *Le Grand livre de Napoléon*, 58.

102 *Correspondance générale*, no. 351 (to Joseph, October 20, 1795), 1:271.

103 Composed toward the end of 1794, *Le Reveil du peuple* was a song hostile to the Jacobins. Because it exhorted the "sovereign people" to hasten to "hand over all these drinkers of blood to the monsters of Tenaro [Hades]," it was very popular among the moderates and the royalists who had just been struck on 13 Vendémiaire.

104 Barras, *Memoirs*, 2:30.

105 *Correspondance générale*, no. 380, 1:282–283.

106 Sorel, *L'Europe et la Révolution française*, 5:53.

107 Thiers, *The History of the French Revolution*, 4:94–95.

108 Quoted in Ferrero, *Bonaparte en Italie*, 31; Guyot, *Le Directoire et la paix de l'Europe*, 127–133.

109 Guyot, *Le Directoire et la paix de l'Europe*, 127–133.

110 The British and the Russians had offered Austria Venice and the legations, on the condition that they continued the war to reconquer Belgium.

111 Quoted in Guyot, *Le Directoire et la paix de l'Europe*, 137.

112 "Instruction pour les représentants du peuple et le général en chef de l'armée d'Italie" (*Correspondance de Napoléon Ier*, no. 53, 1:75–78). These instructions repeat, with a few minor

differences regarding the movements to be carried out at the beginning of the campaign, the suggestions made in the "Mémoire militaire" already cited (no. 50, 1:69–70), and those in the "Instruction militaire pour le général en chef de l'armée des Alpes et d'Italie" (no. 52, 1:71–75).

113 Quoted in Le Doulcet de Pontécoulant, *Souvenirs*, 1:335.

114 *Correspondance de Napoléon Ier*, no. 83, 1:103–104.

115 Reinhard, *Le Grand Carnot*, 2:200–201.

116 Quoted in Tulard, *Napoléon: Ou le mythe du sauveur*, 79–80.

117 Letter from Ritter to Letourneur, February 3, 1796, quoted in Godechot, *Commissaires aux armées*, 1:179.

8. Happiness

1 The authenticity of this scene, which was described by Napoleon on many occasions and by Hortense de Beauharnais (*Mémoires*, 1:42), was contested by Barras (*Memoirs*, 1:311). It is plausible on the condition that it is situated a few days after the date often given, October 9, because Napoleon was not appointed second-in-command of the Army of the Interior until October 11.

2 *Correspondance générale*, no. 351 (to Joseph, October 20, 1795), 1:271.

3 Castelot, *Joséphine*, 111.

4 Napoléon Bonaparte, *Manuscrits inédits*, 21–23.

5 *Correspondance générale*, no. 303 (to Désirée Clary, June 14, 1795), 1:229.

6 Napoléon Bonaparte, *Clisson et Eugénie*, 7, 103–104.

7 Leijendecker, "Un amour inconnu de Bonaparte."

8 This text was probably written in Auxonne, in 1788, and not in 1791, as is supposed by F. Masson (Napoléon Bonaparte, *Manuscrits inédits*, 523–530) and J. Tulard (Napoléon Bonaparte, *Oeuvres littéraires et écrits militaires*, 2:179–186): its content, which is full of allusions to the society of the Old Regime, proves it.

9 Napoléon Bonaparte, *Manuscrits inédits*, 460–461. Alexandre Des Mazis mentions this episode in his *Cahiers*, noting that the young Bonaparte "was of a purity of morals entirely rare in a young man."

10 See, for example, Savant, *Les Amours de Napoléon*.

11 Fleischmann, *Charlotte Robespierre et ses mémoires*, 252.

12 *Correspondance générale*, no. 244 (to Désirée Clary, September 10, 1794), 1:201–202.

13 Ibid., no. 283 (to Désirée Clary, February 4, 1795), 1:218.

14 Ibid., no. 285 (to Désirée Clary, February 12, 1795), 1:219.

15 Las Cases, *Mémorial*, 1:111.

16 Regenbogen, *Napoléon a dit*, 37.

17 Napoléon Bonaparte, *Manuscrits inédits*, 461.

18 Ibid.

19 Bertrand, *Cahiers*, 3:32.

20 *Correspondance générale*, no. 302 (to Désirée Clary, June 7, 1795), 1:228.

21 Ibid., no. 308, 1:232–233.

22 Letter to Thomas Mann, November 29, 1936, quoted by Laurens et al., *Expédition d'Égypte*, 399–400.

23 Masson, *Napoléon et sa famille*, 1:97–98.

24 *Correspondance générale*, no. 297 (to Désirée Clary, May 9, 1795), 1:224.

25 Girod de l'Ain, *Désirée Clary*, 54–55.

26 Ibid.

27 *Correspondance générale*, no. 300 (to Désirée Clary, June 2, 1795), 1:227.

28 Ibid., no. 303 (to Désirée Clary, June 14, 1795), 1:228–229.

29 Ibid., no. 308 (to Joseph, June 24, 1795), 1:232.

30 Girod de l'Ain, *Désirée Clary*, 69–71.

31 *Correspondance générale*, no. 321 (to Désirée Clary, August 10, 1795), 1:247–248.

32 Ibid., no. 337 (to Joseph, September 6, 1795), 1:262.

33 Ibid., no. 317, 1:243.

34 Ibid., no. 320, 1:246.

35 Quoted in Gilles, *Madame Tallien*, 227–228.

36 Merveilleuses: A fashion trend of the time characterized by dissipation and extravagance.

37 Barras, *Memoirs*, 2:64.

38 *Correspondance générale*, no. 333 (to Désirée Clary, August 31, 1795), 1:257.

39 Ibid.

40 Thiébault, *Mémoires*, 2:6.

41 Masson, *Napoléon et les femmes*, 41.

42 Bruce, *Napoleon and Josephine*, 121–129.

43 Barras, *Memoirs*, 1:413–424. She was looking for a husband, and in 1799 she finally married an actor, Honoré Bourdon (known as Neuville), who had long been her lover.

44 *Correspondance générale*, no. 336, 1:260.

45 Ibid.

46 Ibid., 1:262.

47 See ibid., no. 313, 1:239; no. 344, 1:268.

48 Furet, *La Révolution*, 190.

49 *Correspondance générale*, no. 387, 1:285.

50 Marmont, *Mémoires*, 1:93–94.

51 *Correspondance générale*, no. 418 (to Barras, March 23, 1796), 1:300.

52 Wagener, *L'Impératrice Joséphine*, 133.

53 Rose becoming Joséphine, Eugénie became Désirée again. "My compliments to Eugénie and to Julie," he still wrote to Joseph on October 6 (*Correspondance générale*, no. 346, 1:269); two months later, on December 9, "Embrace your wife and Désirée for me" (ibid., no. 374, 1:280).

54 Gourgaud, *Journal*, 2:263–264.

55 These words are those of a contemporary, quoted in Castelot, *Joséphine*, 95.

56 O'Meara, *Napoleon in Exile*, 2:101.

57 Masson, *Napoléon et les femmes*, 51–52; letter to Teresa Tallien, August or September 1795 (J. de Beauharnais, *Correspondance*, nos. 31, 32).

58 Barras, *Memoirs*, 2:63.

59 Bertrand, *Cahiers*, 3:98.

60 Marmont, *Mémoires*, 1:93–94.

61 Las Cases, *Journal*, 1:161.

62 Masson, *Napoléon et les femmes*, 54–55.

63 Gourgaud, *Journal*, 2:263–264.

64 *Correspondance générale*, no. 411, 1:296–297.

65 See Chapter 5.

66 In his *Petit dictionnaire des grands hommes de la Révolution*, published in 1790 (reproduced in Dutourd, *Rivarol*, 200).

67 After Eugène's birth in September 1781, Alexandre had left his wife and child to go on a long excursion in Italy. He is said to have returned to Paris on July 25, 1782. Hortense was born exactly eight months and sixteen days later (Castelot, *Joséphine*, 45–46).

68 Quoted in ibid., 80.

69 Ibid., 63.

70 Coston, *Biographie des premières années de Napoléon*, 2:347–350.

71 Wagener, *L'Impératrice Joséphine*, 142.

72 Las Cases, *Mémorial*, 2:655.

73 Montholon, *Récits*, 1:269.

74 I allude to Tolstoy's *Family Happiness*, the passage where Sergei Mikhailovich offers his definition of happiness to the woman who is already his fiancée.

75 Napoléon Bonaparte, *Clisson et Eugénie*, 19–20.

76 Valéry, *Cahiers*, 1:356.

77 Wagener, *L'Impératrice Joséphine*, 143.

78 Barras, *Memoirs*, 2:58.

79 Jourquin, "Un jour de mars 1796: Le mariage de Napoléon Bonaparte et Joséphine de Beauharnais"; Wagener, *L'Impératrice Joséphine*, 131–132.

80 This was the term used to designate priests who had refused to swear the oath required by the Civil Constitution of the Clergy of 1790, and exercised their ministry clandestinely.

81 Las Cases, *Journal*, 2:302n1.

82 Bonnet, *Histoire de Croissy-sur-Seine*, 296–299.

83 Quoted in Wagener, *L'Impératrice Joséphine*, 130.

84 Ibid., 129.

85 *Correspondance générale*, no. 414, 1:298.

9. That Beautiful Italy

1 The figures are still subject to debate, and many historians suspect Bonaparte of having deliberately underestimated the number of his troops in order to make his victories seem more brilliant. Gilles Candela opts for a real figure of 47,000 men at the beginning of the campaign (*L'Armée d'Italie*, 234–235).

2 "Campagne d'Italie" (*Correspondance de Napoléon Ier*, 29:83–84).

3 In this first version of the text, Carnot prescribed bringing the main effort to bear on the Milan area, with a secondary attack on Acqui and Ceva to pin down the Piedmontese, thus

avoiding as much as possible offending the Piedmontese government, with which the Directory was still hoping to conclude an agreement. Bonaparte, convinced that Lombardy could not be invaded without having first defeated the Piedmontese, got the text changed (Chandler, *Campaigns of Napoleon*, 47–49). See also Clausewitz's classic analysis, *Bonaparte en Italie: La campagne de 1796*, 19–24).

4   To improve the condition of the army, the Directory's civilian representative, Saliceti, had asked the Republic of Genoa for a loan of seven million, and because Genoa was slow in giving a positive response, he had decided, with Schérer's consent, to threaten its borders by sending a brigade to occupy Voltri. This brigade had begun to move before Bonaparte arrived (Lefebvre, *La France sous le Directoire*, 340–341).

5   Although he disapproved of the occupation of Voltri, he had not canceled this operation, whose possible consequences he recognized, as is shown by this letter of April 6 addressed to the Directory: "I have been greatly vexed and extremely unhappy about this movement on Genoa, which is all the more inappropriate because it . . . has awakened the enemy that I would have liked to have surprised at his ease" (*Correspondance générale*, no. 463, 1:324).

6   Béraud, *Bonaparte en Italie*, 41. See Défossé, *Montenotte*.

7   Thiers, *The History of the French Revolution*, 4:370.

8   Thiry, *Bonaparte en Italie*, 45.

9   Bouvier, *Bonaparte en Italie*, 335–338.

10   In this plan, we read: "Everything commands us to seek by all means in our power to make the enemies recross the Po, and to concentrate our greatest efforts in the direction of the area around Milan. This operation seems impossible to carry out unless the French army has previously taken Ceva. The Directory leaves the general-in-chief at liberty to begin operations by attacking the enemies at this point, and, whether he obtains a complete victory over them or they retreat toward Turin, the Directory authorizes him to follow them, to fight them again, and even to bombard this capital, if circumstances make it necessary to do so. The Directory must state here its intentions relative to the sieges that the events of the campaign . . . may make possible. Its resolution is that no siege may be undertaken before the enemy, which might trouble [the French general], has been totally routed and is incapable of attempting anything" (Debidour, *Recueil des actes du Directoire*, 1:721–722).

11   Bouvier, *Bonaparte en Italie*, 255.

12   Clausewitz, *Bonaparte en Italie: La campagne de 1796*, 38.

13   See Bouvier, *Bonaparte en Italie*, 271.

14   *Correspondance générale*, no. 519 (to Barras, April 23, 1796), 1:356.

15   Ibid., no. 522 (to the Directory, April 24, 1796), 1:357.

16   These were General Salliler de La Tour, Colonel Costa de Beauregard, the Piedmontese army's chief of staff, and Captain de Seyssel, Colli's aide-de-camp.

17   Costa de Beauregard, *Un homme d'autrefois*, 332.

18   Ibid., 333–334.

19   *Correspondance de Napoléon Ier*, no. 256 (*Conditions d'une suspension d'armes arrêtée entre les armées française et piémontaise*), 1:199–201.

20   Costa de Beauregard, *Un homme d'autrefois*, 339.

21   Ibid., 340–341.

22 Quoted in Thiry, *Bonaparte en Italie*, 90.

23 See the report submitted by the British ambassador in Turin, quoted in Ferrero, *Bonaparte en Italie*, 33.

24 Clausewitz, *Bonaparte en Italie: La campagne de 1796*, 45.

25 The Agogna, the Terdoppio, and the Ticino.

26 On bridge-building equipment and crossing water courses, see J.-L. Riccioli, "Le franchissement des cours d'eaux pendant la campagne [d'Italie]."

27 Clausewitz suggests the figure of 15,000, asserting that thanks to these reinforcements Bonaparte now had a clear numerical superiority over Beaulieu: almost 45,000 men against 31,000 (*Bonaparte en Italie: La campagne de 1796*, 52–53).

28 *Réimpression de l'ancien Moniteur*, 28:259. On July 31, 1796, the French troops moving from Mantua to Verona covered 85 kilometers in thirty-six hours (Mascilli Migliorini, *Napoléon*, 106), and this exploit was surpassed in 1805 when, on the eve of the battle of Austerlitz, the army corps commanded by Davout covered 160 kilometers in thirty-six hours, at a rate of more than 4 kilometers an hour, carrying thirty kilograms on their shoulders (Damamme, *Les Soldats de la Grande Armée*, 71). For their part, the Austrians were moving slowly: it took them seventy-two hours to cover 80 kilometers (Béraud, *Bonaparte en Italie*, 55). This is one of the main explanations for French superiority: the French army had adopted a cadence of 120 paces a minute, while its adversaries continued to march at "the orthodox rate of seventy paces" (Liddell Hart, *Stratégie*, 228–229).

29 General Laharpe was accidentally killed by his own soldiers in the course of this night engagement.

30 If they did not destroy the bridge, it was, according to Botta, because Beaulieu was counting on using it to return to the right bank of the Adda in the event of a French defeat (Botta, *Histoire d'Italie*, 1:419).

31 He suggests it in his report, writing that "Beaulieu with all his army was in battle formation" (*Correspondance générale*, no. 589 [to the Directory, May 11, 1796], 1:393).

32 "Campagne d'Italie" (*Correspondance de Napoléon Ier*, 29:101).

33 Even the outcome is uncertain. A thousand killed and wounded (Pigeard, *Dictionnaire des batailles de Napoléon*, 488), or fewer than 200, as Bonaparte claims (*Correspondance générale*, no. 589 [to the Directory, May 11, 1796], 1:394)?

34 "Campagne d'Italie" (*Correspondance de Napoléon Ier*, 29:101).

35 Ibid.

36 Did his generals try to dissuade him from doing this, as Carlo Botta asserts (*Histoire d'Italie*, 1:419–420)? On Saint Helena, he was to claim that he sent in the infantry only after having seen his cavalry "forming up on the left bank," but then he was trying to make people believe that the action had been conducted "with all due prudence" ("Campagne d'Italie" [*Correspondance de Napoléon Ier*, 29:101]).

37 "The enemy fire was terrible. The head of the column even seemed to hesitate; a moment of hesitation and all would have been lost! . . . Generals Berthier, Masséna, Cervoni, Dallemagne, brigade leader Lannes, and battalion leader Dupas sensed this, rushed to the van, *and decided the outcome, which still hung in the balance*" (*Correspondance générale*, no. 589 [to the Di-

36 Marmont, *Mémoires*, 1:152.

37 Miot de Melito, *Memoirs*, 1:53. The future General Pelleport wrote, but regarding a later scene he witnessed at the beginning of September 1796: "I saw Masséna and Augereau reporting to Bonaparte on the day's operations and receiving his orders for the following day: the behavior of these two division leaders was very respectful. I mention this circumstance only to suggest the extent of the authority that Bonaparte, from the beginning of his tenure as commander-in-chief, had taken over his lieutenants. One has to refer to this time of comradeship to assess the ascendancy that this man had over the mind of the officers who served under his orders." (Quoted in Sainte-Beuve, "Souvenirs militaires et intimes du général Pelleport," in *Causeries du lundi*, 8:332–333.)

38 *Correspondance de Napoléon Ier*, no. 234 (Proclamation to the army, April 26, 1796), 1:188.

39 Ibid., no. 461, 1:303–304. "Capua in Lombardy": a reference to Hannibal's prolonged R&R in Capua, which led to his troops becoming soft and being defeated by the Romans.

40 Sainte-Beuve, *Causeries du lundi*, 8:333.

41 *Correspondance de Napoléon Ier*, no. 1170 (speech to the Vaubois division, November 7, 1796), 2:103. But in the report he sent to the Directory, he did not condemn those who fled, speaking only of a "panic terror" that had to be connected not with the army's cowardice but with "its inferiority and its exhaustion" (*Correspondance générale*, no. 1059 [November 13, 1796], 1:664–665). Finally he decided to throw the blame entirely on General Vaubois, reproaching him for having "neither character nor the habit of commanding great divisions" (ibid., no. 1062 [to the Directory, November 19, 1796], 1:669), and later on he sent Vaubois away from the front by giving him command of the fortress of Livorno (ibid., no. 1077 [to the Directory, November 24, 1796], 1:677): case closed.

42 Bertrand, *Cahiers*, 2:289.

43 Extract from a letter to General Clarke, who had just arrived from Paris, quoted in Garros and Tulard, *Napoléon au jour le jour*, 109.

44 Ludwig, *Napoleon*, 59.

45 Yavetz, *César et son image*, 184.

46 Englund, *Napoleon*, 103–104.

47 See Las Cases, *Mémorial*, 1:254–255.

48 *Correspondance générale*, no. 836 (to the Directory, August 6, 1796), 1:535; no. 898 (to the Directory, September 9, 1796), 1:574.

49 *Correspondance de Napoléon Ier*, no. 1309 (order of the day for December 21, 1796), 2:194.

50 By decree of the Constituent Assembly of July 30, 1791. The Convention had then rejected various proposals seeking to replace the former military medals with republican decorations, on the ground that any distinction accorded for merit would encourage in the soldiers feelings of ambition, pride, and honor incompatible with republican simplicity and equality (Blaufarb, *The French Army*, 110–111).

51 *Correspondance*, no. 2127 (Decree of August 28, 1797), 3:247–248. It is possible that the distribution of arms as a reward for a brilliant action began well before this decree was issued, as is shown by a document presumed to date from March 6, 1797 (the date is uncertain), in which we read: "All those who have sabers shall have 100 francs in pension on the Mantuan" (ibid., no. 1548, 2:369). It was only in October 1799, shortly before 18 Brumaire, that the

Directory made official this disguised reestablishment of military distinctions (Lentz, "Armes d'honneur," in Tulard, *Dictionnaire Napoléon*, 1:123).

52 On this subject, see Hanson's observations in *Le Modèle occidental de la guerre*, 160–161.

53 This was so true that on June 2, 1797, Bonaparte issued an order that the "veterans" were not to be sacrificed to the benefit of soldiers who had recently arrived to reinforce them (*Correspondance de Napoléon Ier*, no. 1857, 3:88–89).

54 Bertaud, *La Révolution armée*, 285.

55 De Gaulle, *Le Fil de l'épée*, 98.

56 Ibid.

57 Ibid., 102.

58 On these reports on the situation of the different corps of troops, updated every day, see Baron Fain's *Mémoires*, 74–91.

59 Chaptal, *Mes souvenirs*, 151.

60 Lanfrey, *The History of Napoleon the First*, 368–369. The letter to Grenadier Aune is dated January 15, 1800 (*Correspondance générale*, no. 4875, 3:41). In public, Marmont reported, Bonaparte did everything he could to make his authority felt and to maintain distance, "but in private, with his staff, there was a great ease on his part, an affability that went as far as pleasant familiarity" (*Mémoires*, 1:296–297).

61 The armistice with the Duke of Modena was signed on May 17, 1796. There are three versions of this episode: in the first, it was Saliceti who brought Bonaparte the sum of four million on behalf of the Duke of Modena (Las Cases, *Journal*, 1:164–165); in the second, the banker Haller advised him to accept the two million the duke was offering (Bertrand, *Cahiers*, 1:166–167); and in the third it was the duke's illegitimate son who delivered to him, in person, two cases containing "two million in gold, in double sovereigns." According to this last version, Bonaparte did not refuse the money, which he had taken to the army's treasurer to be received by him "on account for the contribution" (*Correspondance de Napoléon Ier*, 32:244).

62 Napoleon adds "that plotters were not so disinterested, and were clever enough to steal a million from this republic" (ibid., 245).

63 Las Cases, *Journal*, 1:165.

64 Marmont, *Mémoires*, 1:308. Napoleon claims on the contrary that when Marmont showed him "a casket of gold and precious items" that had fallen into his hands after the sack of Pavia, he ordered that it be handed over to the army's treasurer (*Correspondance de Napoléon Ier*, 32:244).

65 See Chapter 10.

66 *Correspondance générale*, no. 993, 1:629–630; Bonaparte wrote to the Directory on January 6, 1797: "Those people may have received three million through factitious payments. This company owes the army five million, proceeding from contributions. . . . I have considered the company bankrupt, and I have had its buildings in Livorno and Genoa put under seal. I ask you to issue orders for the arrest of this company's agents in Paris; they are the biggest crooks in Europe; they have put us here in a very difficult situation. I have tried to arrest Flachat and his brother-in-law, . . . but the scoundrels got away" (ibid., no. 1274, 1:779). The af-

fair ended up with the conviction of a few minor figures; Flachat himself was cleared. See Candela, *L'Armée d'Italie*, 267–271.

67 Blanc, *Regnaud de Saint-Jean d'Angély*, 86.

68 Las Cases, *Journal*, 1:164.

69 Branda, *Le Prix de la gloire*, 37–39.

70 See in particular a newspaper called *Le Bulletin de Paris*, edited by a certain "Citizen Sarrazin" who may or may not have been the general of the same name who served at that time in Italy and went over to the enemy in 1810. Only a few issues of this paper were published, in September and October 1797. It was then prohibited. In it appeared reports of this kind: "Milan, August 27. Here and in the surrounding area there is an astonishing number of robbers who stop people on the highways, imposed levies on peasants, and have already burned several fields. About thirty-eight [men] have been arrested. They are a mixture of Frenchmen and Italians. Their leader has taken the name of Buonaparte, while others call themselves Masséna, d'Augereau, and other generals" (September 15, 1797).

71 Hamelin, "Douze ans de ma vie," 29.

72 Bourrienne, *Mémoires*, 2:17–18.

73 *Correspondance générale*, no. 1062 (to the Directory, November 19, 1796), 1:668.

74 Béraud, *Bonaparte en Italie*, 106–117.

75 Clausewitz, *Bonaparte en Italie: La campagne de 1796*, 239.

76 Thiers, *The History of the French Revolution*, 4:523.

77 Gourgaud, *Talks of Napoleon at St. Helena*, 211.

78 On March 10, 1797, the day the march on Vienna began, the Army of Italy numbered 79,100 men; the principal corps of the army, under Bonaparte, 44,100; the Tyrol corps, under Joubert, 19,500; the Victor corps, at Ancona, 6,500; and the garrisons left behind in Lombardy, 9,000 (Clausewitz, *Bonaparte en Italie: La campagne de 1796*, 262). See Candela, *L'Armée d'Italie*, 248.

79 "Campagnes d'Italie" (*Correspondance de Napoléon Ier*, 29:231).

80 Ferrero, *Bonaparte en Italie*, 138.

81 Thiers, *Histoire de la Révolution française*, 9:56.

82 Much later on, Napoleon emphasized the choice of the moment, which was in fact crucial but which also allowed him to justify his imprudence. See "Campagnes d'Italie" (*Correspondance de Napoléon Ier*, 29:231–235). See also his remarks on Antoine-Henri de Jomini's *Traité des grandes opérations militaires*: "The campaign had to begin before the snow melted, so as not to give the Austrian engineers time to construct earthworks at the lower ends of the valleys and to put Palmanova in a condition that could be defended, and also to defeat the archduke before the divisions on the Rhine could reach him" (ibid., 29:357).

83 Thiers, *Histoire de la Révolution française*, 9:70.

84 *Correspondance générale*, no. 1466, 1:884.

85 Ibid., no. 1486, 1:895.

86 Ibid., no. 1484 (March 31, 1797), 1:894.

87 "Campagnes d'Italie" (*Correspondance de Napoléon Ier*, 29:243–244).

88 Ibid.

89 *Correspondance générale*, no. 1488, 1:897.

but precisely success comes to warn us not to make up our minds too quickly." Lodi, he goes on, shows the whole extent of "the psychological power of victory": "Never, certainly, has a feat of arms aroused so much astonishment in Europe as this passage over the Adda.... Perhaps some people will say that the attack on Lodi has no justification from the strategic point of view; Bonaparte could just as well have occupied the bridge the following morning; that is because they have in view only the geometrical laws of strategy. But doesn't psychological influence also have its place in strategy? If there is anyone who still doubts this, that is because he has not been able to grasp war in all its complexity, or to penetrate its soul" (Clausewitz, *Bonaparte en Italie: La campagne de 1796*, 79–81).

60 Thiers, *The History of the French Revolution*, 4:377.

61 Ludwig, *Napoléon*, 60–61.

62 *Correspondance générale*, no. 1062 (to the Directory, November 19, 1796), 1:668–669.

63 "passionate drama": These words are Jomini's, quoted in Fugier, *Napoléon et l'Italie*, 25.

64 *Correspondance générale*, no. 1061 (to General Clarke, November 19, 1796), 1:667.

65 Letter from Gros, quoted in Bosséno, *"Je me vis dans l'histoire,"* 452.

66 On the symbolic erasure over the following weeks of the role actually played at Arcole by Augereau, see Bosséno (ibid., 454–461).

67 Dwyer, *Napoleon*, 5.

68 Thomas, *Essai sur les éloges*, 3:1.

69 The studies collected by Sylvain Menant and Robert Morrissey in *Héroïsme et Lumières* show how much the figure of the military hero was still present in Enlightenment France.

70 On March 30, 1778, when Voltaire, returning from Ferney, was given a triumphal welcome by the people of Paris.

71 Thomas, *Essai sur les éloges*, 3:6.

72 Bernardin de Saint-Pierre, "D'un Élysée," 375–403.

73 Birnbaum, "L'héroïsme n'est plus ce qu'il était," 123–124.

74 As Carlyle understood very well. *Les Héros*, 267–268.

75 See R. Morrissey, *L'Empereur à la barbe fleurie*, 349–351.

76 F. Furet, "Michelet," in Furet and Ozouf, *Dictionnaire critique de la Révolution française*, 2nd ed., 1:1034.

77 Preface to the 1869 edition (Michelet, *Histoire de la Révolution française*, 2:1016n).

78 See de Baecque, *Le Corps de l'histoire*.

79 Joseph Agricol Viala, thirteen years old, had been killed on the banks of the Durance River in July 1793 while fighting the federalists. As for Joseph Bara, aged fourteen, he had been killed in the Vendée on December 7, 1793. Following Robespierre's speech on the Supreme Being, the Convention awarded them the honors of the Pantheon. The ceremony, set for 10 Thermidor, never took place: on that day, Robespierre and his supporters were guillotined.

80 Quinet, "Critique de la Révolution," in *La Révolution*, 55.

81 Tocqueville, *The Ancien Régime and the French Revolution* (bk. 3, chap. 2), 142.

82 On revolutionary subjectivism and its connections with terrorism, see Ph. Raynaud, "Les origines intellectuelles du terrorisme," in Furet et al., *Terrorisme et démocratie*, 35–135.

83 See, for example, Barry, *Discours sur les dangers de l'idolâtrie individuelle dans une république*.

84 Thiers, *The History of the French Revolution*, 5:187.

85 Monge, Correspondance, no. 107 (letter from Monge to his wife, April 9, 1797).

86 Baczko, *Comment sortir de la Terreur*, 353.

87 Stendhal, *La Chartreuse de Parme*, 7.

88 Marmont, *Mémoires*, 1:296.

89 Furet, "Dix-huit Brumaire," 108.

90 Thureau-Dangin, *Royalistes et républicains*, 113.

91 Aron, "La Vᵉ République ou l'Empire parlementaire" (November 1958), in *Une histoire du XXe siècle*, 712.

92 Baczko, *Politiques de la Révolution française*, 531–532.

93 Costa de Beauregard, *Un homme d'autrefois*, 340–341.

94 Nietzsche, *The Genealogy of Morals*, §16.

95 Humboldt, *Journal parisien*, 29.

96 *Correspondance générale*, no. 693 (to Joséphine, June 15, 1796), 1:451.

97 Valéry, *Cahiers*, 2:404.

98 Carlyle, *Heroes and Hero Worship*.

99 Goethe, *Conversations with Eckermann*, 245.

100 Ibid., 246.

101 This point is strongly emphasized by Mascilli Migliorini, *Le Mythe du héros*, 35–36, who also remarks: "These exploits . . . are appreciated especially for the quality of the existential tension that made them possible, for the combative spirit and the vitality that remain the central elements of Napoleon's destiny. . . . That is, *being* like Napoleon clearly takes precedence over *doing* like Napoleon" (11).

13. Saving the Directory

1 Quoted in Madelin, *Histoire du Consulat et de l'Empire*, 2:147.

2 Quoted in Mallet, *Mallet du Pan*, 264. Louis Mandrin (1725–1755) was a famous smuggler, executed in Valence, whose name had become a synonym for bandit.

3 Letter from Mallet du Pan to his father, ibid., 256n1.

4 *Correspondance*, no. 234 (April 26, 1796), 1:187–188.

5 Ibid., no. 453 (May 19, 1796), 1:298.

6 See Thiers, *Histoire de la Révolution française*, 7:24–25.

7 *Correspondance générale*, no. 1023 (October 28, 1796), 1:647–648.

8 Debidour, *Recueil des actes du Directoire*, 4:787–788.

9 Monge, Correspondance, no. 90 (letter from Monge to his wife, October 26, 1796).

10 "prêtraille." In a letter to Carnot, January 28, 1797 (*Correspondance générale*, no. 1331, 1:813).

11 Ibid., no. 1391 (February 19, 1797), 1:846–847.

12 Ibid., no. 1315 (January 22, 1797), 1:802–803.

13 Debidour, *Recueil des actes du Directoire*, 2:332.

14 *Correspondance*, no. 461 (to his brothers-in-arms, May 20, 1796), 1:304.

15 See Chapter 10.

16 Without counting a hundred works of art and 500 valuable manuscripts.

17 Latreille, *L'Église catholique et la Révolution française*, 1:225–234.

18 Pelletier, *Rome et la Révolution française*, 446–449.

19 Quoted in Latreille, *L'Église catholique et la Révolution française*, 1:230.

20 See, for example, Miot de Melito's bitter remarks, *Mémoires*, 1:100.

21 Ferrero, *Bonaparte en Italie*, 92.

22 This legate was none other than Cardinal Mattei, to whom Bonaparte had read the riot act on August 19 (Gendry, *Pie VI*, 2:258–259).

23 *Correspondance générale*, no. 1023 (October 28, 1796), 1:647–648.

24 Bonaparte had reinstated him in office on September 26, and on October 21, in Ferrara, he asked him to go to Rome to see Pius VI on his behalf (Gendry, *Pie VI*, 2:267–269).

25 "Campagnes d'Italie" (*Correspondance de Napoléon Ier*, 29:221–222).

26 *Correspondance générale*, no. 1306, 1:798.

27 Instructions, February 3, 1797 (Debidour, *Recueil des actes du Directoire*, 4:787–788).

28 *Correspondance générale*, no. 1315 (to Cardinal Mattei, January 22, 1797), 1:802–803.

29 *Correspondance de Napoléon Ier*, no. 1499 (decree of February 15, 1797), 2:335.

30 See his letters of February 15 to the Directory (*Correspondance générale*, no. 1379, 1:840) and of February 17 to Joubert (ibid., no. 1383, 1:843).

31 Quoted in Gendry, *Pie VI*, 2:276.

32 Theophilanthropy was a deist movement founded after the Terror had ended. Its founders hoped to see it replace all existing religions. Its credo was reduced to two dogmas—the existence of God and the immortality of the soul—and its worship consisted in purely civil ceremonies. Thanks to the protection given it by the government, which made several religious buildings available to it, philanthropy continued to exist, without ever recruiting many adepts, until 1801.

33 Quoted in Lefebvre, *La France sous le Directoire*, 366–367.

34 *Correspondance générale*, no. 602 (May 16, 1796), 1:401; no. 651 (June 3, 1796), 1:428.

35 Staël, *Dix années d'exil*, 47.

36 The English general George Monk (1608–1670), who betrayed Cromwell and in 1660 helped restore the Catholic Charles II to the throne.

37 Maistre, *Considérations sur la France*, in *Oeuvres*, 276.

38 Quoted in Madelin, *Histoire du Consulat et de l'Empire*, 2:147. Jean-Charles-Dominique de Lacretelle (1766–1855), the former editor of the *Journal de débats*, had been one of the leaders of the "gilded youth" (*jeunesse dorée*) after 9 Thermidor. In 1797 he was one of the royalist party's most influential journalists. Deported after 18 Fructidor, he returned to France after 18 Brumaire and offered his services to Bonaparte, who refused them, saying: "I want nothing to do with him. He's a Bourbonian!"

39 On these various offers, see Mascilli Migliorini, *Napoléon*, 121, 509.

40 Prosper de Barante, *Histoire du Directoire de la République française* (1855), quoted in Mascilli Migliorini, *Napoléon*, 121.

41 Thiers, *Histoire de la Révolution française*, 10:192.

42 Miot de Melito, *Memoirs*, 94.

43 *Correspondance générale*, no. 961, 1:612.

44 The Directory wrote to General Clarke on November 4, 1796: "You know Venice's real and serious offenses against us. People who know the country claim that all the states of the terra

firma, chiefly those of Brescia, Bergamo, and Verona, are revolted by the pride of the Venetian nobles and inclined to arm themselves for liberty. If they were admitted into the Lombard Republic or became its allies, they would lend it new strength. I ask for your observations regarding how difficult or easy it might be to execute this project" (quoted in Landrieux, *Mémoires*, 212n1).

45 On November 15, 1796, the Directory had ordered General Clarke to "go to Venice as an extraordinary envoy for the purpose of proposing a general armistice between the two powers and to agree on the means of beginning peace negotiations" (quoted in Ferrero, *Bonaparte en Italie*, 113). Another mission was entrusted to him: keeping an eye on Bonaparte. The latter made short work of the government's emissary. Having collaborated with him for the Committee of Public Safety in 1795, Bonaparte had seen him at that time as "a good employee," hardworking, competent, and upright (O'Meara, *Napoléon dans l'exil*, 1:324). When Clarke arrived in Milan, Bonaparte had shown him the greatest respect, pretended to share his secrets with him, and flattered the pride of this man infatuated with the nobility of his ancestors (Las Cases, *Mémorial*, 4:420). Bonaparte had succeeded so well in bringing him around that Clarke no longer sent to Paris anything but soothing dispatches in which he swore on his honor that in the whole army the directors had no more zealous or more obedient servant than Bonaparte (see Reiss, *Clarke*, 119–120).

46 Guyot, *Le Directoire et la paix de l'Europe*, 354. Gherardini died suddenly a few days later, on March 24.

47 Quoted in Ferrero, *Bonaparte en Italie*, 132.

48 Chancellor Thugut cynically lays out this strategy in a note reproduced in Ferrero, *Bonaparte en Italie*, 168. The Austrian diplomats had been coveting Venetia for more than fifteen years, and on January 3, 1795, they had even signed with Catherine II a treaty by which Russia secretly promised to support their claims (Sorel, *L'Europe et la Révolution française*, 21–24).

49 Landrieux, *Mémoires*, 85–89 (account of the conversation with Berthier on March 6), and 201–219 (minutes of the meeting on March 9). Landrieux, who claims to have been a double agent, says that he immediately informed the Venetians of the plot against them (ibid., 223–224).

50 *Correspondance générale*, no. 1472 (to the Directory, March 24, 1797), 1:887.

51 Lefebvre, *La France sous le Directoire*, 385.

52 Thiers, *Histoire de la Révolution française*, 9:82–83.

53 This manifesto is reproduced *in toto* in Botta, *Histoire d'Italie*, 2:357–359.

54 See Botta, ibid., 356.

55 *Correspondance générale*, no. 1491 (at Pesaro, April 5, 1797), 1:900.

56 On the spies, secret agents, and agitators in the service of the French in Italy, such as the Piedmontese lawyer Angelo Pico, whose presence in Verona was reported shortly before the massacres, see G. Candela, *L'Armée d'Italie*, 292–299.

57 See Chapter 14.

58 *Correspondance générale*, no. 1514, 1:915.

59 Kérautret, *Les Grands traités du Consulat*, 85–91.

60 He used this image when he blew up at two representatives of the Venetian senate who had come to beg his clemency after the death of Lieutenant Laugier (Botta, *Histoire d'Italie*, 2:409).

61 *Correspondance générale*, no. 1519, 1:922; no. 1527, 1:929.

62 Zorzi, *La République du lion*, 317.

63 Tabet, "Venise, mai 1797," 129–148.

64 Nabonne, *La Diplomatie du Directoire*, 43–44.

65 Signed with Piedmont on April 28, 1796.

66 *Correspondance générale*, no. 1516 (to the Directory, April 19, 1797), 1:917–918.

67 Quoted in Guyot, *Le Directoire et la paix de l'Europe*, 363–364.

68 As we have seen, in July 1796 the Directory had opposed the political enfranchisement of Italy, where the territories taken from Austria would be given back to it if doing so might accelerate the signing of a peace agreement (see above, Chapter 10). In October, it was still only when they were confronted by a fait accompli, and gritting their teeth, that the directors approved the creation of the Cispadane Republic. Moreover, in November the Directory wrote up a new plan without taking the latter's existence into account: France would give up all of its conquests with the exception of Belgium and Luxembourg, the left bank of the Rhine even becoming Imperial territory once again (A. Debidour, *Recueil des actes du Directoire*, 4:287–289). The French government hoped, by showing so much moderation, to win over the English, with whom talks had begun in Lille. The British envoy, Malmesbury, had agreed to plead France's case with his government, on the condition that France demanded nothing more than Belgium. He was committing himself a great deal, because at the same time the English foreign minister was considering a Russian proposal to send 600,000 men to the Rhineland in exchange for substantial subsidies, and when he received Malmesbury's proposals, he had him informed that France, if it wanted peace, would have to give up all of its conquests, with the exception of Avignon and Savoy. The Directory broke off the talks. In January 1797 it adopted a new plan: France still limited its demands to Belgium, but though it did not make the cession of the left bank of the Rhine a condition for peace, it announced its intention to occupy it until the definitive conclusion of peace on the continent (see the note written by Bonaparte and Clarke, and countersigned by Barras on January 23, 1797, in *Correspondance de Napoléon Ier*, no. 1415, 2:267–269). This was before the victory at Rivoli and Wurmser's capitulation at Mantua. After Rivoli, the Directory wrote up new instructions in which Italy was no longer mentioned (Guyot, *Le Directoire et la paix de l'Europe*, 329–330): Did that mean that the French government had always intended to restore its Italian conquests, or, on the contrary, that after this victory it no longer felt capable of imposing anything on Bonaparte so far as their fate was concerned? The fall of Mantua not only led to the French government adopting a harder line—henceforth, it was going to "make the claim to the left bank of the Rhine the unshakable foundation of its policy" (Dufraisse, "Bonaparte a-t-il sacrifié le Rhin," 11)—but also to an almost complete about-face. Another new plan in the middle of February provided, this time, for the defense of "the independence of the Cispadane Republic" and the compensation of the Duke of Modena by offering him territories taken from the pope (Guyot, *Le Directoire et la paix de l'Europe*, 331). Because the Army of Italy was nearing Vienna, French demands inevitably increased, and on April 7—at the time when Bonaparte was reaching Leoben—the Directory changed course once again: whereas for months it had disapproved of the creation of new republics in Italy, now, not content to approve the Cispadane Republic created south of

the Po, it recommended proclaiming another republic in Lombardy, emphasizing that it was "worthy of a great and righteous government . . . to lead other people to happiness" (these instructions of April 7, 1797, are reproduced *in toto* in Ferrero, *Bonaparte en Italie*, 156–161). This amounted to asking Bonaparte to obtain everything from Austria: Belgium, the Rhineland, Lombardy, Modena, and the legations. In exchange for what? On this point as well the Directory constantly changed its mind, sometimes mentioning the secularization, to the benefit of the emperor, of a certain number of German ecclesiastical principalities, sometimes the annexation of Bavaria to Austria, the Elector Palatine being compensated by . . . Lombardy!

69 Letter of January 18, 1797, quoted in Dufraisse, "Bonaparte a-t-il sacrifié le Rhin," 10.

70 Dumolard, *Motion d'ordre sur nos rapports actuels avec l'Italie*, 6–7. The right's campaign against the Venetian "revolution" was orchestrated by Mallet du Pan (see Sayous, *Mémoires et correspondance de Mallet du Pan*, 2:313). Jean-Baptiste Cloots (1755–1794), also known as Anacharsis, or as "the orator of humankind," advocated the establishment of a universal republic, and to govern it an assembly of 10,000 representatives. He was guillotined in 1794, along with the Hébertists.

71 Out of 750 seats, 262 were at stake in the elections of April 1797: the right won 182 (69 percent), the Jacobins 34 (13 percent), and the Directory's candidates only 46 (18 percent). The right henceforth had 330 delegates, or 45 percent of the seats.

72 Quoted in Jourdan, *Napoléon: Héros, imperator, mécène*, 78–79.

73 *Correspondance générale*, no. 1773 (July 11, 1797), 1:1052.

74 "On a great change that has occurred in the relations between the government and the generals of the republican armies, and the quaestors or representatives who supervise them" (Roederer, *Oeuvres*, 3:324–325).

75 See his letters to Barras and Carnot of August 9, 1796 (*Correspondance générale*, no. 839–840, 1:539–540).

76 The letter of support, of July 31, 1796, was signed by Letourneur, Carnot, Reubell, and La Révellière (Debidour, *Recueil des actes du Directoire*, 3:232–233).

77 Letter reproduced in Thiers, *Histoire de la Révolution française*, 8:244–247.

78 *Correspondance générale*, no. 1791, 1:1061. He also demanded, and obtained, that Mallet du Pan, who had launched the royalists' campaign against his policy in Venice, be expelled from Bern, where he was living (Sayous, *Mémoires et correspondance de Mallet du Pan*, 2:307–309).

79 *Correspondance générale*, no. 1741, 1:1036–1037.

80 *Correspondance de Napoléon Ier*, no. 1971, 2:158.

81 Godechot, *La Contre-Révolution*, 282–294.

82 See "Campagnes d'Italie" (*Correspondance de Napoléon Ier*, 29:295).

83 Las Cases, *Journal of the Private Life and Conversations of the Emperor Napoleon at Saint Helena*, 2:146–147.

84 Thiers, *Histoire de la Révolution française*, 9:193.

85 *Bulletin de Paris*, September 16, 1797.

86 Quoted in Miot de Melito, *Memoirs*, 95.

87 *Correspondance de Napoléon Ier*, no. 2010 (July 14, 1797), 3:180–181.

88 *Correspondance générale*, no. 1785, 1:1058.

89 The petition from the officers and soldiers of the divisions led by Masséna, Augereau, Bernadotte, and Sérurier, which Bonaparte announced he was sending in a letter of July 18 (ibid., no. 1798, 1:1064–1065), was published in the *Moniteur universel* for August 12: "Tremble! From the Adige to the Rhine it is only a short step! Tremble! Your iniquities have been counted, and the price is at the end of our bayonets" (*Réimpression de l'ancien Moniteur*, 28:764).

90 Quoted in Lanfrey, *The History of Napoleon the First*, 1:223.

91 Lavalette, *Mémoires*, 1:224–225.

92 Ibid., 226.

93 "proud brigand": Lanfrey, *The History of Napoleon the First*, 1:228.

94 So discreet, in fact, that Carnot, a few days before his fall, still thought it possible to draw him into his camp (see the letter he sent Bonaparte on August 17, in Reinhard, *Le Grand Carnot*, 2:234–235). Bonaparte had Carnot informed that he did not believe "the rumors about him that were being spread" (ibid., 235), but the director's remarks, which incited him to withdraw from public life, were not likely to bring him back to more favorable feelings regarding the right.

95 Quoted in Lanfrey, *The History of Napoleon the First*, 1:232.

96 *Correspondance de Napoléon Ier*, no. 2239 (September 22, 1797), 3:324.

97 *Correspondance générale*, no. 2075 (September 23, 1797), 1:1203–1204. He made identical remarks to Lavalette when he returned from Paris (Lavalette, *Mémoires*, 1:244–245).

98 "Compte rendu par le citoyen Bottot de sa mission en Italie" (A. N. AF III 473, folder nb 2906, p. 14).

99 This conversation with Miot took place in Turin in November 1797. Speaking of the directors, Bonaparte told him: "But do not imagine . . . that I resolved on so doing because of any conformity of ideas with those of the men whom I supported. I did not choose that the Bourbons should return, especially if brought back by Moreau's army and by Pichegru. . . . I do not care to play the part of Monk; I will not play it myself, and I do not choose that others shall do so" (Miot de Melito, *Memoirs*, 112–113).

14. Campoformio

1 See Chapter 13. On January 25, 1797, the Directory had ended up yielding by making Clarke officially subordinate to Bonaparte (Reiss, *Clarke*, 142).

2 Sorel, *L'Europe et la Révolution française*, 5:190.

3 See article 5 of the preliminary agreements of April 18, 1797.

4 French diplomats had found a way of giving "the integrity of the empire" a less restrictive interpretation on the basis of the patent meaning of this formula in article 6: "His Majesty the Emperor and King foregoes all his rights over the Belgian provinces, known as the Austrian Netherlands, and recognizes the limits of France set by the laws of the French Republic." This article explicitly concerns Belgium alone, but by forcing the text a little it could be deduced from it that Austria recognized "the so-called constitutional borders and the annexations, other than those of its *Belgian provinces*" (R. Dufraisse, "Bonaparte a-t-il sacrifié le Rhin," 13). On May 6 the Directory asked Bonaparte to demand the whole of the

left bank, emphasizing that the notion of "borders set by the Republic" did not concern Belgium alone, and reminding him that the empire's (geographical) integrity had already been infringed upon by the treaties signed with the duchy of Württemberg (August 16, 1796) and the margravate of Baden (August 25), both of which were part of the Holy Roman Empire.

5 *Correspondance générale*, no. 1517 (to the Directory, April 22, 1797), 1:919–920.

6 Ferrero, *Bonaparte en Italie*, 199–200.

7 *Correspondance générale*, no. 1517 (to the Directory, April 22, 1797), 1:919–920.

8 Ibid., no. 1561, 1:949.

9 Ibid., no. 1517 (to the Directory, April 22, 1797), 1:920.

10 Ibid., no. 1587 (to the Directory, May 27, 1797), 1:963; Ferrero, *Bonaparte en Italie*, 200–201.

11 *Correspondance générale*, no. 1714 (June 22, 1797), 1:1025.

12 On June 18 he and Clarke still "announced that France will go no farther than what had been foreseen in Leoben, insofar as Austria's acquisitions in Italy are concerned" (Dufraisse, "Bonaparte a-t-il sacrifié le Rhin," 15).

13 *Correspondance générale*, no. 1587 (to the Directory, May 27, 1797), 1:963.

14 He had already mentioned this in a speech given in Milan on May 4. This speech, mentioned in Giuseppe Marelli's *Giornale storico della Repubblica cisalpina* (item 5, folio 39–40, and manuscript item no. 3, folio 18), is also known from the summary Pietro Verri gave of it in a letter of May 6, quoted in Capra, *I progressi della ragione*, 593.

15 See Guyot, *Le Directoire et la paix de l'Europe*, 497.

16 *Correspondance générale*, no. 2243, 1:1298.

17 Ibid., no. 2098, 1:1216.

18 Ibid., no. 775, 1:500.

19 Ibid., no. 758, 1:489.

20 Ibid., no. 1561, 1:948–949.

21 Ibid., no. 1589, 1:965.

22 Ibid., no. 1561, 1:949.

23 Ibid., no. 1600, 1:969–970.

24 Ibid., no. 1561, 1:949.

25 Ibid., no. 2149, 1:1244–1246.

26 Ibid., no. 1212, 1:750–751.

27 Pingaud, *Bonaparte président de la République italienne*, 1:152.

28 *Correspondance générale*, no. 1472, 1:888.

29 "Whether or not Austria, when peace comes, recognizes the independence of its possessions in Italy, it is possible that the love of liberty might have made such progress there that the inhabitants combine their efforts to no longer recognize its yoke" (letter sent by the Directory to Bonaparte on April 7, 1797, reproduced in Ferrero, *Bonaparte en Italie*, 156–161).

30 *Correspondance générale*, no. 1525 (to the Directory, May 1, 1797), 1:925–926.

31 Driault, *Napoléon en Italie*, 26. Was this a sign that in his heart of hearts, if not in his letters to the Directory, he had opted for a unified republic? That is what is suggested in a letter written by Pietro Verri on May 6, 1797, two days after he heard a speech given by Bonaparte in Milan: "Milan will be the capital of a Republic that will include Como, Pavia, Lodi,

Cremona, Casalmaggiore, Bergamo, Crema, Brescia, Reggio, Modena, Bologna, Ferrara, Massa Carrara. A territorial space will be formed all at once, and the French constitution will be adapted to us all. . . . I was present at the speech Bonaparte gave before us and that is the spirit of it. . . . In a few years Italy will probably be a single family" (quoted in Capra, *I progressi della raggione*, 442).

32 On July 28 he announced to the Directory that the Cispadane Republic had requested that it be united with the Cisalpine, and that its request had been granted, without his having had a hand in it (*Correspondance générale*, no. 1827, 1:1084).

33 Quoted in Sorel, *L'Europe et la Révolution française*, 5:178.

34 See the text of this convention signed by Gallo, Bonaparte, and Clarke, in *Correspondance*, no. 1824, 3:63–64.

35 Las Cases, *Mémorial*, 4:419.

36 Ferrero, *Bonaparte en Italie*, 205.

37 Sorel, *L'Europe et la Révolution française*, 5:174.

38 Miot de Melito, *Mémoires*, 1:164–165. *La Quotidienne*, the organ of the royalists in 1797, raised the question in its issue for June 3, 1797: "Truly, when I think about it, despite his giant's drive from Rome to Vienna, his transpadane and cispadane republics, the overthrow of Venice and Genoa, this Buonaparte troubles and worries me. What will become of him? Under the reign of despotism that people call the monarchy, it was very easy to reward a hero; honors, a bit of blue ribbon, were a currency of great [value], and even the sovereign's glances took the place of all favors; but under our excellent democracy, which has completely leveled out people and things, does anyone think that an honorable mention by the two councils, or Chénier's verses, could suffice for a great soul eager for glory? . . . What role will he play once this glorious career is over? He will be made a justice of the peace, or an administrator, or a war representative, or, if you wish, a representative. What a fall, good God, for the conqueror of Italy!!!" (3).

39 "long vacations": Lavalette, *Mémoires*, 1:248.

40 Instructions of May 20, 1797 (Dufraisse, "Bonaparte a-t-il sacrifié le Rhin," 15).

41 Lefebvre, *La France sous le Directoire*, 391.

42 Ultimatum: *Correspondance générale*, no. 1812, 1:1072–1073.

43 Quoted in Ferrero, *Bonaparte en Italie*, 218.

44 The discussions with the English, broken off after the failure of the conferences held in Lille in late 1796, resumed in Lille on July 7, 1797. England seemed prepared to allow France to establish itself in Antwerp and on the Rhine, provided that France's allies compensated it with colonial possessions: Spain would cede it Trinidad and Holland would cede it the Cape.

45 Quoted in Ferrero, *Bonaparte en Italie*, 218.

46 Quoted in Reinhard, *Le Grand Carnot*, 2:234–235.

47 *Correspondance générale*, no. 2009, 1:1166.

48 Las Cases, *Mémorial*, 2:761.

49 Sorel, *L'Europe et la Révolution française*, 5:217.

50 *Correspondance générale*, no. 1973, 1:1147.

51 "Campagnes d'Italie" (*Correspondance de Napoléon Ier*, 29:312).

52 Sorel, *L'Europe et la Révolution française*, 5:225.

53 See Carnot, *Réponse au rapport fait sur la conjuration du 18 Fructidor*, 108–109.

54 *Correspondance générale*, no. 2045, 1:1185–1187.

55 Gourgaud, *Talks of Napoleon at St. Helena*, 1:63.

56 Marmont, *Mémoires*, 1:288.

57 Quoted in Fournoux, *Napoléon et Venise*, 188.

58 In May, Bonaparte had already written, after his first discussions with Gallo: "It seemed to me . . . that what they were reluctant to do was less to grant us the Rhine border than to make any change that would increase the power of the king of Prussia and that would bring down the whole Germany entity" (*Correspondance générale*, no. 1587, 1:962–964). On September 28, after a meeting at which the two men had "argued and repeated themselves at length," they had a long after-dinner conversation, in the course of which Cobenzl mentioned the interest of a Franco-Austrian rapprochement to stop Prussia (ibid., no. 2101, 1:1218–1219).

59 Quoted in Ferrero, *Bonaparte en Italie*, 228–229.

60 Sorel, *L'Europe et la Révolution française*, 5:239.

61 *Correspondance générale*, no. 2116, 1:1229.

62 Instructions of September 29 (Dufraisse, "Bonaparte a-t-il sacrifié le Rhin," 16–18); *Correspondance générale*, no. 2150, 1:1246; Ferrero, *Bonaparte en Italie*, 231–232.

63 *Correspondance générale*, no. 2153 (to the Directory, October 10, 1797), 1:1248–1249.

64 Quoted in Ferrero, *Bonaparte en Italie*, 233–234.

65 The scene is reported by Gourgaud, *Journal*, 1:115.

66 Quoted in Madelin, *Histoire du Consulat et de l'Empire*, 2:192–193.

67 Las Cases, *Journal*, 3:299.

68 Quoted in Lanfrey, *The History of Napoleon the First*, 1:247.

69 Lavalette, *Mémoires*, 1:250–251.

70 Guyot, *Le Directoire et la paix de l'Europe*, 543–545.

71 "This treaty is not a peace, it's a call for another war," Sieyès is supposed to have said (quoted in Zaghi, *Bonaparte e il Direttorio*, 4).

72 *Correspondance générale*, no. 2153 (to the Directory, October 10, 1797), 1:1248–1249.

73 Because he had not reported Pichegru's betrayal, even though he had proof of it.

74 La Révellière-Lépeaux, *Mémoires*, 2:277–278.

75 *Réimpression de l'ancien Moniteur*, 29:56.

76 Lefebvre, *La France sous le Directoire*, 436.

77 See Kérautret, *Les Grands traités du Consulat*, 100–101.

78 Article 20 of the public part of the treaty (ibid., 99).

79 Treaties signed with Prussia on April 5, 1795, and August 5, 1796 (ibid., 16–23, 43–50).

80 Letter of May 27, 1797, to the Directory (*Correspondance générale*, no. 1587, 1:963).

81 Sorel, *L'Europe et la Révolution française*, 5:190–191.

82 Article 1 of the secret part of the treaty (Kérautret, *Les Grands traités du Consulat*, 101).

83 The cession of Belgium to France was solemnly established by article 3 of the public part of the treaty (Ibid., 94–95).

84 Dufraisse, "Bonaparte a-t-il sacrifié le Rhin," 20.

85 Fifth secret article of the treaty (Kérautret, *Les Grands traités du Consulat*, 102).

86 Public articles 5–8 (ibid., 95–96).

87 Sorel, *L'Europe et la Révolution française*, 5:257–258; Ferrero, *Bonaparte en Italie*, 237–252.

88 See D. Alland, "Droit des gens," in Raynaud and Rials, *Dictionnaire de philosophie politique*, 152–157.

89 Rousseau, *Considérations sur le gouvernement de Pologne*, in *Oeuvres complètes*, 3:960.

90 *Du contrat social*, bk. 1, chap. 4, *in Oeuvres*, 3:357.

91 "In most of the countries of Europe, the people's interests and those of the government are very different: patriotism is only a word; citizens are not soldiers: soldiers are not citizens; wars are not quarrels of the nation, they are those of the ministry or the sovereign" (Guibert, *Essai général de tactique*, 165).

92 Ibid., 137.

93 Sorel, *L'Europe et la Révolution française*, 1:89. The War of the Austrian Succession (1740–1748) was provoked by the Pragmatic Sanction (1713), recognized by all European states, by virtue of which the German emperor Charles VI bequeathed to his daughter Maria Theresa the hereditary states of the House of Habsburg. The king of Prussia, Frederick II, whom Austria at that time considered a faithful ally, believed that the accession of Maria Theresa would lead to a long-lasting diminishment of Austria's power, and he took advantage of the circumstances to invade Silesia, which he wanted for himself. France (which had, however, adhered to the Pragmatic Sanction in 1738), and then Spain and Bavaria, took Prussia's side; the Austrians were supported by England and Holland.

94 See Ferrero, *Bonaparte en Italie*, 243–244. However, the Treaty of Campoformio found an unexpected apologist in the person of Louis de Bonald, who saw in it a first step toward a general reorganization of Europe. Under French direction, this reorganization would simplify the political map through the disappearance of small states that were a permanent source of problems and that proceeded, in Germany, from the religious division resulting from the Reformation. It would lead to the creation of great nations that, unified by language, laws, religion, and natural borders, and living, as it were, each in its own space and having nothing to desire abroad, would henceforth only rarely have reasons to engage in conflicts (Bonald, "Du traité de Westphalie et de celui de Campoformio," in *Oeuvres*, 2:411–452).

95 See his letter of November 2, 1797, to the Austrian ambassador in London, quoted in Ferrero, *Bonaparte en Italie*, 237.

96 "Campagnes d'Italie" (*Correspondance de Napoléon Ier*, 29:312–313).

97 Letter of December 23, 1797, quoted in Mascilli Migliorini, *Napoléon*, 515.

15. Parisian Interlude

1 "breakneck speed": *Correspondance générale*, no. 2271, 1:1311.

2 Ibid., no. 2274, 1:1313.

3 Quotation in Espitalier, *Vers brumaire*, 43.

4 "You are in a more favorable situation than the French people," he wrote to the president of the Cispadane congress on January 1797. "You can achieve liberty without revolution and its crimes. The misfortunes that afflicted France before the establishment of the constitution will never be seen among you" (*Correspondance générale*, no. 1243, 1:767); ibid., no. 1081, 1:679.

5 *Correspondance de Napoléon Ier,* no. 1101, 2:64–65. "Above all, repress the small number of men who love liberty only in order to arrive at a revolution," he wrote to the State Congress of Lombardy on December 10, 1796, "they are its greatest enemies. They take every form to realize their criminal designs. The French army will never allow liberty to be covered with crimes in Italy. Repress this revolutionary torrent as soon as it arises; it is a public disease that makes liberty odious. . . . Let the true friends of their country unite and let Lombardy enjoy liberty without experiencing the ills and the crimes of a revolution" (*Correspondance générale,* no. 1125, 1:703–704).

6 See Chapter 14.

7 He told Melzi that in Italy "there [were] even fewer elements of republicanism than in France" (Miot de Melito, *Mémoires,* 1:164).

8 "The Directory . . . believes first, like you, that the primary assemblies must not be allowed to meet . . . , but nothing prevents you from giving them a regular government. . . . So here is what you must do. You will declare that the current administration of Lombardy and the countries included under the name of the Cispadane Republic has neither enough strength nor enough regularity to provide both for the service of the French armies and the welfare of the country's inhabitants; that as a result you have decided it is necessary to establish provisionally a new organization that will improve the country's condition and that of our armies; that, in your view, the best way to achieve that goal is the one that is proposed by the draft constitution presented to the Cispadane Congress. . . . Consequently, you will order that these countries be governed, so long as the French are in Italy, as follows (here you will place before them the draft constitution presented to the Cispadane Congress, which you will call only a set of rules). At the same time, you will declare that for the moment you consider it appropriate to appoint persons who are to fill the positions of all kinds that are indicated in this new organization, or to entrust the choice to whomever you consider appropriate, and you will thus constitute all the parts of the new state. However, it does not seem to us useful that you establish the legislative body. It is only as our withdrawal approaches, if we are fortunate enough to be able to dictate the peace conditions, that you will have it elected in accord with the very real constitution that you will have established. . . . The government must be active in all its parts, but the legislative must, so long as we are there, be manifested by you alone. . . . However, . . . it does not suffice to constitute the people; all the legislation necessary for the new order of things, as well as a general plan for public revenues capable of covering the state's expenses, must also be immediately adapted to these new institutions. Our example should teach us how fatal it is to expect all that from a new legislative body that, for countless different reasons, crawls along for a considerable time in the legislative path and especially in that of finances before being able to walk, and for many years leaves a nascent government in stagnation and always in danger of perishing. Consequently, you will yourself appoint as many committees [of three persons] as you judge necessary to create the legislation that concerns each of the parts of the constitution, justice, administration, finances, the army, the police force, etc. . . . You will then order all the authorities and all the citizens to carry out the rules that you will still publish as general-in-chief of the Army of Italy" (Ferrero, *Bonaparte en Italie,* 156–161).

9 Ibid., 165.

10 Ibid., 194.

11 Latreille, *L'Église catholique et la Révolution française*, 1:228.

12 *Correspondance générale*, no. 741 (to the Directory, July 2, 1796), 1:481.

13 Generally this claim is based on the instructions Bonaparte is supposed to have sent on November 8, 1797, to Serbelloni, one of the directors of the Cisalpine Republic. In this long manifesto, one finds sentences like these: "Your republic must ... prepare its peoples to despise Catholic doctrine, to make them desire the destruction of that religion, and to interest them in overthrowing it entirely. After having alienated the clergy's property, abandon it to the ignominy of charlatanism and the sarcasms of your writers." And at the end: "Incite divisions among the priests, seek out among them the enemies of religion, and you will have apostles of philosophy whose preaching will be more effective than that of a thousand newspapers. Chastise bishops who dare to disturb these missionaries of liberty, and repress the fanatics who refuse to help them" (instruction reproduced *in toto* in Baldassari, *Histoire de l'enlèvement et de la captivité de Pie VI*, 577–580). The authenticity of this document is more than suspect, because it was first published by Pedro Cevallos in his *Politique particulière de Bonaparte à l'égard de la religion catholique*, which appeared in Cadiz in ... 1812! The very tone of these alleged instructions, which is characterized, as the translator of Baldassari's book notes, by a "fanatical hatred of religion," indicates that it is very probably a forgery intended to maintain Spaniards' hostility to the French invader (see the Abbé Lacouture's commentary in Baldassari, 580). The claim that Bonaparte was hostile to Rome is also based on an affair that was much discussed in Milan: that of the *Ballet de papes* (Ballet of the popes), which, despite the archbishop of Milan's protests, was produced on stage with the approval of the French authorities (Gendry, *Pie VI*, 2:278–279). But this play was not performed, as is sometimes said, in the autumn of 1797, but rather in February, after the signature of the peace treaty of Tolentino. It was the way the Milanese Jacobins, who were in fact very anticlerical, had chosen to celebrate the defeat of the papal forces (Pingaud, *Les Hommes d'État de la République italienne*, 156), and Bonaparte no doubt let them do it because it provided an outlet: this play was insulting to the pope, but it sufficed to calm the anticlerical ardor of a part of public opinion (Latreille, *L'Église catholique et la Révolution française*, 1:228).

14 Quoted in Séché, *Les Origines du Concordat*, 1:116.

15 Camille de Jourdan's proposed law regarding freedom of worship, submitted on June 17, had just been adopted by the Council of Five Hundred (July 14) after passionate debates. This resolution became law after its adoption by the Council of Ancients on August 24. But 18 Fructidor was to halt this policy of religious reconciliation before it got off the ground.

16 *Correspondance générale*, no. 1859 (note delivered to Rome's ambassador in Milan, August 3, 1797), 1:1098–1099.

17 Ibid., no. 2214 (to the provisional government of the Ligurian Republic, November 11, 1797), 1:1278–1280.

18 *Réimpression de l'ancien Moniteur*, 29:71–73.

19 Bruce, *Napoleon and Josephine*, 213.

20 Hastier, *Le Grand amour de Joséphine*, 123; Wagener, *L'Impératrice Joséphine*, 166.

21 Bourrienne, *Mémoires*, 2:29.

22 Quoted in *Correspondance générale*, 1:1082n.

23 Ibid., no. 1822 (to Talleyrand, July 26, 1797), 1:1081.

24 Quoted in ibid., 1:1112, note (letter of August 1, 1797).

25 Ibid., no. 1878, 1:1106.

26 Sainte-Beuve, "Talleyrand," *Nouveaux lundis*, 12:40.

27 Talleyrand, *Mémoires et correspondances*, 221.

28 Letter to Olive, May 10, 1797, quoted in Waresquiel, *Talleyrand*, 232.

29 Lacour-Gayet, *Talleyrand*, 269.

30 *Correspondance générale*, no. 1822 (to Talleyrand, July 26, 1797), 1:1081.

31 Quoted in Le Doulcet de Pontécoulant, *Souvenirs*, 2:474–475.

32 *Correspondance générale*, no. 2065 (to Talleyrand, September 2, 1797), 1:1196–1198.

33 Talleyrand, *Mémoires et correspondances*, 224.

34 Quoted in Stendhal, *Vie de Napoléon*, 23–24.

35 *Réimpression de l'ancien Moniteur*, 29:90.

36 Report of the Prussian ambassador, Sandoz-Rollin, quoted in Poniatowski, *Talleyrand et le Directoire*, 414.

37 *Réimpression de l'ancien Moniteur*, 29:90.

38 Guyot, "Du Directoire au Consulat: Les transitions," 7.

39 *Réimpression de l'ancien Moniteur*, 29:90.

40 Waresquiel, *Talleyrand*, 237.

41 Poniatowski, *Talleyrand et le Directoire*, 288–289.

42 See Le Doulcet de Pontécoulant, *Souvenirs*, 2:459. Lucien Bonaparte also says that it is a fable (*Mémoires*, 111).

43 Quoted in Miot de Melito, *Mémoires*, 1:196.

44 J. Lachapelle, "Du culte des théophilanthropes," *Réimpression de l'ancien Moniteur*, 28:762–764.

45 Las Cases, *Mémorial*, 2:781–782.

46 Hyde de Neuville, *Mémoires*, 1:223.

47 Bertrand, *Cahiers*, 1:115.

48 Cherrier, *18 Brumaire et 2 Décembre*, 1:126.

49 See Laurens, *Kléber en Égypte*, 1:93–95.

50 In 1793 Dumouriez had tried to march on Paris. His army having refused to follow him, he had been forced to emigrate.

51 Quoted in Lefebvre, *La France sous le Directoire*, 350.

52 Thus Mme Méchin, who was said to be one of the most beautiful women in Paris, cried, on leaving a banquet given in Bonaparte's honor: "Finally, I have seen General Bonaparte; I have touched his elbow!" (Delécluze, *Souvenirs*, 199).

53 Jean-François Ducis (1733–1816) was known above all for having introduced Shakespeare's tragedies into France by adapting them (not always faithfully). Thérèse Vestris (1729–1808) had made her debut at the Opera in 1751. She belonged to a famous family of dancers.

54 Arnault, *Souvenirs*, 4:29–30.

55 Thiers, *Histoire de la Révolution française*, 9:351–353.

56 *Correspondance générale*, no. 2280 (to Camus, December 26, 1797), 1:1316–1317.

12 A former diplomat had proposed this as early as 1793 (Ducher, *Acte de navigation*). He drew up a proposal that Barère had printed on August 18, 1793 (*Réimpression de l'ancien Moniteur*, 18:85). In 1796 the Directory asked Ducher to write a summary of his project and had it published on June 15, 1796, under the title "Médiation et garantie du roi d'Angleterre" (*Moniteur universel*, 1796, 1:1065–1066).

13 See Coquelle, *Les Projets de descente en Angleterre*.

14 Quoted in Desprez, *Lazare Hoche*, 321–322.

15 The idea of giving the English a taste of their own medicine by inciting a revolt among them had been proposed by Carnot (Service Historique de la Défense [Vincennes], Armée, 11B¹, Première expedition d'Irlande, "Instruction pour l'établissement d'une chouannerie en Angleterre" [1795]).

16 Quoted in Bergounioux, *Essai sur la vie de Lazare Hoche*, 411.

17 Sorel, *Bonaparte et Hoche*, 333.

18 Report by Sandoz-Rollin, the Prussian minister in Paris, March 18, 1798, quoted in Talleyrand, *Correspondance diplomatique*, 207–208n.

19 Miot de Melito, *Mémoires*, 1:165–166.

20 He wrote to the Directory on November 5, 1797, that it would be impossible to succeed without having "good naval officers, numerous, well-commanded troops in order to be able to threaten at several points and to resupply the landing, an intelligent, resolute admiral, [and] thirty million francs in cash" (*Correspondance générale*, no. 2191, 1:1267).

21 Ibid., no. 1908 (to the Directory, August 16, 1797), 1:1118.

22 Ibid., no. 2170, 1:1257.

23 Bourrienne, *Private Memoirs*, 1:155. Moreover, he did not abandon the idea of a combined offensive against British interests and on English soil, even after the Directory had yielded to his arguments and assigned him to invade Egypt, as is shown by a report submitted to the government on April 13, 1798, one month after his appointment as head of the Army of the East. He had to take advantage of being in Egypt, he said, to strengthen the fleet and even make it superior to that of the English, because the expedition to the East would force the latter to disperse their ships from the English Channel to the eastern Mediterranean. Then, in late 1798, the invasion of England would finally become possible: see *Correspondance générale*, no. 2390, 2:80–81.

24 See Magniez, *Histoire de l'idée d'une conquête française de l'Égypte*; Djuvara, *Cent projets de partage de la Turquie*.

25 Jean de Saulx (1555–1629), quoted in Poumarède, *Pour en finir avec la Croisade*, 150.

26 Sully's plan, known under the name of the "Great Design of Henry IV" (Grand dessein d'Henri IV), was inserted into his *Économies royales*. Leibniz's plan (1670–1672) was published in *Oeuvres de Leibniz*, vol. 5. See also Bilici, *Louis XIV et son projet de conquête d'Istanbul*, 78–89.

27 Poumarède, *Pour en finir avec la Croisade*, 127–129.

28 Mantran, *Histoire de l'empire ottoman*, 107–112. The pope's letter (1494) is quoted in Rodinson, *La Fascination de l'islam*, 61–62.

29 Report of the French ambassador in Constantinople, 1606, quoted in Bilici, *Louis XIV et son projet de conquête d'Istanbul*, 39–40.

30 On the Ottoman Empire in the eighteenth century, see Bozarslan, *Histoire de la Turquie*.

31 The Ottomans divided the world into two parts: the "House of Islam," which was subject to Islamic law, and thus at peace, and the "House of War," or all the area that remained to be subjected (Lewis, *The Muslim Discovery of Europe*, 62–63).

32 Rodinson, *La Fascination de l'islam*, 35.

33 Boutant, *L'Europe au grand tournant des années 1680*, 231.

34 See the instructions given the mission's leader, Étienne Gravier d'Ortières, and the complete text of his report (Bilici, *Louis XIV et son projet de conquête d'Istanbul*, 131–140, 188–310).

35 Laurens, *Orientales*, 70–78.

36 "equestrian feudalism": Louca, *L'Autre Égypte*, 29.

37 Report by Baron de Tott, quoted in Charles-Roux, "Le projet français de conquête de l'Égypte," 20.

38 Talleyrand, in his *Mémoire sur les avantages à retirer des colonies nouvelles dans les circonstances présentes*, presented at the Institute on July 3, 1797, was to pay homage to Choiseul, saying that "M. the duke of Choiseul, . . . who foresaw already in 1769 the separation of America from England . . . , sought from that time on the cession of Egypt to France, in order to be ready to replace, with the same products and a more extensive commerce, the American colonies when they escape us" (Talleyrand, *Essai sur les avantages à retirer des colonies nouvelles*, 14). The same arguments and projects are found in a report dated 1770 and written by the French ambassador in Constantinople, the Count of Saint-Priest (*Mémoires*, 134).

39 On these various missions and plans, see Charles-Roux, *La Politique française en Égypte*, 11–16; Charles-Roux, "Le projet français de conquête de l'Égypte," 16–83.

40 Ibid., 84–85. See Laurens, *Les Origines intellectuelles de l'expédition d'Égypte*, 15.

41 Laurens, *Les Origines intellectuelles de l'expédition d'Égypte*, 63–64.

42 It was to counter the offensive mounted by those who wanted to colonize Egypt, who were again very active in the 1780s, that Vergennes sent Volney to the Orient, assigning him to demonstrate that, on the contrary, France had nothing to gain from such an acquisition (Gaulmier, *L'Idéologue Volney*, 30–42). His travels from Alexandria to Beirut between 1783 and 1785 confirmed Volney in his opposition to the colonization of Egypt, and to colonial expansion in general, to which he would have preferred the adoption of a policy of developing French agricultural lands, which were still so neglected. In 1788 (Vergennes had died the preceding year), Volney published a second work in which he predicted in turn the imminent fall of the Ottoman Empire and advised the government to abandon it to its fate, that is, to the Russians: France, he said, had to review the whole of its foreign policy and seek in an alliance with Saint Petersburg the advantages that the alliance with the sultan no longer provided (Volney, *Considérations sur la guerre actuelle des Turcs*, 44–59 and 70ff.).

43 M. Terrasse, "Ottoman," in Tulard, *Dictionnaire Napoléon*, 2:440.

44 Quoted in Marcère, *Une ambassade à Constantinople*, 2:260.

45 Ibid., 2:258–259.

46 *Correspondance*, 29:361–362.

47 Letter of October 27, 1797 (La Jonquière, *L'Expédition d'Égypte*, 1:42–43).

48 Laurens, *Les Origines intellectuelles de l'expédition d'Égypte*, 22.

49 Napoléon Bonaparte, *Manuscrits inédits*, 123–141, 241–248, 319–334.

50 Quoted in Brégeon, *L'Égypte de Bonaparte*, 82–83.

51 *Correspondance générale*, no. 52 (to Sucy, February 17, 1792), 1:103.

52 On Volney's sojourn in Corsica, see Gaulmier, *L'Idéologue Volney*, 129–142.

53 Carré, *Voyageurs et écrivains français en Égypte*, 1:101.

54 See A. Thépot, "Le rêve oriental," in Mistler, *Le Grand livre de Napoléon*, 2:115.

55 Savary, *Lettres sur l'Égypte*, 1:60–61; Volney, *Voyage en Égypte et en Syrie*, 1:15.

56 Savary, *Lettres sur l'Égypte*, 1:43–44; Volney, *Voyage en Égypte et en Syrie*, 1:3, 209–210.

57 Rodinson, *La Fascination de l'islam*, 77–88; Laurens, *Orientales*, 23–33.

58 Condorcet, *Esquisse d'un tableau historique des progrès de l'esprit humain*, 163.

59 We must not be taken in by the "sympathy" or "goodwill" the *philosophes* showed toward Islam. More than to religious beliefs, these were directed to the Arabs, in whom some people saw a faithful image of the natural man. These people, it was said, had remained so simple, pure, sincere, loyal, and hospitable, that they constituted "the best people on Earth" (Savary, *Lettres sur l'Égypte*, 2:27). Around 1730, Boulainvilliers had already painted a similar portrait of the Arabs. Moreover, if he, too, lauded the purity of their customs, it was because he saw in them, not a pledge of gentleness, but on the contrary an explanation for the extraordinary religious fanaticism that had long made them invincible (*Vie de Mahomet*, 2). And if Volney also saw in the Muslim religion the seed of an "ardent and obstinate fanaticism," even more a doctrine that favored the most absolute despotism (*Voyage en Égypte et en Syrie*, 2:237), in eighteenth-century literature we find numerous pages more sympathetic to Islam. The simplicity of Muslim rites and the small number of myths even seemed to indicate a rational dimension in Islam that led some Europeans to see it as an Oriental version of deism. Condorcet admitted it willingly: the Muslim religion was superior to the Christian religion in the tolerance it had generally shown toward non-Christians; but at the same time, he was extremely critical of the Quran's "medley of fables" (*Esquisse*, 160–161). Thus, it cannot be said that the whole of the eighteenth century saw "the Muslim Orient with brotherly, understanding eyes" (Rodinson, *La Fascination de l'islam*, 74). If the comparison between Islam and Christianity turned to the advantage of the former, that was because emphasizing the importance of the Muslim Orient's contribution to the sciences and the arts made it possible to challenge that of Christianity. The *philosophes* admired Islam in proportion to their hostility to the Christian religion. Otherwise, they saw it merely as "superstition."

60 Laurens, "Napoléon, l'Europe et le monde arabe," 367–368.

61 Ibid., 367.

62 See especially Volney, *Voyage en Égypte et en Syrie*, 1:154–162.

63 Sainte-Beuve, *Causeries du lundi*, 7:410.

64 Volney, *Les Ruines*, 74–76, 85–86.

65 Voltaire, *Le Fanatisme, ou Mahomet le prophète*, 36 and 16. It is true that Voltaire changed his point of view: see chaps. 6, 27, and 44 of his *Essai sur les moeurs* and the article "Mahométans" in his *Dictionnaire philosophique*.

66 Bourrienne, *Mémoires*, 2:34.

67 See Laurens, *Orientales*, 162; Bertrand, *Cahiers*, 1:65.

68 "The question of the establishment of the religion of Muhammad still remains uncertain," he said after reading Bayle's article on him in his *Dictionnaire*. "We do not have the information to resolve it. We would have to know the state of Arabia in Muhammad's time. We have little or nothing on that. It is likely that there were civil wars, that the armed people were divided by factions and battle-hardened when Muhammad intervened. Muhammad's conquests are inconceivable. His armies conquered Persia with 45,000 men, Egypt with 19,000; they performed miracles with an unimaginable rapidity. The invasions of the Goths and the Barbarians are understandable; they were achieved with immense armies of 200,000, 300,00, 600,000 men; they occurred one after another. But this little Arab population emerged all at once from its deserts to conquer half the world!" (Bertrand, *Cahiers*, 1:121).

69 See Las Cases, *Journal*, 2:81. In a curious project seeking to relieve Voltaire's tragedy *Mahomet* of its "stains," he also said: "Muhammad was a great man, an intrepid soldier; with a handful of people, he triumphed in the battle of Bender [Badr]; a great captain, eloquent, a great statesman, he regenerated his country and created in the middle of the deserts of Arabia a new people and a new power" ("Observations sur la tragédie de *Mahomet*, par Voltaire," *Correspondance*, 31:488).

70 Napoléon Bonaparte, *Manuscrits inédits*, 335–337.

71 "ideal time": I am paraphrasing, of course, the famous conversation he later had with Mme de Rémusat (*Mémoires*, 1:274).

72 land route: *Correspondance générale*, no. 1379 (to the Directory, February 15, 1797), 1:839.

73 Ibid., no. 1586 (to Delacroix, May 27, 1797) 1:962; no. 1587 (to the Directory, May 27, 1797), 1:963; and no. 1608 (to the Directory June 1, 1797), 1:974.

74 See ibid., no. 1567 (to Baraguey d'Hilliers, May 21, 1797), 1:952; no. 1582 (to Gentili, May 26, 1797), 1:959–960; no. 1583 (to Bourdé, May 26, 1797), 1:960; and the document appended to document no. 1719, 1:1028.

75 Letter of August 16, 1797, to the pasha of Scutari (Shkodër, in Albania), ibid., no. 1909, 1:1118–1119; no. 1840 (July 30, 1797), 1:1090.

76 Talleyrand used this expression in his report of July 10, 1798, *Sur la situation de la République française considérée dans ses rapports extérieurs avec les autres puissances*: "The Mediterranean must be exclusively the French sea" (quoted in Lacour-Gayet, *Talleyrand*, 333–334). The expression soon became common coin: for example, the mathematician Fourier wrote in the introduction to the *Description de l'Égypte* that with the Egyptian expedition "the Mediterranean became a French sea" (*Description*, "Introduction historique," XXXV–XXXVI).

77 The connection between Bonaparte and Choiseul is brought out well by Tabet, "Bonaparte, Venise et les îles ioniennes," and by Pomponi, "Les îles du bassin occidental de la Méditerranée et la 'redécouverte' par la France d'une politique méditerranéenne (1769–1799)."

78 On all this, see the very interesting article, "Questions de paix," that appeared in the *Quotidienne* for May 4, 1797. The author of this article describes the Peace of Campoformio as "partial, onerous, and shaky." The goal, he says, was not achieved for lack of a genuine knowledge of France's interests. The acquisition of Belgium, he predicted, would not compensate for the loss of the colonies, and thus would do nothing to help reestablish France as a commercial power: "The colossus that we will have built," he concluded, "will have feet of clay so

long as the English remain the masters of the conquests they have made in this war." The victory over Austria had settled nothing; it had merely deferred a solution to the problem.

79 See the testimonies by Lavalette (quoted in Mascilli Migliorini, *Napoléon*, 515); Bourrienne, *Mémoires*, 2:44–45; Marmont, *Mémoires*, 1:295; Miot de Melito, *Mémoires*, 1:231; and Arnault, *Souvenirs*, 3:329.

80 Bourrienne, *Mémoires*, 2:44–45.

81 For example, one of them, Matteo Galdi, exhorted the French to colonize Egypt: "So yes, the most magnificent ideas that have long been relegated to the storehouse of philosophical dreams, could be entirely realized . . . the liberation of Greece . . . would come not from the despotic empire of Russia, which would certainly only add to the weight of its chains, but from a generous and powerful nation that would return to it, along with its ancient liberty, its ancient enthusiasm for the sciences and the fine arts. The opening of the Suez isthmus could also be realized; or an attempt could be made to extend the Nile from Alexandria to the Red Sea by improving the ancient canals and digging new ones. In this way the route to the Indies would be abbreviated by half, and navigation not only would be shorter but would take place on the calm waters of a not very turbulent sea, along coasts that are populated and full of pleasures, rich with refreshments of all kinds for the sailors, and easy to reach to escape storms and the boredom of long voyages. Thus, by facilitating communication between Europe and Asia and the whole western coast of Africa, the commerce, political relations, and moral and physical knowledge of the various regions would be multiplied; it would also be easier to penetrate into the heart of Africa, which is still unexplored and unknown. In short, the most remote and most inaccessible parts of the two hemispheres would thus be brought closer together" (*Necessità di stabilire una repubblica in Italia*, in Saitta, *Alle origini del Risorgimento*, 1:276–329, quotation at 312).

82 Monge, quoted in Arnault, *Souvenirs*, 3:329.

83 Quoted in Herold, *Bonaparte en Égypte*, 30.

84 Talleyrand, *Essai sur les avantages à retirer des colonies nouvelles*, 4.

85 Report of February 14, 1798, quoted in La Jonquière, *Expédition d'Égypte*, 1:159–160. See also Talleyrand, *Mémoires et correspondances*, 161–165.

86 Poniatowski, *Talleyrand aux États-Unis*, 237–356.

87 After having read an initial paper at the Institute on July 5, 1797, he had sent three more to the Directory on July 23 (La Jonquière, *L'Expédition d'Égypte*, 1:169–170; Laurens, *L'Expédition d'Égypte*, 24).

88 *Correspondance générale*, no. 1910, 1:1119.

89 Talleyrand, *Correspondance diplomatique*, 124.

90 All these arguments—which had long been made by diplomats and had recently been updated by the heirs of the "interventionist party," Magallon, Verninac, Talleyrand, and so on—are found in the letter Talleyrand sent Bonaparte on September 13, 1797: *Correspondance générale*, no. 2019, 1:1171.

91 He had put forward this idea very early on: "The isle of Malta is of major interest to us," he wrote to the Directory on May 26 (ibid., no. 1580, 1:958), and raised the question again on September 13: "Why shouldn't we seize the isle of Malta? . . . We would be masters of the whole Mediterranean," he wrote to Talleyrand (ibid., no. 2019, 1:1171).

92 Commander Hompesch succeeded Emmanuel de Rohan, who died on July 13, 1797.

93 Masson, *Napoléon et sa famille*, 1:205.

94 On the technical preparation of the landing, see the very important note entitled *Travail pour l'expédition contre l'Angleterre* of December 14, 1797 (*Correspondance*, no. 2388, 3:462–463). The editors of the *Correspondance* gave only the first four paragraphs of this note. The remaining paragraphs were published by La Jonquière, *L'Expédition d'Égypte*, 1:71–73.

95 La Jonquière, *L'Expédition d'Égypte*, 1:74.

96 Having left Constantinople in March 1797, Sultan Selim III's ambassador reached Paris on July 13 and remained there until July 1802.

97 "As for Egypt," he wrote to Bonaparte on September 23, 1797, "if we conquered it, it should be for the Porte, in order to foil the Russian and English intrigues that are so often repeated in that unfortunate country. Such a great service done the Turks would easily commit them to allow us the whole preponderance there along with the commercial advantages we need" (Talleyrand, *Correspondance diplomatique*, 155).

98 Quoted in Lacour-Gayet, *Talleyrand*, 324.

99 Report of February 14, 1798, quoted in La Jonquière, *L'Expédition d'Égypte*, 1:163.

100 See Bertrand, *Cahiers*, 2:305.

101 Talleyrand presented the report in question to the Directory on February 14, 1798; it is reproduced *in toto*, with Bonaparte's annotations, in La Jonquière, *L'Expédition d'Égypte*, 1:154–168.

102 Bourrienne, *Mémoires*, 2:34.

103 Reports of February 20 and 22, quoted in La Jonquière, *L'Expédition d'Égypte*, 1:114–116.

104 *Correspondance générale*, no. 2315, 2:36–37.

105 La Jonquière, *L'Expédition d'Égypte*, 1:185.

106 Ibid., 1:186.

107 Wheeler and Broadley, *Napoleon and the Invasion of England*, 84–85.

108 La Jonquière, *L'Expédition d'Égypte*, 1:136–144.

109 Report dated February 8, reproduced in ibid., 1:133–134.

110 Bainville, *Bonaparte en Égypte*, 12.

17. The Conquest of the Nile

1 One of the remaining two three-deckers, *Le Commerce de Marseille*, had been boarded and searched by the English, and the other, *L'Océan*, was in drydock at Brest.

2 *Correspondance générale*, no. 2496, 2:129.

3 Their number long remained uncertain, varying, depending on the author, from less than 150 to more than 200. After making a close study, Jean-Édouard Goby gave the figure of 151 (*La Composition du premier institut d'Égypte*); Alain Pigeard gave that of 167, the figure generally accepted today (Pigeard, "La Commission des sciences et des arts de l'expédition d'Égypte," in Tranié and Carmigniani, *Bonaparte*, 277–304).

4 La Jonquière, *L'Expédition d'Égypte*, 1:507–528. One month before the fleet's departure, a "Tableau des corps de troupes rassemblés à Toulon, Marseille, Gênes et Civitavecchia," drawn up by the office of the minister of war, Schérer, mentioned 29,402 men "present under arms" (*Correspondance de Napoléon Ier*, no. 2508 [April 14, 1798], 4:61–62).

59 See La Jonquière, *L'Expédition d'Égypte*, 1:39–40. Poussielgue, sent to Malta by Bonaparte, also suggested this to him in his report of February 8, 1798 (ibid., 134).

60 Ibid., 612–613.

61 *Correspondance générale*, no. 2518, 2:142; *Correspondance de Napoléon Ier*, no. 2650, 4:147–148.

62 La Jonquière, *L'Expédition d'Égypte*, 1:577.

63 710 guns for Nelson, 1026 for Brueys (Battesti, *La Bataille d'Aboukir*, 54).

64 "poor general": Bertrand, *Cahiers*, 1:139.

65 See "Campagnes d'Égypte et de Syrie," *Correspondance de Napoléon Ier*, 29:459–460.

66 Thurman, *Bonaparte en Égypte*, 20–21.

67 Pompey's column, constructed in the fourth century to honor Emperor Diocletian, was long thought to mark the site of Pompey's tomb—hence its name.

68 Denon, *Voyage dans la basse et la haute Égypte*, 56.

69 Berthier's report, dated July 6, 1798, is reproduced in La Jonquière, *L'Expédition d'Égypte*, 2:42–49.

70 Laporte, *Mon voyage en Égypte*, 32–33. See also Morand, *Lettres*, 41.

71 The testimony is virtually unanimous on this point: see in particular Captain Gerbaud's notebook (Mangerel, *Le Capitaine Gerbaud*, 212–214).

72 In his report for July 6, Berthier lists 15 dead, 20 drowned, and 60 wounded (La Jonquière, *L'Expédition d'Égypte*, 2:48), and Bonaparte mentioned "30 to 40 men killed and 80 to 100 wounded" (*Correspondance générale*, no. 2593 [to the Directory, July 6, 1798], 2:176). But in a letter, Louis Bonaparte, who was serving as an aide-de-camp to his brother, mentions much higher figures: 100 killed and as many wounded, while the chief warrant officer Boyer, also in a letter, refers to 150 French casualties (Larchey, *Correspondance intime de l'armée d'Égypte*, 4, 39). Doguereau, in his memoirs, mentions 200 killed and wounded (*Journal de l'expédition d'Égypte*, 12). Later Napoleon talked of 300 killed and wounded on the French side, a figure that is obviously exaggerated (*Correspondance de Napoléon Ier*, 29:434).

73 Chateaubriand speaks of a "dreadful slaughter" (*Mémoires d'outre-tombe*, 1:1139).

74 Thurman, *Bonaparte en Égypte*, 24.

75 Quoted in Skakowski, *Les Polonais en Égypte*, 22. More than a century afterward, nothing had changed, as is shown by these lines written by Col. T. E. Lawrence: "The conscripts took their fate unquestioningly: resignedly, after the custom of Turkish peasantry. They were like sheep, neutrals without vice or virtue. Left alone, they did nothing, or perhaps sat dully on the ground. Ordered to be kind, and without haste they were as good friends and as generous enemies as might be found. Ordered to outrage their fathers or disembowel their mothers, they did it as calmly as they did nothing, or did well. There was about them a hopeless, fever-wasted lack of initiative, which made them the most biddable, most enduring, and least spirited soldiers in the world. Such men were natural victims of their showy-vicious Levantine officers, to be driven to death or thrown away by neglect without reckoning" (T. E. Lawrence, *The Seven Pillars of Wisdom* [New York: Doubleday, 1938], 28–29).

76 These quotations are taken from Bonaparte's first proclamation, in Toulon, dated May 10, 1798. Let us note that there are two versions of it: the first is supposed to correspond to

Bonaparte's speech (La Jonquière, *L'Expédition d'Égypte*, 1:461–462); the other is the revised text that was inserted into the *Moniteur universel* (*Correspondance de Napoléon Ier*, no. 2570, 4:96).

77 Proclamation to the army dated June 22, 1798, but made public only on June 28, the day before the landing (ibid., no. 2710, 4:182–183); proclamation, June 22, 1798 (ibid., no. 2710, 4:183).

78 Chateaubriand, *Mémoires d'outre-tombe*, 1:1146.

79 Niello Sargy, *Mémoires*, p. 49.

80 Miot, *Mémoires* (1814), 27–28; Lacorre, *Journal inédit*, 68; letter written by General Dupuy on July 29, 1798 (Petitfrère, *Le Général Dupuy*, 203); Leclerc d'Ostein, *Mémoires*, 28.

81 Norry, *Relation de l'expédition d'Égypte*, 33–34.

82 "Nothing I've seen and suffered has astonished me," wrote Geoffroy Saint-Hilaire to his friend Jussieu on August 12: "I had strongly expected it on leaving Paris. But nevertheless, how many of all those who thought they would find here the delights of the capital of France have had to lower their sights. They never cease to swear at Savary for having described Egypt as an enchanting paradise; they find Volney right about everything; they are correct in that regard" (*L'Expédition d'Égypte*, 44–45).

83 On the birth of this rumor, see Laurens et al., *L'Expédition d'Égypte, 1798–1801*, p. 87.

84 Bourrienne, *Mémoires*, 2:137.

85 Quoted in La Jonquière, *L'Expédition d'Égypte*, 2:166–167.

86 Niello Sargy, *Mémoires*, 56.

87 The expression is Napoleon's (Las Cases, *Mémorial*, 3:54).

88 Joseph Sulkowski, quoted in Laurens et al., *L'Expédition d'Égypte, 1798–1801*, p. 84. Sulkowski was descended from an old family of the Polish nobility and had come to France in 1793, attracted by the French Revolution. He had enlisted in the army and gone to Italy in 1796, where Bonaparte noticed him and made him one of his aides-de-camp.

89 François, *Journal du capitaine François*, 215.

90 Savary, quoted in La Jonquière, *L'Expédition d'Égypte*, 2:108n1.

91 We are not sure whether General Mireur, who is supposed to have publicly opposed the pursuit of the expedition (Morand, *Lettres*, 8), left the column to commit suicide or, having gone off by himself, was killed by Bedouins (La Jonquière, *L'Expédition d'Égypte*, 2:136–138). Sulkowski says that the mutilations he suffered proved that he was killed by Bedouins (Skakowski, *Les Polonais en Égypte*, 41); Desvernois says that the money and weapons found on him proved that he had committed suicide (*Mémoires*, 109–111). The future general Morand, who discusses this episode at length in a letter of July 9, says he cannot decide with certainty (*Lettres*, 53–55).

92 Instructions to the generals of divisions, July 3 (*Correspondance de Napoléon Ier*, no. 2735, 4:199).

93 The expression is used by the ordnance officer Jaubert in a letter to Admiral Bruix dated July 9, 1798 (Larchey, *Correspondance intime de l'armée d'Égypte*, 19). See also Morand's letter of July 8, written in a less decorous style during a halt at Damanhur (*Lettres*, 42), and the journal of cannoneer Bricard (Bricard and Bricard, *Journal*, 312–313).

94 This figure is given by General Desvernois, *Mémoires*, 109.

95 Niello Sargy, *Mémoires*, 58. The figure of 1,500 casualties is surely exaggerated: a list drawn up on December 1, 1800, indicates that 8,915 men are supposed to have died since the beginning of the expedition three and a half years earlier, having been killed in combat or died from their wounds or from illness—that is, about one-fourth of the men involved (Brégeon, *L'Égypte de Bonaparte*, 249–250).

96 "Campagnes d'Égypte et de Syrie" (*Correspondance*, 29:446–447); Las Cases, *Mémorial*, 1:141–142.

97 Murad Bey was one of the two Mamluk leaders who governed Egypt in the Sultan's name; the other was Îbrahîm Bey.

98 Denon and al-Jabartî, *Sur l'expédition de Bonaparte en Égypte*, 30–31.

99 *Correspondance générale*, no. 2625 (to the Directory, July 24, 1798), 2:193.

100 Sulkowski, quoted in Skakowski, *Les Polonais en Égypte*, 51.

101 François, *Journal du capitaine François*, 229.

102 Michalon and Vernet, "Adaptation d'une armée française," 75. The French army had adopted this arrangement in 1776 but had not yet applied it (Brégeon, *L'Égypte de Bonaparte*, 158–159).

103 Sulkowski, quoted by Skakowski, *Les Polonais en Égypte*, 54.

104 Thiers, *Histoire de la Révolution française*, 10:36–37. They waited to open fire until the enemy was "at twenty paces, the optimal distance for effectiveness" (Michalon and Vernet, "Adaptation d'une armée française," 76).

105 Laurens et al., *L'Expédition d'Égypte, 1798–1801*, 87.

106 *Correspondance générale*, no. 2625 (to the Directory, July 24, 1798), 2:193.

107 Benoist-Méchin, *Bonaparte en Égypte*, 103. The Mamluk cavalry was composed of 6,000 to 12,000 men, according to the sources (Herold, *Bonaparte en Égypte*, 122–123).

108 Lacroix, *Bonaparte en Égypte*, 112.

109 The casualty count is uncertain: 2,000 Mamluks killed, according to Bonaparte's report (*Correspondance générale*, no. 2625 [to the Directory, July 24, 1798], 2:194); no more than 1,200 according to Captain Perrée, and less than 800 according to General Damas. Henry Laurens even states that at most about 20 Mamluks died in this battle, almost all the victims being Laurens's footmen who accompanied them, or infantrymen who were attacked in Embabeh (*L'Expédition d'Égypte*, 88–89). On the French side, about 30 men are said to have died, perhaps as many as 50. In his *Campagnes d'Égypte et de Syrie*, Napoleon raises the number of the dead to 10,000 on the Mamluk side and 300 on the French side, which is not very credible (*Correspondance de Napoléon Ier*, 29:450–451).

110 Larchey, *Correspondance intime de l'armée d'Égypte*, 105.

111 Napoleon later returned, apropos of the Mamluks, to "the influence of tactics, order, and movements" ("Notes sur l'art de la guerre," *Correspondance de Napoléon Ier*, 31:321–322).

112 Let us note that at the time of the Crusades it operated more in favor of the Muslim armies, which had a redoubtable weapon in the "Greek fire," whose secret they had learned from the Byzantines (Le Goff, *Saint Louis*, 189–190).

113 See Hanson, *The Western Way of War*.

114 Egypt had been conquered by the Turks in 1517.

115 See Keegan, *A History of Warfare*, 37. He cites the remarks made by Ibn Zabul, the Mamluks' historian, who makes their chieftain say when he was defeated by the Turks in 1516: "You [the Sultan] have brought with you this contrivance artfully devised by the Christians of Europe when they were incapable of meeting Muslim armies on the battlefield. The contrivance is that musket which, even if a woman were to fire it, would hold up such and such a number of men" (37).

116 Lacroix, *Bonaparte en Égypte*, 117–118.

117 Flaubert, *Correspondance*, 1:538 (letter of December 1, 1849, to L. Bouilhet).

118 Quoted in Larchey, *Correspondance intime de l'armée d'Égypte*, 38.

119 *Correspondance de Napoléon Ier*, 29:446–447.

120 Ibid., no. 2635 (to Joseph, July 25, 1798), 4:199–200.

121 Ibid.

122 Quoted in Bainville, *Napoléon*, 125.

123 *Correspondance générale*, no. 3476 (to the Directory, October 17, 1798), 2:543.

124 In his memoirs Chaptal reports this exchange: "One day Napoleon was telling the poet Lemercier how much he regretted that [Lemercier] had not followed him to Egypt. The latter observed that he didn't like places where the rights of man were not recognized. 'Well then,' Bonaparte replied, 'you would have seen a country where the sovereign counts his subjects' lives for nothing, and where a subject counts his own life for nothing, and you would have been cured of your philanthropy'" (*Mes souvenirs sur Napoléon*, 145).

125 Battesti, *La Bataille d'Aboukir*, 50.

126 Bourrienne, *Mémoires*, 2:132.

127 See Marmont, *Mémoires*, 1:389–390. He himself later said he had given this speech: "Well, now we're obliged to do great things: we will do them; [we are obliged] to found a great empire: we will found it. The seas, which we do not control, separate us from our country; but no sea separates us from either Africa or Asia. There are many of us, we have no lack of men from whom to recruit our officers. We have no lack of munitions, we have many of them; if necessary, Champy and Conté can make them for us" ("Campagnes d'Égypte et de Syrie," *Correspondance de Napoléon Ier*, 29:457).

128 Quoted in Battesti, *La Bataille d'Aboukir*, 126.

129 Denon and al-Jabartî, *Sur l'expédition de Bonaparte en Égypte*, 69. The expression "mental illness" (*maladie morale*) is used by Malus (*Agenda*, 92–93).

130 *Correspondance*, no. 3228 (letter to Kléber, September 4), 4:459.

131 Douin, *La Flotte de Bonaparte sur les côtes d'Égypte*.

132 Battesti, *La Bataille d'Aboukir*, 75–81; Maréchal, "Recherches sur un désastre," 137–138.

133 Battesti, *La Bataille d'Aboukir*, 99.

134 Ibid., 96.

135 Ibid., 84–90.

136 In his "Campagnes d'Égypte et de Syrie," he says that on July 7 he had even told Brueys that if he could not anchor safely in the Old Port, he should sail for either Corfu or Toulon (*Correspondance de Napoléon Ier*, 29:436).

137 *Correspondance générale*, no. 2870 (to the Directory, August 19, 1798), 2:298.

138 *Correspondance de Napoléon Ier*, no. 2728 (to Brueys, July 3, 1798), 4:195–196.

139 "contested": see Battesti, *La Bataille d'Aboukir*, 180; "torment": Bourrienne, *Mémoires*, 2:144. "Once he had become first consul," Henry Laurens wrote, "[Bonaparte] was to have removed from the military archives the most compromising documents, and have others altered" (*L'Expédition d'Égypte*, 105–106). On June 17, 1802, Bourrienne asked Fain to give him "all the papers on Egypt that may exist in the government's archives" (AN AF IV 1687). On June 26 and September 20, 1802, Fain delivered two bundles to the first consul. Fain's note explains that these documents "were, on His Majesty's orders, burned in September 1807" (Laissus, *L'Égypte, une aventure savante*, 557).

140 Maréchal, "Recherches sur un désastre," 137. On the copy in General Berthier's register, see La Jonquière, *L'Expédition d'Égypte*, 2:83n6.

141 "In the circumstances in which the army finds itself, it is indispensable to take steps to ensure that the squadron can maneuver in accord with the events that may occur, and be protected from the superior forces the English may have on these seas. The general-in-chief consequently orders the following: Article 1. Tomorrow, Admiral Brueys will bring his whole squadron into Alexandria's Old Port, if the weather permits and if there is the necessary depth. . . . Article 3. He shall send Citizen Ganteaume to the shore to preside over and supervise himself the operation of sounding the port. . . . Article 7. Tomorrow, the admiral will inform the general-in-chief in writing whether the squadron can enter the port of Alexandria, or if it can defend itself, anchored in the Abukir harbor, against a superior enemy squadron, and in the event that neither one nor the other can be executed, he must leave for Corfu" (*Correspondance*, no. 2728, 4:195–196). Napoleon later admitted to Gourgaud that he wanted to see the fleet anchor in Alexandria's port: "it was necessary for the army," he added, "and for the general-in-chief's subsequent plans" (Gourgaud, *Journal*, 2:170).

142 See his letter of July 6 to the Directory (*Correspondance générale*, no. 2593, 2:176).

143 See ibid., no. 2601, 2:181.

144 Barré's report is reproduced in "Campagnes d'Égypte et de Syrie," *Correspondance de Napoléon Ier*, 29:462–463. The letter of July 20 from Brueys to Barré is reproduced in "Campagnes d'Égypte et de Syrie" (ibid., 463–464). Brueys probably did not lack arguments, because Bonaparte himself later asked the same question several times: was it really possible to get into the port at Alexandria ships with high water drafts? Ganteaume's awkward replies tend to point in the same direction (see Battesti, *La Bataille d'Aboukir*, 183–184; Bonaparte, *Correspondance générale*, no. 3871 [to Ganteaume, December 7, 1798], 2:698).

145 Letter quoted in Lachadenède, "L'amiral Brueys à Aboukir," 69. Napoleon later admitted that the accusation was founded: he told Gourgaud that Brueys remained in Abukir after he had gauged the danger of his situation, because he did not dare to take any initiative before receiving from the general-in-chief a letter confirming that the army had taken Cairo (Gourgaud, *Journal*, 2:173–174).

146 *Correspondance générale*, no. 2654 (to Brueys, July 27, 1798), 2:207.

147 In the same letter of July 30, he repeats what he had already written on the twenty-seventh: "The news I am receiving from Alexandria regarding the success of the soundings makes me hope that by now you will have entered the port" (ibid., no. 2676, 2:216). (In the letter he

wrote to the commander of the island, General Chabot, Bonaparte makes no allusion to the impending arrival of the squadron in Corfu (ibid., no. 2748, 2:244–245).

148 Battesti, *La Bataille d'Aboukir*, 82–83.

149 "Campagnes d'Égypte et de Syrie," *Correspondance de Napoléon Ier*, 29:466–467.

150 Casabianca's remarks are reported by Kléber in a letter addressed to Menou on August 15 (Laurens, *Kléber en Égypte*, 1:263).

18. Governing Egypt

1 Compare, e.g., Lord Grenville's remark quoted in Battesti, *La Bataille d'Aboukir*, 123.

2 Charles-Roux, *L'Angleterre et l'expédition française en Égypte*, 1:58.

3 *Correspondance générale*, no. 2884 (to Ganteaume, August 21, 1798), 2:305.

4 Ibid., no. 2857 (to the Directory, August 18, 1798), 2:289–290.

5 In a report to the Directory written on November 21, he admits that his naval resources are absurdly inadequate: "In all, there are, armed, three frigates built in France, two frigates carrying 18-pounders, built in Venice, but which we have shielded in copper, two ships of the line with 64 guns, built in Venice, and six brigantines" (ibid., no. 3755, 2:653).

6 A courier called "Le Simple" had disembarked on that day at Alexandria (see ibid., no. 3112 [to the Directory, September 8–9, 1798], 2:399–400, and no. 3404 [October 7], 2:513). He brought, among other things, a letter from Joseph (ibid., no. 3116 [to Joseph, September 9, 1798], 2:401–402). Other news, the last, was delivered on July 26 by the ship *L'Artémise* (Laurens, *Kléber en Égypte*, 1:161–162).

7 *Correspondance générale*, no. 3380, 2:503.

8 Ibid., no. 3424, 2:523.

9 Ibid., no. 3755, 2:653.

10 Ibid., no. 3948 (to the Directory), 2:729.

11 Ibid., no. 3743 (to Desaix, November 20, 1798), 2:648.

12 Ibid., no. 2860 (to A. Guys, the French consul in Tripoli, August 18, 1798), 2:292.

13 Thus the war representative Jullien succeeded in returning to France at the end of 1798 (Boulay de la Meurthe, *Le Directoire et l'expédition d'Égypte*, 66–67). Louis Bonaparte, who had left Alexandria at the end of October, arrived in Paris on March 11, 1799 (Masson, *Napoléon et sa famille*, 1:239–241). Other couriers also succeeded in reaching their destinations in March or April (La Jonquière, *L'Expédition d'Égypte*, 5:144n1), and toward the middle of May the Directory received a letter that Bonaparte had sent it three months earlier (ibid., 5:145).

14 Boulay de la Meurthe drew up a detailed inventory of these attempts (*Le Directoire et l'expédition d'Égypte*, 228–236, 243–274).

15 A letter from Talleyrand to the French consul in Tripoli, written on April 12, 1799, has led some to believe that Bonaparte communicated regularly with Paris by the overland route through the desert: "Your three letters have reached me by way of Carthage. I thank you for your exactitude in transmitting to me the news that you receive from Egypt, as well as that with which you dispatch to General Bonaparte everything that it is important for him to know regarding European affairs. I ask you to continue this correspondence as much as

whether covert or overt (Gourgaud, *Mémoires pour servir à l'histoire de France sous Napoléon*, 2:251–267). See also, in Bertrand, what he says about the advantages in war of the intolerance, fanaticism, and belligerent character of the Islamic religion (*Cahiers*, 1:120–121, 225).

41 Goethe saw in this precisely a clue to the way in which Napoleon considered "religious matters" (*Conversations with Eckermann*, 316).

42 Volney, *Considérations sur la guerre actuelle des Turcs*, 124–125.

43 "Campagnes d'Égypte et de Syrie," *Correspondance de Napoléon Ier*, 29:479.

44 Quoted in Cherfils, *Bonaparte et l'islam*, 265.

45 See Bertrand, *Cahiers*, 2:55. But he told Las Cases that he had never seriously considered adopting Turkish dress, and still less converting to Islam (Las Cases, *Mémorial de Sainte-Hélène*, 2:529).

46 "Campagnes d'Égypte et de Syrie," *Correspondance de Napoléon Ier*, 29:482–484.

47 Quotations taken from letters from the divan of Cairo, reproduced in Cherfils, *Napoléon et l'islam*, 90–95.

48 Quoted by La Jonquière, *L'Expédition d'Égypte*, 3:8.

49 Sainte-Beuve, *Causeries du lundi*, 1:193.

50 If Bonaparte accorded the Jews the same protection as other communities, it was also the better to control them. The same went for the Copts, whom he accused of dishonesty (*Correspondance générale*, no. 3872 [to Girgès el-Gawhari, intendant-general of Egypt, December 7, 1798], 2:699). With regard to both groups, he showed the same partiality in favor of Islam, simply because it was the dominant religion. The Jewish and Christian religions were protected, but only tolerated and placed under strict surveillance. For example, the Jews: If he organized their community (there were about 5,000, most of them living in Cairo) and chose among them two great priests and seven counselors, that was so that they would be "responsible for the bad conduct and the disorders that the Jews might commit" (*Correspondance de Napoléon Ier*, no. 3258 [order September 7, 1798], 4:474). But the representatives of the Jewish community were not bothered. When a case came up—we do not know why—that involved seven Jews, five men and two women, he had the men decapitated and the women drowned, without taking reprisals against the rest of the community (*Correspondance générale*, no. 4162 [to General Destaing, January 25, 1799], 2:815).

51 Denon and al-Jabartî, *Sur l'expédition de Bonaparte en Égypte*, 51–52.

52 Gourgaud, *Mémoires pour servir à l'histoire de France sous Napoléon*, 2:225–227.

53 Lewis, *Comment l'islam a découvert l'Europe*, trans. Annick Pélissier (Paris: Gallimard, 2005), 186.

54 Louca, *L'Autre Égypte*, 7.

55 Ibid., 5. See also Coller's recent study, *Arab France*.

56 *Correspondance générale*, no. 3129 (to Regnaud de Saint-Jean d'Angély, September 10, 1798), 2:406.

57 Transferred to Cairo, Muhammad al-Kurayyim was executed on September 6; his head was cut off, put on a pike, and displayed throughout the city with this warning: "This is what happens to those who rebel against the French!" (*Correspondance de Napoléon Ier*, no. 3248, 4:469–470).

58 Quoted in Louca, *L'Autre Égypte*, 7.

59 "The Egyptian people," the army's treasurer was later to say, "may seem a very gentle one, but it is secretive, and it is far from liking us, even though it has been treated with more consideration than any other conquered people has ever been. . . . Here we have around us 10,000 hidden enemies for every apparent friend" (Poussielgue, *Lettre . . . à M. Thiers*, 24–25).

60 Laporte, *Mon voyage en Égypte et en Syrie*, 242.

61 Laurens, "Napoléon, l'Europe et le monde arabe," 373–374.

62 *Correspondance de Napoléon Ier*, no. 3785 (to the residents of Cairo, December 21, 1798), 5:221–222.

63 Denon and al-Jabartî, *Sur l'expédition de Bonaparte en Égypte*, 160. This bit of oriental literature was not, however, inferior to its models, if we judge by this call for jihad issued by the Porte against the French: "O you, worshippers of a single God, who believe in the mission of Muhammad son of Abd-Allah! Come together and march into combat under the protection of the All-High! These mad dogs probably imagine that the truly believing people resembles the infidels whom they have fought, whom they have deceived, and whom they have forced to adopt false principles; but they do not know, the accursed, that Islamism is engraved on our hearts" (quoted in Brégeon, *L'Égypte de Bonaparte*, 118–119).

64 *La Décade égyptienne*, 1:6.

65 Arago, "Gaspard Monge," 527–528.

66 Saïd, *Orientalism*, 82, 121.

67 Quoted in Paul Louis Bret, *L'Expédition d'Égypte, une Entreprise des Lumières 1798–1801: Actes du colloque international organisé par l'Académie des inscriptions et belles lettres et l'Académie des sciences, sous les auspices de l'Institut de France et du Muséum d'histoire naturelle, 8–10 juin 1998* (Paris: Technique et Documentation, ca. 1969).

68 André Raymond, in ibid., 105.

69 *Correspondance de Napoléon Ier*, no. 3238 (decree convoking the general divan, September 4, 1798), 4:464–465; instructions given Monge and Berthollet, French representatives to the general divan, October 4, 1798 (*Correspondance générale*, no. 3385, 2:505).

70 Lewis, *The Muslim Discovery of Europe*, 216.

71 Denon and al-Jabartî, *Sur l'expédition de Bonaparte en Égypte*, 154–155.

72 Arago, "Gaspard Monge," 544.

73 Denon and al-Jabartî, *Sur l'expédition de Bonaparte en Égypte*, 168.

74 André Raymond, in Bret, *L'Expédition d'Égypte*, 115–117; Imad Abou Ghazi, "L'expédition française dans les écrits des historiens égyptiens du XX siècle: Implications politiques de l'historiographie," in Humbert, *Bonaparte et l'Égypte*, 129–134.

75 Letters of December 14, 1849, and January 15, 1850 (Flaubert, *Correspondance*, 1:552, 565).

76 The expression is taken from a speech given by Robespierre on January 2, 1792, in opposition to the declaration of war against Austria (*Oeuvres*, 8:1–82).

77 Kléber et al., *L'État-major de Kléber en Égypte*, 54.

78 Doguereau, *Journal*, 23. "Bouillotte" was a new card game, invented a few years before the French Revolution, and very much in fashion (http://academiedesjeux.jeuxsoc.fr/bouil lotte.htm).

79 Letter of June 23, 1799 (Geoffroy Saint-Hilaire, *L'Expédition d'Égypte*, 80–81).

80 On all this, see the letters from the head of the Army of the Orient's clothing workshop, Bernoyer, *Avec Bonaparte en Égypte et en Syrie*, 94–116; Norry, *Relation de l'expédition d'Égypte*, 46; and the information provided by Bret, *L'Égypte au temps de l'expédition de Bonaparte*, 134–135.

81 Letter of the vice-admiral Perrée, in Larchey, *Correspondance intime de l'armée d'Égypte*, 38.

82 Moiret, *Mémoires*, 63–64. The formula of the toast is reproduced in Bourgeois, *Bonaparte et la presse*, 33.

83 Thus Murat wrote to his father on November 6, 1798, that his return to France could only be "very imminent" (*Lettres et documents pour servir à l'histoire de Murat*, 1:25). The quotation is taken from Jacques-François Miot, who was only nineteen years old at the time (*Mémoires* [1804], 92–93).

84 "gloomy conjectures": Morand, *Lettres*, 65; Kléber's letter quoted in Audebaud, *Le Général de division Dugua*, 164.

85 *Correspondance générale*, no. 3878 (December 8, 1798), 2:701.

86 See his letter of October 4, 1798, which he had assigned one of his aides-de-camp to deliver to Bonaparte, published in Brouwet, *Napoléon et son temps*, 3:180.

87 *Correspondance générale*, no. 2676 (to Brueys, July 30, 1798), 2:216.

88 Ibid., no. 3295 (to Poussielgue, September 21, 1798), 3:468–469.

89 The valet Jean-Baptiste Hébert, the major domo Fischer, the squire Vigogne (on the latter, see Méneval, *Napoléon et Marie-Louise*, 1:139), and, after his return from Syria, the Mamluk Roustam Raza, a young Georgian given him by Sheikh el-Bekry. We do not know if Bonaparte's other usual servants, his intendant Charles-Louis Pfister, the valet Jean-Joseph Ambard, and the cooks Louis-Augustin Gallyot and Étienne Collomb (Branda, *Napoléon et ses hommes*, 11), had accompanied him.

90 Joseph Sulkowski and François Croizier were both to die in Egypt.

91 "Campagnes d'Égypte et de Syrie," *Correspondance de Napoléon Ier*, 29:365.

92 Marcel, *Contes du Cheykh êl-Mohdy*, 3:489–491.

93 See Gabriel Madec's study "L'état-major de Bonaparte en Égypte," published as an appendix to the second volume of the *Correspondance générale*, 2:1139–1145; and Dehérain, *Histoire de la nation égyptienne*, 307–310. Let us also mention the presence, around Bonaparte, of another interpreter, the Syrian Élisa Pharaon.

94 Jaubert, quoted in Dehérain, *Histoire de la nation égyptienne*, 309.

95 Quoted in Mme de Rémusat, *Mémoires*, 1:252, 274.

96 J. M. Le Père, "Mémoire sur la communication de la mer des Indes à la Méditerranée, par la mer Rouge et l'isthme de Soueys [Suez]," in *Description de l'Égypte*, "État moderne," 1:133–134. See also Bricard and Bricard, *Journal*, 325–330; Galland, *Tableau de l'Égypte*, 1:46–47.

97 He told Gourgaud: "If Egypt's extraordinary position, which can owe its prosperity only to the extent of the flooding, requires a good administration, the necessity of repressing 20,000 to 30,000 thieves, who escape justice because they take refuge in the immensity of the desert, requires a no less energetic administration" (Gourgaud, *Mémoires pour servir à l'histoire de France sous Napoléon*, 2:221). Here we think of Karl Wittfogel's classic study, *Le Despotisme oriental*, on "hydraulic societies" and the authoritarian, bureaucratic political system they call for.

98 "Campagnes d'Égypte et de Syrie," *Correspondance de Napoléon Ier*, 29:385–386.

99 Barras, *Memoirs*, 4:29–32.

100 Laurens, *L'Expédition d'Égypte*, 188.

101 Bernoyer, *Avec Bonaparte en Égypte et en Syrie*, 58.

102 Clausewitz, *On War*, trans. M. E. Howard (repr., Princeton, NJ: Princeton University Press, 1989), 77.

103 Larchey, *Correspondance intime de l'armée d'Égypte*, 130–131.

104 Carbonnier, "La guerre des Géants sous la toise du Droit," 1084–1085; see also Heller-Roazen, *L'Ennemi de tous*.

105 François, *Journal du capitaine François*, 224; Bonaparte, *Correspondance générale*, no. 3404 (to the Directory, October 7, 1798), 2:513–516.

106 Lockroy, *Ahmed le Boucher*, 15, 135.

107 Ibid., 198.

108 *Correspondance générale*, no. 2699 (to Menou, July 31, 1798), 2:224–225.

109 Ibid., 3171 (to Dugua, September 13, 1798), 2:422.

110 Marcel, *Contes du Cheykh êl-Mohdy*, 3:462–466. Flaubert wrote to his mother on November 23, 1849: "Besides, you could not believe the important role played by the rod here. Blows are handed out with a sublime prodigality, the whole affair accompanied by screams that provide great local color" (*Correspondance*, 1:534).

111 Galland, *Tableau de l'Égypte*, 1:161.

112 *Correspondance générale*, no. 2958 (August 27, 1798), 2:337.

113 *Correspondance de Napoléon Ier*, no. 3105 (order of August 25, 1798), 4:397.

114 *Correspondance générale*, no. 3398 (to Murat, October 6, 1798), 2:510.

115 Ibid., no. 4124 (to Berthier, January 20, 1799), 2:801–802.

116 Ibid., no. 3177 (to Lanusse, September 13, 1798), 2:424; see also no. 3300 (to Dugua, September 23), 2:470–471. Ibid., no. 3425 (to Murat, October 11, 1798), 2:524.

117 *Correspondance de Napoléon Ier*, no. 3570 (November 3, 1798), 5:111.

118 On June 23, 1799, Bonaparte wrote to Kléber: "Hassan Tubar is leaving my custody. He is delivering his son here this evening as a hostage. . . . Hassan Tubar is leaving in a few days for Damietta; he seems to have learned something from his misfortune; besides, his son is our guarantee. I believe he will be very useful to you in organizing Lake Menzaleh, the province of Damietta, communications with El-Arish, and your espionage in Syria" (*Correspondance générale*, no. 4445, 2:960). Bonaparte even returned Hassan Tubar's goods to him (letter to Kléber, July 1, ibid., no. 4500, 2:980).

119 Ibid., no. 3626 (to Berthier, November 6, 1798), 2:602–603.

120 Ibid., no. 2691 (to Zayonchek, July 30, 1798), 2:222.

121 condemned torture: ibid., no. 3656 (to Berthier, November 11, 1798), 2:613. Let us note, however, that two months later he gave quite different instructions to obtain the confession of a village sheikh accused of colluding with the Mamluks (ibid., no. 4110 [to Verdier, January 18, 1799], 2:797).

122 Ibid., no. 2850 (August 16, 1798], 2:286.

123 *Correspondance de Napoléon Ier*, no. 2882 (to Kléber, July 30, 1798), 4:277.

124 Kléber et al., *L'État-major de Kléber en Égypte*, 22–23, 107–109.

125 Laurens, *Kléber en Égypte*, 1:318–319.

126 *Correspondance générale*, no. 2981 (to Kléber, August 28, 1798), 2:346–347.

127 According to Poussielgue, they could not hope to bring in more than 9 to 10 million francs per annum, whereas the army alone required 15 to 16 million (*Lettre . . . à M. Thiers*, 20–22). The *miri* was a property tax based on the product of the harvests and paid in cash or in kind.

128 The head of the clothing service, Bernoyer, has left us an account of one of these expeditions (*Avec Bonaparte en Égypte et en Syrie*, 84–86).

129 Laurens, *L'Expédition d'Égypte*, 125.

130 Denon and al-Jabartî, *Sur l'expédition de Bonaparte en Égypte*, 85.

131 Chalbrand, *Les Français en Égypte*, 103. See also Denon and al-Jabartî, *Sur l'expédition de Bonaparte en Égypte*, 86.

132 Chalbrand, *Les Français en Égypte*, 103–104.

133 Denon and al-Jabartî, *Sur l'expédition de Bonaparte en Égypte*, 99.

134 Brigade leader Detroye, quoted in La Jonquière, *L'Expédition d'Égypte*, 3:279.

135 Denon and al-Jabartî, *Sur l'expédition de Bonaparte en Égypte*, 101.

136 Ibid., 101–102.

137 "Campagnes d'Égypte et de Syrie," *Correspondance de Napoléon Ier*, 29:500.

138 *Correspondance de Napoléon Ier*, no. 3571 (November 3, 1798), 5:112; *Correspondance générale*, no. 3614 (to Destaing, November 4), 2:598.

139 Geoffroy Saint-Hilaire, *L'Expédition d'Égypte*, 75 (letter to his father, October 25, 1798).

140 Denon and al-Jabartî, *Sur l'expédition de Bonaparte en Égypte*, 116–117.

141 Quoted in Laurens, *L'Expédition d'Égypte*, 152.

142 Number for November 27, 1798, quoted in ibid., 161–162. Bonaparte was annoyed when he learned that the mathematician Fourier had resigned from the *Courrier's* editorial board to protest against the general's "weakness." Desgenettes was there: "He is annoyed, and I am going to tell you why," Bonaparte confided to him. "That man, whose opinion I have never asked and never will ask, came here, in my sitting room, to perorate on the revolt, on its causes, on the consequences that have to be feared, and finally, he came to tell me what I had to do. You can well imagine how I listened to him! First I told him that the affair was over, that the rigorous measures he proposed to me were no more politic than human, that cowards always gave this kind of extreme advice, that insurrections could not be judged by having cooperated in them in the muddy streets of Paris (ibid., 433).

143 Quoted in Benoist-Méchin, *Bonaparte en Égypte*, 192.

144 Brégeon, *L'Égypte de Bonaparte*, 205–206. Another version: Bonaparte is supposed to have remained below with Caffarelli, and seeing Berthier interrupt his ascension halfway up, he shouted to him: "Well then! Are you returning to us already? My poor Berthier! *She* is not on top of the pyramid, is she? But *she* isn't below it, either" (Ch. Reybaud, quoted in La Jonquière, *L'Expédition d'Égypte*, 3:18–19).

145 See Collaveri, *Napoléon franc-maçon?*

146 Madelin, *Histoire du Consulat et de l'Empire*, 2:244–245.

147 "beautiful sultanas": Roederer, *Bonaparte me disait*, 15.

148 He speaks of it, in a letter addressed to General Dugua, as a "little accident" (*Revue des études napoléoniennes* 41 [1935]:163–167).

149 Bourrienne, *Mémoires*, 2:174.

150 On September 8 he wrote to the Directory: "I cannot be back in Paris, as I promised you, in October; but it will only be a few months more" (*Correspondance générale*, no. 3112, 2:399–400).

151 Ibid., no. 3948, 2:729.

19. Jaffa

1 "Mémoire sur la situation de la République française considérée dans ses rapports extérieurs avec les autres puissances, présenté au Directoire le 22 messidor an VI [July 10, 1798]" (Talleyrand, *Correspondance diplomatique*, 247–248, 338–339).

2 On Malta, the garrison commanded by General Vaubois resisted until September 4, 1800.

3 Marcère, *Une ambassade à Constantinople*, 2:360.

4 Ibid.

5 Special emissary: See *Projet de mémoire pour servir d'instructions au ministre plénipotentiaire de la République auprès de la Porte ottomane, présenté au Directoire le 26 ventôse an VI [March 16, 1798]*, reproduced in Talleyrand, *Correspondance diplomatique*, 336–338n. We read, after a long development on the decadence of the Ottoman Empire and its imminent "dissolution," these sentences that were to serve as instructions to the French emissary: "Taking in with a glance the commercial system of Europe and especially of the English in India, calculating all the advantages that Egypt may procure, today and in the future, to the French Republic, [the Directory] has resolved to make a landing in Egypt and establish the French nation there. Egypt is, of all the Ottoman provinces, the one in which the Porte's authority is the most precarious. One might even say that it does not have even the shadow of power. Its pasha in Cairo is only the first slave of the [Mamluk] beys. . . . Thus, the conquest of Egypt by France causes no actual prejudice to the Porte" (338).

6 Treaties of alliance were signed with Russia on December 23, 1798, with Britain on January 5, 1799, and with Naples on January 21, 1799.

7 *Correspondance générale*, no. 2904, 2:316.

8 On May 23, when the fleet had just rounded Cap Corse, he asked him to wait until the expedition had passed Sicily before setting out (ibid., no. 2501, 2:133), and a month later he dispatched a frigate to go get Talleyrand in Toulon and take him to Constantinople (no. 2556, 2:159). Convinced that Talleyrand would be there, he even wrote to Ruffin to inform him of his imminent arrival (no. 2592 [July 6], 2:175). He first expressed doubt on August 19: "Is Talleyrand in Constantinople?" he asked the Directory (no. 2870, 2:299). He wrote directly to Talleyrand in Constantinople, calling him "Citizen Ambassador," as if he had received a positive response to his question (no. 2904, 2:316), but in the letter he sent to the Grand Vizier on the same day, he was more circumspect: "Citizen Talleyrand-Périgord," he wrote, "must have arrived. If by some chance he has not . . ." (no. 2906, 2:317). And on August 30, in another letter to the Directory, he limits himself to saying that he "imagines" that Talleyrand has arrived in the Turkish capital (no. 3017, 2:360). In October, completely disillusioned and furious, he wrote to the Directory: "You shall send an ambassador to Constantinople by way of Vienna; that is very essential; Talleyrand must go there and keep his promise" (no. 3404, 2:514).

9 *Correspondance de Napoléon Ier*, 29:474.

10 Kléber et al., *L'État-major de Kléber en Égypte*, 1:289. Denon and Al-Jabartî report his arrival on September 15 (*Sur l'expédition de Bonaparte en Égypte*, 84–85).

11 *Correspondance de Napoléon Ier*, 29:474.

12 *Correspondance générale*, no. 2894 (to Jezzar, August 22, 1798), 2:311–312.

13 Ibid., no. 3647, 2:610–611. In December he sent him an emissary named Beauchamp, the former French consul in Mascate.

14 Instructions of November 4, 1798, quoted in La Jonquière, *L'Expédition d'Égypte*, 3:266–268.

15 See *Correspondance générale*, no. 4235 (to the Directory, February 10, 1799), 2:850. The report was false.

16 Ibid., no. 4235 (February 10, 1799), 2:850. He later explained to Gourgaud why he had to act without delay: "If the French stayed quietly in Egypt, they were going to be attacked by the two armies simultaneously; moreover, it was to be feared that a body of European troops might join them, and that the attack might coincide with internal disturbances. In that case, even if the French had won, they would not have been able to take advantage of their victory. At sea, they had no fleet; on land, the desert 75 leagues wide that separates Syria from Egypt could not be crossed by an army during the hot season. The rules of war thus prescribed that the French general had to forestall his enemies, cross the great desert during the winter, seize all the storehouses the enemy had established on the coasts of Syria, and attack and destroy his troops as they assembled" (Gourgaud, *Mémoires pour servir à l'histoire de France sous Napoléon*, 2:300).

17 *Correspondance de Napoléon Ier*, 29:14. The goal was the Makran, a coastal strip along the Indian Ocean southeast of Iran and southwest of Pakistan. He also told Gourgaud: "With luck, we could be on the Euphrates by midsummer, with a 100,000 auxiliaries, who would have in reserve 25,000 French veterans, the best troops in the world, and numerous artillery units. Constantinople would then be threatened; and if we succeeded in establishing good relations with the Porte, we could cross the desert and march to the Indus in late autumn" (Gourgaud, *Mémoires pour servir à l'histoire de France sous Napoléon*, 2:301).

18 Among the exceptions, Benoist-Méchin (*Bonaparte en Égypte*, 232–234).

19 Bourrienne, *Mémoires*, 2:243–244.

20 The British did not consider a French offensive in India impossible. That is why they had deployed major military forces under the command of Lord Wellesley (the future Wellington) in order to finally defeat Zahman Shah—the British feared a rapprochement between the French and the Afghans—and Tipû Sâhib. The Afghans were driven back to Kabul in January 1799, and the sultan of Mysore was killed in May. Henceforth masters of the Indian subcontinent, the British could turn their attention to the Red Sea and the Persian Gulf. To prevent a French fleet from sailing out of Suez, they occupied the island of Perim, and to prevent them from embarking from Bassorah after having occupied Syria, they sent a squadron to cruise the Persian Gulf (Laurens et al., *L'Expédition d'Égypte, 1798–1801*, pp. 175–178).

21 Quoted in La Jonquière, *L'Expédition d'Égypte*, 3:266–268.

22 *Réimpression de l'ancien Moniteur*, 29:497.

23 Ibid. Henry Laurens also thought that by invading Syria Bonaparte sought to eliminate not only "the threat of the Ottoman armies" but also "the explosion of the empire itself, at

least in its eastern part, by the revolt of its peoples" (Laurens et al., *L'Expédition d'Égypte, 1798–1801*, pp. 180–185).

24 The army sent to Syria consisted of 12,945 men divided as follows: the divisions led by Kléber (2,349), Bon (2,499), Lannes (2,924), Reynier (2,160); cavalry (800), engineers (340), artillery (1,385); 400 guides on foot or on horseback, and 88 camel cavalrymen (figures given by Berthier in his *Relation de la campagne de Syrie* [*Réimpression de l'ancien Moniteur,* 29:842–843]).

25 *Correspondance générale*, no. 4200 (February 3, 1799), 2:832.

26 Ibid., no. 4317, 2:895.

27 Berthier confirms this in his account of the campaign: "March on Syria, punish Jezzar, destroy the preparations for the expedition against Egypt, in the event that the Porte has allied itself with the enemies of France; restore on the contrary [to the Porte] the nomination of the pasha of Syria and its original authority in this province, if it remains friendly to the Republic; return to Egypt immediately afterward to fight the maritime expedition" (*Récit des campagnes du général Bonaparte en Égypte et en Syrie*, 39).

28 Napoléon Bonaparte, *Lettres du Cap de Bonne-Espérance*, in Warden, *Napoléon jugé par un Anglais*, 354.

29 *Correspondance de Napoléon Ier*, no. 3746 (Instructions of December 11, 1798), 5:201–203.

30 *Correspondance générale*, no. 3404 (October 7, 1798), 2:515.

31 See the report of this conversation in *Correspondance de Napoléon Ier*, no. 3944 (February 8, 1799), 5:300–302.

32 To assess this, see the letter in which Bonaparte informs Kléber of the "news" that had arrived from France (*Correspondance générale*, no. 4208 [February 5, 1799], 2:835).

33 Ibid., no. 4231 (to Marmont, February 9, 1799), 2:846.

34 Ibid., no. 4235 (to the Directory, February 10, 1799), 2:850.

35 Ibid., no. 3040 (to Kléber, September 1, 1798), 2:371.

36 Letter to Bonaparte, September 7, 1798 (Laurens, *Kléber en Égypte*, 1:301–302). He handed his powers over to General Manscourt, without waiting for Bonaparte's permission, on September 18.

37 See Bonaparte's conciliatory letter of September 12 (*Correspondance générale*, no. 3151, 2:415), and this other one written on October 4: "Believe . . . in the value that I attach to your esteem and your friendship. I fear that we may be a bit at odds; you would be unjust to doubt how much this pains me. On Egyptian soil, the clouds, when there are any, pass by in six hours; for my part, if there were any, they would have passed in three" (ibid., no. 3384, p. 2:504).

38 As in the portrait inserted at the beginning of the "Campagnes d'Égypte et de Syrie" (*Correspondance de Napoléon Ier*), which Sainte-Beuve "takes literally" (*Causeries du lundi*, 1:185–186), but which has to be read, to understand it correctly, in connection with the devastating pages Napoleon devotes to Kléber's administration in 1799–1800 (*Correspondance de Napoléon Ier*, 30:97–128). See ibid., 29:364–365.

39 "Lazy," pleasure-seeking, greedy, brutal, without any political sense, a mediocre administrator; capable, nonetheless, "of the greatest things," but on the condition that "it was a matter of choosing between glory and dishonor" (Gourgaud, *Journal*, 2:185–186).

40 Laurens, *Kléber en Égypte*, 2:544–545.

41 Reynier complained that he had always been treated less well than his colleagues, that it was a matter of the number of men under his orders, the regions entrusted to his command ("the less agreeable and the ones others would not have wanted"), or the lack of recognition of his successes—"on the occasions when the enemy has been met by my division, no word has been said to testify to the fact that the troops did their duty" (quoted in La Jonquière, *L'Expédition d'Égypte*, 4:186).

42 Villiers du Terrage, *Journal et souvenirs*, 93–94.

43 *Correspondance de Napoléon Ier*, no. 3976 (February 18, 1799), 5:325, and no. 3979 (the same day), 5:326–327.

44 Ibid., no. 3982 (February 19, 1799), 5:328–329.

45 Quoted in La Jonquière, *L'Expédition d'Égypte*, 4:199.

46 Laurens et al., *L'Expédition d'Égypte, 1798–1801*, p. 186.

47 On the return to Egypt of some of these prisoners, see *Correspondance de Napoléon Ier*, no. 3984 (to Dugua, February 21, 1799), 5:329. The next day Bonaparte ordered Reynier to maintain at El-Arish a garrison of 100 Turks who would later be incorporated into the companies of janissaries formed in Cairo, and to recruit "among the Arnauts all the men of goodwill who present themselves" (ibid., no. 3989, 5:332). The same day, he wrote to Dugua: "I have enlisted three or four hundred Maghrebins who are marching with us" (*Correspondance générale*, no. 4251, 2:858).

48 La Jonquière, *L'Expédition d'Égypte*, 4:202–204.

49 "The lemon trees, the forests of olive trees, the unevenness of the terrain represent perfectly the landscape of Languedoc; one would think he was near Béziers" (*Correspondance générale*, no. 4265 [to Desaix, February 27, 1799], 2:867).

50 Ibid., nos. 4260–4261 (to Dugua and to Marmont, February 26, 1799), 2:864–865.

51 "lake of mud": Laporte, *Mon voyage en Égypte et en Syrie*, 160; "parties of Arabs": François, *Journal*, 270.

52 Lacorre, *Journal inédit*, 92.

53 Volney, *Voyage en Égypte et en Syrie*, 1:116–117.

54 Niello Sargy, *Mémoires*, 254–255.

55 Malus, *L'Agenda de Malus*, 134–136.

56 Niello Sargy, *Mémoires*, 255–256.

57 Quoted in Benoist-Méchin, *L'Expédition d'Égypte*, 236. Captain François adds that the pillaging continued for four days, or until March 11 (*Journal*, 274–275); but Bonnefons says it lasted no more than twenty-four hours (*Souvenirs et cahiers sur la campagne d'Égypte*, 45–46).

58 In a note sent by Berthier to the Turkish commander of the fortress, Bonaparte, saying that he was "touched by the misfortunes that the whole city would incur if it allowed itself to be taken by assault," had offered "to save the garrison" and "protect the city" in exchange for a surrender (*Correspondance*, no. 4011 [to Abdallah Aga, March 7, 1799], 5:347).

59 Ibid., 5:222–223.

60 Ibid., 5:223–226.

61 La Jonquière, *L'Expédition d'Égypte*, 5:266–267.

62 *Correspondance générale*, no. 4271, 2:870.

63 See the figures given in La Jonquière, *L'Expédition d'Égypte*, 5:269–270.

64 E. de Beauharnais, *Mémoires et correspondance*, 1:54.

65 Chateaubriand, *Mémoires d'outre-tombe*, 1:1152.

66 Miot, *Mémoires* (1814), 145–148. The first edition, published in 1804, contains a toned-down account of the execution (138). See also the testimonies of Detroye and Peyrusse (in La Jonquière, *L'Expédition d'Égypte*, 5:270, 271) and Bourrienne (*Mémoires*, 2:220–227).

67 Thiers, *Histoire de la Révolution française*, 10:401.

68 Regenbogen, *Napoléon a dit*, 18.

69 The following quotations are taken from bk. 3, chap. 8, "Du droit des nations dans la guerre, et de ce qu'on est en droit de faire et de ce qui est permis, dans une guerre juste, contre la personne de l'ennemi" (Vattel, *Le Droit des gens*, 2:104–122).

70 Ibid.

71 The commander of the fortress, Abdallah Aga, was provisionally spared and sent to Cairo, where, after returning from Syria, Bonaparte ordered him decapitated (*Correspondance générale*, no. 4558 [to Dugua, July 8, 1799], 2:1001).

72 *Correspondance de Napoléon Ier*, no. 3983 (to the commander of the El-Arish fort, February 20, 1799), 5:329.

73 Vattel, *Le Droit des gens*, 2:109.

74 *Archives parlementaires*, 47:131–132 (session of July 24, 1792).

75 Bergen-op-Zoom, besieged by the French (July–September 1747) during the War of the Spanish Succession; Ochakov, on the Black Sea, besieged by the Russians (June–December 1747) during their last conflict with the Turks.

76 Vattel, *Le Droit des gens*, 2:118.

77 "[The prisoners] were bivouacking about twenty-five paces in front of the camp," the administrator Daure wrote. "They were under the guard of only ten guides on foot; every day the small amount of food we could spare was distributed to them, and Bonaparte's intention was to take them to Cyprus. Vice-Admiral Ganteaume, who was always with the army, had received the order to requisition the few ships we had captured in the port, and everything was ready for their departure when an enemy ship, deceived by the signals that we had left floating over the city's towers, entered the port and put itself at our disposal. The crew was arrested, and the captain and a few passengers were taken to Bonaparte's tent. Questioned regarding the motives for their landing, they declared that they were part of the Great Lord's army that was supposed to assemble on the plains of Syria; that they were coming from Constantinople; that war had been declared against France; that all the French who were residing there, as well as in the trading posts of the Levant, had been arrested and thrown in jail; that several had fallen victim to the people's initial fury, and that the goods of all the prisoners had been confiscated. This bad news was to change Bonaparte's policy and dispositions. The Turks, whom he had intended to send to Cyprus, would have been the first nucleus of the group that the Porte proposed to create there. Sent back to the coasts of Jaffa, they would have stirred up against us, not only the whole population, but even the nomadic Arabs who have so cruelly harassed us. Under these circumstances, what was Bonaparte to do?" (Boulos, *Bourrienne et ses erreurs*, 1:72–74).

78 Benoist-Méchin, *Bonaparte en Égypte*, 237–238.

79 La Jonquière, *L'Expédition d'Égypte*, 4:283.

80 Desgenettes, *Histoire médicale de l'armée d'Orient*, 22.

81 Vattel, *Le Droit des gens*, 2:119.

82 That is why, trying to attenuate the horror of what happened at Jaffa, he later went so far as to say that he had executed only those who had broken their promise. That is to forget, of course, the 2,000 other victims, who he even claimed had lost their lives in combat or had gone home. In the *Relation de la campagne de Syrie* published after Bonaparte's return to France, Berthier even hints that those who surrendered were able to go home (*Réimpression de l'ancien Moniteur*, 29:845–846). Rewriting his history on Saint Helena, Napoleon reduced the number of victims to the perjurers of El-Arish alone.

83 Marmont, *Mémoires*, 2:13–14.

84 Stendhal, *Vie de Napoléon*, 27–30.

85 Bourrienne, *Mémoires*, 2:226–227. Desgenettes, who is in general a severe critic of Bonaparte, also said that Jaffa had been "one of those scenes of horror that justify the terrible and necessary laws of war" (*Histoire médicale de l'armée d'Orient*, 45). And Marmont: "What reproaches would be made to a general if out of a false sense of humanity toward his enemies he compromised the safety of his army and his soldiers' lives? In Europe, there are exchange agreements; in order to get back one's imprisoned soldiers and save their lives, one takes care of [the prisoners] one makes. But with barbarians who massacre, there is nothing to do but kill" (*Mémoires*, 2:13).

86 Niello Sargy, *Mémoires*, 328.

87 Bernoyer, *Avec Bonaparte en Égypte et en Syrie*, 147–148.

88 Herold, *Bonaparte en Égypte*, 337.

89 This massacre had been perpetrated on May 19, 1776. See Volney, *Voyage en Égypte et en Syrie*, 1:117–120.

90 *Correspondance générale*, no. 4276, 2:872. Note this variant in the proclamation addressed the same day to the authorities of Jerusalem: "They must know that I am terrible like the heavenly fire against my enemies, clement and merciful toward the people and those who want to be my friends" (ibid., no. 4277, 2:872–873).

91 During the war with Holland (1672–1679) Marshal Luxembourg, who was marching on The Hague, subjected to pillage the town of Swammerdam and another village, Bodegrave (December 1672). Luxembourg's troops indulged in carnage that he was proud of, as we see in a letter to Louvois in which he admits the pleasure he took in seeing the Prince of Orange's castle in flames and the enemy soldiers who had been burned: "I saw some rather nice little piles consumed by the flames that burned as well as the people hidden in the houses." These atrocities had been planned. Luxembourg said he had wanted to inspire a "salutary terror" in the Dutch people (Petitfils, *Louis XIV*, 376–377).

92 In Holland as well, the strategy of terror had an effect contrary to the one sought. In fact, the massacres of 1672 had aroused an anti-French hatred that was not extinguished for a long time, and which Voltaire still witnessed when, half a century later, he visited Holland. After the first moment of stupor and terror, these "examples" that were supposed to disarm the adversary instead galvanized his patriotism and will to resist.

93 See Chapter 20.

94 La Jonquière, *L'Expédition d'Égypte*, 4:283.

95 Six to fifteen a day, according to Larrey, "Mémoire sur la peste qui a régné dans l'armée d'Orient pendant son expédition de Syrie" (Larrey, *Mémoires de chirurgie militaire*, 1:316).

96 Talking about the plague with Las Cases, "he said that its greatest danger and greatest propagation were in fear, and its main seat was in the imagination: in Egypt, everyone whose imagination was struck died. The defense and the wisest remedy were moral courage" (*Mémorial*, 2:432).

97 On Gros's painting, see O'Brien, *Antoine Jean Gros*, 90–117.

98 Bourrienne, *Mémoires*, 2:256–258. Bourrienne also says that this scene took place two months later, after the return from Saint-Jean d'Acre.

99 Desgenettes, *Histoire médicale de l'armée d'Orient*, 49–50.

100 Quoted in La Jonquière, *L'Expédition d'Égypte*, 4:285n1.

101 Battalion leader Detroye, ibid.

102 Ibid.

103 In the booklet for the Salon of 1804 we read that "in order to further dissipate the idea of a sudden and incurable contagion, he [Bonaparte] had opened in his presence a few pestilential tumors and touched several of them" (O'Brien, *Antoine Jean Gros*, 98).

104 On September 24, 1804, during a dinner given for Gros to celebrate the success of the *Pestiférés of Jaffa*, Girodet gave Gros this poem: "Meanwhile the rumor is heard, in this place of misery, / That a guardian angel was seen to show itself there; / Immediately everyone is excited; they all hurry to see it; / And in their dying eyes shines a ray of hope. / Struck blind, in his haste, / One of them lends an attentive ear to his leader: / Without a guide, without a stick, eager to rush there / If the hero speaks to him, he is sure to get well" (Louca, *L'Autre Égypte*, 61).

105 Goethe, *Conversations with Eckermann*, 316.

106 See Friedlaender, "Napoleon as *roi thaumaturge*."

107 This was not plague, but dysentery, typhus, and scurvy; plague had disappeared from the Mediterranean basin in the eighth century and did not reappear until the fifteenth (Le Goff, *Saint Louis*, 189). See Joinville's *Histoire de Saint Louis*.

108 Quoted by Chateaubriand, *Mémoires d'outre-tombe*, 1:1153.

109 Mark 1:40–41.

110 "Campagnes d'Égypte et de Syrie," *Correspondance de Napoléon Ier*, 30:24.

111 Bloch, *Les Rois thaumaturges*, xvi–xxvi (preface by J. Le Goff), 79–86, 185–260, 381–405.

112 O'Meara, *Documents particuliers sur Napoléon Bonaparte*, 111.

113 Faure, *Napoléon*, 106.

114 Ibid.

20. The Return from the Orient

1 Quoted in Bainville, *Bonaparte en Égypte*, 74. Berthier made the same reproach to Bonaparte. In his account, he wrote, imputing the fault to the whole of the army in order not to accuse Bonaparte alone: "The taking of Jaffa had given the French army a confidence that made it at first consider the fortress of Acre with too little regard" (*Récit des campagnes du général Bonaparte en Égypte*, 70).

2 Napoleon set forth the plan worked out by Caffarelli in his "Campagnes d'Égypte et de Syrie" (*Correspondance de Napoléon Ier*, 30:39–40).

3 Ader, *Histoire de l'expédition d'Égypte*, 189–191.

4 François, *Journal*, 310.

5 Miot, *Mémoires* (1804), 240.

6 Quoted in Laurens, *L'Expédition d'Égypte*, 196.

7 Miot, *Mémoires* (1804), 224.

8 Laurens, *Kléber en Égypte*, 2:554–555.

9 Seven ships fell into the hands of the British (Barrow, *Life and Correspondence of Admiral Sir William Sidney Smith*, 1:268n). Captain Stendelet succeeded in saving six others, but he did so by sailing for France, whence, of course, he did not return ("Campagnes d'Égypte et de Syrie," *Correspondance de Napoléon Ier*, 30:32, 37–38).

10 Ibid., 30:51–52. The siege artillery reached Acre only on April 30. Up to then the attackers had only two 32- and 24-caliber carronades, without carriages, that had been found in Haifa, four 6-inch mortars, and thirty-six light artillery pieces (ibid., 40).

11 This massacre took place after the failure of the first French assault, on March 28 (Lockroy, *Ahmed le Boucher*, 254).

12 Contrary to the claim made by Bonaparte, who wrote on April 5 to General Alméras: "All the people are submitting: the Motoâlys, the Maronites, and the Druze are on our side. Damas is only waiting to hear that Saint-Jean d'Acre has been taken to send us its keys" (*Correspondance générale*, no. 4315, 2:894).

13 It was only on April 6 that they saw Jezzar's reinforcements landing at Acre: "about a hundred officers and [experienced] gunners" ("Campagnes d'Égypte et de Syrie," *Correspondance de Napoléon Ier*, 30:43).

14 On William Sidney Smith (1764–1840), see Smith, *Memoirs*; Barrow, *Life and Correspondence of Admiral Sir William Sidney Smith* (esp. 1:235–260); and the article on him in Michaud's *Biographie universelle* (39:465–472).

15 Smith, *Memoirs*, 1:171–172. Captain Krettly says he was also received by Sidney Smith on board the *Tiger* (*Souvenirs*, 58).

16 Bainville, *Napoléon*, 126.

17 See Lavalette's account (*Mémoires et souvenirs*, 1:312).

18 "Campagnes d'Égypte et de Syrie," *Correspondance de Napoléon Ier*, 30:50. On the April 17 meetings, see 30:50. Later on Napoleon exaggerated the support he had received from the Druze, the Shi'ites of the Bekaa, the Christians of Galilee, and the Jews of Palestine, (among whom there was a rumor that "he wanted to restore the temple of Solomon"), and even from Muslims subject to Jezzar's ferocious domination (ibid., 30:36–37).

19 Bernoyer, *Avec Bonaparte en Égypte et en Syrie*, 163.

20 Niello Sargy, *Mémoires*, 286.

21 Lockroy, *Ahmed le Boucher*, 257.

22 Letter of May 30, 1799, reproduced in Barrow, *Life and Correspondence of Admiral Sir William Sidney Smith*, 1:309–310.

23 Bernoyer, *Avec Bonaparte en Égypte et en Syrie*, 164.

24 "Misérable bicoque" (lousy dump): that is what he called Acre in a conversation with Bourrienne (Bourrienne, *Mémoires*, 2:243–244).

25 "Campagnes d'Égypte et de Syrie," *Correspondance de Napoléon Ier*, 30:57.

26 *Correspondance générale*, no. 4315, 2:894.

27 "Campagnes d'Égypte et de Syrie," *Correspondance de Napoléon Ier*, 30:57.

28 Goethe, *Conversations with Eckermann*, 315.

29 Bainville, *Napoléon*, 126.

30 Sainte-Beuve, "Campagnes d'Égypte et de Syrie, par Napoléon," *Causeries du lundi*, 1:195.

31 "Campagnes d'Égypte et de Syrie," *Correspondance de Napoléon Ier*, 30:57.

32 *Correspondance générale*, no. 4346 (May 10, 1798), 2:910–913; *Correspondance de Napoléon Ier*, no. 4138 (May 17, 1799), 5:429–430.

33 Sorel, *L'Europe et la Révolution française*, 5:447.

34 Bourrienne, *Mémoires*, 2:250–251. The 123 leagues from Acre to Cairo were covered in seventeen days—that is, at an average of 7 leagues a day (Desgenettes, *Histoire médicale de l'armée d'Orient* [1802], 110–113).

35 Order of May 28 (*Correspondance de Napoléon Ier*, no. 4158, 5:441–442).

36 *Correspondance générale*, no. 4347 (to Perrée, May 11, 1799), 2:913. On the evacuation of the wounded, see also no. 4350 (to adjutant general Leturcq, May 16, 1799), 2:914; the letters (nos. 4351–4353) sent the same day to adjutants general Boyer and Alméras and to General Dugua (2:914–916); as well as the instructions Berthier gave Lannes the following day (*Correspondance de Napoléon Ier*, no. 4141, 5:431–432).

37 See *Correspondance de Napoléon Ier*, no. 4145 (Berthier to Leturcq, May 19, 1799), 5:433; nos. 4147–4149 (Berthier to Dommartin, May 21), 5:435; *Correspondance générale*, no. 4358 (to Berthier, May 25), 2:918, and especially the instructions Berthier gave adjutant general Boyer on May 24 (*Correspondance de Napoléon Ier*, no. 4150, 5:435–436).

38 Desgenettes, *Histoire médicale de l'armée d'Orient* (1830), 97.

39 *Memoir of a Campaign with the Ottoman Army in Egypt* (London, 1801)—see De Meulenaere, *Bibliographie raisonnée*, 200.

40 Wilson, *History of the British Expedition to Egypt*, 77.

41 This extract, from the military diary of Colonel Vigo-Roussillon, is quoted in Warden, *Napoléon jugé par un Anglais*, 122n1.

42 The first version is that of the "Campagnes d'Égypte et de Syrie" (*Correspondance de Napoléon Ier*, 30:60–61). In his conversations with Doctor O'Meara, Napoleon spoke of only seven sick men (Warden, *Napoléon jugé par un Anglais*, 121–122). He gave the same number to Las Cases (*Mémorial*, 1:136–137), adding that no patient was ultimately finished off, because they had all died by the time the rearguard left Jaffa. See also Bertrand, *Cahiers*, 3:91. The second version is the one Napoleon developed in front of Las Cases (*Mémorial*, 1:135–138). The last version is reported by Bourrienne (*Mémoires*, 2:263–264).

43 Larrey is in fact the only one who denied that a single sick man was poisoned (*Mémoires de chirurgie militaire*, 1:311–312, 355).

44 Bourrienne, *Mémoires*, 2:255.

45 Laurens, *Kléber en Égypte*, 2:543.

46 He said only that he had refused to put an end to the plague victims' lives, while admitting that it was futile to evacuate them: "I pointed out to the superior authority the futility and the dangers of an evacuation of sick men reduced to this extremity" (Desgenettes, *Histoire médicale de l'armée d'Orient* [1802], 99).

47 Desgenettes, *Histoire médicale de l'armée d'Orient* (1830), 245–246.

48 Royer died in Egypt three years later. Bonaparte is said to have opposed his return to France: because he knew too much? (See Dr. Cabanes's study of the affair [ibid., 452–466]).

49 See Bourrienne, *Mémoires*, 2:257; François, *Journal*, 316; Lacorre, *Journal inédit*, 94; Desgenettes, *Histoire médicale de l'armée d'Orient* (1802), 99; Niello Sargy, *Mémoires*, 295–296.

50 See *Correspondance générale*, no. 4363 (to Berthier, May 27, 1799), 2:921.

51 Seven hundred, according to adjutant general Boyer, who was assigned to escort them (*Historique de ma vie*, 1:25–26); 1,700 according to Napoleon ("Campagnes d'Égypte et de Syrie," *Correspondance de Napoléon Ier*, 30:58–59). See the testimony of the head ordnance officer Daure in Boulos, *Bourrienne et ses erreurs*, 1:35–38.

52 Having succeeded in finding in Jaffa a few boats and having several dozen seriously wounded men put on them, the Englishman, after having intercepted the convoy, escorted the wounded himself as far as Damietta (Herold, *Bonaparte en Égypte*, 373–374).

53 *Correspondance générale*, no. 4323 (to Berthier, April 18, 1799), 2:900.

54 See Colonel Vigo-Roussillon's testimony, quoted in Warden, *Napoléon jugé par un Anglais*, 123n.

55 "Campagnes d'Égypte et de Syrie," *Correspondance de Napoléon Ier*, 30:58–61.

56 Desgenettes reduces this figure to 700 (*Histoire médicale de l'armée d'Orient*, 109).

57 Michalon and Vernet, "Adaptation d'une armée française de la fin du XVIIIe siècle à un théâtre d'opérations proche-oriental," 109.

58 "Campagnes d'Égypte et de Syrie," *Correspondance de Napoléon Ier*, 30:62.

59 *Correspondance générale*, no. 4424 (to Ganteaume, June 21, 1799), 2:949–950.

60 Niello Sargy, *Mémoires*, 299.

61 Ibid., 325–326. See also the scientist Redouté, "La dispute entre Desgenettes et Bonaparte à l'Institut d'Égypte, 4 juillet 1799," reproduced in Carmélia Opsomer, "Les manuscrits de Redouté, dessinateur et chroniqueur de l'expédition" (in Bret, *L'Égypte au temps de l'expédition de Bonaparte*, 77).

62 However, he had taken care to have Fourier eliminate from the transcript of the sessions of the Institute of Cairo everything that concerned this dispute, as Fourier is supposed to have told the British general Wilson. The latter in fact jotted, on the back of a letter that Fourier had written him on March 13, 1802: "This man was the secretary of the national Institute: and he removed, on Bonaparte's orders, as he told me, the pages that contained the dispute at the Institute when Desgenettes accused Bonaparte" (Randolph, *Life of General Sir Robert Wilson*, 1:237).

63 *Correspondance générale*, no. 4431 (to Desaix, June 22, 1799), 2:952; see also the letter that he wrote on June 30 to the sultan of Darfur (no. 4492, 2:977–978); ibid., no. 4479 (June 28, 1799), 2:972.

64 Denon and al-Jabartî, *Sur l'expédition de Bonaparte*, 255.

65 See La Jonquière, *L'Expédition d'Égypte*, 5:231n2; Audebaud, *Dugua*, 163. Women were traditionally drowned—as were the two Jewish women whom Bonaparte ordered "thrown into the water" on January 25 (*Correspondance générale*, no. 4162 [to Destaing], 2:815). From Acre, he had also written to Dugua, regarding a "loose woman" Destaing had had arrested, that on his return to Cairo he "would have her drowned" (ibid., no. 4327 [to Dugua, April 19, 1799], 2:901–902).

66 Herold, *Bonaparte en Égypte*, 201.

67 Notably General Donzelot, the commander of Middle Egypt. In Cairo it was the agha of the janissaries who was entrusted with the execution (Bret, *L'Égypte au temps de l'expédition de Bonaparte*, 177–178).

68 He was not the only one; Galland also speaks of a "somewhat violent means" (*Tableau de l'Égypte*, 1:171).

69 *Correspondance générale*, no. 4405 (to the Directory, June 19, 1799), 2:941–942. On the Mahdi, see Brégeon, *L'Égypte de Bonaparte*, 123.

70 *Correspondance générale*, no. 4550 (to Murat, July 7, 1799), 2:999.

71 See Bonaparte's orders to Dugua: ibid., no. 4407 (June 19, 1799), 2:943; no. 4422 (June 21), 2:948–949; no. 4432 (June 22), 2:953. On July 8 he had executed Abdallah Aghâ, the governor of Jaffa, who, after having been earlier spared, had been taken to Cairo (ibid., no. 4558 [to Dugua], 2:1001).

72 Ibid., no. 4527 (July 5, 1799), 2:991.

73 The estimates concerning the army landed at Abukir are uncertain. They vary between 7,000 men (Laurens, *L'Expédition d'Égypte*, 218) and 18,000 (Benoist-Méchin, *Bonaparte en Égypte*, 283). In a letter of July 27 Napoleon mentions the figure of 15,000 men (*Correspondance générale*, no. 4654 [to Desaix, July 27, 1799], 2:1042), whereas Berthier estimates at 11,000 to 12,000 the number of soldiers committed by the Turks on the day of the battle (La Jonquière, *L'Expédition d'Égypte*, 5:407–408). The Turkish order of battle confirms this estimate: slightly less than 13,000 men were occupying the peninsula on July 25.

74 He had been informed on July 15 that an Ottoman fleet was approaching Alexandria on July 12; on the seventeenth, while he was pausing at Terraneh, he wrote to Marmont, telling him to stand fast at Abukir (*Correspondance générale*, no. 4623, 2:1027), whereas the same day the fort's last defenders had laid down their arms, and on the twentieth he still informed him that he was going to send him reinforcements to maintain the fort's resistance (ibid., no. 4627, 2:1029–1030). Only on the evening of July 20 did he learn that the Turks had been in control of the island for the past three days (*Correspondance de Napoléon Ier*, no. 4294 [to Dugua], 5:524).

75 *Correspondance générale*, no. 4622 (July 17, 1799), 2:1026–1027.

76 Marmont, *Mémoires*, 2:28.

77 See *Correspondance générale*, no. 4647 (to Dugua, July 26, 1799), 2:1039–1040; no. 4654 (to Desaix, July 27), 2:1042; no. 4659 (to the Directory, July 28), 2:1045; no. 4669 (to the Directory, August 4), 2:1050; Hourtoulle, "La campagne d'Égypte"; Bernède and Chaduc, *La Campagne d'Égypte*, 90.

78 Or about 3 percent of the 9,000 men Bonaparte threw into the battle. If the wounded are included, 14 percent of the French troops were put out of action. These percentages are

about average for battles of this period. At Austerlitz, for example, the French army was to lose 14 percent of its men, with deaths representing 2 percent of the men sent into battle (Rory Muir, *Tactics and the Experience of Battle in the Age of Napoleon* [New Haven: Yale University Press, 1998]).

79 Letter of August 2, 1799, quoted in Barrow, *Life and Correspondence of Admiral Sir William Sidney Smith*, 1:364.

80 *Correspondance de Napoléon Ier*, no. 4294 (July 20, 1799), 5:524.

81 Quoted in La Jonquière, *L'Expédition d'Égypte*, 5:405.

82 Ibid.

83 *Correspondance générale*, no. 4762 (to the Directory, October 10, 1799), 2:1089–1090; *Correspondance de Napoléon Ier*, no. 4383 ("Retour du général Bonaparte en Europe," October 15, 1799), 5:579–582.

84 *Correspondance générale*, no. 4762 (to the Directory, October 10, 1799), 2:1089. The newspapers delivered to Bonaparte were periodicals published by émigrés, the *Courrier français de Londres* and the *Gazette de Francfort*.

85 Quoted in Marmont, *Mémoires*, 2:32.

86 *Correspondance générale*, no. 4762 (to the Directory, October 10, 1799), 2:1089.

87 The most recent of the newspapers was dated June 10 ("Retour du général Bonaparte en Europe," *Correspondance de Napoléon Ier*, 5:579–582).

88 Arago, "Gaspard Monge," 556.

89 Lucien Bonaparte, *Révolution de brumaire*, 26.

90 Mme de Staël also wrote, in *Dix années d'exil*, that "the two Bonaparte brothers, Joseph and Lucien, . . . wrote to their brother that the state of affairs in France was such that he could hope through his presence to acquire the greatest ascendancy there" (65).

91 Vandal, *L'Avènement de Bonaparte*, 1:271. He himself recognized as much, saying that he was far from assessing at its true value the "civilian merit" of a brother whose aptitude he saw as limited to the "command of armies" alone (Lucien Bonaparte, *Révolution de brumaire*, 29–30).

92 As early as 1817, Rouillon-Petit, the author of a work titled *Campagnes mémorables des Français en Egypte, en Italie, en Hollande, en Allemagne*, wrote that the "precipitous manner in which Bonaparte left Egypt [remains] a political mystery that is known only to a very few persons" (quoted in Massie, *Roger Ducos*, 305). A former representative on the Council of Five Hundred suggests this when he speaks of "secret contacts established within and without, either to inform him regarding the moment when his return from Egypt would be necessary, or to ensure his passage through the enemy fleets" (Bigonnet, *Coup d'état du dix-huit brumaire*, 9). Norvins is more precise: "We cannot explain by what miracle, on the day he sailed, and until his arrival in France, the sea was open for the passage of the four ships that were carrying Bonaparte and his entourage. The historian who wants to solve this problem still hesitates between the hero's luck and *a foreign policy*" (*Histoire de Napoléon*, 1:262). C. Grant Robinson asserted that the hypothesis of a Bonaparte escaping Egypt and arriving miraculously in France was not credible (*England under the Hanoverians* [1948], quoted in Massie, *Roger Ducos*, 305), and Lentz, in his history of the Consulate, mentions the hypothesis, referring to the possible "goodwill of the English navy, because the return of Bonaparte to Paris might mean

both the end of the Egyptian expedition and the beginning of a time of troubles in France" (*Le Grand Consulat*, 46).

93 Proth, *Bonaparte comediante tragediante*, 298–300.

94 Mackesy, *Statesmen at War*, 18.

95 This manifesto is reproduced *in toto* by Berthier, *Récit des campagnes du général Bonaparte en Égypte et en Syrie*, 106–108.

96 Niello Sargy, *Mémoires*, 359.

97 Quoted in Sparrow, *Secret Service*, 189.

98 Marmont had established the contact in Alexandria (*Mémoires*, 2:30–32). The gunner Bricard also mentions this "secret meeting," adding that it delayed for a few days the return to Cairo of the soldiers who had fought at Abukir (*Journal*, 373).

99 Quoted in Douin, "Le retour de Bonaparte," 191.

100 Reybaud, *Histoire scientifique et militaire de l'expédition*, 6:264. Starting in the spring of 1799, Austrian and Russians had resumed the war and attacked French positions in Italy and in Switzerland.

101 Nigulà ibn Yusufal-Turk, *Histoire de l'expédition des Français en Égypte*, 150–151.

102 Laurens, *L'Expédition d'Égypte*, 222.

103 Douin, "Le retour de Bonaparte."

104 Letter quoted in Douin (ibid., 203).

105 Ibid., 203–209.

106 He lied again when he wrote to Nelson on November 8: "The fugitive escaped the *Theseus* and the Turkish squadron that had occupied a position west of Alexandria to intercept him after his probable departure. . . . Unfortunately . . . the *Theseus*, which had left to get supplies, was delayed a few days because of the perversity of the Turkish governor of Baffa" (quoted in Barrow, *Life and Correspondence of Admiral Sir William Sidney Smith*, 1:380).

107 *Correspondance générale*, no. 4470 (to Marmont, June 26, 1799), 2:968.

108 Quoted in Reilly, *Pitt the Younger*, 292.

109 Quoted in La Jonquière, *L'Expédition d'Égypte*, 5:572–573.

110 *Correspondance générale*, no. 4702 (August 12, 1799), 2:1063.

111 See Jomard's testimony in Villiers du Terrage, *Journal et souvenirs*, 225.

112 Bonaparte refused to see her again after she returned to France. He had money given to her and later on arranged her remarriage with a Chevalier de Ranchoup, whom he named consul in Spain (Dupont, *Pauline Fourès*, 221–245).

113 Quoted in La Jonquière, *L'Expédition d'Égypte*, 5:579.

114 *Correspondance générale*, no. 4751 (to Kléber, August 19, 1799), 2:1083.

115 *Correspondance de Napoléon Ier*, no. 4372 (to Menou, August 20, 1799), 5:571.

116 Bourrienne, *Mémoires*, 2:313. See also the note by the aide-de-camp Eugène Merlin regarding the departure from Egypt (Guitry, *L'Armée de Bonaparte en Égypte*, 353–362).

117 "Campagnes d'Égypte et de Syrie," *Correspondance de Napoléon Ier*, 30:94–95.

118 *Correspondance générale*, no. 4757 (to Junot, August 22, 1799), 2:1085.

119 Quoted in La Jonquière, *L'Expédition d'Égypte*, 5:609.

120 "Retour du général Bonaparte en Europe," *Correspondance de Napoléon Ier*, 5:744–745.

121 Regenbogen, *Napoléon a dit*, 15.

21. The Conspiracy

1 As we will see later, permission had been given, but he was not aware of it.

2 Thiers, *The History of the French Revolution*, 5:396.

3 Thiébault, *Mémoires*, 3:60.

4 *Correspondance de Napoléon Ier*, 30:94–95.

5 Stopover in Ajaccio: see Chapter 5.

6 "part of his army": quoted in La Jonquière, *L'Expédition d'Égypte*, 5:166–167.

7 Douin, *La Campagne de Bruix en Méditerranée*.

8 After 18 Fructidor, the government had dismissed Moreau from his command and sent Augereau to Germany. Although it had ultimately capitulated before Bonaparte, at the end of 1798 it had precipitated a showdown by reestablishing the civilian representatives to the armies whose abolition the generals had obtained in 1796. In this measure the generals had seen a genuine *casus belli*. Bernadotte, who became minister of war in July 1799, did what they wanted: in September and October 1799, the civilian representatives were abolished.

9 Vandal, *L'Avènement de Bonaparte*, 1:195–196. On the neo-Jacobinism of 1799, see Gainot, *1799, un nouveau jacobinisme?*

10 Quoted in Vandal, *L'Avènement de Bonaparte*, 1:212.

11 Quoted in Bredin, *Sieyès*, 419.

12 La Révellière-Lépeaux, *Mémoires*, 2:383.

13 That is Louis Madelin's thesis (*Histoire du Consulat et de l'Empire*, 2:302), discussed in Chapter 20.

14 He had been involved, like his brother Joseph, in a crooked scheme connected with maritime insurance.

15 Zweig, *Joseph Fouché*, 112.

16 Vandal, *L'Avènement de Bonaparte*, 1:134–135, 185.

17 Quoted in Kermina, *Bernadotte et Désirée Clary*, 70.

18 Quoted in Höjer, *Bernadotte*, 189.

19 The lack of an upturn in the military operations during the summer was not the only motive that inspired this decision. For months there had been the greatest uncertainty regarding the fate of the Army of Egypt. Rumors were rife, and Paris was hesitating between those who expected to see Bonaparte return via Germany after having taken Constantinople—in June, the government had caused articles to this effect to be published (La Jonquière, *L'Expédition d'Égypte*, 5:178n2)—and those who said he was through (see the articles in the press and the police reports cited in Schmidt, *Tableaux de la Révolution française*, 3:413–447). Rumors soon became suspicions, and then accusations against the Directory that claimed it had deliberately "deported to the deserts of Arabia 40,000 men forming the elite of our armies, General Bonaparte, and with him the best of our scientists, our men of letters, and our artists" (quoted in La Jonquière, *L'Expédition d'Égypte*, 5:179). The question was soon raised in the Councils, where the neo-Jacobins saw in it a new opportunity to harass the government. Reubell rejected these accusations by recalling that Bonaparte had taken the initiative for the expedition; the former director La Révellière, Talleyrand, and even the latter's predecessor as minister, Charles Delacroix, declined any re-

sponsibility (see the documents reproduced in La Jonquière, ibid., 180–181). In vain; no one believed them. The government thus thought it prudent to cover itself in case Bonaparte capitulated or died: What would people say if it had done nothing to help the expeditionary corps? That is why in early September it sent him a second order to return to France. This step cost it little, especially because a report submitted by Talleyrand on September 3 noted the now certain failure of the Egyptian expedition and concluded that an evacuation was necessary (Boulay de la Meurthe, *Le Directoire et l'expédition d'Égypte*, 305). It fell to Talleyrand's successor as minister of foreign affairs, Reinhard, to write this letter dated September 18: "The Executive Directory, General, awaits you, you and the brave men who are with you" (ibid., 316–319).

20 Ibid., 325–329.

21 Quoted in Bainville, *Le Dix-huit brumaire*, 18.

22 Bourrienne, *Mémoires*, 3:19.

23 Quoted in Thiry, *Le Coup d'état du 18 brumaire*, 12–13.

24 Norvins, *Histoire de Napoléon*, 2:4.

25 *Réimpression de l'ancien Moniteur*, 29:853.

26 Boulart, *Mémoires*, 67–68.

27 Marbot, *Memoirs*, 1:30.

28 These letters arrived in France only after 18 Brumaire. As one might imagine, no one heard anything more about them.

29 Crouzet, *La Grande inflation*.

30 See the four volumes in the series *Du Directoire au Consulat*, ed. J.-P. Jessenne et al.; and Bourdin and Gainot, *La République directoriale*.

31 Thiers, *The History of the French Revolution*, 5:435.

32 Quinet, *La Révolution*, 689–690.

33 Talleyrand had said this, but only to the government (see above).

34 Miot de Melito, *Memoirs*, 154.

35 See Chapter 19.

36 Staël, *Considerations on the principal events of the French revolution*, 2:1.

37 Furet, *La Révolution*, 211–212.

38 Staël, *Considerations on the principal events of the French revolution*, 2:6–7.

39 The agent in question is Royer-Collard, in an unsigned report addressed to Louis XVIII on June 14, 1802 (Remacle, *Relations secrètes des agents de Louis XVIII à Paris*, 38).

40 *Correspondance de Napoléon Ier*, 30:303.

41 Ibid., 363.

42 The scene is recounted in Barras, *Memoirs*, 4:32.

43 Quoted in Buchez and Roux, *Histoire parlementaire de la Révolution française*, 38:154.

44 Gohier, *Mémoires*, 1:202.

45 Barras, *Memoirs*, 4:34–40.

46 Bourrienne, *Mémoires*, 4:116–118. Michelet, who had known Collot, confirms the anecdote (*Histoire du XIXe siècle*, 2:375). This scene took place on October 18, not October 17 as Evangeline Bruce states (*Napoleon and Josephine*, 272–273).

47 Letter to Barras, quoted in Wagener, *L'Impératrice Joséphine*, 178.

48 The valet Constant, then in Joséphine's service, states that she wanted to join her husband in Egypt and that she would have made the trip had it not been for an unfortunate accident at Plombières that delayed her departure. When she got better, the French fleet had already been sunk at Abukir; time had passed, and she and Hortense, who had come to her bedside, returned to Paris (Constant Wairy, *Mémoires intimes*, 1:88–89).

49 Gohier, *Mémoires*, 1:199.

50 H. de Beauharnais, *Mémoires*, 1:62.

51 Many historians say, following Barras (*Mémoires*, 4:29), that Bonaparte was met by his brothers before arriving in Paris (Masson, *Napoléon et sa famille*, 1:275–277; Lentz, *Le 18-brumaire*, 213). But contemporaries do not mention this meeting. Bourrienne, who was with Bonaparte (*Mémoires*, 3:36–37; and Gohier, *Mémoires*, 1:199), says on the contrary that Bonaparte arrived in Paris "without having been met by either his wife or his brothers." Christine Reinhard, the wife of the minister of foreign affairs, wrote in a letter of October 20: "Mme Bonaparte and her brother, who had gone to meet him, missed him on the road and came back to Paris after him" (*Lettres*, 90).

52 Bourrienne, *Mémoires*, 4:118–119.

53 Castelot, *Joséphine*, 224.

54 Furet, "Bonaparte," 221.

55 Abrantès, *Souvenirs sur Napoléon*, 48.

56 Roederer, *Oeuvres*, 3:295.

57 Quoted in Fierro et al., *Histoire et dictionnaire du Consulat et de l'Empire*, 8.

58 Ibid.

59 Quoted in Lentz, *Le 18-brumaire*, 217.

60 Quoted in Bredin, *Sieyès*, 446–447.

61 Bainville, *Le Dix-huit brumaire*, 22.

62 Quoted in Ollivier, *Le Dix-huit brumaire*, 158–159.

63 Réal exercised the functions of the Executive Directory's representative to the central administration of the department of the Seine; as such, he had control over the capital's police.

64 Quoted in Buchez and Roux, *Histoire parlementaire de la Révolution française*, 38:162n1.

65 Bertrand, *Cahiers*, 2:278–279.

66 Quoted in Thiry, *Le Coup d'état du 18 brumaire*, 67.

67 Barras, *Memoirs*, 4:59.

68 Bourrienne, *Mémoires*, 3:67.

69 Quoted in L. Bonaparte, *Révolution de brumaire*, 60–63.

70 Bainville, *Le Dix-huit brumaire*, 36.

71 As is shown by the Prussian agent Sandoz-Rollin's note dated November 7, quoted in Poniatowski, *Talleyrand et le Directoire*, 828.

72 Quoted in Thiry, *Le Coup d'état du 18 brumaire*, 79.

73 Cited in Aulard, *Paris pendant la réaction thermidorienne et sous le Directoire*, 5:786.

74 Lavalette, *Memoirs*, 1:389.

22. Brumaire

1 The presidency of the Directorate was held in turns, for one month, by each of its five members.

2 J. de Beauharnais, *Correspondance*, 91.

3 "Bonaparte," he was to write in his memoirs, "agreed to come for dinner at my home, with his family, on 18 Brumaire! . . . I frankly admit that this engagement alone would have made me reject all the warnings that might have been given me regarding the fateful day that was coming" (Gohier, *Mémoires*, 1:228).

4 Constant Wairy, *Memoirs intimes*, 1:80.

5 *Réimpression de l'ancien Moniteur*, 29:883.

6 Buchez and Roux, *Histoire parlementaire de la Révolution française*, 38:168–169.

7 Thiers, *The History of the French Revolution*, 5:424.

8 The reality of this conversation, which Bourrienne claims to have witnessed (*Mémoires*, 3:68–69), was contested by Joseph (see Bessand-Massenet, *Le 18 brumaire*, 103–106, 257). According to him, Bernadotte had asked to be taken to Rue de la Victoire, but seeing what was going on, he turned back. Bernadotte (*Notes historiques sur le 18 brumaire*) states, like Bourrienne, that Joseph came to get him and that the conversation with Napoleon took place. After a close examination of the various testimonies, Höjer decided in favor of the version given by Bourrienne and Bernadotte (Höjer, *Bernadotte*, 191–195).

9 Barras, *Memoirs*, 4:83–84. The version given by Bourrienne differs a little from this one (*Mémoires*, 3:68–69).

10 *Réimpression de l'ancien Moniteur*, 29:883.

11 This oath does not appear in either the *Moniteur* or Buchez, but Roederer mentions it (*Oeuvres*, 3:297), as does Napoléon (*Correspondance de Napoléon Ier*, 30:314).

12 Bourrienne, *Mémoires*, 3:71.

13 Ibid., 3:108.

14 Gohier, *Mémoires*, 1:239.

15 Ibid., 1:235.

16 Bertrand, *Cahiers*, 2:279.

17 Lombard de Langres, *Le Dix-huit brumaire*, 159–163; anonymous, *Mémoires historiques sur le dix-huit brumaire*, 10.

18 According to Roederer, Admiral Bruix carried out this mission alone, without Talleyrand's help (*Oeuvres*, 3:301).

19 Gohier, *Mémoires*, 1:235–236.

20 Quoted in Garnier, *Barras*, 296.

21 Barras, *Memoirs*, 4:xxx.

22 Buchez and Roux, *Histoire parlementaire de la Révolution française*, 38:179.

23 Did Sieyès and Ducos officially resign after Bonaparte claimed they had already handed in their resignations? Lombard de Langres, who witnessed the events, says they did (*Le Dix-huit brumaire*, 157–159). Lanfrey states that the two directors had already resigned when Barras sent in his resignation (*Histoire de Napoléon Ier*, 1:458). But the next day, at Saint-Cloud, when several representatives from the Council of Five Hundred asked where the

as minister of the interior, and Gaudin replaced Lindet as minister of finances. Joseph Lagarde, who had been secretary-general under the Directory, kept his job, and Maret was named
to the new office of *secrétaire d'état*.

21 Dubois-Crancé had proposed to Gohier and Moulin to have Bonaparte arrested on the way
to Saint-Cloud and to have him shot (Norvins, *Histoire de Napoléon*, 2:25).

22 Carnot, *Mémoires*, 2:211.

23 Talleyrand had been the target of a press campaign orchestrated by the Jacobins, who accused him of embezzlement and even of high treason, charging him with having thought up
the expedition to Egypt in order to get Bonaparte out of the way and with having thereby
made things easier for the coalition whose armies were threatening the French borders after
having reconquered Italy. Another affair had clouded the minister's life: a former military
man, a follower of Babeuf named Jorry who had pocketed money intended to cover the
costs of a secret diplomatic mission he had not carried out, took him to court, accusing him
of having had him arrested arbitrarily. Although on July 12 the court threw out Jorry's petition, the damage had been done, and Talleyrand preferred to resign the ministry on his
own initiative before being dismissed (Lacour-Gayet, *Talleyrand*, 338–358).

24 Bourrienne, *Mémoires*, 3:183.

25 "Consuls provisoires," *Correspondance de Napoléon Ier*, 30:331.

26 Fouché says so in his *Memoirs*, 1:89.

27 Zweig, *Fouché*, 124–125.

28 "indelicacy": For example, when Talleyrand told him that thanks to 18 Brumaire he had
amassed a tidy sum of money by buying government bonds, which were then very cheap,
certain that they would go back up after the coup d'état (Lacretelle, *Dix années d'épreuves*,
226–227).

29 Gourgaud, *Journal de Sainte-Hélène*, 1:485.

30 Quoted in Orieux, *Talleyrand*, 369.

31 Talleyrand quoted in Lacour-Gayet, *Talleyrand*, 385; Sainte-Beuve, "Essai sur Talleyrand,"
Nouveaux lundis, 12:41.

32 These words of Napoléon's are quoted in Orieux, *Talleyrand*, 367.

33 Talleyrand, *Mémoires et correspondances*, 233.

34 Bertrand, *Cahiers*, 2:128.

35 Quotation from Gourgaud, *Journal de Sainte-Hélène*, 1:480.

36 See Talleyrand, *Mémoires et correspondances*, 232–233.

37 Mme de Chastenay, quoted in Fierro, *Les Français par eux-mêmes: Le Consulat et l'Empire*,
1137–1139.

38 Pasquier, *A History of My Time*, 2:380.

39 Beugnot, *Mémoires*, 1:309.

40 Gaudin, *Notice historique sur les finances*, 1–8.

41 Bruguière, *Gestionnaires et profiteurs*, 110. However, in 1798 he accepted the position of the
Directory's commissioner for the postal administration.

42 "Where there are neither finances nor the means of creating any, a minister is useless," he is
supposed to have said in 1795 (Crouzet, *La Grande inflation*, 396).

43 Gaudin, *Mémoires*, 1:44–45.

44 Ibid., 1:45–46.

45 Bonaparte refused to accept his resignation, and Gaudin, who always thought anything proceeding from the general was good, resumed his official functions (*Correspondance générale*, no. 5151 [to Gaudin, March 28, 1800], 3:166).

46 Latour, *Le Grand argentier de Napoléon*, 77.

47 Regenbogen, *Napoléon a dit*, 343.

48 Gaudin, *Mémoires*, 3:185.

49 Gaudin, *Notice historique sur les finances*, 13–14. On Gaudin's dress, see the testimony provided by Beugnot, who worked for him (*Mémoires*, 1:310).

50 The list of unseated representatives was appended to article 1 of the law of 19 Brumaire.

51 See Cherrier, *18 brumaire et 2 décembre*, 2:595–597; Lentz, *Le Grand Consulat*, 149–154.

52 *Gazette nationale ou le Moniteur universel*, 1799, 2:206.

53 commissioners: Consular order of November 20 (*Correspondance de Napoléon*, no. 4395, 6:9–10). Article 4 of the law of 19 Brumaire authorized the Consulate "to send delegates with a specific power, within the limits of its own."

54 *Gazette nationale ou le Moniteur universel*, 1799, 2:225–226.

55 See the Army of Holland's reservations, mentioned by Marmont (*Mémoires*, 2:108–109) or these words written by General Treich in Marseille, under the law of 19 Brumaire: "Long live the Republic, more than ever!" The response was swift. Treich and several dozen other officers were dismissed (Lentz, *Le Grand Consulat*, 159–161). See also Thiry, *Le Coup d'état du 18 brumaire*, 200–202; Granger, "L'Opinion de l'armée au lendemain du 18 brumaire," 46–54; Picard, *Bonaparte et Moreau*, 43–49; and Bodinier, "Que veut l'armée? Soutien et résistance à Bonaparte," 65–87.

56 On public opinion and Brumaire, see M. Crook's recent study, *Napoleon Comes to Power*; and the studies collected by J.-P. Jessenne in *Du Directoire au Consulat*, vol. 3: *Brumaire*.

57 On 17 Brumaire, the *tiers consolidé* (public debt, of which only one-third was guaranteed) and *rente provisoire* were valued at 11 francs and 3.75 francs, and on 21 Brumaire at 16.38 and 6.75. The price then stablized at around 20 francs for the former and around 13 francs for the latter.

58 *Le Messager des relations extérieures*, quoted in Aulard, *Paris sous le Consulat*, 1:11–12.

59 See Roederer, *Oeuvres*, 6:396.

60 See Aulard, *Paris sous le Consulat*, 1:17.

61 Quoted in Madelin, *Histoire du Consulat et de l'Empire*, 3:26.

62 Address to the French people on November 12, 1799 (*Correspondance de Napoléon Ier*, no. 4391, 6:7).

63 It is true that it was immediately replaced by a war tax of 25 percent that was added to direct taxes and that, because it affected all taxpayers, "was no more pleasing to the people than the progressive loan had been popular among the well-off" (Lentz, *Le Grand Consulat*, 210).

64 *Gazette nationale ou le Moniteur universel*, 1799, 2:221. The law of 23 Messidor (1799) allowed officials concerned about political assassinations and uprisings to take hostages among nobles, the relatives of émigrés, and those related to the presumed guilty parties, holding them responsible for any resulting damage.

65 Cambacérès, *Mémoires*, 1:490.

66 Thibaudeau, *Le Consulat et l'Empire*, 1:115. On November 15 he also declared, in his response to a deputation of the civil tribunal of the Seine: "We must no longer see Jacobins, Terrorists, moderates, etc., but everywhere Frenchmen" (*Gazette nationale ou le Moniteur universel*, 1799, 2:218).

67 Quoted in Madelin, *Histoire du Consulat et de l'Empire*, 3:24.

68 Quoted in Aulard, *Paris sous le Consulat*, 1:42.

69 "Sur la fausseté de cette maxime: l'autorité qui recule est perdue," *Gazette nationale ou le Moniteur universel* (1799), 2:259.

70 Gourgaud, *Mémoires pour servir à l'histoire de France sous Napoléon*, 1:122.

71 *Gazette nationale ou le Moniteur universel*, 1799, 2:268, 2:258.

72 Lanfrey, *Histoire de Napoléon*, 2:13.

73 General Jourdan's name did not figure on the list that had been drawn up by the consuls as early as November 11 (Aulard, *Registre des délibérations du Consulat provisoire*, 7–8). It was no doubt added afterward, because the sequel proves that Jourdan was one of those proscribed.

74 Bonaparte later accused Sieyès; Cambacérès tells us that Fouché was the first to propose it (*Mémoires*, 1:444–445), and Fouché says that Sieyès asked him to draw up a list of suspects to be deported (*Memoirs*, 1:90–91).

75 Bourrienne, *Mémoires*, 3:133–134, 216.

76 Gourgaud, *Mémoires pour servir à l'histoire de France sous Napoléon*, 1:115–116.

77 Two ships, the *Syrène* and the *Mutine*, which were to take Victor Hugues to Guyana, where he was to serve as governor, were ordered to remain in Rochefort until the thirty-seven deportees arrived (Destrem, *Les Déportations*, 4–6).

78 Reprobation: See the press articles reproduced in Aulard, *Paris sous le Consulat*, 1:23–27. Names struck from the list notably included those of General Jourdan and Xavier Audouin, a judge on the final court of appeal (on the removal of Audouin's name, see *L'Ami des lois* for November 23, quoted in ibid., 1:16–17). For his part, Talleyrand got the name of Jorry, whom he had prosecuted the preceding summer, taken off the list (Lacour-Gayet, *Talleyrand*, 377–379). A counter-order was sent to Victor Hugues in Rochefort on November 22 (Destrem, *Les Déportations*, 6).

79 Vandal, *L'Avènement de Bonaparte*, 1:427.

80 *Correspondance générale*, no. 4771 (November 24, 1799), 2:1094.

81 Ibid., no. 4772 (to J.-F. Beyts, November 24, 1799), 2:1094–1095. A native of Bruges representing the department of the Lys, Beyts was named prefect of Loir-et-Cher on March 1, 1800.

82 Lentz, *Les Coups d'état de Napoléon Bonaparte*, 375.

83 We have different versions of Sieyès's plan: the document "dictated" to Boulay de la Meurthe (*Théorie constitutionnelle de Sieyès*), the outline found by Mignet (*Histoire de la Révolution française*, 2:640–643), the one sketched by Miot de Melito (*Mémoires*, 1:253–255), who said he had obtained it from Regnaud de Saint-Jean d'Angély, and the plan published in the *Moniteur* on December 1 (*Gazette nationale ou le Moniteur universel*, 1799, 2:276–277).

84 Boulay de la Meurthe, *Théorie constitutionnelle de Sieyès*, 40.

85 L. Bonaparte, *Mémoires*, 391.

86 Bastid, *Sieyès et sa pensée*, 254.

87 Roederer, *Oeuvres*, 3:303–304. Thibaudeau gives a different and more complete version of Bonaparte's objections: "The Great Elector, if he limits himself strictly to the functions you assign him, will be the shadow, but the disembodied shadow, of an idle king. Do you know anyone with a character low enough to take pleasure in such antics? . . . It is a great mistake to believe that the shadow of a thing can take the place of reality" (*Le Consulat et l'Empire*, 1:105–106).

88 Montholon, *Récits*, 2:475.

89 Thiers, *Histoire du Consulat et de l'Empire*, 1:94–95.

90 Boulay de la Meurthe, *Théorie constitutionnelle de Sieyès*, 58.

91 His plan has been published by Taillandier, *Documents biographiques sur P. C. F. Daunou*, 174–188.

92 Quoted in ibid., 171.

93 Quoted in Boulay de la Meurthe, *Théorie constitutionnelle de Sieyès*, 61.

94 Staël, *Considerations on the Principal Events of the French Revolution*, 2:15.

95 La Fayette, *Mémoires, correspondance et manuscrits*, 5:159.

96 *Gazette nationale ou le Moniteur universel*, 1799, 2:325–326.

97 Ibid., 2:330.

98 Bourrienne, *Mémoires*, 3:126.

99 This scene is described in comparable terms by La Révellière-Lépeaux, to whom it was recounted by Daunou and by Cambacérès (Vandal, *L'Avènement de Bonaparte*, 1:523).

24. First Steps

1 Furet, *La Révolution*, 222–223. For the position of third consul, Bonaparte hesitated between Le Couteulx de Canteleu, Crétet, Lebrun, Daunou, and Volney; Volney declined the job (Gaulmier, *L'Idéologue Volney*, 243). After consulting Cambacérès, Bonaparte asked Roederer for information on Lebrun, being particularly anxious to know whether he was easy to get along with (Roederer, *Oeuvres*, 3:304–306).

2 Gourgaud, *Journal*, 1:308.

3 It was through his mediation that a few weeks later Louis XVIII tried to enter into contact with Bonaparte. Long afterward, in 1812, the latter told Caulaincourt, advising him not to speak of it to anyone, that Lebrun, "a man who is naturally secretive, unhelpful, hard, and without affection," had been an agent of the Bourbons from the outset (Chrétienne, *Charles-François Lebrun*, 2:602–613).

4 Bourrienne, *Mémoires*, 3:221.

5 Thibaudeau, *Mémoires* (1913), 18; Pasquier, *Mémoires*, 1:239.

6 Quoted in Pinaud, *Cambacérès*, 134.

7 Molé, *Le Comte Molé*, 1:70.

8 Pinaud, *Cambacérès*, 91–99.

9 Quoted in Bory, *Les Cinq girouettes*, 151–152.

10 Chrétienne, *Charles-François Lebrun*, 2:568.

11 Barante, *Souvenirs*, 1:47.

12 Pinaud, *Cambacérès*, 121.

13 According to the *Gazette de France* (Aulard, *Paris sous le Consulat*, 1:55).

14 Article 41 establishes the powers exercised by the first consul alone, without his being obliged to consult his colleagues (the second and third consuls had only a consultative role): "The first consul promulgates the laws; he names and dismisses at will the members of the Council of State, the ministers, the ambassadors, and other leading external agents, the officers of the army and navy, the members of local administrations, and the commissioners of the government in the tribunals. He names all the civil and criminal judges other than the justices of the peace and the judges of appeal courts, without being able to dismiss them." Articles 44–47, 50, and 52 establish the government's powers: appointments, the proposal of laws, the convocation and adjournment of the assemblies, regulatory power, the declaration of war and the signature of peace treaties, and special powers in the event of a "conspiracy against the state."

15 Necker, *Dernières vues de politique et de finance*, 46–59.

16 Bertrand, *Cahiers*, 3:34.

17 For a total of sixty. The Senate was then to co-opt two new members a year for ten years, to reach the number of eighty senators in 1809 (Thiry, *Le Sénat de Napoléon*, 39–50).

18 Bonaparte would have preferred Volney, but the latter had refused, just as he subsequently refused the office of third consul (Guillois, *Le Salon de Madame Helvétius*, 136–137).

19 "Consuls provisoires," *Correspondance de Napoléon Ier*, 30:330; *Correspondance générale*, no. 4811 (to Laplace, December 24, 1799), 2:1113. Bonaparte is supposed to have initially asked the senators, on Joseph's advice, to name Lucien to the Tribunate, but then changed his mind on December 24 (Piétri, *Lucien Bonaparte*, 110–111). Lucien's name is not in the report drawn up by the Senate on December 24 (*Archives parlementaires*, 2nd ser., 1:8–9).

20 When Roederer asked him why he hadn't intervened, he replied: "I don't know enough men capable of forming a good majority, and I didn't want to be involved in a bad composition" (Roederer, *Oeuvres*, 3:330).

21 See Chabaud-Latour's testimony, quoted in Dutruch, *Le Tribunat*, 29–30.

22 "Sur les nouveaux coureurs de bénéfices," *Gazette nationale ou le Moniteur universel*, December 23, 1799, 2:369.

23 Of 60 senators, 37 were former representatives, 26 of whom had been members of the Directory's councils; 279 out of 300 representatives in the Legislative Body—of the remaining 21 representatives, 4 were relatives of Bonaparte, one of Sieyès, and 7 others were members of the Institut—and 74 out of 100 tribunes (Brotonne, *Les Sénateurs du Consulat et de l'Empire*, 1–58; Chevallier, *Histoire des institutions*, 108; Collins, *Napoleon and His Parliaments*, 18–20; Halperin, "La composition du Corps législatif," 40–42). If we add up the members of the three assemblies, former representatives from the period of the Directory occupied 75 percent of the seats, and 85 percent if the members of the earlier assemblies are included.

24 On the creation of the Council of State in 1799, the projects assigned to Sieyès and the changes introduced by Bonaparte, who was particularly eager to avoid a Council that had its own powers, see Durand, *Études sur le Conseil d'État napoléonien*, 58–61; also see, more recently, *Le Conseil d'État*, 1–32.

25 See the lists reproduced in Bourrienne, *Mémoires*, 3:134–161.

26 Woloch, *Napoleon and His Collaborators*, 36–45.

27 Molé, *Le Comte Molé*, 1:53.

28 Thibaudeau, *Mémoires* (1913), 45. Bonaparte is supposed to have told Roederer, who would have liked to wear a senator's garb: "The senate's a tomb . . . just good enough for men who have finished their careers, or who want to write books," and he had him join the Council (Roederer, *Bonaparte me disait*, 13).

29 1 Vendémiaire was the anniversary of the foundation of the Republic, and fell, depending on the year, on either September 21 or September 22. The holidays of January 21 (the execution of Louis XVI), August 10 (the fall of the monarchy), 9 Thermidor, and 18 Fructidor were thus abolished. "We celebrate a victory," Bonaparte had declared, "but we weep over the victims, even if they are our enemies. The holiday of January 21 is immoral. Without judging whether the death of Louis XVI was just or unjust, politic or impolitic, useful or useless, and even in the event that it would be judged just, politic, and useful, it would nonetheless be a misfortune. In such circumstances, forgetting is what is best" ("Consuls provisoires," *Correspondance de Napoléon Ier*, 30:336–337).

30 Thibaudeau, *Le Consulat et l'Empire*, 1:117.

31 Vandal, *L'Avènement de Bonaparte*, 2:30.

32 *Archives parlementaires*, 2nd ser., 1:17 (session of January 3, 1800).

33 Bourrienne, *Mémoires*, 3:243–244.

34 Guillois, *La Marquise de Condorcet*, 172.

35 In an article that was probably written by Bonaparte, published on February 4, 1801, in Roederer's *Journal de Paris* (quoted in Guillois, *Le Salon de Madame Helvétius*, 157).

36 *Archives parlementaires*, 2nd ser., 2:31.

37 Her unpublished work was titled *Des circonstances actuelles qui peuvent terminer la Révolution*. After 18 Brumaire she attempted to influence the constitutional debate by republishing part of Necker's book (*De la Révolution française*) under the title *Examen de la Constitution de l'an III, extrait du dernier ouvrage de M. Necker.*

38 Staël, *Dix années d'exil*, 217.

39 Ibid., 219–220.

40 See Staël, *Correspondance générale*, 4:250n3.

41 See ibid., 255–257.

42 His first impulse had been to tell Miot de Melito, a member of the Tribunate: "My enemies deserve nothing from me but steel" (Miot de Melito, *Memoirs*, 161).

43 Staël, *Dix années d'exil*, 221–222. She retired to her estate in Saint-Ouen. Sieyès, about whom it was said that he was not uninvolved in these incidents, was also sent into exile (Bredin, *Sieyès*, 497–498). The *Moniteur*, which had by that date become the government's official organ, denied that this was so, its editor stating that Sieyès, far from having been exiled, had gone to the home of his friend Clément de Ris "to seek a few days of rest in the country that were necessary for his health" (*Gazette nationale ou le Moniteur universel*, 1800, 1:443).

44 "I shall honor the Republic in the man who governs it," he had said, adding: "having praised up to now only virtue proscribed, I shall show a new kind of courage, that of praising a genius at the heart of power and victory" (*Archives parlementaires*, 2nd ser., 1:35).

45 See in particular his speech of January 5 on the necessity of promising fidelity to the Constitution (ibid., 23–24, and Girardin, *Discours et opinions, journal et souvenirs*, 1:89–93).

46 About thirty, Thibaudeau concluded after making a detailed study of the votes during the legislative session of 1800 (*Mémoires sur le Consulat*, 191–197).

47 Lanfrey, *Histoire de Napoléon*, 2:97.

48 Lacretelle, *Dix années d'épreuves*, 228; Thibaudeau, *Le Consulat et l'Empire*, 1:132–133.

49 *Gazette nationale ou le Moniteur universel*, 1800, 1:417–418; *Journal de Paris*, January 5, 1800 (Roederer, *Oeuvres*, 6:399).

50 Vandal, *L'Avènement de Bonaparte*, 2:53.

51 Mollien, *Mémoires*, 1:255–256.

52 Trinkle, *The Napoleonic Press*.

53 Necker, *Dernières vues de politique et de finance*, 66–67.

54 Staël, *Considérations sur la Révolution française*, 356.

55 Bourrienne, *Mémoires*, 3:214.

56 "Somehow I came to speak with him about the Constitution that he had just given France," wrote the royalist Andigné, whom Bonaparte had received at the Luxembourg. "'The Constitution!,' he said, laughing. He made it sufficiently clear, by the way in which he replied, that he had presented a Constitution to the public only in order to occupy his leisure time, and that he reserved the right to violate it any time his self-interest made him think it appropriate to do so" (quoted in Fierro, *Les Français vus par eux-mêmes: Le Consulat et l'Empire*, 199, from the *Mémoires du comte d'Andigné*, 1:414–429).

57 Bourrienne, *Mémoires*, 3:214.

58 The formula is Paul Valéry's, *Oeuvres*, 1:549.

59 On December 25.

60 Langlois, "Le plébiscite de l'an VIII et le coup d'État du 18 pluviôse an VIII," 60–61; Crook, "Confiance d'en bas, manipulation d'en haut."

61 Number for January 10, 1800, quoted in Langlois, "Le plébiscite," 55.

62 Chateaubriand, *Voyage en Amérique* (1827), quoted in Chateaubriand, *De l'Ancien Regime au Nouveau Monde: Écrits politique*, 95–98.

63 Las Cases, *Mémorial*, 1:250–251.

64 Baczko, *Politiques de la Révolution française*, 608.

65 Fontanes, *Oeuvres*, 1:xvi.

66 Madelin, *Histoire du Consulat et de l'Empire*, 4:95–96.

67 Fontanes, *Oeuvres*, 2:151.

68 Ibid., 2:155.

69 Ibid.

70 Ibid., 2:160.

71 Thiers, *History of the Consulate and the Empire of France under Napoleon*, 1:121.

72 Cambacérès, *Mémoires*, 1:470–471.

73 Quoted in Cabanis, *Le Sacre de Napoléon*, 43. All the graffiti were not removed. For a long time one could read these words on one of the guardhouses at the Place du Carrousel: "On August 10, 1792, the monarchy was abolished: it will never rise again" (Norvins, *Histoire de Napoléon*, 2:53).

74 Vandal, *L'Avènement de Bonaparte*, 2:150–151.

75 Bourrienne, *Mémoires*, 4:3.

76 Quoted in Cabanis, *Le Sacre de Napoléon*, 32.

25. From the Tuileries to Marengo

1 *Correspondance de Napoléon Ier*, no. 4422 (to the French, December 15, 1799), 6:25.

2 See Lentz, "Les consuls de la République: *La Révolution est finie*," 19–37, and the clarification published in the *Moniteur* for January 15, 1800 (*Gazette nationale ou le Moniteur universel*, 1800, 1:456–457).

3 *Correspondance de Napoléon Ier*, no. 4447 (to the French, December 25, 1799), 6:37–38.

4 He had told Roederer, who was assigned to write the proclamation on the basis of the outline Bonaparte had given him: "I have two comments to make; first, you have me promise, and I don't want to make any promises, because I'm not sure I can keep them. Second, you have me promise for the near future; and there are many things for which my ten years will hardly be enough" (Roederer, *Journal*, 6).

5 Though he does not mention the word "peace" in his address to the French people, he mentions it explicitly in his proclamation "to French soldiers" issued on the same day: "Soldiers! By promising the French people peace, I have been your spokesman" (*Correspondance de Napoléon Ier*, no. 4449, 6:38). "accepted . . . responsibility": See Bonaparte's initial dictation and Roederer's draft, which Bonaparte rewrote, in Roederer, *Oeuvres*, 3:328–329. The text composed by Roederer, without differing in content, was more precise and detailed in form.

6 Driault, *Napoléon et l'Europe*, 1:16–23.

7 See Sorel, *L'Europe et la Révolution française*, 6:22–23.

8 Ibid., 6:20.

9 *Correspondance de Napoléon Ier*, no. 4449 (December 25, 1799), 6:38.

10 Ibid., no. 4447 (December 25, 1799), 6:37.

11 Ibid., no. 4649, 6:170–171.

12 Quotation in ibid., 6:9. Out of a theoretical strength of 150,000 men, the Army of Italy had only 28,000 ready to fight (Masséna, *Mémoires*, 6:32–34).

13 *Correspondance de Napoléon Ier*, no. 4482 (to the Burgermaster and Senate of Hamburg, December 30, 1799), 6:58–59. See "Consuls provisoires," ibid., 30:335–336. Hamburg hastened to offer 4.5 million francs to avoid more serious sanctions (see the note Bonaparte sent Talleyrand on January 13, 1800 [ibid., no. 4520, 6:84]). Bourrienne says that part of this sum served to pay off Joséphine's debts and the rest was distributed to those close to Bonaparte (Bourrienne, *Mémoires*, 4:22–34).

14 Quoted in Thibaudeau, *Le Consulat et l'Empire*, 1:168.

15 Kérautret, *Histoire de la Prusse*, 262.

16 The order to retreat had been signed on October 23, 1799.

17 Petrov, "Paul Ier et Napoléon Bonaparte," 247.

18 See the report of an agent named Guttin, dated October 15, 1799, and quoted in Sorel, *L'Europe et la Révolution française*, 6:29–31.

19 *Correspondance générale*, no. 4815 (to Francis II, December 25, 1799), 2:1114–1115; no. 4817 (to George III), 2:1115–1116.

20 Bourrienne, *Mémoires*, 3:183; Gaudin, *Supplément aux mémoires*, 124–128.

21 Driault, *Napoléon et l'Europe*, 1:36.

22 Quoted in Lanfrey, *The History of Napoleon the First*, 1:398. Contacts were broken off in late January 1800.

23 Cambacérès, *Mémoires*, 1:474.

24 Talleyrand, *Memoirs of the Prince de Talleyrand*, 1:209.

25 Lacretelle, *Dix années d'épreuves*, 229.

26 The fund's full name was "Caisse de garantie et d'amortissement" ("Guarantee and Amortization Fund"), and it was entrusted with (1) receiving from the tax collectors-general the guarantees in cash intended to guarantee the bonds that they subscribed for the amount of the taxes to be collected; and (2) amortizing the public debt by redeeming annuity bonds on the stock exchange to make them inalienable (Tulard, *Dictionnaire Napoléon*, 1:347–348). The fiscal administration was created on November 24, the Amortization Fund on November 27, the Bank of France on February 13, 1800, the prefectoral administration on February 17, and the new judicial system on March 18.

27 See Lentz, *Le Grand Consulat*, 195, 357.

28 Gaudin, *Mémoires*, 1:285.

29 Mirabeau, *Entre le roi et la Révolution*, 58–59 (note dated July 3, 1790).

30 Mirabeau acknowledges this in his long note of December 23, 1790, entitled "Survey of the Situation of France and of the Ways of Reconciling Public Liberty with Royal Authority" (ibid., 173–231).

31 See Branda, *Le Prix de la gloire*, 208–209.

32 Remarks made by Bonaparte and reported in Jullien, *Entretien politique sur la situation actuelle de la France*, 42.

33 Branda, *Le Prix de la gloire*, 210.

34 Constitution of Year VIII, articles 60–68.

35 Napoleon defined very well in what way the prefectoral system could be compared with the administration under absolutism and in what way it differed from it: see Las Cases, *Mémorial*, 4:526–527.

36 Marx, *The Holy Family* (Moscow: Foreign Languages, 1956), 166.

37 Ibid.

38 See Garcia de Enterria, *Révolution française et administration contemporaine*, 36n.

39 Ardant, "Napoléon et le rendement des services publics," 181.

40 Lentz, *La Conspiration du général Malet*.

41 See Jourdan, *L'Empire de Napoléon*, 86–88.

42 Tocqueville, *The Ancien Régime and the French Revolution*, 177.

43 Quoted in García de Enterria, *Révolution française et administration contemporaine*, 36n.

44 Vandal, *L'Avènement de Bonaparte*, 2:194–195; Aulard, *Napoléon, 1800–1815*, pp. 1–38; Taine, *The Origins of Contemporary France*, 2:121.

45 See Poussou, "Les conséquences financières et économiques de la guerre d'indépendance américaine pour les royaumes de France et de Grande-Bretagne."

46 England's population was 9 million, France's 28 million.

47 In Year VIII, tax collections in cash did not exceed 113 million francs, out of 266 million to be collected, and it took eighteen months to collect the taxes for this fiscal year (Marion, *Histoire financière de la France*, 4:181–183).

48 Gaudin, *Notice historique sur les finances*, 81–82, 23–44.

49 Marion, *Histoire financière de la France*, 4:173–174.

50 With regard to the suppliers, whom Bonaparte had seen trafficking in everything when he was commanding the Army of Italy, he felt an aversion that was not unrelated to "the popular hatred for men in finance": from this point of view, Bonaparte remained a man of 1793 (Mollien, *Mémoires*, 1:360–361).

51 The order is dated January 27, 1800.

52 Wolff, *Le Financier Ouvrard*, 69–78. According to Ouvrard, it was Lebrun who got the first consul to promise to find an arrangement with him. Bonaparte is supposed to have planned to have him transported to Marseille to be judged by a military commission and shot (*Mémoires*, 1:25–58). Ouvrard also promised to contribute to the financing of the next campaign.

53 Bainville, *Napoléon*, 217.

54 Machiavelli, *Discourses*, in *The Prince and the Discourses* (New York: Random House / Modern Library, 1950), chap. 10, p. 141.

55 Bourrienne, *Mémoires*, 4:40.

56 Gabory, *Napoléon et la Vendée*, 3:68.

57 Chassin, *Les Pacifications de l'Ouest*, 3:444–445.

58 D'Andigné's *Mémoires*, quoted in Fierro, *Les Français vus par eux-mêmes*, 195–200.

59 Hyde de Neuville, *Mémoires*, 1:270–273.

60 Ibid.

61 *Correspondance générale*, no. 4823 (to the inhabitants of the departments of the West, December 28, 1799), 2:1118–1119. Before leaving Paris, d'Andigné decided to make one last attempt and wrote to Bonaparte to beg him to "restore to the throne of his fathers the legitimate heir of the unfortunate Louis XVI" (Fierro, *Les Français vus par eux-mêmes*, 202). The first consul sent him a reply that, though polite, was a flat refusal (*Correspondance générale*, no. 4826 [December 30, 1799], 2:1122).

62 *Correspondance générale*, no. 4872 (to Brune, January 14, 1800), 3:39.

63 Thiébault, *Mémoires*, 3:346.

64 "Consuls provisoires," *Correspondance de Napoléon Ier*, 30:339.

65 Mathieu, *Le Concordat de 1801*, 50–51.

66 Hyde de Neuville, *Mémoires*, 1:300–302; Barras, *Memoirs*, 4:73–80.

67 No document testifies to the presence of Frotté at the École militaire (La Sicotière, *Louis de Frotté*, 1:563).

68 *Correspondance générale*, no. 4944 (to Brune, February 8, 1800), 3:74.

69 Madelin, *Histoire du Consulat et de l'Empire*, 3:190–191.

70 "big Breton": *Correspondance générale*, no. 5046 (to Brune, March 5, 1800), 3:121.

71 Thiers, *History of the Consulate and the Empire of France under Napoleon*, 1:118. Thiers is taking his inspiration from the account of the meeting between Napoleon and Las Cases (*Mémorial*, 2:690).

72 On Saint Helena, however, Bonaparte said that he was thinking of entrusting the Army of the Rhine to Moreau only long enough for Desaix to return from Egypt (in accordance with the capitulation signed by Kléber on January 4), because he had decided at the outset to give the latter the direction of operations in Germany (Bertrand, *Cahiers*, 2:231).

73 Las Cases, *Mémorial*, 1:258. Other reasons for the transfer of Masséna to Italy: First of all, Napoleon said, the choice of Masséna to head the Army of Italy was obvious because he "knew perfectly the valleys of the Appenines ("Marengo," *Correspondance de Napoléon Ier*, 30:397); and then, he said, "the true reason that made me send Moreau to the Rhine after 18 Brumaire and Masséna to Genoa, was that Masséna had not been happy about 18 Brumaire, that he had people around him who were very supportive of the Directory and a little Jacobin, and that his transfer cut all these ties that could be dangerous" (Bertrand, *Cahiers*, 2:373).

74 Thiers, *History of the Consulate and the Empire of France under Napoleon*, 1:132–133.

75 *Correspondance générale*, no. 4786 (to Clarke, head of the cartographic service), 2:1102. The first orders were issued on January 7, followed on the twenty-fifth by more precise instructions regarding the composition and the assembly points of the reserve army (ibid., no. 4903 [to Berthier], 3:54–56), at the time when the disturbances in the west would end in a matter of days, and finally, on March 1, by detailed instructions.

76 *Correspondance de Napoléon Ier*, no. 4651, 6:172.

77 Cugnac, *Campagne de l'armée de réserve*, 1:37–85; "Marengo," *Correspondance de Napoléon Ier*, 30:371.

78 See *Correspondance générale*, no. 2271 (to the Directory, November 26, 1797), 1:1311; and Reinhard, *Le Grand Carnot*, 2:241–245.

79 Gourgaud, *Talks of Napoleon at St. Helena*, 235.

80 "Marengo," *Correspondance de Napoléon Ier*, 30:399–400. Napoléon emphasizes the advantages of crossing the Rhine at Schaffhausen in "Événements des six premiers mois de 1799," ibid., 30:249.

81 See *Correspondance générale*, no. 4804 (to Moreau, December 21, 1799), 2:1109, and the letter in which Moreau writes to Bonaparte, at the same time: "The emperor will sue for peace when we are masters of Bavaria rather than the Cisalpine" (quoted in Picard, *Bonaparte et Moreau*, 143).

82 "It is not impossible, if things continue to go well here," he wrote to Moreau on March 1, "that I might join you for a few days" (*Correspondance générale*, no. 5033, 3:115).

83 "Marengo," *Correspondance de Napoléon Ier*, 30:368. It should be noted that the Constitution of Year VIII does not mention this incompatibility, which was nonetheless implicit in the nature of things, as Napoleon admits.

84 Ibid.

85 The *Moniteur* even had to print a formal denial (*Gazette nationale ou le Moniteur universel*, 1799, 2:357).

86 Chandler, *The Campaigns of Napoleon*, 266.

87 Lanfrey, *The History of Napoleon the First*, 2:14.

88 On March 8 (Picard, *Bonaparte et Moreau*, 156).

89 *Correspondance*, no. 4695, 6:203–204. According to Cugnac, this document was dated March 22, 1800, by mistake. He says it was written and annotated by Dessolles on March 15 (*Campagne de l'armée de réserve*, 1:93–94). See also "Marengo," *Correspondance*, 30:400; and Picard, *Bonaparte et Moreau*, 159–178.

90 As early as February, as is shown by a "Note sur la campagne prochaine" dated February 18 and written by Bourrienne, which mentions the reserve army's entrance into Italy "through Bellinzona, straight toward Milan, in the course of May" (*Correspondance*, no. 4605, 6:137–138). David Chandler favors mid-March (*The Campaigns of Napoleon*, 267).

91 Thiers, *History of the Consulate and the Empire of France under Napoleon*, 1:148. On March 20, Talleyrand reported Bonaparte's new arrangements to the Prussian ambassador, who hastened to inform the Austrians, who did nothing (Picard, *Bonaparte et Moreau*, 178).

92 See *Correspondance de Napoléon Ier*, no. 4694 ("Plan de campagne pour l'armée du Rhin," March 22, 1800), 6:201–203; no. 4695 (to Moreau, March 22), 6:203–204.

93 *Correspondance générale*, no. 5032 (to Berthier, March 1, 1800), 3:113–114.

94 Thibaudeau, *Le Consulat et l'Empire*, 1:261–262. See also Chandler's comments in *The Campaigns of Napoleon*, 269–270.

95 See Picard, *Bonaparte et Moreau*, 210–212.

96 *Correspondance générale*, no. 5245 (May 5, 1800), 3:216.

97 Ibid., no. 5157 (April 1, 1800), 3:168–170.

98 The Austrians seized Mont Cenis on April 8. Soult succeeded in rejoining Masséna in Genoa in early May.

99 "Défense de Gênes par Masséna," *Correspondance de Napoléon Ier*, 30:354–355.

100 *Correspondance générale*, no. 5195 (to Carnot, April 24, 1800), 3:187; no. 5197 (to Moreau, April 24), 3:188.

101 Thiers, *History of the Consulate and the Empire of France under Napoleon*, 1:192. Moreau entered Augsburg on May 28, and Munich the next day.

102 He reproached him for having taken a whole week to cross the Rhine, which gave Kray time to recover; of not having exploited the victory Lecourbe won at Stockach on the third to deal the enemy a death blow; of not having taken advantage, on the sixth, of the fact that part of Kray's army had gone over to the left bank of the Danube at Sigmaringen, to attack and destroy the other half that had remained on the right bank; and finally, of having given up the opportunity to seize Ulm: "That is what happens to generals who are irresolute and act without principles and without plans," he concluded. "Half measures, *mezzo termine*, lose everything in war" ("Marengo," *Correspondance de Napoléon Ier*, 30:401–404, 410–413, quotation at 412). He also said that the campaign of 1800 showed him how exaggerated Moreau's reputation was: "a poor man," "a good division general, a nice fellow capable of leading fifteen or twenty thousand men," who "spent his days smoking and laughing with his aides-de-camp" (Bertrand, *Cahiers*, 1:117–118).

103 Thiers, *History of the Consulate and the Empire of France under Napoleon*, 1:193–194.

104 *Correspondance de Napoléon Ier*, no. 4754, 6:254; the "Basel agreement" is cited in Picard, *Bonaparte et Moreau*, 208.

105 Quoted in ibid., 239.

106 On January 31, Duroc had gone to Switzerland on a mission to reconnoiter the outposts and ways of entering Italy (*Correspondance générale*, no. 4915 [to Moreau, January 31, 1800], 3:61).

107 On the choice of the Splügen Pass, see the "Note pour l'approvisionnement de la réserve" dictated to Bourrienne on February 18 (*Correspondance de Napoléon Ier*, no. 4605, 6:137–138).

108 *Correspondance générale*, no. 5033 (to Moreau, March 1, 1800), 3:115. Note that he mentions the Great Saint Bernard Pass as early as the fifth, in a letter to Masséna (ibid., no. 5048, 3:122–123).

109 See his instructions of March 1 (ibid., no. 5032, 3:113–114).

110 Cugnac, *Campagne de l'armée de réserve*, 1:197–198. See *Correspondance générale*, no. 5206 (to Berthier, April 27, 1800), 3:195; no. 5220 (to Berthier, May 1), 3:202; no. 5229 (to Berthier, May 4), 3:209–210 (in which Bonaparte mentions the possibility of Masséna's capitulation in Genoa).

111 See the report by second lieutenant Tourné on the passes in the Valais, dated March 31, 1800, and reproduced in Cugnac, *Campagne de l'armée de réserve*, 1:99–108, esp. 104–105; and that of Marescot, quoted in Thiers, *History of the Consulate and the Empire of France under Napoleon*, 1:201–202.

112 Bourrienne situates this scene on March 17, and thus at a time when Bonaparte was far from having chosen the Saint Bernard Pass. It cannot have taken place before the end of April, as is indicated by Bourrienne's reference to the siege of Genoa (Bourrienne, *Mémoires*, 4:85–87).

113 "Marengo," *Correspondance de Napoléon Ier*, 30:371.

114 Botta, *Histoire d'Italie*, 4:293–294.

115 The pass is 2,472 meters high, and Martigny is only 469 meters above sea level, Aosta 583 meters.

116 The artillery included about sixty pieces, howitzers and cannons firing four-, eight-, and twelve-pound balls. The cannons weighed more than two tons (Künzi, *Bicentenaire du passage des Alpes*, 12–15).

117 Cugnac, *Campagne de l'armée de réserve*, 1:421.

118 "falling down in the snow": Bulletin of the reserve army (May 24, 1800), quoted in ibid., 1:512.

119 Stendhal, *Aux âmes sensibles*, 26. After having crossed the summit of the pass, he is supposed to have cried, "The Saint Bernard, is that all it is?" (Stendhal, *Vie de Henry Brulard*, 420).

120 Bertrand, *Cahiers*, 2:352. The account of Hannibal's crossing of the Alps is found in Livy's *History of Rome*, bk. 21, chaps. 23–38.

121 Bertrand, *Cahiers*, 2:287; Gourgaud, *Journal*, 2:336.

122 Thiers, *History of the Consulate and the Empire of France under Napoleon*, 1:202. David Chandler claims, on the contrary, that the operation was risky, or would have been had the Austrians been less preoccupied with the outcome of the siege of Genoa and reacted sooner than they did (*The Campaigns of Napoleon*, 276–277).

123 See in particular his note to Berthier, written on May 22 at 11 P.M. (*Correspondance générale*, no. 5353, 3:265).

124 On May 19, having learned that Lannes had not been able to get past the obstacle, he wrote: "This position is on the point of requiring a prompt decision regarding the fate of the army." The next day he mentions again the possibility of a necessary "retrograde movement" of the whole army if it proved impossible to take the fort of Bard (letters quoted in Cugnac, *Campagne de l'armée de réserve*, 1:437, 440).

125 Marmont, *Mémoires*, 2:117–121.

126 *Correspondance générale*, no. 5366 (May 24, 1800), 3:272.

127 Napoleon later explained his success by the Austrians' lack of foresight (Gourgaud, *Journal de Sainte-Hélène*, 2:336).

128 Chandler, *The Campaigns of Napoleon*, 277. See Neipperg, *Aperçu militaire de la bataille de Marengo*, 4.

129 *Correspondance générale*, no. 5398 (to Carnot, June 4, 1800), 3:283.

130 Ibid., no. 5346 (to Moncey), 3:260–261.

131 "You are in a difficult position," he recognizes in a letter to Masséna written on May 14; but he adds: "What reassures me is that you are in Genoa: it is in cases like these that you find that one man is worthy 20,000" (ibid., no. 5300, 3:240).

132 See the accusations made by General Thiébault, *Mémoires*, 3:90–91.

133 Out of the 70,000 Austrian troops who had crossed the Apennines, there remained no more than 40,000 (Thiers, *History of the Consulate and the Empire of France under Napoleon*, 1:228).

134 1,500 soldiers from the Genoa garrison were evacuated by sea along with Masséna, and landed in Antibes; 8,500 more who had left the city with their weapons and were heading for the French border met Suchet's troops within a few days ("Défense de Gênes par Masséna" and "Marengo," *Correspondance de Napoléon Ier*, 30:366, 380).

135 Thiers, *History of the Consulate and the Empire of France under Napoleon*, 1:233.

136 Ibid., 1:233–234.

137 "Marengo," *Correspondance de Napoléon Ier*, 30:380.

138 On Saint Helena, Bonaparte still had very harsh things to day about Masséna, stating that he had committed an error by allowing the Austrians to cut his army in two and throw it back on Genoa, and that once he was under siege he could have hung on for ten additional days with his 16,000 men (who were no more than 8,000, in reality), even if in order to do so he had had to seize the slender rations distributed to the city's people: "A few old men, a few women would have died, but after all, he would have held onto Genoa." He reproached Masséna for having allowed the evacuation by ship of 1,500 survivors, "in order to save his stash" (Gourgaud, *Journal*, 2:449). Regarding Masséna, after having evacuated Genoa he said: "I've had enough of that little devil for a long time" (Thiébault, *Mémoires*, 3:116).

139 "I do not yet see how M. Melas will get out of this: either he will attack Stradella, and he will be defeated and doomed . . . or he will pass over the Po, the Sesia, and the Ticino, and he will not achieve a better result" (*Correspondance générale*, no. 5430 [June 9, 1800], 3:299).

140 At this time the reserve army consisted of 58,000 men, of which 28,000 were on the main front (Chandler, *The Campaigns of Napoleon*, 288).

141 He had lost about 4,000 men in this engagement (Neipperg, *Aperçu militaire sur la bataille de Marengo*, 6).

142 Chandler, *The Campaigns of Napoleon*, 289–290.

143 Neipperg, *Aperçu militaire sur la bataille de Marengo*, 6.

144 Ibid., 13.

145 Ibid., 14.

146 Bourrienne, *Mémoires*, 4:124.

147 M. Dumas, *Souvenirs*, 3:182.

148 Berthier, *Relation de la bataille de Marengo*, 41.

149 Ibid., 44. Napoleon said later that he had told Desaix, who had just arrived and was skeptical about the likelihood of success, that he was, on the contrary, certain that they would win a victory (Las Cases, *Mémorial*, 3:252).

150 Botta, *Histoire d'Italie*, 4:319.

151 *Bulletin de l'armée de réserve* of June 15 (*Correspondance de Napoléon Ier*, no. 4910, 6:361). See also Berthier, *Relation de la bataille de Marengo*, 48; and "Marengo," *Correspondance de Napoléon Ier*, 30:389.

152 Botta, *Histoire d'Italie*, 4:323.

153 Thibaudeau, *Le Consulat et l'Empire*, 1:319.

154 *Correspondance*, no. 4911–4912, 6:362–365.

155 Quoted in Vandal, *L'Avènement de Bonaparte*, 2:450.

26. Works and Days

1 *Correspondance générale*, no. 5476 (to Lucien, June 29, 1800), 3:319.

2 Botta, *Histoire d'Italie*, 4:326.

3 *Correspondance générale*, no. 5440 (to Francis II, June 16, 1800), 3:305.

4 The proposed law allowed parents to double the share of the inheritance of one of their children, thus challenging the principle of strictly equal inheritances, without reestablishing primogeniture.

5 Quoted in Kitchin, *Un journal "philosophique": La Décade*, 71.

6 See Thiers, *Histoire du Consulat et de l'Empire*, 1:167–168; and Roederer's report of the discussions (*Oeuvres complètes*, 3:396–399).

7 Thibaudeau, *Mémoires* (1913), 35.

8 More precisely, the commission made proposals that it transmitted, through the Ministry of Justice, to the first consul, the only person authorized to sign orders of deregistration.

9 La Tour du Pin, *Journal d'une femme de cinquante ans*, 2:217. This commission had been created on March 18, 1800. On July 18, overwhelmed by complaints regarding its laxity and venality, Bonaparte sharply reprimanded the minister of justice (*Correspondance générale*, no. 5535 [to Abrial], 3:343–344).

10 Chastenay, *Deux révolutions*, 358.

11 The list of émigrés, which included almost 150,000 names, had been declared closed starting on December 25, 1799.

12 That is what he told Marc-Antoine Jullien on the day after 18 Brumaire; Jullien had come to ask him what his intentions were (Jullien, *Entretien politique sur la situation actuelle de la France*, 71–72).

13 Quoted in Madelin, *Histoire du Consulat et de l'Empire*, 1:301.

14 Bourrienne, *Mémoires*, 3:216, 220–221; Cambacérès, *Mémoires*, 1:494. See also Chastenay, *Deux révolutions*, 358–359.

15 Napoleon never ceased to repeat that he had imposed this policy despite the repugnance of most of his closest associates (see, for example, Las Cases, *Mémorial*, 2:604–605, 3:33–35).

16 Quoted by G. de Diesbach, "Émigration," in Tulard, *Dictionnaire Napoléon*, 1:717–718.

17 See Thibaudeau, *Mémoires* (1913), 35–36.

18 Letter of May 2, 1800, to Dupont de Nemours (Staël, *Correspondance générale*, 4:271).

19 Thibaudeau, *Mémoires* (1913), 20.

20 Masson, *Napoléon et sa famille*, 1:335.

21 Ibid.; Piétri, *Lucien Bonaparte*, 113–114. Thibaudeau assures us that the matter had gone far beyond simple discussions, and that a plot involving Bernadotte and Lucien had been woven and was to break out the day after Bonaparte left to rejoin the army. He says that the matter was covered up (*Mémoires* [1913], 22–23). Miot de Melito mentions these "rumors" in his memoirs (1:281–282).

22 In May 1800 (see Tulard, *Joseph Fouché*, 122–125).

23 Hyde de Neuville, after the failure of his discussions with Bonaparte, had decided to memorialize in his own way the anniversary of the death of Louis XVI. On the morning of January 21 the Madeleine had been hung with black crepe and the king's testament distributed in Paris.

24 See *Correspondance générale*, no. 5297 (to Fouché, May 14, 1800), 3:239; no. 5333 (May 18), 3:255; and no. 5365 (May 24), 3:271.

25 Girardin, who was a member of the Institute, left a kind of record of these discussions, which he says began as soon as Bonaparte left to go back to the army, and thus long before the rumors of June 20 regarding a defeat in Italy (*Discours et opinions, journal et souvenirs*, 3:175–188). See also Miot de Melito, *Mémoires*, 1:290–301.

26 The philosopher Helvétius's widow died shortly afterward, on August 13.

27 Thiry, *Marengo*, 156.

28 Bourrienne, *Mémoires*, 4:165–166.

29 The *Courrier de Londres*, the émigré's newspaper, mentions the latter in its number for July 1 (see Roederer, *Oeuvres*, 4:411).

30 Joseph Bonaparte contested its authenticity; quoted in Boulos, *Bourrienne et ses erreurs*, 1:268.

31 Senator Clément de Ris was kidnapped on September 23, 1800. According to a legend popularized by Balzac's novel *Une ténébreuse affaire*, Fouché organized a break-in at his friend's château in the Tours area to recover these compromising documents, but his agents had been excessively zealous and kidnapped the senator, seeking afterward to make it look like a crime motivated by financial gain. Historians are in general agreement that it was a criminal kidnapping organized by former *chouans* who were trying, contrary to the thesis made famous by Balzac, to give their crime a political appearance (Rinn, *Un mystérieux enlèvement*; Hauterive, *L'Enlèvement du sénateur Clément de Ris*). On the other hand, Paul Gaffarel thought Balzac had been acting as a historian in accusing Fouché ("L'Affaire Clément de Ris," 704–714).

32 Fouché, *Memoirs*, 1:108.

33 The police directed by Fouché, the services of prefecture directed by Dubois (since the creation of this office on February 17, 1800), the Central Office belonging to the department of

the Seine, the police of the general staff of the fortress (Lefebvre), the police for which Duroc was responsible at the Tuileries (Tulard, *Joseph Fouché*, 121–146), and, Fouché adds, Lucien's police at the Ministry of the Interior (Fouché, *Mémoires*, 1:191).

34 Constant Wairy, *Mémoires intimes*, 1:116–117.

35 Did he suspect Cambacérès of wanting to take his place? A report by the Prussian agent Sandoz-Rollin suggests he did, but nothing proves it (Metzger, "Cambacérès," 551–552).

36 Cambacérès, *Mémoires*, 1:524.

37 Ibid.

38 Bastid, *Sieyès et sa pensée*, 270.

39 Fouché, *Memoirs*, 1:109.

40 Ibid., 107–108.

41 Vandal, *L'Avènement de Bonaparte*, 2:441.

42 Sorel, *L'Europe et la Révolution française*, 6:51.

43 *Correspondance générale*, no. 5625 (to Carnot), 3:379–380.

44 Reinhard, *Le Grand Carnot*, 2:266–269. Berthier being absent, Lacuée took over in the interim.

45 See Thiers, *History of the Consulate and the Empire of France under Napoleon*, 1:263. The Marquise de La Tour du Pin was almost the only person to refer to "the cool reception the people of Paris...gave the news of the Battle of Marengo" (*Journal d'une femme de cinquante ans*, 2:220). Pasquier, on the contrary, speaks in his memoirs of an enthusiasm "at its height" (*Mémoires*, 1:152).

46 Fouché, *Memoirs*, 1:106.

47 Staël, *Dix années d'exil*, 228.

48 Quoted in Madelin, *Histoire de la Révolution et de l'Empire*, 3:291.

49 Staël, *Correspondance générale*, 4:271–300. La Fayette himself, despite his opposition to the regime, could not help admiring the Bonaparte of Marengo (*Mémoires*, 5:164).

50 Bertrand, *Cahiers*, 1:93.

51 *Correspondance générale*, no. 5642 (to Lucien, September 10, 1800), 387–388.

52 Joseph had bought the château, outbuildings, and estate of Mortefontaine on October 20, 1798, while his brother was in Egypt.

53 Roederer, *Oeuvres*, 3:330–331.

54 Rousseau's remains had been transferred to the Pantheon in October 1794.

55 According to Roederer, he said more bluntly: "He's a madman, your Rousseau; he's the one who led us to where we are" (ibid., 3:336).

56 Girardin, *Discours et opinions, journal et souvenirs*, 3:190.

57 Bourrienne, *Mémoires*, 4:170–171.

58 He went to Malmaison on July 9, August 3 and 9, September 17, October 12, and from October 31 to November 2.

59 Fontaine had participated in the repair of the Tuileries; he had been introduced to Bonaparte by David. Percier had just remodeled and decorated the Récamier's town house in Paris. According to other witnesses, it was the painter Isabey who introduced them to Joséphine to carry out the remodeling and embellishment of Malmaison.

60 Wagener, *L'Impératrice Joséphine*, 190. Frédéric Masson thinks she strayed a few more times—for example, with the mysterious gardener she mentioned to her friend Mme de Krény (Masson, *Mme Bonaparte*, 320–321).

61 Las Cases, *Mémorial*, 2:655.

62 Wagener, *L'Impératrice Joséphine*, 204.

63 Ibid., 221–222.

64 Masson, *Napoléon et les femmes*, 123.

65 Niello Sargy, *Mémoires sur l'expédition d'Égypte*, 1:195–199. Compare what Napoleon told Las Cases, *Mémorial*, 3:31. Oddly, he says they next met in 1805, at the time of his coronation in Milan.

66 Vigée-Lebrun, *Souvenirs*, 2:133–134. However, Frédéric Masson describes her as "a dull gossip" (*Mme Bonaparte*, 335).

67 *Correspondance générale*, nos. 5277 and 5322 (to Joséphine, May 11 and 16, 1800), 3:230, 250.

68 Masson, *Napoléon et les femmes*, 113.

69 *Bulletin de l'armée d'Italie* for June 5, 1800 (*Correspondance de Napoléon Ier*, no. 4886, 6:341). Elizabeth Billington (1765/1768–1818) was a famous English soprano, and Luigi Marchesi (1754–1829) the best-known of the Italian *castrati*.

70 Bourrienne, *Mémoires*, 4:167.

71 *Correspondance générale*, no. 5461 (to Lucien, June 21, 1800), 3:313. See also no. 5459 (a letter written the same day to Berthier), 3:313.

72 Gourgaud, *Journal*, 1:305, 2:52–53; Masson, *Napoléon et les femmes*, 115–116.

73 Even though she was a brunette, which he only half liked, as he told Gourgaud (*Journal*, 2:311–312).

74 "My faithful heart will always receive your orders obediently. I shall be your wife, if that is your desire; do not doubt my faith; but I beg you, give me a glance full of love and serenity" (Blangini, *Souvenirs*, 109–110). In 1813 Mme Grassini returned to London, where she became Wellington's mistress.

75 Las Cases, *Mémorial*, 2:655.

76 Bertrand, *Cahiers*, 1:47.

77 Masson, *Napoléon et les femmes*, 166–178.

78 [The Administration de l'Enregistrement was created in 1790. Its task was to collect registration fees and to manage or supervise state property.—Trans.]

79 Constant Wairy, *Mémoires intimes*, 1:121–122.

80 He was endowed, Berlioz said, with a "musical feeling" that we would not necessarily imagine in him. Berlioz recounts an anecdote about him from the time of the Empire: The organizers of a concert having had to replace a singer at a moment's notice, they had also replaced the piece by Paisiello that was supposed to be sung by another composed by Generali; but fearing they would displease the emperor, they attributed this piece to Paisiello, saying that it was work of his youth. Napoleon, who knew Paisiello's work by heart, refused to believe them, and interrupted the concert several times, saying that it was definitely impossible that the piece was by Paisiello (*Critique musicale*, 3:213).

81 *Correspondance générale*, no. 1821 (July 26, 1797), 1:1081.

82 "strategy or deliberate propaganda": That is the thesis defended by David Chaillou in *Napoléon et l'Opéra*.

83 On the Théâtre-Italien, see Mongrédien, "Le Théâtre-Italien de Paris sous le Consulat et l'Empire."

84 J. Mongrédien, "Musique," in Tulard, *Dictionnaire Napoléon*, 2:364.

85 He preferred Spontini's *La Vestale* (1807), which still recalled Gluck's manner.

86 Fleischmann, *Napoléon et la musique*, 86.

87 "Science, and more science, that's what you give us, my friend," he reproached Méhul; "but grace, and gaiety, that's what the French don't have, any more than the Germans do" (quoted in Lecomte, *Napoléon et le monde dramatique*, 455). However, he did not go as far as Rousseau did when he wrote: "There is neither measure nor melody in French music, because the language is not capable of them; French song is only a continual barking, unbearable to the ears of anyone who has not been forewarned; its harmony is crude, without expression, and smelling only of its schoolboy padding; French airs are not airs; French recitative is not recitative. Whence I conclude that the French have no music and cannot have any, or that, if ever they have one, it will too bad for them" (Rousseau, "Lettre sur la musique française," 70).

88 See, in particular, Masson, *Napoléon chez lui*.

89 Méneval, *Napoléon et Marie-Louise*, 1:109–116; Fain, *Mémoires*, 10–15; Masson, *Napoléon chez lui*, 153–160; this antechamber was subsequently made into a map room.

90 He later replaced the Louis XVI desk with a larger one that he had designed himself (Fain, *Mémoires*, 12–13).

91 This place was so protected from any external intrusion that the ushers themselves cleaned and maintained it.

92 Mollien, *Mémoires*, 1:382.

93 He uses the term *moine militaire* (Fain, *Mémoires*, 180).

94 Branda, *Napoléon et ses hommes*, pp. 13, 273–274.

95 See in particular Masson, *Napoléon chez lui*.

96 Fischer went mad in 1809 and died shortly afterward (Fain, *Mémoires*, 192–193). The other Mamluk who had returned from Egypt with Bonaparte, Ibrahim, renamed Ali (this Ali must not be confused with Louis-Étienne de Saint-Denis, who, having become a Mamluk, was also called Ali), entered Joséphine's service, but he was so ill-tempered and sometimes threatening that he had to be sent away (Constant Wairy, *Mémoires intimes*, 1:109–110).

97 Ambard and Hébert did not leave Bonaparte's service: the former became the concierge at Meudon, the latter at Rambouillet (Masson, *Napoléon chez lui*, 67). Ambard committed suicide in 1815 (see their portrait in Constant Wairy, *Mémoires intimes*, 1:106–108).

98 Bourrienne says that Bonaparte had a whole "repertory of pet names": "You're a simpleton, a fool, a brute, an imbecile," to which he added pinches on the ear that were excruciatingly painful and slaps and punches (Bourrienne, *Mémoires*, 3:226–227).

99 Constant Wairy, *Mémoires intimes*, 1:266.

100 Ibid.

101 Ibid., 1:271. He was so sensitive to the cold that a fire was kept going all through the year (1:267).

102 Their names were Landoire and Haugel (Fain, *Mémoires*, 11–12).

103 Bacler d'Albe, who worked in the war depot, came to work in the emperor's office in 1806 (ibid., 39). Yvan was soon replaced by Corvisart, who in 1801 obtained the title "physician to the government" (Tulard, *Dictionnaire Napoléon*, 1:564–566). On Hallé: Constant Wairy, *Mémoires intimes*, 1:262–263.

104 In 1796 Bonaparte had asked his former classmate to join him in Italy to serve as his secretary, because Jacoutot, who had been serving in that capacity, had suddenly died (Fain, *Mémoires*, 26). But Bourrienne, who was waiting until he had been removed from the list of émigrés and thus could not leave France, had had to decline this invitation. The general asked again in March 1797, through the intermediary Marmont, and this time Bourrienne set out and joined Bonaparte at Leoben on April 19 (Bourrienne, *Mémoires*, 1:110–113).

105 Ibid., 1:132–133.

106 Gourgaud, *Journal*, 1:565.

107 He often complained about Maret's lack of assiduity (Cambacérès, *Mémoires*, 1:466).

108 Chardigny, *Les Maréchaux de Napoléon*, 81.

109 Bourrienne, *Mémoires*, 4:188–190.

110 Bonaparte had had Duroc write them down in a document dated April 3, 1800 (ibid., 4:58–60).

111 Fain, *Mémoires*, 46.

112 Cambacérès, *Mémoires*, 1:489.

113 Méneval, *Napoléon et Marie-Louise*, 1:199.

114 Gourgaud, *Journal*, 2:110; Montholon, *Récits*, 2:10.

115 He said "enfin que" for *afin que*, "enfanterie" for *infanteries*, "gabinet" for *cabinet* (Méneval, quoted in Fierro, *Les Français vus par eux-mêmes*, 1034); the same was true for place names: "Èbre" for *Elbe*, "Hysope" for the fortress of Osoppo, "Smolensk" for Salamanca and vice versa (Fain, *Mémoires*, 59). Chaptal adds other examples to the list: "îles Phillipiques" for Philippines, "section" for *session*, "point fulminant" for *point culminant*, "rentes voyageurs" for *rentes viagères*, "armistice" for *amnistie* (Mes souvenirs, 90–91).

116 Méneval, *Napoléon et Marie-Louise*, 1:115, see also 1:235–236; Montholon, *Récits*, 2:265–266.

117 The anecdote is famous: having asked Chaptal, who was then minister of the interior, to write a proposed decree for the creation of a military school in Fontainebleau, he was so little satisfied with the result that, asking Chaptal to sit and take up his pen, he dictated to him, for two solid hours, a new proposal with 517 articles (Chaptal, *Mes souvenirs*, 160).

118 Fain, *Mémoires*, 26–27, 28. He had met Clarke at the cartographic office in 1795, and they had become close during the peace negotiations with Austria in 1797.

119 For instance, he played the role of Bartholo in the *Barber of Seville* (Didelot, *Bourrienne et Napoléon*, 78–80).

120 Gourgaud, *Journal*, 1:565.

121 Bertrand, *Cahiers*, 2:11–12, 415–416.

122 Gaudin, *Supplément aux mémoires*, 192.

123 On the Coulon brothers' bankruptcy, see J. Jourquin, "Bourrienne," in Tulard, *Dictionnaire Napoléon*, 1:305–306. Bonaparte is also said to have received hints that his secretary was maintaining suspicious relations with Mme de Bonneuil, a notorious agent of the princes, and

even that he was the author of a pamphlet in clandestine circulation that declared that Moreau was better than Bonaparte (Didelot, *Bourrienne et Napoléon*, 103–105). Bourrienne was dismissed on November 6, 1802 (*Correspondance générale*, no. 7267 [to Bourrienne], 3:1150).

124 On this initial break between Bonaparte and his secretary, see Bourrienne, *Mémoires*, 5:70–77.

125 Molé, *Le Comte Molé*, 1:96–97.

126 Lavalette, too, had almost paid the price for his defection after Brumaire. He was then Bonaparte's aide-de-camp; he was also his relative by marriage—he had married Émilie de Beauharnais, a niece of Joséphine's with whom Louis was infatuated but whom Bonaparte, refusing to allow his brother to marry that young woman without a dowry, gave in marriage to his aide-de-camp. That was in 1798, before the departure for Egypt. After 18 Brumaire, Bonaparte had told Lavalette that he was naming him to head the new Amortization Fund. Lavalette, having no interest in that kind of job, refused. This was a mistake: "As you wish, I don't want to hear anything more about you!" Bonaparte replied, turning his back on him, and without Eugène's intervention, Lavalette might have been permanently rejected. This time he understood and when Bonaparte suggested that he direct the postal service, he accepted (Lavalette, *Mémoires et souvenirs*, 240–241; Bertrand, *Cahiers*, 1:164).

127 Bourrienne, *Mémoires*, 5:162; Bertrand, *Cahiers*, 2:12.

128 Méneval, *Napoléon et Marie-Louise*, 1:113.

129 Although on November 8 Bonaparte gave Bourrienne a certificate of good and loyal service (Bourrienne, *Mémoires*, 5:182), it was only in March 1805 that he had him given the position of chargé d'affaires for the Hanseatic cities in Hamburg.

130 Fain, *Mémoires*, 30.

131 Even if he did not acquire ministerial rank until 1804 (Lentz, *Le Grand Consulat*, 48–49).

132 Las Cases, *Mémorial*, 3:366–367.

133 He said of Maret, who under the Empire became Duke of Bassano: "There is only one man more witless than M. Maret, and that is the Duke of Bassano" (quoted in Tulard, *Dictionnaire Napoléon*, 2:272).

134 Quoted in Fierro, *Les Français vus par eux-mêmes*, 799.

135 In 1797 after his return from Italy.

136 Barante, *Souvenirs*, 1:393–394; Ernouf, *Maret*, 210–229.

137 Barante, *Souvenirs*, 1:394.

138 Pasquier, *Mémoires*, 1:253–254.

139 Tocqueville, "Discours de M. de Tocqueville, prononcé à la séance publique du 21 avril 1842," 251–269.

140 Ibid., 275.

141 See Woloch, *Napoleon and His Collaborators*, 36–51.

142 We can add to this list Jean-Bon Saint-André, a former member of the Committee of Public Safety in Year II and the future prefect in Mainz, of whom Sainte-Beuve sketched a subtle portrait that illustrates the limits of Tocqueville's thesis (*Nouveaux lundis*, 8:138–189).

143 Talleyrand, *Memoirs of the Prince de Talleyrand*, 1:209.

144 Bertrand, *Cahiers*, 2:117.

145 Durand, "Conseils privés, conseils des ministres, conseils d'administration," 818.

146 About ten such meetings were held each month (Lentz, *Le Grand Consulat*, 44–45).

147 Fain, *Mémoires*, 120–121.

148 Cambacérès, *Mémoires*, 1:480.

149 Bourrienne, *Mémoires*, 4:305.

150 On December 27, 1799.

151 See Maret's letters transmitting to Roederer the first consul's instructions regarding the articles to be written, in Roederer, *Oeuvres*, 3:429.

152 Madelin, *Histoire du Consulat et de l'Empire*, 1:283.

153 It ceased publication after issue no. 73, which appeared on June 3, 1803.

154 On all this, see Mitton, *La Presse française sous la Révolution*, 208–224.

155 Fain, *Mémoires*, 53.

156 Cambacérès recognized this when he referred in his memoirs to the conversations he and Lebrun had with Bonaparte every morning: "He listened to us attentively, occasionally raising an objection that was sometimes real, sometimes apparent, and never failed to remember what he had heard" (*Mémoires inédits*, 1:490). See also Chaptal, *Mes souvenirs*, 55–56.

157 Vandal, *L'Avènement de Bonaparte*, 2:186.

158 Bastid, *Sieyès et sa pensée*, 466–473.

159 Bourdon, *La Réforme judiciaire de l'an VIII*, 1:319–326. Abrial had succeeded Cambacérès as minister of justice.

160 Lentz, *Le Grand Consulat*, 213.

161 Vandal, *L'Avènement de Bonaparte*, 2:186–187.

162 Roederer, *Oeuvres*, 3:381.

163 Thibaudeau, *Mémoires* (1913), 257.

164 See Durand, *Études sur le Conseil d'État napoléonien*, 87–103; Durand, "Napoléon et le Conseil d'État," 146–148. In the various projects worked out by Sieyès, who had the idea of establishing a Council of State, the latter was on the contrary endowed with genuine powers, notably in the matter of legislative initiative (Durand, *Études sur le Conseil d'État napoléonien*, 58–61).

165 Locré, *La Législation civile, commerciale et criminelle de la France*, 1:53–54.

166 Thibaudeau, *Mémoires* (1913), 75. See also Durand, "Napoléon et le Conseil d'État," 153.

167 Molé, *Le Comte Molé*, 1:79–80. The scene described here came later, and concerns the emperor, but the first consul behaved in the same way. Cambacérès, who presided over the Council in Bonaparte's absence, was a very different chairman. Pasquier describes him "always leading the discussion without hampering it, intervening only when it was indispensable to do so, and always in the most luminous way; speaking soberly, . . . he summed up and asked questions with a lucidity that would have forced the least enlightened mind to grasp and understand them" (Pasquier, *Mémoires*, 1:269).

168 Fain, *Mémoires*, 76. See also Méneval, *Napoléon et Marie-Louise*, 1:211–213.

169 Mollien, *Mémoires*, 1:314.

170 Gourgaud, *Journal*, 1:471–472.

171 Las Cases, *Mémorial*, 3:394.

172 Ibid. See also Roederer, *Oeuvres*, 3:381; Gaudin, *Supplément aux mémoires*, 20, 76.

173 He didn't like anyone to be considered his mentor. When he was praising his minister of the treasury, Mollien, someone said to him: "Everybody in Paris, General, thinks as highly of him as you do; it is said that he is your tutor in finances." The result was quick in coming: "The first consul seemed to have completely forgotten me for five months," Mollien reported, whereas before Bonaparte had summoned him every week (Mollien, *Mémoires*, 1:320).

174 Fain, *Mémoires*, 88–90.

175 This observation is made by Molé in *Le Comte Molé*, 1:177; and by Goethe in his *Conversations with Eckermann*, 244.

176 Mollien, *Mémoires*, 1:360.

177 *Revue française*, no. 12 (November 1829), 196–198.

178 Roederer conceded that this system was no doubt not "a model of moral rectitude," but in any case it was able to produce stability (see his two "Mémoires sur le gouvernement de la Chine," *Oeuvres*, 8:98–112). Lentz drew attention to these little-known texts in his "Roederer et le modèle chinois" (1994).

179 See, for example, Voltaire, *Anecdotes sur Pierre le Grand* (Dresden: G. C. Walter, 1748), 281.

180 Durand, "Rome a remplacé Sparte," 173.

181 Mollien, *Mémoires*, 1:262

182 Ibid., 1:283.

183 Las Cases, *Mémorial de Sainte-Hélène*, 3:367.

184 Pelet de la Lozère writes precisely that the Council of State was a "guarantee" against his ministers (*Opinions de Napoléon*, 4).

185 See Durand, *Études sur le Conseil d'État napoléonien*, 125–127.

186 Tocqueville, *L'Ancien Régime et la Révolution*, 1039; on the "economists" or "physiocrats," see bk. 3, chap. 3 (1047–1050).

187 H. de Beauharnais, *Mémoires*, 1:77–78.

188 Bourrienne, *Mémoires*, 3:229; Chaptal, *Mes souvenirs*, 145.

189 H. de Beauharnais, *Mémoires*, 1:77.

190 Bourrienne, *Mémoires*, 4:36–37; Fain, *Mémoires*, 202.

191 Las Cases, *Mémorial*, 3:383.

192 Bourrienne, *Mémoires*, 3:212; Pelet de la Lozère, *Opinions de Napoléon*, 11; Méneval, *Napoléon et Marie-Louise*, 1:210.

193 Goethe, *Conversations avec Eckermann*, 299.

194 The pianist Jean-Népomucène Hummel (1778–1837).

195 Goethe, *Conversations with Eckermann*, 299.

196 Roederer, *Oeuvres*, 3:377.

197 Constant Wairy, *Mémoires intimes*, 1:254–255.

198 Goethe, *Conversations with Eckermann*, 326.

199 Lentz and Macé, *La Mort de Napoléon*, 48.

200 Corvisart cured him of it in 1801 by applying a solution based on sabadilla (a seed from a plant imported from Central America), olive oil, and pure alcohol (Constant Wairy, *Mémoires intimes*, 1:557).

201 Warden, *Napoléon jugé par un Anglais*, 63; Gourgaud, *Journal*, 1:439.

202 Cambacérès, *Mémoires*, 1:562–563. Frédéric Masson speaks, on the contrary, of a "diplomatic illness" to avoid receiving Cardinal Consalvi (*Mme Bonaparte*, 296).

203 Bourrienne, *Mémoires*, 4:339.

204 Las Cases, *Mémorial*, 1:243.

205 Constant Wairy, *Mémoires intimes*, 1:259, 557.

206 Letter from Volney to Bonaparte quoted in Warden, *Napoléon jugé par un Anglais*, 388–389.

207 Bourrienne, *Mémoires*, 4:314. On this ulcer that ended up perforating his stomach, see Lentz and Macé, *La Mort de Napoléon*, 61–69.

27. The Turning Point of 1801

1 See Bonaparte's July 29 letter to Francis II (*Correspondance générale*, no. 5578, 3:361). I return to the "Saint-Julien affair" below.

2 As soon as he took office, Bonaparte had told the minister of foreign affairs, who was at that time Reinhard, that it was indispensable to reestablish "the best relations with the United States" as soon as possible (ibid., no. 4765 [November 10, 1799], 2:1091).

3 An initial American mission had failed: Talleyrand, who was then minister of foreign affairs, had demanded the astronomical sum of 50,000 livres sterling merely to receive the three envoys. This "X, Y, and Z affair," as Talleyrand's emissaries called it, had caused a great stir on both sides of the ocean.

4 Roederer and Fleurieu, the former minister of the navy, seconded Joseph.

5 "right of neutrals": "(1) The flag covers merchandise. . . . (2) The only exception to this rule is war contraband, and this contraband does not include food supplies . . . but solely manufactured weapons and military munitions. . . . (3) The neutral party can go from any port to any port; the only exception to its liberty to sail concerns ports that are actually blockaded, and the only ports actually blockaded are those that are guarded by such a force that there is a serious danger to anyone seeking to break the blockade. (4) The neutral party must allow the ship to be searched to establish its true quality; but . . . if the neutral party is convoyed by a warship, the search may not be conducted, the presence of the military flag being a sufficient guarantee against any kind of fraud" (Thiers, *Histoire du Consulat et de l'Empire*, 2:218).

6 Their representative in Paris, M. de Muzquiz, brought up the subject in a conversation with Bonaparte as early as April 22, 1800 (*Correspondance générale*, no. 5192 [to Talleyrand, April 23], 3:185).

7 Peyre, *La Cour d'Espagne*, 6. A very different and still less flattering portrait is found in Grandmaison, *L'Ambassade française en Espagne*, 185–187.

8 La Parra, *Godoy*, 223–227.

9 Letter to Menou, August 25, 1799 (F. Rousseau, *Kléber et Menou*, 1).

10 Ibid., 76–84.

11 *Correspondance générale*, no. 4689 (to Mazaredo, March 20, 1800), 2:199.

12 Ibid., no. 5148 (to Bruix, March 28, 1800), 3:165.

13 It was only on March 5, 1800, long after the signature of the Convention of El-Arish, that a messenger sent by the consuls, adjutant general Latour-Maubourg, reached Cairo (Laurens, *L'Expédition d'Égypte*, 247).

14 *Correspondance générale*, no. 5295 (to Desaix, May 14, 1800), 3:238.

15 Ibid., no. 5317 (to Talleyrand, May 15, 1800), 3:248.

16 Las Cases, *Mémorial*, 1:155.

17 For the same reason, he was concerned about the possible consequences of bringing the Army of the Orient back to France: he was so afraid that its members would talk that he wrote to Kléber to inform him that the soldiers who returned home would be sent to islands off the coast of southern France, near Marseille and Hyères, "to recover from their fatigue" (*Correspondance de Napoléon Ier*, no. 4721 [to Kléber, April 19, 1800], 6:222–223).

18 *Correspondance générale*, no. 5453 (to Carnot, June 20, 1800), 3:311. However, he ordered the reestablishment, as soon as possible, of communications with Egypt (*Correspondance de Napoléon Ier*, no. 4932, 6:380).

19 "They talked about it, however," Sorel writes. "Bonaparte was still thinking about it, and was inclined to dismember this kingdom in order to drive out the English. The queen of Spain would have helped dethrone her son-in-law in order to give part of his state to her lover. Godoy dreamed of being a real prince, and no longer just a *Prince of Peace*, a prince on parchment, but a prince of the earth, with souls! The Spanish ministers did not consent to the deal, and the matter was postponed once again" (*L'Europe et la Révolution française*, 6:75).

20 Bonaparte had proposed this arrangement involving the retrocession of Louisiana in exchange for "an equivalent expansion of the duchy of Parma in Italy" on July 22 (*Correspondance générale*, no. 5554 [to Talleyrand], 3:351). In addition to Louisiana, Berthier demanded the cession of Florida (which had become Spanish again following the Treaty of Paris of 1783 after being English for two decades), but Madrid refused (Driault, *Napoléon et l'Europe*, 1:104). See Garnier, *Bonaparte et la Louisiane*; Lentz, "Un rendez-vous manqué," 199–232.

21 Plus Mauritius (then called "Isle de France") and Réunion in the Indian Ocean and Saint-Louis du Sénégal on the African coast.

22 See L. Dubois's remarkable book, *Les Vengeurs du nouveau monde*, 237ff.; P. Pluchon, *Toussaint Louverture*; and, more recently, M. S. Bell, *Toussaint Louverture*.

23 See C. L. R. James, *The Black Jacobins: Toussaint Louverture and the San Domingo Revolution* (New York: Dial, 1938).

24 Dubois, *Les Vengeurs du nouveau monde*, 237. See the collection of Toussaint's "correspondence" and speeches in Toussaint-Louverture, *The Haitian Revolution*. Norvins has painted a fine portrait of Toussaint in his *Histoire de Napoléon*, 2:176–180; he asserts that Toussaint learned to read at the age of forty, and then discovered the *Histoire philosophique des deux Indes* by Abbé Raynal, who henceforth became his "prophet" (176).

25 A civil war had been provoked by General Hédouville's decision to divide the command on the island between Toussaint in the north and Rigaud in the south.

26 Signed on August 30, 1798, and June 13, 1799.

27 "Louverture militarized work on the plantations, applying the ideal of discipline and the modes of punishment used in the whole colony's armed forces. Just as soldiers obeyed their officers, the plantation workers had to obey their superiors. Just as soldiers were court-martialed when they did not do their duty, disobedient workers would be punished. Fi-

nally, just as soldiers had no freedom of movement and could not leave their units without incurring *severe punishments*, those who left their dwellings without permission were subject to fines or imprisonment. Louverture sought in this way to eliminate any possibility of escaping from the plantation. . . . As for the worker's status, based on the earlier forms of slavery on the plantations themselves where they were ordered to remain, it was made immutable and permanent. In the end, any attempt made to escape from the past and to invent a different future—other than serving in Louverture's army—was made a criminal offense" (Dubois, *Les Vengeurs du nouveau monde*, 323–324).

28 With one difference, however: in Toussaint's time, plantation workers were paid wages.

29 These commissioners were General Michel, Colonel Vincent, who had been born in the colony and had ties to Toussaint Louverture, and Julien Raimond, who had also been born on the island and had taken an active part in the Revolution and the struggle for emancipation; he had also been a commissioner for the Directory from 1796 to 1798.

30 *Correspondance de Napoléon Ier*, no. 4726 (to Forfait, April 22, 1800), 6:227.

31 This party's offensive against the decree abolishing slavery issued on February 4, 1794, had begun as early as 1795 (Dubois, *Les Vengeurs du nouveau monde*, 265–268).

32 Article 6 of the Constitution of Year III stipulated, "The French colonies are an integral part of the Republic, and are subject to the same constitutional law." "Special system": article 91. On December 27, 1799, Bonaparte asked Admiral Ganteaume for "a proposed regulation for the provisional government of Saint-Domingue, Guadeloupe, and Isles de France and Réunion" (*Correspondance générale*, no. 4820, 2:1117).

33 According to this system, the totality of the island's production was intended for the French market, the island being supplied exclusively by the home country.

34 Napoleon told O'Meara that he had been continually besieged by "former colonists, merchants, and speculators": "In a word, the nation was raging to recover Saint-Domingue and I was obliged to yield to it" (O'Meara, *Napoléon dans l'exil*, 2:129). Joséphine, on the other hand, played no role in the decisions her husband made regarding Saint-Domingue. On all this, see Branda and Lentz, *Napoléon, l'esclavage et les colonies*, 54–60, 105–112. On Joséphine's lack of influence, see also Bénot, *La Démence coloniale sous Napoléon*, 33.

35 Referring to his discussions with the Amis des Noirs, he wrote in his *Mémoires*: "It was our unanimous opinion that the free negroes and mulattos had to be assimilated to the whites by political and civil rights, and that so far as slaves were concerned, they should not be hastily emancipated but gradually given access to the advantages of the civilized condition." After adding that all the abolitionists held the same opinion, both in France and abroad, he wrote: "One can understand why the sudden emancipation declared by the decree of 16 Pluviôse of Year II, which was provoked by Levasseur [de la Sarthe], seemed to us a disastrous measure: it was in politics what a volcano is in physics" (Henri Grégoire, *Memoires de Grégoire ancien évêque de Blois* [Paris: A. Dupont, 1837], 1:390–391).

36 See the transcription of this exchange in Thibaudeau, *Mémoires sur le Consulat*, 116–121.

37 Ibid.

38 Montholon, *Récits*, 1:259–260.

39 "Citizen minister," Bonaparte wrote in this letter of May 10, "I have read with the greatest attention the various reports that you submitted to me on the eve of my departure [for

Dijon and Geneva]. I have found your observations regarding the memorandum I sent you on Saint-Domingue completely correct, especially concerning the freedom we might want to give the blacks. Delete all that from the copy that you are to have made" (*Correspondance générale*, no. 5265, 3:225).

40 See Cambacérès, *Mémoires*, 1:587–588.

41 *Correspondance de Napoléon Ier*, no. 4455 (December 25, 1799), 6:42. He also had these words inscribed on the regimental flags in Saint-Domingue: "Brave black men, remember that the French people alone recognizes your freedom and the equality of your rights" (no. 4456, 6:43). See also the proclamation of May 2, 1800 (no. 4748, 6:251). Let us recall that at this time only France had abolished slavery.

42 Roederer, *Oeuvres*, 3:334.

43 *Correspondance générale*, no. 5860 (to Forfait, December 22, 1800), 3:487.

44 An order of December 25, 1799, already refers to Toussaint Louverture's army as a "national guard of the colony of Saint-Domingue" (*Correspondance de Napoléon Ier*, no. 4456, 6:43).

45 See ibid., no. 5097 (order of September 10, 1800), 6:458–459; no. 5163–5164 (to Roume and to Toussaint Louverture, November 5, 1800), 6:498–499; and no. 5219 (notes for the minister of the navy, December 14, 1800), 6:529–531.

46 According to the report Barbé-Marbois sent Bonaparte on September 11, 1801 (Branda and Lentz, *Napoléon, l'esclavage et les colonies*, 71). Like many other writers, Tocqueville later maintained that the plantation system was on the whole not very productive (*De la démocratie en Amérique*, vol. 1, pt. 2, chap. 10, pp. 320–322).

47 Sixty percent of the sugar plantations and 50 percent of the coffee plantations had been destroyed (Branda and Lentz, *Napoléon, l'esclavage et les colonies*, 95).

48 Ibid., 138.

49 Thomas Pronier, who has studied the evolution of the declarations, initiatives, and decisions made by Bonaparte and the consular government since Brumaire, concludes on the contrary that from the outset he had declared himself in favor of the reestablishment of slavery ("L'implicite et l'explicite dans la politique de Napoléon," in Bénot and Dorigny, *Rétablissement de l'esclavage*, 51–67).

50 President Jefferson was firmly against Louisiana being under French control: "There is on the globe one single spot, the possessor of which is our natural and habitual enemy. It is New Orleans, through which the produce of three-eighths of our territory must pass to market, and from its fertility it will ere long yield more than half of our whole produce and contain more than half our inhabitants. France placing herself in that door assumes to us the attitude of defiance. Spain might have retained it quietly for years. Her pacific dispositions, her feeble state, would induce her to increase our facilities there, so that her possession of the place would be hardly felt by us. . . . Not so can it ever be in the hands of France. The impetuosity of her temper, the energy and restlessness of her character, placed in a point of eternal friction with us, and our character, which though quiet, and loving peace and the pursuit of wealth, is high-minded, despising wealth in competition with insult or injury, enterprising and energetic as any nation on earth, these circumstances render it impossible that France and the U.S. can continue long friends when they meet in so irritable a

position." Thomas Jefferson, letter to the U.S. Minister to France (Robert R. Livingston), April 18, 1802, quoted in Branda and Lentz, *Napoléon, l'esclavage et les colonies*, 17.

51 Driault, *Napoléon et l'Europe*, 1:101–102.

52 Warden, *Lettres de Sainte-Hélène*, 276.

53 *Correspondance générale*, no. 5736 (October 29, 1800), 3:431.

54 Grand Duke Ferdinand III, the archduke of Austria, was the brother of Emperor Francis II.

55 He had General Dupont, whose division had just occupied Florence, ordered "not to make any proclamation or take any step that might make it seem that we want to republicanize Tuscany" (ibid., no. 5707 [to Lacuée, October 22, 1800], 3:416).

56 Michaud, *Biographie universelle*, 15:540. See Baczko, *Politiques de la Révolution française*, 529, 742.

57 On this episode, see B. Baczko, "Turenne au Temple de Mars," in *Politiques de la Révolution française*, 492–534. The ceremony at the Invalides was not the only one: "In the weeks that preceded or followed, the city of Du Puy was authorized to celebrate a fete in honor of the remains of Du Guesclin, and the city of Orléans to erect a statue of Joan of Arc, . . . whereas the monument commemorating Villars's victory at Denain was reconstructed (Madelin, *Histoire du Consulat et de l'Empire*, 4:24).

58 Masson, *Mme Bonaparte*, 277–283, following the account by Jean-Étienne Despréaux.

59 A "decade" was the ten-day period that replaced the week in the revolutionary calendar.

60 Bourrienne, *Mémoires*, 4:5.

61 Masson, *Napoléon et sa famille*, 1:306.

62 Bertrand, *Cahiers*, 1:192.

63 Junot is supposed to have told Bonaparte about this in Egypt (Bourrienne, *Mémoires*, 3:287).

64 Ibid., 3:284–285.

65 "Murat is the son of an innkeeper!" he is supposed to have exclaimed. "In the elevated rank where fortune and glory have placed me, I cannot mix my blood with his blood!" (ibid., 3:289).

66 Masson, *Mme Bonaparte*, 232.

67 Miot de Melito, *Mémoires*, 1:279; Norvins, *Histoire de Napoléon*, 2:52–53.

68 Furet, "Bonaparte," 221.

69 Quoted in Masson, *Napoléon et sa famille*, 1:322.

70 *Correspondance générale*, no. 6382 (to Louis I, July 27, 1801), 3:738.

71 Masson, *Napoléon et sa famille*, 1:340–341. This letter, whose source Masson does not indicate, is not in the recent edition of the complete correspondence between Napoleon and Joseph (ed. Haegelé).

72 July 31, 1800.

73 Miot de Melito, *Mémoires*, 1:314, 290–292.

74 La Fayette, *Mémoires*, 5:167. The proposal had been made by Alexander Hamilton in 1787 (*Works of Alexander Hamilton*, vol. 1, the chapter "Federal Convention").

75 Roederer, *Journal*, 13.

76 Ibid., 12; Miot de Melito, *Mémoires*, 1:294; Bourrienne, *Mémoires*, 4:81–83.

77 Quoted in Roederer, *Oeuvres*, 3:340.

78 Roederer, *Journal*, 12–13.

79 Thibaudeau, *Le Consulat et l'Empire*, 2:3.

80 H. de Beauharnais, *Mémoires*, 1:101. Gabriel Hanotaux, the publisher of Hortense's memoirs, cites in a note on p. 102 an article in the *Journal des défenseurs de la patrie* reporting this rumor, April 10, 1800 (also reproduced in Aulard, *Paris sous le Consulat*, 1:259–260).

81 Toward the end of 1800, she had a glimmer of hope: the treatment prescribed by Corvisart made her menstrual cycle start up again; she had thus not yet reached menopause. It was in order to prolong the effects of this treatment that she went to take the waters at Plombières, which were said to be beneficial for problems of sterility (Masson, *Napoléon et sa famille*, 1:386–387).

82 Bourrienne, *Mémoires*, 5:21–22.

83 Bourrienne, *Mémoires*, 4:74–75. "Save France from its own furies," Louis XVIII wrote in the first of these letters after having heard about 18 Brumaire, "and you shall have fulfilled my heart's deepest wish. Give it back its king, and future generations will bless your memory" (Norvins, *Histoire de Napoléon*, 2:89). This letter, dated December 19, which was supposed to be delivered to Bonaparte through either Joséphine or Berthier, was carried as far as London, but it proved impossible to take it into France safely. The messenger carrying it thus took it back to Mitau (Daudet, *Histoire de l'émigration*, 2:370–373, 401–402). A few months later Louis XVIII tried again, asking Bonaparte to choose between "an empty celebrity" and true glory (Norvins, *Histoire de Napoléon*, 2:89–90). Bonaparte received the two letters at the same time.

84 La Fayette, *Mémoires*, 5:178.

85 *Correspondance générale*, no. 5639 (to the Count of Provence, September 7, 1800), 3:386. Louis XVIII did not give up; on March 22, 1801, he wrote a long letter to the Count of Clermont-Gallerande adopting the substance of those addressed to Bonaparte (Thibaudeau, *Le Consulat et l'Empire*, 2:201–202).

86 Emmisaries: In June 1801 she received at Malmaison the Duchesse de Guiche—who was none other than Mme de Polignac's daughter—an agent of the Count of Artois, who had just come from London and whom Bonaparte had expelled (Gourgaud, *Journal*, 1:229–230).

87 Thiers, *Histoire du Consulat et de l'Empire*, 2:197–198.

88 Talleyrand, *Memoirs of the Prince de Talleyrand*, 1:208–209.

89 See Cabanis, "Un idéologue bonapartiste."

90 On the *Décade*'s "party" in 1800, see Kitchin, *Un journal "philosophique*," 72–78.

91 Fontanes, *Oeuvres*, 2:164.

92 Staël, *Correspondance*, 4:283.

93 Villefosse and Bouissounouse, *L'Opposition à Napoléon*, 147.

94 "I hoped Bonaparte would be defeated," she wrote, "because it was the only way to halt the advance of his tyranny" (Staël, *Dix années d'exil*, 228).

95 Staël, *Correspondance*, 4:302–303.

96 La Fayette, *Mémoires*, 5:166–167.

97 Staël, *De la littérature*, 76–82. Writing that "the nation is destroyed when it is composed only of worshippers of a single man" (282), she explains farther on that enthusiasm for one man is not necessarily a bad thing, especially in democratic societies (328–330).

98 Ibid., 208–209.

99 Claude Fauriel, who was soon to become Sophie de Condorcet's lover and for that reason fall out with Mme de Staël, was also Fouché's secretary; letter addressed by Bonaparte to Daunou on August 17 (*Correspondance*, 4:302–304); Fontanes, *Oeuvres*, 2:161–205.

100 Condorcet was the author of *Tableau historique des progrès de l'esprit humain*, published posthumously in 1795.

101 See the preface to the second edition (Staël, *De la littérature*, 53–64).

102 Chateaubriand, *Mémoires d'outre-tombe*, 1:763–765. The reference is to his "Lettre sur la perfectibilité, lettre au citoyen Fontanes sur la deuxième édition de l'ouvrage de Mme de Staël," published in the *Mercure* for December 22, 1800.

103 The widow of Stanislas of Clermont-Tonnerre, killed by rioters on August 10, 1792, hosted a little group that was "neo-Catholic and tainted with Martinism," frequented by La Harpe (Berchet and Berthier, *Chateaubriand*, 311–312).

104 See Simonetta and Arikha, *Napoleon and the Rebel*.

105 Berchet and Berthier, *Chateaubriand*, 319.

106 Louis de Fontanes, *Chant du 14 juillet 1800* (Paris: A. Leduc, 1926), 5.

107 Ibid.

108 See Madelin, *Fouché*, 1:330.

109 On this subject, see Thibaudeau, *Le Consulat et l'Empire*, 1:405–407.

110 The *Parallèle* is reproduced in Roederer, *Oeuvres*, 3:342–346. Barante suggests that Esménard may have been its author (*Souvenirs*, 1:67).

111 Lucien said this to Roederer (*Oeuvres*, 3:348), and Bourrienne states that Fouché confided it to him (*Mémoires*, 4:218). Thibaudeau also says that the affair had been devised by Napoleon and Lucien (*Le Consulat et l'Empire*, 2:32). See the evidence assembled by F. Piétri in his *Lucien Bonaparte*, 122–123.

112 Fouché, *Memoirs*, 1:120; Roederer, *Oeuvres*, 3:350–353. Cambacérès defends the same thesis (*Mémoires*, 1:539). He suggests that the first consul had gotten wind of the affair, but let it play itself out in order to get rid of Lucien, whom he had decided more than a month before to dismiss (1:538).

113 Roederer, *Oeuvres*, 3:353.

114 Ibid., 350.

115 Miot de Melito, *Mémoires*, 1:340.

116 Bourrienne, *Mémoires*, 4:219.

117 Miot de Melito, *Mémoires*, 1:339–340. See Fouché's account, *Memoirs*, 1:120–122.

118 Girardin, *Discours*, 3:192–194.

119 "We no longer need to torment ourselves finding a successor," he told Roederer, "I've found one, it's Louis: he has none of the faults of his brothers, and he has all their good qualities." Then, Roederer adds, "he pompously praised [Louis] to me, showed me letters from him in which fraternal love is expressed in every line in the tenderest way" (Roederer's remarks are reproduced in Girardin, *Discours*, 3:199). Bonaparte had talked about this with Joséphine— unless she gave him the idea—because a few days later she took Roederer aside, even though she considered him one of her worst enemies, and told him that Bonaparte did not need to have a child because he had Louis, who had an "excellent heart," a "very distinguished mind,"

and loved his elder brother "the way a lover loves his mistress" (Roederer, *Oeuvres*, 3:347). Was she already thinking about marrying Hortense to Louis? We will return to this point (see Chapter 29).

120 These preliminaries are reproduced in Kérautret, *Les Grands traités du Consulat*, 139–142.

121 This was a sanction: Masséna was relieved of his command on August 12, 1800, for having let Kellermann sign an agreement with the Austrians on July 7 that allowed them to retain part of the region of Ferrara.

122 Thiers, *Histoire du Consulat et de l'Empire*, 2:226–277.

123 Ibid., 2:253.

124 Ibid.

125 Bourrienne, *Mémoires*, 4:249. Later on he was to harshly criticize Moreau's victory at Hohenlinden. In his writings on Saint Helena, he calls it a simple "fortunate encounter" (see "Diplomatie, guerre," in *Correspondance de Napoléon Ier*, 30:427–432, and the detailed observations reproduced on 3:438–442). See also Bertrand, *Cahiers*, 1:117–118.

126 The conditions he sent to the French were the return of Malta to the Knights of the Order of Saint John, the restoration of the king of Sardinia in Turin, and a guarantee of the territorial integrity of the kingdoms of Bavaria and the Two Sicilies (Daudet, *Histoire de l'émigration*, 3:164).

127 *Correspondance générale*, no. 5411 (to Talleyrand, June 4, 1800), 3:288.

128 Ibid., no. 5680 (to Talleyrand, September 30, 1800), 3:402–403. On the rapprochement between France and Russia, see F. Petrov, "Paul Ier et Napoléon Bonaparte," 243–258.

129 *Correspondance générale*, no. 5853 (December 21, 1800), 3:484.

130 La Fayette, *Mémoires*, 5:189.

131 See, for example, Las Cases, *Mémorial*, 3:118–119, 124.

132 Driault, *Napoléon et l'Europe*, 1:141–142. This memorandum was dated October 2, 1800.

133 O'Meara, *Napoléon dans l'exil*, 1:311–312; Bertrand, *Cahiers*, 2:292; Bourrienne, *Mémoires*, 4:263. Albert Sorel did not think this was a real project (*L'Europe et la Révolution*, 6:113–115).

134 Sorel, *L'Europe et la Révolution*, 6:53–54.

135 Bonaparte suggested that France officially declare itself the protector of the neutral powers (*Correspondance générale*, no. 5820 [to Talleyrand, December 7, 1800], 3:468).

136 Charlotte Corday, who assassinated Marat; Pâris, Louis XVI's former bodyguard, who assassinated Le Peletier; and Ladmiral, Cécile Renault, and Abbé Poulle, who tried to assassinate, respectively, Collot d'Herbois, Robespierre, and Sieyès.

137 Thiers, *History of the Consulate and the Empire of France under Napoleon*, 2:97. See M. Cottret, *Tuer le tyran?*, 325–362.

138 Gaubert, *Conspirateurs*, 13–126.

139 Ferrero, *Pouvoir*, 199–200.

140 Joseph Aréna's brother, Barthélemy, was the member of the Five Hundred who had struck Bonaparte in the Orangerie at Saint-Cloud. Ceracchi had met Bonaparte in Milan in 1796; he had a bust made that is now preserved in the Nantes Museum.

141 Tulard, *Dictionnaire Napoléon*, 1:513.

142 Barère, whom Demerville had let in on the secret, supposedly feared being compromised and went to see Junot to warn him that an assassination attempt against Bonaparte was being planned (Miot de Melito, *Mémoires*, 1:329–330).

143 Thibaudeau gives a very precise description of this bomb, this *machine infernale*, constructed by Chevalier, who, after being arrested along with twelve of his accomplices, was questioned by Monge (*Le Consulat et l'Empire*, 2:35–36).

144 Warden, *Lettres de Sainte-Hélène*, 128–129.

145 Letter of January 25, 1799, quoted in Lebon, *L'Angleterre et l'émigration*, 267–269. On Sir James Talbot and the Swabian Agency, see Sparrow, *Secret Service*, 280–294.

146 Tulard, *Dictionnaire Napoléon*, 1:344–345. Hyde de Neuville also states that this attack was the work not of a party but rather of "a few obscure *chouans*" (*Mémoires*, 1:360).

147 On this "terrorist moment in *chouannerie*," see Lignereux, "Le moment terroriste."

148 Joséphine and Hortense were with Rapp in a second carriage. Bonaparte having criticized his wife's outfit, she had decided to change it; the general had gone on ahead. This delay probably saved Joséphine's life. Otherwise, because her carriage usually followed that of her husband, it would have been caught in the explosion (H. de Beauharnais, *Mémoires*, 1:79–80).

149 According to a report by Chaptal, the minister of the interior, on January 1, 1801, quoted in Thiry, *La Machine infernale*, 191. According to Fouché, there were twenty dead and fifty-six wounded (*Memoirs*, 1:127n).

150 Thiry, *La Machine infernale*, 169.

151 Bonaparte was encouraged to pursue this line by the prefect of police, Dubois, who, unlike Fouché, "suspected" the Jacobins (Cambacérès, *Mémoires*, 1:542).

152 Miot de Melito, *Memoirs*, 356–357.

153 Roederer attributes the suggestion to himself (*Oeuvres*, 3:360), and so does Cambacérès (*Mémoires*, 1:543). Miot de Melito attributes it to Talleyrand, who, he says, made a proposal that Bonaparte had whispered to him (*Memoirs*, 209).

154 Lanfrey, *Histoire de Napoléon*, 2:261.

155 Roederer, *Oeuvres*, 3:361–362.

156 Ibid., 3:363.

157 Ibid., 3:364. Roederer had told Réal that he would oppose a "mass punishment" (ibid., 3:355).

158 Ibid., 3:364.

159 Of these 130 individuals, some had participated in the September Massacres of 1792, whereas others were former members of the Convention (Choudieu, Talot), well-known figures of revolutionary Paris (Félix Le Peletier, Villain-Daugibny, Thirion, Charles de Hesse, Fournier the American), as well as the Hebertist general Rossignol and Destrem, who had tried to strike Bonaparte at Saint-Cloud. Fifty-five of them were finally incarcerated in state prisons, four were relegated to the Île de Ré, and seventy-one were deported to the Seychelles (Destrem, *Les Déportations du Consulat*). Most of them died in captivity, including Rossignol, despite a rumor that arose long after these events, to the effect that he had succeeded in escaping and had founded in Africa a "kingdom of Muzumbo" of which he had proclaimed himself the dictator, under the name "Aristide I" (see A. de Baecque's

préface to Rossignol, *Vie*). On the genesis of the *sénatus-consulte* of January 4 and the origins of this procedure, see Zacharie, *Le Sénat*, pp. 145–164, 217–229, 239–260.

160 They were guillotined on April 21.

161 Thiers, *Histoire du Consulat et de l'Empire*, 2:336.

162 On these courts, their organization, functioning, and competencies, see Lentz, *Quand Napoléon inventait la France*, 629–630.

163 Thibaudeau, *Le Consulat et l'Empire*, 2:126–127. There are multiple versions of these remarks. For example: "I am a soldier, a child of the Revolution, and have emerged from the breast of the people; I will not allow myself to be insulted like a king"; or "I make bold to say that I am one of those who found states, and not those who let them perish" (Roederer, *Oeuvres*, 3:377).

164 He set forth his conditions in an October 20 letter to Joseph (*Correspondance générale*, no. 5700, 3:411–412).

165 See the separate, secret article of the Treaty of Lunéville (Kérautret, *Les Grands traités du Consulat*, 171).

166 Lanfrey, *Histoire de Napoléon*, 2:249–250.

167 More than eighty prominent royalists were arrested in Paris at the end of January 1801, including Bourmont, Suzannet, and d'Autichamp, the former military leaders of the rebellion in the Vendée and the *chouannerie* (Madelin, *Fouché*, 1:343–347).

168 Zacharie, *Le Sénat*, 304.

169 On the continuity, from this point of view, of the years 1797–1802, see Brown, "War on Brigandage," 661–695; and especially, by the same author, *Ending the French Revolution*.

170 Miot de Melito, *Memoirs*, 218–219.

28. Peace with the Church

1 *Correspondance générale*, no. 5999 (to Chaptal, February 5, 1801), 3:554.

2 Chateaubriand, *Mémoires d'outre-tombe*, 1:752–753.

3 See his *Travels in France*.

4 See Rocquain, *L'État de la France au 18 brumaire*.

5 See the testimony of the Englishman Henry Redhead Yorke, who visited France in 1802 and described the soup kitchens for the poor in Paris (Yorke, *Letters from France*, 2:166–176).

6 On this rather widespread feeling at the time, see X. Martin, *La France abîmée*.

7 *Correspondance générale*, no. 6006 (to Cambacérès and Lebrun, February 10, 1801), 3:557.

8 Dean Paul, *Journal d'un voyage à Paris*, 14–15, 23.

9 On Napoleon's economic ideas, see Lentz's very complete discussion in his *Nouvelle histoire du Premier Empire*, 3:416–442.

10 See the account of his long conversation with Mollien in the latter's *Mémoires*, 1:251–273.

11 On February 20, 1803, he announced that he had thought about the return to order in the monetary domain, and his reflection led to the law of March 18, 1803 (7 Germinal of Year XI), creating the Germinal franc.

12 Was he a Colbertist? He explained his views in his 1801 *Exposé de la situation de la République*: after having enumerated at length the impressive list of things that had been achieved

in all sectors over the past two years, he pointed out that the state could rely on the "national genius" only so far as industry and commerce were concerned, and at most, facilitate private initiatives: "When general peace has restored industry and commerce to all their activity, the duty dearest to the government will be to show them the way, to encourage their work, to remove every obstacle that might hinder their development; it will focus all light on these great interests, and ask for all the counsels of experience; it will establish at its side to consult with them the men who, by positive knowledge, stern probity, and disinterested views, are worthy of the public's confidence and esteem. Happy it will be if the national genius seconds its ardor and its zeal; if, through its care, the Republic's prosperity someday equals its triumphs and its glory!" (*Correspondance de Napoléon Ier*, no. 5874, 7:334–335).

13 Chaptal, *Mes souvenirs*, 30.

14 Chaussinand-Nogaret, *Les Financiers du Languedoc au XVIIIe siècle*; Bergeron, *Banquiers, négociants, et manufacturiers parisiens*; Bruguière, *Gestionnaires et profiteurs de la Révolution*.

15 Bruguière, *Gestionnaires et profiteurs de la Révolution*, 75–76.

16 "other large projects": The reconstruction of the Place Belledour; the construction of a road passing through the Valais and over the Simplon Pass that was intended to facilitate communication between France and the Cisalpine Republic; the construction of several bridges over the Seine and shelters on the Alpine passes.

17 Thiers, *History of the Consulate and the Empire of France under Napoleon*, 1:39.

18 The decree of October 20, 1800, decreased the number of émigrés forbidden to return by more than 100,000, to 52,000. At the same time, individual eliminations from the list continued, so that it was soon reduced to 3,373 names.

19 Chateaubriand, *Mémoires d'outre-tombe*, 1:761–762.

20 "I am not afraid to seek examples and rules in times past," he also said to Mollien. "While preserving everything that the Revolution produced in the way of useful innovations, I am not giving up the good institutions it was wrong to destroy" (Mollien, *Mémoires*, 1:261).

21 See the biographies of Joseph II by François Fejtö and Jean Bérenger, and the classic work by François Bluche, *Le Despotisme éclairé*.

22 Even the time separating the adoption of the law and its rejection by Rome—eight months—proves nothing: Albert Mathiez (*Rome et le clergé français sous la Constituante*) sees in this the proof that the Holy See had concerns other than religion, and that it did not decide to make a break until after having lost all hope of obtaining satisfaction on the other pending issues. That is to forget that in Rome things moved slowly, very slowly. Bonaparte complained about it again in 1801—he who never was able to finish the negotiation on the dates he had successively set—first in February, then on July 14, and finally on August 15. The time of the Church is not that of lay governments. See La Gorce, *Histoire religieuse de la Révolution française*, 1:264–350.

23 Mathiez, *La Révolution et l'Église*, 274.

24 This laconic formula was a merely civil commitment, and its import was entirely negative: those who signed this promise did not commit themselves to "maintain, support, and defend a code that no one, after all, could be required to approve," but solely to "submit and not oppose" (Thibaudeau, *Le Consulat et l'Empire*, 1:152–153).

25 Lanfrey, *Histoire de Napoléon*, 2:342.

26 See what Sismondi says about Chateaubriand's faith after having heard him speak about religion at the home of Mme de Duras in 1813, in Sainte-Beuve, "Sismondi," *Nouveaux lundis*, 6:57–58.

27 Lanfrey, *Histoire de Napoléon*, 2:349. An analysis adopted later by Mathiez, *La Révolution et l'Église*, 270–300.

28 On these debates, see Boulay de la Meurthe, *Histoire de la négociation*, 22–30.

29 The constitutional church had no more than fifty-seven bishops and 7,000 to 8,000 members (ibid., 6–9).

30 Montholon, *Récits*, 2:275.

31 The remarks he made before the Council of State in August 1800 have remained famous: "My policy is to govern men the way most of them want to be governed. That is, I believe, the way to recognize the sovereignty of the people," he declared, and then added that he had been a Catholic in Italy, a Muslim in Cairo, and that he would have reestablished the Temple of Solomon had he had to govern the Jewish people (Roederer, *Oeuvres*, 3:334).

32 Quoted in Boulay de la Meurthe, *Histoire de la négociation*, 55.

33 Lentz, *Le Grand Consulat*, 302–304.

34 Declaration to the Council of State, quoted in Molé, *Le Comte Molé*, 1:76. See also his conversation with Roederer, August 18, 1800 (*Oeuvres*, 3:335).

35 La Fayette, *Mémoires*, 5:184.

36 Pointing to the starry sky one evening, he said to those around him: "Just try to tell me, Messieurs: Who made that?" (Bourrienne, *Mémoires*, 3:232). See also Thibaudeau, *Mémoires sur le Consulat*, 152–153; Las Cases, *Mémorial*, 2:777–780, 3:179–180. But he did not believe in the dogmas of the Christian religion, though he said he was "annoyed" by his disbelief (Bertrand, *Cahiers*, 1:182). On the "divinity" of the sun, see Gourgaud, *Journal*, 1:440–441, 2:269–272, 310–311.

37 O'Meara, *Napoléon dans l'exil*, 1:188.

38 In his diary Roederer tells this anecdote contemporary with the official proclamation of the concordat in the spring of 1802: "When at the end of the acts of the Court of Rome, which were read in the Council of State, the pope threatened rebels with the wrath of Saint Peter and Saint Paul (see the end of the bulls registered that day), the first consul smiled, and the whole Council laughed" (*Journal*, 109–110).

39 Roederer, *Oeuvres*, 3:430.

40 Bourrienne, *Mémoires*, 4:281.

41 Ibid., 281–282.

42 Thibaudeau, *Mémoires sur le Consulat*, 152.

43 "I think each person has to keep to the religion in which he was brought up; that of his fathers," he also told O'Meara on Saint Helena (*Napoléon dans l'exil*, 1:195).

44 See, for example, the report submitted by State Councilor Fourcroy, who resigned himself to the concordat after it was signed, but regretted that in 1790 the Constituent Assembly had failed to seize the opportunity to impose Protestantism on France, because it was "much more tolerant and easier to detach from the government than Catholicism" (Rocquain, *L'État de la France au 18 brumaire*, 154).

45 Quoted in Thiers, *History of the Consulate and the Empire of France under Napoleon*, 3:129–130. In his view, it was not only history that condemned Protestantism: "I love the Catholic religion because it speaks to my soul," he said to Montholon, "because, when I pray, it puts my whole being in action; whereas the Protestant religion speaks only to my reason" (Montholon, *Récits*, 2:174). See also Bourrienne, *Mémoires*, 4:276 (against a French version of Anglicanism); Thibaudeau, *Le Consulat et l'Empire*, 2:181–182; Las Cases, *Mémorial*, 3:181–182 (against the adoption of Protestantism).

46 "Of all civil wars, which is the one that enters most deeply into every heart, that most painfully disrupts families? It is religious war," he replied to those who criticized his policy.

47 Thibaudeau sums it up this way: "The Gallican Church was to retain the enjoyment and exercise of its rights and former practices, without the pope being able to oppose them in any way or do anything contrary to them. In conformity with these liberties, the Gallican Church was to elect its own pastors. It recognized no spiritual jurisdiction in the pope's delegates, or the apostolic prefects and vicars. It was not allowed to send any of the latter to France; the ecclesiastical territorial demarcations determined by the Constituent Assembly were to be preserved. No part of French territory could, insofar as religion was concerned, depend on a foreign bishop, save the purely spiritual relationships maintained with the visible head of the universal church. As the common father of the faithful, the pope was supposed to use the means that his wisdom and charity suggested to pacify the turmoil in the French church. In the brief that he was to send to the Republic, he would recommend the deepest silence concerning the differences of opinion that divided them. The French bishops would again send the pope letters of communion, to which he would respond. In cases where there was only one bishop residing in France for a given diocese, he was to be recognized by all, if he had made the promise of loyalty to the constitution. In the event that [a diocese] had two bishops, one appointed and ordained before 1791, the other elected and ordained afterward, the older bishop would be recognized if he resided in France and if he promised fidelity to the constitution; the other would by rights succeed him. As an exception and to promote peace, the current bishops whose sees had been suppressed could continue in their offices by submitting to the laws; but they could not have successors. The same arrangements were applicable to parish priests" (*Le Consulat et l'Empire*, 2:178–180).

48 Quoted in Lanfrey, *Histoire de Napoléon*, 2:201–202.

49 Quoted in Thiry, *Marengo*, 170.

50 Lanzac de Laborie has well described the persistence, in the years following the Revolution, of feelings hostile to any religious restoration among the people of Paris and especially among the officials and elites of the new regime (*Paris sous Napoléon*, 1:313–335). "With a truly devout minority, a much larger group for whom religion was a habit or a matter of indifference, a society drawn to religion for aesthetic or sentimental reasons, and an intellectual elite violently opposed to religion, the role of the authorities could have been reduced to an impartial neutrality. . . . However that may be, until the promulgation of the concordat, administrative action was continually exercised in a direction hostile to Catholicism" (316).

51 Barante, *Souvenirs*, 1:98–99.

52 The proposed concordat with Spain was the work of the prime minister, Mariano Luis de Urquijo, who had taken advantage of the vacancy of the pontifical throne to carry out a de

facto "nationalization" of the Spanish Church by means of a decree issued on September 5, 1799. Boulay de la Meurthe summed up its principal clauses this way: "Deprive the papacy of all disputed jurisdiction in Spain, abolish its exemptions and the fees levied for the vacancy of benefices, reduce the nuncio to the rank of a simple ambassador, prohibit regular orders from depending on a superior-general residing in Rome and allow bishops to sell convents' property, and finally, recognize the royalty's absolute right of patronage" (*Histoire de la négociation*, 228). As soon as French policy with regard to Rome changed direction when the Consulate took over, Charles IV and Urquijo reversed course: the September 5 decree was abrogated on March 29, 1800 (La Parra, *Manuel Godoy*, 230–232).

53 Boulay de la Meurthe, *Documents sur la négociation du Concordat*, 1:11–12 (letter from Pius VII to Louis XVIII, March 14, 1800).

54 Lentz, *Le Grand Consulat*, 204.

55 The expression is Cardinal Consalvi's, quoted in Thiers, *Histoire du Consulat et de l'Empire*, 2:169.

56 *Correspondance de Napoléon Ier*, no. 4884 (Address to the parish priests of the city of Milan, June 5, 1800), 6:338–340. First printed in Italian, this address was translated into French in September and distributed in France by the *Annales philosophiques*. On July 3, Roederer's *Journal de Paris* printed a shorter version that might be closer to the original: "Italy's natural friends are the French," he is supposed to have declared. "What can you expect from the Protestants, Greeks, and Muslims you have been sent? The French, on the contrary, belong to the same religion as you do. We have had a few quarrels, but all that can be mended and arranged" (Roederer, *Oeuvres*, 6:411). A few days later, on June 18, he attended the *Te Deum* sung in the Milan cathedral to celebrate the victory at Marengo. He wrote to Cambacérès and Lebrun: "Today, despite what our atheists in Paris may say, I am going with great ceremony to the *Te Deum*" (*Correspondance générale*, no. 5449, 3:308).

57 Bonaparte had used this expression in his conversation with Martiniana (Thiry, *Marengo*, 170).

58 Quoted in Mathieu, *Le Concordat*, 3–5.

59 Boulay de la Meurthe, *Documents sur la négociation du Concordat*, 1:26–28 (letter from the pope to Martiniana, July 10, 1800).

60 Spina had been chosen, not by the pope, but by Bonaparte, who thought Martiniana too old to go to Paris, where he demanded that the negotiations take place. He knew Spina, whom he had met in Grenoble as he was returning from Egypt, shortly after the death of Pius VI (Mathieu, *Le Concordat*, 10).

61 Boulay de la Meurthe, *Histoire de la négociation*, pp. 103–127, 149–153.

62 "I know he's a scoundrel," he replied to Volney, who was reproaching him for making use of such servants, "but I need him" (Mathieu, *Le Concordat*, 52). Later Bonaparte refused to name Bernier to the archbishopric of Paris, saying that the services the abbé had rendered did not wipe away the blood he had shed in the Vendée. Bernier obtained the bishopric of Orléans (55).

63 See the text of the first proposal Bernier submitted to Spina, which served as a basis for discussion, in Boulay de la Meurthe, *Documents sur la négociation du Concordat*, 1:113–115.

64 See Bernier's letter of November 30, 1800 (Boulay de la Meurthe, *Documents sur la négociation du Concordat*, 1:145). An initial draft was concluded by Spina and Bernier on November 26 (Mathieu, *Le Concordat*, 109–114). Between that date and the end of January, three other drafts were to be completed.

65 Talleyrand, *Mémoires et correspondances*, 238.

66 Montholon, *Récits*, 2:275.

67 "In general," Cobenzl wrote, "Talleyrand has always shown the greatest ill will toward the reestablishment of the Catholic religion in France; which is rather well explained by the embarrassment that would result from it for him, given his former position as a bishop" (quoted in Lacour-Gayet, *Talleyrand*, 460).

68 Boulay de la Meurthe, *Histoire de la négociation*, 236–239.

69 Ibid., 252–256.

70 This fifth draft is reproduced in Boulay de la Meurthe, *Documents sur la négociation du Concordat*, 1:351–353.

71 "His Holiness," the new version stipulated, "declares that he will recognize as titularies of the archbishoprics and bishoprics preserved by virtue of the new circumscription, only those who are designated to it by the first consul, to the exclusion of all others, whatever their title" (Boulay de la Meurthe, *Histoire de la négociation*, 312).

72 Quoted in ibid., 313. As an additional gesture, the statue of the Virgin from the Sanctuary of Loreto, which had been taken by the French in 1796, was sent back to the pope.

73 See the text of the alternative draft in Mathieu, *Le Concordat*, 145–148.

74 Quoted in Boulay de la Meurthe, *Histoire de la négociation*, 377.

75 Ibid., 376–377.

76 Thiers, *History of the Consulate and the Empire of France under Napoleon*, 3:147.

77 Mathieu, *Le Concordat*, 156.

78 The Neapolitans, who had benefited from French reverses in 1799 to advance as far as Tuscany, had been driven back to Rome by Murat, and on February 18, 1801, they signed an armistice that was converted into a peace treaty a month later. The king of Naples agreed to close his ports to British ships and opened them, notably those in the Gulf of Tarento, to French garrisons.

79 La Parra, *Manuel Godoy*, 295–296.

80 The grand duke of Tuscany, archduke Ferdinand, received in exchange the bishopric of Salzburg.

81 *Correspondance générale*, nos. 5996 and 6018 (to Talleyrand, February 4 and 13, 1801), 3:552–553, 562–563.

82 By the terms of this arrangement, the current Duke of Parma, Ferdinand, would have to abdicate the crown of Parma. At the beginning of March, Bonaparte dispatched an emissary, Moreau de Saint-Méry, to him (see the emissary's instructions in *Correspondance de Napoléon Ier*, no. 5512 [to Talleyrand, April 7, 1801], 7:109–110), but Ferdinand refused (Driault, *Napoléon et l'Europe*, 1:113–115). France had to wait until he died, in October 1802, to seize Parma.

83 On the agreement in Madrid, see *Correspondance générale*, no. 5682 (to Talleyrand, September 30, 1800), 3:403; no. 6335 (to Lucien, June 17, 1801), 712–713.

84 From an unpublished portion of Lucien's memoirs, "Guerre d'Espagne," folio 26v. I thank Marcello Simonetta, who is preparing the complete edition of Lucien's manuscripts, for having sent me this text. See also *Correspondance générale*, no. 6335 (to Lucien, June 17, 1801), 3:712–713.

85 On July 10 Napoleon wrote to Talleyrand, saying that if Godoy, "bought by England, had drawn the king and queen into taking steps contrary to the honor and the interests of the Republic, the last hour of the Spanish monarchy would have sounded" (ibid., no. 6360, 3:726).

86 See the text of the two treaties of June 6 and September 29, 1801, in Kérautret, *Les Grands traités du Consulat*, 184–188, 201–204).

87 L. Bonaparte, "Guerre d'Espagne," folio 27.

88 Driault, *Napoléon et l'Europe*, 1:183. On Lucien's embassy, the best study remains Piétri, *Lucien Bonaparte*, 131–157.

89 Thiry, *La Machine infernale*, 259.

90 Russia demanded, as a precondition for peace, the restitution of Egypt to the sultan, that of Malta to the Knights of St. John, and the independence of Italy (Driault, *Napoléon et l'Europe*, 1:146–148).

91 Watson, *Reign of George III*, 399–405.

92 Bonaparte had informed Menou on October 29, 1800, that help was being sent (*Correspondance générale*, no. 5736, 3:431–432). Ganteaume left Toulon "haunted by the fear of encountering the English fleets; he came back twice . . . before proceeding further [February 19 and April 5, 1801]; finally he set out across the high seas; he traversed the whole Mediterranean without problems; he arrived on the coasts of Egypt; he did not dare leave his men in Alexandria, for fear of finding the English there; he looked further west for a point where he could land and let his troops disembark; he found no such favorable place and returned to Toulon without having done anything [at the end of June]" (Driault, *Napoléon et l'Europe*, 1:184). See the testimony of Savary, whom Bonaparte had sent to supervise the preparations (*Mémoires*, 1:341–345, 353–361).

93 Menou capitulated on August 30.

94 See Bourrienne's remarks in his *Mémoires*, 4:288–292.

95 La Fayette, *Mémoires*, 5:188.

96 Cambacérès, *Mémoires*, 1:561.

97 Thibaudeau, *Mémoires* (1913), 60.

98 Denmark left the League on April 9, Sweden on May 18, and Russia on June 17.

99 As soon as he learned the news, he had this note printed in the *Moniteur*: "It is for history to explain the mystery of this tragic death and to say which country's policy has an interest in causing such a catastrophe" (quoted in Driault, *Napoléon et l'Europe*, 1:171). Also see what he told Las Cases on Saint Helena (*Mémorial*, 3:118–119), and what he told Gourgaud (*Journal*, 2:60).

100 Quoted in Sorel, *L'Europe et la Révolution française*, 6:140.

101 See ibid., 118–138.

102 The next day he signed an order, backdated to April 2, that prepared the integration of Piedmont into France by transforming it into a military division and naming General

Jourdan, who after Marengo had been appointed minister of the Republic in Turin, as "administrator-general of Piedmont" (*Correspondance de Napoléon Ier*, nos. 5525–5526, 7:116–119). The integration of Piedmont into France was officially proclaimed on September 11, 1802.

103 *Correspondance générale*, no. 6206 (to Joseph Bonaparte, April 12, 1801), 3:649; no. 6211 (to Lucien, April 13), 3:652–653.

104 Sorel, *L'Europe et la Révolution française*, 6:105.

105 On the king of Etruria's visit, see H. de Beauharnais, *Mémoires*, 1:98–100; Constant Wairy, *Mémoires intimes*, 1:131–137.

106 Quoted in Thiers, *Histoire du Consulat et de l'Empire*, 3:144.

107 Quoted in Thiry, *Le Concordat et le Consulat à vie*, 62.

108 Boulay de la Meurthe, *Histoire de la négociation*, 424–426.

109 Ibid., 426–428.

110 Quoted in Mathieu, *Le Concordat*, 211. See also the account of this same scene in Cardinal Consalvi's *Mémoires*, written in 1812, 1:348–356.

111 Quoted in Thiry, *Le Concordat et le Consulat à vie*, 77.

112 Boulay de la Meurthe, *Histoire de la négociation*, 436.

113 Ibid., 441–444.

114 On July 7 Bonaparte told Talleyrand that he was confident about the outcome of the negotiation (*Correspondance générale*, no. 6339, 3:725).

115 Boulay de la Meurthe, *Histoire de la négociation*, 452.

116 This document is reproduced in Boulay de la Meurthe, *Documents sur la négociation du Concordat*, 3:201–204.

117 An ex-general of the Servite order and a consultant to the Holy Office, Father Caselli had accompanied Spina to Paris and played, it seems, a major role in ironing out the differences between Paris and Rome: "We have to do something for Bonaparte," he kept repeating to his Roman interlocutors; "we have to help him, he has more religion than people think" (Bertrand, *Cahiers*, 1:182).

118 Thus, it was too late for Bonaparte to be able to congratulate himself on having brought religious peace in the proclamation he addressed to the French people on July 14. He simply inserted this sentence: "The scandal of religious divisions will soon end" (*Correspondance de Napoléon Ier*, no. 5634, 7:193).

119 Quoted in Madelin, *Histoire du Consulat et de l'Empire*, 4:123–124. The version Joseph presented to Bonaparte is reproduced in Boulay de la Meurthe, *Documents sur la négociation du Concordat*, 3:205–210.

120 As soon as he had been informed of the meeting between Bonaparte and Martiniana, Louis XVIII wrote to Czar Paul I, on September 8, 1800, to beg him to intervene and to persuade Pius VII to "resist the insidious proposals of a hypocritical usurper" (Madelin, *Histoire du Consulat et de l'Empire*, 1:99–101). Louis XVIII declared that he was "dismayed" on hearing this news on August 15, 1801: "The current crisis is very violent," he wrote to his brother, the Count of Artois. "I have had forebodings ever since Bonaparte, victorious at Marengo, took advantage of Cardinal Martiniana's imbecility to make overtures to the pope. Now these forebodings have been only too confirmed. . . . It is almost certain that on the pretext of doing

a great service to religion, the monarchy and the clergy of France have been sacrificed." Even though he claimed that his rights would be "no more altered by Pius VII's weakness than those of Philip the Fair were altered by Boniface VIII's violence," the blow was a heavy one, very heavy (Daudet, *Histoire de l'émigration*, 3:258).

121 "We made a better deal than we had expected," he told Mme de Brignole. "[I had] power to make much more considerable concessions" (quoted in Barante, *Souvenirs*, 1:102). In his memoirs, Consalvi wrote that "the price of all these sacrifices, the compensation for all these concessions, the counterweight of all these hardships, was always the certitude of the total extinction of the schism and the constitutional clergy's sincere abandonment" (1:368).

122 The council of the constitutional Church—which in fact no longer existed—was dissolved only on August 16, ten days after the presentation of the Concordat to the Council of State.

123 Thiers, *Histoire du Consulat et de l'Empire*, 3:268. On this session, see Thibaudeau, *Mémoires sur le Consulat*, 158–159.

124 Norvins, *Histoire de Napoléon*, 2:147.

125 "It is false [to say] that I ever repented having made the 1801 concordat," he repeated on Saint Helena. "I never said that the concordat was the greatest error of my reign. . . . I believe today, as I believed in 1801, that the concordat was useful, necessary for religion, for the republic, for the government" (Montholon, *Récits*, 2:270–271).

126 Pradt, *Les Quatre concordats*, 2:137–138.

127 "The Catholic religion is an all-powerful aid to the royalty," he told Montholon. "What would the royalty be if it did not also speak to the imagination and was based on cold reason alone? For why, if the king is only a man like other men, is he born a king, whether he is an imbecile, depraved, or a superior man? The moment that you take away from the royalty the prestige that it receives from the Lord's anointment, it becomes a magistracy; and from that moment on ambition enters the fray, the era of revolutions begins" (Montholon, *Récits*, 2:174).

29. The Top of the Ladder

1 On October 6, 1801.

2 The Helvetic Republic, founded in 1798 after the revolt in the canton of Vaud and the invasion of Switzerland by French troops, was united and modeled on the Directory. It had rapidly declined into an instability and chronic anarchy that became a civil war in 1802. Proponents of unity vs. proponents of a confederacy, cantons vs. cantons, "democrats" vs. "aristocrats": the Swiss, no longer knowing what to do, had called upon Bonaparte to exercise a right of arbitration. Switzerland's political situation not being one of his priorities, so long as the passage from France to Lombardy through the Alps was kept open, he had let the situation deteriorate after having tried in vain, in April 1801, to impose a new constitution that replaced the unitary institutions of 1798 with a confederation. He reopened the issue in 1802 by assigning a commission of four French senators to supervise the drafting of a new constitution: this one, called the "Act of mediation," was promulgated on February 19, 1803, restoring cantonal independence and setting up a confederation.

3 The last stadtholder of the United Provinces, William V of Orange, had been overthrown in 1795. A supporter of England since the American War of Independence and the brother-

in-law of the king of Prussia, he lived in retirement on his estates in the Duchy of Brunswick. Bonaparte sought to obtain a compensation for him in Germany (the abbeys of Corvey and Fulda), but refused to allow this supporter of the English to recover any authority whatever in the Low Countries, as he says here to Roederer.

4 Quoted in Thiry, *La Machine infernale*, 155.

5 Bonaparte proposed to guarantee Prussia's possession of Hanover, which it had just seized.

6 On the beginnings of Alexander's reign, see Rey, *Alexandre Ier*, 131–147.

7 In 1798 Laharpe had been one of those who inspired the revolution in the canton of Vaud that led to French intervention in Switzerland. Stroganov had also had a European tutor, Gilbert Romme, a future member of the Convention.

8 See Rey, *Alexandre Ier*, 135–136.

9 It was still given priority on the day after 18 Brumaire: the law of 19 Brumaire, which established the provisional Consulate, assigned two "legislative commissions" drawn from the Directory's Councils to prepare a civil law code.

10 Carbonnier, "Le Code civil," 1332. On Portalis's role, see Onorio, *Portalis*. Set up in August 1800, the commission, whose other two members were Bigot de Préameneu and Tronchet, had as its "secretary" Malleville, a judge on the Supreme Court (*Correspondance de Napoléon Ier*, no. 5059, 6:440).

11 Sainte-Beuve, "Portalis," in *Causeries du lundi*, 5:475.

12 Letter of September 23, 1799, to Mallet du Pan (Sayous, *Mémoires et correspondance de Mallet du Pan*, 2:398–399).

13 Lentz, *Le Grand Consulat*, 437–438.

14 Madelin, *Histoire du Consulat et de l'Empire*, 4:184. The other sessions were chaired by Cambacérès.

15 Thiers, *Histoire du Consulat et de l'Empire*, 3:299–302.

16 Lanfrey, *The Histoire de Napoleon*, 2:410.

17 Thibaudeau, *Mémoires sur le Consulat*, 412.

18 Cambacérès, *Mémoires*, 1:566–567.

19 From this point of view, noted Alfred Marquiset, who published a stenographic record from 1804 and 1805, all the transcriptions are defective (*Napoléon sténographié*, 20).

20 Thibaudeau, *Mémoires sur le Consulat*, 420–424.

21 Locré, *Législation civile*, 1:93–96. He is supposed to have asked Locré not to hand over the record of these debates for publication.

22 Articles 353–360 of the Civil Code of 1804.

23 Thibaudeau, *Mémoires sur le Consulat*, 441.

24 Ibid., 437, 439–440.

25 Ibid., 447.

26 Ibid., 443–444, 447–448.

27 Carbonnier, "Le Code civil," 1335.

28 "It was for the pre-1789 period to provide most of the rules and the ideas of rules: Who would have been mad enough to reinvent all of civil law in a few months? But it was for the post-1789 period to make the conquests deemed essential, though still fragile: civil status, divorce, the legality of lending at interest, and an absolutism of private property that

simultaneously annihilated feudalism and consolidated the acquisition of national goods" (ibid., 1339). See also Arnaud, Halpérin, and Martinage, "L'esprit des codes napoléoniens," 227–243.

29 Carbonnier, "Le Code civil," 1335.

30 *Correspondance générale*, no. 19416 (to Murat, November 27, 1808), 8:1285.

31 Quoted in Carbonnier, "Le Code civil," 1337.

32 For example, Chaptal, who was later to judge his former master harshly: "It was especially in these meetings that I learned to know the great man to whom we had just entrusted the reins of government. Still young and not very well informed about the various parts of the administration, he brought to the discussion a clarity, a precision, a rational power and a breadth of vision that astonished us. A tireless worker, with inexhaustible resources, he connected and coordinated, with a matchless sagacity, the scattered acts and opinions of a great administrative system. More eager to learn than to affect a knowledge that his military studies and his age had not allowed him to acquire, he often asked that words be defined, inquired about what had existed before his government, and, after having solidly laid his bases, he deduced from them consequences that were always favorable to the present condition" (note by Chaptal quoted in *Mes souvenirs*, 30).

33 Even Mme de Staël could not help "admiring the first consul's facility and perspicacity" in these discussions (*Correspondance*, 4:440). "powerful will": the expression is Jean Carbonnier's ("Le Code civil," 1334).

34 Portalis was assigned to the Direction générale des cultes in the Ministry of the Interior on October 8, 1801.

35 H. de Beauharnais, *Mémoires*, 1:102–103.

36 Henry Kissinger writes, "England's policy was based on throwing its weight as the occasion required to the weaker and more threatened side to redress the equilibrium. . . . England was the one European country whose *raison d'état* did not require it to expand in Europe. Perceiving its national interest to be in the preservation of the European balance, it was the one country which sought no more for itself on the Continent than preventing the domination of Europe by a single power. In pursuit of that objective, it made itself available to any combination of nations opposing such an enterprise. . . . Great Britain's role as the balancer reflected a geopolitical fact of life. The survival of a relatively small island off the coast of Europe would have been jeopardized had all the resources of the Continent been mobilized under a single ruler. [Since William of Orange, England's strategy had been simple: it] would try to maintain a rough balance between the Habsburgs and the Bourbons, so that whoever was weaker would maintain, with British help, the equilibrium of Europe. Ever since Richelieu, the weaker side had been Austria, and therefore Great Britain aligned itself with the Habsburgs against French expansionism" (*Diplomacy*, 72).

37 Notably with Turkey, Bavaria, and Russia.

38 See Cambacérès, *Mémoires*, 1:569–570.

39 *Correspondance générale*, no. 5919 (to General Combis, January 14, 1801), 3:517.

40 See the secret instructions sent to General Combis on January 14, 1801, regarding the Spanish part of Saint-Domingue (ibid., no. 5920, 3:517–518).

41 See ibid., no. 6627 (instructions for General Leclerc, October 31, 1801), 3:837–843.

42 Bourrienne, *Mémoires*, 4:310–311.

43 Branda and Lentz, *Napoléon, l'esclavage et les colonies*, 118–131. A commission chaired by the minister of the navy had been formed on April 6, 1802, to draft new regulations for the colonies (*Correspondance de Napoléon*, no. 6027, 7:430). Its work was communicated to Cambacérès on the 27th to be converted into a *sénatus-consulte* (*Correspondance générale*, no. 6863, 3:956–957). The notes accompanying this letter (3:957–958) show that the commission thought that the reestablishment of the colonial regime in force in 1789 constituted the rule. An exception would be granted in the territories where the law of February 1794 had been "more or less completely" applied. In these cases a list of names would be drawn up, including blacks who had been free before the vote on this law and those who had "helped defend the Republic's territory against its enemies, or who, in one way or another, have served the state." The persons on this list, and only they, would be recognized as free, on the condition that they were property owners or exercised a trade; otherwise they would be "assigned to the property owners" for agricultural work. "Insubordinates" and "vagabonds" would lose their status as free men and could be deported to colonies where slavery had been maintained. The importation of slaves from Africa would resume everywhere, and all blacks would be denied entrance to the national territory.

44 See ibid., no. 6642 (to Talleyrand, November 13, 1801), 3:850–851, for the information to be communicated to the English in order to persuade them to authorize the expedition.

45 Fouché, *Mémoires*, 1:249–251. La Fayette makes the same accusation in his *Mémoires* (5:198, 227–228), as do Generals Thiébault (*Mémoires*, 3:305) and Marbot (*Mémoires*, 1:180–181). For his part, Bourrienne says that Bonaparte wanted chiefly to send away Leclerc, who had, he said, "the gift of displeasing him enormously" (*Mémoires*, 4:309). On Saint Helena, Napoleon himself threw all the responsibility on the colonists while at the same time rejecting, of course, the suspicions that Fouché was to echo (Gourgaud, *Journal*, 1:402–403). Cambacérès also denies that Bonaparte organized this expedition to get rid of the soldiers of the former Army of the Rhine (*Mémoires*, 1:589–590).

46 On the financial speculations surrounding the preparation for the expedition, and the stock market crash they almost caused, see Las Cases, *Mémorial*, 3:363–365.

47 Notably in a report on the situation of the Republic addressed to the Directory in June 1799 (Talleyrand, *Correspondance diplomatique*, 424–433).

48 Thiers, *Histoire du Consulat et de l'Empire*, 3:379.

49 Ibid., 3:319.

50 Quoted in Masson, *Napoléon et sa famille*, 2:89. Did Bonaparte, exasperated by the reproaches made by the "Ideologues," lose his temper to the point of striking Volney? Some historians say that he limited himself to turning his back on him, but Royer-Collard, who was maintaining a secret correspondence with Louis XVIII, says that Bonaparte struck Volney, who had a seizure as a result and lost consciousness (report of June 14, 1802, in Remacle, *Relations secrètes des agents de Louis XVIII*, 44–45).

51 Signed October 8–10, 1801.

52 Kérautret, *Grands traités du Consulat*, 213.

53 In the Tribunate, the text was approved by a vote of 77 to 14, and in the Legislative Body by a vote of 229 to 21.

54 Jourdan and La Martillière had served in Italy, the former in 1800, the latter in 1798 and 1799.

55 The new senators had been co-opted by the Senate from a list of candidates presented by the government, the Tribunate, and the Legislative Body.

56 This was a punishment that was abolished in 1791 and consisted in branding certain offenders with a red-hot iron. It was reestablished in 1801, but only for counterfeiters and arsonists. In 1810 this punishment was made part of the penal code.

57 See Gobert, *L'Opposition des assemblées*, 195–196.

58 Thibaudeau, *Le Consulat et l'Empire*, 2:339.

59 By 65 votes to 13 in the Tribunate, 142 to 139 in the Legislative Body.

60 By 64 votes to 26.

61 By 61 votes to 31.

62 Mme de Staël was not far from thinking as he did on this point, deploring the fact that her friends in the Tribunate had decided to attack the Civil Code, a project that seemed to her to have been worked out by the government in an "impartial" and thus "enlightened" spirit (*Correspondance*, 4:446–447).

63 See Thibaudeau, *Mémoires sur le Consulat*, 216–226.

64 "This year, and the preceding one," Roederer wrote in November 1801, "are the offspring of a great day, 18 Brumaire. Beyond that day lay nothingness or glory; it gave us glory by giving us a man whom it dedicated to the salvation of the country. In the changes that have taken place, this man has seen everything, guided everything; by directing the whole, he has done more in each part than any of those to whom they were specially entrusted. The prodigious strength of his constitution allows him to work eighteen hours a day. . . . While we are contemplating his past works, he is already striding far ahead of us toward the future. No one has preceded him toward a useful idea; happy he who can follow him closely! This head radiant with glory is full of new cares, and works for the interest of all; when your eyes rest on him, his are seeking your needs and your interests. You will still be talking about what he did the past year, when, having arrived at the end of the current year, another 18 Brumaire will demand new expressions of your admiration and your gratitude to him" (*La Seconde année du Consulat de Bonaparte*, in *Oeuvres*, 3:395–396).

65 Thiers, *Histoire du Consulat et de l'Empire*, 3:288.

66 "dogs": Girardin, *Discours et opinions*, 3:235.

67 "a diet of laws": The expression is Portalis's (Thibaudeau, *Mémoires sur le Consulat*, 224).

68 *Correspondance de Napoléon*, no. 5907, 7:356. Article 26 of the Constitution of Year VIII authorized the government to withdraw bills at any point during their discussion in the assemblies.

69 Girardin, *Discours et opinions*, 3:248–249.

70 They claimed that they had not been notified of Daunou's election by the Legislative Body, and they gave General La Martillière the seat to which Daunou had been elected by the two other assemblies.

71 Cambacérès, *Mémoires*, 1:601.

72 See Roederer, *Oeuvres*, 3:427–428.

73 Thibaudeau, *Mémoires sur le Consulat*, 226–229; Thibaudeau, *Le Consulat et l'Empire*, 2:410–417.

74 The tribunes had finally passed eighty-seven bills, the opposition amounting to only 10 to 20 percent of the representatives. Much the same was true of the Legislative Body, where the opposition's votes rarely exceeded 10 percent. (See Durand's analysis in *L'Exercice de la fonction législative*, 66–67).

75 The president was to be elected by indirect voting that passed through three stages: A "Council of state" consisting of only eight members would be chosen by a "Censure commission," consisting of twenty-one members who made all the other choices, itself elected by three electoral colleges representing property owners, commerce and industry, and the clergy and the learned. The drafting of this new constitution had begun in September 1800; at that point Bonaparte was recommending that it be "drawn out" because he did not want to constitute Italy in final form so long as he was not sure of what borders to give the new state (*Correspondance générale*, no. 5628 [to Talleyrand, September 3, 1800], 3:381).

76 Thiry, *Le Concordat et le Consulat à vie*, 165–166.

77 Botta, *Histoire d'Italie*, 4:411.

78 Dard, *Napoléon et Talleyrand*, 49–50.

79 *Correspondance de Napoléon*, no. 5934 (speech to the deputies of the Consulte of Lyon, January 26, 1802), 7:371–373.

80 Thiry, *Avènement de Napoléon*, 46. This bargaining led to the cession of the island of Elba to France on August 26, 1802.

81 The island of Malta, restituted to the Knights, would be occupied by a Neapolitan garrison after the English withdrawal, Russia being called upon to guarantee the accord.

82 Chateaubriand, *Mémoires d'outre-tombe*, 1:835.

83 Lefebvre, *La France sous le Directoire*, 349–350.

84 See the letters Cambacérès sent to Bonaparte during the latter's stay in Lyon (Cambacérès, *Lettres inédites à Napoléon*, 1:21–39), and the letters Bonaparte wrote to him emphasizing the necessity of getting rid of the opponents; otherwise, he suggested, the government would no longer present any bill to be voted upon by the assemblies (for example, *Correspondance générale*, nos. 6721 and 6733 [January 18 and 21, 1802], 3:364, 367).

85 *Sénatus-consulte* of March 13, 1802. Most of those excluded were then appointed to other offices: Chénier became the inspector-general of education, Chazal prefect of Tarbes, Andrieux professor at the Collège de France, and Daunou the director of the National Library. Only Benjamin Constant was not given any consolation prize.

86 He gave the ex-constitutionals two archbishoprics out of ten and ten bishoprics out of fifty. The other prelates were seventeen bishops from the Old Regime and thirty-one new bishops.

87 Quoted in Thiers, *Histoire du Consulat et de l'Empire*, 3:437.

88 The *Déclaration des Quatre Articles* was the work of Bossuet. It limited the pope's authority to spiritual questions, conferred on Church councils an authority superior to that of the sovereign pontiff, asserted the inviolability of the Church of France's liberties, and subordinated pontifical infallibility to the consent of the Universal Church. Louis XIV renounced this Declaration in 1693.

89 Seven nay votes and 15 abstentions against 78 in the Tribunate, 21 nay votes and 51 abstentions against 228 in the Legislative Body (Gobert, *L'Opposition des assemblées*, 246–247).

90 Bernier received the bishopric of Orléans. Later Bonaparte refused to allow him to be made a cardinal, as the pope proposed: "Such a nomination would be frightening, and the red cap placed on Bernier's head would awaken too many memories of the same color" (Cambacérès, *Mémoires*, 1:668).

91 Monsignor de Belloy was ninety-two years old; he had been named bishop of Marseille in 1755.

92 Thiébault, *Mémoires*, 3:274.

93 Ibid., 3:274–275.

94 Here I am using the words Bonaparte addressed after the ceremony to State Councilor Fourcroy who, received in the Tuileries and smelling a fragrance of perfume, said to the first consul: "It smells good here"; to which Bonaparte replied: "It's an odor of sanctity that will purify your old sins" (Roederer, *Oeuvres*, 3:430). Let us add that Bonaparte preferred a minimum of ceremony. It was the privy council that met on April 11, and especially Portalis and Cambacérès, that persuaded him to give this ceremony more importance by having a mass celebrated in it (Roederer, *Journal*, 111).

95 See the memories of Ferdinand de Berthier, quoted in Lentz, *Le Grand Consulat*, 325.

96 Thibaudeau, *Mémoires sur le Consulat*, 163.

97 Picard, *Bonaparte et Moreau*, 352–387.

98 See Masson, *Napoléon et sa famille*, 2:112–113.

99 See the documents collected in Höjer, *Bernadotte*, 216–228.

100 Report of June 10, 1802 (Remacle, *Relations secrètes des agents de Louis XVIII*, 31).

101 On this unconstitutional procedure, see Durand's analyses, "Transformations de l'an X," 71. Bonaparte had long resisted the idea, defended by Fouché (Madelin, *Fouché*, 1:343–347), of a general amnesty, preferring the current system of granting amnesty on a case-by-case basis. He had not changed his mind after the Peace of Amiens. The provisions of the law ordered in council on April 11 after long and bitter debates (Roederer, *Journal*, 111–112) were communicated to the Council of State on the sixteenth and were converted into a *sénatus-consulte* on the twenty-sixth. The *sénatus-consulte* put the émigrés under police surveillance for a period of ten years, returned to their former owners the properties that, not having been sold, had not been assigned to public use, and confirmed all the other sales; finally, it excluded from the benefit of an amnesty about a thousand émigrés, men close to the princes, the leaders of the insurrections in the west, ecclesiastics who had refused to resign as asked by the pope, and several prominent persons accused of treason, such as Pichegru.

102 It was passed on May 1 by 80 votes to 9 in the Tribunate, and 251 votes to 27 in the Legislative Body.

103 See the arguments Bonaparte made before the Council of State, reported by Thibaudeau, *Mémoires sur le Consulat*, 75–91.

104 See Lentz, *Le Grand Consulat*, 394–399.

105 Roederer, *Oeuvres*, 3:441.

106 Madelin, *Histoire du Consulat et de l'Empire*, 4:168.

107 Ibid., 4:15–17.

108 Berry, *Voyages à Paris*, 95–96.

109 Fiévée, *Correspondance*, 1:clxxv. A "caressing and beautiful smile," according to Chateaubriand (*Mémoires d'outre-tombe*, 1:835).

110 Berry, *Voyages à Paris*, 102–104.

111 Chateaubriand, *Mémoires d'outre-tombe*, 1:835–838.

112 See, for example, what Fontanes said to Lucien on this subject, in Masson, *Napoléon et sa famille*, 2:100.

113 Thibaudeau, *Mémoires sur le Consulat*, 241.

114 Thiers, *Histoire du Consulat et de l'Empire*, 3:502–505.

115 *Lettre d'un citoyen à un sénateur* (Roederer, *Oeuvres*, 3:448–449).

116 See Fouché, *Mémoires*, 1:264–266.

117 That is the hypothesis proposed by Stanislas de Girardin, who followed these intrigues closely in the Tribunate (*Discours et opinions*, 3:267–270).

118 Durand, "Transformations de l'an X," 72.

119 Bourrienne, *Mémoires*, 4:362.

120 Thiers, *Histoire du Consulat et de l'Empire*, 3:507. See Bonaparte's message to the Senate, May 9, 1802 (*Correspondance*, no. 6079, 7:460).

121 Clémence Zacharie rightly points out, in her doctoral dissertation on the Senate, that we must speak of a referendum (a vote on a text) in 1799 and of a plebiscite (a vote on a person) in 1802 and 1804 (*Le Sénat*, 415–417).

122 Mme de Staël says that the voters were, in addition to "paid persons," military men and public officials who had no choice but to vote yes (*Correspondance*, 4:510).

123 F. Bluche, "Plébiscite," in Tulard, *Dictionnaire Napoléon*, 2:514.

124 For the most part, the no votes were cast by military men. La Fayette had also voted no, and so had Carnot. To justify his vote, La Fayette had written to Bonaparte that he would grant him the Consulate for life only when "political liberty [is] sufficiently guaranteed" (La Fayette, *Mémoires*, 5:199–200): "He thinks he's in America," the first consul commented dryly (Madelin, *Histoire du Consulat et de l'Empire*, 4:233). The only departments that did not share the quasi-general enthusiasm were those of Corsica. "If all the departments of France had been driven by the same spirit as those of Golo and Liamone," wrote Miot de Melito, who was on assignment in the island at that time, "his rapid rise might have encountered more obstacles." The Corsicans did not pardon him his elevation (Miot de Melito, *Mémoires*, 2:22–23).

125 In addition to the right to designate his successor, it gave him the right to propose successors for the offices of second and third consuls, to name the chairmen of the electoral colleges, and to name justices of the peace and members of municipal governments. It also conferred on him the right to grant pardons and ensured his control over the Senate.

126 Citizens (all Frenchmen living in France who were over twenty-one years old) elected the members of district and department colleges, the former at the rate of one member for 1,500 citizens, the latter at the rate of one member for 1,000 citizens, necessarily chosen among the 600 citizens paying the highest taxes in the department. The function of these colleges was to present candidates for the various offices who were appointed sometimes by the first consul, sometimes by the Senate.

127 But at the same time it faced new competition from the recently created Privy Council, on which sat, along with the consuls, senators, ministers, and major officials of the Legion of Honor.

128 He had mentioned the plan for reforming the Tribunate as early as January; this plan is reproduced in Thibaudeau, *Mémoires sur le Consulat*, 228. Lucien Bonaparte, who had been made a member of the Tribunate on March 27, presented two days later a plan in conformity with his brother's intentions (Masson, *Napoléon et sa famille*, 2:108). On April 1 and 8, 1802, two orders had divided the Tribunate into three, not five, permanent sections, whose creation, accompanied by a new procedure for examining and discussing bills, made it pointless for the Tribunes to meet in plenary session (Gobert, *L'Opposition des assemblées*, 239–243).

129 The constitutional *sénatus-consulte* of August 4, 1802, changed, as Roederer, who was hostile to this change, understood, the very nature of an assembly that had been electoral and now became "the government's most authentic agency for the elections [that it] wanted to make." And he went on: "That was where the overthrow of the representative constitution was. It was then that protests had to be made, and not when the first consul made himself a hereditary emperor. The empire and inherited power did not change the republic at all; the . . . innovations that denatured the Senate handed it over . . . to the absolute power under the so-called consular authority. . . . No one said anything then. Everyone went along with marvelous facility, not out of baseness, not out of self-interest, but out of confidence, out of gratitude, out of affection for the first consul, out of fear that he might be deprived of power by a faction, and—dare I say it?—out of fear that he might become disgusted with a power that was insufficient and disproportionate to his vast designs" (Roederer, *Oeuvres*, 3:417–418).

130 emoluments: A *sénatus-consulte* of January 4, 1803, created the principle of a *sénatorerie* (guaranteed lifelong income) in each jurisdiction of the appeals court, endowed with a revenue of at least 20,000 francs, the holder to be chosen by Bonaparte from a list of three candidates presented by the Senate. Thirty-one *sénatoreries* were created by the end of 1803: "The attribution of *sénatoreries*," Jean Thiry said, "was to arouse ardent competition and guaranteed the government against any rebirth of serious opposition within the assembly" (*Le Concordat et le Consulat à vie*, 266).

131 Quoted in Thibaudeau, *Le Consulat et l'Empire*, 3:17.

132 Quoted in ibid., 3:39–40.

133 Dean Paul, *Journal d'un voyage à Paris*, 103–104.

134 Staël, *Correspondance*, 4:391, 494–495.

135 Hyde de Neuville, *Mémoires*, 1:372–373.

136 Fouché, *Mémoires*, 1:276.

137 Masson, *Mme Bonaparte*, 331–332.

138 Dean Paul, *Journal d'un voyage à Paris*, 104.

139 Thiers, *Histoire du Consulat et de l'Empire*, 3:554.

140 Thiry, *Le Concordat et le Consulat à vie*, 197.

141 The question—"Shall the first consul have the power to designate his successor?"—is supposed to have been suggested to Roederer by Joseph (see Roederer, *Oeuvres*, 3:447–448).

142 Joseph states that his brother feared seeing the regime acquire a stability that would end up making his presence less necessary: "He desires above all that the need for his existence be strongly felt and that this existence be such a great blessing that no one can see anything beyond it without trembling" (quoted in Masson, *Napoléon et sa famille*, 2:126).

143 During the summer of 1801, she even received in Paris the Duchess de Guiche, an emissary sent by the Count of Artois. On Joséphine's relations with the princes' emissaries, see Masson, *Mme Bonaparte*, 237–269.

144 Joseph had understood this so well that he told anyone who would listen that he would never agree to succeed his brother (Roederer, *Oeuvres*, 3:449), who had no intention of asking him to do so.

145 Ibid., 296–297. Necker had just brought up the question in his *Dernières vues de politique et de finance*, wondering about the possibility that Bonaparte might reestablish the hereditary monarchy to his own advantage. Necker didn't much believe in this, and he believed still less in the legitimacy of a successor designated by the first consul, "whose title would someday be supported only by memories, and for a short time, perhaps, by fragile feelings of gratitude" (238–242).

146 Roederer, *Oeuvres*, 3:347.

147 Hortense seems to have seen her stepfather rather than her mother as the origin of this project (H. de Beauharnais, *Mémoires*, 1:104 f.) So does Cambacérès (*Mémoires*, 1:577).

148 Piétri, *Napoléon et le parlement*, 141–142.

149 Masson, *Napoléon et sa famille*, 2:146–164. In London, Jean-Gabriel Peltier, the former editor of the *Actes des apôtres*, was spreading these rumors in his newspaper, *L'Ambigu*. The Peace of Amiens made it possible to prosecute him. The trial took place in England on February 21, 1803; Peltier was sentenced to pay a fine. On July 25, 1802, Otto, the French minister in London, had demanded, on the first consul's orders, wider prosecution of all those who had repeated such rumors (see J.-G. Peltier, *The Trial of John Peltier*, 229–232, and Bourrienne, *Mémoires*, 4:306–307). Peltier's trial proved to be very profitable for him; he acquired new readers and continued to insult and outrage the "odd little Corsican" until the fall of Napoleon (Mitton, *La Presse française*, 224–225).

150 *Correspondance de Napoléon*, no. 6230 (first consul's speech to the Senate coming to announce to him the proclamation of the Consulate for Life, August 3, 1802), 7:551.

151 Fouché, *Mémoires*, 1:276.

152 "You may be sure," she is supposed to have told a member of the Council of State who was a friend of Thibaudeau, "that they have not given up their project of hereditary power, and that it will happen a little sooner or a little later" (Thibaudeau, *Mémoires sur le Consulat*, 309). Here Joséphine is referring, of course, to the first consul's brothers.

153 Girardin, *Discours et opinions*, 3:276, 282–283. "It has been demonstrated," he adds, "for anyone who takes the trouble to read with attention the articles relating to the nomination of the successor, that they have been written in this way only to prepare for hereditary power" (283).

154 Thiry, *Le Concordat et le Consulat à vie*, 220–221.

155 Ibid., 221.

156 Madelin, *Histoire du Consulat et de l'Empire,* 4:232.

157 Cambacérès, *Mémoires,* 1:636.

158 Thiers, *Histoire du Consulat et de l'Empire,* 5:58–59.

159 Furet, "Bonaparte," 216.

160 Bourrienne, *Mémoires,* 2:135.

BIBLIOGRAPHY

Abrantès, Laure d'. *Souvenirs sur Napoléon.* Paris: Plon, 1937.

Ader, Jean-Joseph. *Histoire de l'expédition d'Égypte et de Syrie.* Paris: Ambroise Dupont, 1826.

al-Jabartî, Abd-al-Rahmân. *Journal d'un notable du Caire durant l'expédition française, 1798–1801.* Paris: Albin Michel, 1979.

Anonymous. *Comment s'est formé le génie militaire de Napoléon Ier? Réponse au général Pierron.* Paris: Baudoin, 1889.

———. *Manuscrit venu de Sainte-Hélène d'une manière inconnue.* Paris: Gallimard, 1974.

———. *Mémoires historiques sur le dix-huit Brumaire, contenant les détails exacts et plus circonstanciés que tous ceux qui ont paru jusqu'à ce jour, des séances des deux Conseils, des 18 et 19 brumaire an viii, et des événements remarquables, qui se sont passés dans ces journées, avec les pièces officielles qui s'y rapportent.* Paris: Gauthier, 1800.

Antonetti, Pierre. *Histoire de la Corse.* Paris: Robert Laffont, 1990.

Arago, François. "Gaspard Monge: Biographie lue en séance publique de l'Académie des Sciences, le 11 mai 1848." In *Oeuvres complètes,* 1:427–592. Paris: Gide et Baudry, 1854.

Archives parlementaires: Recueil complet des débats législatifs et politiques des Chambres françaises. 1st ser., 1787–1794. Edited by Mavidal and Laurent. IHRF/Université Paris I. 92 vols. Paris: Dupontthen/CNRS, 1867.

Archives parlementaires: Recueil complet des débats législatifs et politiques des Chambres françaises. 2nd ser., 1800–1860. 127 vols. Paris: Dupont, 1862–.

Ardant, Gabriel. "Napoléon et le rendement des services publics." *Revue de défense nationale* (August–September 1953): 166–181.

Arnaud, André-Pierre, Jean-Louis Halpérin, and René Martinage. "L'esprit des codes napoléoniens." In *L'État moderne,* edited by S. Goyard-Fabre. Paris: Vrin, 2000.

Arnault, Antoine-Vincent. *Souvenirs d'un sexagénaire.* 4 vols. Paris: Dufey, 1833.

Aron, Raymond. *Une histoire du XXe siècle.* Paris: Grand livre du mois, 1997.

Arrighi, Paul. *Histoire de la Corse.* Paris: PUF, 1969.

Asprey, Robert B. *Frédéric le Grand.* Paris: Hachette, 1989.

Aubry, Paul V. *Monge, le savant ami de Napoléon Bonaparte, 1746–1818.* Paris: Gauthier-Villars, 1954.

Audebaud, Christian. *Le Général de division Dugua, 1744–1802: De l'Égypte à Saint-Domingue.* Paris: SPM, 2007.

Aulard, Alphonse. *Napoléon, 1800–1815.* Edited by E. Lavisse and P. Rambaud. Paris: Colin, 1905.

———. *Paris pendant la réaction thermidorienne et sous le Directoire: Recueil de documents pour l'histoire de l'esprit public à Paris.* 5 vols. Paris: Cerf, Noblet et Quantin, 1898–1902.

———. *Paris sous le Consulat: Recueil de documents pour l'histoire de l'esprit public à Paris.* 3 vols. Paris: Cerf, Noblet et Quantin, 1903–1906.

———, ed. (then P. Mautouchet, then M. Bouloiseau). *Recueil des actes du Comité de salut public, avec la correspondance officielle des représentants en mission et le registre du Conseil exécutif provisoire.* 37 vols. Paris: Imprimerie Nationale, 1889–1992.

———, ed. *Registre des délibérations du Consulat provisoire, 20 brumaire–3 nivôse an VIII (11 novembre–24 décembre 1799)*. Paris: Société de l'histoire de la Révolution française, 1894.

Baczko, Bronislaw. *Comment sortir de la Terreur: Thermidor et la Révolution*. Paris: Gallimard, 1989.

———. *Politiques de la Révolution française*. Paris: Gallimard, 2008.

Bainville, Jacques. *Bonaparte en Égypte*. Paris: Éditions de la Seine, 1998.

———. *Le Dix-huit brumaire et autres écrits sur Napoléon*. Paris: B. Giovanangeli, 1998.

———. *Napoléon*. Paris: Gallimard, 2005.

Baldassari, Pietro. *Histoire de l'enlèvement et de la captivité de Pie VI*. Paris: A. Le Clère, 1839.

Balzac. *Une ténébreuse affaire*. Edited by R. Guise. Paris: Gallimard, 1973.

Barante, Amable-Guillaume-Prosper Brugière de. *Souvenirs, 1782–1866*. 5 vols. Paris: Calmann-Lévy, 1890–1895.

Barbaud, Charles. "La maison Bonaparte: L'immeuble et le mobilier." *Revue des études napoléoniennes* 23 (1924): 46–71.

Barras, Paul. *Mémoires de Barras, membre du Directoire*. Edited by G. Duruy. 4 vols. Paris: Hachette, 1895–1896.

———. *Memoirs of Barras, Member of the Directorate*. Edited by George Duruy. Translated by Charles E. Roche. 4 vols. New York: Harper and Bros., 1895.

Barrow, John. *The Life and Correspondence of Admiral Sir William Sidney Smith*. 2 vols. London: Bentley, 1848.

Barry, Étienne. "Discours sur les dangers de l'idolâtrie individuelle dans une république." In *Discours prononcés les jours de décadi dans la section Guillaume Tell*, 4:1–28. Paris: Massot, 1794.

Bartel, Paul. *La Jeunesse inédite de Napoléon*. Paris: Amiot-Dumont, 1954.

Barthes, Roland. *La Chambre claire*. In *Oeuvres complètes*, vol. 3. Paris: Éditions du Seuil, 1993–1995.

Bastid, Paul. *Sieyès et sa pensée*. Paris: Hachette, 1970.

Battesti, Michèle. *La Bataille d'Aboukir, 1798: Nelson contrarie la stratégie de Bonaparte*. Paris: Economica, 1998.

Baubérot, Jean. *Vers un nouveau pacte laïque?* Paris: Éditions du Seuil, 1990.

Beauharnais, Eugène de. *Mémoires et correspondance politique et militaire*. Edited by A. Du Casse. 10 vols. Paris: Michel Lévy frères, 1858–1860.

Beauharnais, Hortense de. *Mémoires*. Edited by J. Hanoteau. 3 vols. Paris: Plon, 1927.

Beauharnais, Joséphine de. *Correspondance, 1782–1814*. Edited by B. Chevallier, M. Catinat, and C. Pincemaille. Paris: Payot, 1996.

Bell, Madison Smartt. *Toussaint Louverture*. Arles: Actes Sud, 2007.

Benoist-Méchin, Jacques. *Bonaparte en Égypte ou le rêve inassouvi*. Paris: Perrin, 1978.

Bénot, Yves. *La Démence coloniale sous Napoléon*. Paris: La Découverte, 1992.

Bénot, Yves, and Marcel Dorigny. *Rétablissement de l'esclavage dans les colonies françaises, 1802: Aux origines d'Haïti*. Paris: Maisonneuve et Larose, 2003.

Béraud, Stéphane. *Bonaparte en Italie: Naissance d'un stratège*. Paris: B. Giovanangeli, 1996.

Berchet, Jean-Claude, and Philippe Berthier. *Chateaubriand, mémorialiste: Colloque du cent cinquantenaire, 1848–1998*. Geneva: Droz, 1999.

Bérenger, Jean. *Joseph II d'Autriche, serviteur de l'État*. Paris: Fayard, 2007.

Bergeron, Louis. *Banquiers, négociants et manufacturiers parisiens du Directoire à l'Empire*. Paris: Éditions de l'EHESS/Mouton, 1978.

———. *L'Épisode napoléonien*. Vol. 1, *Aspects intérieurs, 1799–1815*. Paris: Éditions du Seuil, 1972.

Bergeron, Louis, and Louis Chaussinand-Nogaret. *Grands notables du Premier Empire*. 30 vols. Paris: CNRS/Guénégaud, 1978–2011.

Bergounioux, E. *Essai sur la vie de Lazare Hoche*. Paris: Julien, Lanier, et Cie, 1852.

Berlioz, Hector. *Critique musicale*. Vol. 3, *1837–1838*. Paris: Buchet-Chastel, 2001.

Bernardin de Saint-Pierre, Jacques-Henri. "D'un Élysée" (1784). In *Études de la nature*, 3:375–403. Paris: Crapelet, 1804.

Bernède, Alain, and Gérard-Jean Chaduc. *La Campagne d'Égypte, 1798–1801: Mythes et réalités*. Paris: Musée de l'Armée, 1998.

Bernoyer, François. *Avec Bonaparte en Égypte et en Syrie, 1798–1800: Dix-neuf lettres inédites*. Edited by C. Tortel. Le Poët-Laval: Curandera, 1981.

Berry, Mary. *Voyages à Paris, 1782–1836*. Paris: Roblot, 1905.

Bertaud, Jean-Paul. *La Révolution armée: Les soldats-citoyens et la Révolution française*. Paris: R. Laffont, 1979.

Berthier, Alexandre. *Récit des campagnes du général Bonaparte en Égypte et en Syrie*. Paris: Didot aîné, 1799–1800.

———. *Relation de la bataille de Marengo gagnée le 25 prairial an VIII, par Napoléon Bonaparte, Premier consul, commandant en personne l'armée française de réserve, sur les Autrichiens aux ordres du lieutenant-général Mélas*. Paris: Imprimerie Impériale, 1805.

Bertrand, Henri-Gatien. *Cahiers de Sainte-Hélène*. Edited by P. Fleuriot de Langle. 3 vols. Paris: Sulliver-Albin Michel, 1949–1959.

Bessand-Massenet, Pierre. *Le 18 brumaire*. Paris: Hachette, 1965.

Beugnot, Jacques-Claude. *Mémoires*. 2 vols. Paris: Dentu, 1866.

Bigonnet, Jean-Adrien. *Coup d'état du dix-huit brumaire*. Paris: Bureau du Censeur européen, 1819.

Bilici, Faruk. *Louis XIV et son projet de conquête d'Istanbul*. Ankara: Imprimerie de la société d'histoire turque, 2004.

Birnbaum, Antonia. "L'héroïsme n'est plus ce qu'il était . . . ." *Les Cahiers philosophiques de Strasbourg*, no. 2 (December 1994): 111–124.

Blanc, Olivier. *Regnaud de Saint-Jean d'Angély, l'éminence grise de Napoléon*. Paris: Pygmalion/Gérard Watelet, 2002.

Blangini, Félix. *Souvenirs*. Paris: Allardin, 1834.

Blaufarb, Rafe. *The French Army, 1750–1820: Careers, talent, merit*. Manchester: Manchester University Press, 2002.

Bloch, Marc. *Les Rois thaumaturges: Étude sur le caractère surnaturel attribué à la puissance royale particulièrement en France et en Angleterre*. Paris: Gallimard, 1983.

Bloom, Harold. "Napoleon and Prometheus: The Romantic Myth of Organic Energy." *Yale French Studies* 26 (1961).

Bluche, François. *Le Despotisme éclairé*. Paris: Hachette, 2000.

Bodinier, Gilbert. "Que veut l'armée? Soutien et résistance à Bonaparte." In *Musée de l'armée, Terminer la Révolution*, 65–87. Paris: Economica, 2003.

Bonald, Louis de. "Du traité de Westphalie et de celui de Campoformio." In *Oeuvres*, 2:411–452. Brussels: Société nationale pour la propagation des bons livres, 1845.

Bonaparte, Joseph. *Mémoires et correspondance politique et militaire*. Edited by A. Du Casse. 10 vols. Paris: Perrotin, 1853–1854.

Bonaparte, Lucien. *Mémoires*. Paris: Charles Gosselin, 1836.

———. *Révolution de brumaire, ou relation des principaux événements des journées des 18 et 19 brumaire*. Paris: Charpentier, 1846.

Bonaparte, Napoléon. *Clisson et Eugénie*. Edited by É. Barthet and P. Hicks. Paris: Fayard, 2007.

———. *Correspondance de Napoléon Ier publiée par ordre de l'Empereur Napoléon III*. 32 vols. Paris: Imprimerie impériale, 1869.

———. *Correspondance générale*. 10 vols. Paris: Fayard, 2002–.

———. *Manuscrits inédits, 1786–1791*. Edited by F. Masson and G. Biagi. Paris: Société d'éditions littéraires et artistiques, 1907.

———. *Napoléon inconnu: Papiers inédits (1786–1793), accompagnés de notes sur la jeunesse de Napoléon (1769–1793)*. Edited by F. Masson and G. Biagi. 2 vols. Paris: Ollendorff, 1895.

———. *Oeuvres littéraires et écrits militaires*. Edited by J. Tulard. 3 vols. Paris: Claude Tchou/ Bibliothèque des Introuvables, 2001.

Bonnefons, Antoine-Mathias, and Pierre-Louis Cailleux-Barallier. *Souvenirs et cahiers sur la campagne d'Égypte: Extraits du Carnet de La Sabretache, années 1903–1906–1931–1932*. Paris: Teissèdre, 1997.

Bonnet, Jean-Charles. *Histoire de Croissy-sur-Seine*. Paris: Res Universis, 1991.

Borges, Jorge Luis. "Biographie de Tadeo Isidoro Cruz (1829–1874)." *Sur*, no. 122 (December 1944).

Bory, Jean-Louis. *Les Cinq girouettes ou servitudes et souplesses de Son Altesse Sérénissime le prince archichancelier de l'Empire Jean-Jacques Régis de Cambacérès, duc de Parme*. Paris: Ramsay, 1979.

Bosséno, Christian-Marc. *"Je me vis dans l'histoire: Bonaparte de Lodi à Arcole, généalogie d'une image de légende."* *Annales historiques de la Révolution française*, no. 313 (July–September 1998): 449–465.

Boswell, James. *Account of Corsica*. 2nd ed. London, 1768.

———. *An Account of Corsica: The Journal of a Tour to that Island, and Memoirs of Pascal Paoli*. 2nd ed. London: Printed for Edward and Charles Dilly in the Poultry, 1768.

Botta, Charles. *Histoire d'Italie de 1789 à 1814*. 5 vols. Paris: Dufart, 1824.

———. *L'Île de Corse: Journal d'un voyage*. Edited by D. Carrington. Paris: Hermann, 1991.

Bottot, François-Marie. "Compte rendu par le citoyen Bottot de sa mission en Italie." A. N. AF III 473, plaquette 2906, pièce 14.

Boudon, Jacques-Olivier. *L'Épiscopat français à l'époque concordataire: 1802–1905, origines, formation, nomination*. Paris: Cerf, 1996.

Boulainvilliers, Anne-Gabriel-Henri-Bernard de. *La Vie de Mahomet*. London: n.p., 1730.

Boulart, Jean-François. *Mémoires (1792–1815)*. Paris: La Librairie illustrée, n.d.

Boulay de la Meurthe, Alfred. *Documents sur la négociation du Concordat et sur les autres rapports de la France avec le Saint-Siège en 1800 et 1801*. 6 vols. Paris: Leroux, 1891–1905.

———. *Histoire de la négociation du concordat de 1801*. Tours: Mame, 1920.

———. *Le Directoire et l'expédition d'Égypte: Étude sur les tentatives du Directoire pour communiquer avec Bonaparte, le secourir et le ramener.* Paris: Hachette, 1885.

Boulay de la Meurthe, Antoine-Jacques. *Théorie constitutionnelle de Sieyès: Extraits des mémoires inédits de M. Boulay de la Meurthe; Constitution de l'an VIII.* Paris: Renouard, 1836.

Boulos, A., ed. *Bourrienne et ses erreurs.* 2 vols. Paris: Heideloff and Canel, 1830.

Bourcet, Pierre-Joseph de. *Principes de la guerre de montagnes* [1775]. Paris: Imprimerie Nationale, 1888.

Bourdin, Philippe, and Bernard Gainot. *La République directoriale: Actes du colloque de Clermont-Ferrand, 22–24 mai 1997.* 2 vols. Clermont-Ferrand: Société des études robespierristes; Centre d'histoire des entreprises et des communautés; Centre de recherches révolutionnaires et romantiques, 1998.

Bourdon, Jean. *La Réforme judiciaire de l'an VIII.* 2 vols. Rodez: Carrère, 1941.

Bourgeois, Armand. *Le général Bonaparte et la presse de son époque.* Paris: Champion, 1906.

Bourrienne, Louis-Antoine Fauvelet de. *Mémoires sur Napoléon, le Directoire, le Consulat, l'Empire et la Restauration.* 10 vols. Paris: Ladvocat, 1831.

———. *Private Memoirs of Napoleon Bonaparte, during the Periods of the Directory, the Consulate, and the Empire.* Philadelphia: Carey and Lea, 1831.

Boustamy, Saladin, ed. *The Journals of Bonaparte in Egypt, 1798–1801.* 10 vols. Cairo: Al Arab Bookshop, 1971–1977.

Boutant, Charles. *L'Europe au grand tournant des années 1680: La succession palatine.* Paris: SEDES, 1985.

Bouthillon, Fabrice. "Comme quoi Napoléon n'a jamais existé, ou le révisionnisme en histoire." *Commentaire* 11, no. 43 (Autumn 1988): 769–777.

Bouvier, Félix. *Bonaparte en Italie: 1796.* Paris: Cerf, 1899.

Boyer, F. "Les responsabilités de Napoléon dans le transfert à Paris des oeuvres d'art de l'étranger." *Revue d'histoire moderne et contemporaine* 11 (1964): 241–262.

Bozarslan, Hamit. *Histoire de la Turquie.* Paris: Tallandier, 2013.

Branda, Pierre. *Le Prix de la gloire: Napoléon et l'argent.* Paris: Fayard, 2007.

———. *Napoléon et ses hommes.* Paris: Fayard, 2011.

Branda, Pierre, and Thierry Lentz. *Napoléon, l'esclavage et les colonies.* Paris: Fayard, 2006.

Bredin, Jean-Denis. *Sieyès, la clé de la Révolution française.* Paris: Éditions de Fallois, 1988.

Brégeon, Jean-Joël. *L'Égypte de Bonaparte.* Paris: Perrin, 2006.

Bret, Patrice. *L'Égypte au temps de l'expédition de Bonaparte, 1798–1801.* Paris: Hachette, 1998.

Bricard, Jules, and Alfred Bricard. *Journal du canonnier Bricard, 1792–1802.* Paris: Delagrave, 1891.

Brice, Catherine. *Histoire de l'Italie.* Paris: Perrin, 2002.

Broers, Michael. *The Napoleonic Empire in Italy, 1796–1814: Cultural Imperialism in a European Context?* New York: Palgrave Macmillan, 2005.

———. *The Politics of Religion in Napoleonic Italy: The War against God, 1801–1814.* London: Routledge, 2002.

Brotonne, Léonce de. *Les Sénateurs du Consulat et de l'Empire: Tableau historique des pairs de France (1789–1814–1848); Les sénateurs du Second Empire.* Geneva: Slatkine-Megariotis, 1974.

Brouwet, Émile. *1934, 16 novembre: Napoléon et son temps, catalogue de livres.* Paris: n.p., 1934–1936.

Brown, Howard G. *Ending the French Revolution: Violence, Justice and Repression from the Terror to Napoleon.* Charlottesville: University of Virginia Press, 2006.

———. "From Organic Society to Security State: The War on Brigandage in France, 1797–1802." *Journal of Modern History* 69, no. 4 (December 1997): 661–695.

Bruce, Evangeline. *Napoleon and Josephine: An Improbable Marriage.* London: Phoenix, 1995.

Bruguière, Michel. *Gestionnaires et profiteurs de la Révolution: L'administration des finances françaises de Louis XVI à Bonaparte.* Paris: Olivier Orban, 1986.

Buchez, B.-J., and P.-C. Roux. *Histoire parlementaire de la Révolution française ou Journal des Assemblées nationales depuis 1789 jusqu'en 1815.* 40 vols. Paris: Paulin, 1834–1838.

Bulletin de Paris. September 13–December 18, 1797.

Burgess, Anthony. *La Symphonie Napoléon.* Paris: R. Laffont, 1977.

Buti, Gilbert. "Convois pour l'expédition d'Égypte." *Bonaparte, les îles méditerranéennes et l'appel de l'Orient, Cahiers de la Méditerranée,* no. 57 (December 1998): 173–205.

Cabanis, André. "Un idéologue bonapartiste: Roederer." *Revue de l'Institut Napoléon* (1977): 3–19.

Cabanis, José. *Le Sacre de Napoléon.* Paris: Gallimard, 2007.

Cadet de Gassicourt, Charles-Louis. *Voyage en Autriche, en Moravie et en Bavière, fait à la suite de l'armée française pendant la campagne de 1809.* Paris: l'Huillier, 1818.

Cahiers d'Alexandre Des Mazis. http://napoleonbonaparte.wordpress.com/2007/08/11/les-cahiers-alexandre-des-mazis-ecole-militaire-1/.

Caldwell, Ronald J. *The Era of Napoleon: A Bibliography of the History of Western Civilization, 1799–1815.* 2 vols. New York: Garland, 1991.

Cambacérès, Jean-Jacques-Régis de. *Lettres inédites à Napoléon.* Edited by J. Tulard. 2 vols. Paris: Klincksieck, 1973.

———. *Mémoires inédits.* 2 vols. Edited by L. Chatel de Brancion. Paris: Perrin, 1999.

Camon, Hubert. *Quand et comment Napoléon a conçu son système de manoeuvre.* Paris: Berger-Levrault, 1931.

Candela, Gilles. *L'armée d'Italie: Des missionnaires armés à la naissance de la guerre napoléonienne.* Rennes: Presses Universitaires de Rennes, 2011.

Capra, Carlo. *I progressi della ragione: Vita di Pietro Verri.* Bologne: Il Mulino, 2002.

Caratini, Roger. *Napoléon, une imposture.* Paris: L'Archipel, 2002.

Carbonnier, Jean. "La Guerre des Géants sous la toise du Droit (ca. 1943): Essai d'un examen juridique de la première insurrection de l'Ouest." In *Écrits,* 1077–1109. Paris: PUF, 2008.

———. "Le Code civil." In *Les Lieux de mémoire,* edited by P. Nora, 1:1331–1351. Paris: Gallimard, 1997.

Carlyle, Thomas. *Heroes and Hero Worship.* New York: Lovell Brothers, 1800.

———. *Les Héros.* Paris: Maisonneuve et Larose/Édition des Deux Mondes, 1998.

Carnot, Lazare. *Mémoires, 1753–1823.* Edited by H. Carnot. 2 vols. Paris: Hachette, 1907.

———. *Réponse au rapport fait sur la conjuration du 18 fructidor au Conseil des Cinq-Cents par J.-Ch. Bailleul.* Paris: n.p., 1798.

Carré, Jean-Marie. *Voyageurs et écrivains français en Égypte.* 2 vols. Cairo: Institut français d'archéologie orientale, 1990.

Carrington, Dorothy. "Les Pozzo di Borgo et les Bonaparte (jusqu'en 1793), d'après les mémoires manuscrits de Charles-André Pozzo di Borgo." In *Problèmes d'histoire de la Corse (de l'Ancien*

Régime à 1815): Actes du Colloque d'Ajaccio, 29 octobre 1969, 101–129. Paris: Société des études robespierristes, 1971.

———. *Napoleon and His Parents: On the Threshold of History*. New York: Dutton, 1990.

Carrot, Georges. "Napoléon Bonaparte et le maintien de l'ordre, d'août 1786 à Vendémiaire an IV." *Revue de l'Institut Napoléon*, no. 165 (April 1994): 7–20.

Casanova, Antoine, and Ange Rovère. *La Révolution française en Corse, 1789–1800*. Toulouse: Privat, 1989.

Castelot, André. *Joséphine*. Paris: Perrin, 1964.

Caulaincourt, Armand-Augustin-Louis de. *Mémoires*. 3 vols. Paris: Plon, 1933.

Cevallos Guerra, Pedro. *Política peculiar de Buonaparte en quanto á la Religión Católica: Medios de que se vale para extinguirla y subyugar los Españoles por la seducción ya que no puede dominarles por la fuerza*. Guadalajara: n.p., 1812.

Chaillou, David. *Napoléon et l'Opéra: La Politique sur la scène, 1810–1815*. Paris: Fayard, 2004.

Chalbrand (Colonel). *Les Français en Égypte, ou souvenirs des campagnes d'Égypte et de Syrie par un officier de l'expédition*. Tours: Mame, 1868.

Chandler, David G. *The Campaigns of Napoleon*. New York: Macmillan, 1966.

Chaptal, Jean-Antoine. *Mes souvenirs sur Napoléon*. Edited by P. Gueniffey. Paris: Mercure de France, 2009.

Chardigny, Louis. *Les Maréchaux de Napoléon*. Paris: Tallandier, 1977.

Charles-Roux, François. *Bonaparte, gouverneur d'Égypte*. Paris: Plon, 1936.

———. *L'Angleterre et l'expédition française en Égypte*. 2 vols. Cairo: Société Royale de Géographie d'Égypte, 1925.

———. *La Politique française en Égypte à la fin du XVIIIe siècle*. Paris: n.p., 1906.

———. "Le projet français de conquête de l'Égypte sous le règne de Louis XVI." In *Mémoires présentés à l'Institut d'Égypte*, vol. 14. Cairo: IFAO, 1929.

Chassin, Charles-Louis. *Les Pacifications de l'Ouest, 1794–1801–1815*. 3 vols. Paris: Dupont, 1899.

Chastenay, Victorine de. *Deux révolutions pour une seule vie: Mémoires, 1771–1855*. Paris: Tallandier, 2009.

Chateaubriand, François-René de. *De l'Ancien Régime au Nouveau Monde: Écrits politiques*. Edited by J.-P. Clément. Paris: Hachette, 1987.

———. *Mémoires d'outre-tombe*. Edited by J.-P. Clément. 2 vols. Paris: Gallimard, 1997.

Chaussinand-Nogaret, Guy. *Les Financiers du Languedoc au XVIIIe siècle*. Paris: SEVPEN, 1970.

Cherfils, Christian. *Bonaparte et l'Islam, d'après les documents français et arabes*. Paris: Pedone, 1914.

Cherrier, Emmanuel. *18 Brumaire et 2 Décembre: D'un coup d'état à l'autre; Éléments pour une étude du coup d'état*. 3 vols. Doctoral thesis. Paris: EHESS, 1999.

Chevallier, Jean-Jacques. *Histoire des institutions et des régimes politiques de la France de 1789 à nos jours*. 6th ed. Paris: Dalloz, 1981.

Chrétienne, Valérie, *Charles-François Lebrun (1739–1824)*. 2 vols. Villeneuve d'Ascq: Presses Universitaires du Septentrion, 1998.

Chuquet, Arthur. *La Jeunesse de Napoléon*. 3 vols. Paris: Armand Colin, 1898–1899.

Cini, Marco. *Nascita di un mito: Pasquale Paoli*. Pisa: BFS, 1998.

Clausewitz, Carl von. *Bonaparte en Italie: La campagne de 1796 en Italie*. Paris: Pocket, 1999.

———. *De la guerre.* Paris: Éditions de Minuit, 1955.

———. *La Campagne de 1815 en France.* Paris: Champ libre, 1973.

Code corse, ou recueil des édits, déclarations, lettres patentes, arrêts et règlements publiés dans l'île de Corse depuis sa soumission à l'obéissance du roi. 3 vols. Paris: Imprimerie Royale, 1778.

Colin, Jean. *L'Éducation militaire de Napoléon.* Paris: Teissèdre, 2001.

Collaveri, François. *Napoléon franc-maçon?* Paris: Tallandier, 2003.

Coller, Ian. *Arab France: Islam and the Making of Modern Europe, 1798–1831.* Berkeley: University of California Press, 2011.

Collins, Irene. *Napoleon and His Parliaments, 1800–1815.* London: Edward Arnold, 1979.

Condorcet, Jean-Antoine-Nicolas de Caritat de. *Esquisse d'un tableau historique des progrès de l'esprit humain.* 2 vols. Paris: Dubuisson et Marpon, 1864.

Consalvi, Hercule. *Mémoires du cardinal Consalvi.* 2 vols. Paris: Plon, 1864.

Constant, Benjamin. *De la force du gouvernement actuel de la France et de la nécessité de s'y rallier (1796): Des réactions politiques; Des effets de la Terreur (1797).* Edited by P. Raynaud. Paris: Flammarion, 1988.

———. *De l'esprit de conquête et de l'usurpation.* Montpellier: Archange minotaure, 2003.

———. *Journaux intimes (1804–1807).* In *Oeuvres complètes,* vol. 6, edited by P. Delbouille, S. Balayé, A. Blaeschke, and K. Kloocke. Tübingen: Niemeyer, 2002.

Constant Wairy, Louis. *Mémoires intimes de Napoléon Ier par Constant, son valet de chambre.* Edited by M. Dernelle. 2 vols. Paris: Mercure de France, 2002.

———. *Memoirs of Constant, First Valet De Chambre of the Emperor, on the Private Life of Napoleon, His Family and His Court.* Translated by Elizabeth Gilbert Martin. 4 vols. New York: C. Scribner's Sons, 1895.

Coquelle, Pierre. *Les Projets de descente en Angleterre, d'après les archives des Affaires Etrangère.* Paris: Plon-Nourrit, 1902.

Costa de Beauregard, Charles-Albert. *Un homme d'autrefois.* Paris: Plon, 1886.

Coston, Adolphe de. *Biographie des premières années de Napoléon Bonaparte, c'est-à-dire depuis sa naissance jusqu'à l'époque de son commandement en chef de l'armée d'Italie.* 2 vols. Paris: Marc Aurel frères, 1840.

Cottret, Monique. *Tuer le tyran? Le tyrannicide dans l'Europe moderne.* Paris: Fayard, 2009.

Covin, Michel. *Les Mille visages de Napoléon.* Paris: L'Harmattan, 1999.

Cranmer-Byng, John L. "Lord Macartney's Embassy to Peking in 1793." *Journal of Oriental Studies* 4 (1957–1958): 117–187.

Crook, Malcolm. "Confiance d'en bas, manipulation d'en haut: La Pratique plébiscitaire sous Napoléon (1799–1815)." In *L'Incident électoral de la Révolution française à la Ve République,* edited by Ph. Bourdin, J.-C. Caron, and M. Bernard. Clermont-Ferrand: Université Blaise-Pascal, 2002.

———. *Napoleon Comes to Power: Democracy and Dictatorship in Revolutionary France, 1795–1804.* Cardiff: University of Wales Press, 1998.

Crouzet, François. *La Grande inflation: La monnaie en France de Louis XVI à Napoléon.* Paris: Fayard, 1993.

Cugnac, Jean de. *Campagne de l'armée de réserve en 1800.* 2 vols. Paris: Chapelot, 1900–1901.

Cuoco, Vincenzo. *Essai historique sur la révolution de Naples.* Edited by A. De Francesco. Paris: Les Belles Lettres, 2004.

Damamme, Jean-Claude. *Les Soldats de la Grande Armée*. Paris: Perrin, 1998.

Dard, Émile. *Napoléon et Talleyrand*. Paris: Plon, 1935.

Daudet, Ernest. *Histoire de l'émigration pendant la Révolution française*. 3 vols. Paris: Hachette, 1905–1907.

Dayot, Armand. *Napoléon: Raconté par l'image d'après les sculpteurs, les graveurs et les peintres*. Paris: Hachette, 1895.

Dean Paul, John. *Journal d'un voyage à Paris au mois d'août 1802*. Edited by P. Lacombe. Paris: Picard, 1913.

De Baecque, Antoine. *Le Corps de l'histoire: Métaphores et politique (1770–1800)*. Paris: Calmann-Lévy, 1993.

Debidour, Augustin. *Recueil des actes du Directoire exécutif (procès-verbaux, arrêtés, instructions, lettres et actes divers)*. 4 vols. Paris: Imprimerie Nationale, 1910–1917.

Défossé, Gabriel. *Montenotte, la première victoire de Napoléon Bonaparte, général en chef, commandant l'armée d'Italie, 12 avril 1796*. Cagnes-sur-Mer: EDICA, 1986.

Defranceschi, Jean. *La Corse française (30 novembre 1789–15 juin 1794)*. Paris: Société des études robespierristes, 1980.

———. *La Jeunesse de Napoléon: Les dessous de l'histoire*. Paris: Lettrage, 2001.

———. "Le rôle du lieutenant Bonaparte aux débuts de la Révolution française en Corse." *Revue de l'Institut Napoléon*, no. 134 (1978): 3–20.

De Francesco, Antonino. *L'Italia di Bonaparte: Politica, statualità e nazione nella penisola tra due rivoluzioni, 1796–1821*. Turin: UTET Libreria, 2011.

De Gaulle, Charles. *Le Fil de l'épée*. Paris: Perrin, 2010.

Dehérain, Henri. *Histoire de la nation égyptienne*. Vol. 5, *L'Égypte turque: Pachas et mamelouks du XVIe au XVIIIe siècle; L'expédition du général Bonaparte*. Paris: Société de l'histoire nationale/Librairie Plon, 1934.

Delbeke, Francis. *Action politique et sociale des avocats au XVIIIe siècle*. Louvain: Imprimerie des Trois-Rois, 1927.

Delécluze, Étienne-Jean. *Louis David, son école et son temps: Souvenirs*. Edited by J.-P. Mouilleseaux. Paris: Macula, 1983.

De Meulenaere, Philippe. *Bibliographie raisonnée des témoignages oculaires imprimés de l'expédition d'Égypte (1798–1801)*. Paris: Chamonal, 1993.

Demolins, Edmond. *Les Français d'aujourd'hui: Les Types sociaux du Midi et du Centre*. Paris: Librairie de Paris, 1900.

Denon, Vivant. *Lettres à Bettine*. Arles: Actes Sud, 1999.

———. *Voyage dans la basse et la haute Égypte pendant les campagnes du général Bonaparte*. Edited by R. Brunon. Paris: Pygmalion/Gérard Watelet, 1990.

Denon, Vivant, and 'Abd al-Rahmân al-Jabartî. *Sur l'expédition de Bonaparte en Égypte*. Edited by Mahmoud Hussein. Arles: Actes Sud, 2008.

Description de l'Égypte publiée par les ordres de Sa Majesté l'Empereur Napoléon le Grand. Complete digital version. Le Mans: Harpocrate, 2006.

Desgenettes, René-Nicolas. *Histoire médicale de l'armée d'Orient*. Paris: Croullebois, 1802.

Desprez, Claude. *Lazare Hoche d'après sa correspondance et ses notes*. Paris: Dumaine, 1858.

Destrem, Jean. *Les Déportations du Consulat et de l'Empire*. Paris: Jeanmaire, 1885.

Desvernois, Nicolas-Philibert. *Mémoires.* Edited by A. Dufourcq. Paris: Plon, 1898.

Didelot, Jean. *Bourrienne et Napoléon.* Levallois-Perret: Centre d'études napoléoniennes, 1999.

Djuvara, T. G. *Cent projets de partage de la Turquie.* Paris: Alcan, 1914.

Doguereau, Jean-Pierre. *Journal de l'expédition d'Égypte.* Paris: La Vouivre, 1997.

Dosse, François. *Le Pari biographique.* Paris: La Découverte, 2005.

Douin, Georges. *La Campagne de Bruix en Méditerranée, mars-août 1799.* Paris: Société d'éditions géographiques, maritimes et coloniales, 1923.

——. *La Flotte de Bonaparte sur les côtes d'Égypte: Les prodromes d'Aboukir.* Cairo: Printed by the French Institute of Oriental Archaeology for the Royal Geographical Society of Egypt, 1922.

——. "Le retour de Bonaparte d'Égypte en France." *Bulletin de l'Institut d'Égypte* 23 (1941): 184–216.

Driault, Édouard. *Napoléon en Italie (1800–1812).* Paris: 1906.

——. *Napoléon et l'Europe: La politique extérieure du Premier consul (1800–1803).* Paris: Alcan, 1910.

Dubois, Laurent. *Les Vengeurs du nouveau monde: Histoire de la Révolution haïtienne.* Rennes: Les Perséides, 2005.

Ducher, Gaspard-Joseph-Amand. *Acte de navigation avec ses rapports au commerce, aux finances, à la nouvelle diplomatie des Français, imprimé par ordre de la Convention nationale, décret du 18 août 1793.* 2 vols. Paris: Imprimerie nationale, 1793.

Dufraisse, Roger. "Bonaparte a-t-il sacrifié le Rhin à l'Italie en 1796–1797?" *Le Souvenir napoléonien,* no. 416 (January–February 1998): 5–20.

Dumas, Guy. *La Fin de la République de Venis: Aspects et reflets littéraires.* Rennes: Imprimerie bretonne, 1964.

Dumas, Mathieu. *Souvenirs.* 3 vols. Paris: Gosselin, 1839.

Dumolard, Joseph-Vincent. *Conseil des Cinq Cents: Motion d'ordre sur nos rapports actuels avec l'Italie; Séance du 5 messidor an V.* Paris: Imprimerie Nationale, 1797.

Dumouriez, Charles-François. *La Vie et les mémoires du général Dumouriez.* 4 vols. Paris: Baudouin, 1822–1823.

Dupont, Marcel. *Pauline Fourès, une maîtresse de Napoléon.* Paris: Hachette, 1942.

Durand, Charles. "Conseils privés, conseils des ministres, conseils d'administration de 1800 à 1814." *Revue d'histoire moderne et contemporaine* 17 (July–September 1970): 814–828.

——. *Études sur le Conseil d'État napoléonien.* Paris: PUF, 1949.

——. "Les transformations de l'an X dans les rapports entre le gouvernement et les assemblées." *Revue de l'Institut Napoléon* (1969): 69–78.

——. *L'Exercice de la fonction législative de 1800 à 1814.* Aix-en-Provence: Imprimerie des Croix provençales, 1955.

——. "Napoléon et le Conseil d'État." *Revue de l'Institut Napoléon* (1962): 145–156.

——. "Rome a remplacé Sparte." In *Le Grand livre de Napoléon,* edited by J. Mistler, 1:172–186. Paris: Bibliothèque des Arts, 1968.

Dutourd, Jean. *Rivarol, les plus belles pages.* Paris: Mercure de France, 1963.

Dutruch, Roger. *Le Tribunat sous le Consulat et l'Empire.* Paris: Rousseau, 1921.

Dwyer, Philip G. *Napoleon: The Path to Power, 1769–1799.* London: Bloomsbury, 2007.

Emerson, Ralph Waldo. "Napoléon ou l'homme du monde." In W. E. Channing and R. W. Emerson, *Vie et caractère de Napoléon Bonaparte*, edited by F. Van Meenen, 143–178. Brussels: Van Meenen, 1857.

———. *Representative Men: The Collected Works of Ralph Waldo Emerson*. Cambridge, Mass: Belknap Press of Harvard University Press, 1987.

Englund, Steven. *Napoleon: A Political Life*. Cambridge, Mass.: Harvard University Press, 2004.

Ernouf, Alfred Auguste. *Maret, duc de Bassano*. Paris: Charpentier, 1878.

Espitalier, Albert. *Vers Brumaire: Bonaparte à Paris, 5 décembre 1797–4 mai 1798*. Paris: Perrin, 1914.

Ettori, Fernand. "Pascal Paoli, modèle du jeune Bonaparte." In *Problèmes d'histoire de la Corse (de l'Ancien Régime à 1815): Actes du Colloque d'Ajaccio, 29 octobre 1969*, 89–99. Paris: Société des études robespierristes, 1971.

Fain, Agathon Jean-François. *Mémoires*. Paris: Plon, 1908.

Faure, Élie. *Napoléon*. Paris: Éditions G. Crès, 1921.

Fejtö, François. *Joseph II, un Habsbourg révolutionnaire*. Paris: Perrin, 1982.

Ferrero, Guglielmo. *Bonaparte en Italie (1796–1797)*. Paris: Éditions de Fallois, 1994.

———. *Pouvoir: Les génies invisibles de la cité*. Paris: LGF, 1988.

Fierro, Alfred. *Les Français vus par eux-mêmes: Le Consulat et l'Empire; Anthologie des mémorialistes du Consulat et de l'Empire*. Paris: R. Laffont, 1998.

Fierro, Alfred, André Palluel-Guillard, and Jean Tulard. *Histoire et dictionnaire du Consulat et de l'Empire*. Paris: R. Laffont, 1995.

Fiévée, Joseph. *Correspondance et relations avec Bonaparte Premier consul et Empereur, pendant onze années (1802–1813)*. Paris: Desrez et Beauvais, 1837.

Flaubert, Gustave. *Correspondance*. Vol. 1. [January 1830–May 1851.] Edited by J. Bruneau. Paris: Gallimard, 1973.

Fleischmann, Hector. *Charlotte Robespierre et ses Mémoires*. Paris: Albin Michel, 1910.

Fleischmann, Théo. *Napoléon et la musique*. Brussels: Brepols, 1965.

Fogel, Robert William. *Without Consent or Contract: The Rise and Fall of American Slavery*. New York: W. W. Norton, 1989.

Fogel, Robert William, and Stanley L. Engerman. *Time on the Cross: The Economics of American Slavery*. Boston: Little, Brown, 1974.

Fontanes, Louis-Jean-Pierre. *Oeuvres*. 2 vols. Paris: Hachette, 1839.

Forrest, Alan. "L'Angleterre face à la France napoléonienne." In *Napoléon, le monde et les Anglais: Guerre des mots et des images*, edited by J.-P. Bertaud, A. Forrest, and A. Jourdan. Paris: Éditions Autrement, 2004.

Foucart, Bruno. "Les Salons sous le Consulat et les diverses représentations de Bonaparte." *Revue de l'Institut Napoléon* (1969): 113–119.

Fouché, Joseph. *Mémoires*. 2 vols. Osnabrück: Proff, 1824.

———. *Memoirs of Joseph Fouché*. Philadelphia: J. B. Lippincott Co., 1892.

Fournoux, Amable de. *Napoléon et Venise, 1796–1814*. Paris: Éditions de Fallois, 2002.

Franceschini, Émile. "Saliceti et Napoléon." *Revue des études napoléoniennes* 31 (1930): 131–155.

François, Charles. *Journal du capitaine François, dit le Dromadaire d'Égypte, 1792–1830*. Edited by Ch. Grolleau and J. Jourquin. Paris: Tallandier, 2003.

Friedlander, Walter. "Napoleon as *roi thaumaturge.*" *Journal of Warburg Studies* 4 (1940–1941).

Fugier, André. *Napoléon et l'Italie.* Paris: J.-B. Janin, 1947.

Furet, François. "Bonaparte." In F. Furet and M. Ozouf, *Dictionnaire critique de la Révolution française,* 2nd ed., vol. 1, *Événements,* 216–229. Paris: Flammarion, 1988.

———. "Dix-huit brumaire." In F. Furet et M. Ozouf, *Dictionnaire critique de la Révolution française,* 2nd ed., vol. 1, *Événements,* 101–121. Paris: Flammarion, 1992.

———. *La Révolution: De Turgot à Jules Ferry, 1770–1880.* Paris: Hachette, 1988.

———. *Le Passé d'une illusion: Essai sur l'idée communiste au XXe siècle.* Paris: R. Laffont/Calmann-Lévy, 1995.

Furet, François, Antoine Liniers, and Philippe Raynaud. *Terrorisme et démocratie.* Paris: Fayard, 1985.

Furet, François, and Denis Richet. *La Révolution française.* Paris: Hachette, 1973.

Gabory, Émile. *Napoléon et la Vendée.* 3 vols. Paris: Perrin, 1914.

Gaffarel, Paul. *Bonaparte et les républiques italiennes (1796–1799).* Paris: Félix Alcan, 1895.

———. "L'Affaire Clément de Ris d'après un document inédit." *La Révolution française* 12 (January–June 1887): 704–714.

Gainot, Bernard. *1799, un nouveau jacobinisme? La démocratie représentative, une alternative à Brumaire.* Paris: Comité des travaux historiques et scientifiques, 2001.

Galantini, Federico. *Napoléon et Sarzane: Les origines italiennes de Bonaparte.* Paris: Michel de Maule, 2004.

Galland, Antoine. *Tableau de l'Égypte pendant le séjour de l'armée française: Ouvrage où l'on traite des moeurs, usages et caractère des Égyptiens.* 2 vols. Paris: Galland, 1804.

Garcia de Enterria, Eduardo. *Révolution française et administration contemporaine.* Paris: Economica, 1993.

Garnier, Jean-Paul. *Barras, le roi du Directoire.* Paris: Perrin, 1970.

Garnier, Michaël. *Bonaparte et la Louisiane.* Paris: SPM, 1992.

Gaubert, Henri. *Conspirateurs au temps de Napoléon Ier.* Paris: Flammarion, 1962.

Gauchet, Marcel. *La Religion dans la démocratie, parcours de la laïcité.* Paris: Gallimard, 1998.

———. *La Révolution des pouvoirs: La souveraineté, le peuple et la représentation, 1789–1799.* Paris: Gallimard, 1995.

Gaudin, Martin-Michel-Charles. *Mémoires, souvenirs, opinions et écrits.* 3 vols. Paris: Armand Colin, 1926.

———. *Notice historique sur les finances de France, de l'an VIII (1800) au 1er avril 1814.* Paris: Ange Clo, 1818.

———. *Supplément aux mémoires et souvenirs de M. Gaudin.* Paris: Goetschy, 1834.

Gaulmier, Jean. *L'Idéologue Volney, 1757–1820: Contribution à l'histoire de l'orientalisme en France.* Geneva: Slatkine, 1980.

Gazette nationale ou le Moniteur universel. 1796. 2 vols.

Gazette nationale ou le Moniteur universel. 1799. 2 vols.

Gendry, Jules. *Pie VI, sa vie, son pontificat (1717–1799).* 2 vols. Paris: Picard, 1906.

Geoffroy Saint-Hilaire, Étienne. *L'Expédition d'Égypte, 1798–1802.* Paris: Paleo, 2000.

Geyl, Pieter. *Napoleon: For and Against.* New Haven: Yale University Press, 1949.

Gilles, Christian. *Madame Tallien, la reine du Directoire (1773–1835).* Biarritz: Atlantica, 1999.

Giornale Patriottico di Corsica. Nos. 1–32 (April 3–November 27, 1790). Bastia.

Girard, Philippe. "Napoleon Bonaparte and the Emancipation Issue in Saint-Domingue, 1799–1803." *French Historical Studies* 32, no. 4 (Autumn 2009): 587–618.

Girardin, Stanislas. *Discours et opinions, journal et souvenirs.* 3 vols. Paris: Moutardier, 1828.

Girod de l'Ain, Gabriel. *Désirée Clary.* Paris: Hachette, 1959.

Gobert, Adrienne. *L'Opposition des assemblées pendant le Consulat, 1800–1804.* Paris: Librairie générale de droit et de jurisprudence Ernest Sagot, 1925.

Goby, Jean-Édouard. *La Composition du premier institut d'Égypte.* Cairo: Imprimerie de l'Institut français, 1948.

Godechot, Jacques. *La Contre-révolution, 1789–1804.* Paris: PUF, 1984.

———. "Le babouvisme et l'unité italienne (1796–1799)." In *Regards sur l'époque révolutionnaire,* 269–288. Toulouse: Privat, 1980.

———. *Les Commissaires aux armées sous le Directoire: Contribution à l'étude des rapports entre les pouvoirs civils et militaires.* 2 vols. Paris: Fustier, 1937.

———. "Les Français et l'unité italienne sous le Directoire." In *Regards sur l'époque révolutionnaire,* 303–327. Toulouse: Privat, 1980.

———. *Regards sur l'époque révolutionnaire.* Toulouse: Privat, 1980.

Goethe, Johann Wolfgang von. *Conversations avec Eckermann.* Paris: Gallimard, 1988.

———. *Conversations with Eckermann.* Abridged edition. Translated by John Oxenford. London: Everyman Library, 1930.

Gohier, Louis-Jérôme. *Mémoires.* 2 vols. Paris: Bossange frères, 1824.

Gourgaud, Gaspard. *Journal de Sainte-Hélène, 1815–1818.* 2 vols. Edited by O. Aubry. Paris: Flammarion, 1947.

———. *Mémoires pour servir à l'histoire de France sous Napoléon, écrits à Sainte-Hélène, par les généraux qui ont partagé sa captivité.* 2 vols. Paris: Firmin-Didot et Bossange, 1823.

———. *Talks of Napoleon at St. Helena with General Baron Gourgaud: Together with the Journal Kept by Gourgaud on Their Journey from Waterloo to St. Helena.* Translated by Elizabeth Wormeley Latimer. 2nd ed. Chicago: A. C. McClurg, 1904.

Grandmaison, Geoffroy de. *L'Ambassade française en Espagne pendant la Révolution (1789–1804).* Paris: Plon, 1892.

Granger, J. "L'Opinion de l'armée au lendemain du 18 brumaire." *Revue de l'Institut Napoléon* (1954): 46–54.

Graziani, Antoine-Marie. *Pascal Paoli, père de la patrie corse,* Paris: Tallandier, 2004.

Guibert, Jacques-Antoine-Hippolyte. *Essai général de tactique.* In *Stratégiques,* edited by J.-P. Charnay and M. Burgos. Paris: L'Herne, 1977.

Guillois, Antoine. *La Marquise de Condorcet: Sa famille, son salon, ses amis, 1764–1822.* Paris: Ollendorff, 1897.

———. *Le Salon de Madame Helvétius: Cabanis et les Idéologues.* Paris: Calmann-Lévy, 1894.

Guitry, Paul. *L'Armée de Bonaparte en Égypte, 1798–1799.* Paris: Flammarion, 1898.

Guyot, Raymond. "Du Directoire au Consulat: Les transitions." *Revue historique* III (September–December 1912): 1–31.

———. *Le Directoire et la paix de l'Europe, des traités de Bâle à la deuxième coalition (1795–1799).* Paris: Félix Alcan, 1911.

Hahn, Roger. *Le Système du monde: Pierre-Simon Laplace, un itinéraire dans la science*. Paris: Gallimard, 2004.

Halperin, Jean-Louis. "La composition du Corps législatif sous le Consulat et l'Empire: De la notabilité révolutionnaire à la notabilité impériale." *Revue de l'Institut Napoléon* (1985): 37–57.

Hamelin, Antoine-Romain. "Douze ans de ma vie (1796–1808)." *La Revue de Paris*, 33rd year, vol. 6 (November–December 1926): 5–24, 281–309, 544–566, 811–839; 34th year, vol. 1 (January–February 1927): 46–71.

Hamilton, Alexander. *Works of Alexander Hamilton*. Vol. 1. New York: Haskell House, 1971.

Hanley, Wayne. *The Genesis of Napoleonic Propaganda, 1796 to 1799*. New York: Columbia University Press, 2005.

Hanson, Victor Davis. *Le Modèle occidental de la guerre: La bataille d'infanterie dans la Grèce classique*. Paris: Les Belles Lettres, 2001.

———. *The Western Way of War: Infantry Battle in Classical Greece*. New York: Knopf, 1989.

Harouel, Jean-Louis. *Les Républiques soeurs*. Paris: PUF, 1997.

Hastier, Louis. *Le Grand amour de Joséphine*. Paris: Corréa/Buchet-Chastel, 1955.

Hauterive, Ernest d'. *L'Enlèvement du sénateur Clément de Ris*. Paris: Perrin, 1926.

———. "Lettres de jeunesse de Bonaparte (1789–1792)." *Revue des Deux Mondes* (September–December 1931): 767–792.

Havard, Oscar. *Histoire de la Révolution dans les ports de guerre: I. Toulon; II. Brest, Rochefort*. 2 vols. Paris: Nouvelle librairie nationale, 1911–1913.

Hazareesingh, Sudhir. *La Saint-Napoléon: Quand le 14 juillet se fêtait le 15 août*. Paris: Tallandier, 2007.

Heine, Henri. *De l'Allemagne*. Edited by P. Grappin. Paris: Gallimard, 1998.

Heller-Roazen, Daniel. *L'Ennemi de tous: Le pirate contre les nations*. Paris: Éditions du Seuil, 2009.

Hénin, Michel. *Histoire numismatique de la Révolution française*. 2 vols. Maastricht, 1987.

Herold, J. Christopher. *Bonaparte en Égypte*. Paris: Plon, 1964.

Heuser, Beatrice. *The Evolution of Strategy: Thinking War from Antiquity to the Present*. Cambridge: Cambridge University Press, 2010.

Höjer, Torvald T. *Bernadotte maréchal de France*. Paris: Plon, 1943.

Houdecek, François. "Un projet avorté, Bonaparte chez les Turcs en 1795." *Revue du souvenir napoléonien*, 69th year, no. 464 (April–May 2006): 27–33.

Hourtoulle, François-Guy. "La campagne d'Égypte." *Revue du souvenir napoléonien*, no. 383 (June 1992): 29–38.

Hugo, Victor. *Les Orientales: Les Feuilles d'automne*. Edited by P. Albouy. Paris: Poésie/Gallimard, 1981.

Humbert, Jean-Marcel, ed. *Bonaparte et l'Égypte, feu et lumières*. Paris: Institut du monde arabe/Région Nord-Pas-de-Calais, 2008.

Humboldt, Wilhelm Von. *Journal parisien (1797–1799)*. Arles: Actes Sud, 2001.

Hyde de Neuville, Guillaume. *Mémoires et souvenirs*. 3 vols. Paris: Plon-Nourrit, 1888–1892.

Iung, Théodore. *Lucien Bonaparte et ses mémoires, 1775–1840*. 3 vols. Paris: Charpentier, 1882–1883.

James, C. L. R. *Les Jacobins noirs: Toussaint-Louverture et la Révolution de Saint-Domingue*. Paris: Éditions caribéennes, 1983.

Jessenne, Jean-Pierre, Hervé Leuwers, et al. *Du Directoire au Consulat.* 4 vols. Villeneuve d'Ascq: CRHEN-O (Université Charles de Gaulle-Lille 3), GRHIS (Université de Rouen et Région Haute-Normandie), 1999–2001.

Joffrin, Laurent. *Les Batailles de Napoléon.* Paris: Éditions du Seuil, 2000.

Joinville, Jean de. *Histoire de Saint Louis.* Edited by J. Monfrin. Paris: Les Classiques Garnier, 2010.

Jollivet, Maurice. *La Révolution française en Corse: Paoli–Bonaparte–Pozzo di Borgo.* Paris: Bureaux de la Revue de la France moderne, 1892.

Jomard, Edme-François. *Souvenirs sur Gaspard Monge et ses rapports avec Napoléon.* Paris: Thunot et Cie, 1853.

Joubert, Joseph. *Pensées, essais et maximes, suivis de Lettres à ses amis et précédés d'une notice sur sa vie, son caractère et ses travaux.* 2 vols. Paris: C. Gosselin, 1842.

Jourdan, Annie. *L'Empire de Napoléon.* Paris: Flammarion, 2000.

———. *Napoléon: Héros, imperator, mécène.* Paris: Aubier, 1998.

Jourquin, Jacques. "Un jour de mars 1796: Le mariage de Napoléon Bonaparte et Joséphine de Beauharnais." *Revue du souvenir napoléonien*, no. 406 (March 1996): 20–26.

Julliard, Jacques. *Que sont les grands hommes devenus?* Paris: Perrin, 2010.

Jullien, Marc-Antoine. *Entretien politique sur la situation actuelle de la France, et sur les plans du nouveau gouvernement.* Paris: Léger, 1799.

Kadaré, Ismaïl. *Avril brisé.* Paris: Fayard, 1982.

Keegan, John. *Histoire de la guerre: Du néolithique à la guerre du Golfe.* Paris: Dagorno, 1996.

———. *A History of Warfare.* New York: Vintage, 1994.

Kérautret, Michel. *Histoire de la Prusse.* Paris: Éditions du Seuil, 2005.

———. *Les Grands traités du Consulat (1799–1804): Documents diplomatiques du Consulat et de l'Empire.* Vol. 1. Paris: Nouveau Monde Éditions/Fondation Napoléon, 2002.

Kermina, Françoise. *Bernadotte et Désirée Clary: Le Béarnais et la Marseillaise, souverains de Suède.* Paris: Perrin, 1991.

Kissinger, Henry. *Diplomacy.* New York: Simon and Schuster, 1994.

Kitchin, Joanna. *Un journal "philosophique": La Décade (1794–1807).* Paris: Minard, 1965.

Kléber, Jean-Baptiste, Auguste Damas, Charles Morand, et al. *L'État-major de Kléber en Égypte, 1798–1800, d'après leurs carnets, journaux, rapports et notes.* Edited by St. Le Couëdic. Paris: La Vouivre, 1997.

Knapton, Ernest J. "A Contemporary Impression of Napoleon Bonaparte in 1797." *French Historical Studies* 1, no. 4 (Autumn 1960): 476–481.

Krebs, Léonce, and Henri Moris. *Campagnes des Alpes pendant la Révolution, d'après les archives des états-majors français et austro-sarde.* 2 vols. Paris: Plon-Nourrit, 1891–1895.

Krettly, Élie. *Souvenirs historiques.* Edited by G. Bodinier. Paris: Nouveau Monde Éditions/ Fondation Napoléon, 2003.

Künzi, Frédéric. *Bicentenaire du passage des Alpes par Bonaparte, 1800–2000.* Martigny: Fondation Pierre Gianadda, 2000.

Lachadenède, René de. "L'amiral Brueys à Aboukir." *La Nouvelle revue maritime*, no. 378 (June 1983): 52–71.

Lacorre, Alexandre. *Journal inédit d'un commis aux vivres pendant l'expédition d'Égypte*. Bordeaux: Émile Crugy, 1852.

Lacour-Gayet, Georges. *Talleyrand*. Paris: Payot, 1990.

Lacretelle, Charles de. *Dix années d'épreuves pendant la Révolution*. Paris: Tallandier, 2011.

Lacroix, Désiré. *Bonaparte en Égypte (1798–1799)*. Paris: Garnier, 1899.

La Décade égyptienne: Journal littéraire et d'économie politique. 3 vols. Cairo: Imprimerie Nationale, 1798–1799.

La Fayette, Gilbert du Motier. *Mémoires, correspondance et manuscrits*. 6 vols. Paris: H. Fournier aîné; Leipzig, Brockhaus, 1837–1838.

La Gorce, Pierre de. *Histoire religieuse de la Révolution française*. 5 vols. Paris: Plon-Nourrit, 1922–1923.

La Harpe, Jean-François. "Éloge de Nicolas de Catinat, maréchal de France." In *Choix d'éloges couronnés par l'Académie française, précédé de l'Essai sur les éloges par Thomas*, 2:279–343. Paris: Chaumerot, 1812.

Laissus, Yves. *L'Égypte, une aventure savante, 1798–1801*. Paris: Fayard, 1998.

La Jonquière, Clément de. *L'Expédition d'Égypte, 1798–1801*. 5 vols. Paris: Charles-Lavauzelle, 1899–1907.

Landrieux, Jean. *Mémoires*. Edited by L. Grasilier. Paris: Savine, 1893.

Lanfrey, Pierre. *Histoire de Napoléon Ier*. 5 vols. Paris: Charpentier, 1892–1896.

———. *The History of Napoleon the First*. 2nd ed. London: Macmillan, 1886.

Langlois, Claude. "Le plébiscite de l'an VIII et le coup d'État du 18 pluviôse an VIII." *Annales historiques de la Révolution française* 44 (1972): 43–65, 231–246, 390–415.

Lanzac de Laborie, Léon de. *Paris sous Napoléon*. 8 vols. Paris: Plon, 1905–1913.

La Parra Lopez, Emilio. *Manuel Godoy, la aventura del poder*. Barcelona: Tusquets, 2005.

Laporte, Joseph. *Mon voyage en Égypte et en Syrie: Carnets d'un jeune soldat de Bonaparte*. Paris: PUF/Fondation Martin Bodmer, 2007.

Larchey, Loredan. *Correspondance intime de l'armée d'Égypte interceptée par la croisière anglaise*. Paris: Pincebourde, 1866.

La Révellière-Lépeaux, Louis-Marie de. *Mémoires*. 3 vols. Paris: Plon-Nourrit, 1895.

Larrey, Dominique-Jean. *Mémoires de chirurgie militaire et campagnes*. Vol. 1, *1787–1811: Campagnes de l'Amérique septentrionale, du Rhin, de Corse, des Alpes-Maritimes, de Catalogne, d'Italie, d'Égypte et de Syrie, de Boulogne, d'Ulm et d'Austerlitz, de Saxe, de Prusse, de Pologne, d'Espagne et d'Autriche*. Paris: Tallandier, 2004.

Larrey, Hippolyte. *Madame Mère: Essai historique*. 2 vols. Paris: Dentu, 1892.

Las Cases, Emmanuel de. *Journal of the Private Life and Conversations of the Emperor Napoleon at Saint Helena*. 4 vols. London: H. Colburn, 1825.

———. *Mémorial de Sainte-Hélène*. 4 vols. Edited by A. Fugier. Paris: Garnier, 1961.

La Sicotière, Louis de. *Louis de Frotté et les insurrections normandes, 1793–1832*. 3 vols. Paris: Plon, 1889.

Latour, François. *Le Grand argentier de Napoléon*. Paris: Éditions du Scorpion, 1962.

La Tour du Pin, Henriette-Lucie Dillon de. *Journal d'une femme de cinquante ans (1778–1815)*. 2 vols. Paris: Chapelot, 1913.

Latreille, André. *L'Église catholique et la Révolution française*. 2 vols. Paris: Hachette, 1946–1950.

Laurens, Henry. *Kléber en Égypte, 1798–1800: Kléber et Bonaparte, 1798–1799.* 2 vols. Cairo: IFAO, 1988.

———. *Les Origines intellectuelles de l'expédition d'Égypte: L'orientalisme islamisant en France (1698–1798).* Istanbul: Isis, 1987.

———. "Napoléon, l'Europe et le monde arabe." In *Napoléon et l'Europe,* edited by Thierry Lentz, 366–377. Paris: Fayard, 2005.

———. *Orientales.* Vol. 1, *Autour de l'expédition d'Égypte.* Paris: CNRS, 2004.

Laurens, Henry, Charles C. Gillispie, Jean-Claude Golvin, and Claude Traunecker. *L'Expédition d'Égypte, 1798–1801.* Paris: Armand Colin, 1989.

Laus de Boissy, Louis de. *Bonaparte au Caire, ou mémoires sur l'expédition de ce général en Égypte, avec des détails curieux et instructifs sur cette intéressante partie du globe.* Amsterdam: Société typographique, 1799.

Lavalette, Antoine-Marie Chamans de. *Mémoires et souvenirs.* 2 vols. Paris: Fournier jeune, 1831.

———. *Memoirs of Count Lavallette.* 2 vols. 2nd ed. London: Henry Colburn and Richard Bentley, 1831.

Lawrence, Thomas Edward. *Les Sept piliers de la sagesse.* Paris: Gallimard, 1992.

Lebon, André. *L'Angleterre et l'émigration française de 1794 à 1801.* Paris: Plon, 1882.

Leclerc d'Ostein, François. *Mémoires, campagne d'Égypte.* Brussels: Association belge napoléonienne, 1992.

Lecomte, L.-Henry. *Napoléon et le monde dramatique.* Paris: Daragon, 1912.

Le Conseil d'État: Son histoire à travers les documents d'époque, 1799–1974. Paris: CNRS, 1974.

Le Doulcet de Pontécoulant, Gustave. *Souvenirs historiques et parlementaires.* 4 vols. Paris: Lévy frères, 1861–1865.

Lefebvre, Georges. *La France sous le Directoire, 1795–1799.* Edited by J.-R. Suratteau. Paris: Éditions sociales, 1977.

———. *Napoléon.* Paris: PUF, 1941.

Le Goff, Jacques. *Saint Louis.* Paris: Gallimard, 1996.

Leibniz, Gottfried Wilhelm. "Projet de conquête de l'Égypte présenté par Leibniz à Louis XIV." In *Oeuvres de Leibniz,* edited by A. Foucher de Careil, vol. 5. Paris: Firmin-Didot, 1864.

Leijendecker, Marcel. "Un amour inconnu de Bonaparte." *Revue des études napoléoniennes* 36 (January–June 1933): 52–53.

Lentz, Thierry. *Cent questions sur Napoléon.* Paris: La Boétie, 2013.

———. *La Conspiration du général Malet, 23 octobre 1812, premier ébranlement du trône de Napoléon.* Paris: Perrin, 2012.

———. *Le 18-Brumaire: Les coups d'État de Napoléon Bonaparte.* Paris: Jean Picollec, 1997.

———. *Le Grand Consulat, 1799–1804.* Paris: Fayard, 1999.

———. "Les consuls de la République: *La Révolution est finie.*" In Musée de l'armée, *Terminer la Révolution,* 19–37. Paris: Economica, 2003.

———. *Napoléon.* Paris: Le Cavalier Bleu, 2001.

———. *Nouvelle histoire du Premier Empire.* 4 vols. Paris: Fayard, 2002–2010.

———. *Quand Napoléon inventait la France: Dictionnaire des institutions politiques, administratives et de cour du Consulat et de l'Empire.* Paris: Tallandier, 2008.

———. "Roederer et le *modèle chinois*." *Revue de l'Institut Napoléon*, no. 163 (1994): 45–53.

———. "Un rendez-vous manqué: Napoléon et les États-Unis." In *Napoléon diplomate*, 199–232. Paris: CNRS, 2012.

Lentz, Thierry, and Jacques Macé. *La Mort de Napoléon: Mythes, légendes et mystères*. Paris: Perrin, 2009.

Leopardi, Giacomo. *Le Massacre des illusions*. Edited by M. A. Rigoni. Paris: Allia, 1993.

Levi, Carlo. *Le Christ s'est arrêté à Eboli*. Paris: Gallimard, 2003.

———. *Christ Stopped at Eboli*. Translated by Francis Frenaye. Harmondsworth: Penguin, 2008.

Lévy, Arthur. *The Private Life of Napoleon*. 2nd ed. Translated by Stephen Louis Simeon. New York: C. Scribner's Sons, 1894.

Lewis, Bernard. *The Muslim Discovery of Europe*. New York: Norton, 2001.

Leys, Simon. *The Death of Napoleon*. New York: Farrar, Straus and Giroux, 1991.

———. *Protée et autres essais*. Paris: Gallimard, 2001.

Liddell Hart, Basil Henry. *Stratégie*. Paris: Perrin, 2007.

Lignereux, Aurélien. "Le moment terroriste de la chouannerie: Des atteintes à l'ordre public aux attentats contre le Premier consul." *La Révolution française* 1 (2012).

———. *L'Empire des Français, 1799–1815*. Paris: Éditions du Seuil, 2012.

Livy. *Histoire romaine*. 35 vols. Paris: Les Belles Lettres, 1940–1984.

Lockroy, Édouard. *Ahmed le Boucher: La Syrie et l'Égypte au XVIIIe siècle*. Paris: Ollendorff, 1888.

Locré, Jean-Guillaume. *La Législation civile, commerciale et criminelle de la France, ou commentaire et complément des codes français*. 5 vols. Paris: Treuttel et Würtz, 1827.

Lombard de Langres, Vincent. *Le Dix-huit brumaire: Ou tableau des événements qui ont amené cette journée; Des moyens secrets par lesquels elle a été préparée; des faits qui l'ont accompagnée, et des résultats qu'elle doit avoir*. Paris: Garnery, Catineau et Rat, year VIII [1800].

Loriga, Sabina. *Le Petit X: De la biographie à l'histoire*. Paris: Éditions du Seuil, 2010.

Louca, Anouar. *L'Autre Égypte, de Bonaparte à Taha Hussein*. Cairo: IFAO, 2006.

Ludwig, Émile. *Napoleon*. New York: Boni and Liveright, 1926.

———. *Napoléon*. Paris: Payot, 1928.

Lyautey, Hubert. *Du rôle colonial de l'armée*. Paris: A. Colin, 1900.

Machiavel, Nicolas. *Discours sur la première décade de Tite-Live*. Edited by A. Fontana and X. Tabet. Paris: Gallimard, 2004.

———. *Oeuvres complètes*. Edited by E. Barincou. Paris: Gallimard, 1952.

Mackesy, Piers. *Statesmen at War: The Strategy of Overthrow, 1798–1799*. London: Longman, 1974.

Madelénat, Daniel. *La Biographie*. Paris: PUF, 1984.

Madelin, Louis. *Fouché, 1759–1820*. 2 vols. Paris: Nouveau Monde Éd./Fondation Napoléon, 2002.

———. *Histoire du Consulat et de l'Empire*. 16 vols. Paris: Tallandier, 1974.

Magniez, Émile. *Histoire de l'idée d'une conquête française de l'Égypte*. Paris: Jouve, 1900.

Maistre, Joseph de. *Considerations on France*. Translated by R. A. Lebrun. Cambridge: Cambridge University Press, 1995.

———. *Considérations sur la France*. Brussels: Éditions Complexe, 1988.

———. *Discours à Madame la marquise de Costa, sur la vie et la mort de son fils Alexis-Louis-Eugène de Costa*. Chambéry: Imprimerie savoisienne, 1892.

————. *Oeuvres complètes*. 7 vols. Geneva: Slatkine, 1979.

Mallet, Bernard. *Mallet du Pan and the French Revolution*. London: Longmans, Green, 1902.

Mallet du Pan, Jacques. *Mémoires et correspondance de Mallet du Pan pour servir à l'histoire de la Révolution française*. 2 vols. Edited by A. Sayous. Paris: Amyot et Cherbuliez, 1851.

————. *Mercure britannique ou notices historiques et critiques sur les affaires du temps*. 5 vols. London: Spilsbury, Snowhill, and Fauche, 1798–1800.

Malus, Étienne. *L'Agenda de Malus: Souvenirs de l'expédition d'Égypte, 1798–1801*. Edited by Charles Antoine Thoumas. Paris: Honoré Champion, 1892.

Mangerel, Maxime. *Le Capitaine Gerbaud, 1773–1799*. Paris: Plon-Nourrit, 1910.

Mantran, Robert, ed. *Histoire de l'empire ottoman*. Paris: Fayard, 1989.

Marbot, Jean-Baptiste-Antoine-Marcelin. *Mémoires*. 2 vols. Edited by J. Garnier. Paris: Mercure de France, 2001.

————. *The Memoirs of Baron De Marbot, Late Lieutenant-General in the French Army*. Translated by Arthur John Butler. London: Longmans, Green, 1892.

Marcaggi, Jean-Baptiste. *La Genèse de Napoléon: Sa formation intellectuelle et morale jusqu'au siège de Toulon*. Paris: Perrin, 1902.

Marcel, Jean-Joseph. *Contes du Cheykh Êl-Mohdy, traduits de l'arabe d'après le manuscrit original*. 3 vols. Paris: Dupuy, 1832–1835.

Marcère, Édouard de. *Une ambassade à Constantinople: La Politique orientale de la Révolution Française*. 2 vols. Paris: Alcan, 1927.

Marchand, Louis-Joseph-Narcisse. *Mémoires de Marchand, premier valet de chambre et exécuteur testamentaire de l'Empereur*. 2 vols. Paris: Tallandier, 1991.

Maréchal, Jean-François. "Recherches sur un désastre (Aboukir)." In *La Campagne d'Égypte (1798–1801), mythes et réalités: Actes du colloque des 16 et 17 juin 1998 à l'Hôtel national des Invalides*, 135–145. Paris: Éditions in Forma, 1998.

Marelli, Giuseppe. *Giornale storico della Repubblica cisalpina*. Milan. 1796–1797. Available at Biblioteca Ambrosiana di Milano.

Marion, Marcel. *Histoire financière de la France depuis 1715*. 6 vols. Paris: Rousseau, 1925.

Marmont, Auguste Frédéric Louis Wiesse de. *Mémoires*. 9 vols. Paris: Perrotin, 1857.

Marquiset, Alfred. *Napoléon sténographié au Conseil d'État, 1804–1805*. Paris: Honoré Champion, 1913.

Martin, Andrew. *Napoléon écrivain*. Toulouse: Privat, 2003.

————. *Napoleon the Novelist*. Cambridge: Blackwell, 2000.

Martin, Marc. *Les origines de la presse militaire en France à la fin de l'Ancien Régime et sous la Révolution (1770–1799)*. Vincennes: EMAT-Service historique, 1975.

Martin, P. *Histoire de l'expédition française en Égypte*. Paris: J.-M. Eberhart, 1815.

Martin, Roger, and Alain Pigeard. *Bibliographie napoléonienne*. Dijon: Cléa, 2010.

Martin, Xavier. *La France abîmée: Essai historique sur un sentiment révolutionnaire (1780–1820)*. Bouère: Dominique Martin Morin, 2009.

Martineau, Gilbert. *Lucien Bonaparte, prince de Canino*. Paris: France-Empire, 1989.

Marx, Karl. *La Sainte famille*. In *Philosophie*, edited by M. Rubel. Paris: Gallimard, 1982.

Mascilli Migliorini, Luigi. *Le Mythe du héros*. Paris: Nouveau Monde, 2002.

————. *Napoléon*. Paris: Perrin, 2004.

Masséna, André. *Mémoires*. 7 vols. Paris: J. de Bonnot, 1966–1967.

Massie, Michel. *Le Troisième consul Roger Ducos*. Biarritz: J&D Éditions, 1992.

Masson, Frédéric. *Mme Bonaparte (1796–1804)*. Paris: Ollendorff, 1920.

———. *Napoléon chez lui: La journée de l'empereur aux Tuileries*. Paris: Ollendorff, 1909.

———. *Napoléon dans sa jeunesse, 1769–1793*. Paris: Ollendorff, 1907.

———. *Napoléon et les femmes*. Paris: Borel, 1899.

———. *Napoléon et sa famille*. 13 vols. Paris: Albin Michel, 1927–1930.

Masson de Pezay, Alexandre-Frédéric-Jacques. *Histoire des campagnes de M. le maréchal de Maillebois en Italie pendant les années 1745 et 1746*. 4 vols. Paris: Imprimerie royale, 1775.

Mathieu, François Désirée (Cardinal). *Le Concordat de 1801: Ses origines, son histoire*. Paris: Perrin, 1904.

Mathiez, Albert. *La Révolution et l'Église: Études critiques et documentaires*. Paris: A. Colin, 1910.

———. *Rome et le clergé français sous la Constituante: La Constitution civile du clergé; l'affaire d'Avignon*. Paris: A. Colin, 1911.

Mauguin, Georges. "Saliceti et l'arrestation de Bonaparte à Nice." *Revue des études napoléoniennes* 39 (July–December 1934): 261–263.

———. "Trois lettres du lieutenant Fourès." *Revue des études napoléoniennes* 41 (1935): 163–167.

McErlean, John Michael Peter. "Between Paoli and Bonaparte: Philippe Masseria, an Anglomaniac in Corsica, 1789–1793." In *Proceedings 1986: Consortium on Revolutionary Europe 1750–1850*. Tallahassee: Florida State University, Institute on Napoleon and the French Revolution, 1986.

———. *Napoleon and Pozzo di Borgo in Corsica and after, 1764–1821: Not Quite a Vendetta*. Lewiston, N.Y.: Edwin Mellen Press, 1996.

McLynn, Frank. *Napoleon: A Biography*. New York: Arcade, 2002.

McPherson, James M. *La Guerre de Sécession: 1861–1865*. Paris: R. Laffont, 1991.

Menant, Sylvain, and Robert Morrissey. *Héroïsme et Lumières*. Paris: Champion, 2010.

Méneval, Claude-François de. *Napoléon et Marie-Louise, souvenirs historiques*. 3 vols. Paris: Amyot, 1844.

Mercier, Louis-Sébastien. *Tableau de Paris*. 2 vols. Edited by J.-C. Bonnet. Paris: Mercure de France, 1994.

Metzger, P. "Cambacérès, son rôle comme remplaçant de Bonaparte." *La Révolution française* 43 (July–December 1902): 528–558.

Meyer, Jack Allen. *An Annotated Bibliography of the Napoleonic Era*. New York: Greenwood Press, 1987.

Meyer, Philippe. *Dans mon pays lui-même . . .*. Paris: Flammarion, 1993.

Michalon, Roger, and Jacques Vernet. "Adaptation d'une armée française de la fin du XVIIIe siècle à un théâtre d'opérations proche-oriental (Égypte, 1798–1801)." *Revue internationale d'histoire militaire*, no. 49 (1980): 67–144.

[Michaud, J.-F.] *La Quotidienne ou feuille du jour*. October 22, 1796–September 4, 1797.

Michaud, Louis-Gabriel. *Biographie universelle ancienne et moderne*. New ed., 45 vols. Paris: Michaud, 1843–?.

———. *Lettre d'un Français au général Buonaparte*. Paris, 1799.

Michelet, Jules. *Histoire de la Révolution française*. 2 vols. Edited by G. Walter. Paris: Gallimard, 1952.

———. *Histoire du XIXe siècle*. 3 vols. Paris: Germer Baillière, 1872–1875.

Michon, Georges. *Robespierre et la guerre révolutionnaire, 1791–1792*. Paris: Marcel Rivière, 1937.

Mignet, François-Auguste. *Histoire de la Révolution française depuis 1789 jusqu'en 1814*. 2 vols. Paris: F. Didot, 1824.

Miot, Jacques-François. *Mémoires pour servir à l'histoire des expéditions en Égypte et en Syrie, pendant les années VI, VII et VIII de la République française*. Paris: Demonville, 1804.

———. *Mémoires pour servir à l'histoire des expéditions en Égypte et en Syrie, revue et augmentée d'une introduction, d'un appendice et de faits, pièces et documents qui n'ont pu paraître sous le gouvernement précédent*. Paris: Le Normant, 1814.

Miot de Melito, André François. *Mémoires*. 3 vols. Paris: Michel Lévy frères, 1858.

———. *Memoirs of Count Miot De Melito, Minister, Ambassador, Councillor of State and Member of the Institute of France, between the Years 1788 and 1815*. Edited by Wilhelm A. Fleischmann. Translated by Frances C. Hoey and John Lillie. New York: Scribner's, 1881.

Mirabeau, Honoré-Gabriel Riqueti de. *Mirabeau entre le roi et la Révolution: Notes à la cour suivies de discours*. Edited by G. Chaussinand-Nogaret. Paris: Hachette, 1986.

Mistler, Jean. *Le Grand livre de Napoléon*. 2 vols. Paris: Bibliothèque des Arts, 1968.

Mitton, Fernand. *La Presse française sous la Révolution, le Consulat, l'Empire*. Paris: Guy Le Prat, 1945.

Moiret, Joseph-Marie. *Mémoires sur l'expédition d'Égypte*. Paris: Belfond, 1984.

Molé, Mathieu. *Le Comte Molé, 1781–1855: Sa vie, ses mémoires*. Edited by E.-H.-V. Noailles. 6 vols. Paris: Édouard Champion, 1922–1930.

Mollien, Nicolas François. *Mémoires d'un ministre du Trésor public, 1780–1815*. 3 vols. Paris: Guillaumin, 1898.

Monestier, Louis. *Compte rendu des opérations des commissaires civils envoyés en Corse, avec des observations propres à faire connaître la situation de ce département au 1er avril 1791*. Paris: Imprimerie Nationale, [1792].

Monge, Gaspard. *Correspondance*. Archives de l'École polytechnique, Paris.

Mongrédien, Jean. "Le Théâtre-Italien de Paris sous le Consulat et l'Empire." *Napoleonica: La Revue* 1, no. 7 (2010): 79–87.

Monteagle, H. "La première rencontre de Barras et de Bonaparte." *Revue de l'Institut Napoléon*, no. 69 (October 1958): 141–145.

Montholon, Charles de. *Récits de la captivité de l'empereur Napoléon à Sainte-Hélène*. 2 vols. Paris: Paulin, 1847.

Morand, Charles Antoine. *Lettres sur l'expédition d'Égypte, de l'Italie à la prise du Caire, suivies de son carnet de chef de brigade de Rome à Assouan, 1798–1799*. Paris: La Vouivre, 1998.

Morrissey, Robert. *L'Empereur à la barbe fleurie: Charlemagne dans la mythologie et l'histoire de France*. Paris: Gallimard, 1997.

Moullier, Igor. *Le Ministère de l'intérieur sous le Consulat et le Premier Empire (1799–1814): Gouverner la France après le 18 Brumaire*. Doctoral thesis, Université de Lille, 2004, http://documents.univ-lille3.fr/files/pub/www/recherche/theses/moullier/html/these.html.

Murat, Joachim. *Lettres et documents pour servir à l'histoire de Joachim Murat.* Edited by P. Le Brethon. 7 vols. Paris: Plon, 1908–1914.

Nabonne, Bernard. *La Diplomatie du Directoire et Bonaparte d'après les papiers inédits de Reubell.* Paris: La Nouvelle Édition, 1951.

Napoléon, Charles. *Bonaparte et Paoli: Aux origines de la question corse.* Paris: Perrin, 2000.

Nasica, T. *Mémoires sur l'enfance et la jeunesse de Napoléon Ier jusqu'à l'âge de vingt-trois ans, précédés d'une notice historique sur son père.* Paris: P. Dupont, 1865.

Necker, Jacques. *De la Révolution française.* 2 vols. N.p., n.p., 1796.

———. *Dernières vues de politique et de finance.* Geneva, year X [1802].

———. *Examen de la Constitution de l'an III, extrait du dernier ouvrage de M. Necker.* Paris: Maradan, year VIII [1799].

Neipperg, Adam Albert de. *Aperçu militaire de la bataille de Marengo.* Saint-Amand: Bussière, 1906.

Nicolas le Turc [Nigulà ibn Yusufal-Turk]. *Histoire de l'expédition des Français en Égypte.* Paris: Imprimerie royale, 1839.

Niello Sargy, Jean Gabriel de. *Mémoires sur l'expédition d'Égypte.* Paris: Vernarel et Tenon, 1825.

Nietzsche, Friedrich. *Oeuvres philosophiques complètes.* Vol. 7, *Généalogie de la morale.* Edited by G. Colli and M. Montinari. Paris: Gallimard, 1971.

———. *Oeuvres philosophiques complètes.* Vol. 9, *Fragments posthumes (été 1882–printemps 1884).* Edited by G. Colli and M. Montinari. Paris: Gallimard, 1997.

———. *Oeuvres philosophiques complètes.* Vol. 13, *Fragments posthumes (automne 1887–mars 1888).* Edited by G. Colli and M. Montinari. Paris: Gallimard, 1973.

———. *On the Genealogy of Morals.* Translated by Walter Kaufmann. New York: Vintage Books, 1967.

Norry, Charles. *Relation de l'expédition d'Égypte, suivie de la description de plusieurs monuments de cette contrée.* Paris: Charles Pougens-Magimel, 1799.

Norvins, Jacques Marquet de Montbreton de. *Histoire de Napoléon.* 4 vols. Paris: Furne, 1833.

———. *Mémorial.* 3 vols. Paris: Plon-Nourrit, 1896–1897.

O'Brien, David. *Antoine Jean Gros.* Paris: Gallimard, 2006.

Ollivier, Albert. *Le Dix-huit brumaire.* Paris: Gallimard, 1959.

O'Meara, Barry E. *Documents particuliers sur Napoléon Bonaparte.* Paris: Plancher, 1819.

———. *Napoléon dans l'exil.* 2 vols. Edited by P. Ganière. Paris: Fondation Napoléon, 1993.

———. *Napoleon in Exile: Or, a Voice from St. Helena; the Opinions and Reflections of Napoleon on the Most Important Events of His Life and Government, in His Own Words.* 2 vols. New York: W. Gowans, 1853.

Onorio, Joël-Benoît d'. *Portalis, l'esprit des siècles.* Paris: Dalloz, 2005.

Orieux, Jean. *Talleyrand ou le Sphinx incompris.* Paris: Flammarion, 1970.

Outin, Edmond. *Napoléon fils du comte de Marbeuf . . .* Paris: France-Empire, 2006.

Ouvrard, Gabriel-Julien. *Mémoires sur sa vie et ses diverses opérations financières.* 3 vols. Paris: Moutardier, 1826.

Ozouf, Mona. *La Fête révolutionnaire (1789–1799).* Paris: Gallimard, 1976.

Pairault, François. *Gaspard Monge, le fondateur de Polytechnique.* Paris: Tallandier, 2000.

Pasquier, Étienne-Denis. *A History of My Time: Memoirs of Chancellor Pasquier*. Edited by Duke d'Audiffret-Pasquier. Translated by Charles E. Roche. New York: C. Scribner's Sons, 1893.

———. *Mémoires, histoire de mon temps*. 6 vols. Paris: Plon-Nourrit, 1893–1895.

Payard, Maurice. "Bonaparte et le fournisseur Collot." *Revue des études napoléoniennes* 40 (January–June 1935): 129–143.

Pelet de la Lozère, Jean. *Opinions de Napoléon sur divers sujets de politique et d'administration*. Paris: Firmin Didot, 1833.

Pelletier, Gérard. *Rome et la Révolution française: La théologie et la politique du Saint-Siège devant la Révolution française (1789–1799)*. Rome: École française de Rome, 2004.

Peltier, Jean-Gabriel. *The Trial of John Peltier, for a Libel against Napoleon Buonaparte, First Consul of the French Republic, at the Court of King's Bench, Middlesex, on Monday the 21st of February, 1803*. London: Cox and Baylis, 1803.

Pérès, Jean-Baptiste. *Comme quoi Napoléon n'a jamais existé, ou grand erratum, source d'un nombre infini d'errata à noter dans l'histoire du XIXe siècle*. Edited by G. Davois. Paris: Éditions bibliographique, 1909.

Petiteau, Natalie. *Napoléon, de la mythologie à l'histoire*. Paris: Éditions du Seuil, 1999.

———. *Voies nouvelles pour l'histoire du Premier Empire: Territoires, pouvoirs, identités; Colloque d'Avignon, 9–10 mai 2000*. Paris: La Boutique de l'Histoire, 2003.

Petitfils, Jean-Christian. *Louis XIV*. Paris: Perrin, 2002.

———. *Louis XVI*. 2 vols. Paris: Perrin, 2010.

Petitfrère, Claude. *Le Général Dupuy et sa correspondance (1792–1798)*. Paris: Société des études robespierristes, 1962.

Petrov, Fyodor. "Paul Ier et Napoléon Bonaparte: L'Alliance impossible?" In Musée de l'armée, *Terminer la Révolution*, 243–257. Paris: Economica, 2003.

Peyre, Roger. *La Cour d'Espagne au commencement du XIXe siècle, d'après la correspondance de l'ambassadeur de France Alquier*. Paris: Émile-Paul, 1909.

Picard, Ernest. *Bonaparte et Moreau*. Paris: Plon, 1905.

Picavet, François. *Les Idéologues: Essai sur l'histoire des idées et des théories scientifiques, philosophiques, religieuses, etc., en France depuis 1789*. Paris: Félix Alcan, 1891.

Pierron, Édouard. *Comment s'est formé le génie militaire de Napoléon Ier?* Paris: Librairie militaire de L. Baudoin, 1899.

Piétri, François. *Lucien Bonaparte*. Paris: Plon, 1939.

———. *Napoléon et le parlement, ou la dictature enchaînée*. Paris: Fayard, 1955.

Pigeard, Alain. *Dictionnaire des batailles de Napoléon*. Paris: Tallandier, 2004.

Pillepich, Alain. *Napoléon et les Italiens: République italienne et royaume d'Italie (1802–1814)*. Paris: Nouveau Monde Éditions/Fondation Napoléon, 2003.

Pinaud, Pierre-François. *Cambacérès, 1753–1824*. Paris: Perrin, 1996.

Pingaud, Albert. *Bonaparte président de la République italienne*. 2 vols. Paris: Perrin, 1914.

———. *Les Hommes d'État de la République italienne, 1802–1805: Notices et documents biographiques*. Paris: Éditions Champion, 1914.

Pingaud, Léonce. *Bernadotte, Napoléon et les Bourbons (1797–1844)*. Paris: Plon, 1901.

Pluchon, Pierre. *Toussaint Louverture, un révolutionnaire noir d'Ancien Régime*. Paris: Fayard, 1989.

Pommereul, François-Xavier-Jean de. *Histoire de l'île de Corse*. Nîmes: C. Lacour, 1990.

Pommier, Édouard. *L'Art de la liberté: Doctrines et débats de la Révolution française*. Paris: Gallimard, 1991.

Pomponi, Francis. *Histoire de la Corse*. Paris: Hachette, 1979.

———. *Le Mémorial des Corses*. 6 vols. Marseille: Éditions méditerranéennes du Prado, 1980.

———. "Les îles du bassin occidental de la Méditerranée et la 'redécouverte' par la France d'une politique méditerranéenne (1769–1799)." *Bonaparte, les îles méditerranéennes et l'appel de l'Orient: Cahiers de la Méditerranée*, no. 57 (December 1998): 1–32.

———. "Sentiment révolutionnaire et esprit de parti en Corse au temps de la Révolution." *Annales historiques de la Révolution française* (1971): 56–87.

Poniatowski, Michel. *Talleyrand aux États-Unis, 1794–1796*. Paris: Perrin, 1976.

———. *Talleyrand et le Directoire, 1796–1800*. Paris: Perrin, 1982.

Poumarède, Géraud. *Pour en finir avec la Croisade: Mythes et réalités de la lutte contre les Turcs aux XVIe et XVIIe siècles*. Paris: PUF, 2004.

Poussielgue, Jean-Baptiste-Étienne. *Lettre de M. Poussielgue, ancien administrateur général des finances de l'Égypte, accompagnée de pièces justificatives, à M. Thiers, auteur de l'Histoire du Consulat et de l'Empire*. Paris: G. Pissin, 1845.

Poussou, Jean-Pierre. "Les conséquences financières et économiques de la guerre d'Indépendance américaine pour les royaumes de France et de Grande-Bretagne." In *La France et l'Indépendance américaine*, edited by Ph. Bonnichon, O. Chaline, and Ch.-Ph. De Vergennes, 203–219. Paris: PUPS, 2008.

Pradt, Dominique-Dufour de. *Les Quatre concordats*. 3 vols. Paris: Béchet, 1818.

Prendergast, Christopher. *Napoleon and History Painting*. Oxford: Oxford University Press, 1997.

Prosperi, Adriano. "Otras Indias: Missionari della Controriforma tra contadini e salvaggi." In *America e apocalisse e altri saggi*. Rome: Instituti et Poligrafici Internazionali, 1999.

Proth, Mario. *Bonaparte comediante tragediante*. Paris: A. Le Chevalier, 1869.

Quinet, Edgar. *La Révolution*. Paris: Belin, 1987.

Randolph, Herbert. *Life of General Sir Robert Wilson*. 2 vols. London: John Murray, 1862.

Ransom, Roger L. *Conflict and Compromise: The Political Economy of Slavery, Emancipation and the American Civil War*. Cambridge, Mass.: Cambridge University Press, 1990.

Rao, Anna Maria. "Les républicains démocrates italiens et le Directoire." In *La République directoriale*, edited by Ph. Bourdin and B. Gainot, 2:1057–1090. Paris: Clermont-Ferrand, Société des études robespierristes, Centre d'histoire des entreprises et des communautés, Centre de recherches révolutionnaires (Université Blaise-Pascal/Clermont-Ferrand II), 1998.

Raynal, Guillaume. *La Négresse couronnée, ou moeurs des peuples mises en action, histoire remplie d'événements singuliers, amusants et curieux*. 2 vols. Paris: Cailleau, 1787.

Raynaud, Philippe, and Stéphane Rials. *Dictionnaire de philosophie politique*. Paris: PUF, 1996.

Regenbogen, Lucian. *Napoléon a dit: Aphorismes, citations et opinions*. Paris: Les Belles Lettres, 1998.

Regent, Nikola. "Nietzsche's Napoleon: A Renaissance Man." *History of Political Thought* 33, no. 2 (Summer 2012): 305–347.

Reilly, Robin. *Pitt the Younger, 1759–1806*. London: Cassell, 1978.

Réimpression de l'ancien Moniteur, seule histoire authentique et inaltérée de la Révolution française depuis la réunion des États généraux jusqu'au Consulat (mai 1789—novembre 1799), avec des notes explicatives. 31 vols. Paris: Plon, 1847–1854.

Reinhard, Christine. *Lettres de Madame Reinhard à sa mère, 1798–1815: Une Femme de diplomate.* Paris: Picard, 1900.

Reinhard, Marcel. *Avec Bonaparte en Italie, d'après les lettres inédites de son aide de camp Joseph Sulkowski.* Paris: Hachette, 1946.

———. *Le Grand Carnot.* 2 vols. Paris: Hachette, 1952.

Reiss, René. *Clarke, maréchal et pair de France.* Strasbourg: Coprur, 1999.

Remacle, Albert de. *Relations secrètes des agents de Louis XVIII à Paris sous le Consulat (1802–1803).* Paris: Plon, 1899.

Rémusat, Claire Élisabeth Jeanne Gravier de Vergennes de. *Mémoires (1802–1808).* 3 vols. Edited by P. de Rémusat. Paris: Calmann-Lévy, 1881.

Rey, Marie-Pierre. *Alexandre Ier.* Paris: Flammarion, 2009.

Reybaud, Louis. *Histoire scientifique et militaire de l'expédition française en Égypte.* 10 vols. Paris: Denain, 1830–1836.

Riccioli, J.-L. "Le Franchissement des cours d'eaux pendant la campagne [d'Italie]." http://195.15 4.144.20/fr/hors_serie/1campagne-italie/lesecrits/colloques/eau.html.

Rinn, Charles. *Un mystérieux enlèvement: L'affaire Clément de Ris, 1800–1801.* Paris: Lefrançois, 1910.

Robert, Marthe. *Roman des origines et origines du roman.* Paris: Gallimard, 2002.

Robespierre, Augustin, and Maximilien Robespierre. *Correspondance de Maximilien et Augustin Robespierre.* 2 vols. Edited by G. Michon. Paris: A. Nizet et M. Bastard, 1926–1941.

Rocquain, Félix. *L'État de la France au 18 brumaire, d'après les rapports des conseillers d'État chargés d'une enquête sur la situation de la République.* Paris: Didier, 1874.

Rodinson, Maxime. *La Fascination de l'islam.* Paris: La Découverte, 2003.

Roederer, Pierre-Louis. *Bonaparte me disait: Conversations notées par le comte P.-L. Roederer.* Edited by M. Vox. Paris: Horizons de France, 1942.

———. *Journal du comte P.-L. Roederer.* Edited by M. Vitrac. Paris: Daragon, 1909.

———. *Oeuvres.* 8 vols. Paris: Firmin Didot, 1853–1859.

Rollin, Charles. *Traité des études [De la manière d'enseigner et d'étudier les belles-lettres par rapport à l'esprit et au coeur].* [1726]. 4 vols. Paris: Mame, 1810.

Rossignol, Jean. *Vie de Jean Rossignol, vainqueur de la Bastille.* Edited by A. de Baecque. Paris: Mercure de France, 2011.

Rousseau, F. *Kléber et Menou en Égypte depuis le départ de Bonaparte (août 1799–septembre 1801).* Paris: Picard, 1900.

Rousseau, Jean-Jacques. *Confessions.* Translated by J. M. Cohen. Harmondsworth: Penguin, 1954.

———. *Du contrat social.* Edited by B. de Jouvenel. Paris: Hachette, 1978.

———. "Lettre sur la musique française" [1753]. In *Oeuvres complètes,* vol. 14. Paris: Daliban, 1826.

———. *Oeuvres complètes.* Vol. 1, *Les Confessions, Autres textes autobiographiques.* Edited by B. Gagnebin, R. Osmont, and M. Raymond. Paris: Gallimard, 1959.

———. *Oeuvres complètes.* Vol. 3, *Du contrat social, écrits politiques.* Edited by B. Gagnebin and M. Raymond. Paris: Gallimard, 1964.

———. *The Social Contract: Or, the Principles of Political Rights.* New York: G. P. Putnam's Sons, 1893.

Roustan, Antoine-Jacques. *Défense du christianisme considéré du côté politique où l'on répond en particulier au chapitre viii du quatrième livre du Contrat social.* Amsterdam: Rey, 1764.

Saïd, Edward W. *L'Orientalisme: L'Orient créé par l'Occident.* Paris: Éditions du Seuil, 2005.

———. *Orientalism.* New York: Vintage, 1979.

Sainte-Beuve, Charles-Augustin. *Causeries du lundi.* 16 vols. Paris: Garnier, 1858–1872.

———. *Nouveaux lundis.* 13 vols. Paris: Calmann-Lévy, 1883–1886.

Saint-Priest, François-Emmanuel Guignard de. *Mémoires.* Paris: Calmann-Lévy, 1929.

Saitta, Armando. *Alle origini del Risorgimento: I testi di un celebre concorso, 1796.* 3 vols. Rome: Istituto storico italiano per l'età moderna e contemporanea, 1964.

Savant, Jean. *Les Amours de Napoléon.* Paris: Hachette, 1956.

———. *Les Ministres de Napoléon.* Paris: Hachette, 1959.

Savary, Claude-Étienne. *Lettres sur l'Égypte.* 2 vols. Paris: Onfroi, 1785–1786.

Savary, Jean-Marie-René. *Mémoires.* 8 vols. Paris: Bossange, 1828.

Sayous, André. *Mémoires et correspondance de Mallet du Pan, pour servir à l'histoire de la Révolution française.* 2 vols. Paris: Amyot-Cherbuliez, 1851.

Schmidt, Adolphe. *Tableaux de la Révolution française, publiés sur les papiers inédits du département et de la police secrète de Paris.* 3 vols. Leipzig: Veit, 1870.

Schnettger, Matthias. "*De vasallo non statu Imperii:* Les fiefs impériaux en Italie à l'époque moderne." In *L'Espace du Saint-Empire du Moyen Âge à l'époque moderne,* edited by C. Lebeau. Strasbourg: Presses Universitaires de Strasbourg, 2004.

Séché, Léon. *Les Origines du Concordat.* 2 vols. Paris: Delagrave, 1894.

Sénèque. "Consolation à ma mère Helvia." In *Entretiens: Lettres à Lucilius,* edited by P. Veyne. Paris: R. Laffont, 1993.

Serra, Maurizio. *Malaparte, vies et légendes.* Paris: Perrin, 2012.

Sicard, Augustin. *Les Études classiques avant la Révolution.* Paris: Didier et Perrin, 1887.

Simiot, Bernard. *De quoi vivait Bonaparte.* Paris: Deux Rives, 1952.

Simonetta, Marcello, and Noga Arikha. *Napoleon and the Rebel: Lucien Bonaparte.* New York: Palgrave Macmillan, 2011.

Sismondi, Jean-Charles-Léonard Simonde. *Histoire des Français.* 31 vols. Paris: Treuttel et Würtz, 1821–1844.

Skakowski, Adam Mieczysaw. *Les Polonais en Égypte, 1798–1801.* Kraków: G. Gebethner, 1910.

Smith, William Sidney. *Memoirs of Admiral Sidney Smith.* 2 vols. London: R. Bentley, 1839.

Solomon, Maynard. *Beethoven.* Paris: J.-C. Lattès, 1985.

Sorel, Albert. *Bonaparte et Hoche en 1797.* Paris: Plon-Nourrit, 1896.

———. *L'Europe et la Révolution française.* 8 vols. Paris: Claude Tchou/La Bibliothèque des Introuvables, 2003.

Sparrow, Elizabeth. *Secret Service: British Agents in France, 1792–1815.* Woodbridge: Boydell Press, 1999.

Spillmann, Georges. *Napoléon et l'islam.* Paris: Perrin, 1969.

Staël, Germaine de. *Considerations on the Principal Events of the French Revolution: Posthumous Work of the Baroness de Staël*. New York: James Eastburn and Co., 1818.

———. *Considérations sur la Révolution française*. Edited by J. Godechot. Paris: Tallandier, 1983.

———. *Correspondance générale*. 7 vols. Paris: Champion/Slatkine, 2009.

———. *De la littérature*. Edited by G. Gengembre and J. Goldzink. Paris: Garnier-Flammarion, 1991.

———. *De l'influence des passions sur le bonheur des individus et des nations, suivi de Réflexions sur le suicide*. Edited by Ch. Thomas. Paris: Payot, 2000.

———. *Des circonstances actuelles qui peuvent terminer la Révolution et des principes qui doivent fonder la République en France*. Edited by L. Omacini. Geneva: Droz, 1979.

———. *Dix années d'exil, précédé d'une notice sur la vie et les ouvrages de Madame de Staël, par Mme Necker de Saussure*. Edited by D. Lacroix. Paris: Garnier, n.d.

Stendhal. *Aux âmes sensibles, lettres choisies*. Edited by E. Boudot-Lamotte. Paris: Gallimard, 1942.

———. *La Chartreuse de Parme*. Edited by H. Martineau. 2 vols. Paris: Le Divan, 1927.

———. *Rome, Naples et Florence en 1817*. Edited by P. Brunel. Paris: Gallimard, 1987.

———. *Vie de Henry Brulard*. Edited by B. Didier. Paris: Gallimard, 1973.

———. *Vie de Napoléon*. Cahors: Éditions Climats, 1998.

Szramkiewicz, Romuald, and Jacques Bouineau. *Histoire des institutions, 1750–1914: Droit et société en France de la fin de l'Ancien Régime à la Première Guerre mondiale*. 3rd ed. Paris: Litec, 1996.

Tabet, Xavier. "Bonaparte, Venise et les îles ioniennes: De la politique territoriale à la géopolitique." *Bonaparte, les îles méditerranéennes et l'appel de l'Orient: Cahiers de la Méditerranée*, no. 57 (December 1998): 131–141.

———. "Venise, mai 1797: La Révolution introuvable." In *Venise 1297–1797: La République des Castors*, edited by A. Fontana and G. Saro, 129–148. Fontenay-aux-Roses: ENS éditions, 1997.

Taillandier, A. H. *Documents biographiques sur P. C. F. Daunou*. Paris: Firmin Didot, 1847.

Taine, Hippolyte. *Les Origines de la France contemporaine*. 2 vols. Edited by F. Léger. Paris: R. Laffont, 1986.

———. *The Origins of Contemporary France*. 2 vols. New York: Holt, 1890.

Talleyrand, Charles-Maurice de. *Correspondance diplomatique de Talleyrand: Le Ministère de Talleyrand sous le Directoire*. Edited by G. Pallain. Paris: Plon-Nourrit, 1891.

———. *Essai sur les avantages à retirer des colonies nouvelles dans les circonstances présentes: Lu à la séance publique de l'Institut national le 15 messidor an V*. Paris: Baudouin, [1797].

———. *Mémoires et correspondances*. Edited by E. de Waresquiel. Paris: R. Laffont, 2007.

———. *Memoirs of the Prince de Talleyrand*. Translated by Raphael Ledos de Beaufort. London: Griffith Farran Okeden and Welsh, 1891.

Thibaudeau, Antoine Clair. *Le Consulat et l'Empire, ou Histoire de la France et de Napoléon Bonaparte de 1799 à 1815*. 10 vols. Paris: J. Renouard, 1834–1835.

———. *Mémoires, 1799–1815*. Paris: Plon, 1913.

———. *Mémoires sur la Convention et le Directoire*. 2 vols. Paris: Baudouin frères, 1824.

———. *Mémoires sur le Consulat: 1799 à 1804; Par un ancien conseiller d'État*. Paris: Ponthieu, 1827.

Thiébault, Paul-Charles-François-Adrien-Henri-Dieudonné. *Mémoires*. 5 vols. Edited by F. Calmettes. Paris: Plon, 1893–1896.

Thiers, Adolphe. *Histoire de la Révolution française.* 10 vols. Paris: Furne, 1839.

———. *Histoire du Consulat et de l'Empire.* 20 vols. Paris: Lheureux, 1845–1862.

———. *History of the Consulate and the Empire of France under Napoleon.* Translated by D. F. Campbell. 20 vols. London: H. Colburn, 1845.

———. *The History of the French Revolution.* 5 vols. Translated by Frederic Shoberl. London: R. Bentley, 1838.

Thiry, Jean. *Bonaparte en Italie, 1796–1797.* Paris: Berger-Levrault, 1973.

———. *La Machine infernale.* Paris: Berger-Levrault, 1952.

———. *L'Avènement de Napoléon.* Paris: Berger-Levrault, 1959.

———. *Le Concordat et le Consulat à vie.* Paris: Berger-Levrault, 1956.

———. *Le Coup d'état du 18 brumaire.* Paris: Berger-Levrault, 1947.

———. *Le Sénat de Napoléon (1800–1814).* Paris: Berger-Levrault, 1932.

———. *Marengo.* Paris: Berger-Levrault, 1949.

Thomas, Antoine-Léonard. *Essai sur les éloges.* In *Oeuvres complètes*, vols. 3–5. Paris: Desessarts, 1802.

Thureau-Dangin, Paul. *Royalistes et républicains: Essais historiques sur des questions de politique contemporaine.* Paris: Plon-Nourrit, 1888.

Thurman, Louis. *Bonaparte en Égypte: Souvenirs.* Paris: E. Paul, 1902.

Tocqueville, Alexis de. *De la démocratie en Amérique: Souvenirs—L'Ancien Régime et la Révolution.* Edited by J.-Cl. Lamberti and F. Mélonio. Paris: R. Laffont, 1986.

———. *Democracy in America.* Translated by Arthur Goldhammer. New York: Library of America/Penguin Putnam, 2004.

———. "Discours de M. de Tocqueville, prononcé à la séance publique du 21 avril 1842, et venant prendre séance à la place de M. le comte de Cessac." In *Oeuvres complètes*, vol. 16, *Mélanges*, edited by F. Mélonio, 251–269. Paris: Gallimard, 1989.

———. *Tocqueville: The Ancien Régime and the French Revolution.* Edited by Jon Elster. Translated by Arthur Goldhammer. New York: Cambridge University Press, 2011.

Tolstoy. *La Sonate à Kreutzer; Le Diable; Le Bonheur conjugal.* Edited by S. Luneau. Paris: Gallimard, 1974.

Tomi, Pierre. "Les biens de la famille Bonaparte." *Études corses*, new ser., no. 12 (October–December 1956): 47–52.

Tomiche, Nada. *Napoléon écrivain.* Paris: Armand Colin, 1952.

Toussaint-Louverture, Jean-Dominique. *The Haitian Revolution.* London: Verso Books, 2008.

Tranié, Jean, and Juan Carlos Carmigniani. *Bonaparte: La campagne d'Égypte.* Paris: Pygmalion, 1988.

Trinkle, Dennis A. *The Napoleonic Press: The Public Sphere and Oppositionary Journalism.* Lewiston, N.Y.: Mellen Press, 2002.

Tulard, Jean, ed. *Dictionnaire Napoléon.* 2 vols. Paris: Fayard, 1999.

———. *Joseph Fouché.* Paris: Fayard, 1998.

———. *Le Mythe de Napoléon.* Paris: Armand Colin, 1971.

———. *Napoléon: Le pouvoir, la nation, la légende.* Paris: LGF, 1997.

———. *Napoléon: Ou le mythe du sauveur.* Paris: Fayard, 1987.

———. "Robespierre vu par Napoléon." In *Actes du colloque Robespierre, XIIe Congrès international des Sciences historiques (Vienne, 3 septembre 1965)*, 35–45. Paris: Société des études robespierristes, 1967.

Tulard, Jean, and Louis Garros. *Itinéraire de Napoléon au jour le jour (1769–1821)*. New ed. Revised by J. Tulard and J. Jourquin. Paris: Tallandier, 2002.

Valéry, Paul. *Cahiers*. Vol. 1. Edited by J. Robinson. Paris: Gallimard, 1973.

———. *Oeuvres*. Vol. 1. Edited by J. Hytier. Paris: Gallimard, 1957.

Vandal, Albert. *L'Avènement de Bonaparte*. 2 vols. Paris: Plon, 1907–1915.

Vattel, Emer de. *Le Droit des gens ou principes de la loi naturelle appliqués à la conduite et aux affaires des nations et des souverains*. 2 vols. London: n.p., 1758.

Venturi, Franco. *La rivoluzione di Corsica: Le grande carestie degli anni sessanta; La Lombardia delle riforme*. Vol. 1 of *Settecento riformatore V: L'Italia dei lumi (1764–1790)*. Turin: Giulio Einaudi, 1987.

Vergé-Franceschi, Michel. *Histoire de Corse: Le pays de la grandeur*. 2 vols. Paris: Éditions du Félin, 1996.

———. *Napoléon, une enfance corse*. Paris: Larousse, 2009.

———. *Paoli, un Corse des Lumières*. Paris: Fayard, 2005.

Versini, Xavier. *M. de Buonaparte ou le livre inachevé*. Paris: Albatros, 1977.

Vigée-Lebrun, Élisabeth. *Souvenirs*. 2 vols. Paris: Charpentier, 1869.

Villefosse, Louis de, and Janine Bouissounouse. *L'Opposition à Napoléon*. Paris: Flammarion, 1969.

Villiers du Terrage, René-Édouard de. *Journal et souvenirs sur l'expédition d'Égypte, 1798–1801*. Paris: Plon, 1899.

Volney, Constantin-François. *Considérations sur la guerre actuelle des Turcs*. London: n.p., 1788.

———. *Les Ruines, ou méditation sur les révolutions des empires*. Paris: Parmantier et Froment, 1826.

———. *Tableau du climat et du sol des États-Unis d'Amérique*. 2 vols. Paris: Courcier et Dentu, 1803.

———. *Voyage en Égypte et en Syrie pendant les années 1783, 1784 et 1785, suivi de Considérations sur la guerre des Russes et des Turcs, publiées en 1788 et 1789*. 2 vols. Paris: Parmantier et Froment, 1825.

Voltaire. *Anecdotes sur Pierre le Grand*. In *Oeuvres*, vol. 24, pt. 3 (*Mélanges, 2*). Paris: 1879.

———. *Dictionnaire philosophique*. Edited by A. Pons. Paris: Gallimard, 1994.

———. *Essai sur les moeurs*. Vols. 15–17 of *Oeuvres complètes*. Paris: Lefèvre, 1829.

———. *Le Fanatisme, ou Mahomet le Prophète*. Amsterdam: Estienne Ledet, 1753.

———. *Oeuvres historiques*. Edited by R. Pomeau. Paris: Gallimard, 1957.

Vovelle, Michel. "Nascita e formazione del mito napoleonico in Italia durante il Trienno: La lezione delle immagini." In *1796–1797: Da Montenotte a Campoformio; la rapida marcia di Napoleone Bonaparte*, 11–17. Rome: "L'Erma" di Bretschneider, 1997.

Wagener, Françoise. *L'Impératrice Joséphine*. Paris: Perrin, 2005.

Warden, William. *Napoléon jugé par un Anglais: Lettres de Sainte-Hélène, lettres de W. Warden, chirurgien de S. M. à bord du Northumberland qui a transporté Napoléon Bonaparte à Sainte-Hélène, suivies des Lettres du Cap de Bonne-Espérance, réponses de Napoléon aux Lettres de Warden*. Edited by A. Cabanès. Paris: H. Vivien, 1901.

Waresquiel, Emmanuel de. *Talleyrand, le prince immobile*. Paris: Fayard, 2003.

Watson, J. Steven. *The Reign of George III, 1760–1815*. Oxford: Clarendon Press, 1960.

Wegeler, F. G., and Ferdinand Ries. *Notices biographiques sur Ludwig van Beethoven*. Paris: Dentu, 1862.

Whaley, Leigh Ann. *The Impact of Napoleon, 1800–1815: An Annotated Bibliography*. Lanham, Md.: Scarecrow Press; Pasadena, Calif.: Salem Press, 1997.

Whately, Richard. *Historic Doubts relative to Napoleon Buonaparte*. London: Longmans, Green, 1865.

———. *Peut-on prouver l'existence de Napoléon?* Edited by J.-C. Martin. Paris: Vendémiaire, 2012.

Wheeler, H. F. B., and A. M. Broadley. *Napoleon and the Invasion of England: The Story of the Great Terror*. Chalford: Nonsuch, 2007.

Willis, F. Roy. "Development Planning in Eighteenth-Century France: Corsica's Plan Terrier." *French Historical Studies* 11, no. 3 (Spring 1980): 328–351.

Wilson, Robert Thomas. *History of the British Expedition to Egypt, to Which Is Subjoined a Sketch of the Present State of That Country and Its Means of Defence*. London: T. Egerton, 1802.

Wittfogel, Karl. *Le Despotisme oriental: Étude comparative du pouvoir total*. Paris: Éditions de Minuit, 1964.

Wolff, Jacques. *Le Financier Ouvrard: L'Argent et la politique*. Paris: Tallandier, 1992.

Woloch, Isser. *Napoleon and His Collaborators: The Making of a Dictatorship*. New York: W. W. Norton, 2001.

Woolf, Stuart Joseph. *A History of Italy, 1700–1860: The Social Constraints of Political Change*. London: Methuen, 1979.

Yavetz, Zvi. *César et son image: Des limites du charisme en politique*. Paris: Les Belles Lettres, 1990.

Yorke, Henry Redhead. *Letters from France in 1802*. 2 vols. London: Symonds, 1804.

Young, Arthur. *Arthur Young's Travels in France: During the Years 1787, 1788, 1789*. Edited by Matilda Bethem-Edwards. Cambridge: Cambridge University Press, 2012.

Zacharie, Clémence. *Le Sénat du Consulat et de l'Empire: Vontribution à l'étude du contrôle de constitutionnalité des lois en France*. Paris: Université de Paris II, 2004.

Zaghi, Carlo. *Bonaparte e il Direttorio dopo Campoformio: Il problema italiano nella diplomazia europea, 1797–1798*. Naples: Edizioni scientifiche italiane, 1956.

Zivy, Henry. *Le Treize Vendémiaire An IV*. Paris: Félix Alcan, 1898.

Zorzi, Alvise. *La République du lion: Histoire de Venise*. Paris: Payot, 1996.

Zweig, Stefan. *Joseph Fouché*. Paris: Le Livre de Poche, 2000.

INDEX